BATTLES OF THE 11TH TENNESSEE INFANTRY, CSA
1861-1865

MAP BY HAL JESPERSON

"Forward My Brave Boys!"

Endowed by
TOM WATSON BROWN
and
THE WATSON-BROWN FOUNDATION, INC.

"Forward My Brave Boys!"

A HISTORY OF THE 11TH TENNESSEE VOLUNTEER INFANTRY

C. S. A. 1861–1865

M. Todd Cathey

and

Gary W. Waddey

MERCER UNIVERSITY PRESS | MACON, GEORGIA

MUP/ H908

© 2016 by Mercer University Press
Published by Mercer University Press
1501 Mercer University Drive
Macon, Georgia 31207
All rights reserved

9 8 7 6 5 4 3 2 1

Books published by Mercer University Press are printed on acid-free paper that meets the requirements of the American National Standard for Information Sciences—Permanence of Paper for Printed Library Materials.

ISBN978-0-88146-544-0
Cataloging-in-Publication Data is available from the Library of Congress

Contents

Acknowledgments	viii
Preface	xi
1. "For Tennessee and the South": November 1860–Mid-May 1861	1
2. "Drilling and Otherwise Preparing for War": Mid-May–24 July 1861	14
3. "We Are Ready if They Come": 25 July–Mid-September 1861	30
4. "Cold as the North Pole": Mid-September–23 October 1861	47
5. "The Dad Gumdest Roughest Country in the Southern Confederacy": 24 October–December 1861	68
6. "Well, This Beats Hell": January–October 1862	79
7. "Eager for the Fray": November–December 1862	100
8. "Your Son Until Death": January–July 1863	117
9. "Our Men Have Suffered Awful Today and Gained Nothing": July–September 1863	131
10. "There Was All the Blue-coats We Wished to Shoot At": October–December 1863	142
11. "Three Cheers for the Snowball Colonel": January–May 1864	152
12. "We Will Stay Here": June 1864	170
13. "In Their Fall the Regiment Suffered Great Loss": July 1864	181
14. "Our Line at This Place Was Not Much Stronger than a Good Picket Line": August–September 1864	193

15. "They Had Well Tried to Capture a Red Fox": October–29 November 1864	199
16. "Follow Them into Their Works": 30 November 1864	204
17. "This Was the Most Disorderly Retreat I Experienced": December 1864	229
18. "Barefoot, Ragged, and Hungry": January–May 1865	
19. "Send Other Couriers Those May Be Killed": Post-War	253
Part II: Roster and Biographical Sketches	257
Appendix 1. 2nd Tennessee Infantry Regiment (Redesignated 11th Tennessee), First Organization, 31 May 1861	421
Appendix 2. 11th Tennessee Infantry Regiment, Second Organization, 1 May 1862	423
Appendix 3. "Camp Cheatham and the Boys," By Sergeant W. Jerome D. Spence, 3 July 1861, Camp Cheatham, Robertson County, Tennessee	425
Appendix 4. Killed, Wounded, Captured, and Missing	426
Appendix 5. Members of the 11th Tennessee Infantry Held in Federal Prisoner of War Camps	441
Appendix 6. Members of the 11th Tennessee Infantry on Rolls at the Surrender	446
Appendix 7. Members attending Postwar Reunions	449
Bibliography	451
Index	464

To Rick Robnett

—TC

To the men who served in the 11th Tennessee Volunteer Infantry and their descendants,

who honor their memory

—GW

Acknowledgments

First, we both extend our gratitude to the men of the 11th Tennessee Infantry, several of whom are our ancestors, and all of whom sacrificed in this horrific period of American history known as the Civil War. Next, a research project of this scope and magnitude, taking two men more than twelve years to complete, required the contributions of hundreds of people from all parts of the United States, especially descendants of the men. You know who you are, and we thank all of you who have contributed so much to make this work possible.

We also owe a debt of gratitude to Bart Ridings, our friend, fellow descendant, and 11th Tennessee webmaster, through which has come so much information. We are deeply indebted to Robert Halliburton, who provided much information on Company C and who encouraged us to combine our efforts in writing the history of the 11th Tennessee.

Todd Cathey's Acknowledgments

I thank my wife, Sheila, and kids, Candi and Cole, for enduring countless hours of dad's research, whether in a library, on a battlefield, in a cemetery, or during hours spent on the computer. You are precious to me, and my accomplishments are due to your unwavering support. Words cannot express my gratitude and indebtedness for my lifelong historical journey with my "Civil War companion" and fellow 11th Tennessee descendant, Rick Robnett. For decades, Rick and I have driven thousands of miles to get "on site," where we have discussed, dreamed about, and explored just about every aspect of the Confederate soldier of the Army of Tennessee. Our journeys have taken us to battlefields, cemeteries, museums, libraries, and historical sites all over the country. No briar patch has ever kept us out of an area we wanted to explore. All of those miles and trips count for something, so to you my friend, this book is dedicated. I owe a tremendous debt of gratitude to my writing partner, Gary Waddey. When we began this project, the short sketches contained in *Tennesseans in the Civil War* and *The Military Annals of Tennessee* comprised most of what was known about the 11th. Gary has searched near and far and has filled scores of binders with obscure primary source material, including many unpublished photographs of the soldiers. Over the years, he has remained patient and steady, always willing to track down any lead. His tenacity and thoroughness in research is the sole reason this work contains the level of detail regarding our subject. I am also grateful to my dear friend, the late Rick Koch, who walked the fields of the Chattanooga, Atlanta, and North Carolina campaigns with me. Dave Owens provided information, walked the field, and camped with me in the same location that the 11th Tennessee did at Camp Wildcat, Kentucky. Ray Adkins gave me a tour of the Barboursville, Kentucky, battlefield and read an early draft of that chapter.

Many others provided invaluable help along the way. I am grateful to Pat Walsh for ongoing encouragement and much information on C. H. Yates; Dennis Lampley for information about the history and burial places of many of the Hickman and Dickson County soldiers; Dr. Jack D. Welsh for his research regarding the medical histories of many of the soldiers; Colonel William Slayden and the W. H. Weems Educational Foundation, for support for this project in the very early days of research. Thanks also to Thomas Cartwright, who in my early years I grew to respect as *the* Battle of Franklin historian; to Tim Burgess, the provider of information regarding Reynolds Powell, Jeremiah Batts, and other Battle of Franklin fatalities; to Jamie Gillum for his support and information regarding the 11th Tennessee in the Atlanta Campaign as well as information about the Affair at Spring Hill, Tennessee; to Brian Allison, of "Historic Travellers Rest Plantation" for information regarding the Franklin/Nashville campaign, and to Beth Trescott of the Battle of Franklin Trust, Franklin, Tennessee. Eric Jacobson, whose insight is always deeply appreciated, was also a valuable resource. We are grateful for the easy-going expertise of cartographer Hal Jespersen, who designed our maps, and for Vance Harris, who provided additional information on the unit's participation in the Battle of Tazewell, Tennessee.

Gary Waddey's Acknowledgments

First, I would like to thank my partner, Todd Cathey, for his patience over all these years and his consistent dedication to accuracy and documentation in the process. To Ronnie and Emily Townes, who provided several of the uniformed images of the soldiers and whose dedication to the preservation of Confederate history is unwavering. To Dan Andrews, who has provided encouragement, support, and his wide knowledge of history for the Dickson and Hickman Counties. A special debt of gratitude is reserved for Johnny Ellis, who shared family information and previously unpublished images of his ancestor, Brigadier General James E. Rains. A special thanks also to local historians Paul Clements and Jim Summerville, who encouraged us in this project and contributed much to the published history of Nashville, and to the late Kermit C. Stengel, who never failed to share his vast knowledge of Nashville history and to ask how the project was progressing.

In my primary role of research and documentation, I especially wish to thank Marylin Hughes of the Tennessee State Library and Archives, who frequently went beyond the call of duty to bring to my attention items related to our research that would have otherwise been unknown. Likewise, Von Unruh of the United Methodist Church Archives, Nashville, Tennessee, provided both insight and information on the lives of the regimental chaplains. In addition, I wish to thank the staffs of the many libraries and archives I visited; their assistance was invaluable. These include the Tennessee State Library and Archives in Nashville; the state archives of Georgia, Morrow, Georgia; Alabama, Montgomery, Alabama; and Kentucky Frankfort, Kentucky; the Nashville Room of the Davidson County Public

Library, Nashville, Tennessee; Dickson County Public Library, Dickson, Tennessee; Hickman County Historical Society, Centerville, Tennessee; Robertson County Public Library and Yolanda Reid of the Robertson County Archives, Springfield Tennessee; Humphreys County Public Library, Waverly, Tennessee; Cheatham County Public Library, Ashland City, Tennessee; Williamson County Archives and Historian Rick Warwick, Franklin, Tennessee; and the Chattanooga-Hamilton County Public Library, Chattanooga, Tennessee. The University of Memphis, Memphis Tennessee, provided information about Brigadier General George Washington Gordon; Lincoln Memorial University, Harrogate, Tennessee, for information about the occupation of the Cumberland Gap, and the East Tennessee Historical Society in Knoxville for information about the occupation of East Tennessee.

I conducted much research on the opposing units at both the Wisconsin Historical Society on the campus of the University of Wisconsin at Madison and the Milwaukee Public Library, and I am grateful for their many hours of Yankee hospitality.

We acknowledge the contributions of the United States Military History Institute, Carlisle Barracks, Pennsylvania, and are grateful to the staff members of sites where the men of the 11th Tennessee fought, died, and sometimes remain for allowing us access to their historical collections. These include Cumberland Gap National Park, Cumberland Gap, Tennessee; Stones River National Battlefield, Murfreesboro, Tennessee; Chickamauga-Chattanooga National Battlefield, Fort Oglethorpe, Georgia; the Kennesaw Mountain National Battlefield, Kennesaw, Georgia; and the Carter House and Carnton Plantation of Franklin, Tennessee.

To all of you, and all others who have provided help and information along the way, we are deeply appreciative.

Preface

The American Civil War is perhaps the most defining event in the history of the United States. Now 150 years after the fact, the Civil War still evokes awe, curiosity, discussion, and deep emotion in those of us who have studied this most brutal and obscene of wars. There are scholars, historians, descendants, and hobbyists, among others, who have devoted their entire lives searching for a greater sense of knowledge and understanding regarding this event that forcibly galvanized the United States into the nation it has become.

Thankfully, many of the places the reader will encounter in this book are preserved. It is possible to visit the very spot, in many instances, where the events recorded in these pages occurred. In many cases, the terrain, obstacles, or breastworks are much as they were in the mid-1860s (e.g., John's Valley at Rockcastle, Kentucky; Brock Field at Chickamauga, Georgia; the "Dead Angle" at Kennesaw Mountain, Georgia; or the Carter House, at Franklin, Tennessee). We have visited these places scores of times, never tiring of them, but with each visit our desire to understand more about what happened increases. Even though the events are interesting, events do not occur in a vacuum. More interesting than the events, and more interesting than fiction, are the true stories of the people involved in those events.

Those personal stories are what capture our curiosity and fuel our imaginations. There are those among us who have the blood of Confederate or Federal soldiers flowing through their veins. Many of us long to know more of these sacrificial, often heroic, but always trying times of our ancestors. We, the authors, both descendants of soldiers who served in the 11th Tennessee Infantry, have dedicated much of our lives to recording the personal accounts of our ancestors and their comrades. We have endeavored to tell the soldiers' stories the way they saw and interpreted the events. We have attempted to construct a tapestry, within the larger context of the particular battle or even the war, that weaves hundreds of individual experiences into a single narrative that gives the reader some idea of what life was like, not only in the Confederate Army of Tennessee, but also on the regimental and company level. Here, we have researched and recorded the experiences of the soldiers of the 11th Tennessee Infantry for their posterity. We have attempted to do this fairly and openly and have left their original spelling and punctuation intact. This book contains the record of their deeds, some heroic, some cowardly, some joyous, some sad, some barbaric, some saintly, some atrocious, and some tragic, but nevertheless, it is an account of their contribution during the darkest days of our country's history. This is the story of the 11th Tennessee Volunteer Infantry, Vaughan's (Gordon's) Brigade, Cheatham's Division, Army of Tennessee, in the American Civil War.

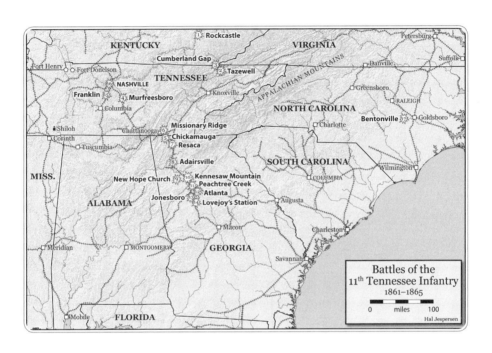

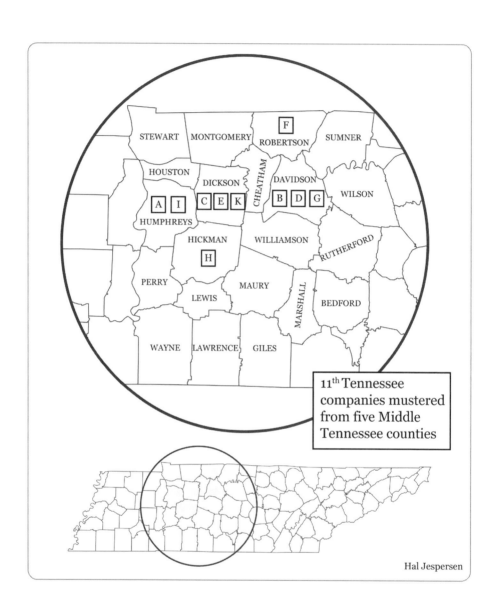

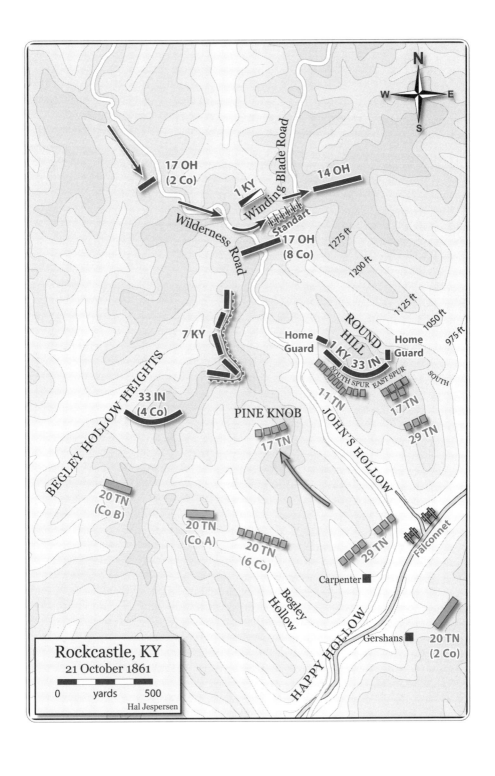

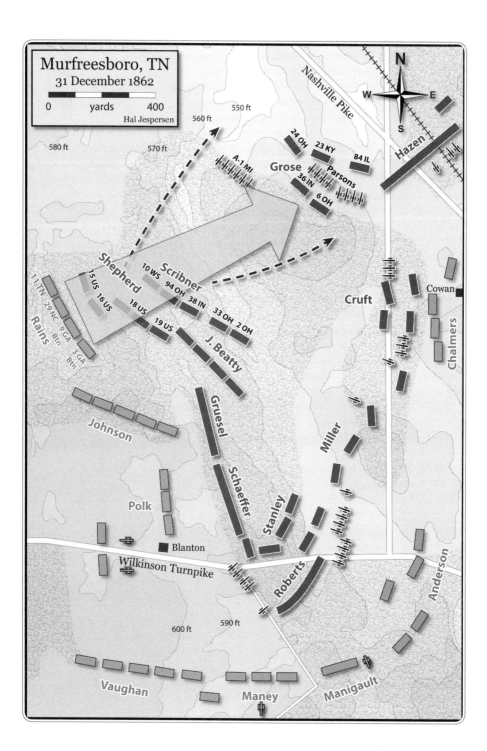

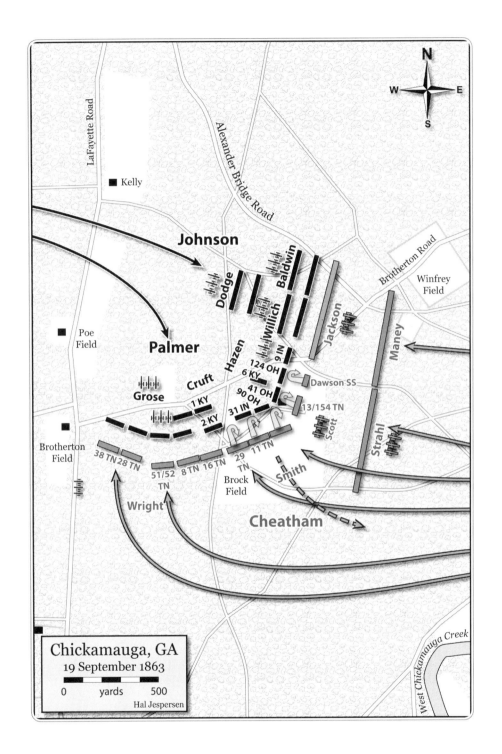

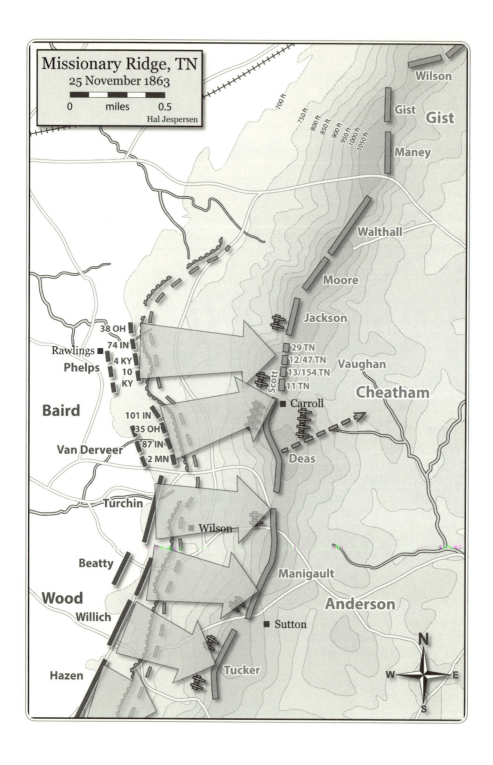

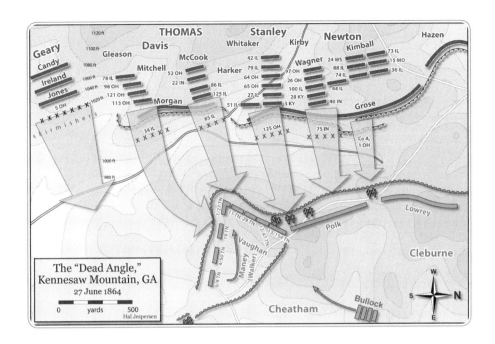
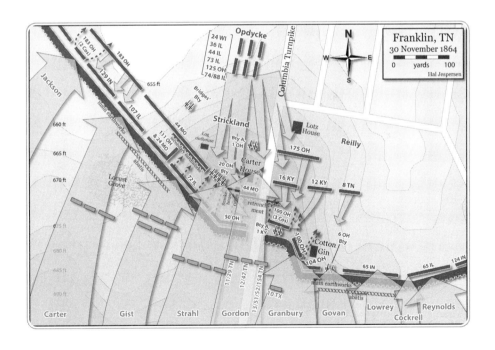

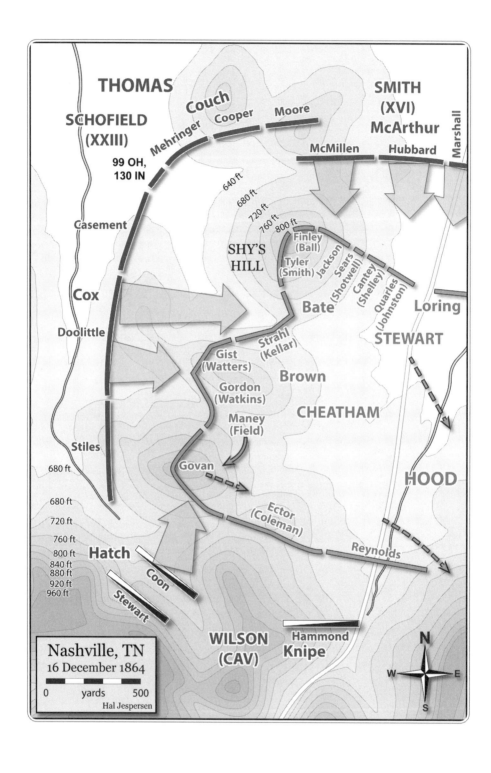

1

"For Tennessee and the South"

November 1860–Mid-May 1861

In the waning days of 1860, the prospect of war loomed heavy on the horizon as Abraham Lincoln was elected president. In his campaign, Lincoln vowed not to interfere with slavery in those states in which it already existed, but he did oppose its expansion. Over the preceding decades, Southern politicians had successfully shrouded the slavery issue and other secessionist viewpoints into states' rights rhetoric, and used states' rights as the platform to inflame the Southern populace.[1] Lately, repeated attempts at compromise between those who wanted to expand slavery and those who didn't had failed. Clement Eaton writes, "The tensions between the North and the South had become so great that the admirable art of compromise, which had hitherto preserved the American experiment of democratic government, failed to function in 1860–1861."[2] With Lincoln's election, South Carolina held the match to the powder keg as she threatened secession.

At this time Tennessee was largely pro-Union, but the heightened sense of militarism spreading across the South did not leave her untouched. On 10 November 1860, Samuel C. Godshall, a prominent Nashville resident and Mexican War veteran, wrote Governor William Henry Gist of South Carolina, offering to raise a battalion of Tennesseans from Davidson and the surrounding counties to go to South Carolina's aid should the need arise. In exchange for his services, the pugnacious Godshall requested a commission to the rank of captain and a subsequent promotion to major if he could raise the proffered battalion.[3]

Tensions escalated, and on Christmas Eve 1860, South Carolina became the first state to secede from the Union. Tennessee became increasingly embroiled in the political morasse, assuring Godshall that his home state would require his services. Within two weeks of South Carolina's secession, third-term Tennessee governor Isham G. Harris, a Democrat and an ardent supporter of slavery, convened

---

[1] Charles Adams, *When in the Course of Human Events: Arguing the Case for Southern Secession* (Lanham, MD: Rowman & Littlefield Publishers, 2000) 12.

[2] Clement Eaton, *A History of the Southern Confederacy* (New York: Free Press, 1965) 23.

[3] Samuel C. Godshall, "Letter to Honorable William H. Gist of South Carolina," 10 November 1860, M268, R160, 11th Tennessee Infantry Service Records, National Archives Records Administration, *Compiled Service Records of Confederate Soldiers Who Served in Organizations from the State of Tennessee*, Washington, DC: National Archives and Records Service, General Services Administration, 1960. Hereafter cited as "11th TISR."

the Tennessee General Assembly. In his 7 January address, Harris charged the Federal government with

> the systematic, wanton, and long continued agitation of the slavery question, with the actual and threatened aggressions of the Northern States and a portion of their people, upon the well-defined constitutional rights of the Southern citizen; the rapid growth and increase, in all the elements of power, of a purely sectional party, whose bond of union is uncompromising hostility to the rights and institutions of the fifteen Southern States, have produced a crisis in the affairs of the country, unparalleled in the history of the past, resulting already in the withdrawal from the Confederacy of one of the sovereignties which composed it, while others are rapidly preparing to move in the same direction.[4]

By February the crisis deepened, and Mississippi, Florida, Alabama, Georgia, Louisiana, and Texas seceded. All eyes turned to see what Virginia, Arkansas, North Carolina, Maryland, Kentucky, Missouri, and Tennessee would do.

Despite the ever-widening breach with the Federal government, not every Tennessean felt the same as Harris and Godshall. Even after the initial states withdrew, most Tennesseans still entertained hopes of peace. Jeremiah Batts, a young man of Robertson County, who later gained the rank of captain in the 11th Tennessee, was in secondary school at the time and never mentioned the impending crisis in his daily diary entries.[5] Felix K. Zollicoffer, a Whig and former Tennessee congressional representative, was elected to serve as a commissioner to the National Peace Conference, held in Washington DC on 4 February. Five days later, on 9 February, Tennesseans went to the polls to decide the question of separation and voted overwhelmingly (557,798 to 69,675) to remain in the Union.[6]

Over the next two months, however, tensions between Tennessee and the Federal government sharply increased. Despite the growing hostility, Union supporters met at the Davidson County Courthouse on 2 April to select representatives for the gubernatorial nominating convention scheduled for 2 May. Among the men appointed as delegates were James E. Rains, John H. Callender, J. Richard McCann, and George W. Darden. All of these men would later hold rank in the 11th Tennessee.[7]

In early April, as the drums of war tapped a cadence of death and destruction to the east, Confederate sentiment in the Volunteer State continued to rise. On 6

---

[4] "Call for a Referendum on a Tennessee Secession Convention" Speech of Governor Isham G. Harris 7 January 1861. AmericanCivilWar.com. http://www.americancivilwar.com/documents/isham_harris.html (accessed 25 April 2015).

[5] Phillip A. Gowan, *Byrns/Jackson: A Record of Their Probationary State*, 3 vols. (Brentwood, TN: P. A. Gowan, 1986) 3:152–59.

[6] Stanley F. Horn, *Tennessee's War: 1861–1865, Described by the Participants* (Nashville: Tennessee Civil War Centennial Commission, 1965) 15.

[7] "Union Meeting in Davidson Country," Nashville (TN) *Daily Patriot*, 2 April 1861.

April Mr. A. M. Waddle presented a large silk Confederate flag to Benjamin F. Cheatham, major general of the 2nd Division of the Tennessee Militia, and Samuel C. Godshall.[8] During this same week, several young men in Nashville, under the direction of Milton O. Brooks, organized the Beauregard Light Infantry.[9]

It wasn't long before the reality of war shook the country. On 12 April, Confederate artillery opened fire on a Federal fort in Charleston Harbor. In response to the Confederate attack on Fort Sumter, Lincoln issued his 15 April call for 75,000 volunteers to march into the South and put down the rebellion. This mandate was the end of Tennessee's alignment with the Union because Tennesseans refused to allow this perceived aggression to go unchecked. Tennessee would neither furnish troops nor allow Federal troops to be funneled across her highways into the cotton states. Governor Harris tersely replied to Lincoln's request for troops by saying, "Your dispatch of the 15th Inst. informing Me that Tennessee is called upon for two Regiments of Militia for immediate service is received. Tennessee will not furnish a single man for the purpose of Coercion, but 50,000 if necessary for the defense of 'our rights and those of our Southern brothers.'"[10]

Harris's statement set off a chain reaction across much of Tennessee, towns across the state began to whir with talk of war and secession. Local newspapers informed the citizenry of war events daily. A headline in the 13 April edition of the Nashville *Daily Gazette* proclaimed, "The Volunteer State in Motion—Her people Ready to Defend the South." Immediately below this column another title announced, "Tennessee Preparing for the Struggle."[11] This article announced the establishment of the Hermitage Guards, a military company under the command of Captain George E. Maney, a prominent Nashville lawyer. In addition, Southern preachers proclaimed the defense and rights of the South from their pulpits. Reverend W. M. Reed, pastor of the First Cumberland Presbyterian Church of Nashville, preached a sermon to his congregation titled "Right of Revolution Proven by the Bible."[12]

Moreover, Nashville merchants literally turned plowshares into swords as they laid aside the fabrication of farm implements and geared up to produce war material. The owners of the Nashville Plow Works, under the direction of Messrs. Sharp and Hamilton, converted their shops into sword-making facilities. The Claiborn Machine Works operated by T. M. Brennan, and Ellis & Moore, also a foundry, shifted production from producing boilers to casting cannons. In addition to the College Hill Arsenal, operated by L. T. Cunningham, the Nashville Arsenal,

---

[8] "A Splendid Flag," Nashville (TN) *Daily Gazette*, 7 April 1861.
[9] "New Military Company," Nashville (TN) *Daily Gazette*, 7 April 1861.
[10] Robert H. White, Steven V. Ash, and Wayne C. Moore, *Messages of the Governors of Tennessee 1857-1869* 8 vols. (Nashville: Tennessee Historical Commission, 1959) 5:272-73.
[11] "Tennessee Preparing for the Struggle," Nashville (TN) *Daily Gazette*, 13 April 1861.
[12] Ibid., 5 May 1861.

and numerous other firms in Davidson County began manufacturing other small arms.[13] The I. M. Singer sewing machine office at 45 College Street made Confederate flags to order;[14] as did Beck & Meyers, "plain and ornamental painters", on Broad Street;[15] and C. D. Benson & Company's Music Store at No. 20 Union Street.[16]

Although support for the Union waned, there were still some who hoped for reconciliation. Reverend John Rains, city treasurer of Nashville and father of James E. Rains (who would later become colonel of the 11th Tennessee), was earnestly opposed to secession. One day Reverend Rains witnessed a group tearing the Stars and Stripes from the Colonnade building at Riddleberger's corner. When the agitators threw the flag into the middle of the street, Rains rushed out, picked it up, and asked aid from the crowd in putting it back. He quickly discovered he was in the minority and had to desist.[17]

Captain Samuel Godshall published an invitation in the 18 April issue of the Nashville *Daily Patriot* to the men of Davidson County to enlist in the Beauregard Light Infantry.[18] J. Richard "Dick" McCann also began taking enlistments in his infantry company, the Cheatham Rifles. The following day, Captain George Maney stepped out of his law office on Cherry Street and addressed a group of gathered citizens about the importance of organizing military companies to prevent an invasion of Tennessee. After Maney's speech, the men who were willing to join his Hermitage Guards gathered in the street and marched in a parade led by a band. The throng returned to Cherry Street where additional speakers made soul-stirring speeches.[19] At 4:00 PM on the same day, a huge fifteen-star Confederate flag bearing the inscription, "A United South—One in Interest and One in Heart," was raised at the corner of Cherry and Church streets.[20]

In Nashville, as in other areas across the South, men and women both participated in the war effort. As men made speeches, marched in the streets, and enlisted in military companies, the women did their part by making, cutting, and sewing cloth for uniforms and flags. Mary Bradford, a young woman living near the

---

[13] Other firms included gun and locksmiths, Fall & Cunningham, McCall & Co., Samuel Vanleer and Co., and Macey & Hamilton; and watch and jewelry maker, W. H. Calhoun. *Tennessee State Gazetteer and Business Directory for 1860-61* (Nashville: John L. Mitchell, 1860) 211, 215, 222, 224; *Nashville City and Business Directory for 1860-61* (Nashville: L. P. Williams & Co., 1860) 70, 129.
[14] Ibid., 23 April 1861.
[15] "Flag of the Confederate States," Ibid., 25 April 1861.
[16] Ibid.
[17] Nashville (TN) *Weekly American*, 10 July 1879.
[18] "Attention, Beauregard Infantry," Nashville (TN) *Daily Patriot*, 18 April 1861.
[19] Ibid., 19 April 1861.
[20] Ibid., 20 April 1861.

Granny White Pike, led a group of local women to begin constructing a first national pattern flag to be presented to a regiment of infantry.

By 20 April, three companies of infantry, the Cheatham Rifles, the Hermitage Guards, and the Beauregard Light Infantry, were completely organized. J. Richard "Dick" McCann was the captain of the Cheatham Rifles. The company elected W. T. Cheatham, first lieutenant; James Everett, second lieutenant; Edward W. Clark, third lieutenant; and Minor Smith, color-bearer. After the organization was complete, the company assembled and marched through the streets of Nashville preceded by Horn's Silver Band.[21] Captain Samuel Godshall completed the formation of the Beauregard Light Infantry. The company, composed mainly of Irishmen, elected Samuel D. Nichol, first lieutenant; B. B. Leake, second lieutenant; Milton O. Brooks, third lieutenant; and W. W. Wetmore, orderly sergeant.[22] Captain George E. Maney finalized the Hermitage Guards. The boys in this company elected James E. Rains, first lieutenant, and Benjamin W. McCann, second lieutenant.[23]

On 22 April, Felix K. Zollicoffer, a former Whig congressional representative, traveled to Charlotte, the seat of Dickson County. There, he spoke on the condition of public affairs and encouraged the young men of Dickson County to rally to the Southern cause. The following day, Zollicoffer spoke on the same subject in Springfield, the seat of Robertson County.[24] Over the course of the next few days, prominent men in both counties responded to Zollicoffer's plea. In Dickson County, William Green began organizing the Dickson Rifles; William J. Mallory began enlisting men around Charlotte into the Dickson County Slashers, and William Thedford began enlisting young men in the area of Burns into a third company of infantry. In Robertson County, in the shadow of the Wessyngton tobacco plantation, James A. Long of Cedar Hill, sought enlistments for the Washington Guards.

On 25 April, Governor Harris delivered a second message to the Tennessee General Assembly in which he again elucidated and endorsed the Southern cause:

> The President of the United States—elected according to the forms of the Constitution, but upon principles openly hostile to its provisions—having wantonly inaugurated an internecine war between the people of the slave and non-slave holding States, I have convened you again at the seat of Government, for the purpose of enabling you to take such action as will most likely contribute to the defense of our rights, the preservation of our liberties, the sovereignty of the State, and the safety of our people; all of which are now in imminent peril by the

---

[21] Nashville (TN) *Daily Patriot*, 21 April 1861, 24 April 1861; Nashville (TN) *Daily Gazette*, 21 April 1861.
[22] "Cheatham Rifles," Nashville (TN) *Daily Patriot*, 21 April 1861.
[23] "The Hermitage Infantry," Ibid., 25 April 1861.
[24] Ibid., 19 April 1861.

usurpations of the authorities at Washington, and the unscrupulous fanaticism which runs riot throughout the Northern States.[25]

Governor Harris was not the only one aroused by the threat of Federal invasion; the people of Davidson County and the citizens of other counties across state were now becoming increasingly agitated as well. In Humphreys County, Josiah E. Pitts began organizing the Waverly Guards, while Hugh R. Lucas sought enlistments for the Gheber Guards.

On 26 April tension further escalated among Tennesseans due to an act of Northern treachery. An armed force of Federal soldiers seized the *C. E. Hillman*, a steamboat owned by a Tennessean, just above Cairo, Illinois, as it made its passage down the Mississippi River from St. Louis. In response, on 29 April, Governor Harris wrote a letter to Abraham Lincoln stating,

> This interruption of the free navigation of the Mississippi river and the seizure of property belonging to the State of Tennessee and her citizens, is aggressive and hostile, and without commenting upon the character and lawlessness of the outrage, it becomes my imperative duty to inquire by what authority the said acts were committed. I have therefore respectfully to request that the President shall inform me whether the same was done under the instructions of the Federal Government, or is approved by said Government.[26]

President Lincoln sent a hasty reply to Governor Harris about the incident. In his rebuttal, Lincoln disavowed any "official information of such seizure."[27] However, the president did say that "assuming the capture was made, and that the cargo consisted chiefly of Munitions of War owned by the State of Tennessee and passing into the control of its governor, this government avows the seizure."[28] Lincoln then justified the confiscation:

> A legal call was made upon the Said Governor of Tennessee to furnish a company of Militia to suppress an insurrection against the United States, which call said Governor responded to by a refusal couched in disrespectful and malicious language—this Government therefore infers that Munitions of War passing into the hands of said Governor, and intended to be used against the United States, and

---

[25] "Senate Journal of the Second Extra Session of the Thirty-Third General Assembly of the State of Tennessee, which Convened at Nashville on Thursday, the 25th Day of April, A. D. 1861," http://docsouth.unc.edu/imls/tennessee/tennessee.html (accessed 25 April 2015).

[26] *Isham G. Harris to Abraham Lincoln*, 29 April 1861, Abraham Lincoln Papers, Series 1, General Correspondence, 1833–1916, Library of Congress. Microfilm Reel 21

[27] *Abraham Lincoln in Reply to Isham G. Harris*, 11 May 1861, Abraham Lincoln Papers, Series 1, General Correspondence, 1833–1916, Library of Congress. Microfilm Reel 22.

[28] Ibid.

the government will not indulge the weakness of allowing it, so long as it has the power to prevent.[29]

Thus, Tennessee was drawn yet closer to the point of the bayonet.

Thomas P. Bateman, another Mexican War veteran and a prominent lawyer in Centerville, the seat of Hickman County, was commissioned by Governor Harris to raise a company of infantry. Bateman circulated the following proclamation through-out the area:

TO ARMS!

> We are now in a state of revolution, and Southern soil must be defended, and we should not stop to ask, Who brought this war? Or, Who is at fault? But let us go and do battle for our native, or adopted soil, and settle the question as to who is to blame.
>
> I have the acceptance of a company to go to the South and fight for Tennessee and the South, provided it can be mustered into service between the 1st and 10th of May next. Come forward and enroll yourselves immediately at my office in the town of Centerville.[30]

Bateman hung the following announcement in his office, which bears the signatures of many men:

> We the undersigned, agree to volunteer for the term of twelve months to serve in the military service of the State of Tennessee, subject to the order of I. G. Harris, Governor of the State of Tennessee, to serve in any part of the South that we may be needed, or on the borders thereof to defend the State of Tennessee, and the rights of the South. April 23rd, 1861.[31]

As the men of Nashville enlisted to defend the South, weapons, uniforms, and other military equipment were highly desired commodities. The Nashville city council took immediate action by appropriating $100,000.00 for the defense of the city.[32] Toward the end of April a large number of boxed muskets were discovered in the warehouse of Fisher, Wheless & Company. These desperately needed long arms, produced at the Harper's Ferry Arsenal in 1826, went immediately to equip the infantry being raised in the city. One newspaper correspondent reported, "They are handy things to have about at this particular time."[33] Due to the scarcity of materials in Nashville, the Beauregard Light Infantry appointed a commissioner to

---

[29] Ibid.

[30] W. J. D. Spence and David L. Spence, *History of Hickman County, Tennessee* (1900; reprint, Columbia, TN: P-Vine Press, 1981) 180.

[31] Ibid.

[32] "Meeting of the City Council," Nashville (TN) Daily Gazette, 25 April 1861. Ibid.

[33] "In Good Time," Ibid.

travel to Louisville, Kentucky, to procure uniforms and equipment for their company.[34] By 26 April, Davidson County alone could field 4,000 troops.[35]

In the opening days of May, many of the companies raised across the state, now fully organized, traveled to Nashville to tender their services to Governor Harris. On 2 May, the 1st Tennessee Infantry regiment was organized. Although the Hermitage Guards was not one of the companies of the 1st Tennessee Regiment, Captain George E. Maney of that company was elected their colonel. Upon Maney's acceptance, he resigned from the Hermitage Guards, and two days later, 1st Lieutenant James E. Rains acceded to the captaincy of the company in his place.[36]

James Edwards Rains was born in Nashville, Tennessee, on 10 April 1833. In 1854, at the age of twenty-one, he graduated from Yale University. Following his formal education, he moved to Cheatham County, Tennessee, where he managed and taught at the Millwood Institute for about two years. After this, Rains returned to Nashville, where he began to practice law. As he gained popularity, he became city attorney and was the associate editor of the Nashville *Banner*. On 22 June 1858, the brilliant young lawyer married Ida Yeatman, and in 1860, won the election of district attorney general for Davidson, Williamson, and Sumner counties. When Rains took command of the Hermitage Guards, he continued drilling the men in preparation for the prospect of war.[37]

On Wednesday, 1 May, men in the 1st Civil District of Dickson County enlisted in William Thedford's Company at Sil Wiley's house.[38] The following day, Thedford held a meeting of interested men at the old voting grounds in Burns in the 4th District of Dickson County to enlist additional men in his company.[39] The junior officers for Captain Thedford's Company were F. F. Tidwell, first lieutenant; Moses H. Meek, second lieutenant; and Josiah Tidwell, third lieutenant.[40] As Thedford worked hard to raise his unit, Captain Josiah Pitts, the son of the well-

---

[34] "The Beauregards," Ibid.

[35] "Military Enthusiasm," Ibid., 26 April 1861.

[36] Nashville (TN) *Daily Patriot*, 4 May 1861.

[37] James E. Rains, M268 R162, 11th TISR; Ezra J. Warner, *Generals in Gray: Lives of the Confederate Commanders* (Baton Rouge: Louisiana State University, 1987) 250; Goodspeed Brothers, *The Goodspeed Histories of Montgomery, Robertson, Humphreys, Stewart, Dickson, Cheatham, Houston Counties of Tennessee* (Columbia, TN: Woodward & Stinson, 1972) 971.

[38] Clayton H. Yates, Kentucky Confederate Pension Application #1574, https://dspace.kdla.ky.gov/xmlui/handle/10602/7359 (accessed 25 February 2015).

[39] J. S. Welch, "Veteran Questionnaire," in Gustavus W. Dyer, John Trotwood Moore, Colleen Morse Elliott and Louise Armstrong Moxley, *Tennessee Civil War Veterans Questionnaires*, 5 vols (Easley, SC: Southern Historical Press, 1985) 5:2157.

[40] Josiah C. Alspaugh, "Reminiscences of Company A, 11th Tennessee," *Confederate Veteran* 18/11 (November 1910): 506.

known Methodist firebrand, Reverend Fountain Elliott Pitts, was completing the organization of the Waverly Guards in Humphreys County.[41] Officers for this unit included James B. Pitts (Josiah's brother), first lieutenant; William I. White, second lieutenant; and William Bowen, third lieutenant.

On the morning of 4 May Captain Dick McCann assembled the Cheatham Rifles and marched them to Camp Harding, an induction center established at the Nashville fairgrounds just west of the state capital.[42] The men took their places, spread out their bedrolls, and made themselves comfortable. Two days later, on 6 May, the Tennessee State Legislature proposed "An Ordinance for the Adoption of the Constitution of the Provisional Government of the Confederate States of America," subject to ratification by the electorate of the state.[43] On this same day, the Waverly Guards left their homes in Humphreys County, and marched to Charlotte, Tennessee, where they spent the night. The following morning they resumed their march toward Nashville. They arrived at Camp Harding on 8 May, where they took oaths to defend the state of Tennessee.[44]

Captain Thomas P. Bateman ordered his Hickman Guards to assemble on 10 May in Centerville. Philip Van Horn Weems, the owner of the renowned Bon Aqua Springs, served as first lieutenant. Other officers included Richard Cross Gordon, as second lieutenant; and Alexander H. Vaughan, another Centerville lawyer, third lieutenant.[45] After uniting at the courthouse on the town square, they marched out of town on their way to Nashville with the fifer playing the jaunty tune "The Girl I Left Behind Me."[46]

Earlier that same morning, Jerome Spence and James H. "Tack" Carothers left their homes at Vernon on the Piney River in Hickman County to join Bateman's Company. Upon leaving their homes at about 10:00 AM, the two recruits stopped at Miss Ella Smith's school where they visited with the girls for about an hour. They then bade the girls farewell and continued their journey to Bon Aqua Springs, where they met up with the remainder of the company. The boys spent the night at the springs agreeably enough, but one of the Hickman County recruits wrote in his journal that evening, "Though our dearest ones were left behind, we tried to [pass]

---

[41] "Departure of Volunteers," Nashville (TN) *Daily Gazette*, 5 May 1861.

[42] Ibid.

[43] Charles A. Miller, *Official and Political Manual of the State of Tennessee* (Nashville: Marshall & Bruce, 1890) 106.

[44] William Carroll Pullen, "Veteran Questionnaire," in Dyer, et al., *Tennessee Civil War Veterans Questionnaires*, 4:1781–82; William C. Pullen, *Reminiscences of a Confederate Soldier*, unpublished manuscript, transcr. and ed. Mary McCrary. Manuscript in possession of Jennie Lee Monroe, McEwen, TN.

[45] John Berrien Lindsley, *Military Annals of Tennessee: Confederate* (1886; facsimile of the first edition, Wilmington, NC: Broadfoot Publishing, 1995) 292.

[46] Spence and Spence, *History of Hickman County, Tennessee*, 180.

the hours away in dreaming of our future happiness with the loved ones of our bosom. The night is sad."[47]

At 6:00 the next morning, the company arose and continued their journey toward Nashville. Although many of the men traveled in horse-drawn buggies, their progress was slow, and at nightfall, they spent the night in a barn on the property of Belle Vue, a farm near the Harpeth River owned by Mrs. DeMoss. After settling in for the evening, several of the boys made speeches before they went to sleep. One observer said, "You had better reckon we had a time of it. Over one hundred slept in the barn."[48] On the following day, the Hickman Guards proceeded a short distance from Belle Vue to the Nashville and Northwestern Railroad and loaded onto a train, which transported them the final few miles into Nashville. While the boys were taking their places in the cars, a great concourse of citizens had gathered to cheer them on. Emotions ran high. The bystanders waved handkerchiefs and Bonnie Blue Flags, while others threw flowers into the transports of their departing defenders. Everyone expected these men to return as heroes from the field of battle; few dreamed of the great horror awaiting them. When the men had settled into the cars, the train slowly pulled out of sight and headed for downtown Nashville. The train gathered speed as it clambered down the rickety tracks toward the state capital. The citizen-soldiers gazed dreamily across the timbered landscape with thoughts miles away.[49]

One by one, the companies of volunteers arrived at Nashville. Almost forty-eight hours after leaving Centerville, the Hickman Guards rolled into the city, reaching downtown Nashville at 10:00 AM. The Waverly Guards met the Hickman Countians at the train depot and escorted them to Camp Harding, where about eight hundred soldiers were already gathered. The members of the Hickman Guards went to their quarters located on the second story of a large shelter. The Beauregard Light Infantry, more commonly known as the "Bull Pups," were on the lower level. One observer stated that you could hear them "growling now and then."[50]

After the Hickman Guards had spent the first night in their new quarters, they awoke to a rainy morning. Despite the unfavorable weather, the boys found various activities to pass the time. George Marable played chuck-a-luck with Billy Bowen, one of his lieutenants. Sam Godshall, captain of the disorderly Bull Pups, had two

---

[47] W. Jerome D. Spence, *The Travels, Troubles, Pleasures and Pastimes of Jerome D. Spence of Dunnington, Tennessee*, 10 May 1861, unpublished diary 10 May–25 November 1861, copy of manuscript in possession of Gary W. Waddey.
[48] Ibid., 11 May 1861.
[49] Ibid.
[50] Ibid., 12–13 May 1861.

of his men on a work detail as a disciplinary measure for some of their earlier misconduct.[51]

The next morning, 14 May, the boys awoke in proper military fashion to the tapping drum of William Kirkland of the Waverly Guards. At this signal, the men rose, cleared the sleep from their eyes, dressed, and cooked breakfast. After breakfast, many activities of the previous day resumed. Foot races, euchre, and wrestling were popular exploits among the men. Some, not content to stay in their encampment, went to explore Nashville. While in their wanderings throughout the state capital, many of the boys bought pistols or bowie knives from local merchants to take with them to the field of battle.[52]

Although these activities were enough to keep most of the men occupied, they were not enough for Godshall's Bull Pups. As was becoming commonplace, two of the Bull Pups were engaged in what one observer called, "a devil of a fight." One of the participants was a small man, the other, a very large fellow armed with a knife. Immediately, their heavyset 1st lieutenant, Sam Nichol, began wading through the crowd that had surrounded the brawlers, casting men to either side. Nichol stepped between the contenders and ordered them to quit. The men disregarded their lieutenant's order and went at it again. Not to be outdone, Nichol threatened to put them under guard if they did not desist. The smaller soldier, regaining some sense, backed off. The large man, however, was drunk and refused to obey. Without hesitation, Nichol seized him by the throat and shoved him backward. In a fit of rage, the drunken soldier lunged at the lieutenant. In one quick motion, Nichol dropped the soldier to the ground and called for a rope. With the rope immediately procured, the lieutenant tied up the loud-mouthed scoundrel and left him harmlessly threatening and swearing on the floor.[53]

Despite their silence for the time being, the incident was not over. Just before noon, some other members of the Bull Pups were engaged in yet another row. Apparently, during the previous fight some contention had arisen between two other parties. Not letting it die, at the first opportunity they resumed their altercation. This time, Captain Godshall and Lieutenant Nichol both intervened to put an end to the scrap. Finally, dinnertime arrived, and the men settled down enough to eat. After the meal was finished, the Cheatham Rifles, the Beauregard Light Infantry, the Waverly Guards, and the Hickman Guards were assembled, medically examined, and sworn into the service of the Provisional Army of the State of Tennessee.[54]

Now officially soldiers, the men collected their effects and marched back to the depot. The boys climbed aboard the awaiting trains. Once the men were aboard,

---

[51] Ibid., 13 May 1861.
[52] Ibid., 14 May 1861.
[53] Ibid.
[54] Ibid.

General Cheatham boarded, and the steam locomotive hissed and chugged away from downtown, crossed the Cumberland River, passed through Edgefield, and continued northwestwardly up the Edgefield and Kentucky Railroad until the pinnacle of the capitol, the crowning jewel of the Nashville skyline, disappeared from the horizon.[55]

As these companies cleared out, other companies arrived at Camp Harding. On 14 May 102 members of the Dickson Rifles, under the command of Captain William Green, arrived in Nashville.[56] Officers for this group included W. J. Mathis, first lieutenant; W. H. Roberts, second lieutenant; and Sanford Hendricks, third lieutenant. Likewise, on 15 May, Captain James E. Rains assembled the Hermitage Guards and marched them to Camp Harding.[57] Three days later, on 18 May, the Dickson Slashers, the second company from Dickson County, arrived by the train of the Nashville and Northwestern Railroad and at 2:30 PM left the depot for Camp Harding. The officers of this company were William J. Mallory, captain; R. A. W. James, first lieutenant; William M. Kirk, second lieutenant; and Samuel Brown, third lieutenant.[58]

Later that night, the Gheber Guards, 90 strong, of Humphreys County arrived by the Northwestern Railroad and took their places at the fairgrounds. They were commanded by Captain Hugh R. Lucas, lieutenants L. Castillo Barfield, Leroy Traylor, John D. Woodward, and John Todd, and by orderly sergeant Nat Scholes.[59]

The Washington Guards comprised men from Robertson County and were commanded by Captain James A. Long. Aside from Long, their officers were Martin V. Morris, first lieutenant, W. H. Winn, second lieutenant, and Samuel J. Alley, third lieutenant.[60]

On the morning of 24 May, the men of Dickson County who had enlisted at Squire James Davidson's house gathered in Burns.[61] As in all of the companies, many of Thedford's men were leaving home for the first time. Leaving home that morning was a heart-wrenching experience for Private Clayton Yates:

> My, that was an awful ordeal, that bright May morning, to bid my dear mother goodbye. We, the family, had set down to breakfast and it was indeed a sad time. When my mother had scarcely poured the coffee she could restrain her grief no

---

[55] Spence, *Travels*, 14 May 1861; Nashville (TN) *Daily Gazette*, 15 May 1861.
[56] "Dixie in Motion," Nashville (TN) *Daily Gazette*, 15 May 1861.
[57] "Gone to Camp," Ibid., 16 May 1861.
[58] "Dixon County Slashers," Ibid., 19 May 1861.
[59] "Three Cheers for the Gallant Sons of Humphreys County," Nashville (TN) *Daily Gazette*, 19 May 1861; Lindsley, *Military Annals*, 291.
[60] Lindsley, *Military Annals*, 292.
[61] Moses Garton, "Veteran Questionnaire," in Dyer et al., *Tennessee Civil War Veterans Questionnaires*, 3:889.

longer, when she exclaimed, "O, how can I give up my boy," so there was little, if any, breakfast partaken of that morning. And I started out for Burns Station. I had gone perhaps 50 yards, looking back I saw that my mother had fainted and they were carrying her into the house. It was then that the fountain of my tears were breaking up, and I wept as I never had before.[62]

When Yates and the other boys arrived in Burns, a great crowd turned out to see them off. As the boys and families said their final goodbyes, Captain Thedford ordered his volunteers to form a line, and in the path of others, they marched down the Charlotte Road toward Nashville. After the company marched about seven miles, they arrived at White Bluff and made camp for the night.[63] The following morning, the men resumed their journey toward Nashville and as they left White Bluff, they continued their march and that afternoon, arrived at Kingston Springs, a small town on the Nashville and Northwestern Railroad. Josiah C. Alspaugh, a recruit of the company stated, "[At Kingston Springs] we were put on board a train of flat cars and carried to Nashville."[64]

---

[62] Clayton H. Yates, "Reminiscences of the Civil War," Mayfield (KY) *Daily Messenger*, date unknown.

[63] Alspaugh, "Company A," 506.

[64] Ibid.

2

"Drilling and Otherwise Preparing for War"

Mid-May–24 July 1861

Late in the evening of 14 May the steam locomotive transporting the Cheatham Rifles, the Beauregard Light Infantry, the Hickman Guards, and the Waverly Guards chugged along to a marked cadence as it snaked over the green rolling hills away from Nashville and moved northward toward the Kentucky state line. By 7:30 PM, the train was in sight of Camp Cheatham, the newly established training grounds for Tennessee troops just outside of Springfield in Robertson County. As the train rolled to a halt, the boys hopped off the cars and unloaded their equipment.[1]

While awaiting orders, the volunteers surveyed the surrounding countryside as the sun began dipping below the western horizon. The campground lay over relatively level spacious fields with a bountiful water supply from nearby Spring Creek. Other landmarks included the buildings of the Kinney distillery, a large wooden rail trestle spanning the creek, and small tents dotting the landscape outlining the camps of the 1st and 3rd Tennessee regiments already present.[2]

Soon, the captains ordered the men to take their equipment to a designated location within the camp. Once there, the boys broke out their gear and set up their tents by companies. William Frazier of the Hickman Guards stated that his company set up 150 tents, and that General Ben Cheatham, commander and namesake of the post, personally assisted them.[3] The men, inexperienced at setting up a military camp, much less doing so in the dark, finally got their quarters in order. After the men had set up their tents, they were free to cook supper. At 9:00 PM, William Kirkland of the Waverly Guards beat his drum, the signal for the boys to get some sleep. Later that night, raindrops pelting the canvas sides of the tents awakened the weary boys. The raw recruits had failed to dig ditches around their tents before going to sleep. With no diversionary channel, the water began running over the ground and soon streamed underneath their tent walls. "So we could stand or sit up all the night or lie down in mud as we chose," said the aggravated Frazier.

---

[1] "Army Correspondence of the Gazette," Nashville (TN) *Daily Gazette*, 19 May 1861.

[2] Colonels Rains, Maney of the 1st Tennessee, and Brown of the 3rd Tennessee would all be promoted to generals as the war progressed; Sam Watkins, *Co. "Aytch" First Tennessee Regiment or a Side Show of the Big Show* (Franklin, TN: Providence House, 2007) 8.

[3] William G. Frazier, "Veteran Questionnaire," in Dyer et al., *Tennessee Civil War Veterans Questionnaires*, 2:853, 2:856.

"I tried both but never slept a wink [the] 1st night."[4] Immediately after breakfast the next morning, the boys dug trenches around their tents to prevent a repeat of the previous night. After the ditches were dug, they spread straw on the ground inside their tents and then covered the straw with blankets on which they slept. As the weeks passed and days grew warmer, the summer sun beat down on the fields, causing the tents to become very warm.[5]

Meanwhile, back at Camp Harding in Nashville, on 16 May, the Hermitage Guards and Dickson Rifles boarded the train of the Edgefield and Kentucky Railroad and headed to Camp Cheatham. A large number of Nashville citizens turned out to witness their departure. According to observers, the scene was very emotional and dry eyes were scarce. Later that day, these companies arrived at Camp Cheatham and set up their encampment in proximity to the other companies.[6]

By Friday, 17 May, after the initial companies had been at Camp Cheatham for only three days, the monotony of camp life had already started nagging the contentious Bull Pups. General Orders forbade whiskey, but as one soldier from Camp Cheatham wrote, "[It] is not a very scarce article here. Although it is contrary to Order No.— I forget which, yet a large amount of it is smuggled in, and sold to the thirsty soldiers."[7] Despite orders to the contrary, one of the Bull Pups had obtained whiskey and became intoxicated. While the remainder of the company ate dinner, this Irishman rose, gaining everyone's attention. As the other soldiers of the company ate, the rogue, who wielded a butcher knife with a ten-inch blade, launched into a tirade. The longer he talked, the more indignant he became. Soon, he began carelessly waving the knife around. One of the officers approached him and demanded the knife. The riotous Irishman informed the officer, "none but a d--- coward gave up his sword."[8] He went on to tell the officer that Cornwallis gave up his sword, but a Bull Pup was better than Cornwallis and "when I give up this knife it will be in your d--- bosom."[9] The drunken Bull Pup continued babbling about his sorrows, placed the tip of the knife against his breast, and drew his right fist high above the hilt to drive the blade deep into his chest. The Bull Pup's fist was above the knife when a nearby comrade intervened. The soldier who stayed the blow received an ugly but relatively minor wound on his hand. The frenzied Irishman, whose life had just been saved, then turned upon him. The soldier

---

[4] Ibid., 2:856.

[5] Frazier, "Veteran Questionnaire," in Dyer et al., *Tennessee Civil War Veterans Questionnaires*, 2:856; W. Jerome D. Spence, *The Travels, Troubles, Pleasures and Pastimes of Jerome D. Spence of Dunnington, Tennessee*, 15 May 1861, unpublished diary 10 May–25 November 1861, copy of manuscript in possession of Gary W. Waddey.

[6] Nashville (TN) *Daily Patriot*, 17 May 1861.

[7] "Letter from Camp Cheatham," Nashville (TN) *Republican Banner*, 2 July 1861.

[8] Spence, *Travels*, 17 May 1861.

[9] Ibid.

managed to escape, as Orderly Sergeant Bill Wetmore intervened, seizing the offender by the wrist, while someone else disarmed him. One of the officers arrested the inebriated soldier, and the sentries hauled him off to the guardhouse. "When he gets sober I do not think he will wish to die, for life is the sweetest of all sweet things. It is sweet even to a Bull Pup," said an observer.[10] After the commotion had subsided and dinner was finished, Captain Bateman took the Hickman Guards out on the parade ground and drilled them for about two hours.[11]

On Saturday, 18 May, Brigadier General R. C. Foster replaced General Cheatham as commander of the camp. Later that day, just as a train was departing, one of the Bull Pups slipped into one of the cars. Lieutenant Samuel Nichol happened to see him and pursued him onto the train to prevent the desertion. Before the train had proceeded very far, the lieutenant had informed the conductor of the situation. Soon the conductor notified the engineer, who stopped the train, and Nichol returned to camp with the would-be deserter in custody.[12]

In the afternoon, one of the Hickman Guards went to the creek to wash his clothes. Due to the ground-in mud, it took him about four hours to get one shirt, one pair of drawers, and one pair of socks clean. When he had finished washing, it was time for supper. After the meal, many of the boys enjoyed fiddling, dancing, and singing by Horatio "Rash" Witty of the Waverly Guards. One of the songs that Witty sang brought tears to the eyes of the homesick soldiers. Although the boys were sad, they were compelled to laugh at the next number, which Witty immediately began. After the revelry of the evening, the boys went to bed. The camp was silent except for the tread of the sentry and the many voices of nature that broke the peace of the still summer night.[13]

The next morning, as was now customary, the men were awakened for roll call and breakfast. Soon after the meal, a heavy rain began and continued through the day. Because of the rain, the boys chose to stay inside or at least near their tents. An observer reported that he heard swearing across the camp and could occasionally hear singing. Some of the men entertained themselves by playing cards. Others read their Bibles, and others thought about loved ones as they wrote letters back home.[14]

Although this was only General Foster's second day as commander of the camp, he had already noticed that absenteeism was a problem among the troops. On 19 May, Foster issued General Order Number 3, which mandated that all absentees

---

[10] Ibid.
[11] Ibid.
[12] Ibid., 18 May 1861.
[13] Ibid.
[14] Ibid., 19 May 1861.

return to camp, and instructed all commanding officers to enforce the order. Later in the evening, Governor Harris visited the camp.[15]

On Tuesday evening, 21 May, the men had gathered around listening to Rash Witty's music. While Witty was singing, the boys heard a noise off in the distance that sounded like two dogs barking. Immediately, the boys sprang from their seats to investigate the commotion. When they arrived at the place of the disturbance, to their astonishment, they saw two members of the Bull Pups imitating barking dogs. One observer said that they "were Bull Pups true to their name."[16] With an audience now gathered around them, the barking Bull Pups, who had stolen the show from Witty, entertained the troops for some time. Subsequently, William Kirkland tapped his drum, the signal for the boys to retire for the evening.[17]

The men arose the next morning at the specified time. As usual after roll call, breakfast was cooked, and the soldiers began eating. While the meal was in progress, Sergeant Spence saw the twenty-two year old Thomas Jenkins, one of the Bull Pups, whom he referred to as "a notorious robber," running up the hill away from a supply wagon carrying a box of oysters. Spence called out, "Hello Jenkins, how much did your oysters cost you?" Jenkins responded, "Cost, hell, I forgot to ask about it. Cost me nothing."[18] Spence alleged that Jenkins was a continual problem. On one occasion, Spence recalled that Jenkins took a bottle of whiskey from Howell Huddleston. On another occasion, Jenkins had the nerve to go into Captain Pitts's marquee tent, and while he was talking with the captain, stole a cup of sugar, took it to his tent, and then returned the empty cup to the chest from where he had taken it. At another time, he stole a knife from a comrade. Upon hearing the fellow offer a fifty cents reward for the knife, Jenkins returned it and took the reward money.[19]

Aside from drill and the other routine activities of the following day, several women passed about the camp selling pies, cakes, and butter. While the women peddled their goods, Andrew Gravitt and George Lancaster of the Hickman Guards contended in a few wrestling matches. Lancaster threw Gravitt first, and then Gravitt threw Lancaster, resulting in a tie. When this match was over, Robert Work and James Lunsford (also of the Hickman Guards) wrestled four or five falls.

---

[15] Jill Garrett and Marise P. Lightfoot, *The Civil War in Maury County, Tennessee* (Columbia, TN: s.n., 1966) 11; Spence, *Travels*, 19 May 1861.

[16] Spence, *Travels*, 21 May 1861.

[17] Ibid.

[18] Ibid., 22 May 1861.

[19] Ibid.; Thomas G. Jenkins, M268 R161, 11th Tennessee Infantry Service Records, National Archives Records Administration, *Compiled Service Records of Confederate Soldiers Who Served in Organizations from the State of Tennessee*, Washington, DC: National Archives and Records Service, General Services Administration, 1960. Hereafter cited as 11th TISR. Although considered by his comrades to be a thief, ironically, Jenkins would be assigned extra duty in the quartermaster department in September 1861.

One soldier reminisced in his diary that evening that "Lunsford got the best of it and Work became insulted."[20]

As companies were organized and sworn into state service, they were forwarded on to Camp Cheatham. By 19 May, two additional companies from Dickson County, the Dickson County Slashers and William Thedford's Company, had arrived from Camp Harding.[21]

On 26 May, at about 7:00 AM, tragedy struck the ranks of the Hickman Guards. A young soldier named Ambrose N. Chamberlain succumbed to illness after a ten-day struggle. Orderlies placed Chamberlain's body inside a coffin, and the boys proceeded to the grave in double file. As the men marched solemnly in procession behind the coffin, no one said a word. One of the soldiers reflected in his journal later that evening, "No kind brother was near to watch his dying struggles; no kind father was near to hear his last request; no kind sister near to smooth his dying pillow. *Oh! He had no pillow*. And no kind mother was near to drop a tear on his silent grave or raise a prayer to Him who rules in behalf of her departed son."[22]

Perhaps a deeper sense of mortality began to grip the men, as they were only sixteen days into their terms of service and had already lost a comrade. Little did they know that before leaving Camp Cheatham, many others would die. These early deaths resulted not from Yankee shot and shell but from a far greater enemy—disease. Private Frazier of the Hickman Guards commented, "Soon the measles broke out in camp. having no hospital. One poor man died at the spring and 8 others of the Hickman county guards died here and were buried here."[23]

By this time, discontentment began to rise in the ranks at Camp Cheatham. One of the Hickman Guards reported, "The orders issued by Gen. R. C. Foster are so very astringent that the boys have become very much dissatisfied, they talk very strong of leaving, not one at a time, but all together."[24] The soldier went on to explain, "He will not permit us to cross the bridge to go to the spring for water. Yesterday, about thirty of the Bull Pups took with the leaving. Several of the Cheatham Riflemen have absconded."[25]

On Monday morning, 27 May, Captain James A. Long who had organized a local Robertson County company at Cedar Hill, received instructions from Adolphus Heiman, assistant adjutant general for General Foster. Heiman instructed Long not to take his eighty-seven-member Washington Guards to Camp Harding

---

[20] Spence, *Travels*, 23 May 1861; Gravitt died a few weeks later at Camp Cheatham, probably from disease.
[21] Nashville (TN) *Daily Gazette*, 19 May 1861.
[22] Spence, *Travels*, 26 May 1861.
[23] Frazier, "Veteran Questionnaire," in Dyer et al., *Tennessee Civil War Veterans Questionnaires*, 2:856.
[24] Spence, *Travels*, 26 May 1861.
[25] Ibid.

in Nashville, but to move directly to Camp Cheatham and join the other nine companies assembled there.[26]

At 9:00 on following morning, as Captain Long's Washington Guards were getting acclimated to the camp, Captain Bateman took the Hickman Guards out to target practice with their antiquated flintlock muskets. Bateman's men fixed their targets and about ninety men took their places on the firing line. The soldiers were to shoot at a target scarcely fifteen yards away. After the boys fired their weapons and the smoke finally cleared, much to their dismay, they discovered that only seven men in the entire company had hit the target.[27]

With the arrival of the Washington Guards, Special Field Order 21, dated 31 May, instructed the ten companies present at Camp Cheatham to constitute into a regiment. At 4:00 PM on this date, the specified ten companies held an election to select their colonel and other regimental field and staff officers.[28] Captain James E. Rains of the Hermitage Guards defeated Captain Josiah Pitts of the Waverly Guards for colonel. The boys elected Captain Thomas P. Bateman of the Hickman Guards as lieutenant colonel over Captain William Green of the Dickson Rifles and Captain Samuel C. Godshall of the Bull Pups. Captain Hugh R. Lucas of the Waverly Guards beat out Captain Dick McCann of the Cheatham Rifles for the position of major. When the election was over, the winners made eloquent speeches amid the cheering of the men. There was some grumbling in the ranks, however. The Cheatham Rifles were miffed at the Hickman Guards because the Cheatham Rifles supported Bateman for lieutenant colonel, but the Hickman Guards did not return the favor by supporting McCann for major.[29]

When the organization was complete, the regiment, initially called the 2nd Tennessee Infantry, was made up strictly of Middle Tennesseans: three companies were from Davidson County, three were from Dickson County, one was from Hickman County, two were from Humphreys County, and one was from Robertson County. On the same day as their organization, Colonel Rains received his first written order as commander of the regiment. Special Order 29 instructed him to proceed at once to Nashville to obtain the necessary requisitions to fully arm and equip his regiment.[30]

Now an organized regiment, the daily routine for the volunteers began at 4:00 AM when they were awakened to answer roll call. After the sergeants had taken roll,

---

[26] Special Order 15, 27 May 1861, MF 109, *Order Book for Confederate Volunteers at Camp Cheatham*, Tennessee Historical Society Miscellaneous Volumes, 1805–1918, Tennessee State Library and Archives, Nashville, TN (hereafter cited as *Order Book*); Nashville (TN) *Daily Gazette*, 19 May 1861.

[27] Spence, *Travels*, 28 May 1861.

[28] Special Order 21, 31 May 1861, MF 109, *Order Book*.

[29] "Military Election," Nashville (TN) *Daily Gazette*, 1 June 1861, "Our Army Correspondants," 5 June 1861; Spence, *Travels*, 31 May 1861.

[30] Special Order 29, 31 May 1861, MF 109, *Order Book*.

they organized a twenty-four hour guard of three reliefs consisting of twelve men each. Also during this time, surgeons attended to the sick, and the boys cooked breakfast. From 4:00–5:00, the officers would drill. At 5:30, everyone ate breakfast and cleaned their cooking utensils. The boys had thirty minutes to eat and put away their mess equipment. At 6:00 AM, they fell into line and marched to the parade ground to rehearse their maneuvers. From 6:00–9:00, the captains drilled their individual companies primarily in skirmishing tactics. One soldier said that the boys executed many of these drills on the "double quick."[31] At 9:00, the officers dismissed their troops and allowed them to rest until noon when they had dinner. After dinner until 4:00 PM, the schedule allowed the boys to use their time as they chose. Some swam in the creek, others read, and others played honest John, euchre, or seven up, while others spent time writing letters home or keeping a diary of their exploits. Regardless of what activity they found for themselves, all except the "sleeping squad would be smoking," reported one Rebel from Camp Cheatham.[32] This soldier went on to say, "The amount of smoking tobacco consumed in this camp is enormous and would of itself, I think, keep the value of the staple from depreciating. It is the soldiers' greatest comfort."[33]

As time passed, the boys became more proficient in light infantry tactics, so the officers added three additional hours, from 4:00–7:00 PM, for advanced battalion or regimental drill. The men were free to spend the remaining time as they wished. Following supper, many gathered around the campfires to sing songs or to tell tales. One volunteer reported, "The fatigue and hardships peculiar to the soldier would be doubly felt if it were not for the 'fun' to be seen after 'business hours.'"[34] The soldier continued,

> Singing, dancing, playing on the banjo, making the fiddle talk, indulging in small doses of mint juleps, without the mint and ice, a sociable game of cards (no betting allowed) are among the principal amusements at night, and to witness the general merriment that prevails through the different tent rows, the observer is naturally inclined to participate. Running too late at night is a habit which so far, few have acquired. The thing was tried on at first, but that institution known as the guard house, prevents a repetition of anything like disorderly conduct. Extra duty also and a place in the work house is terrible to think of.[35]

---

[31] "Letter from Camp Cheatham," Nashville (TN) *Republican Banner*, 2 July 1861.
[32] Ibid.
[33] "Letter from Camp Cheatham"; General Order 25, 11 June 1861, MF 109, *Order Book*.
[34] "Camp Cheatham," Nashville (TN) *Daily Gazette*, 11 June 1861.
[35] Ibid.

Captain William Thedford brought his fiddle with him when he left Burns. While at Camp Cheatham, some of the men composed "The Thedford Song."[36]

Ye Dixie boys of Tennessee
Enlisted soldiers now to be,
Go leave your homes just as they stand
By orders and by strict command.
The first went out from Dixie's land
Was under Thedford's brave command.
'Twas on the twenty-fifth day of May,
I shall never forget that day.
My heart did ache—I felt it smart
To see so many people part.
To see so many volunteers
With broken hearts and falling tears.
Go bid their friends and parents adieu,
Their brothers and their sisters, too [37]
. . .
It was by votes as all may see
That caused their Civil War to be.
Some voted right, some voted wrong,
Some voted Union most too strong.
They elected them a President,
And to this war he gave consent,
Not caring for a ruined land
Nor the blood of fellow man.

As the boys from Burns sat around the campfires at night, they often sang it. Then about 10:00 PM, a hush would envelop the camp as the soldiers turned in for the night.

Perhaps one of the tales told late at night around the campfire was the legend of the Bell Witch. The "witch" as it was called, was a ghost alleged to have preyed on the John Bell family, some forty years earlier in nearby Adams, Tennessee. The spirit, more infamously known as Kate, claimed to be the "witch" of Kate Batts, another early settler of Robertson County. On one occasion, one version of the story claimed the spirit even got the best of General Andrew Jackson as he and an entourage visited the Bells to investigate the paranormal phenomena occurring on

---

[36] Pauline Williams Luff, "A Confederate Military Record of Lieutenant Colonel William Thedford Together With His Descendants," p. 73, Genealogy Room, Dickson County Public Library, Dickson County, TN. According to Pauline Williams Luff, this song was passed down by oral tradition from Private Newton J. Luther of Thedford's Company, to his nephew, Alonzo Luther, of Humphreys County, Tennessee. He in turn passed it to his son Vernon Luther of McEwen, Tennessee.

[37] Two lines following this one are lost.

the Bell farm. John Bell, whom the spirit purportedly murdered, had two grandsons who were members of the Washington Guards. Corporal Reynolds L. Powell was the son of Betsy Bell Powell, the daughter of John Bell, whom "Old Kate" supposedly tormented. The other grandson, Sergeant James Allen Bell, was the son of Richard Williams Bell. After the war, James allowed M. V. B. Ingram to publish his father's alleged manuscript *Our Family Trouble* as part of a larger work entitled *An Authenticated History of the Bell Witch* in 1894. This was the first written account ever published by the family and is believed to be the only 'eyewitness account' ever published.

Generally, the soldiers at Camp Cheatham had plenty (sugar, coffee, flour, rice, potatoes, and dried ham) to eat.[38] Sergeant Spence of the Hickman Guards stated that his company received seventy-five pounds of meat, sixty-five pounds of flour, twelve pounds of coffee, twelve pounds of sugar, twelve pounds of rice, one gallon of vinegar, one gallon of molasses, one quart of salt, twelve candles, and three pounds of soap per day, and sometimes potatoes.[39] Spence observed that the boys "usually come out even, but seldom have too much. It is very tedious dividing, for some of them are very contemptuous."[40] One complaint did arise, however, regarding the food. One poor Rebel reporting to the Nashville *Republican Banner* on conditions at Camp Cheatham, begged the quartermaster to send them some meat. He was careful to specify that he did not want the "solidified lard" that had been coming there. The discontented Johnny wrote, "Out of fifty mouthfuls of that pork, we have but one mouthful of solid meat."[41]

The earlier election for field and staff officers left several company-level positions vacant, so the various companies held elections to fill the empty slots. Since the men elected Rains colonel, the position for captain of the Hermitage Guards was open. This company elected John E. Binns to this position. Major Lucas had been captain of the Waverly Guards, and the men elected John D. Woodward to fill this vacancy. Bateman, who was elected lieutenant colonel of the regiment, left an opening for the rank of captain in the Hickman Guards. The Guards scheduled their election for 3 June to fill this position, but a hard rain necessitated postponement. This gave the candidates more time to campaign. As a result of the bad weather, many of the soldiers spent the evening with their favorite pasttimes: chuck-a-luck, euchre, honest John, and seven up.[42]

---

[38] James Shipp, "Letter to Sister," 25 May 1861, from *Civil War Letters of Hickman County, Tennessee*, comp. and ed. Carol Chessor, Genealogy Room, Hickman County Public Library, Hickman County Tennessee, unpublished compilation of letters written by Hickman County residents during the Civil War.

[39] Spence, *Travels*, 21 May 1861.

[40] Ibid.

[41] "Letter from Camp Cheatham."

[42] Spence, *Travels*, 30 May–3 June 1861.

By the next morning the rain had ceased, so the Hickman Guards convened to hold their election. First Lieutenant P. V. H. Weems and Private Andrew J. Lowe were the candidates for captain. The men elected Weems over Lowe by nineteen votes. This election filled other vacancies in this company as well. The men elected E. A. Dean orderly sergeant over S. G. Jones, William Allen, William Baker, William Brown, and Nat Sugg. Dean received forty-one votes; Jones received thirty-one, Baker twenty-two. The number Brown received is unknown. Allen received two, and Sugg received two. The men also elected Buck White Fourth Corporal over William Webb and one of the Johnsons.[43]

On 31 May, just after the regimental organization occurred, Rains received orders to move the encampment of the regiment. On the afternoon of 4 June, the regiment moved across the creek to a location that Adolphus Heiman, assistant adjutant general for General Foster, had designated.[44] After dinner, the boys collected their equipment and moved across the creek where they established new quarters. Two days later, the men built brush arbors on the front of their tents for shade. After getting their quarters squared away, two men of the Hickman Guards tried their hands at laundry. They made the mistake of boiling their socks with their other clothes, which turned everything a reddish-brown color.

George W. Gordon, a member of the Gheber Guards, accepted the position of regimental drillmaster. Gordon was born on 5 October 1836 in Giles County, Tennessee, and was an 1859 graduate of the Western Military Institute at Nashville. Just before the war, the Nashville and Northwestern Railroad Company had employed Gordon as a civil engineer to aide in the construction of the railroad from Kingston Springs to Johnsonville, Tennessee. This would link Nashville to the Tennessee River by rail. At the time of his enlistment, he was living in a boarding house in Denver, in Humphreys County, Tennessee. Gordon joined the Gheber Guards, and with his earlier training at the Western Military Institute, the "West Point of the South," he proved himself capable of both leading soldiers and expertly drilling them in preparation for battle.[45]

Day after day, Gordon drilled the regiment through *Hardee's Tactics* and gave instruction in military maneuvers. The regiment responded well to Gordon's

---

[43] Ibid., 4 June 1861.

[44] Special Order 29, 31 May 1861, MF 109, *Order Book*.

[45] John Berrien Lindsley, *Military Annals of Tennessee: Confederate* (1886; facsimile of the first edition, Wilmington, NC: Broadfoot Publishing, 1995) 293; Ezra J. Warner, *Generals in Gray: Lives of the Confederate Commanders* (Baton Rouge: Louisiana State University, 1987) 109; L. B. McFarland, "Address of L. B. McFarland at Reunion in Macon, GA," *Confederate Veteran* 20/9 (September 1912): 427; The Nashville and Northwestern Railroad was 75 miles long and ran from Johnsonville on the Tennessee River in Humphreys County, through Dickson and Cheatham Counties, and then on to Nashville. This railroad would be completed by Federal troops and would help supply William T. Sherman's armies in the Atlanta Campaign.

leadership. Not only did Gordon drill the men, but Colonel Rains, who took great delight in his regiment, often drilled them as well. Hour after hour the commands, "present arms," "order arms," "right shoulder shift, arms," would echo across the parade ground, as the soldiers learned to obey each order with exact martial precision. As the men wheeled into column or marched by rank and file, other commands such as "by files left, march"; on the double quick, march;" or guide on the center;" would be executed with alacrity.

Even though Tennessee was gearing up for war, on 8 June 1861, the electorate held the second vote for secession. This time Tennesseans voted 105,000 to 47,000 to declare Tennessee's sovereignty.[46] The vote at Camp Cheatham was a unanimous vote of 2,090 for separation.[47]

While at Camp Cheatham, the Bull Pups organized a company band under the direction of E. L. Williams. Captain McCann wrote, "It is a solace to those who sink down at night to rest on a soldier's bed, to hear their delicious strains.... The sweet song of 'We Miss Thee at Home' is always sung last, to remind him in his dreams that he is missed."[48] The captain concluded by saying, "Then again we hear the enlivening song of 'Dixie,' which drives away all dull care and carries him gently to the land of dreams, and he rests peacefully until the sound of 'Reveille' at five the next morning."[49]

On 9 June, Captain Godshall issued orders forbidding any of his men to swear in camp. Godshall dictated that if an enlisted man was heard swearing he would be fined sixteen cents. An officer would be charged one dollar for the same offense.[50] On the same date, General Foster received word that Mr. Boon, a grocer at Cedar Hill, was enticing the soldiers to his grocery with liquor. Major Lucas, in obedience to orders, took a file of six men to the grocery and closed it down.[51] A few days later, authorities discovered a prostitute dressed in men's clothing in camp. The camp guard arrested her and escorted her away.[52] The following day, 10 June, the armament for the 2nd Tennessee arrived. The regiment received 710 .69 caliber flintlock muskets and 175 percussion rifled muskets.[53]

The longer the soldiers stayed at Camp Cheatham, the more impatient they became with their dull routine. Many of the men were tired of the redundant drilling day in and day out. With the threat of battle growing ever closer in Virginia, the anxiety among the men at Camp Cheatham grew. "Our officers are equally

---

[46] Thomas L. Connelly, *Civil War Tennessee: Battles and Leaders* (Knoxville, TN: The University of Tennessee Press, 1979) 3–4.
[47] "Camp Cheatham," Nashville (TN) *Daily Gazette*, 9 June 1861.
[48] Ibid. 15 June 1861.
[49] Ibid.
[50] Ibid.
[51] Special Order 50, 8 June 1861, MF 109, *Order Book*.
[52] "Our Army Correspondence," Nashville (TN) *Daily Gazette*, 15 June 1861.
[53] Ibid.

impatient," wrote one Reb at Camp Cheatham in early July. "The question is asked a hundred times a day: 'When are we going to Virginia?'"[54] Because of the growing hostility, the men were longing for the possibility of going to the Dominion State to engage the enemy.

The following week was one of increased tension at Camp Cheatham. Whiskey was frequently smuggled into camp and only intensified the soldiers' problems. As the stress of camp life increased, Willis Miller, a member of the Bull Pups, suffered a severe cut on the neck at the hands of E. L. Williams, the company band director. The provost immediately arrested Williams and put him under guard. On another occasion, several men from the Dickson Rifles, with permission, went beyond the guard lines. While on their foray, they went to visit some women a few miles from camp. One of the women identified one of the soldiers as one who had insulted her on a previous occasion, and she attacked him with an axe. Struck on the shoulder, the soldier received a deep and dangerous injury. The other men helped their comrade back to camp, where Dr. J. M. Larkins, the regimental surgeon, attended his wounds. Later in the week, on 15 June, Colonel Rains attempted to illegally by-pass a guard at General Foster's headquarters. In response, the guard attacked Rains with his bayonet. The colonel stood his ground and defended himself by throwing rocks at the guard, inducing the sentry to make a hasty retreat. The following day, by Special Order 57, General Foster placed Colonel Rains under arrest for the offense. The arrest order forbade Rains to leave his encampment for several days.[55]

On 18 June, the first regimental dress parade of the 2nd Tennessee was held. About 700 men of the 2nd Tennessee passed in review before Colonel Rains and Captain James B. Craighead of the 1st Tennessee Infantry.[56] The following day, the Cheatham Rifles and the Bull Pups received coats, pants, and checked and hickory shirts delivered to them by the Soldier's Friend Society, an organization of Nashville women established to aid in the outfitting of the troops.[57] Due to many soldiers sneaking into Cedar Hill to obtain liquor, on 22 June, authorities ordered Captain Mallory to take six armed men, provisioned with one day's rations, and to arrest any soldier from the camp that entered the town.[58]

---

[54] Ibid.
[55] "Our Army Correspondence," Nashville (TN) *Daily Gazette*, 19 June 1861; Special Order 57, 16 June 1861, MF 109, *Order Book*.
[56] "Our Army Correspondence," Nashville (TN) *Daily Gazette*, 19 June 1861.
[57] "Report of Soldiers Friend Society," Nashville (TN) *Daily Patriot*, 19 June 1861.
[58] Special Order 64, 22 June 1861, MF 109, *Order Book*.

The following day, several men of the regiment left camp without permission. Lawrence Kuhn, J. A. Cearnall, Grant Ford, and James Long of the Cheatham Rifles, and James T. Smith of the Hermitage Guards all departed and were absent until 29 June. Edward J. Marsh of the Dickson Rifles left on the same date and did not return until 2 July.[59]

In a letter to his sister on 25 June, Private James Shipp of the Hickman Guards related more about the state of affairs of the 2nd Tennessee at Camp Cheatham. Shipp wrote,

> I have been sick for nearly three weeks with the meassels but I have been going for about a week. Father come to see me last Friday and left on Monday. Ther[e] has been two more deaths in our company since I wrote you before. We have small pox in our regiment. There is talk of us leaving this place this week but I don't believe it for their tow hundred of [the] Regiment sick and we are not drilled and we can not fight until we are. We don't know where we will go to but the[y] speak of going to union city 4 miles of Memphis.[60]

Another soldier echoed Shipp's belief that the regiment would move to West Tennessee due to the "flair up in Missouri, and the prospect of there being a good fight there."[61] The soldier went on to say, "all are ready and eager to move."[62]

The liquor problem in camp continued to worsen. Matthew Chessy, Aaron Stultz, Thomas Fizer, and a soldier by the name of Johnson had allegedly been selling liquor to soldiers in camp. On 24 June, authorities directed Captain Mallory to take a sergeant and three other soldiers to question these men regarding the allegations. Following orders, Mallory warned the accused that if the offenses persisted they would receive legal action.[63]

Meanwhile, Colonel Rains had been busy obtaining the necessary items to fulfill his duties as colonel. In a letter of defense to his wife dated 1 July as to why he had spent so much outfitting himself, the colonel stated that he paid only $165.00 for his horse. Rains told his wife that colonels Maney and Brown had spent about four thousand dollars outfitting themselves, and he had not "spent so many hundreds. I have spent perhaps less than any colonel in the service." Rains then confessed to his wife that he had "nothing to eat last Friday," because his week's rations had given out, and on Saturday he took his meals with Major Lucas for the same reason.[64]

---

[59] Ibid., General Order 49, 10 July 1861, MF 109.
[60] Shipp, "Letter to Sister," 25 June 1861.
[61] "Letter from Camp Cheatham."
[62] Ibid.
[63] Special Order 69, 24 June 1861, MF 109, *Order Book*.
[64] James E. Rains to Ida Rains, 1 July 1861, James Edward Rains Letters 1861–1862, Manuscript Collection MF 64, Tennessee Library and Archives, Nashville, TN.

One evening in late June while the regiment was on dress parade, an altercation broke out between 1st Lieutenant William T. Cheatham and 2nd Lieutenant James Everett of the Cheatham Rifles. The incident grew heated as Everett let loose a string of profanity toward Cheatham. Later, at the quartermaster's tent, Colonel Rains approached Lieutenant Everett about his vulgar language in the presence of his company. Everett defiantly told Rains that he had heard the colonel swear too, and that if the colonel would set a better example he would follow it. Rains told Everett that he would not address his superior officer in that manner, and Everett desisted in further defiant speech. Rains had the lieutenant arrested and filed court martial charges against him.[65]

On 28 June, Edward Clark, a youthful third lieutenant of the Cheatham Rifles, left camp without permission. Clark was absent without leave until 1 July. Upon his return, his captain had him arrested to await court martial.[66]

On 30 June, Major Lucas, Captain Green, and 2nd Lieutenant George Gordon served as members of a military tribunal at Camp Cheatham to hear court martial cases. The following day, Monday, 1 July, a general court martial convened, and the members of the court heard such cases as was brought before it. Private E. L. Williams of the Bull Pups appeared to answer for fighting and disorderly conduct. The court decided that Williams would forfeit one month's pay and perform hard labor for one week.[67]

The court also heard the case against Lieutenant Everett of the Cheatham Rifles. Everett was charged with "improper and unsoldier like conduct in the presence of his entire company," of "disrespectful and contemptuous language toward 1st Lieutenant W. T. Cheatham," and of "disrespectful and contemptuous language toward Colonel Rains." Lieutenant Everett was found guilty of the charges and awaited the disposition of the sentence.[68]

Next, the court heard the case of 3rd Lieutenant Edward W. Clark, who was still under arrest for his absenteeism. The court found Clark guilty and ruled that the army would "drum" the lieutenant out of the service. General Foster intervened in the case and granted the lieutenant clemency due to his youth and ignorance of the rigorous requirements of military discipline. Foster amended the sentence, and instead of releasing him from service, suspended him from duty for two weeks and forfeited his pay for that period. This was a fortunate turn of events for Clark, as the Cheatham Rifles would later elect him to be their captain.[69]

---

[65] Special Order 77, 5 July 1861, MF 109, *Order Book*.
[66] Ibid., General Order 48, 9 July 1861, MF 109.
[67] Ibid., General Order 43, 30 June 1861, MF 109; Special Order 72, 5 July 1861, MF 109.
[68] Ibid., Special Order 77, 5 July 1861, MF 109.
[69] Ibid., General Order 48, 9 July 1861, MF 109.

By 5 July, the state officials had formally changed the numerical designation of the regiment from the 2nd Tennessee to the 11th Tennessee Infantry Volunteers. The following day, in regimental orders, which an officer read aloud before the entire regiment censured 2nd Lieutenant Everett for his use of profanity and disrespectful attitude toward his superiors. After this, the incident was over, and Everett returned to duty.[70]

On 10 July, the court adjudicated several other cases against members of the regiment. Private J. T. Smith of the Hermitage Guards; Lawrence Kuhn, J. A. Cearnall, Grant Ford, and James Long of the Cheatham Rifles; and Edward J. Marsh of the Dickson Rifles were all found guilty of being absent from camp without permission. The court ordered that Kuhn, Cearnall, Ford, and Smith would pass before the regiment with packed knapsacks on their backs for three days at dress parade. Long was ordered to extra duty for one week. The court ordered Marsh to perform one week's hard labor. General Foster again intervened and changed the sentences. Kuhn, Cearnall, Ford, and Smith were to forfeit one month's pay. James Long had to forfeit one week's pay, and Marsh forfeited two weeks' pay and worked at hard labor for one week.[71]

A superior officer had charged Private W. H. Henry, another member of the Cheatham Rifles, with drunkenness and disrespectful language toward a superior officer. The court found Henry guilty. On the following morning, the entire brigade was to be drawn up on the parade field of the 1st Tennessee Infantry, with the 11th Tennessee on the right fronting the Springfield Road. However, Henry escaped before the sentence of dishonorably discharging him before the regiment could be carried out.[72]

On 12 July, the court martial reconvened and the court handed down additional decisions regarding other members of the regiment. James H. McDonald of the Cheatham Rifles was sentenced by the court to carry a fence rail two hours each day for three consecutive days between 2:00 and 4:00 PM. Foster amended his sentence to forfeiture of one month's pay. The court sentenced Jason Figg, also of the Cheatham Rifles, to lose one month's pay and to carry a rail for two hours a day for ten days. Foster also amended his sentence to the forfeiture of one month's pay.[73]

The following week, the court handed down additional disciplinary actions. J. E. Crawford of the Hermitage Guards and J. J. Carter of the Gheber Guards were sentenced to stand on a barrel in front of the guardhouse from 2:00 to 4:00 PM. General Foster changed the sentence to each man losing one month's pay. The court demoted D. Rawley of the Bull Pups from corporal to private. The court ordered Private Charles Cooper of the Waverly Guards to carry a heavy plank from

---

[70] William T. Cheatham, M268 R159, 11th TISR.
[71] General Order 49; General Order 54, 12 July 1861, MF 109, *Order Book*.
[72] Ibid., General Order 51, 11 July 1861, MF 109.
[73] Ibid., Special Orders 84, 12 July 1861, MF 109.

2:00 to 4:00 PM on three consecutive days. The court sentenced Absolum Seals of the Dickson Rifles to carry a packed knapsack one evening before the regiment at dress parade. The court adjudged Private Pleasant Matlock of the Waverly Guards to pay $23.35 in fines. Private Lawrence Kuhn of the Cheatham Rifles had to forfeit one month's pay and be confined in the guard house at night and on Sundays and to stand on a barrel Sunday from 4:00 to 7:00 PM. General Foster amended the sentences for Kuhn, Cooper, and Seals by the forfeiture of two weeks' pay.[74] In the meantime, authorities had recaptured W. H. Henry. On 20 July the brigade assembled on the parade ground of the 1st Tennessee, and the regiment drummed him out of the service.[75]

On 24 July, Colonel Rains received Special Order 108 from General Foster, ranking the seniority of the captains of the 11th Tennessee. Captain Pitts was named the senior captain, followed by McCann, Green, Binns, Mallory, Long, Godshall, Weems, Woodward, and Thedford, in that order. In obedience to orders, the boys quickly packed their belongings and fell into line. All were anxious to depart their camp of instruction. The 11th Tennessee was now composed of 880 fully armed and accoutered troops.[76]

While the regiment was at Camp Cheatham, it had lost fifty-three men and had not yet engaged the enemy on the battlefield. No fewer than twenty of the fifty-three had died, mostly from the measles or smallpox. While others had deserted, the surgeon had discharged several men for medical reasons, and courts had sentenced others to dishonorable discharges. Although new recruits occasionally joined their ranks, the numbers of the 11th Tennessee continually dwindled away. Over the course of the war, more than 1300 men served in the regiment, but their aggregate strength never surpassed their original total of 933.

Also on 24 July, Colonel Rains received Special Order 106, which instructed him to have the regiment ready to leave Camp Cheatham at 6:00 the following morning with cooked rations for forty-eight hours.[77] The regiment would be going by rail via Nashville and Chattanooga to the town of Haynesville in East Tennessee to help stabilize the unrest in the pro-Union section of the state.[78] The following day Rains drew up the regiment at the depot as ordered. Once again, the boys climbed into the railcars. When loaded, the train headed down the tracks back toward Nashville, traversing the same route that had brought the men to Camp Cheatham several weeks before.

---

[74] Ibid., Special Order 103, 19 July 19, 1861, MF 109; Special Order 94, 18 July 1861, MF 109.
[75] Ibid., General Order 56, 19 July 1861, MF 109.
[76] Ibid., Special Order 108, 24 July 19, 1861, MF 109.
[77] Ibid., Special Order 106, 24 July 19, 1861, MF 109.
[78] Lindsley, *Military Annals*, 293; Haynesville is the modern-day Johnson Station, Tennessee.

3

"We Are Ready if They Come"

25 July–Mid-September 1861

After a short journey from Camp Cheatham, the train once again pulled into the busy depot at Nashville. Amid the chaos of civilian and military activity, the boys stepped off the train and saw the porticos of the Tennessee State Capitol looming in the background.[1]

During their layover in Nashville, on 25 July, just four days after the stirring Southern victory at Manassas Junction in Virginia, Rains marched the regiment into the public square where in a splendid presentation ceremony they received their regimental colors. The gathering consisted of family members, friends, acquaintances, and other citizens. The regiment marched through the crowd and formed opposite the City Hotel on the east side of the public square.[2] Preeminent among those present this day was the distinguished Miss Mary Bradford. For some time, she and several other young women had been meeting to construct the regimental colors for the 11th Tennessee, which they made "with a rare degree of elegance."[3] The young women who had sewn the standard had demonstrated their patriotic zeal for the cause. The words "God and Our Country" were handsomely embroidered on the silk fabric, emblazoned on the folds as a memorial to provoke and inspire the troops to their chivalrous and patriotic duty while on the field of battle.[4] As the ceremony began, J. D. B. DeBow, the well-known editor of *DeBow's Review* took the stand to make the presentation speech "on behalf of the ladies and the citizenry of Nashville:"[5]

> Colonel:—I am deputed by some of the fair daughters of Tennessee, interested especially in your fortunes, and in that of the gallant regiment which you have the honor to command, and devoted, as women only can be, to the great cause in which so much of security, liberty and honor are involved, to present to you this

---

[1] James Shipp, "Letter to Sister," 31 July 1861, from *Civil War Letters of Hickman County, Tennessee*, comp. and ed. Carol Chessor, Genealogy Room, Hickman County Public Library, Hickman County Tennessee, unpublished compilation of letters written by Hickman County residents during the Civil War.
[2] "Presentation of a Banner to the Eleventh Regiment," Nashville (TN) *Republican Banner*, 26 July 1861.
[3] Ibid.
[4] Ibid.
[5] L. J. Watkins, "Address of Brig. Gen. James E. Rains," *Confederate Veteran* 16/5 (May 1908): 209.

beautiful standard, which they have caused to be fabricated under their gentle superintendence, and with which they dismiss you to the battle-field, with tearful eyes, yet proud and swelling bosoms.

In all ages of history, it has been the glorious mission of woman to incite, by her approving smiles and plaudits, the most daring feats of heroism, and to sustain by her unswerving constancy the cause of patriotism, when drooping in the dust. The classic page has ever illustrated. The mothers of Sparta, the Cornelias of Rome, belong not only to that age. They re-appear in every period of our first great war of independence, the brilliant results of which may be ascribed as much to her inspiration as to the deeds of the statesman at the council-board or the prowess of the warrior in the field. The ages of chivalry are not past, and woman to-day is as ready to belt the knight for the lists, and crown the victor with the garland, as in the days of Charlemagne or of Richard. Cheered onward by her, man advances to the cannon's mouth as if Deity had lent him armor.

"God and our Country"—what words are these that float out upon the broad and beautiful tissue, which now resists, and now reclines luxuriantly upon the breeze. Like the burning words seen above the cross of Constantine in the sky, they rouse the sensibilities and fire the heart. Without the guidance of the Most High, and without reliance upon His right arm, the battle ceases to be to the strong, and marshalled hosts melt away like morning dew: with that guidance, let the storm lower—it shall harmlessly break; let the din of battle be loud and fierce—it shall not move. "The sun shall not smite thee by day, nor the moon by night." Our Country too, with what proud emotions does it swell the heart! It involves every thought which man treasures–his friends, kindred, home; around it cluster all the memories of an heroic ancestry; the wretch is only oblivious to its claims–the wretch is only laggard at its call. It is ever the theme which fires the poet's imagination, and causes to burn the embers upon the patriot's heart. It is the Eden, from which the curse of perpetual exile leaves man a wanderer and desolate!

And what is it, that God and Country require of us today? It is to go forth, with brave heart and strong arm, to meet and repel an insulting and arrogant foe, who, defiant of all obligations sacred among men, breaks down the forms of government, established by mutual compact and sacrifices, and seeks to overwhelm and crush, with the very power we have aided to establish. Do you refuse this mission? Do your hearts quake at sight of the boastful and swelling columns? Every page in the chronicle of glorious old Tennessee, whether written on the heights of King's Mountain, or on the plains of Chalmette, on the prairies of the West, or in the desperate struggles of Mexico, gives the lie to such an imputation.

In the presence of the sacred shades of your ancestors, remember soldiers, that your swords are drawn in maintainance of a government, which *they* framed by their councils, or cemented by their blood—a government which has been the pride and hope of freemen, throughout the world; and in resisting the infamous purpose of those, who having wickedly subverted that government, seek with bristling bayonets and pompously paraded armies, to force upon you a government which these ancestors struggled against, and repudiated, and which under the mere flimsy guide of democracy, involves the most abject forms of despotism—the despotism of irresponsible masses—of ignorant, prejudiced, unsympathising numbers–of those who proclaim an irrepressible warfare against all that has constituted the wealth, resources, and civilization of the South.

Great God! could a brave and true man hesitate now? With the heel of the despot upon his neck, could he dare breathe the name of Washington, of Sumter, of Henry, or of your own immortal chief, who reposes almost within your sight? Could his martial form appear again at the head of your columns, in battle array, to what and where would it beckon you on? Can you doubt? Which of you would shrink away? rather would it make

"each petty artery in your bodies
As hardy as the Naemean lion's nerve!"

The union which *he* reverenced and illustrated, represented alone, by this flag (the other and older having become symbolic of despotism) "it must and shall be preserved."

"Snatch from the ashes of your sires
The embers of their former fires
And he who in this strife expires
Will add to theirs a name of fear
That tyrany shall quake to hear."

Take the flag. Let it wave proudly upon the breeze; let the sun guild it; let the storm rock it; ever floating, never furled, till the foe perish, and the cause triumph. This is no holiday pageant! Float out glorious sheet! In the hour of carnage, in the day of death, when battles are to be fought and won, be seen, like the tall and quivering plume of Murat, indicating the eager chief who may watch its fortunes, the point where dangers lowers most, and whence the cry first shall come, so recently heard on the great day of Manassas, of Victory, Victory Victory![6]

At this time, Colonel Rains proudly stepped forward seizing the staff of the flag. Then from the balcony of the old City Hotel, he addressed the audience gathered for the occasion. Rains, a the former district attorney, replied to DeBow's address, "in a style exceedingly creditable to his brilliant powers as an orator,"[7]

In behalf of the gallant men before us, I accept these colors and return to you, and through you to the fair donors—and especially to her who has been mainly instrumental in its presentation—our most hearty thanks for the beautiful gift and for the handsome manner in which it has been bestowed.

I feel conscious of the high and sacred trust I assume in receiving from the hands of beauty this holy emblem of freedom and human rights; and had I the least lingering apprehension that its proud folds would wave above one coward heart or trail before a conquering foe, I would refuse to accept the proffered gift. But, sir, I

---

[6] "Presentation of a Banner."
[7] Ibid.

accept it, and can commit it to the keeping of these men with the confident assurance that they will defend it with a valor and a patriotic self-devotion which will infinitely prefer death to dishonor.

Sir, these gallant men are panting for the fray. From the Old Dominion they have suffered the scent of battle and caught the shout of victory, and they are champing at their bits for the fight. You may tell the fair ladies from whom you bear your commission that those men will never disgrace that flag. Tell them that they will prize it as the dearest object of the soldier's affection, the holiest emblem of a just cause, and the grandest incentive to patriotic chivalry. Tell them they will defend it with their stout arms while it floats and cover it with their lifeless forms should it fall. Tell them that in the height of battle, when grim-visaged war shall shake his gory locks, bristle his angry crest, and send his death dealing messengers thick and fast among their ranks, they will turn their eyes to where that banner floats, and, catching a fresh inspiration from its gallant folds, will rush with steadier and stouter heart to the deadly assault. And tell them, too, that they will never forget the fair donors of the standard they bear; that their names will be watchwords for enthusiasm amidst the cry of battle and the shout of victory; that they might mingle with the song of praise for the conquering hero the requiem of sadness for the fallen brave; that they will give keener zest to the soldier's joy when a field has been won, and soothe the dying pangs of those whose blood the victory costs.

To you then, brave men, I commit this banner. To your keeping is confided the sacred badge of an oppressed people's rights. Take it and defend it for the honor of those who bear it; defend it for the love of those who gave it; defend it for the justice of the cause it symbolizes. Let it be to you the guiding star of duty, the never failing proof of valor, the sure harbinger of victory, the everlasting symbol of a patriotic and holy cause. And should it be your good fortune to fling it to the breeze in the face of the foe, there rear with your arms an impenetrable rampart around it, or build with your bodies a sacred mausoleum above it.

No one, sir, of these gallant men, while this flag shall wave above, will begrudge a thousand lives in so holy a cause.

Nowhere can a man fall more gloriously than in defending his own liberties and his country's honor; in no way can he make his name clearer and his memory sweeter to surviving friends; in no way can he invest the sod that shall cover him with a more thrilling interest and shed upon his own dust a more lasting honor than to fall battling for his country's freedom.

You may fall, brave men, in defending the trust you have this day assumed; but if fall you must, you will not fall in vain. You may sleep the silent sleep of death upon some far-off plain, and mingle undistinguished with the dust of thousands more; but your names will live and linger among the people for whom you died. Your memories will be forever enshrined in the great heart of that country upon whose altars and in defense of whose rights you shed your blood. The story of your deeds, recalling as I know it will the well-fought battlefield with all its brilliant associations, and coming emblazoned with the halo of victory, shall awaken an emotion of admiration and love in the Southern mind and send a thrill of sympathy and sadness through the Southern heart as long as our blue mountains shall point to the heavens or our bright water run down to the seas.

And now, my brave boys, with the blessing of the age, the smiles of beauty, and the benedictions of Heaven you go forth to add fresh laurels to the chaplet of Tennessee's glory.

"With one parting look at the bright sun, one prayer to the sky,
One glance at our banner that floats glorious on high,
Rush on, as the young lion bounds on his prey!
Let the sword flash on high! Fling the scabbard away!
Roll on like the thunderbolt over the plain!
We'll come back in glory or we'll come not again."

Once more I return to you our thanks for this proud banner and renew our promise that we will conquer before or fall beneath it.[8]

After the ceremony, the citizens held large dinner in honor of the regiment. Private Clayton Yates of Thedford's Company stated, "The good people of that city [Nashville] treated us to a good dinner and to all the lemonade we could drink."[9]

Military authorities assigned the regiment to the command of Brigadier General Felix Kirk Zollicoffer. Zollicoffer, a former Tennessee Whig Congressman, was given the responsibility of quelling the Unionist uprising in East Tennessee. Men like Senator Andrew Johnson, Representatives Thomas Nelson and Horace Maynard, and the itinerant Methodist preacher, Parson William G. Brownlow had incited Union support. Brownlow protested that Governor Harris had disregarded the wishes of Tennesseans who had overwhelmingly voted pro-Union in February. Brownlow alleged that Harris had instead formed a military alliance with the cotton states. Despite Unionist rhetoric, Confederate authorities hoped that Zollicoffer through sympathetic treatment and a force of arms could nullify this martial spirit.[10]

Despite its hopes, Richmond had given Zollicoffer an impossible task. He was plunged into the middle of this socio-economic, political, and geographical morass of East Tennessee Unionism. Thomas Lawrence Connelly commented that the general had been assigned to command the longest section of the line "with the smallest force and the largest percentage of unarmed men of any district commander in Tennessee."[11] Other issues also plagued Zollicoffer. His area of responsibility lay in the most rugged terrain in Tennessee, the Cumberland and Unaka Mountain ranges. Moreover, this was the "poorest food-producing area in Tennessee,

---

[8] Ibid.

[9] Clayton H. Yates, "Reminiscences of the Civil War," Mayfield (KY) *Daily Messenger*, date unknown.

[10] Robert L. Kincaid, *The Wilderness Road* (Indianapolis, IN: Bobs-Merrill, 1947) 227.

[11] Thomas Lawrence Connelly, *Army of the Heartland* (Baton Rouge: Louisiana State University Press, 1967) 86.

contained the largest amount of Unionist activity, and possessed the worst roads and other lines of communication."[12]

With their new regimental colors in hand and morale at highest peak, the men of the 11th Tennessee boarded the train and left Nashville, and by way of Chattanooga, were bound for Haynesville, the present-day town of Johnson City in East Tennessee. "After a very tiresome railroad travel, we reached this camp," stated a member of the Hermitage Guards.[13] On the expedition, the citizen reaction of the East Tennesseans was different than expected. A sergeant of the regiment reported, "At every village and hamlet between Chattanooga and this place we were greeted with loud hurrahs for Jeff Davis, the waving of flags, with the 'stars and bars' conspicuously displayed from the housetops. This was especially the case at Greeneville and Jonesboro, where crowds assembled to greet the gallant boys."[14]

The 11th Tennessee arrived at Haynesville on Sunday 28 July. They established their quarters at an already existing encampment, Camp Gannt, which they renamed Camp Bradford in honor of Mary Bradford. One of Rains's men described the setting:

> Our present camp is in every respect a location far preferable to Camp Cheatham. We have excellent water and our whole encampment is shaded by a forest of oak trees, through which the rays of the sun scarcely penetrate, and our boys, so dissatisfied and restless under the restraints of Camp Cheatham, are now tolerably well contented, no more desiring to visit Nashville, but still eager to prosecute our journey to the immediate seat of war in Virginia.[15]

While at Haynesville, Captain Woodward of the Gheber Guards resigned, and the company elected George W. Gordon, the former regimental drillmaster, to fill the vacancy.[16] Three days after arriving in Haynesville, James Shipp of the Hickman Guards wrote his sister back in Hickman County:

July 31, 1861

> Dear sister I take the present opportunity to write you a few hurried lines I feel well and hardy at present I have not much of any importance to write but if could see you I could tell you a great many things that I have neither time nor space to write we have left our old camp ground and are on [our] way to virginia but we have camped about 300 miles from camp cheatham in East Tennessee I have passed throu several touns There is a probability that we will leave here in tow or three weeks but we may stay six months We do not know how long Tell Joseph and Caroline and Elizabeth to write to me direct your letters to Camp Bradford it taken

---

[12] Ibid.
[13] "Our Army Correspondence," Nashville (TN) *Daily Gazette*, 3 August 1861.
[14] Ibid.
[15] Ibid.
[16] John Berrien Lindsley, *Military Annals of Tennessee: Confederate* (1886; facsimile of the first edition, Wilmington, NC: Broadfoot Publishing, 1995) 293.

its name from the lady who presented us the flag in Nashville if you direct your letters in maner they will follow me any where just James Shipp the Eleventh Regiment Tennessee Captain Weems company Nothing more at present

Your affectionat

James Shipp[17]

The following day, 1 August, Jerome S. Ridley accepted the position of assistant commissary of subsistence for the regiment.[18]

After several days at Camp Bradford, Rains separated the two battalions of the regiment and assigned them to guard various strategic points along the East Tennessee and Virginia Railroad from Unionist attack. The 1st battalion under command of Lieutenant Colonel Bateman was made up of the Hermitage Guards, the Waverly Guards, the Gheber Guards, the Dickson Rifles, and the Washington Guards. The 2nd battalion, under command of Major Hugh R. Lucas, included the Bull Pups, the Dickson Slashers, the Cheatham Rifles, Thedford's Company, and the Hickman Guards. Headquarters ordered the 1st battalion to Loudon, Tennessee, to guard the 585-yard railroad bridge spanning the Tennessee River. Meanwhile, the 2nd battalion was ordered to Watauga, Tennessee, to guard Carter's Station, the Watauga Bridge, and Midway Station.[19]

Upon arrival at Watauga, the Cheatham Rifles and the Hickman Guards were assigned to Carter's Station guarding the Watauga Bridge. The remaining companies, the Bull Pups, the Dickson County Slashers, and Thedford's Company (under the command of captains Godshall, Mallory, and Thedford) moved to Midway Station to guard the railroad trestle and the Lick Creek Bridge.[20]

On Monday, 12 August, the companies at Carter's Station drilled until they were exhausted. While the men were marching with arms at "a support," John Leeper of the Hickman Guards had his gun to fire accidentally. The muzzle flash burned his shirtsleeve just above the elbow. One observer noted that it "scared him

---

[17] James Shipp, "Letter to Sister," 31 July 1861, from *Civil War Letters of Hickman County, Tennessee*, comp. and ed. Carol Chessor, Genealogy Room, Hickman County Public Library, Hickman County Tennessee, unpublished compilation of letters written by Hickman County residents during the Civil War.

[18] Jerome S. Ridley, M268 R162, 11th Tennessee Infantry Service Records, National Archives Records Administration, *Compiled Service Records of Confederate Soldiers Who Served in Organizations from the State of Tennessee*, Washington, DC: National Archives and Records Service, General Services Administration, 1960. Hereafter cited as 11th TISR.

[19] "Colonel James E. Rains-False Rumors," "From Our Army Correspondence," Nashville (TN) *Republican Banner*, 18 August 1861; Nashville (TN) *Daily Gazette*, 18 August 1861, 23 August 1861.

[20] "From Army Correspondence," Nashville (TN) *Daily Gazette*, 18 August 1861.

as bad as if he had been fired at by a Yankee Doodle."[21] This accidental discharge motivated the boys to be more careful with their weapons. The following morning the boys were on the parade ground again. After drilling for some time, the officers gave them a break. Many of the soldiers walked to a nearby rail fence, and several, still holding their loaded guns, climbed on the fence. Suddenly, a few boys started running from the fence looking back like the enemy was upon them. Seconds later, one of the men pulled off his hat and began waving it around his head. Soon a general rally was made, and a counterattack left three of the enemy killed on the field and five wounded, two mortally, and missing their nest as well. The men took no prisoners because the attackers were wasps instead of Yankees. One observer said they believed they would be "too troublesome to keep under guard." The loss to the battalion was two wounded, caused by their jumping off the fence too quickly. Although this attack was from wasps, the men expected the Unionists in the area to attack at any moment. Should an attack occur, however, everyone believed that the Cheatham Rifles and the Hickman Guards were ready.[22]

Wednesday, 14 August, was a relatively calm day. At about 10:00 that evening, Major Lucas, who was away at Bristol, Tennessee, sent a dispatch to Colonel Rains. The message said that pro-Southerners in the area had captured many arms, and that the Unionists intended to make an attack at Carter's Station and on the Loudon railroad bridge, which served as a strategic link between Knoxville and Chattanooga. Due to the threats, officers placed a picket line a quarter of a mile from their camp. For additional security, each man made his gun ready and slept with it beside him through the night, as though it was his "loved companion."[23]

The next morning, Private William A. Baker and another soldier, both of the Hickman Guards, were walking around camp with their guns in hand. Captain Weems commanded the men to halt. As they did, Baker brought his gun to his shoulder, and the weapon fired. Weems ordered Baker to the guardhouse. Baker protested that the gun went off accidentally. One onlooker sardonically observed, "Accidentally or intentionally [the] poor fellow is now (4 o'clock) in the guardhouse."[24]

Because the men expected an enemy attack, tension remained high around camp. As a result, orders forbade the men to go to the guard line without guns and cartridge boxes. At about 9:00 the next night, after the men had retired for the evening and all was quiet, a shot rang out in the darkness. With nerves on edge, the

---

[21] W. Jerome D. Spence, *The Travels, Troubles, Pleasures and Pastimes of Jerome D. Spence of Dunnington, Tennessee*, 12 August 1861, unpublished diary 10 May—25 November 1861, copy of manuscript in possession of Gary W. Waddey, Nashville, TN.

[22] Ibid., 13 August 1861.

[23] Ibid., 15 August 1861.

[24] Ibid.

soldiers sprang from their tents with guns at the ready. Everyone asked what was going on, but no one seemed to know. The shot had come from one of the pickets at the bridge, so a detail went immediately to strengthen the bridge guard. At the same time, the Hickman Guards formed a line of battle between the camp and the bridge. The men waited anxiously, expecting any moment to see the enemy. Captain Weems and 2nd Lieutenant Vaughan proceeded to the bridge to investigate the shot, while 1st Lieutenant Jones remained behind commanding the company. While standing in line, 3rd Sergeant Thomas D. Thompson asked several of the boys around him for a chew of tobacco. Suddenly, through the shadows of the night, the boys could faintly see about a dozen men with bayonets glimmering in the moonlight coming down the railroad at a fast walk. Someone down the line whispered, "Yonder they come." At that time, the roaring laugh of Captain Weems echoing through the stillness released the tension as he exclaimed, "Boys, by God it's a false alarm. 'Twas only a fellow on the other side of the river shot at an owl." With a sigh of relief, the men returned to their tents.[25]

The following morning just as the men had finished breakfast, another gunshot rang through the camp. The report of the musket was followed by a man crying, "I'm shot, I'm shot." Upon investigation, the men discovered that two soldiers of the Cheatham Rifles had been wounded from the accidental firing of Wash Shouse's gun, of the Hickman Guards. The gun was lying on the ground in his tent, supposedly with no one around, at the time of the discharge. The load fired was a buck and ball cartridge. One buckshot penetrated the shoulder of Nicholas Stewart. The other soldier, Charles A. Ceston was lying in his tent when the 69. caliber ball and buckshot entered the posterior part of his hip. The shot lodged in his thigh, but the ball passed down his leg and exited above his knee. The projectile continued, passing through Ceston's tent, and smashed into a nearby hill. It wasn't until about 4:00 that afternoon when a surgeon arrived by train and attended to Ceston's wounds. By evening he was resting well. The incident was greatly lamented by Shouse, but as an observer stated, "As he was not present at the time of the discharge is of course totally blameless." The night closed with drizzling rain.[26]

By Sunday, 18 August, the rain of the night before had intensified, preventing the companies from performing their typical inspection of arms. Most of the boys remained in their tents through the morning, but some did go to church at about 9:00. As the day passed, the rain cleared. Later in the day, the men assembled by companies for roll call. Not long after this, Captain Weems came running from the depot. The captain called for several soldiers to go with him in pursuit of some men who had thrown rocks at the train and had hit a bystander. Weems led the detail and soon captured the suspects about a mile and a half from the camp. Before long,

---

[25] Ibid., 17 August 1861.
[26] Spence, *Travels*, 17 August 1861; "Accident at Camp Rains," Nashville (TN) *Daily Gazette*, 23 August 1861.

the detachment returned with four intoxicated prisoners. The perpetrators sat under guard, awaiting their dispositions. The assailants were still in custody the next morning.[27] Private Jesse Coble, one of the men on Weems's detail, commented about the affair,

> i was in a spree the other night with 7 more of the boys and hour Captain. we run 4 of the union men about a mile and took them prisoners and fetch them back to camps and kept them under gard too days and knights and tha [they] reliest them with thught [without] punsing [punishing] them. tha was throwing rocks at the cars as tha past along. i will say to you it was fun for me to make the union devils walk bafore at the point of my baonet [bayonet].[28]

While the Cheatham Rifles and the Hickman Guards were encamped at Watauga Bridge, a few of the soldiers became ill. On Sunday, 25 August, the train arrived in camp to transport the debilitated soldiers to the hospital at Knoxville. James Anderson and Jerome Spence were two of the sick. Upon hearing the train whistle, they immediately dressed and boarded one of the cars. Aside from the two soldiers, the car contained wooden crates about eight feet long. Spence and Anderson made themselves comfortable among the boxes. Not long after the train had pulled away from the depot, it appeared that something astonishing had just crossed Anderson's mind. Anderson looked at Spence and said, "Do you know what is in these boxes?" Spence replied that he did not, and inquired as to their contents. Anderson said, "Dead men are in them and I am going to get out of here." The two men, although sick, managed to hop from car to car until they found more suitable accommodations. They completed the hundred-mile journey and arrived in Knoxville at about 11:00 AM. There, they saw the surgeon and were given their furloughs.[29]

Spence and Anderson boarded the East Tennessee and Virginia Railroad at Knoxville and traveled to Chattanooga where they boarded a train of the Nashville and Chattanooga Railroad, which carried them on to Nashville. Dr. Larkins, surgeon of the 11th Tennessee, was on the train with them. Larkins, fearing the death of his wife, had just resigned his commission and was returning to his home in Charlotte, Tennessee.[30] When Dr. Larkins arrived in Charlotte, he discovered that his wife had passed away and that family members had buried her among relatives in the Charlotte Cemetery.

The following day, Private Jesse Coble of the Hickman Guards wrote his family back in Hickman County,

---

[27] Spence, *Travels*, 18 August 1861.

[28] Jesse Coble, to Father and Mother, 26 August 1861, in John Trotwood Moore, *Tennessee, Civil War Records—Middle Tennessee, Civil War Correspondence* (Nashville: Tennessee Historical Records Survey, 1939).

[29] Spence, *Travels*, 24 August 1861.

[30] Ibid., 26 August 1861.

The boys is jenualy well in hour Company. hour mess is all well and in good spirits. I fiel as happy as a judg just now. I have just come don off a mountain that is with my hamper [haver] sack of the best kind of pearches [peaches]…we have been expecting a fight here with the union men. tha say tha talked of coming in on us and therashing us out, but I learn tha air about to give that out.[31]

Meanwhile, the 1st battalion arrived at Loudon, Tennessee, and made their quarters in barracks at an encampment called Camp Foster. A sergeant in the battalion stated, "The object in placing us here was to prevent the Unionists from destroying the railroad bridge, which was strongly apprehended as a retaliatory measure for the arrest of [U. S. Congressman, Thomas A. R.] Nelson."[32]

After the 1st battalion had been there for only a short time, a report reached Brigadier General Zollicoffer that there were three hundred armed Unionists at Kingston, Tennessee. When the news arrived, Colonel Rains left Haynesville and proceeded to Loudon, eighteen miles from Kingston, to take the 1st battalion to put an end to the disruption.[33]

Rains took a special train and reached Loudon within a few hours. At about midnight, the rattling drumroll woke the men as Sergeant S. A. Davidson of the Hermitage Guards entered the barracks and ordered the men to "fall in." One soldier of his company later reminisced that in "a few seconds almost every man in the battalion was on his feet, with gun in hand, eager for any adventure that might turn up."[34] Officers instructed the troops to prepare for a forced march. "This was certainly a misnomer, for never did men enter into a forced march with more eagerness, as all anticipated a skirmish," stated a member of the Hermitage Guards.[35] Second Lieutenant James Sloan, commanding the battalion's advance guard, left ahead of the column to secure a ferry to cross the river. The ferrymen were all "Union men" and initially refused to assist the Confederates across. Nevertheless, "a few bayonets brought them to their senses." Before daylight the entire battalion was across the river and on the march.[36]

The men began to grow weary as the battalion marched. One of the men stated, "We had no time to prepare rations before starting, and as a consequence of the rapid march, upon empty stomachs soon began to tell upon us, and by noon we were glad to halt for a while near a cool spring, and rest our weary limbs."[37]

---

[31] Jesse Coble, to Father and Mother.
[32] Nashville (TN) *Daily Gazette*, 18 August 1861.
[33] James E. Rains to Ida Rains, 15 August 1861, James Edward Rains Letters 1861–1862, Manuscript Collection MF 64, Tennessee Library and Archives, Nashville, TN.
[34] "From Army Correspondence," Nashville (TN) *Daily Gazette*, 18 August 1861.
[35] Ibid.
[36] Ibid.
[37] Ibid.

By this time, 1st Lieutenant Benjamin McCann of the Hermitage Guards was in command of the advance guard. His platoon captured several suspicious suspects who were attempting to warn the citizens at Kingston of the Confederate force headed in their direction. When the battalion was within five miles of Kingston, the men saw a man coming toward them in a buggy. As soon as the man saw the soldiers, he immediately wheeled the buggy around and headed back toward the town. Colonel Rains believed the man would return to the town and warn the citizens, who would then prepare for resistance. The impetuous Rains took off to apprehend him. The colonel rode at full speed to within a mile of Kingston in an attempt to catch the man, but he never saw him again. Later, the men discovered that when the man had gone through the town, he stopped only long enough to tell the citizenry that three thousand soldiers were coming and that the line of troops was four miles long. The man also reported that the soldiers had fired on him and tried to kill him.[38]

On the approach to Kingston, Rains's troops found many homes deserted as the men of the community had abandoned them and fled to the woods. The women of the town were screaming, weeping, and begging for mercy. Soon a delegation of citizens met Rains as his column entered deeper into the town. The story had gotten out that the Southern troops were on the way and that they were going to burn the houses and kill the women and children. As Rains rode at the van of his column, he reassured the citizens who had not deserted their homes that no harm would come to them. Rains's troops entered the town with drums beating and their beautiful silk colors floating in the breeze. As the battalion passed through the town, the soldiers saw more abandoned homes, some with half-eaten meals still on the table. The three hundred Unionists reportedly in the town had fled to the woods and remained there during the stay of the Southern troops. As a result, Rains and his men met no hostile foe. The battalion remained in Kingston for about 18 hours. Rains reported that this visit did great good, as his men behaved with the utmost respect. This soon produced a positive reaction in favor of the South. One of the most violent Unionists, who had fled their approach in the beginning, came within the lines of the battalion and talked with the troops in the friendliest manner.[39]

As Rains's men left Kingston, he detached the Dickson Rifles, under command of Captain William Green, to remain behind to ensure that no further trouble arose. The remaining four companies boarded the steamer *Tennessee*, owned by Captain Doss of that town, and returned to Camp Foster at Loudon.[40] Rains stated, "The boys stood the march very well. They are a noble set of fellows, ever

---

[38] "From Army Correspondence," Nashville (TN) *Daily Gazette*, 18 August 1861; James E. Rains to Ida Rains, 15 August 1861.

[39] James E. Rains to Ida Rains, 15 August 1861.

[40] "From Army Correspondence," Nashville (TN) *Daily Gazette*, 18 August 1861.

ready at any moment to do anything which they are called upon to do, never murmuring and never complaining."[41] Rains reported that the Unionists at Loudon were deeply hostile. For a week to ten days, they had been leaving East Tennessee in groups of ten and heading for Kentucky, where they expected to be armed and organized as an army before returning to Loudon.[42]

Rumors abounded with reports of Unionist activity in the area. On the night of 14 August, three men woke Rains with another report from Kingston. The men reported that about 2,000 Unionists had broken their way through the mountains and were approaching Kingston from Jamestown, Tennessee. Rains discounted this information by saying, "If we were to credit half we hear we would be marching and countermarching all the time."[43]

Within the next day or so, the colonel received orders from Zollicoffer directing him to proceed to Knoxville with his battalion where he would meet and escort a section of artillery to Huntsville, the seat of Scott County. Rains sent the steamer, *Tennessee*, back to Kingston to retrieve the Dickson Rifles, and when the company returned to Loudon, the 1st battalion boarded the train and went to Knoxville.[44]

After their arrival at Knoxville, Private Clayton Yates of Thedford's Company said that they "were supplied with wagons and mules, one to each company."[45] On Saturday, 17 August, rain fell as the second section of the Rutledge Artillery (under command of Lieutenant Mark S. Cockrill) arrived in Rains's camp. The following day, baggage was packed and the companies began escort duty for Cockrill's battery. By 3:00 PM and in a heavy rain, the infantry moved out in advance followed by their baggage wagons and the artillery. The men were thoroughly drenched as they reached the Clinch River. The column crossed the river, climbed the opposite bank, and entered the town of Clinton. Here, the boys took possession of the courthouse, and in an attempt to get out of the rain, more than 350 soldiers crowded into the courthouse and spent the night.[46]

The next morning the boys started on the march again. After trudging through rain all day, that night they camped on a farm where many of the men slept in the barn. The following daybreak, Rains's cold and hungry troops started on the march again. The men had not eaten supper the previous night nor breakfast that morning. After marching all morning, around noon, the column halted in a field

---

[41] James E. Rains to Ida Rains, 15 August 1861.
[42] Ibid.
[43] Ibid.
[44] "From Army Correspondence," Nashville (TN) *Daily Gazette*, 18 August 1861; James E. Rains to Ida Rains, 15 August 1861.
[45] Clayton Yates, "War Reminiscences," Mayfield (KY) *Daily Messenger*, date unknown.
[46] Bradford Nichol, "Civil War Memoir," 18 August 1861, Manuscript Collection MF 1627, Tennessee State Library and Archives, Nashville, TN.

and the men were finally allowed to eat a snack. The battalion remained here until they could ascertain if it would be possible to pass over the mountains and continue on to Huntsville.[47]

By 22 August, Colonel Rains had succeeded in getting his mule-drawn baggage wagons over the mountain.[48] The task was not easy. The men had to lighten the loads in the wagons and double the teams to get them over the mountaintops. On 26 August, Rains's men continued their journey. After marching for three days in the rain, the battalion reached Wheeler's Gap at the foot of the Cumberland Mountains at Jacksboro.[49] Sergeant Preston G. Price of the Hermitage Guards commented that Jacksboro was "the most God forsaken place in East Tennessee. The town comprises some twenty houses, with an old dilapidated court house, which is now used as a hospital by a portion of Col. Battle's regiment stationed there."[50]

After remaining at Jacksboro four or five days, orders came for the battalion to move again. One of the men commented, "After becoming heartily tired of the place, we were ordered to proceed towards Chitwood."[51] Rains wrote his wife back in Nashville to tell about their movements: "I have now got my wagon train and artillery wagons nearly all over the mountains and leave here for Chitwood in the morning. We certainly expect some active work over there, as we are going within four miles of the Kentucky line and another fifteen miles of an encampment of the enemy. We are therefore in the advance, being at least 25 miles further than any Regiment, with four high mountains between us and any other Southern forces."[52] Rains continued, "I will tell you a secret if you promise not to tell anybody. We are going to invade Kentucky and my regiment is in the advance, being already in the line."[53]

The following morning, the boys packed their equipment and headed toward Chitwood, the present-day town of Winfield in Scott County. As the regiment passed over the mountains from Jacksboro, Private W. W. Willard of the Hermitage Guards raised "the first Confederate flag on one of the highest peaks, leaving its folds flying in the breeze to be seen and admired by all passing by."[54] When within about twelve miles of Chitwood, the men established their camp and

---

[47] Ibid., 18–20 August 1861.
[48] James E. Rains to Ida Rains, 25 August 1861.
[49] "From Army Correspondant," Nashville (TN) *Daily Gazette*, 3 September 1861.
[50] Ibid.
[51] Ibid.
[52] James E. Rains to Ida Rains, 25 August 1861.
[53] Ibid.
[54] "From Army Correspondent," Nashville (TN) *Daily Gazette*, 3 September 1861.

called it "Camp Rains."[55] Sergeant Price stated that the route was "undoubtedly the roughest over which a train of wagons ever passed."[56] He continued,

> The road up the mountains is so steep and rocky, that it was with difficulty our wagons reached the top, even after "doubling our teams." After considerable perseverance, we succeeded in reaching the summit. From here the prospect was grand beyond description. The valley below, though somewhat hilly, looked like a level plain. While away off in the distance could be seen mountain rising above mountain, until as far as the eye could reach, the main Cumberland, overtopping all the others, was distinctly visible. The climate is healthy, though for this season, it seems to us, the weather is extremely cool.[57]

The march was not an easy one. "The artillery however, seemed to meet with less difficulty in this passage through the mountains than did our baggage train, they having excellent double teams, while our wagons were heavily laden, with single mule teams, and some of them unbroken,"[58] commented one of the Hermitage Guards. This soldier continued, "We scarcely ever march more than twelve or fifteen miles a day, camping early for the purpose of cooking rations for the next day."[59]

From Chitwood, the 1st battalion received orders to proceed to Huntsville, Tennessee. Second Lieutenant Edward Clark of the Cheatham Rifles complained to his mother, "We are ordered to Huntsville, Scott Co. I tell you it is no joke we have to strike the march for sixty five long miles. I would not mind the march if we did not have to cross the mountains, that is what troubles me. I don't mind walking on level ground, but climbing mountains is not my forte."[60]

Upon arrival, the battalion set up their camp some three to five miles from Huntsville and named it Camp Crawford in honor of one of the men in the Hermitage Guards. One soldier described the camp as being "on a beautiful eminence… near the Kentucky line."[61] Not long after the battalion had made itself comfortable, Rains received an order to make a retrograde movement back toward Jacksboro. In a little while, the men had everything packed up, but headquarters countermanded the order. Rumors were circulating that some 2,000 Unionists were preparing to leave Kentucky and cross the Tennessee line to attack Rains's Battalion.[62]

On Saturday, 31 August, Colonel Rains and Captain Gordon addressed the

---

[55] Ibid.
[56] Ibid.
[57] Ibid.
[58] Ibid.
[59] Ibid.
[60] E. W. Clark to Mother, 31 August 1861, Clark Papers, Tennessee State Library and Archives, Nashville, TN.
[61] "Camp Crawford, Scott County," Nashville (TN) *Daily Gazette*, 10 September 1861.
[62] Ibid.

citizens of the area regarding the purposes of the Confederate government in stationing troops in that area. The following day, several of the Hermitage Guards had a narrow escape when a musket thoughtlessly handled by one of the camp guards went off. The buck and ball load barely missed several bystanders and passed through five different tents. One of the projectiles passed through the pillow of 2nd Lieutenant James Sloan. Fortunately, he had just gotten up, but feathers were scattered in every direction.[63] One of the soldiers writing from camp said, "While in camp here, we are not idle, but employ our time in target shooting and drilling, thus rendering ourselves more proficient in the science of war, and fitting ourselves to be equal to at least double our number of Lincolnites."[64]

While at Camp Crawford, on 2 September, Private James Long of the Cheatham Rifles, who had been detailed to break young mules for the regiment, was thrown from a wagon. In the fall, Long's fibula was broken near the knee. When he arrived at the hospital, the surgeon set the break badly, causing it to heal imperfectly. Afterwards, Long was unable to place his full weight on his leg and was incapable of walking without the aid of a walking stick. He was finally discharged for disability on 12 May 1862 at Knoxville.[65]

Sometime after midnight, in the early morning hours of 7 September, an intoxicated Private Nathaniel T. Ussery of the Washington Guards slipped away from camp and traveled approximately a mile and a half to the two-story log home of Hiram Marcum on Buffalo Creek. Marcum was a known Unionist and allegedly aided many Federal sympathizers from Scott County and the surrounding area to slip past the Confederates and make their way into Kentucky. Ussery, acting on his own and without orders, arrived at the Marcum residence at about 2:00 AM. The drunken soldier kicked open the door, burst inside, and brandished his musket and bayonet. Hiram Marcum, expecting trouble, was hidden in the barn. As Ussery forcibly entered the house, his noise woke the women and children, who began screaming. Ussery told them that thirty-six soldiers surrounded their house and he demanded to know where Marcum was hiding. Ussery told the women that if they did not hand him over, the soldiers would kill the entire family and burn them in the house. Again, the women began to cry for help. One of the Marcum daughters, Didama, found a match and lit a small tallow candle. Ussery began poking at the women with the bayonet on the muzzle of his rifle, and then he then began choking the mother. With her struggling mother gasping for breath, Didama ran up the stairs. Ussery released the mother and ran after the daughter. As he followed the girl up the stairs, he grabbed her by the foot and threatened to cut her throat. Two of the other Marcum daughters, Minerva and Julia, grabbed chopping axes, the only weapons they had in the house. Julia, age sixteen, ran up the stairs, axe in hand, to

---

[63] Ibid.
[64] Ibid.
[65] Private James Long, M268 R161, 11th TISR.

help her sister. Ussery lunged at Julia with his rifle and bayonet. The teenage girl managed to duck under the bayonet while swinging the axe at her assailant. The axe struck Ussery in the face and chest, splitting his chin and cutting him "to the hollow."[66] The blow stunned and seriously injured the soldier. As Ussery staggered, trying to regain his balance, Julia knocked the gun from his hands. Ussery begged the young girl not to chop him anymore. "But I did not stop," stated the sixteen year old.[67] As Julia continued to hack at Ussery with her axe, he managed to pick up his rifle and pull the trigger. The shot blew off the third finger of Julia's right hand. Weakened, Ussery again lunged at Julia with the rifle and bayonet. This time the bayonet struck the left side of her forehead, put out her eye, and penetrated her skull, causing a portion of her brain to protrude from her forehead. At this time, Hiram Marcum, who had finally heard the pleas for help, ran up the stairs and shot Ussery in the shoulder with a pistol. Ussery and Julia both lay bleeding on the floor. Marcum took his unconscious daughter downstairs and laid her on a bed. Julia's brother, Clayburn, went to a nearby neighbor, Mrs. Taylor, to get help. Mrs. Taylor arrived at the Marcum house, and after sunrise went to Rains's camp to report the incident. After Mrs. Taylor explained the situation, Rains sent Captain George W. Gordon and the Gheber Guards to the Marcum residence. By the time the Ghebers arrived, Ussery had died of his wounds. When Captain Gordon saw Julia's condition, he sent for a surgeon who treated her injuries. The Ghebers retrieved Ussery's body and returned to camp.[68]

The following day, Sunday, 8 September, Chaplain Fountain E. Pitts, frequently called "Old Man Eloquent," preached under a large Elm tree. With the Marcum incident fresh on his mind, Pitts delivered a message titled "Righteousness Exalteth a Nation, but Sin is a Reproach to Any People." That evening in the camp of the Rutledge Artillery, Pitts preached again. This message was titled "Marvel Not That I Say Unto You, You Must Be Born Again." One observer stated, "A most impressive service it was, not an eye but had its tear to shed. Many a brave heart returned to his tent resolved to cease swearing and live for God."[69]

---

[66] "Julia Marcum, Scott County's (and the USA's) Only Woman to Receive a Pension for Her Civil War Service," *Scott County Historical Society Newsletter*, Winter 1984, 3. Copy in possession of M. Todd Cathey.

[67] Ibid.

[68] "Julie Marcum," 3; Paul Roy, *Scott County in the Civil War* (Huntsville: Scott County Historical Society, 2001) 329–34; Private Nathaniel T. Usrea, Co. F, states he was "killed by one Markam citizen in a personal conflict" (M269 R163, 11th TISR). Julia Marcum survived her wounds but suffered from the effects for the rest of her life. As a result of her injuries, she was the only woman "as a fighter to receive a U.S. pension: Special Act of Congress 1884." After being awarded her pension, she became a member of the Grand Army of the Republic and after World War I she became a member of the American Legion. She died 9 May 1936 at the age of 91 and was given a military funeral. Roy, *Scott County*, 335.

[69] Nichol, "Memoir," 8 September 1861.

4

"Cold as the North Pole"

Mid-September–23 October 1861

The Cumberland Gap lies at the critical strategic junction of Tennessee, Kentucky, and Virginia. In the opening days of the war, both the Federal and Confederate governments immediately recognized its potential as an invasion route through which Federal forces could march into Tennessee and further into the South. Here, the Wilderness Road, more of a wide rough path than an actual thoroughfare, provided the main route through the Appalachian Mountains from the Kentucky bluegrass region southeasterly into the valley of East Tennessee.[1]

To make things more complicated for Zollicoffer, as early as July, the Federals had brushed aside Kentucky's bid for neutrality by establishing Camp Dick Robinson, just south of Lexington, for the purpose of recruiting, arming, and training Kentucky Unionists. Since the Unionists could no longer effectively recruit troops within Tennessee, by the beginning of August, James and Samuel Carter, two East Tennessee Tories, had established an advanced recruiting station named in honor of the Democratic senator from Greenville, Tennessee. Camp Andy Johnson, as it was called, was located in the small town of Barboursville, Kentucky, only forty miles or so from Cumberland Gap.[2]

Before the Unionists could organize and take the initiative, Zollicoffer moved his scattered units and seized Cumberland Gap, Big Creek Gap, and other strategic points along the Tennessee-Kentucky border. Because of these developments, Zollicoffer informed Rains that he would not be invading Kentucky by way of Chitwood as initially planned. Instead, the general ordered Rains to move back over the Cumberland Mountains and to reunite his two battalions at Cumberland Gap.[3]

Rains arrived at Cumberland Gap a few days ahead of his men, and when his troops arrived, they established their camp at the foot of the mountain on the Tennessee side at a large spring.[4] In a letter to his wife, Rains commended his regiment by saying,

---

[1] Thomas Lawrence Connelly, *Army of the Heartland* (Baton Rouge: Louisiana State University Press, 1967) 14.

[2] Robert L. Kincaid, *The Wilderness Road* (Indianapolis, IN: Bobs-Merrill, 1947) 228.

[3] Ibid., 227.

[4] James E. Rains to Ida Rains, 15 September 1861, James Edward Rains Letters 1861–1862, Manuscript Collection MF 64, Tennessee Library and Archives, Nashville, TN; William G. Frazier, "Veteran Questionnaire," in Gustavus W. Dyer, John Trotwood Moore,

The men have made a noble march from Knoxville, and behaved themselves most excellently, eliciting universal praise along the road. Maj. Lucas commanded the 2nd battalion, in the march. He is a most excellent officer. The poor fellows nearly marched themselves to death, having heard the rumor that the troops were advancing from Camp Robertson [Dick Robinson] on Cumberland Ford. They seemed afraid they might miss the fuss and could not be kept back.[5]

Life at Cumberland Gap was not easy. Private John H. Ward of the Bull Pups recalled that the conditions there during those early days "was quite a trial for soldiers who had no experience in warfare, surrounded by the worst enemies, the bushwhackers of Tennessee and Kentucky, and many of our boys was picked off without warning."[6] Ward continued, "We had been there but a short time before we were relieved of outside picket duty for a while by several companies of Indians, who brought in many scalps."[7]

Reverend S. M. Cherry, chaplain of the 4th Tennessee of Zollicoffer's Brigade recalled the religious status of the men at Cumberland Gap. Cherry stated,

> I remember no chaplain of the Mississippi regiment, but each of the Tennessee regiments had chaplains—Rev. F. E. Pitts, D. D., Eleventh, Rev. John A. Edmondson, Twentieth; and Rev. P. G. Jamison and Rev. J. G. Bolton were privates in the Eleventh Tennessee, and while doing good service as soldiers, they were "instant in season and out of season," as soldiers of the Cross, very few in the army proving more faithful throughout the entire war than did John G. Bolton, who won the confidence of his comrades and kept it for four years because of his fidelity to Christ and his country.[8]

Cherry continued,

> Very few of the commissioned officers were religious. The large proportion of the soldiers were wicked and many were reckless. For more than a year very few manifested any desire to become Christians save the sick or wounded. The boys of the 4th and 11th Tennessee regiments did not take enough interest in religious services to prepare a place of public worship, nevertheless, whenever the weather was cooperative, services were held for all who wished to attend.[9]

Colleen Morse Elliott and Louise Armstrong Moxley, *Tennessee Civil War Veterans Questionnaires* 5 (Easley, SC: Southern Historical Press, 1985) 2:856.

[5] James E. Rains to Ida Rains, 15 September 1861.

[6] John H. Ward, "The Eleventh Tennessee Infantry," *Confederate Veteran* 16/8 (August 1908): 420.

[7] Ibid.

[8] J. William Jones, *Christ in the Camp or Religion in the Confederate Army* (1887; reprint, Harrisonburg, VA: Sprinkle Publications, 1986) 564.

[9] All references to the 4th Tennessee Infantry apply to William Churchwell's regiment. This regiment was also known as the 4th Confederate (Tennessee) and the 34th Tennessee

Strategic conditions worsened in Kentucky as Federal troops on 2 September, under command of General Ulysses S. Grant, moved down into Belmont, Missouri, across from Columbus, Kentucky. In response, General Leonidas Polk, commander of the Western Department made the rash decision to send one of his subordinates, Brigadier General Gideon Pillow, into Kentucky to hold Columbus. Despite Federal recruiting at Camp Dick Robinson, Polk's actions decisively violated Kentucky neutrality. Within three days, both Federal and Confederate troops occupied Kentucky as Grant crossed the Ohio River into Paducah.[10]

By mid-September, numerous infantry units were under Zollicoffer's command: the 16th Alabama, the 14th Mississippi, the 15th Mississippi, the 11th Tennessee, the 17th Tennessee, the 19th Tennessee, the 20th Tennessee, the 34th Tennessee, and Lilliard's Tennessee regiment. The cavalry units were the 1st, 2nd, 3rd, and 4th Tennessee regiments.[11]

On 12 September, in an attempt to stymie Federal recruiting or any advance by troops in the area, Zollicoffer ordered his brigade, now assembled at Cumberland Gap, to move fifteen miles into Kentucky to take possession of and to fortify a forward position at Cumberland Ford.[12] The 20th Tennessee Infantry, commanded by Colonel Joel Battle, moved immediately. Colonel Rains arrived at Cumberland Ford on the evening of 15 September, a day or so ahead of his regiment. In a letter to his wife that evening, Rains stated that he had eaten supper with Colonel Battle and had taken a bath in the Cumberland River. In describing the surroundings to his wife, Rains commented, "It's a decidedly romantic and beautiful place; mountains on all sides of the most tremendous height, and the beautiful the beloved Cumberland came roaring and dashing down from among the mountains, a mere creek, but clear as crystal. The Ford at the place is the only gap through the mountains, and when we get it fortified, it will be impassible by any force the enemy can send against us."[13]

According to Rains, the work of fortification at Cumberland Ford had already begun. The men had started clearing timber from the sides of the mountains and placing artillery at the tops. These batteries commanded a mile and a half down the

---

Infantry. Later the unit received permanent designation as the 34th Tennessee Infantry; Jones, *Christ in the Camp*, 564.

[10] Kent Masterson Brown, *The Civil War in Kentucky: Battle for the Bluegrass State* (Mason City, IA: Savas Publishing, 2000) 9–12; Kincaid, *Wilderness Road*, 228.

[11] United States War Department, *The War of the Rebellion: A Compilation of the Official Records of the Union and Confederate Armies*, 70 vols. in 128 (Washington: Government Printing Office, 1880–1901; reprint, Gettysburg, PA: The National Historical Society, 1972) ser. I, vol. 4, 409. Hereafter cited as *OR*.

[12] *OR*, ser. I, vol. 4, 406.

[13] James E. Rains to Ida Rains, 15 September 1861.

roads to their front. The colonel stated that the cannons "would mow down any column which should attempt to advance through the gap and across the Ford."[14]

The Confederate seizure of Cumberland Gap and Zollicoffer's subsequent advance into Kentucky to occupy Cumberland Ford further restricted the ability of East Tennessee Unionists in crossing the mountains to enlist in the Union army. On Wednesday morning, 16 September, Rains, the senior colonel present, assumed command of the troops gathered at Cumberland Ford. Later that evening, the 1st battalion of the 11th Tennessee arrived after a wearied march, and the 2nd battalion arrived a few days later. On paper, the strength of the regiment at this time totaled 891 men, but only 677 could be mustered present for duty.[15]

Rains's men were elated to enter Kentucky. An officer of the regiment commented that the boys "all seem to feel at home on the banks of the Cumberland."[16] While encamped here, Captain McCann (of the Cheatham Rifles) spent many hours sending letters in bottles down the Cumberland River to his friends back home in Nashville.[17]

On 17 September, at approximately 6:00 PM, Colonel Rains came riding hard into camp from the direction of Camp Andy Johnson in Barboursville. While Rains and an escort of twenty cavalrymen were reconnoitering near that location, the Barboursville Home Guard, commanded by Captain Isaac Black, spotted and fired on Rains's scouting party. As soon as the colonel dismounted, he sent for Colonel Joel Battle. Rains ordered Battle to take eight companies of infantry from the various regiments, including the Bull Pups and the Cheatham Rifles of the 11th Tennessee, and two companies of cavalry, to dislodge the Unionists. By 10:00 PM, Battle had his battalion assembled and had begun the forced march. The men tramped all night, and by 6:00 the next morning, the column was within two miles of Barboursville. Captain Dick McCann stated, "We neared the suburbs of the town, Barboursville, the county seat of Knox County, and whose atmosphere is foul with the stench of Unionism, and every house was decorated with that *old rag*, which has brought so much trouble on this once glorious and happy country."[18]

The Confederates neared the town, feeling their way through a very heavy fog.[19] The cavalry was the lead element of Battle's column, followed by the Bull Pups, the Cheatham Rifles, and the remainder of the infantry.[20] As the Rebels waded through the dense fog, the enemy unexpectedly fired on them. Black had

---

[14] Ibid.
[15] Ibid.; *OR*, ser. I, vol. 4, 409.
[16] James E. Rains to Ida Rains, 15 September 1861.
[17] Ibid.
[18] "Our Army Correspondence," Nashville (TN) *Daily Gazette*, 26 September 1861.
[19] Ibid.
[20] Ibid.

concealed his men on both sides of the road in a cornfield belonging to Mrs. Poe.[21] Battle immediately swung his men from a marching column into a line of battle and pushed forward. The Bull Pups and the Cheatham Rifles were on the right of the battalion. Battle's men advanced, despite being under constant Federal fire. When within range, Battle halted his line and roared, "Brave Tennessee boys, give them thunder!"[22] On his command, hundreds of flintlock muskets clicked as the flints struck downward toward the powder pans and boomed as the powder was touched off, sending a volley whizzing toward the enemy. Smoke from the muskets billowed in front of the battle line. Before the smoke cleared, Battle ordered his men to reload and to continue firing at their obscured foe. A nervous Charley Thomas in Battle's line attempted to dodge the enemy bullets as they whizzed by. Colonel Battle, noticing his repetitive ducking, told his men, "Boys, don't dodge; bullets won't hit you, and if they do, [they] don't hurt."[23] Within a few minutes, the mountain howitzer of the enemy fired a round that came very near Colonel Battle. As the projectile shrieked by, the aged colonel slid from his saddle and hit the ground with a loud grunt. One of the Rebs in Battle's line called out, "Don't dodge, Colonel," to which Battle retorted, "Boys the big ones don't count. I was speaking only of the little bullets. Dodge the cannon."[24]

This exchange no doubt brought some levity to the Rebs receiving the incoming fire. Suddenly, down the line in front of the 20th Tennessee, there was a great commotion. The billowing black powder smoke, hanging thick in the air, obstructed their vision. As a result, several men of the 20th Tennessee, believing the Yankees to be advancing on their position, all fired in the direction of the racket. After the volley, there was no more disturbance. Much to the pleasure of Battle's men, they had either killed or driven back their assailants. Later some of the men discovered the disruption had not been the Yankees, instead it was an old sow spooked by the skirmish. As the frantic swine ran headlong toward the Confederate line, Battle's men riddled her with their buck and ball at close range.[25]

After volleying back and forth for some time, 1st Lieutenant William C. Nichol positioned on the right of the line, led his Cheatham Rifles forward. Nichol's men crossed the Poe cornfield on the "double quick" and routed the

---

[21] "Our Army Correspondence," Nashville (TN) *Daily Gazette*, 26 September 1861; Ray Adkins and Ron Bowling, local historians, on-site interview by Todd Cathey, Barboursville, KY, 14 November 2004.

[22] Bradford Nichol, "Civil War Memoir," 17 September 1861, Manuscript Collection MF 1627, Tennessee State Library and Archives, Nashville, TN.

[23] Ibid.

[24] Ibid.

[25] William J. McMurray, Josiah Roberts Deering, and Ralph J. Neal, *History of the Twentieth Tennessee Regiment Volunteer Infantry, C.S.A.* (1904; facsimile reproduction, Nashville, TN: Elder's Bookstore, 1976) 192–93.

enemy. Nichol's Company managed to capture eight of Black's men in this well-executed maneuver. Corporal D. H. Barry of this company "got his man."[26]

With the enemy routed, the Confederates continued pursuing the Home Guard toward Barboursville. As the Rebels advanced, they came to a bridge over a ravine. The Federals had removed the cross planks, leaving only the sleepers of the bridge intact. Still under fire, the Cheatham Rifles approached the runners and one by one started across. As they traversed the sleepers, they noticed about fifteen of the enemy attempting to escape through the ravine. Quickly, Nichol's men fired a volley into the fleeing Unionists. One member of Nichol's detachment stated, "We poured a galling fire into them that killed some 10 or 12."[27]

Although held back for some time, a portion of the Confederate cavalry flanked the Unionists on the left by fording the Cumberland River. The Barboursville Home Guard saw the line of Rebel troopers crossing the river to encircle them. Black's men realized that their situation was now serious, and they decided that further resistance would lead to disastrous consequences, so they quickly withdrew from the town. As the firing dissipated, Battle continued into the town where he formed his men in a line of battle on the square and sent a detail to search the courthouse and several nearby residences. The search party confiscated thirty or so rifles and burned many of the land records and other important documents of the town. Battle's men stayed the night in Barboursville, and at 10:00 the following morning, began the march back to Cumberland Ford. On the return trip, spirits were high and the victorious men broke off green sprigs and placed them in their hats and in the muzzles of their muskets.[28]

Battle's expeditionary force returned to Cumberland Ford and continued strengthening the fortifications. A member of Zollicoffer's Brigade described,

> We have planted our batteries, two six pounders and two twelve pounders, at the river, three hundred yards distant, with an unobstructable range of a mile, covering the entire road toward Barboursville, so as to render the advance of a very superior force rashly suicidal. In the bottom we have Battle's, Newman's, Cumming's, and Rains's regiments amounting to about 3,500 men, with a fair sprinkling of cavalry, under command of Col. Rains, he being the senior colonel. Seniority is reckoned by priority of organization. We have mounted pickets ranging the neighborhood, and vigilant outposts on the surrounding peaks to prevent a surprise, which renders us comparatively safe.[29]

The regimental returns for 24 September record that the 11th Tennessee had 658 men present for duty.[30] On the same day, General Zollicoffer sent a message to

---

[26] "Our Army Correspondence," Nashville (TN) *Daily Gazette*, 1 October 1861.
[27] "Our Army Correspondence," Ibid., 26 September 1861.
[28] Ibid.
[29] "Cumberland Ford, KY," Nashville (TN) *Republican Banner*, 28 September 1861.
[30] *OR*, ser. I, vol. 4, 425.

Lieutenant Colonel William Mackall, assistant adjutant general at Nashville, reporting on his strategy that the best defense for East Tennessee to be an onward movement into Kentucky toward those who threaten invasion.[31]

The following day, Zollicoffer ordered Colonel Rains to make an expedition to the Laurel Creek Bridge on the London Road, forty-three miles away, to break up another Unionist camp. At once, the colonel began preparing for the assignment. The units placed under Rains's command for the expedition were the 11th Tennessee Infantry, Branner's Cavalry Battalion, and Lieutenant Falconnett's section of the Rutledge Artillery. The 15th Mississippi Infantry and the 1st Tennessee Cavalry Battalion would join the expedition later.[32]

Early the next morning, the men of the 11th Tennessee prepared rations for six days, three of which were cooked.[33] Lieutenant Colonel Thomas P. Bateman, commanding the 11th Tennessee on this excursion, ordered his boys to travel light and to leave their tents behind. By 4:00 AM, Bateman assembled the regiment and in column with Falconnett's cannons, started toward the objective. As the day passed, a deluge fell from the heavens. Sergeant Preston G. Price of the 11th Tennessee stated, "We have heard of equinoxial rains, but never have we seen such a rain as fell that day. The whole heavens seemed a sieve from which the cover had been removed and the water came down in torrents."[34] The boys trudged on through the mud and crossed the swollen streams until they neared Barboursville. There, they took shelter and spent the night in the houses of the residents which had been recently vacated. During their layover, Rains's men visited the home of Green Adams, a member of Congress. While here, the 1st battalion of the 15th Mississippi and the 1st Tennessee Cavalry joined Rains's force. The driving rain continued, so the Confederates remained in the town overnight. The next morning, 28 September, Rains assembled his command and started for Laurel Bridge, still some twenty-four miles away.[35]

When within ten miles of the Laurel Creek Bridge, Rains ordered Colonel McNairy to take his 1st Tennessee Cavalry across Laurel Creek two miles above the bridge. There they were to come in behind the enemy and simultaneously attack with the infantry. Rains directed the 11th Tennessee and the 15th Mississippi straight toward the bridge.[36] One soldier of the 11th Tennessee stated, "We had no idea of the strength of the enemy, nor did our boys seem to care, as they were eager for a fight."[37]

---

[31] Ibid., 202–203.
[32] Ibid., 292.
[33] Ibid.
[34] "Our Army Correspondence," Nashville (TN) *Daily Gazette*, 8 October 1861.
[35] Ibid.
[36] *OR*, ser. I, vol. 4, 292.
[37] "Our Army Correspondence," Nashville (TN) *Daily Gazette*, 8 October 1861.

The infantry, continuing their advance, made contact with the enemy's pickets some distance from the main camp. The 11th Tennessee and 15th Mississippi quickly overran the Unionist pickets and sent them scurrying back to their main lines. With the initial Federal troops routed, Rains restored his line, sent the Waverly Guards forward as skirmishers, and continued the advance. As the 11th Tennessee came within about two miles of the Home Guard encampment, Lieutenant Colonel Bateman thought he observed the enemy in the edge of some woods to the right. Bateman deployed Captain Binns and his Hermitage Guards as skirmishers as they resumed the advance. Binns cautiously led his company into the woods. As the battalion neared the main camp at the bridge, Rains sent a portion of the infantry around a swamp to cut off any line of retreat. Rains hoped this maneuver would induce the Home Guard into one of two options: fight or surrender. At this time, the remainder of 15th Mississippi and the 11th Tennessee formed a line of battle and were given the order to charge the encampment.[38] An officer of the Cheatham Rifles stated, "The command of double quick being given, the Mississippians and Tennesseans tried themselves, and with unearthly yells that made them appear as madmen they rushed wildly on." The officer continued, "There was no line at all, for every man was trying to reach the enemy first."[39] A sergeant of the Hermitage Guards commented, "The undergrowth was so thick that it was almost impossible to force our way through; but we succeeded in scaring up the game, and the cavalry being near chased them beyond London, killing one and taking several prisoners and two of their wagons and teams, with their camp equipage."[40] The enemy, numbering between 600 and 1,500, fled in the face of Rains's pincer attack. Even though the Confederates pursued them, all but three of the Unionists escaped. Aside from the three prisoners, Rains's men captured 8,000 cartridges, 25,000 percussion caps, three kegs of powder, six barrels of salt, two wagons and teams, three other horses, twenty-five pairs of shoes, and several guns.[41] Captain Dick McCann of the Cheatham Rifles said that the cartridges captured in the attack were made in Ohio and excel "by a great degree, those we at present use."[42]

With darkness rapidly coming on, Rains ordered his men to fall back about two miles where they billeted in an open field. The next morning after partaking of a "hearty meal," Rains's men were preparing to return to Cumberland Ford with their spoils of war, when several horsemen arrived to report that the enemy were advancing on their position. After Rains received the news, he rode over to the Hermitage Guards and told them to be ready for an attack as the enemy was only

---

[38] Ibid.
[39] "Camp Buckner, Oct. 3 1861," Ibid., 10 October 1861.
[40] "Our Army Correspondence," Ibid., 8 October 1861.
[41] *OR*, ser. I, vol. 4, 202–203.
[42] "Camp Buckner, Oct. 3 1861," Nashville (TN) *Daily Gazette*, 10 October 1861.

five miles away. One member of the Hermitage Guards, Private Henry Robertson replied, "Well Colonel, they have no advantage of us; we are in five miles of them."[43] Rains formed his men in a line of battle, placing the 1st battalion of the 15th Mississippi on the right and the 11th Tennessee on the left.[44] After remaining in a line of battle for some time, the colonel learned that the information was false. With this new information, Rains returned with his men to Cumberland Ford. Rains praised his men saying,

> They made the most gallant charge, on the Lincoln camp at Laurel Bridge, I ever saw. It was wild and terrifying beyond all description. No troops on earth could have withstood the combined charge of his battalion [McNairy's Cavalry] and my own and the Mississippi Regiment, all of them rushed like lions upon the prey. If the devils had stood, we would certainly have taken the last one of them.[45]

For the next few weeks, the Confederates lay idle in their camps at Cumberland Ford. According to Sergeant Preston G. Price, the regiment took a position some two miles from the camp acting as the advance guard. Colonel Rains named the place Camp Buckner, in honor of his friend, General Simon B. Buckner, commander of the Kentucky State Militia.[46]

On 3 October, Rains said that the "camp was exceedingly quiet today, for the first time since we left Knoxville."[47] The colonel also commented that the health of the regiment was presently very good. Nevertheless, the monotonous day-to-day realities of camp life had set in, replacing the early novelty.[48] On 4 October, the men received rations consisting of six ears of hard corn and no meat.[49] Despite the shortage of food, work on the fortifications continued daily. Every day men worked building breastworks and blockading roads.[50]

On 7 October the replacement for Dr. Larkins, the regimental surgeon who had resigned two months earlier due to the death of his wife, arrived in camp. Doctor John H. Callender became the regimental surgeon, and Dr. James B. Pitts, brother of Chaplain Fountain E. Pitts and uncle of Captain Josiah Pitts, assumed the role of assistant surgeon. For lack of accommodations, Dr. Callender stayed with Colonel Rains in his marquee tent. The following day, Rains wrote to his wife and told her that his regiment was still at Camp Buckner, but preparations were underway for an advance on Lexington and Frankfort. Despite a shortage of supplies, Rains told Zollicoffer that his regiment was ready to move at any moment.

---

[43] "Our Army Correspondence," Ibid., 8 October 1861.
[44] Ibid.
[45] James E. Rains to Ida Rains, 3 October 1861.
[46] Ibid.
[47] Ibid.
[48] Ibid.
[49] Nichol, "Memoir," 4 October 1861.
[50] James E. Rains to Ida Rains, 3 October 1861.

Rains went on to say they were willing to rely on Providence and Major Ridley, regimental commissary, for subsistence. Nevertheless, the general thought it best to postpone the advance. While at Camp Buckner, the boys of the 11th developed an innovative way to mill their corn. They took a tin plate, pierced it full of holes with a nail, and grated the hard corn across the perforations, which produced meal for their cooking.[51]

By early October, nights became cool, so warmer clothing became a necessity for the troops. Later in the month, a rumor circulating around camp had made its way back to Nashville. The rumor intimated that Colonel Rains had a narrow escape during the engagement at Laurel Creek. In a letter to his wife, Rains stated, "I was neither shot in the finger, coat sleeve, nor coat tail, nor was my horse shot. The report was current in camp, and I have frequently been asked if it is true."[52]

Meanwhile, Colonel Theophilus T. Garrard had concentrated a considerable Federal force at Camp Wildcat in the Rockcastle Hills. This position was some thirteen miles northeast of London, where the Mount Vernon Road crosses the Rockcastle River, and about seventy miles northwest of Cumberland Ford. As the Confederates heard about the Yankee threat building to the north, Rains wrote, "I do not believe that my regiment can be whipped…. I have no fear of the glorious 11th. They can whip their weight in wildcats."[53] To stop the impending threat, Zollicoffer devised a strategy to dislodge the Federals fortifying at that location.

At midnight on Wednesday, 16 October, all plans for a movement against Camp Wildcat were complete. The regiments assembled, and the company commanders carefully inspected the condition of the arms and equipment of their men. When all was ready, Zollicoffer's men marched out of Camp Buckner and crossed the Cumberland River by ferry.[54] A couple of hours later, Zollicoffer's troops arrived at the advanced encampment of the 11th Tennessee. After packing their knapsacks,[55] Rains's men fell into line, and the brigade marched out with Lieutenant Colonel Branner's cavalry battalion at the van of the column with 220 troopers. The 11th Tennessee led the infantry with 650 men. The 15th Mississippi, commanded by Colonel Winfield S. Statham, followed with 600 men. The 17th Tennessee, under command of Colonel Tazewell Newman, was next in line with 600 men. Colonel Joel Battle's 20th Tennessee followed with 650 men. Colonel Samuel Powel's 29th Tennessee was next in line, followed by the Rutledge Artillery and the baggage train, ambulances, and rear guard of infantry. The 1st Tennessee

---

[51] "Our Army Correspondence," Ibid., 8 October 1861.
[52] Ibid.
[53] Ibid.
[54] "The Storming of Camp Wildcat," Nashville (TN) *Republican Banner*, 30 October 1861.
[55] Castillo Barfield to Mollie, 4 November 1861, In Lincoln Museum Collection, Abraham Lincoln Library and Museum, Lincoln Memorial University, Harrogate, TN.

Cavalry, commanded by Lieutenant Colonel Frank McNairy, with 280 men, and Lieutenant Colonel William Brazelton's 3rd Tennessee Cavalry Battalion with 280 men, followed the infantry. The remainder of all the commands not taken on the march, including the 16th Alabama Infantry, armed with percussion cap muskets, stayed behind to garrison Camp Buckner under the command of Major A. L. Landis.[56] After marching for approximately two miles, the entire brigade halted and bivouacked the remainder of the night. One soldier of the brigade described the scene:

> This, the scene of our first bivouac in the enemy's country was one of novelty and interest—horses and camp wagons, caissons and cannon scattered in every direction; and the blazing camp fires, casting a lurid glare around and over everything, lent an excitement to the occasion which seemed to be contagious, for, while the bugles sounded and the snare drums rattled, horses were neighing and soldiers were singing and the sapper's axe was ringing in the woods, the welcome note of preparation for supper. It was the only really comfortable night we experienced on the expedition.[57]

On the following morning, the Gheber Guards were the advance company of the brigade.[58] As the men fell into formation, clouds darkened the sky signaling the likelihood of a strong thunderstorm. Despite the chance for showers, Zollicoffer continued his march deeper into enemy territory. The Ghebers moved several hundred yards in front of the brigade building bridges and clearing the route. As the morning passed, the rain came, "and then followed the most wretched and dismal day I ever knew" stated one of the Tennesseans.[59] The soldier went on to say, "All day in the rain we trudged along the penetrating showers drenching us mercilessly."[60] First Lieutenant Castillo Barfield of the Gheber Guards stated, "We marched about 300 yards ahead [of the brigade] built bridges &c.—from early dawn to eve through a hard rain the entire day—I never came so near dying from fatigue in my life."[61] After a hard wet day of marching, the Confederates camped that Thursday night in a forest. One of Zollicoffer's Rebels complained, "There we were without a change of linen or even a dry chip to lay on—leafless branches of the trees affording little or no protection from the rain."[62]

By Friday morning, the rain had stopped, and the sky had cleared. As the Confederate column crept deeper into Kentucky, a lieutenant of the 20th Tennessee described the scene, "When the sunlight appeared its bright rays caused the gun

---

[56] *OR*, ser. I, vol. 52, pt. 2, 176.
[57] "The Storming of Camp Wildcat," Nashville *Republican Banner*, 30 October 1861.
[58] Castillo Barfield to Mollie.
[59] "The Storming of Camp Wildcat," Nashville *Republican Banner*, 30 October 1861.
[60] Ibid.
[61] Castillo Barfield to Mollie.
[62] "The Storming of Camp Wildcat," Nashville *Republican Banner*, 30 October 1861.

barrels to glitter and the winding column presented the appearance of a monster boa-constrictor creeping along the road with its brilliant scales glistening in the sun."[63] Later in the day, "the splendid brass band of the 15th Mississippi Regiment struck up and the soldiers with high hopes and buoyant spirits kept merry time to its delightful measures."[64]

By the end of the day, the men footsore and weary, had reached Laurel Bridge, eighteen miles or so beyond Barboursville. As men made camp, pickets took their places at intervals around the perimeter. After dark, these pickets had a small skirmish with about forty Federal scouts, and succeeded in capturing an "Indiana Hoosier."[65]

The following morning, Zollicoffer placed the 20th and 29th Tennessee regiments, who were unencumbered with knapsacks, in the front of the brigade. Zollicoffer's men once again marched forward. As the brigade made its way deeper into enemy territory, the men passed the grave of the "defunct abolitionist," who had been killed in the action of the previous night and buried by Confederate troops.[66]

At noon, the Rebels marched through London and found it mostly deserted. Zollicoffer halted his column in the middle of town and ordered them to fix bayonets. The troops then continued the march through the village with sunlight gleaming from their weapons. After proceeding about four miles from town, a citizen brought the news that approximately 1,500 of the enemy were marching toward them and were only about three miles ahead.[67] Zollicoffer took the necessary precautions to engage the enemy. "We threw off our knapsacks, drew cartridges and double quicked for several miles," recalled a soldier of the 11th Tennessee.[68] The 29th Tennessee advanced across Laurel Creek while the 20th Tennessee took down every fence within a half mile of their position and formed a line of battle. After the 20th formed their line, following orders, the men concealed themselves in the tall grass, while pickets went out in every direction to ascertain the movement of the Federals. A lieutenant of the 11th Tennessee said, "During the day we formed three lines of battle and double-quicked about two miles instantly expecting an attack."[69] The pickets found no sign of the enemy, and soon the brigade was on the march again.

---

[63] Ibid.
[64] Ibid.
[65] Ibid.
[66] "The Storming of Camp Wildcat," Nashville *Republican Banner*, 30 October 1861. This is believed to be Private Travis Moore of the 1st Kentucky Cavalry.
[67] "The Storming of Camp Wildcat," Nashville *Republican Banner*, 30 October 1861.
[68] Castillo Barfield to Mollie.
[69] Ibid.

As the advance continued, two companies of the 20th Tennessee moved forward through "an almost impenetrable thicket on each side of the road," while the remainder of Zollicoffer's men followed some distance behind.[70] The line of skirmishers eventually reached a cornfield. Suddenly, one of the sergeants on the left of the skirmishers observed a group of men he believed to be the enemy. The skirmish line moved forward slowly. Before the skirmishers had gone a few steps, they fired at a small party of men they saw scampering through the field. As the skirmishers looked deeper into the field, they saw a line of soldiers they identified as an Ohio regiment, but on closer examination, it was discovered that they were the 29th Tennessee, which had moved around them and had gained a position to their front without their knowledge.[71]

As Zollicoffer's men neared Rockcastle, felled trees littered the route, delaying the Confederate advance. The brigade moved a hundred yards at a time clearing the fallen timber from their path. As the column inched forward, a Confederate lieutenant recalled that the men were "tired hungry, and wanting sleep; it was not surprising that a gloom pervaded the entire column, and made every soldier silent and thoughtful."[72] About dusk, the lead elements of the brigade collided with enemy pickets. One of the Confederates present said,

> Our men gave the signal by raising their hats. One of the enemy said "Union." As soon as he spoke, a dozen Rebel bullets whizzed in their direction, killing one man instantly. Upon examination, he proved to be an East Tennessean from Bledsoe County, a shoemaker named Merryman [Private James Mariman, Company B, 1st Kentucky Cavalry]. We left him on the roadside where he remained until after the attack on Wildcat Camp, when our men returning buried the body.[73]

After the enemy pickets withdrew, the remainder of Zollicoffer's men continued their march, passing Mariman's body. An officer of the 11th Tennessee remembered,

> Just as we started through it [the defile leading down to the Little Rockcastle River] we found one of the enemy's pickets lying dead on the roadside. He had been shot by our pickets only a half hour before. We filed around him and went on our way. My feeling[s] were indescribable. He was a well dressed and a fine looking young man. As he lay covered ore with his own gore and dirt where he fell, I thought might not some sunny face be brightening with the ardent hope of hearing his footsteps again and might not some heart be throbbing for this poor miserable

---

[70] "The Storming of Camp Wildcat," Nashville (TN) *Republican Banner*, 30 October 1861.
[71] Ibid.
[72] Ibid.
[73] Ibid.

outcast as many hearts would doubtless have been for us did they know our perilous situation.[74]

As the cavalry vanguard approached the Little Rockcastle River, they discovered that the Yankees, in an attempt to retard their advance, had burned the bridge and cut down trees to blockade the ford. Sappers were called up and sent ahead to remove the downed trees. While the Sappers were clearing the road, the men of the 11th Tennessee rested in the middle of the road. As the men waited, night came and brought with it "the chilling air with its biting breath."[75] Given their dangerous proximity to the enemy, the Confederate officers did not allow the men to build campfires.[76] While they waited, an occasional shot rang out in the distance echoing through the mountains reminding the men of the deadly business to which they must soon attend.

After remaining in the middle of the road for approximately four hours, at 1:00 AM, Zollicoffer ordered the men back into line. At the command, the men stepped forward, moving down the mountain toward the bank of the Little Rockcastle River. A member of the Gheber Guards stated, "We marched on inch by inch—sending out scouts and the word 'alls well' was passed back and then we would move on 40 or 50 or a hundred yds as the case might be. Never in my life did I pass such a night of eager expectancy."[77] As the men bumbled around in the darkness, anxiety gripped them. "We did not know where we were going," expressed a concerned officer of the 11th.[78] Not only did the darkness obscure their path, but when they moved, they were occasionally fired on by the enemy. With the image of the dead Federal, James Mariman, indelibly imprinted in their minds, they were all concerned about who among them would be killed. Despite their fears, the brigade soon reached the river. On the opposite bank lay the Moses Kemper farm.

As a precautionary measure, Zollicoffer ordered Brazelton's Cavalry to cross the river to drive off any enemy possibly concealed in the Kemper cornfield. As Brazelton's men dashed across the river, the enemy sent a volley in their direction. The volley checked Brazelton's advance, and his troopers fell back across the river. Zollicoffer then sent Colonel McNairy across the river with his battalion of cavalry. "Away they went dashing through the leaves and cornstalks and crack! Crack! Went a dozen rifles right among them."[79] McNairy's cavalrymen cheered loudly and charged the enemy. Other troopers dismounted and fired at the enemy who were concealed in the bushes lining the road. Off in the distance could be heard the rattle

---

[74] Castillo Barfield to Mollie.
[75] Ibid.
[76] Ibid.
[77] Ibid.
[78] Ibid.
[79] "The Storming of Camp Wildcat," Nashville (TN) *Republican Banner*, 30 October 1861.

of drums as the Federal alarm echoed through the Rockcastle hills. Everyone in Zollicoffer's Brigade thought a general engagement was on.[80]

General Zollicoffer ordered the 20th Tennessee to cross the river to support McNairy's cavalry. Lieutenant Albert Roberts of that regiment commented,

> We went ahead at a double quick, dashing through the creek nearly waist deep and it caused an involuntary shudder as the chilling element filled our boots and saturated our clothing so that we moved forward with difficulty, charging we knew not where and anticipating a shower of bullets from some direction at any moment. We were halted in the road and a consultation was held, the result of which was that we were ordered back across the creek. Then were ordered to return [making three trips across the river] to guard the cornfield while the cavalry got forage for their horses. Then we were thrown out as skirmishers on the very hill from which the enemy fired on our cavalry and there I think I spent the most wretched and uncomfortable night of my life. I shall certainly never forget it.[81]

When the enemy pickets withdrew from the field, the majority of the brigade crossed the river. At 2:00 on Saturday morning, Zollicoffer's exhausted men halted and spent a miserable night in the fields and woods on the Kemper farm, located in the Hazel Patch Valley, about one and a half miles from the main Federal positions in the Rockcastle Hills. "Finally we bivouacked in an open field and lay upon the wet ground until morning," stated a member of the 11th Tennessee.[82] Colonel Rains and Dr. Callender spread out their blankets and slept in a cabbage patch just north of Kemper's. Lieutenant Albert Roberts of the 20th Tennessee said,

> Before we were ordered down into the road and proceeded on to Wildcat, which some of us from long watching began to believe was a myth. We made a halt in the road for daylight and I remember seeing with no little envious feeling my friends Dr. C. [Callender] and Col. Rains retire to their virtuous blankets in a cabbage patch while mine were back in the wagons several miles behind."[83]

Lieutenant Castillo Barfield of the Gheber Guards stated, "I lay down with 5 of our boys and when I awoke I was trembling like an aspen leaf from the chilling influence of the midnight air."[84] An officer of the Bull Pups commented, "We never passed a colder or more disagreeable night, having no blankets or covering of any sort, nor could we make [a] fire, on account of our being in the neighborhood of the

---

[80] Ibid.
[81] Ibid.
[82] Castillo Barfield to Mollie.
[83] "The Storming of Camp Wildcat," Nashville (TN) *Republican Banner*, 30 October 1861.
[84] Castillo Barfield to Mollie.

enemy."[85] Another soldier tersely but accurately encapsulated the misery of the situation by saying that it was "a miserable night, cold as the north pole."[86]

At dawn the following morning, the men rose. Rations were scarce and could not be prepared. Lieutenant Barfield said that the men ate a piece of bread and meat if they had it.[87] Soon the regiments formed, and Zollicoffer began his attack. The 11th Tennessee led the brigade, and the Bull Pups were the lead unit of the regiment.[88] As the 11th Tennessee moved up the Wilderness Road, they reached the range of hills where the enemy was encamped. At this point, the enemy had again blockaded the road with fallen trees, leaving it impassable. The infantry stopped, and Captain Josiah Pitts strategically deployed the Waverly Guards as skirmishers on the left wing of the brigade.[89] As soon as the skirmishers had taken their positions, the brigade left the road and continued its advance through the woods. Pitts's skirmishers had only gone about 100 yards when they encountered the Yankee picket line. One of the startled Federal pickets, probably belonging to the 7th Kentucky Infantry, hailed a member of the advancing Waverly Guards and asked if he was an Indianian. "No! By God, a Tennessean!" exclaimed the soldier from Humphreys County, as he sent a round of buck and ball whizzing past the head of the Yankee who was already beating a hasty retreat.[90] The Federal soldier, who apparently was uninjured, skedaddled but abandoned his gun, haversack, and other trappings. The report of the musket echoed through the hills and induced the remaining Federal pickets to fall back to their main line. As the Yankees retreated, the 11th Tennessee charged ahead after them. After a short pursuit, the recall was sounded.[91]

After reforming, Zollicoffer's men continued up the Wilderness Road until other obstructions lay in their path. As men cleared the blockades, some of Zollicoffer's officers attempted to find out more about the strength of the Federal positions. A soldier of the 20th Tennessee recalled the story, "An Old Hag, living at the bottom of the hill, was asked if the enemy had any cannon; 'Yes,' she replied, and 'if you go up there they'll give you hell.'"[92] In close proximity to the woman's home, Dr. Callender and the other surgical staff appropriated a few old buildings for a temporary hospital.[93]

---

[85] Nashville (TN) *Daily Gazette*, 1 November 1861.

[86] Deering J. Roberts, "Service with the Twentieth Tennessee," *Confederate Veteran* vol. 33 no. 1 (January 1925): 15.

[87] Castillo Barfield to Mollie.

[88] Nashville (TN) *Daily Gazette*, 1 November 1861.

[89] Ibid.

[90] Ibid.

[91] Ibid.

[92] "The Storming of Camp Wildcat," Nashville (TN) *Republican Banner*, 30 October 1861.

[93] Ibid.

As the other regiments came up, the excellently armed 15th Mississippi, deployed behind the "old hag's" house and moved to the left up a hill toward the enemy's right. Meanwhile, the 11th, 17th, and 29th Tennessee regiments arrived, moved past the old woman's house, marched through a field and halted in the valley. Rains deployed his men in a line of battle and awaited further orders.[94]

After all was ready, Rains moved his men forward while the 17th Tennessee, supported by the 29th Tennessee, moved up the hill to the right. The 20th Tennessee, except for two companies, remained behind to support Rutledge's Battery. The other two companies of the 20th deployed to the extreme left and right flanks of the advancing Confederate line.[95]

As the 11th Tennessee made its way through the thick underbrush, the 1st battalion or right wing of the regiment was deployed to the right and was sent toward Colonel Newman's 17th Tennessee to engage the Federals in position on Round Hill. Meanwhile, the 2nd battalion moved straight ahead.[96] As soon as the 1st battalion of the 11th Tennessee neared the Yankee positions on the summit of Round Hill, Federal infantrymen some 500 yards to their right unleashed a heavy volley. Colonel John Coburn of the 33rd Indiana Infantry reported, "In ten minutes or more the enemy appeared in front of our position to the south at a distance of half a mile in the valley. They were in large numbers, and for half an hour passed by an open space in the road and formed in line. They soon came near us under cover of a wood, which entirely concealed their approach until we were appraised of their immediate presence by firing of musketry."[97]

As the battle commenced in earnest, a Yankee described the scene, "Suddenly, a little after ten o'clock, three unearthly yells broke from the fatal woods, and their echoes were drowned in the sharp rattle of musketry. Protected by the thickets and trees, the enemy had ascended unseen to within a hundred and thirty yards of the hilltop—then forming, were advancing on two sides and in four ranks."[98] One of the Confederates observed, "I was struck with the long range of the enemy's guns and the great force with which the Minnie balls would lop off large twigs and bark trees with a savage crash all around us."[99] "Colonel Rains gallantly led his regiment forward," stated one observer, "though part of the time in a cross-fire from two strong gally-ports of the enemy."[100] Lieutenant Barfield stated, "We had to climb the mountain sides, so precipitous that we took hold on the bushes to help us up....

---

[94] Nashville (TN) *Daily Gazette*, 1 November 1861.
[95] Ibid.
[96] "Our Special Army Correspondence," Ibid., 31 October 1861.
[97] *OR*, ser. I, vol. 4, 208.
[98] Cincinnati (OH) *Gazette*, 23 October 1861.
[99] "The Storming of Camp Wildcat," Nashville (TN) *Republican Banner*, 30 October 1861.
[100] Ibid.

We climbed over logs, rocks, went thru the thickest bushes I ever saw, became entangled in grapevines & greenbriers, & had the confoundest time I generally ever witnessed."[101] Barfield went on to say, "For a time the firing on both sides resembled one universal volcanic eruption or explosion. The mountainsides seemed to be vomiting fire. Pitts company [the Waverly Guards] was thrown forward early in the action as skirmishers & when the fight began in real earnest they got scattered so that several of them came into our ranks & and into the other companies engaged."[102]

Private James F. Gray was advancing as a skirmisher with the Waverly Guards when a minie ball struck his rifle. The bullet passed through the gunstock, bent the barrel, entered his cheek and ranged around his head. Gray, in critical condition, was removed him from the field and taken to the temporary field hospital, which Dr. Callender had set up in the rear.[103] In addition to Gray, Corporal William E. Burns of the Hermitage Guards and B. F. Mayberry of the Waverly Guards sustained injuries.[104] For the most part, however, the Federal volleys were too high. In the struggle, Rains's men attempted to return fire, but their antiquated flintlocks were ineffective at that range, so the boys took cover behind trees.[105]

Meanwhile, the 2nd battalion moved further up John's Hollow. The Cheatham Rifles, commanded by Captain Dick McCann, led this advance, and the Bull Pups, Hickman Guards, Dickson Slashers, and Thedford's Company followed closely behind. The Federal position was heavily fortified and rested on the face of a hill, on a precipitous bluff, which lay at the head of a gorge about a quarter of a mile wide. Captain McCann stated, "The enemy had built numerous breastworks of great strength, and the natural position, made it a second Gibraltar. The principal place of the fortification was on a large mountain whose rock bluffs stood out in bold relief; and on an adjoining mountain were pits dug for their 'sharpshooters' that would keep us off any position we should wish to occupy."[106]

While the battle was in progress, additional Federal units under command of Brigadier General Albin Schoepf, who assumed overall command when he arrived, reinforced Garrard's troops. As Rains's companies tried to move forward in order, they became intermingled. Lieutenant Sam Nichol of the Bull Pups was beside his brother, Lieutenant William Nichol of the Cheatham Rifles, when the latter had a button shot off his uniform. The bullet struck William in the hand, causing a slight wound.[107] As Captain Godshall led his tenacious Bull Pups forward, he received a

---

[101] Castillo Barfield to Mollie.
[102] Ibid.
[103] "The Storming of Camp Wildcat," Nashville (TN) *Daily Gazette*, 30 October 1861.
[104] "Our Special Army Correspondence," Ibid., 31 October 1861.
[105] Ibid., 1 November 1861.
[106] "Our Special Army Correspondence," Ibid., 31 October 1861.
[107] Ibid., 1 November 1861.

shot through the coat and another bullet hit his waist belt, leaving him with a slight wound in the side.[108] In addition, Federal fire wounded two other soldiers from the Bull Pups.[109]

The Federal bullets fell thickly around Rains's men, so they sought cover behind trees, brush, rocks, and anything else that could offer protection. One observer stated, "Col. Rains's men were pretty well 'up' in the skirmish drill and in the 'bullet storm' they hugged the ground like lizards, firing and loading from a recumbent position."[110] The concentrated enemy fire from the ridge kept the 11th Tennessee pinned down. After thirty minutes or so of being unable to move, the 17th Tennessee advanced toward the fort on Round Hill, diverting the Federal fire away from Rains's position. Although bold, Newman's charge was futile as he was unable to breach the Federal defenses. Nevertheless, he stubbornly held his ground, sustaining heavy casualties.[111] Lieutenant Barfield stated, "Newman's Reg. got on the breastworks, but were repulsed from the fact that Raines Reg could not get them—we were within 100 yds of a bluff from 10 to 40 feet high & the top was lined with the enemies sharpshooters."[112]

Meanwhile, as the 2nd battalion of the 11th tried to advance, Federal reinforcements, including artillery, continued falling into line on the Federal right and played on Rains's advancing troops. "Minnie balls, grape and cannister & round shot fell about us as thick as hail. The trees & bushes were riddled in some places," stated a lieutenant of the 11th Tennessee.[113] At this time Major Hugh Lucas, commanding the 2nd battalion, ordered Lieutenant Sam Nichol of the Bull Pups to take twelve men to scout out the Federal position to locate an entrance into the Yankee fort and to determine the strength of the defenders. The lieutenant did as ordered but was unable to find a breach in the Federal defenses.[114]

Unable to continue the advance, Zollicoffer's men temporarily withdrew. Later in the day, Rains and the other colonels again formed their lines of battle and attempted to advance along the London Road. Rains led his men forward once again, this time to the highest point on the hill. The men hid behind rocks, trees, and other natural barriers making their best attempt at maintaining the alignment of their line of battle.[115] One of the Yankees reported, "The Rebels advanced shouting as before, supported by their artillery, at every discharge of which they screamed like fiends. A shell from the first of our guns silenced both their shouts

---

[108] Ibid.
[109] Ibid.
[110] Ibid., 30 October 1861.
[111] "The Storming of Camp Wildcat," Nashville (TN) *Banner*, 30 October 1861; "Our Special Army Correspondence," Nashville (TN) *Daily Gazette*, 31 October 1861.
[112] Castillo Barfield to Mollie.
[113] Ibid.
[114] Nashville (TN) *Daily Gazette*, 1 November 1861.
[115] Ibid.

and their cannonade, and sent them flying again with astonishment and consternation."[116] Sergeant Eastham Tarrant of the 1st Kentucky Cavalry (US) stated, "The enemy now formed in unbroken lines in a semi-circle from around our entire position on the point, in superior numbers, and delivered volley after volley into our ranks. The fire of the enemy at this time was hot and heavy."[117] As the Yankees fired a volley, Lieutenant Sam Nichol shouted to his Bull Pups, "Down boys, down for your life!"[118] At that instance, grape shot came from their front while small arms fire came from both the right and left flanks. Officers in the individual companies of the 11th pointed out targets in the forts to their men who carried the longer-range minie rifles. While these men acted as sharpshooters, the regiment determinedly held its ground, trying to make every shot count.[119] During this fight, Joseph Nesbitt of the Dickson Slashers, then more than forty-five years of age, saw an officer he believed to be the colonel of a Yankee regiment. The supposed colonel was too far off for the range of Nesbitt's old flintlock musket. Nesbitt then turned to J. I. J. Adams of the Dickson Rifles and asked to borrow his Enfield rifled musket, as he desired to shoot at the colonel. Adams could not let him have his Enfield, so Nesbitt decided to put in two charges of powder and "try him anyway." Nesbitt said that he did not know whether he killed the Yankee colonel or not, but he "moved" him. According to Adams, every time that Nesbitt fired a shot he would blow the smoke out of his gun, as was his custom when squirrel shooting at home.[120] Little did Nesbitt know at the time, but his target was probably not a colonel, but was likely General Schoepf himself. Chaplain Artemus Fullerton of the 17th Ohio commented, "General Schoepf was on the hill when the attack commenced and displayed most admirable personal courage. Seeing that the noise disturbed his horse, which he had tied at some distance, he desired a soldier to go and bring the animal to him. The man hesitating to go, General Schoepf went himself and just as he was unfastening the rein a perfect storm of balls flew round him-one passing between his legs and several striking the tree to which his horse was tied.[121]

Zollicoffer's men fell back again. After falling back for the second time, Rains reformed the 11th Tennessee to make a third sortie against the enemy. This time the 20th Tennessee was to advance in support of the 11th. In the meantime, however, Zollicoffer reconsidered and decided not to make another assault. Instead, a little after 4:00 PM, he withdrew his men. As the companies retired, they passed

---

[116] Louisville (KY) *Daily Journal*, 29 October 1861.

[117] Eastham Tarrant, *The Wild Riders of the First Kentucky Cavalry: A History of the Regiment in the Great War of the Rebellion* (Louisville, KY: Press of R. H. Carothers, 1894) 41.

[118] Nashville (TN) *Daily Gazette*, 1 November 1861.

[119] Ibid.

[120] J. I. J. Adams, "The Last Roll," *Confederate Veteran* 6/11 (November 1898): 534.

[121] Boston (MA) *Daily Courier*, 1 November 1861.

the makeshift field hospital where Drs. Callender, Cliffe, and Gentry "had their hands full."[122] As the men passed the hospital, a lieutenant stopped to chat a minute with Dr. Callender. The doctor showed him the bullet he had just "cut out from the back part" of Private James Gray's head. "The ball with its jagged and broken edge was about the ugliest thing I ever saw go through a man's head and not kill him" stated the lieutenant.[123] Despite the intense fire they sustained, the 11th Tennessee only lost about six wounded: James M. Brown of Company E, severely; Corporal William E. Burns of Company D, slightly; Private James F. Gray of Company A, severely; Private Robert Scott of Company E; Private John Hansberry of Company G; and John Brown of Company K, slightly.[124]

That night Zollicoffer's men camped on the same ground that they had the previous night. General Schoepf, content to remain in his strong defensive position, did not attempt to pursue Zollicoffer. During the battle, Zollicoffer had only fully engaged the 11th and 17th Tennessee regiments and a company from the 29th Tennessee and a company of the 20th Tennessee. The next morning the Confederates began a leisurely retreat back to Cumberland Ford over the same road on which they had advanced.

---

[122] "The Storming of Camp Wildcat," Nashville (TN) *Daily Gazette*, 30 October 1861.
[123] Ibid.
[124] Regimental Return, Record of Events, Field & Staff, October 1861, M268, R259, 11th Tennessee Infantry Service Records, National Archives Records Administration, *Compiled Service Records of Confederate Soldiers Who Served in Organizations from the State of Tennessee*, Washington, DC: National Archives and Records Service, General Services Administration, 1960. Hereafter cited as 11th TISR.

5

"The Dad Gumdest Roughest Country in the Southern Confederacy"

24 October–December 1861

By 24 October, Jerome Spence was nearing the Cumberland Gap on return from his sick furlough over what he termed "the dad gumdest roughest country in the Southern Confederacy or anywhere else." As the Confederate positions came into distant view, he observed the fortifications and said, "when an attack is made that it would be ineffectual as the natural advantages are very great."[1]

As Spence's party continued closer to Cumberland Gap, they began hearing reports of Zollicoffer's repulse at Rockcastle. Some of the rumors claimed that the 11th Tennessee lost thirty men at once and that the brigade was cut to pieces. Finally, they passed through the Gap and arrived at the 11th Tennessee's camp on the Rufus Moss farm near Cumberland Ford. The next morning, Spence was in a room with Dr. William Slayden, assistant surgeon of the 11th Tennessee, writing in his journal. As Spence wrote, he estimated three hundred wagons passing the Ford headed on to the Gap. At Cumberland Ford, "a thousand and one tales" of the battle circulated around camp. By sundown, the 20th Tennessee Infantry came in sight on the opposite side of the Cumberland River. Spence stated, "I know nothing of reliable character of the fight but I guess that our boys got most gloriously whipped or baffled at least in their calculations."[2]

Rain poured from the sky on Saturday morning, 26 October. The men of the 11th Tennessee trudged through mud, which was from an inch to two feet deep, crossed the Cumberland River and returned to their camp. The day passed, and then came a dark and dreary night. Before turning in for bed, James Shipp made biscuit dough for breakfast the next morning while one of his comrades sat near the campfire on a burnt chunk of wood writing letters home with smoke from the campfire blowing in his face.[3] The following day the men returned to their general camp routines of "cooking, cursing, and cutting firewood."[4] Spence commented that the looks of the men had changed greatly since he left them at Watauga Bridge two

---

[1] W. Jerome D. Spence, *The Travels, Troubles, Pleasures and Pastimes of Jerome D. Spence of Dunnington, Tennessee*, 24 October 1861, unpublished diary 10 May–25 November 1861, copy of manuscript in possession of Gary W. Waddey.

[2] Ibid., 25 October 1861.

[3] Ibid., 26 October 1861.

[4] Ibid., 27 October 1861.

months earlier, "Their beard has grown considerably and their clothes have become very homely and the boys have patched them to their own notions. William Burchard has patched his on the outside of the seat with the red front of an old boot leg. He is very well pleased with it for it is durable certain. About half the company ought to have something of the same kind for the rear of their pants which have become more holely than sighted."[5]

Throughout the month of September, Spencer Chandler, a citizen of Nashville, spent a great deal of energy raising supplies including socks, shoes, and blankets for the men of the 11th Tennessee. On 1 October, Mr. Chandler in the company of Corporals Abe Bumpass and J. L. Schaffer of the Hermitage Guards left Nashville transporting the much-needed supplies to the men. The officers of the regiment were so appreciative of Chandler's benevolence that they purchased a gold-headed cane and had engraved on the piece, "Presented to Spencer Chandler, by the Eleventh Regiment Tennessee Volunteers, 1861."[6]

On the morning of 29 October, some of the boys of the Hickman Guards were rousted before daylight for fear that a tree that had been burning for some time was about to fall on their tents. Many of the men stood around giving their opinion about which way the tree would fall. Sergeant Thomas Thompson and a friend left camp later that day and went to an eastern hillside a mile and a half to two miles away. On looking back at the camp, the boys reported, "all is in a perfect hallobaloo and uproar of fuss, fun, and fixings."[7] From their vantage point some of the boys could be seen chopping wood, carrying water to use for cooking, talking and laughing in groups. Some were rubbing their guns, some were driving wagons, some were pushing wagons, others were currying their horses, some were cooking, and some were walking about. By the end of the day the burning tree still had not fallen, so those in the endangered tents had to find room in the tents of others for fear that the tree might fall on them that night.[8]

After the expedition to Rockcastle, the Confederates withdrew from Cumberland Ford and fell back to Cumberland Gap. At the same time, General William S. Rosecrans, commanding the 1st Division of the Army of the Ohio, was rumored to be advancing on the Gap from Camp Dick Robinson.[9] On the morning of the 30th, the men of the 11th Tennessee prepared breakfast and made extra meat and biscuits, which they put in their haversacks. Following breakfast, the boys rolled up their tents and sat on the ground awaiting orders to move. While the boys sat, Zollicoffer came up and passed on some orders to an officer. As the men waited

---

[5] Ibid., 28 October 1861.
[6] "An Old Man Caned" Nashville (TN) *Daily Gazette*, 17 November 1861.
[7] Spence, *Travels*, 29 October 1861.
[8] Ibid.
[9] "Rosecrans Advancing on Cumberland Gap," Nashville (TN) *Republican Banner*, 31 October 1861.

around, boredom set in, and the men wondered what they would have to do next. A sergeant of the Hickman Guards commented, "We ignorant soldiers do not know one minute what we will do next, I don't at least and I know nearly as much as any of them and all I know is that we have to do as we are bid."[10] Before long, about two hundred cavalrymen rode up and said that the Lincolnites were advancing and were near Barboursville. As a result, the 11th did not proceed to the Gap that day, but late that evening the men found themselves taking their tents out of the wagons and setting them up again. When the camp was reestablished, Samuel G. Jones and William Lomax of the Hickman Guards took their guns and went to hunt hogs, turkeys, squirrels, or anything else edible. Not long after Jones and Lomax left, the boys in camp heard four shots ring out in the distance. Upon hearing the gunfire, Captain Weems ordered one of his sergeants to "go to where those boys are and tell them to come back to camp, and quit that shooting."[11] The sergeant went to find them as instructed, but while he was wandering alone in the woods, he began to think about all the reports he had heard about Yankees in the area and figured he would be better off back at camp. The sergeant returned only to find that Jones and Lomax had already returned and were having fun at his expense. The two men had killed a squirrel, but one soldier, observing the torn-up meat said, "The musket does not suit squirrel hunting." Suppertime neared, and Wallace Haile made up a game of bull pen.[12]

The following morning the men of the 11th Tennessee expected to start for Cumberland Gap, but again did not. About 10:00 AM, several of the men were engaged in killing and dividing a cow. The boys had great trouble killing the animal, but when the job was over, Thedford's Company and the Hickman Guards shared the beef. Aside from a typical day of routine camp duties little else happened.[13]

On Friday morning, 1 November, the 11th Tennessee received orders to prepare to march. The boys rolled up their tents and cooked two days rations. Finally, when all was ready, the boys formed ranks and began marching. After moving only about two hundred yards, the orders came for the men to halt, stack arms, fall out, and await further orders. While the boys were sitting on the ground waiting for orders, Lieutenant Dick Gordon was "singing one of the thunderingest songs that I ever heard," said an onlooker. The soldier continued, "I do not think Lieutenant Dick will die soon with the blues."[14]

The next morning clouds garrisoned the sky and a chill was noticeable in the damp mountain air. While the men were attending to morning duties, Colonel

---

[10] Spence, *Travels*, 30 October 1861.
[11] Ibid.
[12] Ibid.
[13] Ibid., 31 October 1861.
[14] Ibid., 1 November 1861.

Rains rode up and commanded the regiment to march on toward Cumberland Gap. Some of the boys of the regiment began joking that it did not look right for them to be marching unless rain was falling, for every time the 11th Tennessee marched it was raining. This time would be no different. Shortly after the regiment began its journey over the rough muddy roads toward the Gap, rain began falling. The boys had blankets and oilcloths draped around them, which helped to keep them dry. Although their opinions might change in the forthcoming Middle Tennessee Campaign, one member of the regiment said, "of all muddy places in creation, this is the muddiest."[15]

As the boys made their way over the rough east Kentucky road, they came to a house that appeared to be deserted but had several chickens around. Jerome Spence could not resist the temptation for fresh chicken, so he slipped into an outbuilding to catch one. Spence said, "I figured I had as good a title to them as anybody so I pitched in and caught an old hen."[16] As Spence was coming out of the crib with the hen in hand, someone yelled out, "What in the hell are you doing Spence?"[17] Thinking his captain had already passed, Spence stopped dead in his tracks recognizing his captain's thundering voice. The sergeant sheepishly turned around thinking he was caught red handed only to see Captain Weems coming out of a nearby barn with two hens. The boys of other companies helped themselves to the chickens as well.[18]

As the column neared Cumberland Gap, the soldiers made camp about a mile and a half out. Some of the boys kept dry that night by spending the night on hay in the loft of a stable. From their encampment, the soldiers of the 11th Tennessee could see a bare hill overlooking the road that passed through the Gap. The hill was strongly fortified. The men had placed several pieces of artillery on the summit, awaiting the approach of the Federals. On Sunday morning, 3 November, the regiment resumed its march toward the Gap. The men slogged through mud about four inches deep. At the base of the mountain, the boys had to cross Yellow Creek. Wagons passing through the cut of the Wilderness Road going up to the Gap entirely blocked the road. Finally, after marching all day, the boys passed through the Gap, came to the bottom of it at the Tennessee side and set up their camp. Of the march, Private James Morris Skelton of the Dickson Rifles, wrote his father, Abner Brown Skelton, "We have had a hard muddy time of it for it rained nearly every day and about 300 wagons, 6 or 700 cavalry and 5000 infantry makes a road a little muddy."[19] Lieutenant Barfield commented, "We arrived here today and are

---

[15] Ibid.
[16] Ibid.
[17] Ibid.
[18] Ibid.
[19] James M. Skelton to A. B. Skelton, 5 November 1861, possession of James M. Skelton, Evanston, IL.

snugly encamped in Tenn. on this side of the mountain.... At present we are comfortably situated on the south side of the mountain, which is near 1500 feet high on just the banks of a beautiful hill that leaps from the mountain side above us and turns an old aged mill whose crazy wheel makes strange and varied music for those who are absent."[20] Skelton also commented on the scenery, "This is one of the greatest places for mountain scenery I ever beheld, you can go on top of the mountain & see most any where you want to. We have good water as Tenn affords, sulphur and limestone, both our camps are situated between the 2 springs, so we can have either."[21]

On 5 November, Calvin F. Austin of Thedford's Company took a few minutes from the mundane camp duties to write his cousin, Mrs. E. A. Reeder, back home in Dickson County. In the letter Austin reported, "All the boys is better sadisfied than they have been since we left Thanesville [Haynesville]. I reckon we will take winter quarters here. We are at Cumberland Gap."[22] In another section of the letter, Austin described the setting at the Gap. "I think we have a healthy situation heare, theare is a good sulphur sprng heare and plenty of other water, theare is a spring breaks out of the mountains that turnes a splendid mill and furnace, it is a grand seen."[23] Austin went on to report on the health of some of the boys of his company, "I believe all the boys is getting well but Will Tatum, he has the mumps very bad. Burell Clifton is mending very slow, him and Tatum is going to Knoxville to the Hospitle with the wounded and theare I expect they will get furloughs home. J. J. Brown says he don't want to go home. Silas Tidwel is pestered with rheunatis [rheumatism]. I believe the rest of the boys is able for duty."[24]

Austin who had been sick himself, and had just recently recovered stated, "I was very sick for about a week, but I am able to eat my allowance now." He continued, "The first that I got that I could eat was sum soup of that Jack made of an old hen he got hold of on the road, he made the best soup that I ever eat. I believe Lige Caps said it would have been a heep beter if that bug hadent dropped in it. I believe it helped cure me."[25]

When the fellows of the 11th Tennessee had established their bivouac, they joined the other units of the encampment in the work of fortifying and building breastworks. On Wednesday morning, 6 November, Lieutenant Clint Jones of the Hickman Guards was put in command of a one hundred-man work party. The

---

[20] Castillo Barfield to Mollie.
[21] James M. Skelton to A. B. Skelton, 5 November 1861.
[22] C. F. Austin to E. A. Reeder, 5 November 1861, in John Trotwood Moore, *Tennessee, Civil War Records—Middle Tennessee, Civil War Correspondence* (Nashville, TN: Historical Records Survey, 1939) 48.
[23] Ibid.
[24] Ibid.
[25] Ibid.

group consisted of ten men from each of the ten companies of the regiment. Due to the roughness of the road, the men moved in a scattered formation, each choosing his route. The party climbed to the top of the mountain, which was about a mile from their encampment. When they arrived, they received orders to proceed to the breastworks on the northeast side of the Gap. Lieutenant Jones took about a dozen men to a distant hill and began chopping wood. Corporal Frazier took about ten men and began repairing some of the gabions around the works. Sergeant Spence took the remainder of the men and began throwing up embankments for the fortifications. After a hard day of work, the company returned to the camp.[26]

Zollicoffer's men placed several siege guns at strategic places on the sides of the mountains. The boys placed one cannon, dubbed "Long Tom," at the top of the pinnacle. At this time, the Confederates deemed their fortress at Cumberland Gap to be impenetrable.[27]

The men knew winter was well on the way, so they started building huts to live in for the coming cold weather. When the boys completed their shanties, they named their little village "Rainsville," and they named two of the company streets "Main Avenue" and "Boulevard de Godshall."[28]

Around this time, General Zollicoffer took several of the regiments of his brigade on his ill-fated campaign in the Battle of Fishing Creek. Zollicoffer left the garrison at Cumberland Gap under command of Colonel Rains. Rains kept the 11th Tennessee and a few other units to maintain the post lest this strategic position fall into enemy hands.[29] George W. Gordon of the 11th Tennessee stated, "Here we remained on this duty, and in cantonment, during the winter of 1861–2, with no more important action than an occasional display of our forces on the crest of the mountain on each side of the Gap, and delivering a few shots from our heaviest ordnance as the enemy would appear in our front."[30] During November and December 1861, Lieutenant Colonel Bateman was detached on extra service as the president of a general court martial at Knoxville, Tennessee.[31]

---

[26] Spence, *Travels*, 6 November 1861.

[27] Robert L. Kincaid, "Long Tom," *Kentucky* 17/4 (Winter 1963): 17.

[28] Nashville (TN) *Daily Gazette*, 24 December 1861.

[29] United States War Department, *The War of the Rebellion: A Compilation of the Official Records of the Union and Confederate Armies*. 70 vols. in 128 (Washington: Government Printing Office, 1880–1901; reprint, Gettysburg, PA: The National Historical Society, 1972) ser. I, vol. 4, 520. Hereafter cited as *OR*.

[30] John Berrien Lindsley, *Military Annals of Tennessee: Confederate* (1886; facsimile of the first edition, Wilmington, NC: Broadfoot Publishing, 1995) 293.

[31] Thomas P. Bateman, M268 R159, 11th Tennessee Infantry Service Records, National Archives Records Administration, *Compiled Service Records of Confederate Soldiers Who Served in Organizations from the State of Tennessee*, Washington, DC: National Archives and Records Service, General Services Administration, 1960. Hereafter cited as 11th TISR.

As soon as Rains assumed command of the garrison, Colonel William Churchwell, commander of the 4th Tennessee Infantry, protested. Because Churchwell's commission was from the Confederate States, and Rains's commission was from the State of Tennessee, there was a question of who was the senior officer. Upon hearing the issue, Richmond authorities transferred temporary command of the garrison to Churchwell until they could investigate the dispute. Because of the disagreement, a sense of tension prevailed around the camp until the matter was resolved.[32]

On Friday morning, 8 November, the men of the regiment fell in line for roll call. This was the first time since the regiment's arrival at Cumberland Gap that the company officers had assembled their troops for roll. With things in a lax state, the men had begun wandering off from camp in large numbers and going all over the country. One member of the 11th Tennessee commented that the men of his company did not like the increased discipline very much as they would not behave themselves.[33]

On the same day, Colonel Rains took a detachment of the 11th Tennessee to Cumberland Ford where Bushwhackers had shot a cavalry lieutenant a few days earlier. The location from which the enemy shot the lieutenant was a very rugged rocky peak about a half-mile south of the Ford, near the previous fortifications of the Confederates.[34] Perhaps prophetically, one of the members of the regiment stated of Colonel Rains, "He wants a name and will get one if he ever gets into a fight."[35] Rains and his detachment returned two days later with three prisoners, one having a gunshot wound to the head.[36]

The following Sunday morning, 17 November, those interested gathered at an elbow in the road on the mountainside to hear a sermon from their chaplain, Fountain Pitts. After Pitts began his homily, and had gone on with his arguments "to an interesting part," some horses hitched to a wagon up the mountainside were spooked. The horses took off, galloping at first but increased their pace to full speed as they ran down the winding mountain road nearing the place where the congregation had gathered for worship. Instead of making the all-important turn in the road, the horses kept straight, heading toward the crowd. One of the wagon wheels struck a stump and threw one of the horses into a deep gully, but the other horse continued at full speed into the crowd. By this time, the parson's congregation had scattered in every direction. Corporal Frazier of the Hickman Guards took off running and while looking back, he hung his foot on something. The corporal fell

---

[32] James E. Rains to Ida Rains, 6 November 1861, James Edward Rains Letters 1861–1862, Manuscript Collection MF 64, Tennessee Library and Archives, Nashville, TN.
[33] Spence, *Travels*, 6 November 1861.
[34] Ibid.
[35] Ibid.
[36] Ibid., 16 November 1861.

and about a dozen men ran over him trying to get out of the way of the renegade horse. Of course, this frightened Frazier as he expected to be run over by the wagon. Besides dirtying his Sunday clothes, the corporal was providentially saved from further injury.[37]

Lazy times around camp were spent reading or lounging around. On the evening of 18 November, Dr. Hughes and Chaplain Pitts were reading. Hughes had the *Christian Advocate*, and Pitts had the *Union and American*. While these two were reading, Dr. Slayden, assistant surgeon for the 11th, was busy smoking a pipe about the size of a man's fist.[38]

Work continued the following day as the men were still building huts and throwing up breastworks. Four members of the Hickman Guards were at work and had almost completed house number 4. The men had located the houses for the 11th Tennessee a quarter of a mile east of the Gap under the Virginia Road and approximately two hundred yards from a fine mountain spring.[39] One of the soldiers writing from Cumberland Gap a few days later wrote in a letter to his wife, "We are building our little cabins [we] daub them tight with mud have a little fireplace in them & we can keep comfortable this winter."[40] The following day, Wednesday, 20 November, opened with a very dreary morning. Rain began to fall, once again increasing the already thick mud.[41]

On one occasion during this time, a Confederate soldier was out in the woods on picket duty. He was all alone and perhaps a little edgy thinking about the possibility of Federal troops being in the area. As the soldier watched through the woods for any sign of the enemy, he noticed something dark moving in the distance. The excited Rebel picket, with his mind racing, believed the object to be a masked battery. The Rebel picket steadied his nerves as best he could, took careful aim, fired a round, and skedaddled back to camp. After the frightened picket raised the alarm, an officer sent a reconnaissance patrol to investigate the whereabouts of the enemy. As the patrol arrived at the location of the incident, they discovered that the nervous picket had mistaken a bear for the masked battery. The bear was in the last agonies of death. Another soldier put the animal out of its misery, skinned it, and took the bear back to camp where it was eaten by the soldiers.[42]

On Friday, 22 November, Dr. Pitts gave Sergeant Spence a medical discharge. Spence carried his paperwork first to Colonel Churchwell, who was still commanding the garrison. Churchwell signed the papers. Spence then proceeded to

---

[37] Ibid., 17 November 1861.
[38] Ibid., 18 November 1861.
[39] Ibid., 19 November 1861.
[40] Enoch L. Mitchell, "Letters of a Confederate Surgeon in the Army of Tennessee to His Wife," *Tennessee Historical Quarterly* 5/1 (March 1946): 60.
[41] Spence, *Travels*, 20 November 1861.
[42] Nashville (TN) *Daily Gazette*, 21 November 1861.

Colonel Rains to get him to sign them. Rains became furious that Churchwell had discharged one of his men without his authorization first. Rains took the discharge, tore it in half and threw it in the fire before the sergeant's eyes. Spence commented, "I understand why he treated me so ungentlemanly, twas simply this—Col. Churchwell out managed Rains and got command of this post and Rains has been mad at him ever since. And to see Churchwell's approval above his did not suit a man of Rains' pride."[43] Rains told Spence to get Dr. Callender to examine him, and if Dr. Callender recommended one then he would get a discharge. Enraged, Rains went on to say that Churchwell could not discharge his men.[44]

As the days passed, the mountain air continued to turn colder. By Sunday, 24 November, it was snowing. The ground was muddy and was not yet frozen, so the snow melted as soon as it hit the ground. This gave the boys added incentive to get their houses completed before a big snowfall. One soldier, looking at the snow falling between the mountains said, "It was a beautiful sight, but lonesome."[45] On the same day, while work parties of the 11th Tennessee were continuing to throw up breastworks on the mountain, two members of the 11th accidentally rolled a large stone down the mountainside, which killed one of Colonel Churchwell's men.[46]

On 25 November, Rains wrote his wife in Nashville and said that he was living "very comfortably" in his new house and that his men would soon be moving into theirs. As soon as the boys finished their huts, complete with chimneys, they began to leave their tents and move in.[47] A soldier of the regiment stated, "They are not like home though they are comfortable."[48] Rains also told his wife in the same letter that the matter of rank between him and Colonel Churchwell had been settled. Churchwell was sent to Knoxville as provost marshal of East Tennessee, and Rains was left in command of the garrison at Cumberland Gap.[49]

On 4 December, the Gheber Guards received some much-needed supplies including forty-six coats and fifty-two pairs of pants.[50] Two days later, some friends of Lieutenant Sam Nichol of the Bull Pups presented him with a sword while he was visiting Nashville.[51] Meanwhile, the Confederates continued strengthening their position at Cumberland Gap.

Five days later, one of the soldiers wrote about the improved defenses:

---

[43] Spence, *Travels*, 22 November 1861.
[44] Ibid.
[45] Ibid., 24 November 1861.
[46] James E. Rains to Ida Rains, 25 November 1861.
[47] Ibid.
[48] Spence, *Travels*, 25 November 1861.
[49] James E. Rains to Ida Rains, 25 November 1861.
[50] William Thedford, M268 R163, 11th TISR.
[51] "Presented with a Sword," Nashville (TN) *Daily Gazette*, 7 December 1861.

We have recently had quite an acquisition to our defenses here in the shape of several big guns. Yesterday, Colonel Rains, who is in command here, ordered every man to the entrenchments to witness the firing of all the cannon in the fortifications. In obedience to the above order, we marched to the works where we were stationed so as to see the sight, when everything was ready the signal was given and boom, boom, went the cannon from every direction. Presently the infantry were ordered to fire, and for the space of about fifteen minutes a more incessant rattle of musketry relieved every half minute by the booming cannon, never was heard. [52]

Within another ten days, Rains reported to his wife that everything at Cumberland Gap was quiet and in good order. He stated that his success in the management of the post had thus far been satisfactory, at least to himself.[53]

On 23 December, Rains had his regiment march in a dress parade. After the parade was over, Rains assembled the regiment and Patsy, Rains's "little Irish orderly," presented each man with a New Testament, provided by the Methodist Publishing House in Nashville. The men of the 11th Tennessee looked very sharp as many of them had new uniforms including red kepis.[54] Later that evening Rains commented about the condition of things at Cumberland Gap,

> [I] have a great deal of trouble with furloughs, especially with the cavalry. Applications are numerous and pushed upon me. My own men do not trouble me much about it. They are very quiet, orderly, and well behaved. It is conceded everywhere and by everybody to be the best disciplined and best behaved regiment in the service. They are very much devoted to me, and seem to behave well just to please me, for they know how gratifying it is to me. I am so proud of the regiment now.[55]

While the 11th Tennessee manned the Gap, the citizens of Tazewell filed a petition to Colonel Rains, the commander of the post, regarding various atrocities several Confederate soldiers had committed against the residents, so the citizens of the area requested protection for life and property. Reportedly, a portion of the 3rd Tennessee Cavalry Battalion under command of Lieutenant Colonel Brazelton, which, according to some, were practically undisciplined, was at that time scouting and roaming over Lee County, Virginia, Claiborne, and Hancock counties, Tennessee, and into parts of Kentucky around the Gap. In response, Rains detailed several men of the Hickman Guards (including Warham Easley, Thomas Grimes, Sam Jones, Daniel Montgomery, C. C. Moreau, S. H. Ballard, George Garner, Andrew Lowe, Wash Shouse, Armistead Martin, and J. S. Thompson) under the

---

[52] Ibid., 14 December 1861.
[53] James E. Rains to Ida Rains, 18 December 1861.
[54] Ibid., 23 December 1861.
[55] Ibid.

command of 2nd Lieutenant Alexander H. Vaughan, whom he appointed provost marshal of the town.[56]

For a while, all went well. However, on 27 December at Blair's Creek, about five miles from Tazewell, on the Kentucky Road leading to Cumberland Gap, Lieutenant Vaughan was murdered while attempting to arrest several drunken cavalry troopers who were creating absolute pandemonium in the vicinity. Despite his death, Lieutenant Vaughan's detachment apprehended Joel T. Taylor, George M. Holmes, and John A. Cooter—all from Brazelton's 3rd Tennessee Cavalry Battalion—and took them back to Cumberland Gap where they were placed in chains and kept in the guardhouse to await trial by court-martial. The death of Lieutenant Vaughan was greatly lamented by fellow soldiers and the citizens of Tazewell alike. He was buried in the "Irish Cemetery" at Tazewell, and according to B. F. Shultz, a local resident, "There was sadness in every heart, and no funeral at this place had been so largely attended and no death so universally regretted."[57] As for the suspects, one died from illness and a second made his escape to the enemy's lines. The third, George Holmes, was taken first to Knoxville, then to Bean Station, where he was condemned by court-martial and executed by firing squad.[58]

---

[56] "Acknowledgement," Knoxville (TN) *Register*, 6 February 1862; B. F. Shultz, "Lieut. A. H. Vaughan, Killed in the War," *Confederate Veteran* 8/12 (December 1900): 518.

[57] Shultz, "Lieut. A. H. Vaughan," 518.

[58] A. H. Vaughan, M268 R163, 11th TISR.

6

"Well, This Beats Hell"

January–October 1862

The month of January brought increasingly bitter temperatures to Cumberland Gap. Private J. W. Wynn of the Washington Guards stated, "Some of the most severe hardships we had to undergo was in standing guard, where we were exposed to the wind, sleet and snow, to say nothing of the danger from the rifles of the foe lurking behind rocks and bushes, ready to pick us off without warning."[1]

By 2 January, Lieutenant Colonel Thomas P. Bateman had returned to the regiment after his absence of two months due to his service as the president of a military tribunal convened at Knoxville. On 10 January 1862, a court martial was convened by authority of Special Order Number 15. The purpose of the court martial was to try two soldiers from the Hermitage Guards for desertion. The defendants, Samuel McElroy and Alexander Miller, were charged with leaving the post at Cumberland Gap for fifteen days without the consent of their captain, John Binns, or other superior officer. A detail, which had been sent to Nashville by Colonel Rains specifically for the purpose of arresting deserters, returned with them. Captain William Green of the Dickson Rifles served as president of the proceedings. Lieutenant C. A. Bradshaw of the 4th Tennessee Infantry acted as the judge advocate. Other members of the 11th Tennessee sitting on the court included Captain W. J. Mallory of the Dickson Slashers, Captain George W. Gordon of the Gheber Guards, 1st Lieutenant F. F. Tidwell of Thedford's Company, 2nd Lieutenant J. L. Sloan of the Hermitage Guards, and 1st Lieutenant A. R. M. McDaniel of the Cheatham Rifles. The remaining members of the court were members of the 4th Tennessee Infantry and the 3rd Battalion Tennessee Cavalry. After prosecutors presented the evidence and the hearing was completed, the court found the accused guilty of being absent without leave and of frequently disobeying the orders of their superior officers. Their sentence was to forfeit all pay and allowances due them up to that point and that they pay by cash the cost of their arrest and transportation.[2]

---

[1] Mamie Yeary, *Reminiscences of the Boys in Gray, 1861–1865* (1912; reprint, Dayton, OH: Morningside, 1986) 827.

[2] Special Order 15, Cumberland Gap, Tennessee. 6 January 1862, Samuel M. McElroy, M268 R161, 11th Tennessee Infantry Service Records, National Archives Records Administration, *Compiled Service Records of Confederate Soldiers Who Served in Organizations from the State of Tennessee*, Washington, DC: National Archives and Records Service, General Services Administration, 1960. Hereafter cited as 11th TISR.

After leaving a small force under command of Colonel Rains at Cumberland Gap, Zollicoffer took the remainder of his troops to Jamestown, Tennessee, and then to Mill Springs, Kentucky, a small town on the south bank of the Cumberland River. Here Zollicoffer planned to build a base that would support a forward movement into Kentucky toward London or Danville. To the surprise of his superiors, instead of remaining at Mill Springs, Zollicoffer crossed the Cumberland and began to entrench on the north side of the river at Beech Grove. In response, Federal general, George H. Thomas, encamped at Lebanon, Kentucky, some forty miles from Beech Grove, moved his division southward in an attempt to destroy Zollicoffer's force. Bad weather slowed Thomas's progress, but within a few weeks, he had moved his division to Logan's Crossroads only nine miles north of Beech Grove. By 18 January, the Yankee commander began preparing to attack the Confederates. Meanwhile, General George Bibb Crittenden, Zollicoffer's immediate supervisor, arrived on the field to take command of the Southern forces. In the early morning hours of 19 January before Thomas could attack, the Confederates moved out of their camps and attacked him. The Rebel advance drove back the Federal pickets. In the confusion of the battle, Zollicoffer believed the 19th Tennessee, his leftmost regiment, was firing on another Confederate unit. Zollicoffer ordered the 19th to cease firing as he and an aide rode forward to realign the other troops. Federal Colonel S. S. Fry approached Zollicoffer, who was wearing a long green overcoat concealing his Confederate frock coat. Fry believed Zollicoffer to be the commander of one of the Federal regiments coming in as reinforcements. After a brief discussion, Colonel Fry realized he was talking to a Confederate officer. At that time, he and his regiment opened fire, killing Zollicoffer and his aide. Zollicoffer's body remained in the mud on the Mill Springs Road throughout the battle. By 3:00 PM, the Confederates had been beaten and retreated across the Cumberland River to Mill Springs. After the fighting had ceased, some Federal troops removed Zollicoffer's body and laid it under a large white oak tree nearby.[3] As the news of Zollicoffer's death reached Cumberland Gap, a sense of uneasiness seized the camp. Private James Bryan of the 11th Tennessee commented that a great deal of excitement prevailed in the camp due to Zollicoffer's death.[4]

On 22 January, the detachment of men that Rains had sent as guards to Tazewell, Tennessee, under command of Lieutenant Vaughan, returned to the Gap. The soldiers had received kind treatment from the citizens of the town. Upon their departure, some of the young women of Tazewell presented them with a cat.[5]

---

[3] Kent Masterson Brown, *The Civil War in Kentucky: Battle for the Bluegrass State* (Mason City, IA: Savas Publishing, 2000) 51–69.

[4] James Bryan to Tennie, 22 February 1862, Leigh Collection Book 19:35, United States Military History Institute, Carlisle Barracks, PA.

[5] Knoxville (TN) *Register*, 6 February 1862.

By 4 February, reports circulated in camp that the Federals had moved down to Cumberland Ford. "We don't expect an attack very soon but [we] don't know how soon it may happen," wrote a soldier in a letter to his wife.[6] He went on to say that "it rains every day here very sloppy, muddy, &c, today is cool and cloudy."[7]

Ten days later, on 14 February, a company of the 1st Battalion Kentucky Cavalry (US) made a reconnaissance to Cumberland Gap. In the expedition, the Federal soldiers advanced close to the Confederate positions and attacked the Rebel cavalry who were on picket duty. The Federals reported that they killed five of the Rebels, wounded two, and took two prisoners. In addition to the prisoners, the Yankees also claimed to have captured eight horses, seven sabers, and five double-barreled shotguns.[8] Confederate artillerymen spotted the Federal troops and fired at them. This warm Southern hospitality forced the Federals to fall back to their positions at Cumberland Ford.[9]

On this same day, a nervous Colonel Rains anxiously requested additional troops in order to hold the Gap:

> I am convinced that the enemy will attack us at this place within a week. An attack to-morrow is probable. Their cavalry drove in our pickets to-day about three miles in advance of us. The force, seven regiments, are reported to be at Cumberland Ford, 15 miles in front. The force we have cannot hold the place, being insufficient to man the works. The strength of the position has been greatly exaggerated. On the Kentucky side it is naturally weak and difficult to defend. It has been our policy to give currency to a different opinion of the place, and hence the error. It will require two regiments, in addition to the two now here, to resist the force menacing us. The position should never be abandoned. Its strategic importance cannot be exaggerated. On the Tennessee side it is naturally almost impregnable and art can make it completely so. If abandoned, it cannot be easily retaken.[10]

Because of the Federal probes, a sense of tension prevailed over the camp. A few days later, 1st Lieutenant Dick Gordon of the Hickman Guards wrote a friend that on the morning of 18 February, "the enemy came within sight of our breastworks again, but retreated without firing a shot."[11]

---

[6] Enoch L. Mitchell, "Letters of a Confederate Surgeon in the Army of Tennessee to His Wife," *Tennessee Historical Quarterly* 5/1 (March 1946): 66.

[7] Ibid.

[8] United States War Department, *The War of the Rebellion: A Compilation of the Official Records of the Union and Confederate Armies.* 70 vols. in 128 (Washington: Government Printing Office, 1880–1901; reprint, Gettysburg, PA: The National Historical Society, 1972) ser. I, vol. 7, 417. Hereafter cited as *OR*.

[9] Ibid.

[10] Ibid.

[11] R. C. Gordon to Miss Mary, 18 February 1862, Civil War Collection, Confederate, Box 9 #14, Tennessee State Library and Archives, Nashville, TN.

In a letter written to a friend on 22 February, James M. Bryan, a private in the Hermitage Guards, described the expectation of battle at Cumberland Gap, "It is reported that we will certainly have an attack here tomorrow or next Thursday by General Garrat [Garrard] with 7000 men. Colonel Rains has sent for three more regiments."[12] Again before closing his letter Bryan stated, "You may not be surprised to hear of a fight at this place for Col. Rains is expecting a fight here himself."[13]

Meanwhile, back home in Middle Tennessee, things had significantly worsened. By early February, a joint army-navy force consisting of land troops and a flotilla of seven gunboats, commanded by General Ulysses S. Grant and Flag Officer Andrew H. Foote, had broken the Confederate defensive perimeter across southern Kentucky. The joint operation drove south and east down the Tennessee and Cumberland River corridors. On 6 February, Fort Henry on the Tennessee River capitulated. James Lee McDonough commented, "The fall of Fort Henry opened the Tennessee River as an avenue of penetration all the way to the Alabama and Mississippi state lines."[14] Ten days after the fall of Fort Henry, Confederate authorities surrendered Fort Donelson, a garrison on the Cumberland River, guarding the approach to Nashville. With the demise of Fort Donelson, a Federal invasion of the South through Cumberland Gap to reach Nashville was no longer necessary. From Fort Donelson, Federal troops under Don Carlos Buell headed east toward Nashville. On 25 February, Buell drove a nail in the coffin of the Confederacy as his men entered Nashville virtually unopposed, capturing the vast stores of military goods collected there. As Buell's troops marched east into Nashville, General John Pope and Flag Officer Foote captured the thirty-nine-gun river battery at Island Number Ten just north of Memphis. Meanwhile, Grant continued southward down the Tennessee River toward Pittsburg Landing where he had established his camp by early March. At Pittsburg Landing, Grant's troops lay only twenty miles from the vital rail center of Corinth, Mississippi. Both sides considered Corinth the most strategically important town west of Chattanooga. The town held the intersection for the north-south Mobile and Ohio Railroad and the east-west Memphis and Charleston Railroad, providing a vital lifeline to the western Confederacy.[15]

With things in a critical state, Major General Edmund Kirby Smith arrived in Knoxville on 9 March to assume command of the Department of East Tennessee. When Smith arrived in Knoxville, he set up his headquarters across the street from

---

[12] James Bryan to Tennie.

[13] Ibid.

[14] James Lee McDonough, *War in Kentucky From Shiloh to Perryville* (Knoxville: University of Tennessee Press, 1994) 12.

[15] Ibid., 16–18.

the Bell Hotel and formally assumed his responsibilities.[16] Nothing had prepared Smith for the situation in which he found himself. In a letter to his wife the general confided, "I am overwhelmed with cares and troubles, no one can conceive the actual condition of East Tenn. Disloyal to the core, it is more dangerous and difficult to operate in, than the country of an acknowledged enemy."[17] In a report to the adjutant general on the same day, Smith stated, "I repeat, East Tennessee is an enemy's country. The people are against us, and ready to rise whenever an enemy column makes its appearance."[18]

Things at Cumberland Gap were no less tense. On 7 March a Rebel wrote his wife, "We have been threatened here by the enemy. They have come in sight twice with their bright swords, guns, &c glistening in the sun.... Several days ago they killed one of our men took 8 or 10 horses from the Cavalry too their swords guns, our men had to run. Everything is quiet here now."[19] Sometime during the siege of Cumberland Gap, the Federals captured Private John Brice of the Cheatham Rifles. The Federal authorities suspected Brice of being a spy, but instead of being condemned to death, Federal authorities imprisoned him at Camp Morton, Indiana, where he arrived 30 June 1862.[20]

By mid-March, Rains commanded 4,000 men at Cumberland Gap.[21] On Friday, 21 March the enemy moved up in force from Cumberland Ford. At daylight the following morning, the enemy attacked the Confederate positions with about 7,000 men. The Federal attack began by infantry assault along the Harlan Road.[22] Colonel Rains stated,

> We have had a fight at last. The enemy moved up from the Ford on Friday & attacked us at day light on Saturday morning. The fight lasted all day, closing at sunset. The fire was pretty hot. I was a mark all day, being on horseback, & having to visit all the different positions. Wherever I went they fired at me, & came very near striking me several times. The shells & minnie balls fell very thickly all over the encampment, but only wounded four of our men, none of them Nashville men. One man, of Col Morgan's Regt was killed; the wounded men were from the 3rd & 5th Geo Regts.[23]

---

[16] Joseph H. Parks, *General Edmund Kirby Smith C. S. A.* (Baton Rouge: Louisiana State University Press, 1982) 156–57.

[17] Ibid., 158.

[18] Ibid.

[19] Mitchell, "Letters of a Confederate Surgeon," 67.

[20] John Brice, M268 R159, 11th TISR.

[21] *OR*, ser. I, vol. 10, pt. 2, 308.

[22] James E. Rains to Ida Rains, 26 March 1862, James Edward Rains Letters 1861–1862, Manuscript Collection MF 64, Tennessee Library and Archives, Nashville, TN.

[23] Ibid.

The Federals made one sortie, which the Confederates easily repulsed. After the initial probe, the Yankees pulled back. With their infantry out of the way, the Federal artillery began bombarding the Confederate positions. The Rebel gunners responded in kind, and both sides banged at each other the rest of the day. The 11th Tennessee suffered no casualties in this engagement.[24] In a letter to his wife, Colonel Rains wrote, "It was quite a nice little battle.... It showed the strength of the Gap, & that our works are well built. Had it not been for the new works recently constructed on the mountain top the place would have been easily taken. Our men all behaved well. I believe they would have whipped twenty thousand as easily as they whipped seven thousand."[25]

After giving the details of the battle, the colonel described more of the beautiful surroundings at Cumberland Gap:

> We are having great excitement here at this time over a cave that has been recently discovered. The entrance to it is just above our house. Hundreds visit it daily. Gen Smith & staff visited it last week. I have been in today. It is indeed grand & beautiful. The stalactite formations surpass anything of the kind I ever saw. All conceivable shapes of men & animals & vegetables, are distinctly to be seen. There are towers & statues, pools of clear water, beautiful archades, & splendid chambers. Some of the rooms are said to surpass those of the Mammoth Cave. It is perhaps the most beautiful cave in the world. What a pity you did not see it, but you must come back in the spring, if I remain here until then. Cumberland Gap is a very different place now, from what it was when you were here. It is now an extensive military encampment. The troops are nearly all encamped on the mountains, around the works. We have a fine body of troops here & can not be whipped. It is our purpose never to surrender the place.[26]

Colonel Rains sent a message to General Smith informing him of the situation at Cumberland Gap. In reply, Smith instructed Rains to "keep his men under cover, conserve ammunition, and let the enemy exhaust their artillery."[27] Smith further advised Rains to allow the men to carry their blankets into the works with them. The men would then be well rested in the event of an attack. Smith exhorted Rains to "trust to your bayonets when the ammunition fails." Smith had no reinforcements to send, but he stressed that the Gap must be held to the "last extremity."[28]

In April, Lieutenant Colonel Bateman resigned his commission (for reasons unknown).[29] On 20 April, Howell Webb of the Hermitage Guards was promoted to

---

[24] Ibid.
[25] Ibid.
[26] Ibid.
[27] Parks, *General Edmund Kirby Smith, C. S. A.*, 161.
[28] Ibid.
[29] Thomas P. Bateman, M268, R159, 11th TISR.

fill the vacancy.³⁰ Later in the month, Milton O. Brooks received orders detailing him to Morristown, Tennessee, where he would be the drillmaster for the recruits of the 30th Tennessee Infantry.³¹ By 17 April, Brigadier General Carter Stevenson, recently assigned to the Department of East Tennessee, brought three additional brigades of infantry and superseded Colonel Rains as commander at Cumberland Gap.³²

By the middle of April, the members of the 11th Tennessee began anticipating their release from service, as their one-year commitments would be fulfilled in the opening weeks of May. However, on 17 April, the following message to the contrary was received at brigade headquarters, "Under a late act of Congress the twelve-months' volunteers will be retained in service for two years after their term of enlistment has expired. The Eleventh Regiment Tennessee Volunteers will not, therefore, be discharged, as you suppose."³³

Thus, on 1 May, with their original enlistments fulfilled, the 11th Tennessee reenlisted for two more years pursuant to the act passed by the Confederate Congress. With this reenlistment came a reorganization and reelection of company officers. Rains was re-elected colonel. George W. Gordon defeated Howell Webb for the position of lieutenant colonel. After losing the election, Webb resigned from the service. Thedford retained the rank of major. I. P. Young became Captain of Gheber Guards. P. G. "Gus" Jamison accepted the appointment of chaplain since Pitts had left to take the colonelcy of the 61st Tennessee Infantry. With the organization, the companies were re-lettered. By its excellence in drill the Waverly Guards won the place of Company A.³⁴ The remaining companies were re-lettered accordingly. These new company appellations became the permanent designations throughout the remainder of the war.³⁵

Further to the west, Confederate troops under command of General Albert Sydney Johnston in an effort to protect the Memphis-Charleston Railroad, and to recover the central and western portions of Middle Tennessee, slammed into Grant's Federal forces at Pittsburg Landing on the Tennessee River. The initial Confederate attack of 6 April started successfully but stalled, particularly after the death of Johnston. P. G. T. Beauregard assumed command of the army. During the night, Buell arrived, bringing Grant much needed reinforcements. The following morning, with fresh troops, Grant counterattacked and pushed the Confederates

---

³⁰ Howell Webb, M268 R163, 11th TISR.

³¹ Milton O. Brooks, M268 R159, 11th TISR.

³² Gary Ray Goodson, Sr., *Georgia Confederate 7,000* (Shawnee, CO: Goodson Enterprises, 1995) 26.

³³ *OR*, ser. I, vol. 10, pt. 2, 427.

³⁴ Reddick C. Carnell, "Capt. William I. White," *Confederate Veteran* 31/5 (May 1923): 187.

³⁵ John Berrien Lindsley, *Military Annals of Tennessee: Confederate* (1886; facsimile of the first edition, Wilmington, NC: Broadfoot Publishing, 1995) 293–94.

back, forcing them to retreat to Corinth. Grant continued his drive south. By May, he had possession of Corinth, had sent Buell to take Chattanooga, as he continued down the Mississippi River toward Vicksburg.

Meanwhile, Braxton Bragg and Kirby Smith began joint operations to launch an invasion into Kentucky. The primary objectives of this incursion were to gain new recruits for the Confederacy, to force Buell to abandon his march on Chattanooga, and to relieve some of the pressure that General Ulysses S. Grant was putting on the Mississippi Valley.

After reorganization, the 11th Tennessee, 30th Alabama, 3rd Georgia Battalion, 42nd Georgia, 29th North Carolina, 34th Tennessee, 36th Tennessee, Companies A and E of Cooke's Tennessee Infantry, Captain R. J. Mileham's Company of Virginia Infantry, the 3rd Battalion Tennessee Cavalry, Eufaula (Alabama) Light Artillery, Rhett (Tennessee) Artillery, and Yeizer's (Georgia) Battery were combined to form the Second brigade, commanded by Brigadier General Carter L. Stevenson, listed in the Department of East Tennessee, commanded by Major-General Edmund Kirby Smith.[36]

Not long after the regiment was reorganized, Captain Dick McCann was brought up on court martial charges for insubordination, drunkenness, disrespect for his superiors, and mutinous language in front of the soldiers. Colonel Rains wrote a letter to Brigadier General Stevenson asking that McCann be allowed to resign in lieu of being court martialed. Stevenson acquiesced to the request, and McCann resigned on 23 May 1862.[37] First Lieutenant Edward W. Clark was then promoted to captain and took command of Company B.[38] On 15 June 1862, William B. Maney was officially appointed surgeon of the 11th Tennessee. Dr. Callender had resigned earlier in the year (reason unknown).[39]

In early June, the Federals, commanded by General George W. Morgan, made a flanking maneuver threatening the Confederate position at Cumberland Gap. As a result, on 9 June Rains began evacuating the Gap. During the withdrawal, the Confederates exploded their ammunition, destroyed other stores that they were unable to carry, and pushed their artillery over the precipice. Just before the

---

[36] *OR*, ser. I, vol. 10, pt. 2, 573.

[37] After resigning from the 11th Tennessee Infantry, McCann raised a battalion of cavalry. McCann's command was involved in the raids of John Hunt Morgan in summer 1862. On 23 December 1862, McCann was promoted to major. He and many of his men were captured at Weem's Spring in Hickman County, Tennessee, in 1863. After his capture he and his men were held at the Nashville Penitentiary (Jack C. Vaughan, *Brigadier General Alfred Jefferson Vaughan's Brigade, Army of Tennessee Confederate States of America* [Grand Prairie, TX: Major Jack C. Vaughan, 1959–1960] 616); James E. Rains to General Carter L. Stevenson, 14 May 1862, J. Richard McCann, M268 R161, 11th TISR.

[38] Edward W. Clark, M268 R159, 11th TISR.

[39] William B. Maney, M268 R161, 11th TISR.

evacuation, the men burned timber to create a curtain of smoke to shield their withdrawal. One of Rains's men wrote,

> Cumberland Gap evacuated and everything destroyed. The cannon, the large pieces, and one in particular, "Long Tom", that they had in Mexico, which our side took from the Yankees at Manassas, was spiked and run off the bluff a quarter of a mile high, and all the balls, canister, and grape followed, the powder magazine blown up, one man getting his face burned off him as the Irishman would say; the tents clothing, provisions, cooking utensils, and everything else destroyed.[40]

After abandoning the Gap, Stevenson moved his troops to Clinch Mountain, south of Tazewell, Tennessee, where he prepared to make a stand. Within a few days, General Morgan's men took possession of the Gap, which Stevenson left in ruins.[41]

Meanwhile at Clinch Mountain, the regiment was supplied with shoes. Company A received thirty-four pairs, and Company D received twenty-one pairs.[42] On 23 June several men including privates Yeatman Anderson of Company B, Wiley S. Brown of Company K, James C. McDonald of Company B, and Patrick Walsh of Company G, were detached to the signal corps and sent to Vicksburg, Mississippi.[43]

On 1 July 1862, Henry R. Shacklett was appointed assistant quartermaster for the regiment.[44] Two days later, General Stevenson was shown in command of the 1st division of the Department of East Tennessee, and Colonel Rains in command of the 2nd brigade.[45]

By the early days of August, Brigadier General Morgan began to probe the strength of the Confederate troops south of Cumberland Gap. On 2 August, Morgan sent troops under the command of Colonel John F. DeCourcy to the town of Tazewell in Claiborne County, Tennessee, thirteen miles south of the Gap to gather forage and to reconnoiter the positions of the Rebels in the area. His force

---

[40] John Clark Francis, unpublished manuscript, p. 17, Francis-Martin Family Papers, Alabama Department of Archives and History, Montgomery, AL; stories surrounding the legend of "Long Tom," a large artillery piece, abound at Cumberland Gap. As a result, it is difficult to separate fact from fiction. See Robert L. Kincaid, "Long Tom," *Kentucky* 17/4 (Winter 1963): 17–18.

[41] Parks, *General Edmund Kirby Smith C. S. A.*, 189.

[42] Captain William I. White, M268 R163, 11th TISR; Colonel John E. Binns, M268 R159, 11th TISR.

[43] Yeatman Anderson, M268 R159, 11th TISR; Wiley S. Brown, M268 R159, 11th TISR; James C. McDaniel, M268 R161, 11th TISR; Patrick Walsh, M268 R163, 11th TISR.

[44] Henry R. Shacklett, M268 R162, 11th TISR.

[45] *OR*, ser. I, vol. 6, pt. 2, 719.

succeeded in securing 200 wagon loads of provisions, which his men sent back to Cumberland Gap.

On Tuesday, 5 August, lead elements of both sides met on the outskirts of Tazewell and bantered with each other in light skirmishing. At daybreak the following morning, the 11th Tennessee under command of Lieutenant Colonel Gordon with Colonel Rains commanding the brigade began the advance toward Tazewell. At 7:00 AM, several companies of the 16th Ohio Infantry relieved the 14th Kentucky of picket duty on the hills and ravines surrounding the town. By 7:30, the Federal main force heard scattered firing in Tazewell.

Initially, Rains's Brigade was held in reserve while other units were engaged. As Rains's men awaited their turn to engage the enemy, Private R. M. Gray of the 3rd Georgia Battalion eyed his commander closely: "Our brigade (Rains) had been held in reserve, whilst the demon of war was busy around us, being near him (Rains), I had the curiosity to watch him closely as shell after shell exploded all around him. mounted on a splendid horse not a muscle of his face moved."[46] Finally, the order to advance is given. Gray continues, "So he stood for half an hour, but now our time came…spurting to our front, sword and hat in hand he led us forward, amid the carnage of that day, as regardless of danger as though none existed, and we carried everything before us. We marked the man and from that day until he yielded his young life at Murfreesboro so freely, he was a beloved chief."[47]

As Rains's Confederates advanced in a line of battle, they clashed with the forward companies of the 16th Ohio and completely surrounded the Federal pickets. The Yankees determined not to surrender, but tried to make their escape. As the Ohioans tried to elude the Confederate line of battle, they ran headlong into the 11th Tennessee Infantry. The fleeing Federals were within ten paces of the Southerners when the 11th fired a volley. The volley had little effect on the enemy, but it did kill Captain Joseph Edgar of the 16th Ohio, who was shot in the head, and Sergeant-Major Beatty Smith, who was severely wounded. After the volley, many Federals scattered, trying to extract themselves from their tight position. Two men from Company B, 16th Ohio, Paul Wilder and John McCluggage, attempted their escape through a field and across a road. As the two Federals snuck away, they soon found their route blocked and quickly hid in the bushes to await further developments.[48]

---

[46] R. M. Gray Reminiscences, 1867, unpublished manuscript, Collection Number: 02445-z, The Southern Historical Collection, Louis Round Wilson Library, Special Collections, University of North Carolina, Chapel Hill, NC.

[47] Ibid.

[48] *OR*, ser. I, vol. 16, pt.1, 835–36; 16th Ohio Volunteer Infantry Website, "#12 Anecdotes from the Battle of Tazewell," http://www.mkwe.com/ohio/pages/H011-14.htm (26 April 2015).

Meanwhile, as there was a lull in the fighting, Lieutenant Colonel Gordon moved ahead of the 11th Tennessee to the crest of the ridge to confer with another commander to assess the situation. As Gordon rode up the road, he discovered the two Federal soldiers hiding in the bushes. Gordon, initially failing to recognize them as the enemy, asked them to what regiment they belonged. The two soldiers responded by asking Gordon his rank and regiment. Gordon, at that moment, realizing the two were Yankees, quickly reached for his revolver and demanded their surrender. As Gordon drew his sidearm, both Wilder and McCluggage stepped forward from the bushes, cocked their rifles, and demanded Gordon's surrender. Outnumbered and deciding that discretion was the better part of valor, Gordon grounded his pistol and surrendered. Wilder and McCluggage headed back toward their lines with their prize. Private Wilder led the way to the Federal camp, taking down fences, while Gordon, who was on horseback, followed. Private McCluggage trailed closely behind with instructions to "shoot the Rebel colonel through the heart" if he tried to escape.[49] The party carefully made their way through the Federal lines and arrived at Colonel DeCourcy's headquarters. While the battle progressed, the Yankees allowed Gordon to sit on the ground outside DeCourcy's tent and watch the battle. As the Confederates were moving his way, Gordon hoped that his men would completely rout the Federals so he could make his escape. From Gordon's vantage point, it appeared that his men were on the verge of success. As Gordon's hopes rose, a 3-inch Parrott rifle of Foster's 1st Wisconsin Artillery, double-shotted with canister and supported by Company D of the 16th Ohio, unleashed a deadly barrage into the Rebel ranks. Much to Gordon's chagrin, the Confederate line broke under the heavy fire. Seeing his chances of escape dwindling away, Gordon muttered in disgust, "Well, this beats hell."[50]

With the Confederate attack stalled, the Federals had an opportunity to make an orderly withdrawal. Corporal William Reid of Company C of the 16th Ohio commented,

> [Our] Regiment went on picket this morning and was attacked by a greatly superior force. They attempted to capture our artillery, but we kept them back until the artillery got safely away. We fell gradually back in good order, firing as we retired. We got in a good position behind a fence, where we fought until our last cartridge was gone. Then we retired beyond the town where our batteries were in position. The rebel's tried to plant a battery, but could not do it. Our gunners soon dismounted their cannon. Our loss in this engagement was 2 killed, 15 wounded, and 52 prisoners. They captured our knapsacks so we returned to camp that night

---

[49] Ibid.
[50] Ibid.

meeting our whole Division near Powels River coming to reinforce us. We all returned to the Gap.[51]

Meanwhile, back with the regiment, after some time had passed someone realized that Gordon had not returned from his reconnaissance mission. Major William Thedford, now commanding the 11th Tennessee, detached a search party consisting of eighteen men from Company H under command of 2nd Lieutenant Jacob H. "Jake" Johnson. While Johnson's squad searched for their colonel, they encountered a Federal force of more than double their size. Johnson's Hickman Countians would not run from a fight, and after a spirited clash, they managed to surround and capture the entire force of forty-two Yankees.[52]

One of the captured Federals tells his experience,

> Those of us who fell back into the woods waited there in painful suspense for hours, while a furious skirmish was going on between our men and the enemy, near the edge of town, not more than a quarter of a mile from us, but just over the hill and out of sight. Our artillery and a rebel battery kept up a lively duel until the middle of the afternoon. During this an occasional shell from our cannon, over shooting its mark, crashed through the tree-tops near us.
>
> While we were lying there undecided what to do we could hear a lot of infantry reinforcements passing up a ravine below us. Although we could not see them, on account of the undergrowth, we could plainly hear their conversation; we also heard the officers scolding the men for breaking from the line when a shell struck near them. The day had been hot until along toward night, when a shower of rain cooled the air a little. About five o'clock in the evening when the artillery had ceased firing and only an occasional rifle-shot could be heard, we rose up in a body and moved from the edge of the woods, back far enough, as we thought, to escape any large bodies of the enemy, but to our amazement, as we came out of the heavy timber into a partially open place, we stood in the presence of a force of the vigilant enemy. A glance at their uniforms told us that they were not a part of those we had encountered at the forks of the road, as they wore dark brown, or, as the boys expressed it, "butternut" uniforms, and the men before us were dressed in light grey. The numbers in our front being less apparently than ours, induced some of our fellows to demand a surrender. Short and excited challenges came from both sides, succeeded by some of the wildest shooting ever done by soldiers. We were so close that from the number of shots fired it seemed a miracle that no one was hit. Sergeant H. Tipton, of Co. B, and a big rebel stood so close to each other that but a few steps separated them. Both fired and both missed.
>
> It subsequently proved that these rebels were but the skirmishers of the 11th Tennessee Infantry, who immediately appeared on the scene with fixed bayonets, and with terrific yells charged among us, and, presto, we were prisoners of war. Not

---

[51] Diary of William Warner Reid, Corporal, Company C, 16th OVI, 6 August 1862, http://www.mkwe.com/ohio/pages/Reid-01.htm. (26 April 2015).

[52] W. J. D. Spence and David L. Spence, *History of Hickman County, Tennessee* (1900; reprint, Columbia, TN: P-Vine Press, 1981) 130.

all. Two men, Jonathan Cornel and Thomas Graham, of Co. B, darted back into the woods and concealed themselves in the bushes. Two days afterward, with torn clothing and bruised bodies, they reached our lines at Cumberland Gap. Less than a year afterwards, their names were on the "death roll," and they were laid to rest in honored graves on the banks of the mighty Mississippi.

Forming us in single rank they marched us up on the open ridge, where we met several regiments that were hurrying to the scene of the firing. These formed in open order and faced inward and we marched through under guard. Taking us to an open space at the edge of the forest, near the forks of the road, they formed a circle of guards around us. In a short time we were the objects of curiosity to the thousands that crowded around us. They all wanted to see the "Yanks." The brigade that captured us was under the command of Colonel Rains. He was a gallant soldier and a gentleman. Captain Taneyhill's sword had been taken. Rains had it returned to him.

During the nine days that we were held in captivity, many things came to our notice that left their impressions on our minds, and the years with their varying and often trying circumstances, has done but little to remove it. Many of our rebel captors treated us with marked respect. Two Whetmore brothers, members of the 11th Tennessee and cousins to Capt. Whetmore, of the 9th Ohio Battery, came daily to sit outside of the guard line and chat with us. These two boys had a fair education and were intelligent, and were an exception to the class of men that composed the regiments around us. We saw some of their troops receive pay. They had no elaborate system of pay-rolls, because the majority of the men were too illiterate to sign them. The captain of each company simply reported the number of men present, and procured a proportionate amount of Confederate money, which he distributed without scratch of pen or record. Some of the enemy had blue U.S. clothing, that came from a supply that had been captured from General Banks in Virginia. A chaplain came to preach to us on Sunday, but his sermon was too sectional for the boys, and he was frequently interrupted by embarrassing questions, that, by and by, made the gray-coated divine wrathy, and his discourse tapered off into a tirade of abuse against the "Yankee invader."

The 11th Tennessee Infantry were in bivouac near us. Their guns were stacked in line at the edge of the woods. When they organized, the ladies of Nashville presented them a beautiful silk flag, the "Stars and Bars." It had a scrolled inscription, "God and Our Country." The color-bearer cared for his trust with pride, and kept its silken folds protected with an oil-cloth sheath. Thus encased, it lay on the gun stacks when a soldier in trying to get at his gun without breaking the stack, accidentally shot through the flag. The shot instantly collected a crowd. When the flag was enrolled, strange as it may seem, the only part mutilated was the word "God."[53]

---

[53] Theodore David Wolbach, "16th Ohio Volunteer Infantry: The 'Camp & Field' Articles," *16th Ohio Volunteer Infantry* http://www.mkwe.com/ohio/pages/h015–00.htm (1 March 2015).

By this time, the remaining Federals had completed their withdrawal from the town. One Confederate stated after the Federal retreat, "We reveled in Yankee knap-sacks blankets, overcoats, etc., galore, and many of us foolishly overloaded ourselves."[54] The Federals who had been captured by Johnson's party were exchanged on the field for Gordon ten days later. There were no reported casualties from the 11th Tennessee Infantry in the Battle of Tazewell, Tennessee.

For the next few days, the Confederates maintained their position at Tazewell. While there, on Sunday morning, 10 August, Reverend S. M. Cherry preached on the left wing of the 4th Tennessee and the right wing of the 11th Tennessee. He preached again to the 11th Tennessee that evening.[55]

These were tough times for the boys of the regiment. One Rebel soldier wrote his family on 14 August describing conditions at Tazewell, "We have been fed very poorly for the last month. Sometimes we have been without food for three days at a time and hardly ever have enough to eat. Part of the time we have bread and no meat, then meat and no bread, then neither."[56]

During the middle of August, the army discharged many men of the regiment because they were over the age of thirty-five. This was in compliance with the Conscript Act passed by the Confederate Congress which allowed men above the age of thirty-five to be dismissed from the service. According to available records at least 116 men were discharged from the 11th Tennessee Infantry on 15 August 1862 at Tazewell.[57]

After the successful Confederate advance on Tazewell, the Federal force fell back to their stronghold at Cumberland Gap and Stevenson made plans to encircle them. On 16 August, Stevenson with 9,000 men invested the Gap from the east, south, and southwest. Lieutenant General Edmund Kirby Smith, with an additional 9,000 men, in a joint invasion of Kentucky with Braxton Bragg, arrived at Barboursville, fully drawing the noose around Morgan. By 17 August, Stevenson's force had moved to the north bank of the Powell River, about three miles south of Cumberland Gap. One of Stevenson's Rebs stated,

> We are now within three miles of Cumberland Gap. We arrived here yesterday morning and commenced a siege, and we have the Gap invested from mountain to mountain, our line forming a semi-circle around the gap. The enemy has heavy batteries on the mountain with which they shell us continually, but with very little

---

[54] Joseph Bogle and William L. Calhoun, *Historical Sketches of Barton's (Later Stovall's) Georgia Brigade, Army of Tennessee, C. S. A.* (Dayton, OH: Morningside, 1984) 11–12.

[55] J. William Jones, *Christ in the Camp or Religion in the Confederate Army* (1887; reprint, Harrisonburg, VA: Sprinkle Publications, 1986) 567.

[56] Mills Lane, *Dear Mother, Don't Grieve About Me: If I Get Killed, I'll Only Be Dead: Letters from Georgia Soldiers in the Civil War* (Savannah, GA: Beehive Press, 1977) 179.

[57] Information comes from a compilation of material from individual service records, M268 R159–163, 11th TISR.

harm to us. Our line is very scattering, owing to our limited numbers, but things are so arranged that should the enemy attack at any one point, we can quickly concentrate at that point, and our pickets and skirmishers are well advanced. It is reported that Gen. Kirby Smith (whom we have lost sight of for sometime) is advancing through Big Creek Gap, with the rest of our division and such other troops as he can collect together, and that his aim is to attack Cumberland Gap in the rear.[58]

On 19 August, a correspondent for the Cincinnati *Commercial* reported on Morgan's situation, "This place [Cumberland Gap] is completely surrounded by the enemy. His pickets are within four miles of the Gap, and extend entirely across the mountain."[59] By the end of August, Morgan was facing critical shortages in food and other necessary supplies. To relieve his men's suffering, he sent out foraging expeditions to obtain more food.

While Morgan was cut off from his supply line, the 11th Tennessee was receiving much needed stores. On 25 August, while encamped on the Powell River, Company K received twenty-one short coats and fifty-four pairs of pants.[60] On the same day, one of Stevenson's soldiers described the situation,

> The enemy approached us this morning. They had two regiments of infantry and some artillery with their wagon train. They did not drive our pickets in, but proceeded to load their wagons with oats and green corn which grew just on their picket line, and the infantry and artillery stood in line of battle to protect the men who gathered the corn. They then planted their battery a little nearer to us and shelled our pickets with great fury for a short time, but as we were under cover of thick woods they did not know where to direct their fire.[61]

Reporting on the strength of the Gap, one Rebel commented:

> Cumberland Gap is a very strong hold, being a natural fortification of itself, and the big forts with heavy siege guns mounted in them, and other formidable earthworks makes the place almost impregnable. Our force is about equal in numbers with that of the enemy, with the difference that they have more field artillery than we have, to say nothing of the heavy fort guns that they are using against us; therefore the idea of storming the gap has not been suggested, and would be perfectly insane. Those forts were built by the Confederates, and they are equally effective on either side of the mountain. We would require a force of 5 to 1 to take the Gap by storm, therefore we must starve them out if we get them.[62]

---

[58] William E. Sloan diary, 18 August 1861, Civil War Collection, Confederate Collection, Box 7, Diary 7, Tennessee State Library and Archives, Nashville, TN.

[59] Memphis (TN) *Daily Appeal*, 30 August 1862, quoting the Cincinnati (OH) *Commercial*, 19 August 1862.

[60] Captain F. F. Tidwell, M268 R163, 11th TISR.

[61] William E. Sloan diary, 25 August 1861.

[62] Ibid.

The combined invasion of Kentucky by Bragg and Smith initially went well. Bragg moved up from Chattanooga as Smith left Barboursville and penetrated north toward Lexington. Smith left Stevenson to invest the Gap as he took his Army of Kentucky northward. On 30 August, Smith's men encountered Federal forces under the command of Major General William Nelson at Richmond, Kentucky. Brigadier General Patrick R. Cleburne, an Irish immigrant, led Smith's advance and achieved a one-sided triumph for the Confederates. After Cleburne's solid victory, Smith's Rebels entered Lexington the following day unopposed. Meanwhile, as Smith was facing Nelson at Richmond, Bragg had swept around Buell's army in Tennessee and headed for the Kentucky state line.[63]

Stevenson, who remained at Cumberland Gap, continued his siege operations as ordered. On 2 September the Federals sent another foraging expedition out to the picket line to gather green corn. Two days later, the foragers returned. One Confederate encouraged by this action stated, "The Yankee foraging party returned today to the same place for more forage, but evidently found very little, and that only corn-stalks. The amount of forage that they are getting by these trips out is too small to amount to anything in way of prolonging the siege. It may keep their horses alive a day or two, but that is all."[64]

As the siege continued, Morgan's starving men began deserting into the Rebel lines. One Confederate noted, "The Federal soldiers are deserting daily and coming to us. They report that they are starving in the Gap."[65] With his supplies cut off and men on half rations, Morgan had few other options but to evacuate the Gap. On the evening of 17 September, three months to the day after he had occupied the Cumberland Gap, Morgan blew up his magazines, and, under the cover of darkness, he led his starving men northward up the Warrior's Path toward the Ohio River. Private William W. Stokey of Company C, 11th Tennessee commented, "Morgan evacuated the Gap one night, and the next morning our company, C, was the first company that went through the Gap."[66] Another Rebel stated, "Here we lay until 11 o'clock AM of the 20th when we marched in pursuit of the retreating foe and marching through volumes of dust with very little and very bad water fourteen miles we slept at Cumberland Ford."[67]

At daybreak on 21 September, the 11th Tennessee was on the march with the remainder of Stevenson's Division. As the column moved, the thick dust boiled up all along the way. The lack of drinking water compounded the misery of the men. After marching sixteen miles, they finally arrived at the Goose Creek Salt Works.

---

[63] Parks, *General Edmund Kirby Smith C. S. A.*, 211–27.
[64] William E. Sloan diary, 2 September 1861.
[65] Ibid., 9 September 1861.
[66] Yeary, *Reminisces*, 726.
[67] Nolan Fowler, "Johnny Reb's Impressions of Kentucky in the Fall of 1862," *Register of the Kentucky Historical Society* 48 (July 1950): 206.

After remaining here for a few days, on the morning of 22 September, Stevenson's men again took up the line of march and headed back five miles to a road leading toward Richmond, Kentucky. After marching until midnight, the officers allowed the men to get a couple of hours sleep. After this brief respite, they were back on the move. By sunrise, the regiment had marched twenty-five miles with very little to eat. Stevenson's column was halted and the men allowed to rest, but at noon, the men resumed the march. The men passed through London where they were again allowed to rest. By 25 September, the 11th Tennessee had crossed the Rockcastle River and had passed over Big Hill. One soldier on the march stated, "[We] stopped near a Lime sink which served us with water. Nearly all the water courses are dried from running and standing pools in their beds was our only chance for water and I have frequently seen men getting water out of a pond to cook with and others bathing in it and others watering stock in the same pond."[68] The next day, Stevenson's men marched toward Richmond but turned off, stopping for the night at Gum Springs, fourteen miles from Lancaster. By 28 September the boys had passed through Lancaster and were within two miles of Danville.[69]

The following day, as the 11th Tennessee remained near Danville, Bradford Nichol of the Rutledge Artillery left his camp to visit his two brothers, Will and Sam, both lieutenants in the 11th. Nichol traveled several miles to the 11th Tennessee's camp on the Lancaster Pike but soon had to return to his men as he received orders they were moving over to Camp Dick Robinson about nine miles away.[70]

Early in the morning of 30 September, with colors flying and bands playing, Stevenson's men marched through Danville. Here, Stevenson's column saw Bragg's troops but continued marching another six miles to Harrodsburg. As the men passed through the town, a soldier of Stevenson's Division commented, "Here we received every demonstration of respect from the citizens such as Ladies waving handkerchiefs and small Confederate Flags and giving our ragged boys clothing."[71] As the men continued through the town, they suffered greatly from sore feet, which one Southerner attributed to the "firm and unyielding Pike road."[72] Fifth Sergeant Clayton H. Yates of Company K stated, "It was on these marches that we suffered untold misery. On that raid many of our men and I was among the number, were entirely barefooted marching on the gravel roads, which produced the most excruciating pains that we had during the war. Notwithstanding we were suffering

---

[68] Ibid., 207.
[69] Ibid., 206–207.
[70] Bradford Nichol, "Civil War Memoir," 29 September 1862, Manuscript Collection MF 1627, Tennessee State Library and Archives, Nashville, TN.
[71] Fowler, "Johnny Reb's Impressions," 207.
[72] Ibid.

so, we had scarcely nothing to eat and for two or three days we suffered greatly for water."[73] The column stopped for the night at Eldorado on the Salt River.[74]

On 1 October, the men resumed the march. By evening, the men passed through Lawrenceburg and made camp for the night. The following day, they marched through Rough and Ready, and from there headed five miles toward Louisville, expecting anytime to have contact with the enemy. The Confederates did not encounter the Federals, so the column moved back through Rough and Ready and marched until they were within two miles of Frankfort.[75] Fifth Sergeant Yates of Company K stated,

> We finally arrived at Frankfort, KY., care-worn, foot-sore, and covered with lice, vermin and many of them with the itch. When we got warm, how these body animals would annoy us, but the greatest satisfaction we had then was in scratching our bodies. Some how or other, there was a doctor who invited my company [K] to dinner at a hotel in Frankfort.... That was a fine dinner and we enjoyed it very much, but we could but notice the conduct of the women on the streets when they saw us they turned the backs of their hands upon us and many of them in arder to annoy us, would show union badges which they wore.[76]

Private Stokey of Company C, gives further detail,

> The last day we were camped here the Confederates organized a Confederate State Government of Kentucky, and they fired the cannons which proclaimed a government of one day's existence. We leaving there late that evening. We passed through Frankfort and burned the railroad bridge across the Kentucky River. We could hear the cannons booming at Perryville. That night Bragg's Army and Kirby Smith's Army met and camped so near that the same big spring furnished water for both armies.[77]

After leaving Frankfort in the afternoon, the men marched until 3:00 AM the next morning. After making the fourteen-mile march, Stevenson's men reached Versailles. On the march from Frankfort to Versailles, many of the men of the 11th Tennessee and other regiments fell out of line from exhaustion and were captured by Federal cavalry. Stevenson stayed in Versailles until 8 October. At 2:00 PM on this date, the column headed toward Harrodsburg where the division was reunited with Kirby Smith.[78]

Meanwhile, by 13 September, Buell with his Army of the Ohio had abandoned his advance on Chattanooga and had moved his army northward to

---

[73] Clayton H. Yates, "Reminiscences of the Civil War," Mayfield (KY) *Daily Messenger*, date unknown.
[74] Fowler, "Johnny Reb's Impressions," 207.
[75] Ibid.
[76] C. H. Yates, "War Reminiscences," Mayfield (KY) *Daily Messenger*, date unknown.
[77] Yeary, *Reminiscences*, 726.
[78] Fowler, "Johnny Reb's Impressions," 208.

Glasgow, Kentucky, and then on to Louisville. By the first week of October, Buell left his supply base at Louisville and marched to the southeast to intercept Bragg. On 8 October, Bragg and Buell stumbled into each other on the banks of Doctor's Creek near Perryville. While Stevenson marched his men from Versailles to Harrodsburg, Bragg's Army of the Mississippi was deadlocked in a fierce battle with Buell's Army of the Ohio at Perryville, only about ten miles away. One Confederate stated, "We have heard the incessant roar of artillery all day. A great battle has been going on for two days at Perryville, which is a few miles from Harrodsburg, and the roar of artillery continued tonight until it was dark."[79] Although both armies were battered, the Federals claimed a strategic victory, causing Bragg to lose the critical momentum necessary for a continued advance to the Ohio River. Bragg then withdrew southward from Perryville and joined Smith at Harrodsburg. The combined Confederate armies began a general retreat from Kentucky via Cumberland Gap.[80]

As Bragg's army moved to the southeast, Stevenson's Division served as the rearguard. At Lancaster, on 13 October, Bragg divided his force to accelerate his retreat. Bragg took his Army of the Mississippi toward Cumberland Gap by the most direct route, and Kirby Smith took a more circuitous route over Big Hill.[81]

On 20 October, one of the Confederates stated, "We are still moving toward Cumberland Gap. We have had nothing to eat for six days except parched corn and beef."[82] J. W. Wynn of Company F stated, "I divided my 'one biscuit a day' with my brother in the cavalry, who had nothing."[83] About his experiences in Kentucky, John H. Ward of Company B, wrote, "Passing other engagements in Kentucky, I recall how we suffered from dust and heat and bad water, filling our canteens from ponds at night after raking off the green scum and drinking that the next day; and how we suffered for something to eat until we reached Camp Dick Robinson, where we destroyed great quantities of Federal rations."[84]

Despite the lack of combat in this campaign, the expedition had been very difficult for the men of the 11th Tennessee. Throughout the expedition, the regiment had marched a distance of four hundred miles. Many of the men were barefooted throughout the excursion. Lieutenant Colonel Gordon commented, "In this condition they marched through the burning sands in the beginning of the campaign and through the snow at its close."[85] Gordon continued, "Though we did

---

[79] William E. Sloan diary, 8 October 1861.

[80] *American Civil War Overview*, Chapter VI, The Western Theater: Bragg's Kentucky Campaign, <http://www.civilwarhome.com/kentucky.htm> (1 March 2015).

[81] Fowler, "Johnny Reb's Impressions," 214.

[82] William E. Sloan diary, 20 October 1861.

[83] Yeary, *Reminiscences*, 827.

[84] John H. Ward, "The Eleventh Tennessee Infantry," *Confederate Veteran* 16/8 (August 1908): 420.

[85] Lindsley, *Military Annals*, 295.

but little fighting on this campaign, it was in some respects very severe, especially on account of forced marches, scarcity of commissary stores and quartermaster supplies. On our retreat we were three days without bread, and lived on beef-cattle we had gathered in Kentucky."[86] Sergeant Yates of Company K stated, "When he [Bragg] came out of Kentucky, however, he brought with him a great many beef cattle and the beef we got from this cattle was about all we had to eat at this time."[87] Yates continued, "When a beef was shot down the soldiers began to cut it in small strips, and each strip of beef was given to a soldier and he would hang it on a ram-rod of his gun and hold it over a blazing fire until it got hot and then it was eaten without any salt and frequently without and bread. Although it was cooked in the barbarous way, yet we were hungry and everything that we had to eat was enjoyed by us."[88] Gordon concluded by stating, "These hardships were endured heroically—only as brave and true men could endure."[89]

During the early weeks of October, Major Jerome S. Ridley, acting commissary of dubsistence for the regiment, was assigned to Stevenson's division commissary.[90] Sergeant Gabriel Fowlkes took Ridley's place as regimental commissary.[91] Many of the sick of the 11th Tennessee who were in the hospital at Versailles, along with the medical stewards from the regiment, were abandoned on the withdrawal and were subsequently captured.[92]

In their withdrawal, Smith's troops retraced the steps they had taken on the invasion into Kentucky. They fell back to Big Hill on their regression toward Cumberland Gap. The route up Big Hill, a sixteen-hundred-foot extrusion, was a rugged narrow dirt road. In order to make it up the prominence, wagons were double-teamed, and infantrymen got behind the wagons to help push them up the grueling slope. Problem after problem arose. Smith feared that he would have to abandon much of his artillery and many of his supply wagons because of the delays. However, due to some quick improvisational thinking by General Patrick Cleburne who happened to be with Smith, and the brute unified strength of man and animal, the wagons and artillery were safely muscled over the crest.[93]

After crossing Big Hill, Smith's army moved on to Barboursville without incident. From Barboursville, the column took the Wilderness Road toward Cumberland Gap and arrived by 23 October. Sergeant Yates commented, "When we reached Cumberland Gap I witnessed the sad spectacle of seeing many of our

---

[86] Ibid.
[87] C. H. Yates, "Article Four," Mayfield (KY) *Daily Messenger*, unknown date.
[88] Ibid.
[89] Lindsley, *Military Annals*, 295.
[90] Ridley, Jerome, M268 R162, 11th TISR.
[91] Gabriel Fowlkes, M268 R160, 11th TISR.
[92] M268 R159–63, 11th TISR.
[93] Earl J. Hess, *Banners to the Breeze: The Kentucky Campaign, Corinth, and Stones River* (Lincoln: University of Nebraska Press, 2000) 111–13.

men walk barefooted through snow six inches deep, leaving traces of blood on the snow."[94] In this condition, the ranks of the 11th Tennessee, intermingled with the remainder of the army, snaked along the arduous, meandering path ever closer to the Tennessee line. Smith's troops, including many of the officers, questioned why they were leaving Kentucky. As a result, the army began to doubt Bragg's competence as commanding officer. In a state of hopeless bewilderment, the poorly shod, half-starved boys of the 11th Tennessee stumbled over the wagon ruts of the eroded pot-holed path, ending the unsuccessful Kentucky campaign, which they had sacrificed so much to secure.

The men marched along the rugged road taxed by their burdensome military trappings. Their assorted armament of archaic flintlock rifles, converted percussion muskets, and minie rifles pressed menacingly into their shoulders, while thousands of cups, bayonets, canteens, and other military equipment, clanked one against the other in perfect unison with every agonizing step. Slowly, the Rebel column reached Cumberland Gap. As they trudged through the narrow breach, they passed their former defensive fortifications bristling from the peaks above. Officers on horseback paused by the roadside to check on the welfare of their fatigued troops. As the boys followed this already historic trail in the footsteps of Daniel Boone and other pioneers, they passed the well-known limestone cave on the left, the familiar rushing creek and the notable old mill on the right, and finally entered Tennessee once again.

After passing through the gap, the regiment directed its course back toward Bean Station. As the Rebel ranks left the war-scarred barren wasteland of Cumberland Gap and crossed to the next range of mountains. The men marched on as far as they could and stopped that night to make camp.

The men resumed the relentless march the next day, and eventually reached Tazewell. While the regiment passed through the small town, no doubt many of the men thought of their comrade, Lieutenant Alex Vaughan, who had been brutally murdered at that place several months before. Perhaps Lieutenant Colonel Gordon reminisced about his capture by the two Ohio infantrymen there, scarcely two months earlier. After passing through Tazewell, the army continued its retrograde movement southward. Within a couple of days the gray ranks arrived at Bean Station.

---

[94] Ibid.

7

"Eager for the Fray"

November–December 1862

After a short but much needed rest at Bean Station, the 11th Tennessee once again received marching orders. This time the regiment proceeded southwestwardly to Knoxville. After a long but uneventful journey, the boys reached their destination. While there, the quartermaster obtained shoes and other desperately needed equipment.[1]

By the early days of November, the command had arrived and established camp. The regiment remained at this location for the next several weeks. On Sunday, 2 November, Reverend Cherry, who had ministered to the men so many times before, took another opportunity to preach to the interested members of the 4th and 11th Tennessee regiments.[2] The following Tuesday, 4 November, Colonel Rains was promoted to brigadier general and was given permanent command of the 2nd brigade of Major General Carter L. Stevenson's 1st Division, Department of East Tennessee, commanded by Lieutenant General Edmund Kirby Smith.[3] In light of Rains's promotion, Lieutenant Colonel Gordon was commissioned a full colonel and assumed command of the 11th Tennessee.[4] Likewise, Major Thedford was promoted to fill the vacancy of lieutenant colonel on 7 November.[5] Captain William Green became major, and William H. McCauley ascended to the captaincy of Company C, Green's former command.[6]

On 10 November, A. J. Allen, apparently unaware of Green's promotion, wrote a letter addressing Green as "Captain," asking that Green withdraw his court martial charges:

---

[1] John Berrien Lindsley, *Military Annals of Tennessee: Confederate* (1886; facsimile of the first edition, Wilmington, NC: Broadfoot Publishing, 1995) 295.

[2] J. William Jones, *Christ in the Camp or Religion in the Confederate Army* (1887; reprint, Harrisonburg, VA: Sprinkle Publications, 1986) 570.

[3] James E. Rains, 11th Tennessee Infantry Service Records, National Archives Records Administration, *Compiled Service Records of Confederate Soldiers Who Served in Organizations from the State of Tennessee*, Washington, DC: National Archives Records and Service, General Services Administration, 1960. Hereafter referred cited as 11th TISR. M268 R162.

[4] George W. Gordon, M268 R160, 11th TISR.

[5] William Thedford, M268 R163, 11th TISR.

[6] William Green, M268 R160, 11th TISR; William H. McCauley, M268 R161, 11th TISR.

Lenoirs Station Nov. 10th 1862
Capt,
You having preferred charges against me and these charges having existed for several months, and a court marshal once having been appointed to adjudicate the case, but being dissolved by the public necessity before it could be tried a long time expired before any other steps were taken in the matter. Recently I have demanded a court marshal, which could not be granted to me without detriment to the public service, and as I am now and have been for some time entitled to a discharge from the service by virtue of the conscript law, I hereby respectfully ask a withdrawal of the charges against me.
A. J. Allen
Co. C, 11th Tenn Regt.[7]

At this time, Rains's Brigade consisted of the 11th Tennessee commanded by Gordon; the 29th North Carolina, commanded by Colonel Robert B. Vance; the 42nd Georgia, commanded by Colonel R. J. Henderson; the 3rd Georgia Battalion, commanded by Lieutenant Colonel Marcellus A. Stovall; the 4th Tennessee, commanded by Colonel J. A. McMurray; and the Eufaula Alabama Light Artillery, commanded by Captain W. A. McTyer.[8] On 22 November, Bragg officially combined Smith's Army of Kentucky and his Army of the Mississippi into one army and reorganized his forces. He divided his infantry into three corps under the commands of Leonidas Polk, William J. Hardee, and Edmund Kirby Smith. To this unification and reorganization, Bragg bequeathed a new name, one by which the force would be known the remainder of the war, the Army of Tennessee.[9]

On 29 November, the 11th Tennessee struck camp at Lenoir Station, boarded the train and headed with the brigade westward to Normandy, Tennessee, via Chattanooga, a distance of about 150 miles. At Normandy, the regiment travelled by another train the remaining fifteen miles to Manchester. Upon arrival at Manchester, the boys unloaded their equipment and set up camp. During their stay here, Alex Bell along with his manservant, Charley Bell, a black man, enlisted in Company K. Charley cooked and performed other duties for the men, serving faithfully with the regiment until the surrender at Greensboro, North Carolina.[10]

---

[7] A. J. Allen to Captain William Green, 10 November 1861, possession of Lewis Hooper, Franklin, TN.

[8] United States War Department, *The War of the Rebellion: A Compilation of the Official Records of the Union and Confederate Armies*. 70 vols. in 128 (Washington: Government Printing Office, 1880–1901; reprint, Gettysburg, PA: The National Historical Society, 1972) ser. I, vol. 20, pt. 2, 413. Hereafter cited as *OR*.

[9] Thomas Lawrence Connelly, *Autumn of Glory: The Army of Tennessee 1862–1865* (Baton Rouge: Louisiana State University Press, 1971) 30.

[10] Record of Events, Company D Muster Roll November and December 1862, 11th Regiment Tennessee Infantry Service Records, National Archives Records Administration, Compiled Service Records of Confederate Soldiers Who Served in Organizations from the

During the division's stay at Manchester, chaplains held religious services every evening for the troops despite inclement weather. On the evening of 3 December, Reverend John G. Bolton, a private of Company A, 11th Tennessee, preached in these services. Reverend Cherry followed Bolton's message with an exhortation of his own. The service concluded with four penitents, and Sergeant-Major Edward F. Shropshire of the 39th Georgia Infantry, made a profession of faith in Christ. According to Cherry, this was the first profession of religion that he witnessed in the army.[11]

On Sunday, 7 December, in the midst of falling snow, the boys of the 11th packed their equipment, loaded it on the baggage train, fell into line, and proceeded to the awaiting train. The train transported the regiment with the remainder of the division to McMinnville, Tennessee. The boys stayed at that town only a brief time. Soon, the regiment took up the line of march and proceeded with the division to the small town of Woodberry. From there, they marched to Readyville, where they camped along the banks of the Stones River.[12] By this time, the structure of Rains's Brigade had changed somewhat. The 9th Georgia Battalion, commanded by Major Joseph T. Smith, replaced the 42nd Georgia. In addition, Lieutenant W. A. McDuffie now commanded the Eufaula Alabama Light Artillery. While at Readyville, on 9 December, Milton R. Scholes of Humphreys County joined Company I. The quartermaster had no rifle that he could issue the new recruit. Even so, Scholes fell into line with the other boys of the company and began learning the manual of arms.[13]

In the middle of December, Richmond ordered Bragg to detach General Stevenson with ten thousand troops to Vicksburg, Mississippi to reinforce General John C. Pemberton. As a result, authorities disbanded Smith's Corps and he returned to East Tennessee. Rains's Brigade was not sent to Vicksburg, but instead was assigned to John P. McCown's division, which had temporarily been assigned

---

State of Tennessee, Washington, DC: National Archives Records and Service, General Services Administration, 1960. M268 R159; Chas. Bell *sv. Tennessee Colored Confederate Veteran Pension Applications,* trans. Pat Spurlock (np: sn, 2012) 71; Charley Bell, Alias Charley Harris joined the 11th Tennessee Infantry at Manchester, Tennessee in November 1862. Charley remained a faithful member of the regiment, cooking and serving Alex Bell during the war. Charley remained with the regiment until the surrender of the Army of Tennessee in April 1865. James K. Clifton and Moses Garton both of Company K, attested to Charley's faithfulness to the regiment on his application for pension in June 1921.

[11] Jones, *Christ in the Camp,* 571.

[12] Record of Events, Company D, November and December 1862, M268 R159, 11th TISR.

[13] Milton R. Scholes, Tennessee Confederate Pension Application, 13108, Family Search, https://familysearch.org/pal:/MM9.3.1/TH-1951-20616-19336-80?cc=1874474 &wc=M6ZF-6WL:171467301,175931301 (29 April 2015).

to William J. Hardee's corps. By mid-December Rains's Brigade was composed of the 11th Tennessee, commanded by Gordon; the 29th North Carolina, commanded by Colonel Robert B. Vance; the 42nd Georgia, commanded by Colonel R. J. Henderson; the 3rd Georgia Battalion, commanded by Lieutenant Colonel M. A. Stovall; and the Eufaula Alabama Light Artillery, commanded by Captain W. A. McTyer.[14]

On the afternoon of 21 December, while the regiment remained at Readyville, Reverend Cherry preached to the men of the 11th Tennessee for the last time.[15] Five days later, on 26 December, the Federals began making their move. General William S. Rosecrans, who replaced Don Carlos Buell as commander of the Federal Army of the Cumberland, came out of Kentucky to Nashville. From Nashville, he marched his army (divided into three columns) to Murfreesboro in an effort to stop the Confederate threat in Middle Tennessee. Meanwhile, at midnight 27 December, McCown received orders for his division to begin another westward march. This time, he was to move his troops to Murfreesboro, a quiet town some twelve miles away.[16] As soon as the boys had packed their equipment, they formed ranks and at 2:00 AM began their trek. A cold wet rain fell on the boys as they marched along the rough roads. It took the regiment ten grueling hours to complete the twelve-mile march. After marching in the rain all night, the boys were wet and exhausted when they finally arrived at Murfreesboro about noon the next day.[17]

On Sunday, 28 December, the 11th Tennessee went into line of battle near the town of Murfreesboro. The regiment remained in line for some time but did not engage the enemy. The next day McCown's Division moved from the right of the Rebel lines, forded the Stones River, and took a position on the extreme left flank of Bragg's Army of Tennessee. There, the 11th Tennessee took position in a country lane to the left of the Triune Road.[18]

On the morning of 30 December, the Federal forces extended their lines on the Confederate left and positioned several batteries of artillery. Again, the 11th Tennessee remained in position during the day, protected by rail breastworks. During the evening, due to faulty alignment on the Confederate left, an enemy battery began shelling Rains's command. Shells burst all around sending shrapnel hissing in every direction. Several artillery rounds struck the field works of the

---

[14] *OR*, ser. I, vol. 20, pt. 1, 660.

[15] Jones, *Christ in the Camp*, 571.

[16] Nathaniel Cheairs Hughes, *General William J. Hardee: Old Reliable* (Baton Rouge: Louisiana State University Press, 1965) 139.

[17] Record of Events, Company A, 11 Regiment Tennessee Infantry Company A Muster Roll, November and December 1862, M268 R159, 11th TISR.

[18] *OR*, ser. I, vol. 20, pt. 1, 911.

regiment, but the 11th Tennessee sustained no casualties. [19] While the bombardment was underway, Rains responded by bringing up a section of his artillery. By 4:00 PM, four 3-inch rifled guns of the Eufaula Alabama Light Artillery arrived in position near the Triune Road where they could take the Federal right and artillery in flank. As soon as McTyer's artillerymen had unlimbered their guns, the Federal batteries turned on the Rebel cannoneers. Despite being under severe fire, the Alabama gunners coolly executed their movements. One at a time, their iron muzzles belched fire and steel, hammering away with deadly accuracy at their foe. Within an hour, the Federal battery, which had initially attacked Rains's line, had been forced to change position. The Southern fire dismounted one gun from its carriage, and left several of its cannoneers dead around the derelict field piece. Three of McTyer's gunners were wounded in this action; nevertheless, the resolute Alabamians continued banging at the enemy until they had expended their ammunition. When the ammunition was gone, the Eufaula battery withdrew to the rear, and all was quiet along the line. Soon Lieutenant General Hardee arrived on the scene and corrected the alignment of Rains's Brigade, which prevented them from being enfiladed by enemy artillery fire in the future.[20]

Later that evening, McCown received orders from Hardee that his division was to form in line of battle at 4:30 the next morning. At daybreak, he and Pat Cleburne, whose division was positioned some 500 yards to his rear, were to strike a crushing sledgehammer blow against the Federal right. The remaining left flank of Bragg's army, following the movements of McCown and Cleburne, would then swing to the left in a semicircular movement like a gate on a hinge, driving the Federal right flank before it, in an attempt to bend the enemy back double against the Stones River.[21]

As night fell across the wooded Tennessee countryside, a hush enveloped the armies. Campfires were not permitted on the Confederate side, and the boys tried hard to keep warm as they saw the glimmering fires of the Federals across the way. During the repose, one of the Federal regimental bands struck up a patriotic piece. The tune split the air and brought a challenge to the Rebs. Not letting this go, an obstinate Confederate band responded with one of its patriotic songs. Soon the regimental bands of both armies were dueling back and forth. "Yankee Doodle" was met with "Dixie." "Rally 'Round the Flag" evoked the strains of "The Bonnie Blue Flag." After this strange incident had gone on for some time, a Federal band began

---

[19] Record of Events, Company F, 11th Regiment Tennessee Infantry Company F Muster Roll November and December 1862, M268 R159, 11th TISR; *OR*, ser. I, vol. 20, pt. 1, 773.

[20] *OR*, ser. I, vol. 20, pt. 1, 773, 911; F. W. Weatherbee *Alabama Artillery Units and Their Organization within the Confederate Army* (Carrollton, MS: Pioneer Publishing Company, 1991) 37–38.

[21] *OR*, ser. I, vol. 20, pt. 1, 774.

to play "Home Sweet Home." Soon the Confederate bands joined them, and ironically, both sides played together this familiar melody. Memories of far-off family and friends overflowed in the minds and hearts of the soldiers as the lonely haunting strains of the music wafted through the air of the dark Tennessee night. With heads pressed despondently against the cold damp ground, soldiers—blue and gray alike—spent the next few restless hours contemplating a peace, long since passed. For many it would be their last memory of home or loved ones.[22] After the music was over and all was quiet, the men of the 11th settled in to get some sleep. With the remainder of the regiment trying to sleep despite their shivering in the frigid night, Captain James A. Long of Company F, bivouacked his men one half at a time on picket duty in front of the regiment's position.[23]

Wednesday morning, 31 December, dawned cold, gray, and miserable. An eerie mist hung in the chilly damp air. Dark masses of heavy clouds covered the sky while a wintry wind blew across the fields and through the cedars. In the low areas, fog drifted over the limestone boulders, through the dense thickets, and crept along the floor of the Stones River valley. The sight presented an ominous scene to the recently awakened Rebs as they fitted themselves for the bloody day's work that lay ahead.[24]

At 5:00 AM, the 11th Tennessee was ordered to change their line and to rebuild their battered breastworks three rails deep. As soon as this was completed, the regiment along with the remainder of Rains's Brigade, McCown's Division, and Hardee's Corps, quietly formed in line of battle and loaded their weapons. As the men formed ranks, the 29th North Carolina took position on the extreme left of the brigade with the 11th Tennessee to their right. To the right of the 11th, the 9th Georgia Battalion was positioned, followed by the 3rd Georgia Battalion. The Eufaula Alabama Light Artillery took a position near the Nolensville Road but was not further engaged in the battle. Company F returned from picket duty and took their place on the extreme left of the 11th Tennessee, butting up to the right of the 29th North Carolina. As the regiments formed and the men dressed their ranks, General Rains, splendidly adorned for the day's work, was astride his large black horse, riding down the line inspecting his brigade.[25]

---

[22] James Lee McDonough, *Stones River: Bloody Winter in Tennessee* (Knoxville: University of Tennessee, 1980) 78.

[23] Record of Events, Company F, November and December 1862, M268 R159, 11th TISR.

[24] "Wacoan's 1862 Letter Describes One of Bloodiest Civil War Battles," Waco (TX) *Times Herald*, 23 February 1961.

[25] Record of Events, Company F M268 R159, 11th TISR; *OR*, ser. I, vol. 20, pt. 1, 943; Robert B. Vance, "Twenty-ninth Regiment," in *Histories of the Several Regiments and Battalions from North Carolina in the Great War 1861–1865*, 5 vols., ed. Walter Clark (Raleigh NC: E. M. Uzell Printer, 1901) 2:488.

The Federal forces lay scarcely six to eight hundred yards to the Confederate front. When Rains's Brigade was ready, skirmishers stepped out fifty paces in advance of the main body of troops. By 6:00 AM, the preparations were complete. The men stood quietly for a moment, anticipating orders. When all was ready, Rains called the brigade to attention. Looking at his endeared boys, Rains barked, "Brigade...shoulder arms, right shoulder shift arms, forward, march!" The orders were echoed down the line from battalion to company. Immediately, in one fluid motion, the entire command moved forward. Sergeant James L. George, more affectionately known as "Big Shiney"[26] to his comrades, advanced with the regimental colors, pressing toward the enemy with a dogged determination to drive the invaders from his home state. The rat-a-tat-tat of the drums sounded cadence with each step of Rains's stalwart Southerners. As the Confederates initiated their advance, the excitement grew. Major Joseph T. Smith of the 9th Georgia Battalion stated, "The men being so eager for the fray that it was in a manner impossible to restrain them in order."[27]

As Rains's juggernaut swept toward the extreme Federal right flank, most of the Federal commanders were still completely oblivious to the desperate situation developing in their front. While the Confederates were forming lines of battle and moving to the attack, the Federal troops were building breakfast fires and boiling coffee. The Prussian-born brigadier general, August Willich, seemed totally unaware of the impending predicament and stated in a reply to a dispatch to his division commander, Brigadier General Richard W. Johnson, earlier that morning, "They are all so quiet out there that I guess they are all no more here."[28]

On the extreme right of the Federal line where Rains's Brigade would slam into the unsuspecting Federals, rested two brigades of Johnson's Division, one commanded by Willich, the other commanded by Brigadier General Edmund Kirk. Willich's Brigade anchored the Federal right. The Prussian's position resembled a fishhook as it curved out of the woods and ran along the Franklin Road. Willich's line formed an angle where it intersected with Kirk, who was immediately to his left. Running from the right where they intersected with Kirk's position were two of Willich's infantry regiments, the 39th Indiana and the 32nd Indiana. These regiments were deployed along the Franklin Pike near Gresham Lane. Some of these men found cover behind a split-rail fence. The 49th Ohio was next in line, curving back into a wooded field. Battery A of the 1st Ohio Light Artillery

---

[26] United Daughters of the Confederacy, Captain Thomas Stewart Easley Chapter, *Confederate Soldiers of Hickman County, Tennessee and Their Families* (Centerville, TN: Captain Thomas Stewart Easley Chapter #1814 United Daughters of the Confederacy, 1996) 84.

[27] *OR*, ser. I, vol. 20, pt. 1, 942.

[28] Peter Cozzens, *No Better Place to Die: The Battle of Stones River* (Urbana: University of Illinois Press, 1990) 82.

followed, with the 15th Ohio Infantry on the end of the line, continuing to curve around to the right. The 89th Illinois rested in the rear of the 49th Ohio.[29]

Occasionally, a sharp winter gust flapped the broad red and white folds of the First National pattern flag of the 11th Tennessee. As they moved forward, advancing in four heavy lines of battle, the embroidered words "God and Our Country" floated out to remind them why they were there. Steadily, the Southern masses moved closer and closer to the unsuspecting enemy. On this day, on the fields of Murfreesboro, the men of the 11th Tennessee would affirm with their life's blood the pledge that Rains had made at the presentation of their regimental colors in Nashville some seventeen months earlier. As the martial pageant unfolded, Rains gave the order for his brigade to move on the "double quick step." All along the line, his subordinates echoed the command. With alacrity his men obeyed, their steps immediately quickened, and their hearts pounded harder and harder in their chests with every step nearer to the enemy.

As Rains's Brigade approached the Yankees on the extreme Confederate left, the spatter of musketry erupted to his right as Ector's and McNair's brigades unleashed a cataclysm of fire against Kirk's unsuspecting Federals. With marked precision, the 11th continued to press toward the enemy. Each man's adrenaline was coursing through his veins. Emotions were on edge. Excitement, passion, and tension welled up in every one, almost to the point of uncontrollable fervor. After moving with this intensity for about half a mile, the men eventually reached the Franklin Road. Behind the road lay Willich's uneasy picket line. When the Rebs were in range, Willich's nervous pickets fired at Rains's unstoppable line of battle, then fled. Private W. K. White of Company H stated, we were "ordered to charge, which we did with a yell and a shout."[30] At this moment, Rains's impassioned brigade smashed the Yankee line with unquenchable fury. Captain Long remarked, "During [the] charge we were wheeled to [the] right [we] had not gone more than ¼ of [a] mile before we were fired upon by the enemies advance[,] our men charging them in gallant style[.] Advancing farther the enemy gave way."[31] By the time Rains had launched his attack against Willich, the remainder of McCown's Division, the brigades of Ector and McNair, had utterly shattered Kirk's position further to the right. As Kirk's line melted into confusion, his men began retreating through Willich's position and obscured the latter's field of fire. Lieutenant Colonel Charles T. Hotchkiss of the 89th Illinois described the situation: "At 5:30 o'clock on the morning of December 31, as my men were building fires for cooking, rapid firing was heard on Kirk's front, which was almost instantly followed by the men of his brigade rushing in confusion and indiscriminately through our ranks and over

---

[29] Ibid., 84.
[30] "Wacoan's 1862 Letter," Waco (TX) *Times Herald*, 23 February 1961.
[31] Record of Events, Company F, November and December 1862, M268 R159, 11th TISR.

my men, closely followed by a heavy column of rebel infantry."[32] Another Yankee observer, John Fiske stated, "The Confederate attack was superb and irresistible. Their men rushed forward like an overwhelming torrent, and in a few minutes Johnson's whole division was swept from the field with the loss of eleven guns, and fled in wild disorder toward the Wilkinson road."[33]

With the rout of Kirk, the force of Rains's vehement attack against Willich caused the extreme Federal right to reel backward in confusion. Willich's regiments disintegrated before Rains's undaunted advance. When the attack began, General Willich, who had been away at division headquarters, attempted to get back to his troops. On his return, his horse was shot from under him, and he was captured. Thus, the entire Federal right was struck with panic as blue mobs fled frantically to the rear with the Confederates hot on their trail.[34] Gates P. Thruston, a Federal officer, observed, "On reaching the open and somewhat elevated field in the rear of Johnson's position, I first saw in plain view Hardee's overwhelming force of two divisions extending beyond our right, sweeping over Johnson's two light and unprepared brigades. It was an appalling sight I shall never forget, a noble and thrilling spectacle indeed that a soldier might see once in a lifetime of military service, but it filled my heart with dismay."[35]

Private Milton Scholes of Company I still had no weapon when the battle began. It was not long until he was well equipped and continued the advance with his comrades. One of the Yanks fleeing before the 11th Tennessee tried to find refuge by running into a house. Billy Yank's attempt proved futile as Lieutenant James H. Darden of Company F captured him and carried him to the rear.[36]

The 11th Tennessee was now engaged in a vigorous pursuit of their fleeing opponents. The Rebel objective was simple: to gain the rear of the enemy and the Nashville Turnpike. As the Confederate left wing pivoted forward, a problem occurred with their alignment. McCown's Division, particularly Rains's Brigade, had swung too far to the left in the initial assault, creating a gap in the Rebel line. The seemingly ubiquitous Pat Cleburne saw the predicament and plugged the hole between McCown and Cheatham with his division.

With the displacement of Johnson's entire division, Bragg's objectives were in sight and were now only blocked by the division of Major General Lovell Rousseau.

---

[32] *OR*, ser. I, vol. 20, pt. 1, 310.

[33] John Fiske, *The Mississippi Valley in the Civil War* (New York: Houghton, Mifflin and Co., 1900) 167.

[34] *OR*, ser. I, vol. 20, pt. 1, 304.

[35] Gates P. Thruston, "Personal Recollections of the Battle in the Rear at Stones River, Tennessee," *Sketches of War History 1861–1865: Papers Read Before Ohio Commandery*, The Military Order of the Loyal Legion of the United States (MOLLUS), 8 vols. (Cincinnati OH: By the Commandery, 1888–1908), vol. 6, 223.

[36] Milton Scholes, Tennessee Pension Application, S13108; Record of Events, Company F, November and December 1862, M268 R159, 111th TISR.

The responsibility of removing Rousseau fell to McCown. Rains's Brigade was the strongest in McCown's Division, having suffered only light casualties so far that morning. McCown instructed Rains to take Rousseau, who was near the Nashville Pike, from the flank, while McCown's remaining brigades, those of Ector and McNair, would take the enemy from the front. To accomplish this task, McCown ordered Rains to move his brigade from the left to the right of the division. Without hesitation, Rains obeyed. After getting his brigade into position, he immediately advanced. When Rains had moved his brigade forward at the double quick for a mile or more, completing about one fourth of a circle, he halted and reformed his lines. During this break, the 11th Tennessee took its position on the extreme left of the brigade. The 29th North Carolina was positioned to their right, with the 9th Georgia Battalion coming next, and the 3rd Georgia Battalion positioned on the far right.[37]

Again, when ranks were formed and dressed, Rains directed his men forward over fences and through fields. Now, on the north side of the Wilkinson Road, Rains led his haggard troops into a cedar thicket seeking to finish off their prey and to gain the primary objective, the Nashville Turnpike. Between 8:00 and 9:00 AM, as the 11th Tennessee continued over the rough county, through the cedars and over limestone boulders, they unexpectedly encountered another line of the enemy. By this time, Rains's men were exhausted. Colonel Gordon of the 11th stated, "Suddenly we encountered a new line, hurried from the enemy's left which had not been attacked—well posted in a cedar-brake, and from which we received a deadly fire."[38] Rains's Brigade had come face to face with Captain Ketelta's company of the 15th United States Infantry Battalion, which had been placed some four hundred yards in advance of Shepard's Brigade of US Regulars. Captain Jesse Fulmer of the 15th US described the ensuing engagement:

> A heavy firing between the skirmishers was immediately commenced. Ours were driven back, and the enemy, in two or three lines of battle, hurriedly advanced, with a strong line of skirmishers in front. Our line of battle suffered somewhat by mistaking a body of rebels dressed in our uniform for our troops. When commanded to open fire upon the enemy, the battalion poured in a heavy fire upon them, but were soon compelled to give way to the vastly superior numbers of the enemy. We fired, retreating, until we reached the rear of the position just at that moment taken by the Sixth Regiment Ohio Volunteers. Here we halted to reform our line, but, while so doing, the overwhelming numbers of the rebels, and the fierce onslaught they made on the Sixth Ohio, forced those gallant volunteers to fall back also; whereupon we moved out of the woods, returning the enemy's fire,

---

[37] *OR*, ser. I, vol. 20, pt. 1, 939.
[38] Lindsley, *Military Annals*, 295.

and under cover of Guenther's battery, succeeded in taking a favorable position and reforming our line.[39]

Captain Long of Company F commented, "Here a brisk fight commenced; the enemy retreating, our men pursuing. At this stage of the fight Sergeant J. S. Rosson was wounded; also Private[s] W. R. Miles and W. Elliott."[40]

Continuing to advance, the 11th Tennessee moved past the right of the 15th US. Major Smith of the 9th Georgia explained, "During the momentary check of our right wing, the left of my command, finding but little resistance, still advanced, and thus became separated from my right. A company or more of the left of my command by this means pushed forward with the 11th Tennessee Regiment, which occupied a position to my left, and did not join me again during the day."[41]

As Captain Fulmer stated, Colonel William Grose had ordered the 36th Indiana and the 6th Ohio forward to support Shepard. The two regiments advanced in a "V," and the Rebels advanced on them in overwhelming numbers. Corporal Ebenezer Hanaford of the 6th Ohio recalled, "The line in advance of us, a brigade that had passed us only a few minutes before, had been crushed and beaten back, and were drifting toward us in utter confusion. Organization and discipline were forgotten; they were fleeing for their lives...and almost before I had time to comprehend its meaning, the rebel bullets were hissing all about us."[42] As Shepard's line dissolved, like all the others so far that day, his battered regulars fled to the rear, blocking the field of fire of Grose's 36th Indiana and 6th Ohio. Before Grose's men could fire, the 11th Tennessee and 29th North Carolina were on top of them. These Federals fled to the rear with their other comrades.

With the rout of Shepard, Rains now only had to contend with the final two regiments left in the cedars. Captain Long described the situation facing the 11th Tennessee:

> We pursued them across the fence to [a] break of rocks. The enemy had made a stand about 100 or one hundred and fifty yards, as though they were determined to regain their lost ground. Here we had a brisk and well contested fight. The men (ours) displayed as much coolness as veterans, sight their guns as well, and with as much deliberation as if they were shooting at game. Our fire was too severe for their veterans, [so] they gave way. Our boys ran [with] a shout and pursued them, pouring well directed volleys of musketry, driving them out of the wood[s], into fields and back upon their reserve.[43]

---

[39] *OR*, ser. I, vol. 20, pt. 1, 400.
[40] Record of Events, Company F, November and December.
[41] *OR*, ser. I, vol. 20, pt. 1, 942.
[42] Cozzens, *No Better Place to Die*, 139.
[43] Record of Events, Company F, November and December 1862, M268 R159, 11th TISR.

This assault resulted in the rout of the last Federal troops in the cedars. Grose's units fled out of the woods to the cover of Rousseau's batteries which were posted on a rise in a cotton field by the Nashville Pike. Rains's Confederates continued their advance through the cedars toward the Federal lines that rested on the other side of the dense woods. Lieutenant Pirtle, Rousseau's ordinance officer, described the situation as Rains's Brigade burst from the cedars in pursuit of their beleaguered foe:

> As I looked on, an officer on foot, sword in hand, sprang into view with a shout; in an instant the edge of the timber was alive with a mass of arms, heads, legs, guns, swords, gray coats, brown hats, shirt sleeves, and the enemy were upon us, yelling, leaping, running. Not a shot from them for a few jumps, then one or two paused to throw up their guns, fire and yell, then run forward to try to gain the front.[44]

When Rains's Confederates broke through the woods, the Yankee artillery batteries of Parsons, Guenther, and Van Pelt exploded into action. They seemed to seek vengeance for their comrades who were routed and lost earlier in the day. The 84th Illinois, the 24th Ohio, the 23rd Kentucky, and the 94th Ohio joined the Federal batteries in raking Rains's line. As Colonel Vance of the 29th North Carolina described,

> The enemy formed again on a slight elevation in our front, from which they were soon driven into a cedar thicket, and from thence finally into a large field under cover of their guns, a heavy battery which opened on us at once with shell, grape, and canister, while the enemy's infantry rallied and opened fire from two or three heavy lines of battle. Here was the struggle for the day, and a hard one it was.[45]

Lieutenant Colonel Thedford of the 11th said of the affair, "A charge was immediately ordered, which was obeyed with alacrity, until the advance was checked by the enemy's battery, which rained shot and shell into our ranks."[46] Reverend Cherry stated, "We were exposed to a fearful fire. Never did I see men fall so rapidly."[47] Private White of Company K further described the fierceness of the fight,

> We drove them from field to field, scattering their ranks in confusion and leaving the ground covered with their dead and wounded. But the final desperate struggle was made in a skirt of timber where they had thrown their heaviest forces to stop us on the left. To give you a description of that fight is more than I can do. They fought well and stubbornly, resisted every inch of ground from here on. The missels of destruction, bombs solid balls, grape and cannister shot, and musket balls, were

---

[44] Alfred Pirtle, "Stone River Sketches," *Sketches of War History 1861–1865: Papers Read Before Ohio Commandery*, 6:99–100.
[45] *OR*, ser. I, vol. 20, pt. 1, 939.
[46] Ibid., 943.
[47] Jones, *Christ in the Camp*, 571.

showered upon us as thick as hail, and were returned by our men with equal rapidity.[48]

Rains's Brigade had run headlong into a deadly crossfire. From their position near the Nashville Turnpike, the eight guns of Parson's Batteries H & M of the 4th US Artillery decimated the lines of the exhausted Confederates. Men of the 11th Tennessee began dropping before the concentrated fire of the enemy. The bombardment was so intense that the cedars were riddled by musketry and canister. Treetops and limbs fell to the ground. The brown and yellow leaves that covered the ground were splattered crimson with the blood of Tennessee's native sons. The dead and wounded of the 11th were scattered over the field as the regiment pressed forward. As the minie balls zipped viciously into their ranks, Corporal John Chandler of Company H fell dead. His brother, Joseph, knelt beside his corpse and removed a freshly bloodstained New Testament from the boy's jacket pocket.[49] Sergeant Clayton Yates recalled, "Then it was that the most terrible struggle began. Both sides fought like mad men, each rushing into the very jaws of death. We captured some of the batteries and they retook them from us, killing many of our men and horses."[50] Captain William I. White of Company A stated, "We charged a battery strongly guarded in the enemy's center, the enemy suffered extremely. [We] took the battery but were unable to hold it."[51]

Due to their swift advance, the 11th had captured a battery and a number of prisoners.[52] Rains turned to Sergeant Clint Jones of Company H, and said, "Go take those Yankees to the rear Sergeant."[53] Jones started to the rear with the Federal prisoners. Rains continued to advance. Despite the intense barrage they were facing, the impetuous Rains valiantly moved to the van of his brigade. He was in the immediate front of his cherished old regiment. Rains bolstered the 11th onward. John H. Ward of Company G, of the 11th stated, "General Rains rushed forward and commanded the boys to follow him."[54] The thirty-two-year-old Yale-educated Rains, still astride his handsome black mount, urged his heroic troops on with the

---

[48] "Wacoan's 1862 Letter," Waco (TX) Times Herald, 23 February 1961.

[49] United Daughters of the Confederacy, Confederate Soldiers of Hickman County, 42.

[50] Clayton H. Yates, "Further Reminiscences of the Civil War," Mayfield (KY) Daily Messenger, unknown date.

[51] Record of Events, Company A, November and December 1862, M268 R159, 11th TISR.

[52] Ibid.

[53] James Lunsford, Tennessee Confederate Pension Application 5485, (quote of S. C. Jones), Family Search, https://familysearch.org/pal:/MM9.3.1/TH-1951-20618-18612-91?cc=1874474&wc=M6ZX-4NL:171467301,172409201 (29 April 2015).

[54] John H. Ward, "The Eleventh Tennessee Infantry," Confederate Veteran 16/8 (August 1908): 420.

words, "Forward, my brave boys, forward!"[55] At that time, a minie ball cut the gauntlet of his right hand and then smashed into the young brigadier's chest. Rains's body fell lifelessly to the ground, yet his beautiful steed continued toward the Federal lines. Later, Color Sergeant John R. Rich of the 29th North Carolina saw a Federal officer riding Rains's black horse. This Yankee officer was also shot from the horse, and after that rider fell, the horse continued forward returning to the ranks of the 11th Tennessee and was captured by the men of this regiment.[56]

Despite Rains's fall, Colonel George W. Gordon continued to press the 11th toward the enemy. Amidst the galling fire, Gordon fell dangerously wounded, shot through the thigh and scrotum.[57] About the same time, Captain William H. McCauley of Company C fell with serious injuries. McCauley stated, "At this point I saw General Rains fall from his horse, mortally wounded; and as I turned to mention it to one of my men, a minie ball penetrated three of my ribs, paralyzing my right leg."[58] William Thomas "Pig" Adams, a member of McCauley's Company, was in line by J. I. J. Adams. Almost simultaneously, both men dropped to the ground wounded. A projectile broke J. I. J. Adams's right index finger and struck his left thumb, while another minie ball smashed into "Pig" Adams's right arm and broke it just above the elbow.[59] James M. Rogers, another member of Company C, lost his left arm and right leg.[60] William W. Stokey, a private in Company C stated, "Every commissioned officer in our company was wounded or missing by the end of the day."[61] Other companies of the 11th were cut to pieces as well. James Barr of Company H was shot through the leg twice at the same time and carried off the field.[62] As Private Elisha T. Ridings of Company A was trying to comprehend the

---

[55] L. J. Watkins, "Address of Brig. Gen. James E. Rains," *Confederate Veteran* 16/5 (May 1908): 209.

[56] Vance, "Twenty-ninth Regiment," 2:489.

[57] William B. Maney, "Return of Killed and Wounded in the 11th Tennessee Regiment at the Battle of Stones River, Tennessee, 31 December 1862," *Regimental Surgeon's Log*, Confederate Collection, Manuscript Section, Box 18, Military Units Tenn. Inf. Regt. 11, Medical Records, Tennessee State Library and Archives, Nashville, TN.

[58] William H. McCauley, "Tribute to a Federal Officer," *Confederate Veteran* 7/2 (February 1899): 72.

[59] Maney, Surgeon's Log, "Stones River, TN"; J. I. J. Adams, Tennessee Confederate Pension Application 4073, Family Search, https://familysearch.org/pal:/MM9.3.1/TH-1951-20614-55520-60?cc=1874474&wc=M6Z6-1WL:171467301,171874501 (29 April 2015); William T. Adams, Tennessee Confederate Pension Application 4183, Family Search, https://familysearch.org/pal:/MM9.3.1/TH-1942-20615-1965-40?cc=1874474&wc=M6ZX-SP8:171467301,171883801 (29 April 2015).

[60] Maney, "Return of Killed and Wounded...at the Battle of Stones River."

[61] Mamie Yeary, *Reminiscences of the Boys in Gray, 1861–1865* (1912; reprint, Dayton, OH: Morningside, 1986) 726.

[62] Yeary, *Reminiscences*, 40; Maney, "Return of Killed and Wounded...at the Battle of Stones River."

slaughter, a minie ball struck him over the left eye, passed through the bridge of his nose, and lodged in his upper right jawbone.[63] Ridings, blinded, fell to the ground. His brother, 1st Lieutenant George D. Ridings (of the same company), was shot in the right leg above the ankle and was helped to the rear by some of his men. Sergeant Clayton Yates described the scene: "There were men lying here and there in every shape and every form; some in heaps as if placed that way by friends, while many were wounded and dying, many dying for water, others crying for help, with grape and canister and other missiles of death flying in every direction. It was then that I said, 'O! My God, to be in battle is to be in hell at least for the time being.'"[64]

As soon as Rains fell, "the news, running like wild fire along the whole line produced a temporary confusion."[65] In the chaos, one of Rains's aides turned to Sergeant Clayton Yates of the 11th Tennessee, who was near the general when he fell, and told Yates to tell Colonel Stovall of the 3rd Georgia Battalion to take command of the brigade. Yates went on his errand as commanded and found Stovall sitting behind a huge oak tree. When told of the news of Rains's death, Yates said that Stovall just "sat there as if he did not hear me." Yates repeated himself, and finally Stovall acknowledged him and told him, "I will be there soon." As the party ran to take command of the brigade, Yates said that he noticed that Stovall "could not run very fast."[66] As Yates was on his errand to find Stovall, it was determined that Colonel Vance of the 29th North Carolina was actually senior in rank, and he took command of the brigade. Colonel Vance, seeing that ammunition was low and that the continued assault was futile, commanded the brigade to "fall back both to get ammunition and to shelter themselves from the enemy's batteries, against which they could do nothing."[67]

With Colonel Gordon down, Lieutenant Colonel Thedford assumed command of the 11th Tennessee. Thedford stated, "The enemy opposed our advance with obstinacy, and being strongly reinforced, and our ammunition failing, we retired to the rear."[68] In so doing, the boys of the 11th were forced to abandon their dead and most seriously wounded, leaving them helpless on the field amidst the boulders and cotton. Among them lay the lifeless form of their beloved Rains.

As the 11th Tennessee and the 29th North Carolina retired to get ammunition, they became separated by going to different locations to fill their

---

[63] E. T. Ridings, Pension Application 447, Family Search https://familysearch.org/pal:/MM9.3.1/TH-1951-20611-1227-90?cc=1874474&wc=M6Z6-WWL:171467301,171510601 (29 April 2009); Maney, "Return of Killed and Wounded . . . at the Battle of Stones River TN."

[64] C. H. Yates, "Article Four," Mayfield (KY) *Daily Messenger*, unknown date.

[65] *OR*, ser. I, vol. 20, pt. 1, 938.

[66] Clayton H. Yates, "Further Reminiscences of the Civil War," Mayfield (KY) *Daily Messenger*, unknown date.

[67] *OR*, ser. I, vol. 20, pt. 1, 938.

[68] Ibid., 943.

cartridge boxes. After the 11th Tennessee was resupplied, the regiment was again sent into action with elements of Cleburne's Division. Lieutenant Colonel Thedford wrote, "Collecting the scattered of the regiment and procuring ammunition, we again advanced to the front, and were a third time ordered to charge the enemy. As before, the men obeyed with a shout, and drove the enemy before them until they gained a strong natural position. Here the ground was hotly contested until we were ordered to retire."[69]

As the 11th Tennessee moved up to support the 23rd Tennessee of Cleburne's Division, the men of the 11th took cover behind a fence and poured a heavy fire into the Yankee line. Captain Long stated, "We were again placed on the extreme left and participated in another fight driving the enemy into his strong position. My Co[mpany] was near to a four gun battery from which we had driven horses, [and] killed troops. Falling back on our right we were compelled to retire after having killed the horses connected with the battery, thereby rendering it unfit for service."[70]

The 23rd Tennessee fell back, and its line broke somewhat while crossing the fence sheltering the 11th. With further resistance useless, the 11th retired to the rear intermingled with the 23rd. After reforming, the regiments were again ordered to the front. As they advanced, General Cleburne met them and ordered them to halt and to hold their position.[71]

As night fell over the field, which had been so bitterly contested during the day, the agony of the wounded could not be silenced. Cries for water and help haunted the air. Sergeant Clayton Yates wrote,

> All of that long night, you could hear the wounded crying for water and help, and no tongue or pen can describe that ordeal. We went into battle with about 60 men in my company. That night there was hardly a corporal's guard of us left. Myself and only six men. Early in the morning I had thrown away my knapsack with my blankets, so I had nothing but the cold bare ground to sleep upon, with the canopy of heaven for my covering, and it was indeed very cold. I lay so near the fire that I came nigh burning my new boots off of my feet. My father had just sent me these boots.[72]

In the evening, as some of the boys were looking for their fallen comrades, they came across the body of Colonel George W. Roberts, of the 42nd Illinois. The boys recalled how, earlier in the day, this Yankee colonel heroically but vainly had attempted to stop his men from fleeing in the front of the Tennesseans. Roberts's repeated efforts to restore the Yankee lines in the cedar brake proved futile. His

---

[69] Ibid.

[70] Record of Events, Company F, November and December 1862, M268 R159, 11th TISR.

[71] William Henry Harder, "Memoirs," MF 574, 83, Tennessee State Library and Archives, Nashville, TN.

[72] Yates, "Further Reminiscences."

men could not stand before Rains's advance. Roberts was everywhere conspicuous for his bravery and daring, but his audacity in the face of the overwhelming foe was too much, and about eleven o'clock he fell, killed by a minie ball. With the respect due a true hero, some of the boys of the 11th dug a grave and buried the colonel's body. Other boys of the regiment retrieved a headstone, a large flat rock on which they laboriously scratched and chipped an inscription with a bayonet.[73]

The Battle of Murfreesboro lasted two more days, but the 11th Tennessee was not further engaged. The regiment had suffered many losses on the first day of battle. Private Stokey of Company C stated, "My company went into battle that morning with fifty-two men and came out with myself and eleven comrades left."[74]

In his official listing of the casualties of the 11th, Lieutenant Colonel Thedford recorded eighty-one killed, wounded, and missing. This includes eight officers killed, eight enlisted men killed, ten officers wounded, fifty-four enlisted men wounded, and eleven enlisted men missing. The 11th Tennessee had had its first major engagement. The regiment had suffered substantial casualties but had proven herself faithful. The heavy losses sustained by the regiment attests to her valor and courage, and this reputation would precede her throughout the remainder of the war.[75]

---

[73] Jill Garrett and Marise P. Lightfoot, *The Civil War in Maury County, Tennessee* (Columbia, TN: s.n., 1966) 87–88.

[74] Yeary, *Reminiscences*, 726.

[75] William Thedford, "Report of Operations and Casualties of the 11th Regt. Tenn. Inf. in the Battle of Murfreesboro 31 December 1862," Confederate States Army Casualties: Lists and Narrative Reports, 1861–1865, M836 R4, Tennessee State Library and Archives, Nashville, TN.

8

"Your Son until Death"

January–July 1863

The rising sun of Thursday, 1 January, brought to bear the grim reality of the fierce struggle that had occurred the previous day. The morning was clear, but quite cool. Pickets looked into the cedars for any advance of the enemy. Both sides reconnoitered toward each other's lines, but neither side initiated an attack. The 11th Tennessee remained inactive and occupied its final position of the day of battle.

These first hours of 1863 brought little comfort to the boys as they grieved their comrades lost in the battle the day before. Many wrote letters home attempting to describe what had occurred, yet none could convey the horror of the experience. Private W. K. White of Company H wrote his family back in Hickman County,

> To give you a description of that fight is more than I can do. They fought well and stubbornly, resisted every inch of the ground from here on. The missels of destruction, bombs, solid balls, grape and canister shot, were showered upon us thick as hail.... For eleven long hours this bloody battle raged, until night put an end to the dreadful slaughter. We remained on the field that night with the dead laying all around us, but we were so near worn out that we slept soundly. I never again want to see another battle.[1]

The job of gathering the fallen from the fields was well underway. The reality of the grand struggle, observable in every direction, was inescapable. As the wounded were gathered, the medical stewards took them to field hospitals that surgeons had established in the homes of Murfreesboro residents. The scenes at the hospitals were hideous. Shrieks and cries from the wounded permeated the air. Surgeons converted dining tables into operating tables. Orderlies placed boards on top of barrels to fashion additional surgical beds. Straw was scattered onto the floor of the makeshift operating rooms. As the surgeons hacked off arms and legs, assistants piled the discarded limbs onto army blankets covering the floor. When the severed members filled the blanket, orderlies carried them out and buried them. Reverend Cherry described the sight at one of the hospitals, "The scene was shocking. Hundreds with bleeding wounds shivering around the fires patiently waiting their turn for the surgeons' services. The amputating knives were fast

---

[1] "Wacoan's 1862 Letter Describes One of Bloodiest Civil War Battles," Waco (TX) *Times Herald*, 23 February 1961.

removing maimed limbs which were piled promiscuously by the house."² Aides transported 1st Lieutenant George D. Ridings of Company A to C. S. field hospital #1, which they established in the home of Ms. Grimmage.³ Litter bearers took Captain McCauley to another field hospital that medical personnel had established in the residence of B. W. Henry. Orderlies transported Colonel Gordon to yet another hospital that surgeons had quartered in the residence of Ms. Dromgoole, the wife of the mayor.⁴

In the meantime, the Federals had retrieved the corpse of General Rains from the cotton field. A minister approached General Rosecrans and begged for the body of the fallen brigadier. Rosecrans acquiesced, but warned the preacher that no "infernal secession pow-wow" was to be made in Nashville over it.⁵ The minister retrieved Rains's body. It seems that his body was first taken to the Gresham House hospital where General Benjamin F. Cheatham wept freely at the sight of his fallen friend.⁶ Another disconcerted Rebel described his sentiments, "We saw…the long black casket containing the body our beloved General Rains, which cast a deep gloom over our spirits. His presence in battle had been equal to a regiment of men."⁷

When Private Elisha Ridings of Company A was shot, he was thought to be dead by those of his company who were near him when he collapsed. As a result, his company fell back with the regiment and left Ridings amidst the fallen Yankees. Although seriously wounded, Ridings was not dead. The private lay on the ground unconscious, as blood seeped from the fearful gashes of his head. As night came and the temperature dropped, he was adhered to the earth by his own blood. After lying on the field for hours in this condition, sometime after 10:00 PM, an Ohio

---

² J. William Jones, *Christ in the Camp or Religion in the Confederate Army* (1887; reprint, Harrisonburg, VA: Sprinkle Publications, 1986) 572.

³ George D. Ridings, M268 R162, 11th Tennessee Infantry Service Records, National Archives Records Administration, *Compiled Service Records of Confederate Soldiers Who Served in Organizations from the State of Tennessee*, Washington, DC: National Archives and Records Service, General Services Administration, 1960. Hereafter cited as 11th TISR.

⁴ William H. McCauley, "Tribute to a Federal Officer," *Confederate Veteran* 7/2 (February 1899): 72.

⁵ John Fitch, *Annals of the Army of the Cumberland: Comprising Biographies, Descriptions of Departments, Accounts of Expeditions, Skirmishes, and Battles; Also Its Police Record of Spies, Smugglers, and Prominent Rebel Emissaries…and Official Reports of the Battle of Stone River and of the Chickamauga Campaign*, 5th ed. (Philadelphia, PA: J. B. Lippencott & Co., 1864) 657–58.

⁶ Christopher Losson, *Tennessee's Forgotten Warriors: Frank Cheatham and His Confederate Division* (Knoxville: University of Tennessee Press, 1989) 90; Larry J. Daniel, *Battle of Stones River: The Forgotten Conflict Between the Confederate Army of Tennessee and the Union Army of the Cumberland* (Baton Rouge: Louisiana State University Press, 2012) 170.

⁷ Joseph Hutcheson, "More About Gen. James E. Rains," *Confederate Veteran* 16/8 (August 1908): 391.

infantryman found the gravely wounded soldier and noticed he was still alive. In a grand act of compassion, the Ohioan dressed Ridings's wounds and aided the blinded soldier to the Federal rear where he was given further medical attention and was taken prisoner.[8]

At about 2:00 on the morning of Friday, 2 January, Lieutenant Colonel Thedford, under orders, moved the 11th Tennessee to the vicinity of Murfreesboro.[9] Later that day, Bragg realized that Rosecrans posed a threat to his right flank by holding the high ground on the east side of the Stones River. The obstinate Confederate commander hoped to gain a position from which he could then threaten Rosecrans's left and center with Rebel artillery. Although the 11th Tennessee did not participate, Bragg ordered General John C. Breckenridge to assault the heights with his division and to drive the Federals back. Breckenridge was outraged at what he considered a suicidal charge. Nevertheless, he formed his division and moved forward. Initially, the assault seemed successful, but the advance soon turned disastrous as fifty-eight Federal guns under command of Captain John Mendenhall unleashed their fire and ripped the Southern lines with shot and shell. Breckenridge's attack failed, resulting in heavy losses.

On Saturday, 3 January, Bragg decided that his position was untenable, and a withdrawal was the most feasible alternative of his relatively few options. Bragg marched his army from Murfreesboro to form a new defensive line to the southeast along the Duck River in the area of Shelbyville and Tullahoma, Tennessee.

In the meantime, the boys prepared to abandon the field. Officers detailed several men to load the commissary wagons of the regiment. Private John Ward of Company B was one of the men assigned to this task. The men worked hard loading the supplies until dark. When the wagons were loaded, Ward disappeared into the night to visit one of his lady friends. He was gone until about 1:00 AM. Upon his return, he found everyone else of the company asleep except Captain E. W. Clark. Ward slipped into an old house and fell asleep.[10]

Soon night turned to day, and the men had everything prepared for departure. The men fell in line, and Lieutenant Colonel Thedford marched his battered command down the Shelbyville Pike. The incessant rain and the churning boots of the retreating army turned the road into a quagmire. The boys sloshed through mud

---

[8] E. T. Ridings, Pension Application 447, Family Search https://familysearch.org/pal:/MM9.3.1/TH-1951-20611-1227-90?cc=1874474&wc=M6Z6-WWL:171467301,171510601 (29 April 2009).

[9] Record of Events, Company F Muster Roll November and December 1862, 11th Regiment Tennessee Infantry Service Records, National Archives Records Administration, Compiled Service Records of Confederate Soldiers Who Served in Organizations from the State of Tennessee, Washington, DC: National Archives Records and Service, General Services Administration, 1960. M268 R159.

[10] John H. Ward, "The Eleventh Tennessee Infantry," *Confederate Veteran* 16/8 (August 1908): 420.

an inch deep and sometimes deeper on the pike. Rain fell in torrents, pounding the mud-bespattered soldiers as their column crawled toward the southeast away from Murfreesboro. After marching approximately twenty-eight miles in those conditions, the regiment arrived at their destination and established camp near Shelbyville.

Back in Murfreesboro, as the sun rose, Ward awoke. The private returned to the place his company had been the previous night but was unable to find them. Next, Ward went over to the depot. He was still unable to locate the regiment. When Ward discovered that the regiment had departed, he exulted that he was "master of the situation."[11] Ward recounts his experience,

> Our troops were retiring toward Shelbyville, my home. I caught up with our rear guard of cavalry about six miles out; but I was bound for home, which was not far away. After meeting my good old mother and father and friends, I went to see my sweetheart, who later became my wife. While conversing pleasantly with her I felt something crawling on my neck. Boys, you know what it was [lice]. I slyly put my fingers on it and held it till I got an opportunity to go outdoors and make away with it.[12]

Surgeons sent by train as many of the wounded as possible to Academy Hospital in Chattanooga or to other Confederate hospitals in Georgia, but due to Bragg's hasty retreat from Murfreesboro, the army left behind many of its wounded whom the Federals subsequently captured. As to the gallant and gifted Rains, former Colonel of the 11th Tennessee, George W. Gordon stated,

> It seems but a feeble tribute to his memory to say that he was an ardent patriot, a brilliant orator, and a brave soldier. An impulsive exponent of Southern chivalry, he threw his whole energies and abilities into the struggle for Southern independence. With his high ambition, reckless courage, and impetuous eclat, it was hardly possible that he should survive the casualties of many battles. He fell in the first. If the writer ever knew a man of whom he could say, He was fearless, he thinks that man was Gen. Rains. This term, in its application to most men of conspicuous courage, is but relative; but when applied to him it seems absolute. He appeared rather to invite than to avoid danger; and at the time he was killed he was several hundred feet in advance of his line, and in the immediate front of the Eleventh Regiment as if his best hopes and highest confidence were in his old command.[13]

On Tuesday, 6 January, the body of General Rains was taken back to Nashville and interred the following afternoon in the City Cemetery in the Currin Vault.[14]

---

[11] Ibid.

[12] Ibid.

[13] John Berrien Lindsley, *Military Annals of Tennessee: Confederate* (1886; facsimile of the first edition, Wilmington, NC: Broadfoot Publishing, 1995) 296.

[14] Nashville (TN) *Daily Union*, 8 January 1863.

While the 11th Tennessee was on the march to Shelbyville, Captain McCauley of Company C was having quite a time as a hospital patient and a prisoner of war. McCauley remained in the hospital for about three weeks after the battle. He received good medical care, and though his wound healed well, he was still bedridden. One day a Yankee officer with a detail of six guards rousted the wounded captain. The officer of the detail told him they were taking him to their commander's headquarters. The Federals made the wounded captain walk about a mile and a half until they arrived at General Jefferson C. Davis's command post.[15] There, they left the Rebel captain standing alone. The exerting walk weakened McCauley and caused his wound to bleed again. Soon, General Davis stepped outside his tent. He approached McCauley and asked his name. The captain responded, "My name is McCauley."[16] The captain recalled the remainder of the conversation:

> "What are you doing here?" He asked. I told him I was a captain in the Confederate army, and was offering further explanation, when I saw the officer who had conveyed me there, and pointed him out to the General. He summoned the officer and questioned him; then, with closed fist and pointed finger, said: "There are some men who do not seem to have any sense. I told you to go out into the country and bring in any of our men who might be straggling out from camp." The General took me by the arm, asked me into his marquee, and told me to lie down on his cot. I thanked him, but declined the offer, saying, that my wound was bleeding and that I did not think he would like Rebel blood on his bedding. He asked me to sit on a camp stool which he placed for me. The staff seemed to be busy drawing up reports and maps of the battles. The General asked me whose brigade I was in, and what part of the line. I informed him, and added that we had surprised and routed one line of his men; also that at this point Gen. Rains was killed and I had been wounded. The General's face indicated much interest, and he said: "I placed the line in the cedars, and know the very spot where Gen. Rains fell."[17]

After General Davis had finished with McCauley, he summoned an ambulance to return the wounded Southerner to the hospital. McCauley declined the ambulance because of the nature of his wounds. Davis offered the Rebel captain his horse, which he accepted. McCauley attempted to mount the horse, but the paralysis in his leg caused him considerable difficulty. The Yankee general then took hold of the captain's leg, lifted it over the saddle, and placed it in the stirrup. Davis asked McCauley how he was, shook his hand, and bid him farewell without further incident. McCauley returned to Mr. Henry's house. The captain's wound took some

---

[15] General Jefferson C. Davis commanded the First Division of the Army of the Cumberland.
[16] McCauley, "Tribute," 72.
[17] Ibid.

time to heal. However, when his injuries had healed well enough, the Federals sent McCauley to the provost marshal where he again met up with Colonel Gordon.[18]

In a short time, McCauley and Gordon numbered among a group of Confederate convalescents whom the Federals were shipping from the hospital at Murfreesboro to the penitentiary at Nashville. From there, the Federals transferred McCauley and Gordon to Camp Chase, Ohio. McCauley recalled one of his experiences while at Camp Chase:

> I remained in Nashville but a few days; I was sent to Louisville, where I met a friend who gave me a twenty dollar bill, Bank of Tennessee. This bill I sold to a Yankee sutler, at Camp Chase, Ohio for sixteen dollars in Greenbacks. After being kept at Camp Chase for about a month, we were sent to Philadelphia. I lost my hat enroute, and next day requested the officer in charge to allow a guard to accompany me to buy a new hat. He refused, but offered to get one for me, if I would give him the money. I gave him all I had, a five dollar bill, and he never came back.[19]

By this time, the 11th Tennessee had been encamped at Shelbyville for a couple of weeks. While here, Bragg dissolved Rains's Brigade, temporarily commanded by Colonel Vance, and assigned the different regiments to other brigades. On Wednesday, 21 January, by Special Order Number 15, from army headquarters at Tullahoma, the 11th Tennessee Infantry, under temporary command of Lieutenant Colonel William Thedford, was transferred from Vance's Brigade, McCown's Division, Hardee's Corps and assigned to General Preston Smith's Brigade of Benjamin F. Cheatham's all-Tennessee division of General Leonidas Polk's corps.[20]

The boys of the 11th Tennessee packed their equipment and moved through Shelbyville on the road to Tullahoma. The regiment crossed the Duck River, and marched about two and a half more miles where they joined their new brigade that was encamped in the woods. The 11th established their camp, aligning what tents they possessed in perfect rows. The soldiers attached chimneys to their little shelters that made the winter much more bearable.[21]

Lieutenant General Leonidas Polk, commanding the corps to which the 11th Tennessee was assigned, was born in Raleigh, North Carolina, in 1806. Polk was an 1827 graduate of West Point. After graduation, Polk resigned from the army and

---

[18] Ibid.

[19] Ibid.

[20] United States War Department, *The War of the Rebellion: A Compilation of the Official Records of the Union and Confederate Armies.* 70 vols. in 128 (Washington: Government Printing Office, 1880–1901; reprint, Gettysburg, PA: The National Historical Society, 1972) ser. I, vol. 23, Pt. 2, 613. Hereafter cited as *OR*.

[21] A. T. Fielder, *Captain A. T. Fielder's Civil War Diary Company B, 12th Tennessee Infantry C. S. A. July 1861–June 1865*, ed. M. Todd Cathey (Broken Arrow, OK: Create Space, 2012), 190.

entered the Episcopalian ministry. At the outbreak of the war, Polk again donned a military uniform and was commissioned a major general. On 10 October 1862, he was promoted to the rank of lieutenant general. Although Polk's military performance was sometimes questionable, his men loved and respected him.[22]

The 11th Tennessee's division commander, Major General Benjamin Franklin Cheatham, was born in Nashville in 1820 and was a descendant of the city's founder, James Robertson. During the Mexican War, Cheatham had won a reputation for his service as a captain in the 1st Tennessee Infantry and then as colonel of the 3rd Tennessee. He was especially distinguished in the battles of Monterrey and Vera Cruz. At the threshold of the Civil War, on 9 May 1861, Cheatham was appointed major general in the provisional army of the state of Tennessee. Two months later, he was commissioned a brigadier general in the provisional army of the Confederacy. Cheatham's reputation as a formidable commander resulted from his hard fighting at Shiloh, Perryville, and Murfreesboro.[23]

Preston Smith, commanding the brigade to which the 11th Tennessee had been assigned, was born in Giles County, Tennessee, on 25 December 1823. He obtained his early education in country schools and later attended Jackson College at Columbia. Later, he studied law, and after admission to the bar, moved to Waynesboro, Tennessee, and then to Memphis. In 1861, Smith was commissioned colonel of the 154th Senior Tennessee Infantry, a prewar militia unit, which retained its numerical militia designation when transferred into Confederate service. Smith was seriously wounded while leading the 154th at Shiloh, but he recovered. In the Battle of Perryville, Kentucky, he commanded the division after General Patrick Cleburne was wounded. On 27 October 1862, Smith was promoted to brigadier general and assumed command of the brigade. Smith's Brigade had sustained heavy casualties at Murfreesboro, but with the reorganization of his command at Shelbyville, his brigade now consisted of six Tennessee infantry units, the 11th, 12th, 13th, 29th, 47th, and 154th regiments. This reorganization formed a union whereby the units of this brigade remained together throughout the remainder of the war, although commanders changed and regimental consolidations occurred.[24]

Soon after the 11th joined Smith's Brigade, John W. Harris, acting inspector general of the brigade reported of the 11th Tennessee,

---

[22] Ezra J. Warner, *Generals in Gray: Lives of the Confederate Commanders* (Baton Rouge: Louisiana State University, 1987) 243.

[23] Clement A. Evans, *Confederate Military History*, 12 vols. (1899; reprint, Wilmington, NC: Broadfoot, 1987) 10:302; Losson, *Tennessee's Forgotten Warriors*, 11–16.

[24] Warner, *Generals in Gray*, 283. The 12th and 47th Tennessee regiments were consolidated at the end of October 1862 (Lindsley, *Military Annals*, 309).

The regiment is very well disciplined, and of excellent material. The officers are efficient and well posted in their duties. The arms are well cleaned and in very good order. The armament is about equally divided between the smoothbore musket (cal. .69). The accouterments have been well preserved and are in good order. Cartridge boxes are full, and an average of 51 rounds of ammunition [per soldier] is kept in the regimental ordinance wagons. A sufficient number of [percussion] caps are kept in the boxes.[25]

Harris went on to report, "The clothing is good, generally, but as in all the regiments of the brigade, shoes are badly needed."[26] The regiment had a shortage of cooking utensils, axes, hatchets, and spades and only had fifty-one tents and fourteen flies. Almost half of the men were missing their bayonets and about one-fourth of the men needed new canteens. However, the regiment maintained four two-horse wagons and ambulances, forty-six public animals, and eight four-horse wagons.[27]

With his army safely away from Murfreesboro and reorganized, Bragg established his headquarters and supply base at Tullahoma a small town on the Nashville and Chattanooga Railroad. Hardee's Corps was sent to Wartrace, a town in front of Tullahoma, to establish defenses there, while Polk was ordered to a position on the left wing of the army at Shelbyville. During the six months that the Army of Tennessee remained along this Duck River line, the Confederates constructed a solid system of defensive earthworks, the front of which were protected by an abatis of blackjack thicket.[28] The strongest position at Tullahoma was an earthwork, named Fort Rains in honor of the fallen Brigadier General Rains, which could hold a battalion of infantry.[29] At Shelbyville, Polk stationed a strong advance force to guard Guy's Gap, an important pass on the Shelbyville Pike, with the remainder of his corps in support distance at Shelbyville. Hardee's Corps at Wartrace, held three other important passes, Bellbuckle Gap, Liberty Gap, and Hoover's Gap. Bragg expected that Rosecrans might move against Shelbyville.[30]

Throughout the month of February, cool weather, wind, clouds, snow, and rain were common. During this foul weather, the troops gathered wood for heat and for cooking in addition to standing picket duty, digging entrenchments, and

---

[25] Jack C. Vaughan, *Brigadier General Alfred Jefferson Vaughan's Brigade, Army of Tennessee Confederate States of America* (Grand Prairie, TX: Major Jack C. Vaughan, 1959–1960) 616–17.

[26] Ibid.

[27] Ibid.

[28] Stanley Horn, *Army of Tennessee* (Wilmington, NC: Broadfoot, 1987) 231; William B. Feis, "The Deception of Braxton Bragg: The Tullahoma Campaign, June 23–July 4, 1863," *Blue and Gray Magazine* Vol. X Issue 1 (October 1992): 12.

[29] Michael R. Bradley, *Tullahoma: The 1863 Campaign for Middle Tennessee* (Shippensburg, PA: Burd Street Press, 2000) 30.

[30] Feis, "Deception of Braxton Bragg," 14.

drilling, as the weather permitted.[31] On 23 February, William M. Slayden of the 11th was commissioned assistant surgeon for the regiment.[32] By Thursday, 26 February, rain had caused the Duck River to overflow its banks. Two days later, Private Samuel Cathey of Company A drowned in the flooded river.[33]

The unfavorable weather continued into the opening days of March. On Monday, 2 March, Smith's Brigade had muster roll inspection at 11:00 AM, but by the following day, light sleet and snow covered the Confederate camp. These conditions compounded the misery of the troops. The snow continued to fall the next day, and many soldiers of the brigade were sick with colds and chills.[34] On 5 March, due to their heavy losses in previous battles, the 13th and 154th Tennessee regiments were consolidated under command of Colonel Alfred J. Vaughan of the 13th Tennessee.[35]

A Virginian by birth, Vaughan was an 1851 graduate of the Virginia Military Institute. Prior to the war, Vaughan was a surveyor in California before moving to Mississippi to farm. When the war began, he joined the 13th Tennessee and was elected captain of a company. He was soon elected lieutenant colonel and was later promoted to colonel. Vaughan had already distinguished himself by his conspicuous courage in battle. At both Shiloh and Murfreesboro, he led his regiment to capture a battery of Federal artillery. Though Vaughan had not yet been wounded, several horses had been shot from beneath him.[36]

By 6 March, slightly warmer weather blew in from the South, but one soldier stated, "yet it is quite disagreeable."[37] Rain continued to fall intermittently over the next several days. Early Sunday morning, 8 March, Smith's Brigade was ordered out on picket duty. Smith's regiments left the camp at daylight and marched six miles up the Unionville Pike to counter a Federal advance. The Federals fell back, and the regiments returned to camp in the midst of rain and hail. Later that day, a tornado swept through Shelbyville, destroying a number of houses and injuring several people, but no one of the regiment was killed.[38]

On 26 March, General Cheatham reviewed his division in the evening. Then on Monday, 30 March, Polk held the first general review of his entire corps since the unit had arrived at Shelbyville. The review began at 11:00, and all passed in front of Colonel Johnston, son of the late General Albert Sidney Johnston. The review proceeded in good order. By the afternoon, sleet and snow began to fall again

---

[31] Fielder, *Civil War Diary*, 202.
[32] William M. Slayden, M268 R162, 11th TISR.
[33] Samuel Cathey, M268 R159, 11th TISR.
[34] Fielder, *Civil War Diary*, 202-03.
[35] Roy W. Black, Sr., ed. "William J. Rodgers Memorandum Book," *West Tennessee Historical Society Papers* (1955 vol. 9): 82.
[36] Losson, *Tennessee's Forgotten Warriors*, 166.
[37] Fielder, *Civil War Diary*, 203.
[38] Ibid., 203-04.

and continued through the night. By morning, a heavy snow covered the camps. The following day the boys could hear the rumble of artillery fire from the northwest in the direction of Eagleville. The bombardment only lasted for about an hour, and then subsided. Regardless of the thundering artillery in the distance, Smith's and Maney's brigades gathered on the field for a snowball battle. According to a sergeant in Smith's Brigade, they took Maney's camps, captured twenty men, a stand of colors, and even captured General Maney himself.[39]

Near the beginning of April, the 11th Tennessee had an aggregate 436 men with 415 present for duty. The regimental return listed forty-nine men absent sick, three absent without leave, and none under arrest.[40] On Saturday afternoon, 11 April, and again on 13 April, Smith assembled his brigade in front of General Cheatham. A rumor passed along the ranks said that General Smith bet $1,000 that his regiments would beat the 1st Tennessee of Maney's Brigade drilling. As the troops passed in review on the second occasion, each regiment marched in line of battle. The boys were marching at the double-quick step, and at the command to "charge bayonets," the boys of each regiment let out a tremendous yell as they charged forward. After the review, the regiments retired to camp and had dress parade. As night neared, the cry of a lone whippoorwill off in the distance resounded through the camp. This was the first of the season.[41]

On Thursday, 16 April, the weather was clear. At 12:30 PM, the boys of the 11th Tennessee were called into line to participate in another general review. The men were marched through and beyond Shelbyville, where General Bragg reviewed Cheatham's, Wither's, and McCown's divisions. As Bragg reviewed the troops each band met him with a "delightful tune," he saluted every colonel and raised his cap when opposite the regimental flag.[42] By 5:30 PM, the men had returned to camp and were dismissed.[43]

During this period, there was some attempt to arm many regiments of the Army of Tennessee with a standard rifle, the Enfield, which the Confederacy imported from Great Britain through the blockade. The 12th Tennessee was equipped with Enfields on 20 April. However, from company returns as late as June 1863, the 11th Tennessee was still equipped with a variety of shoulder arms

---

[39] Black, "William J. Rodgers Memorandum Book," 84; Fielder, *Civil War Diary*, 207-08.

[40] Vaughan, *Brigadier General Alfred Jefferson Vaughan's Brigade*, 616.

[41] Black, "William J. Rodgers Memorandum Book," 85; Fielder, *Civil War Diary*, 211-12.

[42] Black, "William J. Rodgers Memorandum Book,"86.

[43] Fielder, *Civil War Diary*, 212.

consisting primarily of .577 caliber Enfield rifles, .58 caliber Springfield rifles, and a number of .69 caliber smoothbore muskets.[44]

Meanwhile, in the Federal prisons, preparations for the exchange of some of the officers of the 11th was underway. On 10 April, Colonel Gordon, who was a prisoner at Camp Chase, was transferred to Fort Delaware, Delaware. Six days later, Captain W. H. McCauley was also transferred from Camp Chase to Fort Delaware. Fort Delaware prison was located on a marshy piece of mosquito-infested land in the Delaware River known as Pea Patch Island. Conditions there were horrible. One Southern captain wrote, "The poor fellows suffering from scurvy are a sad sight. Their legs and feet are so drawn as to compel them to walk on tiptoe, their heels being unable to touch the floor as they walk from their beds to huddle around the stove...."[45] Fortunately, Gordon was only detained at Fort Delaware for about eight weeks while McCauley remained there for only six weeks. On 29 April both of the officers were sent to City Point, Virginia on the James River and exchanged. Gordon and McCauley rejoined the regiment sometime in May.[46]

On Monday, 4 May, General Smith moved his brigade camp two miles down the Duck River and one mile from Shelbyville. The brigade reached the new campground at about 11:00 and began setting up their encampments.[47] The following Monday, 11 May, the brigade was assembled and drilled by General Smith. Later that evening, Chaplain P. G. Jamison, of the 11th Tennessee, preached to the members of the 12th Tennessee Infantry. The chaplain's text was Hebrews 2:3. On the evening of 14 May, Colonel Vaughan drilled the brigade. Drilling was the order of the day. Brigade drill was held two or three times a week, while company and battalion drills were also frequent.[48]

On 14 June, an official detail was issued from Polk's Corps listing the names of delegates to attend a convention at Winchester, Tennessee, to nominate state officers on 17 June. For the 11th Tennessee, Captain James A. Long was appointed the representative of the Robertson County men, surgeon William B. Maney was the delegate for the Davidson County troops, Captain W. H. McCauley represented the Dickson County contingent, Captain Philip Van Horn Weems represented the Hickman Countians, and Captain W. I. White represented the

---

[44] Ibid., 20 April 1863; John E. Binns, Ordnance Received 30 June 1863, M268 R159, 11th TISR; P. V. H. Weems, Ordnance Received 30 June 1863, M268 R163, 11th TISR; F. F. Tidwell, Ordnance Received 30 June 1863, M268 R163, 11th TISR.

[45] Frank Dale, *Delaware Diary: Episodes in the Life of a River* (New Brunswick, NJ: Rutgers University Press, 1996) 89.

[46] G. W. Gordon, M268 R160, 11th TISR; W. H. McCauley, M268 R161, 11th TISR.

[47] Black, "William J. Rodgers Memorandum Book," 87.

[48] Fielder, *Civil War Diary*, 217-28.

Humphreys County men. At the convention, Robert L. Caruthers was nominated and was later officially elected governor of Tennessee.[49]

By the end of June, Rosecrans slipped out of his fortifications at Murfreesboro. The Federal commander sent a diversionary force against Bragg's left at Shelbyville, while he sent the majority of his army against Hardee. Bragg fell for the bait and believed the Federals would launch their attack against Polk. On 24 June, General August Willich's Brigade of McCook's XX Corps dislodged elements of Cleburne's Division from Liberty Gap. Three days later, Bragg ordered the consolidation of his army at Tullahoma. The 11th Tennessee with Smith's Brigade left their winter camps at Shelbyville and moved over the muddy road toward the remainder of Bragg's army. One soldier on the march stated, "The roads are quite muddy the weather very warm and we packing our blankets makes it very disagreeable marching and consequently we get along slow."[50] The boys continued their march some eighteen to twenty miles over hilly, broken ground and waded several streams. About sunset, the brigade made camp on a high hill. Many of the boys cut bushes to lie on and covered themselves with their blankets, getting some much needed rest. During the night, rain pelted the soldiers as they tried to sleep. Early the next morning the boys rose to find the passage clogged with wagons, troops, and artillery. The traffic of thousands—men, horses, wagons, ambulances, and artillery—turned the road into a soup that made marching very difficult. As the boys continued their journey through the mud, showers fell sporadically throughout the day. By 8:00 that evening, the regiment arrived in Tullahoma.[51]

When the 11th arrived, they were immediately ordered out on picket duty. The following morning at about 10:00, lightning split the sky and thunder roared as more rain fell. After two hours of a torrential downpour, the rain ceased and the sun appeared. But before long, another storm blew in and drenched the men again. Rain continued until about 6:00 PM. The next day, 30 June, the regiment was called in from picket duty. In the meantime, Bragg had decided to abandon Tullahoma to dodge a Federal move around his rear. By 9:30 PM, Bragg had the Army of Tennessee en route toward Chattanooga. One of the weary participants stated, "The roads were desperate crowded with soldiers all a stir and going the same direction as ourselves, we traveled very slow and did not reach town a distance of some 3 miles until near midnight—the roads were thronged with soldiers wagons and etc. until it was almost impossible for us to get along the road abounding with mud and water."[52]

---

[49] "Historic Records of Confederate Days," *Confederate Veteran* 16/2 (February 1908): 78.
[50] Fielder, *Civil War Diary*, 233-34.
[51] Ibid..
[52] Ibid., 235-36.

The 11th Tennessee marched slowly all night. After marching through mud and water for twelve hours, the men, hungry, tired, and sleepy, arrived at Alisonia, Tennessee, the current location of Estill Springs in Franklin County. After entering the town, the boys were ordered to stack arms and rest until further orders. The regiment resumed the march again the following day. During this time, Southern troops burned the bridge over the Elk River. At 6:30 the next morning, the 11th Tennessee was on the move again. Three hours later, the regiment had passed through Winchester and had moved on toward Decherd. At Decherd, the column was halted and allowed to rest about half an hour, after which they resumed their places in line and started toward Cowan's Station. The boys reached Cowan's Station around 4:30 that afternoon, halted, and stacked arms a short distance west of the depot where they drew rations. The men camped here for the night, and on the morning of Friday, 3 July, as rain fell again, the men began the strenuous climb up the Cumberland Plateau. Smith's Brigade served as the rearguard of the army and found the roads "awfully torn up and in some places a perfect mire."[53] The trek up the mountain was very steep and slippery, but still the men reached the summit by about 1:00 PM. At sunset, Smith halted his column. The men had only marched about ten miles that day, but according to one of the captains, "all things considered was one of the hardest day's march we have ever done."[54] That night the boys bivouacked on the mountain.

The following day, 4 July, the troops were awakened at 3:00 AM. The boys formed into line, marched for about two miles over a muddy, cut-up road, and then began to descend the mountain. Derelict wagons and various military equipment littered the route. The column entered the Sequatchie Valley and continued their journey to Battle Creek, which they crossed by a pontoon bridge. The men continued to the southeast where they marched up the bank of the Tennessee River and crossed over the river on a pontoon bridge. After marching for another mile and a half, making a total of between eighteen to twenty miles without rations, they stacked arms and camped near the river that night exhausted and very hungry.[55]

While the 11th was crossing the Tennessee River, General John C. Pemberton's half-starved Confederate army, which Grant had cooped up on the banks of the Mississippi River at Vicksburg, capitulated. With this surrender, a number of men including Privates Yeatman Anderson, Wiley S. Brown, J. C. McDaniel, and Patrick Walsh of the 11th Tennessee, who had been detached to Vicksburg the previous summer to work in the signal corps, were also captured.[56]

---

[53] Ibid., 237-38.
[54] Ibid.
[55] Ibid., 238.
[56] Yeatman Anderson, M268 R159; Wiley S. Brown, M268 R159; J. C. McDaniel, M268 R161; and Patrick Walsh, M268 R163, 11th TISR.

On the same day in the eastern theater, Robert E. Lee's Army of Northern Virginia withdrew from the field after three days of bitter fighting at Gettysburg. The fourth of July may have been the day for the independence of the American nation, but it was the death knell for the Southern Confederacy. In this opening week of July, the Federals had won three decisive victories: Gettysburg, Vicksburg, and Tullahoma. The Tullahoma Campaign has never received the attention garnered by Gettysburg or Vicksburg because it was not bought with the price of thousands of lives. Nevertheless, Bragg's loss of Middle Tennessee was a severe blow to the Confederacy. The vast iron and agricultural yields of the region were now in Yankee hands. One Federal commander, August Willich, whose brigade McCown's Division routed on the first day at Murfreesboro, stated that it "must be to every thinking mind evidence that the tide of the rebellion has turned, its hours are measured."[57]

---

[57] *OR*, ser. I, vol. 23, pt. 1, 489.

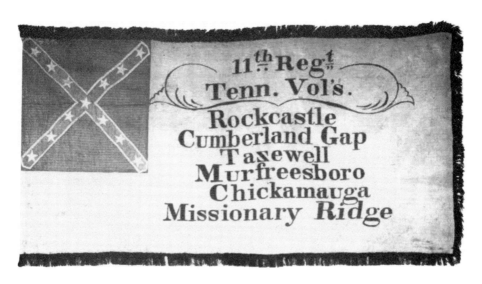

ABOVE: Silk Second National Pattern flag of the 11th Tennessee Volunteer Infantry with battle honors. This flag is believed to have been captured at the Battle of Franklin, Tennessee, 30 November 1864. It was returned by the State of Illinois in 1922. *Courtesy Tennessee State Museum, 73.15.*

BELOW: Dalton Pattern Battle Flag of the 11th Tennessee Volunteer Infantry. It was issued to the Regiment in the spring of 1864. Six color bearers lost their lives carrying this flag forward in the Battle of Franklin, Tennessee, 30 November 1864. Among them were Sgt. Montgomery A. Stokey and Pvt. Peter Edgar Dreux, who was the last to fall that day. His bloodstains are still visible under the upper left star. This flag was not captured. *Courtesy Tennessee State Museum, 3.2.*

James E. Rains had been elected the Nashville city attorney, served as associate editor of the *Nashville Republican Banner* and was elected District Attorney General for Davidson, Williamson and Sumner counties, all prior to age 30. Elected Captain of the Hermitage Guards, later designated Company D of the 11th Tennessee Infantry, this image likely dates to May 1861, and shows early war Tennessee insignia. At the time of his death, the *New York Times* declared he was the "handsomest Confederate." ***Courtesy The Museum of the Confederacy, Richmond, Virginia.***

Brigadier General George W. Gordon. Promoted to colonel of the 11th Tennessee November 1862, and subsequently promoted to brigadier general August 1864. The image appears hastily made during the Atlanta campaign based on the ill fitting sleeves and reflects his signature long hair. Gordon was wounded and captured leading his brigade near the Carter cotton gin in the Battle of Franklin, Tennessee. *Courtesy Alabama Department of Archives and History.*

ABOVE LEFT: A youthful image of James E. Rains likely taken around 1854 during his days as a student at Yale University. *Courtesy Johnny Ellis.* ABOVE RIGHT: Carte de visite of Brigadier General James E. Rains. He had served as colonel of the 11th Tennessee from May 1861 until his promotion to brigadier general in November 1862. Rains was killed leading his brigade in the Battle of Murfreesboro, Tennessee. From a portrait, likely painted after his death. *Courtesy Tennessee State Museum, 2001.15.64.*

BELOW LEFT: Post-war cabinet card image of Brigadier General George W. Gordon. *Courtesy Tennessee State Library and Archives.* BELOW RIGHT: General Gordon gave the dedication address for several Confederate monuments, including Cleburne, Forrest, Sam Davis, and at Franklin, Tennessee. *Courtesy* **Tennesseans 1901–02.**

ABOVE LEFT: Brigadier General George Maney, Company D. Maney raised a company of men, the Hermitage Light Infantry, later Company D of the 11th Tennessee Infantry, and was elected Captain. Shortly thereafter, he resigned after being elected Colonel of the 1st Tennessee Infantry. *Courtesy Ronnie and Emily Townes.* **ABOVE RIGHT**: Colonel Horace Rice of the 11th/29th Tennessee Consolidated Regiment. He was wounded leading the combined regiment during the Battle of Franklin, Tennessee. *Courtesy Gary Waddey.*

BELOW LEFT: Colonel John E. Binns, who following the wounding of Colonel Rice at Franklin, commanded the 11th/29th Tennessee Consolidated Regiment during the Battle of Nashville, Tennessee. Having just finished medical school prior to the war, he later practiced medicine and operated a Drug Store at the corner of 4th and Union, Nashville. *Courtesy Kathleen Binns.* **BELOW RIGHT**: Lieutenant-Colonel William R. Thedford. Having originally raised a company of men from Dickson County, soon designated Company K, Thedford was promoted to lieutenant-colonel in November, 1862. He resigned his commission due to ill health 14 December, 1863. *Courtesy James and Rhonda Rucker.*

ABOVE: Lieutenant-Colonel Thomas P. Bateman. A Mexican War veteran, Bateman was a practicing Attorney in Centerville when he raised the Hickman Guards (Company H). After resigning 1 April 1862, he was later elected a representative to the Tennessee legislature, then in exile in Georgia, and served postwar as a Circuit Court Judge. *Courtesy Hickman County Historical Society.*

BELOW: Broadside of Attorney (later Lieutenant-Colonel) Thomas P. Bateman, used to recruit the Hickman Guards. The circular hung for decades in the Centerville Hotel, owned by regimental veteran 2nd Lieutenant Ephraim A. Dean. *Courtesy Tennessee State Library and Archives.*

ABOVE LEFT: Lieutenant-Colonel James A. Long. Shown here in the early war Tennessee captain's uniform of the Washington Guards (Company F) of Robertson County. Long was killed in the Battle of Jonesboro, Georgia, 1 September 1864. *Courtesy Kerry Elliott.* **ABOVE RIGHT**: Major Jerome S. Ridley, Assistant Commissary of Subsistence. *Courtesy Journal of B. L. Ridley.*

BELOW LEFT: Major Hugh Ross Lucas. A Mexican War veteran, he raised the first company of troops in Humphreys County. A wealthy man, after he was defeated in the election at the reorganization, he tended his plantation in Louisiana, later devastated by Grant's siege of Vicksburg, and postwar accumulated additional lands known collectively as Trinidad. *Courtesy Jonathan T. K. Smith – Wyly Saga.* **BELOW RIGHT**: Major Philip Van Horn Weems. Shown here in the early war Tennessee captain's uniform of the Hickman Guards (Company H). Prior to the war, Weems was the owner of Bon Aqua Springs in Hickman County. *Courtesy David and Frances Hall.*

FUNERAL NOTICE.

Maj. Van WEEMES, of the 11th Regiment, Tennessee Volunteers, died last night at Catoosa Hospital, from wounds received on the 22d instant.

His funeral will take place at 12 o'clock, to-day, from the Methodist Church. Divine services by the Rev. Mr. George.

Griffin, Ga., July 25th, 1864.

ABOVE: A later image of Major Philip Van Horn Weems, shown here in his mid-war uniform of a captain. Known as "the great skirmish officer of the 11th." Weems was seriously wounded in the Battle of Missionary Ridge, Tennessee, prior to losing his life after being wounded during the Battle of Atlanta, Georgia, 22 July 1864. *Courtesy Kerry Elliott.*

BELOW: Funeral notice for Major Philip Van Horn Weems dated 25 July 1864, Griffin, Georgia. *Courtesy Edward Lanham.*

The Captain's Commission of Philip Van Horn Weems. When mortally wounded at Atlanta, his close friend, Colonel George W. Gordon, cut a lock of his hair (upper left) and sent it along with this captains commission to this his family in Hickman County. *Courtesy Philip Van Horn Weems Dodd.*

ABOVE LEFT: Early Regimental Chaplain, Rev. Fountain E. Pitts, D. D. Known to the men as the "Old Man Eloquent," Pitts resigned as chaplain to become "The Fighting Parson," as the Colonel of the 61st Tennessee Infantry. *Courtesy Methodist Archives.* ABOVE RIGHT: Early Regimental Surgeon John H. Callendar. He served as the private secretary of 1860 Presidential candidate John Bell, and served on the faculty of the Shelby Medical College, the Medical College of the University of Nashville, and later Vanderbilt University Medical School. *Courtesy* Tennesseans 1901-02.

BELOW LEFT: Assistant Surgeon Andrew J. Lowe M. D. He later served in the Tennessee legislature. *Courtesy Legislative Composite – 46th General Assembly.* BELOW RIGHT: Surgeon William B. Maney, M. D. Brother of Brigadier General George Maney, his detailed reports of the dead and wounded reflected the toll of war. He surrendered with the Army of Tennessee at Greensboro, North Carolina, and practiced medicine in Nashville postwar, providing charity care to war veterans and the poor. *Courtesy Barry Lamb.*

ABOVE LEFT: Commissary Sergeant Gabriel Fowlkes, Field & Staff. His older brother served in the Federal army. *Courtesy Gary Waddey.* **ABOVE RIGHT**: Sergeant-Major Thomas D. Thompson, Field & Staff. Shown here as a Lieutenant in the 10th Tennessee Cavalry, postwar he served as the physician for the Confederate Veterans Home in Nashville, Tennessee. *Courtesy Jerry Richardson.*

BELOW LEFT: Captain William I. White, Company A. He claimed to be the first man in Humphreys County to enlist in the Confederate army. Never wounded, he resigned 11 February 1865 after consolidation left him with no command. *Courtesy Dennis Hood.* **BELOW RIGHT**: Captain William Hudson McCauley, Company C. Wounded in the Battle of Murfreesboro, Tennessee, he was captured and exchanged. Surrendered at Greensboro, North Carolina, 26 April 1865. *Courtesy McCauley Camp 260, Sons of Confederate Veterans.*

ABOVE LEFT: Captain William D. Eleazer, Company E. Wounded in the Battle of Murfreesboro, Tennessee. Returned to duty and surrendered with the Army of Tennessee at Greensboro, North Carolina. *Courtesy Kevin Matthews.* ABOVE RIGHT: Captain Franklin Fulton Tidwell, Company K. Wounded at Murfreesboro, Chickamauga and in the Atlanta campaign, Captain Tidwell would survive the war and later serve in the Tennessee House of Representatives. *Courtesy Georgia L. Baker.*

BELOW LEFT: Captain Isaac P. Young, Company I. Wounded and captured in the Battle of Murfreesboro, Tennessee, he would also suffer wounds in the battles of Peach Tree Creek and Franklin. *Courtesy Betty DeWitt.* BELOW RIGHT: Captain Jeremiah Batts, Company F. Mortally wounded near the Carter house after penetrating the Federal line in the Battle of Franklin, Tennessee. His dying request was "Tell my mother and sister that I am one of the few that have tried to serve the Lord and I am not afraid to die." *Courtesy Patsy Long.*

ABOVE LEFT: First Lieutenant Richard C. "Dick" Gordon, Company H. Shown here in the early war Tennessee uniform of a 2nd Lieutenant. Gordon entered the war after just having graduated from the University of North Carolina in 1861. He later served two terms in the Tennessee House of Representatives. *Courtesy Hunter and Emmie McDonald.* **ABOVE RIGHT**: First Lieutenant Samuel M. Wilson, Company I. He fought alongside his two brothers, and was wounded in the Battles of Murfreesboro and Franklin, Tennessee. *Courtesy* **Lindsley's Annals of Tennessee—Confederate.**

BELOW LEFT: Second Lieutenant James R. Douglass, Company B. Wounded in the Battle of Murfreesboro, he was mortally wounded in the Battle of New Hope Church, Georgia. *Courtesy Cliff Coss.* **BELOW RIGHT**: Second Lieutenant Robert J. Work, Company H. Wounded in the Battles of Missionary Ridge and New Hope Church. Postwar, he served in the Tennessee legislature. *Courtesy Legislative Composite—47th General Assembly.*

Sergeant John D. Slayden, Company C. Wounded in the Battle of New Hope Church, Georgia, he was later captured in the Battle of Franklin, Tennessee, but escaped. Slayden surrendered with the Army of Tennessee at Greensboro, North Carolina 26 April 1865, and practiced medicine, postwar, in Clarksville, Tennessee. *Courtesy Gary Waddey per license of Picturehistory.com.*

ABOVE LEFT: Fourth Sergeant Darius Rawley, Company G. Captured at Jonesboro, Georgia, 4 September 1864, he spent the remainder of the war in prison at Camp Douglas, Illinois. *Courtesy Vonda Dixon.* ABOVE RIGHT: Fourth Sergeant John W. Jones, Company B. Wounded in the Battle of New Hope Church, Georgia, and wounded and captured in the Battle of Franklin, Tennessee. *Courtesy Carolyn Shofner.*

BELOW LEFT: Fourth Sergeant W. Jerome D. Spence, Company H. His diary and poems prior to discharge provide a detailed account of the daily activity of the Regiment. Shown here as a member of Napier's Battalion, Cavalry. In later years, he wrote *A History of Hickman County* and served in the Tennessee legislature 1891–1893. *Courtesy Gary Waddey.* BELOW RIGHT: Private Joseph Henry Larkins had just turned 18 when he enlisted in Compay C. Wounded at the Battles of Murfreesboro, Tennessee, Chickamauga, Georgia, Adairsville, Georgia, and Bentonville, North Carolina, he was present at the surrender of the Army of Tennessee 26 April, 1865. *Courtesy DePriest family.*

ABOVE LEFT: Private James I. Clark, Company D. Wounded in the Battle of Missionary Ridge, Tennessee. *Courtesy* **Pictures of Company B.** ABOVE RIGHT: Corporal Joseph M. Corbett, Company B. Corbett was wounded in the Battle of Atlanta, Georgia, and captured in the Battle of Franklin, Tennessee. *Courtesy* **Pictures of Company B.**

BELOW LEFT: First Sergeant Joseph Gilman, Company D. Gilman lost an arm in the Battle of Jonesboro, Georgia. *Courtesy* **Pictures of Company B.** BELOW RIGHT: Sergeant James R. Weaver, Company B. Weaver was wounded in the Battles of Chickamauga, Georgia, and Bentonville, North Carolina. *Courtesy* **Pictures of Company B.**

Private Sanford G. M. Jackson, Company F. This image reflects the early war uniform with epaulet. Jackson died of chronic diarrhea at Dalton, Georgia, 30 August 1863. *Courtesy Ronnie and Emily Townes.*

ABOVE: Brothers First Lieutenant Elisha and Private George D. Ridings, Company A. Both were wounded and captured in the Battle of Murfreesboro, Tennessee. *Courtesy Bart Ridings.*

BELOW LEFT: Private Edward Pearl, Company D, shown in the early uniform worn at the Cumberland Gap. *Courtesy Ronnie and Emily Townes.* **BELOW RIGHT:** Postwar image of musician Martin Van Buren Adcock, Company K, Field and Staff. Adcock was transferred to the Regimental band as a drummer in July 1863, and surrendered with the Army of Tennessee in April 1865. *Courtesy Harvey and Mary Adcock.*

ABOVE: Private George Washington Braxton Marable, Company A. His fiddle playing and hot temper, entertained the men at camp. *Courtesy Nina Finley.*

BELOW: Second Lieutenant John W. Phillips, Company K, First Corporal James T. Parker, Company E, and Thomas B. Adcock, Company K, all soldiers from Dickson County, Tennessee. *Courtesy Ron Parker.*

ABOVE LEFT: Mary Bradford presented a silk First National Pattern flag to Colonel Rains, sewn by students of the Nashville Female Academy, at a ceremony on the balcony of the City Hotel in Nashville 25 July 1861. *Courtesy Ridley's* **Battles and Sketches of the Army of Tennessee.**
ABOVE RIGHT: Julia Marcum, whose father was a Unionist pilot, defended herself with an axe on the night of 7 September 1861 from a drunken Private Nathaniel Ussery of Company F. Ussery lost his life, and Julia was critically injured by his bayonet, losing several fingers and the sight in her left eye. She later received a Federal veterans pension. ***Courtesy Scott County, Tennessee, Historical Society.***

BELOW LEFT: Private George Washington Baker, Company C. Captured after the Battle of Murfreesboro, Tennessee, and wounded and captured at the Battle of Franklin, Tennessee. ***Courtesy Debbie Stanfill.*** BELOW RIGHT: Private John T. Batts, Company F. He surrendered with the Army of Tennessee at Greensboro, North Carolina. ***Courtesy Patsy Long.***

First Sergeant John T. Stowers, Company B. Wounded in the left leg, requiring amputation, in the Battle of Atlanta, Georgia, 22 July 1864. Following the war, he worked as a contractor and plasterer, and helped complete construction of the Maxwell House Hotel. *Courtesy Tennessee State Library and Archives.*

ABOVE LEFT: Private William H. H. "Harry" Gordon, Company H. Brother of Brigadier General George W. Gordon, he transferred to the 11th Tennessee from the 8th Texas Cavalry. Killed in the Battle of New Hope Church, Georgia. *Courtesy* **Lindsley's Annals—Confederate.**
ABOVE RIGHT: Private Champion Hayes, Company C. Wounded in the Battle of Peach Tree Creek, Georgia, 20 July 1864. He surrendered with the Army of Tennessee at Greensboro, North Carolina. *Courtesy Clysta Ponic.*

BELOW LEFT: Private James Henry Long Sr., Company F. A tobacco dealer prior to the war, in 1863 he sent his wife a letter detailing what crops should be planted and in which fields. *Courtesy A Collection of Memories.* BELOW RIGHT: Private Milton Sholes, Company I. Wounded in the Battle of Missionary Ridge, Tennessee. *Courtesy Eugene Summers.*

ABOVE: The Great Snowball Battle at Dalton, Georgia, 22 March 1864. The Tennessee troops were led by Colonel George Washington Gordon of the 11th Tennessee. *Courtesy* **Battlefields in Dixie Land.**

BELOW: Carter Family cotton gin, a landmark on the Franklin, Tennessee, battlefield. Brigadier General George Washington Gordon was captured here. *Courtesy* **Heritage Foundation of Williamson County, Tennessee.**

ABOVE: Wooden drum canteen of Private Martin Doherty of Company G. Dogherty was killed in the Battle of Atlanta, Georgia, 22 July 1864. His canteen was picked up as a souvenir by a Federal soldier. *Courtesy Greg Coco Collection.*

BELOW: Snare drum of Musician Martin Van Buren Adcock. Adcock surrendered at Greensboro, North Carolina. *Courtesy Harvey and Mary Adcock.*

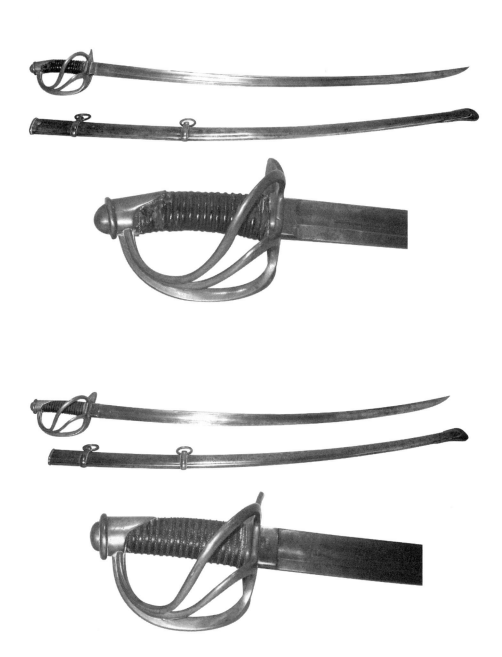

ABOVE: Saber (with handle detail) of Brigadier General George Washington Gordon. *Courtesy Tennessee State Museum, 4.296.*

BELOW: Saber (with handle detail) of Brigadier General James E. Rains. *Courtesy Tennessee State Museum, 4.428.*

ABOVE: The cap box of Private William Henry Harrison Linzy, Company E. *Courtesy Doug Collier.*

BELOW: U.S. Model 1840 Springfield bayonet belonging to Private Joshua C. Cathey, Company E. *Courtesy M. Todd Cathey.*

Return of the Killed and Wounded of the

Name	Wounded	Killed	Rank	Comp.	Regiment	No	Occupation
Gordon W. G.	1		Lt Col		11th Tenn		Civil Engineer
Clark E. W.	2		Capt	B	" "		Clerk
J. P. Young	3		"	J	" "		Farmer
Tidwell J. J.	4		"	K	" "		"
Douglas	5		3rd Lt	B	" "		Stone Mason
Herrew Hugh	6		2nd Lt	D	" "		" "
Beasly R.	7		3rd Lt	A	" "		Farmer
McCauley Wm H	8		1st Lt	C	" "		"
Tidings J	9		1st Lt	A	" "		"
Dean E	10		1st Lt	H	" "		"
Stephens James							

Confederate States Army,

To the A. C. S., 11th Tennessee Infantry.

DATE AND STATION.	REQUIRED, THE ANNEXED SUBSISTENCE STORES:		
	lbs. Fresh Beef.	lbs. Coffee.	lbs. Salt.
	" Pork.	" Sugar.	" Lard.
	" Flour.	galls. Vinegar.	galls. Molasses.
	" Meal.	lbs. Candles.	pecks Potatoes.
	" Rice.	" Soap.	

I Certify, on honor, that the above provisions are for the use of myself and family.

Company

ABOVE: Return of the killed and wounded of the 11th Tennessee at the Battle of Murfreesboro, Tennessee, 31 December 1862. *Tennessee State Library and Archives.*

BELOW: Receipt for Provisions, 11th Tennessee Regiment. *Courtesy Beaman Collection.*

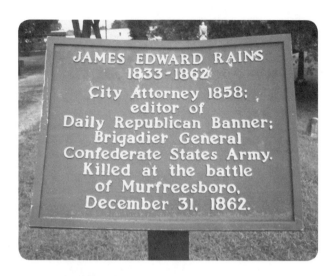

ABOVE: Plaque marking original gravesite of General James E. Rains in the Nashville City Cemetery. His remains were removed to Mt. Olivet Cemetery in 1888. *Courtesy Gary Waddey.*

BELOW: Rains Bivouac, Association of Confederate Soldiers Tennessee Division, Dickson, Tennessee. *Courtesy Ronnie and Emily Townes.*

ABOVE: Frock coat of Capt. William Hudson McCauley, Company C. *Courtesy Dan Andrews.*

BELOW: Return of the Second National colors of the 11th Tennessee to the State of Tennessee by the State of Illinois. The ceremony took place at the unveiling of the Grant Memorial in Washington, D.C. in May, 1922. *Courtesy Library of Congress.*

ABOVE: Stationery of General George Washington Gordon, used during the time he served as Commander of the United Confederate Veterans. *Courtesy University of Memphis.*

BELOW: Post war reunion pin of Private William C. Pullen, Company A. *Courtesy W. L. Etheridge —A History of Tumbling Creek.*

Reunion

of the

11th Tennessee Infantry of the C. S. A.

At the Chamber of Commerce,
Nashville, Tenn., June 14, 1904.

Reunion of the 11th Tennessee Infantry

At a reunion of the 11th Tennessee Infantry of the C. S. A., at the Chamber of Commerce, on June 14, 1904, on motion of Adjt. Mathis Dr. Maney took the chair and Henry Randal was made Secretary.

There being no regular order of business a general love feast was enjoyed, and after a stirring speech from our former Colonel, now Gen. George W. Gordon, Adjt. Mathis moved that the meeting be made a permanent organization and that we meet again at the reunion of the U. C. V. at Louisville, Ky., in 1905, and at all other such reunions as long as they are held.

The motion was carried unanimously.

All members were then requested to come forward and sign their names, which resulted as follows:

OFFICERS.

GEN. GEORGE W. GORDON.....Memphis.
COL. JOHN E. BINNS........Davidson Co.
SURGEON W. B. MANEY........Nashville.
ADJT. WM. J. MATHIS........Nashville.
SERGT. J. R. SAVAGE, Co. G.....Antioch.
CAPT. F. F. TIDWELL, Co. K .....Burns.
LT. J. W. ADCOCK, Co. K.....Burns.
LT. JOHN W. PHILLIPS, Co. K....Gleason.

PRIVATES.

JOHN G. ROGERS, Co. A..... Clarksville.
WM. M. LARK, Co. B ....Nashville.
J. C. MCCAULEY, Co. C............Plant.
J. M. DICKSON, Co. C.........South Side.
GEORGE EPPS, Co. C.........White Bluff.
J. S. JACKSON, Co. C..........Christiana.
J. T. MATHEWS, Co. C............Heath.
W. D. ELEAZER, Co. E ......Beef Range.
T. J. BATTS, Co. F .... Ballinger, Texas.
B. M. JORDAN, Co. F ....Robinson Co.
WM. ELLIOT, Co. F.........Robinson Co.
J. W. BALDWIN, Co. F.,........Nashville.
J. W. FLOWERS, Co. F........ Kentucky.
W. A. ROLER, Co. F..... Kentucky.
B. A. CLIFTON, Co. K............Dickson.
W. M. HOGINS, Co. K.............Burns.
J. C. ALLSPAW, Co. K............ Burns.

After all had signed it was moved and carried that the proceedings be published in folder form and sent to each member present, and that all should use every endeavor to secure the name of every man

Cover and inner pages of the pamphlet printed for the 11th Tennessee reunion held during the Confederate Veterans reunion of Nashville, Tennessee, June 1904. *Courtesy University of Memphis.*

Postwar image of First Sergeant John Turner Stowers, Company B, wearing his wooden leg, the result of his wounds from a minie ball during the Battle of Atlanta, Georgia, 22 July 1864. *Courtesy Tennessee State Library and Archives.*

9

"Our Men Have Suffered Awful Today and Gained Nothing"

July–September 1863

The tide of the "rebellion" may have turned, but the Army of Tennessee was far from beaten. On 5 July, Bragg's forces continued their withdrawal to the southeast. The 11th Tennessee made a short march then halted and set up camp near the Nickajack Cave. There, the men cooked rations and resumed their march the following day. The regiment made another brief march on 7 July and boarded railway cars bound for Chattanooga. The men had marched a distance of ninety miles through mud and nearly continuous rain since their departure from Tullahoma, only six days prior. Arriving at their destination, the regiment established its camp near Chattanooga. Over the next weeks, the duties of the soldiers became monotonous. Company, battalion, and brigade drill, dress parades, building fortifications, standing picket duty, scouting, and marching once again became routine.[1]

Company C, under command of Captain William H. McCauley, shared these wearisome duties with the remainder of the regiment until 13 July. On that date, McCauley was ordered to take his company to guard Brown's Ferry, some six miles below Chattanooga on the Tennessee River. For the next ten days, Company C had an uneventful stay at the ferry. However on 22 July, a contingent of Federal infantry appeared on the opposite bank. McCauley's boys opened fire on the Yanks. For the next few hours, both sides fired across the Tennessee River at each other. The smoke from the rifles partially obscured the view of the enemy. Company C sustained no casualties, while damage to the enemy was unknown. Later that afternoon, the 28th Alabama Infantry of Hindman's Division relieved McCauley's Company. Company C then began its journey to return to the regiment, which it rejoined on 24 July.[2]

On 13 August, pursuant to Special Order Number 3, issued from Cheatham's Division Headquarters, 3rd Lieutenant Ruben F. Beasley of Company A and ten cavalrymen left on assignment to Lafayette, Georgia. Their detail was to arrest for

---

[1] Record of Events, Company F Muster Roll July and August 1863, 11th Regiment Tennessee Infantry Service Records, National Archives Records Administration, Compiled Service Records of Confederate Soldiers Who Served in Organizations from the State of Tennessee, Washington, DC: National Archives Records and Service, General Services Administration, 1960. M268 R159.

[2] Record of Events Co. C, July & August 1863.

desertion 3rd Sergeant Thomas S. Spencer; Corporal Isaac Anderson; privates James Smith, William Bullard, Mitchell Cooley, William R. Morrisett, and Charles W. White of Company A; A. W. Ray of Company I (all were from the 11th Tennessee); and I. M. Cracken, a private of Maney's Sharpshooters Battalion.[3]

On 21 August, Federal gunners of Thomas L. Crittenden's XXI Corps began bombarding Chattanooga from the north bank of the Tennessee River. As the Federal cannons boomed in the distance, shells began falling into the city. Yankee artillery damaged two churches, and wounded and killed several women and children.[4] Meanwhile, as the shelling continued, some of the rounds fell near the 11th Tennessee's encampment. As a result, the regiment struck camp and moved to the foot of Lookout Mountain. After the boys set up their camp, Company F (under command of Captain James A. Long) was sent out on picket duty. The company returned to camp on 7 September.[5]

In the meantime, surgeons sent Private Sanford Jackson of Company F to Oliver Hospital in Dalton, Georgia, because of chronic diarrhea. Jackson, unable to recover, died on 30 August 1863.[6]

On 8 September, Smith formed his brigade, abandoned his bivouac at the base of Lookout Mountain, and began a march in the direction of Lafayette, Georgia. The 29th Tennessee led the way; the 11th was next in line, the 12th/47th followed them, and the 13th/154th brought up the rear. The weather was hot, and the road was dusty, nevertheless the column trudged along and reached McFarland's Gap by about 11:00 AM. Smith halted his men and allowed them to rest until about 7:00 that evening when they resumed the march. At approximately 11:30 PM, Smith halted the brigade and then moved three-quarters of a mile to the southeast, near Chickamauga Creek, where he ordered his men to stack arms, cook rations, and rest the remainder of the night.[7]

The following morning after breakfast Governor Harris delivered a speech to Cheatham's Division. Harris told the boys that he believed they would be engaging the enemy in the next couple of days. Later that same day, an *ad hoc* sharpshooter force for Smith's Brigade was organized. The unit, named Dawson's Battalion

---

[3] Cheatham's Division Headquarters, Special Order No. 3, 13 August 1863, Ruben F. Beazley, M268 R159, 11th Tennessee Infantry Service Records, National Archives Records Administration, *Compiled Service Records of Confederate Soldiers Who Served in Organizations from the State of Tennessee*, Washington, DC: National Archives and Records Service, General Services Administration, 1960. Hereafter cited as 11th TISR.

[4] Christopher Losson, *Tennessee's Forgotten Warriors: Frank Cheatham and His Confederate Division* (Knoxville: University of Tennessee Press, 1989) 100.

[5] Record of Events, Co. F, July & August 1863, M268 R159, 11th TISR.

[6] Sanford G. M. Jackson, M268 R161, 11th TISR.

[7] A. T. Fielder, *Captain A. T. Fielder's Civil War Diary Company B, 12th Tennessee Infantry C. S. A. July 1861–June 1865*, ed. M. Todd Cathey (Broken Arrow, OK: Create Space, 2012) 258-59.

Sharpshooters, was made up of two companies from the 12th/47th Tennessee, one company from the 154th Tennessee, and Company F and one other company (possibly H or C) from the 2nd battalion of the 11th Tennessee. The sharpshooters, numbering 252 men, were commanded by Major J. W. Dawson of the 154th, with Major William Green of the 11th, second in command.[8]

On 10 September, at approximately 8:00 AM, division headquarters called Smith's Brigade into a line of battle. Shortly thereafter, Smith deployed Dawson's Battalion forward as skirmishers. The brigade advanced half a mile to meet the enemy, which the cavalry reported to be advancing in their direction. The regiment along with the brigade remained in position for the next couple of hours. At about 10:00 AM, the brigade was called to attention and each regiment was marched "by the right flank, file right, about one half mile and reformed a line of battle by a change of front forward."[9] Soon Smith ordered his men to stack arms and rest. As soon as the men had made themselves comfortable, Scott's Tennessee Battery, the brigade artillery, passed in front of the regiments and took position on a hill in front of the infantry. Around 7:00 PM, Smith called his brigade to attention, ordered them to take arms, and marched them back to camp. The brigade remained in this location until about 11:30 PM when Smith ordered them into line. The regiments marched out into the road and halted until teamsters got the wagons straightened out. At about midnight, they moved forward on the road toward Rome, Georgia. Soon, they crossed Chickamauga Creek. At about 4:00 AM on 11 September, Smith stopped his column and told his men that he expected a battle before daylight; therefore they were not to wander far from their places.[10] "Most of the men, being very tired, lay right down wherever they halted, many of them in the middle of the road," stated Private William Stokey of Company C.[11] A short time later, some horses broke loose and stampeded. These horses spooked the horses of Scott's battery, which also stampeded. One captain in the brigade stated that Scott's horses tore through the brigade "like a whirlwind."[12] Private Stokey continued,

> As it happened I sat leaning and sleeping against a tree some little distance from the road and because of this precaution was able to see much of the fun which happened later on. It seemed that we had hardly fallen asleep when we were

---

[8] United States War Department, *The War of the Rebellion: A Compilation of the Official Records of the Union and Confederate Armies*. 70 vols. in 128 (Washington: Government Printing Office, 1880–1901; reprint, Gettysburg, PA: The National Historical Society, 1972) ser. I, vol. 30, pt. 2, 115. Hereafter cited as *OR*.

[9] A. T. Fielder, *Captain A. T. Fielder's Civil War Diary Company B, 12th Tennessee Infantry C. S. A. July 1861–June 1865*, ed. M. Todd Cathey (Broken Arrow, OK: Create Space, 2012) 259.

[10] Ibid., 259-60.

[11] Mamie Yeary, *Reminiscences of the Boys in Gray, 1861–1865* (1912; reprint, Dayton, OH: Morningside, 1986) 727.

[12] Fielder, *Civil War Diary*, 260.

aroused by the nearest semblance to our ideas of pandemonium that we ever heard before or since, accompanied by the wild shouting of our comrades who were nearest the noise and knew what it was, yelling to us: "Look out! The artillery is stampeded and is running away."[13]

The private went on to say,

> From my vantage point, being the far side of an old stake and rider fence, to which I ran with an unseemly speed at the first outbreak of the inferno, I could see the other boys less fortunate and only half awake in their frantic efforts to get out of the way of what we all at first thought was a Yankee artillery or cavalry charge. I laugh till this day whenever I think of some of the ludicrous things I saw that night. I saw some of the boys climb impossible trees with the agility, accuracy and speed of squirrels, while others struggled ten deep for the protection of a slender sapling trunk, while one poor fellow ran his cheek into one of the sharp projecting rails of the old stake and rider fence and with extraordinary good fortune missed inflicting upon himself serious injury. Another amusing little incident was a conversation which I overheard between two of my comrades several feet away from me, behind a small tree trunk. One of them my cousin, D. W. Street, it appeared from the argument which carried to me above the tumult, had been the first to reach the tree aforesaid, and the other fellow, whose name I have forgotten, had the incomparable gall to make a successful tackle and separate my cousin from first place at the sapling. It was then I heard my cousin tell the other fellow, in no uncertain words, to "fade" (or words to that effect); that this was his tree, and immediately thereafter I saw the unknown hurled aside as my cousin resumed his position in a loving, embracing attitude next to the tree. At the same time I saw Lieut. Sandy Brown of Company E tear through a puddle of muddy water waist deep, he thinking that the water was only white sand--there being several patches of this close about--and climb a tree with the agility of a monkey. Soon order was restored. The battery was torn up, one soldier of the brigade was killed, and five or six others were wounded.[14]

The regiment remained at Lafayette, Georgia, mainly engaged in post duties, until the evening of 17 September. On the 17th, the regiment left Chattanooga marching for Chickamauga. A private in Company C recalled what happened next,

> We learned that there were cooped up in McLemore's Cove two corps of Yankee soldiers, and one division of our own army was sent ahead to close up the gap by which the Yankees entered the cove, while the division I was in was to wait near the cove for the other division's signal gun, advising us to open up the attack on the Federal soldiers in the cove, whom we hoped we would, with our two divisions, be able to surround and capture with more or less ease. However, we never heard the

---

[13] Yeary, *Reminiscences*, 727.
[14] Ibid.

signal gun, as the Yankees got out of the gap before our other division could hem them in.[15]

On the evening of 17 September, General Preston Smith received orders to move his brigade out on the Ringgold Road to the intersection of Lee and Gordon's Mill Road. From there the brigade moved to Rock Spring Church where it bivouacked for the night in line of battle. Early the following morning the brigade moved forward in the direction of the ford on West Chickamauga Creek below Lee and Gordon's Mills. Colonel Vaughan of the 13th/154th Tennessee Infantry commented that the advance was slow because they had "to wait for Buckner's Corps to pass to the front and effect a crossing of the creek, which they succeeded in doing about dark after heavy skirmishing."[16]

As night fell, the 11th Tennessee with Smith's Brigade, camped in line of battle a half mile south of West Chickamauga Creek. Fourth Sergeant Clayton H. Yates of Company K was a young man about twenty-three years of age at the time. Yates recalled that about dusk, after they had stacked arms, General Cheatham rode up to the regiment and told them that they would attack the enemy in the morning just before daylight. Yates recalled that he dropped down to his knees and began to pray. When he had prayed for an unknown amount of time, "a sweet calm came over me and I dropped into dreamland, the sweetest of my life. And I was no more afraid to go into battle than I am now to go into prayers."[17] While Yates prayed, Granville Johnson of Company H wrote a farewell poem to his family back in Hickman County. The poem closes with the lines "Farewell to you all, my last it may be / But may God whom I reverence and fear / To a home that is blest, in a land that is free, Bring safely the young volunteer."[18]

The morning of 19 September was cool and clear. Frost covered the ground in the early morning hours. Shortly before 6:00 AM, the 11th Tennessee fell into line, marched by the right flank a short distance, and met commissary wagons as they came up with cooked rations. The men drew their allowances and placed them in their haversacks.[19] Even though many men of the 11th Tennessee still carried outdated .69 caliber muskets, their spirits were high as the anticipation of an advance on the enemy filtered down through the ranks. Soon, Gordon reformed the regiment and led them forward in line with the brigade. One by one, the brigades of Cheatham's Division crossed Chickamauga Creek at Dalton's Ford. Jackson's

---

[15] Ibid.

[16] *OR*, ser. I, vol. 30, pt. 2, 106.

[17] Clayton H. Yates, "Saved His Brigade," Mayfield (KY) *Daily Messenger*, 4 November 1912.

[18] "A Sad Reminiscence of the Late War," Centerville (TN) *Hickman Pioneer*, 26 February 1886.

[19] Fielder, *Civil War Diary*, 263-64.

Brigade was first to cross, followed by Smith, Wright, Maney, and Strahl, with each brigade filing to the right and forming in line of battle as they crossed the creek.[20]

As soon as the entirety of the division had crossed, Cheatham moved his men forward about a mile and formed his brigades in line of battle in the rear of Buckner's Corps. As the division rested in this position for some time, the boys heard musketry in the distance to the right. At about midday, Cheatham formed his division again and moved them on the double-quick by the right flank to the support of General Walker, who was heavily engaging the enemy. When Smith's men arrived, they found General Walker's Georgians exhausted. As Cheatham's Division fell into line, Smith formed his brigade on the left of Jackson. Smith aligned his regiments from right to left: Dawson's Battalion Sharpshooters were immediately adjacent to Jackson. The 13th/154th was to their left; the 12th/47th was next in line, followed by the 11th Tennessee, and the 29th Tennessee on the extreme left of the brigade.[21]

As soon as the division was ready, Cheatham moved his Tennesseans forward in a furious charge that drove the enemy back some 600 to 800 yards. As the division advanced, the regiments of Smith's Brigade moved into Brock Field. As they moved forward, the 13th/154th Tennessee wheeled on its right pivot, inadvertently separating from the other regiments of the brigade. At this time, the Federals took cover behind their breastworks from which they had moved that morning.[22] Colonel Charles H. Rippey of the 90th Ohio fronting the 11th Tennessee stated, "The Second Brigade soon became hotly engaged and halted, and before I could move up on to the line, my skirmishers were driven in and I received the fire of one of the enemy's battalions."[23] Colonel Rippey continued, "The fight then opened fiercely with both musketry and artillery. I had gained for my regiment a rather advantageous position on the crest of a swell in the ground along which was some fallen timber and cover. The enemy made four separate attempts to dislodge the regiment from this position, but each time were repulsed with heavy loss."[24]

Gordon led his regiment forward into this hornet's nest. There, the 90th Ohio unleashed a deadly and concentrated fire. As the firefight raged, enemy fire fearfully mangled Granville Johnson of Company H. A grapeshot broke the eighteen-year-old boy's thigh, a minie ball shattered his hand, and a second minie ball pierced his right lung. Johnson lay on the field in agonizing pain.[25] A spent musket ball struck

---

[20] Ibid.

[21] *OR*, ser. I, vol. 30, pt. 2, 106, 110–11, 114.

[22] Ibid., 111.

[23] Ibid., pt. 1, 756.

[24] Ibid.

[25] W. J. D. Spence and David L. Spence, *History of Hickman County, Tennessee* (1900; reprint, Columbia, TN: P-Vine Press, 1981) 130; "John Jefferson Johnson," *Confederate Veteran* 20/9 (September 1912): 432; "A Sad Reminiscence of the Late War," Centerville (TN) *Hickman Pioneer*, 26 February 1886; William B. Maney, "Return of the Killed and

Captain Franklin F. Tidwell of Company K in the side. The captain found himself on the ground but not seriously wounded. A shot in the right ankle left 2nd Lieutenant Richmond McCauley of Company C in much more serious condition. This gunshot caused surgeons to amputate his leg. Another minie ball struck Sergeant Willis Miller of Company B in the head, and he died on the field. Another Yankee minie ball left Sergeant T. L. Fain of Company E with a severe neck wound. As the fight in Brock Field raged, many soldiers of the 11th fell dead or wounded. The battle was so intense that orderlies were unable to move the injured to the rear. As Colonel Gordon urged his men forward, Yankee gunfire hit his horse.[26] Gordon continued on foot, moving the 11th Tennessee forward until they came to a shallow drainage ditch that afforded slight protection from the enemy fire.[27]

To the right of the 11th, a courier from General Smith ordered Colonel William M. Watkins of the 12th/47th Tennessee, to fall back to a fence. Before Watkins's men arrived at the specified location, Captain Donelson, Smith's acting inspector general, ordered Colonel Watkins to return to the front to a position beside the 11th. Watkins moved his men forward and then received another order from General Smith to return to the low fence in their rear. The 12th/47th moved as commanded and found some refuge behind the fence.[28] To the left of the 11th Tennessee, the 29th Tennessee, commanded by Colonel Horace Rice, was stumbling at the double-quick over rough terrain on the southwest side of Brock Field. Due to the terrain, Rice's line was somewhat broken and confused as he brought them to a halt. At this time, the enemy let loose a volley that caused his line to stagger, compounding the confusion. Within minutes, however, Rice regained order in his regiment and continued firing on the enemy. Wright's Brigade, to the left of Rice, did not move up at the same time as Smith's, thus leaving the left flank of the 29th Tennessee exposed to a fearful enfilading fire.[29] Meanwhile, on the extreme right of Smith's Brigade, Dawson's Battalion Sharpshooters, supporting Scott's Battery, were having quite a time of their own. J. W. Wynn, a member of Company F who had been detached to the sharpshooters, stated, "The enemy was pressing us back and we were ordered to lay flat on the ground and not to shoot till they were within twenty-five paces of us. The battery threw grape and canister into

---

Wounded in the 11th Tennessee Regiment at the Battle of Chickamauga, Georgia, 19 September 1863," *Regimental Surgeon's Log*, Confederate Collection, Manuscript Section, Box 18, Military Units Tenn. Inf. Regt. 11, Medical Records, Tennessee State Library and Archives, Nashville, TN.

[26] "Gen. Geo. Gordon, Soldier, Citizen, Statesman, Dead," Memphis (TN) *Commercial Appeal*, 10 August 1911.

[27] Maney, "Return of the Killed and Wounded…at the Battle of Chickamauga, Georgia."

[28] *OR*, ser. I, vol. 30, pt. 2, 106, 111.

[29] Ibid., 114.

the enemy's ranks so fast that they were repulsed at the fifty-yard line."[30] Wynn continued, "The firing from the battery was so heavy that it absolutely swept the earth clean and you could find the different parts of a man's body torn and scattered in different places."[31] Smith's regiments kept steady pressure on the enemy until they had nearly expended their ammunition. About 2:00 PM, a messenger informed the general that ammunition was low. He immediately relayed the information to General Cheatham and added that he could hold the line until reinforced. By 2:30 PM, Strahl's Brigade moved forward to relieve Smith. With Strahl's arrival, Smith withdrew his regiments some 400 yards to the rear, reformed his line, and awaited further orders.[32]

Smith remained in this position until about 6:00 PM when Cheatham once again ordered him to the front. Sergeant Clayton Yates of Company K stated, "In the early days of the war when we were engaged in battle, we were glad when night came, because that meant rest until morning, but in the latter part of the war we did not stop for night."[33] Following orders, the brigade moved to support Deshler's Brigade of Cleburne's Division in a night attack. Yates continued, "So on this occasion we charged upon the enemy in the dark and it was very dark that night...."[34] Cheatham ordered Smith to stay within 200 paces of Deshler's line. Smith moved his brigade into position and advanced through thick undergrowth. After moving forward about 200 yards, musketry erupted on the right flank. Soon, Deshler's Brigade in Smith's front was engaging the enemy.[35]

The darkness of the deep North Georgia woods caused some disorder with a portion of Deshler's men. As a result, these men in their confusion fell back on Smith's Brigade. General Smith met them in person and ordered them to move forward. Deshler's men obeyed. Smith continued to move his brigade to the front when a portion of Deshler's men fell back a second time. Again, General Smith ordered them to advance. However, instead of moving directly to the front, due to obstructions and the irregularity of the ground, they moved obliquely to the left, leaving a gap in the front line. Smith, unaware of this vacuum in his front, continued to move his brigade forward. Once again, he came upon another group of soldiers. Smith, believing them to be another contingent of Deshler's Brigade, rode forward with his aide, Captain Thomas King, to ascertain the reason for the delay. As Smith and King approached the men, Smith addressed a Sergeant Boysen, who, unknown to him, was a Federal soldier. Smith, thinking Boysen was one of Deshler's men, started to strike him with the flat of his sword for disobeying orders.

---

[30] Yeary, *Reminiscences*, 827.
[31] Ibid.
[32] *OR*, ser. I, vol. 30, pt. 2, 107.
[33] Yates, "Saved His Brigade."
[34] Ibid.
[35] *OR*, ser. I, vol. 30, pt. 2, 108.

Boysen, realizing that he was in the presence of a Confederate officer, shot Smith. With Boysen's shooting, other Federal soldiers fired. This gunfire also killed Captain King. Unknowingly, Smith and King had ridden upon a separated portion of the Yankee line. At this time, Colonel Vaughan leading the 13th/154th Tennessee Infantry rode forward. Vaughan also mistakenly believed that these were Deshler's men. Vaughan asked one of the soldiers what regiment he belonged to. The soldier responded by firing at him as well. The bullet missed Vaughan but killed Captain Donelson, who was by his side. Vaughan instinctively ordered some files from the 12th Tennessee to fire on the soldier. The Yankee fell dead before the volley. As the 12th Tennessee fired on the skirmisher, their projectiles fell among the ranks of the Yankee regiments just behind that position. Immediately voices cried out, "Don't shoot, we surrender." Colonel Vaughan ordered the brigade forward as the Yankees grounded their arms. As his men surrounded the Federals, Vaughan spotted the Yankee colors and asked, "Who has those colors?" "The color-bearer," came the reply. Vaughan asked, "To what command do you belong?" The reply came, "To the 77th Pennsylvania Regiment." Vaughan seized the national colors from Corporal W. H. H. Woolslair of Company C, 77th Pennsylvania, and handed them to Captain Carthel of the 47th Tennessee. Immediately, about 200 men of the 77th Pennsylvania and 100 men of the 79th Illinois grounded their arms in surrender. Vaughan ordered Captain Carthel to the rear to report to General Cheatham with the colors and the prisoners. In addition to the number of Federal soldiers apprehended, Vaughan's men rescued several of Deshler's men captured earlier by the enemy. After this engagement, General Cheatham ordered his troops to bivouac in line of battle for the night.[36] J. W. Wynn of Company F stated, "We lay there all night listening to the cries and groans of the wounded and heard them begging to be killed."[37] When quiet finally came, one soldier of the 12th Tennessee stated, "Our men have suffered awful today and gained nothing."[38]

Early on 20 September, Smith's Brigade, temporarily commanded by Vaughan, was held in reserve. At about 9:00 AM, stewards retrieved Granville Johnson of Company H from the field and took him to the field hospital. Though still alive, he was slowly sinking and was able to talk to his companions who had gathered around him. Johnson lingered until Monday morning, 21 September.

---

[36] Ibid., 106–108, 112; Alfred J. Vaughan, ed., *Personal Record of the Thirteenth Regiment, Tennessee C. S. A.* (Memphis, TN: S. C. Toof & Co., 1897) 30–31, 1976 reprint; John Obreiter and David W. Reed, *The Seventy-seventh Pennsylvania at Shiloh: History of the Regiment* (Harrisburg, PA: Harrisburg Publishing Co., 1905) 164; Frederick H. Dyer, "Seventy-seventh Pennsylvania Regiment," in *A Compendium of the War of the Rebellion Compiled and Arranged from Official Records of the Federal and Confederate Armies, Reports of the Adjutant Generals of the Several States, the Army Registers, and Other Reliable Documents and Sources* (Des Moines, IA: The Dyer Publishing Company, 1908) 989.

[37] Yeary, *Reminiscences*, 827.

[38] Losson, *Tennessee's Forgotten Warriors*, 109.

Before he died, he requested that Captain Weems tell his parents that he "fell with his face to the foe—that he was ready to go and meet God and receive his reward—that he had tried to do his duty as a soldier, and wanted to die as one who had no fears of death."[39]

Meanwhile, the rest of the regiment, although in reserve, was close enough to the Federal line that Yankee artillery pounded their position until about 1:00 PM, killing and wounding several men. While in reserve, a spent minie ball knocked Private William Everett Reynolds of Company C to the ground. Litter bearers assisted Reynolds off the field, and he fortuitously fell into the hands of Dr. Read Wilson, a physician who happened to be an old family friend. In the meantime, the Confederates, particularly John B. Hood's division from the Army of Northern Virginia, had exploited a gap in the Federal line and secured victory. Reynolds, hearing the news of the victory, wished to return to the regiment. Dr. Wilson objected to this until he believed Reynolds had recovered sufficiently. Nevertheless, the stimulating news of the Confederate victory inspired Reynolds enough that he hobbled back to the regiment. Late that evening Vaughan was ordered to the extreme right of the Rebel lines. The brigade remained in that position until the morning of 21 September.[40]

Between 2:00 and 3:00 in the afternoon of 21 September, the boys took up the line of march toward Chattanooga. As the brigade was moving forward toward Chattanooga, Vaughan ordered Dawson's Battalion Sharpshooters, now commanded by Major William Green of the 11th Tennessee, due to the death of Major Dawson, to the front. Vaughan deployed the sharpshooters to cover the front of the brigade. Vaughan ordered Green to move as far as the top of Missionary Ridge to determine the position of the enemy.[41]

Soon reports came back that the enemy were in the valley around Chattanooga. At about 3:00 PM Vaughan halted his column, and they camped for the night at Bird's Mill. On the morning of 22 September, Vaughan moved his men on the Shallowford Road in the direction of Chattanooga.[42] W. H. Jones of Company H stated,

> In the night we drove them from their position and about 10 o'clock we were ordered to stack arms, when I heard General Polk tell General [Colonel] Gordon that he could shell Longstreet's left from his right with a Parrot gun. We were ordered to rest but take off nothing. About 4 o'clock in the morning we started in

---

[39] Spence and Spence, *History of Hickman County, Tennessee*, 130; "A Sad Reminiscence of the Late War," Centerville (TN) *Hickman Pioneer*, 26 February 1886.

[40] William E. Reynolds, Veteran Questionnaire, Tennessee Civil War Veterans Questionnaires, Tennessee State Library and Archives, Nashville, TN, 1922. MF 484, R7. Hereafter referred cited as TCWVQ.

[41] *OR*, ser. I, vol. 30, pt. 2, 108.

[42] Ibid.

pursuit of the enemy. I was on skirmish line and went up on Missionary Ridge about 10 o'clock. We thought we were going to Chattanooga that day, but we did not, and the Yankees had a good time to reinforce and they had about ten men to our one.[43]

When the brigade arrived at the foot of Missionary Ridge, Vaughan's men formed a line of battle on the left of General Maney's Brigade and advanced to the top of the ridge. As Vaughan moved his brigade on the double quick up the ridge, even though the enemy manned temporary breastworks on the apex of the ridge, they put up only slight resistance.[44]

---

[43] Yeary, *Reminiscences*, 393–94.
[44] *OR*, ser. I, vol. 30, pt. 2, 109.

10

"There Was All the Blue-coats We Wished to Shoot At"

October–December 1863

The month of October opened with rain, nevertheless, Confederate morale was high as the Rebels laid siege to Chattanooga. In the aftermath of Chickamauga, Bragg arrested General Polk for not launching an attack on the morning of 20 September as ordered. On 2 October, Polk gathered his corps, delivered his farewell address, and then departed for Atlanta. A captain in Polk's command stated, "All appear to be sorry at his leaving, he being very popular among the soldiers of his corps."[1] General Cheatham accepted temporary command of the corps. After the rain cleared away, the next several mornings were cool. By sunrise, low clouds resembling smoke were common in camp as the boys looked across the mountainous terrain. On 5 October, a white frost covered the ground, and the men awoke with their stoppers frozen solidly to their canteens.[2]

On Saturday, 10 October, the men were awakened at 4:00 AM and followed orders to be ready to fall into line under arms at daylight. About an hour later, the order came, and the 11th Tennessee took its place in the breastworks. The men stacked arms and broke ranks but stayed close by. At about 11:30 AM, officers reformed their regiments and the men again took their places in the entrenchments. Down the rear of the works came Jefferson Davis, president of the Confederacy. By his side were Colonel Vaughan, General Cheatham, and an entourage of other generals and distinguished citizens. As the group passed, they halted in front of the colors of each regiment, paused for a moment, and then proceeded to the next regiment.[3]

On 27 October, Bragg recalled General Hardee from the Alabama-Mississippi department and gave him command of Polk's former corps. Bragg then reassigned Polk to Hardee's prior post. During this period, Bragg's ability as a commander once again came into question. His inability to unite his subordinates, his failures at Perryville and Murfreesboro, and his lack of initiative in exploiting the victory at Chickamauga were all points of contention. As a result, General Cheatham took a leave of absence and tendered his resignation, but Confederate authorities in

---

[1] A. T. Fielder, *Captain A. T. Fielder's Civil War Diary Company B, 12th Tennessee Infantry C. S. A. July 1861–June 1865*, ed. M. Todd Cathey (Broken Arrow, OK: Create Space, 2012) 270.
[2] Ibid., 270.
[3] Ibid., 10 October 1863.

Richmond rejected it. Bragg then decided to reorganize the Army of Tennessee. In the restructuring, he broke up Cheatham's Division and placed Vaughan's Brigade in Major General Thomas C. Hindman's division of Lieutenant General James Longstreet's Corps, which had been sent from the Army of Northern Virginia just before the Battle of Chickamauga.[4]

The regiment along with the brigade were to serve as reserves for Longstreet's campaign to relieve Knoxville from the occupation of Federal troops under command of General Ambrose Burnside. On 23 October, Hindman assembled his division in a pouring rain. The 11th Tennessee along with the division formed into lines and headed to the railroad. Rumor had it that the regiment was going to Charleston, about forty miles to the north. Vaughan's Brigade marched in the rain for about two miles and reached the depot at Tyner's Station around noon. At the station, the men tried to find shelter from the rain, which continued until about midnight. As the rain subsided, a cold wind blew in from the north. Many of the boys built fires to bring some relief from their wet, muddy, and chilly surroundings. The following morning, Saturday, 24 October, various regiments boarded the boxcars, and the train began its journey down the tracks at about 8:00 AM. The train moved slowly, stopping from time to time, and finally pulled into the depot at Cleveland, Tennessee, at noon. The shivering men remained in the cars until about 1:00 AM the next morning. At that time, the whistle sounded and the train took off again. Between 2:00 and 3:00 AM, the train pulled into Charleston, Tennessee. The men left the cars, built fires, and slept the remainder of the night. After daybreak, the men drew two days' rations of bacon and hard bread.[5]

On Monday, 26 October, the 11th Tennessee assembled and marched about 600 yards to the bank of the Hiwassee River. The men crossed the river on a makeshift pontoon bridge since the railroad bridge was burned before the battle of Chickamauga. The horses and wagons were ferried across by boat. After crossing the river, the boys walked down the railroad track about two miles, filed off to the right, and then bivouacked for the night. In the early morning hours rain began to fall; nevertheless, the men were up in line and had begun their march down the railroad by 6:00 AM. By 1:30 PM, the column reached Athens, marched through the town, and continued for another two miles where they halted and stayed the remainder of the evening. By 6:00 the next morning, the troops were continuing

---

[4] United States War Department, *The War of the Rebellion: A Compilation of the Official Records of the Union and Confederate Armies*. 70 vols. in 128 (Washington: Government Printing Office, 1880–1901; reprint, Gettysburg, PA: The National Historical Society, 1972) ser. I, vol. 31, pt. 3, 823. Hereafter cited as *OR*. Nathaniel Cheairs Hughes, *General William J. Hardee: Old Reliable* (Baton Rouge: Louisiana State University Press, 1965) 162; Christopher Losson, *Tennessee's Forgotten Warriors: Frank Cheatham and His Confederate Division* (Knoxville: University of Tennessee Press, 1989) 116–17.

[5] Fielder, *Civil War Diary*, 275-76.

their march, taking the road toward Loudon. The troops marched a distance of eight or nine miles, with rain falling intermittently throughout the day. The following day the regiment assembled at 9:00 AM. At this time, the regimental commissary issued rations. After receiving their rations, the boys marched another five miles, reaching the outskirts of the town of Sweetwater. The 11th Tennessee and other regiments remained in this location for about five days but were soon ordered to move to a location where wood was more plentiful. General Jackson, who was temporarily commanding the division, issued an order for the units to drill every day. However, the following day, Thursday, 5 November, officers called the men into line at about 5:00 AM, and orders were given that they would return to their positions on the outskirts of Chattanooga. The men marched back to Sweetwater where they boarded the cars and waited until about 7:00 AM when the trains left for Charleston. The troops reached Athens at approximately 10:00 AM. From Athens, the men returned to their former positions along Missionary Ridge.[6]

Upon arriving at the foot of the ridge, the men set up their camp. "We were stationed under Missionary Ridge without any fortifications except a pile of logs, instead of good fortifications all around Chattanooga to Lookout Mountain," stated a soldier of the 11th Tennessee.[7] The soldier continued,

> One evening about 3:00 or 4:00 o'clock we were getting wood on the side of the ridge when we discovered the enemy coming out of their fortifications, and soon the bugle sounded to fall in line. Their first attack was our picket line, capturing a little knoll just in front of our regiment, about a thousand yards away we expected a continuance of their attack the next morning, but late the next evening they engaged out troops under Lookout Mountain. That night we witnessed the battle above the clouds, saw the flash of the enemies' guns, following closely after the return fire of our men. That night the 12th/47th Tennessee was deployed as skirmishers in the foremost Rebel rifle pits.[8]

On the morning of 23 November, as skirmishing commenced, Captain James A. Long of Company F was sent forward with his company and was engaged during the afternoon. His company remained in the rifle pits throughout the night and was "engaged off and on all day of the 24th" but sustained no casualties.[9] That night his company was relieved by the 12th/47th Tennessee. Captain Long said he slept in a

---

[6] Ibid., 276-80.

[7] William E. Reynolds, Veteran Questionnaire, Tennessee Civil War Veterans Questionnaires, Tennessee State Library and Archives, Nashville, TN, 1922. MF 484, R7. Hereafter referred cited as TCWVQ.

[8] Ibid.

[9] Jack C. Vaughan, *Brigadier General Alfred Jefferson Vaughan's Brigade, Army of Tennessee Confederate States of America* (Grand Prairie, TX: Major Jack C. Vaughan, 1959–1960) 895, 898.

cabin that night.[10] As the night passed, the moon was in eclipse and according to a captain in the 12th Tennessee, "about three o'clock was very nearly total not giving as much light as a large star."[11]

The following morning, Wednesday, 25 November, Vaughan deployed the 11th Tennessee into line of battle. To their front, the 12th/47th Tennessee opened a brisk skirmish with the enemy. The Federals commanded a high position on the left and unleashed a severe enfilading fire on Vaughan's skirmishers. The exploding Yankee shells forced the skirmishers to abandon the rifle pits and to withdraw into some woods about three hundred yards to the rear.[12] The 12th/47th remained in that position until about 9:00 AM. By that time, the Federals had driven the remainder of the Confederate skirmishers back to the main line, so Vaughan ordered the 12th/47th to fall back as well.[13] According to Private J. W. Wynn of Company F, the men were "told to fire at the first attack and retreat."[14] Soon, conflicting orders began coming down from General Bragg's headquarters. Sergeant Clayton Yates of Company C stated, "a courier ran down our line crying, 'Fire one round and fall back,' and here came another saying, 'When the pickets come in fall back to the top of the Ridge.'"[15] Private William E. Reynolds of the 11th Tennessee stated, "Gen. Bragg's command was most heart rending, when he ordered us to hold our fire until the enemy was in close range then fire and fall back to the top of the ridge."[16]

The Yankees made no further advance until about 4:00 PM. At that time, the Federal forces moved forward all along the Confederate front. The Federal assault gained more ground on the Confederate left than on the right. As a result, the Federals were about to outflank Vaughan's Brigade, which was on the right of the division. In an attempt to stymie the enemy, Vaughan's was the last brigade to leave the rifle pits and to withdraw to the crest of the ridge.[17] Reynolds continued, "In a short while, and during the engagement with the picket line, the second order came, fire, reload and fire again and fall back to the top of the ridge. The third command was fire at long range and take position on top of [the] ridge. This proved beyond a

---

[10] Ibid., 898.

[11] Fielder, *Civil War Diary*, 185.

[12] John Hoffman, *The Confederate Collapse at Missionary Ridge: The Reports of James Patton Anderson and His Brigade Commanders* (Dayton, OH: Morningside, 1985) 48–49.

[13] Ibid., 48.

[14] Mamie Yeary, *Reminiscences of the Boys in Gray, 1861–1865* (1912; reprint, Dayton, OH: Morningside, 1986) 827.

[15] C. H. Yates, "Battle of Chattanooga," Mayfield (KY) *Daily Messenger*, 12 November 1912.

[16] Reynolds, Veteran Questionnaire, TCWVQ, MF 484, R7.

[17] Hoffman, *Confederate Collapse*, 49.

doubt, that we should have been on the ridge at first. With this discouraging acknowledgment of a defeat, his command last given was executed."[18]

After firing at the oncoming mass in their front, Vaughan's men left their advanced position and scrambled to the top of the ridge, firing at the Yankees as they gained the crest. During this retreat, a Federal round hit Adjutant Billy Mathis in the arm. Private J. W. Wynn of Company F, picked him up, carried him on his back to the top of Missionary Ridge, and then continued to the rear to the hospital.[19] Reynolds stated, "When we attained the top of the hill, the Federals lay just beneath the brow."[20] Vaughan formed his brigade to the right of Deas's 19th Alabama in the following order; the 11th Tennessee was placed on the extreme left of Vaughan's Brigade. To their right was the 13th/154th Tennessee. Presumably the 12th/47th came next in line with the 29th Tennessee anchoring the right of the brigade.[21]

The Yankees halted at the base of the ridge. The Confederates subjugated those hapless Yankees to a combined withering fire from infantry and artillery. Captain E. B. Parsons of the 24th Wisconsin stated, "[We] were exposed to such a galling fire from their batteries (the nearer we got to the top the safer we were), that General Sheridan, who was right behind us swinging his hat, told us to go for the top of the ridge, which we did, under the most terrific fire of grape, cannister, and schrapnel that you can imagine."[22] Captain F. K. Keil of the 35th Ohio continued, "At first, the lines moved in pretty good order, but as they proceeded they became less distinct; color bearers were generally in advance, and men drifted toward the colors. The long-winded chaps were in the lead; hundreds had to slow up to gain breath. Regiments vied with each other as to which should reach the summit and gain the rebel works."[23] Soon the enemy came into range. From behind their breastworks, Vaughan's men unleashed a deadly fire that stopped the Federal advance and caused it to move slightly to the left. Sergeant Clayton Yates of Company C stated, "But my, when we got on top of that mountain we thought we were safe, but the battle was just begun; as we stood on that mountain we could see them advancing three columns deep. I never saw such bravery before nor since. Our cannon on the mountain cut great swaths through their line but they closed up like some mighty machine with scarcely a warble and on they came, cut down like grass before the scythe filling up the chasm...."[24] Another of Vaughan's Rebs stated, "The

---

[18] Reynolds, Veteran Questionnaire, TCWVQ, MF 484, R7.
[19] Yeary, *Reminiscences*, 827.
[20] Reynolds, Veteran Questionnaire, TCWVQ, MF 484, R7.
[21] Hoffman, *Confederate Collapse*, 51.
[22] Milwaukee (WI) *Sunday Telegram*, 18 March 1888.
[23] F. W. Keil, *The Thirty-fifth Ohio Regiment: A Narrative of Service from August, 1861 to 1864* (Fort Wayne, IN: Archer Housh & Co. 1894) 171.
[24] Yates, "Battle of Chattanooga."

enemy like blue clouds by tens of thousands were advancing while our artillery was playing on them from every available point on the ridge and mowing them down by the hundreds still on they come and when within range of our Enfields we mowed them down with fearful havoc."[25]

Vaughan ordered his regiments to concentrate their fire upon this point in the line. Soon Colonel Gordon noticed that Deas's brigade had given way, thus leaving the left flank of his regiment and that of Vaughan's entire brigade in the air. At once, Gordon took what measures he could to fill this wide vacuum on his left. Private Reynolds explained further:

> Col. G. W. Gordon our commander, called for volunteers to assume the space as guards. Twelve of us, Tom and Roff [Marshall R.] Martin, Little, and Big Jim Schmittou, and myself, the other boys I don't remember, took position at the old house, Bragg's headquarters, the exact location the monument now stands. We were in forty or fifty feet of the federal line, but the hill was so abrupt as to obstruct plain view, but as there was a sag in the ridge and about one hundred yards to our right and in front of where we had just left, laying down beneath the brow of the ridge in plain view there was all the blue-coats we wished to shoot at. And we sure did make use of the time, but only for a short while when their three lines of battle moved forward promptly, cutting our guard off from our command.[26]

The scene now turned critical as Federal regiments began appearing on the left of Vaughan's line. Near the area where Gordon had sent the small detachment, the Federals gained a foothold on the top of the ridge and planted a couple of stands of colors on the spur near the Carol House.[27] In the ensuing tumult, the twelve-man detail came under a heavy fire. Reynolds recalled, "Roff Martin received a fractured leg. And Tom his brother, stayed with him, both were captured, the fracture resulting in his death. Little Jim Schmittou and myself being cut off from our command, made our way to a temporary bridge across Chattanooga Creek."[28]

When Vaughan discovered that he was about to be flanked, he ordered Colonel Gordon to withdraw the 11th Tennessee from their breastworks and to mount an assault to retake the spur captured by the Yankees. Gordon immediately obeyed. He formed his regiment in line of battle and made a determined advance against the ever-strengthening Federal position. As the 11th Tennessee made their charge, the Federal line began to waver. At that time, the Federals met the 11th with a wall of deadly rifle fire. This effective volley enabled the blue-coated foe to maintain their position without giving ground.[29]

---

[25] Fielder, *Civil War Diary*, 285.
[26] Reynolds, Veteran Questionnaire, TCWVQ, MF 484, R7.
[27] Hoffman, *Confederate Collapse*, 51.
[28] Reynolds, Veteran Questionnaire, TCWVQ, MF 484, R7.
[29] Hoffman, *Confederate Collapse*, 51.

As the 11th Tennessee charged, the color-bearers of the regiment fell one by one, as they pressed forward in the face of a withering fire. As Captain P. V. H. Weems advanced, leading Company H into the hellish vortex, he fell from an incapacitating abdominal wound.[30] When he fell, some of his men carried him off the field. Colonel Judson W. Bishop of the 2nd Minnesota Infantry described the Confederate counterattack, "Hardly had a lodgment been gained in the works when the enemy's reserves made a furious counter-attack upon our men, yet in confusion."[31] The regiment closed with the Federals, and vicious hand-to-hand fighting ensued, with neither side willing to give ground. Private James S. Jackson of Company E of the 11th Tennessee stated that "while the flag was bullet ridden and the staff shot in two twice and seven color bearers fell bearing it, the flag was not captured at Missionary Ridge, but boons [borne] off the field."[32] Colonel Bishop continued, "The attack was promptly met by a charge *en masse* by the crowd, which, after a few minutes of desperate hand-to hand fighting, cleared the ridge, leaving the place in our undisputed possession, with between two and three hundred prisoners captured in the melee."[33] The Yankees had stymied the ferocious attack of the 11th, and Gordon knew that any further advance would be suicidal. Now the tables were turned and only the most heroic and obstinate resistance allowed the 11th to hold their position. When Vaughan saw that Gordon's attack had floundered, he ordered the 13th/154th regiments to leave their breastworks and rush to the aid of the 11th. The Federals at this location heavily reinforced their line, and hammered Vaughan's beleaguered regiments with artillery. Despite the intense firestorm, Vaughan's battered regiments held. In the vicious firefight that followed, Major William Green fell mortally wounded while directing his men.[34] Vaughan knew that his mauled units would not be able to delay the Yankee assault at this location much longer. To decrease the needless sacrifice of life, he ordered his regiments to fall back out of the range of the Federal artillery.[35]

As soon as his regiments had cover from the Federal batteries, he halted and reformed his line perpendicular to the ridge. Vaughan, who had gained laurels for his well-executed charges at Perryville, Shiloh, and Chickamauga, again dared to do

---

[30] William B. Maney, "Return of the Killed and Wounded in the 11th Tennessee Regiment at the Battle of Missionary Ridge, Tennessee, 24 November 1863," *Regimental Surgeon's Log*, Confederate Collection, Manuscript Section, Box 18, Military Units Tenn. Inf. Regt. 11, Medical Records, Tennessee State Library and Archives, Nashville, TN.

[31] J. W. Bishop, *The Story of a Regiment; Being a Narrative of the Service of the Second Regiment, Minnesota Veteran Volunteer Infantry, In the Civil War of 1861–1865* (1890; reprint, St. Paul, MN: North Star Press, 2000) 38.

[32] James S. Jackson, "Veteran Questionnaire," in Dyer et al., *Tennessee Civil War Veterans Questionnaires*, 3:1212.

[33] Ibid.

[34] Maney, "Return of the Killed and Wounded…at the Battle of Missionary Ridge."

[35] Hoffman, *Confederate Collapse*, 51.

the unthinkable. When his brigade was reformed, he ordered another advance toward the oncoming Federal deluge. As Vaughan's entire brigade advanced, they soon met the enemy, who were rapidly advancing in their front. Vaughan halted his brigade, and when the enemy was no more than forty yards away, he ordered his men to fire. Remaining steady and in obedience to their orders, Vaughan's Tennesseans unleashed a volley of death into the Yankee line. The Federal line staggered, then broke, and momentarily fell back until heavily reinforced. By this time, darkness was beginning to fall across the Chattanooga Valley. To compound the situation, Vaughan's regiments were out of ammunition.[36] Captain Keil of the 35th Ohio recalled, "After a short but sharp contest the rebels gave way and withdrew down the woody slopes on the south side of the mountain."[37] Seeing that further resistance was useless, Vaughan withdrew his brigade in order to the foot of Missionary Ridge in the direction of Chickamauga Station.[38]

By this time, the small bridge that Reynolds and "Little Jim" Schmittou had reached was jammed with the military equipment of a routed army. Reynolds stated that the bridge "was guarded against everything except wagons and army vehicles, so it was after midnight before we could get over the bridge, after crossing the bridge we observed camp fires all along, so I remarked we had better lay down and get some sleep and rest, as we expected a renewal of battle the next day."[39] By this time, Private Wynn was returning from taking Adjutant Mathis to the rear. Upon his return to the top of the ridge he stated, "I found myself in the midst of Yankees, but in the excitement and smoke from battle I leisurely worked my way out and then proved myself master of the art of running."[40]

The next morning Reynolds and Schmittou awoke to find that the remainder of the army had continued to fall back from this position. Reynolds continues his story,

> Jim decided to come home as he thought we were in rear of the enemies' line and he could slip through home. And as he bade me goodbye, we were surprised by a squad of cavalry, right on us. Jim surrendered, but I made my escape, was under fire of about twelve men for about two hundred yards, when I dropped into an excavation, made by the old run of the creek, they thought I fell from their gun fire. When Jim reached prison he wrote to my folks he saw me fall, and thought I was dead.[41]

---

[36] Ibid., 51–52.
[37] Keil, *Thirty-fifth Ohio*, 171–72.
[38] Hoffman, *Confederate Collapse*, 52.
[39] Reynolds, Veteran Questionnaire, TCWVQ, MF 484, R7.
[40] Yeary, *Reminiscences*, 827.
[41] Reynolds, Veteran Questionnaire, TCWVQ, MF 484, R7.

As the regiments of the Army of Tennessee retreated from the crest of Missionary Ridge, the glory of the victory at Chickamauga was lost. A private in the 11th stated,

> With men demoralized, disheartened, and worn out from fatigue and hunger, the entire army straggled into Dalton, Georgia our next wintering quarters, under the leadership of one of the ablest generals of the south, Joseph E. Johnston. We always felt safe under his care and never knew when we were going to fight or retreat, but we always forced the enemy to fight us in our trenches. It was often when we passed a wagon mired up or broken down, the general remark would be we will form a line of battle until Johnston can start this wagon.[42]

Captain James A Long of Company F wrote, "Retreated to this place (Dalton, GA). A number of my men were barefooted. Marched the entire distance over frozen ground." [43] The regiment lost nine killed and fifty-one wounded at Missionary Ridge.[44]

The strain of the war had taken its toll on the regiment. On returns submitted around 10 December 1863, Gordon recorded the strength of the 11th Tennessee as 340 present with an effective strength of 269, weapons for 267, and 35 rounds of ammunition per man. This was very different from the original returns of 880 present at the beginning of the war. This was a loss of 540 in only twenty-nine months. After Missionary Ridge, Vaughan's entire brigade only mustered 997 effectives.[45]

Shortly after arriving at Dalton, headquarters promoted Captain James A. Long of Company F to major to fill the vacancy created when Major Green was killed. Then on 14 December Lieutenant Colonel William Thedford resigned his position due to health concerns.[46]

---

[42] Ibid.
[43] Vaughan, *Brigadier General Alfred Jefferson Vaughan's Brigade*, 905.
[44] Maney, "Return of the Killed and Wounded...at the Battle of Missionary Ridge."
[45] *OR*, ser. I, vol. 31, pt. 3, 825.
[46] James A. Long, 11th Tennessee Infantry Service Records, National Archives Records Administration, Compiled Service Records of Confederate Soldiers Who Served in Organizations from the State of Tennessee, Washington, DC: National Archives Records and Service, General Services Administration, 1960. Hereafter referred cited as 11th TISR. M268 R161.

11

"Three Cheers for the Snowball Colonel"

January–May 1864

Vaughan's Brigade camp lay about two miles from the train depot at Dalton.[1] Here the soldiers constructed mud-daubed cabins called "shebangs" to withstand the winter cold. Reporting on their conditions, one of the soldiers stated, "We have plenty of dry leaves and grass for beds with two blankets apiece. We sleep very comfortable."[2] After the men had time to get settled into their new camp, on 27 January, Vaughan held brigade dress parade.[3]

On Saturday, 30 January, Johnston held a grand review of the Army of Tennessee. At 7:30 AM, with falling rain and a southerly wind, Vaughan formed his brigade by regiments and in turn, each passed in front of the commanding general.[4] Approximately two weeks later, on Thursday, 11 February, Vaughan again held dress parade for his brigade. On this occasion, as the men stood in formation, an order was read informing them that their brigade would once again be assigned to Cheatham's Division, Hardee's Corps.[5] The men's spirits soared, as they knew they would once again fight under "Mars Frank." The following morning, officers called the 11th Tennessee into line, and the regiment with the brigade relocated to Cheatham's Division camp. By 10:00 AM, the regiment had reached its new billet, and the men took their places in the shanties that were already there. In the evening, the division commander visited each regiment, and as the highly esteemed Cheatham entered the individual camps of the Tennesseans, a hearty cheer went up.[6]

While the Army of Tennessee was settling in for the winter at Dalton, further to the west, a Federal force had penetrated into east-central Mississippi. This move precipitated General Leonidas Polk's withdrawal into Alabama. In an effort to counter the Federal offensive, Hardee readied his corps to move to Demopolis,

---

[1] Peter Marchant to Susan Marchant, 16 December 1864, Letters of Captain Peter Marchant, http://freepages.military.rootsweb.ancestry.com/~bsdunagan/letters.html (30 April 2015).

[2] Ibid.

[3] A. T. Fielder, *Captain A. T. Fielder's Civil War Diary Company B, 12th Tennessee Infantry C. S. A. July 1861–June 1865*, ed. M. Todd Cathey (Broken Arrow, OK: Create Space, 2012) 27 January 1864.

[4] Ibid., 304.

[5] Ibid., 307.

[6] Ibid.

Alabama, to reinforce Polk. After preparations were made, around midnight on the 19th, the 11th Tennessee with Cheatham's Division were assembled and headed toward the depot at Dalton. After a ninety-minute march, the boys entered the town, broke ranks, and built fires with what kindling they could obtain. The men spent the night shivering around their small fires. Finally, at 7:30 AM, officials gave the order for the men to board a train. After all had taken their places, the whistle sounded, and the train chugged off toward the south. Although the men were in boxcars, the temperature was extremely cold causing them a great deal of suffering. By 5:00 PM, the train rolled into Atlanta. When the train jerked to a stop, the men dismounted and again built what small fires they could to protect themselves from the bitter cold.[7]

The men waited around, huddling together in the frigid temperatures. At 9:30 PM, their transport train arrived. The men climbed into the boxcars with each car holding approximately fifty men. A little after sunrise on Saturday morning, the trains pulled into LaGrange, Georgia. After a two-hour delay, the train pulled out again, this time heading west toward Alabama. Before crossing the state line, at about 11:00 AM, the trains stopped at West Point, Georgia. At 8:30 the following morning, the men boarded the cars, and the train departed. After a twelve-hour ride, Montgomery, the former capital of the Confederacy was reached.[8]

As soon as the men dismounted the train, they made their way down to the boat landing where they stacked arms and drew rations. At about 11:30 AM, after the rations were distributed, the boys filed onto the steamboat *Jeff Davis*. The men crowded the decks as the boat took off on a 110-mile journey to Selma. Almost twenty-one hours later, the steamer reached its destination. When the boat glided into the dock at about 9:00 AM, the men disembarked, marched to the edge of town, halted, and stacked arms. After a wait of an hour and a half, officers called the boys into line and went through the town to the train depot. As evening approached, a portion of Vaughan's Brigade was loaded onto a train and headed out on the final leg of the journey. The remainder of the brigade spent the night and was loaded on a train for Demopolis the following morning. By noon, the second train had completed the fifty-two-mile journey, and the brigade was reunited.[9]

While at Demopolis, authorities detailed the 29th Tennessee Infantry, under command of Colonel Horace Rice, as the provost guard. The 29th commandeered the town courthouse as headquarters. While Rice's men were on duty, they met a Confederate captain from Louisiana, Peter Edgar Dreux, who had been confined to the guardhouse. Before the war, Dreux had been a student at the Kentucky Military Institute, but when the war began, he enlisted in the Confederate army and served as a sergeant in Company B, Pointe Coupee Light Artillery, a Louisiana battery

---

[7] Ibid., 309.
[8] Ibid., 309-310.
[9] Ibid., 310-311.

from New Orleans. In April 1862, the Yankees captured Dreux and the remainder of his unit at Island Number 10, an island garrison mounting artillery in the Mississippi River between Tennessee and Missouri. The Federals sent the captives to prison at Camp Douglas in Chicago, Illinois. Dreux was later exchanged at Vicksburg, Mississippi, on 20 September 1862 and was assigned to the engineering department the following August.[10] While stationed in Demopolis, the captain was involved in a conflict with a higher-ranking officer over the placement of some breastworks. The officer had Dreux arrested and confined in the guardhouse until a court martial could be convened. Rice and his men took a keen interest in Dreux, so much so that when Cheatham's Division returned to Dalton, members of the 29th Tennessee released the captain from jail and allowed him to join their regiment as a private in Company G.[11]

While remaining at Demopolis, on Wednesday evening 24 February, General Leonidas Polk rode to the various brigades of Cheatham's Division. When Polk came to Vaughan's, he told the men that General Nathan B. Forrest had turned back the Federal push at Okolona, Mississippi, and as a result, Cheatham's Division would return to the Army of Tennessee at Dalton. The following day at 3:00 PM, officers called the boys into line and they headed to the depot. Three hours later the train arrived, and within fifteen minutes, the men were on board headed back toward Selma. The train reached Selma at 11:15 PM. As soon as the men disembarked, they spread out their blankets and settled down for the night. The following day, Friday, 26 February, the regimental commissary issued bacon and crackers. Not long after obtaining rations, half of the brigade was loaded onto a steamboat and headed for Montgomery. The following day, the remainder of the brigade was loaded onto the steamboat *Le Grande*. By 4:30 PM, the boat's bell rang, and the steamer pulled away from the dock headed toward Montgomery. From Montgomery, the men were transported by a train back to Dalton where they arrived on Monday, 29 February, at about 7:00 PM.[12] One of Cheatham's soldiers commented about their experience, "This trip was a great benefit to us in the way of recreation. At every station crowds of ladies, old men and children gathered to see us and the waving of handkerchiefs and cheers of men and boys gave us a new stimulus, bringing back to our minds the early days of the war, and we returned to camp refreshed and inspired for the coming decisive campaign."[13]

---

[10] P. E. Dreux, M320 R59, Pointe Coupee Light Artillery, Compiled Service Records of Confederate Soldiers Who Served in Organizations From the State of Louisiana, National Archives Microfilm Publications, Washington, DC.

[11] C. D. M'Amy, "Brave P. E. Drew and His Fate," *Confederate Veteran* 2/3 (1894): 85.

[12] Fielder, *Civil War Diary*, 311-13.

[13] N. McLeod Johnson and E. McLeod Johnson, *A History of Henry County, Tennessee: Descriptive, Pictorial Reproductions of Old Papers and Manuscripts* (Paris, TN: McLeod, 1934) 66.

When Cheatham's men returned to their camps at Dalton, they found their shanties destroyed. One of Cheatham's men alleged that Brigadier General John R. Jackson's Brigade of Walker's Division had torn them up and used them for firewood. This soldier recalled that they were "very wrathy on account of it."[14]

On the night of 22 March, a heavy snow of at least four inches fell and blanketed the Confederate camps. Colonel Gordon stated, "It was too cold to drill or to indulge in the usual out-door games, 'stag dances,' etc., tents being too small for these purposes. And as most of the 'boys' were young men, naturally there was an accumulation of physical energy constantly sought issue in athletic exercises."[15] After breakfast, some of the boys began throwing snowballs at one another. Before long entire companies among the Tennessee brigades were shelling each other with snowballs. That night, W. J. Crook of Vaughan's Brigade recalled the event:

> We learned this morning that the South Carolinians had determined to wipe out the Tennesseans in a mock battle with snowballs. Gists brigade formed in front of the 16th South Carolina under command of the lieutenant colonel of the 16th. Our brigade and a portion of Maney's, all Tennesseans, formed under command of Colonel Gordon of the 11th Tennessee Regiment. We charged Gist's men. The fight was determined furious. Victory alternated first with one side and then the other. Charge after charge was made by the Tennesseans, but their thinned and broken ranks would be compelled to give way before overwhelming numbers.
>
> We reformed our lines and at the sound of the bugle the charge was again advanced. It was irresistible, we carried everything before us. [We] captured a large number of officers and men with several stands of colors, still driving the South Carolinians through the streets of their own encampment.[16]

The brigades making up Cheatham's Division (Vaughan's, Wright's, Strahl's, and Maney's) were encamped on one side of a deep wet-weather branch. Across the depression and about three hundred yards away were the camps of Walker's Georgia division. After the victorious Tennesseans had defeated the South Carolinians, they determined to take vengeance on the Georgians for their earlier crime of using their shanties as firewood, and so turned their attention to Walker's men. Soon, some of the Tennesseans and Georgians were bombarding each other with snowballs. News of the fight spread throughout the respective camps as men of both states flooded to reinforce their comrades. Soon the two divisions were deadlocked in the contest.[17] Colonel Gordon reminisced, "As news spread through the camps that a fight was

---

[14] Ibid., 66.

[15] George W. Gordon, "The Famous Snowball Battle," in *Personal Record of the Thirteenth Regiment, Tennessee Infantry, C. S. A.*, ed. Alfred J. Vaughan (1897; reprint, Memphis, TN: Frank and Gennie Myers and Burke's Book Store, 1976) 89.

[16] W. J. Crook to Hattie, 22 March 1864, W. J. Crook Papers, Kennesaw Mountain National Military Park, Kennesaw, GA.

[17] Gordon, "The Famous Snowball Battle," 89–90.

on hand between the Georgians and the Tennesseans, division pride and State pride became excited, the small fights ceased, and reinforcements poured in to both sides of the State forces until all interest was absorbed in one grand battle between Georgians and Tennesseans, in which several thousand men were now engaged, making the heavens wild with shouts and the air striped with the tracks of flying snow-balls."[18]

At this time, a member of the 11th Tennessee ran to Colonel Gordon's quarters and entreated him to lead the division. The messenger told Gordon that the Tennesseans thought they could win if they had a mounted commander to lead them. The colonel, whose interest was already piqued, needed no additional persuasion and asked his body servant to saddle his horse. By the time his servant had saddled the horse, the courier had fashioned a flag out of a thirty-six-inch square dirty bandanna handkerchief.[19] Gordon stated,

> I mounted my horse, a beautiful dappled iron grey, and with the bandanna flag flying to the breeze, I charged to the field—my horse leaping logs, ditches and other obstructions and running faster as I approached the excited scene. When I checked up in front of the Tennesseans, (now in battle array) and waving my flag, such a tremendous shout shook the air that the very atmosphere seemed to quiver around and above us. Excitement was now intense, and the men wildly impatient to make the charge.[20]

Immediately after Gordon arrived on horseback to lead his troops, a major of General W. H. T. Walker's staff arrived to lead the cheering Georgians. The Tennesseans answered the Georgians with another earth-shaking cheer. As the excitement continued to build, observers by the hundreds gathered on surrounding hills and housetops to watch the Georgians and Tennesseans go at it. Gordon ordered his men to "fill their pockets, bosoms and hands with balls, and the ordnance officers to follow the line with all the ammunition their details could carry."[21] When all was ready, Gordon gave the order to charge. The colonel stated, "With a shout that signaled victory, and an impetuosity that seemed irresistible, we dashed upon the brave Georgians, and for a few minutes the struggle was fierce and furious, desperate and doubtful."[22] Colonel James Cooper Nisbet of Steven's Brigade of Walker's Division stated, "It was the first snow-ball of fighting proportions, one half of my Regiment ever saw; consequently, they did not understand making ammunition with deftness and celerity."[23]

---

[18] Ibid., 90.
[19] Ibid., 91.
[20] Ibid., 91–92.
[21] Ibid., 92.
[22] Ibid., 92.
[23] James Cooper Nisbet, *Four Years on the Firing Line* (Chattanooga, TN: Imperial Press, 1914) 269.

Gordon, the superb horseman, galloped headlong into the ranks of the Georgians carrying his improvised standard. As the colonel approached their line of battle, they pummeled both horse and rider with hundreds of snowballs. One of Cheatham's men stated, "Though they resisted stubbornly, we drove them out and captured their general [Brigadier General Jackson]. It was a stirring scene; the air filled with flying snowballs the orders of the officers and the yells of the men seemed much like real war."[24]

Colonel Gordon recalled the scene as the Tennesseans advanced on the Georgians,

> The momentum of the charging column was too great, however, to be successfully resisted, more especially when it outflanked both wings of the enemy, which soon gave way. The center then being flanked, and at the same time being sorely pressed in front, also gave way, and his entire army fled in great confusion. The rout on the field was now complete, and the enemy was not only driven therefrom, but through his own camp and into the woods beyond. The object of the campaign (victory) being now accomplished, I ordered the pursuit to cease and the men to return to their camps.[25]

While the victorious Tennesseans withdrew, some of them pilfered the mess equipment of the Georgians. Colonel Stevens described, "I was captured, dragged from my horse, and carried a prisoner to Cheatham's Division, where I was paroled. The victorious Tennesseans looted in the meantime our camp; a desperate charge to capture Cheatham's camp was repulsed; then to recover our camp kettles, frying pans, etc., called for diplomacy of high order, as we could not recapture them with snowballs."[26]

Instead of hard feelings existing between the Tennesseans and the Georgians, the snowball episode ever after unified the two divisions with a bond of mutual respect for each other. Because of the triumph, Gordon gained indomitable fame. From that time onward, he was known as the "Snowball Colonel."[27] Gordon stated, "The writer never afterward passed or met the Georgia division, that its men did not greet him with shouts, often with 'Three cheers for the Snowball Colonel.' 'Colonel' was my rank at that time and 'The Snowball Colonel' was the designation they ever afterward gave me. This 'snowball battle' seems to have made a deep and indelible impression on all the soldiers who took part in, or who witnessed it."[28] Although wounded in three different battles and captured three times during the war, Gordon

---

[24] Johnson and Johnson, *A History of Henry County*, 66.
[25] Gordon, "The Famous Snowball Battle," 92.
[26] Nisbet, *Four Years*, 269.
[27] Gordon, "The Famous Snowball Battle," 93.
[28] Ibid.

later mused that he gained more notoriety in this snowball battle than in all the other battles in which he participated during the war.[29]

After the Tennesseans defeated the Georgians, Cheatham's most pugnacious brigades, Maney's and Vaughan's, decided to go at it. Colonel Hume Feild of the 1st Tennessee rode out to take command of Maney's Brigade, while Gordon reformed Vaughan's for the grand championship. When all was ready, both Gordon and Feild gave the command to charge. Both lines of battle moved rapidly toward each other. When the two lines clashed, "the shock was tremendous," stated a member of the 11th Tennessee.[30] As the two lines collided, men fell, others were dragged from the field, some lost coats or hats and some suffered black eyes and bruises. At least one soldier, Jimmie White, of the 1st Tennessee was killed in the wild melee when a caisson ran over him.[31] All of this occurred amidst the wildest shouts. As Gordon led Vaughan's Brigade, he inadvertently rode too deep into Maney's lines. Seeing an opportunity, many of Maney's Tennesseans surrounded Gordon's horse. In the melee, the colonel was drug to the ground and seized by Maney's men. As they were dragging him to the rear, several of his own men grabbed hold of his legs and tried to recapture him. In this tug-of-war, the opposing pulling forces suspended the colonel in mid-air. Gordon felt that his situation had become critical, and told his men to stop the "d–n foolishness."[32] Gordon, by vigorous "kicking, cussing, and yelling" finally got his men to release him.[33] As they let go of their commander, he was left a prisoner in the hands of the enemy but fortunately without serious injury. In the meantime, however, Gordon's men had captured Colonel Feild, and as neither side had a leader, the men ceased fighting and entered into negotiations for an exchange of prisoners. Gordon stated, "By the time the exchange was effected, the ardor of the combatants, had greatly cooled, and neither side seemed disposed to renew the contest."[34]

The participants of both brigades acquiesced to a draw. The scene closed as "the last beams of the setting sun gilded the icy branches of the leafless trees with the beauteous tints of the rainbow, the soldiers returned to their camps from the white field of the great 'snowball battle,' and retired that night with the fadeless memory of a glorious day."[35]

As General Johnston continued efforts to resupply his army, on 31 March army quartermasters issued a number of .54 caliber Austrian rifles and their oddly

---

[29] Ibid.
[30] George C. Porter, "Eleventh Tennessee," Nashville (TN) *Banner*, unknown date.
[31] S. R. Watkins, "Snow Battle at Dalton—Little Jimmie White," *Confederate Veteran* 1/9 (September 1893): 262.
[32] Gordon, "The Famous Snowball Battle," 95.
[33] Ibid.
[34] Ibid.
[35] Ibid.

shaped four-sided bayonets to several members of the 11th Tennessee. The armament of the regiment now consisted of .577 caliber Enfields, .58 caliber Springfields, and .54 caliber Austrian rifles.[36]

As spring came on officers posted pickets miles out from camp to prevent spies from infiltrating the Confederate lines. On one occasion, Private William E. Reynolds of Company C was on picket duty. While Reynolds was at his post, he noticed a group of "polk stalks" about six feet high. When the private was relieved of duty, he gathered all the stalks he could carry in his arms and made his way back to his shanty. He retrieved a 10-gallon camp kettle, filled it with water, and told his eager messmates to get their bacon, mark it, and drop it into the water. Reynolds and his comrades then stripped the polk leaves from the stalks and crammed them into the kettle. After the concoction was cooked, the men ate until they were completely full. After the meal, Reynolds fell asleep and did not wake until he was called on to go out on picket duty again. When he was awakened, he noticed that his mouth was very sore. His messmates experienced the same phenomenon. Reynolds recalled that their mouths were in so much pain they could barely eat for the next several days.[37]

On 6 April, there were promotions among the officers of Company F. 1st Lieutenant James H. Darden accepted the promotion to captain to fill the vacancy created when James A. Long was earlier promoted to major. Brevet Second Lieutenant Jeremiah Batts was subsequently promoted to first lieutenant.[38] Brigade returns for 30 April, show Vaughan's Brigade commanded by Brigadier General Alfred J. Vaughan and made up of the 11th Tennessee commanded by Colonel Gordon, the 12th/47th Tennessee Consolidated commanded by Colonel William M. Watkins, the 29th Tennessee commanded by Colonel Horace Rice, and the 13th/154th Tennessee Consolidated commanded by Colonel Michael Magevney, Jr.[39]

---

[36] F. F. Tidwell, 11th Tennessee Infantry Service Records, National Archives Records Administration, Compiled Service Records of Confederate Soldiers Who Served in Organizations from the State of Tennessee, Washington, DC: National Archives Records and Service, General Services Administration, 1960. Hereafter referred cited as 11th TISR. M268 R163. P. V. H. Weems, Service Records, W. I. White, Service Records, I. P. Young Service Records, M268 R163, 11th TISR.

[37] William E. Reynolds, Veteran Questionnaire, Tennessee Civil War Veterans Questionnaires, Tennessee State Library and Archives, Nashville, TN, 1922. MF 484, R7. Hereafter referred cited as TCWVQ.

[38] James H. Darden, 11th Tennessee Infantry Service Record, M268 Roll 160; Jeremiah Batts, M268 R159, 11th TISR.

[39] United States War Department, *The War of the Rebellion: A Compilation of the Official Records of the Union and Confederate Armies.* 70 vols. in 128 (Washington: Government Printing Office, 1880–1901; reprint, Gettysburg PA: The National Historical Society, 1972) ser. I, vol. 38, pt. 3, 638. Hereafter cited as *OR*.

Approximately a month later, on 7 May, headquarters made additional promotions. James A. Long, who had recently accepted an appointment to major, was promoted to lieutenant colonel. On this same day, Captain Philip Van Horn Weems, who had just returned to duty from his severe abdominal wound received at Missionary Ridge, was promoted to major.[40]

Throughout the day, as some of the 11th Tennessee received promotions, the Federals under command of General William T. Sherman abandoned their winter camps around Chattanooga and began advancing on the Southern positions near Dalton. As Sherman's bluecoats moved south, the infamous one-hundred-day Campaign for Atlanta was initiated. To counter Sherman's movements, the 11th Tennessee and the remainder of Cheatham's Division abandoned their winter quarters at Dalton and took up a position on the crest of Rocky Face Ridge along with other elements of the Army of Tennessee. On the crest of the ridge, the boys fashioned a crude line of works built from large rocks found on the top. Cheatham's left was anchored above the railroad at Mill Creek Gap while the remainder of his line extended along Rocky Face Ridge and joined with Stevenson's Division of Georgians and Alabamians.[41]

Two days later, Major General James B. McPherson's Federal Army of the Tennessee stealthily passed undetected through the unguarded Snake Creek Gap some fourteen miles south of Dalton as he headed to secure Johnston's rear and the rail line at Resaca. Advance forces of General Leonidas Polk's corps, hurrying from Alabama, met McPherson. Cantey's Brigade of Polk's Corps heavily engaged with the enemy. Vaughan's Brigade was sent to their position as reinforcements. With Vaughan's arrival, McPherson was unable to capture Resaca and was compelled to withdraw back to Snake Creek Gap. This delaying action gave Johnston the time needed to move the Army of Tennessee south, thus foiling Sherman's attempt to entrap his army.[42]

By 13 May, Johnston had his army firmly entrenched in a commanding position northwest of Resaca. Vaughan's Brigade was positioned near the extreme left of the Rebel line astride the road to Snake Creek Gap. While there, headquarters had detailed several of the boys from Company C to build a defensive position for an artillery battery from Mobile, Alabama. As they worked, an enemy battery, which was stationed about one thousand yards away, continuously banged at them. One of the Federal rounds screamed overhead and exploded in the rear killing and wounding fourteen artillery horses. Soon the Alabama battery was in position. According to Private Reynolds of Company C, who was working on the

---

[40] James A. Long, M268 R161, 11th TISR; Philip Van Horn Weems, M268 R163, 11th TISR.

[41] Christopher Losson, *Tennessee's Forgotten Warriors: Frank Cheatham and His Confederate Division* (Knoxville: University of Tennessee Press, 1989) 143.

[42] Ibid., 144.

fortifications, the Mobile gunners loaded their field piece and fired a round. Whether by coincidence or by proficiency the first round disabled the gun and scattered the Yankee artillerymen.[43]

During this time, the 13th/154th Tennessee, under command of Lieutenant Colonel John W. Dawson, took an advance position as the brigade skirmishers. Even though they were under artillery fire, Dawson deployed his men to the front while the remainder of the brigade kept their heads down and erected breastworks. As the day progressed, Vaughan's men braced themselves for an attack as the Federals twice pressed Dawson's skirmish line. While the Federals engaged Dawson, General Johnston, who happened to be with Vaughan at the time, was intently watching the battle unfold. As Dawson's skirmishers punished the attacking Yankees, Johnston turned to Vaughan and asked, "What command is that in your front?" Vaughan proudly responded, "That is the 13th/154th Tennessee, Vaughan's Brigade, Cheatham's Division." Johnston, the wily old veteran, lauded Vaughan's troops as he stated that he had never seen skirmishers "behave better, or handled with more skill."[44]

The following day, Sherman's army renewed the advance and the 11th Tennessee firmly held their line in the face of a determined assault. As the Yankees made their move, Company D of the 11th hotly engaged the enemy. Five of the seven casualties sustained by the 11th Tennessee were from this company alone. Private A. J. Robinson was wounded in the lower left thigh, Private Andrew Stout was also shot in the left thigh, Private William Kyle was wounded in the left temple, Sergeant Joe Gilman was wounded in the left arm, and Private William D. Bowers was killed on the field. Private Thomas Shortle of Company G received a wound in the left arm, and Private Wallace Haile of the regimental band received a contused wound in the left groin.[45]

By 15 May, Sherman had failed to take Resaca but did succeed in outflanking Johnston's line. In the meantime, officers deployed Company F of the 11th on picket duty. After more skirmishing during the day, Johnston began withdrawing his army across the Oostanaula River and headed south about sixteen miles toward Adairsville. As the Confederates withdrew, troops set fire to the bridges across the river in hopes of delaying the Federal advance. In the confusion, word of the

---

[43] Reynolds, Veteran Questionnaire, TCWVQ, MF 484, R7.

[44] Alfred Vaughan, ed., *Personal Record of the Thirteenth Regiment, Tennessee Infantry, C. S. A.* (1897; reprint, Memphis, TN: Frank and Gennie Myers and Burke's Book Store, 1976) 32.

[45] William B. Maney, "Return of the Killed and Wounded in the 11th Tennessee Regiment at the Battle of Resaca, New Hope, and Other Places in May 1864," *Regimental Surgeon's Log*, Confederate Collection, Manuscript Section, Box 18, Military Units Tenn. Inf. Regt. 11, Medical Records, Tennessee State Library and Archives, Nashville, TN.

withdrawal never reached Company F. Private John W. Wynn of that company recalled,

> At the Battle of Resaca one night my whole company, officers and all, were put on picket. Gen. Johnston was retreating, burning bridges behind him, and our company was forgotten and at daylight we found ourselves between the enemy and three burning bridges. We found two of the bridges down and the other wet ever few feet with turpentine and fired. This was our only escape and we succeeded in jumping the flames without damage to ourselves and regained our army about noon.[46]

As the Confederates withdrew through Calhoun toward Adairsville, the 11th Tennessee was engaged in skirmishing on 16 May at Calhoun and on the 17th at Adairsville. At Adairsville, Cheatham deployed Vaughan's, Maney's, and Wright's brigades of his division astride the road about three miles north of the town. As Colonel Frank Sherman's Federal brigade (the advance guard of Howard's IV Corps) approached the town, Cheatham's artillery and sharpshooters hammered them. Howard, under intense pressure from General William T. Sherman, and believing this brigade fronted a lesser number of mounted infantry, urged the colonel to move on. Frank Sherman made several futile attempts to dislodge Cheatham's Rebs and in the process sustained many needless casualties. In the ensuing fight, the 11th was deployed near an eight-sided brick structure called the "Octagon House." Many soldiers of the 1st Tennessee of Maney's Brigade occupied the interior of the structure. Sherman launched several repeated assaults against this position.[47] As the Yankees came up, Vaughan's and Maney's men shot them down. As in all the times before, the 11th held their line, but not without losses. In the fight, Sergeant Orval Jamison of Company I was shot in the thigh. A Yankee bullet hit Private Martin Dogherty of Company G in the shoulder. Private Joe Larkins of Company E suffered a severe wound in the left thigh. Private W. D. House of Company K suffered a slight flesh wound on the scalp. Corporal George H. French of Company I received a severe flesh wound through both buttocks, and Private W. L. Baker of Company E was mortally wounded, shot through the bowels.[48]

Displeased with Colonel Sherman's lack of success, General Howard arrived on the scene to ascertain the delay. As Howard approached, he too received a warm reception by Cheatham's artillery. Much to his chagrin, Howard learned that he did not face a small contingent of mounted infantry, but instead, he faced some of the hardest fighters of the entire Army of Tennessee, Cheatham's Division. When Howard assessed the situation, he wasted no time in deploying his entire corps in extended battle order. As soon as his men were ready to attack, Howard received

---

[46] Mamie Yeary, *Reminiscences of the Boys in Gray, 1861–1865* (1912; reprint, Dayton, OH: Morningside, 1986) 827.

[47] Losson, *Tennessee's Forgotten Warriors*, 146–47.

[48] Maney, "Return of the Killed and Wounded…at the Battle of Resaca."

word from his immediate superior, General George H. Thomas, to delay his advance. Once again, the 11th Tennessee with Cheatham's other regiments suffered light casualties while making Sherman pay dearly for every inch of ground gained. As was becoming commonplace, Johnston's Rebels were successful in thwarting the Federal advance in the face of overwhelming odds.[49]

Late that night, Vaughan's, Maney's, and Wright's brigades withdrew with the army. The following day, 18 May, Hardee's Corps went southward toward Kingston with the army's ambulances and supply trains. As General Sherman continued his flanking maneuvers, he headed his army down the Adairsville Road toward Cassville. Upon arrival, Howard's IV Corps formed on the Federal right opposite Hardee. By mid-afternoon, Sherman and Johnston once again squared off with each other. Johnston met with his lieutenants, and they agreed that this position was untenable. The Army of Tennessee fell back southward once again, this time across the Etowah River. While in camp, Private Martin F. Long wrote his father back in Robertson County,

> Mr. Samuel Long—May 20, 1864
> Camp near Etowa River, Ga.
> Dear Father and Mother,
> It is with pleasure that I avail myself of the present opportunity to write you a few lines, to let you know how I am getting along. My health is fine, and I am doing as well as any person could under the present circumstances. Our company is in fine health. The health and spirits of Johnston s Army is better, I believe, than I ever saw, & I think that when a general engagement takes place between the two armies it will surely meet with success. Pa, I reckon you have heard of our retreat by this time. On our retreat we have had some pretty hard skirmishing and shells fell pretty thick around us, but got into no general engagement. None of our company hurt. Jo Larkin was shot through the thigh in a skirmish, but his wound is not of a serious nature. I saw the [?] two or three days ago. None of the boys were hurt in Robertson Company. Tom Cobb came out safe, also James Darden has been with us for the last day or two. He is in fine health. Excellent health and is in the notion of fighting the Yankees till the last pea in the pot is gone. I wrote you a letter some times since in which I gave the names of those wounded at Missionary Ridge. John Baldwin and Irvine Parish died of wounds received there. Polk Bartlett is improving. I do not think he will ever be able to use his left arm. He told me to tell his folks how he was getting along & tell them old that Robertson is his home after this war; I suppose. Tell G. T. Martin, G. S. is at Raymond (MS). Tell him Tom has come back to. I want you to write to me soon and tell me who is dead and who wants to marry and cannot get to marry. Tell Mary Ann that Tom had a severe chill on the 20th instant and was sent to the hospital yesterday morning but I think he will return soon. Pa, I would like to have some money if you have any. Tenn

---

[49] Albert Castel, *Decision in the West: The Atlanta Campaign of 1864* (Lawrence: University of Kansas Press, 1992) 193–94.

money is worth 4 for one. So if you a silver watch like John Batts, I can get four or five hundred dollars. So if watches are any like [?] [?] they was when I left, you would make mine by send me one of [?] in the place of Tenn money, through their might be more danger of its being captured. If you have Confed send it, but do not buy more of the old issue for it is only [?] it. Pa, I told you the first part of my letter that I joined the [?] [?] [?] Their was five slightly wounded but prove that you [?] [?] hardly[?]. We are not retreating because we are whipped. You mark what I tell you. Pa, [?] [?] [?].

I get as much to eat as I want. You all need not think anything else. We get [?] lbs. bacon [?] [?] [?][?] [?] meat and bread. [?] [?] [?] as for vegetables, we do not get them and [?] [?] [?] we do not expect the [?]. Pa, I want you to write to me. I have not received a letter from Tennessee since last Nov. and tell what is the reason. What has transpired since you last wrote. We are not getting furloughs now, [?] when reenlisting [?] [?] if a soldier furnishes a recruit he gets a 40 day furlough. I expect to come home when the war closes if it is the good Lord s will to spare me, and if I fall it will be in defense of what I think is right and well. Pa, I will bring my letter to a close for it is getting dark. Give my love to all friends and receive a portion yourself. So nothing more this. Martin. Read it if you can. I have not time look for mistakes.[50]

This would be the last words the Longs would receive from their son. He would be killed the following month on the Kennesaw Line.[51]

By 23 May, as Sherman inched closer to Atlanta, he crossed the Etowah as well, and in the spirit of Julius Caesar crossing the Rubicon River in pursuit of Gnaeus Pompeius Magnus toward Rome, he christened the Etowah the "Rubicon of Georgia." As Sherman cast the die, he fully committed to take Atlanta or to be destroyed in the process.[52]

After crossing the Etowah, the 11th Tennessee with the army occupied a strong defensive position near Allatoona Pass for several days. Instead of attacking Johnston here, Sherman headed southwest toward Dallas, abandoning his approach down the railroad. Johnston quickly moved to block Sherman's advance. On 23 May, the 11th Tennessee with the remainder of Cheatham's Division left their camp, marching seven miles on the Dallas Road. The following day, Cheatham

---

[50] Martin F. Long to Samuel Long, 20 May 1864. Possession of Jim Brooks.

[51] William B. Maney, "Return of the Killed and Wounded in the 11th Tennessee Regiment at the Battle of Kennesaw Mountain, Georgia, in the month of June 1864," *Regimental Surgeon's Log*, Confederate Collection, Manuscript Section, Box 18, Military Units Tenn. Inf. Regt. 11, Medical Records, Tennessee State Library and Archives, Nashville, TN.

[52] James Lee McDonough and James Pickett Jones, *War So Terrible: Sherman and Atlanta* (New York: W. W. Norton & Company, 1987) 141.

moved his division to a position near New Hope Church, a small log Methodist meeting house located at a crossroads about two miles northeast of Dallas.[53]

While Johnston's army remained near New Hope Church, Cantey's Alabama brigade occupied a position on the main line about 250 yards southwest of the church. Vaughan's Brigade took a position behind them in support. While in this position, for three or four nights Cantey's pickets believing the enemy was advancing on them, opened up a heavy fire about midnight. Each time Cantey's men opened fire, Vaughan's Brigade was ordered up into position, and each time it was a false alarm. Second Lieutenant W. D. Eleazer of Company E stated, "When things would quiet down, Vaughan's men got to guying Cantey's men for shooting at the lightening bugs."[54] First Lieutenant Preston G. Price of Company D, wrote an article to the Chattanooga *Daily Rebel*, then operating out of Atlanta, stating that Cheatham's Division would donate a ton of printer's ink to black out the tails of the lightning bugs to keep Cantey's men from shooting at them.[55]

Later in the day, the regiment with the division was marched to the southeast. By 6:00 PM on 24 May, they had returned to the line and took a position with their right resting near New Hope Church while their left occupied a ridgeline covering the road leading into Dallas.[56]

On 25 May, Joe Hooker launched an attack against Hood's Corps near New Hope Church. Cheatham's men took positions along the Powder Springs Road, but the following day, they were recalled to New Hope Church and placed in line between Hood's Corps on the left and Polk's Corps on the right. Not long after taking position, Cheatham's skirmish line heavily engaged the enemy all along his division front. After dark, Cheatham was ordered to advance toward the enemy and drive them from Elsberry Ridge, a prominence southwest of New Hope Church, where the enemy had gained an advantageous position.[57]

At 3:00 AM, the brigade, with the exception of the 13th/154th Tennessee, left their position and moved out with the division. The 13th/154th Tennessee, under the able command of Major J. W. Crook, forming a strong skirmish line, was left behind to hold the position. Vaughan ordered Crook to hold this position "at all hazards."[58]

Cheatham, accompanied by his staff and escort, led the way for his division. General Vaughan, along with his staff and escort, followed Cheatham. Vaughan's

---

[53] Losson, *Tennessee's Forgotten Warriors*, 149.

[54] W. D. Eleazer, "Fight at Dead Angle in Georgia," *Confederate Veteran* 14/7 (July 1906): 312.

[55] Ibid.

[56] Losson, *Tennessee's Forgotten Warriors*, 149.

[57] Chatham Coffee, "May 27, 1864—Battle of Pickett's Mill," Memphis (TN) *Daily Appeal*, 12 June 1864.

[58] Ibid.

men, following on the heels of their commander, formed the lead infantry of the division. Strahl's Brigade was drawn up next in line, followed by Wright's Brigade, commanded by the unostentatious John C. Carter. George E. Maney, whose arm was still in a sling from his wound at Missionary Ridge, led his brigade as they brought up the rear.[59]

As the first rays of morning pierced the darkness, Cheatham's men reached their objective. Upon arrival, Cheatham deployed the division in line of battle. Vaughan marched his depleted brigade by the left flank and occupied the left of the line. Strahl, followed and occupied the center, and Carter was posted on the right. Maney was ordered to assume a position in the rear of Vaughan, acting as reserve. Skirmishers deployed to the front, and Major P. V. H. Weems, known as "the great skirmish officer of the 11th," commanded the skirmish line.[60] Weems advanced with his skirmishers until he intersected "Bate's skirmishers on a line perpendicular to his."[61] At this time, Weems halted his advance, but in doing so, he inadvertently left part of the brigade "uncovered." Weems immediately sent word to Vaughan about this development. Vaughan responded quickly, telling Weems to resume his advance. As soon as Bate's skirmish line cleared his, Weems ordered his men forward. At this time, General Cheatham waved his headquarters flag, signaling his brigades to advance. Vaughan's Brigade moved forward, following in the steps of Weems's skirmishers. Even though part of his brigade lacked the frontal protection of his skirmish line, Vaughan, realized there was no time to waste. The brigade commander strained his voice as he shouted "forward!" As they had done a thousand times before, at Vaughan's command, his boys stepped out in perfect unison.[62]

Vaughan had aligned his regiments from left to right: the 29th Tennessee occupied the extreme left of the brigade; the 11th Tennessee was on their right, occupying the center; and the 12th/47th Tennessee was on the right of the brigade. Vaughan's Brigade moved toward the Federal line, intent on dislodging the enemy from their strategic position. Weems's line neared the enemy's position, but before his skirmishers had fired a shot, the heavy Federal skirmish line let loose with a well-aimed volley, which raked Vaughan's left. Immediately, Vaughan's men responded in kind, the two lines exchanging a heavy cascade of fire. Despite the "dreadful conflict" which ensued, the enemy found the impetus of 29th and 11th regiments "irresistible."[63] While the 29th and 11th regiments continued their push, a cheer arose in the 29th, the 11th picked it up, and it was continued by the 12th/47th Tennessee. As Weems's skirmishers on the left drove the enemy,

---

[59] Ibid.
[60] Ibid.
[61] Ibid.
[62] Ibid.
[63] Ibid.

Cheatham checked his alignment. Cheatham was securely connected with Bate on the left but on the right, he discovered that a three-quarter-mile gap existed between his right and General Leonidas Polk's left. Cheatham hurriedly extended his line to the right as far as he could, and Hardee managed to send reinforcements to fill the breach.[64]

While Cheatham reconnected his right flank to the remainder of the Confederate line, Vaughan managed to drive the Federals back. Even though their position had been wrested from their control, the Yanks would not give up easily. Despite their dislodgement, they maintained enough unit cohesion to unleash a deadly volley into Vaughan's left flank. Captain Chatham Coffee, a nearby witness, stated that this was one "of the most tremendous and precisely directed volleys of musketry I ever beheld."[65] As a result, the Yankees caught the 29th Tennessee, the leftmost regiment of Vaughan's Brigade, in a terrific enfilading fire. With the fire on his left flank intensifying, Vaughan, accompanied by his staff, raced on horseback to supervise the 29th and 11th regiments. By the time of his arrival, the Federals had engulfed the 12th/47th Tennessee in the ferocious fire as well. Even though terrific, the devastating deluge caused "but a temporary waiver in the heretofore unbroken line."[66] To add to the confusion, Vaughan's men believed their own troops were firing on them. Some of the men frantically yelled, "It is your friends firing on you by mistake."[67] Officers quickly considered what to do. Soon they discovered that the fire was not "friendly" but was from the enemy, who had moved at an angle perpendicular to Vaughan. With this discovery, Vaughan pushed forward again, driving the enemy back once more.[68]

The Yankees fell back, but again stubbornly contested every inch of ground. As soon as they could sufficiently reform, the bluecoats turned and once again delivered a volley into Vaughan's left flank. Colonel Horace Rice commanding the 29th Tennessee, who was said to be "cool under the most embarrassing circumstances,"[69] wheeled the 29th to the left to deal with the flanking fire. While Rice with the 29th Tennessee took care of the threat to the left, Colonel Gordon and the 11th Tennessee poured a heavy volume of fire into the Federals who had the misfortune to face his regiment. To Gordon's right, Colonel William Watkins, commanding the 12th/47th Tennessee, urged his men forward. While the 29th Tennessee confronted the enemy on the flank and the remainder of Vaughan's men

---

[64] Losson, *Tennessee's Forgotten Warriors*, 149; Coffee, "Battle of Pickett's Mill."
[65] Coffee, "May 27, 1864—Battle of Pickett's Mill."
[66] Ibid.
[67] Ibid.
[68] Ibid.
[69] Ibid.

gained the crest, Maney hurriedly sent the 6th and 9th Tennessee regiments of his brigade forward to support Vaughan.[70]

As Vaughan's men pressed forward, Captain John W. Harris, Vaughan's Brigade inspector, "was shot through the heart within fifty feet of the enemy's line."[71] Not long after Harris went down, Harry Gordon of the 11th Tennessee, the younger brother of Colonel Gordon, who had just transferred to Company H from the 8th Texas Cavalry, received a mortal wound. As young Harry lay in critical condition, Colonel Gordon raced to his side. With his life slipping from his body, Harry told his brother to "tell Father that I died in a glorious cause."[72]

As Vaughan's men continued pushing the enemy, Major James Purl of the 12th/47th Tennessee fell seriously wounded with a broken thigh. Further down the line, Lieutenant Hamilton of the 29th Tennessee fell dead within a "musket length" of the Federals. Despite their casualties, Vaughan's men finally succeeded in gaining the crest. As they reached the top, officers ordered them to lie down in order to escape "the terrible fire of the enemy's sharpshooters."[73]

Even though the men were lying down, the enemy sharpshooters still played heavily on them. Major A. K. Blevins of the 29th Tennessee, who had replaced the gallant Weems on the skirmish line, was killed. Within an hour, the 11th lost several men. A Yankee sharpshooter managed to kill 5th Sergeant Sterling Capps of Company K. Capps was one of a few specially chosen men who, equipped with deadly English Whitworth rifles, made up Cheatham's sharpshooters, the equivalent of today's snipers. An observer stated, "Kapps…whose unerring aim had made so many Yankees bite the dust, fell victim to the service, in which he was himself an expert."[74] Besides Gordon and Capps, Private George K. Freeman of Company C, 5th Sergeant Joseph P. Skelton of Company H, and Private William McKelvy of Company A, were all killed on the field. Private Thomas Rochelle of Company H and Private David Gentry of Company K were both shot through the bowels and died the following day. Second Lieutenant James R. Douglass of Company B was shot through the arm and both lungs. Lieutenant Douglass died on 29 May. Corporal Pat Cronan of Company A was shot in the shoulder. Second Lieutenant R. J. Work of Company H was shot in the right leg. Private Absolom Hooper of Company I, was shot in the penis and in the upper left thigh. In all, in

---

[70] Ibid.

[71] Ibid.

[72] Coffee, "May 27, 1864—Battle of Pickett's Mill"; John Berrien Lindsley, *Military Annals of Tennessee: Confederate* (1886; facsimile of the first edition, Wilmington, NC: Broadfoot Publishing, 1995) 298.

[73] Coffee, "May 27, 1864—Battle of Pickett's Mill."

[74] Ibid.

the fighting at New Hope Church, the regiment lost eight killed and seventeen wounded.[75]

While the regiment was slugging it out with the Federals in North Georgia, Private Alex L. Bartlett of Company F, now a patient in Ward A of Stout Hospital in Madison, Georgia, due to a gunshot wound, along with J. M. Burditt, Company C, 50th Tennessee, submitted a letter of complaint to Army of Tennessee Medical Director, Dr. S. H. Stout, decrying their lack of adequate medical treatment. Bartlett wrote,

> Stout Hospital Ward A Madison Ga May 25th 1864.
> Dr. [S.] H. Stout,
> Dear Sir
> having ben wounded at missionary Ridge we have ben stopping at Marietta until a few weeks ago and then we were sent to this place and being very much dissatisfied for we get but little attention neither Medical or any other way we ask you for a transfer. If yo will bee so kind as to grant it sened them to this Hospital. One to J. M. Burditt of Co. C 50th Tenn Reg. to Westpoint Ga and the other to A. L. Bartlett of co F 11th Tenn reg to Montgomery Ala please send them as soon as yo get this.
> Your obedient servant
> A. L. Bartlett J. M. Burditt.[76]

Dr. Stout assigned the case to be investigated. Surgeon Glenn reported on 28 May, "I have fully investigated the charge.... The men deny that they had ever been neglected in any way or have complained." However, when the letter was produced, the men apparently confessed that it was simply a ruse attempting to get transferred closer to their homes.[77]

---

[75] Maney, "Return of the Killed and Wounded...at the Battle of Kennesaw Mountain."

[76] Bonnie P. Harris, *The Confederate Hospitals of Maidson, Georgia: Their Records and Histories 1861–1865* (Buckhead, GA: Bonnie P. Harris, 2014) 183.

[77] Ibid., 165.

12

"We Will Stay Here"

June 1864

After the Battle of New Hope Church, on Saturday, 4 June, in a violent rainstorm, the Army of Tennessee fell back toward the south. The following day at 5:00 PM, Cheatham's Division assembled and continued the march further south toward Marietta. Not long after the march was underway, rain began to fall again, making the roads very muddy. After marching about ten miles through the rain and darkness, the column took a road to the left for about two more miles, and then they halted and bivouacked for the night. The following morning, the officers rousted the men from their sleep. Soon they fell into line, and the entire brigade moved about a mile out where it went on picket duty. The following day, Thursday, 9 June, as Vaughan's Brigade remained on outpost duty, the Yankee pickets fired on them, and a steady firefight continued between the pickets for some time.[1] On Saturday, 11 June, a cannonball struck and killed Corporal Abe Bumpass of Company B while he was on the picket line. William B. Maney, regimental surgeon of the 11th, reported that the artillery round killed him without breaking the skin.[2] Later in the day, Lowrey's Brigade of Cleburne's Division relieved Vaughan's Brigade on outpost duty.[3]

As soon as his men left the picket line, Vaughan directed them to the ordnance trains where they restocked their ammunition. After filling their cartridge boxes, the men marched a half-mile in a heavy rain and then made camp for the night.[4]

Tuesday morning, 14 June, Hardee, Polk, and Johnston went to the top of Pine Mountain to inspect the Confederate fortifications in that area. When the generals were within about one hundred yards of the position held by the 11th Tennessee, a Federal battery fired on the officers. While the first round did no

---

[1] A. T. Fielder, *Captain A. T. Fielder's Civil War Diary Company B, 12th Tennessee Infantry C. S. A. July 1861–June 1865*, ed. M. Todd Cathey (Broken Arrow, OK: Create Space, 2012) 337-38.

[2] William B. Maney, "Return of the Killed and Wounded in the 11th Tennessee Regiment at the Battle of Kennesaw Mountain, Georgia, in the month of June 1864," *Regimental Surgeon's Log*, Confederate Collection, Manuscript Section, Box 18, Military Units Tenn. Inf. Regt. 11, Medical Records, Tennessee State Library and Archives, Nashville, TN.

[3] Fielder, *Civil War Diary*, 338-39.

[4] Ibid.

damage, a second round fired from a three-inch Parrott rifle passed completely through General Polk's chest, killing him instantly. The death of the bishop-general saddened many men of the rank and file. Although Polk was no great military strategist, he had gained the admiration of his men.[5]

On 15 June, Sherman flanked Johnston's line on Pine Mountain, and heavier fighting resumed. Later in the day, Federal skirmishers pressed against Cheatham's entire front.[6] As darkness fell, Colonel Gordon took his regiment out on picket duty to relieve the 12th Tennessee.[7] By 17 June, the 11th Tennessee with Cheatham's Division had fallen back to positions near Marietta. In the evening, Sherman launched a heavy attack on Johnston's left, and Cheatham was sent to reinforce the line.[8] In this attack, made primarily by Federal cavalry and artillery, Private J. T. Innis of Company I received a severe wound to the head.[9]

The following day, the 11th Tennessee and Cheatham's Division moved once again. This time, they fell back four miles toward Marietta and made camp for the night. Late in the afternoon of 19 June, Cheatham sent Vaughan's Brigade to reinforce Cleburne's Division.[10] As the Yankees attacked their line, Private G. L. Redden of Company K suffered a severe flesh wound in the foot, and Private George Martin of Company H was wounded in the hand.[11] Cheatham's men remained in this position and began fortifying. By 18 June, Johnston had established his formidable Kennesaw Mountain line. The Confederate line stretched about eight miles and ran from the summit of Big Kennesaw Mountain, over to Little Kennesaw, down to Pigeon Hill, and over to a small hill, later to be known as Cheatham's Hill, and continued on over to the Kolb farm and beyond.[12]

At Kennesaw Mountain, Sherman hoped he could duplicate the Federal success at Missionary Ridge. In the attempt, he devised a bold plan involving a two-pronged attack against Johnston. General George Henry Thomas, "the Rock of Chickamauga," led the main assault against Cheatham and Cleburne. Sherman chose to attack this point in the Confederate line because he believed the position was weak along Hardee's front, especially at a salient angle where Cheatham's two right brigades, Maney and Vaughan, joined. Losson describes,

---

[5] Fielder, *Civil War Diary*, 339; Christopher Losson, *Tennessee's Forgotten Warriors: Frank Cheatham and His Confederate Division* (Knoxville: University of Tennessee Press, 1989) 151.

[6] Losson, *Tennessee's Forgotten Warriors*, 152.

[7] Fielder, *Civil War Diary*, 339-40.

[8] Losson, *Tennessee's Forgotten Warriors*, 152.

[9] Maney, "Return of the Killed and Wounded...at the Battle of Kennesaw Mountain."

[10] Fielder, *Civil War Diary*, 341-42; Losson, *Tennessee's Forgotten Warriors*, 152.

[11] Maney, "Return of the Killed and Wounded...at the Battle of Kennesaw Mountain."

[12] Losson, *Tennessee's Forgotten Warriors*, 152.

Cheatham's position was vulnerable in large measure because of an angle along his line, where his right brigades under Vaughan and Maney linked. Vaughan's Brigade extended from the right of Cheatham's line, where it connected with Cleburne, to the angle, and faced to the northwest. Four companies of Maney's First and Twenty-seventh (Consolidated) Tennessee Regiment were aligned in the same direction as Vaughan's troops, but the remainder of his regiments faced to the southwest as the angle bent back to the left.[13]

Later this position would be known by the chilling sobriquet, the "Dead Angle."[14]

Of Vaughan's Brigade, the 13th/154th Tennessee (Vaughan's rightmost regiment) linked with Lucius Polk's Brigade of Cleburne's Division. Behind the 13th/154th rested two guns of Mebane's Tennessee Battery commanded by Lieutenant Luke E. Wright. Posted to the left of the 13th/154th Tennessee was the 12th/47th Tennessee. The 29th Tennessee was to the left of the 12th/47th, and the 11th Tennessee was to the left of the 29th Tennessee anchoring the left of Vaughan's Brigade.[15] To the left of the 11th, Maney's Brigade, commanded by Colonel Francis Walker, intersected with Vaughan's. The 1st/27th Tennessee rested just to the left of the 11th and took their place in the bend in the Confederate line.[16] While occupying this point, General Vaughan received orders that the safety of the army depended upon holding this position, and that it must be held if it required the sacrifice of every man in the brigade. Vaughan passed the order on to his men and received the unanimous response, "We will stay here."[17]

Across the valley, several Yankee batteries were posted on a high incline just to the southwest of the position held by the 11th Tennessee. To keep their line from being enfiladed, the Rebels dug sectional ditches and placed headlogs on the top of the trenches for added protection.[18] On 16 and 17 June, Captain W. J. Crook of the 13th Tennessee was on the picket line commanding the brigade skirmishers. Crook reported that he "was never subject to a heavier fire."[19] A soldier of Vaughan's Brigade wrote to a loved one back in Tennessee, "Continued and sharp skirmishing is kept up between the armies day and night. Many are killed and wounded on both

---

[13] Ibid., 153.

[14] W. D. Eleazer, "Fight at Dead Angle in Georgia," *Confederate Veteran* 14/7 (July 1906): 312.

[15] William E. Reynolds, Veteran Questionnaire, Tennessee Civil War Veterans Questionnaires, Tennessee State Library and Archives, Nashville, TN, 1922. MF 484, R7. Hereafter referred cited as TCWVQ.

[16] Losson, *Tennessee's Forgotten Warriors*, 156.

[17] Alfred Vaughan, ed., *Personal Record of the Thirteenth Regiment, Tennessee Infantry, C. S. A.* (1897; reprint, Memphis, TN: Frank and Gennie Myers and Burke's Book Store, 1976) 34.

[18] Reynolds, Veteran Questionnaire, TCWVQ, MF 484, R7.

[19] W. J. Crook to Hattie, 20 June 1864, W. J. Crook Papers, Reference: TN6, Kennesaw Mountain National Military Park, Kennesaw, GA.

sides but there's nothing of a decided character to either side gained it is a natural as well as needful result of the close proximity of the contending forces."[20] As the boys of the 11th sat in their trenches, minie balls passed over them making a lot of noise but doing little damage. On Saturday, 18 June, a heavy rain fell and continued through Tuesday, 21 June. The rain fell so hard that it made the roads almost impassable.[21] To compound the situation, fatigue gripped the troops. A captain in the brigade stated that he had "not slept in a house or tent in the last forty-five days."[22] The captain continued, "I have not slept with my over-clothing off but one night during the time and some of the nights have passed without me closing my eyes in sleep such toil and such vigilance I have never known before."[23]

As the days passed, the fighting between the skirmishers increased. On 21 June a hot firefight broke out between the pickets. One officer reported after the skirmishing that "several of our brigade were killed and wounded mostly from the 11th and 29th Tennessee regiments."[24] Private Martin F. Long of Company F was shot through the lungs and died two days later. Private John C. Crow of Company K suffered a severe fracture of the left leg. Private W. H. Stewart of Company K was dangerously wounded in the lower portion of the right thigh. Late that night, litter bearers brought Stewart to the surgeon in critical condition. The surgeons believed the private was in such a serious condition that amputation of the limb was necessary to prevent death. Dr. Maney performed the operation and hoped that Stewart would be able to remain at the field hospital. The young soldier's condition failed to improve, and he was evacuated to Atlanta two days after his surgery. Stewart died upon reaching Atlanta. Also on 21 June, Private R. C. Eubanks of Company E was slightly wounded in the left thigh. Private I. W. Powel of Company F received a "severe flesh wound" in the lower left thigh. Private William T. Jackson of Company E was shot in the lower right arm. Private B. J. Smith of Company C received "a contused wound" in the left side. Privates Steve Williams of Company E and Jordan Trotter of Company I were both "killed on the field."[25]

The following day at approximately 1:00 PM, the Federals assaulted the Confederate picket line and drove the pickets back. The Rebel pickets were reinforced, and a heavy skirmish involving both small arms and artillery ensued for some time. In this engagement, Sergeant Mark Gorman of Company B was wounded in the left knee.[26]

---

[20] Ibid.
[21] Fielder, *Civil War Diary*, 341-42; W. J. Crook to Hattie, 20 June 1864.
[22] W. J. Crook to Hattie, 20 June 1864.
[23] Ibid.
[24] Fielder, *Civil War Diary*, 342.
[25] Maney, "Return of the Killed and Wounded…at the Battle of Kennesaw Mountain."
[26] Ibid.

Later in the day, Major Philip Van Horn Weems wrote a somber note to his brothers back in Hickman County,

> Camp near Marietta, Georgia June 23, 1864
>
> …I am without clothes, money, or horses. I am now a major of my regiment and the position, if not pride, demands I should look as respectable as possible.… I have nearly recovered from my wound [the abdominal injury received at Missionary Ridge], so nearly I can undergo the most arduous fatigues. We have not been out of hearing of the guns for 40 days. Most of the time they shell us and are sharp shooting all the time.[27]

Weems closed his letter, "Goodbye my brothers, I hope to see you once again, but the daily risks I am under leaves me but little chance of hope. I have been favorably mentioned in headquarters reports. In fact, my qualifications are overestimated. I am on outpost duty in consequence."[28]

Back on the main line, construction on the entrenchments continued. The men dug deep sectional trenches, and threw up strong dirt embankments in front. On top of the embankments, the men secured headlogs, which allowed Vaughan's men to stand straight up in the trenches and fire through improvised gun ports between the embankment and the log without exposing themselves unnecessarily. In front of the breastworks, the boys felled trees, sharpened the limbs toward the enemy, and strategically placed *cheveaux-de-frise* or abatis to retard any advance of the enemy. Artillerymen placed their batteries in camouflaged strategic positions all along the line.[29]

As the sun rose on Monday morning, 27 June, so did the thermometer. After breakfast, as had become commonplace, many of the men in the main line arranged blankets across the support timbers of the entrenchments to provide some semblance of shade. While most of the men in the regiment remained in the works, a few of the boys topped the hill and went down to the wagons to wash clothes and to perform other duties.[30]

In the meantime, a strong detail from the 11th Tennessee was serving on the skirmish line. Among these were men from Companies A, B, and G.[31] Soon, the Federal batteries let loose, hammering Vaughan's line. Along with them the pickets opened up for a while, then the firing died away, and all became quiet. "It was but the dead calm that precedes the storm," stated one observer.[32] During the lull in the

---

[27] "Philip Van Horn Weems, C.S.A., Hero of the Confederacy, Killed at Atlanta Was Beloved Kinsman," *Weemsana* XXIX/1 (July 1983): 6.

[28] Ibid.

[29] Losson, *Tennessee's Forgotten Warriors*, 154.

[30] Sam Watkins, *Co. "Aytch" First Tennessee Regiment or a Side Show of the Big Show* (Franklin, TN: Providence House, 2007) 175.

[31] Maney, "Return of the Killed and Wounded…at the Battle of Kennesaw Mountain."

[32] Watkins, *Co. "Aytch,"* 173.

picket firing, the men of the 11th Tennessee could easily see the enemy forming for their attack on the crest of the hill across the valley. The "calm" did not last long, and the ominous "storm" approached. One soldier commented, "It seemed that the arch-angel of Death stood and looked on with outstretched wings, while all the earth was silent."[33] Then, between 10:00 and 11:00 AM, a heavy cannonading opened, pounding Vaughan's line. Solid shot and shrapnel bounced around, striking the headlogs and knocking dirt and rocks into the air. Not long after the Yankee artillery barrage begun, the Federals began their advance, once again driving toward the Confederate picket line.[34]

As the pageant unfolded, the Rebels removed their blankets from the support beams, and the men returned from their mundane duties in the rear to take their places in the breastworks. Across the way, bayonets glistened in the sunlight and flags fluttered as Federal units of McCook's and Harker's brigades marched down the hill and formed a line of battle in the valley opposite the "Angle" and the 11th Tennessee. The 85th Illinois deployed as skirmishers for McCook's Brigade and were supported by the 125th Illinois, 86 Illinois, 22nd Indiana, and 52nd Ohio.[35] To McCook's left, the 125th Ohio were deployed as skirmishers in front of Harker's Brigade with the 51st Illinois, 3rd Kentucky, 27th Illinois, 65th Ohio, 64th Ohio, 79th Illinois, and 42nd Illinois in column behind them.[36] The advancing Federals quickly reached the Confederate skirmish line where portions of Companies A, B, and G of the 11th Tennessee, in the face of overwhelming odds, abandoned their position and raced to the protection of the main line. Not all of the men on the skirmish line were able to escape. Captain James G. Stephens, Sergeant John J. Flynn, Private John Glenn of Company G, and Private William S. Holland of Company A hesitated too long and were captured.[37]

After overrunning the pickets, the Federals continued toward the main Confederate line. As the Yankees attacked the Confederate works, a savage slaughter took place in front of this hinge in Cheatham's alignment, which has since been known as the "Dead Angle." "[The] Dead Angle, which was known as the 'Devil's Elbow,' was a sharp turn in the main line where the Yankees shot at us from

---

[33] Ibid.

[34] Ibid.

[35] United States War Department, *The War of the Rebellion: A Compilation of the Official Records of the Union and Confederate Armies*. 70 vols. in 128 (Washington: Government Printing Office, 1880–1901; reprint, Gettysburg PA: The National Historical Society, 1972) ser. I, vol. 38, pt. 1, 718, 721, 724, 727, 729. Hereafter cited as *OR*.

[36] Ibid., 361, 363, 364, 365.

[37] James G. Stevens, M 268 R162; John J. Flynn, M 268 R160; John Glenn, M 268 R160; William S. Holland, M 268 R160, all from 11th Tennessee Infantry Service Records, National Archives Records Administration, *Compiled Service Records of Confederate Soldiers Who Served in Organizations from the State of Tennessee*, Washington, DC: National Archives and Records Service, General Services Administration, 1960. Hereafter cited as 11th TISR.

three directions, but we killed ten of them to where we lost one," stated Zachary Heath of the 13th Tennessee.[38] Lieutenant W. D. Eleazer of Company E stated that the enemy made the assault with "five lines of battle in close column, and charged with blind determination up to the foot of our works."[39]

As the Federal troops advanced up the slope, a dense abatis in front of the Confederate works slowed their advance. As the Yankees struggled to get through the obstacles, the 1st/27th Tennessee Infantry of Maney's Brigade and the 11th Tennessee Infantry of Vaughan's Brigade unleashed a withering fire on the assaulting Federal columns. Colonel Gordon described the ensuing battle, "The Eleventh was one of the regiments that occupied the 'Dead Angle,' near Kennesaw Mountain, when this salient in our line was so gallantly charged by the enemy with a column of three or four lines, one brigade front, June 27th, 1864."[40]

Anxiety gripped the Rebels in the "Angle" as they watched the oncoming Federal masses but they were ordered to reserve their fire until the Yankees were within about sixty yards of the main line. Closer and closer the sea of blue came toward the waiting nervous defenders in the works. As they neared the abatis, one obstinate Yankee officer turned his back toward the Confederates to give some final instructions to his unit. As he faced his men, encouraging them to great acts of heroism, Cheatham's stalwart veterans screamed a cry of defiance as they unleashed a thundering volley into the very faces of the relentless attackers. The brave Yankee commander was cut down in mid-sentence along with over half of his men. This initial volley mowed down most of the Yankees in the front. The survivors turned to flee but were fronted by the subsequent oncoming waves of their comrades.[41]

Despite the confusion that followed the volley, the assaulting masses regained some semblance of order and continued toward the works as Vaughan's Tennesseans reloaded. The assaulting masses advanced until they reached the abatis that retarded their progress. Colonel Gordon recalled, "In this charge the first line of the enemy came with guns uncapped, to take us with the bayonet; but when it reached our dense abatis, extending thirty yards in front of our line, well fortified and provided with head-logs, they halted and staggered with considerable confusion."[42] While the Federals struggled to clear the obstacles, the boys of the 11th Tennessee poured a devastating fire into them, tearing huge holes in their lines. Colonel Gordon commented, "Their other lines closed up on their first, and

---

[38] Mamie Yeary, *Reminiscences of the Boys in Gray, 1861–1865* (1912; reprint, Dayton, OH: Morningside, 1986) 323.

[39] Eleazer, "Fight at Dead Angle," 312.

[40] John Berrien Lindsley, *Military Annals of Tennessee: Confederate* (1886; facsimile of the first edition, Wilmington, NC: Broadfoot Publishing, 1995) 299.

[41] Losson, *Tennessee's Forgotten Warriors*, 155.

[42] Lindsley, *Military Annals*, 299.

in this condition we swept them down with great slaughter...."[43] Regardless of the massacre that was occurring, the Federals persistently came on. Federal valor this day would only be surpassed by the assault of the Army of Tennessee on the Federal works at Franklin, Tennessee, four months later. Sam Watkins of the 1st/27th Tennessee, positioned just to the left of the 11th, described the ferocity of the battle:

> My pen is unable to describe the scene of carnage and death that ensued in the next two hours. Column after column of Federal soldiers were crowded upon that line.... Yet still the Yankees came. It seemed impossible to check the onslaught, but every man was true to his trust, and seemed to think that at that moment the whole responsibility of the Confederate government rest on his shoulders.
>
> The sun beaming down on our uncovered heads, the thermometer being one hundred and ten degrees in the shade, and a solid line of blazing fire right from the muzzles of the Yankee guns being poured right into our very faces, singeing our hair and clothes, the hot blood of our dead and wounded spurting on us, the blinding smoke and stifling atmosphere filling our eyes and mouths, and the awful concussion causing the blood to gush out of our noses and ears, and above all, the roar of battle, made it a perfect pandemonium.[44]

Still the Yankees advanced, and Cheatham finally ordered his masked batteries to open fire. The Rebel gunners now joined the infantry in the deadly task of defending the hill. The Confederate fire was now terrible, and it eviscerated the oncoming lines with the devastating effects of canister, grape, and musketry. Section blasts from canister ripped huge holes in the Federal lines with savage ferocity. The Southern infantrymen fired so rapidly that the barrels of their rifles became overheated. One soldier in the angle reported that his gun frequently became so hot that he had to exchange it for the gun of a dead comrade. Opposite the angle, one desperate Federal of the 3rd Kentucky recalled, "The concussion from the enemy's cannon [facing Smith's Battery] nearly unjointed my neck and the heat from them burnt my face."[45] Fronting Vaughan, losses were particularly high in McCook's Brigade. Losson writes,

> Two Ohio regiments lost half their force, and one of these lost 153 men in twenty minutes. McCook, himself, was mortally wounded near the Confederate works, and the colonel who replaced him was killed five minutes later by a shot through the heart. The lead ranks of the assaulting party melted away as the Tennesseans continued their withering fire. One of McCook's Illinois regiments had nearly 60

---

[43] Ibid.
[44] Watkins, *Co. "Aytch,"* 175.
[45] John W. Tuttle, diary, Kennesaw Mountain National Battlefield, Reference: KY-1, 18-19.

men killed within a few moments, and the officer contingent of several Federal units was nearly extinguished.⁴⁶

Somehow, despite the maelstrom unleashed by Vaughan's and Maney's Tennesseans, some of the Federals still managed to break through the abatis and scale the parapet of the Confederate trenches. Here savage hand-to-hand fighting broke out. Confederates swung clubbed muskets as the Yankees lunged at them with bayonets. One Reb in the angle recalled that the men on both sides threw rocks and beat each other in the faces with sticks. Sam Watkins of the 1st/27th Tennessee said, "The rocks came in upon us like a perfect hail storm, and the Yankees seemed very obstinate, and in no hurry to get away from our front, and we had to keep up the firing and shooting them down in self-defense. They seemed to walk up and take death as cooly as if they were automatic or wooden men...."⁴⁷ To the right of the 11th, one intrepid Yankee color-bearer neared Vaughan's works and lost his regiment's colors to Sergeant W. J. Woltz of the 29th Tennessee.⁴⁸

As the face-to-face fighting dwindled away, the boys of the 11th resumed firing into the oncoming bluecoats, who were now struggling to climb over their own dead to reach the Rebel line. Musketry rattled and artillery jarred the ground with each deafening discharge of the guns. By this time, most of the Yankees realized the utter futility of continuing to try to take the Confederate works. Many of the Federals attempted to find any type of cover possible. Some vainly attempted to hide behind trees while others flattened themselves on the ground under the crest. Still, Vaughan's men played on them with horrible effect.⁴⁹ The Federals were pinned down. One officer of the 98th Ohio who was suppressed in front of the 11th Tennessee recalled that it was certain "death to take your face out of the dust."⁵⁰

Soon the Federal attack was over. The boys of the 11th looked through the gun ports of their trench and were completely awestruck by the carnage that lay on the field just a few feet in front of them. Sam Watkins said that he later learned that "in some places they were piled up like cord wood, twelve deep."⁵¹ Colonel Gordon recalled seeing eleven bodies piled around one large tree.⁵² Watkins commented that he thought the only reason the Yankees did not take the Rebel line was their inability to climb over the bodies of their dead.⁵³ Colonel Henry B. Banning of the 121st Ohio Infantry, after having 144 of his brave men lost at the angle later wrote,

---

⁴⁶ Losson, *Tennessee's Forgotten Warriors*, 157.
⁴⁷ Watkins, *Co. "Aytch,"* 176.
⁴⁸ Chattanooga (TN) *Daily Rebel*, 28–29 June 1864; Memphis (TN) *Daily Appeal*, 1 July 1864.
⁴⁹ Lindsley, *Military Annals*, 299.
⁵⁰ *OR*, ser. I, vol. 38, pt. 1, 693.
⁵¹ Watkins, *Co. "Aytch,"* 175.
⁵² Lindsley, *Military Annals*, 299.
⁵³ Watkins, *Co. "Aytch,"* 175.

"We fought the flower of the Southern army, being Cheatham's Division, of Hardee's Corps."[54] Private Reynolds of Company C stated, "The battle only lasted a very short while but the enemy was so crippled and confused as to not be able to get away from under the crest of the hill, so they entrenched in this situation."[55]

Tuesday, 28 June, opened clear and warm. Sharpshooting commenced along the line. At about 9:00 AM, the Federals began a crossfire with artillery on the exposed Confederate position. The incessant Yankee banging did little if any damage. Late in the evening, Vaughan ordered his colonels to keep one-third of their men on watch at all time, but the night passed without incident.[56]

The following day, the sun continued to bake the unburied bodies of the dead that lay before the Dead Angle. A soldier of the 9th Tennessee positioned down the line to the left from the 11th stated, "I don't suppose those of us in the ditches the next day after the battle will every forget the scent arising from the decomposed bodies."[57] On the 29th, both sides agreed to a truce from 9:00 AM to 4:00 PM to allow the Federals to bury their dead. Unarmed guards from each side were stationed facing toward the battlefield to prevent the passing of anyone except the burial parties. When the cease-fire was called, William E. Reynolds of Company C was placed as a guard on the battlefield. Reynolds stated that he saw "men in piles, three and four deep, in a space not over twenty or thirty yards wide and less than one hundred yards long. I was informed that there were a thousand dead Yankees removed from this little spot."[58] Approximately 415 dead Federal soldiers were removed from Vaughan's front alone. Soldiers removed another 385 dead Federals from the front of Maney's Brigade, just to the left of Vaughan.[59] Regardless of the sentries, many of the soldiers from both sides met each other and exchanged tobacco, newspapers, and coffee.[60]

After the truce, the killing resumed. Private James M. Larkins of Company E was shot through the stomach and bowels. He died at 10:00 the following morning.[61] The Federals, who were pinned under the crest with no chance of escape, began digging a tunnel under the Confederate works at the angle. Reynolds stated,

---

[54] *OR*, ser. I, vol. 38, pt. 1, 704.

[55] Reynolds, Veteran Questionnaire, TCWVQ, MF 484, R7.

[56] Fielder, *Civil War Diary*, 344.

[57] John Holland Bittick, "Veteran Questionnaire," in Dyer et al., *Tennessee Civil War Veterans Questionnaires*, 1:323.

[58] Reynolds, Veteran Questionnaire, TCWVQ, MF 484, R7.

[59] Edwin L. Drake, ed., *The Annals of the Army of Tennessee and Early Western History* (Nashville, TN: A. D. Haynes, 1878) 116.

[60] Bittick, "Veteran Questionnaire," in Dyer et al., *Tennessee Civil War Veterans Questionnaires*, 1:323.

[61] Maney, "Return of the Killed and Wounded…at the Battle of Kennesaw Mountain."

At this place they went to digging a tunnel under us. The distance having been measured by one of their soldiers, who tied a string to his foot, jumped over their works, threw up his hands and asked to be surrendered. He came upon our works, which was only thirty or forty feet apart, placed his foot on the string and broke it, and his command hauled it in...We could hear them digging and the supposition was, they aimed to blow up our line on the fourth of July.[62]

As the lines lay deadlocked, men from either side were afraid to move. "Our line diverged to nearly a triangle, so close that we could not have a guard out from the point to our company about one hundred yards, our company placed one man just outside of our line so he could see over the crest of the hill, and only remained there during the night," stated Private Reynolds of Company C.[63] At about 2:30 AM on 30 June, the pickets of the 11th came in from outside the works and reported that the enemy was coming. Federal officers could be heard in the night giving orders. Reynolds continued, "This excited a belief with our men that the enemy was making ready to charge us, so shooting commenced at this close point and extended for a hundred yards up the line."[64] The firestorm lasted about thirty minutes then died down because it was thought it was a false attack. Brigadier General Cantey's men, who had been engaged in the "Lightning Bug Battle" at New Hope Church, were always looking for a chance to get even with Cheatham's men for their constant harassing. When Cantey's men thought that Cheatham's boys had been spooked into a false attack, they could not let the opportunity for retribution pass. One Alabamian wrote in an article to the *Chattanooga Daily Rebel* that they would "divide ink" with Cheatham's Division.[65]

A few days later, General Joseph E. Johnston in the company of Generals Hardee and Cheatham rode up to the angle. General Johnston told the boys that he would furnish the ammunition to shoot at the lightening bugs as long as we would do as good execution.[66] The attack had not been false. The Federals had actually made an unsuccessful attempt to relieve their men who were pinned down under the crest. From this point on, "below and all the way to the angle, was protected by turpentine balls and casting them over between the lines that we might see any movement of the enemy."[67]

At Kennesaw Mountain, Sherman handed Johnston the clearest victory of the Atlanta Campaign. Soon, Sherman resorted to his old tactics and outflanked the Kennesaw line, forcing Johnston to fall back across the Chattahoochee River and to prepare to defend the key city of Atlanta. As the Army of Tennessee withdrew, the

---

[62] Reynolds, Veteran Questionnaire, TCWVQ, MF 484, R7.
[63] Ibid.
[64] Ibid.
[65] Eleazer, "Fight at Dead Angle," 312.
[66] Ibid., 312.
[67] Reynolds, Veteran Questionnaire, TCWVQ, MF 484, R7.

11th Tennessee Infantry was assigned to cover the retreat of the army from that position.[68]

At about 10:00 PM on 2 July, Vaughan ordered all of his regiments into line and moved them out of their trenches at the "Dead Angle" except the 11th Tennessee. Vaughan left the 11th Tennessee in the works to screen their movement. As the remainder of Vaughan's men moved out, Gordon's boys set fire to turpentine balls, threw them out toward the enemy's line, and began firing their weapons to cover the withdrawal of the brigade. Within a few hours, the 11th abandoned their position as well and started south toward Marietta to rejoin the brigade. After marching all night, the regiment had moved about nine miles from their fortifications at the "angle." By early morning, Gordon halted his column and allowed his exhausted men to stack arms and get some rest.[69]

---

[68] Ibid.
[69] Fielder, *Civil War Diary*, 345-46.

13

"In Their Fall the Regiment Suffered Great Loss"

July 1864

Just before sunrise on Monday, 4 July, the 11th Tennessee with Cheatham's Division deployed in a line of battle and moved toward the front, taking their place to the west of Vining Station, just below Marietta. The boys of the 11th took their position, forming a reserve line behind an artillery battery. Once in place, the men began throwing up a series of breastworks. As the day wore on, the sun beat down on Gordon's men in what Vaughan referred to as "one of the hottest days of the season."[1] Throughout the morning, General Vaughan and his staff had directed the construction of the breastworks. Sometime between 12:00 and 1:00 PM, the general and his cohort made their way about 150 yards to the rear where they sat down under the shade of a "large spreading oak tree" and began eating their scanty rations.[2]

Throughout the morning, the artillery of both sides fired at each other, and occasionally the infantrymen would take a shot at an enemy soldier who came into view. While Vaughan and his staff ate, Sam Watkins, a private in the 1st/27th Tennessee, was standing on the breastworks leveling off a section with a spade. As Watkins worked, a Yankee sharpshooter fired at him. The bullet missed him, but struck William A. Graham of the same regiment in the chest.[3] In the meantime, back behind the lines, General Vaughan decided to smoke his pipe. Due to a scarcity of matches, he took out a sunglass to light his tobacco. Lieutenant Colonel Beverly Dyer, Vaughan's inspector general, bet the general a drink of pine-top whiskey that he would not be able to light his pipe with the sunglass. Vaughan accepted the wager and found a place under the oak tree where the sun was shining through the dense foliage and proceeded to focus the sun's ray on his tobacco. Just as Vaughan drew the sunlight onto the tobacco, a Federal shell screamed into the air, arched over the line of the 11th Tennessee, and headed to the rear. Vaughan, unaware of the impending danger, continued lighting his pipe as the Federal shell came down on top of him. The shell detonated, tearing off Vaughan's foot and

---

[1] Alfred Vaughan, ed., *Personal Record of the Thirteenth Regiment, Tennessee Infantry, C. S. A.* (1897; reprint, Memphis, TN: Frank and Gennie Myers and Burke's Book Store, 1976) 85.

[2] Ibid.

[3] Sam Watkins, *Co. "Aytch" First Tennessee Regiment or a Side Show of the Big Show* (Franklin, TN: Providence House, 2007) 184.

leaving a huge crater in the dirt. Lieutenant Colonel Dyer, who was standing over the general's shoulder, received seventeen flesh wounds and had almost all of his clothing torn off. General Vaughan later recalled, "The shock from the explosion of the shell was very severe, yet the tearing away of my leg was accompanied by neither pain nor the loss of much blood."[4] As those nearby rushed to aid the general, they discovered a cut on Vaughan's other leg about four inches long and down to the bone. Surprisingly, the shell blast tore neither his pants nor underclothing in the location of the wound. As attendants hurried to take the general to the field hospital, he refused to move until they recovered his pipe and sunglass.[5] Once at the field hospital, Vaughan's wound was dressed by Drs. Godwin, Mauzy, and Kidden of Wright's Brigade.[6] After his wound was dressed he was sent south to another hospital.

Within a half hour, the commotion subsided, and about that time officers called Vaughan and Maney's brigades to attention and marched them quickly two to three miles to the left. There they formed a line of battle and threw forward skirmishers in preparation for an attack.[7]

At daybreak the following day, commanders relocated Vaughan's Brigade further to the left. After marching the distance of seven or eight miles in the scorching July sun, the 11th Tennessee arrived on the bank of the Chattahoochee River and many of the men jumped into the water to bathe and swim. As night fell the regiment remained in reserve as Federal artillery boomed and picket firing occurred off in the distance.[8]

At 7:00 the next morning, the boys moved to the right, where they took their place in the main line. The line at this point consisted of very strong, well-prepared entrenchments, which "negroes" had erected under the supervision of Southern engineers. Throughout the day and into the next, sharp firing occurred between the pickets. At about 1:00 AM, 8 July, Vaughan's men were relieved of outpost duty by Tyler's Brigade. The 11th Tennessee retired to the rear where officers allowed the boys to go swimming again in the Chattahoochee River. At about 6:00 that evening, the regiment formed and moved with the brigade across pontoon bridges that engineers had extended across the river. The regiment crossed the Chattahoochee and marched another six miles or so toward the southwest where they stayed the rest of the night.[9]

---

[4] Vaughan, *Personal Record of the Thirteenth Regiment*, 87.
[5] Ibid., 86–87.
[6] *Chattanooga Daily Rebel* (Griffin GA), 9 July 1864.
[7] A. T. Fielder, *Captain A. T. Fielder's Civil War Diary Company B, 12th Tennessee Infantry C. S. A. July 1861–June 1865*, ed. M. Todd Cathey (Broken Arrow, OK: Create Space, 2012) 346.
[8] Ibid., 346–47.
[9] Ibid., 347–48.

On 9 July, General Johnston again withdrew the Army of Tennessee. The 11th took its place in line at daylight and countermarched to a position on the south side of the river near its position of the previous day. The men lay around throughout the day until they were called into line later that evening. The boys began a march to the south, taking a road toward Atlanta. Soon the column came to the railroad and took the road west toward Powder Springs. After marching about two miles down this road, the column halted and the boys camped for the night.[10]

Reports dated 10 July showed Vaughan's Brigade was temporarily commanded by Colonel Michael Magevney Jr. and was made up of the 11th Tennessee, commanded by Colonel Gordon; the 12th/47th Tennessee Consolidated, commanded by Colonel William M. Watkins; the 29th Tennessee, commanded by Colonel Horace Rice; and the 13th/154th Tennessee Consolidated, commanded by Major William J. Crook.[11]

On 14 July, Private Joseph W. Jackson of Company F, the former railroad pumper for the Kentucky and Edgefield Railroad in Robertson County, wrote his parents back home in Cedar Hill.

> July 14, 1864
> Dear Parents,
> I thank God that I have the privilege of seating myself this sultry July evening to drop you a few lines. I wrote you on the 17th and 22nd of June last, and also another, 23rd of May, and this will make the third letter that I have started since we left Dalton, Ga., and I have written near a dozen since Christmas, but I fear you have not received them. Since my last, we have received the mournful intelligence of the death of two of our comrades and friends, Mr. M. F. Long and Wily Powell. They were wounded on the 21st whilst we were on skirmish, and Mart, who was wounded in the breast, died on the 23rd of June. He was perfectly resigned, and died in the faith, whilst Wily Powell died on the 26th in Atlanta. G. J. Morris died on the 14th; he died in Macon from the effects of measles.
>
> Since we left Dalton we have lost five men, three dead, two captured; John W. Winn and George Allen. We have three at the hospital: Wes Winn, Hiram Morgan, and Ben Jordan. We have had but three slightly wounded; John Batts, Sam Baldwin, and myself. I was slightly wounded in the head, but it disabled me but two or three days, and I do thank God that he has been with and protected me on this severe, bloody and protracted campaign.
>
> On the 27th of June the enemy, as you have learned through northern channels, made an unsuccessful attempt to carry our works by assault in front of our division (Cheatham). He came and some say 7 and others say 4 lines of battle; the enemy approached within a very few steps of our works and our boys mowed them

---

[10] Ibid., 348.

[11] United States War Department, *The War of the Rebellion: A Compilation of the Official Records of the Union and Confederate Armies*. 70 vols. in 128 (Washington: Government Printing Office, 1880–1901; reprint, Gettysburg, PA: The National Historical Society, 1972) ser. I, vol. 38, pt. 3, 654. Hereafter cited as *OR*.

down by hundreds. They were literally piled upon one another on the left of our brigade, and right of Nancy Creek on a field of ground of but one or two acres, there were from seven hundred to one thousand dead Yankees. They lay there for two days and were becoming very offensive when we got up an armistice and they were buried. But I suppose, dear parents, you are growing tired of such as this, but I must, before I quit speaking of our army, say something of our boys, and something of the condition of our army. We are all still in the finest of spirits, and place the greatest confidence in the scar worn veteran that leads us in all our march from Dalton to this place. I have heard nothing of a disparing character, and all say and believe that the time is coming when we will send Sherman and his vandals howling back to their cold and passionateless home in the north. We may have to fall back beyond Atlanta. If we do, I think it will be for the best and if they should succeed in defeating our armies, if we survive then, we may have to and will eventually gain our independence and as for the campaign in Virginia, I think that it is in a manner closed, and the illustrious Ulysses has suffered a more signal defeat than any of his predecessors. But before this reaches you, something I think will be done, and I pray God, if it is consistent with His Holy will, be with us and sustain us in this, our time of need, and this is the prayer of this whole contingent. I never saw a people so humble. We have preaching in our brigade where we are still daily.

Dear parents, I heard of the sad end of our neighbor, Robert Gossett, who, as the Yankee paper said, was hung on the 9th of the month at Nashville, on the charge of bushwacking. I feel for his father, and mother and sisters.

I suppose, dear Papa, you have laid by your crop before this, and from all accounts, you have had a good season, and of course you have a good crop. I was glad to hear of your going to farming, for it is the most sure of all occupations and of late it has proven to be the most profitable. The next letter you write, I want you to tell me how you are getting on with your stock, bees, etc., tell me how you are getting on generally, and dear Mother, I want you to tell me all about the garden, cows, chickens, etc., and I want you to write every opportunity without fail.

Well, as it is growing late, I must also give my love to all my relatives, to my dear grandparents, and uncles and aunts, cousins and friends. I want you to remember me in all your prayers, and I feel that we will meet again on earth; if not, we will meet in heaven, where there will be no more parting, as was. Kiss all my brothers and sisters, and tell them not to forget their brother Joe. I must close. No more, but remain, every your affectionate son.

J. W. Jackson[12]

These were the last words the Jacksons ever received from their son. Joe Jackson would die eight days later assaulting the Federal positions on Bald (Leggett's) Hill in the 22 July fighting at Atlanta.[13]

---

[12] J. W. Jackson to parents, 4 July 1864, Martha Farmer Anthony Collection, Box 1, Tennessee State Library and Archives, Nashville, TN.

[13] William B. Maney, "Return of the Killed and Wounded in the 11th Tennessee Regiment at the Battle of Atlanta, Georgia, 22 July 1864," *Regimental Surgeon's Log*,

Sherman followed Johnston across the Chattahoochee, and for the next several days, both armies prepared for battle. On 17 July, news perceived as tragic by the Tennesseans arrived in camp. Joe Johnston had been relieved of command, and Richmond authorities promoted John Bell Hood in his place as commander of the Army of Tennessee. Jefferson Davis, a long-time rival of Johnston, was dissatisfied with the general for not making a northward offensive and for giving up so much ground. According to one soldier of the brigade, "Johnston was the most popular general that was ever in command of this department and his removal gives great dissatisfaction among the army all appear to be sorry to part with him."[14]

Richmond wanted a fighter, and a fighter they got. Hood was certainly not afraid to expend his precious troops assaulting the positions of the enemy. Morale among the Tennesseans plummeted, as they were aware of the incredible casualty rates incurred by troops under Hood's command earlier in the war. At Antietam, for example, Hood's 1st Texas regiment lost 82 percent of their men, believed to be the highest of any regiment in the entire war, North or South.[15] Van Buren Oldham, a member of the 9th Tennessee stated his opinion on the matter:

> Whatever Johnston has done to deserve such treatment by the Dep[artment] is left a secret. He alludes to nothing that would enlighten us in his farewell address. We feel (and it is the common feeling of the army that he has been the object of gross injustices) that Gen[eral] Bragg and Pres[ident] Davis are alone responsible for the evil which is likely to result.... A battle is expected tomorrow or next day. Gen[eral] Hood will probably teach the army other tactics than fortifying.[16]

Hood's promotion to army command necessitated some changes for the Tennesseans. Hood temporarily assigned command of his former corps to General Cheatham on 19 July, a position that Cheatham reluctantly accepted. General George Maney, the original captain of the Beauregard Light Infantry, now one of Cheatham's Brigade commanders, temporarily took command of Cheatham's Division.[17]

That same day at 7:00 AM, the regiments were assembled and marched by "the rights of companies to the front some 400 yds. and formed line of battle on the line marked out by our engineer corps."[18] Cheatham's Division took their place in line to the left of Walker's Georgians. As was now commonplace, the troops immediately

---

Confederate Collection, Manuscript Section, Box 18, Military Units Tenn. Inf. Regt. 11, Medical Records, Tennessee State Library and Archives, Nashville, TN.

[14] Fielder, *Civil War Diary*, 350.
[15] *OR*, ser. I, vol. 19, pt. 1, 933.
[16] Civil War Diaries of Van Buren Oldham, 18 July 1864, Special Collections, University of Tennessee at Martin, ed. Dieter Ullrich, http://www.utm.edu/departments/special_collections/E579.5%20Oldham/text/vboldham_indx.php (1 March 2015).
[17] *OR*, ser. I, vol. 38, pt. 3, 663, 661.
[18] Fielder, *Civil War Diary*, 350-51.

began digging defensive fortifications. Before long however, the boys moved about 400 yards to the left. When they arrived at this position, they resumed digging entrenchments.[19]

After Sherman had crossed the Chattahoochee, he moved his army to the southeast, along the northern edge of Atlanta. According to Cheatham's Division historian Craig Losson, Sherman's purpose was to cut the Georgia Railroad, a line providing access to Virginia and the Carolinas through Decatur.[20]

By this time, Hood deployed the Army of Tennessee about a mile south of Peachtree Creek through heavily wooded high ground. Colonel Michael Magevney, a former schoolteacher in Ireland who immigrated to Memphis in 1854 and rose to command the 154th Tennessee, now commanded Vaughan's Brigade.[21] Magevney's men took their place on the left of Cheatham's Division, which Maney was commanding. The thirty-three-year-old Hood, whose left arm hung useless from a wound at Gettysburg and whose right leg had been amputated due to a wound at Chickamauga, wasted no time in attacking Sherman, whose legions were divided. George H. Thomas, "The Rock of Chickamauga," commanding the Army of the Cumberland, had his men spread out over a six-mile front. Moreover, he was separated from John McAllister Schofield, commanding the Army of the Ohio, by more than two miles. With Sherman's troops divided and spread out, Hood prepared for the offensive using the same plan to attack Sherman along Peachtree Creek that Johnston had devised.[22]

On Wednesday, 20 July, after a meeting with his corps commanders, Hood moved his men out of their works to attack the Federal forces. Cheatham, commanding Hood's former corps, was to move to the right of the army to scout out a good defensive position that would block Schofield and McPherson from coming to Thomas's aid. Hardee's men, in the center of the Confederate line, were to attack Thomas. Hardee was to engage with his right and then subsequently commit his other brigades, rolling the battle to the left. When Hardee was fully engaged, A. P. Stewart's corps (positioned to Hardee's left) was to join him in destroying Thomas's Army of the Cumberland.[23]

In Hardee's Corps, Magevney's troops were on the right of Maney's line. Before the battle could commence, however, a number of complications arose. Confederate cavalry advancing down the Georgia Railroad at a rapid pace observed

---

[19] Ibid.

[20] Christopher Losson, *Tennessee's Forgotten Warriors: Frank Cheatham and His Confederate Division* (Knoxville: University of Tennessee Press, 1989) 174.

[21] Damian Shiels, "Irish Colonels: Michael Magevney, Jr., 154th Tennessee Infantry," *Irish in the Civil War*, http://irishamericancivilwar.com/2011/03/21/irish-colonels-michael-magevney-jr-154th-tennessee-infantry/ (March 2011; accessed 1 March 2015).

[22] Thomas Lawrence Connelly, *Autumn of Glory: The Army of Tennessee 1862–1865* (Baton Rouge: Louisiana State University Press, 1971) 439.

[23] Ibid., 440.

McPherson. Hood ordered Cheatham to extend his line one division length to the right to block the railroad. Likewise, Hardee and Stewart were to move their corps half of a division length to the right to keep the line connected.[24] That morning, the 11th Tennessee, with the brigade assembled, marched to the right about a mile to make the necessary adjustments in their alignment. Each delay that occurred rendered the plan less likely to succeed. As 2:00 PM approached, the regiments under Magevney's command moved forward in line of battle and in conjunction with Wright's Brigade composing the front line. The brigades of Maney (Carter) and Strahl followed in support. The 11th Tennessee moved forward some distance and halted. Following orders, the men loaded their weapons. When this was complete, skirmishers deployed to the front. When all was ready, the regiment with the Rebel line continued to advance.[25] According to a member of Company C, the 11th Tennessee "charged down a long slope, crossed a little branch or creek and continued up an incline for about thirty or forty yards."[26] At the top of the rise, the regiment came face to face with the enemy's concealed breastworks. The breastworks were "completely covered up with leaves, we could not see them, and so well protected by every available addition, it was impossible to break their lines."[27] As the 11th Tennessee advanced on the works, casualties began to mount with Company C taking the highest losses of the regiment as it moved forward. Lieutenant N. B. Dickson was shot through the right hand, and Corporal John Dickson was shot in the back. Sergeant William T. Weakley was dangerously wounded in the neck, and Private C. L. Hayes was shot in the right shoulder. Company H was hit hard as Privates Alfred B. Darden was shot in the left shoulder, John Southerland was hit in the groin. G. W. Martin received a slight wound in the left side, and Armistead W. Martin was missing in action. As Captain Isaac P. Young led Company I forward, he was hit in the scalp. Privates Cullen French, John Rushing, and J. H. Webb were wounded as well. In Company F, William Roland was shot in the head and died the following day. W. J. Newton also of Company F was killed on the field, and Fred Morgan was missing in action.[28]

The inability of the regiment to break the Federal line at this point left the men with but three choices: "surrender, retreat five hundred to a thousand yards under heavy gunfire or lay down in this little stream, until the cover of night,"

---

[24] Losson, *Tennessee's Forgotten Warriors*, 174.

[25] Fielder, *Civil War Diary*, 351-52.

[26] William E. Reynolds, Veteran Questionnaire, Tennessee Civil War Veterans Questionnaires, Tennessee State Library and Archives, Nashville, TN, 1922. MF 484, R7. Hereafter referred cited as TCWVQ.

[27] Ibid.

[28] Maney, "Return of the Killed and Wounded…at the Battle of Atlanta."

explained Private Reynolds.²⁹ Reynolds and his comrades chose the latter and lay down in the stream. The 11th Tennessee remained pinned down in the creek by heavy fire. For five hours, the men of the regiment "lay in this water while it ran red with comrades' blood."³⁰ Private Reynolds further described the situation,

> To remain in such a position for four or five hours and dare to raise the head so much as a foot and a half, seemed to be days. One poor fellow, James McClennan [McClelland], laying by my side was suffering from rheumatism took chances to change his position, raised his head not exceeding one and a half foot, received a bullet well aimed that instantly ended his life. At last the hour arrived when we could stealthily extricate ourselves.³¹

Sometime around 10:00 PM, the brigade under the cover of darkness retired back into their works. In all, the 11th Tennessee suffered 2 killed, 3 missing in action, and 23 wounded in fighting at Peachtree Creek on 20 July.³²

Later that night, at about 4:00 AM, the boys were aroused after only a few hours of sleep. The regiment, with the remainder of Hardee's Corps, was ordered on a fifteen-mile night march from their works along Peachtree Creek. The men trudged through downtown Atlanta and then turned northeast on Fayetteville Road. The troops marched along dusty roads all night with empty canteens. As the sun rose, the day grew increasingly warm. Many of the men suffered greatly due to heat and exhaustion. By noon, Hardee's men had reached their destination.³³

In the meantime, while Hardee's Corps was on the march, Major General James B. McPherson moved his Federal Army of the Tennessee westward from Decatur, Georgia, and reached the outskirts of Atlanta. The next night, at 2:00 AM, the 11th Tennessee assembled and marched out with the brigade to the left then proceeded southward down the road toward Macon. After marching down this road for seven to eight miles, the boys followed the road to Decatur for approximately two more miles. The column filed past General Hardee and was ordered to rest for ten to fifteen minutes. After a short break, the boys were called to attention and were placed to the left of Cleburne's Division.³⁴

On Friday, 22 July, at about 12:15 PM, the Battle of Atlanta opened as Major General William Bate's division launched an attack against the Federal left. At 12:45 PM, Cleburne's Division moved forward and began its attack. With Maney's (Cheatham's) division in support, Cleburne advanced toward the left flank of Giles Smith's Federal division, which was entrenched along the Flat Shoals Road near Bald (Leggett's) Hill. Cleburne's Division struck Smith with such force that it drove

---

²⁹ Reynolds, Veteran Questionnaire, TCWVQ, MF 484, R7.
³⁰ Ibid.
³¹ Ibid.
³² Maney, "Return of the Killed and Wounded…at the Battle of Atlanta."
³³ Fielder, *Civil War Diary*, 352-54.
³⁴ Ibid.

the entire Federal division north to Bald Hill and reached further success when they captured eight guns of the 2nd Illinois and 2nd US Light Artillery, the entire 16th Iowa Infantry regiment, and forced Morrill's Brigade, the right of Dodge's XVI Corps to fall back to the north. At approximately 2:00 PM, Federal Major General James B. McPherson passed in front of one of Cleburne's units and was killed. Major General John A. Logan assumed command of the Federal Army of the Tennessee.[35]

At 3:00 PM, Maney moved from Cleburne's support to make an attack of his own against the Federals on Bald Hill from the southwest. As the 11th Tennessee advanced with Magevney's Brigade, Major Philip Van Horn Weems probably leading the 11th's skirmish line forward, including his old company (H), moved against a house in a ravine to dislodge a contingent of Federal troops. Weems's detachment ran into more Federals than was expected. As the several hundred Federal troops unleashed a withering fire on Weems's skirmishers, the gallant major climbed up on a fence, waved his sword over his head, and gave repeated orders for his men to advance.[36] While urging his men forward, a Yankee bullet perforated Weems's bowels, leaving him mortally wounded and in excruciating pain.[37] The conspicuous fearlessness displayed by Major Weems on this horrific field of battle is just a sample of the arresting heroism exhibited by the 11th Tennessee Infantry as a whole through the entire course of the war.

As Hood flung his Army of Tennessee against the staunch Federal defenders of Mortimer D. Leggett's division on Bald Hill, Colonel Gordon continued bravely leading the 11th Tennessee forward from the southwest through a cornfield. Soon, Gordon fell wounded, though not seriously, and attendants took him to the rear.[38] Command of the regiment then devolved to Lieutenant Colonel James A. Long, who continued leading the 11th against the Ohioans of Colonel Benjamin F. Potts's brigade. As the 11th Tennessee and other regiments of the brigade smashed into the Federal works, savage fighting ensued. The 12th/47th Tennessee and the 13th/154th regiments (led by the color bearer of the 12th) swept over the breastworks on the right, while the 11th and 29th Tennessee regiments struck the left. Private Reynolds of Company C explained, "One night we were called to form a line of march, and after the worry and fatigue of the night's march, we formed a line of battle, striking the enemy's extreme left flank an enfilading charge. The 11th Tennessee regiment being on the left flank of our line, charged so fast as to swing

---

[35] William R. Scaife, *The Campaign for Atlanta* (Atlanta, GA: William R. Scaife, 1985) 62.

[36] P. V. H. Weems, "Veteran Questionnaire," in Gustavus W. Dyer, John Trotwood Moore, Colleen Morse Elliott and Louise Armstrong Moxley, *Tennessee Civil War Veterans Questionnaires* 5 (Easley, SC: Southern Historical Press, 1985) 5:2155–156.

[37] Maney, "Return of the Killed and Wounded…at the Battle of Atlanta."

[38] Ibid.

around in front of the enemy direct face to face."[39] Private Reynolds continued, "We passed through a little sag thickly set with Sweetgum bushes, and up a slant from one to two hundred yards planted in corn, it was about knee high."[40] In this charge across the cornfield, Lieutenant William C. Nichol was seriously wounded by a minie ball that struck him in the knee. As Nichol lay helpless in the field, the thermometer reached 104 degrees. Word was sent to Nichol's brother, a staff officer on General Walker's staff. As soon as he could, he went to find his brother. Nichol with a companion traversed the cornfield under heavy enemy fire until they located the wounded lieutenant. William Nichol was in unbearable pain and was mumbling incoherently. When a lull in the firing occurred, the two men carried Nichol to Dr. William B. Maney, regimental surgeon for the 11th. The ball was imbedded in Nichol's knee joint and Dr. Maney thought the case to be hopeless, but he amputated the leg to relieve the pain. After Dr. Maney removed the mangled limb, Nichol was sent to Waycross, Georgia, for additional medical attention.[41]

Meanwhile, back on the field, the regiment "failed to take their fortifications and was ordered to fall back in line with the main line. We then captured the enemy's trenches. When the battle was over, there was not a stalk of corn standing, and the bushes was a perfect frazzle. We lost several good men killed, one a former messmate, Corporal Dod McNeilly of Charlotte."[42] Lieutenant Jacob H. "Jake" Johnson, commanding Company H, was killed on the field in this charge.[43] After repeated attempts to dislodge their Yankee counterparts from Bald Hill, Leggett's bluecoats stood firm. In the evening, the Confederates withdrew back to their entrenchments.

The regiment lost heavily in the Battle of Atlanta. According to surgeon William B. Maney's records, the 11th Tennessee Infantry lost a colonel, a major, six lieutenants, fifteen sergeants, seven corporals, and twenty-seven privates, or a devastating total of fifty-seven killed and wounded in the 22 July Battle of Atlanta.[44]

That night at the field hospital, Major Weems appended his will by scratching a codicil into a little black book. The major bequeathed to his brother Joseph his Bon Aqua Springs plantation and three slaves. He requested for three of his slaves—Angeline, Alfred, and Horace—to be freed. He left the remainder of his estate to his brother, Nathaniel Chapman Weems, except for his body servant Daniel, whom he left to Colonel Gordon. Weems also asked his brother Joseph to

---

[39] Reynolds, Veteran Questionnaire, TCWVQ, MF 484, R7.
[40] Ibid.
[41] Bradford Nichol, "Civil War Memoir," 22 July 1864, Manuscript Collection MF 1627, Tennessee State Library and Archives, Nashville, TN; Maney, "Return of the Killed and Wounded...at the Battle of Atlanta."
[42] Reynolds, Veteran Questionnaire, TCWVQ, MF 484, R7.
[43] Maney, "Return of the Killed and Wounded...at the Battle of Atlanta."
[44] Ibid.

erect a monument at their mother and father's grave in the Weems's family cemetery behind his boyhood home. He gave his horse to Miss Lucy Baltzwell Fowlkland of Green County, Alabama. His vest in which he was wounded at Missionary Ridge, he left to his two brothers. He left his clothes to Preston G. Price and his boots to E. A. Dean. He left his plate and silverware to Captain F. F. Tidwell; his sword he left to James M. Bullock of the 2nd Alabama Cavalry. Weems was loaded onto the railroad boxcar and transported south to Griffin to the Catoosa Hospital.[45]

Other wounded were distributed to hospitals in Griffin, Georgia, as well. Corporal James H. Yates and Sergeant Jacob Shouse of Company H were admitted to the Quintard Hospital. Sergeant C. N. Croswell; privates Stephen Echols, W. H. Weeks, and Henry Collins, of Company I; John H. Bartlett of Company F; and Gus Smith of Company B were admitted to the Pim Hospital.[46]

Major Weems died in excruciating pain on the night of 24 July from the wounds he had received in the Battle of Atlanta two days before. After his death, a lock of his hair was cut and sent home along with his captain's commission. The following morning, Weems's body was moved from the Catoosa hospital to the Methodist church, and at 12:00 PM Reverend George held his funeral service. Afterward, Weems's body was interred in the cemetery at Griffin, Georgia. Of the loss of Weems and Johnson, Colonel Gordon stated, "These were brave and popular officers, and in their fall the regiment suffered great loss." After Weems's death, Captain John E. Binns was promoted to major.[47]

After the Battle of Atlanta, the Confederates and Federals were engaged in a month-long stalemate. During this time, both sides hammered away at each other from entrenched positions. Sherman's men began pounding Atlanta into rubble with their artillery.

On 27 July, Cheatham returned to command his division when General Stephen D. Lee arrived to take permanent command of Hood's old corps. Two days later Cheatham was again given temporary command of one of Hood's three army corps because General A. P. Stewart had been struck in the head by a spent bullet in fighting at Ezra Church on 28 July. While Cheatham commanded Stewart's Corps, his division continued to be commanded by Brigadier General George Maney. Vaughan's Brigade continued under the temporary command of Colonel Michael

---

[45] Philip Van Horn Weems, will, 22 July 1864, in *Hickman County Tennessee Wills*, comp. and ed. by Olgia Dotson (Nunnelly, TN: O. Dotson, 1983) 2–3; P.V.H. Weems, funeral notice, 25 July 1864, possession of Edward J. Lanham, Brooks, GA.

[46] *Chattanooga Daily Rebel* (Griffin, GA), 24 and 27 July 1864.

[47] "Philip Van Horn Weems, C.S.A., Hero of the Confederacy, Killed at Atlanta Was Beloved Kinsman," *Weemsana* XXIX/1, (July 1983):7; P. V. H. Weems, funeral notice, 25 July 1864; John Berrien Lindsley, *Military Annals of Tennessee: Confederate* (1886; facsimile of the first edition, Wilmington, NC: Broadfoot Publishing, 1995) 299.

Magevney Jr. The brigade composed of the 11th Tennessee, commanded by Colonel George W. Gordon; the 12th/47th Tennessee Consolidated, by Captain William S. Moore; the 29th Tennessee, by Colonel Horace Rice, and the 13th/154th Tennessee Consolidated by Lieutenant Colonel Beverly L. Dyer.[48]

By August, Colonel Gordon had returned to duty from his 22 July wound at Atlanta. By mid-August he had been promoted to brigadier general and was given permanent command of Vaughan's old brigade. With Gordon's promotion, Lieutenant Colonel James A. Long assumed command of the 11th Tennessee.[49] At this time the 12th/47th Tennessee was commanded by Lieutenant Colonel Josiah N. Wyatt, the 13th/154th Tennessee by Major William J. Crook, and the 29th Tennessee by Colonel Horace Rice.[50]

---

[48] *OR*, ser. I, vol. 38, pt. 3, 661.

[49] Lindsley, *Military Annals*, 299; Long was officially promoted to lieutenant colonel on 5 September 1864, but the rank was to have taken effect on 13 December 1863. His rank was posthumously confirmed 5 January 1865.

[50] *OR*, ser. I, vol. 38, pt. 3, 668–69.

14

"Our Line at This Place Was Not Much Stronger Than a Good Picket Line"

August–September 1864

Following his victories around Atlanta, Sherman continued to tighten his hold around the strategic city. Nevertheless, the Federal commander was frustrated because he had not been able to pound and starve Atlanta into submission. In a final attempt, the Yankee general sent his armies in a wide sweep west and south far below Atlanta to cut the railroads to Macon and West Point. Sherman realized that these areas were not heavily fortified, and in order for Hood to effectively counter his movements, the Confederate commander would have to pull a substantial portion of his troops from Atlanta's defenses.

Initially, Hood believed the Federals were giving up on Atlanta but finally realized Sherman's intentions. In a counter movement, Hood sent Lieutenant General William J. Hardee and two corps, Hardee's Corps under the command of Major General Patrick Cleburne and Stephen D. Lee's corps (both under the overall command of Hardee), toward Jonesboro on the night of 30 August. At this time, the 11th Tennessee, commanded by Lieutenant Colonel James A. Long, was in Gordon's Brigade, Cheatham's Division (commanded by Brigadier General George E. Maney), Hardee's Corps (commanded by Major General Patrick R. Cleburne). The number of acting commanders gives an indication of how depleted the Army of Tennessee had become under Hood's leadership during the fight for Atlanta.

The 11th Tennessee with Hardee's Corps began their night march through East Point and Rough and Ready. At 3:00 AM, Brown's Division, which was at the head of Hardee's column, encountered Federal pickets at the bridge near John Chamber's mill. Rather than risk a night battle, Hardee detoured to the east, entering Jonesboro on the Morrow Station Road. This redirection caused considerable delay, and it was well into the afternoon of 31 August before Hardee's Corps was in line at Jonesboro. The bulk of Stephen D. Lee's corps went by the Mount Zion Baptist Church and Rough and Ready, where they followed the railroad and arrived at Jonesboro behind Hardee's Corps later in the afternoon.[1]

The Federal commander, O. O. Howard, had deployed his Army of the Tennessee in entrenchments along the Flint River, ready to receive a Confederate assault. Hardee wasted little time and was on the move to attack Howard's Federals

---

[1] William R. Scaife, *The Campaign for Atlanta* (Atlanta, GA: William R. Scaife, 1985) 108–109.

by 3:00 PM. Lieutenant General Stephen D. Lee's corps was deployed to the right, and Hardee's Corps (commanded by Pat Cleburne) was deployed on the left. Cleburne was to move to attack a line held by Union Brigadier General Thomas E. Ransom's XVI Corps, which had good positions behind a wide, marshy ravine. After Cleburne's attack was in progress, Lee was to make a headlong assault on Logan's XV Corps, which held positions east of the river.[2]

Cleburne's left division, commanded by the Baptist preacher from Mississippi, Brigadier General Mark P. Lowrey, advanced with Granbury's Brigade on the left, Lowrey's Brigade, commanded by Colonel John Weir, in the center, and Mercer's Brigade, commanded by Colonel Charles Olmstead on the right, while Govan's Arkansas brigade was held in reserve. As Grandbury's men advanced on the left, they clashed with units of Kilpatrick's dismounted Federal cavalry, driving the Yankee troopers across the river, and pursued them to the west side. Cleburne's other brigade commanders, Lowrey and Mercer, followed Grandbury in a spectacular advance, but this shift to the west created a gap between Cleburne and Bate. In the midst of all of this, Stephen D. Lee, having heard the firing on the Confederate left, perceived that Cleburne's attack was well under way and moved into position for his frontal assault. As Lee's troops moved forward, they initially overran the Federal skirmish line but were unsuccessful in penetrating the main line. With the entire Confederate attack in motion, Maney, commanding Cheatham's Division, moved his brigade (commanded by Colonel George Porter) and Gordon's Brigade, including the 11th Tennessee, to fill the gap between Cleburne and Bate. By the time Maney and Gordon's brigades went in to the attack, Bate's Division had already been repulsed. At this time, the Federal fire was concentrated on the two lone Tennessee brigades. As a result, they were repulsed before they reached the enemy's works.[3]

In the attack, the 11th Tennessee suffered four men wounded, all from artillery fire. Shell fragments hit Private James W. Flowers of Company F in the left side of the head and hit Private John J. Nave (also of Company F) in the right elbow. Private Charles Moore of Company I received a severe wound to the left leg by a shell fragment, and Private E. A. Harrison of Company D was wounded in the lower left arm by a piece of shrapnel.[4] As the other Confederate troops withdrew, Maney pulled his division back as well. When the 11th Tennessee returned to the

---

[2] Ibid., 109.

[3] Scaife, *Campaign for Atlanta*, 109; United States War Department, *The War of the Rebellion: A Compilation of the Official Records of the Union and Confederate Armies*. 70 vols. in 128 (Washington: Government Printing Office, 1880–1901; reprint, Gettysburg, PA: The National Historical Society, 1972) ser. I, vol. 38, pt. 3, 709. Hereafter cited as *OR*.

[4] William B. Maney, "Return of the Killed and Wounded in the 11th Tennessee Regiment near Atlanta during the month of August 1864," *Regimental Surgeon's Log*, Confederate Collection, Manuscript Section, Box 18, Military Units Tenn. Inf. Regt. 11, Medical Records, Tennessee State Library and Archives, Nashville, TN.

main line at approximately 10:00 PM, the boys began digging entrenchments.[5] When Maney arrived at headquarters, unknown events transpired that apparently led to his resignation or dismissal from command. Brigadier General John C. Carter then took command of Cheatham's Division.[6]

Carter's men were awakened early the next morning and moved forward to occupy a line of works cleared when Lowrey's troops had moved to the right. This shift occurred because of Hood's summoning Lee's Corps back to Atlanta. The morning was set up for disaster. Hood's retrieval of Lee further reduced the number of Hardee's already outnumbered Confederates. Three full Federal corps were in Jonesboro with another three within striking distance. Hardee stretched his thin line to the breaking point. Hardee's right was held by Cleburne's Division, which was refused back at the Warren House, forming a salient in the Confederate line. Govan's Brigade of Cleburne's Division held the position at this salient angle. The 11th Tennessee with Gordon's Brigade was held in reserve several hundred yards south of the Warren House and Govan's angle.[7]

At about 4:00 PM on 1 September, the Federals began their assault. Their attack fell first against the railroad cut on the right of the Confederate line held by Colonel Ellison Capers's 24th South Carolina Infantry. The Union troops broke the line west of the rail cut, but Capers rallied his South Carolinians and restored the line. A little further to the west, Morgan's 2nd division of Jefferson C. Davis's XIV corps fiercely attacked the angle held by Daniel C. Govan's Arkansas brigade. Govan rebuffed the first sortie against his line. The Federals did not stop with that failure and renewed their advance against the angle. Govan's men could not resist the continued onslaught of the Federal division. Govan's Brigade fought hard, but this time his line was overrun, and a tide of Yankees poured through the gap. Govan, six hundred of his men, and eight pieces of artillery were captured.[8] Watching the events transpire from a distance, Private Reynolds of Company C stated, "Our line at this place was not much stronger than a good picket line. And on our right wing, the enemy charged our line and captured a considerable space."[9]

The situation was now critical as this breach in the Confederate line threatened disaster. Cleburne, immediately sizing up the situation in his front, sought help from Brigadier General Gordon.[10] At once, Gordon ordered his boys forward. As the 11th advanced on the heretofore-victorious Yankees, the casualties

---

[5] *OR*, ser. I, vol. 38, pt. 3, 711.

[6] Ibid., 712.

[7] Ibid., 743; The officers are still referring to Gordon's Brigade as Vaughan's in their official reports.

[8] Ibid., 742–43.

[9] William E. Reynolds, Veteran Questionnaire, Tennessee Civil War Veterans Questionnaires, Tennessee State Library and Archives, Nashville, TN, 1922. MF 484, R7. Hereafter referred cited as TCWVQ.

[10] *OR*, ser. I, vol. 38, pt. 3, 729.

mounted. Lieutenant Colonel James A. Long was shot through the left leg near the knee and later died at the hospital of pyemia (blood poisoning). Captain James Darden was mortally wounded, shot through the pelvis, as he gallantly led Company F into the fray. Two lieutenants fell in the advance and a number of enlisted men. As he raced toward the Federal breakthrough, 1st Sergeant Joe Gilman of Company D was shot in the left arm, his second wound of the Atlanta Campaign. Sergeant William Willard of Company D was shot through the base of the skull. Willard was evacuated to Griffin, Georgia, and died shortly after arriving. Private Gustavus Balthrop of Company F was shot through the lung. Despite the losses, Gordon's furious counter-punch drove the Federals back and restored the thin gray line. The 11th Tennessee lost a total of eighteen wounded and three killed in the two-day fight at Jonesboro.[11] Gordon's Brigade maintained their new position in line the remainder of the day and held the enemy in check until nightfall. Gordon's attack was successful and possibly saved Hardee's entire corps from annihilation.

As night covered the field, the Yankees were finally in a position to flank Hardee's line, but fortunately, for the Confederates, it was too late to attempt the opportunity. Hardee abandoned his entrenchments and moved his beleaguered corps down the railroad, seven miles south, to Lovejoy Station. As the remainder of the corps evacuated the works, Gordon's Brigade was called upon again and was ordered to cover Hardee's withdrawal. When the other units of Hardee's Corps had passed safely to the south, Gordon skillfully withdrew his brigade.[12] Private William Reynolds of Company C stated, "[We] held the position until late at night, when we were ordered to place our hand on, and follow our guide, and not to utter a word. While it was excessively dark, I could observe men we were passing. It was said we passed through the enemy's lines."[13] In the meantime, back in Atlanta, Hood abandoned the city, destroyed his supply trains, and moved to join Hardee at Lovejoy Station.[14]

Upon arrival at Lovejoy Station, the Confederates began carving out entrenchments for defensive purposes. An officer of the brigade stated, "[The] next morning [2 September] we began fortifying, about 2 o'clock PM the enemy appeared

---

[11] William B. Maney, "Return of the Killed and Wounded in the 11th Tennessee Regiment at Jonesboro and Lovejoy Station in September 1864," *Regimental Surgeon's Log*, Confederate Collection, Manuscript Section, Box 18, Military Units Tenn. Inf. Regt. 11, Medical Records, Tennessee State Library and Archives, Nashville, TN.

[12] John Berrien Lindsley, *Military Annals of Tennessee: Confederate* (1886; facsimile of the first edition, Wilmington, NC: Broadfoot Publishing, 1995) 300.

[13] Reynolds, "Veteran Questionnaire," in Dyer et al., *Tennessee Civil War Veterans Questionnaires*, vol 5: extra page 6.

[14] Lindsley, *Military Annals*, 300.

in our front but finding us ready they only planted batteries and shelled our line with but little effect."[15] Private Reynolds recalled,

> Here I was on picket duty, the enemy with two lines of battle came against us. Our line consisted of one man every four or five feet. We allowed the enemy to drive us back to the main line. I shall never forget the words of old Frank Cheatham, when he came among the boys and exclaimed, "go back and drive the enemy from your picket posts and never allow two lines of Yankees to break your lines." We did as ordered, but soon they reinforced and again charged, driving us back until they gained the top of the hill above us about two hundred yards. Our entrenchment crossed a sag and that evening a rain came up and filled our trenches with water the place where my company occupied, here we stood in mud and water, those of us who was not too tired. I sat down against the side of the ditch and enjoyed the most pleasant sleep of my life, to awake [the] next morning perfectly benumbed, having no use of my lower extremities."[16]

In the three days of fighting at Lovejoy Station, the 11th Tennessee sustained a loss of three killed and five wounded.[17]

From Lovejoy Station, Hood moved his army approximately twenty miles east to Palmetto where an attempt at reorganization took place. The condition of Cheatham's entire division was at a crucial stage. These gallant regiments, which at one time had boasted a strength of near one thousand men each, were by this time reduced to only a few hundred. The regiments of Gordon's Brigade were no different. As a result, the 11th and 29th Tennessee Infantry regiments were consolidated into one unit due to their heavy losses in the fighting around Atlanta. Colonel Horace Rice of the 29th Tennessee was given command of the consolidated regiment.[18] On 5 September, Captain John E. Binns of Company D was promoted to major to fill the vacancy left by Van Weems, who had been mortally wounded at Atlanta on 22 July. With this promotion, Binns became second in command of the 11th/29th Consolidated. After Captain James H. Darden's fall, 1st Lieutenant Jeremiah Batts of Company F was promoted to captain and took command of the Robertson County company.[19]

On 25 September, President Jefferson Davis visited the Army of Tennessee at Palmetto. Hood tried to blame the failures of the battles for Atlanta, particularly

---

[15] Peter Marchant to Susan Marchant, 15 September 1864, Letters of Captain Peter Marchant, http://freepages.military.rootsweb.ancestry.com/~bsdunagan/letters.html.

[16] Reynolds, Veteran Questionnaire, TCWVQ, MF 484, R7.

[17] Ibid., Maney, "Return of the Killed and Wounded…at Jonesboro."

[18] Lindsley, *Military Annals*, 300.

[19] Binns, 11th Tennessee Infantry Service Records?, National Archives Records Administration, *Compiled Service Records of Confederate Soldiers Who Served in Organizations from the State of Tennessee*, Washington, DC: National Archives and Records Service, General Services Administration, 1960; Jeremiah Batts, M268 R160, 11th TISR. Batts's promotion was official 11 September 1864.

Peachtree Creek, Atlanta, and Jonesboro on Lieutenant General Hardee. Davis acknowledged that Hardee commanded the best troops in the army, and on 28 September Hardee was relieved of command. Ben Cheatham took command of Hardee's Corps, which necessitated several changes in the command structure of his former division. John C. Brown was given command of the division. Cheatham's former brigades were reduced from five to four. Marcus J. Wright's brigade was disbanded. John C. Carter was assigned to permanent command of Maney's former brigade. Gordon retained command of Vaughan's old brigade; Otho Strahl continued to command his brigade, and States Rights Gist continued to command his brigade of South Carolinians and Georgians.[20]

---

[20] Christopher Losson, *Tennessee's Forgotten Warriors: Frank Cheatham and His Confederate Division* (Knoxville: University of Tennessee Press, 1989) 197; When Wright's Brigade was disbanded, the 51st/52nd Tennessee Regiment was transferred to Gordon's Brigade.

15

"They Had Well Tried to Capture a Red Fox"

October–29 November 1864

With the fate of Atlanta sealed and the Army of Tennessee reorganized, Hood began a bold move to the north in an attempt to draw Sherman out of Georgia. Sherman initially took the bait, following Hood as far as Gadsden, Alabama, but shortly headed to the southeast, where in a rare twist of events, the two opposing armies marched away from each other, Sherman beginning his march to the sea, and Hood setting out on his Middle Tennessee Campaign.

As Hood began a withdrawal from Georgia, he moved his army back toward Dalton where they captured a Federal post garrisoned by the 44th United States Colored Troops. The 11th/29th participated in tearing up the railroad there. From Dalton, the Army of Tennessee headed west toward Alabama.[1] Once Hood crossed into Alabama, he directed the army toward Gadsden, where he met with General P. G. T. Beauregard, the new military commander of the West. At that time, Gadsden was a small town of only about 400 people. Hood's army of 35,000 men engulfed the tiny village. Cheatham's Corps camped in the area now bordered by 4th, 5th, Broad, and Chestnut Streets.[2]

From Gadsden, the majority of Hood's army continued on to Decatur, but the 11th/29th Tennessee was detached with the remainder of Gordon's Brigade to Blountsville, where they were to escort a convoy of 700 supply wagons across Sand Mountain. The brigade reached Blountsville, and after the convoy's arrival, left to rejoin the army. According to one of the soldiers, the wagon train was from fifteen to twenty miles long, with a few men assigned to guard each wagon. General Gordon described the condition of the animals pulling the wagons, "Most of the teams in this train were poor, jaded, and apparently half-starved; but after several days of hard marching the men often pulling and pushing the wagons through creeks and bogs, over the hills and the mountains, we successfully rejoined the army near Courtland, and on time."[3]

On 13 November, Colonel Horace Rice led the 11th/29th across the Tennessee River and passed on through Florence. The soldiers marched through

---

[1] John Berrien Lindsley, *Military Annals of Tennessee: Confederate* (1886; facsimile of the first edition, Wilmington, NC: Broadfoot Publishing, 1995) 300.

[2] Etowah County Centennial Commission, *History of Etowah County, Alabama* (Gadsden, AL: Etowah County Centennial Commission, 1968) 48.

[3] Lindsley, *Military Annals*, 300.

the town with bands playing and bivouacked in the fields beyond. The Army of Tennessee remained at Florence for some time, but by 21 November, Hood was back on the march. On this date, a heavy snow fell as the 11th/29th marched up the Waynesboro Road. Snow continued falling all day, throughout the night, and into the next day as the boys crossed into Tennessee. General Gordon commented that the snow beat the soldiers in the face "as if to say go back"; nevertheless, they trudged dutifully onward. By the end of the day, the regiment had marched eighteen miles. The boys took up the line of march again the following day, and after marching about fourteen miles, by 4:00 PM Hood's column entered the deserted town of Waynesboro.[4]

Many of the men had no shoes or coats, and the cold weather compounded their misery. Colonel Rice, commanding the 11th/29th Consolidated, detailed Captain William I. White of Company A, to cross the Tennessee River and to make his way back home to Humphreys County to obtain some of these desperately needed supplies. While White was on his journey, the Yankees heard of his assignment and determined to capture him. The Federals failed, and White returned to the regiment after the Battle of Nashville saying, "They had well tried to capture a red fox."[5]

Meanwhile, over the next couple of days, Cheatham's men marched another fifty miles or so, and by 26 November, despite heavy rain, were within two and a half miles of Columbia. On Sunday, 27 November, Cheatham moved his corps to the right above Columbia on the Duck River. There, some skirmishing occurred with Federal forces in the town. The Federals, under command of General John M. Schofield, were troops that Sherman had detached to General Thomas just before he returned to Georgia from Alabama to begin his infamous "March to the Sea." Schofield had two corps under his command, the XXIII Corps of the Army of the Ohio under command of General Jacob Cox and the IV Corps of the Army of the Cumberland, commanded by General David Stanley. As the Confederates prepared to cross the river, unforeseen delays hindered their progress. The Federals abandoned Columbia during the night, and the Confederates took possession of the town the following day.[6]

At about sunrise on the morning of 29 November, General John C. Brown, commanding Cheatham's old division, formed his troops, the rearmost in

---

[4] Ibid.; United States War Department, *The War of the Rebellion: A Compilation of the Official Records of the Union and Confederate Armies.* 70 vols. in 128 (Washington: Government Printing Office, 1880–1901; reprint, Gettysburg, PA: The National Historical Society, 1972) ser. I, vol. 45, 1, 730. Hereafter cited as *OR*.

[5] W.I. White, "Veteran Questionnaire," in Gustavus W. Dyer, John Trotwood Moore, Colleen Morse Elliott and Louise Armstrong Moxley, *Tennessee Civil War Veterans Questionnaires* 5 (Easley, SC: Southern Historical Press, 1985) vol. 5:2178.

[6] *OR*, ser. I, vol. 45, 1, 730–31.

Cheatham's Corps, and marched them from their encampment on the Mooresville Turnpike toward the Duck River. Brown maneuvered his men through cedar brakes and pathless woods, eventually arriving at Davis's Ford, where his men crossed the river on a pontoon bridge. After crossing the river and having contact with some Yankee skirmishers, Cheatham expected an attack against his left flank. To prepare for such an eventuality, he divided his corps into two parallel columns so that his men could instantly maneuver into two lines of battle if an attack occurred. Cleburne's and Bate's divisions made up the main column, and Brown's Division formed the supporting column. Cheatham marched his corps another five or six miles through fields, woods, and over rough ground, eventually arriving at Rutherford Creek. Soon after his men were in motion, Cheatham rode over to Brown and ordered him to detach Gist's Brigade and about half of Strahl's as pickets. After crossing Rutherford Creek, Brown's Division moved up the Rally Hill Turnpike toward Spring Hill.[7]

Hood's intention was to beat Schofield to Spring Hill. If he could cut off their route of retreat up the Columbia Turnpike, he thought he could capture Schofield's army before they could join Thomas at Nashville.

Before the Civil War, Spring Hill was a relatively obscure town. The little village had gained some notoriety as the place where Dr. George Peters had killed the high-profile Confederate cavalry commander General Earl Van Dorn for having an affair with his wife, the infamous (but reputedly beautiful) Jessie McKissick Peters. Now two armies were engulfing the small village.

Cleburne's men formed the van of the Confederate infantry. Around 4:00 PM, Cleburne's men moved through fields just south of Spring Hill toward the Columbia Pike. As they moved forward, they came under a heavy fire from the Federals in the location now known as Bradley's Knoll. There, a brigade of Federals, commanded by Colonel Luther P. Bradley, made a determined stand against Cleburne's respected veterans, distinguished by their unique blue and white "Hardee Pattern" regimental colors. As Cleburne's legions passed his front, Bradley's men released a destructive fire into Cleburne's rightmost element, a brigade of Alabamians and Mississippians led by Mark P. Lowrey. Cleburne, who was arguably the most able infantry commander in the army, would have none of this. In response, his legions crushed Bradley's Brigade. As Bradley's men fell back, Cleburne halted to reform his troops. As Cleburne reformed, he received word from his corps commander, General Benjamin F. Cheatham, to wait for support.[8]

It was almost dark when the 11th/29th Tennessee with the remainder of Gordon's Brigade arrived by way of the Rally Hill Turnpike and deployed to

---

[7] R. A. Brock, "Lost Opportunity at Spring Hill," *Southern Historical Society Papers* (Richmond, VA: Virginia Historical Society, 1959) 537–38.

[8] Eric Jacobson and Richard Rupp, *For Cause & for Country: A Study of the Affair at Spring Hill and the Battle of Franklin* (Franklin, TN: O'More Publishing, 2007) 106–117.

Cleburne's right, in a line that generally followed along the McCutcheon's Creek bottom.⁹ At that time Brown's Division formed the right flank of the Confederate infantry. As his men took position in the creek bottom, Brown could see Yankee activity on the grounds of the Martin Cheairs home, "Ferguson Hall," just to his front. There was at least a battery of artillery supported by Yankee infantry at that location. In addition, it seemed that the Federal line extended from the home north through the City cemetery and then continued further north and east, extending past his right flank. Forrest's cavalry was in position on the high ground northeast of Brown. Brown received word to form a line of battle and to "take Spring Hill." This is yet a second example of confusion in the Confederate command as communications among the high-level commanders began breaking down.

As night fell, Bate's Confederate division was only a few yards from actually cutting the pike when Cheatham, who was unaware of Hood's directive to Bate, ordered him to move to the right, away from the pike, to join with Cleburne's left flank or be placed under arrest. Adding to the increasing confusion of the Army of Tennessee's high command, Brown only had about half of his division present as Gist's Brigade and the half of Strahl's, which had been detached as pickets had not returned. Nevertheless, Brown deployed his men in line of battle as ordered. As his brigades were maneuvering into position, Brown noticed that Forrest's troopers were gone, and that his right flank was unprotected. Half of his division was missing. Forrest, who was to support his right flank and rear, due to orders, had relocated to another part of the field. To make matters worse, Brown had no artillery support. Brown, not realizing that the Federal left he was ordered to attack was only lightly held, saw the situation as disastrous if he launched an attack. Brown, in an attempt to decide what to do, called a meeting of his brigade commanders who were present. Gordon, Carter, and Strahl all agreed that an attack would be catastrophic. When Brown informed Cheatham, he concurred.¹⁰ Hood, now aware of the predicament, suspended the attack until Gist's Brigade was in position and A. P. Stewart's Corps arrived on the field. In the meantime, Hood told Brown to be ready to move at a moment's notice.¹¹

Gist's Brigade arrived not long after sundown and assumed a position on Brown's right. A. P. Stewart's Corps came up well after dark and took a position to the right and rear of Brown's line. After the arrival of Stewart's Corps, Hood issued no further attack orders. During the night, Schofield's entire army slipped past the

---

⁹ William E. Reynolds, Veteran Questionnaire, Tennessee Civil War Veterans Questionnaires, Tennessee State Library and Archives, Nashville, TN, 1922. MF 484, R7. Hereafter referred cited as TCWVQ.

¹⁰ Jamie Gillum, *Twenty-five Hours to Tragedy: The Battle of Spring Hill and Operations on November 29, 1864 Precursor to the Battle of Franklin* (Spring Hill, TN: James F. Gillum, 2014) 305–306.

¹¹ Brock, "Lost Opportunity," 538.

Confederate line. Private William E. Reynolds of Company C of the 11th Tennessee stated, "[I] was close enough to see the enemy marching along the pike...."[12] Hood's plan to destroy Schofield's army had failed.

---

[12] Reynolds, Veteran Questionnaire, TCWVQ, MF 484, R7.

16

"Follow Them into Their Works"

30 November 1864

The following morning, 30 November, Hood awoke to discover that Schofield had slipped out of his trap and was continuing northward to join Thomas at Nashville. Upon hearing the news, Hood, according to one observer, became "as wrathy as a rattlesnake."[1] James Lee McDonough and Thomas Connelly wrote, "Hood was enraged to learn at daylight that he had underestimated what Schofield could accomplish, discovering the Union commander had eluded him while he slept."[2] The irate Hood immediately summoned his corps commanders to "Rippavilla," the Nathaniel Cheairs house on the Columbia Pike. There, in an early morning conference, Hood lashed out in fury toward his subordinates, blaming others for the catastrophe but accepting none of the blame for himself. Hood, who went to bed the previous evening—even though it should have been apparent to any thinking man that his plan was not being executed—pointed the finger at Cleburne, Brown, and Cheatham. Everyone in Hood's command knew that a great opportunity had been lost. As a result, two emotions prevailed in the Army of Tennessee that day, disappointment and anger.

Hood ordered his men in immediate pursuit of Schofield. Nathan Bedford Forrest rode out with his cavalry at the van of the army to harass General George D. Wagner's Yankee division, the rear guard of Schofield's fleeing Federals. Following Forrest, Stewart's Corps filed onto the Columbia Pike leading the infantry as it headed north. One Rebel of Walthall's Division said, "When daylight came we were marched onto the pike and saw the signs of a panic stricken army. Wagons had been abandoned. Some of the teams had been shot to keep the mules from falling into our hands. Men had thrown away their guns and knapsacks."[3] Cheatham formed his infantry and followed Stewart. The 11th/29th Tennessee took their position in the line of march at approximately 10:00 AM.[4] Stephen D. Lee's corps,

---

[1] Wiley Sword, *Embrace An Angry Wind: The Confederacy's Last Hurrah: Spring Hill, Franklin, and Nashville* (New York: HarperCollins Publishers, 1992) 156.

[2] James Lee McDonough and Thomas L. Connelly, *Five Tragic Hours: The Battle of Franklin* (Knoxville: University of Tennessee, 1983) 53.

[3] Washington Bryan Crumpton, *A Book of Memories 1842–1920* (Montgomery, AL: Baptist Mission Board, 1921) 96.

[4] William E. Reynolds, Veteran Questionnaire, Tennessee Civil War Veterans Questionnaires, Tennessee State Library and Archives, Nashville, TN, 1922. MF 484, R7. Hereafter referred cited as TCWVQ.

which was coming up from Columbia, arrived at Spring Hill by 9:00 AM and brought up the rear of the army some distance behind Cheatham.

As the morning passed, Hood spewed his venom toward everyone with whom he had contact. The blustering Hood rode up to John C. Brown as his division was moving to the north, and perhaps as a grim harbinger of coming events brusquely stated,

> I wish you to bear in mind this military principle: that when a pursuing army comes up with the retreating enemy he must be immediately attacked. If you have a brigade in front as advance guard, order its commander to attack as soon as he comes up with him. If you have a regiment in advance and it comes up with the enemy, give the colonel orders to attack him; if there is but a company in advance, and if it overtakes the entire Yankee army, order the captain to attack forthwith; and if anything blocks the road in front of you today, don't stop a minute, but turn out into the fields or woods and move on to the front.[5]

Within a few hours, Schofield's army had reached Franklin, some fifteen miles north of Spring Hill. The Yankees were unable to pass through the town and escape Hood because of recent damage to both bridges over the Harpeth River. While his engineers, under the oversight of Captain Twining, were working to get a pontoon bridge over the river, Schofield gave orders for the XXIII Corps of the Army of the Ohio (commanded by General Jacob D. Cox) to begin strengthening the existing entrenchments around the town. Cox commandeered the brick home of Fountain Branch Carter for his headquarters. One of the Carter's sons, Tod, was a captain in the rapidly approaching Army of Tennessee. Federal officers ordered the Carter family, including their servants and another son, former Lieutenant Colonel Moscow Carter of the 20th Tennessee Infantry, into the basement in the unlikely event that Hood should attack.

The Army of Tennessee continued its pursuit, marching rapidly toward Franklin. Gunfire erupted some distance in its front as Forrest's troopers made contact with Wagner's Federals along a cedar-lined range of hills two miles south of the town. After a brief skirmish, Wagner's men fell back, abandoning the high ground to Forrest. Within earshot of the gunfire, Hood's Infantry hurried forward.

The Federal rear guard filed down Winstead and Breezy hills. As they withdrew, Wagner deployed two of his brigades, Conrad's and Lane's, some five hundred yards in advance of the Federal main line at an apex along a small rise. Wagner's remaining brigade, commanded by Colonel Emerson Opdyke, refused to obey orders and continued marching up the pike, taking a position in reserve approximately two hundred yards north of Fountain Carter's 1830 Federal-style house.

---

[5] Sword, *Embrace an Angry Wind*, 157.

Soon, the Southern infantry arrived along the Winstead-Breezy Hill range. Hood and his subordinate officers gathered on the crest of Winstead Hill overlooking Franklin. There, they observed that the Federals had three defensive lines of breastworks. The first Federal line consisted of Conrad's and Lane's advanced brigades. Half a mile to their rear lay the formidable main line consisting of trenches, headlogs, and some abatis with the Columbia Pike running through its center. A third line, known as the smokehouse line, lay another seventy yards to the rear of the main line and ran parallel to the Carter smokehouse and other outbuildings in the Carter yard.

As the Rebel infantry came up, Stewart's Corps headed to the east to form the extreme right of the Confederate line. As Stewart's Corps deployed, they moved toward the Lewisburg Pike, forming some 500 yards to the south of Carnton, the 1826 plantation home of John and Carrie McGavock. Cheatham's Corps followed, with Cleburne's Division moving to the right behind Stewart with his left resting on the Columbia Pike. Brown filed to the left with his right resting on the Columbia Pike, forming to the left of Cleburne. Bate swung his division further to the left, moving through a pass between a range of hills to the west and moved toward the Carter's Creek Pike. After moving into position, Stewart's and Cheatham's corps of the Army of Tennessee and the entrenched Federal IV and XXIII corps faced each other.

Few in the Federal army really thought Hood would make a frontal attack against three lines of prepared defenses. However, on the slopes of Winstead Hill, Hood announced, "We will make the fight."[6] Private William E. Reynolds of Company C of the 11th Tennessee wrote, "There are so many sad, as well as pleasant thoughts, that make my war history. But my vocabulary is insufficient to attempt to adjust the uncalled for mistake committed.... But here at Franklin, one of the saddest and gravest mistakes, the grossest blunder that will ever paint the pages of history, records the bloody massacre at Franklin, Tenn."[7] Although no one questions Hood's bravery, a private of the 11th Tennessee offered his perspective of his commander: "Hood was a brave man, and could satisfactorily fill the place of a captain or a colonel, but his brains as a general, and especially as a leader was insufficient."[8] Private Reynolds went on to say, "I was near General Hood when he and his staff came on the hill, and heard him say, these temporary breastworks would have to be overcome. I didn't hear what the officers said but from his expression, I am satisfied they objected to this move."[9] George W. Gordon was one of the Confederate generals on Winstead Hill near Hood. Gordon removed his field glasses from their case and carefully examined the enemy's position. After

---

[6] Ibid., 178.
[7] Reynolds, Veteran Questionnaire, TCWVQ, MF 484, R7.
[8] Ibid.
[9] Ibid.

discussions with Cheatham, Brown, and the other brigade commanders, Gordon left the company of officers and moved to the foot of the hill where he formed his brigade.[10]

As the stir of regiments, brigades, and divisions moved to get into position, the four brigades of Brown's Division formed on the left of the Columbia Pike leading into Franklin while Cleburne's three brigades formed to the right of the pike. The alignment of Brown's Division consisted of a two-brigade front. Gist's and Gordon's brigades were placed in the front line with Brown's remaining brigades, Carter's and Strahl's, following two hundred yards in support. Gordon's Brigade was on the right front of the division with his right wing resting on the Columbia Pike. Strahl's Brigade was immediately to his rear. Gordon's Brigade was aligned with the 13th/154th/51st/52nd Tennessee Consolidated as the right guide of the brigade, beside the 10th Texas Infantry, which was the extreme left of Grandbury's Brigade of Cleburne's Division. To the left of the 13th/154th/51st/52nd was the 12th/47th Tennessee. The 11th/29th Tennessee was to their left with Company F of the 11th being the left-most company of the regiment.[11] Wiley M. Crook of Gordon's Brigade stated, "The 13th Tennessee regiment to which I belonged was placed just left of the pike, being the right wing of [Brown's] division. The whole ground between our line and the Federals could plainly be seen from our position. We could see the enemy's lines of defense and the open plain between us and knew we were to attack by a charge on them in their works."[12]

Private Reynolds described the Federal position from his point in the line of the 11th Tennessee,

> We could see with the naked eye the first line we would come to, was logs, the next was about one hundred yards beyond, well excavated ditches, head-logs and small trees with their limbs trimmed to two or three feet long, in front of the entanglement. The last line was only twelve or twenty feet behind this, all well supplied with men and across the river in rear of their line of battle was a considerable hill [Fort Granger] that was well fortified with cannon. They could engage our line all the way from where we formed our line, up to a short space of their men by shooting over their line of battle.[13]

Reynolds went on to say that "no commander except a crazy man would have had the least thought of making this charge after looking at their invincible fortifications and seeing how easy it would be to put in a pontoon bridge above the

---

[10] "Address of General Gordon," *Confederate Veteran* 8/1 (January 1900): 6–7.

[11] John Berrien Lindsley, *Military Annals of Tennessee: Confederate* (1886; facsimile of the first edition, Wilmington, NC: Broadfoot Publishing, 1995) 301.

[12] Wiley M. Crook, "Autobiography and Reminiscences," http://www.tngenweb.org/records/chester/bios/crook/crook01.htm.

[13] Reynolds, Veteran Questionnaire, TCWVQ, MF 484, R7.

town, and go on and leave them, to surrender when they saw they had to."[14] One despondent Reb of Gordon's Brigade stated, "I felt more keenly than in any other battle that I would never survive the impending danger into which I was entering."[15] In order to secure some sense of hope, the soldier placed a small testament in his left breast pocket and a little hymn book in his right in the hopes that those precious books given to him at the beginning of the war by his mother would protect him in some way from the Yankee bullets.[16]

Gordon was busy getting his men formed and aligned for this suicidal charge. From Winstead Hill, a lieutenant of General Chalmers's staff noticed the young brigadier and asked Captain Wigfall of Hood's staff who he was. The captain stated that he was General Gordon. The lieutenant responded that he had "often seen General Gordon with the Army of Northern Virginia and that is not him."[17] Wigfall replied that he was General Gordon of Tennessee. Gordon was mounted on a very beautiful iron-gray horse, and according to those who saw him that day, "looked every inch the ideal soldier."[18] Gordon was a superb horseman and wore a new uniform. His 1840 heavy cavalry saber bounced at his side. Another Confederate officer described Gordon, saying, "His eyes were dark, quickly melting to tenderness at another's woes, but on occasions flashing with the suppressed lightning of passion. His brown hair, while a soldier unwittingly neglected, would sometimes hang in golden brown to his shoulders, suggesting the cavalier of the Charles I age."[19] In a few minutes, Gordon completed the formation of his brigade and awaited orders to move forward.

Earlier in the war, Gordon had allowed his hair to grow longer than military regulations allowed. In a postscript to one particular order, General Cheatham, jesting with Gordon, told his adjutant, Major John Ingram, to "tell Gordon to cut off that hair."[20] Major Ingram delivered the directive adding the addendum as ordered. Gordon responded, "Tell General Cheatham I will carry out his military order, but tell him it is none of his business how I wear my hair."[21] The length of Gordon's hair became a joking matter between the young brigadier and Cheatham, his commanding officer.

As the twenty-eight-year-old Gordon, one of the youngest generals in the army, formed his brigade on the west side of the Columbia Pike, he knew from his

---

[14] Ibid.

[15] Crook, "Autobiography and Reminiscences."

[16] Ibid.

[17] James Dinkins, *Personal Recollections and Experiences in the Confederate Army by an Old Johnnie* (1897; reprint, Dayton, OH: Morningside, 1975) 235.

[18] Ibid.

[19] L. B. McFarland, "Address of L. B. McFarland at Reunion in Macon, GA," *Confederate Veteran* 20/9 (September 1912): 430.

[20] Ibid., 428.

[21] Ibid.

earlier experiences that the Federal works were formidable, particularly where the Columbia Pike crossed them. When he had finished surveying the works, Gordon ordered his men to fix bayonets. The bayonets rattled and pinged against the rifle muzzles as these stalwart Southerners, veterans of Murfreesboro, Chickamauga, Missionary Ridge, and the Atlanta Campaign, pushed and twisted them into place. As they waited, Cheatham finally sent the fateful word. At approximately 4:00 PM, a courier delivered Cheatham's directive to begin the assault and instructed Gordon to go over the works "even if he had to be pulled over by his hair."[22]

The young general felt that a "desperate and death-dealing struggle was about to ensue."[23] At the command, Gordon's Brigade jolted forward in "double column at half distance."[24] Private Martin Van Buren Adcock of Company K tapped away on his snare drum as Gordon's columns impudently stepped down from Winstead Hill into the valley below. This was Adcock's twenty-eighth birthday, and he must have wondered as he stared at enemy in his front, if it would also be the day he died. The tattered shreds of the frayed St. Andrews Cross regimental flag of the 11th Tennessee undulated in the gentle breeze, as did all the colors of Brown's Division, which contrasted sharply with the flapping blue and white regimental standards of Cleburne's Division just to their right. As the men stepped forward, one of Brown's bands struck up "Dixie," the martial strains shattering the air, only to be answered by "The Bonnie Blue Flag" from one of Cleburne's bands. A soldier of Gordon's Brigade stated, "As General Hood sent his couriers right and left with orders to advance, our regimental band cheered us with the soul-stirring strains of Dixie as we moved forward with banners sweetly kissing the breezes of heaven, and our rebel yell rending the air as though it echoed in the portals of Paradise."[25]

Eighteen brigades, comprising more than one hundred veteran regiments of the Army of Tennessee's infantry, marched forward with parade ground precision. Their regimental colors, tattered from the fighting of the Atlanta Campaign, flapped and fluttered in the late November breeze. Cheatham's Division historian Craig Losson wrote, "The impetuosity displayed along both sides of the road was also triggered by the long-standing rivalry between Cleburne's Division and Cheatham's old unit."[26] Major James D. Porter of Cheatham's staff commented that this was the first occasion that Cleburne and Cheatham's divisions "had met side by side in full view of each other, in an open field, with the advantages for desperate work equally balanced between them. For years each had contended for the right to wear the name of the crack division of that army, and the faces of both men and

---

[22] Ibid.
[23] "Address of General Gordon," 7.
[24] Ibid.
[25] Crook, "Autobiography and Reminiscences."
[26] Christopher Losson, *Tennessee's Forgotten Warriors: Frank Cheatham and His Confederate Division* (Knoxville: University of Tennessee Press, 1989) 221.

officers seemed to say, 'Here is the field upon which that right shall be decided.'"[27] One participant described the scene, "It presented the most magnificent and spectacular military pageant ever witnessed by that veteran army, or perhaps any other during that great international war. It presented a scene so imposing and thrilling in its grandeur that the sense of ensuing danger was lost in the sublime emotions inspired by the surpassing martial panorama."[28]

After the initial march, Gordon halted his regiments in column about four hundred yards from Lane's short advanced line and formed two lines of battle. Gordon, on his gray mount, rode down the length of his brigade checking his line. When he was satisfied with the preparatory alignment, he halted his horse in the center of his brigade and made a speech. Gordon told his veterans that Granbury's Brigade of Cleburne's Division was beside them, but he reminded his boys that they were "Tennesseans on Tennessee soil and we must not suffer ourselves to be outdone this day even by such gallant fighters as the Texas Brigade."[29] Gordon then dismounted, and the youthful brigadier took position, not in the rear of his brigade as regulations specified, but in the front.[30] When Gordon had taken his place he barked, "Shoulder arms!"..."Right shoulder shift arms!"..."Brigade forward!"..."Guide center!"..."Quick time!"..."March!" At Gordon's command, his scrappy Tennesseans stepped forward and raised an earthshaking cheer.[31]

Before Brown's and Cleburne's divisions lay Wagner's advanced Federal brigades of Conrad and Lane. Their division commander, George Wagner, had refused to allow them to retire behind the main line of works even when it was apparent that Hood was actually attacking. In response to a request to retire for fear of being overrun, Wagner, allegedly under the influence of whiskey, declined by sending word by a courier, "Tell them to fight—fight like hell."[32] Thus, Wagner made a grave mistake. Gordon said, "They had thrown out a detached battalion [actually two brigades], I judge about 600 yards from the main line. This detached command was drawn up in a straight line about the apex of the main line. I had been studying their position through field glasses for about two hours prior to our attack and had discovered the weakness of the position."[33]

Colonel John Q. Lane's Federal brigade lay right in Gordon's path. Lane's Brigade consisted of the 100th Illinois, the 40th and 57th Indiana, the 28th Kentucky, and the 26th and 97th Ohio. Lane's men nervously watched and waited.

---

[27] Ibid.

[28] "Address of General Gordon," 7.

[29] "Gen. Geo. Gordon, Soldier, Citizen, Statesman, Dead," Memphis (TN) *Commercial Appeal*, 10 August 1911.

[30] Dinkins, *Personal Recollections*, 235.

[31] "Gen Geo. Gordon, Soldier, Statesman, Dead."

[32] Jacob D. Cox, *The Battle of Franklin, Tennessee, November 30 1864: A Monograph* (New York: Charles Scribner's Sons, 1897) 337.

[33] "Gen Geo. Gordon, Soldier, Citizen, Statesman, Dead."

W. W. Gist of the 26th Ohio stated, "The suspense and nervous strain became greater and greater as…the lines of gray came nearer and nearer. We stood up part of the time, and part of the time we sat down with our guns resting on the rails or logs in front.… Nearer and nearer the Confederates approached with the precision of dress parade, and our hearts beat rapidly."[34]

As Gordon's Brigade advanced across the fields toward Franklin, rabbits darted and coveys of quail whirred before his intrepid line of battle. Levi T. Schofield, a Federal officer, described the Confederate assault,

> It was a grand sight, such as would make a lifelong impression on the mind of any man who could see the resistless, well-conducted charge. For the moment we were spellbound with admiration, although they were our hated foes; and we knew that in a few brief moments, as soon as they reached firing distance, all that orderly grandeur would be changed to bleeding, writhing confusion, and that thousands of those valorous men of the South, with their chivalric officers, would pour out their life's blood on the fair fields in front of us.[35]

As Gordon's men continued their advance, the ground trembled beneath their steady tread. One onlooking Federal stated, "At their approach, the earth grew tremulous beneath the tread of many feet and sounded like a low, rumble of distant thunder."[36] Finally, the Federals of Lane's Brigade could stand it no longer. Gordon stated, "The Federal advance realizing that we were outflanking them on both sides fired a single volley and fled back to the main line."[37] When the Federals abandoned their advance line, the Confederates rushed forward behind them. Brigadier General Gordon further described, "My command took advantage of a tactical mistake on the part of the Federals…to rush upon their breastworks under cover of their own retreating men. We were not so far apart when the race began. Some of the fleetest of my command caught up with the slowest of the Federals and we had a running fight with them across the field from there to the Yankee breastworks."[38]

Now the race for the main line was on. Conrad's and Lane's brigades were running for their very lives toward the main Federal works, with Gordon's Tennesseans and Grandbury's Texans pursuing closely behind. As the gray line surged forward, Gordon's and Grandbury's unit cohesiveness disintegrated. It was a mad footrace to the main line as both sides struggled to gain the advantage over the other. During this frenzied race, someone in the Confederate line yelled, "Follow

---

[34] David R. Logsdon, comp., *Eyewitnesses at the Battle of Franklin* (Nashville, TN: Kettle Mills Press, 2000) 15–16.

[35] Levi T. Schofield, *The Retreat from Pulaski to Nashville, Tenn.; Battle of Franklin, Tennessee, November 30th, 1864* (Cleveland, OH: Press of the Caxton Co., 1909) 18.

[36] William J. K. Beaudot, *The 24th Wisconsin Infantry in the Civil War* (Mechanicsburg, PA: Stackpole Books, 2003) 336.

[37] "Address of General Gordon," 7.

[38] "Gen Geo. Gordon, Soldier, Citizen, Statesman, Dead."

them into their breastworks." Gordon and others picked up the idea, and from a thousand voices the cry "Go into the works with them," and "Follow them in, Follow them in," were repeated over and over again.[39]

Here, Wagner's blunder proved near fatal for the Federals. With each passing minute, the problem intensified exponentially for the Federals in the main line, as they had to hold their fire for fear of hitting their own oncoming men. Impending and probable disaster loomed. Colonel Horace Rice, leading the 11th/29th Tennessee, ran as fast as he could, his men running with him, immediately behind the fleeing Yankees of Lane's routed brigade.

In the confusion of the advance, the Confederate lines intermingled as the units near the Columbia Pike all raced toward the narrow breach in the Federal line just in front of the Carter House. Gordon and the extreme right of his brigade veered to the right, crossing the Columbia Pike, mixing with Grandbury's Texans, and the left of Cleburne's Division veered to the left, co-mingling with the Tennesseans. At this time, Gordon saw General Cleburne riding fast from the left making his way through the interspersed Tennesseans and Texans. Gordon abruptly stopped to let Cleburne pass, lest Cleburne's horse trample him.[40]

With nail-biting anxiety, before all of their men could clear the works, the Federals in the main line could hold their fire no longer and unloaded a deadly volley indiscriminately into the oncoming mass of gray interspersed with the blue-coated forms of their own comrades. The deafening rattle of musketry shattered the tranquility of the fields skirting the town of Franklin. With this volley, it seemed as if the very pandemonium of hell was unleashed as the deadly missiles tore into the Southern ranks. General Gordon said, "perhaps, [when we were] within a hundred paces of their main line and stronghold…it seemed to me that hell itself had exploded in our faces. Men fell right and left fast and thick and the field was covered at this point with a mantle of dead and dying men."[41] From this point on, for the Federals, it was load and fire as fast as possible. A few seconds later, incoming Federal fire hit Cleburne's horse. Private James C. Brandon of Cleburne's escort company dismounted to let the general have his horse. As Cleburne was in the process of mounting this horse, Federal fire hit it. The resolute Irishman continued forward on foot, disappearing in the smoke of battle. Federal fire decimated the right of Gordon's Brigade as they headed toward a salient angle in the Federal line near the Carter's gin house. A Federal officer behind the main line stated, "I saw then, that waving line of shining bayonets as it rushed toward the

---

[39] "Address of General Gordon," 7.
[40] Ibid.
[41] Ibid.

works with that defiant rebel yell, and the mad and murderous conflict that followed."[42]

A Confederate described the charge,

> As we screamed out the charging yell, the Yankee troops rose up from behind their works, and their rifles fell into a horizontal line; the Federal artillerists sprung to their guns; we instinctively pulled our hat-brims down as though to protect our faces, and dashed into the open. Instantly, we were met by a storm of bullets and canister that caused us to stagger as our dead and wounded comrades fell against us. We wavered badly, then gathered ourselves and pushed on, firing as we went.[43]

The soldier continued,

> The powder smoke hung on the field; through rifts in it we could see the Federal gunners spring nimbly to and fro from the Napoleon guns. The responsive flash of the guns as the lanyards were pulled would be followed by the rip of canister as it flew past and through us, tearing great gaps in our ranks, cracking men's bones as pipe stems, and knocking brave men dead with great holes in their bodies. The zip, zip, zip, of flying rifle-balls was a mighty and steady hum, as though the empty cylinders of countless threshing machines were revolving at full speed all around us.[44]

General Gordon added, "It seemed and sounded as though all the demons in hell had been let loose at once and were bent on our destruction. Grape, shrapnel, shells, bullets, canister—everything that was used in war to kill men with—the whole air seemed to be full of it. I declare to you sir, it seemed to me that I could have swung out my hat, or my hand, and caught it full of bullets."[45]

The chaos and bedlam of battle engulfed the remnants of the 11th/29th Tennessee as they neared the main line. Regiment upon regiment of Federal infantry unleashed a firestorm of death from behind the protection of their breastworks. White sulfurous powder smoke, hanging heavy in the late November afternoon, shrouded the scene obscuring the macabre reality of what was occurring over the remainder of the field. Immediately to the right and left of the 11th/29th Tennessee, the deep stentorian roar of Federal artillery preceded double and triple charges of canister that thudded into their thinning rows like scythes chopping

---

[42] *George Washington Gordon: Memorial Addresses Delivered in the House of Representatives and the Senate of the United States Sixty-Second Congress* (Washington, DC: Prepared Under the Direction of the Joint Committee on Printing, 1913) 16-17.

[43] W. H. Newlin, *A History of the Seventy-third Regiment of Illinois Infantry Volunteers: Its Services and Experiences in Camp, on the March, on the Picket and Skirmish Lines, and in Many Battles of the War, 1861–65. Embracing an Account of the Movement from Columbia to Nashville, and the Battles of Spring Hill and Franklin* (1890; reprint, Denver: University of Denver, N.D.) 476–77.

[44] Ibid., 477.

[45] "Gen. Geo. Gordon, Soldier, Citizen, Statesman, Dead."

through wheat. Just to the east of the Columbia Pike, the 12-pounder Napoleon guns of the 6th Ohio battery commanded by Captain Aaron P. Baldwin were firing into the oncoming Confederates. At this point along the line it was said that the "dead lay in windrows," "like snowdrifts in winter time."[46] In order to mow down the "dense forest of humanity, he loaded his guns to the muzzle with triple rounds of canister and dummies, or stockings filled with bullets." Baldwin stated that at every discharge of his pieces there were two sounds—"first the explosion and then the bones."[47] Minie balls zipped into their ranks. Taxed by the overwhelming losses, lieutenants and sergeants vainly attempted to close the gaps in their decimated lines to maintain at least some semblance of order. One Confederate described, "We advanced, stumbling over our dead and wounded. The latter shrieked as we trod on their mangled limbs."[48] The boys of the 11th/29th Tennessee, or what was left of them, continued moving on the double quick, surging toward the breach where the Columbia Pike passed through the Federal works arching around the southern perimeter of Franklin.

Meanwhile, as Gordon's Rebels chased the routed Yankees toward the main line, the 13th/154th Tennessee followed closely behind the 57th Indiana of Lane's Brigade. The color bearer of the 57th Indiana fell to the ground. As he fell, one of Gordon's men rushed to pick up the Yankee banner. No sooner had this soldier confiscated the flag than Yankee fire hit him.[49] Nearer to the Federal main line, just to the left of the Columbia Pike, enemy fire hit the color bearer of the 11th/29th Tennessee. As he fell, another member of the regiment picked up the sacred banner and carried it forward. A Yankee round hit this man too. As this scene played out repeatedly, eventually Sergeant Montgomery A. Stokey of Company C, with impetuous valor now carried the colors of the 11th. As the sergeant neared the main line, he reportedly suffered three bullet wounds to the head.[50] After Stokey fell, Peter Edgar Dreux, the engineer captain from Louisiana, whom members of the 29th Tennessee had freed from jail at Demopolis, Alabama, only eight months earlier, seized the tattered colors. Dreux, who was just to the west of the Columbia Pike, moved forward with reckless abandon. In an éclat of valor, he lunged over the main line of works carrying the war-torn, bullet-ridden colors into the smoke-filled vortex of battle with portions of the 11th/29th going with him. Dreux, the sixth color bearer of the day, struggled to step over the bodies of his already-fallen

---

[46] Newlin, *History of the Seventy-third Regiment*, 478; Schofield, *Retreat from Pulaski to Nashville*, 139.

[47] Schofield, *Retreat from Pulaski to Nashville*, 139.

[48] Newlin, *History of the Seventy-third Regiment*, 478.

[49] Crook, "Autobiography and Reminiscences."

[50] Mamie Yeary, *Reminiscences of the Boys in Gray, 1861–1865* (1912; reprint, Dayton, OH: Morningside, 1986) 728.

comrades.[51] "We charged right up to the breastworks, and leaped the ditch in front of them," stated General Gordon.[52] As the former artilleryman, turned engineer, turned infantryman, scaled the parapet and jumped to cross the bodies in the ditch, a bullet struck him in the chest, violently hurling his body backward into the trench. Falling into the trench with the other dead, Dreux's hands continued to grasp the flagstaff. As he fell backward, the banner wrapped around his body, and his red artillery kepi slid to the back as the weight of his head pressed the kepi against the dirt embankment.[53]

Passing Dreux, the left wing of Gordon's pugnacious brigade furiously smashed the Yankee line. One of the Rebels in this assault reminisced, "The breastworks were covered with head rails beneath which the Yankee sharpshooters poked their guns to fire upon us. But they recoiled as our men swarmed up over the breastworks, and clubbing their guns knocked them down and bayoneted them as fast as they leaped over."[54] Lieutenant Thoburn of the 50th Ohio, a Federal unit on the Columbia Pike stated, "They swept on like a resistless flood, coming in through our front line on the Columbia Pike, and just to the left of where our regiment was stationed.... After passing through, they swept down in our rear carrying everything before them."[55] S. B. Miller of the 100th Ohio, one of the units that bore the brunt of the overlapping brigades of Gordon and Grandbury, stated,

> The awful roar, the whistling lead, the shouts, shrieks, and groans checked many a strong man as if paralyzed at the thought of the certain fate before him. I saw three Confederates standing within our lines, as if they had been dropped unseen from the sky. They stood there for an instant, guns in hand, neither offering to shoot nor surrender—dazed as in a dream. I raised my gun, but instinctively I felt as if about to commit murder—they were hopeless, and I turned my face to the foe trying to clamber over our abatis. When I looked again the three were down—apparently dead; whether shot by their own men or ours, who could tell?[56]

Another Federal soldier added:

> The Confederates came on with a terrible dash, coming into the main works with Conrad's and Lane's men. It was so impetuous that they covered the main line on

---

[51] C. D. M'Amy, "Brave P. E. Drew and His Fate," *Confederate Veteran* 2/3 (1894): 85.

[52] "Gen. Geo. Gordon, Soldier, Citizen, Statesman, Dead."

[53] M'Amy, "Brave P. E. Drew," 85; J. A. Chalaron to Mary V. Nichols, 18 December 1897, Britt Collection, Box 3, File #10, Tennessee State Library and Archives, Nashville, TN.

[54] "Gen. Geo. Gordon, Soldier, Citizen, Statesman, Dead."

[55] Logsdon, *Eyewitnesses at the Battle of Franklin*, 29.

[56] Marshall P. Thatcher, *A Hundred Battles in the West: St. Louis to Atlanta, 1861–1865, the Second Michigan Cavalry, with the Armies of the Mississippi, Ohio, Kentucky, and Cumberland with Mention of a Few of the Famous Regiments and Brigades of the West* (Detroit, MI: self-published, 1884) 207.

the pike for about three hundred yards. Just at that moment General Stanley arrived from Schofield's headquarters which was on the north side of the river and stated "that the situation was the most critical he had ever known in any battle." Victory seemed almost within the Confederate grasp. Schofield's center was broken, two four gun batteries had fallen into Confederate hands, and it was only necessary for them to press the advantage they had gained to complete their success.[57]

"The courageous Confederates moved as steadily and resistlessly as a tidal wave, sweeping before them the enemy from their first line of works, and we charged on their last line, resulting in the greatest human slaughter of the Civil War, considering numbers engaged," stated a member of the 13th/154th Tennessee.[58]

On the left of Gordon's Brigade, Private Wiley M. Crook continued advancing with Company I of the 13th/154th Tennessee. Crook remembered,

> I never shall forget an incident which occurred a few minutes before the color-sergeant fell, and I thought was dead. I had just shot my gun and was reloading, when a Federal captain, in ten feet of me, with his pistol shot one of my comrades, and another one of them raised his gun to shoot this Federal captain, when he threw up his hands to surrender. A Southern lieutenant, not seeing the captain shoot our man, and thinking his man ought not to shoot an enemy with his hands up, knocked the gun down, and pointed the Federal captain to the rear.[59]

Crook went on to say, "Near and around this spot of which I speak the dead and dying were actually in heaps. God only knows how any of us ever escaped."[60]

As Private Crook and his company passed over the last line of works near the Columbia Pike across from the old cotton gin, he saw a comrade just ahead of him get hit as he picked up the colors of the 57th Indiana. As the colors fell once again, Crook rushed forward to grab the Yankee banner. As he took hold of the flag, it became immediately apparent that he was unable to handle both his gun and the flag. In the wild melee, Crook discarded his gun and decided to return to the supposed safety of the works a few yards to the rear with his prized trophy. As Crook approached the works, he was surprised to discover that there were still many Yankees there who had not abandoned the ditch who were "still firing at our men, who had stopped at the embankment."[61]

A section of Battery A, 1st Ohio Light Artillery, had been placed in the breach of the Columbia Pike. Their gunners abandoned their pieces and fled before

---

[57] Milwaukee (WI) *Sunday Telegraph*, 10 November 1881.
[58] Crook, "Autobiography and Reminiscences."
[59] W. M. Crook, "W. M. Crook's Heroism at Franklin," *Confederate Veteran* 5/6 (June 1897): 303.
[60] Ibid.
[61] Ibid.

the torrent coming toward them. In addition to the artillerymen, the 50th Ohio, the 44th Missouri, and the 72nd Illinois melted away and fled to the rear as well. Illinois sergeant Alex C. Nicholson stated, "the 44th Missouri and 72nd Illinois began to run like h—l from their riflepits."[62]

Another Federal described the Confederate assault,

> The rebel charge was so impetuous, as well as so heavy, that it was scarcely checked by the advance works, held too long by the two brigades aforesaid [Conrad and Lane], but swept over them like a torrent, hurling back our men in tumultuous rout, taking many prisoners and driving the residue right through the center of our main line, which not merely opened to receive them, but kept widening after they had rushed past. In an instant the wings next to the pike, of the 2d and 3d Divisions of the 23d (Cox) Corps, recoiled before the enemy's charge; the hill was lost, eight of our guns taken, and the rebel flag planted in triumph on our breastworks, as the exulting victors, having passed over them, hastily formed on the inside, intending to follow up their triumph. Caissons, as well as men, streamed wildly to the bridges, supposing the day to be utterly lost, and nothing to do but save from the wreck as much as possible.[63]

By this time, where the Columbia Pike crossed the Federal works near the Carter office and smokehouse, the Federal center fully collapsed as Gordon's Rebels poured through the gap, with Strahl's men following only yards behind. It appeared that the Confederate breakthrough was successful as company after company of Federals broke and fled to the rear, streaming down the Columbia Pike, leaving an ever-widening chasm in their wake. Elements of Gordon's Brigade led by Colonel Horace Rice of the 11th/29th Tennessee surged forward over the breastworks, past the smokehouse line, through the breach in the Columbia Pike, with hopes to expand their breakthrough. Interspersed with Gordon's Tennesseans were elements of Cleburne's men, particularly Grandbury's Texans. It was at this point that arguably the most brutal, vicious, and obscene fighting of the entire war occurred. While the Civil War is known for its brutality, no charge during the entire war was more barbaric than this that occurred at Franklin. It was as if hell disgorged its bowels into the yard of the Carter House, with both sides intent on the utter and complete annihilation of the other. Men seemed transformed into demons as they grappled in brutal hand-to-hand combat. One combatant recalled, "Franklin was the hardest, bloodiest and most wicked fight I was ever in; in fact it was the only time I ever saw the bayonet and butts of muskets used; and, let me tell you, both were used freely here."[64]

As Gordon's men swarmed through the gap in the Federal line, they captured the 1st Kentucky, a four-gun battery to the left of the Carter smokehouse. At the

---

[62] Newlin, *History of the Seventy-third Regiment*, 427.
[63] Ibid., 471.
[64] Ibid., 449–50.

time of its capture, one of the Yankee gunners had already made off with the friction primers. Gordon's men turned the guns to clear out the trenches of Federals. However, despite their best efforts, without the friction primers, they could not fire the guns.

With streams of Yankees pouring to the rear to escape the Confederate attack, and just as it looked like the Confederates had secured a permanent lodgment in the Federal line, disaster struck. The men of Opdyke's Brigade, the 36th, 44th, 73rd, 74th, 88th Illinois, 125th Ohio, and 24th Wisconsin regiments (who were in reserve a few hundred yards north of the Carter House because of Opdyke's refusal to obey orders) had stacked arms to have their first meal of the day and their first rest in two days. As these men prepared to cook coffee and bacon, they noticed their routed counterparts flooding to the rear. Major Thomas Motherspaw of the 73rd Illinois swung into his saddle, as did the "boy colonel," Lieutenant Colonel Arthur McArthur of the 24th Wisconsin. Earlier in the war, McArthur had already gained renown for his action at Missionary Ridge. When Motherspaw's infantrymen saw their major mount his horse, they instinctively left their campfires and grabbed their arms and accouterments. With the words "Up Wisconsin!" McArthur's men followed suit, as did other regiments of Opdyke's Brigade. Without orders, the 73rd Illinois started forward. Opdyke, immediately sent his adjutant to halt the move, Motherspaw replied that his men could not be stopped, and with this, Opdyke mounted his horse as well, and with the words "First brigade forward to the works," his Yankees rushed to the south to engage the victory-hungry Tennesseans.[65]

As the 73rd Illinois moved forward, a fence in the Carter yard impeded their progress as did the frantic Federals who had already been routed and were headed to the rear. Captain George W. Patten of Company I, 73rd Illinois described what a difficult time they had in navigating the obstacles to get to the front. Captain Patten wrote, "In our front, between us and the works, were two paling fences, the most formidable of which was heavy oak-paling nailed to heavy oak stringers with large nails, and on the side on which we must approach. Beyond this was what every man in the regiment knew was the safest place on the field—the breastworks."[66] Patten continued, "By the time they reached the oak paling fence, the balls of the enemy were striking very fast, and reminded one of a boy rattling a stick on a picket-fence as he runs along it. The getting over or through that fence in the face of that fire was one of the most, if not the most, terrible experiences the 73rd Regiment ever had."[67] One of the Federals present recounted, "It was too high to climb over; the palings were so thick they could not be broken with the butt of the gun, or the foot in kicking, and the nails were so large and so firmly fixed in the heavy oak bars that

---

[65] Beaudot, *24th Wisconsin Infantry*, 337; Newlin, *History of the Seventy-third Regiment*, 434.

[66] Newlin, *History of the Seventy-third Regiment*, 461–62.

[67] Ibid., 462.

it seemed impossible to get through."[68] Finally, the Federals broke through the fence and surged forward. After clearing the fence, Private Charles W. McNichols of the 73rd Illinois wrote, "I well remember what a badly demoralized mob we met just in the yard at the Carter House.... It was a fight, nearly, to get to the front [through the fleeing Federal ranks], they wildly struggling to the rear, and we crowding to the front."[69] Eventually, as Opdyke's men cleared the obstacles they gained speed and momentum as they and the Confederates determinedly raced toward each other.

As the two sides collided, it was like two ocean waves crashing together. As the two sides clashed, insanity ensued. Men were screaming, and hitting each other with anything and everything that could be fashioned as a weapon. Men used hatchets, picks, guns, swords, bayonets, shovels, and anything else they had. Blood and gore splattered over everyone and everything as men smashed the life out of each other. The ground turned into a bloody mess. As the men swung their muskets with wild force, heads burst open, spraying their contents. Moscow Carter stated that after the battle he scraped up more than a half-bushel basket of human brains around his home.[70] Carter stated, "The whole place was dyed [red] with blood."[71] Hideous arterial wounds spurted blood with each beat of the heart. Ghastly abdominal wounds abounded as men were disemboweled by the bayonet.

It was here that men from both sides found it impossible to describe the realities and horror that occurred. A Federal of the 73rd Illinois stated, "Description or imagination is hardly equal to the task of picturing the scene at this time."[72] The soldier went on to say, "The contending elements of hell turned lose would seem almost as a Methodist love-feast compared to the pandemonium that reigned there the space of ten or twenty minutes."[73]

As Opdyke moved forward, now on foot and engulfed by his brigade, he turned his revolver around and used it as a club until the barrel wedge dropped out. Part of Opdyke's men went around the rear of the Carter House, while the others continued in front. Two of his regiments, the 73rd Illinois, led by Major Thomas Motherspaw, and portions of the 24th Wisconsin led by Lieutenant Colonel Arthur McArthur, who urged his men on with the words, "give 'em hell, twenty-fourth," went to the front or east side of the house and hurried forward into the death-grapple.[74] As McArthur rode forward, his horse was shot from under him and he

---

[68] Ibid.
[69] Ibid., 440
[70] Logsdon, *Eyewitnesses at the Battle of Franklin*, 111.
[71] Moscow Carter Interview, unknown newspaper article in the McGavock-Cowan scrapbook 1992.59, Battle of Franklin Trust, Franklin, TN.
[72] Newlin, *History of the Seventy-third Regiment*, 462.
[73] Ibid.
[74] Beaudot, *24th Wisconsin Infantry*, 337.

took a shot in the right shoulder. McArthur regained his composure and continued forward, inspiring his men with his gallantry.[75]

As Lieutenant Colonel McArthur headed to the front, he saw a Confederate major, possibly Major A. T. Meeks of the 2nd Arkansas Infantry of Daniel C. Govan's Brigade of Cleburne's Division, carrying the colors of his regiment, leading his men forward through the breach in the line. As the two officers saw each other, they sought each other out. As McArthur approached, the Rebel major shot him in the chest. McArthur went down. Thinking his nemesis was dead; the Confederate major turned his back and waved his men forward through the gap. In the meantime, McArthur struggled to his feet and ran his opponent through with his sword. As the Rebel major fell, he got off one last shot that hit McArthur in the knee.[76]

At the head of the melee, Company C of the 11th Tennessee passed over the main line, and headed to the yard of the Carter House. Sergeant John D. Slayden, of this company crossed the main line of works, continued for several more yards, and crossed the parapet of the smokehouse line. As Slayden jumped into the ditch with the Yankees, he saw that his situation was hopeless. In a last desperate act of self-preservation, the sergeant fell to the bottom of the entrenchment, mixed with the bodies of already fallen comrades, and played dead.[77] Nearby, George and Wiley Baker, two brothers from Dickson County, also privates in Company C, scaled the Yankee parapet together. A bullet hit Wiley as he went over the works. His brother George made it over, but a Federal soldier, wielding his musket as a club beat him to the ground. Surprisingly, neither Wiley nor George was killed, but the Federals did capture George.[78] A minie ball hit the Irish-born John Sheridan of Company G in the right knee as he crossed the third line of works.[79] Captain I. P. Young was hit in the hip by a minie ball as he led Company I forward into the fray.[80]

Private McNichols of Company B, 73rd Illinois of Opdyke's Brigade stated, "We opened fire and just before we got to the rear line of works, we saw a reb on top of the outer line, with his gun clubbed ready to strike one of our men who had

---

[75] Ibid., 337–38.

[76] Douglas MacArthur, *Reminiscences* (New York: McGraw-Hill, 1964) 10. It is not completely proven that A. T. Meeks was the one with whom McArthur struggled.

[77] Reynolds, Veteran Questionnaire, TCWVQ, MF 484, R7.

[78] Wiley J. Baker, Tennessee Confederate Pension Application 5240, Family Search https://familysearch.org/pal:/MM9.3.1/TH-1942-20618-28069-70?cc=1874474&wc=M6ZX-WWP:171467301,172279702 (1 May 2015).

[79] John Sheridan, Tennessee Confederate Widows Pension Application 2429, Family Search https://familysearch.org/pal:/MM9.3.1/TH-1942-20613-3877-29?cc=1874474&wc=M6Z6-2TG:171467101,171689201 (1 May 2015).

[80] John D. Young, "In Memoriam: Life and Character of Captain I. P. Young," Unknown Newspaper clipping, 1909, copy in possession of Todd Cathey, Broken Arrow, OK.

failed to get out when the others ran; we pulled down on his 'bread basket' and saw him throw up his hands and fall backwards."[81] Private John W. Wynn of Company F, 11th Tennessee, aimed at one of the Yankees and fired. The Federal fell to the ground. The Yankee behind him pointed his gun at Wynn, but the private from Robertson County sprang past the muzzle of his gun with one leap and grasped it with his left hand. Wynn hoisted his rifle as a club with his right hand and ordered the Yankee to surrender, and the Federal eagerly complied. As Wynn raised his Enfield to club the Yankee, a bullet struck it, slightly bending the barrel. Wynn used the captured Federal's gun the remainder of the battle. While these events were transpiring, three of Wynn's comrades, one on each side and one behind him were shot dead. After the incident, Wynn jumped into the trench to get whatever protection he could from the hail of Yankee lead coming his way. Wynn recounted, "We would drop and load and rise and fire. The second man on my right while I was down was shot through the head and fell dead across my body."[82]

A Confederate bullet fired from close range hit Lieutenant Colonel Porter Olson in the chest while he was at the head of the 36th Illinois Infantry of Opdyke's Brigade. In the midst of the battle raging around him, he asked Lieutenant Hall of Company E, 36th Illinois, to take him to the rear. The lieutenant, with the assistance of Sergeant Yarnell of Company G, carried Olson to the rear of the Carter House, where Yarnell wrenched a shutter from the house, which they used as a litter. As the two men carried their commander toward an ambulance, Olson cried, "Help me dear Lord," and died.[83]

General Gordon gave the credit for breaking the Federal line to Colonel Horace Rice, leading the 11th/29th regiment. Gordon stated, "The credit of leading the men who broke the main line…belongs to my friend and comrade and colonel, Horace Rice."[84] After breaking the line, Colonel Rice received a severe wound as he crossed to the inside of the Federal main works.[85] Despite their colonel's wounding, the momentum of the attack carried on. The survivors of the 11th/29th Tennessee penetrated the Federal interior as deep as the Carter House. Their bodies identified the high water mark of the Confederate attack. General Gordon stated that some of the men of the 11th/29th Tennessee were killed fifty or more yards within the enemy's line.[86]

Twenty-four-year-old Captain Jeremiah Batts and his brother-in-law, Corporal Reynolds Leftrick Powell, of Company F of the 11th were two of these

---

[81] Newlin, *History of the Seventy-third Regiment*, 440–41.
[82] Yeary, *Reminiscences*, 827–28.
[83] Elmer Dickenson, "The Olsen Monument," http://kendallkin.org/records/military/civil-war-records/the-olson-monument.html (accessed 2 March 2015).
[84] "Address of General Gordon," 8.
[85] Lindsley, *Military Annals*, 302.
[86] "Address of General Gordon," 8.

killed within the enemy's line. The men were near each other at the head of the remnants of their company. Powell climbed onto the front steps of the Carter House where he was killed, probably bayoneted to death by an infantryman of Company K, 73rd Illinois.[87] Moscow Carter said that after the battle relatives from Robertson County came for his body.[88] Captain Batts was mortally wounded nearby. A Federal soldier of Company I, 73rd Illinois wrote,

> When we made the charge, part of my regiment went on the west and part on the east of the Carter House, and as we were passing I saw a Confederate officer about 100 feet from the east door of the Carter House and ordered him to surrender. He was about 10 feet from me, and looked at me and said: "I will die first." One of the boys told me to take aim, and if I missed, he would shoot him. My comrade fired, but the officer paid no attention to it, as he was not hit. I had a 16 shooter and fired. The officer threw up his hands and came near falling; I let him have another shot, and he reeled, staggered on to near the east door and fell....[89]

---

[87] Newlin, *History of the Seventy-third Regiment*, 642.

[88] Frank H. Smith, "Interview with Col. M. B. Carter" in *History of Maury County* reproduced in Rick Warwick, comp. and ed., *Williamson County: Civil War Veterans Their Reunions and Photographs* (Nashville, TN: The Heritage Foundation of Franklin and Williamson County, 2007) 55. The identification of Reynolds Powell as the Confederate soldier killed on the steps of the Carter House is based on several pieces of evidence. First, as far as the author can ascertain, Company F of the 11th Tennessee was the only unit comprising men from Robertson County in near proximity of the Carter House in the Battle of Franklin. This is important because, according to Moscow Carter's diary, whatever the soldier's identity, relatives from Robertson County retrieved the body after the battle. Second, Reynolds Powell and his brother-in-law, Captain Jeremiah Batts, were both from Robertson County and lost their lives at Franklin; however, Powell was apparently killed on the spot, while Batts was mortally wounded and died on 9 December 1864. Third, family members retrieved both Powell's and Batts's bodies and returned them to Cedar Hill, Tennessee, where they remain interred side by side in the Batts's Family Cemetery, thus fitting the description of Moscow Carter's diary entry.

[89] This account comes from Private James D. Remington, Company I, 73rd Illinois. If Remington is to be believed, this account may give the details of the mortal wounding of Captain Jeremiah Batts of Company F, 11th Tennessee, from Robertson County. As Remington was passing back through Franklin after the Battle of Nashville, several Federal soldiers who had been wounded and captured by the Confederates at Franklin told him that the Confederate officer he shot in the yard of the Carter House was Captain Tod Carter, whose father owned the house. After the war, Remington read that Captain Carter was killed a few hundred yards west of the house. In an attempt to determine the accuracy of the story, Remington wrote Colonel Moscow Carter, the elder brother of Captain Tod Carter who was living at the Carter House at the time of the battle. Moscow Carter responded, "Franklin, Tenn., Nov. 18, 1884. J. D. Remington. Dear Sir: In reply to yours of the 11th Inst, will say that I lost a brother in the battle of Franklin, Nov. 30, 1864. He was a member of Gen. Tom Smith's staff, with the rank of Captain. Was mortally wounded, 300 or 400 yards from the

Within the space of twenty minutes, the Yankees managed to push the Confederates back over the works, but the Southerners still managed to maintain their hold on the main Federal line. The infernal fighting was over. The Carter yard resembled a slaughter pen with the dead, dying, and wounded scattered all about. More than forty-seven dead men, not counting the wounded, lay in the Carter's front yard. Near the Federal 20th Ohio Battery in the Carter's backyard, more than eighteen dead horses and mules were scattered about the yard.[90]

While the butchery was taking place in the Carter yard, General Gordon with other elements of his Tennessee brigade had crossed the Columbia Pike and had struck the Federal works in the salient angle just west of the Carter's cotton gin. After passing through the infernal barrage of musketry and canister, General Gordon stated, "We reached the works with but few men, and these were well-nigh exhausted, having charged at full speed for more than a half a mile."[91] Despite their fatigue, some of Gordon's men went over the works. Those who did were bayoneted or clubbed to death with muskets.[92]

As he approached the works, Gordon immediately comprehended the desperate situation. In the cotton gin salient, the breastworks were seven to eight feet high. Over these works, the men of both sides literally stabbed at each other over and between the head logs. Others pulled people over the top by the hair or by their uniforms. They threw rocks and dirt clods and sticks at each other. They screamed. Many of the men's ears bled from the concussion of the musketry and cannons that were so close. One Tennessean said that blood ran in streams making rivulets as it flowed to the ditches.[93]

As the violence ensued and the units around the Columbia Pike and cotton gin salient squeezed into the breach as they moved forward, some members of the 49th Tennessee of Quarles's Brigade moved into the ditch near the gin house with Gordon. John M. Copley was one of these men. Copley stated,

> A Federal officer on his horse, at the head of a line of infantry, came dashing up to the works in our front, and one of our soldiers in the ditch, about ten feet from my left, raised his gun and fired, shooting him off his horse. Among the first whom I

---

house, in the field in front of the locust thicket, and considerably to your right. He was brought to the house as soon as the firing ceased, and died about 36 hours afterwards. The man you refer to as falling near the east door, I remember being there the next morning. He was a Tennessee soldier, and was, I think, from Robertson County. His name I heard, but have forgotten." This exchange was printed in "The Fight at Franklin," *National Tribune*, 11 December 1884.

[90] "Memorial Addresses on George Washington Gordon," 18; David Fraley, "Carter House Tour," 5 September 2010.

[91] "Gen. Geo. Gordon, Soldier, Citizen, Statesman, Dead."

[92] Ibid.

[93] *The Valley of Death: Franklin November 30, 1864*, Digital Video Disc, (LotzHouse.com, 2011) Chapter 1.

saw in the ditch, upon their feet and unhurt were Gen. George W. Gordon, Lieutenant Colonel Atkins, commander of our regiment, and Captain Williams of an Alabama regiment. These men appeared to be undaunted, and a look of stoic determination had settled upon their weather-beaten faces....

The slaughtering...could be seen down the line as far as the Columbia and Franklin pike, and where the works crossed the pike...our troops were killed by whole platoons. Our front line of battle seemed to have been cut down by the first discharge, for in many places they were lying on their faces in almost as good order as if they had lain down on purpose; but no such order prevailed amongst the dead who fell in making the attempt to surmount the cheval-de-frise, for hanging on the long spikes of this obstruction could be seen the mangled and torn remains of many of our soldiers who had been pierced by hundreds of minie balls and grape shot.... The ditch was full of dead men, and we had to stand and sit upon them. The bottom of it, from side to side, was covered with blood to the depth of the shoe soles.[94]

In the midst of the carnage, Gordon realized it was utter madness and certain death to go over the works as he and his men were outnumbered four to one. Instead of scaling the Federal works, he yelled for his men to get in the ditch in front of the parapet. For a while, Gordon's men could stand in relative safety, but soon, Federal soldiers from another part of the line noticed them and began firing into them. Moreover, by this time, as Strahl's Brigade, which formed Brown's second line of battle, was charging in from behind them, they were caught in a murderous crossfire from three sides. Gordon described the helplessness of their situation: "All we could do was to crouch there in the ditch and listen to the bullets sing about us."[95] The Yankees on the other side of the works began poking the muzzles of their rifles through the space between the parapet and the head logs trying to hit someone without unduly exposing themselves. One of the Confederates said, "Very little effective work could be done that way of course, I caught and pushed aside a handful of the Federal guns myself, and saw others doing the same thing."[96] A few of the Confederates tried the same thing, but with little result.

Eventually, many of Gordon's men had had all they could stand. They could not take being caught in the three-way crossfire any longer. These men started begging General Gordon to surrender to the Yankees. Although the thick powder smoke draping the field prevented Gordon from seeing very far in any direction, he urged his men to hold on, hoping at any time to receive reinforcements. As the crossfire continued, these hardened veterans of many fields of battle finally reached

---

[94] John M. Copley, *A Sketch of the Battle of Franklin, Tenn. With Reminiscences of Camp Douglas*, 1893; reprint, Broken Arrow OK: Create Space, 2012) 24–25.
[95] "Gen. Geo. Gordon, Soldier, Citizen, Statesman, Dead."
[96] Ibid.

the limits of their endurance. Some of the boys began putting their hats on the ends of their bayonets and raising them above the earthworks as a sign of surrender. Through the thick smoke of battle, the Federals mistook the hats on the bayonets as heads, and survivors stated that the rifle fire cut off many of the bayonets. At this, some of the boys began yelling at the Federals in order to get their attention. Finally, one soldier near Gordon "yelled out in a voice that carried even through the din of battle: 'Cease firing you _____ fools! We'll surrender if you give us a chance.'" [97] Gordon stated that almost immediately afterwards he "heard the command cease firing given on the Federal side of the breastworks, and our men began leaping up and going over inside the Yankee lines, giving up their arms as they went."[98]

As the men were going over the rifle pits to surrender, Gordon dropped back into the outer ditch. One of his men saw him and asked the general if he was not going to surrender. Gordon told him "no." The general said he was going to try to stay in the ditch until nightfall, which was close at hand, and then try to slip back to safety. The young rebel told his commander he would stay with him. Gordon reported that the two crouched among the "dead and dying and waited."[99]

While the Federals were allowing the Tennesseans to surrender, the powder smoke began to clear, and as it did, Gordon looked around. For the first time, the general caught a view of the field. The brigadier stated, "I tell you, it was awful. I believe a man could have walked back from the front of those breastworks for a hundred yards along the line of our charge and stepped on a dead man every time he put his foot down."[100]

After those interested in surrendering had cleared the works, the Federals began firing again, this time among the dead and wounded in front of the breastworks. The general and his partner soon discovered it would be certain death to try to remain in the outer ditch. Gordon happened to have a pocket-handkerchief with him, "a rather unusual thing in those days," the general said. The two men tied the handkerchief to the end of the soldier's bayonet and then hoisted it above the parapet as a token of surrender. Again, the firing stopped, and the general and his partner climbed over the works into the custody of the Yankees.[101]

As soon as General Gordon steadied himself on the Federal side of the breastworks, he found himself in the presence of two Yankee soldiers, an officer and an enlisted man. The Federal enlisted man started cursing Gordon and swung viciously at the general's head with the butt of his musket. Fortunately for Gordon, the Federal officer threw up his sword and with a rash of oaths toward the enlisted

---

[97] Ibid.
[98] Ibid.
[99] Ibid.
[100] Ibid.
[101] Ibid.

man, blocked the blow, causing it to glance off Gordon's shoulder. Gordon received a painful, but relatively minor injury.[102] Captain James Dinkins stated,

> General George W. Gordon followed the enemy into his last works, where his men and those of the enemy fought with such desperation that Gordon's command was almost annihilated. They were within five feet of each other. Nothing but a bank of earth divided them. The enemy's position on both the right and the left enabled him, therefore, to enfilade Gordon's line. It was madness to continue the struggle, and some of Gordon's men attempted to retreat, every one of whom were killed.[103]

By 5:00 PM, darkness began engulfing the field. After only forty-five minutes of fighting, the 11th Tennessee had suffered tremendous casualties, and the Confederate situation had gone from near victory to utter hopelessness. Across the turnpike, Bate had not connected to Brown's left, leaving Brown's flank "in the air." To the right of the turnpike, Gordon's right wing had failed to dislodge the enemy from the main line in the salient angle by the gin house. In that area, the intense Federal fire had annihilated his legions, and the few survivors who had not surrendered lay cowering in the outer ditch. On Gordon's left, his troops had actually broken the Federal line, but in sight of victory, Opdyke's counter charge had brutally beaten them back to the Federal main line where they tenaciously held on. The bodies of the 11th Tennessee lay strewn around the Carter House yard. Reynolds Powell's body lay on the front steps of the Carter House; Captain Jeremiah Batts lay wounded close by, and Peter Dreux's hands still clutched the staff of the regimental colors in the Federal main line as his blood dripped onto the flag. Those who had broken the main line continued to hold it, although a heavy crossfire from both flanks and in front inundated them. Finally, darkness covered the ghastly field.

To the west of the pike, a private of the 73rd Illinois stated, "We dropped behind the inside works, and began firing as fast as we could load. Just at our right there was a section of a battery [the 20th Ohio], brass pieces, which gave the enemy canister as long as it held out."[104] These four guns alone fired 169 rounds into the Confederate-held parapets, sending dirt, head logs, and bodies flying.[105]

As the Federals regained the smokehouse line, Sergeant Ford of the 24th Wisconsin saw his captain, Sam Philbrook, come up to this line. Philbrook noticed one of his privates from Company D, an Irish immigrant named "Mike," who had a thick brogue, dodging and ducking the oncoming hail of Confederate bullets. Philbrook looked down at the Irish soldier and said "Mike quit dodging your head there, stand up and take it like a man."[106] No sooner had these words left his mouth

---

[102] Ibid.
[103] Dinkins, *Personal Recollections*, 237.
[104] Newlin, *History of the Seventy-third Regiment*, 441.
[105] Sword, *Embrace an Angry Wind*, 208.
[106] Beaudot, *24th Wisconsin Infantry*, 340.

than a Southern bullet struck Philbrook in the middle of his forehead. According to Sergeant Ford, the gruff, unrepentant Irishman growled, "Why the devil in hell don't you stand up and take it like a mon?"[107]

By 5:30 PM, the November sun had completely set under the western horizon. The silver crescent moon and starry sky provided negligible light. Except for muzzle flashes, the scene was dark. As the fighting continued, each muzzle flash lit up the scene for a millisecond. One observer watching the battle from Hood's command post on Winstead Hill stated, "Great clouds of smoke overhung both lines, and we could only see the continued flashes of the guns."[108] One historian reminisced that it must have been like something from the pen of Dante.[109] The brief light that flashed each time a musket was fired elicited a scene of grotesque figures moving back and forth in the darkness. A member of the 24th Wisconsin commented, "The guns foul and choked, launched a spitting fire into the darkness, for an instant lighting up the gloom, revealed the choked and powder-begrimed faces of the men, who, haggard and wan looked like hideous specters evoked from the regions of despair."[110]

As the night advanced, the charges made by the Confederates increased in number, but decreased in ferocity. A Federal of the 73rd Illinois recalled, "By ten o'clock it would seem to a close observer from our lines that it was hardly possible for the officers to rally the men to make even a semblance of an assault. When they did make a move in our direction, they were met with such a galling fire that they soon returned, and by 10:30 all was quiet in our front, except the wails and moans of the dying."[111]

Later that night as the Federals abandoned Franklin, General Gordon's captors were marching him to Nashville. Gordon left word with a citizen of Franklin to tell General Cheatham that he [Gordon] had been captured but was not seriously wounded.[112] After the firing had died away, a cold front passed through, sending the temperature plummeting from the forties into the twenties, making it even more uncomfortable for the exhausted, wounded, and dying soldiers. The cries of the suffering wounded hauntingly echoed across the field, and the able-bodied began searching for their dead and wounded comrades. One Confederate reminisced that many of the fallen were literally "shot to pieces," and throughout that horrible night, many of the wounded "crawled off the field," many with "one

---

[107] Ibid, 341.
[108] Dinkins, *Personal Recollections*, 236.
[109] Beaudot, *24th Wisconsin Infantry*, 342.
[110] Ibid.
[111] Newlin, *History of the Seventy-third Regiment*, 465.
[112] "Gen. Geo. Gordon, Soldier, Citizen, Statesman, Dead."

leg trailing on the earth behind them, others with shattered shoulders or torn entrails, or ghastly flesh wounds, or with smashed jaws, or with eyes shot out."[113]

---

[113] Newlin, *History of the Seventy-third Regiment*, 479.

17

"This Was the Most Disorderly Retreat I Experienced"

December 1864

The sunrise of 1 December, ripped back the cover of darkness to expose the scene of slaughter, which had occurred the previous evening. Throughout the morning, the search for the living among the dead continued. That morning, General Cheatham came to view his massacred corps. As he surveyed the damage, the citizen with whom Gordon had talked saw Cheatham and relayed his message as instructed. The corps commander expressed surprise at Gordon's capture and stated, "If the Yankees captured Gordon they dragged him over the breastworks by the hair of the head."[1]

One Confederate wrote, "Franklin was the only battle-ground I ever saw where the faces of the majority of the dead expressed supreme fear and terror. Dead men's faces were drawn away. Their eyes were wide open and fear-staring. Their very attitude as they lay prone upon the ground, with extended, earth-clutching fingers, and with their faces partially buried in the soil, told the tale of mental agony they had endured before death released them."[2] Another shocked Rebel stated, "When daylight dawned on Franklin, Tenn., December 1, 1864, the scene was indescribable."[3] W. E. Reynolds of Company C stated, "[The] next morning I viewed the battleground, and between the middle and outside lines which was about one hundred yards apart, our dead was scattered promiscuously, but at this entanglement, I could have walked on men, for a space of about twenty or thirty yards wide as far as I could see."[4] One Rebel, surveying the pitiful scene stated, "Thousands lay upon that field, dead and dying. You could see squads of these

---

[1] ""Gen. Geo. Gordon, Soldier, Citizen, Statesman, Dead," Memphis (TN) Commercial Appeal, 10 August 1911.

[2] W. H. Newlin, *A History of the Seventy-third Regiment of Illinois Infantry Volunteers: Its Services and Experiences in Camp, on the March, on the Picket and Skirmish Lines, and in Many Battles of the War, 1861–65. Embracing an Account of the Movement from Columbia to Nashville, and the Battles of Spring Hill and Franklin* (1890; reprint, Denver: University of Denver, N.D.) 479.

[3] James Dinkins, *Personal Recollections and Experiences in the Confederate Army by an Old Johnnie* (1897; reprint, Dayton, OH: Morningside, 1975) 238.

[4] William E. Reynolds, Veteran Questionnaire, Tennessee Civil War Veterans Questionnaires, Tennessee State Library and Archives, Nashville, TN, 1922. MF 484, R7. Hereafter referred cited as TCWVQ.

veterans who had fought together kneeling down around the body of some dying comrade, and their grief was so great that they wept like women."⁵

The horror was now visible for everyone to see. As Franklin residents, mostly unaccustomed to the sights of a battlefield, began to emerge from their homes, they were horrified at the scenes they encountered. Carrie Snyder, who happened to be visiting in Franklin, recoiled in shock, "God forgive me for ever wanting to see or hear a battle!"⁶ As Mrs. Snyder walked the field, she recounted, "You had to look twice as you picked your way among the bodies to see which were dead and which were alive and often a dead man would be lying partly on a live one, or the reverse—and the groans, the sickening smell of blood!"⁷ Hardin Figures, a fifteen-year-old resident of Franklin, recorded his experience as he walked down the Columbia Pike with a family slave nearly his own age. He observed,

> Just about daylight, and after I learned that our troops were in possession of the town, I started out to go over the battlefield, accompanied only by one of our slaves, a little younger than myself. The first dead person that I found was a little Yankee boy, about my own age, lying in the middle of the street with his hands thrown back over his head, pale in death. The sight of this boy somehow impressed me more than the thousands of dead men I was to look upon.⁸

As he continued his tour down the Columbia Pike a hundred yards or so past the Carter House, he observed, "In front of the Yankee battery which faced the Columbia Pike, you would find a man with his head shot off. Others had arms and legs shot off, and some were cut in twain, or almost so."⁹ Figures concluded, "Men, shot and wounded in every part of the body, were crying out for help, telling their names and calling for friends to help them. It was…a weird and gruesome sight."¹⁰ Even a veteran of many fields of battle such as General Cheatham was unprepared for the horror that lay before him. As Cheatham surveyed the battlefield, "great big tears ran down his cheeks and he sobbed like a child."¹¹ Cheatham later recalled, "Just at daybreak, I rode upon the field, and such a sight I never saw and can never

---

⁵ Byron Bowers, "Reminiscences of Byron Bowers," Franklin (TN) *Review Appeal*, 24 February 1972.

⁶ Marshall P. Thatcher, *A Hundred Battles in the West: St. Louis to Atlanta, 1861–1865, the Second Michigan Cavalry, with the Armies of the Mississippi, Ohio, Kentucky, and Cumberland with Mention of a Few of the Famous Regiments and Brigades of the West* (Detroit, MI: self-published, 1884) 327.

⁷ Ibid.

⁸ H. P. Figures, "A Boy's Impressions of the Battle of Franklin," *Confederate Veteran* 23/1 (January 1915): 6.

⁹ Ibid.

¹⁰ Ibid.

¹¹ W. J. Worsham, *The Old Nineteenth Tennessee Regiment: June 1861–April 1865* (Knoxville, TN: Paragon Printing Co., 1902), 146.

expect to see again. The dead were piled up like stacks of wheat or scattered about like sheaves of grain. You could have walked all over the field upon dead bodies without stepping on the ground."[12]

In the yard of the Carter House, where the sledgehammer blow of Gordon's Brigade fell, the sights were unimaginable. An observer noted, "Right in front of the Carter House, on the margin of the pike, there was a locust tree, then about five inches in diameter.... A Yankee soldier standing behind this tree was shot through the head instant death and rigidity following. His left shoulder was against the tree, his head had dropped on his bosom, his gun in his left hand had kept him from falling on the left side, and his heavy iron ramrod in his right hand supported him on that side, and there he was standing in that position dead."[13] Cheatham observed, "In front of the Carter House, the bodies lay in heaps.... It was a wonder that any man escaped alive."[14] Cheatham closed his recollection with the chilling words, "I never saw anything like that field, and never want to again."[15] One of Cheatham's artillerymen recalled,

> From what I had heard...the slaughter was great and at dawn of day I hit the pike road to go and see for myself. I had gone but a few hundred yards when I came to a dead Federal picket. He was a little round-faced boy, shot in the thigh and bled to death.... He had corded his thigh with his own suspender. As I went on up the pike the dead pickets lay thicker.... I [walked]...on to within about fifty or one hundred yards of the works.... I had never seen Confederate carnage so thick.... Standing in the gap in the breastworks, where the turn-pike road passed through, I think there must have been two thousand dead Confederates in sight.
>
> The dead, cold and stiff bodies were laying in every conceivable posture, all with ghastly faces and glassy eyes. Some lay with faces up and some with faces down. Some in a sitting attitude, braced with the dead bodies of their comrades. Some lay with two or three bodies on them. Sometimes you could see a company commander lying with sword in one hand and hat in the other. Sometimes you could see a man who had a heavy martial frown, then again you could see others who wore a pleasing smile....
>
> At the gap where the works went through...were laying a Confederate and a Federal soldier, both with bayonets sent through their bodies. It was plain to see that they were each others victims; they both had hands on their guns. Close by a Georgia colonel and a Federal major lay, their positions indicating that they had slain each other with pistols...."[16]

---

[12] Thatcher, *Hundred Battles in the West*, 399.
[13] Figures, "A Boy's Impressions," 7.
[14] Thatcher, *Hundred Battles in the West*, 399.
[15] Ibid.
[16] David R. Logsdon, comp., *Eyewitnesses at the Battle of Franklin* (Nashville, TN: Kettle Mills Press, 2000) 79–80.

As the eyewitnesses recalled, men were in every conceivable position, some remaining in upright positions, braced in these unnatural states, due to leaning against a tree, embrasure, and the bodies of the other dead. Almost without exception, surgeons used many homes and outbuildings in Franklin as makeshift hospitals, and surgeons were overwhelmed with the numbers of casualties requiring their services. Attendants recovered Colonel Horace Rice and took him from the field to the home of Mrs. Sallie Gault Carter on Third Avenue.[17]

J. A. Chalaron of Bouanchaud's Louisiana Battery [formerly Pointe Coupee Light Artillery] was walking the field searching for comrades when he discovered the body of his former schoolmate, Peter Dreux, the final color bearer of the day for the 11th/29th Tennessee. Druex's body was immediately to the left of the Columbia Pike and on "top of the highest pile of our dead."[18] Chalaron described Dreux's position, "He had died in the act of springing over his dead comrades who had preceded him in the charge and whose bodies filled the ditch far above the crest of the earthwork."[19] Dreux remained on his back with his red artillery kepi on his head and pressed against the pile of dead below. His hands maintained their clutched position although someone of the regiment had already removed the bloodstained flag and staff from his hands. Chalaron and a detail from Dreux's old artillery unit removed the young man's body from the pile of dead in the trench and buried him near a large white oak tree about 150 yards outside the works, near the Columbia Pike and to the left facing Franklin. The other soldiers of the 11th/29th were buried side by side by companies in large trenches between the earthworks and Dreux's grave.[20]

The burial details were fast at work. One of Gordon's men, W. S. Chapman, an acting company commander of the 12th Tennessee, was instructed to go down to the breastworks with what remained of his company (eight men) and to act as a burial detail. When they laid out their dead together, they were ordered to take the "dead of the enemy to the breastworks, cover them with blankets, if any could be found, and throw enough dirt over all to prevent nauseating odors to reach the citizens living nearby."[21] Chapman was instructed by Captain Patterson to gather and stack the guns and hang the cartridge boxes with them. Chapman stated, "I went down with my remnant company and we went to work."[22] Details buried the

---

[17] Sam Davis Elliott, ed., *Doctor Quintard, Chaplain C. S. A. and Second Bishop of Tennessee: The Memoir and Civil War Diary of Charles Todd Quintard* (Baton Rouge: Louisiana State University Press, 2003) 106.

[18] J. A. Chalaron to Mary V. Nichols, 18 December 1897, Britt Collection, Box 3, File #10, Tennessee State Library and Archives, Nashville, TN.

[19] Ibid.

[20] Ibid.

[21] W. S. Chapman, "A Boast and a Challenge," *Confederate Veteran* 34/8 (August 1926): 301.

[22] Ibid.

Yankees in the earthworks, but for the Confederates, trenches were dug "two and a half feet deep and wide enough for two to lay side by side. A piece of oilcloth or blanket was spread over their faces and covered up. Every one that could be identified a small piece of plank was placed on their head with their names on it."[23]

The Army of Tennessee had been all but annihilated at Franklin. Particularly hard hit was Cheatham's Corps. A member of the 29th Tennessee stated that Company G of that regiment went into the battle with eighteen men. Fifteen of these men were killed on the field. Another man was shot through the bowels and died on 1 December, leaving only two men in the company.[24] This same soldier reported that there were only seventy men present in Gordon's entire brigade to answer roll on 1 December.[25] Lieutenant John K. Shipley of the 29th Tennessee was the ranking officer present after the battle, and he took command of the brigade.[26] The fight at Franklin had thoroughly decimated Cheatham's Corps. Cheatham lost two of his three division commanders: Cleburne was killed and Brown was wounded. His brigade commanders were ravaged as well. Strahl, Carter, Gist, and Grandbury were all killed, and Gordon was wounded and captured.

Confederate surgeons opened the courthouse and used it as a field hospital for Brown's Division. Attendants recovered Sergeant M. A. Stokey's body and buried him near where he fell.[27] Litter bearers conveyed Captain Batts to one of the field hospitals, but he died on 9 December. The young captain's dying words were, "Tell my mother and sisters that I am one of the few that have tried to serve the Lord, and I am not afraid to die."[28] Since Major General Brown, commanding the division, was dangerously wounded, Colonel C. C. Hurt of the 9th Tennessee regiment temporarily commanded the division. The regiment suffered horribly. A private in Company C stated, "Our company numbered fourteen in going into the fight, but only four of us were numbered [the] next morning with the living."[29] Conservative estimates rate the strength of the survivors of the 11th Tennessee at approximately 150 before the battle. The loss of the 11th Tennessee is estimated at approximately 81 killed, wounded, and captured, bringing the regimental losses to a minimum of 54 percent, though the actual numbers could be higher. According to William E. Reynolds, Company C suffered 71 percent casualties.[30] Historian James McDonough says, "if one compares the total number of men killed in each army,

---

[23] Ibid.
[24] C. D. M'Amy, "Brave P. E. Drew and His Fate," *Confederate Veteran* 2/3 (1894): 85.
[25] Ibid.
[26] Ibid.
[27] Mamie Yeary, *Reminiscences of the Boys in Gray, 1861–1865* (1912; reprint, Dayton, OH: Morningside, 1986) 728.
[28] Jeremiah Batts, tombstone inscription, Batts Family Cemetery, Springfield, TN.
[29] Reynolds, Veteran Questionnaire, TCWVQ, MF 484, R7.
[30] Ibid.

using the commonly accepted figures, the Bluecoats had more than a nine-to-one edge."[31]

Lee's and Stewart's corps moved behind the Federals toward Nashville. Cheatham's Corps, too badly mauled by the previous day's fight, remained behind at Franklin. Perhaps the impact of the battle may be demonstrated by the terse words of a member of Cheatham's Corps, "Today spent in burying the dead, caring for the wounded, and reorganizing the remains of our corps."[32]

Meanwhile, over the next few days, those who were not seriously injured and those who had been separated from their units in the battle began to reassemble. By the time the brigade began the march to Nashville, they numbered 511. Lieutenant Colonel William M. Watkins took command of the brigade, and Major John E. Binns assumed command of the 11th/29th Tennessee.[33]

On the morning of 2 December, Ben Cheatham formed his emaciated corps and marched it north up the Franklin Pike toward Nashville. Private William E. Reynolds commented, "With regret and sadness, we disposed of sacrificed comrades, as best we could, and took up our line of march to Nashville, God only knows for what purpose, as our army had been reduced to so few that we were unable to cope with those of the enemy that had concentrated from various posts along the way to Nashville."[34]

As Cheatham's Corps advanced up the turnpike and neared John Overton's "Traveler's Rest," several ladies lined the road to cheer the troops. Cheatham's men must have thought that there was little to cheer about because they had just left behind one-third to one-half of their comrades in graves or hospitals back in Franklin. Among the women present was Mary Bradford, who was instrumental in making the first regimental colors of the 11th Tennessee. Others present were Becky Allison, Mary Hadley, and Buck Correy. After marching all day, the corps bivouacked within five miles of the city on a farm owned by Mr. Regan.[35]

In the meantime, Colonel David C. Kelly, with a portion of Forrest's Cavalry, blockaded the Cumberland River at Bell's Mill just outside of Nashville. Kelly's

---

[31] James Lee McDonough, *Nashville: The Western Confederacy's Final Gamble* (Knoxville: University of Tennessee Press, 2004) 110.

[32] United States War Department, *The War of the Rebellion: A Compilation of the Official Records of the Union and Confederate Armies*. 70 vols. in 128 (Washington: Government Printing Office, 1880–1901; reprint, Gettysburg, PA: The National Historical Society, 1972) ser. I, vol. 45, 1, 731. Hereafter cited as *OR*.

[33] Tennessee Civil War Centennial Commission, *Tennesseans in the Civil War: A Military History of Confederate and Union Units with Available Rosters of Personnel*, vol. 1 of 2, (Nashville, TN: Civil War Centennial Commission, 1964) 1:198.

[34] Reynolds, Veteran Questionnaire, TCWVQ, MF 484, R7.

[35] W. D. Gale to wife, "Letter to Wife after Hood's Defeat Before Nashville," 19 January 1865, Civil War Collection: Confederate Collection, Box 9, Letters, Folder 7, Gale William Dudley, Tennessee State Library and Archives, Nashville, TN.

cavalry was fighting it out on the river with Federal gunboats such as the heavily armed, ironclad *Carondelet*. While Kelly was interrupting traffic on the Cumberland, Hood had established his headquarters at "Traveler's Rest" and deployed his shattered infantry regiments along the heights ringing Nashville. On 3 December, Cheatham's Corps moved out on the extreme right of the Confederate line near the Murfreesboro Pike. When their lines were marked, the boys began digging entrenchments. The men remained in this location (with only occasional skirmishing) until 15 December.[36]

The weather during the first week of December had been mild, that changed the night of 8 December. The temperature dropped, and mixed precipitation began to fall, worsening through the night. By the next morning, sleet and snow blanketed the ground. Rain, freezing rain, and sleet continued for the next week, and the ground became so icy it was nearly impossible for man or beast to move about.[37] This halted work on the fortifications and compounded the misery of Cheatham's men, who like the rest of the army, were scantily clad and poorly equipped. A large number were without shoes. In order to compensate, many of the boys took green beef hides and cut out moccasins. The boys wrapped the hairy side of the skins against their feet and then sewed them together.[38]

While pickets kept a vigilant watch on the Federal lines in Nashville, visitors to the army were common occurrences. On one occasion, two boys visited the camps of Cheatham's Corps. As the boys stopped at one of the fires to warm themselves, they noticed one of the soldiers frying eggs, using the half of an old canteen. The young man, John Cook, was amazed as he observed Cheatham's ragged troops. Cook noticed that not one of these Confederates had an overcoat. The boy recalled, "One poor fellow had no shoes, his feet being wrapped in blue rags, evidently cut from the uniform of a dead Federal soldier. Another had no trousers, unless the white domestic overalls he wore could be thus designated."[39] Cook further described the state of Cheatham's men:

> I recall now how wonderful it seemed to me that men could be fond to fight for a government that could not or would not clothe and feed them; and on this point I have never ceased to wonder. This trouserless soldier was with a single exception the best natured Confederate in the camp. The exception was the one without shoes. He did little else than tell funny stories, and he laughed at his own jokes as heartily as any of his auditors. And his laugh—it was one of the merriest, jolliest, laughs I have ever heard; and his eyes—they were just brimming over with fun.

---

[36] Ibid.

[37] Stanley Horn, *The Decisive Battle of Nashville* (Knoxville: University of Tennessee Press, 1986) 43.

[38] Yeary, *Reminiscences*, 64.

[39] John C. Cook, "A Boy at the Battle of Nashville," *Taylor-Trotwood Magazine* 6/3 (November 1909): 102.

Sometimes in my sleep the form of this happy-go-lucky confederate comes to haunt my dreams, and I see that mirthful face, those merry eyes, and my ears catch again the joyous ripple of his infectious laugh. Perhaps he is still laughing, but if so it is in that other and happier world beyond the stars, where the monstrous apparitions of war and famine and freezing cold come not to affright the soldier's soul, for the day after the Battle of Nashville I saw him lying cold and stiff in the embrace of death.[40]

As the boys continued their journey, Cook noticed another Confederate who occasionally slipped his hand into his haversack to take out a long slender piece of something that he thought might be molasses candy. Hoping to get a piece of the homemade candy, the boy approached the soldier. His excitement, however, quickly melted to disappointment when the supposed pieces of candy turned out to be strips of dried pumpkin.[41]

On 10 December, Watkins's command was as follows: the 11th/29th Tennessee commanded by Major John E. Binns; the 12th/47th Tennessee commanded by Captain C. N. Wade; and the 13th/51st/52nd/154th Tennessee commanded by Major John T. Williamson.[42] On 14 December, 1st Lieutenant Thomas B. Adcock, J. W. Redden, G. H. Petty, and John Majors, all of Company K, received furloughs home to Dickson County, issued by Major Binns.[43]

By 15 December, the temperature had risen enough to melt the ice, which had delayed the Federal attack. Although the ice was gone, the land turned into a thick mud. A heavy fog blanketed the countryside in the early morning hours of 15 December. This curtain of fog allowed the Federals to get into position, and Yankee batteries from Fort Negley and other positions began shelling the Confederate lines. General Thomas, the overall Federal commander at Nashville, sent Brigadier General Charles Cruft's provisional division against the Confederate left and began the assault with the black soldiers of Colonel Charles Thompson's Colored Brigade. Up to this point, Thompson's soldiers had served on construction and garrison duty along the Nashville and Northwestern Railroad, which ran west from Davidson County through Cheatham, and Dickson counties, terminating at Johnsonville on the Tennessee River in Humphreys County. Nevertheless, on this day they had the horrible misfortune to be hurled against the surviving veterans of Cleburne's Division, now commanded by Brigadier General James A. Smith. The right of Smith's line was anchored by a crude but strongly built lunette, occupied by artillery

---

[40] Ibid.
[41] Ibid.
[42] *OR*, ser. I, vol. 45, pt. I, 667.
[43] Thomas B. Adcock, M268 R159; J. W. Redden, M268 R162; G. H. Petty, M268 R162; and John Majors, M268 R161, all in 11th Tennessee Infantry Service Records, National Archives Records Administration, *Compiled Service Records of Confederate Soldiers Who Served in Organizations from the State of Tennessee*, Washington, DC: National Archives and Records Service, General Services Administration, 1960. Hereafter cited as 11th TISR.

and the survivors of Grandbury's Texas Brigade commanded by Captain E. T. Broughton.

The 11th/29th Tennessee and the remainder of Brown's Division (now commanded by General Mark P. Lowrey), supported by a battery of artillery, occupied the extreme right of the Confederate line just east of the Nolensville Pike, southeast of Grandbury's lunette, and on a rise overlooking the Nashville and Chattanooga Railroad. As two of Cruft's remaining four brigades wrapped around the Confederate line to the left, Lieutenant Colonel Charles H. Grosvenor was fronted by Grandbury's veterans, and Colonel Thomas J. Morgan's 1st Colored Brigade made up the extreme Federal left fronting Lowrey's (Brown's) Division across the Nashville and Chattanooga railroad.[44]

At 7:00 AM, Morgan's regiments marched out the Murfreesboro Pike and took their place on the extreme left of the Federal line. The 14th US Colored Infantry deployed as skirmishers and advanced until they met a devastating fire from the Confederate picket line. At this time, the 17th and 44th US Colored Infantry regiments advanced and drove in the Confederate skirmishers. As Morgan's regiments continued forward, they neared the Confederate line held by Watkins's Brigade. A member of the 13th Tennessee reported that the "teeth and eyes shining in the black faces of these negroes were a good mark to shoot at from behind our breastworks."[45] Morgan's black soldiers steadily advanced when they were met with a sheet of fire from Lowrey's indignant Rebels. An observer stated, "I heard an awful roar of musketry and artillery, and looking back over my shoulder I saw fully one half of that negro brigade melt away."[46] This observer went on to say that once he "had seen ripened wheat go down before the cradles of the reapers, and the dropping of these dusky men forcibly reminded me of that scene."[47] A soldier of Watkins's Brigade stated, "On our [right] flank where I was with General Cheatham's Tennessee division, we held our lines unbroken, hurling back overwhelming numbers through the day."[48] Once the Confederates had stymied Morgan's assault, the black soldiers retreated in broken order out of the range of Lowrey's canister. They took up a position near the Rains House, and sharp skirmishing was kept up until after dark. The 17th US Colored Infantry alone lost eighty-four men killed and wounded in this attack.[49] Losses for the 11th Tennessee

---

[44] *OR*, ser. I, vol. 45, pt. 1, 534–39.

[45] Wiley M. Crook, "Autobiography and Reminiscences," http://www.tngenweb.org/records/chester/bios/crook/crook01.htm.

[46] Cook, "A Boy at the Battle of Nashville," 105.

[47] Ibid.

[48] Crook, "Autobiography and Reminiscences."

[49] *OR*, ser. I, vol. 45, pt. 1, 539.

were very light. Private John A. Carroll of Company A was wounded, and Private Eugene Harrison of Company D was hit by a minie ball in the left thigh.[50]

John Cook, one of the boys who had been with Cheatham's men the previous day, walked over that section of the field following the battle and commented, "We halted only a few minutes at the spot where we had seen the negro soldiers slaughtered the day before. It was a gruesome sight.... The ground was thickly dotted with the slain, and here and there the bodies lay in huge heaps as if whole companies had been killed at a single volley. The wounds of the slaughtered negroes must have literally rained showers of blood, for the very earth was dyed red with it."[51]

On the left of Hood's line things were not going quite as well. Hood's left flank was composed of a series of five redoubts garrisoned with artillery and infantry of A. P. Stewart's corps. Two Federal brigades attacked Redoubt Number 5, on the extreme left of the Confederate line. A battery of artillery and a company of infantry manned this redoubt. The Federal brigades soon took the redoubt. As soon as the Federals successfully took Redoubt Number 5, they received a salvo from Redoubt Number 4, garrisoned by Lumsden's Alabama Battery and a company of the 29th Alabama Infantry. The Alabama defenders of Redoubt Number 4 fought stubbornly for three hours before the Federals forced them to give way. One by one, Redoubts 1, 2, and 3 capitulated as well.[52]

With the collapse of his redoubts on the left, during the night Hood moved his headquarters to "Lealand," the home of Judge John Lea, and redeployed his infantry along a shorter, more compressed line. Cheatham's Corps, on Hood's left, was anchored on Compton's Hill. Stewart's Corps was in the center behind a stone wall. Lee's Corps was on Hood's right, ensconced across the Franklin Pike on Peach Orchard Hill.

As Cheatham's men assumed their positions on Compton's Hill and farther west in the dark, the engineers marked the line. The boys began digging entrenchments to protect themselves from the imminent Federal attack. Lieutenant Colonel William Shy, commanding the 20th Tennessee of Tyler's Brigade, Bate's Division, was on the crest of Compton's Hill. Further to his left and over on the next hill, the 11th/29th Tennessee were preparing defenses with the other regiments of Watkins's Brigade, only 511 men strong. Throughout the night, Cheatham's Rebels worked hard to build adequate field fortifications. However, as the sun began to rise, the Confederate infantrymen discovered that the engineers had marked their line off too far back from the military crest of the hill, making

---

[50] Cook, "A Boy at the Battle of Nashville," 105; John Carroll, M268 R159, 11th TISR; Eugene Harrison, M268 R160, 11th TISR.

[51] Cook, "A Boy at the Battle of Nashville," 105.

[52] William R. Scaife, *Hood's Campaign for Tennessee* (Atlanta, GA: W. R. Scaife, 1986) 54–55.

their defense precarious at best. This meant that the Federals would be able to advance without fear of Confederate fire until they were right on top of the Confederate works. This was particularly evident in the position held by the 20th Tennessee.[53]

Early in the morning, the Federals began their advance. Yankee artillery moved into strategic positions to demolish the Confederate line. Once in place, the Federal cannoneers opened a fearful crossfire as they began relentlessly pounding Compton's Hill. One battery alone fired over 560 rounds.[54] W. D. Gale of General Stewart's staff, observing from headquarters located on a hill overlooking Nashville, described the events of the day, "The enemy adapted their line to ours, and about 9:00 AM began the attack on Cheatham, trying all day to turn him."[55] Gale went on to say,

> We could see the whole line in our front every move attack and retreat. It was magnificent. What a grand sight it was! I could see the Capitol all day, and the churches. The Yanks had three lines of battle everywhere I could see, and parks of artillery playing upon us and raining shot and shell for eight mortal hours. I could see nearly every piece in our front, even the gunners at work. They made several heavy assaults upon General [Stephen D.] Lee's line near John Thompson's, and one in front of Mrs. Mullin's.[56]

As the Federal artillery pounded the Confederate works, the 11th Tennessee started taking a few casualties. First Sergeant Marcus Gorman of Company G was hit by a shell fragment, and Private Joshua B. Butler of Company K was wounded in the leg.[57] Late in the afternoon, when the artillery bombardment ceased, the Federal infantry began their assault against Cheatham's Corps on the Confederate left. With Federal infantry, under command of Colonel William L. McMillan, advancing straight up Compton's Hill, Shy's men made a determined stand but were unable to hold in the face of such overwhelming odds. Lieutenant Colonel Shy received a fatal gunshot wound to the forehead at almost point-blank range.[58]

As Shy's men gave way under pressure, the Confederate line further down and to the left, manned by Watkins's Brigade, held for a while. Nevertheless, as Federal

---

[53] Ross Massey, *Nashville Battlefield Guide* (Nashville, TN: Tenth Amendment Publishing, 2007) 121.

[54] Horn, *Decisive Battle*, 118.

[55] W. D. Gale to wife, "Letter to Wife after Hood's Defeat Before Nashville."

[56] Ibid.

[57] Marcus Gorman, M268 R160, 11th TISR; J. B. Butler, Tennessee Confederate Pension Application 14044.Family Search, https://familysearch.org/pal:/MM9.3.1/TH-1942-20619-20120-79?cc=1874474&wc=M6ZF-NM9:171467301,176050201 (1 May 2015).

[58] Wiley Sword, *Embrace An Angry Wind: The Confederacy's Last Hurrah: Spring Hill, Franklin, and Nashville* (New York: HarperCollins Publishers, 1992) 373.

troops poured through the shattered defenses on the crest of Compton's Hill, the right of the Yankee line (under command of Colonel Charles C. Doolittle) started toward Lowrey's position while Federal cavalry gained the left flank and rear of the Confederate line.[59]

Brigadier General Jacob D. Cox, commanding Schofield's 3rd Division, described Lowrey's works as a strong work "revetted with timber, with embrasures for cannon, and a parapet high enough to defilade the interior."[60] Cox sent his 1st Brigade under Colonel Charles C. Doolittle forward for the work at hand. The commander of the 12th Kentucky Infantry (US), one of Doolittle's five regiments, stated that Lowrey's men fired a number of "severe volleys" but because of the angle at which they were firing, the majority of the projectiles passed overhead.[61] As Doolittle's seemingly innumerable Yankees neared Lowrey's works and as they were being flanked from behind by Federal cavalry, Lowrey's veterans knew they must extricate themselves from this ever-tightening noose. To the right of the 12th Kentucky, two of Doolittle's other regiments, the 8th Tennessee (US) and the 100th Ohio regiments, scaled Lowrey's parapet just as Turner's Mississippi artillerymen were loading their battery. In the face of Doolittle's overwhelming advance, the Rebel gunners abandoned their fully loaded pieces. The spoils for the victorious Yankees were eight pieces of artillery and about 300 prisoners.[62]

The situation for members of the 11th/29th Tennessee became desperate. W. E. Reynolds of Company C stated, "Soon the enemy was firing into our rear and left flank. We were then ordered to fall back, or rather we assumed the notice to take care of ourselves. Here we were nearly surrounded, the main line having give way, throwing us in the shape of a horse shoe."[63] Wiley M. Crook of the 13th Tennessee said, "The brigade of my regiment was not driven out of our works but was forced out by Day's [Reynolds's] brigade giving way on the end of this horseshoe circle, and Vaughan's [Watkins's] brigade was endangered by the Yankee's attempt to get behind us. We were ordered to retreat from out this trap. This was the most disorderly retreat I experienced [in] my service in the Confederate army."[64]

W. D. Gale further explained, "Here was a scene which I shall not attempt to describe, for it is impossible to give you any idea of an army frightened and routed. Some brave effort was made to rally the men and make a stand, but all control over

---

[59] *OR*, ser. I, vol. 45, pt. 1, 414–15.

[60] Jacob D. Cox, *March to the Sea: Franklin and Nashville* (New York: Charles Scribners Sons, 1913) 116.

[61] *OR*, ser. I, vol. 45, pt. 1, 417.

[62] Ibid., 407; 414–19.

[63] Reynolds, Veteran Questionnaire, TCWVQ, MF 484, R7.

[64] Crook, "Autobiography and Reminiscences." Cook is mistaken about Deas's Brigade. Reynolds's Arkansas Brigade of Walthall's Division occupied this position. Deas's Brigade was with Stephen D. Lee's Corps on Peach Orchard Hill.

them was gone, and they flatly refused to stop, throwing down their guns, and indeed everything that impeded their flight, and every man for himself."[65] Brigadier General Lowrey found himself in the same predicament as the rest of his men. Lowrey stated, "At first, I saw no chance for myself or any considerable portion of my division to escape capture."[66] Even though Lowrey's favorite warhorse, named "Rebel," was killed, the general made it through to safety.[67]

A cornfield overgrown with crab grass lay behind the position of Watkins's Brigade. Due to the snow that had fallen days before and the subsequent rise in temperature, the melted snow made the field very wet and muddy. A member of the 13th/154th Tennessee described, "The land was a stiff clay soil and the mud with the grass worked up in a mortar around our feet in such weight as to retard our progress."[68] As the remnants of the 11th/29th Tennessee fled southwestwardly from their defensive positions toward the Granny White Pike, they had to pass through this field. Lieutenant William D. Slayden, commanding Company C, ran through the field and had his shoes sucked off his feet as he struggled through the mire.[69] Lieutenant Slayden was not the only member of the 11th Tennessee to lose his shoes in this field. Private William C. Pullen of Company A explained, "When the line broke on our right, every fellow was for him-self. We fell back through a large field. Running through, my shoes stuck in the deep mud, and were pulled off my feet. The cannon balls were plowing the mud from every direction, but we reached the top of the next hill with out further difficulty. I went from there to Franklin with only my socks on my feet."[70] Captain W. J. Crook of the 13th/154th Tennessee grabbed the colors of the 13th and ordered his company to make a stand in the edge of the cornfield in an attempt to check the pursuit of the Federals thus allowing many of the men of the brigade to catch up before being captured. Crook's Company fired a few volleys at the oncoming Yankees, but as the enemy advanced closer, the minie balls began striking the corn stalks around Crook's men. Seeing that further resistance was futile, it was every man for himself as the men jumped across a swollen stream and continued the retreat to the Granny White Pike.[71]

Not all the members of the regiment were able to escape. Private James Shipp of Company H was killed. Private Gustavus Goad of Company D was wounded by a minie ball and captured. Private A. G. Stout of Company D was captured, as were

---

[65] W. D. Gale to wife, "Letter to Wife after Hood's Defeat Before Nashville."

[66] Mark P. Lowrey, "Autobiography," Civil War Miscellaneous Collection, United States Army Military Institute, Carlisle Barracks, Pennsylvania.

[67] Ibid.

[68] Crook, "Autobiography and Reminiscences."

[69] Reynolds, Veteran Questionnaire, TCWVQ, MF 484, R7.

[70] William C. Pullen, "Reminiscences of a Confederate Soldier," unpublished manuscript, transcr. and ed. by Mary McCrary. Original in possession of Jennie Lee Monroe, McEwen, TN.

[71] Crook, "Autobiography and Reminiscences."

Sergeant Griffin Nichols of Company H and Private James Newton of Company F. Private J. F. Jones of Company G was captured, and after his surrender his arm was broken in two places by a Federal soldier.[72]

The majority of the 11th/29th made it to the Granny White Pike and continued over the hill to relative safety. In the meantime, W. E. Reynolds and another member of the 11th Tennessee thought they could make their way over to the Franklin Pike. The two soldiers took off but had not gone far when they heard a voice from behind them calling for their surrender. They turned around to see a Yankee infantryman just across the creek with his rifle leveled at them. Reynolds's comrade raised his hands, but Reynolds took flight. The Federal soldier, who was only a few feet away from the fleeing Reb, fired but somehow missed him. Reynolds continued running. Reynolds remembered,

> [I] came to where the creek ran so close to the bluff that [it] gave me such a delay, that my pursuer had reloaded and fired again just across the creek, here I decided to climb the bluff, about two-thirds the way up the hill, I was so tired that I decided to rest and reload my gun, here the greedy reprobate came very near claiming his victim, the ball scalped a tree by my side. When I had reloaded I steadied my gun by the side of a sapling, peeping through the sights of my gun, with the exclamation "Lord, grant me the great desire of my heart, let me see him pay the penalty he so courageously attempted on me." But the Lord knew best, so I waved my hand goodbye and was soon out of sight.[73]

Reynolds continued,

> After traveling a considerable part of the night, I sat down by the side of the Franklin Pike and ate a small piece of dry bread and tainted beef, I fell asleep to awake the next morning to find our lieutenant William Slayden who had been in command of the company, but was now a straggler like the rest of us. Lieutenant [Slayden] had lost his shoes in his retreat through the field of tough mud. He was crippling along in great distress, sore, tired, and hungry.[74]

When over the hill in relative safety, the boys continued their weary retreat from the Granny White Pike over to the Franklin Pike and then made their way southward. A soldier described the retreat from the Granny White Pike, "We

---

[72] United Daughters of the Confederacy, Captain Thomas Stewart Easley Chapter, Confederate Soldiers of Hickman County, Tennessee and Their Families (Centerville, TN: Captain Thomas Stewart Easley Chapter #1814, United Daughters of the Confederacy, 1996) 177; Gustavus Goad, M268 R160, 11th TISR; A. G. Stout, M268 R162, 11th TISR; Griffin Nichols, M268 R162, TISR; James Newton, M268 R162, TISR; J. F. Jones, Tennessee Confederate Pension Application, 8500, Family Search, https://family-search.org/pal:/MM9.3.1/TH-1951-20623-60601-82?cc=1874474&wc=M6ZX-RMS:171467301,174059701 (1 May 2015).

[73] Reynolds, Veteran Questionnaire, TCWVQ, MF 484, R7.

[74] Ibid.

descended the southern slope and entered the deep valley, whose shadows were darkened by approaching night. The woods were filled with retreating men. I joined the crowd and finally made my way to the Franklin Pike."[75] By sunrise the next morning, the survivors of the 11th/29th Tennessee had crossed the Harpeth River and had made it to Franklin where they were finally able to get a little rest after two days of battle and two nights without sleep.[76]

After Hood's defeat at Nashville, he headed the ghost of the Army of Tennessee south in a withdrawal from the Volunteer State. On Saturday, 17 December, as the army passed through Franklin, many of the wounded from the Battle of Nashville along with those who had been wounded in the Battle of Franklin weeks earlier, were abandoned as Hood continued southward. By nightfall, the 11th/29th had reached Spring Hill. On Sunday morning, Cheatham's men began moving south from Spring Hill. In the afternoon, when they were about two and a half miles from the town, Cheatham deployed his corps and skirmished with Yankee cavalry for an hour or so. After the Federal threat had abated, Cheatham moved his corps to the south side of Rutherford Creek and established camp for the night. The following day, still on the banks of Rutherford Creek, Cheatham's men fought the Federals for several hours. In the afternoon Cheatham withdrew his corps toward Columbia and fell back across the Duck River. On Tuesday, 20 December, the 11th/29th marched approximately twenty-three miles before arriving in Lynnville, a small town south of Columbia. The following day the regiment made it to Pulaski, and by Friday, the regiment had marched another thirty miles. The following day, Christmas Eve, the 11th/29th made camp only ten miles from the Tennessee River.[77]

Christmas Day found the regiment on the march at daylight. Private William C. Pullen of Company A stated, "We continued falling back toward the Tennessee River through the rain, snow and sleet. My socks were completely worn out by this time, and as I walked on the frozen ground, my feet left blood-stained prints."[78] After some difficulty due to high water, the men finally managed to cross Shoal Creek a short distance from the river. As soon as they had crossed, orders came to build breastworks to protect the bridge spanning the river in the event that the Yankees should attempt to follow them. Private Pullen continued, "Our difficulties were not over with, by any means, yet. When we reached the river, we found we had to make a pontoon bridge, and had to carry plank nearly all night."[79] When the pontoon across the Tennessee River was complete, the 11th/29th along with the remainder of Cheatham's Corps crossed the river. The boys made the march on to

---

[75] W. D. Gale to wife, "Letter to Wife after Hood's Defeat Before Nashville."
[76] Crook, "Autobiography and Reminiscences."
[77] *OR*, ser. I, vol. 45, pt. 1, 73, 170, 731–32.
[78] Pullen, "Reminiscences of a Confederate Soldier."
[79] Ibid.

Tuscumbia, Alabama, passed through the town, and continued their march for approximately ten more miles. That night the regiment camped near Cane Creek, where they slept in the mud. On Wednesday, 28 December, the regiment marched sixteen miles to Barton's Station and arrived near Bear Creek.[80]

At daylight on Friday, 30 December, the regiment came up to Bear Creek to cross, but due to the high water and the lack of boats, Cheatham had his men to cross the creek on the railroad bridge. This was accomplished by 2:00 PM. From this location, the regiment headed toward Iuka, Mississippi. The men passed through Iuka on this same day and made camp three miles beyond the town. The following morning, New Year's Eve, the regiment continued marching and made Corinth by nightfall.[81]

During this time, Lieutenant Thomas B. Adcock, J. W. Redden, G. H. Petty, and John Majors, who had been home on furlough to Dickson County, attempted to return to the army but were fired on by Federal gunboats each time they attempted to cross the Tennessee River. The men stayed on the riverbank trying to cross for eight days, and with provisions running out, they were forced to return home.[82]

---

[80] *OR*, ser. I, vol. 45, pt. 1, 73, 731–32.

[81] Ibid.

[82] Thomas B. Adcock, Tennessee Pension Application 6814, Family Search https://familysearch.org/pal:/MM9.3.1/TH-1951-20622-23603-87?cc=1874474&wc=M6ZX-NTL:171467301,173260201 (1 May 2015).

18

"Barefoot, Ragged, and Hungry"

January–May 1865

For the first nine days of January 1865, the brigade was encamped within a few miles of Corinth, Mississippi. While here, Major W. J. Crook of the 13th/51st/52nd/154th Tennessee Consolidated confided to a friend, "[I] have passed unharmed through the trying and disastrous campaign just ended—which I am sorry to say was the most unfortunate and disastrous of the war." The despondent Crook continued, "I am gloomy more so than [at anytime] during the war."[1]

Rations were slim at Corinth. To make up for the shortage, some of the soldiers took matters into their own hands. As Private William C. Pullen of Company A describes,

> We went into camp at Corinth, Mississippi, where we remained two weeks. Being with out food, several of the boys volunteered to investigate a place where they might get a nice ham, or a middling would have been acceptable to a hungry squad of soldiers. At last they found an old log smoke house containing a number of jars. They opened one and gulped down the contents—apple butter, and hurried away with the unopened jars because they were afraid of alarming a watch dog. We saw them returning to camp and hastened to greet and assist them with their load, but great was our disappointment when we opened the jars and found the contents to be lard.[2]

While the Army of Tennessee was encamped at Corinth, Colonel John E. Binns approved furloughs for Charles B. Darden, T. B. Darden, Jim Bartlett, and W. W. Hornberger to go home to Robertson County. The two-hundred-mile journey took the men almost twenty days. Charles Darden stated they would not have made it then if not for the aid of some of the Dickson County men who went home after the Battle of Nashville. Although they were eventually able to get home, they were unable to return to the army due to Federal patrols.[3]

---

[1] W. J. Crook to Hattie 4 January 1865, W. J. Crook Papers, Kennesaw Mountain National Military Park, Kennesaw, GA.

[2] William C. Pullen, "Reminiscences of a Confederate Soldier," unpublished manuscript, transcr. and ed. by Mary McCrary. Possession of Jennie Lee Monroe, McEwen, TN.

[3] Charles B. Darden, Tennessee Confederate Pension Application 14956, Family Search, https://familysearch.org/pal:/MM9.3.1/TH-1951-20621-55231-81?cc=187447 4&wc=M6ZF-KM9:171467301,176151201 (1 May 2015).

On 10 January the remnants of the regiment left their camp at Corinth and started toward Tupelo. The boys of the 11th/29th marched about fifteen miles, entering Rienzi by evening. The men spent the next three days on the march to Tupelo. Many of the roads were almost impassable, so they had to use alternate routes. Cheatham sent his wagon train toward Tupelo from Saltillo by way of Verona, and the infantry passed through the swamp around Tupelo, finally entering the town by 3:00 PM.[4]

General P. G. T. Beauregard inspected the Army of Tennessee for the first time in two months while it was in Tupelo. No longer could he be misled by half-true reports about the status of the army. As Beauregard saw firsthand the condition of the troops, he decried, "If not a disorganized mob in the strict sense of the word, it was no longer an army."[5] Hood voluntarily submitted his resignation to Beauregard, and it was accepted. General Richard Taylor was named temporary commander of the army.[6]

On 25 January the 11th/29th, with the remainder of Cheatham's Corps, left Tupelo on foot and marched to West Point, Mississippi, where they arrived three days later. Within a few days, the men left West Point by train headed to Meridian, where they arrived the next day. Around the beginning of February, the 11th/29th Tennessee with the brigade was encamped about a mile north of Meridian. Before dawn on Sunday morning, 12 February, the boys were marched to the railroad where they boarded a train. When the men were aboard, they were sent to McDowel's Landing. At the landing the men left the train and boarded the steamboat *Marengo*, which transported them to Demopolis, Alabama. On Monday, 13 February, at Demopolis, the boys boarded another train and reached Selma by 3:30 PM. When the troops arrived at Selma, they assembled and marched through the town and down to the docks. The steamers *Cherokee*, *St. Cloud*, and *Harry J. King* were moored at the landing. The wagons and baggage of Cheatham's Corps were loaded onto the *Cherokee*, and the remnants of Watkins's Brigade boarded the *Harry J. King*. At about 5:00 PM, the boats left the dock and headed for Montgomery.[7]

---

[4] United States War Department, *The War of the Rebellion: A Compilation of the Official Records of the Union and Confederate Armies*. 70 vols. in 128 (Washington: Government Printing Office, 1880–1901; reprint, Gettysburg, PA: The National Historical Society, 1972) ser. I, vol. 45, pt. 1, 732. Hereafter cited as *OR*.

[5] Alfred Roman, *The Military Operations of General Beauregard In the War Between the States 1861–1865 Including a Brief Personal Sketch and a Narrative of His Services in the War With Mexico, 1846-8*, vol. 2 (1884; reprint, New York: Da Capo Press, 1994) 332.

[6] *OR*, ser. I, vol. 45, pt. 2, 784–85.

[7] A. T. Fielder, *Captain A. T. Fielder's Civil War Diary Company B, 12th Tennessee Infantry C. S. A. July 1861–June 1865*, ed. M. Todd Cathey (Broken Arrow, OK: Create Space, 2012) 399-403.

After a seventeen-hour journey, the steamboat churned up to the wharf at Montgomery. The boys disembarked, formed ranks, and marched toward the railroad depot. Some of the men reported seeing icicles hanging from the eaves of houses as the regiment went through the town. After arriving at the depot, the men learned that the train would not arrive until the next day, so they looked for sleeping quarters and found refuge in a car shed where they spent the night. Throughout the night, thunder roared and lightning split the sky. Rain fell in torrents, but the men stayed dry in their makeshift barracks.[8]

By 8:00 the next morning, the men had awakened, drawn rations for two days, and boarded a train for Columbus, Georgia. As they continued their journey, the weather began clearing up, and by noon, conditions had completely cleared. By 7:00, the train had arrived at Columbus. The men left the cars and hurried to the depot where the ladies of the city had prepared refreshments. After a two-hour break, the boys were back on the train headed for Macon.[9]

At 4:30 PM on 16 February, the convoy arrived in Macon. General Lowrey, who was still commanding the division, told the troops they would not be leaving before morning, so they relaxed from their journey. The next morning the boys boarded the cars and headed toward Milledgeville, Georgia. By 12:30 PM, the train arrived at Midway, a town about two miles from Milledgeville. There, the men received three days' rations. After drawing supplies, the troops loaded their baggage onto wagons and marched on to Milledgeville where they arrived at approximately 3:00 PM. After a thirty-minute rest, a crossing over the Oconee River was found. The men crossed the river and made camp about a mile farther out.[10]

Before daylight the next morning, the men were up, had cooked breakfast, and were on the march toward Augusta. On this lovely spring-like day, the regiment marched nineteen miles and then bivouacked for the night. By 19 February, after a continual march through Sparta, Mayfield, and Camak, the brigade once again boarded a train, which transported them the rest of the way to Augusta. As the train passed through Augusta, the town clock struck 2:00 AM. The train crossed the Savannah River and stopped after proceeding another mile. The boys disembarked and made camp. The next morning Colonel Watkins assembled the brigade; the commissary issued the boys three days' rations, and the quartermaster issued them new Enfield rifles. The men were told to be ready to move by 7:00 the following morning. From Augusta, the men marched seventy miles to Newberry, South Carolina.[11]

On 24 February, Richmond reinstated General Joe Johnston as the commander of the Army of Tennessee. As soon as Johnston took command, he

---

[8] Ibid., 403.
[9] Ibid., 404.
[10] Ibid., 404-405.
[11] Ibid., 405.

began the task of reassembling all the troops that he could. His plan was to move against Sherman who was moving northward to join Grant in Virginia.[12]

By 25 February, Cheatham's men were within eighty miles of Charlotte, North Carolina, as they had swung northward through South Carolina into North Carolina. Sherman's intention was to move to Goldsboro, North Carolina, and from there to join Grant, who had Lee's Army of Northern Virginia besieged at Petersburg, Virginia. As Sherman moved toward Goldsboro, his corps were separated and were moving by different routes. Johnston, aware of Sherman's movements, assembled a force of about 15,000 men at Smithfield, some fifteen miles south of Raleigh.[13]

On 2 March, Cheatham's Corps crossed the Enoree River at Jones's Ferry and marched within four miles of Unionville. The next day the men moved through Unionville to Skeift's Ferry on the Broad River. By 20 March, Cheatham's men passed through Chester and arrived at the Smithfield depot.[14] At this time, Captain F. F. Tidwell was commanding the 11th/29th Tennessee Infantry Consolidated.[15]

Meanwhile, Johnston had devised a plan where his army would attack Sherman's XIV Corps, commanded by General Henry W. Slocum, while it was separated from the remainder of the army. As the plan unfolded, Johnston moved the parts of his army that were present to Bentonville, North Carolina, a small town south of Smithfield. On the morning of 19 March Johnston deployed his forces, placing Stewart's Corps on the right and Bragg's Corps on the left astride the Fayetteville-Goldsboro highway.[16]

The battle was initiated as Hampton's cavalry struck Slocum's column. Slocum deployed his men and advanced against the cavalrymen as they fell back through Bragg's Corps. Soon, Slocum's men engaged with Bragg. Although Slocum was not fully committed, his advance was thrown back, as was an attack against Stewart's Corps. In the early afternoon, General Hardee led a strong countercharge supported by Stewart. In this attack, Hardee's sixteen-year-old son, Willie, was mortally wounded. Hardee's attack pushed Slocum's XIV Corps back approximately a mile where it rallied on the Federal XX Corps, and together the two Federal corps made a determined stand, halting the Confederate advance.[17]

The Federals spent the next day strengthening their position and attempting to ascertain the disposition of Johnston's army. In the meantime, Cheatham, whose

---

[12] Losson, *Tennessee's Forgotten Warriors*, 245–46.
[13] Stanley Horn, *Army of Tennessee* (Wilmington, NC: Broadfoot, 1987) 425.
[14] *OR*, ser. I, vol. 47, pt. 1, 1082.
[15] Ibid., pt. 3, 735.
[16] Horn, *Army of Tennessee*, 425.
[17] Ibid.

entire corps had been delayed in Salisbury due to railway transportation issues, finally managed to get his corps to Mitchener's Station by 5:00 PM on 20 March.[18]

The next morning, because of the previous delays, Cheatham set a grueling pace for his men as they made the twenty-mile march to join Johnston, who was still facing Sherman at Bentonville. Not long after noon, the 11th/29th Tennessee with Watkins's Brigade, now commanded by Colonel William P. Bishop of the 29th Tennessee, arrived on the field. As the brigade arrived, the exhausted Tennesseans raised a hearty cheer at the sight of "Old Joe." Colonel Bishop reported to General Johnston and respectfully told the general that even though his men were exhausted from the forced march, they were ready for duty. The 11th/29th with the brigade was held in position near the Mill Creek Bridge at Johnston's headquarters on the John Benton farm. Bishop's men were allowed to rest while the remainder of the division, as they arrived, were put in line further to the right.[19]

As Bishop's exhausted Tennesseans rested near the Benton home, they were jarred from their lethargy by a vicious attack of the 64th Illinois Infantry. Johnston, his staff, his cavalry escort, and Bishop's men put up what fight they could in the overwhelming face of the enemy, but were driven back. Two men of the 11th Tennessee were wounded in this attack. Sergeant James R. Weaver of Company B suffered an injury, and Private Joseph H. Larkins of Company E was shot in the calf. Although the men of the 64th Illinois were armed with Henry repeating rifles, their attack was eventually stymied, but not before Johnston's headquarters was pilfered. Before long, the 64th Illinois was forced to retreat by Cumming's Brigade of Georgians.[20]

Although the Battle of Bentonville was technically a Confederate victory, it failed to achieve the desired outcome of destroying Slocum's detached XIV Corps. Sherman's army was now within striking distance, and with its back against Mill Creek, the Army of Tennessee withdrew from Bentonville to Smithfield. On 31 March 1865, Watkins's Brigade was shown to be commanded still by Colonel William P. Bishop and the 11th/29th by Captain F. F. Tidwell. The 12th/47th Tennessee was commanded by Captain James R. Oliver, and the 13th/51st/52nd/154th Tennessee was commanded by Major Marsh M. Patrick.[21]

---

[18] Mark L. Bradley, *Last Stand in the Carolinas: The Battle of Bentonville* (Campbell, CA: Savas Woodbury, 1996) 375.

[19] John Berrien Lindsley, *Military Annals of Tennessee: Confederate* (1886; facsimile of the first edition, Wilmington, NC: Broadfoot Publishing, 1995) 438.

[20] Bradley, *Last Stand*, 380; James R. Weaver, Tennessee Confederate Pension Application 11275, Family Search, https://familysearch.org/pal:/MM9.3.1/TH-1942-20611-41225-47?cc=1874474&wc=M6ZF-HWL:171467301,175551201 (1 May 2015); Joseph Henry Larkins, Tennessee Confederate Pension Application, 4739, Family Search, https://familysearch.org/pal:/MM9.3.1/TH-1942-20616-8088-14?cc=1874474&wc=M6ZX-Q36:171467301,171930601 (1 May 2015).

[21] *OR*, ser. I, vol. 47, pt. 3, 735.

On Friday, 7 April 1865, the 11th/29th Tennessee was camped with the brigade about four miles northeast of the Smithfield depot. Later in the day, General Johnston reviewed the troops. After the review, rumors circulated through camp that many of the regiments of the army were to be restructured. Men and officers alike speculated as to which commanders would be retained and which would be relieved of command. The following day, 9 April 1865, as Lee surrendered the Army of Northern Virginia to Ulysses S. Grant at Appomattox Court House, Virginia, Johnston officially reorganized the Army of Tennessee. The 11th/29th along with the survivors of the 12th, 13th, 47th, 50th, 51st, 52nd, and 154th Tennessee regiments were combined to form the 2nd Tennessee Infantry Regiment Consolidated under command of Lieutenant Colonel George W. Pease. The survivors of the 11th Tennessee formed companies F and K of the 2nd Tennessee Consolidated. After the reorganization, the brigade was composed of the 1st, 2nd, 3rd, and 4th Tennessee Consolidated regiments under command of Brigadier General Joseph B. Palmer. With the surplus of generals, Cheatham was reduced from corps command and returned to command his old division in Hardee's Corps.[22]

On Monday, 10 April, under clouds and rain, Palmer's Brigade with the division was ordered into line. By 5:00 PM, the division was moving toward Raleigh, North Carolina. The following day, the brigade marched about twenty miles. On 12 April the men were on the march by 7:00 AM and moved into Raleigh from the east between 8:00 and 9:00 AM. The Rebel column marched up to the capitol, filed right beside the iron fence and then turned west heading for Greensboro.[23]

On Tuesday, 18 April, some of the soldiers of Lee's Army of Northern Virginia, who had been surrendered nine days earlier, began filtering through North Carolina. With the capitulation of Lee's Army, it became obvious that further resistance to Federal arms was useless. As a result, Joe Johnston met William Sherman at Bennett's farm at Durham Station to discuss surrender terms.

While Johnston was negotiating peace terms with Sherman, back in Greensboro in the camps of the Army of Tennessee, the potential for peace and the news of Lincoln's assassination were the main topics of conversation. The men had their hopes set on returning home.

With the news of the possibility for peace terms near at hand and the thought of the boys getting to return home, Captain A. T. Fielder of the 2nd Tennessee Consolidated stated, "A general joy seems to beam from almost every face at the

---

[22] Ibid., pt. 1, 1062; Fielder, *Civil War Diary*, 7–9 April 1865; Tennessee Civil War Centennial Commission, *Tennesseans in the Civil War: A Military History of Confederate and Union Units with Available Rosters of Personnel*, vol. 1 of 2 (Nashville, TN: Civil War Centennial Commission, 1964) 1:198; *OR*, ser. I, vol. 47, pt. 1, 1083; Losson, *Tennessee's Forgotten Warriors*, 246.

[23] Fielder, *Civil War Diary*, 421-22.

prospect of peace and the thoughts of home and meeting loved ones from whom they have long been separated."[24] On Thursday afternoon, 27 April, an official announcement was made that the terms of surrender had been agreed upon. The men would be required to sign an obligation not to bear arms against the United States after which they would be marched by their units to their respective states and there be disbanded.[25]

On Friday, 28 April, the commanding general ordered his corps commanders to "make out their muster rolls in duplicate and to collect all cannon, limbers, caissons, forges, and draft animals, as well as four-fifths of the soldiers' small arms, ammunition, and accouterments."[26] At about noon the following day, the assembly was sounded and every man of the 2nd Tennessee Infantry Consolidated was ordered to get his rifle and to buckle on his cartridge box.[27] As the men gathered and formed a final line, Captain Edward W. Clark removed the tattered, bloodstained battle flag of the 11th Tennessee from its staff. Some of the men cut strips from their beloved banner and others cut out a few of the stars for souvenirs. When the men had collected their keepsakes, Captain Clark wrapped the remains of the flag around his body and beneath his clothing for safekeeping.[28] After the flag had been safely put away, the men formed ranks and marched to a nearby ordnance train where they stacked their Enfield rifles and turned in their cartridge boxes. According to the terms of the surrender, every fifth man was allowed to retain his musket and accouterments. When the last rifle had been stacked, the men returned to their respective camps and broke ranks.[29]

On 2 May, after the men received their paroles, Cheatham's Division assembled and marched westward to Salisbury, North Carolina.[30] Here, on 5 May, Cheatham drew up his division for their last inspection. As "Old Frank" passed down the line, with tears streaming down his face, he said goodbye to his few remaining veterans. At this point Cheatham left his division and headed south, and his men continued the march toward Asheville, North Carolina.[31]

From Asheville, the survivors of the 11th Tennessee walked to Greenville, Tennessee. At Greenville, they boarded a train, which transported them to

---

[24] Ibid., 425.

[25] *OR*, ser. I, vol. 47, pt. 1, 1084.

[26] Mark L. Bradley, *This Astounding Close: The Road to the Bennett Place* (Chapel Hill, NC: University of North Carolina, 2000) 224.

[27] Fielder, *Civil War Diary*, 426-30.

[28] Lindsley, *Military Annals*, 306.

[29] Fielder, *Civil War Diary*, 426-30.

[30] James K. Clifton, "Veteran Questionnaire," in Gustavus W. Dyer, John Trotwood Moore, Colleen Morse Elliott and Louise Armstrong Moxley, *Tennessee Civil War Veterans Questionnaires* 5 volumes (Easley, SC: Southern Historical Press, 1985) 2:517.

[31] Fielder, *Civil War Diary*, 431.

Nashville by way of Chattanooga.[32] All along the way, Cheatham's Tennesseans departed as they reached their points of demarcation. Private J. S. Welch of Company K stated that he and many of the men were "barefoot, ragged, and hungry."[33] Welch further stated that on the return trip home, Yankee soldiers stopped them several times.[34] The members of the 11th Tennessee stayed together as far as Nashville. In Nashville, the regiment was disbanded. The survivors of the three Nashville companies went to their homes, while the Robertson County men headed north toward Springfield, and the Dickson, Hickman, and Humphreys County companies headed west down the Nashville and Northwestern Railroad. Welch and the other members of the Dickson County companies arrived back in Burns on 20 May. After bidding their comrades goodbye, many headed up the Charlotte Road toward their homes in the north end of the county. The Humphreys County men continued toward Waverly. For some reason, William Carroll Pullen and the Humphreys County men did not arrive home until 23 May.[35]

In the meantime, Captain William I. White, who had been relieved of command at the consolidation because there was no one left in his company, went to Augusta, Georgia. While there, a group of seventy-five crippled soldiers persuaded him to lead them in an assault on the quartermaster's headquarters for clothing. White stated they had "nothing but their crutches to make the charge with but we won and they got the clothing. I got an overcoat."[36] From Augusta, White and his infirmary corps received transportation to Atlanta, and from there, they walked to Dalton. White stated it took ten days for the crippled soldiers to make the one-hundred-mile journey. From Dalton, White made his way to Chattanooga where he caught a train to Nashville. At Nashville, he boarded a train of the Nashville and Northwestern Railroad to his home in Humphreys County. He arrived on 25 May.[37]

As the remaining armies across the South capitulated, soldiers who were prisoners of war (such as General Gordon) were released. Those men confined in hospitals were released as soon as their physical condition allowed.

---

[32] W. M. White, "Veteran Questionnaire," in Dyer et al., *Tennessee Civil War Veterans Questionnaires*, 5:2179.

[33] J. S. Welch, "Veteran Questionnaire," ibid., 5:2157.

[34] Ibid.

[35] William Carroll Pullen, "Veteran Questionnaire," in Dyer et al., *Tennessee Civil War Veterans Questionnaires*, 4:1782.

[36] White, "Veteran Questionnaire," ibid., 5:2178.

[37] Ibid.

19

"Send Other Couriers Those May Be Killed"

Post-War

As the men returned home, they found conditions to be vastly different from what they were four years earlier. Their lands had been devastated. The Hickman County courthouse, which had stood proudly as the Hickman Guards marched out of Centerville on 10 May 1861, had been razed by Federal troops in 1864. The Northwestern Railroad, on which General Gordon had worked before the war as a civil engineer, had been completed from Kingston Springs in Cheatham County through Dickson and Humphreys counties. It had also been transformed into a military railroad that carried supplies from Johnsonville on the Tennessee River to Nashville and then southward to Chattanooga to supply Sherman's Atlanta Campaign. If the deprivations and damages of four years of war were not enough, these men were now subjugated to the harshness and humiliation of post-war Reconstruction.

After Reconstruction was over, and the last of the occupying Federal soldiers withdrew from Tennessee, the South began getting back on her feet. As the nation healed, a number of former members of the 11th Tennessee held political office. In the late 1880s many joined veterans' organizations such as United Confederate Veterans. This organization was made up of local camps or "bivouacs" often named after respected commanders. The veterans of Dickson County formed the James E. Rains Bivouac Number 4, naming their camp after their fallen commander. Members of the 11th Tennessee in Nashville joined the Frank Cheatham Bivouac Number 1, and those in the Clarksville area joined the Forbes Bivouac Number 21. The highly esteemed General George W. Gordon served as the commander-in-chief of the United Confederate Veterans from 1910 until his death in 1911.

There were at least two reunions for the survivors of the 11th Tennessee. The first was held on 24 September 1885 at the former home of Major Van Weems, Bon Aqua Springs, which by this time had become a well-known health resort.[1] The second reunion was held on 14 June 1904 at the Nashville Chamber of Commerce as part of the annual United Confederate Veteran's reunion. At this meeting, a motion was made and passed that the members of the 11th Tennessee would meet again at the United Confederate Veteran reunion to be held at

---

[1] "The Reunion," Centerville (TN) *Hickman Pioneer*, 2 October 1885.

Louisville, Kentucky, in 1905. The motion further stated that the survivors of the regiments would meet "at all other such reunions as long as they are held."[2]

Throughout the war, more than 1300 men served with the 11th Tennessee Infantry. Only eighty-nine were still listed on the rolls at the surrender, and fewer were actually present at the surrender. Most of the surviving veterans of the 11th Tennessee suffered from long-term rheumatism from exposure to the elements while in the army, long-term pain from a badly set broken bone, or some other lifelong effect of an injury. Other effects of the war were long lasting as well. After the war, Turner Halliburton of Company C carried an umbrella with him everywhere he went. Halliburton stated that he was wet all during the war and he would not be wet after the war. According to family tradition, another member of the 11th Tennessee, Charlie Halliburton, refused to wear blue, the color of the uniforms of his former enemies, in the postwar years.[3]

After the war, General Gordon lived a very active public life. He was released from Fort Warren prison in Boston Harbor in July 1865. Once home, he attended Cumberland University Law School at Lebanon, Tennessee. Upon graduation, he practiced law in Pulaski, Tennessee, with the firm of Rose and Gordon before moving to Memphis, Tennessee. Gordon married Ora S. Paine in September 1876, but she died a few weeks after their marriage. In 1899, Gordon married Minnie Hannah (1861–1928). Gordon practiced law in Memphis, serving as a district attorney until 1883, at which time he was appointed as a railroad commissioner for the state of Tennessee. In 1885 he was appointed to a position with the Department of the Interior and served four years among the Indians in Arizona and Nevada. Returning to Memphis in 1892, he was named Superintendent of Memphis Public Schools. In 1906, he was elected to the US House of Representatives for the 10th Congressional District of Tennessee, and he served from 4 March 1907 until his death in 1911 (he was reelected in 1908 and 1910). Gordon was the last Confederate general living in Tennessee and the only Confederate general left in Congress. He served as commander-in-chief of the United Confederate Veterans. General Gordon gave the dedication address for many Confederate monuments, including those for General Patrick Cleburne in Helena, Arkansas, in 1891; the monument on the square at Franklin, Tennessee, in 1899; and the Sam Davis monument in Pulaski, Tennessee, in 1906. Always eager to see his boys, he was present at the 14 June 1904 reunion of the 11th Tennessee Infantry in Nashville. General Gordon had ties with the first Ku Klux Klan and was the first Grand Dragon of the Realm of Tennessee. He authored the Klan's *Precept*, a book describing its organization, purposes, and principles. As General Gordon lay dying,

---

[2] Reunion Pamphlet of the 11th Tennessee Infantry of the C.S.A. 14 June 1904, George W. Gordon Collection. University of Memphis Libraries' Preservation and Special Collections Manuscript number 117, box 1, folder 5, scrapbook page 30.

[3] Interview with family historian Robert Halliburton, 5 September 1998

his final thoughts were on the war. On 9 August 1911, with the words, "send other couriers, those may be killed,"[4] he passed from this life. He was buried in full Confederate uniform and with a Confederate flag in Elmwood Cemetery, Memphis, Tennessee.

Gordon had a special bond with the boys with whom he had shared so much in the war. They were his boys. Sergeant Clayton Yates recalled an incident after the war:

> At a reunion of his old brigade at Dickson, Tenn. In 1875, when his old regiment was formed in line, he was mounted on a fine white horse standing in front, and I said to him: "General Gordon, we all want to shake hands with you." He dismounted and came forward and passed down in line grasping every man by the hand, tears streamed down his face and he could not speak. But those tears spoke volumes which every one of us read.
>
> General Gordon is an orator and a most magnetic speaker, and at that reunion he was orator of the day. When he repaired to the grand stand and he was introduced he had scarcely begun to speak when it began to rain. We were in the park and I was afraid the people would disperse, for I knew that he would say all things that I wanted the whole world to hear. He had only been speaking a few minutes, when suiting the action to his words, he drew from his breast our old flag, tattered, torn, bloody, and riddled with bullets. He said "When I am dead I want this flag placed under my head." I never witnessed such a scene as the one which followed. There were thousands of men crying like their hearts were broken.[5]

On 24 January 1940, the last known living veteran of the 11th Tennessee Infantry, Private William E. Reynolds of Company C, passed away. Now, only headstones, memoirs, monuments, a few photos, and even fewer artifacts are all that have endured the ravages of time to remind us of the deeds, hardships, and battles in which our ancestors participated.

On many fields of conflict, several now state or national military parks, visitors may go and stand in the exact places where these brave men fought. The rugged cliffs of Wildcat, Kentucky, have changed little since October 1861. From the valley below "Hoosier Knob," visitors can stand where the battalions of the 11th Tennessee were pinned down under their first exposure to heavy fire from the enemy. At Murfreesboro, Tennessee, one can walk out of the wood line near the

---

[4] L. B. McFarland, "Address off L. B. McFarland at Reunion in Macon, GA," *Confederate Veteran* 20/9 (September 1912): 427–31; "Bivouac 18 A.C.S. and Camp 28, U. C. V." *Confederate Veteran* 5/11 (November 1897): 567; "Tributes to Gen. George W. Gordon," *Confederate Veteran* 19/10 (October 1911): 499; Clement A. Evans, *Confederate Military History*, 12 vols. (1899; reprint, Wilmington, NC: Broadfoot, 1987) vol 10 507–08; Memphis (TN) *Commercial Appeal*, 10 August 1911.

[5] C. H. Yates, "C. H. Yates' War Experiences," Mayfield (KY) *Daily Messenger*, unknown date.

park headquarters and see where General Rains and his men were decimated by murderous artillery and small arms fire. At Chickamauga, one may struggle through the briars and thickets to the opening where the 11th Tennessee was locked in fierce combat as they sought cover in the shallow gully just south of Brock field. On Cheatham's Hill near Kennesaw Mountain, Georgia, Civil War enthusiasts can go to the exact spot where the men of the 11th Tennessee and their comrades of the 1st/27th Tennessee held the "Dead Angle" in the face of overwhelming odds and mercilessly cut the enemy to pieces. At Franklin, Tennessee, one can still walk in the yard of the Carter House and see where the 11th Tennessee and other members of Gordon's Brigade broke the Federal main line, or see the front steps of the Carter House where Corporal Reynolds Powell of Company F was bayoneted to death. The visitor can go to Confederate cemeteries, such as the one at Griffin, Georgia, or Franklin, Tennessee, and see the graves of scores of men who lie in repose since their final battle.

In 1870, General Gordon said, "One of the noblest duties of the living is to represent the virtues and memories of the dead."[6] Although at that time, General Gordon was speaking of the responsibility of the surviving veterans to venerate the memory of their fallen comrades, we the authors, both of whom are descendants of veterans of the 11th Tennessee, have written this work to consign their deeds and their memories to posterity.

---

[6] George. W. Gordon, unknown commemoration address, George W. Gordon collection. University of Memphis Libraries' Preservation and Special Collections Manuscript number 117, box 1, folder 5.

[1] Adams, John Isaac Johnson, Pvt., Co. C, *Courtesy Cheryl Adams;* [2] Adcock, Jesse W., Lt., Co. K, *Courtesy Ron Parker;* [3] Adcock, Martin Van Buren, Musician, Co. K, F&S, *Courtesy Harvey and Mary Adcock;* [4] Adcock, Thomas B., 1st Lt., Co. K, *Courtesy Ron Parker;* [5] Adkisson, Thomas J., 1st Lt., Co. E, A, F&S, *Courtesy Bob Mazoll*

[1] Alspaugh, Josiah Clifton, 2nd Sgt., Co. K, *Courtesy Dickson County Historical Society;* [2] Anderson, Jerome B., Chaplain, F&S, *Courtesy United Methodist Archives;* [3] Anglin, Martin Van Buren, Pvt., Co. K, H, *Courtesy Janet Dansie;* [4] Austin, Charles D. Van Buren, 4th Sgt., Co. K, *Courtesy Dickson County Historical Society;* [5] Baker, George Washington, Pvt., Co. C, *Courtesy Debbie Stanfill*

[1] Baker, William H., Bvt. 2nd Lt., Co. I, *Courtesy Bob Baker;* [2] Barr, John Hassell, Pvt., Co. H, *Courtesy Mary Beale;* [3] Bartlett, John H., Pvt., Co. F, *Courtesy* **A Circle of Memories;**
[4] Bateman, Thomas Pool, Lt. Colonel, Co. H, F&S, *Courtesy Hickman County Historical Society;*
[5] Batts, Jeremiah, Capt., Co. F, *Courtesy Patsy Long*

[1] Batts, John Thomas, Pvt., Co. F, *Courtesy Patsy Long;* [2] Batts, Thomas Jefferson, Pvt., Co. F, *Courtesy Phillip Gowan;* [3] Baxter, William Martin Sr., 4th Sgt., Co. H, *Courtesy Heritage Foundation of Williamson County;* [4] Bell, Alexander H., 4th Sgt., Co. K, *Courtesy Barry Nelson* [5] Binkley, William H., Pvt., Co. E, *Courtesy Kevin Matthews*

[1] Binns, John E., Colonel, Co. D., F&S, *Courtesy Kathleen Binns;* [2] Callendar, Dr. John Hill, Surgeon, F&S, *Courtesy* **Tennesseans 1901-02;** [3] Clark, James I., Pvt., Co. D, *Courtesy* **Photographs of Company B, Confederate Veterans;** [4] Clifton, James Kirby Jr., Pvt., Co. K, *Courtesy Dickson County Historical Society;* [5] Coble, Jesse, 5th Sgt., Co. H, *Courtesy Joyce Mayberry*

[1] Cochran, Samuel, Pvt., Co. H, *Courtesy Hickman County Historical Society*; [2] Cooley, Robert W., Pvt., Co. A, *Courtesy Humphreys County Historical Society*; [3] Corbett, Joseph M., Cpl., Co. B, *Courtesy* **Photographs of Company B, Confederate Veterans**; [4] Darden, Charles Berry, Musician, Co. F, F&S, *Courtesy Phillip Gowan*; [5] Darden, Thomas Berry, Pvt., Co. F, *Courtesy Phillip Gowan*

[1] Dean, Ephraim A., 2nd Lt., Co. H, *Courtesy Hickman County Historical Society;* [2] Dickson, John McCauley, Cpl., Co. C, *Courtesy Kevin Matthews;* [3] Douglass, James R., 2nd Lt., Co. B, *Courtesy Cliff Coss;* [4] Eleazer, William D., Capt., Co. E, *Courtesy Kevin Matthews;* [5] Elliott, William M., Pvt., Co. F, *Courtesy Ronald Duane Elliott*

[1] Epps, George P. Young, Pvt., Co. C, *Courtesy Tony England;* [2] Estes, William Garrett, Pvt. Co. K, *Courtesy Michael Hood;* [3] Fain, Tyree L., 3rd Lt., Co. E, *Courtesy Bobby Jo Fain;* [4] Fowlkes, Gabriel, Commissary Sgt., Co. H, F&S, *Courtesy Gary Waddey;* [5] Frazier, William Gamblin, 3rd Cpl., Co. H, *Courtesy Hickman County Historical Society*

[1] Fuqua, Jesse Jerome Jr., Pvt., Co. A, *Courtesy Marion Rochelle;* [2] Gafford, James Knox Polk, Pvt., C. E, *Courtesy Gary Mathis;* [3] German, Dr. Daniel II, Surgeon, F&S, *Courtesy Heritage Foundation of Williamson County;* [4] Gilman, Joseph, 1st Sgt., Co. D, *Courtesy* **Photographs of Company B, Confederate Veterans;** [5] Glenn, Patrick, Pvt., Co. G, *Courtesy Humphreys County Historical Society*

[1] Gooch, James William M., 5th Sgt., Co. F, *Courtesy* **A Circle of Memories**; [2] Goodwin, Henry H., Corp., Co. G, *Courtesy Tyler Smith*; [3] Gordon, George Washington, Brigadier General, Colonel, Co. I, F&S, *Courtesy Tennessee State Library & Archives* [4] Gordon, Richard Cross, 1st Lt., Co. H, *Courtesy Hunter and Emmie McDonald*; [5] Gordon, William H. H., Pvt., Co. H, *Courtesy* **Lindsley's Annals of Tennessee**

[1] Gray, James W., Pvt., Co. K, *Courtesy Heritage Foundation of Williamson County;* [2] Gray, William C., Pvt., Co C, *Courtesy Mary Lou Dawson;* [3] Halliburton, Charles, Pvt., Co. C, *Courtesy Robert K. Halliburton;* [4] Halliburton, Turner H., Pvt., Co. C, *Courtesy Robert K. Halliburton;* [5] Handlin, John N., 2nd Cpl., Co. C, *Courtesy United Methodist Archives*

[1] Harbison, John M., Pvt., Co. H, *Courtesy W. L. Ethridge, Sr.*, **A History of Tumbling Creek;** [2] Harvey, Onesiphorus S., Pvt., Co. C, *Courtesy Mary Lou Dawson;* [3] Hayes, Champion Lafayette, Pvt., Co. C, *Courtesy Clysta Ponic;* [4] Hayes, William A., Pvt., Co. C, *Courtesy Cora Hunt;* [5] Hooper, William H., Pvt., Co. H, *Courtesy Hickman County Historical Society*

[1] Hornberger, Wiley W., Pvt., Co. F, *Courtesy Yolanda Reid, Robertson County Archives;*
[2] Howe, Peter, Pvt., Co. G, *Courtesy Lawrence Dillard;* [3] Jackson, Joseph William Green, Pvt., Co. F, *Courtesy Phillip Gowan;* [4] Jackson, Sanford G. M., Pvt., Co. F, *Courtesy Ronnie and Emily Townes;* [5] Jamison, Purvoyant G., Chaplain, F&S, *Courtesy Richard Jamison*

[1] Johnston, Samuel Milton, Pvt., Co. F, *Courtesy Jim Brooks;* [2] Jones, John Wesley, 4th Sgt., Co. B, *Courtesy Carolyn Shofner;* [3] Jones, Samuel Green, Pvt., Co. H, *Courtesy* **Legislative Composite—46th General Assembly;** [4] Larkins, Joseph Henry, Pvt., Co C, E, *Courtesy DePriest family;* [5] Linzy, William Henry H., Pvt., Co. E, *Courtesy Doug Collier*

[1] Long, James A., Lt. Colonel, Co. F, F&S, *Courtesy Kerry Elliott*; [2] Long, James Henry, Pvt., Co. F, *Courtesy* A Collection of Memories; [3] Lowe, Andrew J., Asst. Surgeon, Co. H, F&S, *Courtesy* Legislative Composite—46th General Assembly; [4] Lucas, Hugh Ross, Major, Co. I, F&S, *Courtesy Jonathan K. T. Smith*, Wyly Saga; [5] Maney, General George B., Captain, Co. D, *Courtesy Ronnie and Emily Townes*

[1] Maney, Dr. William Brown, Surgeon, Major, F&S, *Courtesy Barry Lamb;* [2] Marable, George Washington Braxton, Pvt., Co. A, *Courtesy Nina Finley;* [3] McCauley, John Carl, Pvt., Co. C, *Courtesy Humphreys County Historical Society;* [4] McCauley, William H., Capt., Co. C, *Courtesy* **Lindsley's Annals of Tennessee—Confederate;** [5] McCrary, Joseph, Pvt., Co. A, *Courtesy Betty Callis*

[1] Meek, Moses Harvey, 2nd Lt., Co. K, *Courtesy Hardy Morgan;* [2] Nichols, Griffin, Sgt., Co. H, *Courtesy Hickman County Historical Society;* [3] Parker, James T., Cpl., Co. E, *Courtesy Ron Parker;* [4] Pearl, Edward, Pvt., Co. D, *Courtesy Ronnie and Emily Townes;* [5] Phillips, John W., 2nd Lt., Co. K, *Courtesy Ron Parker*

[1] Pitts, Rev. Fountain E., Chaplain, F&S, *Courtesy United Methodist Archives;* [2] Plant, John Harrison, Pvt., Co. A, *Courtesy Humphreys County Historical Society* [3] Pullen, William Carroll, Pvt., Co. A, *Courtesy W. L. Ethridge, Sr.,* **A History of Tumbling Creek;** [4] Rains, James E., Brigadier General, Colonel, Co. D., F&S, *Courtesy The Museum of the Confederacy, Richmond, Virginia;* [5] Rawley, Darius N., 4th Sgt., Co. G, B, D, *Courtesy Vonda Dixon*

[1] Reynolds, William Evrette, Pvt., Co. C, *Courtesy Cleo Hogan;* [2] Rice, William Bartlett, Pvt., Co. I, *Courtesy Joyce Mayberry;* [3] Ridings, Elisha T., Pvt., Co. A, *Courtesy Bart Ridings;* [4] Ridings, George D., 1st Lt., Co. A, *Courtesy Bart Ridings;* [5] Ridley, Jerome S., Major, Asst. Commissary of Subsistence, F&S, *Courtesy* **Journal of B. L. Ridley**

[1] Rogers, James Monroe, Cpl., Co. C, *Courtesy Forbes Bivouac photo—Montgomery County Library;* [2] Rogers, John Gilbert, Cpl., Co. A, *Courtesy Forbes Bivouac photo—Montgomery County Library;* [3] Rooker, John Wesley, 2nd Cpl., Co. E, *Courtesy United Methodist Archives;* [4] Rye, Thomas, Pvt., Co. C, *Courtesy Humphreys County Historical Society;* [5] Scholes, Milton R., Pvt., Co. I, *Courtesy Eugene Summers*

[1] Seals, E. Holloway Morris, Pvt., Co. E, *Courtesy Conrad Murray;* [2] Shacklett, Henry Rector, Asst. Quartermaster, Co. E, F&S, *Courtesy Sarah Foster Kelly;* [3] Shaffer, Josiah L., 4th Sgt., Co. D, B, *Courtesy* **Nashville Banner** *July 11, 1918;* [4] Shouse, Jacob Washington, 4th Sgt., Co. H, *Courtesy Mary Beth Shouse Pruett;* [5] Skelton, James Morris, Bvt. 2nd Lt., Co. C, *Courtesy Jim Skelton*

[1] Slayden, John Daniel, Sgt., Co. C, *Courtesy* **Lindsley's Annals of Tennessee—Confederate**; [2] Slayden, Dr. William Marshall, Asst. Surgeon, Co. C, F&S, *Courtesy Humphreys County Historical Society;* [3] Sloan, James Lloyd, 2nd Lt., Co. D, *Courtesy Grand Masonic Lodge of Tennessee;* [4] Spence, John David, Pvt., Co. H, *Courtesy Barry Dunagan* [5] Spence, W. Jerome D., 4th Sgt., Co. H., *Courtesy Gary Waddey*

[1] Stowers, John Turner, 1st Sgt., Co. B, *Courtesy Tennessee State Library and Archives* [2] Sugg, Nathan Rufus, Pvt., Co. H, *Courtesy Nancy Sugg;* [3] Tarkington, George Washington, Pvt., Co. H, *Courtesy Ova Lee Sawyer* [4] Tarkington, John Henry Clay, 4th Cpl., Co. H., *Courtesy Ova Lee Sawyer;* [5] Thedford, William R., Lt. Col., Co. K, F&S, *Courtesy James and Rhoda Rucker*

[1] Thompson, Thomas D., Sgt. Major, Co. H, F&S, *Courtesy Jerry Richardson;* [2] Tidwell, Franklin Fulton, Capt., Co. K, *Courtesy Georgia L. Baker;* [3] Traylor, Thomas B., 2nd Lt., Co. A, *Courtesy* **Confederate Veteran Magazine;** [4] Trogdon, Alfred Winslow, Pvt., Co. A, *Courtesy Mary Sue Anderson Johnson,* **Like Leaves on Trees**

[1] Weaver, James R., Sgt., Co. B, *Courtesy* **Photographs of Company B, Confederate Veterans;**
[2] Weems, Corder Terrell, Pvt., Co. K, *Courtesy Dickson County Historical Society;* [3] Weems, Philip Van Horn, Major, Co. H, F&S, *Courtesy David and Frances Hall;* [4] Welch, John Shadrach, Pvt., Co. K, *Courtesy Dianne Breyfogle*—**Welch Family of Dickson County and Beyond**

[1] White, William I., Capt., Co. A, *Courtesy Dennis Hood;* [2] Wilson, Daniel W., 1st Sgt., Co. I, *Courtesy David Wilson;* [3] Wilson, John D., Pvt., Co. I, *Courtesy David Wilson;* [4] Wilson, Samuel M., 1st Lt., Co. I, *Courtesy* **Lindsley's Annals of Tennessee—Confederate**

[1] Winn, William Hunley, 2nd. Lt., Co. F, *Courtesy* **GenealogyMagazine.com**; [2] Work, John H., Pvt., Co. H, *Courtesy Kevin Work;* [3] Work, Robert J., 2nd Lt., Co. H, *Courtesy* **Legislative Composite—47th General Assembly;** [4] Wyatt, William M., 2nd Lt., Co. I, *Courtesy* **Bakerville Review Abstracts, Vol. III**

[1] Yates, Clayton, 3rd Sgt., Co. K, *Courtesy Pat Walsh;* [2] Young, Isaac Pavatt, Capt., Co. I, *Courtesy Betty DeWitt*

Part II

Roster and Biographical Sketches

Note: * Indicates soldier was listed on the roll at the surrender at Greensboro, NC., 26 April 1865. It does not necessarily mean he was present.

-A-

Adams, John Isaac Johnson; Private, Company C: Born 3 November 1841. Sworn into service 14 May 1861 at Nashville. Issued a Belgium musket, and later an Enfield rifle. Wounded in the hand in the Battle of Murfreesboro, TN., 31 December 1862, the shot breaking his index finger and striking the left thumb. Absent in hospital at Chattanooga, TN., 22 April – 1 May 1863. Given sick furlough to Dickson Co. Married (1) Nancy "Nannie" Moore, 11 March 1858. Following her death in 1894, he married (2) Nancy Taylor, 11 January 1901. Resided at Danielsville, Dickson Co., TN., later at Erin, Houston Co., TN. Occupation: teacher. Served as Magistrate, Tax Assessor, and Clerk of Houston Co., TN. Local preacher of the Methodist Church. Member, Knights of Pythias and Royal Arch Masons. When applying for a pension, he was declared a deserter by the Pension Board. Several members of the 11th Tennessee wrote letters on his behalf, including J. M. Skelton, who reported he had listed him on furlough, and Captain McCauley, who called him a model soldier. On his own behalf, Adams stated he would "rather his bones be bleaching on the battlefield of Stones River than die with the charge [of deserter] and [have it] go down to succeeding generations." Buried Moore Cemetery, Houston Co., TN..[1]

Adams, Jeams; Private, Company D: No further.

Adams, L. A.; Private, Company G: Born in Dickson Co., TN. Died at Coolidge, TX., age sixty-five.[2]

Adams, William Thomas "Pig"; Private, Company C: Born 11 July 1844. Sworn into service 14 May 1861 at Nashville. Issued a minie musket. Right arm broken above elbow by a minie ball in the Battle of Murfreesboro, TN., 31 December 1862. Captured and sent to U. S. Hospital #7, Louisville, KY. Sent to Camp Morton, IN., 23 February 1863. Later exchanged and rejoined unit. Age 18 on roll dated 8 May 1863, at Shelbyville, TN. Resided at Edgewood, Dickson Co., TN. Married (1) Ann Elizabeth May.

---

[1] Byron and Barbara Sistler, Early Middle Tennessee Marriages vol. 1 (Nashville TN: Byron Sistler and Associates, 1988) 2; "J. I. J. Adams," *Confederate Veteran* vol. 6 no. 11 (November 1898): 534; W. H. McCauley, Record Book-11th Tennessee Infantry, Company C, Guns and Equipment Tennessee State Library and Archives, Army of Tennessee Records, Record Group 4, Box 3, series 5: Miscellaneous Material no.19; Thedford, "Report of Operations"; J. I. J. Adams, Tennessee Pension Application, 4073, Tennessee State Library and Archives; Irene Adams Proctor, *The Adams Family Kith and Kin: From Halifax County, Virginia to Yellow Creek Valley and Grices Creek, Houston County, Tennessee: A Narrative Account: History, Biography, Genealogy, and Legend* (Baltimore: Gateway Press, 2000) 93-147.

[2] "Members of Joe Johnston Camp, No. 94, Mexia, Tex. Deaths from July, 1911 to July, 1912," *Confederate Veteran* vol. 20 no. 12 (December 1912): 579.

Following her death, he married (2) Laura Gray. Died 2 December 1928. Buried Edgewood Cemetery, Dickson Co., TN. Veterans Questionnaire Vol. 1, 173-74..[3]

Adcock, Jesse W.; Lieutenant, Company K: Born 25 April 1836, possibly in Ireland. Sworn into service 25 May 1861 at Nashville. Age 26 on roll dated 15 August 1861. Appointed second sergeant 17 February 1862. At the Battle of Missionary Ridge, TN., 25 November 1863, a bullet struck his knapsack and lodged in his back on the left side of the spine. Promoted to first sergeant at the consolidation of the Tennessee regiments near the end of the war. Later promoted to lieutenant. Surrendered with the Army of Tennessee, 26 April 1865 as a member of Company K, 2nd Consolidated Tennessee Infantry. Paroled 1 May 1865. Married Mazura Elizabeth Fussell, 31 January 1867. Baptist. Present at the 14 June 1904 reunion of the 11th Tennessee Infantry in Nashville. Died 7 October 1923. Buried Wills Cemetery, Dickson Co. Tennessee Pension Application S3575.[4]

Adcock, Martin Van Buren; Musician, Company K, Field & Staff: Born in Dickson Co., TN., 30 November 1836. Resided at Burns, TN. Sworn into service, 25 May 1861 at Nashville. Age 25 on roll dated 15 August 1861 at Midway, TN. On detached service as wardmaster at the Knoxville, TN. hospital from 2 May 1862. Admitted to Fairground Hospital #2 in Atlanta, GA., for catarrhus, 20 March 1863. Returned to duty 24 April 1863. Transferred to regimental band 1 July 1863 as a drummer. During the second year of the war he was wounded at the base of the brain by the careless handling of an Enfield rifle in the hands of a guard, causing a concussion. Sent to Marietta, GA., hospital, 6 August 1863. Sent to hospital in Kingston, GA., 1 September 1863. Surrendered and paroled with Company K, 2nd Consolidated Tennessee Infantry, 26 April 1865. After the war, he married Susan Brown Cathey, the widow of Private Archy Cathey of the 11th Tennessee, who had died during the war. Attended the reunion of the 11th Tennessee Infantry at Bon Aqua Springs, TN., 24 September 1885. Died 6 May 1913. Buried Adcock Cemetery, Dickson Co., TN..[5]

Adcock, Thomas Benton; First Lieutenant, Company K: Born 20 November 1841 on Little Beaver Dam Creek in Dickson Co., TN. Sworn into service on 25 May 1861 at Nashville. Contracted measles at Camp Cheatham. Age 21 on roll dated 15 August 1861 at Midway, TN. Was first sergeant by July 1862. Promoted to first lieutenant, 1 May 1863. Furloughed home by Colonel Binns on 14 December 1864 at Nashville. After the Battle of Nashville, Adcock, J. W. Redden, G. H. Petty, and John Majors attempted to return to the army, but were fired upon by Federal gunboats at the Tennessee River. The men stayed on the river bank trying to cross for eight days, and with provisions running out, were forced to return home. Took oath 10 January 1865 at Nashville. Height 5'10", fair complexion, brown hair, blue eyes. Resident of Dickson, Dickson Co., TN. Married Sarah Richardson. Attended the reunion of the 11th Tennessee Infantry at Bon Aqua Springs, TN., 24 September 1885. Died 15 October 1917. Buried Alf Richardson Cemetery, Dickson Co., TN. Pension Application S6814.[6]

---

[3] William T. Adams, Tennessee Pension Application, 4183; William Nesbitt, *The Primal Families of the Yellow Creek Valley* (Vanleer TN: W. J. Nesbitt,1985) 110; William Thomas Adams, "Veteran Questionnaire" vol. I, 173; Veteran Questionnaire states that he was shot in the head at Murfreesboro and lost the use of his right arm, although the surgeon's records do not support this claim.

[4] Jesse W. Adcock, Tennessee Pension Application, 3575; Maney, *Surgeon's Log*, "Missionary Ridge, TN"; Byron and Barbara Sistler, *1880 Census, Dickson County, Tennessee* (Nashville TN: B. Sistler & Associates, 1993) 1; Barbara Beasley, "Jesse W. Adcock and the Civil War" in *The Heritage of Dickson County, Tennessee, 1803-2006*, Dickson County Heritage Book Committee, (Waynesville NC: County Heritage Inc., 2007) 150-51; *Reunion Pamphlet of the 11th Tennessee Infantry of the C.S.A.* 14 June 1904.

[5] Martin V. Adcock, Tennessee Pension Application, 6246; Jack D. Welsh, *Two Confederate Hospitals and Their Patients* (Macon GA: Mercer University Press, 2005) Patient Roster, Fair Ground Hospital #2, 2; "The Reunion," *Hickman Pioneer*, 2 October 1885.

[6] Jill Knight Garret and Iris H. McClain, *Dickson County Tennessee Cemetery Records* Pt. 1 (Columbia, TN: s.n., 1967) 213; Jill Knight Garret, *Dickson County Handbook* (Easley, SC: Southern Historical Press, 1984) 199; John W. Redden, Tennessee Confederate Pension Application, 3010; "The Reunion," *Hickman Pioneer*.

Adkisson, James Paul; Private, Company A: Born in 1845 in the extreme western portion of Davidson Co., TN., which later become Cheatham Co. Brother of First Lieutenant Thomas J. Adkisson. Enlisted 17 July 1863 at Shelbyville, TN. Detached to the quartermaster department, 17 July 1863. Discharged 16 October 1863 by surgeon's certificate of disability. After the war he owned a farm located along River Road. Married Nannie Hollingsworth. Later relocated to West Nashville, building a home on Charlotte Pike near White Bridge Road. Buried Adkisson Cemetery, located within the River Road farm.[7]

Adkisson, Thomas Jefferson; First Lieutenant, Company E, A, Field & Staff: Born 23 December 1837 in the extreme western portion of Davidson Co., TN., which later became Cheatham Co. Brother of Private James P. Adkisson. Occupation: farmer. Their father, Samuel W. Adkisson, was born in Virginia and became skilled in Mathematics and Engineering. He supervised the construction of the tunnel now known as the "Narrows of the Harpeth" and Newsom's Mill. Sworn into service 18 May 1861 in Company E at Nashville. Age 22 on roll dated 16 August 1861 at Watauga Bridge, TN. Given thirty day furlough from 11 December 1861. Transferred to Company A at the reorganization on 1 May 1862. Appointed quartermaster sergeant, 1 May 1862 and assigned to the Field & Staff. Detached to the provost marshal (Captain Josiah Pitts) at Bristol, TN., 23 May to 24 June 1862. Promoted to first lieutenant of Company K, 2nd Consolidated Tennessee Infantry, April 1865. Surrendered with the Army of Tennessee, at Greensboro, NC., 26 April 1865. Paroled 1 May 1865. After the war he returned to the family farm in Cheatham Co., near the Narrows of the Harpeth. Relocated to Ashland City, TN. in 1880 as owner of the Ashland City Mills. Married Tennie J. Hale in 1886. Politically a Democrat, he was elected as superintendent of public instruction for Cheatham Co. from 1877 to 1884. Member, Christian Church and the Cheatham Bivouac. Died 19 March 1921. Buried Forest Hills Cemetery, Ashland City, TN.[8]

Agnew, I. P.; Private, Company E: No further.

Akles, James; Private, Company C: Enlisted 14 May 1861 at Nashville. Deserted 25 July 1861.

Albright, W. C.; Rank unknown, Company K: Died 26 November 1863 at the Medical College Hospital, Atlanta, GA. Buried Oakland Cemetery, Atlanta, GA.

Alderson, A. J.; Third Corporal; Company C, E: Born c. 1842. Sworn into service in Company C, 14 May 1861 at Nashville. Transferred to Company E, at the reorganization, 1 May 1862. Age 21 on roll dated 14 May 1863. In the Battle of Missionary Ridge, TN., his right thigh bone was broken, and he was left on the field and captured 25 November 1863. Forwarded to the U. S. Military Prison at Louisville, KY. then to Rock Island Prison, IL.[9]

Alderson, William L.; Third Sergeant, Company E: Born c. 1839. Enlisted 18 May 1861 at Nashville. Age 23 on roll dated 16 August 1861 at Watauga Bridge, TN. Elected fourth corporal. Was fourth sergeant by July 1862. Promoted to third sergeant, 10 October 1863.[10]

Alexander, Alex; Private, Company B: Enlisted 10 May 1861 at Nashville. Hospital cook at Bean Station, TN., February 1863. Age 31 on roll dated 2 June 1863 at Shelbyville, TN. Hospital cook in

---

[7] Bob Matzoll, electronic mail correspondence, Adkisson and Sloan Family Historian, Rochester Michigan, 27 February 2001; Sarah Foster Kelley, *West Nashville, It's People and Environs* (Nashville TN: West Nashville Founders Museum, 1987) 123.

[8] Kelley, *West Nashville*, 143; Goodspeed Brothers, *Goodspeed's Histories of Montgomery, Robertson, Humphreys, Stewart, Dickson, Cheatham, Houston Counties of Tennessee*, (Columbia TN: Woodward and Stinson, 1972) 1358; Dennis Dozier Hale and James E. Garrett, Jr., *Tombstone Records of Cheatham County, Tennessee* (Nashville TN: Cata/List Services, 1987) 123.

[9] Captain W. H. McCauley Camp #260 Sons of Confederate Veterans, *Confederate Graves of Dickson County Tennessee Soldiers* (Dickson TN: Dale's Quick Print, 2003) 5; Maney, *Surgeon's Log*, "Missionary Ridge TN."

[10] McCauley Camp 260, *Confederate Graves*, 5.

Chattanooga, TN., 25 April 1863. Also served as a cook at Buckner Hospital, Newnan, GA., as of 31 December 1863.

Alexander, Francis M.; Private, Company A: Born c. 1834. Resided Waverly, Humphreys Co., TN. Occupation: tailor. Enlisted 1 May 1862 at Cumberland Gap, TN. Absent sick at hospital, Bean Station, TN., 26 October 1862. Detailed to Quartermaster department, 17 July 1863 as a teamster herding stock. Listed as a deserter and captured near Chattanooga, TN., 13 September 1863. Took oath and was paroled 29 September 1863.[11]

Alexander, Robert Preston; Private, Company A: Born 24 January 1841 in Maury Co., TN. Sworn into service 10 May 1861 at Nashville. Detached as a guard at hospital in Cleveland, TN., 25 December 1862. Deserted February 1864. Married Martha Yarbrough. Died 26 June 1911 in Humphreys Co., TN. Buried Ebenezer Methodist Church Cemetery, Hustburg, Humphreys Co., TN.[12]

Allen, Andrew Jackson; First Sergeant, Company C: Born 11 September 1823 in Montgomery Co., TN. Sworn into service 14 May 1861 at Nashville. Elected first sergeant at the organization. Returned to rank of private, 1 May 1862 at reorganization. Discharged at Lenoir Station, TN., 14 November 1862 by the conscript act. Occupied postwar as a grocer. Married to E. Allen. Died 8 August 1915. Buried in the Jarrell Cemetery, Montgomery Co., TN.[13]

Allen, Benjamin; Private, Company F: Admitted to Fairground Hospital #1, Atlanta, GA., 1 March 1864 for pneumonia. Sent to another hospital 23 September 1863.[14]

Allen, Christian Felix; Private, Company F: Enlisted 18 May 1861 at Cedar Hill, TN. Recorded as deserting at Readyville, TN., 15 December 1862. Captured at Tullahoma, TN., 1 July 1863. Sent to U. S. Military Prison at Louisville, KY. Forwarded to Camp Chase, OH., 20 July 1863. Transferred to Camp Douglas, IL., 24 August 1863. Released 15 May 1865. Complexion fair, hair light, eyes blue, height 5'8".

Allen, George; Private, Company F: Occupation: farmer. Enlisted 1 August 1861 at Camp Bradford, TN. Seriously wounded in the left thigh with the ball coming out of the left buttock in the Battle of Chickamauga, GA., 19 September 1863. Sent to hospital and captured after May 1864. Took oath 19 June 1864. Complexion dark, hair dark, eyes hazel, height 5'7". Ordered to be released north of the Ohio River.[15]

Allen, Julius D. (Alley); Private, Company F: Enlisted 18 May 1861 at Cedar Hill, TN. Teamster from 13 September – 31 December 1861. Furloughed home 19 January – 8 February 1862 by order of Colonel Rains. Served as a nurse at Big Springs Hospital.

Allen, Myrick R.; Private, Company unknown: No further.

Allen, William; Private, Company H: Sworn into service 10 May 1861 at Nashville. Deserted at Camp Cheatham, TN., 25 July 1861.

Allen, William B.; Private, Company B: No further.

Allen, William D.; Private, Company D: Sworn into service 14 May 1861 at Nashville. Died 18 September 1861. Buried in the Bethel Cemetery, Knox Co., TN.

---

[11] Susy A. Johnson, United States Census Office, *1860 Census, Humphreys County, Tennessee* (Rosell, IL: The Author, 1976) 52.

[12] Jill Knight Garrett, Virginia Wood Alexander, and Evelyn B. McAnally, *Confederate Soldiers and Patriots of Maury County, Tennessee* (Columbia, TN: Captain James Madison Sparkman Chapter, United Daughters of the Confederacy, 1970) 9; Gladys P. Anderson and Jill Knight Garrett, *Humphreys County, Tennessee, Cemetery Records*, vol. 1 (Columbia: s.n., 1966) 113.

[13] Anita Whitefield Darnell, Mary Lewis Roe Jones, Ann Evans Alley, Robert D. Davidson, and Cleo Hogan, *Cemetery Records of Montgomery County, Tennessee*, vol. 1, (Clarksville, TN: Ideal Publishing County, 1965) 13; Georgia L. Baker, *1860 Census for Dickson County, Tennessee with Index* (Nashville, TN: Richland Press, 1998) 164.

[14] Welsh, *Two Confederate Hospitals*, Patient Roster Fairground Hospital #1, 7.

[15] Maney, *Surgeon's Log*, "Chickamauga GA."

Alley, Benjamin M.; Private, Company F: Born in 1830. Enlisted 18 May 1861 at Cedar Hill, TN. Admitted to Fairground Hospital Number 1 with Asthma, 31 March 1864. Received at Confederate hospital, Atlanta, GA., and transferred to Madison, GA., 7 May 1864. Returned to duty from Stout Hospital, Madison, GA., 30 July 1864. Deserted 25 January 1865. Captured at Spring Hill, TN., 8 February 1865. Took oath. Complexion fair, hair brown, eyes blue, height 5'6".[16]

Alley, J. R.; Private, Company A: No further.

Alley, Samuel J.; Brevet Second Lieutenant, Company F: Enlisted 18 May 1861 at Cedar Hill, TN. Elected third lieutenant, 21 May 1861. Brevetted second lieutenant by September 1861. Dropped from roll 1 May 1862.

Allison, A. B.; Private, Company C, E: Born c. 1840. Sworn into service 14 May 1861 at Nashville. Transferred to Company E, at the reorganization, 1 May 1862. Age 23 on roll dated 8 May 1863 at Shelbyville, TN.[17]

Allison, William L.; Sergeant, Company E: Born c. 1834. No further.[18]

Allsbrook, Alfred M.; Private, Company F: Enlisted 18 May 1861 at Cedar Hill, TN. Wife followed him to Cumberland Gap. On detached service as a hospital steward, October 1861 to January 1862.[19]

*Alspaugh, Josiah Clifton; Second Sergeant, Company K: Born in Forsyth Co., NC., 8 January 1836. Relocated to Dickson Co., TN., residing at Burns. Sworn into service 25 May 1861 at Nashville. Age 25 on roll dated 15 August 1861 at Midway, TN. Elected second sergeant at organization. Detached as a hospital steward at Hospital #3, Knoxville, TN., 1 May 1862 to March 1863. Contracted asthma and suffered a general breakdown from heat in Johnston's 1864 Georgia campaign. Surrendered with the Army of Tennessee as a member of Company K, 2nd Consolidated Tennessee Infantry, 26 April 1865. Paroled 28 April 1865. Married Mary Zenab "Zenie" Austin about 1876 at Burns, TN. Present at the 14 June 1904 reunion of the 11th Tennessee Infantry in Nashville. Submitted article, "Reminiscences of Company A, 11th Tennessee," published in the *Confederate Veteran*, vol. 18 no. 11 (November 1910): 506. Attended the 50th Anniversary of the Battle of Franklin, TN., 30 November 1914. Died 22 December 1918. Buried in the Austin Cemetery, Dickson Co., TN.[20]

Anderson, Andrew O.; Private, Company B: Born c. 1838. Father had served as Mayor of Nashville from 1856-1857. Married Mary Ann Todd, 24 January 1855. Sworn into service 10 May 1861 at Nashville. Discharged at Cumberland Gap, TN., 1 November 1861 for chronic asthborlmia.[21]

Anderson, C.; Private, Company C: Captured 9 January 1863 at Middleton, TN. Sent to U. S. Military Prison at Louisville, KY.

Anderson, Isaac C.; First Corporal, Company A: Born c. 1842. Enlisted 10 May 1861 at Nashville. Promoted to first corporal, 1 January 1863. Reported to have deserted 28 August 1863 at Chattanooga, TN.[22]

Anderson, James F.; Private, Company H: Born in Hickman Co., TN. Occupied prewar as a farmer. Sworn into service 14 May 1861 at Nashville, age 22. Discharged 22 November 1861 due to a chronic infection of the kidneys and urinary organs. Complexion fair, hair light, eyes blue.

---

[16] Harris, *Confederate Hospitals*, 401, 356, 200.
[17] McCauley Camp 260, *Confederate Graves*, 5.
[18] Ibid.
[19] Rains, "Letter to Ida," 4 October 1861.
[20] Warwick, *Williamson County Civil War Veterans*, 62; *Reunion Pamphlet*, 14 June 1904; Josiah Clifton Alspaugh, *Tennessee* Confederate Pension Application, 9325.
[21] Peggie Dobson-Sides, *1860 Davidson County, Tennessee, Census* (Nashville, TN: P. Dobson-Sides, 2000) 521; Byron Sistler and Barbara Sistler, *Davidson County Marriages 1838-1863*, (Nashville, TN: Byron Sistler & Associates, 1985) 5.
[22] Johnson, *1860 Census of Humphreys County*, 52.

Anderson, James H.; Private, Company H: Sworn into service 14 May 1861 at Nashville. On detached duty at Cleveland, TN. from November 1862 through February 1863. Deserted 29 March 1863.

Anderson, Jerome Bonaparte; Chaplain, Field & Staff: Born 11 July 1830 in Giles Co., TN. Converted and joined the Methodist Church, September 1845. Married Emily F. Batts, 23 October 1860. Brother-in-law of soldiers Jeremiah and John Thomas Batts. Living near Camp Cheatham, he served as chaplain of the regiment for a short period of time during training. Died 1 December 1902. Buried in the Maplewood Cemetery, Pulaski, Giles Co., TN.[23]

Anderson, John W.; Private, Company G, B: Occupied prewar as a laborer. Sworn into service 10 May 1861 at Nashville in Company G. Discharged on surgeon's certificate of disability September 1861. Re-enlisted at Cumberland Gap, TN., 28 October 1861. Transferred to Company B at the reorganization, 1 May 1862. Age 21 on roll dated 30 May 1863. Wounded in the right hip in the Battle of Missionary Ridge, TN., 25 November 1863. In hospital at Marietta, GA.[24]

Anderson, Joseph B.; Private, Company A: Born c. 1830. Occupation: farmer. Enlisted 6 May 1863 at Shelbyville, TN. Age 34 on roll dated 6 May 1863.[25]

Anderson, William G.; Private, Company E: Born 11 March 1842 in Paducah, KY. Died 1 August 1862.[26]

Anderson, Yeatman; Fourth Corporal, Company G, B: Sworn into service 10 May 1861 at Nashville in Company G. Elected fourth corporal at organization. At reorganization, 1 May 1862, returned to the rank of private and transferred to Company B. Age 18 on roll dated 30 May 1863. Detached to signal corps in June 1862 and sent to Vicksburg, MS. by order of General Stevenson. Captured at the fall of Vicksburg, MS., 4 July 1863. Paroled 13 July 1863 by an officer of the 20th Illinois Infantry. Rejoined the 11th Tennessee Infantry after parole. Captured again 4 September 1864 near Atlanta, GA. Sent to U. S. Military Prison at Louisville, KY. Forwarded to Camp Douglas, IL.

Andrews, Christopher; Private, Company D: Sworn into service 11 May 1861 at Nashville. Discharged 15 August 1862 at Walden's Ridge, TN. by authority of the conscript law.

*Andrews, David L.; Third Corporal, Company F: Occupation: farmer. Enlisted 18 May 1861 at Cedar Hill, TN. Slightly wounded in the left ankle in the Battle of Chickamauga, GA., 19 September 1863. Promoted to third corporal by January 1864. Surrendered as a member of Company F, 2nd Consolidated Tennessee Infantry at Greensboro, NC., 26 April 1865. Paroled 28 April 1865.[27]

Andrews, Elijah S.; First Corporal, Company A: Occupation: farmer. Sworn into service 10 May 1861 at Nashville. Elected first corporal at the organization. Reduced to the rank of private, 1 May 1862 at the reorganization. Wounded through the right side of the chest in the Battle of Murfreesboro, TN., 31 December 1862. Captured and sent to U. S. General Hospital #7 at Louisville, KY., 15 February 1863. Died 14 April 1863 of plural pneumonia. Buried 18 April 1863 at Cave Hill Cemetery, Louisville, KY., Confederate Section O, Lot 260 #112.[28]

Anglen, John W.; Third Sergeant, Company K: Born 5 May 1833. Occupation: farmer. Married Martha E. Harris, 12 December 1855. Sworn into service 25 May 1861 at Nashville. Age 25 on roll dated 15 August 1861 at Midway, TN. Elected third sergeant at organization. On detached duty at the brigade hospital, 1 November 1861. Absent on sick furlough to Dickson Co., TN., 11 December 1861

---

[23] R. J. Craig, "Obituary of Jerome B. Anderson," *Journal of the Tennessee Methodist Conference*, 1902: 41-42.

[24] Maney, *Surgeon's Log*, "Missionary Ridge TN."

[25] Johnson, *1860 Census of Humphreys County*, 79.

[26] McCauley Camp 260, *Confederate Graves*, 5.

[27] Maney, *Surgeon's Log*, "Chickamauga GA."

[28] Ibid., "Stones River TN."

for thirty days. Discharged 15 February 1862 for disability. Listed as a Constable in 1870. Died 20 August 1907. Buried in the Union Cemetery, Dickson, TN.[29]

Anglin, A. J.; Private, Company H: Enlisted 1 December 1862 at Manchester, TN. Deserted with the evacuation of Chattanooga, TN., 8 September 1863, taking his gun and equipment. Captured near Chattanooga, TN., 12 September 1863.

Anglin, Martin Van Buren.; Private, Company K, H: Born in December 1843 in Dickson Co., TN. Sworn into service 25 May 1861 in Company K at Nashville. Age 18 on roll dated 15 August 1861 at Midway, TN. Transferred to Company H at the reorganization, 1 May 1862. Deserted when Chattanooga was evacuated, 8 September 1863, taking his gun and equipment. Captured near Chattanooga, 12 September 1863. Took oath. Married Margret Peggy Tidwell, 27 August 1864. Died 22 April 1927 in Whitney, Hill Co., TX. Buried Whitney Memorial Park Cemetery, Whitney, Hill Co., Tx.[30]

Arnold, John.; Private, Company I: No further.

*Atwood, T. H.; Private, Company I: Enlisted 7 January 1863 at Shelbyville, TN. Joined by reason of substitute. Wounded at the Battle of Franklin, TN., 30 November 1864. Sent to Way Hospital, Meridian MS., 7 January 1865. Surrendered as a member of Company F, 2nd Consolidated Tennessee Infantry, 26 April 1865. Paroled 1 May 1865.[31]

Austin, Calvin Franklin; Private, Company K: Born 21 September 1836. Sworn into service 25 May 1861 at Nashville. Age 24 on roll dated 15 August 1861 at Midway, TN. Captured in the Battle of Missionary Ridge, TN., 25 November 1863. Forwarded to the U. S. Military Prison at Louisville, KY. for exchange. Sent to Rock Island Prison, IL., 9 December 1863. Took oath at Nashville, TN., 2 December 1865. Complexion fair, hair dark, eyes blue, height 5'11". Married Lurana Elizabeth Adams, 9 December 1877. Present at the 24 September 1885 reunion of the 11th Tennessee Infantry at Bon Aqua Springs, TN. Died 27 February 1894. Buried 2 March 1894 in the Austin Cemetery, Burns, Dickson Co., TN.[32]

*Austin, Charles D. Van Buren; Fourth Sergeant, Company K: Born 22 October 1843 in Dickson Co., TN. Occupation: farmer. Sworn into service 25 May 1861 at Nashville. Sent to hospital January 1864. Suffered a scalp wound in an unknown battle and later suffered a severe flesh wound in the right calf in the Battle of Lovejoy Station, GA., 2 September 1864. Surrendered 26 April 1865 as fourth sergeant in Company K, 2nd Consolidated Tennessee Infantry. Paroled 1 May 1865. Relocated to Texas from 1902 to 1911, returning to reside at Cumberland Furnace, Dickson Co., TN. Died 17 June 1926. Buried in the Cumberland Furnace Cemetery, Dickson Co., TN. Pension Application S14841.[33]

Austin, George Wyatt; Private, Company K: Born c. 1837 in Dickson Co., TN. Enlisted 23 July 1863 at Shelbyville, TN. Age 36 on roll dated 9 May 1863 at Shelbyville, TN. On duty with the pioneer corps. Took oath 7 January 1865. Complexion dark, hair dark, eyes hazel, height 5'10". Died in 1905. Buried in Stewart Co., TN.[34]

Austin, M. V.; Private, Company K: Born c. 1844. Enlisted 21 September 1861 at Cumberland Ford, KY.

Averitt, Paul M. C.; Sergeant, Company C: Born in June 1837 in Hickman Co., TN. Sworn into service 14 May 1861 at Nashville. Issued a minie musket. Promoted to first corporal, 1 August 1862. Age

---

[29] Georgia L. Baker, *1870 Census for Dickson County, Tennessee, with Index* (Nashville TN: Richland Press, 2001) 78; Sistler and Sistler, *1880 Census of Dickson County*, 3.

[30] McCauley Camp 260, *Confederate Graves*, 6; Ancestry.com, "Martin VanBuren Anglin," http://trees.ancestry.com/tree/10668473/person/473114254 (16 August 2014).

[31] A. W. Trogdon, "Interesting Letter," *Waverly Sentinel*, unknown date.

[32] "The Reunion," *Hickman Pioneer*.

[33] Maney, *Surgeon's Log*, "September 1864"; Jill Knight Garrett, and Iris H. McClain, *Dickson County, Tennessee, Cemetery Records* vol. 1 (Columbia TN: s.n., 1967) 248.

[34] McCauley Camp 260, *Confederate Graves*, 6.

26 on roll dated 8 May 1863 at Shelbyville, TN. Promoted to sergeant by November 1863. Wounded by a gunshot wound in the side and hip in the Battle of Franklin, TN., 30 November 1864. Taken prisoner and sent to Camp Chase, OH. Sent for exchange 6 March 1865. Applied for admission to the Confederate Soldiers Home from Dickson Co., TN. in 1907.[35]

Averitt, Walter; Private, Company E: Born in 1832 in Dickson Co., TN. No further.[36]

-B-

Baggett, Stephen; Private, Company I, A: Sworn into service 20 May 1861, at Nashville, in Company I. Transferred to Company A, 11 May 1862. Age 27 on roll dated 6 May 1863. Reported missing since the Battle of Missionary Ridge, TN., 25 November 1863. Captured near Chickamauga, GA. Sent to U. S. prison at Louisville, KY., 9 December 1863. Forwarded to Rock Island Prison, IL., 13 December 1863.

Bailey, John Calvin; Private, Company E: Born in 1829 in Virginia. No further.[37]

Bailey, Matthew Patrick. "Pat"; Private, Company E: Born in 1829 in Virginia. No further.[38]

*Baker, Charles; Private, Company H: Enlisted 10 January 1863 at Shelbyville, TN. Surrendered with the Army of Tennessee as a member of Company F, 2nd Consolidated Tennessee Infantry Regiment. Paroled 1 May 1865.

Baker, George Washington; Private, Company C: Born 12 January 1837. Brother of Private Wiley Johnson Baker. Enlisted 14 May 1861 at Nashville. Issued a minie musket. Later issued an Enfield rifle. Left sick in Murfreesboro, TN., 4 January 1863. Captured 9 January 1863. Sent to City Point, VA., 11 February 1863. Exchanged and rejoined regiment, 2 March 1863 at Shelbyville, TN. Age 26 on roll dated 8 May 1863 at Shelbyville, TN. Admitted to General Hospital #9 in Richmond, VA. Given sick furlough 4 August 1864. Clubbed after he and his brother went over the rifle pits at the Battle of Franklin, TN., 30 November 1864. Taken prisoner on the Confederate retreat from Nashville on 17 December 1864. Took oath 1 January 1865. Fair complexion, light hair, gray eyes, 5'4". Married Emily Jane Finch, 26 December 1866. Died 27 April 1887. Buried in the Averitt Cemetery, Vanleer, Dickson Co., TN.[39]

Baker, James; Private, Company G, B: Occupation: laborer. Sworn into service 10 May 1861 at Nashville in Company G. Listed as a teamster, September 1861 through January 1862. Transferred to Company B, 1 May 1862. Age 21 on roll dated 30 May 1862 at Shelbyville, TN. Wounded in the left hand in the Battle of Missionary Ridge, TN., 25 November 1863. Severely wounded in the right thigh by a shell fragment at the Battle of Jonesboro, GA., 1 September 1864. Admitted to Fairground Hospital No. 2, Vineville, GA., 3 September 1864 for vulnus sclopecticum. Returned to duty 14 September 1864. Took oath at Nashville. Fair complexion, light hair, blue eyes, 5'9".[40]

Baker, O.; Private, Company A: Captured 15 April 1865. Confined at Knoxville, TN. Sent to Chattanooga, TN., 17 April 1865.

Baker, O. D.; Rank unknown, Company H: Buried in the Confederate section of Oakland Cemetery, Atlanta, GA.[41]

---

[35] McCauley, *Record Book, Company C.*
[36] McCauley Camp 260, *Confederate Graves*, 6.
[37] McCauley Camp 260, *Confederate Graves*, 6.
[38] Ibid.
[39] McCauley, *Record Book, Company C*; McCauley Camp 260, *Confederate Graves*, 6; Tennessee Widow's Pension 1811. Additional information from Dennis J. Lampley and Deborah Stanfill, 12 June 2002.
[40] Maney, *Surgeon's Log*, "Missionary Ridge TN"; Welsh, *Confederate Hospitals*, Patient Roster, Fair Ground Hospital #2, 8; Maney, *Surgeon's Log*, "September 1864."
[41] www.geocities.com/collegepark/grounds/7235/oakland~index.htm.

Baker, Robert S.; Private, Company E: Born in 1832 in Dickson Co., TN. Killed in battle near Calhoun, GA., 15 May 1864.[42]

Baker, S. G.; Private, Company H: Enlisted 13 February 1863 at Shelbyville, TN. Deserted 2 July 1863.

Baker, Stephen; Private, Company C: Born c. 1832. Married Missouri Hudson, 7 January 1855. Enlisted 24 February 1863 at Shelbyville, TN. by the conscript act. On sick leave at hospital, 13 April 1863. Died 30 April 1863 of typhoid fever at the Quintard Hospital at Rome, GA. Buried in Rome, GA.[43]

*Baker, Wiley Johnson; Private, Company C: Born in Dickson Co., TN., 16 March 1839. Occupation: farmhand. Sworn into service 14 May 1861 at Nashville. Issued a Springfield rifle. Left sick at Murfreesboro, TN., 4 January 1863. Captured 7 January 1863. Forwarded to Nashville, TN., 1 February 1863. Sent to City Point, VA., 11 February 1863. Exchanged and rejoined the regiment, 2 March 1863. Suffered a gunshot wound after going over the rifle pits with his brother, George, in the Battle of Franklin, TN., 30 November 1864. Surrendered as a member of the 2nd Consolidated Tennessee Infantry, 26 April 1865 at Greensboro, NC. Married Nancy E. Simmon, 26 February 1868 in Dickson Co., TN. Pension Application S5240.[44]

Baker, William Alderson: Lieutenant, Company H: Born 25 November 1829. Sworn into service 14 May 1861 at Nashville. Reported sick at Readyville, TN. Promoted to first sergeant, 23 January 1864. Wounded through the bowels in the Battle of Jonesboro, GA., 1 September 1864. Surgeon William B. Maney thought the wound was mortal, and recorded his rank as lieutenant. Captured and listed in the Floyd House Hospital, Macon, GA., 3 October 1864. Recovered and took oath 6 January 1865 at Nashville. Fair complexion, light hair, hazel eyes, 5'10". Died 17 January 1879. Buried in the Baker Cemetery, Shady Grove, Hickman Co., TN.[45]

Baker, William F.; Private, Company E: Enlisted 21 July 1861 at Camp Cheatham. Age 19 on roll dated 16 August 1861 at Watauga Bridge, TN.

Baker, William Henry; Brevet Second Lieutenant, Company I: Born 15 April 1840 in Humphreys Co., TN. Occupation: farmer. Enlisted 30 September 1861 at Cumberland Ford, KY. Age 23 on roll dated 6 May 1863. On extra duty in the quartermaster department as a teamster from November 1861 to January 1862. Promoted to third lieutenant, 1 May 1862. Brevetted second lieutenant by January 1863. During the Battle of Jonesboro, GA., 1 September 1864, he was thought to be mortally wounded, shot through the bowels, losing the right index finger to the wrist joint, and his arm was broken between the elbow and shoulder, losing about 1½ inches of bone. Admitted to the Ocmulgee Hospital in Macon, GA., 17 November 1864. He was taken prisoner by the Federals while in the hospital. Paroled and released without shoes or coat. A comrade loaned him five dollars to get some shoes and someone gave him a jacket. Arrived home, 1 May 1865. Lived at Galaville where he served as postmaster, on upper Sugar Creek, Hickman Co., TN., where he served as a Magistrate. Died 13 May 1921. Buried in the Thornton Cemetery, Hickman Co., TN.[46]

Baker, William J.; Private, Company C: Born in 1844 in Dickson Co., TN. No further.[47]

---

[42] McCauley Camp 260, *Confederate Graves*, 6; Lindsley, *Annals*, 338.

[43] Baker, *1860 Census for Dickson County*, 27.

[44] Wiley J. Baker, Tennessee Confederate Pension Application, S5240; McCauley, *Record Book, Company C*.

[45] Mary Sue Anderson, *Like Leaves on Trees* (Waverly TN: Privately Published, 1969) 82; United Daughters of the Confederacy, *Confederate Soldiers of Hickman County*, 9; Maney, *Surgeon's Log*, "September 1864".

[46] Maney, *Surgeon's Log*, "September 1864"; United Daughters of the Confederacy, *Confederate Soldiers of Hickman County*, 9; W. H. Baker, Tennessee Confederate Pension Application, S615; Personal correspondence with descendant Bobby Baker, 31 March 2000.

[47] McCauley Camp 260, *Confederate Graves*, 7.

Baker, William L.; Private, Company E: Born in 1842 in Dickson Co., TN. Occupation: farmer. Enlisted 23 July 1861 at Camp Cheatham. Age 19 on roll dated 14 May 1863. In hospital July and August 1863 at Catoosa Springs, AL. Carried a .58 cal. Springfield rifle in the war. Wounded through the bowels in the Battle of Adairsville, GA., 17 May 1864, the wound thought to be mortal by Regimental Surgeon William B. Maney. Captured and recovered. Listed as taking the oath on 1 January 1865 at Nashville, TN. on U. S. records. Dark complexion, brown hair, hazel eyes, 5'8".[48]

*Baldwin, David W.; Private, Company F: Born 22 October 1843 in Caldwell Co., KY. Occupation: farmer. Enlisted 1861 in Company B, Starnes 4th Tennessee Cavalry. Enlisted in the 11th Tennessee Infantry 15 August 1862 at Cumberland Gap, TN. Wounded severely in the left arm in the Battle of Missionary Ridge, TN., 25 November 1863. Sent to hospital, returned to regiment. Surrendered as a member of Company F, 2nd Consolidated Tennessee Infantry, 26 April 1865, at Greensboro, NC. Paroled 1 May 1865. Married 28 August 1894. Resided at Clay, Webster Co., KY. Died 5 September 1918. Pension Application Kentucky 38.[49]

Baldwin, James W.; Private, Company F: Enlisted 23 March 1862 at Cumberland Gap, TN. He was originally part of a unit that was surrendered at Fort Donelson, TN. After his capture and release he joined the 11th Tennessee Infantry. Captured again on 3 July 1863 at Petersburg, TN. Sent to the U. S. Military Prison at Louisville, KY. Forwarded to Camp Morton, IN where he arrived 7 August 1863. Released on oath 18 May 1865. He was present at the 14 June 1904 reunion of the 11th Tennessee Infantry in Nashville.[50]

Baldwin, James Wesley; Private, Company I: Born 18 November 1840. Originally enlisted as a private in Company E, 50th Tennessee Infantry, which was organized on Christmas Day, 1861 at Fort Donelson. Having escaped the surrender of Fort Donelson on 16 February 1862, he enlisted with the 11th Tennessee at Cumberland Gap, TN., 23 March 1862. On extra duty at the Knoxville Hospital, 3 June 1862 to February 1863. About March 1863, transferred to Maney's Battalion Sharpshooters. Age 30 on roll dated 6 May 1863 at Shelbyville, TN. Admitted to Way Hospital at Meridian, MS, 15 January 1865 due to a wound. Following the war, he resided in Carthage, TN. before relocating to Nashville, where he was engaged in the grocery business. Married to Effie. Member of the Methodist Church. Died 27 March 1917 after a lingering illness of 17 years. Buried in the Mount Olivet Cemetery, Nashville, Davidson Co., TN.[51]

Baldwin, John G.; Private, Company F: Occupation: farmer. Enlisted 18 May 1861 at Cedar Hill, TN. Given sick furlough 17 August 1861. Wounded in the left arm by a spent minie ball in the Battle of Chickamauga, GA., 19 September 1863. Wounded in the left shoulder in the Battle of Missionary Ridge, TN., 25 November 1863, and died shortly thereafter. Buried in the Confederate Cemetery, Marietta, GA.[52]

Baldwin, Samuel P. "Sam;" Private, Company F: Born c 1839. Occupation: farmer. Enlisted 18 May 1861 at Cedar Hill, TN. Wounded in the knee in the Battle of New Hope Church, GA., 27 May 1864. Killed in the Battle of Atlanta, GA., 22 July 1864.[53]

Ballard, Sam Houston. "Hugh;" Private, Company H: Sworn into service 14 May 1861 at Nashville. Died 14 September 1864 of a severe flesh wound in right hip and buttock received in the Battle of Jonesboro, GA., 1 September 1864.[54]

---

[48] Maney, *Surgeon's Log*, "May 1864."

[49] Ibid., "Missionary Ridge TN."

[50] *Reunion Pamphlet*, 14 June 1904. David C. Allen, *Winds of Change: Robertson County, Tennessee in the Civil War* (Nashville TN: Land Yacht Press, 2000) 183.

[51] *Nashville Banner*, 27 March 1917.

[52] Maney, *Surgeon's Log*, "Chickamauga GA"; Maney, *Surgeon's Log*, "Missionary Ridge TN"; Jackson, "Letters to Parents," 1 January 1864; 14 July 1864.

[53] Maney, *Surgeon's Log*, "May 1864."

[54] Ibid., "September 1864."

Balthrop, David; Private, Company E: Born in 1828 in Dickson Co., TN. No further.[55]

Balthrop, Gustavus J.; Private, Company F: Born in 1842 in Robertson Co., TN. Occupation: farmer. Enlisted 18 May 1861 at Cedar Hill, TN. Wounded in the left leg below the knee in the Battle of Chickamauga, GA., 19 September 1863. Sent to hospital. Mortally wounded in the Battle of Jonesboro, GA., 1 September 1864. Shot through the right lung, his ribs were separated by the ball, resulting in much suffering. Taken to the Floyd House Hospital, where he was attended to by two members of the regiment. Died 9 November 1864. Buried in the Riverside Cemetery, Macon, GA.[56]

Balthrop, William T.; Private, Company C: Born in 1841. Died 29 July 1861.[57]

Banks, H. T.; Private, Company G: Captured at Murfreesboro, TN., 18 September 1863. Received at the U. S. Military Prison at Louisville, KY., 21 September 1863. Sent to Camp Chase, OH., then to Camp Morton, IN. Released upon taking oath 14 February 1865.

Banks, Robert; Private, Company E: Occupation: farmer. Shot through the base of the brain in the Battle of Jonesboro, GA., 1 September 1864. Died at Griffin, GA.[58]

Barfield, Castillo M.; First Lieutenant, Company I: Born 1834. Said to have been the most educated man in Humphreys Co., TN. Sworn into service 20 May 1861 at Nashville. Elected first lieutenant at organization. On sick leave 29 July to October 1861. Defeated for the position of first lieutenant in reorganization, 1 May 1862. Dropped from roll, 1 May 1862. Resided in Louisville, KY. after the war. Occupied as an advertising agent. Died 10 March 1914, in Louisville, Jefferson Co., KY. Buried Cave Hill Cemetery, Louisville, Jefferson Co., KY.[59]

Barnes, James H.; Private, Company F: Born c 1842. Brother of Private John T. Barnes. Nephew of Captain Jeremiah Batts, Jr. Enlisted 18 May 1861 at Cedar Hill, TN. Killed in the Battle of Franklin, TN., 30 November 1864, age 22. Buried in the McGavock Confederate Cemetery, Franklin, TN., section 59, grave 115.[60]

Barnes, John T.; Private, Company F: Born c 1846. Brother of Private James H. Barnes. Nephew of Captain Jeremiah Batts, Jr. Enlisted 25 July 1863 at Chattanooga, TN. No further.[61]

Barr, James Forrest; Private, Company H: Born in 1839 in Hickman Co., TN., where his family owned a large cotton plantation on the Duck River near Centerville, TN. Brother of Private John H. Barr. Occupation: farmer. Sworn into service 14 May 1861. Wounded badly through the thigh, being shot twice at the same time, in the Battle of Murfreesboro, TN., 31 December 1862. Sent to hospital in Chattanooga, TN. Sent on to Fairground Hospital #1 for vulnus sclopeticum, 8 January 1863. Forwarded to Fairground Hospital #2, 15 February 1863. Furloughed 11 April 1863. Discharged from duty 3 November 1863. Took oath 29 January 1864. Complexion dark, hair light, eyes hazel, height 5'8". Married Minnie White, the daughter of Private William K. White of Company H, and thirty-two years younger. Barr lived his last days in the Confederate Home in Austin, TX. He is buried with the Confederate dead near the State Capitol in Austin, TX.[62]

---

[55] McCauley Camp 260, *Confederate Graves*, 7.

[56] Maney, *Surgeon's Log*, "Chickamauga GA"; Maney, *Surgeon's Log*, "September 1864"; Mrs. T.H. Plant, "Letter to John Christian Balthrop," 13 November 1864 in John Trotwood Moore, *Tennessee, Civil War Records – Middle Tennessee, Civil War Correspondence*, (Nashville TN: Historical Records Survey June 1, 1939. Tennessee Historical Records Survey) 104.

[57] Garrett and McClain, *Dickson County Cemetery Records*, vol. 1, 258.

[58] Maney, *Surgeon's Log*, "September 1864."

[59] Garrett, *Humphreys County, Tennessee, 1850 Census*, 21; *Louisville Courier Journal*, 12 March 1914.

[60] Jane Irish Nelson, Jane's Genealogy Jigsaw: Military Ancestors. http.//freepages.genealogy. rootsweb/ ~irishgirl/military/south (26 August 2005).

[61] Ibid.

[62] United Daughters of the Confederacy, *Confederate Soldiers of Hickman County*, 12; Maney, *Surgeon's Log*, "Stones River TN"; Yeary, *Reminiscences*, 40; Welsh, *Confederate Hospitals*, Patient Roster, Fair Ground Hospital #1, 18; Patient Roster Fair Ground Hospital #2, 11; Claire Masters, "True Son of

Barr, John Hassell; Private, Company H: Born 11 April 1845 in Goodrich, Hickman Co., TN. Occupation: farmer. Brother to Private James F. Barr. Enlisted 16 April 1863 at Shelbyville, TN. Wounded severely in the face in the Battle of New Hope Church, GA., 27 May 1864. Admitted to Asylum Hospital, Madison, GA., 30 May 1864. Returned to duty 15 July 1864. Wounded in the left shoulder in the Battle of Peachtree Creek, GA., 20 July 1864. Gangrene developed in the shoulder and he was hospitalized eight to ten months before being paroled at Gainesville, AL., 10 May 1865. Married Letitia Whitson. He attended at least two Confederate Veteran Reunions: 1906 in New Orleans, LA., and 1911 in Little Rock, AR. Died 22 December 1932 in Columbia, TN. Buried in the Centerville Cemetery, Hickman Co., TN.[63]

Barron, W. J.; Assistant Surgeon, Field & Staff: Commission given 6 August 1863, at Chattanooga, TN.

Barry, D. H.; Corporal, Company B: Sworn into service 10 May 1861 at Nashville. Discharged under the conscript law, 12 August 1862.

Barry, James T.; Private, Company B: Enlisted 21 August 1861 at Carter's Station, TN. Discharged under conscript law, 12 August 1862 at Walden's Ridge (Tazewell), TN.

Barry, William A.; Private, Company D: Born 21 September 1844. Sworn into service 11 May 1861 at age 16 at Nashville. Discharged on account of age. He became a prominent Nashville businessman, employed by the Fourth National Bank and the Bank of Commerce. A graduate of the medical department of the University of Nashville in 1876, but never practiced as a physician. Elected to one term on the Nashville City Council, and held the position of secretary as a member of the Hermitage Club. He was for many years a member of the Independent Order of the Odd Fellows, where, like his father, he was elected Grand Master of the Order for all of TN. In his later years he was a stock broker and partner in the firm of Searight and Barry. Member of the Cheatham Bivouac. Died 21 September 1895. Buried in the Mount Olivet Cemetery, Nashville, Davidson Co., TN.[64]

Bartlett, Alex L.; Private, Company F: Occupation: farmer. Enlisted 25 August 1862 at Cumberland Gap, TN. Left arm broken in the Battle of Missionary Ridge, TN., 25 November 1863. Sent to hospital at Marietta, GA. Received at Confederate hospital, Atlanta, GA., 7 May 1864 with vulnus sclopeticum. Sent to Confederate hospital, Madison, GA., 8 May 1864. Transferred to Greensboro Hospital 5 June 1864. Buried in the Bartlett Cemetery, Robertson Co., TN.[65]

Bartlett, James T.; Private, Company F: Born 24 August 1827. Occupation: farmer. Uncle of Private John H. Bartlett, with whom he rode a horse to join the regiment at Cumberland Gap, where he enlisted 25 August 1862. Not wounded during the war. Present at least through February 1864. Married Mary Ann Speer. Died 24 May 1909. Buried in the Bartlett Cemetery, Robertson Co., TN.[66]

*Bartlett, John H.; Private, Company F: Born in 1834. Built a store near a ford of Sturgeon Creek, on a hill surrounded by cedar trees, and gave the village "Cedar Hill" its name, residing nearby. Nephew of Private James T. Bartlett. Enlisted 25 August 1862 at Cumberland Gap, TN. Wounded in the right

---

the Confederacy: The Story of Reagan Barr" *Waco Heritage and History* vol. 27 no. 1 (Winter 1997): 5-13.

[63] John Hassell Barr, Tennessee Pension Application, 13873; Maney, *Surgeon's Log,* "May 1864"; Maney, *Surgeon's Log,* "20 July 1864"; Harris, *Confederate Hospitals,*424, 90 ; United Daughters of the Confederacy, *Confederate Soldiers of Hickman County,* 12.

[64] William A. Barry, Application, United Confederate Veterans, Tennessee Division, Frank Cheatham Bivouac No. 1, Nashville, Tennessee, Records and Correspondence, Tennessee State Library and Archives. Confederate Collection. Box 20, VII-D-1-2, Box 1, f. 5 and vol. II; *Nashville Banner,* 21 September 1895.

[65] Maney, *Surgeon's Log,* "Missionary Ridge TN.;" Harris, *Confederate Hospitals,* 401, 357, 201.

[66] Jean M. Durrett, Diane Reid Williams, and Yolanda G. Reid, *Robertson County, Tennessee, Cemetery Records* (Springfield, TN: Springfield Printing, 1987) 70; J.S. Bartlett notes, Robertson County Library, Springfield, Tennessee.

arm in the Battle of Atlanta, GA., 22 July 1864. Admitted to the Pim Hospital, Griffin, GA., 22 July 1864. Surrendered as a member of Company F, 2nd Consolidated Tennessee Infantry at Greensboro, NC., 26 April 1865. Paroled 1 May 1865. Died in 1900. Buried in the Bartlett Cemetery, Robertson Co., TN.[67]

Bateman, Thomas Pool; Lieutenant-Colonel, Company H, Field & Staff: Born 30 November 1828 in Williamson Co., TN. Worked on his father's farm near the Williamson-Davidson Co. border. At age 17 he took a job at the Lafayette Furnace, chopping wood at the coaling grounds. A Mexican War veteran, he enlisted 17 September 1847 at Centerville, TN. in Company K, 3rd Tennessee Infantry, and served throughout the war, until discharged with the rank of corporal on 24 July 1848 at Memphis, TN. Upon returning, he attended school in Maury Co., then in 1850 entered into the Franklin, TN. law firm of Campbell and McEwen. Licensed to practice the following year, he established a law firm at Centerville, TN. In full sympathy with the Southern cause, he raised a company of infantry, the Hickman Guards (Company H), in Centerville, TN., 1 May 1861, and was elected captain at the organization. Elected lieutenant-colonel, 28 May 1861. Listed on detached service, November and December 1861, as president of general court martial at Knoxville, TN. Rejoined the command, 2 January 1862. Resigned 1 April 1862. Later elected to represent Hickman Co. in the Tennessee Legislature in exile in GA. After the war he returned to the practice of law in Centerville. In January 1867 he formed a partnership with Judge Elijah Walker and relocated his law office to Savannah, Hardin Co., TN. In 1873, he was appointed to succeed Judge Walker as Circuit Court Judge, holding this position until his retirement in 1886. Described as a man of vigorous mind with a strong and practical common sense, well grounded in the law, of unimpeachable honesty and firmness, with a high sense of fairness and justice. He was 6' tall, heavy set, but well proportioned, slightly stoop shouldered, gray eyes, dark hair and beard that became solid white in old age. A frugal lifelong bachelor, he amassed an estate of more than a quarter of a million dollars. In his later years, he lived in Nashville, where he died 23 March 1913. Buried Mount Olivet Cemetery, Nashville, TN.[68]

Bates, John; Private, Company B: Sworn into service 10 May 1861 at Nashville. Discharged at Camp Cheatham, 10 July 1861.

Batts, Benjamin F.; Corporal, Company F: Enlisted 18 May 1861 at Cedar Hill, TN. Died at the General Hospital in Knoxville, TN., 2 September 1861 of pneumonia. Buried in the Bethel Cemetery, Knox Co., TN.[69]

Batts Jeremiah "Jerrie;" Captain, Company F: Born 27 November 1840 in Robertson Co., TN. Brother of Private John T. Batts. Enlisted 18 May 1861 at Cedar Hill, TN. Elected third sergeant at the organization. Promoted to first sergeant by July 1862. Brevetted second lieutenant by January 1864. Promoted to captain of Company F, 10 September 1864. Mortally wounded in the Battle of Franklin, TN., 30 November 1864. Died 9 December 1864. His dying request was, "Tell my mother and sister that I am one of the few that have tried to serve the Lord and I am not afraid to die." Member of the Methodist Episcopal Church South. Buried in the Batts Family Cemetery, Cedar Hill, Robertson Co., TN.[70]

*Batts, John Thomas; Private, Company F: Born 27 April 1832, in Robertson Co., TN. Brother of Captain Jeremiah Batts. Enlisted 18 May 1861 at Cedar Hill, TN. On sick furlough September through December 1861. Detached as a nurse at Hospital #1 at Knoxville, TN., 24 June 1862 through April

---

[67] Maney, *Surgeon's Log*, "Battle of Atlanta GA.;" *Chattanooga Daily Rebel*, 27 July 1864.

[68] John A. Pitts, *Personal and Professional Reminiscences of an Old Lawyer* (Kingsport TN: Southern Publishers, 1930) 22, 147-54; Andrew P. Hitt, *Short Life Sketches of Some Prominent Hardin Countians* (Savannah TN: FundCo., 1988) 55-56.

[69] Bernice W. Gordon, *Index to Confederate Cemeteries, Tennessee* (Memphis TN: United Daughters of the Confederacy, Tennessee Division, n.d.) 1.

[70] Personal correspondence with Mr. Tim Burgess, Battle of Franklin Historian, 13 May 2001; Durrett, Williams, and Reid, *Robertson County Cemetery Records*, 71.

1863. On provost duty 25 August 1863. Slightly wounded just prior to 14 July 1864. Surrendered with the Army of Tennessee as a member of Company F, 2nd Consolidated Tennessee Infantry, 26 April 1865. Paroled 1 May 1865. Married Virginia Draughon, 13 September 1866. Following her death in 1870, married Mary J. Adams, 23 October 1870. They later relocated to Kentucky. He was a Mason, a member of the Knights of Honor fraternity, and the Methodist Episcopal Church South. Politically, he was a Democrat. Died 20 January 1911 in Christian Co., KY.[71]

Batts, Thomas Jefferson; Private, Company F: Born 10 May 1846. Brother of Private William R. Batts. Enlisted 1 June 1863 at Shelbyville, TN. Wounded in the Battle of Chickamauga, GA., 19 September 1863. Sent to hospital at Newnan, GA. Surrendered with the Army of Tennessee, 26 April 1865 at Greensboro, NC., as a member of Company F, 2nd Consolidated Tennessee Infantry. Paroled 1 May 1865. Present at the 14 June 1904 reunion of the 11th Tennessee Infantry in Nashville. Later relocated to Ballinger, Runnels Co., TX. Died 18 February 1910. Buried in the Evergreen Cemetery, Ballinger, Runnels Co., TX.[72]

Batts, William Riley; Private, Company F: Born c. 1844. Brother of Private Thomas J. Batts. Occupation: farmer. Enlisted 4 February 1863 at Shelbyville, TN. Drove wagons and hauled supplies in April, 1864. Wounded in the left leg below the knee in the Battle of Chickamauga, GA., 19 September 1863. Sent to hospital. Wounded in the Battle of Franklin, TN., 30 November 1864. Captured at Franklin, TN., 17 December 1864. Received at the U. S. Military Prison at Louisville, KY., 2 January 1865. Forwarded to Camp Chase, OH., where he died 28 January 1865. Buried Camp Chase Cemetery, Row 25, Number 9, Grave 932.[73]

Baxter, William Martin, Sr.; Fourth Sergeant, Company H: Born 9 August 1836 near Franklin, Williamson Co., TN. Later moved to Centerville, Hickman Co., TN. Sworn into service 14 May 1861 at Nashville. Appointed fourth sergeant, 1 January 1862. Reduced to private August 1862. Shot in the head in the Battle of Murfreesboro, TN., 31 December 1862. Took oath October 1864. Complexion fair, hair brown, eyes blue, height 5'6". Married Artimesia Murray on 9 September 1867 at Pinewood, Hickman Co., TN. Served as a Hickman Co. Trustee. Active in the Cumberland Presbyterian Church at Pinewood. Died 10 July 1915. Buried in the City Cemetery, Centerville, Hickman Co., TN.[74]

Beasley, Francis M.; Third Corporal, Company A: Born c. 1841. Occupation: laborer. Brother of Second Lieutenant Reuben Beasley and Private William S. Beasley, Jr. Sworn into service 10 May 1861 at Nashville. Elected third corporal at organization. At reorganization, 1 May 1862, rank reduced to private. Age 21 on roll dated 6 May 1863 at Shelbyville, TN. Dangerously wounded in the Battle of Missionary Ridge, TN., 25 November 1863. Left on the field and captured. Sent to U. S. Hospital #3 in Nashville, TN. Transferred to the Provost Marshal, 8 February 1864.[75]

Beasley, Reuben F.; Second Lieutenant, Company A: Born c. 1839. Occupation: farmer. Brother to Third Corporal Francis M. and Private William S. Beasley. Sworn into service 10 May 1861 at

---

[71] Deane Porch, *Robertson County, Tennessee, Census: 1850* (Nashville TN: Porch, 1968) 109. Jackson, "Letter to Parents," 14 July 1864; Electronic mail correspondence with Jane Irish Nelson, Batts Family genealogist, 22 January 2002.

[72] Electronic mail correspondence with C. W. Simmons, Batts descendant, 14 December 2001; *Reunion Pamphlet*, 14 June 1904.

[73] Maney, *Surgeon's Log*, "Chickamauga GA"; Jackson, "Letter to Parents," 14 July 1864; Find-a-Grave, Camp Chase, Ohio, William R. Batts, http://www.findagrave.com/cgi-bin/fg.cgi?page=gr&GSln=Batts&GSfn=William& Gsiman=1&GScid=40165&GRid=6286584&. (2 August 2014).

[74] William Martin Baxter, Tennessee Pension Application, 12480; Hickman County Historical Society, *Hickman County, Tennessee History 1807-1993* (Dallas TX: Taylor Publishing Co., 1993) 80-81; United Daughters of the Confederacy, *Confederate Soldiers of Hickman County*, 20; Spence, *History*, 453.

[75] Maney, *Surgeon's Log*, "Missionary Ridge TN"; Jill K. Garrett, *Humphreys County, Tennessee, 1850 Census* (Columbia TN: N.P. 1962) 9; Maney, *Surgeon's Log*, "Stones River TN"; Maney, *Surgeon's Log*, "Battle of Atlanta GA."

Nashville. Elected second sergeant at organization. Promoted to third lieutenant at the reorganization, 1 May 1862. Wounded slightly in the left side in the Battle of Murfreesboro, TN., 31 December 1862. Age 23 on a roll dated 26 May 1863 at Shelbyville, TN. Detailed 13 August 1863 with a detachment of ten cavalrymen to go to Lafayette, GA. to arrest certain named deserters of the 11th Tennessee Infantry and Maney's Sharpshooter Battalion. Promoted to second lieutenant by January 1864. Shot through the chest in the Battle of Atlanta, GA., 22 July 1864. Supposed to be mortally wounded by the regimental surgeon. Sent to Way Hospital, Meridian, MS., 14 January 1865. Recovered and paroled at Meridian, MS., 12 May 1865 by the colonel of the 20th Wisconsin Volunteers.[76]

Beasley, William S., Jr.; Private, Company A: Born c. 1835. Brother of Third Corporal Francis M. and Second Lieutenant Reuben F. Beasley. Enlisted 12 September 1861 at Knoxville, TN. Detailed as a teamster in the quartermaster department, 1 January 1862. Deserted 19 April 1863 at Shelbyville, TN.[77]

Beech, Stephen C.; Private, Company I: Born c. 1841. Sworn into service 20 May 1861 at Nashville. Died of disease at home in Humphreys Co., TN., 25 December 1861.

Beech, Thomas H.; Brevet Second Lieutenant, Company D: Born c. 1844. Sworn into service 11 May 1861 at Nashville. Age 19 on roll dated 5 May 1863 at Shelbyville, TN. Promoted to first sergeant by July 1863. Brevetted second lieutenant by September 1863. Suffered a slight flesh wound in the right calf in the Battle of Jonesboro, GA., 31 August 1864. Killed in the Battle of Franklin, TN., 30 November 1864, age 20.[78]

Bell, Alexander Hamilton; Fourth Sergeant, Company K: Born 17 August 1841 in Cheatham Co., TN. Grandson of pioneer industrialist Montgomery Bell. Sworn into service 25 May 1861 at Nashville. Age 20 on a roll dated 15 August 1861 at Midway, TN. On sick furlough since 27 December 1861 by order of Colonel James E. Rains. Later returned to the Regiment. Promoted to fifth sergeant 3 May 1863 at Shelbyville, TN. Promoted to fourth sergeant by September 1863. Captured near Marietta, GA., 3 July 1864. Sent to Camp Morton, IN. Took oath 17 February 1865. Hair brown, eyes hazel, height 6' 3/4". Died 8 August 1908. Buried in the Bell Cemetery, Cheatham Co., TN.[79]

Bell, Charley (a.k.a. Charley Harris); N/A, Company K: One of four known black men to serve with the 11th Tennessee Infantry. Born 1843 in Dickson Co., TN. Joined Company K with his master, Alexander H. Bell, November 1862 at Manchester, TN. Served as a cook, and was engaged in waiting on the soldiers of the company. He remained with Company K after the capture of Alexander Bell, and was present until the surrender at Greensboro, NC., 26 April 1865. Returning home to Dickson Co., TN. after the war, he changed his name to his father's last name, Harris. Married Rutha Jane. Occupation: railroad worker. Applying for a Colored Man's Pension in June 1921, the validity of his service was attested to by other members of Company K including H. C. Tidwell, Moses Garton, J. K. Shelton, and J. K. Clifton. Died 14 May 1925 in Dickson Co., TN. Cause of death unknown, but contributed to by senility. Buried Dickson Co., TN.[80]

Bell, James Allen; Second Sergeant, Company F: Born in Robertson Co., TN., 24 December 1834. Educated in the common country schools, began farming on his own at age sixteen and purchased a small farm in 1858. He served as Justice of the Peace in 1860. Enlisted 18 May 1861 at Cedar Hill, TN. Elected second sergeant at organization. Age 27 on roll dated 4 May 1862 at Cumberland Gap, TN. Discharged on certificate of disability. The captain of Company F stated on his certificate: "He has acted well and truly the part of the soldier . . . I have unbounded confidence in his patriotism and devotion to the interest of his country." Married in 1865 to Eugenia Chambers. In 1872 he was elected president of the Robertson County Agricultural and Mechanics Association. A Democratic member of the Tennessee House of Representatives, 39th General Assembly, 1875-77. Member of the Methodist Church. In 1877

---

[76] Maney, *Surgeon's Log*, "Stones River TN"; Maney, *Surgeon's Log*, "Battle of Atlanta GA."
[77] Garrett, *Humphreys County, Tennessee, 1850 Census*, 9.
[78] Lindsley, *Annals*, 303; Dobson-Sides, *1860 Davidson County Census*, 599.
[79] McCauley Camp 260, *Confederate Graves*, 8.
[80] Charley Bell, alias Charley Harris, Colored Man's Application for Pension, 27 June 1921, 68.

he moved to Adairville, KY. and entered the tobacco trade. In the 1890's he allowed the manuscript of his father, Richard Williams Bell, titled *Our Family Trouble*, the only known eyewitness account of the Bell family encounters with the Bell Witch, to be published. Died 21 November 1908. Buried Greenwood Cemetery, Adairville, Logan Co., KY. Pension Application Kentucky 2034.[81]

Bell, Montgomery; First Sergeant, Company K: Son of John I. Bell of Pennsylvania. Born in AL. Sworn into service 25 May 1861, at Nashville. Given thirty day sick furlough from 16 December 1861. Discharged by virtue of the conscript act, 12 August 1862 at Tazewell, TN. Died in 1865 or 1866.[82]

Berry, W. G.; Private, Company K: Born c. 1835. Enlisted 8 October 1861 at Camp Buckner, KY. On extra duty in the quartermaster department at Bean Station, TN., as forage master, 8 October 1861. Transferred to General Buford's Cavalry, 16 November 1862.

Bibb, Epaminondas "Pam"; Sergeant, Company H: Born 6 May 1841 in Dickson Co., TN. Resided at Leatherwood (Jones Valley), Hickman Co., TN. Occupation: farmer. Enlisted 8 August 1861 at Knoxville, TN. Wounded in the left side by an artillery shell fragment in the Battle of Murfreesboro, TN., 31 December 1862. Appointed sergeant 23 January 1864. Admitted to Fair Ground Hospital #2, Atlanta, GA., 1 March 1864 for vulnus sclopeticum. Returned to duty 14 March 1864. After the Battle of Nashville, TN. in December 1864, he was cut off from his command and joined the 9th Tennessee Cavalry Battalion until the end of the war. He was surrendered at Charlotte, NC. in 1865. Died 24 June 1912 in Maury Co., TN. Buried in the Leatherwood (Jones Valley) Cemetery, Hickman Co., TN.[83]

Binkley, James P.; Private, Company E: Born c. 1837. Enlisted 1 September 1861 at Knoxville, TN. On 12 January 1863 recorded as having been court martialed and undergoing punishment. Sent to hospital 14 February 1864. Admitted to Fairground Hospital No. 2, Atlanta, GA., for ascites. Returned to duty 11 March 1864. Captured 4 July 1864 near Marietta, GA. Received at the U. S. Military Prison at Louisville, KY. Sent to Camp Morton, IN., 13 July 1864. Took oath 11 May 1865. Complexion dark, hair black, eyes black, height 5' 9".[84]

Binkley, Joseph S.; Private, Company E: Born in 1843 in Dickson Co., TN. No further.[85]

Binkley, William Henry; Private, Company E: Born in Dickson Co., TN., 20 November 1840. Married Anna Jane Matthews, 9 January 1862. Enlisted 20 January 1862 at Cumberland Gap, TN. Patient at Academy Hospital in Chattanooga, TN., 30 April 1863. Age 20 on roll dated 14 May 1863 at Shelbyville, TN. Admitted to Fairground Hospital No. 1 Atlanta, GA., for chronic diarrhea on 4 June 1863. Returned to duty 29 June 1863. Captured by a squad of Federal cavalry at the foot of Missionary Ridge just before the battle, 25 November 1863. Carried to Chattanooga and forced to take oath or go to prison. Occupied as a blacksmith and farmer in Dickson and Montgomery counties, TN. Married (1) Anne Matthews and (2) Sarah A. Matthews. Died 3 January 1928. Buried 4 January, in Big Springs Cemetery, Charlotte, Dickson Co., TN. Pension Application S5207.[86]

---

[81] A note of interest: James Allen Bell's grandfather was the famous John Bell, who was allegedly "haunted" by the Bell witch, and as the story goes was killed by her 20 December 1820. His father Richard Williams, described as the best educated of the Bell children, wrote a manuscript entitled *Our Family Trouble*, describing the spirit, especially its gentle treatment of his mother, and was buried with John Bell on the Bell place in Adams, Tennessee. It was our James Allen Bell who finally allowed someone outside the family to see his father's manuscript.

[82] McCauley Camp 260, *Confederate Graves*, 8.

[83] E. Bibb, Tennessee Confederate Pension Application, S10023; Welsh, *Confederate Hospitals*, Patient Roster, Fair Ground Hospital #2, 15; United Daughters of the Confederacy, *Confederate Soldiers of Hickman County*, 22.

[84] Welsh, *Confederate Hospitals*, Patient Roster, Fair Ground Hospital #2, 15.

[85] McCauley Camp 260, *Confederate Graves*, 8.

[86] William H. Binkley, Tennessee Confederate Pension Application, 5207; Sara Binkley Tarpley, family historian, electronic mail correspondence, 24 March 2001.

Binns, John Esselman; Colonel, Company D, Field & Staff: Born 30 June 1838 in Marshall Co., TN., son of William A. and Mary Guinn (Garrett) Binns. Moved to Davidson Co. with his family when he was a child. Father was a physician and surgeon. Educated in the private schools of Nashville. At age 15, he worked for the mercantile house of H.S. French & Son. Graduated with a degree in medicine from the University of Nashville in 1861. With the threat of Civil War looming, Binns, age 22, enlisted in the Hermitage Guards on 11 May 1861 at Nashville. This company would become Company D of the 11th Tennessee Infantry. Binns was elected captain of Company D after the election of James E. Rains to colonel in May, 1861. Binns was promoted to major on 5 September 1864, after the fall of Major P. V. H. Weems in the Battle of Atlanta on 22 July 1864. Promoted to lieutenant-colonel. According to Cheatham Bivouac application he was later promoted to full colonel. Took oath 7 May 1865 at Augusta, GA. Fair complexion, dark hair, blue eyes, 5'8". He was present at the 24 September 1885 reunion of the 11th Tennessee Infantry at Bon Aqua Springs, Hickman Co., TN., and at the 14 June 1904 reunion held at the Chamber of Commerce in Nashville. Died 1 May 1914. Buried at Mount Olivet Cemetery, Nashville, TN.[87]

Bird, John; Private, Company D: Arrested 29 October 1862. Shipped to U. S. Military Prison at Louisville, KY., 31 October 1862.

Birmingham, Martin S.; Private, Company G: Born c. 1832 in Ireland. Occupation: day laborer. Married with two young sons at the outbreak of the war. Sworn into service 10 May 1861 at Nashville. Deserted 26 June 1861. Age 26 on roll dated 30 May 1863 at Shelbyville, TN.[88]

Biter, William Andrew Jackson; Private, Company C: Born 25 January 1835 in Dickson Co., TN. Occupation: farm hand. Enlisted 4 September 1861 at Knoxville, TN. Listed as a teamster from 25 September to 10 October 1861. Hospital attendant 3 March to April 1862. Wounded with the left arm broken in the middle third, in the Battle of Murfreesboro, TN., 31 December 1862. Sent to hospital and captured, 5 January 1863. Sent to U. S. Military Prison at Louisville, KY. Forwarded to Camp Butler, IL. Paroled and returned to the regiment between April and July 1863. Discharged 1 September 1863 by surgeon's certificate. Married Lucy Jane Baggett Harvey of Montgomery Co., TN., 18 October 1864. Resided in Gum Springs, Montgomery Co., TN. Died from a gunshot wound in an altercation, 29 August 1898 at Palmyra, Montgomery Co., TN.[89]

Bivins, Ashley B.; Private, Company I: Born c. 1836. Occupied as a laborer prewar. Sworn into service 20 May 1861 at Nashville. On indefinite sick furlough since 23 November 1861.[90]

Black, William A.; Private, Company G, B, D: Sworn into service 10 May 1861 at Nashville in Company G. Transferred to Company B at the reorganization, 1 May 1862. Transferred to Company D, 1 July 1862. Deserted at Murfreesboro, TN. after the battle. Captured 5 January 1863. Sent to Gratiot Street Military Prison in St. Louis, MO. Arrived 21 January 1863. Released 12 February 1863 upon taking oath.

Black, William J.; Private, Company F: Enlisted 18 May 1861 at Cedar Hill, TN. Died at Cumberland Gap, TN., 13 December 1861.

Blackburn, William Henry; Private, Company K, H: Born 1 December 1839 in Dickson Co., TN. Sworn into service 25 May 1861 at Nashville in Company K. Age 23 on roll dated 15 August 1861 at Midway, TN. Transferred to Company H, 1 May 1862. Captured at Nickajack Creek, Marietta, GA., 5 July 1864. Sent to U. S. Military Prison at Louisville, KY. Sent to Camp Douglas, IL., 16 July 1864, where he caught a fever which caused his lips to turn black. Complexion fair, hair brown, eyes blue, height 5'9". Discharged 15 May 1865. Being unable to walk, he was carried home. Veteran

---

[87] John E. Binns, Cheatham Bivouac Application; "The Reunion," *Hickman Pioneer*; *Reunion Pamphlet*, 14 June 1904.

[88] Dobson-Sides, *1860 Davidson County Census*, 814.

[89] Maney, *Surgeon's Log*, "Stones River TN"; Montgomery County Historical Society, *Montgomery County, Tennessee, Family History Book 2000* (Paducah KY: Turner Pub. Co., 2000) 138-139.

[90] Johnson, *1860 Census of Humphreys County*, 42.

Questionnaire vol. 1, 328. Attended the reunion of the 11th Tennessee Infantry at Bon Aqua Springs, Hickman Co., TN., 24 September 1885. Died 4 March 1925. Buried in the Daniel Cemetery Dickson Co. TN.[91]

    Blackwell, Micajah (Michael); Private, Company C: Born 1828 in GA. Married (1) Sarah Rebecca Crain, 25 November 1845. Father of Private William J. Blackwell. Occupation: farmer. Enlisted 4 February 1863 at Shelbyville, TN. Age 33 on roll dated 8 May 1863 at Shelbyville, TN. Captured on retreat from Tullahoma to Chattanooga, 2 July 1863. Married (2) Sarah McClelland. Died in 1869, supposedly of smallpox. Buried in the Browning Cemetery, Dickson Co., TN.[92]

    Blackwell, William J.; Private, Company C: Son of Private Micajah Blackwell. Enlisted 4 March 1863 at Shelbyville, TN. Deserted 26 April 1863.

    Bledsoe, William Thomas "Tom"; Private, Company C: Born July 1836. Enlisted 25 March 1863 at Shelbyville, TN. Issued an Enfield rifle. Age 25 on roll dated 8 May 1863 at Shelbyville, TN. Admitted to Ocmulgee Hospital, Macon, GA., 8 April 1864. Died 16 February 1893. Buried at Stoney Point Church Cemetery, Vanleer, Dickson Co., TN.[93]

    Bolton, Rev. John G.; Private, Company A: Born in Humphreys Co., TN., 22 February 1841. Reared on a farm. At age 18 he was licensed to preach and was serving the Lebanon Circuit when he joined the army. Sworn into service, 10 May 1861 at Nashville. Detached to quartermaster department at Bean Station, TN., March through April, 1862. Detached as brigade postmaster 7 November 1862. After leaving the 11th, he was chaplain for the 50th Tennessee Infantry. Captured at the Battle of Franklin, TN., 30 November 1864. Sent to Federal prison at Johnson's Island, OH. for two months. Married Hettie J. Williams, 7 February 1868. A minister of the Methodist Episcopal Church for thirty-two years and member of the Tennessee Methodist Conference, he was a Knights Templar and belonged to the K. of H. Died at Franklin, TN., 22 November 1891. Buried at Mount Hope Cemetery, Franklin, Williamson Co., TN. A published eulogy proclaimed "He was every inch a true man, an appreciative, reliable friend, a courageous soldier of the cross, a wise counselor, a refined gentleman, a pure Christian, an effective sensible preacher, and a really lovable character."[94]

    Bone, John J.; Private, Company E: Born 1835 in Dickson Co., TN. Died c. 1863.[95]

    Bouglies, Victor; Sergeant, Company G, B: Sworn into service 10 May 1861 in Company G at Nashville. Transferred to Company B at the reorganization, 1 May 1862. Promoted to fourth corporal by January 1863. Age 27 on roll dated 30 May 1863 at Shelbyville, TN. Promoted to third corporal by September 1863. Appointed to second corporal by January 1864. Dr. Maney has him listed as a sergeant by July 1864. Killed in the Battle of Atlanta, GA., 22 July 1864.[96]

    Bowen, William M. "Billy"; Third Lieutenant, Company A: Born 2 May 1842. Sworn into service 10 May 1861 at Nashville. Elected third lieutenant at the organization. Resigned 1 September 1861. Died 16 March 1862.[97]

---

    [91] W. H. Blackburn, Tennessee Confederate Pension Application, S7829; "The Reunion," *Hickman Pioneer.*

    [92] Georgia L. Baker, *1850 Census for Dickson County, Tennessee, with Index* (Nashville TN: Richland Press, 2001) 91.

    [93] McCauley, *Record Book, Company C*; Garrett and McClain, *Dickson County Cemetery Records*, vol. 1, 2.

    [94] Goodspeed Brothers, *Goodspeed's History of Maury, Williamson, Rutherford, Wilson, Bedford, & Marshall Counties of Tennessee* (Columbia TN: Woodward & Stinson, 1971) 908; *Nashville Union and Dispatch,* 3 December 1864; W. A. Turner, "Obituary of John G. Bolton," *Journal of the 79th Session Tennessee Conference of the Methodist Episcopal Church South* (19-25 October 1892): 43-44; Garrett, Alexander, and McAnally, *Confederate Soldiers and Patriots,* 30.

    [95] McCauley Camp 260, *Confederate Graves,* 9.

    [96] Maney, *Surgeon's Log,* "Battle of Atlanta GA."

    [97] Jamie Ault Grady, *Bowens of Virginia and Tennessee; Descendants of John Bowen and Lily McIlhaney* (Knoxville TN: s.n., 1969) 163.

Bowers, William D.; Private, Company D: Occupation: clerk. Sworn into service 11 May 1861 at Nashville. Absent on sick furlough October 1861. Rejoined the unit by re-enlistment 14 November 1862. Age 22 on roll dated 5 May 1863 at Shelbyville, TN. Killed on the field in the Battle of Resaca, GA., 14 May 1864.[98]

Bowker, John Allen; Private, Company E: Born in 1835 in Dickson Co., TN.[99]

Bowker, Joseph Alston; Private, Company E: Born in 1838 in Dickson Co., TN. Sworn into service 18 May 1861 at Nashville. Age 21 on roll dated 6 August 1861 at Watauga Bridge, TN. Deserted at Cumberland Gap, TN., 28 May 1862. Captured 11 June 1862. Arrived at Camp Morton, IN., 11 June 1862. Died at Camp Morton in 1863.[100]

*Bowles, M. W.; Private, Company B, D: Sworn into service 10 May 1861 in Company B at Nashville. Acting ordinance sergeant, 3 September 1861 to January 1862. Transferred to Company D, 1 December 1862. Age 38 on roll dated 5 May 1863. Surrendered with the Army of Tennessee on 26 April 1865 at Greensboro, NC. as a member of Company C, 2nd Consolidated Tennessee Infantry. Paroled 1 May 1865.

Boyle, Patrick; Private, Company E, G: Sworn into service 18 May 1861 in Company E at Nashville. Age 38 on roll dated 16 August 1861 at Watauga Bridge, TN. Transferred to Company G at the reorganization, 1 May 1862. Discharged by virtue of the conscript act at Tazewell, TN., 13 August 1862.

Bradley, Jefferson Casewell; Private, Company H: Born 1813 in NC. Member of the Tennessee State Militia in 1844 and a member of Company K, 3rd Tennessee Infantry in the Mexican War. Fifty-five years of age at the beginning of the war and the owner of a farm at Little Lot, Hickman Co., TN. Married to Lucinda Overby. First Civil War service was as a substitute for Samuel G. Delk in Company C, 9th Tennessee Cavalry, before transferring to the 11th Tennessee Infantry due to age. Discharged 1 May 1862 on a surgeon's certificate of disability. He was present at the 24 September 1885 reunion of the 11th Tennessee Infantry at Bon Aqua Springs, Hickman Co., TN. Buried in the Harrington Cemetery, Little Lot, Hickman Co., TN.[101]

Brake, James D.; Private, Company F: Born in Montgomery Co., TN. Occupation: farmer. Sworn into service 18 May 1861 at Cedar Hill, TN. Left sick in hospital at Knoxville, TN., 13 September 1862. Discharged 19 November 1862 with the disease of pulmonary consumption, age 24, sandy hair.

Brake, Thomas W.; Private, Company F: Enlisted 18 May 1861 at Cedar Hill, TN. On extra duty driving a port team.

Branch, Alex; Private, Company D: Sworn into service 11 May 1861 at Nashville. Wounded 10 September 1862 at Cumberland Gap, TN. Deserted at the siege of Cumberland Gap. Age 40 on roll dated 5 May 1863 at Shelbyville, TN.

Brann, Martin; Private, Company G: Captured at Versailles, KY., 12 October 1862. Shipped on the steamboat *Belle Creole*, 18 November 1862 from the U. S. Military Prison in Louisville, KY. to Cairo, IL.

Brazell, Henry; Private, Company K: Born c. 1844. Enlisted 13 December 1862 in Dickson Co., TN., by Captain F. F. Tidwell. Age 19 on roll dated 1 May 1863 at Shelbyville, TN.[102]

---

[98] Maney, *Surgeon's Log*, "May 1864."
[99] McCauley Camp 260, *Confederate Graves*, 9.
[100] Ibid.
[101] Spence, *History*, 178; United Daughters of the Confederacy, *Confederate Soldiers of Hickman County*, 25; "The Reunion," *Hickman Pioneer*; Electronic mail correspondence with Linda Gordon Smith, great granddaughter of J. C. Bradley, 1 July 1999; United Daughters of the Confederacy, Captain Thomas Stewart Easley Chapter, *Hickman County, Tennessee Cemetery Records* part 2 (Centerville TN: Captain Thomas Stewart Easley Chapter, 1814, United Daughters of the Confederacy, 1989) 136.
[102] McCauley Camp 260, *Confederate Graves*, 10.

Brazzell, James; Private, Company K: Born 1839 in Dickson Co., TN. Sworn into service 25 May 1861 at Nashville. Had the measles while at Camp Cheatham. Age 25 on roll dated 15 August 1861 at Midway, TN. Feet badly frozen in the Kentucky campaign. On sick furlough to his home in Tennessee City, Dickson Co., TN. for thirty days from 13 September 1862. Could not travel to keep up with the army and was cut off from his command near Elk River in route to Chattanooga. Took oath 7 January 1864 at Nashville. Complexion fair, hair brown, eyes gray, height 6'4". Resided postwar at McEwen, Humphreys Co., TN.[103]

Brazell, John; Private, Company E: Sworn into service 18 May 1861 at Nashville. Deserted at Camp Cheatham, TN., 1 June 1861.

Brazell, John James; Private, Company K: Born 1839 in Dickson Co., TN. Died in 1861 at Camp Cheatham, TN.[104]

*Brennon, Bartley; Private, Company I, G: Sworn into service 20 May 1861 at Nashville in Company I. Transferred to Company G at the reorganization, 1 May 1862. Wounded on retreat from Versailles, KY., left and captured. Rejoined the unit by January 1863. Age 23 on roll dated 30 May 1863. Detached as a railroad guard, 25 August to October 1863. Surrendered with the Army of Tennessee, 26 April 1865 at Greensboro, NC., as a member of Company C, 2nd Consolidated Tennessee Infantry. Paroled 1 May 1865.

Brennon, John; Private, Company G: Enlisted 3 June 1861 at Camp Cheatham. Discharged by court martial, 20 July 1861. Age 40 on roll dated 30 May 1863.

Brice, John; Private, Company B: Sworn into service 10 May 1861 at Nashville. Captured by General George Morgan's men at Cumberland Gap, TN. Sent to Camp Morton, IN., arriving 30 June 1862. Suspected of being a spy by Federal authorities. Age 18 on letter of certification, 27 August 1862. Forwarded to Johnson's Island, OH., then to City Point, VA. for exchange on 28 September 1863. Complexion fair, hair auburn, eyes gray.

Brooks, Milton O.; Second Lieutenant, Company G: Born c. 1837. Occupation: clerk. Sworn into service 10 May 1861 at Nashville. On detached service at Morristown, TN. as the drill master for recruits of the 30th Tennessee Infantry, March through April 1862. Applied to be a permanent drill master, 27 March 1862, his application being signed by all ten captains of the 11th Tennessee recommending him. Acting sergeant-major July through August 1862. Wounded in the right leg slightly in the Battle of Murfreesboro, TN., 31 December 1862. Taken prisoner. Paroled 18 January 1863. Returned to unit at Shelbyville, TN. Age 22 on roll dated 30 May 1863. Temporarily detached to General Wheeler, 14 August 1863. Promoted to second lieutenant, 29 April 1864. Took oath, 23 December 1864. Complexion fair, hair light, 5'7". Postwar occupation: printer for the *Nashville American*. During the war, his mother, Ann L. Ferguson Brooks, was described as a "Southern Nightingale," who smuggled medical supplies out of Nashville and operated as a nurse in the hospitals of Nashville, Chattanooga, Atlanta, Griffin, and other Southern towns. Milton attended the reunion of the 11th Tennessee Infantry at Bon Aqua Springs, Hickman Co., TN., 24 September 1885.[105]

Brown, Aaron; Private, Company K: Born c. 1841. Sworn into service 25 May 1861 at Nashville. Died 27 June 1861.[106]

Brown, Alexander Youree "Sandy"; First Lieutenant, Company E: Born 7 August 1839. Occupation: laborer. Sworn into service 18 May 1861 in Nashville. Appointed second lieutenant, 16 August 1861. Age 22 on roll dated 16 August 1861 at Watauga Bridge, TN. Elected first lieutenant at reorganization, 1 May 1862. Shot through the bowels in the Battle of Missionary Ridge, TN., 25 November 1863. Thought to be dead by the Confederates, he was captured and sent to U. S. Military Prison at Louisville,

---

[103] James Brazzell, Tennessee Confederate Pension Application, S4312.

[104] McCauley Camp 260, *Confederate Graves*, 10; Lindsley, *Annals*, 306.

[105] Sistler and Sistler, *1880 Census of Davidson County*, 55; Maney, *Surgeon's Log*, "Stones River TN"; "The Reunion," *Hickman Pioneer*.

[106] McCauley Camp 260, *Confederate Graves*, 10.

KY. Sent to Rock Island, IL., 7 December 1863 and arrived on the 9 December. Took oath 25 May 1865. Complexion dark, hair dark, eyes gray, 5'7". Resided at Charlotte, Dickson Co., TN.[107]

Brown, Jackson J. "Jack"; Private, Company K: Born in 1839 in Dickson Co., TN. No further.[108]

Brown, James A. "Jim"; First Sergeant, Company H: Born 1829 in Williamson Co., TN. Son of Neill Smith Brown, former Governor of Tennessee and Minister to Russia. Nephew of Confederate Major General and later Governor John C. Brown. Sworn into service 14 May 1861 at Nashville. Elected first corporal at organization. Later promoted to first sergeant. Buried in the Plunkett Cemetery, Hickman Co., TN. Pension Application S11109.[109]

*Brown, James Madison; First Sergeant, Company C: Born 2 March 1830 in Dickson Co., TN. Sworn into service, 18 May 1861 at Nashville. Age 26 on roll dated 16 August 1861 at Watauga Bridge, TN. Elected third sergeant at organization. Severely wounded in the Battle of Rock Castle, KY., 21 October 1861. Reduced to private, August 1862. Forge master since 3 May 1862. Promoted to first sergeant after February 1864. Surrendered with the Army of Tennessee, 26 April 1865 as a member of Company C, 2nd Consolidated Tennessee Infantry. Paroled 1 May 1865. Returning to Dickson Co., he married Mary J. Stuart on 7 December 1866. Died 1885. Buried in the Stuart Cemetery, Dickson Co., TN.[110]

Brown, John Joshua; Private, Company K: Born 11 December 1841 in Dickson Co., TN. Resided at Burns, TN. Sworn into service 25 May 1861 at Nashville. Age 20 on roll dated 15 August 1861. Wounded in the right side in the Battle of Rock Castle, KY., 21 October 1861. Discharged at Dalton, GA., in December 1863. Took oath at Chattanooga, TN., 12 March 1864. Complexion dark, hair brown, eyes blue, 6'4". Attended the reunion of the 11th Tennessee Infantry at Bon Aqua Springs, Hickman Co., TN., 24 September 1885. Pension.[111]

Brown, Robert J.; Private, Company A: Sworn into service, 10 May 1861 at Nashville. Absent on sick furlough for thirty days from 13 January 1862. Rejoined regiment in November 1862 by recruitment. Deserted 11 March 1863 at Shelbyville, TN.

Brown, Russell; Private, Company I: Born 20 December 1829 in Davidson Co., TN. Sworn into service, 20 May 1861 at Nashville. Detached from the regiment to man a siege gun at Cumberland Gap. Wounded in the action at Cumberland Gap, TN., by the discharge of a cannon, made deaf in left ear and lost sight in left eye. Discharged 15 August 1862 at Tazewell, TN., by order of the conscript act. Later served one month in the 10th Tennessee Cavalry. Lived at McEwen, Humphreys Co., TN.[112]

Brown, Samuel; Private, Company I: Born 1828 in Humphreys Co., TN. Occupation: farmer. Sworn into service, 20 May 1861 at Nashville. Discharged 15 August 1862 at Tazewell, TN. by order of the conscript act. Resided at McEwen, TN. Pension Application S8972.[113]

Brown, Thomas; Private, Company D: Sworn into service, 11 May 1861 at Nashville. Deserted at Camp Cheatham, TN.

---

[107] Maney, *Surgeon's Log*, "Missionary Ridge TN."

[108] McCauley Camp 260, *Confederate Graves*, 10.

[109] James A. Brown's service records report that he died 10 August 1862 at the C. S. General Military Hospital #4 in Wilmington NC of Febris Remittens. Buried in the town cemetery. This data is apparently incorrect given the above information; *Confederate Soldiers of Hickman County*, 28; James A. Brown, Tennessee Confederate Pension Application, S11109.

[110] Baker, *1850 Census for Dickson County*, 76; Baker, *1860 Census for Dickson County*, 69; Garrett and McClain, *Dickson County Cemetery Records* vol. 1, 21.

[111] J. J. Brown, Tennessee Confederate Pension Application, 12116; "The Reunion," *Hickman Pioneer*; McCauley Camp 260, Confederate Graves, 10.

[112] Russell Brown, Tennessee Pension Application, 1794.

[113] Samuel Brown, Tennessee Pension Application, 8972; Johnson, *1860 Census of Humphreys County*, 90.

Brown, W. J.; Private, Company A: Sworn into service 20 May 1861 at Nashville. Captured at the Battle of Murfreesboro, TN., 31 December 1862. Sent to Camp Douglas, IL. Forwarded to City Point, VA. Exchanged and returned to the 11th Tennessee by July 1863. Deserted on march from Sweetwater, TN. to Chattanooga, TN., 10 November 1863. Captured again by the Federals. Not wanting to endure another imprisonment, he joined the Federal Frontier forces, serving as a wagon driver, and was never allowed to have a gun. Resided at Waverly, Humphreys Co., TN. Occupation: day laborer. Applied to the Confederate Soldiers Home.[114]

Brown, W. L.; Rank unknown, Company A: Wounded and captured in the Battle of Franklin, TN., 30 November 1864.

Brown, Wiley S.; Private, Company K: Enlisted 13 December 1862 in Dickson Co., TN. Sent to hospital, returning to duty prior to the end of April, 1863. Captured 19 December 1864 at Columbia, TN. Sent to the U. S. Military Prison at Louisville, KY. Forwarded to Camp Chase, OH., 28 January 1865. Died of pneumonia 1 April 1865. Buried 1/3 mile from Camp Chase, grave #1794.[115]

Brown, William F.; Private, Company G: Occupation: laborer. Enlisted 3 June 1861 at Camp Cheatham, TN. Age 23 on roll dated 30 May 1863 at Shelbyville, TN. Wounded in the Battle of Missionary Ridge, TN., 25 November 1863. Left on the field and captured. Sent to U. S. Military Prison at Louisville, KY. Transferred to Rock Island, IL., 26 January 1864.

Brown, William J; Private, Company A: Sworn into service 10 May 1861 at Nashville. Captured at the Battle of Murfreesboro, TN., 31 December 1862. Sent to Camp Douglas, IL. Contracted smallpox and died in Rock Island Prison, 11 March 1863. Buried in the Oak Woods Cemetery, Chicago, IL.[116]

Brown, William Spencer; Private, Company H: Born c1840 in Hickman Co., TN. Occupation: brick mason. Sworn into service 14 May 1861 at Nashville. Absent at hospital at Knoxville, TN., from 10 April 1862. Re-enlisted in the 11th Tennessee Infantry, 3 May 1862. Height 6'1", fair complexion, blue eyes, light hair. Age 24 on roll dated 3 May 1862. Detached to General Stevenson's signal corps at Vicksburg, MS. from August 1862. Captured at the capitulation of Vicksburg, 4 July 1863. Paroled at Vicksburg, 6 July 1863. Deserted 1 November 1863.[117]

Browning, John Alvin; Private, Company I: Born 17 April 1843 in Stewart Co., TN. Sworn into service, 20 May 1861 at Nashville. Age 20 on roll dated 6 May 1863. Missing since the Battle of Missionary Ridge, TN., 25 November 1863. Joined Page's Company, 16th Kentucky Cavalry. Captured 11 February 1865 near Hartford, KY. Sent to prison in Louisville, KY., then to Camp Chase, OH. Married Hannah Fannie Duncan, 23 December 1868 in Hardin Co., KY. Resided Louisville, KY. Died 21 July 1896 at Franklin Cross Roads, Hardin Co., KY. Pension Application Kentucky 4628.

Browning, William J.; Private, Company G: Sworn into service 10 May 1861 at Nashville. Discharged 27 August 1862 at Tazewell, TN. by order of the conscript act.

Bruce, Jonathan M.; Private, Company A: Enlisted 23 July 1861 at Camp Cheatham. Age 27 on roll dated 6 May 1863 at Shelbyville, TN.

Bruce, Thomas N.; Private, Company A: Enlisted 23 July 1861 at Camp Cheatham. Deserted 17 June 1862 at Cumberland Gap, TN.

Bryan, Edward W.; Second Lieutenant, Company F: Born 24 July 1840 in Montgomery Co., TN. Relocated to Robertson Co., TN. Occupation farmer. Enlisted 18 May 1861 at Cedar Hill, TN. Detailed to Montgomery Co., TN. for sixty days, from 2 November 1864. Elected second lieutenant from the rank of private by Special Field Order 137/11. Received twenty-four votes which was a majority

---

[114] W. J. Brown, Confederate Soldiers Home Application.
[115] McCauley Camp 260, *Confederate Graves*, 10.
[116] Find-A-Grave, "Oak Woods," http://www.findagrave.com/cgi-bin/fg.cgi?page=gr&GSln=Brown&GSiman=1&GSsr=81&GScid=173554&GRid=37530729& (16 August 2014).
[117] United Daughters of the Confederacy, *Confederate Soldiers of Hickman County*, 30.

in the election. Deserted 30 December 1864. Took oath at Nashville, 22 April 1865. Complexion fair, hair light, eyes blue, height 6'3". Married Rebecca Grady in 1867. Politically he was a Democrat.[118]

Bryan, Jake "Colonel"; N/A., Company F: One of four known black men to serve with the 11th Tennessee Infantry. Born in Sumner Co., TN. Enlisted in the 11th Tennessee in May 1861. Served as a cook. Remained with the regiment throughout the war and served Brigadier General Gordon and his staff during the latter part of 1864 until he was captured at some point during the Tennessee campaign. After the war, he lived near Guthrie, KY. Tennessee Pension Application S1486.[119]

Bryan, James F.; Private, Company G, B: Sworn into service 10 May 1861 in Company G. Transferred to Company B, 1 May 1862 at the reorganization. Age 21 on roll dated 2 June 1863 at Shelbyville, TN. Deserted at Chattanooga, TN., 9 September 1863. Captured and took oath, 10 September 1863. Apparently rejoined the regiment and was surrendered as a member of Company C, 2nd Consolidated Tennessee Infantry, 26 April 1865. Paroled 1 May 1865.

Bryan, James Melvin; Private, Company F: Born 4 March 1843 in Montgomery Co., TN. Occupation: farmer. Enlisted 18 May 1861 at Cedar Hill, TN. Left in the hospital at Bean Station, TN., 4 August 1862. Age 19 on roll dated 20 October 1862. Discharged 1 November 1862 at Knoxville, TN., for disability due to rheumatism in the left knee. Height 6'4", complexion fair, eyes blue. Married Nannie Jane Manion, 5 November 1867 in Todd Co., KY. Resided at Guthrie, Todd Co., KY., where he died 27 December 1885. Pension Application Kentucky 4206.

Bryan, Martin W.; Sergeant, Company F: Born 1831 in Montgomery Co., TN. Occupation: merchant. Enlisted 19 July 1861 at Camp Cheatham. Age 30 on roll dated 31 January 1862. In February 1862 served as a courier for Colonel Rains, taking private dispatches to the War Department in Richmond, VA. While engaged in this service he was exposed to ice and snow and contracted neuralgia of the head. In later life he eventually lost his sight. Complexion dark, eyes dark, hair dark. Captured and sent to prison at Johnson's Island, OH., where he was discharged 25 July 1865.[120]

Bryan, Montgomery T.; Private, Company F: Enlisted 1 April 1862 at Cumberland Gap, TN. Wounded in the Battle of Atlanta, GA., 22 July 1864.[121]

Bryant, Ephraim; Private, Company D: No further.

Bryant, J. W.; Private, Company K: Enlisted 17 December 1862 in Dickson Co., TN. Died 26 March 1863, age 30 years.

Bryant, S. B.; Private, Company B: Sworn into service 10 May 1861 at Nashville. Deserted at Knoxville, TN., 8 September 1861.

Bryant, Thomas R.; Private, Company D, B: Born in Lincoln Co., TN. Sworn into service 11 May 1861 at Nashville in Company D. Transferred to Company B by July 1862. Served as a carpenter. Discharged for disability at Loudon, TN., 1 December 1862. Apparently rejoined unit. Wounded in the Battle of Chickamauga, GA., 19 September 1863. Wounded again in the Battle of Peachtree Creek, GA., 20 July 1864. Discharged at Atlanta, GA., by Dr. Maney. Resided in Nashville. Died 12 March 1905. Buried in Mount Olivet Cemetery, Nashville, TN.[122]

Bullard, William; Private, Company A: Sworn into service 10 May 1861 at Nashville. Age 29 on roll dated 21 August 1863. Deserted 21 August 1863 near Chattanooga, TN. and captured the same day by the 1st U. S. Cavalry Division at Stevenson, AL. Complexion fair, eyes blue, hair light.

Bumpass, Abram B. "Abe"; Third Corporal, Company D, B: Born c. 1840. Occupation: clerk. Sworn into service 11 May 1861 at Nashville. Elected third corporal. Served as Forage Master. Sent to

---

[118] Goodspeed Brothers, *Goodspeed's Histories of Montgomery, Robertson, Humphreys, Stewart, Dickson, Cheatham, Houston Counties*, 1134.

[119] Jake Bryan, Tennessee Pension Application, S1486.

[120] Martin W. Bryan, Tennessee Confederate Pension Application, S165.

[121] Jackson, "Letter to Parents," 14 July 1864.

[122] W. W. Clayton, *History of Davidson County* (Nashville TN: Charles Elder, 1971) 187; Thomas R. Bryant, Tennessee Confederate Pension Application, S4493.

Nashville, TN. for supplies 20 September 1861. Transferred to Company B by July 1862, and returned to the rank of private. Age 23 on roll dated 2 June 1863. In hospital at Atlanta, GA., 23 December 1863. Killed by a cannon ball without breaking the skin on the skirmish line at Kennesaw Mountain, GA., 11 June 1864.[123]

Bunn, William T.; Private, Company A: Born c. 1832. Occupation: laborer. Missing in action in the Battle of Murfreesboro, TN., 31 December 1862.[124]

Bunnell, Theodore Adolphus; Private, Company I: Born 2 February 1844 in Montgomery Co., TN. Enlisted 1 April 1861 in Company A, Captain Bonment's Artillery. Later transferred to the 50th Tennessee Infantry. After falling ill with the measles and recovering, he joined the 11th Tennessee on 5 March 1862 at Cumberland Gap, TN. Age 19 on roll dated 6 May 1863 at Shelbyville, TN. On extra duty as a cook for the company, November 1863 through February 1864. Wounded three times in the Battle of Franklin, TN., 30 November 1864. Sent to the hospital and unable to return to the regiment. Took oath 5 April 1865. Complexion fair, hair light, eyes blue, height 6' 3". Married Elenora Charley Blake, 15 February 1872. Member of Forbes Bivouac and the Masonic Order. Politically a Democrat. Died 19 March 1919. Buried in the McEwen Cemetery, Humphreys Co., TN.[125]

Burch, Thomas; Private, Company H: Born 15 December 1835 in Pearson Co., NC. Occupation: day laborer. Sworn into service 14 May 1861 at Nashville. Left in hospital in KY., 15 October 1862. Frequently was color bearer. Suffered a slight flesh wound in the calf in the Battle of Lovejoy Station, GA., 2 September 1864. Deserted 17 December 1864. Complexion fair, eyes grey, hair brown, height 5' 10". Postwar he relocated to Humphreys Co., TN., where he farmed in the Cherry Bottom community.[126]

Burchard, Abram Valentine; Private, Company H: Born 2 June 1844. Brother of First Sergeant William J. Burchard. Enlisted 1 December 1862 at Manchester, TN. Captured in the Battle of Missionary Ridge, TN., 25 November 1863. Forwarded to U. S. Military Prison in Louisville, KY. on 7 December 1863. Sent to Rock Island, IL. Later served in the 10th Tennessee Cavalry. Took oath 18 May 1865. Complexion fair, hair auburn, eyes hazel, height 5' 11". Married (1) Alice Huddleston, (2) Zianna Huddleston. Died in 1905. Buried in the Huddleston Cemetery, Hickman Co., TN.[127]

Burchard, William J.; First Sergeant, Company H: Born 27 January 1843 in Hickman Co., TN. Brother of Private Abram V. Burchard. Sworn into service 14 May 1861 at Nashville. Acting provost sergeant November 1861 through January 1862. Admitted to Fair Ground Hospital #1, Atlanta, GA., for dysentery 19 April 1863. Returned to duty 11 May 1863. First sergeant by July 1863. Later joined the cavalry. Following the war, he lived in Martin, TN. Married Margaret Montgomery, 14 December 1871. Died in Weakley Co., TN., 3 December 1916. Buried in the Eastside Cemetery in Martin, Weakley Co., TN.[128]

---

[123] Maney, *Surgeon's Log*, "Kennesaw Mountain GA"; Dobson-Sides, *1860 Davidson County Census*, 176.

[124] Johnson, *1860 Census of Humphreys County*, 131; Thedford, "Report of Operations."

[125] M. R. Scholes, Tennessee Confederate Pension Application, S13108; Goodspeed Brothers, *Goodspeed's Histories of Montgomery, Robertson, Humphreys, Stewart, Dickson, Cheatham, Houston Counties*, 1209-10; Anderson and Garrett, *Humphreys County, Cemetery Records*, 171; William H. Shelton, "Forbes Bivouac #21 of Clarksville," *Montgomery County Genealogical Journal* vol. 7 no. 1 (September 1977): 23.

[126] Maney, *Surgeon's Log*, "September 1864"; United Daughters of the Confederacy, Thomas Stewart Easley Chapter No. 1814, *Hickman County, Tennessee United States Census, 1860* (Centerville TN: Thomas Stewart Easley Chapter No. 1814, United Daughters of the Confederacy, 1982) 150; Electronic mail correspondence with descendant, Gail Tomlinson, 12 November 2002.

[127] Spence, *History*, 498; United Daughters of the Confederacy, *Confederate Soldiers of Hickman County*, 33.

[128] Welsh, *Confederate Hospitals*, Patient Roster, Fair Ground Hospital #1, 39; United Daughters of the Confederacy, *Confederate Soldiers of Hickman County*, 34.

Burk (Burke), Peter; Private, Company E, G: Enlisted 18 May 1861 in Company E at Nashville. Age 22 on roll dated 16 August 1861 at Watauga Bridge, TN. Transferred to Company G at the reorganization, 1 May 1862 at Cumberland Gap, TN. Sent to Fairground Hospital No. 2, Atlanta, GA., with lumbago. Returned to duty 1 May 1863. Wounded in the right leg in the Battle of Chickamauga, GA., 19 September 1863. Deserted at Chattanooga, TN., 11 November 1863. Captured and sent to U. S. Military Prison at Louisville, KY. Took oath 28 November 1863. Complexion dark, hair black, eyes gray, height 5' 10".[129]

Burkhart, B. F.; Private, Company E: Enlisted in Company B, 50th Tennessee Infantry at Fort Donelson, TN., 9 September 1861. Transferred to Company E of the 11th Tennessee Infantry by General Order 38. Wounded in the Battle of Chickamauga, GA. Admitted to Fairground Hospital No. 1 at Atlanta, GA., 24 September 1863 for vulnus sclopeticum. Sent to another hospital 25 September 1863. Transferred to Company B, 50th Tennessee Infantry, 18 February 1864.[130]

Burnett, E. F.; Private, Company D, B: Sworn into service 11 May 1861 in Company D at Nashville. Transferred to Company B. Discharged under the conscript law, 15 August 1862 at Walden's Ridge, TN. Died in May 1928.[131]

Burnett, Thomas J.; Private, Company D: Sworn into service 11 May 1861 at Nashville. Deserted at Murfreesboro, TN., 4 January 1863. Applied for pension in Miller Co., AR. in 1914. Died 15 January 1918.

Burns, Bryant; Private, Company C: Sworn into service 14 May 1861 at Nashville. Listed as a teamster from 13 September to 28 September 1861. Given sick furlough 9 October 1862. Issued a minie musket. Listed as a deserter November 1862. Rejoined from desertion after December 1862. Deserted again 29 April 1863. Shown to be present after July 1863. Age 27 on roll dated 8 May 1863 at Shelbyville, TN. Complexion dark, hair dark, eyes hazel, height 5' 6 ½". Took oath 19 June 1864.[132]

Burns, William E.; First Corporal, Company D: Sworn into service 11 May 1861 at Nashville. Discharged 15 August 1862 at Walden's Ridge, TN. by order of the conscript act.

Burton, John W.; Private, Company G: Sworn into service 10 May 1861 at Nashville. Deserted 1 August 1861.

Burton, N. G.; Private, Company B: Born in Greene Co., KY. Occupation: farmer. Sworn into service 10 May 1861 at Nashville. Discharged 11 May 1862 at Cumberland Gap, TN. by virtue of the conscript law. Age 45 on record dated 11 May 1862. Complexion fair, eyes black, hair gray.

Butler, Joshua B.; Private, Company K: Born 1842 in Maury Co., TN. Enlisted 23 January 1863 in Dickson Co., TN. Age 19 on roll dated 1 May 1863 at Shelbyville, TN. Wounded in the neck by a shell fragment in the Battle of Jonesboro, GA., 1 September 1864. Wounded in the leg in the Battle of Nashville, TN., 16 December 1864. Was in the hospital in North Carolina near the end of the war. Took oath 9 January 1865. Complexion fair, hair brown, eyes gray, height 5' 8".[133]

---

[129] Welsh, *Confederate Hospitals*, Patient Roster, Fair Ground Hospital #2, 26; Maney, *Surgeon's Log*, "Chickamauga GA."
[130] Welsh, *Confederate Hospitals*, Patient Roster, Fair Ground Hospital #1, 40.
[131] Joseph McCrary, Tennessee Pension Application, 16241.
[132] McCauley, *Record Book, Company C.*
[133] J. B. Butler, Tennessee Pension Application, 14044; Maney, *Surgeon's Log*, "September 1864."

-C-

Caffrey, John; Private, Company D, G: Sworn into service 11 May 1861 in Company D at Nashville. Age 28 on roll dated 5 May 1863 at Shelbyville, TN. Transferred to Company G by July 1862. Missing in action in the Battle of Missionary Ridge, TN., 25 November 1863. Sent to U. S. Military Prison. Forwarded to Rock Island, IL., 7 December 1863. Forwarded to Camp Douglas, IL., 25 January 1865.

Cagle, Charles B.; Private, Company H: Born 28 August 1841 in Hickman Co., TN. Sworn into service 14 May 1861 at Nashville. Home on sick furlough August, 1861. Present through December 1863. Married Sarah Blackwell, 7 May 1871. Died 1 July 1914. Buried in the Chessor Cemetery, Hickman Co., TN.[134]

Caldwell, William H.; Fourth Sergeant, Company I: Born c. 1841. Sworn into service 20 May 1861 at Nashville. Home recovering from illness, August, 1861. In August 1862 rank was reduced to private. Age 22 on roll dated 6 May 1863 at Shelbyville, TN. Captured in the Battle of Jonesboro, GA., 1 September 1864. Sent to U. S. Military Prison in Louisville, KY. then to Camp Douglas, IL., 29 October 1864. Took oath 24 June 1865. Complexion light, hair dark, eyes blue, height 5' 6". Relocated to Ward, Lonoke Co., AR. following the war, where he practiced medicine. Married. Died March 1887. Pension Application Arkansas Widow 5803.

Callender, John Hill; Surgeon, Field & Staff: Born 28 November 1832 near Nashville, TN., son of Mary Sangster and Thomas Callender. His grandfather, James Thompson Callender, had been exiled from Scotland because of his advanced democratic doctrines expressed in his *Political History of Great Britain*. In his early life John Hill Callender was a student in the literary department of the University of Nashville. He studied law, was briefly in business and finally decided on a career in medicine. He received his degree from the University of Pennsylvania in 1855 and became a member of the Medical Society of Tennessee in the same year. Within a few months he became joint proprietor and editor of the *Nashville Patriot*. On 24 February 1858, he married Della Jefferson Ford, great grand-niece of Thomas Jefferson. Also, in 1858 he became a founder and member of the faculty of the Shelby Medical College in Nashville, as Professor of *Materia Medica* and Therapeutics. Callender was also interested in politics and was a member of the National Union Convention that nominated John Bell for the presidency in 1860. During the campaign that followed, he was Bell's private secretary. Dr. Callender was appointed surgeon of the 11th Tennessee Infantry, 11 September 1861. He remained in this position until he resigned in February 1862. Following the war he was on the editorial staff of the Nashville *Union and American* until 1869, and he accepted the chair of *Materia Medica* and therapeutics in the Medical Department of the University of Nashville and later Vanderbilt University. In 1870, Dr. Callender began more than twenty-five years' service as medical superintendent of the Tennessee Hospital for the Insane. He gained a national reputation as an alienist, and was summoned by the U.S. Government as an expert witness in the trial of Charles J. Guiteau, the assassin of President James Garfield. In 1894 he was active in organizing the faculty of the University of Nashville and served as its dean until his death, 3 August 1896. Buried at Mount Olivet Cemetery, Nashville, TN.[135]

Calus, Patrick; Private, Company I: Resident of Jefferson Co., KY. prior to enlisting. Complexion fair, hair dark, eyes gray, 5' 7". Surrendered at Augusta, GA., 1 May 1865. Took oath 16 May 1865.

---

[134] Coble, "Letter to Father," 16 August 1861; Norman G. Durham, *The Cagle Family of Hickman County, Tennessee* (Sanford NC: N.G. Durham, 1994) 5; Jill Knight Garrett and Iris Hopkins McClain, *Sacred to the Memory: Cemetery Records of Hickman County*, vol. 1 (Columbia TN: P-Vine Press, 1982) 39.

[135] Philip May Hamer, *Centennial History of the Tennessee Medical Association* (Nashville TN: Tennessee State Medical Association, 1930) 149-50.

Campbell, C. E.; Private, Company B: Sworn into service 10 May 1861 at Nashville. Discharged 15 August 1862 at Walden's Ridge (Tazewell), TN.

Cannon, John T.; Private, Company A: Born c. 1842. Sworn into service 10 May 1861 at Nashville. Died 28 June 1861 at Camp Cheatham with the measles.[136]

Capes, Elijah "Lige"; Private, Company K: Sworn into service 25 May 1861 at Nashville. Age 23 on roll dated 15 August 1861 at Midway, TN. Discharged 1 July 1862 by procuring a substitute.

Capps, Sterling F.; Fourth Sergeant, Company K: Occupation: farmer. Sworn into service 25 May 1861 at Nashville. Age 26 on roll dated 15 August 1861 at Midway, TN. Forage Master, 1 May 1862 through December 1862. Promoted to fourth sergeant by July 1863. Made fifth sergeant September 1863. Wounded in the right thigh in the Battle of Missionary Ridge, TN., 25 November 1863. Sent to hospital. Assigned to Cheatham's division sharpshooters commanded by Lieutenant John M. Ozanne. Issued a Whitworth rifle. Killed in the Battle of New Hope Church, GA., 27 May 1864 while performing sharpshooting duties.[137]

Capps, William; Private, Company B: Enlisted 10 May 1861 at Nashville. Age 20 on roll dated 25 June 1863 at Shelbyville, TN. Captured in Davidson Co., TN. in July 1864. Sent to U. S. Military Prison. Took oath 18 July 1864. Complexion light, hair dark, eyes hazel, height 5' 8".

Carbide, James N.; Second Corporal, Company A: Sworn into service 10 May 1861 at Nashville. Promoted to second corporal. Reduced back to the rank of private, 13 September 1861. Discharged by providing a substitute, 1 August 1862 at Bean Station, TN. Captured at Chattanooga, TN., 1 April 1865. Took oath 29 May 1865. Complexion fair, hair dark, eyes blue, height 5' 8".

Carbide, Joseph M.; Private, Company B: Sworn into service 10 May 1861 at Nashville. Teamster for General Rains, September through December 1862. Age 20 on roll dated 2 June 1863 at Shelbyville, TN. Captured in the Battle of Franklin, TN., 30 November 1864. Sent to the Provost Marshal at Nashville. Forwarded to the U. S. Military Prison at Louisville, KY. Arrived at Camp Douglas, IL., 6 December 1864. Released 24 March 1865. Complexion fair, hair brown, eyes brown, height 5' 5".

Carothers, James Howell "Tack"; Third Sergeant, Company H: Born in 1833. Married Ophelia M. Hassell, 17 August 1859 in Maury Co., TN. Sworn into service, 14 May 1861 at Nashville. Appointed corporal, 28 October 1861. Promoted to third sergeant, 24 March 1862. Reduced to private August 1862. Regimental wagon master, 1 May 1862 through August 1863. Captured in Hickman Co., TN., 23 January 1864. Unaware of his capture, Confederate records have him listed as deserting, 9 February 1864. Sent to Nashville, then to the U. S. Military Prison in Louisville, KY. Sent to Rock Island, IL., 3 February 1864. Transferred to Boule's Wharf, VA., where he was exchanged, 5 March 1865. Admitted to Jackson Hospital, Richmond, VA., 7 March 1865. Entered Way Hospital, Meridian, MS., 24 March 1865. Paroled. Moved to Gatesville, Coryell Co., TX. around 1876. Died 31 August 1905 in Gatesville, TX. and buried in the Gatesville City Cemetery. Texas Confederate Widows Pension 18373.[138]

Carper, John; Private, Company B: Born c. 1843 in TN. Sworn into service 10 May 1861 at Nashville. Deserted 1 August 1861 at Haynesville, TN.[139]

Carroll, James Jackson; Private, Company K: Born in Bedford Co., TN., 11 September 1840. Occupation: farmer. Enlisted 27 December at Readyville, TN. Wounded in the elbow and lost the use of his arm in the Battle of Murfreesboro, TN., 31 December 1862. Discharged 27 March 1863 at Rome, GA., due to wounds sustained. Age 19, complexion fair, hair dark, eyes hazel, height 5' 7". Resided at

---

[136] Johnson, *1860 Census of Humphreys County*, 129; Shipp, "Letter to Sister," 25 June 1861.

[137] "Battle of Pickett's Mill," *Memphis Daily Appeal*; Maney, *Surgeon's Log*, "Missionary Ridge TN"; Maney, *Surgeon's Log*, "May 1864."

[138] United Daughters of the Confederacy, *Confederate Soldiers of Hickman County*, 36; *Hickman County News*, 19 October 1905, Byron Sistler and Barbara Sistler, *Maury County Tennessee Marriages 1852-1867* (Nashville TN: B. Sistler, 1986) 6.

[139] Dobson-Sides, *1860 Davidson County Census*, 441.

Graham's Station in Hickman Co., TN. Died 9 December 1923. Buried in the Willow Springs Cemetery, Hickman Co., TN.[140]

Carroll, John; Private, Company A: Born 11 September 1840 in Bedford Co., TN. Wounded on the first day of the Battle of Nashville, TN., 15 December 1864. Captured at Franklin, TN., 17 December 1864. Admitted to U. S. General Hospital #1 at Nashville, TN. on 26 December 1864. Transferred to Provost Marshal, 15 February 1865. Sent to U. S. Military prison in Louisville, KY. on 15 February 1865. Sent to Camp Chase, OH., 17 February 1865. Transferred to Point Lookout, MD., 26 March 1865. Released 4 June 1865. Died 9 December 1923.

Carter, D. E.; Private, Company B: Sworn into service, 10 May 1861 at Nashville. Deserted 29 December 1861 at Cumberland Gap, TN.

Carter, Green W.; Private, Company A, I: Sworn into service 10 May 1861 in Company A at Nashville. Transferred to Company I at the reorganization, 1 May 1862. Left as hospital nurse at Murfreesboro, TN., 31 December 1862. Captured 5 January 1863. Sent to Camp Butler, IL., 11 March 1863. Returned to unit by April 1863. Married Annie O'Guin.[141]

Carter, Joseph Jeff; Private, Company I, G: Occupation: farmer. Sworn into service 20 May 1861 in Company I at Nashville. At hospital in Richmond, KY., 1 October 1862. Captured 29 November 1862 at Richmond, KY. Returned to unit. Transferred to Company G, 1 March 1863. Wounded in the left side in the Battle of Chickamauga, GA., 19 September 1863. Sent to Foard Hospital in Marietta, GA., as a nurse, 1 October 1863. Killed in the Battle of Lovejoy Station, GA., 2 September 1864.[142]

Casey, John; Private, Company I, G: Sworn into service 20 May 1861 in Company I at Nashville. Transferred to Company G, 1 May 1862 at the reorganization. Discharged by virtue of the conscript act, 15 August 1862 at Tazewell, TN.

Cathey, Archibald "Archy"; Private, Company K: Born 1841 in Dickson Co., TN. Brother of Private Elias N. Cathey and first cousin of Private Joshua C. Cathey. Occupation: farmer. Married Susan E. Brown, 1 February 1860. Enlisted 1 December 1862 in Dickson Co., TN. Present through February 1864. Family history indicates he died during the war at Chattanooga, TN.[143]

Cathey, Elias Newton; Private, Company K: Born in Dickson Co., TN., 18 August 1839. Brother of Private Archibald Cathey and first cousin of Private Joshua C. Cathey. Occupation: farmer. Sworn into service 25 May 1861 at Nashville. Age 22 on roll dated 15 August 1861 at Midway, TN. Absent sick 15 September 1863. Returned for duty by February 1864. After affliction was assigned to duty as cook. Admitted to Ocmulgee Hospital in Macon, GA., for syphilis. Was on furlough in North Georgia when captured. Took oath at Chattanooga, TN., 30 March 1865. Married Lucindy M. Brown, 10 February 1866. Died 11 July 1927. Buried in the Stuart Cemetery, Dickson Co., TN. Complexion fair, hair dark, eyes gray, height 5' 6".[144]

Cathey, James N.; Private, Company K: Enlisted 1 December 1861 in Dickson Co., TN. Died at Fair Ground Hospital #2 in Atlanta, GA., 3 April 1863 of febris typhoid.

Cathey, John; Private, Company A: Born c. 1827. Brother of Private Samuel Cathey. Sworn into service 10 May 1861 at Nashville. On 20 day furlough from 14 January 1862. Discharged 14 August

---

[140] James Jackson Carroll, Tennessee Pension Application, 968; McCauley Camp 260, *Confederate Graves*, 12; United Daughters of the Confederacy, *Hickman County, Tennessee Cemetery Records* part 2, 346.

[141] Anderson and Garrett, *Humphreys County Cemetery Records* vol. 2, 171.

[142] Maney, *Surgeon's Log*, "Chickamauga GA"; Maney, *Surgeon's Log*, "September 1864."

[143] Byron Sistler and Barbara Sistler, *Dickson County Tennessee Marriages 1857-1870* (Nashville TN: B. Sistler, 1988) 4; Byron and Barbara Sistler, *1850 Census, Tennessee* vol.1 (Evanston IL: Byron Sistler and Associates, 1974) 300.

[144] Garrett, *Dickson County Handbook*, 201; E. N. Cathey, Tennessee Pension Application, 5359; Baker, *1850 Census for Dickson County*, 300.

1862 at Tazewell, TN. Captured at Richland Creek, TN., 16 May 1863. Sent to prison at Point Lookout, MD. Took oath 14 September 1864.[145]

Cathey, Joshua C.; Private, Company E: Born c. 1842. First cousin of Private Archibald Cathey and Private Elias N. Cathey. Occupation: farmer. Married Mary Ann Hood, 23 June 1858. Their first son, Martin Cathey, was born in April 1861, with Joshua being sworn into service on 18 May 1861 at Nashville. Age 21 on roll dated 16 August 1861 at Watauga Bridge, TN. On sick furlough since 5 November 1861. Listed as deserting at Cumberland Gap, TN., 7 October 1862. Buried at Missionary Ridge Baptist Church Cemetery, Bon Aqua, Hickman Co., TN. Grave unmarked.[146]

Cathey, Morris R; Private, Company K: Born c. 1828. Married M. A. F. Lewallen, 23 August 1859. Enlisted 1 December 1862 in Dickson Co., TN. Age 35 on roll dated 1 May 1863 at Shelbyville, TN. Admitted to Fair Ground Hospital #2, Atlanta, GA., 12 September 1863 with chronic diarrhea. Returned to duty 13 September 1863. Surrendered with the Army of Tennessee, 26 April 1865, as a member of Company K, 2nd Consolidated Tennessee Infantry. Paroled 1 May 1865.[147]

Cathey, Samuel Morris; Private, Company A: Born c. 1838. Brother of Private John Cathey. Enlisted 10 May 1861 at Nashville. Drowned in the Duck River near Shelbyville, TN., 28 February 1863.[148]

Cathey, William James; Private, Company K: Born 1841 in Dickson Co., TN. Enlisted 1 December 1862 at Manchester, TN. Admitted to Fair Ground Hospital #2, Atlanta GA., with febris typhoides, from which he died 26 March 1863. Buried in Oakland Cemetery, Atlanta, GA.[149]

Cavanaugh, James; Private, Company G: Enlisted 3 June 1861 at Camp Cheatham. Wounded at Camp Buckner, KY., 20 September 1861. In hospital at Knoxville, 4 November 1861. Age 23 on roll dated 30 May 1863 at Shelbyville, TN. Attendant in hospital from 6 August 1863 through 4 November 1863. On sick furlough from 4 November 1863 in Flewellen Hospital, Cassville, GA. Wounded late in the war and admitted to Way Hospital, Meridian, MS., 9 February 1865. Surrendered in Macon, GA. Took oath 12 May 1865. Complexion dark, hair black, eyes hazel, height 5' 7".

Cearnall, John A.; Private, Company A: Sworn into service 10 May 1861 at Nashville. Deserted 17 June 1862 at Cumberland Gap, TN. Re-enlisted from desertion 15 November 1862 at Lenoir Station, TN. Present through February 1864.

Ceston, Charles A.; Private, Company B: Sworn into service 10 May 1861 in Nashville. Shot by an accidental discharge of "Wash" Shouse's gun at Carter's Station, TN., 17 August 1861, and later died from the wound.[150]

Chamberlain, Andrew (Ambrose) N.; Private, Company H: Born c. 1839. Sworn into service 14 May 1861 at Nashville. Died 20 May 1861 at Camp Cheatham, Robertson Co., TN.[151]

Chamberlain, D. P.; Private, Company H: Born c. 1845. Sworn into service in Company H, 11th Tennessee. Later joined Company C, 9th Tennessee Cavalry Battalion. No further.[152]

---

[145] Johnson, *1860 Census of Humphreys County*, 21.

[146] Sistler and Sistler, *Dickson County Marriages*, 4; Baker, *1850 Census for Dickson County*, 300.

[147] Welsh, *Confederate Hospitals*, Patient Roster, Fair Ground Hospital #2, 33; Sistler and Sistler, *Dickson County Marriages*, 4; Baker, *1850 Census for Dickson County*, 300.

[148] Johnson, *1860 Census of Humphreys County*, 21.

[149] Welsh, *Confederate Hospitals*, Patient Roster, Fair Ground Hospital #2, 33; McCauley Camp 260, *Confederate Graves*, 12.

[150] Spence, *Travels*, 17 August 1861.

[151] Byron Sistler and Barbara Sistler, *1880 Census Hickman County, Tennessee* (Nashville TN: Byron Sistler & Associates, 1999) 12; United Daughters of the Confederacy, *Confederate Soldiers of Hickman County*, 40.

[152] Sistler and Sistler, *1880 Census of Hickman County*, 12; United Daughters of the Confederacy, *Confederate Soldiers of Hickman County*, 40.

Chambers, John; Private, Company F: Enlisted 18 May 1861 at Cedar Hill, TN. Brigade teamster from 13 August to 17 December 1861. Detached July 1863 through 25 November 1863 as a teamster for the brigade.

Chandler, James G; Private, Company H: Born c. 1839. Occupation: farm laborer. Sworn into service 14 May 1861 at Nashville. Died at Camp Cheatham, Robertson Co., TN., 1 June 1861, with measles.[153]

Chandler, John E.; Second Lieutenant, Company G: Sworn into service 10 May 1861 at Nashville. Elected third lieutenant at the organization, Promoted to second lieutenant 5 October 1861. Relieved of duty 1 May 1862 at the reorganization and dropped from the roll.

Chandler, John H.; Second Corporal, Company H: Born in 1838. Married Cynthia Adeline Flowers about 1860. Enlisted 25 July 1861 at Camp Cheatham. Appointed second corporal by August 1862. Killed in the Battle of Murfreesboro, TN., 31 December 1862.[154]

Chandler, Joseph K.; Second Corporal, Company H: Occupation: farmer. Sworn into service 14 May 1861 at Nashville. Appointed third corporal in August 1862. Promoted to second corporal by November 1862. Wounded in the thigh in the Battle of Murfreesboro, TN. Sent to hospital in Chattanooga, TN. Admitted to Fairground Hospital No. 1, Atlanta, GA., for vulnus sclopeticum, 8 January 1863. Sent to another hospital 15 February 1863. Furloughed 4 April 1863. Wounded in the right thigh in the Battle of Missionary Ridge, TN., 25 November 1863. Admitted to Fairground Hospital No. 2 at Atlanta, GA., 25 May 1864. Killed in the Battle of Jonesboro, GA., 1 September 1864.[155]

Chaney, Daniel M.; Private, Company G: Born 4 August 1846 at Spotsylvania, VA. Enlisted in Company G, then transferred to Benjamin W. McCann's cavalry. Captured at Augusta, Carroll Co., OH., 26 July 1863. Sent to Camp Chase, OH., 28 July 1863. Transferred to Camp Douglas, IL., 22 August 1863. Released from Point Lookout, MD., 9 June 1865. Resided in Nashville following the war, where he was occupied as a carpenter and mechanics hand. Member Cheatham Bivouac. Died after 1920.[156]

Chapman, M. G.; Private, Company C: Sworn into service 14 May 1861 at Nashville. Deserted 3 July 1861.

Cheatham, Ephriam Foster; Major, Quartermaster, Field & Staff: Born in Springfield, Robertson Co., TN. in 1833. Son of General Richard Cheatham. Prior to the war, he was a partner in the firm of M. and E. F. Cheatham, the largest wholesale merchants of Nashville. Regimental Quartermaster in 1861. Under a commission from Governor Isham G. Harris, he was assigned to General S. R. Anderson's brigade, and in 1862 was transferred to I. B. Wharton's Texas Cavalry. He was later transferred to John Hunt Morgan's command and took part in Morgan's raid and captured, held at Camp Chase, OH. and later at Fort Delaware. Following the war, in 1867 he served as clerk of the Tennessee State Senate at the time his brother, Edward S. Cheatham, was speaker of that body. Major Cheatham later became a cotton planter in Arkansas and lived for a period in New York. He returned to Nashville in the late 1890's. Genial in disposition, kind hearted and generous, he was well informed and always took a deep interest in politics and all other public affairs. Died at Tennessee Hospital, 3 June 1911. Buried at Mount Olivet Cemetery in Nashville, Davidson Co., TN.[157]

---

[153] United Daughters of the Confederacy, *Hickman County Census 1860*, 149; Shipp, "Letter to Sister," 25 June 1861.

[154] United Daughters of the Confederacy, *Hickman County Census 1860*, 151, United Daughters of the Confederacy, *Confederate Soldiers of Hickman County*, 42.

[155] Maney, *Surgeon's Log*, "Missionary Ridge TN"; Welsh, *Confederate Hospitals*, Patient Roster, Fair Ground Hospital #1, 51; Welsh, *Confederate Hospitals*, Patient Roster, Fair Ground Hospital #2, 34; United Daughters of the Confederacy, *Confederate Soldiers of Hickman County*, 42.

[156] Daniel M. Chaney, Cheatham Bivouac Application.

[157] *Nashville Daily Gazette*, 21 June 1861.

Cheatham, William T.; First Lieutenant, Company B: Born c. 1832. Sworn into service 10 May 1861 at Nashville. Elected first lieutenant at the organization. Resigned 6 July 1861.

Chessey, Matthew; Private, Company F: Deserted at Readyville, TN., 15 December 1862.

Chester, Claiborne B.; Sergeant, Company C: Born c. 1840 in Dickson Co., TN. Brother of Sergeant John A. Chester. Sworn into service 14 May 1861 at Nashville. Promoted to sergeant in August 1862. Arm broken in the Battle of Murfreesboro, TN., 31 December 1862. Supposed to have been captured.[158]

Chester, John A.; Fourth Sergeant, Company C: Occupation: farmer. Brother of Private Claiborne B. Chester. Sworn into service 14 May 1861 at Nashville. Issued a minie musket. Elected fourth sergeant at the organization. Lost rank and reduced to private at the reorganization, 1 May 1862. In quartermaster department as a wagon master, 5 May through July 1862. Age 29 on roll dated 8 May 1863. Teamster in the quartermaster department, 25 April 1863 through February 1864. Killed by a guard in Atlanta, GA., 18 August 1864.[159]

Chester, Joseph; Private, Company K: Sworn into service 25 May 1861 at Nashville. On duty as wagon master since 12 August 1862. Transferred to the 49th Tennessee Infantry, 18 December 1862.

Chichester, Cyrus; Private, Company E: Born 25 December 1815. Married Jane Mallory, sister of Captain William J. Mallory, on 5 July 1848. Occupied as a jailor in 1850. Sworn into service 18 May 1861 at Nashville. Age 48 on roll dated 16 August 1861 at Watauga Bridge, TN. On extra duty as a teamster March 1861 through January 1862. Discharged in August 1862 at Tazewell, TN. Occupied postwar as a carpenter and mechanic. Died 20 October 1890. Buried in the City Cemetery, Charlotte, Dickson Co., TN.[160]

Choate, John; Private, Company A: Born 1841 in Humphreys Co., TN. Sworn into service 10 May 1861 at Nashville. Wounded in the Battle of Murfreesboro, TN., 31 December 1862. The projectile entered the left leg just above the knee and ranged upward and had to be cut out of the buttock. Bullet removed by Assisstant Regimental Surgeon William M. Slayden. Suffered permanent disability from the wound. Deserted 29 September 1863 at Chattanooga, TN. Returned to McEwen, Humphreys Co., TN. and resumed farming. Buried in the McEwen Cemetery, Humphreys Co., TN.[161]

Choate, Smith E.; Fourth Corporal, Company E: Born 1839 in Dickson Co., TN. Occupation: farmhand. Sworn into service 18 May 1861 at Nashville. Age 22 on roll dated 16 August 1861 at Watauga Bridge, TN. Promoted to fourth corporal by March 1862. Reduced to private by August 1862. Cut off from command in the Battle of Nashville, TN., 16 December 1864 and captured. Took oath 29 January 1865. Complexion dark, hair dark, eyes gray, height 5' 11". Married Francis Williams, 20 December 1866. Postwar occupation: sawmill worker. Resided at McEwen, Humphreys Co., TN. Died in May, 1913.[162]

Chrisman, Lafayette C.; Private, Company C: Enlisted 1 August 1861 at Knoxville, TN. Issued a Belgium musket. Wagon master from 1 August through 31 December 1861. Discharged 10 August 1862 at Tazewell, TN.[163]

Church, Charles H.; Private, Company H: Enlisted 3 February 1863 at Shelbyville, TN. Deserted 9 March 1863.

---

[158] McCauley Camp 260, *Confederate Graves*, 12.

[159] McCauley, *Record Book, Company C*.

[160] Baker, *1850 Census for Dickson County*, 32; Sistler and Sistler, *1880 Census of Dickson County*, 111.

[161] John Choate, Tennessee Pension Application, 4445; Anderson and Garrett, *Humphreys County Cemetery Records*, vol. 1, 172.

[162] Smith E. Choate, Tennessee Pension Application, 13980; Georgia L. Baker, *1860 Census for Dickson County, Tennessee with Index* rev. ed. (Nashville TN: Richland Press, 2007) 140; Baker, *1870 Census Dickson County*, 109.

[163] McCauley, *Record Book, Company C*.

Clardy, George W.; Private, Company K: Sworn into service 25 May 1861 at Nashville. Age 22 on roll dated 15 August 1861. On extra duty as a teamster 20 September 1862 through December 1863.

*Clark, Edward White; Captain, Company B: Born 14 October 1832. Occupation: clerk. Sworn into service 10 May 1861 at Nashville. Elected third lieutenant at the organization. Appointed second lieutenant in August 1861. Elected first lieutenant 10 May 1862. Promoted to captain of Company B, 23 May 1862. Wounded in the right thigh in the Battle of Murfreesboro, TN., 31 December 1862. Wounded again in 1864. Granted a leave of absence for 60 days, Special Order #16, 21 January 1865. Surrendered with the Army of Tennessee, 26 April 1865 as the Captain of Company C, 2nd Consolidated Tennessee Infantry. Paroled 1 May 1865. Member of the Episcopal Church. Died 25 July 1868. Buried in the Mount Olivet Cemetery, Nashville, Davidson Co., TN. "He was as noble and gallant a soldier as ever drew saber for the lost cause."[164]

Clark, George N.; Private, Company F: Born at Carter, Sullivan Co., TN. Occupation: farmer. Enlisted 18 May 1861 at Cedar Hill, TN. Discharged 23 November 1862 on a surgeon's certificate of disability for phetisis pulmonabis, age 20. Complexion fair, eyes blue, hair light, height 5' 10".

Clark, James Ira; Private, Company D: Born in Warren Co., TN., 8 May 1831. Occupation: laborer. Married Mary L. Bryan, 12 December 1855. Sworn into service 11 May 1861 at Nashville. On extra duty as brigade quartermaster, September through December 1862. Age 33 on roll dated 5 May 1863 at Shelbyville, TN. Wounded in the upper left thigh in the Battle of Missionary Ridge, TN., 25 November 1863. Sent to hospital. Gangrene caused muscles to be eaten away. Discharged in August 1864 because of wound. Complexion fair, height 5' 10", eyes blue. Postwar, he lived in South Nashville and was occupied as a carpenter. Member of the Frank Cheatham Camp No. 35 and a member of Company B, United Confederate Veterans. Died 22 May 1901. Buried in his uniform at Mount Olivet Cemetery, Nashville, Davidson Co., TN.[165]

*Clifton, Burill Alexander; First Corporal, Company K: Born 18 January 1842 in Dickson Co., TN. Brother of Private Josiah Clifton and Private James K. Clifton, Jr. Sworn into service 25 May 1861 at Nashville. Contracted measles while at Camp Cheatham in June 1861. Elected third corporal at the organization. Age 19 on roll dated 15 August 1861 at Midway, TN. Absent on sick furlough to home in Dickson Co., TN. from 6 November 1862 for 30 days due to typhoid fever. Wounded in the right elbow in the Battle of Murfreesboro, TN., 31 December 1862. Promoted to second corporal by July 1863. Wounded in the breast in the Battle of Atlanta, GA., 22 July 1864. Appointed first corporal by the end of the war. Surrendered with the Army of TN., 26 April 1865 as a member of Company K, 2nd Consolidated Tennessee Infantry. Paroled 1 May 1865. Resided at Dickson, Dickson Co., TN. Married 25 August 1867 to his cousin, Cynthea Adeline Bullock. Present at the 14 June 1904 reunion of the 11th Tennessee Infantry in Nashville. Died 5 July 1919. Buried in the Union Cemetery, Dickson, Dickson Co., TN.[166]

*Clifton, James Kirby, Jr.; Private, Company K: Born in Dickson Co., TN., 23 December 1844. Brother of Corporal Burrill A. Clifton and Private Josiah Clifton. Occupation: farmer. Enlisted November 1862 at Manchester, TN. Age 18 on roll dated 1 May 1863 at Shelbyville, TN. In Floyd House Hospital or Ocmulgee Hospital at Macon, GA., for debilitas, 28 November 1863. Surrendered 26 April 1865 as a member of Company K, 2nd Consolidated Tennessee Infantry. Paroled 1 May 1865. Returned to farming. Married Tennessee (Tennie) Ann Dudley, 3 August 1865. Attended the reunion of

---

[164] Maney, *Surgeon's Log,* "Stones River TN"; *Nashville Union and Dispatch,* 28 July 1868.

[165] James Ira Clark, Tennessee Confederate Pension Application, S1005; *Biographical Sketches,* 27; Maney, *Surgeon's Log,* "Missionary Ridge TN"; "James I. Clark," *Confederate Veteran,* vol. 9 no. 6 (June 1901): 274.

[166] B. A. Clifton, Tennessee Confederate Pension Application, S1309; Garrett, *Dickson County Handbook,* 201; Ruth Clifton Gill, "Pioneer Family of Burril Alexander Clifton January 18, 1842-July 5, 1919" in *The Heritage of Dickson County, Tennessee, 1803-2006,* Dickson County Heritage Book Committee, (Waynesville NC: County Heritage Inc., 2007) 190; *Reunion Pamphlet,* 14 June 1904.

the 11th Tennessee Infantry at Bon Aqua Springs, Hickman Co., TN., 24 September 1885. Died 18 October 1925. Buried in the Clifton Cemetery, Dickson Co., TN. Pension Application S7112.[167]

Clifton, Josiah W.; Private, Company K: Born 2 May 1838 in Dickson Co., TN. Brother of Corporal Burill Clifton and Private James K. Clifton, Jr. Sworn into service 25 May 1861 at Nashville. Died 9 August 1861. Buried Clifton Cemetery, Dickson Co., TN.[168]

Clohasey, John; Private, Company G: Enlisted 3 June 1861 at Camp Cheatham. Wounded in the Battle of Murfreesboro, TN., 31 December 1862. Sent to hospital. Detached as a nurse to a hospital in Rome, GA., 15 June 1863. Died in Polk Hospital, Rome, GA., 30 October 1863 from the effects of a wound in the head received at the hands of an unknown person. Buried in the Myrtle Hill Cemetery, Rome, GA.

Coble, Jesse; Fifth Sergeant, Company H: Born 2 June 1835. Married (1) Margaret Chandler, 27 July 1854. Sworn into service 14 May 1861 at Nashville. Elected fifth sergeant at the reorganization, 1 May 1862. Deserted 29 March 1863. Married (2) Alta Bates. Died 14 March 1917. Buried in the Chandler Cemetery, Hickman Co., TN.[169]

Cochran, John A.; Private, Company H: Born in 1830. No further.[170]

Cochran, John F.; Private, Company H: Born c. 1827. Sworn into service 14 May 1861 at Nashville. On extra duty as a teamster January 1862. Deserted 12 August 1864, at Atlanta, GA. Captured in Hickman Co., TN. Complexion dark, hair dark, eyes dark, height 5' 10". Ordered to be released north of the Ohio River.[171]

Cochran, Samuel; Private, Company H: Born 9 November 1832. Occupation: farmer. Sworn into service 14 May 1861 at Nashville. Deserted 20 January 1864. Married Sallie Nichols 22 November 1866. Died at his home on Dunlap Creek, Hickman Co., TN., 30 January 1914.[172]

Cohen, William Patrick; Private, Company D: Enlisted 11 May 1861 at Nashville. Discharged 15 August 1862 at Walden's Ridge (Tazewell), TN. by the conscript law.

Coleman, George W.; First Corporal, Company A: Occupation: farmer. Sworn into service 11 May 1861 at Nashville. Wounded in leg at Murfreesboro, TN., 31 December 1862 and captured. Sent to U. S. General Hospital No. 7, 15 February 1863. Forwarded to Camp Morton, IN., 25 February 1863, then to City Point, VA. for exchange. Rejoined the regiment. Wounded in the left arm in the Battle of Chickamauga, GA, 19 September 1863. Promoted to first corporal, 20 October 1863. Deserted 7 January 1865. Complexion fair, hair light, eyes blue, height 5' 10". Took oath at Fort Donelson, TN., 14 February 1865.[173]

Coleman, H. Clay; Musician, Field & Staff: Enlisted 1 November 1862 at Dalton, GA. Present through December 1863.

Collier, Arthur; Private, Company I: Born 1826 in Stewart Co., TN. Enlisted 6 February 1863 at Shelbyville, TN., age 37. Deserted 28 April 1863. Died in 1885 in Lawrence Co., AR.

---

[167] J. K. Clifton, Tennessee Confederate Pension Application, S7112; "The Reunion," *Hickman Pioneer*; Sistler and Sistler, *1880 Census of Dickson County*, 13; Garrett and McClain, *Dickson County Cemetery Records*, vol. 1, 80; Barbara Clifton Whittington, "John J. Clifton" in *The Heritage of Dickson County, Tennessee, 1803-2006*, Dickson County Heritage Book Committee, (Waynesville NC: County Heritage Inc., 2007) 190-91.

[168] McCauley Camp 260, *Confederate Graves*, 13.

[169] United Daughters of the Confederacy, *Confederate Soldiers of Hickman County*, 49.

[170] United Daughters of the Confederacy, *Confederate Soldiers of Hickman County*, 50; United Daughters of the Confederacy, *Hickman County Census 1860*, 226.

[171] United Daughters of the Confederacy, *Hickman County Census 1860*, 226.

[172] Hickman County Historical Society, *Hickman County History*, 124-25.

[173] Thedford, "Report of Operations"; Maney, *Surgeon's Log*, "Chickamauga GA."

Collier, Christopher Columbus; Private. Company C: Born 18 May 1826 in Dickson Co., TN. Brother of Private George W. Collier. Merchant in Charlotte, TN. postwar. Died 9 September 1899. Buried in the Collier Cemetery, Charlotte, Dickson Co., TN.[174]

Collier, George Washington; Private, Company I: Born 22 February 1828 in Stewart Co., TN. Brother of Private Christopher C. Collier. Occupation: farmer. Sworn into service 20 May 1861 at Nashville. On sick furlough since 25 July 1861. Discharged by surgeon's certificate of disability of pulmonary consumption, 14 November 1861 at Cumberland Gap, TN., age 26. Complexion dark, eyes dark, hair light, height 5' 9". Died 12 May 1892. Buried in the Collier Cemetery, Charlotte, Dickson Co., TN.

Collins, Andrew; Private; Company C: Enlisted 27 June 1862 at Thorn Hill, TN. Issued a flintlock musket. Left sick at Murfreesboro, TN., 4 January 1863 when the regiment withdrew to Shelbyville. Captured 7 January 1863. Sent to Nashville, then to City Point, VA., 15 February 1863 for exchange. Rejoined unit. Age 17 on roll dated 8 May 1863 at Shelbyville, TN. Given sick leave to East Tennessee, 1 June 1863. Killed in the Battle of Chickamauga, GA, 19 September 1863.[175]

Collins, Hazard; Private, Company I: Enlisted 27 June 1862 at Thorn Hill, TN. Issued a flintlock musket. Age 19 on roll dated 6 May 1863 at Shelbyville, TN. Wounded in the Battle of Atlanta, GA., 22 July 1864. Sent to hospital. Deserted 1 January 1865. Took oath 20 March 1865.[176]

Collins, Henry M. Clay; Private, Company I: Born 10 April 1832 in Stewart Co., TN. Occupation: farmer. Enlisted in May 1861. Wounded in the middle third of the right arm in the Battle of Atlanta, GA., 22 July 1864. Sent to the field hospital, arrived around nightfall and the wound was dressed the same day. Sent to Pim Hospital, Griffin, GA., 22 July 1864, where he remained for six weeks, before being sent to a hospital in Augusta, GA. Here gangrene set in, which disabled him, and he remained hospitalized until the early part of winter, at which time he received a sixty day furlough home. While at home he had to sleep in the woods to keep Federal soldiers from finding him. At the end of his furlough he was unable to return to the Army due to being cut off by the enemy. Married Fredonia Scholes, 25 March 1866. Resided at Tennessee Ridge, Houston Co., TN. Died 21 April 1915. Pension Application S2262, S5576 and W6075.[177]

Collins, Insley; Private, Company A: Enlisted 19 June 1862 at Thorn Hill, TN. Absent on sick furlough since 1 August 1862. Deserted 1 March 1863 at Shelbyville, TN.

*Collins, James; Private, Company I: Occupation: farmer. Sworn into service 20 May 1861 at Nashville. Age 25 on roll dated 6 May 1863. Wounded in the ankle and captured in the Battle of Missionary Ridge, TN., 25 November 1863. Sent to U. S. General Hospital No. 1 at Nashville, TN., 16 February 1864 with a gunshot wound to the right chest and fractured ribs. Sent to the U. S. Military Prison at Louisville, KY., 20 February 1864. Sent to Fort Delaware, Delaware, 29 February 1864. Exchanged 20 October 1864. Rejoined unit and was surrendered, 26 April 1865 as a member of Company F, 2nd Consolidated Tennessee Infantry. Paroled 1 May 1865.[178]

Collins, Jones; Private, Company H: Born 1834. Sworn into service 14 May 1861 at Nashville. Deserted when Chattanooga was evacuated 8 September 1863. Married Sarah E. Allen. Postwar Occupation: night watchman at the Pinewood Mills. Died in Hickman Co., TN. Buried in the Petty Cemetery there.[179]

---

[174] McCauley Camp 260, *Confederate Graves*, 13.

[175] McCauley, *Record Book, Company C*; Maney, *Surgeon's Log*, "Chickamauga GA."

[176] McCauley, *Record Book, Company C*; Maney, *Surgeon's Log*, "Battle of Atlanta GA."

[177] Henry M. Collins, Tennessee Confederate Pension Application, S5576; Maney, *Surgeon's Log*, "Battle of Atlanta GA.;" *Chattanooga Daily Rebel*, 27 July 1864.

[178] Maney, *Surgeon's Log*, "Missionary Ridge TN."

[179] United Daughters of the Confederacy, *Confederate Soldiers of Hickman County*, 51; Spence, *History*, 205; United Daughters of the Confederacy, *Hickman County Census 1860*, 95; United Daughters of the Confederacy, *Hickman County, Tennessee Cemetery Records* part 2, 75.

Conell, Joseph M; Fourth Sergeant, Company D, F: Sworn into service 11 May 1861 at Nashville. Promoted to fourth sergeant by November 1862. Captured in the Battle of Murfreesboro, TN., 31 December 1862. Exchanged and returned to unit as a private in Company F. Admitted to Fairground Hospital No. 2, Atlanta, GA., 12 November 1863 for vulnus sclopeticum.[180]

Conlan, Edward; Private, Company G: Born in Ireland 7 January 1832. Immigrated to the United States in 1849. Admitted to U.S. citizenship 19 May 1856. Enlisted 3 June 1861 at Camp Cheatham. On extra duty as a teamster September 1861. Arrested for civil process at Knoxville, TN., 10 September 1861. Discharged by virtue of the conscript act, August 1862.

Conley, Austin; Private, Company G: Enlisted 3 June 1861 at Camp Cheatham. Discharged by the conscript act 28 August 1862 at Tazewell, TN.

Conley, John; Private, Company D: Sworn into service 11 May 1861 at Nashville. Age 27 on roll dated 5 May 1863 at Shelbyville, TN. Deserted on the retreat from Chattanooga, TN., September 1863.

Connell, Hiram D.; Private, Company F: Sworn into service 18 May 1861 at Cedar Hill, TN. Admitted to Fair Ground Hospital #1, Atlanta, GA., for anasarca 19 May 1863, and died there the following day, 20 May 1863. Buried in Oakland Cemetery, Atlanta, GA.[181]

Connell, James Morgan; Private, Company F: Born 11 October 1827. Occupation: farmer. Enlisted 21 May 1861 at Cedar Hill, TN. Brigade forage master, July through August 1862. Left leg broken just above the ankle in the Battle of Chickamauga, GA., 19 September 1863. The wound was a compound fracture which also dislocated the ankle, and was so severe that he was unable to put the affected foot on the ground for two years. Admitted to Fair Ground Hospital #2, Atlanta, GA., on 12 November 1863 for vulnus sclopeticum. Present through February 1864. Resided at Turnersville, Robertson Co., TN. Pension Application S37.[182]

Connell, John; Private, Company D: Deserted near Chattanooga around 10 September 1863. Took oath at Chattanooga, TN.

Conners, Patrick; Private, Company E, G: Sworn into service 18 May 1861 in Company E at Nashville. Transferred to Company G at the reorganization on 1 May 1862 at Cumberland Gap. Discharged at Tazewell, TN., 13 August 1862 by the conscript act.

Connor, Martin; Private, Company C, G: Sworn into service 14 May 1861 at Nashville in Company C. Transferred to Company G at the reorganization, 1 May 1862. Discharged 13 August 1862 at Tazewell, TN. by the conscript act.

Connor, Patrick D.; Private, Company B, G: Born in 1832 in Ireland, immigrating to the United States in 1839. Became a naturalized citizen, 22 May 1856. Occupation: laborer. Sworn into service 10 May 1861 in Company B. Transferred to Company G at the reorganization, 1 May 1862. Deserted 16 May 1862.[183]

*Cook, C. A.; Private, Company I: Sworn into service 20 May 1861 at Nashville. Surrendered with the Army of Tennessee, 26 April 1865 as a member of Company F, 2nd Consolidated Tennessee Infantry. Paroled 1 May 1865.

*Cook, E. D.; Third Sergeant, Company I: Occupation: farmer. Sworn into service 20 May 1861 at Nashville. Elected first corporal at the reorganization, 1 May 1862. Promoted to fifth sergeant by March 1863. Promoted to third sergeant by July 1863. Wounded in the lower third of the left arm at the Battle of New Hope Church, GA., 27 May 1864. Admitted to Asylum Hospital in Madison, GA., 30 May

---

[180] J. M. Connell, Ledger 4L223 vol. 1 Fairground Hospital #2, Hospital Register, September 1862-October 17, 1863, Samuel Stout H. Ledgers, Microfilm Reel 2, Item A. Samuel H. Stout Papers, The Center for American History, The University of Texas at Austin.

[181] Welsh, *Confederate Hospitals*, Patient Roster, Fair Ground Hospital #1.

[182] Maney, *Surgeon's Log*, "Chickamauga GA"; Welsh, *Confederate Hospitals*, Patient Roster, Fair Ground Hospital #1, 40; J. M. Connell, Tennessee Confederate Pension Application, S37.

[183] Dobson-Sides, *1860 Davidson County Census*, 688; Mary Sue Smith, *Davidson County Naturalization Records 1803-1906* (Nashville TN: Byron Sistler & Assoc., 1997) 215.

1864. Returned to duty 8 July 1864. Wounded in the Battle of Franklin, TN., 30 November 1864. Surrendered as a member of Company F, 2nd Consolidated Tennessee Infantry, with the Army of Tennessee, 26 April 1865 at Greensboro, NC.[184]

Cook, John F.; Private, Company unknown: Enlisted 8 May 1861 at Nashville. Took oath 24 April 1865. Complexion fair, hair dark, eyes blue, height 5' 10". No further.

Cooley, Mitchell M.; Private, Company A: Born c. 1839. Sworn into service 10 May 1861 at Nashville. Left wounded on the field at Murfreesboro, TN., 31 December 1862 and later captured. Sent to the U. S. Military Prison, Louisville, KY. Forwarded to City Point, VA. for exchange. Rejoined the regiment. Deserted at Chattanooga, TN. August, 1863. Captured in Huntsville, AL. Paroled in Stevenson, AL., 25 August 1863. Age 23, complexion fair, hair dark, eyes blue, height 5' 8". Married. Occupation: farmer. Died in 1875. Buried in the Union Chapel Cemetery, Humphreys Co., TN.[185]

Cooley, Robert William; Private, Company A: Born in 1841. Occupation: farmer. Sworn into service 10 May 1861 at Nashville. Left with the wounded in C. S. Hospital #1 at Murfreesboro, TN. and captured. Sent to U. S. prisons in Nashville, TN.; Louisville, KY.; and City Point, VA., where he was exchanged. Rejoined company. Detailed as a cook, November through December 1863. Surrendered at Johnsonville, TN. Took oath 15 May 1865. Complexion fair, hair dark, eyes blue, height 5' 10". Married Mary Ann Waggoner, who died in 1869. He married in 1870 (2) Victoria Wyly Napier, widow of Lieutenant-Colonel Thomas Alonzo Napier, who had died in the Battle of Parkers Crossroads, TN., 31 December 1862. Victoria died in 1881, and was buried with Napier. He married (3) Livina Miller Crockett Jobson in 1887. Resided in Humphreys Co., TN., where he was sheriff in 1868-70, tax collector in 1870, marshal in 1885, mail carrier in 1886, and a member of the Masonic Lodge at Hustburg. Later relocated to Memphis, TN., where he died on 2 May 1903. Buried in the Elmwood Cemetery, Memphis, TN.[186]

Cooper, Charles; Private, Company A: Sworn into service 10 May 1861 at Nashville. Deserted on the march to Jacksboro, TN., 19 August 1861. Arrested by U. S. authorities at Bowling Green, KY., 9 December 1862. Sent to Camp Chase, OH., 22 March 1863. Age 35, complexion light, hair light brown, eyes blue, height 5' 10".

Cooper, Oliver; Private, Company D: Sworn into service 11 May 1861 at Nashville. Sick at Bean Station, TN. from June through December 1862. Age 25 on roll dated 5 May 1863. Captured in the Battle of Missionary Ridge, TN., 25 November 1863. Sent to the U. S. Military Prison at Louisville, KY. Forwarded to Rock Island, IL., 9 December 1863. Took oath 21 February 1865. Complexion fair, hair light, eyes blue, height 5' 5".

Corbett, Joseph Martin; Corporal, Company B: Born in Nashville, TN., 21 December 1842. Sworn into service at Nashville on 1 May 1861. Wounded in the right hand in the Battle of Atlanta, GA., 22 July 1864. Promoted to corporal before the end of the war. Captured at the breastworks in the angle by the cotton gin with General George W. Gordon in the Battle of Franklin, TN., 30 November 1864. Paroled from prison at Camp Douglas, IL. in July 1865. Operated a grocery store in South Nashville. Member of Company B, United Confederate Veterans. Admitted to the Tennessee Confederate Veterans Home, December 1908. Attended the 50th Anniversary of the Battle of Franklin, TN., 30 November 1914. Died 6 November 1929. Buried at Mount Olivet Cemetery, Nashville, Davidson Co., TN.[187]

---

[184] Maney, *Surgeon's Log*, "May 1864"; Harris, *Confederate Hospitals*, 75, 87; Trogdon, "Interesting Letter."

[185] Johnson, *1860 Census of Humphreys County*, 4; Betty F. Clifton, *1870 Census of Humphreys County, Tennessee* (Taylorsville CA: B.F. Clifton, 1979) 2.

[186] Johnson, *1860 Census of Humphreys County*, 79; "R. N.[W.] Cooley," *Confederate Veteran* vol. 11 no. 9 (September 1903): 422.

[187] United Confederate Veterans, *Biographical Sketches and Pictures of Company B, Confederate Veterans of Nashville, Tennessee* (Nashville TN: Foster & Webb, 1902; reprint Beverly Pearson Barnes,

Corbitt, James A.; Private, Company B: Sworn into service 10 May 1861 at Nashville. Discharged August 1861 at Carter's Station, TN.

Corbitt, James N.; Second Corporal, Company A: Born c. 1843. No further.[188]

Corder, Moses P.; Third Lieutenant, Company G: Born c. 1839 in Tennessee. Occupation: carpenter. Sworn into service 10 May 1861 at Nashville. Promoted to fourth sergeant by August 1861. Appointed to third lieutenant, 5 October 1861. Relieved of duty at the reorganization, 1 May 1862.[189][58]

Corlis, Patrick.; Private, Company G: Born 7 March 1844 in Galway, Ireland. Occupation: laborer. Enlisted 3 June 1861 at Camp Cheatham. Patient in Ocmulgee Hospital, Macon, GA., 22 February 1865 for syphilis. Returned to duty 3 April 1865. Paroled 12 May 1865 in Augusta, GA. Lived at the Tennessee Confederate Soldiers Home from 28 September 1892. Died 30 April 1893. Buried in the Soldiers Home Cemetery, grave # 7.[190]

Corn, P. S.; Rank unknown, Company B: Died 3 October 1863 at Fair Ground Hospital #2, Atlanta, GA. Buried in the Oakland Cemetery, Atlanta, GA.

Cosgrove, W. J.; First Corporal, Company B: Sworn into service 10 May 1861 at Nashville. Elected first corporal at the organization. Discharged 11 May 1862 at Cumberland Gap, TN.

Cox, Samuel A.; Private, Company K: Born 1841 in Arkansas. Enlisted 16 June 1862 at Thorn Hill, TN. Died at Bean Station, 27 September 1862.[191]

Cox, William J.; First Sergeant, Company K: Born 1835 in Arkansas. Enlisted 25 May 1861 at Nashville. Elected first sergeant at the organization. Died 27 June 1861 at Camp Cheatham, TN.

Crawford, Charles C.; Private, Company D: Sworn into service 11 May 1861 at Nashville. Promoted to third sergeant by July 1862. On detached service as a nurse at Knoxville, TN., November 1861. Age 24 on roll dated 5 May 1863.

Crawford, John E.; Private, Company D: Sworn into service 11 May 1861 at Nashville. Wounded in the Battle of Murfreesboro, TN., 31 December 1862. Captured 5 January 1863. Arrived Gratiot Street Prison, St. Louis, MO., 21 January 1863. Took oath.

*Crim, Henry Clay; Fourth Sergeant, Company A: Born in Humphreys Co., TN., 1 September 1838. Occupation: merchant. Sworn into service 10 May 1861 at Nashville. Elected fourth sergeant at the organization. Age 21 on roll dated 6 May 1863 at Shelbyville, TN. Wounded in the right elbow in the Battle of New Hope Church, GA., 27 May 1864. Bones fractured badly and had cut a main artery. The civilian surgeon wanted to amputate the arm, but Dr. Maney, regimental surgeon, would not allow it. Patient at Concer Hospital, Montgomery, AL., 15 November 1864. Surrendered at Citronelle, AL. under command of Lieutenant General Richard Taylor, 4 May 1865. Paroled at Meridian, MS., 15 May 1865. Married. Postwar Occupation: clerk. Buried in the Marable Cemetery, Humphreys Co., TN.[192]

Crim, James H.; Private, Company H: Enlisted 14 December 1862 at Waverly, TN. by Lieutenant McAdoo. Deserted 14 September 1863 near Chattanooga, TN. Captured 15 September 1863 at Chattanooga, TN. Forwarded to the Provost Marshal in Nashville. Sent to the U. S. Military Prison at

---

1974) 26; Maney, *Surgeon's Log*, "Battle of Atlanta GA"; *Nashville Daily Press*, 3 December 1864; Warwick, *Williamson County Civil War Veterans*, 62; Joseph M. Corbitt, Tennessee Pension Application, 8895.

[188] Johnson, *1860 Census of Humphreys County*, 79.

[189] Dobson-Sides, *1860 Davidson County Census*, 164.

[190] Judith A. Strange, *The Tennessee Confederate Soldiers Home: Marching Out of the Midst into the Light: Roster One and Roster Two, The Tennessee Confederate Veterans Home* (Nashville TN: Tennessee Tracers Limited, 1996) 6.

[191] McCauley Camp 260, *Confederate Graves*, 14.

[192] Henry C. Crim, Tennessee Confederate Pension Application, 3104; Maney, *Surgeon's Log*, "May 1864"; Johnson, *1860 Census of Humphreys County*, 54; Marjorie H. Fischer, and Ruth Blake Burns, *1880 Census, Humphreys County, Tennessee* (Vista CA: RAM Press, 1987) 92; Anderson and Garrett, *Humphreys County Cemetery Records*, vol. 1, 38.

Louisville, KY. around 25 September 1863. Complexion fair, hair light, eyes blue, height 5' 9". Released and joined the Federal Army.

Critz, John M.; Lieutenant, Company unknown: Born at Thompson Station, TN., 18 December 1837. Enlisted in Company G, 2nd Tennessee Infantry at Thompson's Station. Transferred to the 11th Tennessee and promoted to lieutenant. After the war he moved to Arkansas and engaged as a planter. A member of the Omer R. Weaver Camp, United Confederate Veterans. Died April 1917. Buried in the Oakland Cemetery, Little Rock, Arkansas.[193]

Crocker, J. G.; Private, Company B: Enlisted 10 May 1861 at Nashville. In hospital at Richmond, KY., 6 October 1862. Taken prisoner 18 September 1862 at Laurel Bridge, KY.

Crocker, John M.; Private, Company B: Born c. 1837. Occupation: farm laborer. Married Tennessee Williams, 31 July 1860. Captured 13 July 1863 at Franklin, TN. Forwarded to the U. S. Military Prison at Louisville, KY., 16 July 1863. Transferred to Fort Delaware, DE., where he died 23 May 1864. Buried at Finn's Point National Cemetery, Salem, NJ.[194]

Cronan, Patrick.; Second Corporal, Company A: Born c. 1836. Occupation: laborer. In 1860, he lived on the farm of William S. Beasley. Sworn into service 10 May 1861 at Nashville. Elected second corporal, 13 September 1861. Age 23 on roll dated 6 May 1863. Wounded in the left leg in the Battle of Missionary Ridge, TN., 25 November 1863. Wounded in the Battle of New Hope Church, GA., 27 May 1864. Admitted to Foard Hospital, 31 May 1864. Transferred to to Asylum Hospital, Madison, GA., 20 June 1864 with a gunshot wound to the left shoulder. Received a thirty day medical furlough 11 July 1864. Returned to duty. Killed in the Battle of Franklin, TN., 30 November 1864, age 28. Buried in the McGavock Confederate Cemetery, Franklin, TN., Section 54, Grave #50.[195]

Crooker, Jacob P.; Third Sergeant, Company K, G: Born c. 1840 in IN. Sworn into service 25 May 1861 in Company K at Nashville. Age 21 on roll dated 15 August 1861 at Midway, TN. Transferred to Company G, 27 November 1861. Promoted to third sergeant. Deserted 9 May 1862. Captured and sent to Camp Morton, IN.[196]

Crosswell, C. N. "Jim"; Second Sergeant, Company A: Sworn into service 20 May 1861. Promoted to third sergeant 14 October 1862. Promoted to second sergeant by July 1863. Wounded in the left side of the face in the Battle of Atlanta, GA., 22 July 1864. Admitted to the Pim Hospital, Griffin, GA., 22 July 1864. Killed in the Battle of Franklin, TN., 30 November 1864. Died at Dr. Hunter's. Buried in the Unknown Section of the McGavock Confederate Cemetery, Franklin, TN.[197]

Crosswell, Nimrod B.; Private, Company I: Born c. 1838. Occupation: farmer. Enlisted 20 May 1861 at Nashville. Wounded through the right arm just below the elbow in the Battle of Murfreesboro, TN., 31 December 1862. Sent to Cleveland, TN. hospital. Age 22 on roll dated 6 May 1863. Wounded in the left hand in the Battle of Chickamauga, GA., 19 September 1863. Retired from service 26 August, 1864.[198]

---

[193] "John M. Critz," *Confederate Veteran* vol. 25 no. 10 (July 1917): 324.

[194] Dobson-Sides, *1860 Davidson County Census*, 85; Finn's Point National Cemetery Salem, Salem County, New Jersey, interment.net/data/us/nj/salem/finns/ (26 July 2014).

[195] Johnson, *1860 Census of Humphreys County*, 79; Maney, *Surgeon's Log*, "Missionary Ridge TN"; Maney, *Surgeon's Log*, "May 1864"; Harris, *Confederate Hospitals*, 438, 48, 81, 88, 287; Helen H. Hudgins and Helen Potts, *McGavock Confederate Cemetery* (Franklin TN: Franklin Chapter #14 United Daughters of the Confederacy, 1989) 32.

[196] Deane Porch, *1850 Census of the City of Nashville, Davidson County, Tennessee* (Fort Worth TX: American Reference Publications, 1969) 62.

[197] Maney, *Surgeon's Log*, "Battle of Atlanta GA"; *Chattanooga Daily Rebel*, 27 July 1864; Personal correspondence with Mr. Tim Burgess, Battle of Franklin Historian, 13 May 2001; Trogdon, "Interesting Letter."

[198] Dobson-Sides, *1860 Davidson County Census*, 34; Maney, *Surgeon's Log*, "Stones River TN"; Maney, *Surgeon's Log*, "Chickamauga GA."

Crow, John Campbell; Private Company K: Born 28 February 1846 in Dickson Co., TN. Occupation: farmer. Enlisted 26 March 1863 at Columbia, TN. Age 18 on roll dated 1 May 1863. Wounded in the upper third of the left leg at Kennesaw Mountain, GA., 21 June 1864. Surrendered 11 May 1865 at Augusta, GA. Relocated to Texas in 1877. Died 27 August 1939. Buried in Lonestar Cemetery, Clarksville, Red River Co., TX. Pension Application Texas 25460.

Crow, Manley B.; Private, Company K: Born 1828 in Dickson Co., TN. Enlisted 4 February 1863 at Shelbyville, TN., age 35. Died at Chattanooga, TN., 3 April 1863. Buried in the Confederate Cemetery, Chattanooga, TN.

Crowder, William H; First Sergeant, Company F: Enlisted 18 May 1861 at Cedar Hill, TN. Elected first sergeant at the organization. Reduced to private. Deserted 17 May 1862 at Cumberland Gap, TN.

Crunk, William Castleberry; Third Corporal, Company E: Born c. 1837. Married Sally C. Morrisett, 24 July 1855. Occupation: carpenter. Sworn into service 18 May 1861 at Nashville. Elected third corporal at the organization. Age 25 on roll dated 16 August 1861 at Watauga Bridge, TN. Badly wounded in the shoulder at Murfreesboro, TN., 31 December 1862 and abandoned on the field. He made his way back to his home in Dickson Co. where he was recovering from his wounds when a Federal unit came through Charlotte, TN. and captured him, 26 September 1863. Sent to the U. S. Military Prison at Louisville, KY., 9 October 1863. Forwarded to Camp Morton, IN. While imprisoned, his wife died. Since he did not return to his unit after a reasonable time he was listed as a deserter. Released on oath, 18 May 1865. Complexion dark, hair black, eyes black, 5" 9 1/4". Married (2) E. E. Shelton, 23 July 1869.[199]

Cruthers, J. M.; Private, Company B: Captured at Winchester, TN., 4 July 1863. Sent to the U. S. Military Prison at Louisville, KY., 21 July 1863. Forwarded to Camp Chase, OH., 27 July 1863. Released 17 November 1863.

Cunningham, H. D.; Private, Company C: Sworn into service 14 May 1861 at Nashville. Issued a minie musket. Later issued a Springfield rifle. Age 25 on roll dated 8 May 1863 at Shelbyville, TN. Patient in Ocmulgee Hospital, Macon, GA., 22 July 1864.[200]

Curren, Patrick; Private, Company F: Sworn into service 18 May 1861 at Cedar Hill, TN. On detached service as a driver for Rutledge's Tennessee Artillery from 12 September 1862.

Curtis, John; Private, Company C, D: Born c. 1832 in Rutherford Co., TN. Occupation: hotel cook. Married Sarah Francis Still, 1 July 1857. Sworn into service 14 May 1861 in Company C at Nashville. Issued a minie musket. Transferred to Company D, 4 March 1863. Deserted 22 April 1863 at Shelbyville, TN. Complexion fair, hair dark, eyes blue, height 5' 8".[201]

Curtis, S. J.; Private, Company A: Sworn into service 1 May 1861 at Nashville. Deserted at Shelbyville, TN., 17 April 1863.

Curtis, Samuel; Private, Company C, A: Sworn into service 14 May 1861 in Company C at Nashville. Transferred to Company A at the reorganization, 1 May 1862.

-D-

Dailey, Edward; Private, Company D: Enlisted 14 June 1863 at Shelbyville, TN. Deserted on the retreat from Chattanooga, TN., 10 September 1863.

---

[199] Baker, *1860 Census for Dickson County*, 139; Baker, *1870 Census for Dickson County*, 76; Personal correspondence with Billy New, great grandson, 20 May 2002.

[200] McCauley, *Record Book, Company C*.

[201] Dobson-Sides, *1860 Davidson County Census*, 2; McCauley, *Record Book, Company C*, Sistler and Sistler, *Davidson County Marriages 1838-1863*, 53.

Dalton, William M.; Corporal, Company G, B: Sworn into service 10 May 1861 in Company G at Nashville. Transferred to Company B, 1 May 1862. Deserted 1 November 1862 at Lenoir Station, TN.

Darden, Alfred Britton; Private, Company H: Born in 1842. Brother of Privates Henry G. and James P. Darden. Occupation: farmer. Sworn into service 14 May 1861 at Nashville. Wounded in the left shoulder in the Battle of Peachtree Creek, GA., 20 July 1864. Admitted to Ocmulgee Hospital, Macon, GA., for vulnus sclopeticum. In General Hospital No. 3 at Augusta, GA., 7 November 1864. Listed as deserting 18 December 1864. After the war, he resided in Hickman Co., TN., but later relocated to Gatesville, Coryell Co., TX. in 1891. Returning to Hickman Co., he died there in 1901. Buried in the Darden Cemetery, Hickman Co., TN.[202]

Darden, Charles Byrns; Musician, Company F, Field & Staff: Born 4 March 1842 in Cedar Hill, Robertson Co., TN. Brother of Private Thomas Berry Darden. Occupation: farmer. Enlisted 18 May 1861 in Company F at Cedar Hill, TN. Appointed Regimental Musician (fifer) and transferred to Field & Staff, 21 May 1862. Also assisted in caring for the wounded and assisted in the hospital service. Present through February 1864. Married Adline Virginia Bartlett, 30 January 1868. Member of the Methodist Episcopal Church South and a Democrat. Died 1 October 1922. Buried in the Bartlett Cemetery, Cedar Hill, Robertson Co., TN.[203]

Darden, George W.; Second Sergeant, Company F: Enlisted 18 May 1861 at Cedar Hill, TN. Appointed second sergeant by August 1862. Reduced in rank to private by December 1862. Wounded in the Battle of Jonesboro, GA., 1 September 1864. Admitted to Way Hospital, Meridian, MS., 29 January 1865. Surrendered at Citronelle, AL., by Lieutenant General Richard Taylor, 4 May 1865. Paroled at Mobile, AL., 20 May 1865.[204]

Darden, Henry G.; Private, Company H: Born 20 October 1823. Brother of Privates Alfred B. and James P. Darden. Served in the Mexican War. Sworn into service 14 May 1861 at Nashville. Discharged 1 May 1862 by virtue of the conscript act. Resided in Hickman Co., TN. Married Martha Cotham. Died 26 March 1896. Buried in the Darden Cemetery, Hickman Co., TN.[205]

Darden, James H.; Captain, Company F: Occupation: farmer. Enlisted 18 May 1861 at Cedar Hill, TN. Detached as prisoner guard to Knoxville, TN., December 1861. Promoted to first corporal, 9 January 1862. Elected second lieutenant, April 1862. Appointed first lieutenant, 1 May 1862 at the reorganization. Promoted to captain of Company F, 6 April 1864. Mortally wounded, shot through the pelvis, in the Battle of Jonesboro, GA., 1 September 1864. Died at Hood Hospital, Cuthbert, GA., 8 September 1864. Buried in the Confederate Cemetery, Griffin, GA.[206]

Darden, James P.; Private, Company H: Brother of Privates Alfred B. and Henry G. Darden. Enlisted 6 February 1863 at Shelbyville, TN. Admitted to Fairground Hospital #1 in Atlanta, GA., 19 May 1863 for rubeola. Returned to duty 7 July 1863. Received in the Confederate hospital in Atlanta, GA., 16 June 1864. Forwarded to Confederate hospital in Madison, GA., 16 June 1864. Admitted to Asylum Hospital, Madison, GA., 17 June, 1864 with vulnus sclopeticum. Captured in the Battle of

---

[202] United Daughters of the Confederacy, *Confederate Soldiers of Hickman County,* 58; Maney, *Surgeon's Log,* "20 July 1864"; Mrs. Alfred Britton Darden, Texas Confederate Widows Pension Application, McLennan County, Texas (rejected).

[203] Goodspeed Brothers, *Goodspeed Histories of Montgomery, Robertson, Humphreys, Stewart, Dickson, Cheatham, Houston Counties,* 1140; Charles B. Darden, "Veteran Questionnaire," vol. 2, 635-36. Tennessee Pension Application 14956.

[204] Maney, *Surgeon's Log,* "September 1864."

[205] United Daughters of the Confederacy, *Confederate Soldiers of Hickman County,* 59.

[206] United Daughters of the Confederacy, *Hickman County Census 1860,* 31; Maney, *Surgeon's Log,* "September 1864."

Nashville, TN., 16 December 1864. Sent to U. S. Military Prison in Louisville, KY. Forwarded to Camp Chase, OH., 4 January 1865.[207]

Darden, James P.; Private, Company H: Sworn into service 14 May 1861 at Nashville. Wounded in the thigh in the Battle of Murfreesboro, TN., 31 December 1862. Sent to the hospital in Chattanooga, TN. Forwarded to Fairground Hospital #2 in Atlanta, GA. Sent to Convalescent Camp, 28 November 1863.[208]

Darden, Thomas Berry; Private, Company F: Born 24 January 1838. Brother of Musician Charles Byrns Darden. Enlisted 18 May 1861 at Cedar Hill, TN. Detached as a prison guard to Knoxville, TN., December 1861. Died 30 November 1905. Buried in the Darden Cemetery, Cedar Hill, Robertson Co., TN.[209]

Dark, Samuel T.; Private, Company A: Sworn into service 10 May 1861 at Nashville. Sick in hospital at Tazewell, TN., 28 April 1862. Deserted 26 February 1863 near Shelbyville, TN. Later, operated with DuVal McNairy's Scouts and was killed by Federal cavalry 26 January 1865 on Tumbling Creek, Humphrey, Co., TN.

Daughtry, George Robert; Private, Company G: Born 10 January 1837 in NC. Sworn into service 10 May 1861 at Nashville. On extra duty for the brigade hospital, driving a wagon team since April, 1862. Captured at Atlanta, GA., 3 September 1864. Sent to the U. S. Military Prison in Louisville, KY. Forwarded to Camp Douglas, IL. Released 9 March 1865. Complexion fair, hair dark, eyes black, height 5' 9 ½". Married Mary Louisa Ray. Resided at Auburn, Logan Co., KY. Died 8 June 1880 at Franklin, Simpson Co., KY. Pension Application Kentucky 1279. Buried in the Greenwood Cemetery, Franklin, Simpson Co., KY.

Davidson, Calvin; Private, Company K: Born c. 1815. Married Malinda Anglin of Maury Co., TN., 3 August 1841. Sworn into service 25 May 1861 at Nashville. Age 46 on roll date 15 August 1861 at Midway, TN. Died at Cumberland Gap, TN., 7 April 1862.

Davidson, Edmond A.; Private, Company H: Born c. 1828. Occupation: farmer. Married. Enlisted 11 February 1863 at Shelbyville, TN. Deserted late 1863.

Davidson, George C.; Private, Company C: Born c. 1843. Enlisted 5 March 1861 at Nashville. Deserted 6 April 1863.[210]

*Davidson, Green H.; Private, Company K: Born 15 August 1842. Enlisted 20 December 1862 in Dickson Co., TN. Patient in Ocmulgee Hospital, Macon, GA., 19-23 July 1864. Examined 1 September 1864 at Confederate hospital, Madison, GA., for measels and diarrhea. Received furlough from Hospital #3. Surrendered with the Army of Tennessee as a member of Company K, 2nd Consolidated Tennessee Infantry on 26 April 1865. Paroled 1 May 1865. Died 15 March 1926. Buried in the Union Cemetery, Dickson, Dickson Co., TN.[211]

Davidson, John.; Private, Company I: Sworn into service 20 May 1861 at Nashville. Discharged 15 August 1862 at Tazewell, TN. by the conscript act.

Davidson, John W.; Private, Company K: Born 1842 in Dickson Co., TN. Sworn into service 25 May 1861 at Nashville. Age 20 on roll dated 15 August 1861 at Midway, TN. On extra duty as a teamster September through October 1861. Missing in the Battle of Missionary Ridge, TN., 25 November 1863.

Davidson, S. A.; First Sergeant, Company D: Sworn into service 11 May 1861 at Nashville. Discharged 15 August 1862 at Tazewell, TN.

---

[207] Welsh, *Confederate Hospitals*, Patient Roster, Fair Ground Hospital #1, 71; Harris, *Confederate Hospitals*, 375, 80, 430; *Nashville Daily Press*, 22 December 1864.
[208] Welsh, *Confederate Hospitals*, Patient Roster, Fair Ground Hospital #2, 47.
[209] Durrett, Williams, and Reid, *Robertson County Cemetery Records*, 76.
[210] Baker, *1860 Census for Dickson County*, 23.
[211] Harris, *Confederate Hospitals*, 232; Jill Knight Garrett, Ruth Burns, and Iris H. McClain. *Dickson County, Tennessee, Cemetery Records* rev. ed. 2 vols. Vol. 1, (Vista CA: Ram Press, 1991) 98.

Davis, C. J.; Private, Company F: Captured in the Battle of Murfreesboro, TN., 31 December 1862. Sent to Camp Douglas, IL. Forwarded to City Point, VA.

Davis, J. T.; Private, Company E: Died 24 May 1864 at Rock Island Prison, IL. Buried at Rock Island Prison grave #1121.[212]

Davis, John B.; Private, Company G: Sworn into service 10 May 1861 at Nashville. Discharged for disability June 1861.

Dean, Ephraim Andrews; Second Lieutenant, Company H: Born 31 July 1838 in Williamson Co., TN. Family moved to Lick Creek, Hickman Co., TN. in 1843. Occupation: farmer. Sworn into service 14 May 1861 at Nashville. Elected first sergeant at the organization. Promoted to third lieutenant, 27 December 1861 at the death of Lieutenant Alexander H. Vaughan. Wounded in the right thigh at the Battle of Murfreesboro, TN. The ball ranged through the knee and against the joint. Recovered after surgery, but with a stiff leg and without amputation. Sent to hospital in Rome, GA. Resigned 29 March 1863. Married Sue Anderson, October, 1865. Occupied as a farmer until he was elected to three terms as Sheriff of Hickman Co. 1872-1878. Relocated to Centerville in 1882, and built the Centerville Hotel a year later for the cost of $10,000. Kept Lieutenant-Colonel Bateman's recruiting poster for Company H on display in the hotel office. Later relocated to Bon Aqua where he served as postmaster and was a stockholder in the Bon Aqua Springs Company. Died 28 October 1917. Buried in the Anderson Chapel Cemetery, Hickman Co., TN.[213]

DeBow, H. B.; Rank unknown, Company unknown: Color bearer. Captured at Missionary Ridge, TN., 25 November 1863.[214]

DeBow, John D; Private, Company B: Occupation: printer. Sworn into service 10 May 1861 at Nashville, age 29. Deserted 10 May 1862 at Cumberland Gap, TN.[215]

DeGarris, William; Corporal, Company G: Sworn into service 10 May 1861. Discharged for disability 20 June 1861.

Dickens, Isaac W.; Private, Company G, B: Sworn into service 10 May 1861 in Company G at Nashville. Transferred to Company B at the reorganization on 1 May 1862. Deserted 10 May 1862 at Cumberland Gap, TN.

Dickens, Thomas P.; Private, Company G, B: Sworn into service 10 May 1861 in Company G at Nashville. Transferred to Company B at the reorganization, 1 May 1862. Took oath 6 January 1865. Complexion fair, brown hair, gray eyes, 5' 10".

Dickson, James C.; Rank unknown, Company unknown: Born 19 October 1840 near Omega, TN. Occupation: farmer. Enlisted in the 11th Tennessee in the fall of 1862. Captured and sent to Camp Douglas, IL. After the war he returned home and resumed farming. Married Fredonia Adams 11 October 1874.[216]

Dickson, John McCauley; Corporal, Company C: Born 14 June 1842 in Dickson Co., TN. Brother of Lieutenant Newton B. Dickson. Joined the Methodist Church at age 13. Enlisted 14 May 1861 at Nashville with his brother Newton. The two boys enlisted against their father's advice, who seeing they were determined to go, counseled them to "obey your superiors." Issued a minie musket. Wounded in the Battle of Atlanta, GA., 22 July 1864. Wounded a second time in the Battle of Jonesboro, GA., 1

---

[212] United States, Commissioner for Marking Confederate Graves. *Register of Confederate Dead, Rock Island, Illinois,* (s.l.: U.S. War Dept., 1912) 10.

[213] E. A. Dean, Tennessee Pension Application, 11452; Maney, *Surgeon's Log,* "Stones River TN"; United Daughters of the Confederacy, *Confederate Soldiers of Hickman County,* 61; Goodspeed Brothers. *The Goodspeed Histories of Lawrence, Wayne, Perry, Hickman & Lewis Counties, Tennessee* (Columbia TN: Woodward & Stinson, 1975) 913-14.

[214] "H. R. DeBow," *Confederate Veteran,* vol. 13 no. 10 (October 1905) 445.

[215] Dobson-Sides, *1860 Davidson County Census,* 515.

[216] Goodspeed Brothers, *Goodspeed Histories of Montgomery, Robertson, Humphreys, Stewart, Dickson, Cheatham, Houston Counties,* 1390.

September 1864. Admitted to Floyd House Hospital at Macon, GA., 9 November 1864 of a gunshot wound to the left foot, fracturing the leg. Admitted to Way Hospital at Meridian, MS., 27 March 1865. Paroled 9 June 1865 at Grenada, MS. Height 5'8", complexion light, eyes gray. In 1869, purchased a farm in Southside, Montgomery Co., TN. Member of the Forbes Bivouac of the Association of Confederate Soldiers. Present at the 14 June 1904 reunion of the 11th Tennessee Infantry in Nashville. Co-founder of the Southside Methodist Episcopal Church. Described as one of the most widely known and respected men of Montgomery Co. Charter member of the McAllister Lodge, Free and Accepted Masons and was repeatedly elected Master of the lodge. Married Martha E. Batson, 5 February 1868. Died 27 July 1915. Buried in the Southside Cemetery, Montgomery Co., TN.[217]

Dickson (Dixon), Newton Berryman; First Lieutenant, Company C: Born 6 January 1836 in Dickson Co., TN. Brother of Corporal John McCauley Dickson. Occupation: school teacher. Sworn into service 14 May 1861 at Nashville. Promoted to second sergeant. Sixty-three days later brevetted second lieutenant (3 July 1862). Promoted to second lieutenant 7 November 1862. Left sick at Murfreesboro, TN. Captured, exchanged, and rejoined company. Wounded in the right hand in the Battle of Peachtree Creek, GA., 20 July 1864. Admitted to Catoosa Hospital, Griffin, GA., 22 July 1864. Promoted to first lieutenant of Company F, 2nd Consolidated Tennessee Infantry. Surrendered with the Army of Tennessee at Greensboro, NC. Paroled 1 May 1865. Later changed spelling of last name to Dixon. Resided at Herndon, KY., where he died 31 July 1919. Buried in the Dixon Cemetery, Christian Co., KY. Pension Application Kentucky 2383.[218]

Dickson, William Henry; Private, Company C: Born in Dickson Co., 9 April 1836. Joined the Cumberland Presbyterian Church at age 17. Married Penina Waynick. Enlisted 14 May 1861 at Nashville. Issued a minie musket. Captured in the Battle of Missionary Ridge, TN., 25 November 1863. Sent to the U. S. Military Prison at Louisville, KY., 7 December 1863. Forwarded to Rock Island, IL. Took oath 28 April 1865. Complexion fair, hair dark, eyes blue, 5' 8". Resided at Van Leer, Dickson Co., TN. Died of influenza, 12 December 1918. Buried in Union Cemetery, Dickson, TN. Pension Application S7211.[219]

Dillan, Pat; Private, Company D: Sworn into service 11 May 1861 at Nashville. Deserted.

Divaney, Matthew; Second Lieutenant, Company C, G: Occupation: laborer. Sworn into service 14 May 1861 in Company C at Nashville. Teamster from 13 September through 31 December 1862. Transferred to Company G at the reorganization, 1 May 1862. Appointed third lieutenant, 1 May 1863. Promoted to second lieutenant by November 1863. Killed in the Battle of Atlanta, GA., 22 July 1864.[220]

Doak, J. D; Private, Company C: Issued a minie musket. No further.[221]

Dobins, Byron; Private, Company A: Sworn into service 10 May 1861 at Nashville. Discharged by the conscript act, 14 August 1862 at Tazewell, TN.

Dodson, Napoleon Bonaparte "Poney"; Private, Company C: Born 24 February 1836 at Charlotte, Dickson Co., TN. Occupation: farmer. Sworn into service 14 May 1861 at Nashville. Issued a minie musket. Wounded in the right side of the head near Atlanta, GA., 28 July 1864. Killed in the Battle of

---

[217] McCauley, *Record Book, Company C*; *Reunion Pamphlet*, 14 June 1904; *Chattanooga Daily Rebel*, 25 July 1864; J. M. Dickson, Application, United Confederate Veterans, Tennessee Division, Forbes Bivouac No. 21, Clarksville, Tennessee, Records and Correspondence, Tennessee State Library and Archives. Confederate Collection. Box 20, VII-D-1-2, Box 1, f. 5 and vol. II; *Clarksville Leaf Chronicle*, 27 July 1915.

[218] Maney, *Surgeon's Log*, "20 July 1864"; Electronic mail correspondence from Ken Matthews, 26 October 2001.

[219] Nesbitt, *Primal Families*, 210; McCauley, *Record Book, Company C*; W. H. Dickson, Tennessee Confederate Pension Application, S7211; *Dickson County Herald*, 20 December 1918; Garrett and McClain, *Dickson County Cemetery Records*, vol. 1, 99.

[220] Maney, *Surgeon's Log*, "Battle of Atlanta GA."

[221] McCauley, *Record Book, Company C*.

Franklin, TN., 30 November 1864, age 28. It is believed that his brother Private Jerome A. Dodson of the 49th Tennessee Infantry brought his body back home to Charlotte, TN. Buried in the Speight Cemetery, Dickson Co., TN.[222]

Doherty, Martin; Third Corporal, Company E, G: Occupation: laborer. Sworn into service 18 May 1861 in Company E at Nashville. Age 28 on roll dated 16 August 1861 at Watauga Bridge, TN. Transferred to Company G at the reorganization, 1 May 1862. Promoted to third corporal by July 1862. Reduced in rank to private 1 November 1862. Wounded in the left wrist in the Battle of Missionary Ridge, TN., 25 November 1863. Wounded in the shoulder in the Battle of Adairsville, GA., 17 May 1864. Killed in the Battle of Atlanta, GA., 22 July 1864.[223]

Dooley, Thomas; Private, Company E: Sworn into service 18 May 1861 at Nashville. Age 40 on roll dated 16 August 1861 at Watauga Bridge, TN. Discharged 20 May 1861 at Cumberland Gap, TN. due to the conscript act.

Dossett, William; Private, Company D: Enlisted 11 May 1861 at Nashville. Discharged 27 October 1862 near Knoxville, TN.

Dotson, Thomas Glen; Second Sergeant, Company E: Sworn into service 18 May 1861 at Nashville. Elected second sergeant at the organization. Age 23 on roll dated 16 August 1861 at Watauga Bridge, TN. Reduced in rank to private by July 1862. Buried in the Dotson-Brummit Cemetery, Charlotte, Dickson Co., TN.

Doughton, William C., Jr.; Private, Company C: Born 1846 in Montgomery Co., TN. Enlisted April 1862 at Shelbyville, TN. Age 18 on roll dated 8 May 1863. Wounded in the left side of head and captured in the Battle of Missionary Ridge, TN., 25 November 1863. Right arm paralyzed. Sent to U. S. Military Prison at Louisville, KY. Forwarded to Rock Island, IL. In Jackson Hospital, Richmond, VA. with debilitas, 2 March 1865. Paroled at Meridian, MS., 29 April 1865. Resided at Nunnelly, Hickman Co., TN. Relocated to Mt. Pleasant, TX. by 1909.[224]

Douglass, James R.; Second Lieutenant, Company B: Married Susan E. Green, 19 May 1860. Occupation: store clerk. Sworn into service 10 May 1861 at Nashville. Brevetted second lieutenant, 10 May 1862. Promoted to second lieutenant, 23 May 1862. Wounded severely in the face and left ear in the Battle of Murfreesboro, TN., 31 December 1862. Age 26 on roll dated 2 June 1863 at Shelbyville, TN. Wounded through the left arm and both lungs in the Battle of New Hope Church, GA., 27 May 1864. Died 29 May 1864.[225]

Douglass, Victor; Rank unknown, Company B: No further.

Drake, Joseph D.; Private, Company C: Enlisted 11 July 1861 at Camp Cheatham. Age 19 on roll dated 8 May 1863 at Shelbyville, TN. Deserted 28 November 1864. Took oath 29 January 1865 at Nashville. Complexion fair, hair light, eyes blue, 5' 5".

Draughon, George W.; Private, Company F: Occupation: farmer. Enlisted 21 May 1861 at Cedar Hill, TN. Deserted at Readyville, TN., 15 December 1862. Returned. Present July 1863. Killed in the Battle of Lovejoy Station, GA., 2 September 1864.[226]

Driscall, James; Private, Company C, G: Sworn into service 14 May 1861 at Nashville. Transferred to Company G at the reorganization, 1 May 1862. Discharged at Tazewell, TN., 14 August 1862 by the

---

[222] McCauley, *Record Book, Company C*; Maney, *Surgeon's Log*, "28-31 July 1864"; Electronic mail correspondence with Mark Choate, 6 September 2000.

[223] Maney, *Surgeon's Log*, "Missionary Ridge TN"; Maney, *Surgeon's Log*, "May 1864"; Maney, *Surgeon's Log*, "Battle of Atlanta GA."

[224] W. C. Daughton, Tennessee Pension Application, 9248.

[225] John Trotwood Moore. *Tennessee Records of Cheatham County, Marriage Liscence [Sic]*, vol. A 1856-1897, (Nashville TN: The Survey: Works Progress Administration, 1937) 11; Maney, *Surgeon's Log*, "Stones River TN"; Maney, *Surgeon's Log*, "May 1864."

[226] Maney, *Surgeon's Log*, "September 1864."

conscript law. Returned. Captured near Dallas, GA., 1 June 1864. Sent to the U. S. Military Prison at Louisville, KY. Forwarded to Rock Island, IL.

Dudley, Harry F.; Private, Company H: Enlisted 14 May 1861 at Nashville. Died 14 June 1861 at Camp Cheatham of the measles.[227]

*Duke, John C.; Private, Company G: Occupation: farmer. Enlisted 3 June 1861 at Camp Cheatham. Age 35 on roll dated 30 May 1863 at Shelbyville, TN. Wounded in the back in the Battle of New Hope Church, GA., 27 May 1864. Admitted to Ocmulgee Hospital, 5 June 1864 with a gunshot wound. Surrendered with the Army of Tennessee as a member of Company F, 2nd Consolidated Tennessee Infantry.[228]

Dunn, A. J.; Private, Company F: Nurse at the Confederate Hospital #1 at Murfreesboro, TN. Captured shortly after the Battle of Murfreesboro.

Dunn, Edward; Private, Company G: Born in Ireland c. 1833. Occupation: railroad laborer. Enlisted 4 June 1861 at Camp Cheatham. Age 28 on roll dated 30 May 1863 at Shelbyville, TN. Wounded in the left arm in the Battle of Missionary Ridge, TN., 25 November 1863. Admitted to Fair Ground Hospital #2, Atlanta GA., 26 February 1864. Sent to receiving and distributing hospital, 27 February 1864. Discharged from service on 24 August 1864, totally disqualified for duty. Took oath 12 May 1865 at Macon, GA. Complexion dark, hair dark, eyes hazel.[229]

–E–

Eanes, John T.; Private, Company B: Born c. 1836 in GA. Occupation: printer. Married Sarah E. Francis, 2 July 1859. Sworn into service 10 May 1861 at Nashville. Absent without leave, 15 October 1862. Listed as a deserter at Readyville, TN., 1 December 1862. Captured.[230]

Easley, John A.; Private, Company H: Born in 1838. Sworn into service 14 May 1861 at Nashville. Discharged 2 April 1862.[231]

Easley, James D.; Private, Company H: Born in Hickman Co., TN. Occupation: merchant. Mexican War Veteran. Enlisted 8 August 1861 at Nashville. Discharged at Cumberland Gap, TN., 14 December 1862 for disability. Complexion light, hair light, eyes blue, 5' 5".

Easley, Warham David; Musician, Company H, A: Born 8 July 1840 in Hickman Co., TN. Sworn into service 14 May 1861 at Nashville in Company H. Transferred to Company A at the reorganization, 1 May 1862. Died at Bean Station, TN., 22 June 1862.[232]

Echols, John S.; Private, Company I: Born c. 1840. Brother to Corporal Robert and Private Stephen Echols. Killed in the Battle of Murfreesboro, TN., 31 December 1862.[233]

Echols, Robert M.; First Corporal, Company I: Born c. 1837. Brother to Privates John and Stephen Echols. Enlisted 20 May 1861 at Nashville. Promoted to fourth corporal by July 1862. Appointed third corporal by March 1863. Promoted to first corporal by July 1863. Admitted to Fair Ground Hospital #1, Atlanta, GA., on 8 July 1863 for chronic diarrhea. Returned to duty 15 August 1863. Captured at White Oak Creek, TN., 7 February 1865. Sent to the U. S. Military Prison at Louisville, KY. Forwarded to

---

[227] Shipp, "Letter to Sister," 25 June 1861.
[228] Maney, *Surgeon's Log*, "May 1864."
[229] Dobson-Sides, *1860 Davidson County Census*, 326; Maney, *Surgeon's Log*, "Missionary Ridge TN"; Welsh, *Confederate Hospitals*, Patient Roster, Fair Ground Hospital #2, 55.
[230] Dobson-Sides, *1860 Davidson County Census*, 468; Sistler and Sistler, *Davidson County Marriages 1838-1863*, 66.
[231] United Daughters of the Confederacy, *Confederate Soldiers of Hickman County*, 68.
[232] Ibid., 71.
[233] Johnson, *1860 Census of Humphreys County*, 33; Anderson and Garrett, *Humphreys County Cemetery Records* vol. 2, 291; Maney, *Surgeon's Log*, "Stones River TN."

Camp Chase, OH. Took oath 13 May 1865. Complexion dark, hair dark, eyes blue, 5' 11 ½ ". Occupation: miller.[234]

Echols, Steven C.; Private, Company I: Brother to Private John and Corporal Robert Echols. Enlisted 1 December 1861 at Fort Donelson, TN. Present through December 1861. Admitted to Pim Hospital, Griffin, GA., 22 July 1864.[235]

Edwards, R. H.; Private, Company B: Sworn into service 10 May 1861 at Nashville. Discharged 11 May 1862 at Cumberland Gap, TN. by the conscript law.

Edwards, Wiley; Fourth Sergeant, Company F: Born 9 February 1843 in Robertson Co., TN. Enlisted 18 May 1861 at Cedar Hill, TN. Appointed corporal. Promoted to fourth sergeant. Discharged 15 December 1862 at Murfreesboro, TN. Resided in Adams, Robertson Co., TN.

Egan, James; Private, Company D: Sworn into service 11 May 1861 at Nashville. Discharged 15 August 1862 at Tazewell, TN. by the conscript law.

Egan, Michael; Sergeant, Company D: Born c. 1822 in Co. Galway, Ireland. Sworn into service 11 May 1861 at Nashville. Appointed sergeant by July 1862. Discharged 15 August 1862 at Tazewell, TN. by the conscript law. Married Winifred Murray, 11 August 1863 at the Church of Our Lady in Louisville, KY., where they resided after the war. Occupation: laborer. Died 20 June 1907 in Louisville, KY. Pension Application Kentucky 2103.

*Eleazer, William Doake "Billy"; Captain, Company E: Born 18 July 1839 in Montgomery Co., TN. Occupation: farmer. Sworn into service 18 May 1861 at Nashville. Age 22 on roll dated 16 August 1861 at Watauga Bridge, TN. Elected second lieutenant at the reorganization, 1 May 1862. Wounded in the thigh in the Battle of Murfreesboro, TN., 31 December 1862. Sent to hospital at Chattanooga, TN. Later promoted to captain, and was the last captain of Company E. Surrendered as a member of Company C, 2nd Consolidated Tennessee Infantry at Greensboro, NC., 26 April 1865. Paroled 1 May 1865. Resided at Cumberland Furnace, Dickson Co., TN. Married Dolly H. Dodson, 30 January 1867. Occupation: merchant. Present at the 14 June 1904 reunion of the 11th Tennessee Infantry in Nashville. Died 3 April 1917 due to paralysis of the right side. Buried in the Brumit Cemetery, Dickson Co., TN.[236]

Elliott, A. J.; Private, Company D: Born 13 June 1820 in Montgomery Co., TN. Occupation: farmer. Sworn into service 11 May 1861 at Nashville. Discharged under the conscript law, 12 August 1862 at Tazewell, TN. Resident of Montgomery Co., TN. Resided at the Tennessee Confederate Soldiers Home from 18 August 1904. Died 24 June 1912. Buried in Soldiers Home Cemetery grave # 254.[237]

Elliot, James; Private, Company D: Sworn into service 11 May 1861 at Nashville. Discharged under the conscript law.

Elliott, W. C.; Private, Company C: Captured at Somerset, KY., 14 August 1863. Sent to U. S. Military Prison at Louisville, KY. Transferred to Camp Chase, OH., 3 September 1863. Transferred to Rock Island, IL. Patient in Blackie Hospital, Augusta, GA., 18 November 1864.

Elliott, William.; Private, Company D: Enlisted 12 August 1861 at Loudon, TN. Wounded in the leg severely in the Battle of Murfreesboro, TN., 31 December 1862. Captured at Murfreesboro, TN., 5 January 1863. Patient in U. S. Hospital #1 at Murfreesboro. Quartered at Mrs. Grimmage's home. Sent to U. S. Military Prison at Louisville, KY. Forwarded to Fort McHenry, MD. Transferred to Fortress Monroe, VA. for exchange. Exchanged and sent to C. S. General Hospital in Petersburg, VA., 19 June

---

[234] Welsh, *Confederate Hospitals*, Patient Roster, Fair Ground Hospital #1, 83; Johnson, *1860 Census of Humphreys County*, 33; Clifton, *1870 Census of Humphreys County*, 180.

[235] Johnson, *1860 Census of Humphreys County*, 33; *Chattanooga Daily Rebel*, 27 July 1864.

[236] Maney, *Surgeon's Log*, "Stones River TN"; Sistler and Sistler, *1880 Census of Dickson County*, 21; *Reunion Pamphlet*, 14 June 1904; John T. Matthews, Tennessee Pension Application, 4243; Electronic mail correspondence with descendant Kevin Matthews, 4 February 2002.

[237] Strange, *Soldiers Home*, 68; A. J. Elliott, Confederate Soldiers Home Application.

1863. Transferred to smallpox hospital, 3 August 1863. Admitted to Episcopal Church Hospital, Williamsburg, VA., 7 March 1864 for gunshot wound. Transferred to hospital in Augusta, GA., 17 March 1864. Surrendered at Sweetwater, TN., 15 May 1865. Took oath, 22 May 1865. Complexion fair, hair light, eyes blue, height 5' 10". Present at the 14 June 1904 reunion of the 11th Tennessee Infantry.[238]

Elliott, William Meredith; Private, Company F: Born 10 October 1843 in Robertson Co., TN. First cousin to Privates Charles W. and William B. Woodruff. Enlisted 13 July 1861, at Camp Cheatham, TN. Wounded and captured 31 December 1862 at the Battle of Murfreesboro, TN. Released from prison 12 July 1863. Returned to duty with regiment. Received a gunshot wound fracturing both bones of right leg. Given sixty day furlough from Confederate hospital, Madison, GA., 14 July 1864. Paroled 12 May 1865. Resided at Carmel, Montgomery Co., TN. Occupation: farmer. Married Louisa Jane Gower on 29 December 1870. Member, Ed Crockett Bivouac, United Confederate Veterans. Attended the 1904 reunion of the 11th Tennessee. Died at the family home place near Stroudsville, 13 November 1930. Buried in the Head's Freewill Baptist Church Cemetery in Robertson Co., TN.[239]

Ellis, John M.; Private, Company F: Sworn into service 18 May 1861 at Cedar Hill, TN. Deserted before July 1862.

Ellis, Thomas J.; Private, Company F: Enlisted 18 May 1861 at Cedar Hill, TN. Wounded late 1863 or early 1864. Patient in Ocmulgee Hospital, Macon, GA., 30 April 1865.

Ely, A.; Private, Company F: Enlisted 25 August 1861 at Cumberland Gap, TN. No further.

Emery, N. R.; Private, Company A: Enlisted 18 February 1863 at Shelbyville, TN. Captured 27 June 1863 at Shelbyville, TN. Sent to U. S. Military Prison at Louisville, KY. Forwarded to Camp Chase, OH., on 6 July 1863. Sent to Fort Delaware, Delaware, 14 July 1863. Paroled 30 July 1863. Admitted to General Hospital, Petersburg, VA., where he died of chronic diarrhea 17 August 1863.

Emery, William L.; Private, Company A: Enlisted 12 September 1861 at Knoxville, TN. Sick in hospital at Shelbyville, TN. on 29 April 1863 age 27. Took oath 20 January 1864. Complexion fair, hair brown, eyes gray, height 5' 5".

Epps, George Peterson Young; Private, Company C: Born 12 January 1838 in Mississippi. Enlisted 25 June 1861 at Camp Cheatham. Worked in the Adjutant's office 2 – 13 September 1861. Issued a minie musket. Hospital attendant from 21 March 1862. Teamster from 24 September 1862. Left in charge of sick at Murfreesboro, TN., 4 January 1863. Captured at Murfreesboro, TN. in January 1863. Sent to Fort McHenry, MD., 14 February 1863. Exchanged and rejoined unit, 2 March 1863. Age 25 on roll dated 8 May 1863. After the Battle of Nashville, TN. in December 1864 he traveled with the army to Corinth, MS., where he was furloughed to Jackson, TN. He was then unable to return to his command. Took oath, 19 January 1865. Complexion fair, hair light, eyes gray, height 5' 4". Attended the reunion of the 11th Tennessee Infantry at Bon Aqua Springs, Hickman Co., TN., 24 September 1885 and was also present at the 14 June 1904 reunion of the 11th Tennessee Infantry in Nashville. Resided at White Bluff, TN. Buried in the Southerland Cemetery, Dickson Co., TN.[240]

Estes, Joshua G.; Private, Company I: Born 16 April 1838. Brother of Private Solomon Estes. Married Elizen Thomas. Died in Hickman Co., TN., 17 October 1918. Buried in the Tidwell Cemetery in Hickman Co., TN.[241]

Estes, Solomon; Private, Company K: Born 1844. Brother of Private Joshua G. Estes. Enlisted 20 December 1862 in Dickson Co., TN. Age 18 on roll dated 1 May 1863 at Shelbyville, TN. Killed in the Battle of Missionary Ridge, TN., 25 November 1863.[242]

---

[238] *Reunion Pamphlet,* 14 June 1904.

[239] Harris, *Confederate Hospitals,* 234, 213; Electronic mail correspondence with descendant Johnny Long, 26 June 1999; *Reunion Pamphlet,* 14 June 1904.

[240] McCauley, *Record Book, Company C*; Garrett, *Dickson County Handbook,* 204; George Epps, Tennessee Pension Application, 526; "The Reunion," *Hickman Pioneer*; *Reunion Pamphlet,* 14 June 1904.

[241] United Daughters of the Confederacy, *Confederate Soldiers of Hickman County,* 75.

Estes, William Garrett; Private, Company K: Born 1826. Enlisted 10 December 1862 in Dickson Co., TN. Age 38 on roll dated 1 May 1863 at Shelbyville, TN. Married (1) Margaret Austin and (2) Sydney E. Lankford. Died 1884 in Hickman Co., TN.[243]

Ethridge, William T.; Private, Company I: Born in Humphreys Co., TN., 10 December 1838. Resided at McEwen, TN. Enlisted 25 September 1861 at Nashville. Discharged for disability due to rupture on right side at Cumberland Gap, TN., 25 October 1861. Complexion fair, eyes blue, hair light, height 6'. Married. Occupation: farmer. Died 17 June 1918. Buried in the Young Cemetery, Bold Springs, Humphreys Co., TN.[244]

Ethridge, William; Private, Company K: Enlisted 1 December 1862 at Manchester, TN. Age 22 on roll dated 1 May 1863. Killed in action near Atlanta, GA., 1 August 1864.[245]

Eubanks, Raford Crumpler "Rafe"; Private, Company E: Born 21 November 1841. Brother of Private Robert G. Eubanks. Occupation: farmer. Enlisted 19 September 1861 at Camp Buckner, KY. Age 19 on roll dated 14 May 1863 at Shelbyville, TN. Given furlough 11 March 1864. Wounded in the left thigh at Kennesaw Mountain, GA., 21 June 1864. Admitted to Fair Ground Hospital #1, Atlanta, GA., 21 June 1864 for vulnus sclopeticum. Sent to another hospital 8 July 1864. Killed in the Battle of Franklin, TN., 30 November 1864, age 23. Buried in the McGavock Confederate Cemetery, Franklin, TN., Section 55, Grave #53.[246]

Eubanks, Robert G.; Private, Company E: Brother of Private Raford C. Eubanks. Occupation: farmer. Enlisted Feb, 8, 1863 at Shelbyville, TN. age 18. Killed in the Battle of Jonesboro, GA., 1 September 1864.[247]

Evans, J. C.; Private, Company F: Enlisted September, 1863 at Chattanooga, TN. Present through December 1863. No further.

Everett, James; First Lieutenant, Company B: Sworn into service 10 May 1861 at Nashville. Elected first lieutenant at organization. Resigned 10 May 1862.

Ewing, John A.; Private, Company I: Sworn into service 20 May 1861 at Nashville. At hospital in Knoxville, TN., 20 April 1862. On extra duty November 1861 through January 1862 as a carpenter.

–F–

*Fain, Tyree Lindsey; Third Lieutenant, Company E: Born in Dickson Co., TN., 5 September 1839. Occupation: farmer. Sworn into service 18 May 1861 at Nashville, age 22. Extra duty as a teamster September 1861 through January 1862. Promoted to first sergeant at the reorganization, 1 May 1862. Later promoted to third lieutenant. Wounded in the right side of the face at the Battle of Murfreesboro, TN., 31 December 1862. The bullet was extracted from under the left ear, with the wound causing interference with speech and swallowing. Wounded in the neck in the Battle of Chickamauga, GA., 19 September 1863. Bullet entered the right side of the neck and came out at the top of the spinal column

---

[242] United Daughters of the Confederacy, *Confederate Soldiers of Hickman County*, 75; Maney, *Surgeon's Log*, "Missionary Ridge TN."

[243] United Daughters of the Confederacy, *Confederate Soldiers of Hickman County*, 75.

[244] William T. Saunders, Tennessee Pension Application, 9904; Anderson and Garrett, *Humphreys County Cemetery Records* vol. 2, 42.

[245] William B. Maney, *Regimental Surgeon's Log*, "Return of the Killed and Wounded in the 11th Tenn. Regt. near Atlanta 28-31 July 1864."

[246] Maney, *Surgeon's Log*, "Kennesaw Mountain GA"; Welsh, *Confederate Hospitals*, Patient Roster, Fair Ground Hospital #1, 87; Garrett, *Dickson County Handbook*, 204; Hudgins and Potts, *McGavock Cemetery*, 32; Baker, *1860 Census for Dickson County*, 169.

[247] Garrett, *Dickson County Handbook*, 204; Baker, *1860 Census for Dickson County*, 169.

one and a half inches to the left, causing a partial paralysis of the right arm. Detached as army supply train wagon master, November 1863 through February 1864. Wounded in the left leg in the Battle of Peachtree Creek, GA., 20 July 1864. Surrendered as a member of the 2nd Tennessee Consolidated Infantry, 26 April 1865. Complexion fair, hair light, eyes gray, height 5' 11". Married Elizabeth Tinsley. Postwar occupation: farmer. Member of the Christian Church and Forbes Bivouac. Died of congestive chill, 18 October 1919. Buried in the Southside Cemetery, Montgomery Co., TN.[248]

Farley, John; Private, Company F: Born in Pennsylvania. Occupation: laborer. Enlisted 18 May 1861 at Cedar Hill. Discharged 26 November 1861, on surgeon's certificate, age 61. Complexion dark, hair gray, eyes dark, height, 5' 5". Died at Bank Hospital on 6 April 1862. Buried in the Oakland Cemetery, Atlanta, GA.

Farley, Thomas; Private, Company C, G: Sworn into service 14 May 1861 at Nashville in Company C. Transferred to Company G at the reorganization, 1 May 1862. Discharged by the conscript act at Tazewell, TN., 14 August 1862.

Farrell, James; Rank unknown, Company F: Admitted 21 March 1864 to C. S. General Hospital #21 at Richmond, VA. for pneumonia. Age 18. No further.

Farrell, John; Private, Company K: Born in Ireland. Occupation: laborer. Sworn into service 25 May 1861 at Nashville, age 58. Discharged 12 May 1862 by the conscript act. Complexion light, hair sandy, eyes hazel, height 5' 4".

Ferguson, Clement M.; Private, Company F: Enlisted 18 May 1861 at Cedar Hill, TN. Discharged 17 August 1862 at Tazewell, TN.

*Ferguson, George Simon; Private, Company A: Born 1837 in Hickman Co., TN. Later moved to Humphreys Co., TN. Occupation: apprentice carpenter. Sworn into service 10 May 1861 at Nashville. Deserted 12 February 1863 at Shelbyville, TN. Reenlisted from desertion by July 1863. Wounded in the Battle of Missionary Ridge, TN., 25 November 1863. Surrendered as a member of Company F, 2nd Consolidated Tennessee Infantry, 26 April 1865. Married Cora A. Stacy. Occupied as a farmer after the war.[249]

Ferguson, Jasper A.; Private, Company A: Born c. 1841. Married. Occupation: farmer. Enlisted 12 September 1861 at Knoxville, TN. Died at Cumberland Gap, TN., 10 February 1862.[250]

Ferris, Martin; Private, Company D: No further.[251]

Fielder, James Knox Polk; Private, Company H: Born in Maury Co., TN., 28 November 1837. Later moved to Hickman Company. Sworn into service 14 May 1861 at Nashville. Detached as a cook for hospital at Tazewell, TN. since 22 March 1862. Transferred to the 8th Texas Cavalry, 27 April 1864. Attended the reunion of the 11th Tennessee Infantry at Bon Aqua Springs, Hickman Co., TN., 24 September 1885. Died 21 January 1900, in Greene Co., AR. Pension Application, Arkansas Widow, Greene Co., AR. 1901.[252]

Fields, James; Private, Company D: Born c. 1832 in Tennessee. Occupation: farm laborer. Sworn into service 11 May 1861 at Nashville. On extra duty as a blacksmith from January 1862. Absent without leave since 15 December 1862. Discharged at Readyville, TN.[253]

Fields, Samuel H.; Private, Company D: Born c. 1834 in Tennessee. Occupation: laborer.

---

[248] Maney, *Surgeon's Log*, "Chickamauga GA"; Maney, *Surgeon's Log*, "20 July 1864"; T. L. Fain, Tennessee Pension Application, 7244.

[249] Johnson, *1860 Census of Humphreys County*, 5; Clifton, *1870 Census of Humphreys County*, 28; Anderson and Garrett, *Humphreys County Cemetery Records* vol. 2, 267.

[250] Johnson, *1860 Census of Humphreys County*, 57.

[251] Clayton, *History of Davidson County*, 187.

[252] "James Polk Fielder," *Confederate Veteran* vol. 8 no. 7 (July 1900): 328; "The Reunion," *Hickman Pioneer*; Jack D. Welsh, *Arkansas Confederate Pension Applications by Veterans of Tennessee Units*, (Oklahoma City OK: J.D. Welsh, 1994) 2.4; *Hickman County News*, 9 March 1899.

[253] Dobson-Sides, *1860 Davidson County Census*, 88.

Figg, Jason; Musician/Corporal, Company B: Born in Alabama. Occupation: printer. Sworn into service 10 May 1861 at Nashville. Elected third corporal by January 1863. Age 21 on roll dated 2 June 1863 at Shelbyville, TN. Promoted to second corporal by September 1863. Promoted to first corporal by January 1864. Killed in the Battle of Atlanta, GA., 22 July 1864.[254]

Fitzgerald, Edward; Private, Company C: Born c. 1837. Sworn into service 14 May 1861 at Nashville. Died from disease 23 June 1861, age 24.

Fitzgerald, James; Private, Company D: No further.[255]

Fitzgerald, Michael; Private, Company I, G: Sworn into service 20 May 1861 at Nashville in Company I. Transferred to Company G by July 1862. Age 26 on roll dated 30 May 1863 at Shelbyville, TN. Provost duty in brigade since 1 June 1863. Wounded in the Battle of Franklin, TN., 30 November 1864 by an artillery shell fragment which fractured his right ankle and apparently injured his left arm. Captured at Franklin, TN., 17 December 1864. Sent to U. S. Military Prison at Louisville, KY. Forwarded to Camp Chase, OH., 25 January 1865. Sent to Wayside Hospital or Hospital #9 in Richmond, VA., 7 March 1865. Forwarded to Chimborazo Hospital #2, Richmond, VA., 10 March 1865 for amputation of left forearm from wound. Sent to Yandell Hospital, Meridian, MS., 4 April 1865.

Fitzgerald, Thomas; Private, Company D: Sworn into service 11 May 1861 at Nashville. Discharged by conscript law 15 August 1862 at Tazewell, TN.

Fitzgivens, E.; Private, Company B: Sworn into service 10 May 1861 at Nashville. Discharged 1 August 1861 at Carter's Station, TN.

Fitzhugh, John A.; Private, Company B: Born c. 1845 in Tennessee. Occupation: farm laborer. Sworn into service 10 May 1861 at Nashville. Teamster from 3 September 1861 through December 1862. Deserted 15 February 1863 at Shelbyville, TN.[256]

Fitzmorris, Patrick; Private, Company G: Enlisted 3 June 1861 at Camp Cheatham. Discharged by the conscript law at Tazewell, TN., 31 August 1862.

Flaherty, Roger; Private, Company E, G: Sworn into service 18 May 1861 in Company E, age 20. Transferred to Company G at the reorganization, 1 May 1862. Killed in the Battle of Atlanta, GA., 22 July 1864.[257]

Flarity, Patrick; Private, Company I: Born c. 1840 in Ireland. Employed as a construction worker on the Nashville and Northwestern Railroad in Humphreys Co., TN. Sworn into service 20 May 1861 at Nashville. Died 19 April 1862 at Cumberland Gap, TN.[258]

Fleming, John; Private, Company B: Sworn into service 10 May 1861 at Nashville. Discharged under the conscript act, 12 August 1862 at Tazewell, TN., age 42.

Fleming, Patrick; Private, Company G: Enlisted 3 June 1861 at Camp Cheatham. Discharged under the conscript law at Tazewell, TN., 16 August 1862.

Flemings, Lawrence; Private, Company C: Sworn into service 14 May 1861. Died 1 December 1861.

Fletcher, William J.; Sergeant, Company G: Sworn into service 10 May 1861. Regimental clerk for Colonel Rains, September through November 1861. Discharged for disability 10 December 1862.

Flowers, James W.; Private, Company F: Born in Montgomery Co., TN. in 1840. Occupation: farmer. Sworn into service 18 May 1861 at Cedar Hill, TN. Wounded in the left side of the forehead by a shell fragment in the first day of the Battle of Jonesboro, GA., 31 August 1864. Captured on the second day of the Battle of Nashville, TN., 16 December 1864. Sent to the U. S. Military Prison in Louisville, KY. Forwarded to Camp Chase, OH., 4 January 1865. Transferred to Point Lookout, MD.,

---

[254] Ibid., 510.
[255] Clayton, *History of Davidson County*, 187.
[256] Dobson-Sides, *1860 Davidson County Census*, 72.
[257] Maney, *Surgeon's Log*, "Battle of Atlanta GA."
[258] Johnson, *1860 Census of Humphreys County*, 164.

17 February 1865 for exchange. Took oath at Columbus, KY. Resided postwar in Nashville. Present at the 14 June 1904 reunion of the 11th Tennessee Infantry in Nashville. Died 3 September 1914 at Paducah, KY. while visiting his daughter.[259]

Floyd, Harrison; Private, Company H: Born in 1833. Married. Occupation: farmer. Sworn into service 14 May 1861 at Nashville. Detached as a teamster at Morristown, TN., March through December 1862. Absent wounded December 1863. Killed on the skirmish line in the Battle of Jonesboro, GA.[260]

Flym, Martin; Private, Company D: Sworn into service 11 May 1861 at Nashville. Left with the wounded at Murfreesboro, TN., where he was captured and later exchanged. Returned to regiment by July 1863. Captured again near Kennesaw Mountain, GA., 3 July 1864. Sent to the U. S. Military Prison at Louisville, KY. Transferred to Camp Morton, IN., 14 July 1864. Released on oath 20 May 1865. Hair dark, eyes blue, height 5' 8".

Flynn, John J.; Fourth Sergeant, Company G: Enlisted 3 June 1861 at Camp Cheatham. Appointed fourth corporal by July 1862. Reduced in rank to private, 15 November 1862. Age 27 on roll dated 30 May 1863 at Shelbyville, TN. Admitted to Fair Ground Hospital #1, Atlanta, GA., on 22 August 1863 for rheumatism. Returned to duty 12 September 1863. Promoted to fourth sergeant by September 1863. Captured in the Battle of Kennesaw Mountain, GA., 27 June 1864. Sent to the U. S. Military Prison at Louisville, KY. Transferred to Camp Morton, IN., 13 July 1864. Released on oath 20 May 1865. Hair dark, eyes blue, height 5' 5".

Folia, Thomas; Private, Company G: Born in 1825 in Ireland. Enlisted 4 June 1863 at Shelbyville, TN. Absent sick at hospital since 8 September 1863. Admitted to Fairground Hospital #2 in Atlanta, GA., for ulcus. Returned to duty 21 September 1863. Died 31 October 1864.[261]

Ford, Benjamin Franklin Lafayette; Corporal, Company B: Sworn into service 10 May 1861 at Nashville. Corporal by 11 June 1861. Discharged 1 September 1861 at Knoxville, TN. by a surgeon's certificate of disability.[262]

*Ford, Jesse Manley; Private, Company E: Born 17 February 1834 in Dickson Co., TN. Sworn into service 18 May 1861, age 26. Surrendered as a member of Company C, 2nd Consolidated Tennessee Infantry, 26 April 1865. Paroled 1 May 1865. Died 15 August 1913. Buried in the Greenwood Cemetery, Montgomery Co., TN.

Ford, Matthew Washington; Private, Company G, B, K: Born 1835 in Rutherford Co., TN. Occupation: farmer. Sworn into service 10 May 1861 in Company G at Nashville. Transferred to Company B at the reorganization, 1 May 1862. Transferred to Company K, 29 December 1862. Age 27 on roll dated 2 June 1863 at Shelbyville, TN. Captured near Marietta, GA., 3 July 1864. Sent to the U. S. Military Prison at Louisville, KY. Forwarded to Camp Morton, IN., 13 July 1864. Released on oath 20 May 1865. Hair dark, eyes dark, height 5' 7". Resident at the Tennessee Confederate Soldiers Home from 3 November 1904. Died 6 June 1914. Buried in Soldiers Home Cemetery grave # 290.[263]

Ford, W. L. Grant; Private, Company B: Sworn into service 10 May 1861 at Nashville. Deserted 12 June 1862 at Cumberland Gap, TN. Arrested by William A. Cole and delivered to Richmond, VA. on 7 July 1863. Cole was paid $30.00 for apprehending Ford.

Foster, William B.; Private, Company A: Born c. 1836. Occupation: farmer. Married. Sworn into service 10 May 1861 in Nashville. Discharged by providing a substitute.

---

[259] J. W. Flowers, Tennessee Pension Application, 11794; Maney, *Surgeon's Log*, "August 1864"; *Reunion Pamphlet*, 14 June 1904.

[260] United Daughters of the Confederacy, *Confederate Soldiers of Hickman County*, 76.

[261] Johnson, *1860 Census of Humphreys County*, 159; Welsh, *Confederate Hospitals*, Patient Roster, Fair Ground Hospital #2, 64.

[262] *Nashville Daily Gazette*, 11 June 1861.

[263] Strange, *Soldiers Home*, 69.

Fowler, G. W.; Private, Company A: Enlisted 6 May 1863 at Shelbyville, TN., age 22.

Fowlkes, Gabriel; Commissary Sergeant, Company H, Field & Staff: Born 27 January 1833 in Hickman Co., TN. Brother served in the Union Army. Sworn into service 14 May 1861 at Nashville. Elected second sergeant at the organization. Reduced in rank to private by August 1862. Acting commissary sergeant from 1 October 1862 to August 1863. Transferred to Field & Staff, September 1863. Surrendered at Johnsonville, TN., 13 May 1865. Married (1) Senona McMinn in 1869 and (2) Anna McClanahan in 1888. Died 7 January 1898 in Hickman Co. Buried in the Temple Cemetery, Pinewood, Hickman Co., TN.[264]

Foy, Thomas; Private, Company I: Born c. 1817 in Ireland. Employed as a worker on the Nashville and Northwestern Railroad. Sworn into service 20 May 1861. Discharged 15 August 1862 at Tazewell, TN. by the conscript act.

Frazier, William Gamblin; Third Corporal, Company H: Born in Perry Co., TN., 2 January 1835. Resided in Coble, Hickman Co., TN. Sworn into service 14 May 1861 at Nashville. Elected third corporal at the organization. Discharged for disability, 15 April 1862 at Cumberland Gap, TN., age 26. Complexion dark, hair dark, eyes blue, height 6'. Later enlisted in Company I, 10th Tennessee Cavalry Battalion and was elected first lieutenant. Returned to Hickman Co., after the war. Married Millie Evaline Rice Garrett in 1867. Died at his son's home on 31 May 1923 in Wilson, AR. Buried in the Shouse Cemetery, Hickman Co.[265]

Freeman, George Kennard; Private, Company C: Born c. 1840 in Dickson Co., TN. Occupation: day laborer. Sworn into service 14 May 1861 at Nashville. Issued a Belgium musket. Wounded in the head in the Battle of Murfreesboro, TN., 31 December 1862. Captured at Murfreesboro, TN., 10 January 1863. Sent to Fort McHenry, MD. 14 February 1863. Forwarded to Fortress Monroe, VA. Exchanged and rejoined unit, 2 March 1863. Age 23 on roll dated 8 May 1863 at Shelbyville, TN. Killed in the Battle of New Hope Church, GA., 27 May 1864.[266]

Freeman, Samuel; Private, Company D: Sworn into service 11 May 1861 at Nashville. On extra duty as a teamster, October through November 1861. Captured February 1862 at Nashville when it fell into Union hands.

French, Cullen E.; Private, Company I: Born c. 1829. Occupation: laborer. Married. Enlisted 15 May 1861 in Germantown, TN. Transferred to the 11th Tennessee Infantry from the 5th Tennessee Infantry, 31 August 1863. On extra duty as a cook from November 1863 through February 1864. Killed in the Battle of Franklin, TN., 30 November 1864. Buried in the McGavock Confederate Cemetery, Franklin, TN., section 55 grave #51.[267]

French, George H.; Third Corporal, Company I: Born in Stewart Co., TN., 27 January 1839. Brother of Private Robert J. French. Occupation: farmer. Enlisted 20 May 1861 at Nashville. Age 23 on roll dated 6 May 1863 at Shelbyville, TN. Appointed third corporal, 1 August 1863. Wounded through the buttocks in the Battle of Adairsville, GA., 17 May 1864. Wounded in the Battle of Atlanta, GA., 22 July 1864. Admitted to Ocmulgee Hospital, Macon, GA. Captured in the Battle of Franklin, TN., 30 November 1864. Sent to the U. S. Military Prison in Louisville, KY. Forwarded to Camp Douglas, IL., 3 December 1864. Released from Point Lookout, MD., 26 June 1865. Complexion light, hair brown, eyes blue, height 5' 9". Resided at Tennessee Ridge, Houston Co., TN. Pension Application S15068.[268]

---

[264] United Daughters of the Confederacy, *Confederate Soldiers of Hickman County*, 80.

[265] William Gamblin Frazier, Tennessee Pension Application, 12028; United Daughters of the Confederacy, *Confederate Soldiers of Hickman County*, 81.

[266] Baker, *1860 Census for Dickson County*, 123; McCauley, *Record Book, Company C*; Maney, *Surgeon's Log*, "Stones River TN"; Maney, *Surgeon's Log*, "May 1864."

[267] Hudgins and Potts, *McGavock Cemetery*, 32.

[268] Laura Willis and Betty Sellers, *Stewart County, Tenn. Census of 1850* (Melber KY: Simmons Historical Publications, 2000) 41; G. H. French, Tennessee Confederate Pension Application, S15068;

French, Robert J.; Private, Company I: Born c. 1836. Brother of Corporal George H. French. Sworn into service 20 May 1861 in Nashville. Given indefinite sick furlough 7 July 1861. Re-enlisted in the company, 20 January 1863 at Shelbyville, TN. Age 27 on roll dated 6 May 1863 at Shelbyville. Admitted to Fair Ground Hospital #2, Atlanta, GA, 7 July 1863 for acute diarrhea. Returned to duty 15 July 1863. Missing since the Battle of Missionary Ridge, TN., 25 November 1863. Captured 4 February 1864 in Stewart Co., TN. Sent to the U. S. Military Prison at Louisville, KY. Forwarded to Camp Morton, IN., 12 May 1864. Transferred for exchange 15 March 1865.[269]

Frizzell, William G. "Billy"; Fourth Corporal, Company H: Born in 1840. Enlisted in Company H, 11th Tennessee. Died at Danville, TN. of the measles on 31 January 1862. Buried in an unmarked grave on Blue Creek in Humphreys Co., TN.[270]

Fuqua, Jesse Jerome, Jr.; Private, Company A: Born in Hickman Co., TN., 6 February 1830. Brother of Musician William T. Fuqua. Married Elmeda Pullen, sister of Private W. C. Pullen, prior to the war. Resided near McEwen, Humphreys Co., TN. Occupation: farmer. Enlisted 12 September 1861 at Knoxville, TN. Listed as a teamster. Discharged by the conscript act at Tazewell, TN., 14 August 1862. Re-enlisted in the 10th Tennessee Cavalry. In this service he was detailed to make wagons and coffins. Later assigned to pick up deserters and stragglers. Complexion dark, hair dark, height 5' 10". After the war he followed the calling of his father and served as a Primitive Baptist minister. Died 31 July 1909. Buried in the Vineyard Cemetery, Humphreys Co., TN.[271]

*Fuqua, William Thomas; Musician, Company A: Born 22 July 1834 in Hickman Co., TN. Brother of Private J. J. Fuqua. Their father, a Primitive Baptist minister had organized Harmony Baptist Church in 1844. Sworn into service 10 May 1861 at Nashville. Sick in hospital at Tazewell, TN. since 28 April 1862. Transferred to hospital at Bean Station, TN., 10 August 1862. Age 25 on roll dated 6 May 1863 at Shelbyville, TN. Wounded in the Battle of Chickamauga, GA, 19 September 1863. Surrendered as a member of Company K, 2nd Consolidated Tennessee Infantry, 26 April 1865. Paroled 1 May 1865. Relocated to Kentucky in 1866. Married Mary E. Singleton, 13 March 1889 in Graves Co., KY. Died 15 January 1919 at Farmington, Graves Co., KY., and buried there in the Harmony Primitive Baptist Church Cemetery. Pension Application Kentucky 2122.[272]

-G-

Gafford, James Knox Polk; Private, Company E: Born 1 September 1841. Brother of Private William Jefferson Gafford. Enlisted 22 July 1861 at Camp Cheatham, age 20. Deserted and captured 26 November 1863 near Ringgold, GA. Sent to U. S. Military Prison at Louisville, KY., 9 December 1863. Transferred to Rock Island, IL., 13 December 1863. Enlisted December 1863 in Company F, 2nd U.S. Volunteer Infantry, and was placed on frontier service. Mustered out of Union Service, 7 November 1865. Died 27 December 1912. Buried in the Centerpoint Cemetery, Dickson Co., TN.[273]

Maney, *Surgeon's Log*, "May 1864"; Maney, *Surgeon's Log*, "Battle of Atlanta GA"; *Nashville Daily Press*, 3 December 1864.

[269] *Census Stewart County, Tennessee: 1850*, 41; Welsh, *Confederate Hospitals*, Patient Roster, Fair Ground Hospital #2, 66.

[270] United Daughters of the Confederacy, *Confederate Soldiers of Hickman County*, 81.

[271] Johnson, *1860 Census of Humphreys County*, 125; Anderson and Garrett, *Humphreys County Cemetery Records* vol. 1, 40; Anderson and Garrett, *Humphreys County Cemetery Records* vol. 2, 85; J. J. Fuqua, Tennessee Confederate Pension Application, S10403.

[272] Garrett, *Humphreys County, Tennessee, 1 850 Census*, 105; Johnson, *1860 Census of Humphreys County*, 126.

[273] Personal correspondence with Mr. Tim Burgess, Battle of Franklin Historian, 13 May 2001.

Gafford, William Jefferson "Bud"; Private, Company E: Born 1839 in Dickson Co., TN. Brother of Private James K. Polk Gafford. Occupation: farmer. Sworn into service 18 May 1861 at Nashville, age 22. Teamster since 17 August 1862. Captured at the Battle of Missionary Ridge, TN., 25 November 1863. Sent to the U. S. Military Prison at Louisville, KY. Transferred to Rock Island, IL., 9 December 1863. Took oath 11 April 1865. Complexion dark, hair dark, eyes hazel, height 6' 4". Died in 1905. Buried in the Bud Gafford Cemetery, Dickson Co., TN.

Gaither, William B.; Private, Company H: Captured 5 July 1864 at Marietta, GA. Sent to the U. S. Military Prison at Louisville, KY. Forwarded to Camp Douglas, IL., 26 July 1864. Died 21 October 1864.

Gallaway (Galliway), Henry; Sergeant, Company K: Enlisted 16 July 1861 at Camp Cheatham. Killed at Woodson's Cross Roads, TN. (near Cumberland Gap) 7 September 1862.

Gallop, William T.; Private, Company C: Captured at Union City, TN., 11 October 1863. Died at Camp Douglas, IL., 3 November 1864 of erysiphales. Placed in vault of C. H. Jordon, Undertaker. Buried Oak Woods Cemetery, Chicago, IL.[274]

Galloway, J. W.; Private, Company K: Killed by his own men while in front of the line at Cumberland Gap, TN.[275]

Gardner, Charles Napoleon; Private, Company F: Born in Robertson Co., TN., 29 September 1842. Occupation: farmer. Father was a large slaveholder. Enlisted 18 May 1861 at Cedar Hill, TN. Wounded in the neck in the Battle of Chickamauga, GA., 19 September 1863. Captured at the Battle of Missionary Ridge, TN., 25 November 1863. Sent to the U. S. Military Prison at Louisville, KY., 7 December 1863. Forwarded to Rock Island, IL., 9 December 1863. Released from prison 6 March 1865. Paroled at Richmond, VA. Arrested by Federal Authorities at Nashville, TN. and compelled to take the oath, 24 April 1865. Complexion fair, hair light, eyes gray, height 5' 10". Relocated to Kentucky around 1877, residing at Pembroke, Christian Co., KY. Occupation: farmer. Returned to Tennessee in July 1927, residing near Adams. Died 15 March 1935. Buried at the Red River Baptist Church Cemetery, Adams, Robertson Co., TN.[276]

Gareo, R. William O.; Private, Company I: Born 1828 in Ireland. Occupation: railroading. Captured in the Battle of Jonesboro, GA., 31 August 1864. No further record.[277]

Garland, Jesse; Private, Company E: Occupation: farm worker. Sworn into service 18 May 1861 at Nashville, age 27. In convalescent camp at Knoxville, TN., September through December 1862. Last recorded military record at Cuthbert, GA., 21 September 1864 where he received clothing. In 1880 he was listed as a pauper living in the poor house.[278]

Garner, George Washington Fly; Sergeant, Company H: Born 7 April 1841 in Maury Co., TN. Sworn into service 14 May 1861 at Nashville. Wounded in the chest resulting in the breaking of two ribs around Chattanooga, TN. Admitted to St. Mary's Hospital at LaGrange, GA., 8 July 1864 with a gunshot wound. Captured in the Battle of Nashville, TN., 16 December 1864. Sent to U. S. Military Prison at Louisville, KY. Forwarded to Camp Chase, OH., 29 January 1865. Taken from Camp Chase to Richmond where he was paroled. Occupied as a farmer postwar. Married Mary Jane Harrington, 26 September 1867. Attended the reunion of the 11th Tennessee Infantry at Bon Aqua Springs, Hickman

---

[274] Find-A-Grave, "Oak Woods," http://www.findagrave.com/cgi-bin/fg.cgi?page=gr&GSln= Gallop&GSiman= 1&GScid=173554&GRid=7111386& (16 August 2014).

[275] Garrett, *Dickson County Handbook*, 205.

[276] Charles N. Gardner, Tennessee Pension Application, 16459; Maney, *Surgeon's Log*, "Chickamauga GA"; Durrett, Williams, and Reid, *Robertson County Cemetery Records*, 51.

[277] Johnson, *1860 Census of Humphreys County*, 65.

[278] Baker, *1860 Census for Dickson County*, 160; Sistler and Sistler, *1880 Census of Dickson County*, 24.

Co., TN., 24 September 1885. Died in Dyer Co., TN., 30 November 1919, and buried in the Rehobeth Church Cemetery there. Pension Application S13554.[279]

Garner, Samuel W.; Private, Company H: Born c. 1839. Enlisted 5 August 1861 at Nashville. Discharged 1 December 1861 on a surgeon's certificate of disability. Later joined Company D, 9th Tennessee Cavalry. Killed 2 July 1863 during an attack on a Federal stockpile on Hurricane Creek, Humphreys Co., TN.[280]

Garrett, James P.; Private, Company I: Enlisted 20 May 1861 at Nashville. Deserted 8 May 1862 at Cumberland Gap, TN. Joined Captain James T. Gillespie's Company of Tennessee Cavalry (subsequently became Company I, 63rd Tennessee Infantry, a.k.a. 74th Tennessee Infantry) 12 July 1862. Returns of 12 May through 31 August 1862 show him under arrest for desertion of the 11th Tennessee.

Garrett, Joseph; Private, Company I: Enlisted 20 May 1861 at Nashville. Died at Cumberland Gap, TN., 22 April 1862.

*Garton, Moses; Private, Company E: Born 24 July 1841. Occupation: farmer. Enlisted 1 September 1861 at Knoxville, TN. Age 19 on roll dated 14 May 1863 at Shelbyville, TN. Wounded seven times during the war. Wounded in the side below the first rib in the Battle of Adairsville, GA., 17 May 1864. The most severe was in the face in the Battle of Peachtree Creek, GA., 20 July 1864. The ball fractured the cheek bone, broke the jawbone, and passed out the rear of the right ear. Admitted to Floyd Hospital at Greensboro, GA., for this wound. Surrendered as a member of Company C, 2nd Consolidated Tennessee Infantry, 26 April 1865. Paroled 1 May 1865. Resided at Spencer Mill, Dickson Co., TN. Attended the reunion of the 11th Tennessee Infantry at Bon Aqua Springs, Hickman Co., TN., 24 September 1885. Died 19 April 1922. Buried in the Martin Garton Cemetery, Dickson Co., TN. Pension Application S2553.[281]

Gary, Peter; Private, Company B: Enlisted 10 May 1861 at Nashville. Deserted 1 September 1861 at Knoxville, TN.

Gee, William K.; Private, Company H: Enlisted 14 May 1861 at Nashville. Took oath 29 December 1864. Complexion fair, hair light, eyes gray, height 5' 8".

Gentry, David C.; Private, Company K: Occupation: farmer. Enlisted 3 March 1863 at Columbia, TN. Wounded in the left foot in the Battle of Chickamauga, GA., 19 September 1863. Shot through the bowels in the Battle of New Hope Church, GA., 27 May 1864. Died 28 May 1864.[282]

George, James L. "Big Shiney"; Sergeant/Color Bearer, Company H: Born 1838. Occupation: farmer. Enlisted 8 August 1861. Promoted to corporal around July 1862. Regimental color-bearer July 1862 through April 1863. Wounded in the right thigh in the Battle of Missionary Ridge, TN., 25 November 1863. Received at Confederate hospital in Atlanta, GA., for a gunshot wound. Forwarded to Confederate hospital, Madison, GA., 8 May 1864. Admitted to Confederate hospital, Madison, GA., 9 May 1864. Took oath 22 October 1864. Complexion fair, hair light, eyes blue, height 6'.[283]

German, Dr. Daniel, II; Surgeon, Field & Staff: Born 19 March 1831 near Franklin, Williamson Co., TN. Received his early education in the schools of Franklin. Began the study of medicine in 1850, graduating from the University of Pennsylvania medical school in 1854. Served as surgeon of the 11th Tennessee from the beginning of the war until around the middle of 1862, when he was put in charge of

---

[279] George W. F. Garner, Tennessee Confederate Pension Application, S13554; United Daughters of the Confederacy, *Confederate Soldiers of Hickman County*, 83; "The Reunion," *Hickman Pioneer*; *Nashville Daily Press*, 22 December 1864.

[280] United Daughters of the Confederacy, *Confederate Soldiers of Hickman County*, 82.

[281] Moses Garton, "Veteran Questionnaire" vol. 3, 888-89; Maney, *Surgeon's Log*, "20 July 1864"; Moses Garton, Tennessee Confederate Pension Application, S2553; Garrett, *Dickson County Handbook*, 205; "The Reunion," *Hickman Pioneer*.

[282] Maney, *Surgeon's Log*, "Chickamauga GA"; Maney, *Surgeon's Log*, "May 1864."

[283] United Daughters of the Confederacy, *Confederate Soldiers of Hickman County*, 84; Maney, *Surgeon's Log*, "Missionary Ridge TN;" Harris, *Confederate Hospitals*, 358, 401.

a Confederate hospital in Franklin, TN. Later joined Roddy's cavalry division in late 1862 or early 1863 and served that unit throughout the rest of the war as chief surgeon. Following the war he resumed his medical practice in Franklin. Married Frances Adelicia McEwen, 14 January 1869. Politically a Democrat. Member of the Masonic Order and the Methodist Episcopal Church. Died in 1911. Buried at Rest Haven Cemetery, Williamson Co., TN.[284]

Gibbons, Patrick; Private, Company I: Born in Trigg Co., KY. Occupation: blacksmith. Sworn into service 20 May 1861 in Nashville. Discharged 12 September 1862 for disability due to a bad structure at the neck of the bladder caused by violent gonorrhea. Complexion dark, hair black, eyes gray, height 5' 6", age 27.

Gill, George Washington "Wash"; Second Sergeant, Company H: Born 28 December 1836 in Hickman Co., TN. Married Mary Priscilla Fowlkes. Enlisted 14 May 1861 at Nashville. Elected third sergeant at the reorganization, 1 May 1862. Was promoted to second sergeant by July 1863. Deserted and captured 26 July 1864 at Atlanta, GA. Took oath 26 August 1864. Complexion light, hair dark, eyes blue, height 5' 10". Resided postwar in Arkansas and later, Oklahoma. Died 11 September 1916 in Oklahoma. Buried in the Blackburn Cemetery, Norman, Cleveland Co., OK. Pension Application Arkansas, Sebastian Co., 1914 and later applied in Oklahoma.[285]

Gilman, Joseph Warren; First Sergeant, Company D: Born in Davidson Co., TN., 22 June 1842. Sworn into service 11 May 1861 at Nashville. Promoted to second sergeant by July 1862. Age 35 on roll dated 5 May 1863. Promoted to first sergeant by September 1863. Wounded in the lower half of the left arm in the Battle of Resaca, GA., 14 May 1864. Wounded in the Battle of Jonesboro, GA., 1 September 1864. Right ulna fractured near elbow. Lower one third of arm amputated. Paroled at Augusta, GA., 1 May 1865. Member of the Cumberland Presbyterian Church. For thirty years he was one of the most popular engineers on the Nashville, Chattanooga, and Saint Louis Railroad, retiring shortly before his death. Member of Company B, United Confederate Veterans. Died at his home, 7 February 1908. His funeral was held at the First Presbyterian Church in Nashville. Buried at Mount Olivet Cemetery, Nashville, TN. Members of the Frank Cheatham Bivouac attended his funeral as a body. A group of Confederate veterans fired a salute over his grave at the service.[286]

Gilman, Thomas A.; Fourth Sergeant, Company D: Enlisted 11 May 1861 at Nashville. Promoted to first corporal by July 1862. Age 20 on roll dated 5 May 1863 at Shelbyville, TN. Sent to hospital at Rome, GA., 25 October 1863. Promoted to fourth sergeant by September 1863. Given medical discharge 26 August 1864.

Glenn, John; Private, Company G: Brother of Private Patrick Glenn. Enlisted 3 June 1861 at Camp Cheatham. Left sick at Versailles, KY., 6 October 1862. Captured at Huntington, TN., 4 February 1863. Sent to Fort McHenry, MD., 14 February 1863. Exchanged and returned to unit. Captured in the Battle of Kennesaw Mountain, GA., 27 June 1864. Sent to the U. S. Military Prison at Louisville, KY. Transferred to Camp Douglas, IL., 14 July 1864. Died of pneumonia at Camp Douglas, 5 May 1865.[287]

Glenn, Patrick; Private, Company G: Born in Ireland. Brought to America at age seven. Resided at Denver, Humphreys Co., TN. Brother of Private John Glenn. Enlisted 3 June 1861 at Camp Cheatham.

---

[284] Hudson Alexander, *Physicians of Williamson County, A Legacy of Healing 1797-1997* (Franklin TN: Bob Canaday, 1998) 34, 51, 64-65; Goodspeed Brothers, *Goodspeed's History of Maury, Williamson, Rutherford, Wilson, Bedford, & Marshall Counties of Tennessee*, 983.

[285] Welsh, *Arkansas Pension Applications by Tennessee Veterans*, 2.8; Joe L. Todd, *Tennessee's Confederate Veterans in Oklahoma* (Oklahoma City OK: Archives Division, Oklahoma Historical Society, 1996) 6.

[286] "Joseph W. Gilman," *Confederate Veteran*, vol. 16 no. 3 (March 1908): 137; Maney, *Surgeon's Log*, "May 1864"; Maney, *Surgeon's Log*, "September 1864"; *Nashville Banner*, 8 February 1908.

[287] Patrick Glenn, Tennessee Pension Application, 9716.

Age 23 on roll dated 30 May 1863. Captured in the Battle of Nashville, TN., 16 December 1864. Took oath at Paducah, KY.[288]

Glover, Joseph; Private, Company A: Enlisted 1 August 1861 at Bean Station, TN. Died in hospital at Knoxville, TN., 15 November 1862. Buried in the Bethel Cemetery there.[289]

Goad, Gustavus; Private, Company D: Occupation: clerk. Enlisted 10 December 1863 at Dalton, GA. Complexion fair, hair brown, eyes blue, height 5' 9". Slight flesh wound of the scalp on the left side of the head in the Battle of Peachtree Creek, GA., 20 July 1864. Left side of skull fractured by a shell fragment near Atlanta, GA., 31 July 1864. Supposed to be mortally wounded but recovered. Wounded in the Battle of Nashville, TN., 15 December 1864 by a conical ball. Captured and sent to prison. Soldier's mother, Delilah Goad, wrote Major General George Thomas to ask the pardon and release of her son from prison. The general replied that "sufficient clemency has already been shown the prisoner in commuting the sentence of the Military Commission from death to imprisonment. This application is therefore not granted." Took oath 25 February 1865.[290]

Godshall, Samuel Chester; Captain, Company G: Born c. 1827 in Delaware. Resided in Philadelphia, PA., prior to moving to Nashville around 1845. First worked for the Tennessee Marine and Fire Insurance Company. On 26 May 1846, he enlisted under Captain R. C. Foster of Company L, 1st Tennessee Infantry Regiment (the "Bloody First") at Nashville. He served with gallantry throughout the Mexican War. Promoted to corporal then sergeant. During this service he served as a correspondent to one of the Nashville papers and wrote interesting accounts of his regiment's marches and battles. Discharged 23 May 1847 at New Orleans, LA. After the Mexican War, Godshall entered the mercantile business and later the boot and shoe business. Married Aramathia H. Webb, 27 September 1849. Three of their children (Frederick age 8, Douglas age 6, and Eugene age 4) died within hours of each other and were all three buried on 22 May 1860, victims of scarlet fever. A fourth child died just three weeks later of the same ailment, with all buried at the Nashville City Cemetery. Godshall organized the first infantry company in the state of Tennessee for Confederate service. His company was sworn into service on 10 May 1861 at Nashville. Elected captain at organization. Relieved of duty and discharged under the conscript law May 1862. He was a prominent member of the Odd Fellows. Died in Nashville, 5 October 1866 of cholera, with the funeral held at the First Baptist Church, the Reverend R. B. C. Howell presiding. Buried in the Nashville City Cemetery.[291]

Godwin, J. M.; Private, Company H: Sworn into service 14 May 1861 at Nashville. Discharged 10 September 1862 on a surgeon's certificate of disability. Rejoined the regiment. Killed in the Battle of Nashville, TN., 16 December 1864. Buried in Confederate Circle at Mt. Olivet Cemetery, Nashville, TN.[292]

Goff, Anderson; Private, Company F: Enlisted 18 May 1861 at Cedar Hill, TN. Teamster from 3 October to 13 December 1861. Died 20 March 1862 at the General Hospital in Knoxville, TN. Buried in the Bethel Cemetery, Knox Co., TN.[293]

Goff, Patrick; Second Sergeant, Company G: Occupation: laborer. Enlisted 3 June 1861 at Camp Cheatham. Extra duty in the Commissary Department since 22 July 1862. Appointed third sergeant, 1 February 1863. Age 28 on roll dated 30 May 1863 at Shelbyville, TN. Promoted to second sergeant by July 1863. Shot through the right lung in the Battle of Missionary Ridge, TN., 25 November 1863. Sent

---

[288] Glenn, Pension Application.
[289] Gordon, *Confederate Cemeteries*, 36.
[290] Maney, *Surgeon's Log*, "20 July 1864"; Maney, *Surgeon's Log*, "28-31 July 1864."
[291] Dobson-Sides, *1860 Davidson County Census*, 781; Reid Brock, Thomas O. Brock, and Tony Hays, *Volunteers-Tennessee in the War with Mexico, A-L*, vol. 1 (Nashville TN: Kitchen Table Press, 1986) 112; *Union and American*, 6 October 866; *Nashville Daily American*, 18 August 1885.
[292] United Daughters of the Confederacy, *Confederate Soldiers of Hickman County*, 86.
[293] Gordon, *Confederate Cemeteries*, 4.

to hospital. Killed in the Battle of Franklin, TN., 30 November 1864. Buried in the McGavock Confederate Cemetery, Franklin, TN., section 55 grave #52.[294]

Gooch, James William Monroe; Fifth Sergeant, Company F: Born 10 September 1839. Resided at Cedar Hill, TN. where he enlisted 18 May 1861. Elected second corporal at the organization. Drummer July through November 1862. Promoted to fifth sergeant by December 1862. Surrendered as a member of Company F, 2nd Consolidated Tennessee Infantry on 26 April 1865 at Greensboro, NC. Paroled 1 May 1865. Quoted as saying that he and Private James T. Bartlett were the only two of his company not wounded during the war out of 100 men, and that only thirteen of the company came back from the war. Member of the Methodist Church. Married Alice Adams in 1873. For a number of years, he was a member of the Robertson Co. Court. Died 9 May 1906. Buried in the Bartlett Cemetery, Robertson Co., TN.[295]

Goodrich, J. P.; Private, Company B: Sworn into service 10 May 1861 at Nashville. Discharged 16 August 1861 at Carter's Station, TN.

Goodwin, George Buchanan; Musician, Company B: Born 5 September 1821, in Davidson Co., TN., he was the son of George Moses Goodwin and Jane Trindle Buchanan. He married Martha Ann Barnes on 3 February 1842, in Davidson Co., TN. Sworn into service 10 May 1861 at Nashville. Died at Summit Hospital at Knoxville, TN., 4 June 1862. Buried in the Bethel Cemetery, Knox Co., TN.[296]

Goodwin, Henry H.; Third Corporal, Company G, B, D: Sworn into service 10 May 1861 in Company G. Elected third corporal at the organization. Transferred to Company B at the reorganization, 1 May 1862. Transferred to Company D, 1 July 1862. Absent without leave since 11 November 1862. Returned by March 1863. Age 22 on roll dated 2 June 1863 at Shelbyville, TN. Captured 3 July 1864 near Kennesaw Mountain, GA. Sent to the U. S. Military Prison at Louisville, KY. Forwarded to Camp Morton, IN., 14 July 1864. Released upon taking oath 22 March 1865.

Goodwin, J. L. C.; Private, Company B: Sworn into service 10 May 1861 at Nashville. Killed in Nashville, 10 December 1861 in a personal encounter.

Goodwin, John; Private, Company K: Born 1826 in Dickson Co., TN. Sworn into service 10 May 1862 in Dickson Co. Age 38 on roll dated 1 May 1863 at Shelbyville, TN. Admitted to Fair Ground Hospital #2, Atlanta, GA., 15 July 1863 for pneumonia, and died 21 July 1863. Buried in the Oakland Cemetery, Atlanta, GA.

Goodwin, Ruben; Fourth Corporal, Company K: Sworn into service 25 May 1861 at Nashville. Appointed fourth corporal, 1 May 1863. Captured 2 September 1864 at Jonesboro, GA. Sent to the U. S. Military Prison at Louisville, KY. Forwarded to Camp Douglas, IL., 29 October 1864. Took oath 16 May 1864.

Gordon, Brigadier General George Washington; Colonel, Company I, Field & Staff: Born 5 October 1836 at Brick Church, Giles Co., TN. Brother of Private W. H. H. "Harry" Gordon. Lived in Texas and Mississippi before returning to Tennessee to attend the Western Military Institute at Nashville under future Confederate General Bushrod Johnson. Graduated from the Western Military Institute in 1859 with a degree in Civil Engineering. Employed as a surveyor for the planned westward extension of the Nashville and Northwestern Railroad. During this time, he lived at a boarding house near the Tennessee River at Denver, Humphreys Co., TN. At the outbreak of the war, he joined the Gheber Guards in Humphreys Co. Due to his military training, Gordon was assigned to be drill-master for the regiment. He was promoted to captain of Company I, 1 August 1861. He was subsequently promoted to lieutenant-colonel at the regimental reorganization, 1 May 1862. Captured in the Battle of Tazewell, TN., but was soon exchanged and rejoined the regiment 15 August 1862. Promoted to colonel, 7

---

[294] Maney, *Surgeon's Log*, "Missionary Ridge TN"; Hudgins and Potts, *McGavock Cemetery*, 32.

[295] Bartlett notes, Robertson County Library, Springfield, Tennessee.

[296] Find-A-Grave Memorial, "Bethel Confederate Cemetery," http://www.findagrave.com/cgi-bin/fg.cgi?page=gr&GSln=Goodwin&GSfn=G&GSiman=1&GScid=9207&GRid=88182696& (15 August 2014); Gordon, *Confederate Cemeteries*, 12.

November 1862, and was wounded through the thigh and groin in the Battle of Murfreesboro, TN., 31 December 1862. Captured 5 January 1863, at a Murfreesboro hospital. Sent to Camp Chase, OH., 25 March 1863. Transferred to Fort Delaware, Delaware, 10 April 1863, age 26. Forwarded to City Point, VA. for exchange, which took place 29 April 1863. Rejoined the 11th Tennessee Regiment at Shelbyville, TN. Wounded in the left hip in the Battle of Atlanta, GA., 22 July 1864. Promoted to brigadier general dating from 15 August 1864. Wounded and captured in the Battle of Franklin, TN., 30 November 1864. Sent to Fort Warren, MA. Released July 1865. Complexion fair, hair brown, eyes hazel, height 5' 8". Postwar, he attended Cumberland University Law School at Lebanon, TN. Upon graduation, he practiced law in Pulaski, TN. with the firm of Rose and Gordon before moving to Memphis, TN. Married Ora S. Paine in September 1876, who died a few weeks after their marriage. Married (2) Minnie Hannah (1861-1928). Practiced law in Memphis until 1883 at which time he was appointed as a railroad commissioner for the State of TN. In 1885 he was appointed to a position with the Department of the Interior and served four years among the Western Indians. Returning to Memphis, in 1892 he was named Superintendent of Memphis Public Schools. Elected in 1906 to the U. S. House of Representatives for the 10th Congressional District of Tennessee, serving from 4 March 1907 until his death in 1911. He was the last Confederate General living in the State of Tennessee and the only Confederate General left in Congress. Served as Commander-in-Chief of the United Confederate Veterans. Present at the 14 June 1904 reunion of the 11th Tennessee Infantry in Nashville. General Gordon gave the dedication address for many Confederate monuments, including those for General Patrick Cleburne in Helena, AR. in 1891, the monument on the square at Franklin, TN. in 1899, and the Sam Davis monument in Pulaski, TN. in 1906. General Gordon had ties with the first Ku Klux Klan and was the first Grand Dragon of the Realm of Tennessee. He authored the Klan's *Precept*, a book describing its organization, purposes, and principles. Died 9 August 1911 of primary uremia; contributing factor, nephritis, and was buried in full Confederate uniform and with a Confederate flag in Elmwood Cemetery, Memphis, TN. His 1840 heavy cavalry saber is on display at the Tennessee State Museum in Nashville.[297]

Gordon, Richard Cross "Dick"; First Lieutenant, Company H: Born at Cottage Hill, Hickman Co. (now Maury Co.), TN., 25 February 1837. Obtained his secondary school education at the preparatory school of Professor Nathaniel Cross in Nashville, living at the time in the Felix Zollicoffer home, as Mrs. Zollicoffer, the former Pocahontas Gordon, was his cousin. Attended the University of North Carolina where he was in the Chi Psi fraternity, graduating in 1861. Sworn into service 14 May 1861 at Nashville. Elected second lieutenant at the organization. Elected first lieutenant at the reorganization, 1 May 1862. Resigned 14 February 1863 for acute rheumatism in the right hand and left knee. Married Mary Camp Webster, 20 August 1863. Occupied as a farmer, he also provided much service to the Maury County Courts. Elected in 1892 to the Tennessee State House of Representatives representing Maury Co. and reelected in 1894. A Democrat and a member of the Methodist-Episcopal Church. Resided at Cross Bridges, Maury Co., TN., where he died 8 April 1903. Funeral services were held at the St. Peters Church in Columbia. Buried at the Rose Hill Cemetery, Columbia, TN.[298]

---

[297] "Record of Gen. Gordon," 427-31; "Bivouac 18, A.C.S. and Camp 28 U.C.V.," 566; "Tributes to Gen. George W. Gordon"; Warner, *Generals*, 109-10; Maney, *Surgeon's Log*, "Stones River TN"; Stewart Sifakis, *Who was Who in the Confederacy: A Biographical Encyclopedia of More Than 1,000 Confederate Participants* (New York NY: Facts on File, 1988) 110; Evans, *Confederate History* vol. 10, 507-08; Maney, *Surgeon's Log*, "Battle of Atlanta GA"; Jack D. Welsh, *Medical Histories of Confederate Generals* (Kent OH: The Kent State University Press, 1995) 82; *Nashville Daily Press*, 3 December 1864; "Autographs From An Old Album," *Confederate Veteran*, 32 no. 4 (1924): 129; *Reunion Pamphlet*, 14 June 1904.

[298] Hunter McDonald, Unpublished Manuscript (4 January 1966, Nashville TN) Tennessee State Library and Archives Manuscript Division AC NO. 1132; Robert M. McBride, Don M. Robison, and Ilene J. Cornwell, *Biographical Directory of the Tennessee General Assembly* vol. 2 1861-1901 (Nashville

Gordon, W. G.; Private, Company H: Enlisted 13 February 1863 at Shelbyville, TN. Deserted 20 January 1864 or 1865.

Gordon, William Henry Harrison "Harry"; Private, Company H: Occupation: farmer. Brother of Brigadier General George W. Gordon. Transferred from Company A, 8th Texas Cavalry (Terry's Texas Rangers). Killed on the skirmish line in the Battle of New Hope Church, GA., 27 May 1864. Buried in the Oakland Cemetery, Atlanta, GA.[299]

Gorman, Marcus; First Sergeant, Company E, G: Sworn into service 18 May 1861 in Company E at Nashville. Age 27 on roll dated 16 August 1861. Transferred to Company G at the reorganization, 1 May 1862. Appointed third corporal, 1 November 1862. Promoted to third sergeant by July 1863. Promoted to first sergeant after February 1864. Wounded by an artillery shell in the Battle of Nashville, TN., 16 December 1864. Captured at Franklin, TN., 18 December 1864. Sent to the U. S. Military Prison at Louisville, KY., 4 January 1865. Forwarded to Camp Chase, OH., 9 January 1865. Complexion florid, hair brown, eyes gray, height 5' 5".

Gorman, Mark; Sergeant, Company B: Occupation: laborer. Wounded in the left knee at Kennesaw Mountain, GA., 23 June 1864.[300]

Gorman, Patrick; Private, Company K, G: Married Bridget Tearney, 30 May 1859. Sworn into service 25 May 1861 at Nashville in Company K. Age 22 on 16 August 1861 roll at Watauga Bridge, TN. Transferred to Company G at the reorganization, 1 May 1862. Admitted to Fair Ground Hospital #1, Atlanta, GA., 22 September 1863 for vulnus sclopeticum. Sent to another hospital on 23 September 1863. Listed as deserting at Chattanooga, TN., 11 November 1863. Captured 12 November 1863. Sent to the U. S. Military Prison at Louisville, KY. Complexion dark, hair dark, eyes blue, height 5' 9".[301]

Gossett, John Calvin; Private, Company H: Born 1838. Sworn into service 14 May 1861. Died 28 June 1862 at Bean Station, TN. Buried in the Bethel Cemetery, Knoxville, TN.[302]

Gossett, William Howell; Private, Company F: Occupation: farmer. Enlisted 18 May 1861 at Cedar Hill, TN. Teamster 1 June 1862. Wounded in the left leg below the knee in the Battle of Chickamauga, GA., 19 September 1863. Driving Confederate government wagons and hauling supplies, 24 April 1864. Sent to hospital at Griffin, GA. Captured in Itawamba Co., MS., 1 January 1865. Sent to the U. S. Military Prison at Louisville, KY. Forwarded to Camp Chase, OH., 16 January 1865. Complexion florid, hair dark, eyes blue, height 5' 11".[303]

Gotton, James W.; Private, Company F: Captured at Alexandria, TN., 25 April 1863. Sent to the U. S. Military Prison at Louisville, KY. Forwarded to City Point, VA.

Graig, James Polk; Rank unknown, Company unknown: Born 17 September, 1844 in Williamson Co., TN. Enlisted at the end of 1862 at Murfreesboro, TN. Wounded in the right wrist in the Battle of Nashville, TN., 16 December 1865. Following the war, resided at Bolivar, TN. Attended the reunion of the 11th Tennessee Infantry at Bon Aqua Springs, Hickman Co., TN., 24 September 1885.[304]

Graig, John C.; Third Sergeant, Company K: Sworn into service 25 May 1861 at Nashville. Promoted to first corporal, 16 November 1861. Elected third sergeant by July 1862. Missing in action in the Battle of Murfreesboro, TN., supposed killed.

TN: The Tennessee State Library & Archives and The Tennessee Historical Society, 1979) 346; "Death's Harvest," *Columbia Herald*, 10 April 1903.

[299] United Daughters of the Confederacy, *Confederate Soldiers of Hickman County*, 86; Maney, *Surgeon's Log*, "May 1864."

[300] Maney, *Surgeon's Log*, "Kennesaw Mountain GA."

[301] Sistler and Sistler, *Davidson County Marriages 1838-1863*, 85; Welsh, *Confederate Hospitals*, Patient Roster, Fair Ground Hospital #1, 105.

[302] Spence, *History*, 469; United Daughters of the Confederacy, *Confederate Soldiers of Hickman County*, 87; Gordon, *Confederate Cemeteries*, 14.

[303] Maney, *Surgeon's Log*, "Chickamauga GA"; Jackson, "Letter to Parents," 14 July 1864.

[304] James Polk Graig, Tennessee Pension Application, 3227; "The Reunion," *Hickman Pioneer*.

Gravitt, Andrew W.; Private, Company H: Born c. 1838. Occupation: saddler. Enlisted in Company H. Died at Camp Cheatham in June 1861.[305]

Gray, George A.; Private, Company K: Sworn into service 25 May 1861 at Nashville. Age 22 on roll dated 15 August 1861 at Midway, TN. Served as a steward at Gilmer Hospital, Marietta, GA., August 1863. Captured near Marietta, GA., 3 July 1864. Sent to the U. S. Military Prison at Louisville, KY. Forwarded to Camp Morton, IN., 13 July 1864. Admitted to U. S. Army Pest (smallpox) Hospital in Indianapolis, IN., in March 1865. Released from hospital, 10 March 1865. Released on oath, 20 May 1865. Complexion dark, hair dark, eyes hazel, height 5' 7".

Gray, James; Private, Company K: Sworn into service 25 May 1861 at Nashville. Deserted at Camp Cheatham, 23 July 1861. Returned to the regiment, 8 December 1861 at Cumberland Gap, TN. Age 26 on roll dated 1 May 1863 at Shelbyville, TN. Captured at Marietta, GA., 3 July 1864. Sent to the U. S. Military Prison at Louisville, KY. Forwarded to Camp Morton, IN., 13 July 1864. Died 14 February 1865 from chronic diarrhea. Buried in Crown Hill Cemetery, Indianapolis, IN.[306]

Gray, James Franklin; Private, Company A: Born c. 1835. Sworn into service 10 May 1861 at Nashville. Wounded in the Battle of Rockcastle, KY., 21 October 1861. Admitted to Ocmulgee Hospital at Macon, GA., 21 May 1864 for unknown reason. Killed in the Battle of Franklin, TN., 30 November 1864. Buried in the McGavock Confederate Cemetery, Franklin, TN., Section 54, Grave #49.[307]

Gray, James M.; Private, Company H: Occupation: farmer. Sworn into service 14 May 1861 at Nashville. Wardmaster at Knoxville, TN. hospital from 21 October 1862. Wounded in the left hand in the Battle of New Hope Church, GA., 27 May 1864. Admitted to Asylum Hospital, Madison, GA., 30 May 1864. Returned to duty 8 July 1864. Captured in the Battle of Atlanta, GA., 22 July 1864. Sent to the U.S. Military Prison at Louisville, KY. Forwarded to Camp Chase, OH., 31 July 1864.[308]

Gray, James W.; Private, Company K: Sworn into service 25 May 1861 at Nashville. Extra duty as a teamster, 18 August 1862. Blacksmith 1 September 1862. Age 31 on roll dated 1 May 1863 at Shelbyville, TN. Admitted to the S. P. Moore Hospital, Griffin, GA, 28 June 1864. Deserted and captured 3 July 1864 near Marietta, GA. Sent to the U. S. Military Prison at Louisville, KY. Forwarded to Camp Morton, IN., 13 July 1864. Released on oath 1 May 1865.[309]

Gray, Joseph; Rank unknown, Company H: From Perry Co., TN. No further.

Gray, Samuel B.; Quartermaster Sergeant, Company H: Born 1838. Sworn into service 14 May 1861 at Nashville. Detailed to the quartermaster department September and October 1861. Killed in the Battle of Chickamauga, GA., 19 September 1863.[310]

Gray, William C. "Billy"; Private, Company C: Occupation: farmer. Captured after the Battle of Murfreesboro, TN., 6 January 1863. Sent to City Point, VA., 11 February 1863. Forwarded to Fort McHenry, MD., 15 February 1863. Exchanged and rejoined company. Wounded in the back in the Battle of New Hope Church, GA., 27 May 1864.[311]

Green, Michael; Third Sergeant, Company G: Sworn into service 10 May 1861 at Nashville. Promoted to first corporal by March 1862. Promoted to third sergeant by July 1862. Killed in the Battle of Murfreesboro, TN., 31 December 1862.

Green, Robert W.; Private, Company G: Sworn into service 10 May 1861 at Nashville. Discharged 10 August 1862 by the conscript law.

---

[305] United Daughters of the Confederacy, *Hickman County Census 1860*, 120; United Daughters of the Confederacy, *Confederate Soldiers of Hickman County*, 88.

[306] Information from personal phone call from Neil Brown, 4 September 2003.

[307] Johnson, *1860 Census of Humphreys County*, 125; Hudgins and Potts, *McGavock Cemetery*, 32.

[308] Maney, *Surgeon's Log*, "May 1864;" Harris, *Confederate Hospitals*, 75, 87, 424.

[309] *Chattanooga Daily Rebel*, 28 June 1864.

[310] Welsh, *Confederate Hospitals*, Patient Roster, Fair Ground Hospital #1, 80; United Daughters of the Confederacy, *Confederate Soldiers of Hickman County*, 89.

[311] Maney, *Surgeon's Log*, "May 1864."

Green, Samuel Marion; Private, Company C: Born in Maury Co., TN., 7 October 1838. Sworn into service, 14 May 1861 at Nashville. Issued a minie musket. Captured between Murfreesboro and Chattanooga, TN. Taken to Nashville and took oath. Transferred to the 4th Tennessee, 20 December 1862. Died 25 January 1926. Buried in the Anderson Cemetery, Cheatham Co., TN.[312]

Green, William H. "Bill"; Major, Company C, Field & Staff: Born 1829 in Dickson Co., TN. Occupation: cabinet maker. Married Rebecca E. Massie, 3 July 1852. Sworn into service 14 May 1861 at Nashville. Elected captain of Company C at the organization. Promoted to major, 7 November 1862. Age 33 on roll dated 8 May 1863 at Shelbyville, TN. Detached to Dawson's Battalion Sharpshooters during the month of September, 1863. Killed in the Battle of Missionary Ridge, TN., 25 November 1863.[313]

*Greer, Daniel Webster "Web"; Private, Company F: Born 5 May 1839. Occupation: blacksmith. Enlisted 18 May 1861 at Cedar Hill, TN. Wounded in the right lumbar region in the Battle of Atlanta, GA., 22 July 1864. Surrendered as a member of Company F, 2nd Consolidated Tennessee Infantry at Greensboro, NC., 26 April 1865. Paroled 1 May 1865. Resided at Holmansville, Robertson Co., TN. Member of the Harmony Primitive Baptist Church. Died 4 March 1910. Buried in the Norfleet Cemetery, Robertson Co., TN.[314]

Greer, Richard T. "Dick"; Private, Company E, H: Born 1829. Married. Resided in the Shady Grove community along Leatherwood Creek, Hickman Co., TN. Sworn into service, 18 May 1861 in Company E at Nashville. Transferred to Company H, 1 May 1862 at the reorganization. Died at Bragg Hospital, Newnan, GA., 14 November 1863 of chronic diarrhea. Buried in the Confederate section, Oak Hill Cemetery, Newnan, GA.[315]

Gregg, J. P.; Private, Company K: Enlisted 1 December 1862 in Dickson Co., TN. Age 20 on roll dated 1 May 1863 at Shelbyville, TN. Present through 31 October 1863. Killed in battle after September 1864.[316]

Grenille, A. W.; Private, Company H: Sworn into service 14 May 1861 at Nashville. Died 14 July 1862.

Griffin, William; Private, Company I: Enlisted 14 October 1861 at Cumberland Ford, KY. Discharged 15 August 1862 at Tazewell, TN. by authority of the conscript law.

Griffis, Francis M.; Private, Company B: Sworn into service 10 May 1861 at Nashville. On extra duty as a teamster September 1861 through January 1862. Absent without leave 31 December 1862. Listed as a deserter at Shelbyville, TN., 15 January 1863. Present July 1863. Took oath 22 December 1864. Complexion dark, hair dark, eyes hazel, 5' 7".

Grimes, Daniel W.; N/A, Company C: One of four known black men to serve with the 11th Tennessee Infantry. Born in Charlotte, Dickson Co., TN., 2 February 1845. Servant of John A. Wynn. Served with the 11th Tennessee until Wynn was fatally wounded in the Battle of Franklin, TN., 30 November 1864. Daniel returned to Springfield, TN. with Wynn's body. Lived at Cedar Hill, Robertson Co., TN. after the war. Wife's name was Mary. Occupation: farmer. Died 8 February 1935 in Springfield, TN., aged 90, of chronic nephritis. Buried in the Mount Olive Cemetery, Springfield, Robertson Co., TN.[317]

---

[312] Samuel Green, Tennessee Pension Application, 15442; McCauley, *Record Book, Company C*.

[313] Baker, *1850 Census for Dickson County*, 98; Baker, *1860 Census for Dickson County*, 15; Maney, *Surgeon's Log*, "Missionary Ridge TN."

[314] Maney, *Surgeon's Log*, "Battle of Atlanta GA"; Durrett, Williams, and Reid, *Robertson County Cemetery Records*, 67; Gregory, G. Poole, *Robertson County Obituaries and Death Records 1803-1930* (Nashville TN: Land Yacht Press, 1993) 105.

[315] *Hickman County News*, 9 March 1899; United Daughters of the Confederacy, *Confederate Soldiers of Hickman County*.

[316] Lindsley, *Annals*, 306.

[317] Daniel W. Grimes, Colored Man's Pension Application No. 228.

Grimes, John Preston "Press"; Private, Company E: Born in Dickson Co., TN., 16 October 1847. Sworn into service 18 May 1861 at Nashville. Age 18 on roll dated 16 August 1861 at Watauga Bridge, TN. Deserted. Returned 25 December 1862. Wounded through the thigh in the Battle of Chickamauga, GA., 19 September 1863. Admitted to Fair Ground Hospital #1, Atlanta, GA., 24 September 1863. Sent to another hospital 25 September 1863. Sent to hospital in Montgomery, AL. Teamster 20 February to 31 March 1864. Surrendered as a member of Company C, 2nd Consolidated Tennessee Infantry, with the Army of Tennessee at Greensboro, NC., 26 April 1865. Paroled 1 May 1865. Married Doney Stokes. Member of the Oak Grove Free Will Baptist Church. Politically a Democrat. Died 16 October 1935 at daughter's home on Johnson Creek. Buried in the Jackson Cemetery, Dickson Co., TN.[318]

Grimes, Thomas J.; Private, Company E: Born 1 January 1840 in Dickson Co., TN. Resided at Kingston Springs, Cheatham Co., TN. Sworn into service 18 May 1861 at Nashville. Age 21 on roll dated 16 August 1861 at Watauga Bridge, TN. Extra duty in quartermaster department October 1861, November and December 1862, and February and March 1864. Surrendered at Chester, SC. in April 1865. Paroled 1 May 1865.[319]

Grimes, Thomas R.; Musician, Company H, Field & Staff: Sworn into service 14 May 1861 in Company H at Nashville. On sick furlough since 10 September 1861. Away with regimental band at Dalton, GA., September through 15 December 1862 by orders of General Stevenson. Appointed musician and transferred to the Field & Staff, 1 November 1862. Deserted 1 February 1865. Took oath 16 February 1865. Complexion dark, hair dark, eyes hazel, 5' 9".

Griner, Lewis P.; Private. Company H: Sworn into service 14 May 1861. Discharged 20 March 1862.

Griner, W. J.; Private. Company H: Born in Hickman Co., TN. Occupation: farmer. Enlisted 25 July 1861 at Nashville. Discharged 15 April 1862 at Cumberland Gap, TN., age 24. Complexion dark, hair dark, eyes gray, 5' 6".

Grubbs, Joseph P.; Chief Musician, Company F, Field & Staff: Born 31 July 1829 in Louisa Co., VA. Relocated to Kentucky in 1839, residing at West Fork, Christian Co., KY. Enlisted 18 May 1861 in Company F at Cedar Hill, TN. Appointed Chief Musician and transferred to the Field & Staff, 10 August 1861. Hospitalized for 5 days following the Battle of Franklin, TN., 30 November 1864 due to a carbuncle on the hand. Obtained furlough and traveled to Charlotte, TN., remaining for a period of 3 weeks. Returned on horseback with arm in a sling, along with Adjutant Wm. J. Mathis, to the Regiment at Corinth, arriving around 1 January 1865. Transferred to the quartermaster department and accompanied the wagons from Corinth, MS. to Augusta, GA. Surrendered and paroled at Augusta, GA., 10 May 1865. Resided at West Fork, Christian Co., KY. Pension Application Kentucky 757.[320]

Guilford, Edward J.; Captain, Company G, Field & Staff: Enlisted 3 June 1861 at Nashville. Elected second lieutenant of Company G at the organization. Appointed regimental quartermaster, 5 October 1861 and transferred to the Field & Staff. Elected captain of Company G at the reorganization, 1 May 1862. Elected quartermaster at the resignation of E. A. Hornbeak around December 1862. Left his command at Bean Station, TN. in July 1862 on a surgeon's certificate of disability. Traveled to Knoxville where he remained until March 1863 during which time he did not report to his commanding officers as

---

[318] Goodspeed Brothers, *Goodspeed's Histories of Montgomery, Robertson, Humphreys, Stewart, Dickson, Cheatham, Houston Counties*, 1339; J. P. Grimes, Tennessee Confederate Pension Application, S16568; Welsh, *Confederate Hospitals*, Patient Roster, Fair Ground Hospital #1, 109; *Dickson County Herald*, 25 October 1935; Marian G. Harris, "Grymes (Grimes)" in *The Heritage of Dickson County, Tennessee, 1803-2006, Dickson County Heritage Book Committee*, (Waynesville NC: County Heritage Inc., 2007) 246-47.

[319] T. J. Grimes, Tennessee Pension Application, 10106.

[320] Stephen D. Lynn, *Confederate Pensioners of Kentucky: Pension Applications of the Veterans & Widows, 1912-1946* (Baltimore MD; Sebree KY: Gateway Press 2000) 105.

requested to do so. Left Knoxville and proceeded to West Tennessee by way of Shelbyville. Remained at Shelbyville for a period, still not reporting to his company, then continued on. Last heard from near Paducah, KY. Declared unfit for command and dropped from the roll.

Gunn, Edward W.; Second Lieutenant, Company F: Born 25 December 1840. Resided at Cedar Hill, Robertson Co., TN., where he enlisted 18 May 1861. Elected fourth sergeant at the organization. Reduced to private. Captured at Richmond, KY. in late 1862. Exchanged. Promoted to second sergeant by January 1864. Shot through the body and the foot in the Battle of Atlanta, GA., 22 July 1864. Listed as second lieutenant, Company F, 2nd Consolidated Tennessee Infantry. Surrendered with the Army of Tennessee, 26 April 1865 at Greensboro, NC. Paroled 1 May 1865.[321]

Gunn, Miles A.; Private, Company F: Born 1834. Enlisted 12 August 1861 at Loudon, TN. On sick furlough since 13 September 1861. Missing in action in the Battle of Murfreesboro, TN., 31 December 1862. Rejoined unit. Wounded in the left hip in the Battle of Franklin, TN., 30 November 1864. Captured at Franklin on 17 December 1864. Sent to the U. S. Military Prison at Louisville, KY. Forwarded to Camp Chase, OH., 17 January 1865. Sent to Jackson Hospital, Richmond, VA. where he died 15 May 1865. Buried in grave #127 at the Hollywood Cemetery, Richmond, VA.[322]

Gunn, William Bowling; Private, Company F: Born 25 August 1843. Enlisted 18 May 1861 at Cedar Hill, TN. Died at Camp Cheatham, 26 July 1861. Buried in the Gunn Cemetery, Robertson Co., TN.

Guthrie, Rodger; Private, Company G: Enlisted 3 June 1861 at Camp Cheatham. Age 24 on roll dated 30 May 1863 at Shelbyville, TN. Captured in the Battle of Nashville, TN., 16 December 1864. Sent to the U. S. Military Prison at Louisville, KY. Forwarded to Camp Chase, OH. Took oath 12 May 1865. Complexion dark, hair brown, eyes dark, 5' 10".[323]

Guy, John F.; Private, Company G: Sworn into service 10 May 1861 at Nashville. Discharged by the conscript law 10 August 1862 at Tazewell, TN.

-H-

Hadley, Jerome J.; Private, Company G: Sworn into service 10 May 1861 at Nashville. Discharged by the conscript law, 1 August 1861.

Haffy, John; Private, Company D: Sworn into service 11 May 1861 at Nashville. On sick furlough since 25 May 1861.

Haile, George Washington; Private, Company A: Born 23 July 1843 in Hickman Co., TN. His father had been a captain in the 97th Regiment, Tennessee State Militia. Enlisted 25 November 1862 at Lenoir Station, TN. Captured in the Battle of Missionary Ridge, TN., 25 November 1863. Sent to the U. S. Military Prison at Louisville, KY. Forwarded to Rock Island, IL., 9 December 1863. Complexion fair, hair dark, eyes gray, 5' 8". Postwar, resided in Humphreys Co., TN. where he married Mary Anne Turner, 2 May 1868. Occupation: farmer. Relocated to Des Arc, AR. in 1872, and died there, 16 May 1901. Buried in the Haile Cemetery, Snell, Cleburne CO., AR. Pension Application, Arkansas Widow, Cleburne Co., 1904.[324]

Haile, William Wallace; Musician (Drummer), Company B, Field & Staff: Born c. 1838 in TN. Occupied as a painter and musician prior to the war. Sworn into service 10 May 1861 in Company B and was appointed a musician at the organization. Under arrest in Knoxville, TN., April 1862. Transferred to McCann's Cavalry Battalion, 8 February 1863. Transferred back to the Field & Staff of the 11th

---

[321] Maney, *Surgeon's Log*, "Battle of Atlanta GA"; E. W. Gunn, Tennessee Pension Application, 9572.
[322] Poole, *Robertson County Obituaries and Death Records*, 107.
[323] *Nashville Daily Press*, 22 December 1864.
[324] Welsh, *Arkansas Pension Applications by Tennessee Veterans*, 2.11.

Tennessee from the 2nd Tennessee Regiment. Shot in the arm by accident, 7 December 1863. Sent to hospital in Atlanta, GA. Wounded in the left groin in the Battle of Resaca, GA., 14 May 1864.[325]

Hakewessell, Felix; Private, Company I: Born c. 1825 in Germany. Employed as a construction worker on the Nashville and Northwestern Railroad in Humphreys Co., TN. Sworn into service 20 May 1861 at Nashville. Discharged by the conscript law, 15 August 1862 at Tazewell, TN.[326]

*Hale, Joseph D.; Private, Company A: Born c. 1841. Occupation: farmer. Sworn into service 1 May 1861 at Nashville. Wounded in the head in the Battle of Murfreesboro, TN., 31 December 1862. Age 22 on roll dated 6 May 1863 at Shelbyville, TN. Wounded in the left shoulder while on picket duty, 23 November 1863 at Missionary Ridge, TN. Admitted to Floyd Hospital, 28 November 1863 for a gunshot wound. Surrendered as a member of Company F, 2nd Consolidated Tennessee Infantry with the Army of Tennessee, 26 April 1865. Paroled 1 May 1865.[327]

Hale, Rufus A.; Private, Company A: Born c. 1837. Sworn into service 10 May 1861 at Nashville. Died 12 April 1862 at Cumberland Gap, TN.[328]

Hall, Benjamin Franklin "Tobe"; Private, Company K: Born in Dickson Co., TN., 7 November 1839. Resided in Burns, TN. Occupation: farmer. Sworn into service 25 May 1861 in Nashville. Suffered from rheumatism at Camp Cheatham. Age 21 on roll dated 15 August 1861 at Midway, TN. On indefinite sick furlough from 13 September 1861, during which he married Mary Brown, 20 March 1862. Developed typhoid fever. Given a medical discharge by Dr. Maney at Shelbyville, TN. in January 1863. Forced to take oath to avoid going to a Federal prison. Attended the reunion of the 11th Tennessee Infantry at Bon Aqua Springs, Hickman Co., TN., 24 September 1885. Died 28 March 1909. Buried in the Hall Cemetery, Burns, Dickson Co., TN.[329]

Hall, Joseph J.; Private, Company G: Born in Delaware Co., PA. Occupation: apothecary. Enlisted 20 June 1861 at Camp Cheatham. Discharged December 1861 for chronic rheumatism, age 22. Complexion light, hair dark, eyes dark, 5' 6".

Halliburton, Charles "Charley"; Private, Company C: Born in Dickson Co., TN., 29 November 1840. Uncle of Private Turner Halliburton. Sworn into service 14 May 1861 at Nashville. On extra duty as a teamster, 14 January 1862. Issued a Belgium musket. Age 22 on roll dated 18 May 1863 at Shelbyville, TN. Wounded in the left leg by a conical ball during the Battle of Franklin, TN., 30 November 1864, requiring amputation at the middle third of the leg. Captured at Franklin, TN. following the retreat of the Confederate Army of Tennessee on 17 December 1864. Sent to the U. S. General Hospital #1 at Nashville. Following his recovery, he was transferred to the U. S. Military Prison at Louisville, KY., and was later forwarded to Camp Chase, OH., 12 March 1865, and then transferred to Point Lookout, MD., 25 March 1865. Released 5 June 1865. Married Mary Oliver in 1887 at Gibson Co., TN. According to his grandson, Charles would never allow his family to wear blue clothing. Died 21 April 1897 in Memphis, TN. Believed to be buried in the Ragan Cemetery, Dickson Co., TN.[330]

Halliburton, John Calvin; Private, Company C: Born 1843. Occupation: farmhand. Enlisted 7 December 1862 at Waverly, TN. in Napier's Battalion Cavalry, later Company E, 10th Tennessee

---

[325] Dobson-Sides, *1860 Davidson County Census*, 486; Maney, *Surgeon's Log*, "May 1864."

[326] Johnson, *1860 Census of Humphreys County*, 150.

[327] Johnson, *1860 Census of Humphreys County*, 83; Thedford, "Report of Operations"; Maney, *Surgeon's Log*, "Missionary Ridge TN."

[328] Johnson, *1860 Census of Humphreys County*, 52.

[329] B. F. Hall, Tennessee Pension Application, 6146; "The Reunion," *Hickman Pioneer*; Sistler and Sistler, *1880 Census of Dickson County*, 27; Garrett and McClain, *Dickson County Cemetery Records* vol. 1, 174; Martha Hall Barfield, "John Hall Family" in *The Heritage of Dickson County, Tennessee, 1803-2006, Dickson County Heritage Book Committee*, (Waynesville NC: County Heritage Inc., 2007) 250.

[330] Robert K. Halliburton, Personal Records on ancestor, Charles Halliburton, 5 September 1998; McCauley, *Record Book, Company C.*

Cavalry. Transferred to the 11th Tennessee Infantry, 1 August 1863 at Chattanooga, TN. In hospital at Kingston, GA. in August 1863. Died 17 April 1864 at Dalton, GA. of chronic diarrhea.[331]

Halliburton, Turner Howard; Private, Company C: Born 8 October 1841 in Dickson Co., TN. Nephew of Private Charles Halliburton. Enlisted 4 September 1861 at Knoxville, TN. Issued a minie musket, and later a Springfield rifle. Age 23 on roll dated 8 May 1863 at Shelbyville, TN. Captured in the Battle of Franklin, TN., 30 November 1864. Sent to the U. S. Military Prison at Louisville, KY. Forwarded to Camp Douglas, IL., 6 December 1864. Forwarded to Point Lookout, MD. Released 27 June 1865. Complexion light, hair brown, eyes gray, 5' 6". Married Virginia A. Boaz, 7 November 1866. Member of the Forbes Bivouac, Association of Confederate Soldiers. Died at his home in Clarksville, Montgomery Co., TN., 28 January 1898, and buried in the Greenwood Cemetery there.[332]

Hamilton, James G.; Private, Company unknown: Took oath at Fort Delaware, Delaware, 10 June 1865. Complexion fair, hair light, eyes gray.

Hamilton, William A.; Musician, Company C: Sworn into service 25 May 1861 at Nashville. Age 23 at Midway, TN., 15 August 1861. Present through 30 April 1862. No further.

Hamlet, Robert; Private, Company B: Sworn into service 10 May 1861 at Nashville. Detached to the quartermaster department, September through December 1862. Age 27 on roll dated 2 June 1863. Took oath at Chattanooga, TN., 14 July 1864. Complexion light, hair dark, eyes hazel, 5' 8".

Hammon, Samuel; Private, Company K: Born in Dickson Co., TN., 10 October 1845, residing near Spencer's Mill. Enlisted at Spring Hill, TN., 1 November 1864. Captured in the Battle of Nashville, TN. Sent to the U. S. Military Prison at Louisville, KY. Transferred to Camp Chase, OH., 4 January 1865. Took oath 13 May 1865. Complexion fair, hair dark, eyes blue, 5' 10". Died 28 June 1928. Buried in the Hammon Cemetery, Dickson Co., TN.[333]

Hanah, Joseph; Private, Company A: Enlisted 20 March 1863 at Shelbyville, TN. Age 32 on roll dated 6 May 1863 at Shelbyville, TN.

Hanan, Michael, Private, Company D: Sworn into service 11 May 1861 at Nashville. Wounded in the head at the Battle of Murfreesboro, TN., 31 December 1862 and captured. Sent to Camp Butler, IL. Paroled and rejoined the regiment. In hospital at Rome, GA., 20 May 1863. Captured at Atlanta, GA., 28 July 1864. Sent to Camp Chase, OH. Released 14 May 1865. Complexion dark, hair dark, eyes dark, 5' 7".

Handlin, John Nathaniel; Second Corporal, Company C: Born 27 August 1843 in Henry Co., TN. Sworn into service 14 May 1861 at Nashville. Elected second corporal at the organization. Demoted to third corporal by January 1863. Age 19 on roll dated 8 May 1863 at Shelbyville, TN. Listed as deserting on the retreat from Tullahoma to Chattanooga, 2 July 1863. Married Georgia Shelton, 13 March 1864. Licensed to preach in the Methodist Episcopal Church on 13 February 1869 and served in churches as a local minister in the Yellow Creek vicinity of Dickson Co., TN. Received into the Tennessee Conference on 7 October 1877 and was ordained an elder in 1879. Given the Beaver Dam charge for his first work, he would serve in the ministry for over forty years. For additional income, he split rails, cut wheat and oats, and picked cotton for .50 cents a hundred pounds. In 1917 he was superannuated and still preached occasionally. Stated if he had his life to live over he would be a pastor again. Following the death of his first wife in 1919, he married Dora Myers Davidson, 15 March 1922. Described as "tall, slender though well-proportioned, lithe, and energetic. His eye was keen and piercing, modified by a twinkle which

---

[331] Robert K. Halliburton, Personal Records of relative, John Calvin Halliburton, 5 September 1998.

[332] Robert K. Halliburton, Personal Records of ancestor, Turner Halliburton, 5 September 1998; McCauley, *Record Book, Company C*; "Turner Halliburton," *Confederate Veteran* vol. 6 no. 3 (March 1898): 110; *Nashville Daily Press*, 3 December 1864.

[333] Samuel Hammon, Tennessee Confederate Pension Application No. S3793; Other information provided by historian, Dennis Lampley; *Nashville Daily Press*, 22 December 1864.

betokened a kind and loving heart." Died at his home in Waverly, TN., 13 December 1937, age 94. Buried in the Marable Cemetery, Humphreys Co., TN.[334]

Handlin, Thomas J.; Corporal, Company C: Sworn into service 14 May 1861 at Nashville. Issued a minie musket, and later reissued a Belgium musket. Deserted on the retreat from Tullahoma to Chattanooga, 2 July 1863. Captured in Dickson Co., TN., 19 December 1863. Sent to the U. S. Military Prison at Louisville, KY. Forwarded to Rock Island, IL., 17 January 1864.[335]

Hannah, Benjamin Franklin; Private, Company E, A: Born 6 January 1843 in Davidson Co., TN. Enlisted 18 October 1861 in Company E, at Cumberland Ford, KY. Transferred to Company A at the reorganization, 1 May 1862. Sick in hospital at Bean Station, TN., 26 October 1862. Age 22 on roll dated 6 May 1863 at Shelbyville, TN. Wounded in the Battle of Chickamauga, GA., 19 September 1863. Struck on the left nipple over the heart by a spent minie ball. Unconscious for several hours and disabled for five or six days. Wounded on the head and in the leg in the Battle of Missionary Ridge, TN., 25 November 1863. Captured near Atlanta, GA. on the Eddewall Road, 4 July 1864. Sent to Camp Douglas, IL. Took oath, 14 July 1864. Released from Camp Douglas, 13 May 1865. Complexion ruddy, hair dark, eyes gray, 5' 8". Resided at Shacklett and later Kingston Springs, both in Cheatham Co., TN. Buried in the Scott Cemetery, Cheatham Co., TN.

Hansberry, John; Private, Company G: Enlisted 3 June 1861 at Camp Cheatham. Wounded in the Battle of Rockcastle, KY., 21 October 1861. Discharged 13 August 1862 at Tazewell, TN. by virtue of the conscript act.

Harbison, John; Private, Company F: Enlisted 17 October 1861 at Nashville. Present through April 1862. No further.

Harbison, John M.; Private, Company H: Born 1839. Sworn into service 14 May 1861 at Nashville. Brigade teamster, 1 May 1862. Wounded and captured September 1863 near Chattanooga, TN.[336]

Hargrove, D.; Sergeant, Company E: Given medical furlough 11 December 1863. No further.

Harlow, John; Private, Company G: Born c. 1837 in Tennessee. Occupation: carpenter. Sworn into service 10 May 1861 at Nashville. Discharged on surgeon's certificate, 10 September 1861.

*Harper, John H.; Sergeant-Major, Company B, Field & Staff: Sworn into service 10 May 1861 in Company B at Nashville. Elected second corporal at the organization. Promoted to sergeant-major, 1 November 1862 and transferred to the Field & Staff. Age 28 on roll dated 2 June 1863 at Shelbyville, TN. Acting Adjutant since 25 November 1863. Surrendered as sergeant-major of the 2nd Consolidated Tennessee Infantry with the Army of Tennessee, 26 April 1865. Paroled 1 May 1865.

Harris, B. E. W.; Private, Company A: Born c. 1816 in Virginia. Captured 14 April 1865 at Knoxville, TN. No further.

Harris, George; Private, Company H: Born 1841. Enlisted in Company H, 11th TN. Buried in the Oakland Cemetery, Atlanta, GA.[337]

*Harris, Thomas Jefferson; Private, Company K: Born 14 March 1847 in Dickson Co., TN. Enlisted 20 December 1864. Contracted diarrhea at Bentonville, NC. Surrendered with the Army of Tennessee, 26 April 1865 at Greensboro, NC. Resided near Burns, TN. Died 4 March 1936. Buried in the Union Cemetery, Dickson, Dickson Co., TN.[338]

Harris, William; Private, Company K: Born 1842 in Dickson Co., TN. Sworn into service 25 May 1861 at Nashville. Age 18 on roll dated 15 August 1861 at Midway, TN. Died 17 September, 1861 at the hospital in Knoxville, TN.

---

[334] John N. Handlin, Tennessee Confederate Pension Application, S16360; Gladys P. Anderson and Jill Knight Garrett, *Humphreys County, Tennessee, Cemetery Records* vol. 1 rev. ed. (s.l.: Gladys P. Anderson and Jill Knight Garrett, 1978) 88.
[335] McCauley, *Record Book, Company C*.
[336] United Daughters of the Confederacy, *Confederate Soldiers of Hickman County*, 97.
[337] Ibid., 98.
[338] T. J. Harris, Tennessee Pension Application, 9308; *Dickson County Herald*, 1 March 1936.

Harrison, Eugene A.; Private, Company G, A, D: Occupation: mechanic. Sworn into service 10 May 1861 in Company G at Nashville. Transferred to Company A, 1 May 1862. Transferred to Company D, 1 July 1862. Age 23 on roll dated 5 May 1863. Wounded in the lower left arm by a shell fragment on the first day of the Battle of Jonesboro, GA., 31 August 1864. Wounded by a conical ball in the left thigh on the first day of the Battle of Nashville, TN., 15 December 1864. Captured at Franklin, TN., 18 December 1864. Sent to the U. S. Military Prison at Louisville, KY. Forwarded to Camp Chase, OH., 9 January 1865. Paroled or exchanged and rejoined unit. Surrendered as a member of Company C, 2nd Consolidated Tennessee Infantry with the Army of Tennessee, 26 April 1865. Paroled 1 May 1865.[339]

Harrison, John M.; Private, Company unknown: Sworn into service 15 May 1861 at Nashville. Deserted 15 December 1864. Complexion fair, hair light, eyes hazel, 5' 9".

Harrison, Tobe; Private, Company D: No further.[340]

Harrison, William Henry; Private, Company F: Enlisted 18 May 1861 at Cedar Hill, TN. Captured and released on oath 27 January 1864.

Harvey, Onesiphorus (Oney) S. "Tip"; Private, Company C: Born in Dickson Co., TN., 15 April 1840. Resided in Montgomery Co., TN. Sworn into service 14 May 1861 at Nashville. Issued a minie musket. Captured at Murfreesboro, TN., 5 January 1863. Exchanged and rejoined company. Captured at the Battle of Missionary Ridge, TN., 25 November 1863. Sent to the U. S. Military Prison at Louisville, KY. Forwarded to Rock Island, IL. Released 19 May 1865. Married Mary Frances Hickerson, 24 June 1866 at Charlotte, TN. Member of the Baptist Church. Died 20 September 1920. Buried in the Mount Zion Cemetery, Montgomery Co., TN.[341]

Haslem, William B.; Private, Company D: Sworn into service 11 May 1861 at Nashville. Transferred to Felt's Company, Nashville Infantry Battalion, and elected lieutenant. No further.[342]

Hassell, Alfred Britton; Private, Company H: Born 1845 in Hickman Co., TN. Half-brother of soldiers, Artin, Joseph, and Zebulon Hassell. Enlisted 6 February 1863 at Shelbyville, TN. Surrendered as a member of Company K, 2nd Consolidated Tennessee Infantry with the Army of Tennessee at Greensboro, NC., 26 April 1865. Paroled 1 May 1865. Married Temperance "Tempy" Caroline Truett, 11 September 1866.[343]

Hassell, Artin; Private, Company H: Born 1828 in Hickman Co., TN. Occupation: Blacksmith. Brother of Joseph and Zebulon Hassell, and half-brother of Alfred Hassell. Mexican War veteran. Married Martha Gardner, 18 December 1845, and remarried prior to 1860. Sworn into service 14 May 1861 at Nashville. Discharged 1 May 1862 with surgeon's certificate. After serving with the 11th Tennessee, he later served in Company C, 9th Tennessee Cavalry Battalion. Married (3) Mary O'Guinn Harrington, 13 April 1863. Died 24 September 1868, having been stabbed in a personal conflict with former Sergeant Griffin Nichols at Shady Grove, Hickman Co., TN.[344]

Hassell, Joseph H.; Private, Company H: Born 20 June 1840 in Hickman Co., TN. Brother of Artin and Zebulon Hassell and half-brother of Alfred Britton Hassell. Married Hannah Parthenia Harrington. Enlisted 8 February 1863 at Shelbyville, TN. Deserted 1 December 1864. Took oath 19 January 1865.

---

[339] Maney, *Surgeon's Log*, "August 1864."
[340] Clayton, *History of Davidson County*, 187.
[341] McCauley, *Record Book, Company C*; O. S. Harvey, Tennessee Pension Application, 7159; *Clarksville Leaf Chronicle*, 24 September 1920.
[342] Clayton, *History of Davidson County*, 187.
[343] Information from Sarah Armistead, 1 March 2002.
[344] United Daughters of the Confederacy, *Confederate Soldiers of Hickman County*, 99; Spence, *History*, 34, 54; Sarah Armistead, *The Hassell Family of Hickman County and Their Descendants* (s.l.: s.n.) 43.

Complexion light, hair light, eyes hazel, 6' 1". Died 27 December 1870. Buried Harrington Cemetery, Hickman Co., TN.[345]

Hassell, Zebulon; Second Corporal, Company H: Born 21 December, 1837 in Hickman Co., TN. Brother of Artin and Joseph Hassell, and half-brother of Alfred B. Hassell. Sworn into service 14 May 1861 at Nashville. Appointed second corporal, 1 December 1861. Reduced back to private. Brigade teamster since 1 August 1862 by command of General Stevenson. Captured in the Battle of Vicksburg, MS., 4 July 1863. Paroled and rejoined the 11th Tennessee. Surrendered as a member of Company K, 2nd Consolidated Tennessee Infantry with the Army of Tennessee at Greensboro, NC., 26 April 1865. Paroled 1 May 1865. Married Nancy Seline Totty, 26 October 1865. Died 28 June 1907. Buried Hassell Cemetery, Hickman Co., TN.[346]

Hawkins, George N.; Private, Company F: Enlisted 18 May 1861 at Cedar Hill, TN. In hospital at Knoxville, TN., 13 September 1861. No further.

Hawkins, Martin; Private, Company C, G: Sworn into service 14 May 1861 in Company C at Nashville. Discharged at Tazewell, TN., 15 August 1862 by order of the conscript act. Later rejoined the 11th Tennessee. Captured in the Battle of Missionary Ridge, TN., 25 November 1863. Sent to the U. S. Military Prison at Louisville, KY. Forwarded to Rock Island, IL., 7 December 1863. Died of diarrhea, 23 December 1863. Buried south of prison barracks in grave #52.

Hawkins, William F.; Private, Company F: Enlisted 1 August 1861 at Camp Bradford. Died in hospital at Chattanooga, TN., 1 March 1863. Buried in the Confederate Cemetery, Chattanooga, TN.

*Hayes, Champion Lafayette "Champ"; Private, Company C: Born 8 April 1837 in Rutherford Co., TN. Brother of Private William A. Hayes. Occupation: farmer. Sworn into service 14 May 1861 at Nashville. Issued a Belgium musket. Paid an additional $4 for work performed on the medical house at Cumberland Gap, 1-16 December 1861. Admitted to Asylum Hospital, Madison, GA., 4 July 1864. Returned to duty 15 July 1864. Wounded in the right shoulder in the Battle of Peachtree Creek, GA., 20 July 1864. Spent four months in the hospital. Surrendered as a member of Company F, 2nd Consolidated Tennessee Infantry with the Army of Tennessee at Greensboro, NC., 26 April 1865. Paroled 1 May 1865. Married Margaret Jane Lloyd, 11 December 1865. Resided at Vanleer, Dickson Co., TN. where he returned to farming after the war. Member of the Cumberland Presbyterian Church. Later relocated to Clarksville, Montgomery Co., TN. where he died 28 March 1927. Buried in the Hayes Cemetery near Vanleer, Dickson Co., TN. Pension Application S6620.[347]

Hayes, William Abraham; Private, Company C: Born 10 July 1843 in Dickson Co., TN. Brother of Private C. L. Hayes. Enlisted in the 11th Tennessee in May 1861. Never wounded during the war. Captain McCauley permitted a furlough home in July 1864. While there, he caught influenza and was never able to rejoin his command. Married Mary Fredoney Potts, 13 January 1872. Resided at Cumberland Furnace, Dickson Co., TN. Died 1931. Buried in the Potts Cemetery, Dickson Co., TN.[348]

Hayes, William Hartwell; Private, Company C: Born 4 December 1837 in Dickson Co., TN. Married Sarah A. Hamlett, 20 March 1857. Sworn into service, 14 May 1861 at Nashville. Issued a minie musket. Deserted on the retreat from Tullahoma to Chattanooga, TN., 2 July 1863. Died 16 May 1922. Buried in the Hayes Cemetery, Fairview, Williamson Co., TN.[349]

---

[345] Information from Sarah Armistead, 1 March 2002.
[346] Ibid.
[347] C. L. Hayes, Tennessee Confederate Pension Application, 6620; McCauley, *Record Book, Company C*; Maney, *Surgeon's Log*, "20 July 1864"; Harris, *Confederate Hospitals*, 85, 90, 448; Garrett, *Dickson County Handbook*, 207.
[348] W. A. Hays, Tennessee Pension Application, 16330.
[349] McCauley, *Record Book, Company C*; Additional information from descendant, Jerry Anderson, and historian Dennis Lampley, 12 June 2002.

Hays, John; Private, Company A: Captured in the Battle of Missionary Ridge, TN., 25 November 1863. Sent to the U. S. Military Prison at Louisville, KY. Transferred to Rock Island, IL., 13 December 1863. Took oath, 22 May 1865. Complexion light, hair brown, eyes blue, 5' 3", age 48.

Hays, Silas; Private, Company B: Sworn into service 10 May 1861 at Nashville. Discharged at Camp Cheatham, 10 July 1861.

Heath, Burril; Private, Company E: Enlisted 22 July 1861 at Camp Cheatham. Age 23 on roll dated 16 August 1861 at Watauga Bridge, TN. Deserted at Cumberland Gap, TN., 10 May 1862.

Heath, John; Fourth Corporal, Company E: Born 1837. Occupation: farmer. Sworn into service 18 May 1861 at Nashville. Age 24 on roll dated 16 August 1861 at Watauga Bridge, TN. Appointed fourth corporal by July 1862. Killed in the Battle of Missionary Ridge, TN., 25 November 1863.[350]

Heckman, Charles E.; Hospital Steward, Company B: Born c. 1830 in Nova Scotia, Canada. Occupation: druggist. Sworn into service 10 May 1861 at Nashville. Hospital steward throughout entire service history. Captured near Nashville, TN., 17 December 1864. Sent to Camp Douglas, IL. Discharged 17 May 1865. Complexion fair, hair brown, eyes hazel, 5' 9".[351]

Hedgecock, Joseph; Private, Company A: Born 3 October 1830 in Humphreys Co., TN. Sworn into service 10 May 1861 at Nashville. Left in hospital at Knoxville, TN., 11 September 1861. Captured between Knoxville and Loudon, TN. Took oath at Knoxville and rejoined company. Left with the wounded after the Battle of Murfreesboro, TN. and captured. Sent to Camp Morton, IN., 25 February 1863. Forwarded to City Point, VA., 12 April 1863. Exchanged and rejoined company. Age 29 on roll dated 6 May 1863 at Shelbyville, TN. In hospital at Rome, GA., 17 June 1863. Deserted on the march from Sweetwater, TN. back to Chattanooga, 10 November 1863. Resided at McKenzie, Carroll Co., TN. Died 14 July 1908. Buried in Enon Cemetery, Carroll Co., TN.[352]

Helpin, Lawrence; Private, Company G: Enlisted 3 June 1861 at Camp Cheatham. Died January 1862 in General Hospital at Knoxville, TN.

Henderson, Hugh H.; Private, Company E: Born 17 July 1844 in Toronto, Canada. Relocated to Tennessee at age 4, residing at Charlotte, Dickson Co., TN. Occupation: stone cutter. Sworn into service 18 May 1861 at Nashville. Age 18 on roll dated 16 August 1861 at Watauga Bridge, TN. Left as a nurse after the Battle of Murfreesboro, TN. Captured 5 January 1863. Sent to City Point, VA. and exchanged. Hit with a ball in the Battle of Peachtree Creek, GA., 20 July 1864 and ordered to the rear by General Manigault Captured at Atlanta, GA. and sent to prison at Nashville, TN. Became ill there and was taken care of by a man named Rise Porter. Took oath 25 October 1864. Complexion dark, hair blonde, eyes blue, 5' 10". Resided in Charlotte, TN. and later Cheatham Co., TN. Returned to the occupation of stone cutter. Married Elizer J. Dawson, 7 February 1866. Admitted to the Confederate Soldier's Home, 30 March 1916. Died 9 January 1925. Buried in the Confederate Soldier's Home Cemetery grave #418. Pension Application 9281.[353]

Hendricks, Sanford; Brevet Second Lieutenant, Company C: Born c. 1830. Occupation: farmer. Married L. E. Cording, 6 May 1855. Sworn into service 14 May 1861 at Nashville. Brevetted second lieutenant at the organization. Defeated in the election at the reorganization, 1 May 1862. Dropped from roll.[354]

Hendrix, James; Private, Company G: Enlisted 23 November 1861 at Camp Buckner, KY. Wounded in the Battle of Murfreesboro, TN., 31 December 1862. No further.

---

[350] Maney, *Surgeon's Log*, "Missionary Ridge TN."
[351] Dobson-Sides, *1860 Davidson County Census*, 507.
[352] Joseph Hedgecock, Tennessee Pension Application, 3992.
[353] Baker, *1860 Census for Dickson County*, 157; Sistler and Sistler, *1880 Census of Dickson County*, 95.
[354] Baker, *1860 Census for Dickson County*, 157.

Hendrix, William A.; Private, Company I: Born c. 1834. Sworn into service 20 May 1861. Died at home in Humphreys Co., TN., 9 July 1861.[355]

Henley, Thomas J.; Private, Company H: Born 9 November 1839. Sworn into service 14 May 1861 at Nashville. Deserted when Chattanooga was evacuated 8 September 1863. Died ca. 1895. Buried in the Milan Cemetery in Hickman Co., TN.[356]

Henressy, Nicholas; Private, Company D: Sworn into service 11 May 1861 at Nashville. Transferred to Rutledge's Tennessee Artillery, 5 September 1861.

Henry, William H.; Private, Company B: Sworn into service 10 May 1861 at Nashville. Drummed out of service 6 July 1861 at Camp Cheatham.

Herring, Michael; Private, Company E: Sworn into service 18 May 1861 at Nashville. Discharged 10 August 1862 at Tazewell, TN. by the conscript act. Later captured in Kentucky and exchanged, 16 October 1862. No further.

Heverin, Hugh J.; First Lieutenant, Company D: Born 1 November 1839 in Co. Armagh, Ireland. Immigrated to the United States in 1851, landing in New York, becoming a resident of Nashville shortly thereafter. Occupation: store clerk. Sworn into service 11 May 1861 at Nashville. Elected fourth corporal at the organization. Appointed second lieutenant at the reorganization, 1 May 1862. Wounded in the shoulder at the Battle of Murfreesboro, TN., 31 December 1862. Sent to hospital in Atlanta, GA. Returned to duty. Wounded in the middle third of the left arm at Missionary Ridge, TN., 24 November 1863. Suffered a severe flesh wound between the left shoulder and neck in the Battle of Atlanta, GA., 22 July 1864. Later promoted to first lieutenant. Discharged 9 May 1865 at Augusta, GA. Occupied as a stone mason and contractor. Served as a jailor for Dickson Co., TN., an elected position. Became a U.S. citizen, 3 July 1874 and married Mary Cox on 1 November of the same year. Member of the Catholic church. Served as an attendant at the smallpox hospital during the outbreak of 1899. Member of the Cheatham Bivouac. Died 7 February 1900 after gangrene set in following the removal of his left thumb. Buried Calvary Cemetery, Nashville, TN.[357]

Hickey, Andrew; Private, Company B, G: Occupation: laborer. Sworn into service 10 May 1861 in Company B at Nashville. Wounded in the Battle of Murfreesboro, TN., 31 December 1862. Age 32 on roll dated 2 June 1863 at Shelbyville, TN. Deserted near Missionary Ridge, TN., 8 September 1863. Captured and sent to Camp Morton, IN., 27 February 1863. Took oath 27 September 1863. Complexion light, hair sandy, eyes blue, 5' 8".[358]

Hicks, James H; Private, Company unknown: Took oath 10 June 1865. Complexion light, hair dark, eyes gray, 6'. No further.

Hilton, John B; Private, Company B: Sworn into service 10 May 1861 at Nashville. Deserted 1 December 1862 at Readyville, TN.

*Hogan, Martin; Private, Company D, G: Sworn into service 11 May 1861 in Company D at Nashville. Transferred to Company G at the reorganization, 1 May 1862. Admitted to Fair Ground Hospital #2, Atlanta, GA., 12 September 1863. Returned to duty 14 September 1863. Wounded through the small and two next toes in the Battle of Atlanta, GA., 22 July 1864. Surrendered as a member of Company C, 2nd Consolidated Tennessee Infantry with the Army of Tennessee at Greensboro, NC., 26 April 1865. Paroled 1 May 1865.[359]

Hogin, William Millington; First Sergeant, Company K: Born 18 December 1843. Resided at Burns, Dickson Co., TN. Enlisted 29 November 1861 in Company B, 49th Tennessee Infantry. Enlisted in the

---

[355] Johnson, *1860 Census of Humphreys County*, 37.

[356] United Daughters of the Confederacy, *Confederate Soldiers of Hickman County*, 103.

[357] Maney, *Surgeon's Log*, "Stones River TN"; Maney, *Surgeon's Log*, "Missionary Ridge TN"; Maney, *Surgeon's Log*, "Battle of Atlanta GA"; Hugh J. Heverin, Cheatham Bivouac Application; Smith, Davidson County Naturalization Records, 92-3.

[358] Maney, *Surgeon's Log*, "Stones River TN."

[359] Ibid., "Battle of Atlanta GA."

11th Tennessee, 16 July 1862 at Thorn Hill, TN. Age 19 on roll dated 1 May 1863 at Shelbyville, TN. Appointed first sergeant by May 1863. Present at least through February 1864. Rejoined the 49th Tennessee in the spring of 1864. Wounded in the shoulder 28 July 1864. Sent to the hospital at Macon, GA. Received a 60 day furlough. Reported back to the Army of Tennessee at Florence, AL. Captured at the Battle of Franklin, TN., 30 November 1864. Forwarded to Camp Douglas, IL., then to Point Lookout, MD. where he was paroled 27 June 1865. Postwar occupation: farmer. He was present at the 14 June 1904 reunion of the 11th Tennessee Infantry in Nashville. Died 20 September 1922. Buried in the Union Cemetery, Dickson, Dickson Co., TN.[360]

Holland, William S.; Private, Company A: Born in Humphreys Co., TN., 27 September 1841. Sworn into service 10 May 1861 at Nashville. Age 22 on roll dated 6 May 1863 at Shelbyville, TN. Captured in the Battle of Kennesaw Mountain, GA., 27 June 1864. Sent to the U. S. Military Prison at Louisville, KY. Forwarded to Camp Douglas, IL., 26 July 1864. Paroled 13 May 1865. After the war, he relocated to Nashville where he worked as a dry goods merchant and lived above the store located at 817 Fourth Avenue South. Wife named Susan.[361]

Holt, Isaac L.; Private, Company C: The 23 August 1863 *Nashville Daily Press and Times* reports that he was arrested for being in Confederate service after taking the oath of allegiance. No further.[362]

Hooper, Absolom Brack "Dink"; Private, Company I: Born in 1840 in Perry Co., TN. Occupation: farmer. Enlisted 15 September 1861 at Waverly, TN. in Captain Frank Maney's Artillery. Wounded at Fort Donelson, TN. as he fell, crushing his left shoulder and dislocating the elbow. Transferred to the 11th Tennessee Infantry after the Battle of Murfreesboro, joining at Shelbyville, TN. Wounded in the penis and in the left thigh in the Battle of New Hope Church, GA., 27 May 1864. Captured at Covington, GA., 22 July 1864. Sent to the U. S. Military Prison at Louisville, KY. Forwarded to Camp Chase, OH., 3 August 1864. Transferred to New Orleans, LA., 2 May 1865. Resided at Betsytown, Dickson Co., TN. postwar. Husband of 1) Leona Parker and 2) Missouri Rushing. Died 27 April 1932 at Danville, Stewart Co., TN. Buried in the Hooper Cemetery, Turkey Creek, Humphreys Co., TN.[363]

Hooper, John; Private, Company D: Sworn into service 11 May 1861 at Nashville. Discharged for disability for paralysis of left arm. Complexion light, eyes blue, hair light, 5' 8".

Hooper, Simeon Homes; Private, Company I: Born in 1816 in Tennessee. Sworn into service 20 May 1861 at Nashville. Discharged by the conscript act, 18 August 1862 at Tazewell, TN. Died in 1892. Buried in the Hooper Cemetery, Humphreys Co., TN.

Hooper, William H.; Private, Company H: Born 15 July 1835 in Bedford Co., TN. Sworn into service 14 May 1861 at Nashville. After the Battle of Nashville, TN., 16 December 1864, he was cut off from his command and unable to rejoin it. Took oath 13 January 1865. Complexion fair, hair light, eyes gray, 5' 8". Married Pamela Ann Moss. Attended the reunion of the 11th Tennessee Infantry at Bon Aqua Springs, TN., 24 September 1885. Died in Hickman Co., TN., 5 December 1912, and buried in the Hooper Cemetery there.[364]

Hornbeak, Eli Adam; Assistant Quartermaster, Company H, Field & Staff: Born 3 June 1831. Brother of Private Samuel M. and Musician Frank B. Hornbeak. Occupation: merchant. Appointed assistant quartermaster, 1 June 1861. Resigned from this position 10 October 1861. Appointed fourth corporal, 14 May 1862. Later served as a captain in the 9th Battalion Tennessee Cavalry and was wounded at Kennesaw Mountain, GA. Died 25 August 1886 at Hornbeak, Obion Co., TN. Buried Hornbeak City Cemetery, Hornbeak, Obion Co., TN.

---

[360] *Reunion Pamphlet,* 14 June 1904.

[361] W. S. Holland, Tennessee Pension Application, 13751.

[362] *Nashville Daily Press and Times,* 23 August 1863.

[363] Absolom Hooper, Tennessee Pension Application, 2128; Maney, *Surgeon's Log,* "May 1864"; *Humphreys County Cemetery Records* vol. 1, 136.

[364] United Daughters of the Confederacy, *Confederate Soldiers of Hickman County,* 103; W. H. Hooper, Tennessee Pension Applications, 7369, and 10024; "The Reunion," *Hickman Pioneer.*

Hornbeak, Francis Buchanan "Frank"; Musician, Company H, A, Field & Staff: Born 2 October 1841 in Centerville, TN. Brother to Asst. Quartermaster Eli A. and Private Samuel M. Hornbeak. Sworn into service 14 May 1861 in Company H at Nashville. Transferred to Company A and elected first sergeant at the reorganization, 1 May 1862. Appointed musician and transferred to the Field & Staff, 1 January 1863. Age 24 on roll dated 6 May 1863 at Shelbyville, TN. Transferred from the band back to Company H, 16 October 1863. Later a member of Gantt's 9th Battalion Cavalry. Married 1) Emma A. Cash Jul 1, 1866 and 2) Jennie Jones, 24 April 1890. Died 12 April 1905 at Hornbeak, Obion Co., TN. Buried Hornbeak City Cemetery, Obion Co., TN.[365]

Hornbeak, Samuel M; Private, Company H: Born c. 1838. Brother to Assistant Quartermaster Eli A. and Private Frank B. Hornbeak. Sworn into service 14 May 1861 at Nashville. Discharged 2 April 1862. Later transferred to Company D, 9th Tennessee Cavalry Battalion.[366]

Hornberger, James P.; Private; Co., F: Born c 1839. Resided in Montgomery Co., TN. for a period prior to the war. Brother of Private Wiley W. Hornberger. Enlisted 18 May 1861 at Cedar Hill, TN. Died 2 July 1861.

Hornberger, Wiley W.; Private, Company F: Born in Stewart Co., TN., 30 August 1839. Brother of Private James P. Hornberger. Resided in Orlinda, Robertson Co., TN. Occupation: farmer. Enlisted 18 May 1861 at Cedar Hill, TN. Wounded in the shoulder in the Battle of Murfreesboro, TN., 31 December 1862, taking four or five days to recover. Wounded in the scalp in the Battle of Chickamauga, GA., 20 September 1863. Furloughed home from Corinth, MS. after the Battle of Nashville, TN. Cut off from his command, he attempted to return to the regiment, but was captured near the Tennessee River. Paroled at Meridian, MS. Resided at Barren Springs, TN. postwar. Member of the Ed Crockett Bivouac, Springfield, TN. Died 19 June 1919. Buried Elmwood Cemetery, Springfield, Robertson Co., TN.[367]

Horrigan, Timothy; Private, Company G: Enlisted 3 June 1861 at Camp Cheatham. Deserted 28 August 1861.

House, James W.; Private, Company unknown: Entered service in Rutherford Co., TN. in November 1864. Took oath 28 December 1864. Complexion fair, hair light, eyes gray, 6'. No further.

House, John W.; Private, Company K: Sworn into service 25 May 1861 at Nashville. Age 20 on roll dated 15 August 1861 at Midway, TN. Entered Fairground Hospital #2, Atlanta, GA., 7 July 1863 for scorbutus. Returned to duty 27 July 1863. Captured near Marietta, GA., 3 July 1864. Sent to the U. S. Military Prison at Louisville, KY. Forwarded to Camp Douglas, IL., 14 July 1864. Died 18 November 1864 of smallpox. Buried Oak Woods Cemetery, Chicago, IL.[368]

House, William Duke; Private, Company K: Born 1 February 1838 in Williamson Co., TN. Occupation: farmer. Sworn into service 25 May 1861 at Nashville. Age 24 on roll dated 15 August 1861 at Midway, TN. On extra duty in the quartermaster department as a teamster since 15 March 1862. Wounded in the scalp in the Battle of Adairsville, GA., 17 May 1864. This injury later caused his eyes to fail. Captured near Marietta, GA., 3 July 1864. Sent to the U. S. Military Prison at Louisville, KY. Forwarded to Camp Douglas, IL., 14 July 1864. Paroled 13 May 1865. Resided near Martin, Weakley

---

[365] United Daughters of the Confederacy, *Confederate Soldiers of Hickman County*, 104.
[366] Ibid.
[367] Maney, *Surgeon's Log*, "Stones River TN"; W. W. Hornberger, Tennessee Pension Applications, 12550 and 4287.
[368] Welsh, *Confederate Hospitals*, Patient Roster, Fair Ground Hospital #2, 96; Find-A-Grave, "Oak Woods," http://www.findagrave.com/cgibin/fg.cgi?page=gr&GSln=House&GSiman=1&GScid=173554&GRid=37804110&(16 August 2014).

Co., TN. Member of the Methodist Episcopal Church South. Died 10 May 1929. Buried Oak Hill Cemetery, Weakley Co., TN.[369]

Howe, Peter; Private, Company G: Enlisted 3 June 1861 at Camp Cheatham. On extra duty in the Commissary Department from September 1861 through January 1862. Discharged by virtue of the conscript act, 19 August 1862 at Tazewell, TN.

Huddleston, James H.; Private, Company H: Sworn into service 14 May 1861 at Nashville. Teamster since 1 November 1861. Admitted to Fair Ground Hospital #1, Atlanta, GA., 7 July 1863 for ulcus. Returned to duty 26 July 1863. Transferred to Company G, 10th Tennessee Cavalry, 17 July 1863.

Huddleston, William Howell; Private, Company H: Born November 1842 in Hickman Co., TN. Enlisted in Company H. Married May Louise Pettus. Died in April 1886 in Hickman Co., TN. and buried in the Centerville Cemetery.[370]

*Hudgins, Francis Marion "France"; Private, Company E: Born in Dickson Co., TN. in 1842. Sworn into service 10 May 1861 at Nashville. Wounded in the hand in the Battle of Murfreesboro, TN., 31 December 1862. Sent to hospital at Chattanooga, TN. Age 19 on roll dated 14 May 1863 at Shelbyville, TN. Wounded in the head in the Battle of Franklin, TN., 30 November 1864, and captured there 17 December 1864. Sent to the U. S. Military Prison at Louisville, KY., 1 January 1865. Forwarded to Camp Chase, OH., 2 January 1865. Released from Camp Chase, 12 March 1865. Apparently rejoined company. Surrendered as a member of Company C, 2nd Consolidated Tennessee Infantry with the Army of Tennessee at Greensboro, NC., 26 April 1865. Paroled 1 May 1865. Married Missouri F. Proctor, 6 January 1867. Occupation: farmer. Died in 1917. Buried in the Hudgins Cemetery, Owl Hollow, Dickson Co., TN.[371]

Hudson, David; Private, Company D: Sworn into service 11 May 1861 at Nashville. Discharged 15 August 1862 by the conscript act at Tazewell, TN. Captured near Nashville, TN., 15 September 1862. Confined in the penitentiary. Forwarded to the military prison at Alton, IL. Transferred to City Point, VA.

Hudson, Robert Anderson; Private, Company C: Born c. 1826. Occupation: farmer. Enlisted 18 February 1863 at Shelbyville, TN., age 37. Captured in the Battle of Missionary Ridge, TN., 25 November 1863. Sent to the U. S. Military Prison at Louisville, KY. Forwarded to Rock Island, IL., 7 December 1863. Took oath 20 January 1865. Complexion light, hair dark, eyes gray, 5' 8". Married Sarah Elizabeth Bone, 19 May 1866. Resided at Ruskin, Dickson Co., TN. Died c. 1902. Widows Pension Application #873.

Hudson, William B.; Private, Company C: Born 8 October 1832 in Tennessee. Enlisted 24 February 1863 at Shelbyville, TN. Captured in the Battle of Missionary Ridge, TN., 25 November 1863. Sent to the U.S. Military Prison at Louisville, KY. Forwarded to Rock Island, IL., 7 December 1863. Took oath 28 April 1865. Complexion fair, hair brown, eyes gray, 5' 7". Died 28 November 1898. Buried in the Adams Cemetery, Dickson Co., TN.

Huffman, William; Private, Company D: Sworn into service 11 May 1861 at Nashville. Discharged for disability 24 September 1861.

Huggins, A. J.; Private, Company B: Sworn into service 10 May 1861 at Nashville. Discharged under the conscript law, 15 August 1862 at Tazewell, TN.

---

[369] Maney, *Surgeon's Log*, "May 1864"; William Duke House, "Veteran Questionnaire" vol. 3, 1155; Daughters of the American Revolution, James Buckley Chapter. *Weakley County Cemetery Listings*, vol. 2 (Sharon TN: The Chapter, 1980) 186.

[370] United Daughters of the Confederacy, *Confederate Soldiers of Hickman County*, 106.

[371] F. M. Huggins, Tennessee Confederate Pension Application, S11368; *Nashville Daily Press*, December 22, 1864.

Hughes, Edward W.; Private, Company F: Enlisted 18 May 1861 at Cedar Hill, TN. Present through January 1862. On sick furlough since 19 January 1862. Died at Shelbyville, TN. Buried Willow Mount Cemetery, Shelbyville, TN.[372]

Hughes, Frederick J.; Private, Company C: Born c. 1826 in KY. Occupation: blacksmith. Married Margaret Baldwin, 11 December 1846. Sworn into service 14 May 1861 at Nashville. Issued a minie musket. Blacksmith from 19 October 1861 to January 1862. Discharged under the conscript act at Tazewell, TN., 15 August 1862.[373]

Hughes, George W.; Private, Company C: Born c. 1837. Occupation: day laborer. Sworn into service 14 May 1861 at Nashville. Issued a minie musket. On detached duty as a provost guard at Atlanta, GA. September through October 1863. Captured in Dickson Co., TN., 20 August 1864. Took oath 26 September 1864. Complexion dark, hair dark, eyes blue, 5' 10".[374]

Hundley, Elisha Thomas; First Corporal, Company D: Enlisted 11 May 1861 at Nashville. On extra duty in quartermaster department July through August 1862. Age 21 on roll dated 5 May 1863 at Shelbyville, TN. Appointed fourth corporal by July 1863. Sent to hospital at Rome, GA., 3 July 1863. Admitted to Ocmulgee Hospital in Macon, GA., 13 August 1864 for a gunshot wound. Promoted to first corporal by September 1863. Captured in the Battle of Jonesboro, GA., 2 September 1864. Sent to the U. S. Military Prison at Louisville, KY. Sent to Camp Douglas, IL., 29 October 1864. Took oath 15 May 1865. Complexion fair, hair brown, eyes hazel, 5' 5".

Hundley, John Lafayette; Brevet Second Lieutenant, Company D: Born between 1832 and 1837. Married Mary Jane Manley, 9 June 1852. Sworn into service 11 May 1861 at Nashville. Brevetted second lieutenant, 1 May 1862. Age 26 on roll dated 5 May 1863 at Shelbyville, TN. Resigned 11 September 1863 due to inability to get along with company and regiment.[375]

*Hunt, Andrew Washington; Musician, Company A, Field & Staff: Born 17 March 1839 at Nunnelly, Hickman Co., TN. Sworn into service 10 May 1861 at Nashville. Clerk in Commissary Department from July 1861 to January 1862. Transferred to band and to the Field & Staff, 10 March 1863. Age 22 on roll dated 6 May 1863 at Shelbyville, TN. Surrendered as a member of Company K, 2nd Consolidated Tennessee Infantry with the Army of Tennessee at Greensboro, NC., 26 April 1865. Paroled 1 May 1865. Married Kate Cotham, 4 October 1876. Died 27 May 1926 in Bloomfield, MO.[376]

Hunt, B. B.; Private, Company A: Sworn into service 10 May 1861 at Nashville. Deserted at Camp Cheatham, 23 May 1861.

Hunter, James Pitts; Second Corporal, Company E: Born in 1842 in Dickson Co., TN. Both parents had died by 1850, after which he lived with his maternal grandfather, Caleb Rooker. Occupation: farmhand. Sworn into service 18 May 1861 at Nashville. On sick furlough at Knoxville, TN. since 22 March 1862. Age 19 on roll dated 14 May 1863 at Shelbyville, TN. Promoted to second corporal, 10 October 1863. Killed in the Battle of Atlanta, GA., 22 July 1864.[377]

Hurley, James; Private, Company I: Sworn into service 20 May 1861 at Nashville. Discharged by the conscript law, 18 August 1862 at Tazewell, TN.

Hurley, Jeremiah; Fourth Sergeant, Company G: Enlisted 3 June 1861 at Camp Cheatham. Discharged by the conscript law, 16 August 1862 at Tazewell, TN. Apparently rejoined the regiment at a later date. Killed in the Battle of Franklin, TN., 30 November 1864, age 38. Buried in the Unknown section of the McGavock Confederate Cemetery.[378]

---

[372] Allen, *Winds*, 109.
[373] McCauley, *Record Book, Company C*.
[374] McCauley, *Record Book, Company C*; Baker, *1860 Census for Dickson County*, 13.
[375] Sistler and Sistler, *Davidson County Marriages 1838-1863*, 113.
[376] United Daughters of the Confederacy, *Confederate Soldiers of Hickman County*, 108.
[377] Maney, *Surgeon's Log*, "Battle of Atlanta GA."
[378] Personal correspondence with Mr. Tim Burgess, Battle of Franklin Historian, 13 May 2001.

Hust, Francis O.; Private, Company I: Born c. 1841. Occupation: farmer. Sworn into service 20 May 1861 at Nashville. Elected fourth sergeant at the reorganization, 1 May 1862. Discharged 7 January 1863 by providing a substitute in the person of S. A. Stennett.[379]

Hutchins, William; Private, Company D: Sworn into service 11 May 1861 at Nashville. Deserted 22 April 1863. Arrested at Chattanooga, TN. for desertion and held July through August 1863. Captured at Cleveland, TN., 29 November 1863. Forwarded to the U. S. Military Prison at Louisville, KY. Forwarded to Rock Island, IL., 1 January 1864.

Hutchinson, James O.; Private, Company F: Sworn into service 18 May 1861 at Cedar Hill, TN. Died 8 July 1861.

Hutton, Zachariah Drummond "Zach"; Private, Company E: Born in Dickson Co., TN., 11 May 1845. Occupation: barber. Sworn into service 18 May 1861 at Nashville. Age 18 on roll dated 16 August 1861 at Watauga Bridge, TN. Discharged on surgeon's certificate of disability at Camp Buckner, KY., 5 October 1862. Complexion light, hair light, eyes light, 5' 8". Postwar occupation: farmer. Accidentally struck and killed by a passenger train 6 August 1892. Described as a sober, hard-working, Christian gentleman. Married. Buried in the Mount Olivet Cemetery, Section 10, Nashville, TN.

Hyde, Joseph; Private, Company I: Sworn into service 10 May 1861 at Nashville. Deserted between Nashville and Knoxville 23 July 1861.

-I-

Innis, J. T.; Private, Company I: Occupation: farmer. Sworn into service 20 May 1861 at Nashville. Age 23 on roll dated 6 May 1863 at Shelbyville, TN. Wounded severely in the head at Kennesaw Mountain, GA., 17 June 1864. Sent to Atlanta from R. & D. Hospital, Marietta, GA 16 June 1864.[380]

Irwin, Thomas; First Lieutenant, Company G: Born 14 March 1836 in County Kilkenny, Ireland. Came to Nashville in 1858. Occupation: printer for the *Nashville Republican Banner*. Sworn into service 10 May 1861 at Nashville. Elected second lieutenant at the reorganization, 1 May 1862. Later promoted to first lieutenant. Suffered a gunshot wound in the left side of his back by a minie ball, left on the field, and captured in the Battle of Missionary Ridge, TN., 25 November 1863. Sent to General Field Hospital at Bridgeport, AL., 10 December 1863. Forwarded to the U. S. Military Prison at Louisville, KY., 28 February 1864. Sent to Camp Chase, OH. Transferred to Fort Delaware, Delaware, 21 March 1864. Later sent to Morris Island, SC. and then to Fort Pulaski, GA., and back to Fort Delaware. Took oath 12 June 1865. Complexion light, hair light, eyes blue, height 5' 7". Resumed his occupation as a printer after the war. Married Ellen O'Connor, 8 September 1866. Member of the Catholic Church and the Cheatham Bivouac. Died 9 December 1894. Buried in Calvary Cemetery, Nashville, TN.[381]

Ivey, W. O.; Private, Company H: Admitted to Fair Ground Hospital #1, Atlanta, GA., 15 May 1864 for diarrhea. Sent to another hospital on 17 May 1864.[382]

---

[379] Johnson, *1860 Census of Humphreys County*, 36.

[380] Maney, *Surgeon's Log*, "Kennesaw Mountain GA"; *Daily American*, 7 August 1892; Chattanooga Daily Rebel, "List of Soldiers Sent to Atlanta from R. & D. Hospital, Marietta, GA," 16 June 1864.

[381] Maney, *Surgeon's Log*, "Missionary Ridge TN"; Thomas Irwin, Cheatham Bivouac Application; *Nashville Banner*, 10 December 1894.

[382] Welsh, *Confederate Hospitals*, Patient Roster, Fair Ground Hospital #1, 142.

-J-

Jackson, Epps; Private, Company E: Sworn into service 18 May 1861. Age 27 on roll dated 16 August 1861 at Watauga Bridge, TN. Died at Chattanooga, TN., 24 December 1862 of chronic diarrhea.

Jackson, Green P.; Private, Company E: Born in 1825 in Dickson Co., TN. Died c.1885. Buried in the Jackson Cemetery, Dickson Co., TN.[383]

Jackson, Green P. Rev.; Private, Company E: Born 27 March 1840 in Dickson Co., TN. Died 9 March 1918. Buried in the Mt. Olivet Cemetery, Nashville, Davidson Co., TN.[384]

Jackson, James; Private, Company B: Sworn into service 10 May 1861 at Nashville. Detached to Rutledge's Tennessee Artillery Battery 1 November 1861 through 2 January 1862. No further.

*Jackson, James P.; Private, Company E: Occupation: farmer. Sworn into service 18 May 1861 at Nashville. Age 26 on roll dated 16 August 1861 at Watauga Bridge, TN. Wounded below the right knee in the Battle of Missionary Ridge, TN., 25 November 1863. Admitted to Fair Ground Hospital #2, Atlanta, GA., 26 November 1863 for vulnus sclopeticum. Sent to receiving and redistributing hospital, 26 January 1864 to be sent to Covington, GA. Later rejoined company. Wounded in the lower third of the of the right arm in battle near Atlanta, GA., 4 August 1864. Surrendered as a member of Company C, 2nd Consolidated Tennessee Infantry with the Army of Tennessee at Greensboro, NC., 26 April 1865. Paroled 1 May 1865.[385]

Jackson, James Shelton; Private, Company E: Born in Dyer Co., TN. in 1842. Enlisted 18 December 1862 at Readyville, TN. Age 19 on roll dated 14 May 1863 at Shelbyville, TN. Deserted 13 December 1864. Took oath 13 January 1865. Complexion fair, hair light, eyes hazel, height 6'. He was present at the 14 June 1904 reunion of the 11th Tennessee Infantry in Nashville. Died 20 January 1923. Buried in the Holden Cemetery, Rutherford Co., TN.[386]

Jackson, Joseph William Green "Jo"; Private, Company F: Born 26 October 1844. Prior to the war, he held a job with the railroad as a "pumper," using a mule to pump water into a high tower for use by the Kentucky and Edgefield Railroad that ran through Cedar Hill. On 8 June 1861 he joined the Cedar Hill Cadets, with whom he drilled prior to joining the 11th. He was present at Camp Cheatham on 25 July 1861 to see the 11th Tennessee off. Enlisted 1 July 1863 at Chattanooga, TN. Several letters were written to family members during the war which describe the Atlanta Campaign and mention numerous other soldiers. Slightly wounded on the head resulting in disability for two or three days just prior to 14 July 1864. Killed in the Battle of Atlanta, GA., 22 July 1864. The bullet entered near the corner of his mouth and came out the back of his head. Buried on the battlefield, his body was later returned to his home and interred in the Jackson Cemetery, Adams, Robertson Co., TN. Longtime Congressman Joseph W. Byrns would later be named in his honor.[387]

Jackson, Sanford Gilpin Marion; Private, Company F: Born 22 September 1836. Married Mary Ann Patience Barnes, 10 September 1857. Enlisted 4 November 1862 at Lenoir Station, TN. In hospital at Chattanooga in early 1863. Returned to duty before 12 July 1863. Died of chronic diarrhea at Oliver Hospital, Dalton, GA., 30 August 1863. His body was returned to Robertson Co. and buried in the Jackson Cemetery outside Adams, TN. His widow never remarried.

Jackson, Sylvanus; Private, Company D: Sworn into service 11 May 1861 at Nashville. Discharged 15 August 1862 at Tazewell, TN. by the conscript law.

---

[383] McCauley Camp 260, *Confederate Graves*, 27.
[384] Ibid.
[385] Maney, *Surgeon's Log*, "Missionary Ridge TN"; Welsh, *Confederate Hospitals*, Patient Roster, Fair Ground Hospital #2, 102; Maney, *Surgeon's Log*, "August 1864."
[386] James S. Jackson, Tennessee Pension Application, 14768; *Reunion Pamphlet*, 14 June 1904.
[387] Maney, *Surgeon's Log*, "Battle of Atlanta GA."

Jackson, William T.; Second Sergeant, Company E: Born 17 February 1838. Wife's name was Ellen. Occupation: farmer. Enlisted 19 September 1861 at Camp Buckner, KY. Elected second sergeant at the reorganization, 1 May 1862. Wounded in the lower third of the left arm at Kennesaw Mountain, GA., 21 June 1864. Captured in the Battle of Franklin, TN., 30 November 1864. Sent to the U. S. Military Prison at Louisville, KY. Forwarded to Camp Douglas, IL., 3 December 1864. Took oath at Point Lookout, MD., 28 June 1865. Complexion fair, hair light brown, eyes hazel, height 5' 7". Transportation given to his residence in White Bluff, TN. Buried in the Gibbs Cemetery, Cheatham Co., TN.[388]

James, Robert A. W.; Major, Company E, Field & Staff: Born c. 1836. Occupation: clerk. Sworn into service 18 May 1861 at Nashville. Elected first lieutenant at the organization. Age 21 on roll dated 16 August 1861 at Watauga Bridge, TN. Elected captain at the reorganization, 1 May 1862. Promoted to major and transferred to the Field & Staff of the 11th/29th Tennessee Infantry Consolidated. Listed as being in the Ocmulgee Hospital in Macon, GA., 28 February 1865 for syphilis. Surrendered 30 April 1865 at Macon, GA. Complexion fair, hair brown, eyes gray, height 5' 11".[389]

James, Thomas; Private, Company C: Born c. 1828. Occupation: farmer. Married C. J. Selfe, 25 September 1851. Sworn into service 14 May 1861 at Nashville. Issued a minie musket. Discharged by the conscript law, 15 August 1862 at Tazewell, TN.[390]

Jamison, Orville O.; Fourth Sergeant, Company I: Brother of Chaplain P. G. and Private W. A. Jamison. Occupation: farmer. Sworn into service 20 May 1861 at Nashville. Appointed first corporal, 15 January 1862. Promoted to fourth sergeant, 1 August 1863. Wounded in the thigh in the Battle of Adairsville, GA., 17 May 1864. Wounded in the Battle of Franklin, TN., 30 November 1864.[391]

Jamison, Purvoyant Gustavus "Gus"; Chaplain, Company I, Field & Staff: Born 12 July 1837 at Waverly, Humphreys Co., TN. The third son of Downs and Sarah Jamison. Brother of Sergeant Orville O. and Private W. A. Jamison. Admitted on trial as a Methodist minister October 1860. Served in the Yellow Creek Circuit just prior to the war. Sworn into service 20 May 1861 at Nashville. Appointed chaplain, 15 May 1862 at Cumberland Gap, TN. Resigned as chaplain, 26 March 1864 due to his services being unsatisfactory. Seriously wounded in the Battle of Franklin, TN., 30 November 1864. Federal record states that he deserted, 15 December 1864 at Nashville, TN. This would later prove false. Took oath, 7 February 1865. Complexion fair, hair brown, eyes hazel, height 5' 11". This was later proven false by affidavits submitted by Gen. George W. Gordon and others who attested to his faithful service. Ordained deacon in 1867, and married Margaret Damesworth that same year. Ordained Elder in 1868 by Bishop Holland McTyeire. Gifted as a poet. Relocated to Northern Alabama around 1869, and later to Missouri about 1900. Served as a school teacher for several years. Resident, Missouri Confederate Veterans Home, Higginsville, MO. Died of paralysis, 1 February 1915. Buried Anniston Cemetery, Anniston, Mississippi Co., MO.[392]

Jamison, William A. "Will"; Private, Company I: Brother of Sergeant Orville O. and Chaplain P. G. Jamison. Sworn into service, 20 May 1861 at Nashville. Died at Camp Cheatham, 5 July 1861.

Jarnagin, T. C.; Private, Company C: Born c. 1840. Occupation: farm hand. Sworn into service, 14 May 1861 at Nashville. Issued a minie musket. Captured in Dickson Co., TN. in June 1864. Took oath at Louisville, KY., 20 June 1864. Complexion light, hair sandy, eyes blue, height 5' 6".[393]

---

[388] Maney, *Surgeon's Log*, "Kennesaw Mountain GA"; Haile and Garrett, *Tombstone Records of Cheatham County*,14; *Nashville Daily Press*, 3 December 1864.

[389] Baker, *1860 Census for Dickson County*, 152.

[390] McCauley, *Record Book, Company C*; Baker, *1860 Census for Dickson County*, 4.

[391] Maney, *Surgeon's Log*, "May 1864"; Trogdon, "Interesting Letter"; Johnson, *1860 Census of Humphreys County*, 41.

[392] W. J. Ward, "Gone Home," Unknown Missouri Newspaper, 1915, papers of Richard Jamison, Seaford, DE; Trogdon, "Interesting Letter."

[393] McCauley, *Record Book, Company C*; Baker, *1860 Census for Dickson County*, 77.

Jarrell, R. F.; Second Lieutenant, Company I: Sworn into service 20 May 1861 at Nashville. Elected third lieutenant, 19 September 1861. Promoted to second lieutenant before the reorganization, 1 May 1862. Defeated in election, 1 May 1862. Dropped from roll.

Jenkins, Thomas G.; Private, Company G, K: Sworn into service 25 May 1861 in Company G. Transferred to Company K in July 1861. Age 22 on roll dated 15 August 1861 at Midway, TN. On extra duty in the quartermaster department, 30 September 1861 through 30 April 1862. No further.

Jennings, Edward; Private, Company K, G: Sworn into service 25 May 1861 in Company K at Nashville. Age 27 on roll dated 15 August 1861 at Midway, TN. Transferred to Company G at the reorganization, 1 May 1862. Deserted and later captured. Held at Memphis, TN. Complexion light, hair auburn, eyes blue, height 5' 7".

Jentry, Thomas P.; Private, Company K: Born in Dickson Co., TN. Sworn into service 25 May 1861 at Nashville. Age 18 on roll dated 15 August 1861 at Midway, TN. Discharged 1 November 1861 for disability resulting from chronic bronchitis. Complexion light, hair light, eyes blue, height 6".

Johnson, Granville M. Jr.; Private, Company H: Born 1833 in Tennessee. Sworn into service 14 May 1861 at Nashville. Brother to Lieutenant Jacob and Private John J. Johnson. Wounded 19 September 1863, shot through the right thigh and through the lungs, in the Battle of Chickamauga, GA. He lay between the lines throughout the night and was taken to a field hospital the next morning. Still able to talk, he sent final words to his family, then died, 20 September 1863. Buried among the unknown dead of Chickamauga.[394]

Johnson, Jacob H. "Jake"; First Lieutenant, Company H: Born in 1838. Occupation: farmer. Brother to Private Granville M., Jr. and Private John J. Johnson. Sworn into service 14 May 1861 at Nashville. Elected second lieutenant at the reorganization, 1 May 1862. Along with 18 men, while searching for Colonel George W. Gordon after he was captured at Tazewell, TN., captured 42 Federal soldiers, who were later exchanged for Gordon. Promoted to first lieutenant by July 1863. Killed in the Battle of Atlanta, GA., 22 July 1864.[395]

Johnson, James; Second Corporal, Company D: Occupation: laborer. Sworn into service 10 May 1861 at Nashville. Elected second corporal at the reorganization, 1 May 1862. Left sick at Versailles, KY., 6 October 1862. Age 22 on roll dated 30 May 1863 at Shelbyville, TN. Wounded in the head in the Battle of Missionary Ridge, TN., 24 November 1863. Sent to hospital. Wounded in the Battle of Franklin, TN., 30 November 1864. Captured at Franklin, TN., 17 December 1864. Sent to the U. S. Military Prison at Louisville, KY. Forwarded to Camp Douglas, IL. Took oath 8 May 1865. Complexion fair, hair brown, eyes gray, height 5' 6".[396]

Johnson James S.; Private, Company E: Enlisted 18 December 1862 in Company E. Deserted 13 December 1864. Took oath 3 January 1865.

Johnson, James T.; Private, Company D: Born 28 January 1848 in Dickson Co., TN. Sworn into service 11 May 1861 at Nashville. Age 32 on roll dated 5 May 1863 at Shelbyville, TN. Deserted while on picket duty at Missionary Ridge, TN., 12 November 1863. Captured and sent to the U. S. Military Prison at Louisville, KY. Took oath 25 November 1863. Complexion fair, hair sandy, eyes blue, height 5' 5". Died 2 May 1934.[397]

Johnson, John Jefferson; Private, Company H: Born 27 October 1826. Brother of Private Granville and Lieutenant Jacob H. Johnson. In 1846 he enlisted in Company A of the "Hickory Guards", 1st

---

[394] United Daughters of the Confederacy, *Confederate Soldiers of Hickman County*, 111; Maney, *Surgeon's Log*, "Chickamauga GA"; "John Jefferson Johnson," 432.

[395] United Daughters of the Confederacy, *Confederate Soldiers of Hickman County*, 111; Maney, *Surgeon's Log*, "Battle of Atlanta GA"; "John Jefferson Johnson," 432.

[396] Maney, *Surgeon's Log*, "Missionary Ridge TN"; *Nashville Daily Press*, 20 December 1864.

[397] James T. Johnson, Tennessee Pension Application, 16601.

Tennessee Infantry. A veteran of the Mexican War, he fought in the Battle of Vera Cruz. Married Sarah Harris. Died May 1912 at White Bluff, TN.[398]

Johnson, Peter; Private, Company D: Occupation: laborer. Sworn into service 11 May 1861 at Nashville. On extra duty as a nurse in Wilson Hospital at Atlanta, GA., 1 August through 30 September 1862. Age 26 on roll dated 5 May 1863 at Shelbyville, TN. Wounded in the left thigh in the Battle of Missionary Ridge, TN., 25 November 1863. Sent to hospital. Deserted 16 December 1864 at Nashville. Complexion fair, hair dark, eyes blue, height 5' 2".[399]

Johnson, Thomas; Private, Company D: Sworn into service, 11 May 1861 at Nashville. Age 28 on roll dated 5 May 1863 at Shelbyville, TN. Detailed to the telegraph department, 10 March 1863 through February 1864 at Huntsville, AL. No record after February 1864.

Johnson, William; Private, Company A: Enlisted 12 September 1861 in Company A, at Knoxville, TN. Age 21 on roll dated 6 May 1863 at Shelbyville, TN. Captured in the Battle of Missionary Ridge, TN., 25 November 1863. Sent to the U. S. Military Prison at Louisville, KY. Forwarded to Rock Island, IL., 6 December 1863. No further.

Johnston, Samuel Milton; Private, Company F: Born 10 March 1817. Occupation: carpenter. Enlisted 18 May 1861 at Cedar Hill, TN. Discharged for disability, 2 May 1862. Complexion fair, hair gray, eyes blue, height 5' 10", age 45. Died in 1874.

Jones, Edward B.; Private, Company F: Born in Montgomery Co., TN. Brother of First Lieutenant Thomas B. Jones and Private Lentulus Jones. Occupation: farmer. Enlisted 18 May 1861 at Cedar Hill, TN. Died 28 July 1861 at Academy Hospital in Chattanooga, TN. Complexion fair, hair auburn, eyes blue, height 6', age 22.[400]

Jones, F. A.; Private, Company H: Enlisted 8 February 1863 at Shelbyville, TN. Admitted to Fair Ground Hospital #1, Atlanta, GA., 19 May 1863 for rubella, and died of chronic diarrhea there 1 July 1863. Buried in the Oakland Cemetery, Atlanta, GA.

Jones, George M.; First Sergeant, Company A: Sworn into service 10 May 1861 at Nashville. Elected second sergeant at the reorganization, 1 May 1862. Later promoted to first sergeant. Age 28 on roll dated 10 May 1863. Deserted 16 December 1864.

Jones, George W.; Private, Company F: Enlisted 12 August 1861 at Loudon, TN. Captured at Tullahoma, TN., 1 July 1863. Sent to the U. S. Military Prison at Louisville, KY. Forwarded to Camp Chase, OH., 21 July 1863. Sent to Camp Douglas, IL., 24 August 1863. Complexion dark, hair brown, eyes black, height 6'.

Jones, Harris; Private, Company H: Born in 1824. No further.[401]

Jones, John A.; Private, Company H: Enlisted 26 February 1863 at Shelbyville, TN. Deserted 9 February 1864.

Jones, John Wesley; Fourth Sergeant, Company B: Born 17 July 1837 in Davidson Co., TN. Occupation: farmer. Sworn into service, 10 May 1861 at Nashville. Promoted to fifth sergeant by March 1863. Promoted to fourth sergeant by February 1864. Admitted to Asylum Hospital, Madison, GA., 30 May 1864. Returned to duty from Asylum Hospital, 15 July 1864. Wounded in the hand in the Battle of New Hope Church, GA., 27 May 1864. Wounded and captured in the Battle of Franklin, TN., 30 November 1864. Sent to the U. S. Military Prison at Louisville, KY. Forwarded to Camp Douglas, IL., 3 December 1864. Complexion fair, hair brown, eyes gray, height 5' 8". Married Margaret Virginia Neely (Jennie), 24 May 1866. Residing at Beechville, Williamson Co., TN. in 1870. Applied for admission to

---

[398] United Daughters of the Confederacy, *Confederate Soldiers of Hickman County*, 112; Garrett, *Dickson County Handbook*, 208; "John Jefferson Johnson," 432.

[399] Maney, *Surgeon's Log*, "Missionary Ridge TN."

[400] Electronic mail correspondence with William L. Jones, 17-19 October 2002.

[401] United Daughters of the Confederacy, *Confederate Soldiers of Hickman County*, 113.

the Tennessee Confederate Soldiers Home in 1897. Member of the Cheatham Bivouac. Died 2 May 1907. Buried in Mount Olivet Cemetery, Nashville, TN.[402]

Jones, Joseph T.; Private, Company B, G: Born in Davidson Co., TN. in 1840. Sworn into service 10 May 1861 in Company B at Nashville. Nurse in hospital at Richmond, KY., July through 6 October 1862. Captured at Richmond, KY. upon the withdrawal of the army and exchanged at Nashville, TN. Age 21 on roll dated 2 June 1863 at Shelbyville, TN. Transferred to Company G by July 1863. Wounded in the right eye by the explosion of a shell in the Battle of Missionary Ridge, TN., 25 November 1863. Patient in Cannon Hospital Union Springs, AL., July through August 1864. Wounded after surrender and capture in the Battle of Nashville, TN., 16 December 1864, having his arm broken in two places by a Federal soldier. Sent to the U. S. Military Prison at Louisville, KY. Forwarded to Camp Chase, OH., 4 January 1865. Enlisted in the United States Army, 22 April 1865, but rejected due to disabilities. Resided at Adairville, Logan Co., KY. Died 2 February 1924 at the Little Sisters of the Poor, Louisville, KY. Buried St. Louis Cemetery, Louisville, KY.[403]

Jones, Lentulus A. "Lynn"; Private, Company F: Brother of First Lieutenant Thomas B. Jones and Private Edward B. Jones. Occupation: farmer. Resided in Montgomery Co., TN. Enlisted 18 May 1861 at Cedar Hill, TN. Wounded in the left arm in the Battle of Missionary Ridge, TN., 25 November 1863. Admitted to Fair Ground Hospital #2, Atlanta, GA. on 27 November 1863 for vulnus sclopeticum. Given a medical furlough 8 December 1863. At 7' 4", he was possibly the tallest soldier in the Army of Tennessee. No further.[404]

Jones, Samuel G.; Private, Company H: Born 28 November 1840 in Hickman Co., TN. Brother of First Lieutenant William Clinton Jones. Attended Centerville Academy. Sworn into service 14 May 1861. Wounded severely in the chest in the Battle of Murfreesboro, TN., 31 December 1862. Sent to Confederate Hospital #1 at Murfreesboro, TN. Captured and sent to Nashville, 17 April 1863. Forwarded to the U. S. Military Prison at Louisville, KY, 23 April 1863. Sent to City Point, VA., 27 April 1863. Paroled 30 April 1863. Returned to his command, but was unfit for service, and was furloughed home. Captured while on furlough in Hickman Co., TN. by Lieutenant Horton, 27 January 1864. Sent to the U. S. Military Prison at Louisville, KY. Forwarded to Rock Island, IL., 11 February 1864. Took oath 24 April 1865. Complexion fair, hair light, eyes blue, height 5' 11', age 23. Married Mary J. Webb, 16 May 1870. Relocated to Humphreys Co., TN. in 1875. Engaged in general farming. He was a member of the Methodist Church, a Master Mason, and a Democrat. Member of the Tennessee House of Representatives, 46th General Assembly, 1889-91, representing Humphreys Co. Died at Sycamore Landing, Humphreys Co., TN., 4 February 1900.[405]

Jones, Thomas B.; First Lieutenant, Company F: Brother of Private Lentulus and Private Edward B. Jones. Enlisted 18 May 1861 at Cedar Hill, TN. Brevetted second lieutenant, 1 April 1862. Promoted to second lieutenant by November 1863. Promoted to first lieutenant, 9 April 1864. Killed in the Battle of Atlanta, GA., 22 July 1864.[406]

Jones, W. J.; Private, Company E, A: Enlisted 8 October 1861 in Company E at Camp Buckner, KY. Transferred to Company A at the reorganization, 1 May 1862. Detailed as a teamster in the

---

[402] Maney, *Surgeon's Log*, "May 1864"; Harris, *Confederate Hospitals*, 424, 90; John Wesley Jones, Cheatham Bivouac Application; *Nashville American*, 3 May 1907.

[403] J. T. Jones, Tennessee Pension Application, 8500 and Kentucky 1762; Lynn, *Confederate Pensioners of Kentucky*, 134; *Nashville Daily Press*, 22 December 1864.

[404] Maney, *Surgeon's Log*, "Missionary Ridge TN"; Electronic mail correspondence, William L. Jones, 17-19 October 2002; Welsh, *Confederate Hospitals*, Patient Roster, Fair Ground Hospital #1, 151.

[405] Goodspeed Brothers, *Goodspeed's Histories of Montgomery, Robertson, Humphreys, Stewart, Dickson, Cheatham, Houston Counties*, 1236.

[406] Jackson, "Letter to Parents," 14 July 1864; Electronic mail correspondence, William L. Jones, 17-19 October 2002.

quartermaster department, 23 March 1863 through December 1863. Deserted sometime in January or February 1864.

Jones, William Clinton "Clint"; First Lieutenant, Company H: Born 17 October 1835 in Hickman Co., TN. Brother of Private Samuel Jones. Occupation: farmer. Sworn into service 14 May 1861. Promoted to first lieutenant 8 June 1861. Absent at Knoxville, TN. as a drill officer March through April 1862. Reduced in rank to first sergeant April 1862. Left as a nurse at Confederate Hospital #1 at Murfreesboro, TN. and captured 3 January 1863. Sent to the U. S. Military Prison at Louisville, KY. Forwarded to Camp Butler, IL. Exchanged and returned to the company. Promoted to second lieutenant by November 1863. Wounded through the buttock in the Battle of Missionary Ridge, TN., 25 November 1863. Promoted to first lieutenant by August 1864. Wounded in battle near Atlanta, GA., 6 August 1864. Shot in upper part of right leg. Admitted to Ocmulgee Hospital Macon, GA., 28 February 1865 for a gunshot wound. Released 3 March 1865. Paroled at Gainesville, AL. Married Mary E. Walker, 7 March 1867. In 1875 he relocated to Humphreys Co., TN. and for many years lived on the Buffalo River near Bakerville. After his first wife's death he married Ellen Link. Late in life he moved to Waverly, where he experienced failing health. Member of the Methodist Episcopal Church South and was a Royal Arch Mason. Died 17 June 1910 in Humphreys Co., TN. Buried Wyly Cemetery, Waverly, Humphreys Co., TN.[407]

Jones, William H.; Private, Company H: Born 6 February 1842 at Centerville, TN. Sworn into service 14 May 1861 at Nashville. Present with cavalry commander Nathan B. Forrest at the Battle of Missionary Ridge, 25 November 1863. Present with company through February 1864. Took oath at Chattanooga, TN., 5 May 1865. Complexion fair, hair light, eyes gray, height 6'1". Following the war he resided in Brandy, TX.[408]

Jones, William H. H.; Private, Company B: Born 3 August 1840 in Davidson Co., TN. Sworn into service 10 May 1861 at Nashville. Age 23 on roll dated 2 June 1863 at Shelbyville, TN. Wounded by an artillery shell fragment on the left side of the head near the eyes in the Battle of Kennesaw Mountain, GA., 27 June 1864. His wound left him blind in one eye. Captured soon after the evacuation of Kennesaw Mountain near Marietta, GA., 3 July 1863. Sent to the U. S. Military Prison at Louisville, KY. Forwarded to Camp Douglas, IL., 16 July 1864. Discharged 15 May 1865. Later resident of Samburg, Obion Co., TN. Applied to the Tennessee Confederate Soldiers Home in 1899.[409]

Jones, William S.; Private, Company I: Sworn into service 20 May 1861 at Nashville. Died 25 November 1861 at Cumberland Gap, TN.

Jones, William Washington; Private, Company E: Born in 1832 in Dickson Co., TN. Sworn into service 18 May 1861 at Nashville. Discharged on surgeon's certificate of disability 27 November 1861. Buried in the Seals Cemetery, Dickson Co., TN.

*Jordan, Benjamin M.; Private, Company F: Enlisted 12 September 1861 at Knoxville, TN. Listed as regimental blacksmith from 3 March 1862. In hospital just prior to 14 July 1864. Surrendered as a member of Company K, 2nd Consolidated Tennessee Infantry, 26 April 1865 at Greensboro, NC. He was present at the 14 June 1904 reunion of the 11th Tennessee Infantry in Nashville.[410]

Jordan, Berry M.; Private, Company K: Occupation: farmer. Sworn into service 25 May 1861 at Nashville. Age 21 on roll dated 1 May 1863. Shot through the head and killed in the Battle of Chickamauga, GA., 19 September 1863.[411]

---

[407] Goodspeed Brothers, *Goodspeed's Histories of Montgomery, Robertson, Humphreys, Stewart, Dickson, Cheatham, Houston Counties*, 1235-36; Maney, *Surgeon's Log*, "Missionary Ridge, TN"; Maney, *Surgeon's Log*, "August 1864"; United Daughters of the Confederacy, *Confederate Soldiers of Hickman County*, 114; Waverly Newspaper, 18 June 1910.

[408] Yeary, *Reminiscences*, 393-94.

[409] William H. H. Jones, Tennessee Pension Application, 2560.

[410] Jackson, "Letter to Parents," 14 July 1864; *Reunion Pamphlet*, 14 June 1904.

[411] Maney, *Surgeon's Log*, "Chickamauga GA."

Jordan, Montgomery; Private, Company E: Sworn into service 18 May 1861 at Nashville. Present through August 1863. No further.

Joyce, Richard; Private, Company G: Enlisted 3 June 1861 at Camp Cheatham, TN. Discharged under the conscript act, 16 August 1862 at Tazewell, TN.

Joyce, Thomas; Private, Company E, G: Born c. 1835 in Ireland. Occupation: day laborer. Sworn into service 18 May 1861 in Company E at Nashville. Age 27 on roll dated 16 August 1861 at Watauga Bridge, TN. Transferred to Company G at Cumberland Gap, TN. Discharged 13 August 1862 at Tazewell, TN. under the conscript law.[412]

-K-

Karney, Pat; Private, Company B: Enlisted 10 May 1861 at Nashville. Discharged by the conscript law at Tazewell, TN., 12 August 1862.

Keenan, Robert; Private, Company I, G: Sworn into service 20 May 1861 in Company I at Nashville. Transferred to Company G at the reorganization, 1 May 1862. Captured in the Battle of Missionary Ridge, TN., 25 November 1863. Sent to the U. S. Military Prison at Louisville, KY. Forwarded to Rock Island, IL., 7 December 1863. Forwarded to Camp Douglas, 25 January 1864.

Kelleher, Patrick; Private, Company D: Sworn into service 11 May 1861 at Nashville. Deserted from hospital in Nashville, 25 July 1861.

Kelly, Jeremiah; Private, Company G: Enlisted 3 June 1861 at Camp Cheatham. Discharged by the conscript law 19 August 1862 at Tazewell, TN.

Kelly, John; Private, Company G: Sworn into service 14 May 1861 in Company C at Nashville. Transferred to Company G at the reorganization, 1 May 1862. Discharged by the conscript act, 14 August 1862 at Tazewell, TN.

*Kemp, John; Second Lieutenant, Company H: Sworn into service 14 May 1861 at Nashville. Elected fourth corporal at the reorganization, 1 May 1862. Promoted to third corporal by January 1863. Appointed fifth sergeant, 10 June 1863. Wounded in the Battle of Chickamauga, GA., 19 September 1863. Admitted to Fair Ground Hospital #1, Atlanta, GA., 24 September 1863 for vulnus sclopeticum. Sent to another hospital 28 September 1863. Admitted to Confederate hospital, Madison, GA., 24 December 1863. Furloughed 30 December 1863. Admitted to Blackie Hospital, Madison, GA., 29 January 1864. Held rank of second lieutenant in Company K, 2nd Consolidated Tennessee Infantry. Surrendered with the Army of Tennessee, 26 April 1865.[413]

Kennedy, John; Private, Company B: Sworn into service 10 May 1861 at Nashville. Discharged due to the conscript act, 12 August 1862 at Tazewell, TN.

Kennedy, Patrick; Private, Company E: Sworn into service 18 May 1861 at Nashville. Age 30 on roll dated 16 August 1861 at Watauga Bridge, TN. Transferred at the reorganization, 1 May 1862 at Cumberland Gap, TN.

Kennedy, Patrick; Private, Company G: Sworn into service 10 May 1861 at Nashville. Discharged 13 August 1862 by the conscript act at Tazewell, TN.

Kephart, Fountain Elliott Pitts; Private, Company E: Born in 1838 in Dickson Co., TN. Sworn into service 18 May 1861 at Nashville. Age 22 on roll dated 16 August 1861 at Watauga Bridge, TN. Deserted at Cumberland Gap, TN., 10 May 1862. Died 20 September 1914. Buried in the Greenwood Cemetery, Dickson Co., TN.[414]

---

[412] Dobson-Sides, *1860 Davidson County Census*, 356.

[413] Welsh, *Confederate Hospitals*, Patient Roster, Fair Ground Hospital #1, 155; Harris, *Confederate Hospitals*, 401, 109.

[414] Garrett, Burns, and McClain, *Dickson County Cemetery Records* vol. 1, rev. ed., 50.

Kerley, E. R.; Private, Company D: Sworn into service 11 May 1861 at Nashville. Discharged for disability.

Kernell, Samuel H.; Private, Company B: Sworn into service 10 May 1861 at Nashville. Present with company at least through February 1864. Took oath 22 December 1864. Complexion dark, hair dark, eyes gray, height 5' 7".

Kessell, Samuel A.; Private, Company G, B, D: Sworn into service 10 May 1861 in Company G at Nashville. Transferred to Company B at the reorganization, 1 May 1862. Transferred to Company D, 1 July 1862. Sent to hospital in Richmond, KY. Deserted 14 February 1863 at Shelbyville, TN. Captured near Chattanooga, TN., 10 September 1863.

Keys, James A.; Musician, Company D: Born c. 1845 in Michigan. Resident of Williamson Co., TN. in 1860. Sworn into service 11 May 1861 at Nashville. Elected musician. Discharged 15 August 1862 by the conscript act at Tazewell, TN.[415]

Kimbro, George W.; Private, Company K: Sworn into service 25 May 1861 at Nashville. Age 28 on roll dated 15 August 1861 at Midway, TN. On extra duty in the quartermaster department, 30 September 1861 through 30 April 1862. Discharged by the conscript act, 12 August 1862 at Tazewell, TN.

King, Festus; First Corporal, Company E, G: Sworn into service 18 May 1861 in Company E at Nashville. Age 22 on roll dated 16 August 1861 at Watauga Bridge, TN. Transferred to Company G at the reorganization, 1 May 1862. Promoted to second corporal by July 1863. Appointed first corporal by November 1863. Deserted near Chattanooga, TN. Captured and sent to the U. S. Military Prison at Louisville, KY, 9 November 1863. Took oath 25 November 1863. Complexion dark, hair black, eyes gray, height 5' 8".

King, Martin; Private, Company E: Sworn into service 18 May 1861 at Nashville. Age 38 on roll dated 16 August 1861 at Watauga Bridge, TN. Transferred at the reorganization, 1 May 1862 at Cumberland Gap, TN.

King, Martin; Private, Company G: Sworn into service 10 May 1861 at Nashville. Discharged by the conscript act, 1 August 1862 at Tazewell, TN.

King, Martin; Private, Company A: Sworn into service 20 May 1861 at Nashville. Discharged by the conscript act, 18 August 1862.

Kinsbro, J. C.; Private, Company A: Enlisted 6 May 1863 at Shelbyville, TN., age 25. No further.

Kirby, Richard; Private, Company D: No further.[416]

Kirk, William Montgomery; Second Lieutenant, Company E: Born 11 July 1838 at Charlotte, Dickson Co., TN. Occupation: farmer. Married Sarah Hendrick, 25 December 1860. Sworn into service 18 May 1861 at Nashville. Age 22 on roll dated 16 August 1861 at Watauga Bridge, TN. Elected second lieutenant at the organization. Dismissed from service. Later served in the cavalry, but was discharged due to poor health. Listed as Sheriff of Dickson Co., TN. in 1880. Relocated to Hickman, Fulton Co., KY. where he died, 28 August 1905. Buried in the City Cemetery, Hickman, Fulton Co., KY. Pension application Kentucky Widow 407.[417]

Kirkland, William H.; Musician, Company A, Field & Staff: Sworn into service 10 May 1861 at Nashville. Appointed musician (bugler) in Company A. Transferred to the Field & Staff, 15 April 1862.

---

[415] Williamson County Archives, *1860 Census of Williamson County, Tennessee* (s.l.: Williamson County Archives, 2003) 3.

[416] Clayton, *History of Davidson County*, 187.

[417] McCauley Camp 260, *Confederate Graves*, 29; Sistler and Sistler, *1880 Census of Dickson County*, 118; Donald L. Livingston, *Fulton Countians in the Civil War: Biographical Sketches of the Men from Fulton County, Kentucky, and Surrounding Area Who Participated in Our Nation's Civil War, 1861-1865: Unit Histories and Muster Rolls* (s.l.: D.L. Livingston, 1985) 37; Lynn, *Confederate Pensioners of Kentucky*, 140.

Age 26 on roll dated 6 May 1863 at Shelbyville, TN. Deserted 18 December 1864. Took oath 9 February 1865. Complexion fair, hair brown, eyes hazel, height 5' 7".

Kleiser, Jonas M.; Musician, Field & Staff: Enlisted 1 November 1862 at Dalton, GA. as a musician. Appointed sutler, January 1863 and dropped from the roll. Took oath, 30 May 1865. Complexion fair, hair dark, eyes dark, height 5' 8".

Knight, Thomas H.; Private, Company A: Sworn into service 10 May 1861 at Nashville. Died 6 July 1861 at home in Humphreys Co., TN.

Knott, James R.; Private, Company H: Born c. 1825 in VA. Occupation: farmer. Married to Mary L. Sworn into service 14 May 1861 at Nashville. Discharged 1 May 1862 by the conscript act.[418]

Kuhn, Lawrence B.; Private, Company B: Born c. 1842. Occupation: apprentice printer. Sworn into service 10 May 1861 at Nashville. Deserted 25 November 1861 at Cumberland Gap, TN.[419]

*Kyle, William D.; Private, Company D, B: Occupation: mechanic. Sworn into service 11 May 1861 in Company D. Transferred to Company B. Age 30 on roll dated 2 June 1863 at Shelbyville, TN. Captured and exchanged. Wounded in the left temple in the Battle of Resaca, GA, 14 May 1864. Shot through the right hand in the Battle of Jonesboro, GA., 1 September 1864. Shot through the right hand. Surrendered with the Army of Tennessee, 26 April 1865 as a member of Company C, 2nd Consolidated Tennessee Infantry.[420]

-L-

Lancaster, George W.; Private, Company H: Born in 1842. Brother of Privates J. S. J., Samuel, and Thomas Lancaster. Occupation: farm hand. Sworn into service 14 May 1861 at Nashville. Discharged 10 October 1862 on a surgeon's certificate of disability. Took oath 16 January 1864. Complexion dark, hair dark, eyes blue, height 5' 10".[421]

Lancaster, Jarrott S. J. "Rockie"; Private, Company H: Born c. 1834. Brother of Privates George, Samuel, and Thomas Lancaster. Occupation: farmer. Married to Rachael C. Sworn into service 14 May 1861 at Nashville. Admitted to Fair Ground Hospital #2, Atlanta, GA., 15 July 1863 for chronic diarrhea. Returned to duty, 1 August 1863. Killed in the Battle of Chickamauga, GA., 19 September 1863. Age 30.[422]

Lancaster, Samuel M.; Private, Company H: Born in 1844 in Hickman Co., TN. Brother of Privates George, J. S. J., and Thomas Lancaster. Enlisted 1 December 1862 at Manchester, TN. Wounded in the head by a shell fragment at the Battle of Murfreesboro, TN., 31 December 1862. Sent to hospital in Chattanooga, TN. Rejoined Company by September 1863. Furloughed home. Captured 12 August 1864 at Atlanta, GA. Sent to the U. S. Military Prison at Louisville, KY. Took oath, 26 August, 1864. Complexion light, hair dark, eyes blue, height 5' 11". Resided at Lynn Grove, Calloway Co., KY. Occupation: farmer. Died 28 December 1930. Tennessee Pension Application S5970.

Lancaster, Thomas C.; Private, Company H: Born in Hickman Co., TN. in 1839. Brother of Privates George, J. S. J. and Samuel Lancaster. Enlisted 8 August 1861 at Nashville. He had heart and nervous trouble rendering him unfit for service. Admitted to Fair Ground Hospital #1, Atlanta, GA., 5 July 1863 for febris intermittens. Returned to duty 18 July 1863. At Hood Hospital, Cuthbert, GA., 28

---

[418] United Daughters of the Confederacy, *Hickman County Census 1860*, 213.

[419] Dobson-Sides, *1860 Davidson County Census*, 454.

[420] Maney, *Surgeon's Log*, "May 1864"; Maney, *Surgeon's Log*, "September 1864."

[421] United Daughters of the Confederacy, *Confederate Soldiers of Hickman County*, 118.

[422] United Daughters of the Confederacy, *Hickman County Census 1860*, 153; Welsh, *Confederate Hospitals*, Patient Roster, Fair Ground Hospital #2, 114; Maney, *Surgeon's Log*, "Chickamauga GA."

November 1864. On detached service May and June 1864 at the military prison at Atlanta, GA., commanded by Captain A. Hurtel. Retired by a board of physicians at Augusta, GA. in March 1865.[423]

Landers, Adam; Private, Company A: Sworn into service 10 May 1861 at Nashville. Nurse in Hospital #2 at Knoxville, TN., 15 December 1862 through May 1863. Age 30 on roll dated 6 May 1863. On detached service as a nurse at Academy Hospital in Chattanooga, TN., 17 July through August 1863. Killed in the Battle of Missionary Ridge, TN., 25 November 1863.

Lane, Abraham; Private, Company G: Captured at Dunlap, TN., 21 August 1863. Sent to Camp Chase, OH., 1 September 1863.

Lane, Jacob E.; Private, Company E: Enlisted 24 February 1863 at Shelbyville, TN. Died 16 April 1863 in hospital at Shelbyville, TN. Buried Willow Mount Cemetery, Shelbyville, Bedford Co., TN.

Lane, Thomas; Second Lieutenant, Company E: Born in Dickson Co., TN. in 1839. Occupation: farmer. Sworn into service 18 May 1861 at Nashville. Age 25 on roll dated 16 August 1861 at Watauga Bridge, TN. Elected fourth sergeant at the organization. Elected second lieutenant at the reorganization, 1 May 1862. Sick at Readyville, TN., 7 December 1862. Wounded in the Battle of Peachtree Creek, GA., 20 July 1864. A spent ball struck the left leg in the calf and penetrated three to four inches. Incapacitated three to four months. Admitted to Catoosa Hospital, Griffin, GA., 22 July 1864. Given a furlough from the hospital. Before the furlough expired the army had relocated. Took oath 21 January 1865. Complexion fair, hair light, eyes gray, height 5' 11".[424]

Lankford, John Newton Henry; Private, Company K: Born c. 1838. Brother of Privates Lawrence and Robert Lankford. Occupation: farmhand. Married Margaret Marsh 10 May 1861. Sworn into service 25 May 1861 at Nashville. Age 24 on roll dated 15 August 1861 at Midway, TN. Died 14 February 1862 at Cumberland Gap, TN.[425]

Lankford, Lawrence D. R.; Private, Company K: Born c. 1835. Brother of Privates John and Robert Lankford. Occupation: farmhand. Married Harriet M. Parker, 19 July 1860. Enlisted 4 February 1863 at Shelbyville, TN. Age 22 on roll dated 1 May 1863 at Shelbyville, TN. Deserted and captured 3 July 1864 at Marietta, GA. Sent to the U. S. Military Prison at Louisville, KY. Forwarded to Camp Douglas, IL., 16 July 1864. Died 16 December 1864. Buried in the Oak Woods Cemetery, Chicago, IL.[426]

Lankford, Robert Henry; Private, Company K: Born c. 1836. Brother of Privates John and Lawrence Lankford. Married Louisa Partee Tate, 26 April 1856. Enlisted 25 May 1861 at Nashville. Age 25 on roll dated 15 August 1861 at Midway, TN. On extra duty as a teamster, October 1861. Working on post commissary house, January 1862. On indefinite sick furlough from 15 February 1862. Returned to duty by November 1862. Captured 3 July 1864 at Marietta, GA. Sent to the U. S. Military Prison at Louisville, KY. Forwarded to Camp Douglas, IL. Died 17 December 1864 of small pox. Buried in the Oak Woods Cemetery, Chicago, IL.[427]

Lark, William; Private, Company G, D: Born 25 January 1842 in Winchester, TN. Sworn into service 10 May 1861 in Company G at Nashville. Transferred to Company D in December 1861. Age 24 on roll dated 5 May 1863 at Shelbyville, TN. Shot through the left hand in the Battle of New Hope Church, GA., 27 May 1864. Received at Confederate hospital, Atlanta, GA., 28 May 1864. Sent to

---

[423] Welsh, *Confederate Hospitals*, Patient Roster, Fair Ground Hospital #1, 161; T. C. Lancaster, Tennessee Pension Application, 4172.

[424] *Chattanooga Daily Rebel*, 27 July 1864; Thomas Lane, Tennessee Pension Application, 4368.

[425] Strange, *Soldier's Home*, 124; Baker, *1860 Census for Dickson County*, 51; McCauley Camp 260, *Confederate Graves*, 29.

[426] Baker, *1860 Census for Dickson County*, 51; Find-A-Grave, "Oak Woods," http://www.findagrave/com/cgi-bin/fg.cgi?page=gr&GSln=Lankford&GSiman=1&GScid=173554& GRid=381345 17& (16 August 2014).

[427] Baker, *1860 Census for Dickson County*, 52; McCauley Camp 260, *Confederate Graves*, 30; Find-A-Grave, "Oak Woods," http://www.findagrave.com/cgi-bin/fg.cgi?page=gr&GSln=Lankford&GSiman=1&GScid=173554&GRid=38134519& (16 August 2014).

Confederate hospital Madison, GA., 29 May 1864. Deserted Blackie Hospital, Madison, GA., 6 June 1864. Captured in the Battle of Franklin, TN, 30 November 1864. Took oath 22 December 1864 at Nashville. Sent to the U. S. Military Prison at Louisville, KY. Paroled May 1865. Complexion dark, hair dark, eyes hazel, height 5' 4". He was present at the 14 June 1904 reunion of the 11th Tennessee Infantry in Nashville. Lived at the Tennessee Confederate Soldiers Home from 24 July 1908. Died May 21, 1922. Buried in the Soldiers Home Cemetery, grave #387.[428]

Larkin, Joseph N.; Private, Company unknown: Enlisted 15 November 1862 at Nashville. Deserted 3 July 1863. Took oath 4 February 1865. Complexion dark, hair dark, eyes hazel, height 5' 4".

Larkins, James Martin; Private, Company E: Born 20 October 1840 in Dickson Co., TN. Occupation: farmer. Sworn into service 18 May 1861 at Nashville. Age 20 on roll dated 16 August 1861 at Watauga Bridge, TN. Teamster in the quartermaster department January through December 1862. Shot through the stomach and bowels at Kennesaw Mountain, GA., 29 June 1864. Died 30 June 1864 at 10:00 a.m.[429]

Larkins, Dr. James Monroe; Surgeon, Field & Staff: Born 29 June 1818 in Dickson Co., TN. Attended Tracey Academy in Charlotte, TN. Began study of medicine in 1843, graduating from the Medical College of Louisville in 1846. Returning to Dickson Co. to practice medicine, his patients were largely among the employees and slaves of the iron works located there. Plagued by ill health all of his life. Married 1) D. Jane Coldwell, 23 December 1847. Opposed to slavery in principle, but considered Lincoln's call for troops without the consent of Congress an act of tyranny, and thus heartily entered into the rebellion. Appointed surgeon in the 11th Tennessee Infantry by Governor Isham G. Harris, 8 June 1861 with the rank of major. While serving at Camp Cheatham, he conceived the idea of using hospital tents instead of wooden huts then in use. Remaining with the regiment until his commission expired, he returned home due to the death of his wife, 21 August 1861. Rejoining the army, but refusing a commission, he worked as a post surgeon under Dr. Samuel H. Stout, Medical Director for the Army of Tennessee. Took a leave of absence in November 1864 and was trying to rejoin the army at Marietta, GA. when news of the surrender came. Following the war, with the iron works in ruin, he relocated to Clarksville, TN. Married 2) Emma V. Bagwell, 10 February 1866. Royal Arch Mason. Died 11 May 1887. Buried in the Charlotte Cemetery, Charlotte, Dickson Co., TN.[430]

Larkins, Joseph Henry; Private, Company C, E: Born in Dickson Co., TN., 12 April 1843. Sworn into service 14 May 1861 in Company C. Transferred to Company E, at the reorganization, 1 May 1862. On sick furlough, 25 July through December 1861. Wounded in the shoulder in the Battle of Murfreesboro, TN., 31 December 1862. Age 21 on roll dated 8 May 1863 at Shelbyville, TN. Wounded in the left breast in the Battle of Chickamauga, GA., 19 September 1863. Wounded in the Battle of Adairsville, GA., 17 May 1864, the ball entering the top of the thigh, ranged downward, and came out the calf of the leg. Hospitalized just over six months at Macon, GA. due to this wound. Rejoined his company as soon as he was able to lay aside the crutches. Wounded in the calf in the Battle of Bentonville, NC., 21 March 1865. Surrendered with the Army of Tennessee, 26 April 1865 at Greensboro, NC. as a member of Company C, 2nd Consolidated Tennessee Infantry. Married Elizabeth Corlew. Resided in Charlotte, Dickson Co., TN. Died 29 November 1905. Buried Leech Cemetery, Charlotte, Dickson Co., TN.[431]

---

[428] Harris, *Confederate Hospitals*, 369, 142, 424; Strange, *Soldiers Home*, 124; *Reunion Pamphlet*, 14 June 1904.

[429] Maney, *Surgeon's Log*, "Kennesaw Mountain GA"; McCauley Camp 260; *Confederate Graves*, 30.

[430] *Semi-Weekly Tobacco Leaf* (Clarksville TN) 13 May 1887.

[431] Joseph Henry Larkins, Tennessee Confederate Pension Application, S4739.

Latham, John B.; Private, Company C: Born c. 1838. Occupation: farmer. Sworn into service 14 May 1861 at Nashville. Issued a Belgium musket. Died of disease 3 December 1863 at Murfreesboro, TN.[432]

Lawler, Michael J.; Brevet Second Lieutenant, Company G: Born c. 1837. Sworn into service 10 May 1861 at Nashville. Elected second corporal at the organization. Breveted second lieutenant at the reorganization, 1 May 1862. Deserted 14 January 1863. Resided postwar in Louisville, KY. Occupation stone-cutter. Died 11 January 1920 at Louisville, Jefferson Co., KY and buried there in the St. Louis Cemetery.[433]

*Lawrence, Belfield F.; Private, Company E: Born 11 February 1836. Enlisted 17 October 1862 at Lenoir Station, TN. Brigade teamster, 17 October 1862 through April 1863. Age 26 on roll dated 14 May 1863 at Shelbyville, TN. Regimental ordnance teamster, July 1863 through February 1864. Surrendered with the Army of Tennessee, 26 April 1865 at Greensboro, NC., as a member of Company C, 2nd Consolidated Tennessee Infantry. Died 27 April 1922. Buried in the Freemont Church of Christ Cemetery, Obion Co., TN.[434]

*Lawrence, Joseph B. "Joe"; Private, Company E: Born in Montgomery Co., TN., 15 November 1833. Resided in Dickson Co., TN. Occupation: farmer. Sworn into service 18 May 1861 at Nashville. Age 27 on roll dated 16 August 1861 at Watauga Bridge, TN. Wounded on the right top side of the head, fracturing the skull, in the Battle of Murfreesboro, TN., 31 December 1862. Sent to the hospital in Chattanooga, TN. Shot between the eyes at Missionary Ridge, TN., 23 November 1863. The ball broke the nose and came out under the jaw. Wounded dangerously a third time near Atlanta, GA., 29 July 1864. Shot through the upper portion of the right thorax, breaking two ribs, the ball passing out about four inches above the left nipple. Surrendered with the Army of Tennessee, 26 April 1865 at Greensboro, NC. as a member of Company C, 2nd Consolidated Tennessee Infantry. Married Sarah Dowden, 2 March 1870. Postwar occupation: farmer. Died 28 March 1919. Buried Jackson Chapel Methodist Church Cemetery, Charlotte, Dickson Co., TN., where his grave stone reads, "A Brave Soldier is Buried Here."[435]

Lawrence, William Henry Harrison; Private, Company E: Born in Montgomery Co., TN. in 1840. Sworn into service, 18 May 1861 at Nashville. Age 20 on roll dated 16 August 1861 at Watauga Bridge, TN. Wounded in the head in the Battle of Murfreesboro, TN., 31 December 1862. Brigade teamster, 11 January through April 1863. Regimental ordnance teamster, July through August 1863. Division ordnance teamster, September through October 1863. Wounded through the right lung, thought to be mortal, in the Battle of Atlanta, GA., 22 July 1864. Wounded in the shoulder in the Battle of Franklin, TN., 30 November 1864. Took oath, 31 March 1865. Complexion fair, hair dark, eyes hazel, height 5' 10". Resided at Hornbeak, Obion Co., TN.[436]

Leak, James L.; Private, Company B: Born 16 March 1825. Sworn into service, 10 May 1861 at Nashville. Discharged 12 August 1862 at Tazewell, TN. under the conscript law. Resident of Davidson Co., TN. Occupied as a printer. Applied to the Confederate Soldiers Home.[437]

Leake, Berry B.; Private, Company G: Born 6 July 1838 in Davidson Co., TN. Sworn into service, 10 May 1861 at Nashville. Discharged May 1861 for disability. Later joined the 11th (Gordon's) Tennessee Cavalry Battalion, serving as a lieutenant, and was later attached to the 15th Tennessee Cavalry Regiment (also known as the 9th). Participated in Morgan's raid into OH., where he was

---

[432] McCauley, *Record Book, Company C*; Baker, *1860 Census for Dickson County*, 68.

[433] *Louisville Courier Journal*, 13 January 1920.

[434] Obion County Genealogical Society, *Cemeteries of Obion County, Tennessee* vol. 2 (Union City TN: Obion County Genealogical Society, 1986) 49.

[435] Maney, *Surgeon's Log*, "Stones River TN"; Maney, *Surgeon's Log*, "Missionary Ridge TN"; Maney, *Surgeon's Log*, "28-31 July 1864"; Joseph B. Lawrence, Tennessee Pension Application, 6949.

[436] W. H. H. Lawrence, Tennessee Pension Application, 16694.

[437] James L. Leak, Confederate Soldiers Home Application.

captured at Salineville, OH., 26 July 1863. Remained in prison until released in May 1865. Postwar, resided in Nashville, TN. Occupation: Insurance agent. Member of the Cheatham Bivouac. Applied to the Confederate Soldiers Home in 1898, and was living there when he died, 5 February 1914.[438]

Leek, Alfred H.; Private, Company H: Born in 1844. Occupation: farm laborer. Enlisted 10 January 1863 at Shelbyville, Bedford Co., TN., and died there 15 April 1863.[439]

Leeper, John Henry; Private, Company H: Born 22 November 1840. Sworn into service 14 May 1861 at Nashville. On sick furlough, 6 November through December 1861. Captured 22 May 1863 at Murfreesboro, TN. Sent to the U. S. Military Prison at Louisville, KY. Forwarded to Baltimore, MD. Exchanged and rejoined company. Present at least through February 1864. Took oath 22 October 1864. Complexion fair, hair brown, eyes blue, height 5' 8". After the war was on the Board of Directors of the Bank of Lobelville, Perry Co., TN. In the late 1880s he built a water mill on the Buffalo River that provided a gristmill, sawmill, and a limited amount of electrical power to the surrounding area of Lobelville. Died 24 January 1923. Buried Leeper Cemetery, Lobelville, Perry Co., TN.[440]

Leggitt, R. A.; Private, Company H: Deserted 3 August 1863. Captured at Shelbyville, TN. Took oath and released.

Lewis, James A.; Private, Company A: Born 22 April 1837 in Dickson Co., TN. Resided at Dresden, Weakley Co., TN. Sworn into service 10 May 1861 at Nashville. Attendant at hospital at Tazewell, TN. from 28 April 1862. At Henry Hospital in Atlanta, GA., 18 June to 1 July 1862 as a nurse. Age 28 on roll dated 6 May 1863 at Shelbyville, TN. Seriously wounded in the left breast in the Battle of Franklin, TN., 30 November 1864. Hospitalized for two weeks. Given a sixty day furlough to go home. At end of furlough was cut off from command. Took oath 15 February 1865 to avoid going to prison. Complexion dark, hair dark, eyes hazel, height 6'. Married Sarah R. Ridings, 20 December 1865. Postwar, he resided in Humphreys Co., TN., where he farmed and served as a magistrate. Member of the Primitive Baptist Church. Died 23 February 1913. Buried in the Ridings Cemetery on White Oak Creek, Humphreys Co., TN. Pension Application S10019.[441]

Lewis, William; Musician, Company B, Field & Staff: Sworn into service 10 May 1861 in Company B at Nashville. Appointed musician and transferred to the Field & Staff at the reorganization, 1 May 1862. Age 26 on roll dated 2 June 1863. Present at least through February 1864.

Linebaugh, Benjamin E.; Corporal, Company F: Born 21 June 1830 in Russellville, KY. Moved to Springfield, Robertson Co., TN. in 1839. Occupation: saddle maker. Enlisted 18 May 1861 at Cedar Hill, TN. Discharged at Tazewell, TN., 25 August 1862. Married Louisa B. Miles, 11 January 1866. Politically a Democrat, member of the Cumberland Presbyterian faith and a Mason. In April 1895, shortly after the death of his wife, he became deranged and stabbed a man who had brought him food. He was brought to Springfield and placed in the care of officers. Died 18 November 1901. Buried in the Red River Baptist Church Cemetery, Robertson Co., TN.[442]

---

[438] Berry B. Leake, Cheatham Bivouac Application; Berry B. Leake, Confederate Soldiers Home Application.

[439] United Daughters of the Confederacy, *Confederate Soldiers of Hickman County*, 121; United Daughters of the Confederacy, *Hickman County Census 1860*, 69.

[440] United Daughters of the Confederacy, *Confederate Soldiers of Hickman County*, 121; James Lunsford, Tennessee Confederate Pension Application, 5485; Bowen, Mary Stewart and Melissa Snyder Bowen, *Perry County, Tennessee Cemetery Records*, vol. 1 (Linden TN: M.N. Bowen, 1992) 146; "Letters to Jill, Letter from Mrs. H. P. Leeper, Nashville," *River Counties*, Jill Garrett ed., vol. 3, 1974: 195.

[441] Goodspeed Brothers, *Goodspeed's Histories of Montgomery, Robertson, Humphreys, Stewart, Dickson, Cheatham, Houston Counties*, 1240-41; J. A. Lewis, Tennessee Confederate Pension Application, S10019; Anderson and Garrett, *Humphreys County Cemetery Records*, vol. 2, 27; Clifton, *1870 Census of Humphreys County*, 179.

[442] Goodspeed Brothers, *Goodspeed's Histories of Montgomery, Robertson, Humphreys, Stewart, Dickson, Cheatham, Houston Counties*, 1168-69; *Nashville Weekly American*, 9 April 1895.

Linzy, William Henry Harrison; Private, Company E: Born in Dickson Co., TN. in March 1841. Occupation: farmer. Sworn into service, 18 May 1861 at Nashville. Age 21 on roll dated 16 August 1861 at Watauga Bridge, TN. In mid-February 1862, while on picket duty at Cumberland Gap, he came down with "brain fever" which was brought on by exposure, leaving him unconscious at times. He remained incapacitated in camp about ten days, then was sent to the Confederate hospital at Tazewell, TN., where he was attended to by Drs. Shacklett and Slayden. On sick furlough at Knoxville, TN., 22 March 1862, remaining in the hospital until the following May. Throughout the remainder of the war he would relapse into this condition and be unfit for duty for three to four weeks. Wounded through the right arm and left on the field in the Battle of Missionary Ridge, TN., 25 November 1863. Captured and sent to Rock Island, IL. He was exchanged in 1865 in Richmond. According to great grandson, Doug Collier, Linzy saw the fires of Richmond burning from James Island before his exchange. Started for North Carolina and discovered that the 11th Tennessee had surrendered, so he headed back home to Dickson County Home Guards captured him, placing him in another camp until he took the oath of allegiance in late May, 1865. Complexion fair, hair dark, eyes gray, height 5' 6". Died 7 June 1927. Buried in the Greenwood Methodist Church Cemetery, Dickson Co., TN.[443]

Loftin, Thomas; Private, Company H: Born c. 1829. Occupation: farmer. Enlisted 8 February 1863 at Shelbyville, TN. Present through May 1863.[444]

Lomax, William E.; Private, Company H: Born c. 1840 in Hickman Co., TN. Occupation: farmer. Sworn into service 14 May 1861 at Nashville. Nurse in hospital in Knoxville, TN., September 1861. Discharged 8 April 1862 at Cumberland Gap, TN. Complexion fair, hair light, eyes blue, height 5' 7".[445]

*Long, Alfred "Alf"; Private, Company E: Born 23 January 1842 in Humphreys Co., TN. Occupation: farmer. Enlisted 19 September 1861 at Camp Buckner, KY. Age 19 on roll dated 14 May 1863 at Shelbyville, TN. Wounded in the Confederate works near Atlanta, GA., 31 July 1864, having just come in from picket duty, hit in the right leg three inches below the knee. The ball ranged down and around the large bone, splintering it, lodging just below the calf of the leg. Surgery to remove the ball was performed there. Removed to the hospital at Columbus, GA. until November 1864, at which time he was given a sixty-day furlough. Rejoined the command before the time had expired. Surrendered with the Army of Tennessee as a member of Company C, 2nd Tennessee Consolidated Infantry at Greensboro, NC., 26 April 1864. Captain W. D. Eleazer of Company E stated that Long was a great deal above the average soldier. Married Mary A. Binkley, 27 August 1870. Occupation: farmer. Died 17 February 1905. Buried Big Springs Cumberland Presbyterian Church Cemetery near Charlotte, Dickson Co., TN.[446]

Long, Felix G.; Private, Company unknown: Born 28 February 1826 in Davidson Co., TN. Occupation: farmer. Sworn into service May 1861 at Nashville. Discharged June 1862. Later served with the Stinson Guards. Resided at the Tennessee Confederate Soldiers Home from 13 April 1892, and died there 18 February 1895. Buried Tennessee Confederate Soldiers Home Cemetery, grave #15.[447]

Long, James; Private, Company B: Born in Nashville. Occupation: carpenter. Sworn into service 10 May 1861 at Nashville. In hospital at Knoxville, TN., 3 September 1861 due to being thrown from a wagon the day before, receiving an injury to the right leg whereby the fibula was broken near the upper

---

[443] W. H. H. Linzy, Tennessee Confederate Pension Application, S3104; Doug Collier, electronic mail correspondence, Great Grandson to W. H. H. Linzy, 28 December 2001; Maney, *Surgeon's Log*, "Missionary Ridge TN"; Garrett, *Dickson County Handbook*, 210.

[444] Jill Knight Garrett, and Catherine Kelly Gilliam, *1850 Census of Hickman County, Tennessee* (Columbia TN: 1967) 27.

[445] United Daughters of the Confederacy, *Confederate Soldiers of Hickman County*, 123.

[446] Maney, *Surgeon's Log*, "28-31 July 1864"; Alfred Long, Tennessee Confederate Pension Application, S4809; Sistler and Sistler, *1880 Census of Dickson County*, 40; Garrett and McClain, *Dickson County Cemetery Records*, vol. 1, 36.

[447] Strange, *Soldiers Home*, 5; Felix G. Long, Confederate Soldiers Home Application.

extremity, complicating the knee joint. The bones were badly set, and as a result weight could not be placed on that leg without using a crutch for support. Discharged 12 May 1862 at Knoxville, TN. Complexion dark, hair dark, eyes gray, height 5' 11", age 26.

Long, James A.; *Lieutenant-Colonel, Company F, Field & Staff:* Born 10 December 1825. Occupation: school teacher, and farmer at the family home just prior to the war. Enlisted 21 May 1861 at Cedar Hill, TN. Elected captain of Company F at the organization. Promoted to major, 21 March 1862 and transferred to the Field & Staff. Assumed duties of lieutenant-colonel, 14 December 1863. Long was officially promoted to lieutenant-colonel on 5 September 1864 but the rank was to have taken effect on 13 December 1863. His rank was posthumously confirmed 5 January 1865. Wounded in the Battle of Jonesboro, GA., 1 September 1864, being shot through the left leg near the knee. Died in the hospital of pyemia, 17 September 1864. Originally buried in the Confederate Cemetery, Forsyth, GA. His body may have been reinterred as a headstone exists for him in the Long Cemetery, Robertson Co., TN.[448]

Long, James H.; *Private, Company A:* Born 24 November 1831 in Maury Co., TN. Resided Humphreys Co., TN. Enlisted May 1861. Admitted to Asylum Hospital, Madison, GA., 4 July 1864. After the war he returned home to Humphreys Co., TN. and resumed farming. Married Sarah Elizabeth Dodson in 1869. Politically, he was a Democrat.[449]

Long, James Henry, Sr.; *Private, Company F:* Born 9 April 1828. Brother of Private Martin Frey Long. Occupation: farmer and tobacco dealer. Married Sarah Farmer, 14 October 1851. Served as a constable, 1854-56, and as a revenue collector in 1856-57. Enlisted 4 December 1862 at Manchester, TN. In late 1863, he sent a letter to his wife giving her instructions on managing their farm and included a detailed map indicating what crops to plant in each field. Present at least through February 1864. A member of the Free and Accepted Masons and the Methodist Episcopal Church South. Politically a Democrat.[450]

Long, Martin Frey; *Private, Company F:* Brother of Private James Henry Long, Sr. Occupation: farmer. Married 14 October 1851. Member of the Free and Accepted Masons. Enlisted 20 November 1862. Wrote parents 20 May 1864 from camp near Etowah, GA. Shot through the lungs while on the picket line at Kennesaw Mountain, GA., 19 June 1864. Died 23 June 1864. Buried in the Confederate Cemetery, Marietta, GA.[451]

Love, Jacob; *Rank unknown, Company A:* Died at Shelbyville, TN.[452]

Lowe, Andrew J.; *Assistant Surgeon, Company H, Field & Staff:* Born 8 November 1833. A practicing physician in the Whitfield community of Hickman Co., TN. prior to the war, he held a school of medical instruction in his home 1858-1859. Included as his students were future soldiers Samuel G. Jones, William Burchard, and W. Jerome D. Spence. Sworn into service 14 May 1861 at Nashville. On detached service in hospital at Tazewell, TN., 20 March through April 1862. Assistant surgeon, hospital at Bean Station, TN., 1 May 1862 through April 1863. Later served as surgeon for the 10th TN Cavalry (CS). Married Rachel Jones Carothers. Member of the Masonry and politically a Democrat. Served as a Representative in the Tennessee State Legislature, 46th General Assembly, from 7 January through 7

---

[448] Maney, *Surgeon's Log*, "September 1864."

[449] Harris, *Confederate Hospitals*, 85, 448; Goodspeed Brothers, *Goodspeed's Histories of Montgomery, Robertson, Humphreys, Stewart, Dickson, Cheatham, Houston Counties*, 1241-42.

[450] Goodspeed Brothers, *Goodspeed's Histories of Montgomery, Robertson, Humphreys, Stewart, Dickson, Cheatham, Houston Counties*, 1170; Allen, *Winds*, 67-69.

[451] Lindsley, *Annals*, 304; Maney, *Surgeon's Log*, "Kennesaw Mountain GA"; Jackson, "Letter to Parents," 14 July 1864.

[452] Lindsley, *Annals*, 303.

May 1889 at which time he resigned due to ill health. Died 21 June 1889. Buried in the Carothers Cemetery, Lowe's Bend, Hickman Co., TN.[453]

Lowe, Henry; Private, Company H: Sworn into service 14 May 1861 at Nashville. Died 10 July 1861 at Camp Cheatham.

Lucas, Hugh Ross; Major, Company I, Field & Staff: Born in 1827. Served in the Mexican War. As a youth he took up the tanners trade and later acquired a partnership interest in a large tanyard, located on Little Turkey Creek in Humphreys Co., TN. Elected to the Tennessee House of Representatives 1853-55, representing Humphreys and Benton Counties. Member of the Whig party. Married Artemis "Missie" Wyly in 1854. The couple had two children before she died, 21 August 1858. Purchased an ownership interest in Major Thomas K. Wyly's Fairfield Plantation on Walnut Bayou near Tallulah, LA. He raised the first company of Confederates in Humphreys Co. Sworn into service 20 May 1861 at Nashville. Elected captain of the company (later became Company I) at the organization. Promoted to major, 28 May 1861. On detached service as a member of a general court martial held in Knoxville, TN., November-December, 1861 to try those connected with the 9 November 1861 burning of the Virginia and East Tennessee Railroad bridge over Lick Creek, Greene Co., TN. Defeated in the election at reorganization, 1 May 1862. On furlough, he visited his plantation in Louisiana, where he was captured and imprisoned at Fort Delaware. Located twenty miles west of Vicksburg, his plantation was devastated during the siege of Vicksburg and the latter course of the war. Upon release from prison, he returned to his plantation, Algodon, where he remained for the rest of his life, acquiring several other plantations known collectively as Trinidad. He served as a Louisiana state senator, 1880-1884. Described as a handsome, brawny man. Died in 1898. Buried in the Cross Cemetery, Tallulah, LA.[454]

Lundy, William Thomas; Private, Company G: Sworn into service 10 May 1861 at Nashville. Discharged under the conscript act, 10 August 1862 at Tazewell, TN.

Lunn, John A.; Rank unknown, Company C: Born in 1838 in Hickman Co., TN. Married 1)Mollie White in 1861. Also served in Company F, 17th Tennessee Infantry. Married 2) Callie Sparkman in 1879. Died 14 November 1926 at the Confederate Soldier's Home in Nashville, TN. Pension Application 6297.[455]

*Lunsford, James; Private, Company H: Born in Hickman Co., TN. in 1843. Sworn into service 14 May 1861 at Nashville. Served as a member of the regimental color guard. On detached service as a guard at a general hospital at Cleveland, TN., November 1862 through January 1863. Had a broken arm 6 August 1864. Service record states subject deserted 5 January 1865. Complexion fair, hair brown, eyes hazel, height 5' 9". Took oath 28 January 1865. However, Lunsford and other witnesses state that he was with the army until the end. He was incapacitated by chronic diarrhea during the Battle of Bentonville, NC., March, 1865. Resident of Bakerville, Humphreys Co., TN. Died at Waverly, TN., 19 April 1915.[456]

*Luther, George Martin; Private, Company K: Sworn into service, 25 May 1861 at Nashville. Age 20 on roll dated 15 August 1861 at Midway, TN. Surrendered with the Army of Tennessee at Greensboro, NC., 26 April 1865 as a member of Company K, 2nd Consolidated Tennessee Infantry.

Luther, Newton Jackson; First Corporal, Company K: Sworn into service 25 May 1861 at Nashville. Elected fourth corporal at the organization. Age 19 on roll dated 15 August 1861 at Midway, TN. Promoted to first corporal by July 1862. Captured 3 July 1864 at Marietta, GA. Sent to the U. S. Military Prison at Louisville, KY., 13 July 1864. Forwarded to Camp Douglas, IL., 14 July 1864. Took oath and released 6 June 1865. Complexion light, hair light, eyes gray, height 5' 11".

---

[453] United Daughters of the Confederacy, *Confederate Soldiers of Hickman County*, 125; Spence, *History*, 278.

[454] Cameron Judd, *The Bridge Burners* (Johnson City TN: Over Mountain Press, 1996) 106; Jonathan K. T. Smith, *The Wyly Saga* (Memphis TN: Padmoor Press, 1981) 31-32.

[455] United Daughters of the Confederacy, *Confederate Soldiers of Hickman County*, 126.

[456] James Lunsford, Tennessee Pension Application, 5485.

Lynch, W. B.; Private, Company B: Occupation: mechanic. Sworn into service 10 May 1861 at Nashville. Detached to the quartermaster department at Morristown, TN., 17 June 1862 through April 1863. Age 23 on roll dated 2 June 1863 at Shelbyville, TN. Wounded in the Battle of Peachtree Creek, GA., 20 July 1864. Died of wounds in hospital.[457]

Lyons, Jeremiah; Private, Company G: Enlisted 3 June 1861 at Camp Cheatham. Wounded in the right forearm in the Battle of Murfreesboro, TN., 31 December 1862. Captured and sent to Camp Morton, IN. Exchanged by April 1863. In Petersburg, VA. hospital, 12 April 1863. Rejoined company by May 1863. Age 32 on roll dated 30 May 1863. In hospital at Rome, GA., 17 June 1863. Deserted near Chattanooga, TN., 11 November 1863. Captured 12 November 1863. Forwarded to the U. S. Military Prison at Louisville, KY. Complexion dark, hair dark, eyes blue, height 5' 6".[458]

–M–

Mahoney, James; Private, Company G: Enlisted 3 June 1861 at Camp Cheatham. Discharged by the conscript act, 15 August 1862 at Tazewell, TN.

Mahoney, John; Private, Company G: Born c. 1838 in Ireland. Occupation: railroad laborer. Enlisted 4 June 1861 at Camp Cheatham. Deserted 24 April 1863.[459]

Majors, John P.; Private, Company K: Occupation: farmer. Enlisted 20 December 1862 in Dickson Co., TN. Age 20 on roll dated 1 May 1863 at Shelbyville, TN. Admitted to Fair Ground Hospital #2, Atlanta, GA., 12 September 1863 for acute dysentery. Returned to duty 14 September 1863. Wounded in the lower right leg and in the lower right thigh in the Battle of New Hope Church, GA., 27 May 1864. Furloughed by Colonel Binns, 14 December 1864 at Nashville, TN. Shortly after the Battle of Nashville, Majors, T. B. Adcock, J. W. Redden, and G. H. Petty attempted to return to the army but each time they attempted to cross the Tennessee River, they were fired on by Federal gunboats. The men stayed on the river bank trying to cross for eight days, and with provisions running out, they were forced to return home. Took oath 10 January 1865. Complexion fair, hair light, eyes blue, height 5' 7".[460]

Malia, Martin; Private, Company I, G: Sworn into service 20 May 1861 in Company I. Transferred to Company G at the reorganization, 1 May 1862. Age 31 on roll dated 30 May 1862 at Shelbyville, TN. Wounded in the side at the Battle of Murfreesboro, TN., 31 December 1862. Admitted to Ocmulgee Hospital, Macon, GA. for a gunshot wound, 22 July 1864. Surrendered with General Richard Taylor at Citronelle, AL. Paroled at Meridian, MS., 14 May 1865.

Mallory, William James; Captain, Company E: Born 11 April 1828 in Virginia. Fought in the Mexican War, enlisting in Company H, 3rd Tennessee Infantry, 24 September 1847 with the rank of private. Discharged 24 July 1848 at Memphis, TN. Lived on the farm of brother-in-law Cyrus Chichester in 1850 as a blacksmith. Sworn into service in Company E of the 11th, 18 May 1861 at Nashville. Elected captain at the organization. Age 33 on roll dated 16 August 1861 at Watauga Bridge, TN. Resigned 1 May 1862 at Cumberland Gap, TN. Dropped from the roll. After the war he operated the Mallory and Leech general store and a saloon in Charlotte, TN. A Democratic member of the

---

[457] Maney, *Surgeon's Log*, "20 July 1864."
[458] Ibid., "Stones River TN."
[459] Dobson-Sides, *1860 Davidson County Census*, 326.
[460] Welsh, *Confederate Hospitals*, Patient Roster, Fair Ground Hospital #2, 123; Maney, *Surgeon's Log*, "May 1864"; John W. Redden, Tennessee Confederate Pension Application, S3010.

"Forward My Brave Boys!"

Tennessee House of Representatives, 43rd General Assembly, 1885-1887, representing Dickson Co. Died 8 December 1889. Buried in the Charlotte Cemetery, Dickson Co., TN.[461]

Malugin, William G.; Private, Company A: Born c. 1832. Sworn into service 14 May 1861 at Nashville. Took oath 22 October 1864. Complexion dark, hair black, eyes dark, height 5' 10". Married E. M. Shaw, 22 December 1866.[462]

Maney, George Earl; Brigadier General, Company D: Born 24 August 1826 in Franklin, TN. in the Maney/Gaut House on Second Avenue. Son of Thomas Maney and Rebecca Southall. Brother of Surgeon William B. Maney. George Maney attended the Nashville Seminary and was graduated from the University of Nashville in 1845. He served as a second lieutenant in the 1st Tennessee Infantry in the Mexican War and later a first lieutenant in the 3rd U.S. Dragoons. After the Mexican War, Maney became an attorney in Nashville and practiced law from 1850 until 1861. Married Betty C. Crutcher in 1853. At the outbreak of the Civil War, Maney was primarily instrumental in raising the Hermitage Light Infantry, later Company D of the 11th Tennessee Infantry and was subsequently elected captain on 1 May 1861 at Nashville. Elected colonel of the 1st Tennessee Infantry Regiment, 8 May 1861. Maney subsequently rose to the rank of brigadier general, 16 April 1862 for gallantry in the Battle of Shiloh. He later temporarily commanded Cheatham's Division during the latter part of the Atlanta Campaign. Paroled at Greensboro, NC., 1 May 1865. Following the war, he was president of the Tennessee and Pacific Railroad. He was nominated to be minister to Ecuador, and in 1876 was a Republican candidate for governor, until he withdrew his name. Maney was later minister resident to Colombia, Bolivia, Paraguay, and Uruguay. He retired to Washington, DC, 30 June 1894 and lived there until his death, 9 February 1901. Buried Mount Olivet Cemetery, Nashville, Davidson Co., TN.[463]

Maney, William Brown; Surgeon, Major, Field & Staff: Born 12 December 1834 in Williamson, Co., TN. Son of Judge Thomas and Rebecca Southall Maney. Brother of Brigadier General George W. Maney. Attended the Pennsylvania Medical College and also the Medical Department of the University of Nashville, where he was graduated in 1857. Enlisted in Company A, 1st Tennessee Infantry Regiment in Nashville in April 1861 and obtained the rank of corporal. Appointed assistant surgeon of the 11th Tennessee regiment sometime between 1 August 1861 and 1 October 1861. Commissioned surgeon 15 February 1862. Left attending the wounded after the Battle of Murfreesboro, TN., 31 December 1862. Captured 2 January 1863. Sent to City Point, VA. Exchanged and rejoined the regiment. At the close of the Atlanta Campaign, he was exhausted and contracted typhoid fever. Sent to the hospital at Albany, GA. where he was in bed for six weeks. Rejoined the army at the Tennessee River on the retreat from Middle Tennessee in December 1864. Surrendered with the Army of Tennessee at Greensboro, NC., 26 April 1865, with the rank of major. Took oath at Nashville, TN., 12 June 1865. Complexion fair, hair light, eyes blue, height 6' 2". His marriage to Elizabeth Stone in 1867 produced three children, two of whom died in infancy, and the other died before reaching adulthood. Following the war he practiced medicine in Nashville for many years, then relocated to Phillips Co., AR. Later practiced medicine in Austin, TX. He returned to Nashville in 1889. The couple lived above his medical practice in the Maney building which he built on Church Street and were both active in Confederate Veteran affairs. He held the office of surgeon as a member of the Cheatham Bivouac, while Bettie Maney was one of the founding members and first treasurer of the United Daughters of the Confederacy. During his later years, Dr. Maney provided much charitable care to the poor and to Confederate veterans. He was present at the 14 June 1904 reunion of the 11th Tennessee Infantry in Nashville. Member, Christ Church

---

[461] Baker, *1850 Census for Dickson County,* 33; Garrett, *Dickson County Handbook,* 210; McBride, Robison, and Cornwell. *Biographical Directory,* 592; Brock, Reid, Thomas O. Brock, and Tony Hays. *Volunteers-Tennessee in the War with Mexico, L-Z* vol. 2 (Nashville TN: Kitchen Table Press, 1986) 16.

[462] United Daughters of the Confederacy, *Hickman County Census 1860,* 61; United Daughters of the Confederacy, *Confederate Soldiers of Hickman County,* 142.

[463] http://www.libarts.ucok.edu/history/faculty/roberson/spr2001/1493suppl/ch18/GeorgeEarl Maney; Warner, *Generals,* 210; *Nashville Daily Patriot,* 4 May 1861.

Episcopal, Nashville, TN. Died within a few days of his wife on 22 February 1920. Buried in the Mount Olivet Cemetery, Nashville, Davidson Co., TN.[464]

Manley, Benjamin Franklin; Private, Company K: Born in Bedford Co., TN., 31 January 1844. Resided in Dickson Co., TN., then moved to McEwen, Humphreys Co., TN. Enlisted 31 December 1861. Age 19 on roll dated 1 May 1863 at Shelbyville, TN. Wounded in the shoulder by flying debris broken by a cannon ball in the Battle of Peachtree Creek, GA., 20 July 1864. Surrendered with the Army of Tennessee as a member of Company K, 2nd Consolidated Tennessee Infantry at Greensboro, NC., 26 April 1865. Married Tennessee Dunnagan. Occupation: farmer. Lived in Oklahoma one year in 1908.[465]

Manley, Frank; Private, Company D: Sworn into service 11 May 1861 at Nashville. Attached to Hospital #2 at Knoxville, TN., 20 June 1862. Discharged 15 August 1862 by the conscript act at Tazewell, TN.

Manley, Hugh H.; Private, Company K: Sworn into service 25 May 1861 at Nashville. Age 25 on roll dated 15 August 1861 at Midway, TN. Died 17 August 1861.

Manley, James; Private, Company D: Enlisted 11 May 1861 at Nashville. Age 20 on roll dated 5 May 1863 at Shelbyville, TN. On extra duty in the quartermaster department 18 July 1863 through November 1863. Complexion dark, eyes gray, hair black. Paroled 15 June 1865 at Mobile, AL.

Manley, Pat; Private, Company D: Enlisted 11 May 1861 at Nashville. Discharged for disability after November 1861.

Marable, George Washington Braxton; Private, Company A: Born 21 August 1846 at Erin, Humphreys Co. (later Houston Co.), TN. Occupation: farmer. Sworn into service 10 May 1861 at Nashville. Frequently played his fiddle in camp. Discharged 29 March 1862 by the conscript act at Tazewell, TN. Married Elizabeth Jane Nolen, 12 July 1866 in Montgomery Co., TN. Died 12 July 1884 from a gunshot wound at Erin, Houston Co., TN. Buried in the Marable Cemetery, Shiloh, Montgomery Co., TN.[466]

Marane, Christopher Columbus; Private, Company H: Born 29 May 1839 in Burke Co., NC. Relocated to Tennessee at age 9. Left the army at Dalton, GA. deserting, 20 January 1864. Released north of the Ohio River. Resided at the County Charity Farm, Hickman Co., TN. Admitted to the insane asylum on several occasions. Died after 1911.

Maroney, Matthew H.; Private, Company H: Born c. 1830. Occupation: engineer. Married Louisa Hunter. Sworn into service, 14 May 1861 at Nashville. Deserted 29 March 1863.[467]

Marsh, Rev. Aquilla; Brevet Second Lieutenant, Company K: Born in 1838 in Dickson Co., TN. Occupation: farmer. Age 22 in 1860. Sworn into service, 25 May 1861 at Nashville. Elected fourth sergeant at the organization. Age 23 on roll dated 15 August 1861 at Midway, TN. Promoted to third sergeant by September 1861. Brevet second lieutenant at the reorganization, 1 May 1862. Resigned 12 July 1862 at Bean Station, TN. due to poor health. Died c. 1910. Buried at Fort Graham, TX.[468]

Marsh, Elijah J.; Musician, Company C: Born c. 1823. Occupation: farmer. Married Polly Harris, 18 April 1844. Sworn into service, 14 May 1861 at Nashville. Fifer in the regimental band. Discharged 25 September 1861.[469]

Marsh, George W.; Private, Company K: Born in 1841 in Dickson Co., TN. Sworn into service, 25 May 1861 at Nashville. Discharged for disability, 24 July 1861.

---

[464] W. H. H. Lawrence, Tennessee Pension Application, 16694; William B. Maney, Cheatham Bivouac Application; *Reunion Pamphlet*, 14 June 1904; *Nashville Banner*, 23 February 1920; Evans, *Confederate Military History* vol. 10, 619.

[465] Benjamin Manley, Tennessee Pension Applications, 7145, 11776; Sistler and Sistler, *1880 Census of Dickson County*, 41.

[466] Johnson, *1860 Census of Humphreys County*, 52.

[467] United Daughters of the Confederacy, *Hickman County Census 1860*, 91.

[468] McCauley Camp 260, *Confederate Graves*, 32; Baker, *1860 Census for Dickson County*, 672.

[469] Baker, *1860 Census for Dickson County*, 106

Marsh, James Solomon; Private, Company A: Born c. 1830 in Humphreys Co., TN. Occupation: farmer. Married to Jane. Sworn into service, 10 May 1861 at Nashville. Discharged for disability 4 February 1862 at Cumberland Gap, TN. Age 36, complexion dark, eyes gray, hair dark, height 6'.

Marsh, James T.; Private, Company C: Sworn into service 18 May 1861 at Nashville. Age 18 on roll dated 16 August 1861 at Watauga Bridge, TN. Deserted at Cumberland Gap, TN., 28 May 1862.

Marsh, William C.; Private, Company E: Occupation: farmer. Sworn into service 18 May 1861 at Nashville. Age 37 on roll dated 16 August 1861 at Watauga Bridge, TN. Discharged 27 April 1862 at Cumberland Gap, TN. due to a disease of the lymphatic gland. Captured 6 February 1863 in Hickman Co., TN. Sent to the U. S. Military Prison at Louisville, KY. Forwarded to Camp Chase, OH., 25 February 1863. Exchanged 28 March 1863. Complexion light, eyes blue, hair light, height 6'.

Martin, Armistead W. R.; Private, Company H: Born c. 1842. Occupation: farm laborer. Sworn into service, 14 May 1861 at Nashville. Wounded through the bowels in the Battle of Peachtree Creek, GA., 20 July 1864. Admitted to S. P. Moore Hospital, Griffin, GA., 22 July 1864. Died of wounds.[470]

Martin, Cave Johnson; Brevet Second Lieutenant, Company K: Born 1 August 1833. Sworn into service 25 May 1861 at Nashville. Elected first corporal at the organization. Age 28 on roll dated 15 August 1861 at Midway, TN. Breveted second lieutenant, 16 November 1861 at the resignation of M. H. Meek. Dropped from roll at the reorganization, 1 May 1862. Apparently rejoined the Regiment. Admitted to Moore Hospital (Gen. Hospital #24) Richmond, VA., 28 February 1865 for chronic diarrhea. Died 8 November 1881. Buried Martin Cemetery, Dickson Co., TN.

Martin, G. W. Jr.; Private, Company H: Enlisted 8 February 1863 at Shelbyville, TN. Wounded in the hand at Kennesaw Mountain, GA., 19 June 1864.[471]

*Martin, George W.; Private, Company H: Born c. 1844. Occupation: farm laborer. Sworn into service 14 May 1861 at Nashville. Forage master October 1861 through January 1862. On detached service in Virginia, March through April 1862, as post horseler. Appointed brigade farrier, 1 May 1862. Wounded in the right breast in the Battle of Missionary Ridge, TN., 25 November 1863. Wounded in the lower third of the left fibula in the Battle of Peachtree Creek, GA., 20 July 1864. Admitted to Way Hospital Meridian, MS., 9 February 1865. Surrendered as a member of Company K, 2nd Tennessee Consolidated Infantry, 26 April 1865.[472]

Martin, J. L.; Private, Company C: Issued a minie musket. No further.[473]

Martin, James Thomas; Private, Company C: Born 15 May 1838 in Dickson Co., TN. Brother of Private Marshall R. Martin. Occupation: wood chopper. Sworn into service 14 May 1861 at Nashville. Age 27 on roll dated 8 May 1863 at Shelbyville, TN. Slightly wounded on the left breast and right thigh and captured in the Battle of Missionary Ridge, TN., 25 November 1863. Sent to the U. S. Military Prison at Louisville, KY., 7 December 1863. Forwarded to Rock Island, IL., 9 December 1863. Took oath 24 May 1865. Hair black, eyes hazel, height 5' 11". Resided at Slayden, Dickson Co., TN. Died 1 September 1914. Buried Baker-Smith Cemetery, Cumberland Furnace, Dickson Co., TN. Pension Application S7215.

Martin, John; Private, Company A: Sworn into service 10 May 1861 at Nashville. Deserted 17 June 1862 at Cumberland Gap, TN.

Martin, John; Private, Company G: Born in Ireland. Occupation: carpenter. Sworn into service 10 May 1861 at Nashville. Received a kick in the side in August 1861 which produced a hernia. On extra

---

[470] United Daughters of the Confederacy, *Confederate Soldiers of Hickman County*, 143; Lindsley, *Annals*, 305; Maney, *Surgeon's Log*, "20 July 1864"; United Daughters of the Confederacy, *Hickman County Census 1860*, 64; *Chattanooga Daily Rebel*, 27 July 1864.

[471] Maney, *Surgeon's Log*, "Kennesaw Mountain GA."

[472] United Daughters of the Confederacy, *Hickman County Census 1860*, 35; Maney, *Surgeon's Log*, "Missionary Ridge TN"; Maney, *Surgeon's Log*, "20 July 1864."

[473] McCauley, *Record Book, Company C*.

duty as a carpenter, October 1861 through January 1862. Discharged 10 May 1862 for disability, age 49. Complexion ruddy, eyes blue, hair light.

Martin, John S.; Private, Company H: Enlisted 10 January 1863 at Shelbyville, TN. Died 2 April 1863 at Academy Hospital in Chattanooga, TN. of chronic dysuria.

Martin, Marshall Rudolph "Roff"; Private, Company C: Born 1842 in Dickson Co., TN. Brother of Private James T. Martin. Occupation: farmer. Sworn into service 14 May 1861 at Nashville. Admitted to G. F. Hospital in Chattanooga, TN., 1 February 1862 for a gunshot wound to the ankle. Issued a minie musket. Age 21 on roll dated 8 May 1863. Right ankle broken, left on the field, and captured in the Battle of Missionary Ridge, TN., 25 November 1863. Forwarded to U. S. general Hospital #1 at Nashville, 16 February 1864. Leg amputated at lower one third, 10 March 1864. Died in U. S. custody in Nashville of chronic diarrhea, 25 March 1864. Buried in grave #6929 in the City Cemetery, Nashville, TN. Later moved to Mount Olivet Cemetery, Nashville, TN.[474]

Mason, Benjamin Francis; Private, Company D: Sworn into service 11 May 1861 at Nashville. Age 20 on roll dated 5 May 1863 at Shelbyville, TN. Admitted to Ross Hospital, Mobile, AL., 14 February 1865 for syphilis primaria. Returned to duty 26 February 1865.

Mason, Bennet; Private, Company B: Born 25 March 1835 in Davidson Co., TN. Sworn into service 10 May 1861 at Nashville. Age 28 on roll dated 2 June 1863 at Shelbyville, TN. On extra duty as a nurse in Hospital #2 at Knoxville, TN., May to July 1862. Shot through the left hand in the Battle of Kennesaw Mountain, GA., 27 June 1864. Shot just above the heart in the Battle of Atlanta, GA., 22 July 1864. Shot over the left eye in the Battle of Franklin, TN., 30 November 1864. Furloughed and was unable to return to the army. Took oath 22 December 1864. Complexion dark, hair light, eyes gray, height 5' 10". Married Mary E. Chambers, 9 January 1873. Resident of White Bluff, Dickson Co., TN., where he died 29 March 1910.[475]

Massey, William; Private, Company I: Born c. 1841. Sworn into service, 20 May 1861 at Nashville. Discharged, 15 July 1861 at Camp Cheatham for disability due to a wasted leg resulting from a wound to the knee joint.[476]

*Mathis, John T.; Private, Company E: Sworn into service 18 May 1861 at Nashville. Age 18 on roll dated 16 August 1861 at Watauga Bridge, TN. On extra duty in the quartermaster department. Surrendered as a member of Company C, 2nd Consolidated Tennessee Infantry.

*Mathis, William James "Billy"; Adjutant, Company C., Field & Staff: Born 29 April 1837 in Charlotte, TN. Occupation: clerk. Father was sheriff of Dickson Co. in 1860. Sworn into service 14 May 1861 in Company C at Nashville. Elected first lieutenant at the organization. Defeated at the reorganization, 1 May 1862 but was appointed adjutant. Age 24 on roll dated 8 May 1863 at Shelbyville, TN. Wounded in the left arm just above the wrist in the Battle of Missionary Ridge, TN., 25 November 1863. Sent to hospital at Atlanta, GA. Gangrene set in causing the contraction of fingers and "perishing" of the hand. Resigned commission, 24 August 1864. Surrendered with the 2nd Consolidated Tennessee Infantry, 26 April 1865 at Greensboro, NC. Returning from the war he resumed work as a clerk. Married Sarah E. Larkins, 10 September 1868. For many years he was a leading merchant in Dickson, TN., conducting a general store on the corner of Main and Railroad Streets. In 1870 he was elected deputy clerk of the Dickson Co. court. Relocated for a period to Nashville, TN., where he engaged in the same business until his health failed and he returned to Dickson Co. Attended the reunion of the 11th Tennessee Infantry at Bon Aqua Springs, Hickman Co., TN., 24 September 1885, and he was also

---

[474] Baker, *1860 Census for Dickson County*, 72; McCauley, *Record Book, Company C*; Maney, *Surgeon's Log*, "Missionary Ridge TN"; Timothy L. Burgess, *Confederate Deaths and Burials Nashville, Tennessee 1861-1865* (Nashville TN: Author's Corner, 2012) 39; McCauley Camp 260, *Confederate Graves*, 32.

[475] Bennet Mason, Tennessee Pension Application, 2366, 3197.

[476] Johnson, *1860 Census of Humphreys County*, 43.

present at the 14 June 1904 reunion of the 11th Tennessee Infantry in Nashville. Died at Charlotte, TN., 30 November 1924. Buried in the Roberts Cemetery, Charlotte, Dickson Co., TN.[477]

Matlock, Pleasant; Private, Company A: Born c. 1842. Sworn into service 10 May 1861 at Nashville. Age 20 on roll dated 6 May 1863 at Shelbyville, TN. Occupation postwar: farmer.[478]

Matthews, Drewy N. "Drew"; Corporal, Company E: Born c. 1845 in Coahoma Co., MS. First cousin to Private John T. Matthews. Relocated to Dickson Co., TN. prior to 1858. Sworn into service 18 May 1861 at Nashville. Age 16 on roll dated 16 August 1861 at Watauga Bridge, TN. Discharged under the conscript act, 10 August 1862 at Tazewell, TN. Returned home for several months, then enlisted in Company A, 50th Tennessee Infantry, receiving a $50.00 bounty for joining. Promoted to corporal during 1863. Died 13 September 1863 along with twelve other soldiers in a train collision at Etowah, GA. as troops were being transported in the buildup prior to the Battle of Chickamauga. Said to have been scalded by steam from the damaged locomotive. Believed to have been buried along with the other accident victims in the Confederate Cemetery at Marietta, Cobb Co., GA.[479]

*Matthews, John T.; Private, Company E: Born in Montgomery Co., TN., 6 April 1838. First cousin to Private Drew Matthews. Sworn into service 14 May 1861 at Nashville. Contracted the measles at Camp Cheatham. Age 18 on roll dated 16 August 1861 at Watauga Bridge, TN. On extra duty as a teamster in the quartermaster department September 1861 through April, 1862. Became ill in the spring of 1862 with bowel and stomach trouble (chronic diarrhea). Surrendered as a member of the 2nd Consolidated Tennessee Infantry at Greensboro, NC., 26 April 1865. Following the war, he worked as a farm laborer and made cross ties. Married (1) Arabella Combs on 30 October 1867 and after her death (2) Tennie Broom. Resided at Heath, Dickson Co., TN. Present at the 14 June 1904 reunion of the 11th Tennessee Infantry in Nashville. Died 15 November 1908. Buried in the Rock Springs Cemetery, Dickson Co., TN.[480]

Maury, John; First Corporal, Company G: Occupation farmer. Sworn into service 10 May 1861 at Nashville. Discharged 14 August 1862 at Tazewell, TN. for disability. Reenlisted 26 December 1862. Age 37 on roll dated 30 May 1863 at Shelbyville, TN. Promoted to first corporal by July 1863. Killed in the Battle of Missionary Ridge, TN., 25 November 1863.[481]

Maxey, William O.; Sergeant-Major, Company A: Transferred from Captain Harris' Cavalry Company of Colonel McNairy's Battalion, 4 October 1861 at Camp Buckner, KY. Promoted to sergeant-major, 4 November 1861. On sick furlough since 9 December 1861. Discharged by virtue of the conscript act for being over age.

Mayberry, Benjamin Franklin "Frank"; Private, Company A: Enlisted 24 July 1861 at Camp Cheatham. On sick furlough September 1861. Reenlisted in the 11th Tennessee 1 May 1862 at Cumberland Gap, TN. Age 22 on roll dated 6 May 1863 at Shelbyville, TN. Occupation: laborer. Wounded seriously through both legs in the Battle of Missionary Ridge, TN., 25 November 1863. Received at Confederate hospital Atlanta, GA., 7 May 1864 for vulnus sclopeticum. Forwarded to

---

[477] Robert E. Corlew, *A History of Dickson County from Earliest Times to the Present* (Nashville TN: Dickson County Historical Society and Tennessee Historical Commission, 1956) 83; William James Mathis, Tennessee Confederate Pension Application, S11184; Maney, *Surgeon's Log*, "Missionary Ridge TN"; Goodspeed Brothers, *Goodspeed's Histories of Montgomery, Robertson, Humphreys, Stewart, Dickson, Cheatham, Houston Counties*, 1341-42; *Garrett, Dickson County Handbook*, 211; "The Reunion," *Hickman Pioneer, Reunion Pamphlet*, 14 June 1904; *Dickson Herald*, 5 December 1924.

[478] Johnson, *1860 Census of Humphreys County*, 89.

[479] McCauley Camp 260, *Confederate Graves*, 33; Correspondence with relative Kevin Matthews, 4 February 2002.

[480] *Reunion Pamphlet*, 14 June 1904.

[481] Maney, *Surgeon's Log*, "Missionary Ridge TN."

Confederate hospital in Madison, GA., 8 May 1864. Admitted to Confederate hospital, Madison, GA., 9 May 1864. Furloughed from Blackie Hospital, Madison, GA., 23 June 1864.[482]

McAnally, Michael; Private, Company G: Enlisted 3 June 1861 at Camp Cheatham. On detached service as a nurse in General Hospital at Knoxville, TN. from 4 November 1861 to April 1863. Age 28 on roll dated 30 May 1863 at Shelbyville, TN. Detached to Academy Hospital at Chattanooga, TN., April through June 1863. Detached to the relocated Academy Hospital at Marietta, GA., July 1863 through April 1864. Wounded in the Battle of Franklin, TN., 30 November 1864. Captured at Franklin, TN., 17 December 1864. Sent to the U. S. Military Prison at Louisville, KY., 11 January 1865. Forwarded to Camp Chase, OH., 14 January 1865. Took oath 13 May 1865. Complexion fair, hair light, eyes blue, height 5' 5".

McBride, James; Private, Company G: Born 14 March 1818 in County Donegal, Ireland. Enlisted 3 June 1861 at Camp Cheatham. Discharged under the conscript act at Tazewell, TN., 28 August 1862. Although over age, he returned unofficially and fought in the ranks at the battles of Murfreesboro, TN. and Chickamauga, GA. Following the war, he became a resident of Chattanooga, Hamilton Co., TN., where he worked as a laborer. Applied to the Tennessee Confederate Soldiers Home in 1900.[483]

McCaleb, Alton; Private, Company H: Enlisted 11 February 1863 at Shelbyville, TN. Deserted 20 January 1864.

McCaleb, J. B.; Private, Company H: Sent to Fair Ground Hospital #2, Atlanta, GA. for febris remittens. Sent to another hospital. No further.

*McCaleb, Thomas P.; Private, Company K: Born 1831 in Hickman Co., TN. Resided in Hampshire, Maury Co., TN. Occupation: farmer. Sworn into service 25 May 1861 at Nashville. Age 28 on roll dated 15 August 1861 at Midway, TN. Wounded in the leg in the Battle of Cumberland Gap, TN. Admitted to Fair Ground Hospital #2, Atlanta, GA., 7 July 1863 with febris remittens. Surrendered with the Army of Tennessee, 26 April 1865 as a member of Company K, 2nd Consolidated Tennessee Infantry. Lived in the Tennessee Confederate Soldiers Home from 20 December 1911. Died 6 July 1914. Buried at the Tennessee Confederate Soldiers Home Cemetery grave #293.[484]

McCaleb, W.; Private, Company H: Admitted to Fair Ground Hospital #1, Atlanta, GA., 12 September 1863 for erysipelas. Sent to hospital in LaGrange, GA., 16 September 1863.

McCann, Benjamin W.; First Lieutenant, Company D: Born 21 April 1837 in Davidson Co., TN. Brother of Captain J. R. "Dick" McCann. Sworn into service 11 May 1861 at Nashville. Elected first lieutenant at the organization. Defeated for reelection at the reorganization, 1 May 1862. Dropped from roll. Later served in McCann's Cavalry Battalion. Captured at Weems Springs, Hickman Co., TN., 19 August 1863. Held at Camp Morton, IN., July 1864. Exchanged at City Point, VA. about two months before the war ended. Surrendered by General Howell Cobb at Macon, GA. Paroled at Augusta, GA, 1 May 1865. After the war, he held the office of Water Tax Collector of Nashville during the 1870s, also serving two terms as the Davidson Co. Registrar. Member of the Cheatham Bivouac. Attended the reunion of the 11th Tennessee Infantry at Bon Aqua Springs, Hickman Co., TN., 24 September 1885. Admitted to the Tennessee Confederate Soldiers Home, 5 July 1906. Died 12 April 1911. Buried at Mount Olivet Cemetery, Nashville, TN.[485]

---

[482] Ibid.; Harris, *Confederate Hospitals*, 357, 401, 146.

[483] Nathaniel Cheairs Hughes, Jr. and John C. Wilson, *The Confederate Soldiers of Hamilton County, Tennessee: An Alphabetical Listing of the Confederate Soldiers Who Lived at One Time in Hamilton County, Tennessee* (Signal Mountain TN: Mountain Press, 2001) 114; James McBride, Confederate Soldiers Home Application.

[484] Welsh, *Confederate Hospitals*, Patient Roster, Fair Ground Hospital #2, 127; Thomas P. McCaleb, Tennessee Pension Application, 10058; Strange, *Soldiers Home*, 100.

[485] "The Reunion," *Hickman Pioneer*; Benjamin W. McCann, Cheatham Bivouac Application; Benjamin W. McCann, Confederate Soldiers Home Application.

McCann, Joseph Richard "Dick"; Captain, Company B: Born 15 December 1828. Relocated to Tennessee in 1829. Brother of First Lieutenant Benjamin W. McCann. Enlisted 15 June 1846 in Nashville as a private in Captain R. C. Foster's Company "L" 1st Tennessee Infantry Regiment in the Mexican War. Discharged 7 September 1846 at Camargo, Mexico on a surgeon's certificate of disability. McCann raised a company of infantry and was sworn into service on 10 May 1861 in Company B at Nashville. Height 5' 10," eyes hazel, light complexion. Elected Captain at the organization. Resigned 23 May 1862 at Cumberland Gap, TN. in lieu of being court martialed for charges of incompetency, drunkenness, disrespect to superiors, and mutinous language in the presence of soldiers. Allowed to raise a battalion of partisan cavalry in the summer of 1862 to operate within the lines of the enemy, obtaining intelligence and interrupting his lines of communication and supply. Accompanied General John Hunt Morgan on his Kentucky raid in the summer of 1862 and operated with Wheeler against the movements of Rosecrans' army later in 1862. Named major of the 9th Tennessee Cavalry Regiment, 23 December 1862, which operated with Morgan on his raid into Indiana and Ohio. Captured along with many of his men 19 August 1863 at Weems Spring, Hickman Co., TN. and held for a time in the Nashville penitentiary before being sent to Johnson's Island. Specially exchanged just before the close of the war. After taking the oath, he was put on trial for his life twice at Knoxville, TN. during 1865 and 1866. McCann was said to have been a "gentleman of genial manners, brilliant conversational powers, warm in his attachments and uncompromising in the zeal of his friendship." In his last illness this latter trait was forcibly illustrated by his raising his prostrate form from his bed and putting on his clothes, and against the advice of his physicians, inviting his friends into his room, telling them he was always glad to see them. Died 15 June 1880. Buried Mount Olivet Cemetery, Nashville, TN.[486]

McCarty, William; Private, Company G: Sworn into service 10 May 1861 at Nashville. Admitted to Fair Ground Hospital #2, Atlanta, GA, 21 April 1863 for constipation. In General Hospital at Atlanta, GA., 23 April 1863. Returned to duty 1 May 1863. Age 26 on roll dated 30 May 1863 at Shelbyville, TN. Deserted near Chattanooga, TN., 11 November 1863 and captured there the following day.

McCauley, George Dallas Jefferson "Jeff"; Private, Company C: Born 21 November 1844 in Montgomery Co., TN. Brother of Private John Carl and Captain William H. McCauley. Occupation: farmer. Enlisted 21 November 1861 at Charlotte, Dickson Co., TN. as a private in Company B, 49th Tennessee Infantry. Captured at Fort Donelson, TN., 16 February 1862. Imprisoned at Camp Douglas, IL. Listed as sick when exchanged with his regiment at Vicksburg, MS., 20 September 1862. Admitted to Ross Hospital, Mobile, AL., 4 October 1863 for fever. Returned to duty 18 October 1863. Transferred by exchange in early 1864 to the 11th Tennessee. Wounded in the upper third of the right arm in battle near Atlanta, GA., 4 August 1864. Detailed to hospital service where he remained until the end of the war. Surrendered at Atlanta, GA., 7 May 1865. Subscribed to the oath of allegiance at Nashville, TN., 12 May 1865. Complexion fair, hair dark, eyes blue, height 5' 11". Married 1) Nancy Adaline Albright, 26 October 1866 in Montgomery Co., TN. Relocated to Texas, where he married 2) Lillie S. Aiken, 11 June 1890 in Stonewall Co., TX. Member of the Masonry. Died 30 August 1897 in Bell Co., TX. Buried Salado Cemetery, Bell Co., TX.[487]

McCauley, John Carl; Private, Company C: Born 17 February 1840 in Montgomery Co., TN. Brother of Private George D. and Captain William H. McCauley. Resided at Waverly, Humphreys Co., TN. Sworn into service 14 May 1861 at Nashville. Issued a minie musket. Detached to hospital at Knoxville, TN., 25 June 1862 through July 1863. Detached to a hospital in Cleveland, TN., 10 August 1863 through at least February 1864. Paroled at Atlanta, GA, but the parole was declared no good at Chattanooga, TN. Sent to Nashville, TN. where he stayed in the penitentiary one night. Took oath 12 May 1865, and released the following day. Complexion fair, hair light, eyes blue, height 5' 10". Married 16 June 1867 to Lula Eugenia Yarbrough. Occupation: farmer. Present at the 14 June 1904 reunion of

---

[486] *Nashville Daily American*, 16 June 1880.

[487] McCauley Camp 260, *Confederate Graves*, 33; Maney, *Surgeon's Log*, "August 1864"; Lillie McCauley, Texas Confederate Widows Pension, 49119, Brown County, Texas.

the 11th Tennessee Infantry in Nashville. Member of the Masonry. Died 27 January 1924. Buried in the Ebenezer Cemetery, Humphreys Co., TN.[488]

McCauley, Richmond M. "Richard"; Second Lieutenant, Company I: Born in Montgomery Co., TN., 24 September 1838. Occupation: farmer. Sworn into service 20 May 1861 at Nashville. Elected second lieutenant at the reorganization, 1 May 1862. Age 24 on roll dated 6 May 1863 at Shelbyville, TN. Wounded in the right leg by a grapeshot ball while charging a Federal line in the Battle of Chickamauga, GA., 19 September 1863. Sent to a hospital in Marietta, GA. Right leg amputated above the ankle at Floyd House Hospital. Resided at Hustburg, Humphreys Co., TN. following the war. Married Elizabeth Virginia Moore, 25 June 1871. Member of the Methodist Episcopal Church and a Democrat politically. Died 15 November 1917. Buried in the Ebenezer Cemetery, Humphreys Co., TN.[489]

*McCauley, Wiley M.; First Lieutenant, Company I: Born 24 September 1834 in Montgomery Co., TN. Sworn into service 20 May 1861 at Nashville. Elected second sergeant at the reorganization, 1 May 1862. Promoted to first lieutenant, 1 May 1863. Reduced in rank to private, 1 August 1863. Admitted to Ocmulgee Hospital Macon, GA., 22 July 1864. Surrendered with the Army of Tennessee, 26 April 1865, as a member of Company F, 2nd Consolidated Tennessee Infantry. Died 18 September 1903.

*McCauley, William Hudson; Captain, Company C: Born 15 October 1837 in Montgomery Co., TN. Prior to the war he taught school and was proprietor of a country store. Sworn into service 14 May 1861 at Nashville. Promoted to third sergeant by August 1861. Elected first lieutenant at the reorganization, 1 May 1862. Promoted to captain, 7 November 1862. Wounded in the right side in the Battle of Murfreesboro, TN., 31 December 1862. Captured at Murfreesboro Hospital 5 January 1863. Sent to Camp Chase, OH., 25 March 1863. Transferred to Fort Delaware, Delaware, 16 April 1863. Forwarded to City Point, VA. for exchange. Exchanged 29 April 1863. Complexion fair, hair dark, eyes blue, height 5' 10", age 24. Admitted to Ocmulgee Hospital, Macon, GA., 18 March 1865 for gonorrhea. Returned to duty 3 April 1865. Captain of Company F, 2nd Consolidated Tennessee Infantry. Absent on sick leave at the surrender of the Army of Tennessee. Surrendered at Augusta, GA., 15 May 1865, and took oath the same day. Postwar he was a successful business owner in Montgomery Co., TN., purchasing a partial interest in the flour and woolen operations of Peacher's Mills. He joined the Masonic Order in 1868, later becoming a Knights Templar in commandery #8 at Clarksville, TN. Member of the Church of Christ and Forbes Bivouac, Clarksville, Montgomery Co., TN. Died 1 August 1922. Buried in the Dickson Union Cemetery, Dickson Co., TN.[490]

McClanahan, Leander Boykin; Private, Company H: Born 13 June 1832 in Hickman Co., TN. Brother of Private Mortimer B. McClanahan. Enlisted 8 August 1861 at Carter's Station, TN. Discharged 31 August 1861. Later joined Company D, 9th Tennessee Cavalry Battalion.[491]

McClanahan, Mortimer Benton; Private, Company H: Born 18 December 1839 in Hickman Co., TN. Brother of Private Leander B. McClanahan. Sworn into service 14 May 1861 at Nashville. Left sick at Camp Cheatham while the regiment traveled to Knoxville, TN. Became ill on march from Camp Cummins to Cumberland Gap. Treated for rheumatism by Dr. Lowe at Camp Cummins and Cumberland Ford. Placed on crutches for one year and never fully recovered. Discharged 1 October 1861

---

[488] John C. McCauley, Tennessee Pension Application, 11837; McCauley, *Record Book, Company C*; *Reunion Pamphlet*, 14 June 1904.

[489] Maney, *Surgeon's Log*, "Chickamauga GA"; Richmond M. McCauley, Pension Application No. 320; Goodspeed Brothers, *Goodspeed's Histories of Montgomery, Robertson, Humphreys, Stewart, Dickson, Cheatham, Houston Counties*, 1211-12; Anderson and Garrett, *Humphreys County Cemetery Records* vol. 1, 124.

[490] W. H. McCauley, Tennessee Confederate Pension Application, S14603; Maney, *Surgeon's Log*, "Stones River TN"; Garrett, *Dickson County Handbook*, 212.

[491] United Daughters of the Confederacy, *Confederate Soldiers of Hickman County*, 132.

at Cumberland Ford, KY. Later served in Company I, 10th Tennessee Cavalry. Never married. Died in Nashville, TN., 1897. Lived in Beechville, Williamson Co., TN.[492]

McClelland, James Robert; Private, Company C: Born 1829 in Dickson Co., TN. Occupation: wood chopper. Married prior to the war. Sworn into service 14 May 1861 at Nashville. Issued a minie musket. Age 34 on roll dated 8 May 1863 at Shelbyville, TN. Shot through the brain in the Battle of Peachtree Creek, GA., 20 July 1864. Died 21 July 1864.[493]

McClenden, Jesse; Private, Company D, B: Sworn into service 11 May 1861 in Company D at Nashville. Later transferred to Company B. Deserted 15 February 1863 at Shelbyville, TN.

*McCollum, Benjamin F.; Second Lieutenant, Company A: Born c. 1838. Married to Helen. Sworn into service 10 May 1861 at Nashville. Elected fourth corporal at the organization. On extra duty in the quartermaster department. Promoted to first corporal by July 1862. Appointed first sergeant, 1 January 1863. Age 22 on roll dated 6 May 1863. Elected second lieutenant, 3 March 1864. Wounded in the right forearm in battle near Atlanta, GA., 11 August 1864. Admitted to Floyd House Hospital, Macon, GA., 9 November 1864 for a gunshot wound to the middle third of the right forearm and fractured lower fibula. Admitted to Way Hospital for wound, 5 February 1865. Admitted to Ocmulgee Hospital, Macon, GA., 16 April 1865 for a gunshot wound to the ankle. Surrendered by General Richard Taylor. Took oath 18 May 1865 at Grenada, MS.[494]

*McConnell, Joseph "Ive"; Third Sergeant, Color Bearer, Company D: Occupation: bar keeper. Sworn into service 11 May 1861 at Nashville. Appointed fourth sergeant by July 1862. Captured in the Battle of Murfreesboro, TN., 31 December 1862. Exchanged. Age 33 on roll dated 5 May 1863 at Shelbyville, TN. Promoted to third sergeant by November 1863. One of the color bearers wounded in the Battle of Missionary Ridge, TN., 25 November 1863. Left on the field and captured. Sent to the U. S. Military Prison at Louisville, KY. In U. S. General Hospital #1, 16 February 1864, for a gunshot wound to the clavicle. Forwarded to Rock Island, IL., 22 June 1864. Exchanged. In Jackson Hospital Richmond, VA., 2 March 1865. Admitted to Pettigrew Hospital (General Hospital #3) at Raleigh, NC., 11 April 1865. Surrendered with the Army of Tennessee on 26 April 1865 as a member of Company C, 2nd Consolidated Tennessee Infantry.[495]

McCord, W. M.; Private, Company A: Enlisted 6 May 1863 at Shelbyville, TN., age 25. No further.

McCracken, M.; Private, Company H: Joined 5 April 1862 by transfer. No further.

McCrary, John W.; Private, Company A: Sworn into service 10 May 1861 at Nashville. Died at hospital in Chattanooga, TN., 29 June 1863. Buried in the Confederate Cemetery, Chattanooga, TN.

McCrary, Joseph; Private, Company A: Born 1 October 1843 at Bon Aqua, Hickman Co., TN. Relocated at age three months to the Big Bottom Community of Humphreys Co. His father was a skilled wagon maker, who produced the first wagon to be built in Humphreys Co. Joseph worked with his father and on the farm prior to volunteering for the army at Waverly. Sworn into service 10 May 1861 at Nashville. Age 22 on roll dated 6 May 1863 at Shelbyville, TN. Listed as deserted 17 September 1863 near Chattanooga. Captured at Chattanooga with Private James Crim and was held as a prisoner of war for ten days. Returned home on parole after taking the oath. His brother, Marquis Lafayette McCrary, was a member of Maney's 24th Tennessee Sharpshooters. Following the war he studied medicine under Dr. Alexander Coke, and practiced medicine for thirty years in the Big Bottom Community in addition to farming and teaching school. Married 1) Emma Herbison. Her chronic illness inspired him to become a doctor. Following her death, he married 2) Susan Field and they adopted her nephew. He married 3) Mary Azalee (Eliza) Etheridge, the couple later relocating to Bold Springs,

---

[492] M. B. McClanahan, *Tennessee Pension Application*, 751.

[493] McCauley, *Record Book, Company C*; Lindsley, *Annals*, 303; Maney, *Surgeon's Log*, "20 July 1864."

[494] Maney, *Surgeon's Log*, "August 1864."

[495] Maney, *Surgeon's Log*, "Missionary Ridge TN"; Dobson-Sides, *1860 Davidson County Census*, 545.

Humphreys Co., TN. where he practiced medicine until just a few months before his death. Died at his home 29 July 1937. Buried Young Cemetery, Bold Springs, Humphreys Co., TN. Pension Application 16241.[496]

McCrary, Thomas L.; Private, Company A: Sworn into service 10 May 1861 at Nashville. Deserted 17 April 1863 at Shelbyville, TN.

*McDaniel, Alexander R. M.; First Lieutenant, Company B: Born c. 1828. Brother of Second Lieutenant Jesse C. McDaniel. Occupation: carpenter. Sworn into service 10 May 1861 at Nashville. Elected second lieutenant at the organization. Appointed first lieutenant, 10 June 1862. Wounded in the right hip in the Battle of Missionary Ridge, TN., 25 November 1863. Admitted to Catoosa Hospital, Griffin, GA., 22 July 1864. Admitted to Fair Ground Hospital #2, Vineville, GA., 7 September 1864 for acute diarrhea. Admitted to Fair Ground Hospital #1, Vineville, GA., 3 November 1864 with acute diarrhea. Returned to duty 12 November 1864. Surrendered with General Richard Taylor 13 May 1865.[497]

McDaniel, Jesse C.; Second Lieutenant, Company B: Born 17 August 1841 in Davidson Co., TN. Brother of First Lieutenant A.R.M. McDaniel. Occupation: printer. Sworn into service 10 May 1861 at Nashville. Elected fourth corporal at the organization. Promoted to third corporal by July 1862. Detached to signal corps, 20 July 1862 and sent to Vicksburg, MS. Captured at the surrender of Vicksburg, 4 July 1863. Took oath 5 July 1863 and paroled there. Given a two month furlough, after which he reported to Parole Camp at Demopolis, AL. for two weeks, then reported to the signal officer at General Bragg's headquarters atop Missionary Ridge, Chattanooga, TN. Later promoted to second lieutenant. Surrendered with the signal corps of the Army of Tennessee, 26 April 1865. Member of the Cheatham Bivouac. Lived at the Tennessee Confederate Soldiers Home from 17 December 1897. Died 5 February 1914. Buried in the Soldiers Home Cemetery grave #281.[498]

McDonald, James C.; Private, Company B: Sworn into service 10 May 1861 at Nashville. Deserted 15 October 1862 at Versailles, KY.

McElhaney, James; Private, Company B: Sworn into service 10 May 1861 at Nashville. Deserted 1 July 1861 at Camp Cheatham.

McElroy, Samuel C.; Private, Company D: Sworn into service 11 May 1861 at Nashville. Court martialed along with Private Alexander Miller, 14 January 1862 at Cumberland Gap, TN. for desertion and general insubordination. Wounded in the Battle of Murfreesboro, TN., 31 December 1862. Admitted to Fair Ground Hospital #1, Atlanta, GA., 6 January 1863 for vulnus sclopeticum. Sent to Gate City Hospital, Atlanta, GA., 11 January 1863. Age 19 on roll dated 5 May 1863 at Shelbyville, TN. Deserted at Missionary Ridge, TN., 12 November 1863.

*McElyea, Marcus L.; Fourth Corporal, Company A: Born c. 1832. Apprenticed as a blacksmith to the father of Musician Thomas J. Moss in 1850. Married Georgia Ann Plant. Sworn into service 10 May 1861 at Nashville. Elected fourth corporal by July 1862. Received at Confederate hospital, Atlanta, GA., 10 June 1864. Forwarded to Confederate hospital, Madison, GA., 11 June 1864. Returned to duty 8 July 1864. Wounded in the middle of the left thigh and through the right arm in the Battle of Atlanta, GA., 22 July 1864. Admitted to Way Hospital Meridian, MS., 24 January 1865 for a wound. Surrendered by

---

[496] Clifton, *1870 Census of Humphreys County*, 47; Fischer and Burns, *1880 Census of Humphreys County*, 30; Anderson and Garrett, *Humphreys County Cemetery Records* vol. 2, 155, 300; *Waverly Sentinel*, 5 August 1937.

[497] Porch, *Census of Nashville:1850*, 52; Maney, *Surgeon's Log*, "Missionary Ridge TN"; Welsh, *Confederate Hospitals*, Patient Roster, Fair Ground Hospital #2, 129; *Chattanooga Daily Rebel*, 27 July 1864; Welsh, *Confederate Hospitals*, Patient Roster, Fair Ground Hospital #1, 184.

[498] Porch, *Census of Nashville:1850*, 52; Strange, *Soldiers Home*, 36; Jesse C. McDaniel, Cheatham Bivouac Application.

General Richard R. Taylor at Citronelle, AL., 4 May 1865. Paroled at Meridian, MS., 15 May 1865. Worked as a farmer and blacksmith after the war.[499]

McGill, Calvin; Private, Company A: Enlisted 26 March 1863 at Shelbyville, TN. Age 21 on roll dated 6 May 1863 at Shelbyville, TN. Present through February 1864. No further.

McGill, John D.; Second Lieutenant, Company A: Sworn into service 10 May 1861 at Nashville. Elected second lieutenant at the reorganization, 1 May 1862. Age 25 on roll dated 6 May 1863 at Shelbyville, TN. Deserted from picket post 17 November 1863 at Missionary Ridge, TN. Captured and sent to the U. S. Military Prison at Louisville, KY., 17 December 1863. Took oath 18 December 1863. Complexion fair, hair light, eyes gray, height 5' 11".

McGill, W. L.; Private, Company A: Enlisted 6 May 1863 at Shelbyville, TN. Age 27 on roll dated the same day. No further.

McGuire, P.; Private, Company B: Sworn into service 10 May 1861 at Nashville. Deserted 10 August 1861 at Knoxville, TN.

McIntosh, Green M.; Private, Company B: Sworn into service 10 May 1861 at Nashville. Age 27 on roll dated 2 June 1863 at Shelbyville, TN. Captured in the Battle of Missionary Ridge, TN., 25 November 1863. Sent to the U. S. Military Prison at Louisville, KY., 7 December 1863. Forwarded to Rock Island, IL., 9 December 1863.

McKelvey, William; Private, Company A: Occupation: farmer. Enlisted 13 November 1862 at Lenoir Station, TN. Wounded in the arm in the Battle of Murfreesboro, TN., 31 December 1862. Age 20 on roll dated 6 May 1863. Killed in the Battle of New Hope Church, GA., 27 May 1864.[500]

McKinnon, James; Private, Company A: Sworn into service 10 May 1861 at Nashville. Deserted at Camp Cheatham, 28 May 1861.

McLaughlin, Alex R.; First Corporal, Company D: Sworn into service 11 May 1861 at Nashville. Elected second corporal by September 1863. Promoted to first corporal by January 1864. Captured in the Battle of Nashville, TN., 16 December 1864. Sent to the U. S. Military Prison at Louisville, KY., 1 January 1865. Sent to Camp Chase, OH., 2 January 1865. Complexion florid, hair brown, eyes blue, height 5' 8".

McLeod, Norman A.; Private, Company D: Born 26 April 1818 in Canada. Occupation: laborer. Sworn into service 11 May 1861 at Nashville. Absent on sick furlough November 1861. Discharged under the conscript act at Tazewell, TN., 15 August 1862. After discharge, he enlisted 22 November 1862 at Knoxville, TN. in Company K, 19th Tennessee Infantry as a substitute for G. O. Faw. Absent in hospital from 24 October 1863 until February 1864, when he returned for duty. Captured 17 May 1864 at Calhoun, GA. Forwarded to the U. S. Military Prison at Nashville, 24 May 1864 and sent to Louisville, KY. the following day. Forwarded to Rock Island, IL., 27 May 1864. Took oath of allegiance, 11 October 1864. Complexion dark, hair light, eyes dark, height 5'7", age 47. Enlisted in the U. S. Army but was rejected by the mustering officer. Released May 1865. Lived in the Tennessee Confederate Soldiers Home from 13 April 1892. Died 10 September 1904. Buried at the Soldiers Home Cemetery, grave #122.[501]

McLemay, John; Private, Company G: Occupation: laborer. Suffered a slight flesh wound in the right scalp in the Battle of Peachtree Creek, GA., 20 July 1864.[502]

McMahan, Allison W.; Private, Company E: Born in 1843 in Dickson Co., TN. Occupation: farmer. Sworn into service 19 September 1861 at Camp Buckner, Kentucky. Wounded in the left shoulder in the Battle of Peachtree Creek, GA., 20 July 1864. Admitted to Ocmulgee Hospital at Macon, GA., 5 August 1864 for a gunshot wound in the back. Deserted 7 December 1864. Took oath at

---

[499] Harris, *Confederate Hospitals*, 430, 375,150; Maney, *Surgeon's Log*, "Battle of Atlanta GA"; Johnson, *1860 Census of Humphreys County*, 69; Fischer and Burns, *1880 Census of Humphreys County*, 37.

[500] Thedford, "Report of Operations"; Lindsley, *Annals*, 303; Maney, *Surgeon's Log*, "May 1864."

[501] Strange, *Soldiers Home*, 5.

[502] Maney, *Surgeon's Log*, "20 July 1864."

Nashville 13 January 1865. Complexion fair, hair dark, eyes gray, height 6' 1". Married L. V. (Louiza) Dunnagen 24 September 1876.[503]

McMahon, Bryan; Private, Company G: Enlisted 3 June 1861 at Camp Cheatham. Deserted December 1861.

*McNailus, James; Private, Company E, G: Sworn into service 18 May 1861 at Nashville in Company E. Age 24 on roll dated 16 August 1861 at Watauga Bridge, TN. Transferred to Company G at the reorganization, 1 May 1862. Surrendered with the Army of Tennessee, 26 April 1865 as a member of Company C, 2nd Consolidated Tennessee Infantry.

McNamara, Patrick; Private, Company G: Enlisted 3 June 1861 at Camp Cheatham. Discharged at Tazewell, TN., 31 August 1862 by the conscript act.

McNeilly, Hugh J.; Third Corporal, Company C: Born November 1842 in Dickson Co., TN. Sworn into service 14 May 1861 at Nashville. Elected third corporal at the organization. Issued a Springfield rifle. Age 20 on roll dated 8 May 1863. Killed in the Battle of Atlanta, GA., 22 July 1864.[504]

McNeilly, William Donald "Dodd"; Corporal, Company C: Born in 1844 in Dickson Co., TN. No further.[505]

McNutt, Alex D.; Private, Company G: Born c. 1840. Occupation: printer. Sworn into service 10 May 1861 at Nashville. On detached service in Knoxville, TN. in the *Knoxville Register* imprinting office, 4 June 1862 through April 1863. Age 24 on roll dated 30 May 1863 at Shelbyville, TN.[506]

Meadows, W. T.; Private, Company I: Born c. 1836. Occupation: carpenter. Enlisted 14 October 1861 at Cumberland Ford, KY. On extra duty in the quartermaster department October 1861 through December 1862. Age 26 on roll dated 6 May 1863 at Shelbyville, TN. Deserted 1 September 1863.[507]

Meek, Howard Turner; Private, Company K: Born in Dickson Co., TN. Brother of Second Lieutenant Moses Harvey Meek. Occupation: farmer. Sworn into service 25 May 1861 at Nashville. Age 20 on roll dated 15 August 1861 at Midway, TN. Discharged 14 September 1861 for disability due to a fractured spine which occurred two years earlier. Complexion light, hair light, eyes blue height 5' 6". Married Mary Jane Cochran Turnbull. Died in Arkansas about 1879.[508]

Meek, Moses Harvey; Second Lieutenant, Company K: Born in Dickson Co., TN., 25 July 1839. Brother of Private Howard Turner Meek. Resident of Burns, TN. Sworn into service 25 May 1861 at Nashville. Elected second lieutenant at the organization. His motto was "keep going." Age 23 on roll dated 15 August 1861 at Midway, TN. Discharged 14 September 1861 on a surgeon's certificate of disability due to typhoid fever. Married Martha J. Gentry, 25 February 1862. Postwar occupation: farmer and stockman specializing in sheep and cattle. Died 27 September 1929. Buried in the Meek Cemetery, Burns, Dickson Co., TN.[509]

---

[503] Ibid.

[504] McCauley Camp 260, *Confederate Graves*, 34; McCauley, *Record Book, Company C*; Lindsley, *Annals*, 303; Maney, *Surgeon's Log*, "Battle of Atlanta GA."

[505] McCauley Camp 260, *Confederate Graves*, 34.

[506] Dobson-Sides, *1860 Davidson County Census*, 554.

[507] Johnson, *1860 Census of Humphreys County*, 43.

[508] Ernest Everett Blevins, "Howard Turner Meek Pioneer and Private Company K, 11th Tennessee Confederate States" in *The Heritage of Dickson County, Tennessee, 1803-2006*, Dickson County Heritage Book Committee, (Waynesville NC: County Heritage Inc., 2007) 315.

[509] M. H. Meek, Tennessee Confederate Pension Application, S15597; Sistler and Sistler, *1880 Census of Dickson County*, 44; Garrett, *Dickson County Handbook*, 211; Jill Knight Garrett, Ruth Burns, and Iris H. McClain, *Dickson County, Tennessee, Cemetery Records* rev. ed. 2 vols. Vol. 1, (Vista, CA: Ram Press, 1991). 32; Phillip Bradley Jones, "Moses Meek" in *The Heritage of Dickson County, Tennessee, 1803-2006*, Dickson County Heritage Book Committee, (Waynesville NC: County Heritage Inc., 2007) 316; Ernest Everett Blevins, "Moses Harvey Meek Pioneer and 2nd Lieutenant Company K, 11th Tennessee Confederate States" in *The Heritage of Dickson County, Tennessee, 1803-2006*, Dickson County Heritage Book Committee, (Waynesville NC: County Heritage Inc., 2007) 316.

Menefee, James; Private, Company D, B: Sworn into service 11 May 1861 in Company D at Nashville. Transferred to Company B at the reorganization, 1 May 1862. Age 25 on roll dated 5 May 1863 at Shelbyville, TN. Killed in the Battle of Franklin, TN., 30 November 1864, age 26.

Menefee, Nicholas S.; Private, Company B: Born 25 November 1839 in Davidson Co., TN. Sworn into service 10 May 1861 at Nashville. Member of the regimental color guard. On sick furlough at Knoxville, TN., 2 March 1862. Age 23 on roll dated 2 June 1863 at Shelbyville, TN. Captured near Chattahoochee, GA., 4 July 1864. Sent to the U. S. Military Prison at Louisville, KY. Forwarded to Camp Douglas, IL., 16 July 1864. Released 16 June 1865. Complexion dark, hair black, eyes gray, height 5' 6". Postwar resident of Nashville. Occupation: printer. Admitted to the Tennessee Confederate Soldiers Home, 4 August 1900. Died 28 September 1923. Buried in the Soldiers Home Cemetery, grave #399.[510]

Merrill, James C.; Private, Company K: Occupation: farmer. Killed on the field in the Battle of Peachtree Creek, GA., 20 July 1864.[511]

Merritt, James K. P.; Private, Company G: Born 1834 in Rutherford Co., TN. Resided at Clarksville, TN. Enlisted 3 June 1861 at Camp Cheatham. Listed as deserting 8 February 1862. Returned to regiment. Wounded in the leg in the Battle of Tazewell, TN., 6 August 1862.[512]

Miles, William R.; Private, Company F: Enlisted 18 May 1861 at Cedar Hill, TN. Wounded in the thigh at the Battle of Murfreesboro, TN., 31 December 1862. Admitted to Fair Ground Hospital #1, Atlanta, GA., 22 February 1863 for vulnus sclopeticum. Received medical furlough 18 March 1863. Returned to company. On detached duty at a hospital, 7 August 1863. Surrendered at Atlanta, GA., 7 May 1865. Took oath, 12 May 1865. Complexion fair, hair dark, eyes gray, height 5' 11".

Miller, Alexander C.; Private, Company C: Sworn into service 11 May 1861 at Nashville. Deserted near Murfreesboro, TN., 5 January 1863 and captured the same day. Sent to Gratiot Street Prison, St. Louis, MO., 21 January 1863. Took oath 12 February 1863.

Miller, Edward Hall; Fifth Sergeant, Company B: Born in Wilson Co., TN., 25 January 1842. Sworn into service, 10 May 1861 at Nashville. Elected fourth corporal by July 1862. Promoted to second corporal by January 1863. Age 20 on roll dated 2 June 1863 at Shelbyville, TN. Promoted to first corporal by November 1863 and later to fifth sergeant. Captured in the Battle of Missionary Ridge, TN., 25 November 1863. Admitted to U. S. Hospital #3 in Chattanooga, TN., 26 November through 18 December 1863 for acute dysentery. Sent to the U. S. Military Prison at Louisville, KY. Forwarded to Rock Island, IL., 1 January 1864. Resided in Nashville, TN. postwar. Married Millie Hunt, December 1865. Relocated to California in 1887. Mason, and member of the United Confederate Veteran Camp 770 in Los Angeles. Died 10 September 1922 in Los Angeles, CA.[513]

Miller, E. Luther; Private, Company H: Born 1836 in Hickman Co., TN. Sworn into service 14 May 1861 at Nashville. Wounded in the shoulder in the Battle of Murfreesboro, TN., 31 December 1862. Captured at Murfreesboro, 9 March 1863. Took oath in Columbia, TN. Resided at Palestine in Lewis Co., TN. Pension Application S7667.[514]

Miller, G. W.; Private, Company B: Sworn into service 10 May 1861 at Nashville. Deserted 20 March 1863.

*Miller, H. C.; Private, Company B: Sworn into service, 10 May 1861 at Nashville. Discharged at Tazewell, TN., 15 August 1862 by the conscript act. Apparently rejoined the regiment. Surrendered with the Army of Tennessee, 26 April 1865 as a member of Company C, 2nd Consolidated Tennessee Infantry.

---

[510] Nicholas S. Menefee, Confederate Soldiers Home Application.
[511] Maney, *Surgeon's Log*, "20 July 1864."
[512] J. K. P. Merritt, Tennessee Pension Application, 9882.
[513] "Edward Hall Miller," *Confederate Veteran*, vol. 30 no. 12 (December 1922): 472.
[514] E. L. Miller, Tennessee Pension Application, 7667.

Miller, H. C.; Private, Company D: Sworn into service 11 May 1861 at Nashville. Discharged due to the conscript act.

Miller, James Guinn; Rank unknown, Company C: Enlisted in Company C, 11th Tennessee Infantry. Married to Amanda. Died February 1903 in Forney, TX.[515]

Miller, Joseph H. "Jo"; Private, Company B: Sworn into service 10 May 1861 at Nashville. Discharged 1 November 1861 at Cumberland Gap, TN. Married to Mary E. Died 3 April 1916. Pension Application, Arkansas, Crawford Co., 1915.[516]

Miller, Willis D.; Fourth Sergeant, Company G, B: Occupation: clerk. Sworn into service 10 May 1861 in Company G at Nashville. Transferred to Company B at the reorganization, 1 May 1862. Wounded in the neck in the Battle of Murfreesboro, TN., 31 December 1862. Sent to hospital in Atlanta, GA. Age 22 on roll dated 30 May 1863 at Shelbyville, TN. Shot in the head and died on the field in the Battle of Chickamauga, GA., 19 September 1863.[517]

Mitchell, Ballard; Private, Company K: Sworn into service 25 May 1861 at Nashville. Age 27 on roll dated 15 August 1861 at Midway, TN. Discharged 11 December 1862 for disability.

Mitchell, John W.; Private, Company G, B, D: Born March 1837 in Dickson Co., TN. Sworn into service 10 May 1861 in Company G at Nashville. Transferred to Company B at the reorganization, 1 May 1862. Transferred to Company D, 1 March 1863. Age 23 on roll dated 21 June 1863 at Shelbyville, TN. Captured near Kennesaw Mountain, GA., 3 July 1864. Sent to the U. S. Military Prison at Louisville, KY. Forwarded to Camp Douglas, IL., 16 July 1864. Took oath, 10 May 1865. Complexion dark, hair brown, eyes gray, height 5' 3". Lived at the Tennessee Confederate Soldiers Home from 24 June 1893. Died 11 July 1911. Buried in the Soldiers Home Cemetery, grave #232.[518]

Mitchell, Lawrence; Private, Company C, G: Sworn into service 14 May 1861 in Company C at Nashville. Transferred to Company G at the reorganization, 1 May 1862. Discharged by the conscript act at Tazewell, TN., August 1862.

Mitchell, R. H.; Private, Company I: Sworn into service 20 May 1861 at Nashville. Discharged by the conscript act, 18 August 1862 at Tazewell, TN.

Mobley, Benjamin Ballinger; Private, Company H: Born 23 April 1840 in Hickman Co., TN. Sworn into service 14 May 1861 at Nashville. Wounded in the Battle of Murfreesboro, TN., 31 December 1862, having one finger on the left hand shot away and all others wounded. Sent to hospital in Chattanooga, TN. Had his arm in a sling for two to three weeks. Sent to hospital in Ringgold, GA. for approximately one month. Transferred to the 9th Tennessee Cavalry Battalion during the fall of 1864. Was with Wheeler harassing Sherman on the March to the Sea. Paroled at Charlotte, NC. by J. H. Akins, cavalry officer. Resided on the Duck River, Hickman Co., TN. Married Jackie T. Coleman, 2 June 1898. Died 28 December 1914 in Hickman Co., TN.[519]

Mobley, T. J.; Private, Company I: Enlisted 1 February 1864 at Dalton, GA. Surrendered with the Army of Tennessee, 26 April 1865 as a member of Company F, 2nd Consolidated Tennessee Infantry.

Montgomery, Daniel; Third Corporal, Company H: Sworn into service 14 May 1861 at Nashville. Promoted to third corporal, 24 March 1862. Killed in the Battle of Jonesboro, GA., 1 September 1864 due to a severe wound in the breast and arm.[520]

Moody, Henry; Private, Company I: Born 27 February 1835 in Stewart Co., TN. Sworn into service, 20 May 1861 at Nashville. On extra duty as a teamster, 15 August through October 1861. Overheated in the Battle of Murfreesboro, TN., 31 December 1862. According to the soldier this caused

---

[515] "J. G. Miller," *Confederate Veteran* vol. 11 no. 7, (July 1903): 334.
[516] Welsh, *Arkansas Pension Applications by Tennessee Veterans*, 3.15.
[517] Maney, *Surgeon's Log*, "Stones River TN"; Maney, *Surgeon's Log*, "Chickamauga GA."
[518] Strange, *Soldiers Home*, 14.
[519] United Daughters of the Confederacy, *Confederate Soldiers of Hickman County*, 147. Pension Application 9228.
[520] Lindsley, *Annals*, 305; Maney, *Surgeon's Log*, "September 1864."

"bloody bowels." Age 27 on roll dated 6 May 1863. Present at least through February 1864. Wounded slightly in the wrist in one battle. On a list of Rebel deserters to report to the Provost Marshal at Fort Donelson, TN. Complexion dark, hair dark, eyes gray, height 6' 2". Resident of Erin, Houston Co., TN. Pension Application S2240.[521]

Moore, Charles R.; Private, Company I: Occupation: farmer. Sworn into service 20 May 1861 at Nashville. On extra duty as a teamster, 15 August 1861 through January 1862. Wounded in the arm in the Battle of Murfreesboro, TN., 31 December 1862. Left as a nurse in the Murfreesboro hospital and captured, 5 January 1863. Sent to the U. S. Military Prison at Louisville, KY. Forwarded to Camp Butler, IL., 14 March 1863. Sent to City Point, VA. for exchange. Admitted to Pim Hospital, Griffin, GA., 22 July 1864. Wounded through the middle third of the left leg in the first day of the Battle of Jonesboro, GA., 31 August 1864. Took oath 17 January 1865. Complexion dark, hair dark, eyes gray, height 5' 6".[522]

Moore, James; Second Corporal, Company D: Sworn into service 1 May 1861 at Nashville. Age 27 on roll dated 5 May 1863 at Shelbyville, TN. Promoted to third corporal by September 1863. Promoted to second corporal by January 1864. Admitted to Quintard Hospital, Griffin, GA., 22 July 1864. Took oath at Nashville, TN., 28 December 1864. Complexion fair, hair light, eyes gray, height 5' 4".[523]

Moore, William H.; Private, Company G: Enlisted 3 October 1861 at Camp Buckner, KY. In hospital since 26 December 1862. Age 21 on roll dated 30 May 1863 at Shelbyville, TN. No further.

Moran, Patrick; Private, Company G: Born c. 1838 in Ireland. Renounced allegiance to Queen Victoria, 5 April 1859. Enlisted 3 June 1861. Discharged by court martial 20 July 1861.[524]

Moreau, Christopher Columbus; Private, Company H: Born c. 1839 in NC. Occupation: day laborer. Enlisted 8 August 1861 at Nashville. Deserted 20 January 1864.[525]

Morgan, Fred; Private, Company F: Occupation: farmer. Enlisted 18 May 1861 at Cedar Hill, TN. Wounded through the hand in the Battle of Peachtree Creek, GA., 20 July 1864. Died 18 August 1864 at General Hospital #2 in Eufaula, AL.[526]

Morgan, Hiram R.; Private, Company F: Born 2 March 1840 in Carroll Co., TN. Enlisted 2 July 1862 in Woodard's Cavalry. Transferred to the 11th Tennessee Infantry, 26 December 1862 at Readyville, TN. Received in Confederate hospital, Atlanta, GA., 3 July 1864. Forwarded to Confederate hospital Madison, GA., 4 July 1864. Admitted to Way Hospital Meridian, MS. for a wound, 17 January 1865. Paroled at Corinth, MS. Resided at Cedar Hill, Robertson Co., TN.[527]

Moriarty, Patrick; Private, Company G: Born in Ireland. Occupation: teacher. Enlisted 3 June 1861 at Camp Cheatham. Discharged May 1862 for disability due to a severe cold. Complexion fair, hair black, eyes dark, height 5' 7", age 38.

Morris, G. J.; Private, Company F: Enlisted 4 November 1862 at Lenoir Station, TN. Admitted to Fair Ground Hospital #1, Atlanta, GA., 12 September 1863 for debilitus. Returned to duty 20 September 1863. Died 14 June 1864 from the effects of measles at Macon, GA.[528]

Morris, Martin V.; First Lieutenant, Company F: Enlisted 18 May 1861 at Cedar Hill, TN. Elected first lieutenant at the organization. On detached service as a provost guard at a hospital in Cleveland, TN., 26 December 1862 through February 1863. Sent to the hospital, 31 August 1863. Resigned 16 October 1863 due to poor health resulting from tuberculosis.

---

[521] Henry Moody, Tennessee Pension Application, 2240.
[522] *Chattanooga Daily Rebel*, 27 July 1864; Maney, *Surgeon's Log*, "August 1864."
[523] *Chattanooga Daily Rebel*, 27 July 1864."
[524] Smith, *Davidson County Naturalization Records*, 64.
[525] United Daughters of the Confederacy, *Hickman County Census 1860*, 1.
[526] Lindsley, *Annals*, 304; Maney, *Surgeon's Log*, "20 July 1864."
[527] Jackson, "Letter to Parents," 14 July 1864.
[528] Lindsley, *Annals*, 304; Welsh, Confederate Hospitals, Patient Roster, Fair Ground Hospital #1, 192; Jackson, "Letter to Parents," 14 July 1864.

Morrisett, William Richard "Dick"; Private, Company A: Born 16 April 1840. Sworn into service, 10 May 1861 at Nashville. Age 24 on roll dated 6 May 1863 at Shelbyville, TN. Deserted August 1863 near Chattanooga, TN. Captured at Huntsville, AL., 21 August 1863. Sent to the U. S. prison at Maysville, AL., 28 August 1863. Enlisted in the Federal Army. Married Margaret A. Warren, 2 August 1866. Occupation: farmer. Died 20 October 1920. Buried Jackson Cemetery, Plant, Humphreys Co., TN.[529]

Morrison, Allen; Private, Company H: Sworn into service 14 May 1861 at Nashville. On extra duty as a blacksmith November 1861 through January 1862. Discharged under the conscript act, 1 May 1862.

Morton, James; Private, Company B: Sworn into service 10 May 1861 at Nashville. On extra duty as a nurse at Hospital #2 at Knoxville, TN., 1 May through 31 July 1862. Discharged 1 November 1862 at Lenoir Station, TN.

*Moss, Thomas J.; Musician, Company A: Born c. 1842. Sworn into service 10 May 1861 at Nashville. Left sick at Readyville, TN., 20 December 1862. Age 23 on roll dated 6 May 1863 at Shelbyville, TN. Promoted to third sergeant, 20 October 1863. Musician for Company K, 2nd Consolidated Tennessee Infantry. Surrendered with the Army of Tennessee, 26 April 1865.

Munford, H. H. "Tip"; Private, Company H: Sworn into service 14 May 1861 at Nashville. Died 1 July 1862.[530]

Murphey, James G.; Private, Company F: Born 16 June 1818 in Logan Co., KY. Resident of Cedar Hill, Robertson Co., TN. Enlisted 25 June 1861 at Camp Cheatham. On sick furlough home, 19 January 1862. Admitted to the Tennessee Confederate Soldiers Home, 8 April 1899. Died 1900. Buried in the Confederate Soldiers Cemetery, Grave #73.

Murphey, John R.; Third Corporal, Company F: Born 11 February 1842. Enlisted 18 May 1861 at Cedar Hill, TN. Appointed third corporal by November 1862. Captured 1 July 1863 at Tullahoma, TN. Sent to the U. S. Military Prison at Louisville, KY. Forwarded to Camp Chase, OH., 20 July 1863. Complexion fair, hair light, eyes blue, height 5' 9". Lived at the Tennessee Confederate Soldiers Home from 9 January 1909. Died 6 July 1909. Buried in the Soldiers Home Cemetery, grave #191.[531]

Murphree, David D.; Private, Company H: Sworn into service 14 May 1861 at Nashville. Sick at Chattanooga, TN., November through December 1862. Captured in the Battle of Missionary Ridge, TN., 25 November 1863. Sent to the U. S. Military Prison at Louisville, KY., 10 December 1863. Forwarded to Rock Island, IL., 1 January 1864. Took oath, 18 May 1865. Complexion light, hair auburn, eyes gray, height 5' 9", age 21. Resided in Arkansas postwar. Pension Application, Arkansas, Yell Co. (1901).[532]

Murphree, W. R.; Private, Company unknown: Surrendered at Nashville, 17 June 1865. Complexion fair, hair light, eyes gray, 5' 11".

Murrell, F. M.; First Corporal, Company F: Sworn into service 10 May 1861 at Nashville. Appointed first corporal, 22 June 1862. Died at Cumberland Gap, TN., 28 October 1862.

Murrell, James C.; Private, Company K: Born in 1844 in Dickson Co., TN. Brother of Richard C. Murrell. Occupation: farmer. Sworn into service 25 May 1861 at Nashville. Age 17 on roll dated 15 August 1861 at Midway, TN. Killed in action as a teamster near Atlanta, GA., 31 July 1864.[533]

Murrell, Richard Crow; Rank unknown, Company H: Born 11 October 1837 in Dickson Co., TN. Brother of Private James C. Murrell. Resided in Centerville, Hickman Co., TN. Discharged at Columbus, MS. in 1863. Married.[534]

---

[529] Fischer and Burns, *1880 Census of Humphreys County*, 80.

[530] *Hickman County News*, 9 March 1899.

[531] Strange, *Soldiers Home*, 88.

[532] Welsh, *Arkansas Pension Applications by Tennessee Veterans*, 3.18.

[533] Maney, *Surgeon's Log*, "28-31 July 1864"; Garrett, Alexander, and McAnally, *Confederate Soldiers and Patriots*, 254.

[534] R. C. Murrell, Tennessee Pension Application, 10865; United Daughters of the Confederacy, *Confederate Soldiers of Hickman County*, 151.

Murrell, T. M.; Rank unknown, Company B: No further.

Musgraves, David; Fourth Sergeant, Company E: Born c. 1836. Occupation: laborer. Sworn into service 18 May 1861 at Nashville. Age 26 on roll dated 16 August 1861 at Watauga Bridge, TN. Promoted to second corporal by July 1862. Promoted to fourth sergeant, 8 October 1863. Wounded in the shoulder in the Battle of Missionary Ridge, TN., 25 November 1863. On detached service in the Nitre Bureau at Selma, AL., 17 February 1864.[535]

Myatt, Burrell; Private, Company A: Enlisted 12 September 1861 at Knoxville, TN. Detached as a guard for the hospital at Cleveland, TN., 25 December 1862 through April 1863. Age 22 on roll dated 6 May 1863 at Shelbyville, TN. Took oath 29 December 1864. Complexion dark, hair dark, eyes hazel, height 5' 11".

-N-

Nall, Rufus F.; Private, Company E: Sworn into service 18 May 1861 at Nashville. Age 20 on roll dated 16 August 1861 at Watauga Bridge, TN. On extra duty in the quartermaster department as a teamster, September 1861 through April 1862. Deserted May 1862 at Cumberland Gap, TN.

Napier, Robert Henry; Private, Company E: Born c 1841 in Charlotte, Dickson Co., TN. Brother of Confederate Partisan Ranger, Thomas Alonzo Napier, who he lived with in Benton Co., TN., while he studied law. After having migrated from North Carolina with his family and 100 slaves, their grandfather served as a lieutenant under Andrew Jackson in the Creek War. They settled on Barton's Creek in Dickson Co. and built one of the first brick houses in Middle Tennessee. The Napier family operated numerous iron foundries in Tennessee and Alabama. Robert enlisted 18 May 1861 at Nashville. Age 18 on roll dated 16 August 1861 at Watauga Bridge, TN. Complexion dark, hair dark, eyes blue, height 5' 7". Wounded in the left thigh in the Battle of Murfreesboro, TN., 31 December 1862 and captured. Sent to the U. S. Military Prison at Louisville, KY. Forwarded to Camp Morton, IN., 5 November 1863. Released from Camp Morton upon taking the oath of allegiance in May 1865. Married Margaret "Maggie" Humble Wyly McCown, widow of Charles McCown, April 1877. Lived near Reynoldsburg, Humphreys Co., TN. Later moved to Nashville, TN. Worked as a night watchman for the N. C. & St. L. Railroad. Died 27 January 1916.[536]

Naughton, Michael; Private, Company G: Born in Ireland. Discharged from Captain McClung's Artillery, 1 April 1863. Enlisted 3 April 1863 at Chattanooga, TN. Age 38 on roll dated 30 May 1863. Sent to General Hospital (location not listed), 9 February 1864. Captured at Macon, GA., 20 April 1865. Took oath 6 May 1865 at Chattanooga, TN. Complexion dark, hair black, eyes gray, height 5' 8".

Nave, John J.; Third Corporal, Company F: Enlisted 18 May 1861 at Cedar Hill, TN. Promoted to fourth corporal by July 1862. Appointed third corporal by September 1863. On sick furlough, 21 July through December 1863. Admitted to Fair Ground Hospital #2, Vineville, GA., 2 September 1864 for vulnus contusio. Returned to duty 17 September 1864.

Nealey, Martin; Private, Company G: Occupation: laborer. Wounded severely through the middle 1/3 of right thigh in the Battle of Peachtree Creek, GA., 20 July 1864.[537]

*Neblett, R. P.; Musician, Company C, Field & Staff: Born 1835 in Montgomery Co., TN. Resided near Charlotte, Dickson Co., TN. Sworn into service 14 May 1861 in Company C at Nashville. Issued a minie musket. Transferred to the brass band and Field & Staff, 16 January 1863. Age 29 on roll dated 8 May 1863. Admitted to Fair Ground Hospital #2, Atlanta, GA., 15 July 1863 for pneumonia. Received

---

[535] Baker, *1860 Census for Dickson County*, 1006; Maney, *Surgeon's Log*, "Missionary Ridge TN."

[536] Robert Henry Napier, Tennessee Pension Application, 6921; *Nashville City Directory* (Marshall & Bruce Company, 1900); Smith, *Wyly Saga*, 29-30.

[537] Maney, *Surgeon's Log*, "20 July 1864."

a sick furlough 4 August 1863. Surrendered with the Army of Tennessee at Greensboro, NC., 26 April 1865 as a member of Company K, 2nd Consolidated Tennessee Infantry. Died c. 1914. .[538]

Neighbors, Jacob W.; Private, Company F: Enlisted 18 May 1861 at Cedar Hill, TN. Discharged 21 August 1861.

*Nelson, Moses A.; First Lieutenant, Company G, B: Born 11 May 1838 in Bedford Co., TN. Sworn into service 10 May 1861 in Company G at Nashville. Promoted to first sergeant by March 1862. Transferred to Company B at the reorganization, 1 May 1862. Age 24 on roll dated 21 June 1863 at Shelbyville, TN. Appointed second lieutenant, 8 April 1864. Promoted to first lieutenant, 15 April 1864. Wounded in the lower third of the left arm in the Battle of Atlanta, GA., 22 July 1864. Wounded in the Battle of Franklin, TN., 30 November 1864. Surrendered with the Army of Tennessee at Greensboro, NC., 26 April 1865 as a member of Company C, 2nd Consolidated Tennessee Infantry. Resided in Chattanooga where he was a saloon keeper in 1890 and a member of the Nathan Bedford Forrest Camp, United Confederate Veterans. Relocated to Nashville in 1891 and joined the Cheatham Bivouac. Occupied as the steward of the Capital Club. Died at his home in Estill Springs, TN., 18 July 1913.[539]

Nesbett, Semus O.; Private, Company E: Sworn into service 18 May 1861 at Nashville. Age 35 on roll dated 16 August 1861 at Watauga Bridge, TN. Discharged under the conscript law August 1862 at Tazewell, TN.

Nesbitt, Joseph T.; Private, Company E: Born 1812 in Dickson Co., TN. Brother of Private William A. Nesbitt and uncle of Private William J. Nesbitt. Occupation: stone mason. Married Caroline J. Burns, 20 October 1838. Sworn into service 18 May 1861 at Nashville. Age 49 on roll dated 16 August 1861 at Watauga Bridge, TN. Issued a flintlock rifle. Due to his advanced age, he served as a hospital nurse, but was wounded once. Discharged under the conscript act, August, 1862. Married 2) Louise Bailey. Lived at the Tennessee Confederate Soldiers Home from 17 February 1893. Died 23 August 1898. Buried in the Soldiers Home Cemetery, grave #47.[540]

Nesbitt, William A. "Buck"; Private, Company E: Born 21 April 1814. Brother of Private Joseph T. Nesbitt and uncle of Private William J. A. Nesbitt. Occupation: farmer. Sworn into service 18 May 1861 at Nashville. Age 47 on roll dated 16 August 1861 at Watauga Bridge, TN. Discharged under the conscript act at Tazewell, TN. in August 1862. Complexion fair, blue eyes, gray hair, height 5' 11". In his later life he loved to recount his Civil War experiences, talking for hours on the subject and once related how he had "toted a cannon for one hundred yards." Never married. Died 24 August 1898. Buried Adams/Nesbitt Cemetery, Yellow Creek, Dickson Co., TN.[541]

Nesbitt, William John Allen; Private, Company C: Born in Dickson Co., TN., 14 February 1840. Nephew of Private Joseph T. and Private William A. Nesbitt. Occupation: farmer. Sworn into service 14 May 1861 at Nashville. Discharged 13 October 1861 on a surgeon's certificate of disability due to chronic pulmonary complaint. Complexion light, hair dark, eyes dark, height 5' 7". The following August he joined Company E, 11th Tennessee Cavalry. Later captured and sent to Rock Island, IL., where he suffered from lung disease (phthisic). His father, Robert S. Nesbitt, was a strong Southern sympathizer, and their home was burned to the ground by Federal "Bushwackers" in 1863. Released upon joining Company G, 3rd United States regiment on 28 February 1865, becoming a "Galvanized

---

[538] McCauley, *Record Book, Company C*; Welsh, *Confederate Hospitals*, Patient Roster, Fair Ground Hospital #2, 143; R. P. Neblett, Tennessee Confederate Pension Application, 6518.

[539] Maney, *Surgeon's Log*, "Battle of Atlanta GA"; "M. A. Nelson," *Confederate Veteran* vol. 21 no. 10 (October 1913): 503; Hughes and Wilson, *Confederate Soldiers of Hamilton County*, 120; Moses A. Nelson, Cheatham Bivouac Application.

[540] "J.I.J. Adams," 534; William J. Nesbitt, *West from Edrom: An Account of the Nesbitt Family of Tennessee* (Warner Robins GA: s.n., 1968) 25-26; James G. Patey, *The Patey-Skelton Family* (Charleston SC: J.G. Patey, 2002) 83; Strange, *Soldiers Home*, 11.

[541] Garrett and McClain, *Dickson County Cemetery Records* vol. 1, 27; Nesbitt, *West from Edrom*, 27; Patey, *Patey-Skelton*, 84.

Yankee" serving in Kansas and Colorado. Mustered out 28 December 1865. Returned home to Yellow Creek in Dickson Co., TN. and married Sallie Sligh on 31 August 1868. Politically a Democrat. Died 2 April 1921. Buried in the Sil Adams/Nesbitt Cemetery, Dickson Co., TN.[542]

Newton, Henry W.; Private, Company F: Enlisted 1 July 1861 at Camp Cheatham. Wounded by a minie ball striking the right toe in the Battle of Franklin, TN., 30 November 1864. Captured at Franklin, TN., 17 December 1864. Admitted to U. S. General Hospital #1 at Nashville, 26 December 1864. Escaped 6 April 1865 en route to the U. S. Military Prison at Louisville, KY. Complexion fair, hair light, eyes blue, height 6'.

Newton, James M.; Private, Company F: Enlisted 1 June 1863 at Shelbyville, TN. Captured in the Battle of Nashville, TN., 16 December 1864. Sent to the U. S. Military Prison at Louisville, KY., 2 January 1865. Forwarded to Camp Chase, OH., 6 January 1865. Complexion florid, hair light, eyes blue, height 5' 7".

Newton, Wiley J.; Private, Company F: Enlisted 1 June 1863 at Shelbyville, TN. Admitted to Fair Ground Hospital #1, Atlanta, GA., on 12 September 1863 for febris remittens. Returned to duty 18 September 1863. Killed in the Battle of Peachtree Creek, GA., 20 July 1864.[543]

Nichol, Samuel Denton; First Lieutenant, Company G: Born 6 August 1830 in Nashville, TN. Brother of Second Lieutenant William C. Nichol. Baptized in the First Presbyterian Church on 19 August 1833. As a boy he attended the old Hume School conducted by his uncle, Professor Alfred Hume. Sworn into service 10 May 1861 at Nashville. Elected first lieutenant at the organization. Relieved of duty under the conscript act at the reorganization, 1 May 1862. He suffered financially after the war, and it was written in 1876 that he lost all his property.

Nichol, William C.; First Lieutenant, Company B: Brother of First Lieutenant Samuel D. Nichol. Baptized in the First Presbyterian Church on 19 August 1833. Occupation: clerk. Sworn into service 10 May 1861 at Nashville. Elected first sergeant at the organization. Brevetted second lieutenant, 23 May 1862. Promoted to first lieutenant, 6 April 1864. Wounded in the Battle of Atlanta, GA., 22 July 1864 due to a gunshot wound which fractured the right knee joint. His half-brother, Major Bradford Nichol of Rutledge's Battery, carried him from the field to the surgeon where his leg was amputated. During the retreat from Atlanta, Bradford Nichol carried him to Waycross, GA., where he regained his strength. Admitted to Ocmulgee Hospital Macon, GA., 6 October 1864. After the war, he would work in Nashville as a clerk and bookkeeper. In 1867 he was deputy clerk of the Davidson Co. Court. Later became deranged from the effects of losing his leg and had to be put in the asylum. Died unmarried, 2 July 1869. Buried Mount Olivet Cemetery, Nashville, TN.[544]

Nichols, Griffin; Sergeant, Company H: Born in 1844. Occupation: farmer. Enlisted 1 October 1861 at Camp Buckner, KY. Wounded and captured in the Battle of Murfreesboro, TN., 31 December 1862. Later exchanged. Wounded in the head in the Battle of Missionary Ridge, TN., 25 November 1863. Captured in the Battle of Nashville, TN., 16 December 1864. Sent to the U. S. Military Prison at Louisville, KY., 2 January 1865. Forwarded to Camp Chase, OH., 4 January 1865. Took oath 6 May 1865. Complexion fair, hair brown, eyes gray, height 5' 8". In 1868 because of constant teasing, Nichols stabbed and killed Artin Hassell, another former member of the 11th Tennessee, at Henry G. Nichols' store at Shady Grove, Hickman Co., TN. Married Melinda Alice Savage 24 September 1868. Later moved to Birchtree Township, MO.[545]

---

[542] Nesbitt, *West from Edrom*, 80; Patey, *Patey-Skelton*, 84; Goodspeed Brothers, *Goodspeed's Histories of Montgomery, Robertson, Humphreys, Stewart, Dickson, Cheatham, Houston Counties*, 1348-49; Baker, *1860 Census for Dickson County*, 24.

[543] Lindsley, *Annals*, 304; Welsh, *Confederate Hospitals*, Patient Roster, Fair Ground Hospital #1, 206.

[544] Maney, *Surgeon's Log*, "Battle of Atlanta GA"; Nichol, "Memoir," 22 July 1864.

[545] United Daughters of the Confederacy, *Confederate Soldiers of Hickman County*, 152; Spence, *History*, 34, 54; *Nashville Daily Press*, 22 December 1864.

Nichols, Henry C.; Private, Company C: Born c. 1840. Occupation: farm hand. Sworn into service 14 May 1861 at Nashville. Issued a minie musket. Teamster from 12 October through 31 December 1861. Taken prisoner at Versailles, KY., 8 October 1862. Exchanged and rejoined company, 17 February 1863 at Shelbyville, TN. Age 23 on roll dated 8 May 1863 at Shelbyville, TN. Captured in the Battle of Missionary Ridge, TN., 25 November 1863. Sent to the U. S. Military Prison at Louisville, KY., 7 December 1863. Forwarded to Rock Island, IL., 9 December 1863. Died at Rock Island, 3 March 1864 of variola. Buried in grave #705.[546]

Nix, James C.; Private, Company A: Born c. 1826. Occupation: farmer. Enlisted 19 September 1861 at Knoxville, TN. Discharged 10 December 1862. After discharge, he returned home and resumed farming.[547]

Nolan, Levi H.; Private, Company A: Sworn into service 10 May 1861 at Nashville. Died 1 June 1862.[548]

Noll, Nicholas; First Sergeant, Company E: Sworn into service 18 May 1861 at Nashville. Elected first sergeant at the organization. Age 35 on roll dated 16 August 1861 at Watauga Bridge, TN. Discharged 18 August 1862 under the conscript act at Tazewell, TN. Captured at Nashville, TN., 24 September 1862.

Norman, Henry Haywood; Musician, Company D, Field & Staff: Born 27 June 1841 at Columbia, Maury Co., TN. Sworn into service 11 May 1861 in Company D at Nashville. Appointed drummer, 1 September 1861 and transferred to the Field & Staff. Returned to Company D, July 1863. Admitted to Ocmulgee Hospital at Macon, GA., 14-18 June 1864. Deserted and captured near Kennesaw Mountain, GA., 3 July 1864. Sent to the U. S. Military Prison at Louisville, KY., 12 July 1864. Forwarded to Camp Douglas, IL., 6 July 1864. Took oath and released, 13 March 1865. Complexion fair, hair dark, eyes gray, height 5' 7". Married Elizabeth Mildred "Minnie" Houge, 22 October 1874. Resided at Nashville, TN. Occupation: tinner. Died 4 August 1902. Buried Mount Olivet Cemetery, Nashville, Davidson Co., TN.

Northington, Samuel; First Corporal, Company F: Resided at Clarksville, TN., where his father was a cabinet maker. Enlisted 7 October 1861 at Camp Buckner, KY. Promoted to first corporal by July 1862. Wounded in the Battle of Chickamauga, GA. and sent from the field hospital to the Confederate hospital at Griffin, GA. Killed in the Battle of Atlanta, GA., 22 July 1864.[549]

Norvell, William; Private, Company D: Sworn into service 11 May 1861 at Nashville. Age 27 on roll dated 5 May 1863 at Shelbyville, TN. At Knoxville, TN. in the telegraph department from 10 May 1863. Captured sixty miles from Mobile, AL., 7 January 1864. Sent to Fort Warren, MA. Released 3 February 1865 upon taking oath.

-O-

Oakley, Cutis Alexander; Private, Company C: Born in Dickson Co., TN., 2 March 1842. Occupation: farm hand. Sworn into service 14 May 1861 at Nashville. Discharged 25 April 1862. Later served in the 10th Tennessee Cavalry and the 12th Kentucky Cavalry. Wounded in the arm, side, and ankle at the July 1864 Battle of Harrisburg (Tupelo), MS. Paroled at Gainesville, AL., 21 May 1865.

---

[546] Baker, *1860 Census for Dickson County*, 3; McCauley, *Record Book, Company C.*
[547] Clifton, *1870 Census of Humphreys County*, 30.
[548] Johnson, *1860 Census of Humphreys County*, 105.
[549] Jackson, "Letter to Parents," 14 July 1864; Maney, *Surgeon's Log*, "Battle of Atlanta GA."

Postwar occupation: farmer. Resided at Smyrna, Rutherford Co., TN. Member of the Cheatham Bivouac. Died 10 January 1914. Buried in the Leech Cemetery, Dickson Co., TN.[550]

O'Brien, Michael; Private, Company I, G: Sworn into service 20 May 1861 in Company I at Nashville. Transferred to Company G, 28 February 1863. Age 24 on roll dated 6 May 1863 at Shelbyville, TN. Admitted to Fair Ground Hospital #1, Atlanta, GA., 22 September 1863 for vulnus contusion, and forwarded to another hospital the following day. Deserted 17 December 1864. Took oath at Nashville, 9 January 1865. Complexion fair, hair light, eyes blue, height 5' 5".[551]

O'Connell, John; Private, Company E, G: Enlisted 24 September 1861 at Camp Buckner, KY. in Company E. Transferred to Company G, 1 May 1862 at Cumberland Gap, TN. Left Sick at Versailles, KY., 6 October 1862. Deserted 8 October 1862.

O'Conner, ?; Rank unknown, Company E: Killed in the Battle of Missionary Ridge, TN., 25 November 1863.[552]

O'Guinn, James C. "Poke"; 2nd Corporal, Company I: Born c. 1839. Brother of Private Robert N. O'Guinn. Occupation: farmer. Sworn into service 20 May 1861 at Nashville. Elected fourth corporal, 25 April 1863. Age 23 on roll dated 6 May 1863 at Shelbyville, TN. Appointed second corporal by July 1863. Medical records indicate he was killed in the Battle of Atlanta, GA., 22 July 1864.[553]

O'Guinn, Robert Newton; Private, Company I: Born 1844 in Humphreys Co., TN. Enlisted 9 December 1862 at Readyville, TN. Age 18 on roll dated 6 May 1863 at Shelbyville, TN. Contracted measles and had a relapse. In hospital in Rome, GA., 1 July through October, 1863. Captured in the Battle of Jonesboro, GA., 2 September 1864. Sent to the U. S. Military Prison at Louisville, KY. Forwarded to Camp Douglas, IL., 1 November 1864. Released 13 June 1865. Resided at Erin, Houston Co., TN. and later Phifer, Humphreys Co., TN. Died 28 August 1934. Buried Averitt Cemetery, Humphreys Co., TN.[554]

O'Leary, Tim; Private, Company B: Sworn into service 10 May 1861 at Nashville. Sick at Atlanta, GA., 17 June 1862. Deserted November 1862.

Oliver, Olenthius D.; Private, Company A: Born c. 1838 in Arkansas. Lived with his sister Martha and brother-in-law Dr. J. B. Wilkerson in Humphreys Co., TN. at the outbreak of the war. Sworn into service 10 May 1861. Deserted 16 December 1861.[555]

O'Neal, Henry Daniel; Private, Company A: Born c. 1842 in Ireland. Occupation: laborer. Enlisted 12 September 1861 at Knoxville, TN. Wounded in the arm in the Battle of Murfreesboro, TN., 31 December 1862. Captured. Sent to U. S. General Hospital #7 for a wound in the right elbow. Forwarded to Camp Morton, IN., 25 February 1863. Age 20 on roll dated 6 May 1863. Took oath in Nashville, 16 December 1863. Complexion dark, hair brown, eyes gray, 5' 10". Postwar occupation: railroad contractor.

O'Neal, Michael; Private, Company G: Enlisted 3 June 1861 at Camp Cheatham. Discharged under the conscript act, 16 August 1862 at Tazewell, TN.

Orm, John; Private, Company G: Occupation: laborer. Enlisted 3 June 1861 at Camp Cheatham. Left after the Battle of Murfreesboro, TN. to care for the wounded. Captured 9 January 1863. Sent to

---

[550] Baker, *1860 Census for Dickson County*, 18; C. A. Oakley, Cheatham Bivouac Application; C. A. Oakley, Tennessee Pension Application, 14086.

[551] Welsh, *Confederate Hospitals*, Patient Roster, Fair Ground Hospital #1, 209.

[552] Lindsley, *Annals*, 304.

[553] Lindsley, *Annals*, 305; Maney, *Surgeon's Log*, "Battle of Atlanta GA"; Johnson, *1860 Census of Humphreys County*, 33.

[554] Johnson, *1860 Census of Humphreys County*, 48.

[555] Johnson, *1860 Census of Humphreys County*, 85; Clifton, *1870 Census of Humphreys County*, 24; Thedford, "Report of Operations"; Maney, *Surgeon's Log*, "Stones River TN."

Camp Morton, IN. Exchanged 27 February 1863. Returned to duty by March 1863. Age 28 on roll dated 30 May 1863 at Shelbyville, TN. Killed in the Battle of Atlanta, GA., 22 July 1864.[556]

Orr, Carson T.; Private, Company E: Born in Giles Co., TN. No further.

Osborn, William J.; Private, Company E, A: Sworn into service 10 May 1861 in Company E at Nashville. Age 29 on roll dated 16 August 1861 at Watauga Bridge, TN. Transferred to Company A at the reorganization, 1 May 1862. Discharged by the conscript act at Tazewell, TN., 10 September 1862.

Osborne, John B.; Private, Company E, A: Born in Davidson Co., TN. in 1832. Enlisted 24 July 1861 in Company E at Camp Cheatham. Age 27 on roll dated 16 August 1861 at Watauga Bridge, TN. Transferred to Company A at the reorganization, 1 May 1862. Suffered a flesh wound after being struck on the knee by a rock thrown up from a cannon ball, knocking him from the breastworks in the Battle of Kennesaw Mountain, GA., 27 June 1864. Captured the same day and remained disabled for some time. Sent to the U. S. Military Prison at Louisville, KY. Forwarded to Camp Douglas, IL., 14 July 1864. Took oath 13 May 1865. Complexion dark, hair dark, eyes gray, height 5' 6".[557]

Owen, J. D.; Private, Company C: No further.

Owen, Jesse L.; Private, Company C, E: Born 7 December 1842 in Dickson Co., TN. Sworn into service 14 May 1861 in Company C at Nashville. Transferred to Company E, at the reorganization, 1 May 1862. Wounded and captured in the Battle of Missionary Ridge, TN., 25 November 1863. Sent to Rock Island, IL., 20 December 1863. Released from prison in February or March 1865. Sent to Richmond, VA. following parole but not exchanged until the close of the war. Resided at Clarksville, Montgomery Co., TN. and later moved to West Nashville. Occupation: railroading. Member of the Forbes Bivouac of the Association of Confederate Soldiers.[558]

Owens, Blythia Fuqua; Color Sergeant, Company I: Born 1840 in Humphreys Co., TN. Occupation: laborer. Sworn into service 20 May 1861 at Nashville. Elected fourth corporal at the organization. Age 21 on roll dated 6 May 1863. Served as sergeant of the regimental color guard. Wounded by a minie ball through the right shoulder in the Battle of Atlanta, GA., 22 July 1864. Admitted to Yandell Hospital in Meridian, MS., 2 April 1865. Sent to Way Hospital Meridian, MS., 29 March 1865. Paroled in AL. Married Mary Jane Miller, 26 October 1867. Died 27 February 1898 at Rutherford, Gibson Co., TN.[559]

Owens, James M.; First Corporal, Company C, E: Sworn into service 14 May 1861 in Company C at Nashville. Assigned to work on medical house, 1 - 15 December 1861. Transferred to Company E, at the reorganization, 1 May 1862. Reduced in rank to private, 18 November 1862. Left sick at Manchester, TN. Captured in the Battle of Missionary Ridge, TN., 25 November 1863. Sent to the U. S. Military Prison at Louisville, KY., 10 December 1863. Forwarded to Rock Island, IL., 11 December 1863.

Owens, William; Private, Company I: Sworn into service 20 May 1861. Age 22 on roll dated 6 May 1863 at Shelbyville, TN. Died 6 July 1863.

-P-

Page, Robert B.; Private, Company B, E: Sworn into service 10 May 1861 in Company B at Nashville. Transferred to Company E, at the reorganization, 1 May 1862. Present through August 1863. No further.

---

[556] Maney, *Surgeon's Log*, "Battle of Atlanta GA."
[557] J. B. Osborne, Tennessee Pension Application, 2529.
[558] J. L. Owen, Tennessee Pension Application, 11568; Jesse L. Owen, Forbes Bivouac Application.
[559] Maney, *Surgeon's Log*, "Battle of Atlanta GA"; James Lunsford, Tennessee Confederate Pension Application, 5485; B. F. Owens, Tennessee Pension Application, 956.

Parish, Thomas M.; Fourth Sergeant, Company F: Occupation: farmer. Enlisted 18 May 1861 at Cedar Hill, TN. Promoted to fourth sergeant by July 1863. Wounded in the left hand in the Battle of Missionary Ridge, TN., 25 November 1863. Sent to hospital.[560]

Parke, Thomas P.; Private, Company I: Died 11 February 1864 at Rock Island Prison, IL. Buried in grave # 323 at Rock Island Prison.[561]

Parker, Dan M.; Private, Company H: Sworn into service 14 May 1861 at Nashville. Discharged 4 July 1861.

Parker, James T.; First Corporal, Company E: Born 29 December 1837. Occupation: farmer. Sworn into service 18 May 1861 at Nashville. Age 23 on roll dated 16 August 1861 at Watauga Bridge, TN. Promoted to first corporal by August 1861. Reduced in rank by July 1862. Wounded in the left hip and right ankle in the Battle of Atlanta, GA., 22 July 1864. Took oath 30 June 1865 at Montgomery, AL. Complexion fair, hair black, eyes gray, height 5' 11". Relocated to Texas. Died 23 June 1900. Buried in the Brook's Cemetery, Paluxy, TX.[562]

Parnell, John C.; Private, Company E: Occupation: farmhand. Sworn into service 18 May 1861 at Nashville. Age 20 on roll dated 16 August 1861 at Watauga Bridge, TN. Deserted near Shelbyville, TN., 17 January 1863.

Parrish, Robert A.; Private, Company G: Born c. 1827 in Williamson Co., TN. Occupation: music teacher. Married Columbia A. Branch, 2 January 1849. Sworn into service 10 May 1861 at Nashville. Discharged for disability 16 January 1862. Complexion dark, hair black, eyes hazel, height 5' 8", age 34.[563]

Patrick, J. B.; Private, Company B: Sworn into service 10 May 1861 at Nashville. Deserted 1 July 1861 at Camp Cheatham.

Patterson, Joseph James; Private, Company C: Born 27 August 1843 in Dickson Co., TN. Occupation: farmhand. Sworn into service 14 May 1861 at Nashville. Issued a Belgium musket. Captured in the Battle of Murfreesboro, TN., 31 December 1862. Sent to Camp Douglas, IL., 15 May 1863. Forwarded to City Point, VA. for exchange, 21 May 1863. Returned to unit. Captured on the retreat from Middle Tennessee at the Elk River December 1864. Took oath to avoid returning to prison. Resided at Ellis Mills, Houston Co., TN. Died 24 July 1935. Buried Patterson Cemetery #1, Houston Co., TN.[564]

Patterson, Joseph K.; Private, Company H: Born c. 1840. Occupation: farmer. Sworn into service 14 May 1861 at Nashville. Killed in the Battle of Murfreesboro, TN., 31 December 1862. Buried in the Confederate Circle, Evergreen Cemetery, Murfreesboro, Rutherford Co., TN.[565]

Patterson, W. H.; Musician, Company C, Field & Staff: Born c. 1833. Sworn into service 14 May 1861 in Company C at Nashville. Appointed drummer for company at the organization. Captured in the Battle of Murfreesboro, TN., 31 December 1862. Sent to City Point, VA. for exchange. Returned to company by March 1863. Age 26 on roll dated 8 May 1863 at Shelbyville, TN. Transferred to the

---

[560] Maney, *Surgeon's Log*, "Missionary Ridge TN."

[561] Office of the Commissioner for Marking Graves of Confederate Dead, comp., "Register of Confederate Dead Rock Island Illinois" (Washington DC: War Department, 1912).

[562] Baker, *1860 Census for Dickson County*, 61; Maney, *Surgeon's Log*, "Battle of Atlanta GA"; Electronic mail correspondence with Ron Parker, Bedford, Texas, Family Historian, 27 July 2003.

[563] Dobson-Sides, *1860 Davidson County Census*, 700; Sistler and Sistler, *Davidson County Marriages 1838-1863*, 169.

[564] McCauley, *Record Book, Company C*; Baker, *1860 Census for Dickson County*, 8; Sistler and Sistler, *1880 Census of Dickson County*, 242.

[565] Maney, *Surgeon's Log*, "Stones River TN"; Confederate Circle of Heroes, Evergreen Cemetery, Murfreesboro, Tennessee http://www.tngenweb.org/rutherford/confed4.htm.

regimental band, 1 November 1863. Present at least through February 1864. Died 30 April 1891. Buried in the Union Cemetery, Dickson, Dickson Co., TN.[566]

Peach, Fountain E.; Private, Company B: Born 29 June 1841. Occupation: plumber. Sworn into service 10 May 1861 at Nashville. Age 26 on roll dated 2 June 1863 at Shelbyville, TN. Captured in the Battle of Jonesboro, GA., 1 September 1864. Took oath 23 December 1864. Complexion fair, hair brown, eyes blue, height 5' 8". Died of senility, 13 September 1910, age 70. Buried at Mount Olivet Cemetery, Nashville, TN.

Pearl, Edward; Private, Company D: Sworn into service 11 May 1861 at Nashville. Deserted at the evacuation of Cumberland Gap, TN. Enlisted in the 2nd Tennessee Cavalry (US), 1 August 1862 at Jacksboro, TN. Listed as a laborer, later working as an ambulance teamster. Discharged in 1865.

Peaters, C. D.; Sergeant, Company I: Occupation: farmer. Suffered a severe flesh wound in the middle 1/3 of the left thigh in the Battle of Atlanta, GA., 22 July 1864.[567]

Peck, Giles; Private, Company B: Sworn into service 10 May 1861 at Nashville. Age 27 on roll dated 2 June 1863 at Shelbyville, TN. Captured in the Battle of Nashville, TN., 16 December 1864.

Peck, James; Private, Company D: Captured near Nashville, 24 December 1864. Sent to the U. S. Military Prison at Louisville, KY. Forwarded to Camp Chase, OH., 6 January 1865. Enlisted in the U. S. Army, 22 April 1865.

Peck, John; Private, Company B: Wounded in the Battle of Franklin, TN., 30 November 1864. Captured at Franklin, TN., 17 December 1864.

Peeler, Samuel; Private, Company A: Born c. 1843. Enlisted 12 September 1861 at Knoxville, TN. On extra duty as a teamster, December 1861 through January 1862. Sick in hospital at Tazewell, TN. since 28 April 1862. Discharged under the conscript act, 14 August 1862 at Tazewell, TN.[568]

Pemberton, John; Private, Company E: Pension Application, Arkansas, Garland Co., 1913.[569]

Pentecost, A. M.; Private, Company A: Sworn into service 10 May 1861 at Nashville. Discharged for disability May 1861.

Perry, Marshall; Private, Company I: Born c. 1844. Sworn into service 20 May 1861 at Nashville. Died 1 December 1861 at Knoxville, TN.[570]

Perry, Thomas; Private, Company G: Enlisted 6 July 1861 at Camp Cheatham. Listed as absent without leave March through April 1862. Hanged for murder and robbery.[571]

Pettis, Eggleston; Private, Company unknown: Deserted 1 March 1863. Took oath at Nashville, TN., 31 March 1863. Complexion fair, hair light, eyes blue, height 6' 1".

Petty, G. H.; Private, Company K: Furloughed by Colonel John E. Binns, 14 December 1864 at Nashville. Following the Battle of Nashville, Petty, T. B. Adcock, J. W. Redden, and John Majors attempted to return to the army but each time they attempted to cross the Tennessee River, they were fired on by Federal gunboats. The men stayed on the river bank trying to cross for eight days, and with provisions running out, they were forced to return home.[572]

Petty, John M.; Private, Company K: Sworn into service 25 May 1861 at Nashville. Wardmaster at the Old State Hospital at Nashville, 20 June 1861. Did not return to regiment. Age 28 on roll dated 15 August 1861 at Midway, TN.

Petty, Thomas Benton; Third Sergeant, Company H: Sworn into service 14 May 1861 at Nashville. Appointed third sergeant, 10 June 1863. Wounded in the Battle of Chickamauga, GA. Sent to the hospital. Died of wounds, 9 January 1864. Buried in the Oakland Cemetery, Atlanta, GA.

---

[566] Garrett and McClain, *Dickson County Cemetery Records* vol. 1, 132.
[567] Maney, *Surgeon's Log*, "Battle of Atlanta GA."
[568] Johnson, *1860 Census of Humphreys County*, 127.
[569] Welsh, *Arkansas Pension Applications by Tennessee Veterans*, 3.23.
[570] Johnson, *1860 Census of Humphreys County*, 122.
[571] Lindsley, *Annals*, 305.
[572] John W. Redden, Tennessee Pension Application, 3010.

Phenix, J. C.; Private, Company I: Sworn into service 20 May 1861 at Nashville. Deserted 12 May 1862 at Cumberland Gap, TN.

Phillips, John W.; Second Lieutenant, Company K: Born in Tallahachie Co., MS., 1 May 1840. Occupation: farmer. Sworn into service 25 May 1861 at Nashville. Elected second corporal at the organization. Age 21 on roll dated 15 August 1861 at Midway, TN. Promoted to second lieutenant at the reorganization, 1 May 1862. Wounded by a minie ball through the left lung in the Battle of Peachtree Creek, GA., 20 July 1864. Admitted to Catoosa Hospital, Griffin, GA., 22 July 1864. Part of eleventh and twelfth ribs removed at the hospital at Lauderdale Springs, MS. Took oath 14 May 1865. Resided in Gleason, Weakley Co., TN. Present at the 14 June 1904 reunion of the 11th Tennessee Infantry in Nashville. Died 8 June 1916. Buried in the Mount Zion Cemetery, Weakley Co., TN.[573]

Pinkston, John; Private, Company G: Enlisted 28 August 1861 at Midway, TN. Deserted. Rejoined from desertion and under arrest, 22 July 1862. Deserted 18 October 1862 en route to the Battle of Rockcastle, KY.

Pinkston, S. P.; Private, Company H: Enlisted 13 February 1863 at Shelbyville, TN. Present at least through May 1863. No further.

Pitts, Fountain Elliott; Chaplain, Field & Staff: Born in Georgetown, KY., 4 July 1808. Brother of Asst. Surgeon James B. Pitts and father of Captain Josiah H. Pitts. Professed religion in 1820 and licensed to preach in 1824 at age sixteen. Considered one of the leading ministers of the Methodist Episcopal Church South. Served as pastor of McKendree Methodist Church, Nashville's founding Methodist congregation, from 1833-1835, and again from 1843-1845. During 1835, he traveled to South America and founded a mission in Buenos Aires and neighboring cities. Known for his inspirational sermons, he won the sobriquet of "the old man eloquent." Elected Chaplain of the 11th Tennessee, 19 June 1861 at Camp Cheatham, and joined the regiment 27 October 1861 at Cumberland Ford, KY. Absent on sick leave from 6 December 1861 through January 1862. Resigned his commission, 1 May 1862 at the reorganization. Organized and became colonel of the 61st Tennessee Infantry. Fighting alongside his men, he was nicknamed the "fighting parson." Following the war Pitts resumed ministerial duties, and was pastor of West End Methodist Church in Nashville at the time of his death from pneumonia, 22 May 1874. Buried in Mount Olivet Cemetery, Nashville, TN.[574]

Pitts, James B.; Assistant Surgeon, Company A, Field & Staff: Born c. 1830. Brother of Chaplain Fountain E. Pitts. Obtained his medical training at the University of Nashville, graduating in 1853, and was a practicing physician in Humphreys Co., TN. prior to the war. Married to Sophia. Sworn into service 10 May 1861 at Nashville. Elected first lieutenant at the organization. Detailed as surgeon for the post hospital 16 October 1861 through January 1862 at Cumberland Gap, TN. Appointed assistant surgeon, 10 February 1862 and transferred to the Field & Staff. Appointed surgeon of the 61st Tennessee, 27 December 1862. Following the war he returned to his practice of medicine in Waverly, Humphreys Co., TN.

Pitts, Josiah Henry; Captain, Company A: Born in 1828. Son of Chaplain Fountain E. Pitts. Resident of Nashville for many years. Served in the Mexican War. He later migrated to California in search of gold, and later returned to Nashville. Married Martha Lawrence Sneed of Nashville, 30 January 1856. Relocated to Humphreys Co., TN. Sworn into service 10 May 1861 at Nashville. Elected captain of the company at the organization. Resigned 3 May 1862. Captured near Lagardo, TN., 8 May 1863. Sent to Fort Delaware, Delaware. Forwarded to Johnsons Island, OH., 18 July 1863. Took oath 19 February 1865. Died 18 December 1896 at the age of 68 at his home at Sartarem, Brazil, South America.[575]

---

[573] Maney, *Surgeon's Log*, "20 July 1864"; *Chattanooga Daily Rebel*, 27 July 1864; John W. Phillips, Tennessee Pension Application, 24; *Reunion Pamphlet*, 14 June 1904.

[574] *Nashville Union and American*, 24 May 1874.

[575] *Christian Advocate*, 25 February 1897.

Pitts, Lewis L.; Private, Company G, B, D: Occupation: clerk. Sworn into service 10 May 1861 in Company G. Transferred to Company B at the reorganization, 1 May 1862. Age 20 on roll dated 20 June 1863 at Shelbyville, TN. Transferred to Company D, 1 July 1863. Wounded in the face by a shell fragment in the Battle of Chickamauga, GA., 19 September 1863. Admitted to Fair Ground Hospital #1, Atlanta, GA., on 22 September 1863 for vulnus sclopeticum, and sent to another hospital the following day. Captured near Kennesaw Mountain, GA., 4 July 1864. Sent to the U. S. Military Prison at Louisville, KY. Forwarded to Camp Douglas, IL.[576]

Plant, John Harrison; Private, Company A: Born in Stewart Co., TN., 8 February 1837. Sworn into service 10 May 1861 at Nashville. Sick with pneumonia for about two weeks at Cumberland Gap, TN. Sent to hospital at Tazewell, TN. Discharged for disability due to fistula in rectum and rupture in left groin. Resided in Humphreys Co., TN. Died 13 November 1921. Buried in the J. Warren Cemetery, Plant, Humphreys Co., TN.[577]

Plunkett, John W.; Private, Company H: Born in 1835. Sworn into service 14 May 1861 at Nashville. Regimental teamster, 7 August 1862 through February 1863. Deserted 22 April 1863 at Shelbyville, TN. Took oath at Nashville, TN., 15 January 1864. Complexion fair, hair light, eyes blue, height 5' 4".

Polk, Henry Atlas; Fifth Sergeant, Company F: Born in Robertson Co., TN., 17 April 1836. Relative of President James K. Polk and Confederate General's Lucius Polk and Leonidas Polk. Occupation: farmer. Enlisted 18 May 1861 at Cedar Hill, TN. Promoted to fifth sergeant by July 1862. Reduced in rank by November 1862. Wounded in the upper left arm and left hand in the Battle of Atlanta, GA., 22 July 1864. Admitted to the Ladies Hospital Montgomery, AL., 15 November 1864. Married Nancy Katherine Ryburn, 1 March 1870. Resided in Robertson Co., TN. following the war, later relocating to Texas after 1876. Died 6 January 1888 in Waxahachie, TX. Buried in the City Cemetery, Waxachie, Ellis Co., TX.[578]

Poore, John M.; Private, Company H: Sworn into service 14 May 1861 at Nashville. Discharged 4 July 1861.

Porch, William Silous "Babe"; Private, Company C: Born 24 June 1839 in Davidson Co., TN. Sworn into service 14 May 1861 at Nashville. Issued a minie musket. Married Aley "Alcie" Jane Street, 4 September 1861. Wounded in the arm during the Battle of Murfreesboro, TN., 31 December 1862. Furloughed from the Confederate Hospital in Shelbyville, TN., February 1863. While attempting to return to the regiment, he was stopped in Columbia, TN. and told by Captain DeMoss of the 10th Tennessee Cavalry, that he could not get through the enemy lines. He took up temporary service with Company A, 10th Tennessee Cavalry. Captured in Dickson, TN., 20 November 1863. Forwarded to Camp Morton, IN. Released upon taking oath on 22 May 1865. Resided at Slayden, Dickson Co., TN. Died 1 October 1916. Buried in the Schmittou Cemetery, Dickson Co., TN.[579]

Poter, Charles P.; Private, Company A: Sworn into service 10 May 1861 at Nashville. Age 24 on roll dated 6 May 1863 at Shelbyville, TN. Deserted 1 September 1863 near Chickamauga, GA. Captured 13 September 1863. Sent to the U. S. Military Prison at Louisville, KY. Took oath 29 September 1863.

Poter, Columbus W.; Private, Company A: Sworn into service 10 May 1861 at Nashville. Absent sick at Bean Station, TN. since 26 October 1862. Age 22 on roll dated 6 May 1863 at Shelbyville, TN. Admitted to Fair Ground Hospital #1, Atlanta, GA., 22 August 1863 for debilitus and diarrhea. Returned to duty 25 August 1863. Captured in the Battle of Missionary Ridge, TN., 25 November 1863.

---

[576] Maney, *Surgeon's Log*, "Chickamauga GA"; Welsh, *Confederate Hospitals*, Patient Roster, Fair Ground Hospital #1, 222.

[577] John H. Plant, Tennessee Pension Application, 5470.

[578] Maney, *Surgeon's Log*, "Battle of Atlanta GA."

[579] Sistler and Sistler, *1880 Census of Dickson County*, 248; McCauley, *Record Book, Company C*; McCauley Camp 260, *Confederate Graves*, 41; Michael Cotten, *The Williamson County Cavalry: A History of Company F, Fourth Tennessee Cavalry Regiment, CSA* (Goodlettsville TN: M. Cotten, 1994) 241.

Sent to the U. S. Military Prison at Louisville, KY. Took oath 18 July 1864. Hair dark, eyes gray, height 5' 6".

Poter, Thomas Y.; Private, Company A: Enlisted 23 July 1861 at Camp Cheatham. Sick in hospital at Tazewell, TN. since 28 April 1862. Age 26 on roll dated 6 May 1863 at Shelbyville, TN. Deserted 14 September 1863 at Chattanooga, TN.

Porter, Samuel M.; Private, Company E: Occupation: farmhand. Sworn into service 18 May 1861 at Nashville. Age 19 on roll dated 16 August 1861 at Watauga Bridge, TN. On sick furlough at Knoxville, TN. since 22 March 1862. Under arrest January through February 1863 and undergoing punishment. Deserted by March 1863. Resided in Arkansas. Pension Application, Arkansas, Woodruff Co., 1906.[580]

Powell, John William "Wiley"; Private, Company F: Occupation: farmer. Enlisted 18 May 1861 at Cedar Hill, TN. Detached as a guard at Rome, GA., March through April 1863. Suffered a severe wound in the lower third of the left thigh on the skirmish line at Kennesaw Mountain, GA., 21 June 1864. Died 26 June 1864 in Atlanta, GA. Buried in the Oakland Cemetery, Atlanta, GA.[581]

Powell, Joseph R.; Private, Company F: Enlisted 18 May 1861 at Cedar Hill, TN. Died at home 21 July 1861.

Powell, R.; Rank unknown, Company F: Died at Camp Cheatham.[582]

Powell, Reynolds Leftrick; Second Corporal, Company F: Born 25 May 1841, son of Professor Richard Powell and Elizabeth "Betsy" Bell Powell. Betsy was the daughter of John Bell of Adams, TN., and was alleged to have been mercilessly tormented by the demonic entity known as the Bell Witch. Enlisted 18 May 1861 at Cedar Hill, TN. Elected fourth corporal at the organization. Appointed second corporal by November 1862. Wounded in the left arm in the Battle of Chickamauga, GA., 19 September 1863. Sent to hospital in Griffin, GA. Killed in the Battle of Franklin, TN., 30 November 1864, age 23. Buried in the Batts Family Cemetery, Cedar Hill, Robertson Co., TN.[583]

Pratt, Henry P.; Second Lieutenant, Company K: Elected second lieutenant, 10 August 1862. Present at least through November 1862. No further.

Price, James; Private, Company K, G: Sworn into service 25 May 1861 in Company K at Nashville. Age 32 on roll dated 15 August 1861 at Midway, TN. Transferred to Company G by May 1863. Deserted 17 June 1863.

Price, John R.; First Corporal, Company I: Born c. 1826. Married to Martha. Sworn into service 20 May 1861 at Nashville. Elected first corporal at the organization. Died of disease 24 December 1861 at home in Humphreys Co., TN.[584]

Price, Preston, Gano; First Lieutenant/Ensign, Company D, B: Born 9 June 1834 in Scott Co., KY. Educated in Georgetown, KY. Relocated to Frankfort, KY. at age 18 to become a printer. Relocated to Nashville, TN. where he remained until the outbreak of the war. Occupation: printer both before and after the war. Sworn into service 11 May 1861 in Company D at Nashville. Correspondent for the regiment while at Camp Cheatham. Elected third sergeant at the organization. Promoted to second Sergeant by November 1862. Transferred to Company B by May 1863. Age 26 on roll dated 5 May 1863 at Shelbyville, TN. Appointed Ensign and first lieutenant, 18 April 1864 after the color sergeant fell in the Battle of Missionary Ridge, TN. Recommended by Colonel George W. Gordon for his exemplary conduct and his more than ordinary devotion to the cause. Resigned 12 October 1864 to join a Kentucky regiment. Surrendered at Augusta, GA, 1 May 1865. Took oath 22 May 1865. Postwar, he returned to Nashville, and in 1867 married Bell Brothers. Member of the Baptist Church and active in Sunday

---

[580] Welsh, *Arkansas Pension Applications by Tennessee Veterans*, 3.26.

[581] Maney, *Surgeon's Log*, "Kennesaw Mountain GA"; Jackson, "Letter to Parents," 14 July 1864.

[582] Lindsley, *Annals*, 304.

[583] Maney, *Surgeon's Log*, "Chickamauga GA"; Lindsley, *Annals*, 304; Personal correspondence with Mr. Tim Burgess, Battle of Franklin Historian, 13 May 2001.

[584] Garrett, *Humphreys County, Tennessee, 1850 Census*, 103; Johnson, *1860 Census of Humphreys County*, 106.

school work. Member of the Cheatham Bivouac. With health failing, he relocated in 1888 to live with his son in Dyersburg, TN. Died 18 May 1912. Buried Zion Hill Cemetery, Dyer Co., TN.[585]

Price, Richard; Private, Company K: Sworn into service 20 May 1861 at Nashville. Died 28 July 1861 at Camp Cheatham.

Price, W. Henry; Private, Company I: Born c. 1835. Occupation: farmer. Sworn into service 20 May 1861 at Nashville. Killed in the Battle of Murfreesboro, TN., 31 December 1862.[586]

Priestly, Lafayette M.; Private, Company A: Sworn into service 10 May 1861 at Nashville. On extra duty in the quartermaster department as Assistant Adjutant General, March through April 1862. Discharged 14 August 1862 under the conscript act at Tazewell, TN.

Primm, William D. S.; Private, Company I: Born c. 1840. Sworn into service 20 May 1861 at Nashville. On extra duty in the quartermaster department July through October 1862. Age 23 on roll dated 6 May 1863 at Shelbyville, TN. At hospital in Atlanta, GA. since 1 July 1863. Returned to duty by September 1863. Took oath at Nashville, TN., 5 January 1865. Complexion dark, hair brown, eyes hazel, height 5' 9". Occupation: farmer.[587]

Proctor, William; Private, Company F: Enlisted 12 September 1861 at Knoxville, TN. On extra duty in the quartermaster department July through August 1862. Captured at Tullahoma, TN., 1 July 1863. Sent to the U. S. Military Prison at Louisville, KY. Forwarded to Camp Chase, OH., 22 July 1863. Transferred to Camp Douglas, Chicago, IL., where he died 4 October 1863. Buried in grave #721, Oak Woods Cemetery, Chicago, IL.[588]

Puckett, Andrew A.; Private, Company G: Born c. 1841. Occupation: laborer. Married Sally. Sworn into service 10 May 1861 at Nashville. Age 22 on roll dated 30 May 1863 at Shelbyville, TN. Wounded in the right foot in the Battle of Missionary Ridge, TN., 25 November 1863. Captured in the Battle of Franklin, TN., 30 November 1864. Sent to the U. S. Military Prison at Louisville, KY. Forwarded to Camp Douglas, IL., 3 December 1864. Took oath 24 March 1865. Complexion fair, hair brown, eyes brown, height 5' 6".[589]

Pullen, James L.; Private, Company A: Born c. 1840. Brother of Private William C. Pullen. Sworn into service 10 May 1861 at Nashville. Attendant at hospital at Tazewell, TN. since 28 April 1862. Age 20 on roll dated 6 May 1863 at Shelbyville, TN. Deserted 24 February 1865. Took oath 15 April 1865 at Nashville. Complexion fair hair dark, eyes blue, height 5' 9". Married Francis E. Cannon, 1 March 1866.[590]

*Pullen, William Carroll; Private, Company A: Born 24 January 1842. Brother of Private James L. Pullen. Resided in Humphreys Co., TN. near McEwen. Sworn into service 10 May 1861 at Nashville. Sick in hospital at Tazewell, TN., 28 April 1862. Age 23 on roll dated 6 May 1863 at Shelbyville, TN. Wounded in the Battle of Lovejoy Station, GA., 2 September 1864. Surrendered with the Army of Tennessee at Greensboro, NC., 26 April 1865. Occupation: farmer. Married to Sarah E. Died 25 June 1935. Buried in his Confederate uniform in the Bethpage Cemetery, Humphreys Co., TN.[591]

---

[585] "Preston G. Price," *Confederate Veteran*, vol. 20 no. 11 (November 1912): 531.

[586] Garrett, *Humphreys County, Tennessee, 1850 Census*, 17; Lindsley, *Annals*, 305.

[587] Johnson, *1860 Census of Humphreys County*, 74; Fischer and Burns, *1880 Census of Humphreys County*, 152.

[588] Find-A-Grave, "Oak Woods," http://www.findagrave.com/cgi-binfg.cgi?page=gr&GSln= Proctor& GSiman= 1&GScid=173554&GRid=38248096& (16 August 2014).

[589] Maney, *Surgeon's Log*, "Missionary Ridge TN"; Sistler and Sistler, *1880 Census of Davidson County*, 395.

[590] Johnson, *1860 Census of Humphreys County*, 125.

[591] Anderson and Garrett, *Humphreys County Cemetery Records*, 49; Fischer and Burns, *1880 Census of Humphreys County*, 181; William C. Pullen, Tennessee Pension Application, 14766.

-Q-

Quarles, Pinkney M.; Private, Company F: Born c 1831. Resided in Montgomery Co., TN. Enlisted 18 May 1861 at Cedar Hill, TN. Extra duty in the quartermaster department July through August 1862. Killed in the Battle of Franklin, TN., 30 November 1864, age 33. Buried in the McGavock Confederate Cemetery, section 59, grave 15.[592]

Quinn, Michael; Private, Company C, G: Sworn into service 14 May 1861 in Company C at Nashville. Transferred to Company G at the reorganization, 1 May 1862. Wounded in the thigh and arm in the Battle of Murfreesboro, TN., 31 December 1862. Sent to hospital. Died from wounds 11 January 1863.

-R-

Ragsdale, Mathias Wilburn; Private, Company H: Born c. 1828. Occupation: wagon-maker. Enlisted 6 February 1863 at Shelbyville, TN. Captured in the Battle of Chickamauga, GA., 19 September 1863. Sent to the U. S. Military Prison at Louisville, KY. Forwarded to Camp Douglas, IL., 2 October 1863. Took oath 12 May 1865. Complexion dark, hair brown, eyes brown, height 5' 9".[593]

Rains, James Edwards; Brigadier General, Colonel, Company D, Field & Staff: Born 10 April 1833 in Nashville, TN., one of fifteen children born to the Reverend John and Lucinda Cartwright Rains. Rev. Rains, a local Methodist minister, owned a modest saddlery shop in which James and his brothers worked in their youth. Producing harness by day and studying at night, he showed an intellectual capacity beyond that of his peers with formal schooling. This talent caught the eye of a benevolent citizen, who loaned Jim Rains $400 to attend Yale University, from which he graduated second in his class of 1854. Upon his return to Middle Tennessee he served as the headmaster of the Millwood Institute of the Sycamore Powder Mills in Cheatham Co., near Ashland City until 1857, and obtained his law license during this time. In 1858, he became the associate editor of the *Nashville Republican Banner*. That same year, on 22 June, he married Ida Laura Yeatman, the daughter of a wealthy merchant, and though only twenty-five years of age, was elected the Nashville city attorney. Politically a Whig and like his father an opponent of secession, in 1860 he was elected district attorney general for Davidson, Williamson, and Sumner Counties. At the outbreak of the Civil War, Rains enlisted as a private in the military service of the State of Tennessee, 4 May 1861 at Nashville in the Hermitage Guards, a unit then being organized by then fellow attorney and later Brigadier General, George E. Maney. Rains was elected first lieutenant of the Hermitage Guards (Company D), on 23 April 1861. Immediately upon Gorge E. Maney's acceptance of the colonelcy of the 1st Tennessee Infantry, Rains was elected captain to fill the vacancy. At the organization of the 11th Tennessee Infantry on 31 May 1861 at Camp Cheatham, Rains was unanimously elected colonel of the regiment. Serving with distinction in the Kentucky Campaign, he was promoted to brigadier general, 4 November 1862. Rains was shot through the heart and killed instantly while leading his men against a Federal battery in the Battle of Murfreesboro, TN., 31 December 1862. His last known words as he was urging his troops to advance in this ill-fated charge were, "Forward, my brave boys! Forward!" After Rains' death his body was conveyed to the Nashville City Cemetery where it was interred in the Currin Vault on 7 January 1863. Rains' body was moved to

---

[592] Lindsley, *Annals*, 304; Personal correspondence with Mr. Tim Burgess, Battle of Franklin Historian, 13 May 2001.

[593] United Daughters of the Confederacy, *Hickman County Census 1860*, 32.

the Yeatman Plot in the Mount Olivet Cemetery, Nashville, TN. in 1888. The Tennessee State Museum has on display Rains' 1840 model heavy cavalry saber.[594]

Randall, David A.; Private, Company H, A: Sworn into service 14 May 1861 in Company H at Nashville. Transferred to Company A at the reorganization, 1 May 1862. Captured in the Battle of Murfreesboro, Tennessee, 31 December 1862. Sent to the U. S. Military Prison at Louisville, KY. Forwarded to Camp Douglas, IL. Exchanged and rejoined company by July 1863. Captured in the Battle of Missionary Ridge, Tennessee, 25 November 1863. Sent to the U. S. Military Prison at Louisville, KY. Forwarded to Rock Island, IL. Died at Rock Island, 8 August 1864 of cholera morbus. Buried in the Confederate Cemetery at Rock Island, grave #1395.

*Randall, William Henry; Private, Company A: Born in Davidson Co., Tennessee, 14 February 1844. In the service of the Confederate government making saddles at Trenton, GA. prior to enlisting, 10 October 1863 at Chattanooga, TN. Knocked down by a spent ball in the Battle of Kennesaw Mountain, GA., 27 June 1864. Surrendered with the Army of Tennessee, 26 April 1865 as a member of Company F, 2nd Consolidated Tennessee Infantry. Occupied as a lumber dealer and later served as a Sheriff's deputy in Nashville. Relocated to Lynnville, Giles Co., TN. prior to entering the Tennessee Confederate Soldiers Home, where he died, 10 October 1926. Buried in the Nashville City Cemetery. Member of the Cheatham Bivouac. Pension Application S9291.[595]

Ratliff, William Newton; Private, Company H: Born 7 April 1847 in Hickman Co., TN. Sworn into service 14 May 1861 at Nashville. Extra duty as a teamster September 1861 through December 1861. Absent sick at Tazewell, TN., 28 April 1862. Discharged under the conscript act, 1 May 1862. Married Mary Elizabeth Garner, 31 December 1878.[596]

Rawley, Darius N.; Fourth Sergeant, Company G, B, D: Sworn into service 10 May 1861 in Company G at Nashville. Elected first corporal in the organization. Transferred to Company B in the reorganization, 1 May 1862. Transferred to Company D by July 1863. Elected fifth sergeant by September 1863. Promoted to fourth sergeant by January 1864. Captured at Jonesboro, GA., 4 September 1864. Sent to the U. S. Military Prison at Louisville, KY., 28 October 1864. Sent to Camp Douglas, IL., 1 November 1864. Took oath 31 January 1865. Complexion fair, hair brown, eyes hazel, height 5' 8". Died in Nashville of cholera 17 September 1866. Burtied Mt. Olivet Cemetery, Nashville, TN.

Ray, A. W.; Private, Company I: Arrested in Lafayette, GA for desertion.

Rearden, Martin; Private, Company K, G: Sworn into service 25 May 1861 in Company K at Nashville. Age 38 on roll dated 15 August 1861 at Midway, TN. Transferred to Company G at the reorganization, 1 May 1862. Discharged under the conscript act at Tazewell, TN., 15 August 1862.

Reaves, James; Private, Company I: Sworn into service 20 May 1861 at Nashville. Discharged for disability 10 October 1861.

Redden, G. L.; Private, Company K: Enlisted 13 December 1862 in Dickson Co., TN. Age 20 on roll dated 1 May 1863 at Shelbyville, TN. Wounded in the Battle of Missionary Ridge, TN., 25 November 1863. Took oath 17 June 1865 at Montgomery, AL. Complexion fair, hair light, eyes blue, height 6'.

Redden, J. Liberty; Sergeant, Company E, K: Occupation: farmer. Sworn into service 18 May 1861 in Company E at Nashville. Age 20 on roll dated 16 August at Watauga Bridge, TN. Transferred to Company K at the reorganization, 1 May 1862. Wounded in the chest in the Battle of Chickamauga, GA., 19 September 1863. Promoted to the rank of sergeant. Wounded in the left ear in the Battle of

---

[594] Evans, *Confederate Military History*, vol. 10, 329-31. Warner, *Generals*, 250-51; Goodspeed Brothers, *Goodspeed's Histories of Montgomery, Robertson, Humphreys, Stewart, Dickson, Cheatham, Houston Counties*, 971; *Nashville Daily Union*, 8 January 1863.

[595] William Henry Randall, Tennessee Pension Application, 9291; William Henry Randall, William Henry Randall, Cheatham Bivouac Application; *Nashville City Directory*, 1926, 619.

[596] United Daughters of the Confederacy, *Confederate Soldiers of Hickman County*, 170.

New Hope Church, GA., 27 May 1864. Wounded severely in the foot at Kennesaw Mountain, GA., 19 June 1864. Admitted to Confederate Hospital at Corinth, MS., 5 January 1865 for chronic diarrhea. Sent to another hospital, 8 January 1865.[597]

Redden, John Wiley; Private, Company K: Born 27 November 1843 in Dickson Co., TN. Occupation: farmer. Enlisted 13 December 1862 in Dickson Co. and joined the army at Readyville, TN. Wounded in the shoulder in the Battle of Murfreesboro, TN., 31 December 1862. Wounded in the neck in the Battle of Missionary Ridge, TN., 25 November 1863. Wounded on the skirmish line near Atlanta, GA. in the right lumbar region by an artillery shell, 28 July 1864. Furloughed by Colonel John E. Binns, 14 December 1864 at Nashville, TN. After the Battle of Nashville, Redden, T. B. Adcock, G. H. Petty, and John Majors attempted to return to the army but each time they attempted to cross the Tennessee River, they were fired on by Federal gunboats. The men stayed on the river bank trying to cross for eight days, and with provisions running out, they were forced to return home. Took oath 10 January 1865. Complexion fair, hair light, eyes blue, height 5' 10". Resided in Dickson Co., TN. Attended the reunion of the 11th Tennessee Infantry at Bon Aqua Springs, Hickman Co., TN., 24 September 1885. Pension Application S3010.[598]

Reddick, John Bell; First Lieutenant, Company D: Born c. 1836 in Tennessee. Occupation: plasterer. Married Catherine M. Felts, 6 October 1857. Sworn into service 11 May 1861 at Nashville. Brevetted second lieutenant by March 1862. Elected first lieutenant at the reorganization, 1 May 1862. Deserted by May 1863.[599]

*Reece, Griffith; Private, Company K: Born 12 December 1835. Sworn into service 20 December 1862. Age 30 on roll dated 1 May 1863 at Shelbyville, TN. Surrendered with the Army of Tennessee at Greensboro, NC., 26 April 1865 as a member of Company K, 2nd Consolidated Tennessee Infantry. Died 26 March 1899. Buried in the Jane Jones Cemetery, Fairview, Williamson Co., TN.[600]

Reeder, John H. L.; Second Corporal, Company K: Born in Mississippi in 1843. Sworn into service, 25 May 1861 at Nashville. Age 19, on roll dated 15 August 1861 at Midway, TN. Promoted to third corporal by July 1862. Appointed second corporal by March 1863. Received injuries from a drunken comrade during the war which resulted in a depression of his skull. Wounded in the Battle of Franklin, TN., 30 November 1864. Took oath at Chattanooga, TN., 30 March 1865. Complexion dark, hair dark, eyes blue, height 5' 10". Following the war he returned home and studied medicine. In 1876 he married Almira A. Walp. Died 3 December 1899. Buried in the Hall Cemetery, Burns, Dickson, Co., TN. Pension Application S1262.[601]

Rees, A. John; Private, Company G: Born 1842 in England. Occupation: printer. Captured at the Battle of Murfreesboro, TN., 31 December 1862. No further.[602]

Reeves, Flavius Jospehus.; Private, Company H: Sworn into service 14 May 1861 at Nashville. Wounded through the left thigh in the Battle of Chickamauga, GA., 19 September 1863. Admitted to Fair Ground Hospital #1, Atlanta, GA. for vulnus sclopeticum. Sent to another hospital, 28 September 1863. Admitted to Confederate hospital, Madison, GA., 24 December 1863. Returned to duty, detailed

---

[597] Maney, *Surgeon's Log*, "Chickamauga GA"; Maney, *Surgeon's Log*, "May 1864"; Maney, *Surgeon's Log*, "Kennesaw Mountain GA"; Welsh, *Confederate Hospitals*, Patient Roster, Fair Ground Hospital #2, 164.

[598] Maney, *Surgeon's Log*, "Missionary Ridge TN"; Maney, *Surgeon's Log*, "28-31 July 1864"; "The Reunion," *Hickman Pioneer*.

[599] Sistler and Sistler, *Davidson County Marriages 1838-1863*, 181; Dobson-Sides, *1860 Davidson County Census*, 598.

[600] McCauley Camp 260, *Confederate Graves*, 42.

[601] Garrett, *Dickson County Handbook*, 215; J. H. L. Reeder, Tennessee Pension Application, 1262.

[602] Dobson-Sides, *1860 Davidson County Census*, 491.

in hospital, 12 April 1864. Returned home 5 June 1865. Resident of Lyles, Hickman Co., TN. Pension Application S11474.[603]

Reeves, William J.; Private, Company H: Brother of F. J. Reeves. Sworn into service 14 May 1861 at Nashville. Wounded in the Battle of Murfreesboro, TN., 31 December 1862. Discharged 8 April 1863.

Reynolds, Robert D.; Private, Company D: Sworn into service 11 May 1861 at Nashville. On extra duty in the brigade quartermaster September through December 1862. Age 24 on roll dated 5 May 1863. Deserted while on picket duty 12 November 1863. Captured at Chattanooga, TN., 12 November 1863. Sent to the U. S. Military Prison at Louisville, KY. Took oath 20 November 1863. Complexion light, hair dark, eyes gray, height 5' 8".

Reynolds, John; Private, Company D: No further.[604]

Reynolds, William Evrette; Private, Company C: Born in Dickson Co., TN. on the date James K. Polk was elected President, 12 November 1844. His grandfather, John Reynolds, had served throughout the Revolutionary War and was present at the surrender of Cornwallis to George Washington. His father had been the superintendent for one of the Dickson Co. iron manufacturers, and owned a large farm in Stewart Co., TN. along with ten slaves. Enlisted 10 June 1863 at Shelbyville, TN. Knocked down by a spent ball in the Battle of Chickamauga, GA., 19 September 1863. Captured in the Battle of Franklin, TN., 30 November 1864. Took oath at Nashville, 18 January 1865. Following the war, he returned to Stewart Co. and engaged in farming. Complexion dark, hair brown, eyes hazel, height 5' 10". Married Nannie F. Mann, 29 April 1868. In April 1876, after a period of ill health, he was persuaded to enter medical school and graduated from Vanderbilt University in 1877. Practiced medicine in Mound Bottom, TN. for seventeen years. In 1894, he relocated to Hopkinsville, KY., where he practiced medicine, serving as the City Physician for the years 1912-1913. Wrote many papers on medicine that were published, some in the *Southern Medical Journal.* Served as a physician with the U. S. Army during World War I, assigned to duty at Pennymoor, VA. in charge of the Influenza hospital. Served as the commander of the Ned Merriweather Camp, United Confederate Veterans, Hopkinsville, KY. Died 24 January 1940. Buried Riverside Cemetery, Hopkinsville, Christian Co., KY.[605]

Rhodes, Granville M.; Private, Company H: Enlisted 10 January 1863 at Shelbyville, TN. Deserted 2 January 1865. Took oath at Nashville, 11 March 1865. Complexion dark, hair brown, eyes hazel, height 6' 1".

Rhodes, James; Private, Company K, H: Born in Maury Co., TN., 15 April 1831. Occupation: farmer. Sworn into service, 25 May 1861 in Company K at Nashville. Age 27on roll dated 15 August 1861 at Midway, TN. On extra duty in the quartermaster department, 30 September 1861 through 30 April 1862. Transferred to Company H at the reorganization, 1 May 1862. Wounded in the left arm in the Battle of Chickamauga, GA., 19 September 1863. Wounded in the right thigh in the Battle of Missionary Ridge, TN., 25 November 1863. Admitted to Pettigrew General Hospital #13 in Raleigh, NC., 22 March 1865 for rheumatism. Admitted to C. S. General Hospital #3 at Greensboro, NC., April 1865. Resided in Linden, Perry Co., TN.[606]

Rhodes, Robert; Private, Company G: Sworn into service 10 May 1861 at Nashville. Discharged under the conscript act, 10 August 1862 at Tazewell, TN.

Rice, Daniel; Private, Company C: Born in Strasbourg City, France, 12 October 1838. Immigrated to New Orleans, LA. in 1851. Later moved to Philadelphia, PA., where he was engaged in the saloon

---

[603] Welsh, *Confederate Hospitals*, Patient Roster, Fair Ground Hospital #1, 234; Harris, *Confederate Hospitals*, 401; F. J. Revves, Tennessee Pension Application, 11474.

[604] Clayton, *History of Davidson County*, 188.

[605] Reynolds, "Veteran Questionnaire," vol. 5, 1829-33; William H. Perrin, *A History of Christian County, Kentucky* (Chicago IL: F. A. Battey, 1884) 620.

[606] James Rhodes, Tennessee Pension Application, 4099; Maney, *Surgeon's Log,* "Chickamauga GA."

business for six months., before relocating to Wilmington, DE. From there he moved to Charlotte, Dickson Co., TN. and began a business as a traveling merchant in Dickson and Humphreys Counties. Transferred from the 4th Tennessee Regiment to Company C, 11th Tennessee, 20 December 1862, swapping a quarter of beef with another soldier of the 11th Tennessee to trade places with him. In commissary department since 20 December 1862. Age 24 on roll dated 8 May 1863 at Shelbyville, TN. Captured in the Battle of Missionary Ridge, TN., 25 November 1863. Sent to the U. S. Military Prison at Louisville, KY. Forwarded to Rock Island, IL., 8 December 1863. Took oath 18 May 1865. Complexion fresh, hair dark, eyes blue, height 5' 8". Following the war he returned to Charlotte, TN. and later moved to Johnsonville, Humphreys Co., TN. While there, he was shot by Tom Warren. The projectile passed entirely through his body. Surviving, he again moved to Charlotte, TN. Around 1868, he began a general merchandise business in Tennessee City, Dickson Co., TN. and served as the first postmaster there. Married Blanch Ann Harrow Long, 26 April 1868. Politically a Democrat. Died 11 March 1898. Buried in the Rice Cemetery, Tennessee City, Dickson Co., TN.[607]

Rice, David H.; First Lieutenant, Company K: Sworn into service, 25 May 1861 at Nashville. Age 25 on roll dated 15 August 1861 at Midway, TN. Promoted to second lieutenant, 15 August 1861. Absent sick at Bean Station, TN. since, 27 October 1862. Elected first lieutenant at the reorganization, 1 May 1862. Deserted 7 February 1863.

Rice, William Bartlett; Private, Company I: Born 22 November 1842 in Humphreys Co., TN. Occupation: blacksmith. Sworn into service 25 September 1861. Discharged for disability at Cumberland Gap, TN., 25 October 1861. Later joined the Cavalry Company of Henon Cross. Resided at Bold Springs, Humphreys Co., TN. Died 7 October 1932. Pension Application S11260.[608]

Rich, Peter; Private, Company G, B: Sworn into service 10 May 1861 in Company G. Transferred to Company B at the reorganization, 1 May 1862. Deserted 17 June 1862 at Cumberland Gap, TN.

*Richardson, Andrew J.; Private, Company E: Born In Dickson Co., TN., 24 March 1843. Occupation: farmer. Enlisted 26 January 1863 at Shelbyville, TN. Wounded in the middle third of the left thigh, just above the knee, in the Battle of Atlanta, GA., 22 July 1864. Gangrene set in and disabled him for the next five months. In hospital at Forsythe, GA. Surrendered with the Army of Tennessee, 26 April 1865 at Greensboro, NC. as a member of Company C, 2nd Consolidated Tennessee Infantry. Following the war he returned home to Humphreys Co. and married Mary E. Burgie, 26 December 1869. Following her death he married Philah Burgie, 19 August 1883. Member of the Methodist Church. Died 19 September 1930. Buried in the family burial grounds near McEwen, Humphreys Co., TN.[609]

Richardson, Benjamin W.; Private, Company K: Born 8 August 1842. Sworn into service, 25 May 1861 at Nashville. Died 1 August 1861.[610]

Richardson, M. Turner; Rank unknown, Company E: Killed in the Battle of Jonesboro, GA., 1 September 1864.[611]

*Richardson, William Turner; Private, Company K: Born 7 December 1843. Sworn into service, 25 May 1861 at Nashville. Age 18, on roll dated 15 August 1861 at Midway, TN. Captured in the Battle of Missionary Ridge, TN., 25 November 1863. Sent to the U. S. Military Prison at Louisville, KY. Forwarded to Rock Island, IL., 8 December 1863. Exchanged and rejoined company. Surrendered with

---

[607] Goodspeed Brothers, *Goodspeed's Histories of Montgomery, Robertson, Humphreys, Stewart, Dickson, Cheatham, Houston Counties*, 1352; Jill Garrett, *A History of Humphreys County, Tennessee: A Supplement* (s.l.: Fischer & Burns, 1988) 402.

[608] W. B. Rice, Tennessee Pension Application, 11260.

[609] Maney, *Surgeon's Log*, "Battle of Atlanta GA"; Goodspeed Brothers, *Goodspeed's Histories of Montgomery, Robertson, Humphreys, Stewart, Dickson, Cheatham, Houston Counties*, 1262-63; A. J. Richardson, Tennessee Confederate Pension Application, S9501.

[610] McCauley Camp 260, *Confederate Graves*, 42.

[611] Lindsley, *Annals*, 304.

the Army of Tennessee at Greensboro, NC., 26 April 1865. Married Emily Catherine Alspaugh in 1866. Died 20 March 1892. Buried in the Alf Richardson Cemetery, Dickson Co., TN.[612]

Richardson, William T.; Sergeant, Company C, E: Sworn into service, 14 May 1861 at Nashville. Worked on the medical office at Cumberland Gap, TN., 1 through 14 December 1861. Transferred to Company E, at the reorganization, 1 May 1862. Appointed first corporal, 18 November 1862. Later promoted to sergeant. Wounded in the right leg in the Battle of Atlanta, GA., 22 July 1864. Leg amputated in the middle third. Later died of wounds. Buried in the Confederate Cemetery, Forsyth, GA.[613]

Rickman, Wiley; Private, Company H: No further.[614]

Ridings, Elisha T.; Private, Company A: Born 23 February 1839 in Hardeman Co., TN. Relocated to Humphreys Co., TN. in infancy. Brother of First Lieutenant George D. Ridings. Enlisted 8 September 1862 at Cumberland Gap, TN. Wounded in the face at the Battle of Murfreesboro, TN., 31 December 1862, the minie ball striking over the left eye, passing through the bridge of the nose, and destroying the upper jawbone. Sent to the U. S. Military Prison at Louisville, KY., 21 April 1863. Exchanged and returned to company. Age 24 on roll dated 6 May 1863 at Shelbyville, TN. Nurse at Foard Hospital Newnan, GA., November through December 1863. Wounded in the Battle of Franklin, TN., 30 November 1864 by a minie ball in the right thigh. Captured at Franklin, TN., 17 December 1864. Admitted to U. S. General Hospital # 1 at Nashville, TN., 25 December 1864. Forwarded to the U. S. Military Prison at Louisville, KY. Transferred to Camp Chase, OH., 18 January 1865. Resided postwar at Tennessee Ridge, Houston Co., TN. Married Mary E. McIntosh, 1 December 1867. Ordained as a minister in the Primitive Baptist Church, 12 October 1878. Died 16 July 1900. Buried in the McIntosh Cemetery, Houston Co., TN. Pension Application S447.[615]

Ridings, George Dillard; First Lieutenant, Company A: Born at Bolivar, Hardeman Co., TN., 4 September 1832. Brother of Private Elisha T. Ridings. Sworn into service 10 May 1861 at Nashville. Elected third lieutenant, 13 September 1861 to replace William Bowen. Elected first lieutenant at the reorganization, 1 May 1862. Wounded in the right leg above the ankle in the Battle of Murfreesboro, TN., 31 December 1861. Captured at Confederate States Hospital #1 at Murfreesboro, TN. while quartered at Ms. Grimmage's. Sent to the U. S. Military Prison at Louisville, KY. Forwarded to Fort McHenry, MD., 18 May 1863. Transferred to Fort Delaware, DE, 13 June 1863. Exchanged and rejoined company. Received at Confederate hospital, Atlanta, GA., 9 May 1864 for debilitas. Admitted to Blackie Hospital, Madison, GA., 10 May 1864. Furloughed from Blackie Hospital, Madison, GA., 1 July 1864. Wounded in the Battle of Jonesboro, GA., 1 September 1864. Admitted to Ocmulgee Hospital, Macon, GA., 8 September 1864 for a gunshot wound which fractured the tibia of the right leg. Following the war he returned home to Humphreys Co., TN. and resumed medical studies. Married Sarah Serena Balthrop, 4 February 1866. Graduated from the medical department of the University of Nashville in 1870 and practiced as a physician. Died 5 September 1884. Buried in the Ridings Family Cemetery near White Oak Creek, Humphreys Co., TN.[616]

---

[612] Garrett, *Dickson County Handbook*, 215.

[613] Maney, *Surgeon's Log*, "Battle of Atlanta GA."

[614] United Daughters of the Confederacy, *Confederate Soldiers of Hickman County*, 173.

[615] Thedford, "Report of Operations"; Maney, *Surgeon's Log*, "Stones River TN"; E. T. Ridings, Tennessee Confederate Pension Application, S447; Electronic mail correspondence with Bart S. Ridings, descendant, 15 February 2001; *Nashville Daily Press*, 22 December 1864.

[616] Thedford, "Report of Operations"; Maney, *Surgeon's Log*, "Stones River TN"; Harris, *Confederate Hospitals*, 362, 134, 401, 148, 422, 225; Goodspeed Brothers, *Goodspeed's Histories of Montgomery, Robertson, Humphreys, Stewart, Dickson, Cheatham, Houston Counties*, 1263; Anderson, and Garrett, *Humphreys County, Tennessee, Cemetery Records* vol. 1, 43; Electronic mail correspondence with Bart S. Ridings, descendant, 15 February 2001.

Ridley, Jerome S.; Major/Assistant Commissary of Subsistence, Field & Staff: Appointed captain and Assistant Commissary of Subsistence, 1 August 1861. On detached service in Atlanta, GA., July 1863 through February 1864. Later promoted to the rank of major on the staff of Major General Carter L. Stevenson.

Riley, Edward; Private, Company C: Sworn into service 14 May 1861 at Nashville. Discharged 4 July 1861 at Camp Cheatham.

Riley, Michael; Private, Company K: Sworn into service 25 May 1861 at Nashville. Age 47 on roll dated 15 August 1861 at Midway, TN. Discharged by the conscript act, 12 August 1862 at Tazewell, TN.

Roberts, W. F.; Private, Company G: Captured at Chaplain Hills, KY. Died at the General Hospital in Harrodsburg, KY.

Roberts, William H.; Second Lieutenant, Company C: Born in Dickson Co., TN., 4 September 1829. Occupation: farmer. Sworn into service 14 May 1861 at Nashville. Elected second lieutenant at the organization. Defeated in the reelection at the reorganization, 1 May 1862. Dropped from the roll. Apparently re-enlisted and was later captured. Sent to Rock Island Prison, IL. Exchanged at City Point, VA. While being conveyed back to his command, the train derailed near Liberty, VA., crushing his right foot and cutting a huge gash in his knee. Died 13 September 1908. Buried in the Roberts Cemetery, Dickson Co., TN.[617]

Robertson, A. Jack; Private, Company D: Occupation: laborer. Sworn into service 11 May 1861 at Nashville. Age 19 on roll dated 5 May 1863 at Shelbyville, TN. Received a flesh wound in the Battle of Resaca, GA., 14 May 1864. Admitted to Confederate hospital, Madison, GA., 18 May 1864. Wounded in the Battle of Atlanta, GA., 22 July 1864. Died of wounds 28 July 1864.[618]

Robertson, David L.; Private, Company C: Born 1836. Occupation: farm hand. Enlisted 5 March 1863 at Shelbyville, TN. Died from disease, 23 March 1863.[619]

Robertson, H. H.; Private, Company B: Sworn into service, 10 May 1861 at Nashville. Discharged under the conscript act, 15 August 1862 at Tazewell, TN. Captured in Kentucky. Exchanged 16 October 1862.

Robertson, Henry H.; Private, Company D: Sworn into service 11 May 1861 at Nashville. Discharged under the conscript act. Killed at Egypt, MS.[620]

Robinson, James; Private, Company B: Born in Barbour Co., KY. Occupation: farmer. Sworn into service 10 May 1861 at Nashville. Discharged 11 May 1862 at Cumberland Gap, TN on a certificate of disability due to old age. Complexion fair, hair gray, eyes blue, height 5' 6", age 45.

Robinson, W. D.; Private, Company G: Sworn into service 10 May 1861 at Nashville. Discharged for disability June 1861.

Rochelle, Thomas Jasper; Private, Company H: Born c1842 in Wake Co., NC. Moved in the 1850s with his family to Gray's Bend in Hickman Co., TN. Occupation: farmer. Sworn into service 14 May 1861 at Nashville. Captured in the Battle of Murfreesboro, TN., 31 December 1862. Admitted to U. S. General Hospital # 7 at Louisville, KY. 15 February 1863. Admitted to the Episcopal Church Hospital at Williamsburg, VA., 12 April through 7 May 1863. Sent to Camp Morton, IN., then to City Point,

---

[617] William H. Roberts, Tennessee Pension Application, 5296; McCauley Camp 260, *Confederate Graves*, 43.

[618] Harris, *Confederate Hospitals*, 401; Maney, *Surgeon's Log*, "May 1864"; Maney, *Surgeon's Log*, "Battle of Atlanta GA."

[619] Lindsley, *Annals*, 303.

[620] Ibid.

VA. for exchange. Wounded in the left arm in the Battle of Missionary Ridge, TN., 25 November 1863. Shot through the bowels in the Battle of New Hope Church, GA., 27 May 1864. Died 28 May 1864.[621]

Rogers, George E.; Private, Company C: Born c. 1838. Brother of Corporal James Monroe Rogers. Occupation: farmer. Sworn into service 14 May 1861 at Nashville. Issued a minie musket. Left with the wounded at Murfreesboro, TN. Captured 5 January 1863. Sent to the U. S. Military Prison at Louisville, KY. Forwarded to Fort McHenry, MD., 25 May 1863. Later exchanged and rejoined company. Attendant at hospital at Newnan, GA., 1 September 1863 through February 1864. Surrendered with the Army of Tennessee at Greensboro, NC., 26 April 1865 as a member of Company F, 2nd Consolidated Tennessee Infantry.[622]

Rogers, James Monroe; Corporal, Company C: Born 29 January 1842 in Dickson Co., TN. Brother of Private George E. Rogers. Sworn into service 14 May 1861 at Nashville. Issued a minie musket. Wounded and captured in the Battle of Murfreesboro, TN., 31 December 1862. Right leg and left arm were both broken. Sent to the U. S. Military Prison at Louisville, KY. Forwarded to Fort McHenry, MD., 24 May 1863. Both leg and arm amputated in hospital in Petersburg, VA., 5 June 1863. Transferred to White Oak Hospital, 31 August 1863. Surgeon asked for artificial limb 11 March 1864. Relocated to Montgomery Co., TN. shortly after the war, serving as County Registrar from 1870 to 1894. Buried in Greenwood Cemetery, Clarksville, Montgomery Co., TN.[623]

Rogers, John Gilbert; Third Corporal, Company A: Born 28 October 1839 in Dickson Co., TN. Serving as a student physician and living in the home of Dr. J. B. Pitts prior to the war. Sworn into service 10 May 1861 at Nashville. Sick at hospital at Knoxville, TN. since, 10 August 1862. Promoted to third corporal by July 1862. Detailed to the quartermaster department, 23 December 1862. Age 23 on roll dated 6 May 1863 at Shelbyville, TN. Wounded in the left shoulder in the Battle of Missionary Ridge, TN., 25 November 1863. Wounded again in the Battle of Atlanta, GA., 22 July 1864, suffering a flesh wound in the right buttock. Admitted to Way Hospital Meridian, MS., 29 January 1865 for debilitis. Sent to Unionville, AL., where he lived on charity. Surrendered with Lieutenant General Richard Taylor at Citronelle, AL., 4 May 1865. Paroled at Meridian, MS., 15 May 1865. Following the war he relocated to Clarksville, Montgomery Co., TN. resuming his work as a practicing physician there for over forty years. Present at the 14 June 1904 reunion of the 11th Tennessee Infantry in Nashville, TN. Died 14 July 1917 near Lone Oak, Montgomery Co., TN. Buried in the Greenwood Cemetery, Clarksville, Montgomery Co., TN.[624]

Rogers, Robert M.; Private, Company B: Died 28 June 1864 at Rock Island Prison, IL. Buried in Rock Island Prison grave #1276.[625]

Roland, William Andrew; Private, Company F: Born 25 November 1841 at Cedar Hill, Robertson Co., TN. Occupation: farmer. Enlisted 18 May 1861 at Cedar Hill, TN. Left upper maxillary bone fractured in the Battle of Peachtree Creek, GA., 20 July 1864. Hospitalized at Lauderdale Springs, MS. Although his jaw was broken, it was never set, causing much suffering over the years. Surrendered with Lieutenant General Richard Taylor at Citronelle, AL., 4 May 1865. Married to Patia Ann Barnes. Owned and operated a gristmill at Barlow, KY. and farmed as well. Present at the 14 June 1904 reunion of the 11th Tennessee Infantry in Nashville, TN. Around 1918, he relocated to Bandana, KY., where he

---

[621] United Daughters of the Confederacy, *Confederate Soldiers of Hickman County*, 173; Electronic mail correspondence with John B. Rochelle, Gray, Tennessee, 19 August 2001; Maney, *Surgeon's Log*, "Missionary Ridge TN"; Maney, *Surgeon's Log*, "May 1864."

[622] Baker, *1860 Census for Dickson County*, 2; McCauley, *Record Book, Company C*.

[623] McCauley, *Record Book, Company C*; James Monroe Rogers, "Veteran Questionnaire" vol. 5, 1876-77.

[624] Johnson, *1860 Census of Humphreys County*, 55; John G. Rogers, Forbes Bivouac Application; Maney, *Surgeon's Log*, "Missionary Ridge TN"; Maney, *Surgeon's Log*, "Battle of Atlanta GA"; *Reunion Pamphlet*, 14 June 1904; *Clarksville Leaf Chronicle*, 16 July 1917. Pension Application 15002.

[625] Office of the Commissioner, "Register of Confederate Dead."

died, 5 December 1922. Buried in the Old Barlow Cemetery, Section 5, Barlow, Bristol Co., KY. Pension Application Kentucky 976.[626]

Rooker, James; Private, Company K: Sworn into service 25 May 1861 at Nashville. Age 39 on roll dated 15 August 1861 at Midway, TN. Discharged under the conscript act, 12 August 1862 at Tazewell, TN.

Rooker, James B.; Private, Company E: Born c. 1825. Brother of Second Corporal John Wesley Rooker. Occupation: farmer. Married Mary Jane Ashley Williams, 15 December 1847. Enlisted 24 December 1862 at Readyville, TN. Received at Confederate hospital, Atlanta, GA., 8 May 1864, Sent to Confederate hospital, Madison, GA., 9 May 1864. Admitted to Confederate hospital, Madison, GA., 10 May 1864. Deserted 12 December 1864. Took oath at Nashville, TN. Complexion fair, eyes hazel, height 6' 1".[627]

Rooker, Rev. John Wesley; Second Corporal, Company E: Born 7 July 1836 in Dickson Co., TN. Occupation: farmer. Sworn into service May 1861 at Nashville. Elected second corporal at the organization. Age 24 on roll dated 16 August 1861 at Watauga Bridge, TN. Listed in the Bragg Hospital, Newnan, GA., November through December 1863. Wounded in the right leg in the charge during the Battle of Atlanta, GA., 22 July 1864. In Lee Hospital, Columbus, GA., September through October 1864, where his leg was amputated. Served in hospital duty after his leg healed. Surrendered with Lieutenant General Richard Taylor at Citronelle, AL., 4 May 1865. Complexion fair, hair light, eyes hazel, height 6', age 28. Paroled at Mobile, AL. in June 1865. Following the war received a license to preach in the Methodist Episcopal Church South. In October, 1870, he was admitted on trial to the Tennessee Annual Conference. Later served many charges in Middle Tennessee. Ordained a deacon by Bishop D. S. Doggett in 1872, and an elder by Bishop E. M. Marvin in 1874. Married Priscilla Mallard, 24 June 1875. Following her death, he married Elizabeth Collier of Sumner Co., TN. Died 18 November 1913. Buried in the City Cemetery at Gallatin, Sumner Co., TN.[628]

Ross, William; Private, Company E: Captured at Adamsville, TN., 3 October 1863. Died in the military prison at Alton, IL., 20 January 1864 of pneumonia and small pox. Buried in the Confederate Cemetery, Alton, IL.

Rosson, Joseph S.; Third Sergeant, Company F: Born 1842 in Robertson Co., TN. Age 18 in 1860 census. Enlisted 18 May 1861 at Cedar Hill, TN. Promoted to third sergeant by July 1862. Wounded in the left lung at the Battle of Murfreesboro, TN., 31 December 1862. Captured and sent to the U. S. Military Prison at Louisville, KY. Forwarded to Camp Butler, IL., 14 March 1863. Recovery from the wound took several months. Married Charlotte Williams, 17 January 1867. Around 1868, they relocated to Montgomery Co., TN. Member Forbes Bivouac, Clarksville, TN. and the Sadlersville Baptist Church. Died 6 March 1912. Buried in the Greenwood Cemetery, Clarksville, Montgomery Co., TN.[629]

Roy, William; Private, Company I: Born c. 1835. Occupation: railroad worker. Sworn into service 20 May 1861 at Nashville. Deserted 18 August 1863 near Chattanooga, TN.[630]

Ruffin, Robert E.; Private, Company F: Born c 1843. Enlisted 18 May 1861 at Cedar Hill, TN. Wounded in the lower left thigh in the Battle of Atlanta, GA., 22 July 1864. Admitted to Way Hospital at Meridian, MS., 1 February 1865. Surrendered with Lieutenant General Richard Taylor at Citronelle, AL., 4 May 1865.[631]

---

[626] Maney, *Surgeon's Log*, "20 July 1864"; *Reunion Pamphlet*, 14 June 1904.

[627] Baker, *1850 Census for Dickson County*, 1; Baker, *1860 Census for Dickson County*, 131; Harris, *Confederate Hospitals*, 360, 401.

[628] Maney, *Surgeon's Log*, "Battle of Atlanta GA"; John W. Rooker, Tennessee Pension Application, 250; P. A. Sowell, "Rev. John Wesley Rooker," *Journal of the Tennessee Conference* (1914): 69-70.

[629] Maney, *Surgeon's Log*, "Stones River TN."

[630] Johnson, *1860 Census of Humphreys County*, 159.

[631] Maney, *Surgeon's Log*, "Battle of Atlanta GA."

Rushing, Clinton; Private, Company A: Born c. 1843. Sworn into service 10 May 1861 at Nashville. Discharged under the conscript act, 14 August 1862 at Tazewell, TN.[632]

Rushing, John H.; Private, Company I: Age seventeen at the time he was wounded in the scalp during the Battle of Peachtree Creek, GA., 20 July 1864. Wounded again two days later in the Battle of Atlanta, GA., 22 July 1864, shot through the left inferior maxillary, through the right thigh, along with a severe wound through the left hypochondriac region. He was surrendered at Johnsonville, TN., 22 May 1865. Took oath 24 May 1865. Complexion fair, hair light, eyes blue, height 5' 8". Resided in Whitton, Mississippi Co., AR. Pension Application Arkansas 23974.[633]

Rushing, William H.; Private, Company I: Born 1841 in Humphreys Co., TN. Occupation: farmer. Sworn into service 20 May 1861 at Nashville. Caught measles at Camp Cheatham and returned home in June 1861. Discharged at Loudon, TN. by surgeon J. M. Larkins, 12 August 1861 for disability. Complexion fair, hair light, eyes blue, height 6', age 20. Took oath when taken in front of the U. S. Marshal in Waverly, TN. When applying for a pension, a letter was received indicating he was not worthy of the benefit. His family was supported by public charity.

Rust, J.; Private, Company F: Enlistment date is unknown. Served in the 11th Tennessee until he was transferred to Company A, 9th Kentucky Infantry, 5 April 1864. Mortally wounded in the Battle of Resaca, GA., 27 May 1864.

Rust, Lewis R.; Private, Company F: Enlisted 25 September 1863 at Chattanooga, TN. Transferred to Company A, 9th Kentucky Infantry, 26 April 1864. No further.

Rust, William H.; Private, Company F: Resident of Logan Co., KY. Enlisted 18 May 1861 at Cedar Hill, TN. Transferred to Company A, 9th Kentucky Infantry, 26 April 1864.

Rye, Thomas; Private, Company C: Born 10 June 1836 in Montgomery Co., TN. Married Martha Francis West. Enlisted 2 March 1863 at Shelbyville, TN. Left at hospital in Rome, GA. On sick leave from 13 April 1863. Age 28 on roll dated 8 May 1863 at Shelbyville, TN. Furloughed to Dickson Co., 28 May 1863. Captured by the Federals and taken to Fort Donelson, TN. Resided on Yellow Creek, Houston Co., TN. Occupation: farmer. Following his first wife's death in 1883, he married Sarah Alley Frost, 4 December 1885. Died 9 August 1920. Buried in the Cooksey Cemetery, Houston Co., TN.[634]

–S–

Sanders, Robert W.; Private, Company A: Born 1 May 1840 in Humphreys Co., TN. Occupation: farmer. Enlisted in 1861. Married Eliza J. Peeler in 1865. Politically a Democrat, he served as magistrate in Humphreys Co., TN. for many years.[635]

Sanders, Z. T.; Private, Company B: Died 11 January 1913. Pension Application Arkansas, Hempstead Co., 1916.[636]

Satterfield, John S.; Private, Company H: Born in Hickman Co., TN. Occupation: farmer. Sworn into service 14 May 1861 at Nashville. Discharged 8 April 1862 on a certificate of disability due to prolonged pneumonia, age 18. Complexion fair, hair dark, eyes dark, height 5' 10".

Saunders, Liberty; Private, Company A: Brother of Privates Robert and William Saunders. Occupation: farmer. Enlisted 12 September 1861 at Knoxville. Absent sick at Versailles, KY., 9 October

---

[632] Garrett, *Humphreys County, Tennessee, 1850 Census*, 55.

[633] Maney, *Surgeon's Log*, "20 July 1864"; Welsh, *Arkansas Pension Applications by Tennessee Veterans*, 4.6.

[634] Jill Knight Garrett, *A History of Humphreys County, Tennessee*, vol. 2 (Columbia TN: Jill Knight Garrett, 1963) 334.

[635] Goodspeed Brothers, *Goodspeed's Histories of Montgomery, Robertson, Humphreys, Stewart, Dickson, Cheatham, Houston Counties*, 1266.

[636] Welsh, *Arkansas Pension Applications by Tennessee Veterans*, 4.7.

1862. Deserted 13 February 1863 when he took advantage of an exchange of prisoners and refused to report to his command. Rejoined from desertion in March 1863 at Shelbyville, TN. Deserted again by the end of April 1863. Died in prison.[637]

Saunders, Robert W.; Private, Company A: Born c. 1839. Brother of Privates Liberty and William Saunders. Sworn into service 10 May 1861 at Nashville. Died 1 June 1861.[638]

Saunders, William V.; Private, Company A: Born c. 1842. Brother of Privates Liberty and Robert Saunders. Sworn into service 10 May 1861 at Nashville. Died 8 July 1861 at his home in Humphreys Co., TN.[639]

*Savage, James Richard; First Sergeant, Company G: Born 1838 in Davidson Co., TN. Enlisted 3 June 1861 at Camp Cheatham. Promoted to second sergeant by July 1862. Age 22 on roll dated 30 May 1863 at Shelbyville, TN. Promoted to first sergeant by July 1863. Admitted to the Quintard Hospital, Griffin, GA., 22 July 1864. Surrendered with the Army of Tennessee, 26 April 1865 at Greensboro, NC. as a member of Company C, 2nd Consolidated Tennessee Infantry. Resided at Antioch, Davidson Co., TN., twelve miles outside Nashville on the Murfreesboro Pike. Married to Mary E. Savage. Charter member of the Frank Cheatham Bivouac. Present at the 14 June 1904 reunion of the 11th Tennessee Infantry in Nashville. Died 1 June 1916. Buried in the Hamilton Chapel Cemetery, Davidson Co., TN.[640]

Sayers, Charles P.; First Sergeant, Company B, Field & Staff: Sworn into service 10 May 1861 at Nashville. Elected fourth sergeant at the organization. Appointed first (orderly) sergeant 22 June 1862 when Sergeant Nichol was promoted to lieutenant. Appointed musician and transferred to the Field & Staff, 1 November 1862. Age 24 on roll dated 2 June 1863 at Shelbyville, TN. Wounded in the Battle of Franklin, TN., 30 November 1864. Captured at Franklin, TN., 17 December 1864. Sent to the U. S. Military Prison at Louisville, KY. Forwarded to Camp Chase, OH., 3 April 1865. Took oath 9 May 1865. Complexion dark, hair dark, eyes blue, height 5' 10".

*Schmittou, James L. V. "Big Jim"; Sergeant, Company C: Born 11 January 1840 in Dickson Co., TN. Occupation: farmer. Sworn into service 14 May 1861 at Nashville. Issued a minie musket. Worked in the surgeon's office at Cumberland Gap, TN., 1 – 11 December 1861. Wounded in the Battle of Atlanta, GA., 22 July 1864. Wounded through the right forearm in the Battle of Lovejoy Station, GA., 4 September 1864. Promoted to corporal then sergeant of Company F, 2nd Consolidated Tennessee Infantry. Paroled 28 April 1865. Resided at Woods Valley, Dickson Co., TN. following the war. Married Eliza Lucretia Edwards, 24 December 1871. Member of the Forbes Bivouac, Clarksville, TN. Died 8 May 1897. Buried in the Edwards Cemetery, McAllister's Crossroads, Montgomery Co., TN.[641]

Schmittou, James O. L. V. "Little Jim"; Private, Company C: Born 14 March 1842 in Dickson Co., TN. Sworn into service 14 May 1861 at Nashville. Issued a flintlock musket. Worked in the surgeon's office at Cumberland Gap, TN., 1 – 11 December 1861. Captured in the Battle of Missionary Ridge, TN., 25 November 1863. Sent to the U. S. Military Prison at Louisville, KY. Forwarded to Rock Island, IL., 8 December 1863. Released 14 October 1864 upon enlistment as a private in Company C, 3rd United States Infantry for service on the western frontier. Discharged 29 November 1865 at Fort Leavenworth, Kansas. Eyes hazel, hair light, complexion fair, height 5' 9". Married Nancy Elizabeth

---

[637] Garrett, *Humphreys County, Tennessee, 1850 Census*, 107; Lindsley, *Annals*, 303.

[638] Garrett, *Humphreys County, Tennessee, 1850 Census*, 107; Johnson, *1860 Census of Humphreys County*, 127.

[639] Garrett, *Humphreys County, Tennessee, 1850 Census*, 107; Johnson, *1860 Census of Humphreys County*, 127.

[640] *Chattanooga Daily Rebel*, 27 July 1864; *Reunion Pamphlet*, 14 June 1904; *Nashville Banner*, 3 June 1916; James R. Savage, Cheatham Bivouac Application.

[641] J. L. V. Schmittou, Forbes Bivouac Application; McCauley, *Record Book, Company C*; Maney, *Surgeon's Log*, "September 1864"; *Clarksville Leaf Chronicle*, 24 May 1897.

Batson, 8 April 1866. Occupation: farmer. Died 10 December 1922. Buried in the Marion Church Cemetery, Montgomery Co., TN.[642]

Scholes, John T.; Private, Company I: Born c. 1839. Brother of Private Milton R. and First Sergeant Nathaniel Scholes. Enlisted 25 October 1861 at Nashville. Discharged 5 November 1862 at Lenoir Station, TN. on a surgeon's certificate of disability. Upon his return home, he was mistaken for his older brother Nat by Federal troops in Humphreys Co. and was shot by firing squad.[643]

Scholes, Milton R.; Private, Company I: Born 7 March 1844 in Humphreys Co., TN. Brother of Private John T. and First Sergeant Nathaniel Scholes. Occupation: farmer. Enlisted 9 December 1862 at Readyville, TN. Age 19 on roll dated 6 May 1863 at Shelbyville, TN. Wounded in the leg at Missionary Ridge, TN., 25 November 1863. Buried his brother Nat Scholes after he died from wounds received in the Battle of Atlanta, GA. Following the Battle of Franklin, TN., 30 November 1864, he was allowed to return home to Humphreys Co. to collect shoes. Cut off from the army after the Battle of Nashville, TN., 16 December 1864 and unable to return. Surrendered at Johnsonville, TN., 22 May 1865. Took oath 24 May 1865. Complexion fair, hair dark, eyes hazel, height 5' 9". Last surviving Confederate soldier in Humphreys Co. prior to his death in August 1938, age 94. Buried in the Milton Scholes Cemetery, White Oak Creek, Humphreys Co., TN.[644]

Scholes, Nathaniel H. "Nat"; First Sergeant, Company I: Born c. 1833. Brother of Privates John T. and Milton R. Scholes. Occupation: farmer. Sworn into service 20 May 1861 at Nashville. Elected first sergeant at the organization. Not reelected at the reorganization. Reduced in rank to private. Wounded in the left arm in the Battle of Murfreesboro, TN., 31 December 1862. Sent to the hospital in Normandy, TN., 31 December 1862. Age 29 on roll dated 6 May 1863 at Shelbyville, TN. Wounded through the bowels in the Battle of Atlanta, GA., 22 July 1864. Died of wounds 28 July 1864, and buried by his brother, Milton.[645]

Scott, Jo.; Private, Company B: Sworn into service 10 May 1861 at Nashville. Discharged 10 July 1861 at Camp Cheatham. No further.

*Scott, Robert T.; Private, Company E: Born in what became Cheatham Co., TN., c. 1843. Enlisted 8 October 1861 at Camp Buckner, KY. Wounded in the Battle of Rockcastle, KY., 21 October 1861. Detailed to the quartermaster department, 15 December 1862. Age 22 on roll dated 3 May 1863 at Shelbyville, TN. Detailed as a teamster, 5 May 1863 and again on 17 July 1863. On extra duty with the 3rd Regiment Engineers under Captain J. B. Richey, Assistant Quartermaster. Paroled at Catawba Bridge, SC., 5 May 1865.[646]

Scrivner, Alexander T.; Private, Company D: Born c. 1825 in Tennessee. Married Sarah W. Meadows, 20 September 1860. Sworn into service 11 May 1861 at Nashville. Discharged for disability.[647]

Scrivner, John A.; Private, Company D: Born between 1825 and 1830 in Smith Co., TN. Sworn into service 11 May 1861 at Nashville. Laborer and mechanic. Discharged 15 August 1862 at Tazewell, TN. by the conscript act. Resident of Nashville, TN.

Seaborn, Oliver; Private, Company B: Sworn into service 10 May 1861 at Nashville. Discharged under the conscript act at Tazewell, TN. Rejoined the regiment. Killed in the Battle of Chickamauga,

---

[642] McCauley, *Record Book, Company C*; Darnell, Jones, Alley, Davidson, and Hogan, *Cemetery Records of Montgomery County* vol. 2, 96; *Clarksville Leaf Chronicle*, 11 December 1922.

[643] Anderson and Garrett, *Humphreys County Cemetery Records*, vol. 2, 46.

[644] M. R. Scholes, Tennessee Pension Application, 13108; Anderson and Garrett, *Humphreys County Cemetery Records*, vol. 2, 46; *Waverly Democrat-Sentinel*, August 1938.

[645] Johnson, *1860 Census of Humphreys County*, 32; Maney, *Surgeon's Log*, "Stones River TN"; Maney, *Surgeon's Log*, "Battle of Atlanta GA."

[646] Robert E. Dalton and Lynette H. Dalton, *Cheatham County Census: 1860* vol. 1 (Memphis TN: Robert E. Dalton and Lynette H. Dalton, 1986) 90.

[647] Dobson-Sides, *1860 Davidson County Census*, 719; Sistler and Sistler, *Davidson County Marriages 1838-1863*, 193.

GA., 19 September 1863. Originally buried in the Castleman Cemetery, Davidson Co., TN., he was reinterred in the Mt. Juliet Cemetery, Wilson Co., TN. by the Corps of Engineers due to the construction of Percy Priest Dam and Reservoir.[648]

  Seales, E. Holloway Morris; Private, Company E: Born c. 1829 in NC. Relocated to Tennessee prior to 1850. Occupation: farmer. Married Elizabeth J. Austin, 24 December 1848. Sworn into service 18 May 1861 at Nashville. Age 27 on roll dated 16 August 1861 at Watauga Bridge, TN. Deserted at Cumberland Gap, TN., 11 June 1862.[649]

  Seals, Absolum; Private, Company C: Born c. 1826. Occupation: farmhand. Married Mary F. Hase, 23 June 1854. Sworn into service 14 May 1861 at Nashville. Discharged at Tazewell, TN., 15 August 1862 under the conscript act.[650]

  Seals, Jacob; Private, Company C: Born c. 1820. Occupation: farm hand. Sworn into service 14 May 1861 at Nashville. Issued a flintlock musket. Discharged at Tazewell, TN., 15 August 1862 under the conscript act.[651]

  Sears, John; Private, Company K: Born c 1825 in Tennessee. Sworn into service 25 May 1861 at Nashville. Age 38 on roll dated 15 August 1861 at Midway, TN. Discharged at Tazewell, TN., 12 August 1862 under the conscript act. Married Paralee Lankford, 9 February 1875. Occupation: laborer.[652]

  Self, Abraham; Sergeant, Company C: Born 17 January 1833. Sworn into service 14 May 1861 at Nashville. Teamster from 8 September 1861 through 25 December 1861. Elected sergeant at the reorganization, 1 May 1862. Issued an Enfield rifle. Left in charge of some of the wounded men at Murfreesboro, TN., and captured there 5 January 1863. Sent to City Point, VA., 24 March 1863 for exchange, and rejoined the company. Age 30 on roll dated 8 May 1863 at Shelbyville, TN. Married to Ophelia T. Died 26 October 1901. Buried in the Edgewood Cemetery, Dickson Co., TN.[653]

  Self, J. W.; Private, Company C: Born c. 1839. Occupation farm-hand. Sworn into service 14 May 1861 at Nashville. Issued a flintlock musket. Age 23 on roll dated 8 May 1863 at Shelbyville, TN. Sick at hospital from 28 May 1863. Had not returned to duty by December 1863. No further.[654]

  Sensing, John Henry; Private, Company C: Born 10 April 1838. Sworn into service 14 May 1861 at Nashville. Issued a Belgium musket. Killed in the Battle of Murfreesboro, TN., 31 December 1862.[655]

  Sevier, James; Private, Company G, B, D: Sworn into service 10 May 1861 in Company G at Nashville. Transferred to Company B at the reorganization, 1 May 1862. Transferred to Company D, 1 July 1862. Wounded severely at the Battle of Murfreesboro, TN., 31 December 1862. Died of wounds 17 January 1863.

  Shacklett, Henry Rector; Assistant Quartermaster, Company E, Field & Staff: Born 2 July 1833 in extreme western Davidson Co. TN., the area later became part of Cheatham Co. Resided in West Nashville. Sworn into service 18 May 1861 in Company E at Nashville. Age 25 on roll dated 16 August 1861 at Watauga Bridge, TN. Appointed assistant quartermaster, 10 June 1862. Surrendered at Gainesville, AL. with General Nathan Bedford Forrest. Following the war, he was a practicing physician in the area surrounding the Narrows of the Harpeth. Married 1) Amelia Ann Dunn, 20 December 1865.

---

[648] Lindsley, *Annals*, 303.
[649] Baker, *1850 Census for Dickson County*, 131; Baker, *1860 Census for Dickson County*, 67.
[650] Baker, *1860 Census for Dickson County*, 5.
[651] McCauley, *Record Book, Company C*; Baker, *1860 Census for Dickson County*, 64.
[652] *Dickson County Census, 1860*, 49.
[653] McCauley, *Record Book, Company C*; Garrett and McClain, *Dickson County Cemetery Records* vol. 1, 40.
[654] McCauley, *Record Book, Company C*; Baker, *1860 Census for Dickson County*, 5.
[655] McCauley, *Record Book, Company C*; McCauley Camp 260; *Confederate Graves*, 44.

Upon her death, he married 2) Emma Agnes Nicks. Served as the postmaster at Shacklett, TN., 1897-1901. Died 20 June 1906. Buried in the Dog Creek Cemetery, Shacklett, Cheatham Co., TN.[656]

Shaffer, Josiah Love; Fourth Sergeant, Company D, B: Born 6 November 1840 in Nashville, TN. Attended the Western Military Institute. Occupation: clerk in the Davidson Co. register's office. Sworn into service 11 May 1861 in Company D at Nashville. Elected second corporal at the organization. Transferred to Company B at the reorganization, 1 May 1862. Promoted to fifth sergeant by July 1862. Taken prisoner, 30 September 1862 in Kentucky. Apparently released and rejoined unit. Appointed fourth sergeant by November 1862. Transferred to Colonel Starnes' 4th Tennessee Cavalry Regiment until assigned to John Hunt Morgan's Cavalry where he remained in active service until captured in Ohio and held prisoner until the end of the war. Married Sarah Shivers, sister of Private William Henry Shivers. Employed by the Nashville Post Office for over forty years. Member of the Cheatham Bivouac, Troop C, Forrest Cavalry. Killed in the Dutchman's Curve train collision near Belle Meade 9 July 1918. Buried in the Mount Olivet Cemetery, Nashville, Davidson Co., TN.[657]

Shaver, Jesse; Private, Company A: Born c 1831 in Humphreys Co., TN. Occupation: farmer. Married to Mary. Sworn into service 10 May 1861 at Nashville. Discharged on a surgeon's certificate, 5 November 1861. Complexion light, hair auburn, eyes gray, height 5' 8", age 31.[658]

Shaver, Matthew M.; Private, Company A: Born c. 1840. Sworn into service 10 May 1861 at Nashville. Wounded severely in the bowels and captured in the Battle of Murfreesboro, TN., 31 December 1862. Sent to Camp Douglas, IL., where he died in prison from smallpox.[659]

Shaver, Michael Jr.; Private, Company A: Born c. 1835. Occupation: farmer. Married. Sworn into service 10 May 1861 at Nashville. Listed as missing in action in the Battle of Murfreesboro, TN., 31 December 1862. Age 27 on roll dated 6 May 1863 at Shelbyville, TN.[660]

Shea, John; Second Corporal, Company D: Sworn into service 11 May 1861 at Nashville. On detached duty at Hospital #2 in Knoxville, TN., 1 May through 31 July 1862. Admitted to Fair Ground Hospital #1, Atlanta, GA., 24 January 1863 for gonorrhea. Sent and admitted to Fair Ground Hospital #2, Atlanta, GA., 15 February 1863 for vulnus sclopeticum. Returned to duty 20 April 1863. Promoted to second corporal by July 1863. Deserted while on picket duty 12 November 1863 at Missionary Ridge, TN. Captured and sent to the U. S. Military Prison at Louisville, KY. Took oath, 25 November 1863. Complexion dark, hair black, eyes gray, height 5' 7".

Shelton, John; Private, Company C: Born 29 July 1831 in Dickson Co., TN. Occupation: mill-hand and farmer. Married Sarah A. "Lovy" Lloyd, 25 December 1856. Issued a Belgium musket. Enlisted 18 February 1863 at Shelbyville, TN. Issued a Belgium musket. Age 32 on roll dated 8 May 1863 at Shelbyville, TN. Having left his wife and children with his wife's father to join the army, as the Army of Tennessee neared Nashville on Hood's Tennessee campaign, he found out that they had been burned out by the Federals. He was given a furlough, 14 December 1864 to return to his home, where he was captured by the Federal Home Guard and was unable to rejoin his command. Took oath 28 December 1864, but was not released from prison until May 1865. Complexion light, hair dark, eyes hazel, height 5' 10". Resided at Woods Valley, Dickson Co., TN. Later a resident of the Tennessee Confederate Soldiers Home from 21 June 1893. Died 28 March 1904. Buried in the Soldiers Home Cemetery grave #118. Pension Application S72.[661]

---

[656] Haile and Garrett, *Tombstone Records of Cheatham County*, 41; Kelley, *West Nashville*, 142; H. R. Shacklett, Tennessee Pension Application, 7613.

[657] *Nashville Banner*, 10 July 1918.

[658] Johnson, *1860 Census of Humphreys County*, 31.

[659] Garrett, *Humphreys County, Tennessee, 1850 Census*, 31; Thedford, "Report of Operations."

[660] Garrett, *Humphreys County, Tennessee, 1850 Census*, 31; Johnson, *1860 Census of Humphreys County*, 35; Thedford, "Report of Operations."

[661] Strange, *Soldiers Home*, 14; Baker, *1860 Census for Dickson County*, 74; Sistler and Sistler, *1880 Census of Dickson County*, 234.

Shepard, J. A.; Private, Company D: Discharged on surgeon's certificate 14 September 1861.

Shepard William; Private, Company D: Sworn into service 11 May 1861 at Nashville. Age 31 on roll dated 5 May 1863 at Shelbyville, TN. No further.

*Sheppard, I. B.; Private, Company K: Surrendered with Lieutenant General Richard Taylor at Citronelle, AL. No further.

Sherer, John D.; Private, Company D: Deserted and captured at Chattanooga, TN., 12 November 1863. Sent to the U. S. Military Prison at Louisville, KY., 18 November 1863. Took oath 20 November 1863.

Sheridan, John; Private, Company G: Born 12 June 1841 in Balinrobe, County Mayo, Ireland. Came to Tennessee in 1859. Enlisted 3 June 1861 at Camp Cheatham. Admitted to St. Mary's Hospital at Dalton, GA., 28 December 1862 through 3 January 1863 for erysiphales. Age 28 on roll dated 30 May 1863 at Shelbyville, TN. Wounded in the thigh by a minie ball on the third line of breastworks at the Battle of Franklin, TN., 30 November 1864, the ball entering the right leg above the knee, cutting veins and tearing leaders. Captured at Franklin, TN., 17 December 1864 as the Army of Tennessee withdrew from the state. Admitted to U. S. General Hospital #1 at Nashville, TN., 23 December 1864. Sent to the U. S. Military Prison at Louisville, KY., 4 January 1864. Forwarded to Camp Chase, OH., 9 January 1865. Took oath 12 May 1865 at Camp Chase. Complexion dark, hair black, eyes brown, height 5' 8". Married Sarah A. Flynn, 14 July 1868. Left crippled by his war injury, he worked as a section boss of street maintenance for the City of Nashville. Member of the Catholic Church. Died 16 February 1908 of Bright's disease. Buried Calvary Cemetery, Nashville, Davidson Co., TN. Widows Pension Application 2429.[662]

*Sherlock, John; Private, Company G: Enlisted 3 April 1863 at Chattanooga, TN. Age 38 on roll dated 30 May 1863 at Shelbyville, TN. Sent to the hospital, 8 November 1863. Admitted to the Ocmulgee Hospital, 8 - 15 April 1864 for chronic diarrhea. Surrendered with the Army of Tennessee, 26 April 1865 at Greensboro, NC. as a member of Company C, 2nd Consolidated Tennessee Infantry.

Sherrod, Richard T.; Private, Company F: Enlisted 18 May 1861 at Cedar Hill, TN. Discharged 10 September 1862 at Tazewell, TN. Re-enlisted 30 June 1863 at Shelbyville, TN. Killed in the Battle of Chickamauga, GA., 19 September 1863.[663]

Shipp, James; Private, Company H: Born in 1841. Sworn into service 14 May 1861 at Nashville. Discharged 2 April 1862. Later joined the 10th Tennessee Cavalry Battalion and was promoted to the rank of lieutenant. Killed in the Battle of Nashville, TN., 15 or 16 December 1864.[664]

Shivers, William Henry; Private, Company D, B: Born 1837. Sworn into service 11 May 1861 in Company D at Nashville. Transferred to Company B at the reorganization, 1 May 1862. Age 26 on roll dated 5 May 1863 at Shelbyville, TN. Captured 22 December 1864 at Columbia, TN. Took oath and released 30 March 1865. Complexion fair, hair brown, eyes gray, height 5' 11". Married Donia Robertson, 6 January 1869. Relocated to Dallas, TX., where he died 18 August 1917. Pension Application - Texas Widow.

Shortle, Thomas; Private, Company G: Occupation: laborer. Sworn into service 10 May 1861 at Nashville. On extra duty in the quartermaster department, 30 April through August 1862. Age 21 on roll dated 30 May 1863 at Shelbyville, TN. Driving an ambulance July through December 1863. Wounded through the middle left arm in the Battle of Resaca, GA., 14 May 1864. Deserted 14 December 1864. Complexion fair, hair brown, eyes hazel, height 5' 4".[665]

Shouse, Jacob Washington "Wash"; Fourth Sergeant, Company H: Born 17 June 1836 in Hickman Co., TN. Occupation: farmer. Married Parthenia Shipp, 9 May 1856. Enlisted 8 August 1861 at Nashville. On sick furlough September through October 1861. Appointed fourth sergeant, 26 February 1862.

---

[662] *Nashville Banner*, 17 February 1908.
[663] Maney, *Surgeon's Log*, "Chickamauga GA."
[664] United Daughters of the Confederacy, *Confederate Soldiers of Hickman County*, 177.
[665] Maney, *Surgeon's Log*, "May 1864."

Wounded in the elbow in the Battle of Atlanta, GA., 22 July 1864. Admitted to Quintard Hospital, Griffin, GA., 22 July 1864. Took oath October 1864. Complexion fair, hair light, eyes blue, height 5' 10". Attended the reunion of the 11th Tennessee Infantry at Bon Aqua Springs, Hickman Co., TN., 24 September 1885. Died after 1910.[666]

Sigel, Martin; Private, Company A: Captured 3 July 1863 at Elk River, TN. Forwarded to Nashville, 10 July 1863. Sent to the U. S. Military Prison at Louisville, KY., 14 July 1863. Forwarded to Camp Chase, OH. then transferred to Camp Douglas, IL. Enlisted in the U. S. Navy.

Sikes, James; Private, Company I: Born c. 1844. Occupation: farmer. Brother of Private William T. Sikes. Enlisted 6 February 1863 at Shelbyville, TN. Age 19, on roll dated 6 May 1863 at Shelbyville, TN. Admitted to Pim Hospital, Griffin, GA., 22 July 1864. Married to Mary.[667]

Sikes, William T.; Private, Company I: Sworn into service 20 May 1861 at Nashville. Age 21 on roll dated 6 May 1863 at Shelbyville, TN. Absent in hospital at Forsyth, GA., 15 September 1863. At hospital in Marietta, GA., 8 February 1864. No further.

Sills, Samuel; Private, Company E: Enlisted 19 September 1861 at Camp Buckner, KY. Deserted at Cumberland Gap, TN., 11 June 1862.

Simpson, George W.; Third Sergeant, Company A: Sworn into service 10 May 1861 at Nashville. Promoted to third sergeant, 1 July 1862. Age 27 on roll dated 6 May 1863 at Shelbyville, TN. Deserted 8 October 1863 at Chattanooga, TN. Captured at Stevenson, AL.

Skelton, James Morris; Brevet Second Lieutenant, Company C: Born 23 December 1834 in Dickson Co., TN. Brother to Sergeant Joseph P. Skelton. Occupation: dry goods clerk. Enlisted 14 May 1861 at Nashville. Hospital attendant, 28 February 1862. Absent on sick leave, 9 October 1862. Captured at Versailles, KY., 10 October 1862. Apparently exchanged and rejoined company. Brevetted second lieutenant, 2 May 1863. Age 28 on roll dated 8 May 1863. Resigned commission, 9 March 1864 due to bad heath resulting from chronic diarrhea. Joined Company A, 12th Tennessee Cavalry. Postwar, he resumed work in merchandising. Married Lenora Shelton, 15 February 1865. Relocated to Howell Co., MO. in the fall of 1870 and returned to Tennessee in 1872. Politically a Democrat. Died 6 November 1927. Buried at his home place, near Omega, Houston Co., TN.[668]

Skelton, Joseph P.; Fifth Sergeant, Company A: Born c. 1838. Brother to Lieutenant James Morris Skelton. Occupation: farmer. Sworn into service 10 May 1861 at Nashville. On detached service as a wardmaster since 28 April 1862 at Tazewell, TN. Elected fifth sergeant at the reorganization, 1 May 1862. Captured in the Battle of Murfreesboro, TN., 31 December 1862. Sent to Camp Douglas, IL., 31 March 1863. Exchanged and rejoined company. Age 22 on roll dated 6 May 1863 at Shelbyville, TN. Wounded in the head in the Battle of Missionary Ridge, TN., 25 November 1863. In hospital at Marietta, GA. Killed in the Battle of New Hope Church, GA., 27 May 1864.[669]

Slayden, Hartwell Marable; Private, Company C: Born 25 January 1845 in Dickson Co., TN. Youngest brother of Sergeant John D. and Assistant Surgeon William M. Slayden. Occupation: farmer. Sworn into service 14 May 1861 at Nashville. Discharged 4 July 1861. Died 1890 in Eastland, TX.[670]

---

[666] United Daughters of the Confederacy, *Confederate Soldiers of Hickman County*, 178; Maney, *Surgeon's Log*, "Battle of Atlanta GA"; *Chattanooga Daily Rebel*, 27 July 1864; "The Reunion," *Hickman Pioneer*.

[667] Baker, *1860 Census for Dickson County*, 77; *Chattanooga Daily Rebel*, 27 July 1864; Baker, *1870 Census for Dickson County*, 90.

[668] Patey, *Patey-Skelton*, 160; Electronic mail correspondence with Faye Wilson Keele, Family Historian, 10 May 2001; Goodspeed Brothers, *Goodspeed's Histories of Montgomery, Robertson, Humphreys, Stewart, Dickson, Cheatham, Houston Counties*, 1401-02. Veteran Questionnaire vol. 5, 1970-71.

[669] Johnson, *1860 Census of Humphreys County*, 78; Electronic mail correspondence with Faye Wilson Keele, Family Historian, 10 May 2001; Maney, *Surgeon's Log*, "Missionary Ridge TN"; Maney, *Surgeon's Log*, "May 1864"; Lindsley, *Annals*, 303.

[670] Interview with Francis Osborn, family genealogist, 31 May 2006.

Slayden, John Daniel; Sergeant, Company C: Born 16 June 1841 in Dickson Co., TN. Brother of Private Hartwell M. and Assistant Surgeon William M. Slayden. Occupation: farmer, civil engineer, and doctor. Sworn into service 14 May 1861 at Nashville. Promoted to second corporal by July 1862. Issued a minie musket. Age 22 on roll dated 8 May 1863 at Shelbyville, TN. Promoted to sergeant by July 1863. Received a gunshot wound in the left hand in the Battle of New Hope Church, GA., 27 May 1864. Sent to Oliver Hospital, Philadelphia, MS. Captured in the Battle of Franklin, TN., 30 November 1864, escaping shortly thereafter. Surrendered with the Army of Tennessee, 26 April 1865 at Greensboro, NC. as a member of Company F, 2nd Consolidated Tennessee Infantry. Following the war he resumed study at the medical college at Nashville and did further study at the Jefferson Medical College in Philadelphia. Married Augustine M. Russell of Shreveport, LA., 27 August 1881 in Pekin, IL. Resided in Clarksville, TN. Politically a Democrat. Member of the Masonic order, the Episcopal Church, and the Forbes Bivouac of the Association of Confederate Soldiers. Died 24 March 1922. Buried in the Greenwood Cemetery, Clarksville, Montgomery Co., TN.[671]

Slayden, William Marshall; Assistant Surgeon, Company C, Field & Staff: Born 11 April 1834 on Yellow Creek in Dickson Co., TN. Older brother of Sergeant John D. and Private Hartwell M. Slayden. Graduated from the Medical School of the University of Nashville in 1858, and began his medical practice in the Bold Springs community of Humphreys Co., TN. Sworn into service, 14 May 1861 at Nashville in Company C. Hospital steward, 1 August 1861 through 15 October 1861. Elected second lieutenant at the reorganization, 1 May 1862. Promoted to first lieutenant, 7 November 1862. Promoted to assistant surgeon, 23 February 1863 and transferred to the Field & Staff. Age 29 on roll dated 8 May 1863 at Shelbyville, TN. Wounded in battle near Atlanta, GA., 5 August 1864 from a shot through the hand. Resigned commission, 11 February 1865 because Company C had only one man present for duty. Married Amanda White in 1867. Member of the Masonic Lodge and Methodist Episcopal Church. Died 13 October 1904. Buried in the Wyly Cemetery, Waverly, Humphreys Co., TN.[672]

Sloan, James Lloyd; Second Lieutenant, Company D: Born 17 January 1841 on Walden's Ridge in Rhea Co., TN. His father was of Irish descent and came to Tennessee from New York, and upon his death, the family relocated to Nashville. A year later they moved to Virginia where he learned the printers trade. The family moved back to Nashville in 1854. Educated in the public schools of Nashville. Occupation: iron and brass molder. Sworn into service 11 May 1861 at Nashville. Elected orderly sergeant at the organization, and later promoted to third lieutenant and second lieutenant. Married Sarah Wills Corbitt, 8 January 1862 while his regiment was stationed at Cumberland Gap, TN. Some records indicate he was not reelected at the reorganization, 1 May 1862, and was dropped from roll. Being a molder, his services were demanded by the Confederate Government in manufacturing munitions of war, and he was detailed to the Ordnance Department after two years of service with the 11th Tennessee. Resided in Hickman Co., TN. immediately following the war, where he studied law in Centerville and was admitted to the bar. Relocating to Linden, Perry Co., TN. in 1869, he remained there for the remaining years of his life. Active in community affairs, he helped to build the First Methodist Church of Linden, where a room is dedicated to him, and named Sloan's Chapel. A devoted Mason, he was a member of the Masonic Lodge #210 of Linden, and in 1904, was chosen as Grand Master of Masonic Order for the State of Tennessee. Died 26 August 1906. Buried Mount Olivet Cemetery, Nashville, Davidson Co., TN.[673]

---

[671] John D. Slayden, Tennessee Pension Application, 15601; McCauley, *Record Book, Company C*; Maney, *Surgeon's Log*, "May 1864"; John D. Slayden, Forbes Bivouac Application; Goodspeed Brothers, *Goodspeed's Histories of Montgomery, Robertson, Humphreys, Stewart, Dickson, Cheatham, Houston Counties*, 1353-54.

[672] Maney, *Surgeon's Log*, "August 1864"; Goodspeed Brothers, *Goodspeed's Histories of Montgomery, Robertson, Humphreys, Stewart, Dickson, Cheatham, Houston Counties*, 1269-70; Anderson and Garrett, *Humphreys County Cemetery Records* vol. 1, 95.

[673] United Daughters of the Confederacy, *Confederate Soldiers of Hickman County*, 180.

Smith, Augustus T.; Private, Company B, D: Born c 1840. Occupation: waggoner. Sworn into service 10 May 1861 at Nashville. Age 23 on roll dated 2 June 1863 at Shelbyville, TN. Admitted to Pim Hospital, Griffin, GA., 22 July 1864. Killed in the Battle of Franklin, TN, 30 November 1864.[674]

Smith, Alexander; Private, Company F: Enlisted 18 May 1861 at Cedar Hill, TN. Discharged 17 August 1862 at Tazewell, TN.

Smith, B. J.; Private, Company C: Born c. 1838. Brother of Corporal William J. Smith. Occupation: farmer. Sworn into service 14 May 1861 at Nashville. Issued a minie musket. Age 25 on roll dated 8 May 1863 at Shelbyville, TN. Took oath 28 December 1863. Complexion dark, hair dark, eyes hazel, height 5' 8". Apparently rejoined unit. Wounded in the left side at Kennesaw Mountain, GA., 21 June 1864.[675]

Smith, Elias P.; Private, Company G, B: Sworn into service 10 May 1861 in Company G at Nashville. Transferred to Company B at the reorganization, 1 May 1862. Deserted 20 March 1863 at Shelbyville, TN., and captured. Sent to the U. S. Military Prison at Louisville, KY. Forwarded to Camp Chase, OH., 5 May 1863. Released 26 May 1863. Complexion fair, hair light, eyes blue, height 5' 8", age 19.

Smith, Gus; Private, Company B: Occupation: butcher. Wounded in the right hand in the Battle of Atlanta, GA., 22 July 1864.[676]

Smith, J. T.; Private, Company B: Sworn into service 10 May 1861 at Nashville. Died at Nashville, TN., 1 July 1861.

Smith, James; Private, Company A: Born in Kentucky, his family relocating to Tennessee at his age one. Enlisted 3 September 1861 at Knoxville, TN. Age 23 on roll dated 6 May 1863 at Shelbyville, TN. Deserted 28 August 1863. Died 24 December 1934. Pension Application S16405.[677]

Smith, James T.; Private, Company B: Admitted to Fair Ground Hospital #1, Atlanta, GA., 12 September 1863 for acute diarrhea. Sent to the Confederate hospital in LaGrange, GA., 15 September 1863. Mortally wounded in the Battle of Franklin, TN., 30 November 1864 by a minie ball penetrating the right lung. Captured by the enemy and transferred to U. S. General Hospital #1 at Nashville, 27 December 1864. Died 26 April 1865, age 22. Buried in the Nashville City Cemetery, grave #11669. Later removed to Confederate Circle, Mt. Olivet Cemetery, Nashville, Davidson Co., TN.

Smith, Jasper; Private, Company I: Enlisted 30 September 1861 at Nashville. Died 5 May 1862 at Tazewell, TN.

Smith, John T.; Private, Company A: Sworn into service 10 May 1861 at Nashville. Discharged for disability 29 June 1861 at Camp Cheatham.

Smith, Lewis; Private, Company A: Deserted 23 July 1864. Captured at Barbour Co., KY. Took oath 31 July 1864. Complexion light, hair dark, eyes hazel, height 5' 8".

Smith, Oliver W.; Private, Company F: Enlisted 18 May 1861 at Cedar Hill, TN. Discharged 2 August 1861.

Smith, Patrick S.; Private, Company H: Sworn into service 14 May 1861 at Nashville. Nurse at hospital at Tazewell, TN., since April 1862. Discharged by the conscript act, 1 May 1863.

Smith, R. J.; Private, Company B: Sworn into service 10 May 1861 at Nashville. Discharged under the conscript act, 15 August 1862 at Tazewell, TN.

Smith, Richard S.; First Lieutenant, Company G, B: Sworn into service 10 May 1861 in Company G at Nashville. Elected third sergeant at the organization. Promoted to second sergeant by March 1862. Transferred to Company B at the reorganization, 1 May 1862. Captured 17 June 1862 while scouting eight miles west of Cumberland Gap, in Claiborne Co., TN. Said to be a spy in citizen's clothing.

---

[674] Lindsley, *Annals*, 303; *Chattanooga Daily Rebel*, 27 July 1864.

[675] Baker, *1860 Census for Dickson County*, 10; McCauley, *Record Book, Company C*; Maney, *Surgeon's Log*, "Kennesaw Mountain GA."

[676] Maney, *Surgeon's Log*, "Battle of Atlanta GA."

[677] James Smith, Tennessee Pension Application, 16405.

Escaped 22 November 1862 and returned to company. Promoted to first lieutenant. Deserted at Shelbyville, TN., 20 March 1863 and captured. Sent to the U. S. Military Prison at Louisville, KY. Forwarded to Camp Chase, OH., 5 May 1863. Sent to Camp Morton, IN., 18 June 1863. Complexion dark, hair black, eyes black, height 5' 8", age 24.

Smith, Thomas; Private, Company A, B: Sworn into service 10 May 1861 in Company A at Nashville. Transferred to Company B at the reorganization, 1 May 1862. Wounded severely in the neck in the Battle of Murfreesboro, TN., 31 December 1862. Age 23 on roll dated 5 May 1863. Present through February 1864.[678]

Smith, Thomas; Private, Company D: Sworn into service 11 May 1861 at Nashville. On sick furlough since 13 September 1861. No further.

Smith, Thomas; Private, Company unknown: Captured at Clarksville, TN., 15 March 1863. No further.

Smith, Thomas Frazier; Private, Company H: Born 1 July 1837 in Hickman Co., TN. Sworn into service 14 May 1861 at Nashville. Wounded severely in the abdomen and captured in the Battle of Murfreesboro, TN., 31 December 1861, the ball entering near the navel and came out near the spine. Forwarded to U. S. General Hospital #7 at Louisville, KY. for a gunshot wound. Transferred to Camp Morton, IN. Exchanged and rejoined company by September 1863. Married Mary S. Russell, 13 July 1865. Died at Little Lot, Hickman Co., TN., 9 April 1896.[679]

Smith, Walter S.; Private, Company A: Sworn into service 10 May 1861 at Nashville. Wounded in the Battle of Franklin, TN., 30 November 1864.[680]

Smith, William; Private, Company A: Enlisted 2 July 1861 at Camp Cheatham. Age 25 on roll dated 6 May 1863 at Shelbyville, TN. Deserted 9 September 1863.

Smith, William J.; Corporal, Company C: Born c. 1834. Brother of Private B. J. Smith. Occupation: teacher. Enlisted 30 December 1862 at Shelbyville, TN. Age 29 on roll dated 8 May 1863 at Shelbyville. Maney lists rank as corporal. Wounded in the upper one third of the left arm in battle near Atlanta, GA., 3 August 1864. Killed in the Battle of Franklin, TN., 30 November 1864. Buried in the McGavock Confederate Cemetery, Franklin, TN., section 54 grave number 47.[681]

Soard, H. A.; Private, Company D: Born c. 1815 in Tennessee. Occupation: mason. Discharged on a surgeon's certificate of disability.[682]

Soard, William; Private, Company D: Enlisted 11 May 1861 at Nashville. Discharged under the conscript act.

Sord, William J.; Private, Company D: Enlisted 11 May 1861 at Nashville. On sick furlough since 2 January 1862. No further.

Southerland, John; Private, Company H: Occupation: farmer. Transferred from Company G, 10th Tennessee Cavalry, 13 December 1862. Received at Confederate hospital, Atlanta, GA., 17 June 1864 for febris intermittens. Sent to Confederate hospital, Madison, GA., 16 June 1864. Admitted to Asylum Hospital, Madison, GA., 17 June 1864 for vulnus sclopeticum. Return to duty 8 July 1864. Wounded in the right forearm in the Battle of Chickamauga, GA., 19 September 1863. Wounded in the right side of the groin in the Battle of Peachtree Creek, GA., 20 July 1864. Took oath 29 December 1864. Complexion dark, hair light, eyes gray, height 5' 8".[683]

---

[678] Maney, *Surgeon's Log*, "Stones River TN."

[679] Thomas F. Smith, Tennessee Pension Application, 1316; United Daughters of the Confederacy, *Confederate Soldiers of Hickman County*, 181.

[680] Trogdon, "Interesting Letter."

[681] Maney, *Surgeon's Log*, "August 1864"; Hudgins and Potts, McGavock Cemetery, 32; Baker, *1860 Census for Dickson County*, 10.

[682] Dobson-Sides, *1860 Davidson County Census*, 346.

[683] Maney, *Surgeon's Log*, "Chickamauga GA"; Harris, *Confederate Hospitals*, 375, 430, 80, 87; Maney, *Surgeon's Log*, "20 July 1864."

Southerland, W. A.; First Corporal, Company H: Sworn into service 14 May 1861 at Nashville. Elected first corporal at the reorganization, 1 May 1862. Captured in the Battle of Missionary Ridge, TN., 25 November 1863. Sent to the U. S. Military Prison at Louisville, KY., 4 December 1863. Forwarded to Rock Island, IL., 6 December 1863. Exchanged and rejoined company. Admitted to Jackson Hospital in Richmond, VA., 7 March 1865 for debilitas. Deserted 10 March 1865. Took oath 12 April 1865. Complexion fair, hair dark, eyes blue, height 5' 9".

Spears, Samuel C.; Private, Company K: Enlisted 10 January 1863 at Shelbyville, TN. Regimental teamster, 13 March 1863 through December 1863. Wife's name was Mary E. Died 29 May 1914. Pension Application, Arkansas Widow 23618, Washington Co., 1914.[684]

Spence, David Moore Lee; Private, Company H: Born 27 April 1840 in Hickman Co., TN. Brother to Sergeant W. Jerome D. Spence. Grandfather was a Revolutionary War soldier. Enlisted with the 11th when he accompanied his brother who was returning from furlough. Detailed as a hospital steward since 1 May 1862 at Bean Station, TN. Discharged 31 October 1862. During 1863, helped raise and served as first lieutenant of Nicks' Cavalry Company. Captured, then escaped while being transported by train. Remained in Hickman Co., TN., until shortly after the war before relocating to Louisville, Jefferson Co., KY., where he married Amelia D. Meek. Occupation: salesman and merchandising agent. Died 15 July 1882 in Louisville, KY. Buried in Cave Hill Cemetery, Section A, lot 508, Louisville, Jefferson Co., KY.[685]

Spence, John David; Private, Company H: Born 6 December 1844. Enlisted 8 February 1863 at Shelbyville, TN. Deserted 10 December 1864. Took oath at Columbia, TN., 13 January 1865. Complexion fair, hair sandy, eyes blue, height 5' 3". Died 30 October 1903 in Dyer Co., TN. Buried in the Church Grove Cemetery, Newbern, Dyer Co., TN.

Spence, William Jerome Dorris; Fourth Sergeant, Company H: Born 21 May 1838 near Lobelville, Perry Co., TN. Son of Dr. John Lycurgus Spence, an early physician of Hickman Co. Brother to Private David M. L. Spence. Enlisted 27 April 1861 at Vernon, Hickman Co., TN. Sworn into service 14 May 1861 at Nashville. Elected fourth sergeant at the organization. Sick with measles for several weeks at Camp Cheatham. Wardmaster of Zollicoffer's brigade hospital at Cumberland Gap, November, 1861. Discharged on surgeon's certificate, 28 November 1861 for an organic disease of the lungs. Complexion dark, hair dark, eyes hazel, height 5' 2". Kept a detailed daily diary and composed several poems during his service with the 11th Tennessee Infantry. Regaining his health, he later helped Alonzo T. Napier recruit and form a cavalry battalion during the spring and summer of 1862 and made several trips to the Confederate army encamped at Corinth, MS. delivering mail. Negotiated several prisoner exchanges under a flag of truce at Nashville. Promoted to captain in Napiers Battalion, Cavalry upon Napier's promotion to lieutenant colonel. Discharged from the cavalry service due to disability in late November 1862. Arrested near Waverly, TN. as a spy in early 1864 and imprisoned at Nashville until April 1864. Released upon taking oath. Married Alice Rebecca Carothers in 1866. Politically a Democrat and a prohibitionist, he served as a member of the Tennessee House of Representatives, 1891-1893, sponsoring legislation prohibiting the sale of alcohol to minors. Author, *Spence's History of Hickman County, Tennessee*, published in 1900 and a book of poems, *Sense and Nonsense, Facts and Fancies, Truth and Traditions, In Rhyme*, published in 1907. Mason. Resided at Vernon, Hickman Co., TN. Died 14 November 1921. Buried in the City Cemetery, Centerville, Hickman Co., TN.[686]

Spencer, Jesse; Private, Company A: Sworn into service 10 May 1861 at Nashville. Discharged for disability.

---

[684] Welsh, *Arkansas Pension Applications by Tennessee Veterans*, 4.12.
[685] United Daughters of the Confederacy, *Confederate Soldiers of Hickman County*, 181.
[686] Ibid., 182; Pension Application 14806.

Spencer, Thomas S.; Third Sergeant, Company A: Born c. 1842. Sworn into service 10 May 1861 at Nashville. Elected third sergeant at the organization. Deserted at Chattanooga, TN. Captured at Stevenson, AL., 21 August 1863. Paroled.[687]

Spillers, William; Private, Company G: Born c. 1832 in Tennessee. Worked as a clerk for a steamboat company. Sworn into service 10 May 1861 at Nashville. Discharged for disability August, 1861 for loss of left arm due to syphalitic disease.[688]

Sroffe, George W.; Musician, Company E: Raised in Iowa. Wounded in the Battle of Franklin, TN., 30 November 1864. Captured at Franklin, TN., 17 December 1864. Admitted to U. S. General Hospital #1 at Nashville. Sent to the U. S. Military Prison at Louisville, KY., 6 January 1865. Forwarded to Camp Chase, OH., 9 January 1865. Complexion dark, hair dark, eyes dark, height 5' 7".

Stanfield, James F. M.; Third Corporal, Company I: Born c. 1843. Sworn into service 20 May 1861 at Nashville. Elected third corporal at the organization. In hospital at Knoxville, TN., 3 June 1862 through February 1863. Transferred to Company A, Maney's Battalion Sharpshooters. No further.

Stennett, S. A.; Private, Company I: Enlisted 17 March 1863 at Shelbyville, TN. as a substitute for John Hust. Deserted 30 April 1863.

Stephens, James G.; Captain, Company G: Occupation: clerk. Enlisted 3 June 1861 at Camp Cheatham. Elected first sergeant at the organization. Elected first lieutenant at the reorganization, 1 May 1862. Wounded through both thighs in the Battle of Murfreesboro, TN., 31 December 1863. Age 27 on roll dated 30 May 1863. Promoted to captain, 7 March 1864. Wounded and captured in the Battle of Kennesaw Mountain, GA., 27 June 1864. Sent to the U. S. Military Prison at Louisville, KY., 14 July 1864. Released on oath 15 June 1865. Complexion florid, hair dark, eyes hazel.[689]

Stevens, William M.; Private, Company G: Occupation: farmer. Enlisted 3 June 1861 at Camp Cheatham. Captured in the Battle of Murfreesboro, TN., 31 December 1862. Sent to Camp Douglas, IL., 31 March 1863. Exchanged and returned to company by April 1863. Age 23 on roll dated 30 May 1863. Received at Confederate hospital, Atlanta, GA., 10 June 1864 with pneumonia. Sent to Confederate hospital, Madison, GA., 11 June 1864. Returned to duty from Blackie Hospital, Madison, GA., 8 July 1864. Wounded in the left arm in the Battle of Peachtree Creek, GA., 20 July 1864. Deserted 17 December 1864. Complexion dark, hair brown, eyes black, height 5' 6".[690]

Stewart, Charles; Private, Company A: Sworn into service 10 May 1861 at Nashville. Discharged 14 August 1862 under the conscript act at Tazewell, TN.

Stewart, Michael; Rank unknown, Company D: Died of wounds received in battle.[691]

Stewart, Nicholas P.; Private; Company B: Sworn into service 10 May 1861 at Nashville. Detached to the quartermaster department at Morristown, TN., as a teamster, 1 January 1862 through April 1863. Age 27 on roll dated 2 June 1863 at Shelbyville, TN. Wounded in the right forehead in the Battle of Jonesboro, GA., 1 September 1864. Died 21 September 1864. Buried in the Confederate Cemetery, Forsyth, GA.[692]

*Stewart, Robert; Private, Company B: Sworn into service 10 May 1861 at Nashville. Detached as brigade teamster, 1 January 1862 through December 1862. Age 25 on roll dated 21 June 1863. In hospital at Marietta, GA., 26 November 1863 through February 1864. Surrendered with the Army of Tennessee, 26 April 1865 as a member of Company C, 2nd Consolidated Tennessee Infantry.

Stewart, William H.; Private, Company K: Born in 1844. Occupation: farmer. Enlisted 20 December 1862 in Dickson Co., TN. Age 18 on roll dated 1 May 1863 at Shelbyville, TN. Mortally wounded in the lower third of the right thigh at Kennesaw Mountain, GA., 21 June 1864. Surgeon

---

[687] Johnson, *1860 Census of Humphreys County*, 53.
[688] Dobson-Sides, *1860 Davidson County Census*, 442.
[689] Maney, *Surgeon's Log*, "Stones River TN."
[690] Ibid., "20 July 1864;" Harris, *Confederate Hospitals*, 374, 150, 430.
[691] Lindsley, *Annals*, 304.
[692] Maney, *Surgeon's Log*, "September 1864."

William B. Maney recorded, "[He was] brought in late at night with complete prostration. Gave stimulants and operated by flaps in the morning of the 22nd. Case critical but was certain death would ensue soon if not amputated. Patient young but extremely delicate. In hopes that the patient could remain here but was forced to have him sent to Atlanta [the] day after operating. Patient died on reaching Atlanta three days after operating. Died 4 July 1864."[693]

Stokes, Andrew Jackson "Jordan"; Corporal, Company C: Born 3 August 1837 in Trigg Co., TN. Sworn into service 14 May 1861 at Nashville. Issued a Belgium musket. On daily duty as a color bearer, 1 August 1861 through April 1862. Age 25 on roll dated 8 May 1863 at Shelbyville, TN. Promoted to corporal by July 1863. Captured in the Battle of Missionary Ridge, TN., 25 November 1863. Sent to the U. S. Military Prison at Louisville, KY., 9 December 1863. Forwarded to Rock Island, IL., 11 December 1863. Complexion fair, hair brown, eyes blue, height 6' 1". Took oath 24 April 1865. Married Fannie Farmer, 24 January 1867 at Port Royal, Robertson Co., TN. Attended the reunion of the 11th Tennessee Infantry at Bon Aqua Springs, Hickman Co., TN., 24 September 1885. Died 27 July 1907 Earlington, Hopkins Co., KY. Buried in the Oakwood Cemetery, Earlington, Hopkins Co., KY. Pension Application Kentucky Widows 1937 Hopkins (1912).[694]

Stokey, Montgomery Alexander; Fourth Sergeant, Company C: Born 18 March 1839. Brother of Private William W. Stokey. Sworn into service 14 May 1861 at Nashville. Elected first corporal at the organization. Issued a minie musket. Elected fourth sergeant at the reorganization, 1 May 1862. Age 24 on roll dated 8 May 1863. Killed carrying the colors of the 11th Tennessee in the Battle of Franklin, TN., 30 November 1864, age 25. Buried in the McGavock Confederate Cemetery, Franklin, TN., section 54 grave #48.[695]

Stokey, William W.; Private, Company C: Born 14 February 1841. Brother of Fourth Sergeant Montgomery A. Stokey. Sworn into service 14 May 1861 at Nashville. Issued a minie musket. Age 22 on roll dated 8 May 1863 at Shelbyville, TN. Present through February 1864. Married Melissa Murpo. Died 20 June 1911. Buried in the Greenwood Cemetery, Dallas, Dallas Co., TX.[696]

Story, W. C.; Private, Company I: Born in Lincoln Co., TN. Occupation: farmer. Sworn into service 20 May 1861 at Nashville. Discharged for disability 6 May 1862. Complexion fair, hair light, eyes blue, height 5' 10", age 51.

*Stout, Andrew Graham; Private, Company D: Born c. 1846. Brother of First Lieutenant Samuel V. D. Stout. Occupation: clerk. Enlisted 20 December 1863 at Dalton, GA. Wounded in the middle left thigh in the Battle of Resaca, GA., 14 May 1864. Captured in the Battle of Nashville, TN., 16 December 1864. Sent to the U. S. Military Prison at Louisville, KY., 4 January 1865. Forwarded to Camp Chase, OH., 17 February 1865. Surrendered with the Army of Tennessee, 26 April 1865 as a member of Company C, 2nd Consolidated Tennessee Infantry.[697]

Stout, Ira Abraham; Rank unknown, Company D: Father of Private Andrew G. and First Lieutenant Samuel Van Dyke Stout. Brother of Samuel Hollingsworth Stout, Medical Director of the Army of Tennessee. Occupation: carriage maker. His grandfather, Abraham Stout, was a captain in the Revolutionary War and an original member of the Society of the Cincinnati. His father, Samuel Van

---

[693] Lindsley, *Annals*, 306; Maney, *Surgeon's Log*, "Kennesaw Mountain GA."

[694] McCauley, *Record Book, Company C*; "The Reunion," *Hickman Pioneer*; Lynn, *Confederate Pensioners of Kentucky*, 224.

[695] Baker, *1860 Census for Dickson County*, 25; McCauley, *Record Book, Company C*; Lindsley, *Annals*, 303; Hudgins and Potts, *McGavock Cemetery*, 32; Yeary, *Reminiscences*, 728.

[696] McCauley, *Record Book, Company C*; Yeary, *Reminiscences*, 726-28; Baker, *1860 Census for Dickson County*, 26; Find-a-grave, "William W. Stokey," http://www.findagrave.com/cgi-bin/fg.cgi?page=gr&GSln=Stokey&GSfn=W&GSby=1841&GSbyrel=in&GSdyrel=all&GSst=46&GScntry=4&GSob=n&GRid=98657236&df=all& (10 October 2013).

[697] Porch, *Census of Nashville: 1850*, 98; Dobson-Sides, *1860 Davidson County Census*, 714; Maney, *Surgeon's Log*, "May 1864"; *Nashville Daily Press*, 22 December 1864.

Dyke Stout, migrated from Pennsylvania to Nashville, establishing the first carriage factory of the city. A long time public servant, he was elected Mayor of Nashville in 1841 and was elected to eighteen one year terms as Alderman. Ira served as a private in Captain Grundy's Company in the Seminole War and served in the quartermaster's department during both the Mexican War and the Civil War.[698]

Stout, Phil A.; Second Sergeant/Color Bearer, Company B, H: Operated a blacksmith shop at the corner of Broad and Vine Streets in Nashville, TN. Sworn into service 10 May 1861 at Nashville. Elected second sergeant at the organization. Left in hospital at Versailles, KY., and captured 12 October 1862. Exchanged. Transferred to Company H, 1 April 1863. Color corporal July 1863 through February 1864. Took oath 22 December 1864. Complexion light, hair sandy, eyes gray, height 5' 7", age 30.[699]

Stout, Samuel Van Dyke; First Lieutenant, Company B: Born c. 1843. Brother of Private Andrew G. Stout. Brother of Samuel Hollingsworth Stout, Medical Director of the Army of Tennessee. Sworn into service 10 May 1861 at Nashville. Elected third sergeant. Promoted to second lieutenant, 10 May 1862. Promoted to first lieutenant, 23 May 1862. Deserted at Chattanooga, TN., 9 September 1863. Captured 10 September 1863. Took oath 22 February 1864. Complexion dark, hair light, eyes blue, height 5' 10".[700]

Stowers, John Turner; First Sergeant, Company B: Born in Nashville, TN., 2 March 1839. Occupation: mechanic. Sworn into service 10 May 1861 at Nashville. Elected fourth sergeant by July 1862. Elected third sergeant by November 1862. Age 24 on roll dated 2 June 1863. Promoted to second sergeant by January 1864. Later promoted to first sergeant. Wounded by a minie ball in the left leg in the Battle of Atlanta, GA., 22 July 1864, requiring the leg to be amputated below the knee. Remained within the Confederate lines in Alabama until the end of the war. Paroled at Columbus, MS. and returned to Nashville. Following the war, he was occupied as a plasterer and contractor, performing those skills in the completion of Nashville's Maxwell House Hotel. Married Mary Tilford of Wilson Co., TN., 2 May 1867. Relocated to West Nashville, which was at that time a separate town, around 1893. Charter member of the Frank Cheatham Bivouac No. 1, Nashville, TN. Member of the West Nashville Methodist Church. On his pension application, he was asked whether the disability was continuing, he wrote, "My leg is still shot off." A widower for fifteen years, he died at the home of his daughter 12 October 1925.[701]

Stratton, John H.; Musician, Company B: Born 9 July 1840 in Giles Co., TN. Sworn into service 10 May 1861 at Nashville. Wounded in the Battle of Cumberland Gap in the spring of 1862, losing a small portion of his skull. Served with a cooking detail and in the hospital corps. Left at the Confederate hospital in Versailles, KY., 12 October 1862. Captured and exchanged. Age 27 on roll dated 2 June 1863 at Shelbyville, TN. Appointed fourth corporal, 1 October 1863. Elected third corporal by January 1864. Left at Pulaski, TN., on the retreat from Nashville late December 1864 with chronic diarrhea. Took oath 11 January 1865. Complexion dark, hair black, eyes hazel, height 5' 9". Pension Application S5453.

Street, Andrew J.; Private, Company C: Born 1844 in Dickson Co., TN. Brother of Sergeant David W. Street. Occupation: farmhand. Enlisted 17 January 1863 at Shelbyville, TN., and listed as age 18 on roll dated 8 May 1863 taken there. Admitted to Fair Ground Hospital #2, Atlanta, GA., 27 February 1864, for chronic diarrhea. Returned to duty, 7 March 1864. Captured at the Battle of Franklin, TN 30 November 1864. Returned home with William C. Reynolds, who took the oath at Nashville 18 January

---

[698] Porch, *Census of Nashville: 1850*, 98; Will Thomas Hale and Dixon Merritt, *A History of Tennessee and Tennesseans* (Chicago IL: Lewis Publishing, 1913) 901; Jill Knight Garrett and Iris H. McClain, *Old City Cemetery Nashville, Tennessee Tombstone Inscriptions* (Columbia TN: Jill Knight Garrett and Iris H. McClain, 1971) 91.

[699] John P. Campbell, *Nashville Business Directory*, 1859.

[700] Porch, *Census of Nashville: 1850*, 98; Garrett and McClain, *City Cemetery*, 106.

[701] John T. Stowers, Cheatham Bivouac Application; Maney, *Surgeon's Log*, "Battle of Atlanta GA"; Kelley, *West Nashville*, 221. Pension Application 4.

1865. Resided in Sylvia, Dickson Co., TN. and later Kingston Springs, Cheatham Co., TN. Died 10 July 1933.[702]

Street, David W.; Sergeant, Company C: Born c. 1836. Brother of Private Andrew J. Street. Sworn into service 14 May 1861 at Nashville. Hospital attendant, 21 March through October 1862. Captured after the Battle of Murfreesboro, TN., 10 January 1863. Admitted to U. S. General Hospital #3, 1 February 1863. Sent to City Point, VA. for exchange, rejoining company, 2 March 1863 at Shelbyville, TN. Age 26 on roll dated 8 May 1863. Promoted to corporal by July 1863. Surrendered with the Army of Tennessee, 26 April 1865 at Greensboro, NC. as a member of Company F, 2nd Consolidated Tennessee Infantry.[703]

Street, John Calvin; Private, Company C: Born c. 1839. Brother of Private William H. Street. Occupation: farmer. Sworn into service 14 May 1861 at Nashville. Died from disease, 9 August 1861.[704]

Street, Thomas M.; Private, Company C: Born 29 April 1841. Occupation: farmhand. Sworn into service 14 May 1861 at Nashville. Died from disease 30 July 1861. Buried in the Street Cemetery, Dickson Co., TN.[705]

Street, William H. Private; Company C: Born c. 1842. Brother of Private John C. Street. Occupation: farmer. Sworn into service 14 May 1861 at Nashville. Issued a Belgium musket. Age 22 on roll dated 8 May 1863 at Shelbyville, TN. Present through February 1864. Died in 1907.[706]

Stroud, John W. Private; Company F: Enlisted 18 May 1861 at Cedar Hill, TN. Captured in Kentucky. Paroled and went home.

Stroud, Joseph W.; Third Corporal, Company F: Enlisted 18 May 1861 in Cedar Hill, TN. Promoted to third corporal by July 1863. Wounded in the Battle of Chickamauga, GA., 19 September 1863. Died at the Medical College Hospital in Atlanta, GA., 16 October 1863. Buried in the Oakland Cemetery, Atlanta, GA.

Stuart, James M.; Private, Company C: No further.

Stuart, John Minor; Private, Company E: Born in Dickson Co., TN., 16 February 1834. Sworn into service 18 May 1861 at Nashville. Age 27 on roll dated 16 August 1861 at Watauga Bridge, TN. Hospital warden at Knoxville, TN., 14 May 1862 through February 1863. Admitted to Fair Ground Hospital #2, Atlanta, GA., 20 March 1863. Returned to duty, 25 April 1863. Captured May, 1864 at Cassville, GA. Sent to the U. S. Military Prison at Louisville, KY. Forwarded to Rock Island, IL., 25 May 1864. Resided at Burns, TN. Married Clarissa Spicer, 27 December 1865. Died 15 January 1918. Buried in the Stuart Cemetery, Burns, Dickson Co., TN.[707]

Sudberry, David R.; Private, Company C: Captured at Knoxville, TN., 20 December 1863. Sent to the U. S. Military Prison at Louisville, KY. Forwarded to Rock Island, IL., 27 January 1864.

Sugg, Joseph H. L.; Private, Company C: Born c. 1845. Occupation: farmhand. Sworn into service 14 May 1861 at Nashville. Issued a Belgium musket. Discharged at Tazewell, TN., 15 August 1862 under the conscript act.[708]

Sugg, Nathaniel Rufus "Nat"; Private, Company H: Born 26 February 1845 on Flat Creek, Bedford Co., TN. Moved to Dickson Co. in early childhood. Occupation: farmer. Sworn into service 14 May

---

[702] Baker, *1850 Census for Dickson County*, 129; Baker, *1860 Census for Dickson County*, 25; Welsh, *Confederate Hospitals*, Patient Roster, Fair Ground Hospital #2, 189. Pension Application 14959.

[703] Baker, *1860 Census for Dickson County*, 25.

[704] Ibid., 29.

[705] Garrett and McClain, *Dickson County Cemetery Records* vol. 1, 25; Baker, *1860 Census for Dickson County*, 26.

[706] McCauley, *Record Book, Company C*; McCauley Camp 260, *Confederate Graves*, 47; Baker, *1860 Census for Dickson County*, 29; Sistler and Sistler, *1880 Census of Dickson County*, 122.

[707] Welsh, *Confederate Hospitals*, Patient Roster, Fair Ground Hospital #2, 190; J. M. Stuart, Tennessee Pension Application, 8316.

[708] McCauley, *Record Book, Company C*; Baker, *1860 Census for Dickson County*, 122.

1861 at Nashville. Regimental teamster, 10 July 1862 through February 1863. Deserted 22 April 1863. Name appears on Federal roll of prisoners of war released at Nashville, TN. upon taking oath, 15 January 1864. Complexion fair, hair brown, eyes blue, height 5' 8". Enlisted in 9th Battalion (Gantt's) Tennessee Cavalry, C.S.A., 15 September 1864; made sergeant, 1 November 1864; Federal records shows he came into their hands, 9 March 1865; subscribed to Oath of Allegiance, 17 April 1865. Married 1) Milbury Petty of Hickman Co., and 2) Mary Buford, native of Mobile, AL., 3) Mrs. Jennie (Cash) Shouse, a native of Hickman Co. Farmer. Clerk, circuit court, Dickson Co., beginning in 1886 to an undetermined date. Resided In Hickman Co., TN. Member Methodist Church and Mason, being a member of the Pinewood Lodge. Census taker in 1880. Died at Dickson, Dickson Co., TN., 23 January 1919. Buried in the Union Cemetery, Dickson, Dickson Co., TN.[709]

Sullivan, S.; Rank unknown, Company unknown: Died at the Confederate General Hospital in Knoxville, TN., 12 November 1862. Buried in the Bethel Cemetery, Knox Co., TN.

Sullivan, Timothy; Private, Company G: Enlisted 3 June 1861 at Camp Cheatham. Age 30 on roll dated 30 May 1863. Deserted near Chattanooga, TN., 11 November 1863.

Sutton, Joseph; Private, Company D: Sworn into service 11 May 1861 at Nashville. Killed in the Battle of Murfreesboro, TN., 31 December 1862.

Swayne, John; Private, Company K: Sworn into service 25 May 1861 at Nashville. Discharged 17 November 1861 for disability.

Sykes, Robert; Fourth Sergeant, Company D, B: Born 4 March 1820 in GA. Occupation: carpenter. Married Martha E. Powell, 2 October 1854. Sworn into service 11 May 1861 in Company D at Nashville, TN. Elected fourth sergeant at the organization. Transferred to Company B at the reorganization, 1 May 1862. Discharged under the conscript law, 15 August 1862 at Tazewell, TN. Died 3 September 1906. Buried in the Mt. Olivet Cemetery, Nashville, TN.[710]

-T-

Talley, James A.; Private, Company F: Enlisted 25 May 1861 at Cedar Hill, TN. Died 26 July 1861.

Tarkington, George Washington; Private, Company H: Born in Hickman Co., TN., 17 April 1844. Brother of Corporal John H. C. Tarkington. Enlisted 19 May 1863 at Shelbyville, TN. Later served as a private in the 10th Tennessee Cavalry. Surrendered at Citronella, AL. by Lieutenant General Richard R. Taylor, 4 May 1865. Married Mary Pillow Totty, 26 December 1866. Resided in the Little Lot community of Hickman Co. before relocating to Cooke Co., TX. and later Sentinel, OK. Attended the reunion of the 11th Tennessee Infantry at Bon Aqua Springs, Hickman Co., TN., 24 September 1885. Died 3 May 1916. Buried in Sentinel Co., OK.[711]

*Tarkington, John Henry Clay; Fourth Corporal, Company H: Born in Hickman Co., TN., 15 November 1842. Brother of Private George W. Tarkington. Occupation: farmer. Sworn into service 14 May 1861 at Nashville. Wounded in the right arm in the Battle of Murfreesboro, TN., 31 December 1862. Promoted to fourth corporal, 26 February 1863. Wounded through the middle third of both thighs in the Battle of Missionary Ridge, TN., 25 November 1863. Wounds considered mortal. Transferred to "sappers and miners." Later served in the 10th Tennessee Cavalry. Surrendered at Broad River, NC. while detailed as a pontoon teamster. Paroled 5 May 1865 at Catawba Bridge, SC. Eyes gray, hair light, complexion fair, 6'. Married Mary Jane Gardner, 30 December 1865 at Little Lot, Hickman Co., TN.

---

[709] McBride, Robison, and Cornwell, *Biographical Directory*, vol. 2, 875-76.
[710] *Nashville City Directory*, 1857, 203; Sistler and Sistler, *Davidson County Marriages 1838-1863*, 211; *Nashville Banner*, 3 September 1906.
[711] "The Reunion," *Hickman Pioneer*; Spence, History, 192.

Served as a magistrate in 1899 and for several years as a member of the Hickman Co. Court (1900). Relocated to Nashville in 1907, residing in the city while also owning a farm on Hydes Ferry Pike. Member of the Frank Cheatham Bivouac. Stricken with an acute attack of asthma, he died within an hour on 15 December 1912 in Nashville. Buried in Mount Olivet Cemetery, Nashville, TN.[712]

Tatom, James K. P.; Private, Company K: Born 13 October 1844. Brother of Private William B. Tatom. Entered service 13 December 1862 in Dickson Co., TN. Absent sick from 14 July 1863. Member of the Masonic Order. Died 24 September 1908. Buried Wills Cemetery, Dickson Co., TN.[713]

Tatom, Montgomery B.; Private, Company K: Sworn into service 25 May 1861. Age 16 on roll dated 15 August 1861 at Midway, TN. Discharged by virtue of conscript act at Tazewell, TN., 12 August 1862.

Tatom, William B.; Private, Company K: Born 11 May 1840. Brother of Private James K. P. Tatom. Sworn into service 25 May 1861. Age 20 on roll dated 15 August 1861 at Midway, TN. Given indefinite sick furlough, 6 November 1862. Rejoined the regiment before the end of the month. Died 8 December 1903. Buried in the Wills Cemetery, Dickson Co., TN.

Taylor, Edmund D.; Private, Company A: Born 25 March 1843. Sworn into service 10 May 1861 at Nashville. Age 20 on roll dated 6 May 1863 at Shelbyville, TN. Detached as provost guard at hospital in Rome GA., 1 May 1863. Wounded at the Battle of Franklin, TN., 30 November 1864. Listed as a prisoner of war and paroled at Meridian, MS., 12 May 1865. Married Margaret Teas. Died 8 August 1885. Buried in the Bryant Cemetery, Humphreys Co., TN.[714]

Taylor, James Andrew Jackson; Private, Company E: Born 8 April 1834. Enlisted in Company E on 7 August 1861. Paroled on 26 April 1865. Living at Short, MS. after the war. Died 13 August 1906 in Burnsville, MS. Buried Mt. Gillead, Iuka, Tishomingo Co., MS.[715]

Taylor, John D.; Second Lieutenant, Company E: Occupation: farmhand and living on the farm of Captain William D. Eleazer. Sworn into service 18 May 1861 at Nashville. Age 22 on roll dated 16 August 1861 at Watauga, TN. Elected second lieutenant, 19 April 1862. Armed with an Enfield rifle. Later listed again as a private. Left as a hospital nurse at Murfreesboro, TN., and captured. Sent to Camp Chase, OH., 27 February 1863 then to Camp Morton, IN. Took oath and was discharged July 1864, to remain north of the Ohio River. Complexion light, hair dark, eyes hazel, 5'10".[716]

Taylor, Manoah "Whack"; Private, Company C: Born c. 1838. Occupation: farmhand. Sworn into service 14 May 1861 at Nashville. Age 21 on roll dated 8 May 1863 at Shelbyville, TN. Discharged 5 July 1861. Married Nancy C. Gilmore 30 January 1864.[717]

Taylor, Skelton; Third Sergeant, Company E: Sworn into service 18 May 1861 at Nashville. Age 20 on roll dated 16 August 1861 at Watauga Bridge, TN. Died at Tunnel Hill, GA., 21 September 1863 of pneumonia.

Teaster, Charles D.; Fifth Sergeant, Company I: Born c. 1841. Brother of Private John T. Teaster. Sworn into service 20 May 1861 at Nashville. Age 21 on roll dated 6 May 1863 at Shelbyville, TN. Promoted to third corporal August 1862. Promoted to second corporal by March 1863. Promoted to fifth sergeant 1 August 1863. Wounded in the Battle of Atlanta, GA., 22 July 1864. Died at Academy

---

[712] J. H. Tarkington, Tennessee Pension Application, 11555; Maney, *Surgeon's Log*, "Missionary Ridge TN"; Spence, *History*, 192; Sarah Peery Armistead, Ova Lee Peery Sawyer, Lorraine Peery Russell, Penny Russell Boyer, and Theresa Tarkington-Kersey, *Tarkingtons of Tennessee: Genealogy of John G. Tarkington* (Brentwood TN: S.P. Armistead, 2001) 338.

[713] Garrett and McClain, *Dickson Cemetery Records* vol. 1, 226.

[714] Trogdon, "Interesting Letter."

[715] Andrew Jackson Taylor, Mississippi Confederate Grave Registry, http://mscgr.homestead.com (1 August 2014).

[716] Baker, *1860 Census for Dickson County*, 124.

[717] Ibid., 144.

Hospital, Forsyth, GA., 13 August 1864 of pyaemia. Buried in the Confederate Cemetery, Forsyth, GA.[718]

Teaster, John Thomas; Private, Company I: Born c. 1839 in North Carolina. Brother of Sergeant Charles D. Teaster. Sworn into service 20 May 1861 at Nashville. Age 24 on roll dated 6 May 1863 at Shelbyville, TN. Assigned to extra duty as a teamster in the quartermaster department, 17 March 1863 to September 1863. Married Sarah Kemp. Occupation: farmer.[719]

Thedford, William R.; Lieutenant-Colonel, Company K, Field & Staff: Born in 1823 in TN. Married Sophronia Edwards, who died 13 May 1859. Sworn into service 25 May 1861 at Nashville. Age of 37 on roll dated 15 August 1861 at Midway, TN. Elected captain of Company K at the organization. Elected to the rank of major, 1 May 1862 at the reorganization. Promoted to lieutenant-colonel, 7 November 1862. Commanded the regiment from 31 December 1862 to May 1863, while Colonel George W. Gordon was a prisoner of war. Resigned for health reasons, 14 December 1863. Died 13 October 1865 in Dickson Co., TN. Buried in the A. J. Donnegan Cemetery, Dickson Co., TN.[720]

Thomas, James D.; Third Corporal, Company K: Sworn into service 25 May 1861 at Nashville. Age 19 on roll dated 15 August 1861 at Midway, TN. Elected fourth corporal summer 1862. Promoted to third corporal by March 1863. Captured near Marietta, GA., 3 July 1864. Sent to Camp Douglas, IL.

Thomas, Minor B.; Brevet Second Lieutenant, Company K: Occupation: farmer. Sworn into service 25 May 1861 at Nashville. Age 20 on roll dated 15 August 1861 at Midway, TN. Brevetted from private to second lieutenant, 1 May 1862. Wounded 16 June 1864. Captured near Clifton, TN., 7 July 1864. Sent to Camp Chase, OH. Arrived 6 August 1864. Died of smallpox, 11 October 1864. Buried at Camp Chase Cemetery Row 10, Number 20, Grave 293.[721]

Thomason, Benjamin W.; Private, Company C: Sworn into service 14 May 1861 at Nashville. Issued a minie musket. Age 20 on roll dated 8 May 1863 at Shelbyville, TN. Captured at Clarksville, TN., 23 December 1863. Sent to Fort Delaware, DE. Discharged 29 February 1864.[722]

Thompson, Francis M.; Third Sergeant, Company K: Occupation farmer. Enlisted 10 August 1861, at Camp Mallory, TN. Age 20 on roll dated 15 August 1861 at Midway, TN. Promoted to fourth sergeant by July 1862 and to third sergeant by January 1863. Wounded in the middle third of the left forearm at Missionary Ridge, TN., 24 November 1863. Sent to Fairground Hospital No. 1, 26 November 1863 with vulnus sclopeticum. Forwarded to another hospital, 27 November 1863. Later captured. Paroled at Meridian, MS., 11 May 1865.[723]

Thompson, J. Stewart; Private, Company H: Born 1843 in Nunnelly, Hickman Co., TN. Occupation: farmer. Enlisted 12 September 1861, at Knoxville, TN. Detached as provost guard at hospital in Rome, GA., January through August, 1863. Shot in the Battle of Missionary Ridge, TN., 25 November 1863, the bullet fracturing his right thigh. Left on the field and captured on the same date. Died 18 January 1864 in U. S. Hospital #4, Chattanooga, TN.[724]

Thompson, James; Private, Company B: Sworn into service 10 May 1861 at Nashville. Listed as deserted 1 July 1861 at Camp Cheatham. Age 28 on roll dated 2 June 1863 at Shelbyville, TN.

Thompson, John; Private, Company B: Listed in General Hospital at Knoxville, TN., 13 September 1861. Listed as deserted at Knoxville, TN. on roll dated January 1862.

---

[718] Maney, *Surgeon's Log*, "Battle of Atlanta GA"; Johnson, *1860 Census of Humphreys County*, 46.

[719] Anderson and Garrett, *Humphreys County Cemetery Records* vol. 1, 198; Johnson, *1860 Census of Humphreys County*, 46; Fischer and Burns, *1880 Census of Humphreys County*, 41.

[720] Luff, "Lt. Col. William Thedford Together with his Descendants," 72.

[721] Baker, *1860 Census for Dickson County*, 79.

[722] McCauley, *Record Book, Company C*.

[723] Maney, *Surgeon's Log*, "Missionary Ridge TN"; Welsh, *Confederate Hospitals*, Patient Roster, Fair Ground Hospital #1, 280 (erroneously listed as T. M. Thompson).

[724] United Daughters of the Confederacy, *Confederate Soldiers of Hickman County*, 189; Maney, *Surgeon's Log*, "Missionary Ridge TN."

Thompson, Samuel C.; Private, Company A: Born c. 1825. Occupation: farmer. Married to Donna. Joined by conscript act, 20 February 1863, at Shelbyville, TN.[725]

Thompson, Thomas; Private, Company I: Sworn into service 20 May 1861 at Nashville. Age 21 on roll dated 6 May 1863 at Shelbyville, TN. Died 7 July 1861 in Humphreys Co., TN.

Thompson, Thomas Douglas; Sergeant-Major, Company H, Field & Staff: Born 1841 in Vernon, Hickman Co., TN. Enlisted in Company H in 1861. Served as secretary to Colonel James E. Rains, then appointed *aide-de-camp* in November 1862. Originally third sergeant, later promoted to sergeant-major. Colonel Rains wrote a letter to G. W. Jones of the Confederate House of Representatives recommending that Sergeant-Major Thompson be made a cadet. In the letter, Colonel Rains praises Sergeant-Major Thompson for meritorious service by valor and efficiency. The letter was forwarded from the congressman to President Jefferson Davis. Served with Colonel Rains after he was promoted to Brigadier General and until Rains's death at Murfreesboro, TN., 31 December 1862. Afterwards, served for a period under General William B. Bate, and later joined the 10th Tennessee Cavalry. Following the war, he returned to his home in Hickman Co. and became a medical doctor. Relocated to Nashville, residing at 1212 McGavock Street, where for many years he was a physician for the Confederate Soldiers Home of Tennessee in Nashville. Died 17 April 1917 in Nashville, TN. Buried in the Petty Cemetery, Hickman Co., TN.[726]

*Thompson, William Turner "Tas"; Private, Company K: Born in Dickson Co., TN., 28 February 1845. Occupation: farmer. Enlisted 23 March 1863 at Shelbyville, TN., and age 18 on roll dated 1 May 1863. Wounded in the lower lip on skirmish line near Atlanta, GA., 31 July 1864. Listed as a member of Company K, 2nd Consolidated Tennessee Infantry at the surrender of the Army of Tennessee. Paroled 26 April 1865 at Greensboro, NC. Married Mary Josephine Anderson. Resided at Waverly, Humphreys Co., TN. Died 25 July 1925. Buried in the Anderson Cemetery, Hurricane Mills, Humphreys Co., TN.[727]

Tidwell, Benjamin O.; Second Corporal, Company K: Cousin to Second Lieutenant Hickman and Captain Franklin F. Tidwell. Sworn into service 25 May 1861 at Nashville. Age 20 on roll dated 15 August 1861 at Midway, TN. Became second corporal by July, 1862. Died at Lumpkin Hospital, Rome GA., 16 April 1863. Buried in the Myrtle Hill Cemetery, Rome, GA.

Tidwell, Edmund Mansel; Private, Company K: Born in 1833. Married Amanda Emmino Tate, 29 February 1859. First cousin to Captain F. F. Tidwell and Second Lieutenant Hickman Tidwell. Enlisted 12 December 1862. Age 30 on roll dated 1 May 1863. Listed as a teamster. Died 17 March 1863 in Cheatham's division hospital, age 30. Buried in Burns, TN.

*Tidwell, Franklin Fulton; Captain, Company K: Born 26 July 1840 in Dickson Co., TN. Brother of Second Lieutenant Hickman Tidwell and cousin to Second Corporal Benjamin Tidwell and Private Edmund M. Tidwell. Occupation: farmer. Sworn into service 25 May 1861 at Nashville. Age 21 on roll dated 15 August 1861 at Midway, TN. Elected first lieutenant, 15 August 1861. Promoted to captain, 1 May 1862. Slightly wounded in the neck during the Battle of Murfreesboro, TN., 31 December 1862. Admitted to Fairground Hospital No. 2, Atlanta, GA., 15 July 1863 with chronic diarrhea. Returned to duty 27 July 1863. Wounded in the side by a spent minie ball in the Battle of Chickamauga, 19 September 1863. Wounded again in the Atlanta Campaign, 9 July 1864. Captain Tidwell was shown to be in command of the 11th/29th Consolidated Tennessee Infantry in the Battle of Bentonville, NC., 21 March 1865. He became ill with typhoid fever in Greensboro, NC. and was delirious at the close of the war, treated in a private home by a private physician. Listed as a prisoner of war in Greensboro, 30 May 1865. Subsequently sent to Washington, DC, where on 13 July 1865 he reported to the provost marshal.

---

[725] Johnson, *1860 Census of Humphreys County*, 131.

[726] Thomas Douglas Thompson, Tennessee Pension Application, 13103; "Dr. Thomas D. Thompson," *Confederate Veteran* vol. 25 no. 7 (July 1917): 323.

[727] W. T. Thompson, Tennessee Pension Application, 3598; Maney, *Surgeon's Log*, "28-31 July 1864"; Garrett, *Cemetery Records of Humphreys County, Tennessee*.

Paroled and given transportation to Nashville. Following the war he engaged in teaching school on Jones Creek and later engaged in merchandising. Owned and operated a hotel in Burns, TN. Married Magdaline Knox Petty, 1 March 1866. Census taker in 1880. Present at the 24 September 1885 reunion of the 11th Tennessee Infantry at the Bon Aqua Springs, Hickman Co., TN., and at the 14 June 1904 reunion in conjunction with the Confederate Veterans reunion held at the Chamber of Commerce in Nashville. A Royal Arch Mason, Charlotte Lodge, and politically a Democrat, he was elected at age 68 to serve in the Tennessee House of Representatives 1909-11. Died 20 February 1911. Buried with full Masonic honors in the Dickson Union Cemetery, Dickson Co., TN.[728]

Tidwell, Hickman C. Second Lieutenant, Company E: Born 16 August 1843. Brother of Captain Franklin F. Tidwell and cousin to Second Corporal Benjamin Tidwell and Private Edmund M. Tidwell. Occupation: farmer. Sworn into service 18 May 1861 at Nashville. Age 17 on roll dated 16 August 1861 at Watauga Bridge, TN. Elected second lieutenant, 16 August 1861. On duty as a herdsman since 1 July 1862. Assigned as orderly to Lieutenant-Colonel Thedford, 1 February 1863. Admitted to Fair Ground Hospital #2, Atlanta, GA. on 15 July 1863 for chronic diarrhea. Returned to duty 27 July 1863. Shown as second lieutenant of Company C, 2nd Consolidated Infantry. Absent on sick furlough 12 March 1865. Died 9 May 1865 in Greensboro, NC.

Tidwell, Josiah; Brevet Second Lieutenant, Company K: Born 26 April 1838. Occupation: farmer. Sworn into service 25 May 1861 at Nashville. Elected third Lieutenant, 25 May 1861, then later brevetted to second lieutenant. Age 23 on roll dated 1 May 1863. Resigned July 1861. Died 19 March 1874. Buried in the White Cemetery, Spencer Mill, Dickson Co., TN.[729]

Tidwell, Silas; Private, Company K: Enlisted 10 August 1861, at Camp Mallory. Age 20 on roll dated 15 August 1861 at Midway, TN. Killed in the Battle of Lovejoy Station, GA., 2 September 1864 from a shot through the right brain.[730]

Totty, Thomas S.; Private, Company E: Born in Hickman Co., TN., 13 July 1829. Sworn into service 18 May 1861, at Nashville. Age 26 on roll dated 16 August 1861 at Watauga Bridge, TN. Listed as a teamster. Ill with typhoid fever at Cumberland Ford, KY. in the latter part of 1861, resulting in near blindness. Drove an ordnance wagon under the management of Dr. Shackelford and Thomas Adkisson, at most times barely seeing well enough to drive. Surrendered 26 April 1865 at Greensboro, NC. as a member of Company C, 2nd Consolidated Tennessee Infantry. Paroled 1 May 1865. Left in a hospital in North Carolina at the time of the surrender. Upon discharge he walked part of the way home arriving during the last days of May 1865. Resided at Edgewood, Dickson Co., TN. Married to Tennessee J. Totty. Totally blind for the last twenty-five years of his life. Died 5 June 1919. Buried in the Edgewood Cemetery, Yellow Creek, Dickson Co., TN.[731]

Tracy, Thomas; Private, Company G: Occupation: laborer. Enlisted 3 June 1861 at Camp Cheatham. Age 26 on roll dated 30 May 1863 at Shelbyville, TN. Wounded slightly in the side at Chickamauga, GA., 19 September 1863. Mortally wounded through the lungs at Missionary Ridge, TN., 25 November 1863. Left on the field and captured. Died in the hands of the enemy 3 December 1863.[732]

---

[728] Maney, *Surgeon's Log*, "Stones River TN"; Maney, *Surgeon's Log*, "Chickamauga GA"; Goodspeed Brothers, *Goodspeed's Histories of Montgomery, Robertson, Humphreys, Stewart, Dickson, Cheatham, Houston Counties*, 1357; Garrett, *Dickson County Handbook*, 202; F. F. Tidwell, Tennessee Pension Application, 12310; McBride, Robison, and Cornwell, *Biographical Directory*, vol. 3, 662-63; "The Reunion," *Hickman Pioneer*, Reunion Pamphlet, 14 June 1904.

[729] Garrett, *Dickson County Handbook*, 220.

[730] Maney, *Surgeon's Log*, "September 1864."

[731] Garrett and McClain, *Dickson County Cemetery Records* vol. 1, 41; Thomas S. Totty, Tennessee Pension Application, 2438.

[732] Maney, *Surgeon's Log*, "Chickamauga GA"; Maney, *Surgeon's Log*, "Missionary Ridge TN."

Traylor, LeRoy M.; Second Lieutenant, Company I: Born c. 1827. Occupation: farmer. Sworn into service 20 May 1861 in Nashville. Elected second lieutenant at the organization. Age 37 on roll dated 6 May 1863 at Shelbyville, TN. Defeated and lost rank in the reorganization, 1 May 1862, at which time he was dropped from the roll. Later served as a second lieutenant in Napier's Cavalry Battalion.[733]

Traylor, Thomas B.; Second Lieutenant, Company A: Born 31 October 1841 in Humphreys Co., TN. Resided at Waverly and occupied as a carpenter. Sworn into service 10 May 1861 at Nashville. Elected second lieutenant at the organization. Defeated and lost rank in the reorganization of 1 May 1862. At the end of his one year enlistment, he organized a company as a part of Napier's Battalion, later the 10th Tennessee Cavalry, serving under generals Forrest and Wheeler. Captured and exchanged after 30 days at Camp Morton, IN. Captured while on scout duty in Humphreys Co. and sent to Camp Chase, OH., where he was held until February 1865. Upon release, Captain Traylor reported for duty and served with his command until paroled with General Forrest, at Gainesville, AL., 10 May 1865. Married Adda McNeil in 1868. Postwar he became a successful merchant and served as justice of the peace, chairman of the county court, and in 1878 was elected clerk of the circuit court of Humphreys Co. Politically a Democrat. Member of the Masonic order and the Presbyterian Church. Died 7 June 1900. Buried in the Marable Cemetery, Waverly, Humphreys Co., TN. [734]

Treanor, James; Private, Company G: Born 1823 in Ireland. Occupation: day laborer. Enlisted 3 June 1861 at Camp Cheatham. Discharged by virtue of conscript law near Tazewell, TN., 19 August 1862.[735]

Trogdon, Alfred Winslow; Private, Company A: Born 15 March 1837 in Humphreys Co., TN. Sworn into service 10 May 1861 at Nashville. Listed as a cook. Captured on retreat from Murfreesboro, TN., 5 January 1863. Sent to Camp Buckner, IL., 11 March 1863. Transferred to City Point, VA., where he was exchanged. Rejoined the 11th Tennessee Infantry by 1 May 1863. Wounded at the Battle of Franklin, TN., 30 November 1864 by a shot entering the left hip, lodging in the right hip. Left lying on the battlefield for several hours in the cold and rain before help came. Hospitalized for two days at Franklin, then taken to the home of John Hunter who lived nearby. The bullet was never removed and was the cause of his death many years later. Home on furlough until the close of the war. Took the oath of allegiance, 14 February 1865. Dark complexion, dark hair, grey eyes, height 6'. His older brother, John W. Trogden, 24th Battalion Tennessee Sharpshooters, made Alfred promise that should he not return from the war, Alfred would take care of his family. John died at Cheatham's division hospital at Shelbyville, TN., 13 June 1863. Alfred kept his promise and married Caroline Turner Trogdon, his sister-in-law, 8 October 1865. After her death, he married 2) Sarah Jane Curtis 4 December 1870. Occupation: carpenter. Died 23 November 1919. Buried in the Anderson Cemetery on Blue Creek, Humphreys Co., TN.[736]

Trotter, George W.; Private, Company I: Born c. 1841. Brother of First Sergeant Jordan J. Trotter. Sworn into service 20 May 1861 at Nashville. Age 21 on roll dated 6 May 1863. Listed as a deserter and captured near Rough and Ready, GA., 31 August 1864. Took the oath 20 September 1864. Light complexion, dark hair, 5'10".[737]

Trotter, Jordan J.; First Sergeant, Company I: Born c. 1839. Brother of Private George W. Trotter. Occupation: farmer. Sworn into service 20 May 1861 at Nashville. Age 24 on roll dated 6 May 1863 at

---

[733] Johnson, *1860 Census of Humphreys County*, 58.

[734] Evans, *Confederate Military History* vol. 10, 756-57; Anderson and Garrett, *Humphreys County Cemetery Records*, 38; Goodspeed Brothers, *Goodspeed's Histories of Montgomery, Robertson, Humphreys, Stewart, Dickson, Cheatham, Houston Counties*, 1274-75.

[735] Dobson-Sides, *1860 Davidson County Census*, 285.

[736] Anderson and Garrett, *Humphreys County Cemetery Records* vol. 1, 53; Johnson, *1860 Census of Humphreys County*, 87; Fischer and Burns, *1880 Census of Humphreys County*, 186; Garrett, *History of Humphreys County*, 396; Johnson, *Leaves*, 22, 51-52; Pension Application 2635.

[737] Johnson, *1860 Census of Humphreys County*, 39.

Shelbyville, TN. Promoted from private to first sergeant at the reorganization, 1 May 1862. Returned to ranks as a private, 1 May 1863. Killed in action at Kennesaw Mountain, GA., 21 June 1864.[738]

Tuberville, Joseph L.; Private, Company A: Enlisted 6 May 1863 at Shelbyville, TN., age 25. Took oath 15 January 1864. Fair complexion, light hair, grey eyes, 5'7".

Tucker, Whil; Private, Company H: Enlisted 14 May 1861 at Nashville. Died 8 July 1861.

Turner, A. L.; Private, Company C: Issued a Belgium musket. No further.[739]

Turner, Dillard; Private, Company C: Born c. 1836. Occupation: day laborer. Married 10 July 1856 to Eugenia (Emma) Darthula Hays. Enlisted 4 September 1861 at Knoxville, TN. Issued a minie musket. Listed as a deserter 25 January 1863. Age 27 on roll dated 8 May 1863.[740]

Turner, George L.; Private, Company A: Sworn into service 10 May 1861 at Nashville. On sick furlough since 2 November 1861. Reenlisted at Normandy, TN., 1 December 1862. Age 19 on roll dated 6 May 1863 at Shelbyville, TN.

Turner, George T.; Private, Company C: Born c. 1842. Occupation: farmer. Enlisted 14 May 1861, at Nashville. Age 21 on roll dated 8 May 1863 at Shelbyville, TN. Listed as a teamster. On provost guard duty 2 August 1863. Wounded in the Battle of Franklin, TN., 30 November 1864. Captured at Franklin, TN., 17 December 1864. Arrived at Camp Chase, OH., 8 March 1865 and discharged 10 March 1865. Fair complexion, light hair, blue eyes, height 6'2".[741]

–U–

Ussery, Nathaniel T.; Private, Company F: Enlisted 18 May 1861 at Camp Cheatham. Died 7 September 1861, during a 2 a.m. raid on the Scott Co., TN. home of Union sympathizer Hiram Marcum, who was providing assistance to East Tennesseans attempting to flee the state and join the Union forces in Kentucky. Wielding an axe, Marcum's sixteen year old daughter, Julia, split open his chin and chest, resulting in fatal wounds.

–V–

Vailes, William Henry H.; Private, Company E: Occupation: day laborer. Sworn into service 18 May 1861 at Nashville. Age 21 on roll dated 16 August 1861 at Watauga Bridge, TN. Listed as a teamster. Deserted at Cumberland Gap, TN., 21 May 1862.

Van Hook, J. W.; Private, Company F: Occupation: physician. Enlisted 1 April 1862 at Cumberland Gap, TN. Mortally wounded through the abdomen at the Battle of Chickamauga, GA., 19 September 1863. Died at Field Hospital #20, 20 September 1863, age 28.[742]

Vaughan, Alexander H.; Brevet Second Lieutenant, Company H: Sworn into service 14 May 1861 at Nashville. Elected second lieutenant at the organization. Appointed Provost Marshal of Tazewell, TN. While attempting to arrest a member of the 3rd Battalion Tennessee Cavalry for disorderly conduct, he was killed by five cavalrymen of that unit 27 December 1861. John A. Cooter, Joel T. Taylor, and George M. Holmes, all of Company F, 3rd Battalion Tennessee Cavalry, were tried and convicted of the

---

[738] Maney, *Surgeon's Log*, "Kennesaw Mountain GA"; Johnson, *1860 Census of Humphreys County*, 39.

[739] McCauley, *Record Book, Company C.*

[740] Electronic mail correspondence with Faye Keele, Turner family genealogist, 10 May 2001; McCauley, *Record Book, Company C.*

[741] Baker, *1860 Census for Dickson County*, 69.

[742] Maney, *Surgeon's Log*, "Chickamauga GA."

crime, the others escaping. Buried in the Irish Cemetery, Tazewell, TN. Citizens grateful for his service constructed a stone memorial at the site of his grave, one of the earliest of the Civil War.[743]

Vaught, William E.; Private, Company B: Sworn into service 10 May 1861 at Nashville. Age 28 on roll dated 26 June 1863 at Shelbyville, TN. Received at Confederate hospital, Atlanta, GA., 10 June 1864. Forwarded to Confederate hospital, Madison, GA., 11 June 1864. Returned to duty from Stout Hospital, 18 June, 1864. Captured 3 July 1864 at Marietta, GA. Sent to Camp Douglas, IL. Discharged 17 July 1864. Later enlisted in the Sixth U. S. Volunteer Infantry.[744]

*Vineyard, Morgan H.; Private, Company K: Born circa 1845. Occupation: farmer. Enlisted 13 December 1862 at Dickson, TN. Age 18 on roll dated 1 May 1863 Shelbyville, TN. Wounded seriously through the face in the Battle of Chickamauga, GA., 19 September 1863. Surrendered and paroled with the Army of Tennessee, 26 April 1865.[745]

Voss, J. E.; Private, Company K: Listed as a prisoner of war on roll dated 17 May 1865 at Columbus, MS.

-W-

Waggoner, Calvin J.; Second Sergeant, Company I: Born c. 1835. Sworn into service 20 May 1861 at Nashville. Discharged 14 September 1862 at Cumberland Gap by reason of substitute. Occupied as a store clerk after the war.[746]

Walker, John; Private, Company D: Sworn into service 11 May 1861 at Nashville. Listed as a carpenter. Discharged 15 August 1862 at Tazewell, TN. by the conscript act.

Wall, John R.; Private, Company E: Born c. 1840. Occupation: farmhand. Sworn into service 18 May 1861 at Nashville. Age 21 on roll dated 16 August 1861 at Watauga Bridge, TN. Deserted. Returned from desertion 14 January 1863. Assigned to extra duty in the quartermaster department and as a courier from 18 January through 31 January 1864.[747]

Wallace, George; Private, Company A: Enlisted 6 May 1863 at Shelbyville, TN. and listed as age 22 on the roll of that date.

*Walsh, Patrick. (Welch); Private, Company G: Enlisted 3 June 1861 at Camp Cheatham. Detached for hospital duty at Knoxville, TN., October 1862. Age 32 on roll dated 30 May 1863 at Shelbyville, TN. Detached by orders of General Stevenson. Captured at Vicksburg, MS., 4 July 1863. Paroled by Major John C. Fry, 20th Ohio Volunteer Infantry. Rejoined the 11th Tennessee. Detached as a teamster, driving an ambulance, February 1864 through 1 July 1864 near Marietta, GA. Surrendered and paroled with the Army of Tennessee at Greensboro, NC., 26 April 1865.

Walters, Frank; Private, Company D: Enlisted 25 May 1863 at Shelbyville, TN. Killed by Southern troops in the retreat from Shelbyville.

Ward, Hugh; Second Sergeant, Company D: Born in County Donegal, Ireland. Occupation: mason. Sworn into service 11 May 1861 at Nashville. Discharged under the conscript act, 6 May 1862. Height 5'3", fair complexion, blue eyes.

Ward, John Henry; Private, Company G, B: Born 29 August 1839 at New York, New York. Sworn into service in Company G, 10 May 1861 at Nashville. Age 22 on roll dated 30 May 1863 at Shelbyville, TN. Transferred to Company B at the reorganization, 1 May 1862. Captured on the second day of the Battle of Nashville, 16 December 1864. Sent to Camp Douglas, IL., arriving 4 January 1865. Took oath

---

[743] B. F. Shultz, "Lieut. A. H. Vaughan, Killed in the War." *Confederate Veteran* vol. 8 no. 12 (December 1900): 518.
[744] Harris, *Confederate Hospitals*, 374, 430, 189.
[745] Baker, *1860 Census for Dickson County*, 38; Maney, *Surgeon's Log*, "Chickamauga GA."
[746] Johnson, *1860 Census of Humphreys County*, 51; Clifton, *1870 Census of Humphreys County*, 23.
[747] Baker, *1860 Census for Dickson County*, 89.

12 June 1865. Hair light, eyes blue, 5' 7". Married, 17 December 1866 in Bedford Co., TN., to Tabitha W. Webb. Resided in Nashville. Occupation: merchant. Member of the Cheatham Bivouac. Died 30 December 1907. Buried Houston-Whitworth Cemetery, Bedford Co., TN.[748]

Ward, William A.; Private, Company C: Born c. 1843. Occupation: farmer. Sworn into service 14 May 1861 at Nashville. Issued a minie musket. Detached on provost guard, 28 January 1863 to Rome, GA. Age 22 on roll dated 8 May 1863 at Shelbyville, TN.[749]

Warfield, Henry C.; Second Lieutenant, Company F: Born 8 August 1842 in Robertson Co., TN. Enlisted 25 June 1861 at Camp Cheatham. Promoted from private to second sergeant around January 1864. Wounded on the second day of the Battle of Jonesboro, GA., 1 September 1864 by a ball that fractured his right humerus bone two inches below the head. Promoted to second lieutenant, 15 September 1864. Paroled 14 May 1865 at Meridian, MS. Died 9 March 1915. Buried in the Gunn Cemetery, Adams, Robertson Co., TN. Pension Application S10109.[750]

*Warren, William J. "Henry"; Private, Company K: Enlisted 21 July 1861 at Camp Cheatham. Age 18 on roll dated 15 August 1861 at Midway, TN. Wounded in the Battle of New Hope Church, GA., 27 May 1864 in the lower third of the right leg. Admitted 30 May 1864 to Fairground Hospital No. 1, Atlanta, GA. with vulnus sclopeticum. Furloughed 30 June 1864. Surrendered with the Army of Tennessee, 26 April 1865, as a member of Company K, 2nd Consolidated Tennessee Infantry. Paroled 1 May 1865.[751]

Waynick, George; Private, Company C: Born c. 1845. Occupation: farm hand. Enlisted 25 March 1863. Listed as deserting 21 April 1863.[752]

*Weakley, William Thomas; Fifth Sergeant, Company C: Born 15 April 1842 in Montgomery Co., TN. Occupation: farmer. Sworn into service 14 May 1861 at Nashville. Issued a minie musket. Age 20 on roll dated 8 May 1863. Promoted to fifth sergeant by July 1862. Shot through the top right shoulder and neck, the ball coming out under the left ear, in the Battle of Peachtree Creek, GA., 20 July 1864. Treated at Burnsville, GA. Put on detached service. Paroled 12 May 1865 at Augusta, GA. Resided at Beefrange, Dickson Co., TN. Member of the Methodist Church and a Mason. Died 5 January 1920. Buried in the Mount Zion Church Cemetery, Montgomery Co., TN. Pension Application S6626.[753]

Weaks, William Henry; Private, Company I: Born 15 October 1839 in Stewart Co., TN. Occupation: farmer. Sworn into service 20 May 1861 at Nashville. Wounded in the right hip on Clinch Mountain, TN. Age 24 on roll dated 6 May 1863 at Shelbyville, TN. Wounded in the right elbow in the Battle of Atlanta, GA., 22 July 1864. Sent to hospital at Macon, GA. then sent to Augusta, GA. In the hospital two to three months. While returning to his command, he was injured in the shoulder and elbow in a train wreck in MS. Wounded in the Battle of Franklin or Nashville, TN. Captured at Franklin, TN., 17 December 1864. Sent to U.S. prison in Louisville, KY., then to Camp Chase, OH. Took oath 16 May 1865. Light complexion, Light hair, height 6'. Occupation: farmer. Married Margaret Clementine Summers. Resided at Trinity, Humphreys Co., TN. Buried Summers Cemetery, Humphreys Co., TN.[754]

---

[748] Ward, "Eleventh Tennessee," 420; *Nashville Banner*, 31 December 1907; Helen C. Marsh, Timothy R. Marsh, and Timothy J. Edwards, *Official Marriages of Bedford County, Tennessee, 1861-1880* vol.1 (Greenville SC: Southern Historical Press, 1996) 49; *Nashville Daily Press*, 22 December 1864.

[749] Baker, *1860 Census for Dickson County*, 177; McCauley, *Record Book, Company C*.

[750] H. C. Warfield, Tennessee Confederate Pension Application, S10109; Maney, *Surgeon's Log*, "September 1864."

[751] Maney, *Surgeon's Log*, "May 1864"; Welsh, *Confederate Hospitals*, Patient Roster, Fair Ground Hospital #1, 294.

[752] Baker, *1860 Census for Dickson County*, 6.

[753] McCauley, *Record Book, Company C*; Maney, *Surgeon's Log*, "20 July 1864"; Darnell, Jones, and Alley, *Cemetery Records of Montgomery County* vol. 1, 20.

[754] Maney, *Surgeon's Log*, "Battle of Atlanta GA"; Pension Application S4023.

BIOGRAPHICAL ROSTER

Weaver, Charles H.; Private, Company D, B: Sworn into service 11 May 1861 in Company D at Nashville. Later transferred to Company B. Age 21 on roll dated 2 June 1863 at Shelbyville, TN. Captured at the Battle of Franklin, TN., 30 November 1864. Sent to Camp Douglas, IL., arriving 3 December 1864. Took oath and was discharged 12 May 1865.

*Weaver, James R.; Sergeant, Company B: Born in Huntsville, AL., 20 February 1841. Sworn into service 10 May 1861, at Nashville. Age 21 on roll dated 2 June 1863 at Shelbyville, TN. Promoted from private to second corporal, 22 June 1862. Wounded in the right foot at the Battle of Chickamauga, GA., 19 September 1863. Sent to hospital in Macon, GA. Promoted to sergeant, 1 October 1863. Wounded in the Battle of Bentonville, NC., 21 March 1865. Surrendered with the Army of Tennessee on 26 April 1865, and paroled 1 May 1865 as part of the 2nd Consolidated Tennessee Infantry. Postwar occupation: furniture maker and finisher. Member of Company B United Confederate Veterans and Cheatham Bivouac. Attended the 50th Anniversary of the Battle of Franklin, TN., 30 November 1914.[755]

Webb, Howell; Lieutenant-Colonel, Company D, Field & Staff: Born c. 1837. Occupation: attorney. Sworn into service 11 May 1861 at Nashville. Appointed Adjutant, 31 May 1861. Promoted to third lieutenant, and subsequently brevetted second lieutenant. Promoted to lieutenant-colonel, 20 April 1862, defeated in reorganization, 1 May 1862. Assistant Inspector General of the Staff of General Carter Stevenson, Spring 1862 until December 1863. Captured. Prisoner at Johnson's Island, OH., 1 January 1864.[756]

Webb, J. H.; Private, Company I: Occupation: farmer. Sworn into service 20 May 1861 in Nashville. Age 21 on roll dated 1 May 1863 at Shelbyville, TN. Wounded in the left side in the Battle of Peachtree Creek, GA., 20 July 1864. Sent to hospital 22 July 1864 in Macon, GA. Captured and sent to Camp Douglas, IL.[757]

Webb, Norman; Private, Company B: Died 9 August 1862.

Webb, William C.; Private, Company H: Sworn into service 14 May 1861 at Nashville. Wounded severely, including a broken right leg at the Battle of Murfreesboro, TN., 31 December 1862. Sent to U. S. General Field Hospital #3. Died 10 June 1863.

Weems, Corder Terrell; Private, Company K: Born in Dickson Co., TN., 22 March 1841. Brother of Private George W. Weems. Occupation: farmer. Sworn into service 25 May 1861 at Nashville. Age 21 on roll dated 15 August 1861 at Midway, TN. Detached on provost duty to Rome, GA. from 29 January 1863 to May 1863. Wounded in the Battle of Resaca, GA., 14 May 1864 and sent to the hospital. Seriously wounded in the Battle of Atlanta, GA., 22 July 1864, the minie ball entered his right arm and continued through the right side and split. One piece went through the right lung, the other penetrated the muscles of the back near the spine. The arm was not amputated as the wound was thought to be mortal. Admitted to St. Mary's Hospital, West Point, MS., 4 January 1865. Paroled 12 May 1865. Returned to reside in Dickson Co., TN. Married (1) Arminta Donnegan, 25 October 1869, (2) Roseana Frances Yates, 15 October 1876. Attended the reunion of the 11th Tennessee Infantry at Bon Aqua Springs, Hickman Co., TN., 24 September 1885. Died 1 August 1918. Buried in the Weems Cemetery, Dickson Co., TN..[758]

---

[755] James R. Weaver, Tennessee Pension Application, 11275; Maney, *Surgeon's Log*, "Chickamauga GA"; Warwick, *Williamson County Civil War Veterans*, 62; James R. Weaver, Cheatham Bivouac Application.

[756] Dobson-Sides, *1860 Davidson County Census*, 511; Joseph H. Crute, Jr. *Confederate Staff Officers*, (Powhattan VA: Derwent Books, 1982) 184; "Autographs," 131.

[757] Maney, *Surgeon's Log*, "20 July 1864."

[758] Baker, *1860 Census for Dickson County*, 45; Maney, *Surgeon's Log*, "Battle of Atlanta GA."; C. T. Weems, Pension Application, S1112; "The Reunion," *Hickman Pioneer*; Find-a-grave, "Corder Terrell Weems," http://www.findagrave.com/cgi-bin/fg.cgi?GSsr+20055&GRid=56984461&. (11 October 2013).

Weems?, Daniel; N/A., Company H: One of four known black men to serve with the 11th Tennessee Infantry. Daniel was the body servant of Major Philip Van Horn Weems. Upon Weems' fatal wounding in the Battle of Atlanta, GA., 22 July 1864, Daniel was bequeathed to Brigadier General George Washington Gordon, Weems' commander and close personal friend.[759]

Weems, George W.; Private, Company K: Born in 1842. Brother of Private Corder T. Weems. Enlisted 13 December 1862 in Dickson Co., TN. Age 19 on roll dated 1 May 1863 at Shelbyville, TN. Died in Forsyth Co., GA., 10 November 1863. Buried in the Confederate Section, City Cemetery, Forsyth, GA.[760]

Weems, Philip Van Horn; Major, Company H, Field & Staff: Born 6 November 1837. The youngest son of William Loch Weems (IV) and Anne Burchett Weems. Owner of the Bon Aqua Springs, a once famous health resort in Hickman Co., TN., which was purchased by William Loch Weems in 1837. P. V. H. Weems inherited the resort and farming operation at his father's death in 1852. In May, 1861, he enlisted as a private in the Hickman Guards, and was sworn into service 14 May 1861 at Nashville. Elected first lieutenant at the organization. Elected captain, 6 June 1861. Absent with leave December 1861, returning 15 January 1862. Reelected captain at the reorganization, 1 May 1862. Detailed for court, 27 May 1863 at Shelbyville, TN. Wounded seriously in the abdomen in the Battle of Missionary Ridge, TN., 25 November 1863. Promoted to major and transferred to the Field & Staff, 7 May 1864. Mortally wounded in the Battle of Atlanta, GA., 22 July 1864. Died 24 July 1864 at Catoosa Hospital. His funeral was held at the Methodist Church in Griffin, GA., 25 July 1864, with services conducted by Reverend George. Originally buried in the Confederate Cemetery at Griffin, GA. After the war his brothers had him disinterred and his remains returned to his home at Bon Aqua Springs, TN., the body being reinterred 31 January 1885 in the Weems Family Cemetery in Bon Aqua, Hickman Co., TN. One legend states that the body was placed in a vinegar barrel and returned home by wagon, however the body was returned by train to Bon Aqua.[761]

Weems, W. T.; Private, Company K: Sworn into service 25 May 1861 at Nashville. Discharged 25 June 1861 for disability.

Welch (Welsh), James; Private, Company C, G: Sworn into service 14 May 1861 in Company C at Nashville. Transferred to Company G at the reorganization, 1 May 1862. Discharged by surgeon's certificate for disability at Tazewell, TN., 26 August 1862.

Welch, John; Private, Company D, G: Occupation: laborer. Sworn into service 11 May 1861 in Company D at Nashville. Later transferred to Company G. Age 26 on roll dated 11 May 1863 at Shelbyville, TN. Shot in the hand in the Battle of New Hope Church, GA., 27 May 1864. Wounded on the left side of the scalp in battle near Atlanta, GA., 2 August 1864. Took oath 11 January 1865. Complexion fair, light hair, grey eyes, height 5' 9". Attended the reunion of the 11th Tennessee Infantry at Bon Aqua Springs, Hickman Co., TN., 24 September 1885.[762]

Welch, John Shadrack G.; Private, Company K: Born 7 October 1842. Sworn into service 25 May 1861 at Nashville. Age 17 on roll dated 15 August 1861 at Midway, TN. Wounded in the left shoulder in the Battle of Nashville, TN., 16 December 1864. Brought home by friends after the army left Tennessee, and was unable to do much for six months. Resided at Burns, Dickson Co., TN. Member of the Primitive Baptist Church. Died 18 August 1927. Over 400 people attended the funeral. Buried in the Martin Garton Cemetery in Dickson Co., TN. Veteran Questionnaire Vol. 5, 2156-57.[763]

---

[759] "Philip Van Horn Weems," 7.

[760] Baker, *1860 Census for Dickson County*, 45.

[761] United Daughters of the Confederacy, *Confederate Soldiers of Hickman County*, 202; Maney, *Surgeon's Log*, "Missionary Ridge TN"; Maney, *Surgeon's Log*, "Battle of Atlanta GA"; "Philip Van Horn Weems," 7; *Hickman Pioneer*, 30 January 1885; Veteran Questionnaire Vol. 5, 2155-56.

[762] Maney, *Surgeon's Log*, "August 1864"; "The Reunion," *Hickman Pioneer*.

[763] John Welch, Tennessee Confederate Pension Application, S4084; Garrett, *Dickson County Handbook*, 221; Garrett and McClain, *Dickson Cemetery Records* vol. 1, 158.

Wells, Lawrence; Private, Company D, B: Born 11 May 1836 in Dinwiddie Co., VA. Occupation: wood workman and machinist. Married Eliza Kinkade, 15 March 1858. Sworn into service 11 May 1861 in Company D at Nashville. Transferred to Company B. Listed as a carpenter. Age 25 on roll dated 5 May 1863 at Shelbyville, TN. Wounded in the left thigh in the Battle of Peachtree Creek, GA., 20 July 1864. Sent to Catoosa Hospital, Griffin, GA., 22 July 1864. Forwarded to a hospital in Forsyth, GA., then to Ocmulgee Hospital, Macon, GA. While on crutches tried to rejoin the Army of Tennessee on Hood's advance, arriving in the neighborhood of Franklin, TN. the night before Hood retreated from Nashville. Captured and took oath 27 December 1864. Complexion fair, hair light, grey eyes, 6'1". Occupied as a carpenter for the Nashville, Chattanooga, & St. Louis Railroad. Member of the Cheatham Bivouac. Died 29 December 1892.[764]

Wetmore, Oldham B.; Private, Company G: Born c. 1844 in OH. Brother of Third Sergeant William S. C. Wetmore. Enlisted 19 June 1861 at Camp Cheatham. Age 17 on roll dated 30 May 1863 at Shelbyville, TN. Discharged by virtue of the conscript act, 15 August 1862.

Wetmore, William C. S. "Bill"; Third Sergeant, Company G, B: Born in 1840 in Kentucky. Brother of Private O. B. Wetmore. Sworn into service in Company G, 10 May 1861 at Nashville. Transferred to Company B at the reorganization, 1 May 1862. Deserted and captured 20 March 1863 at Shelbyville, TN. and sent to Camp Chase, OH., 4 May 1863. Released 9 May 1863. Fair complexion, light hair, hazel eyes, 5'5".[765]

Wheat, Solomon; Private, Company A: Born c. 1843. Sworn into service 10 May 1861 at Nashville. Died 11 March 1862 at Cumberland Gap, TN.[766]

Whelan, John; Private, Company G: Born 1834 in Ireland. Became a naturalized citizen, 21 May 1856. Married Mary Dowling, 1 June 1859. Occupation: laborer. Sworn into service 10 May 1861 at Nashville. Age 26 on roll dated 10 May 1861. Wounded in the knee in the Battle of Murfreesboro, TN., 31 December 1862. Sent to General Hospital at Atlanta, GA., 23 April 1863. Returned to his company May 1863. Captured in the Battle of Missionary Ridge, TN., 25 November 1863. Sent to the U. S. Prison at Louisville, KY., then on to Rock Island Prison, IL., 9 December 1863.[767]

White, Charles W.; Private, Company A: Sworn into service 10 May 1861 at Nashville. Deserted 13 February 1863, by taking advantage of an exchange of prisoners and refused to report to his command. Listed as rejoining the 11th Tennessee in March or April, 1863. Age 22 on roll dated 6 May 1863 at Shelbyville, TN. Listed as deserting again 28 August 1863 near Chattanooga, TN.

White, George W.; Private, Company B: Sworn into service 10 May 1861 at Nashville. Left in hospital at Versailles, KY. and taken prisoner October 1862. Apparently exchanged. Age 21 on roll dated 2 June 1863 at Shelbyville, TN.

White, William Izma; Captain, Company A: Born 29 January 1832 in Humphreys Co., TN. Resided at Waverly, TN. Claims to have been the first man in Humphreys Co. to enlist in the Confederate army. Sworn into service 10 May 1861 at Nashville. Elected 2nd lieutenant at the organization. Promoted to captain, 3 May 1862. Age 28 on roll dated 6 May 1863 at Shelbyville, TN. Missed the Battles of Franklin and Nashville while on special assignment. Resigned 11 February 1865 because the regiment was consolidated with other units leaving him with no command. Sent to Augusta, GA. to be discharged. Returned to his home in Waverly after the war and was engaged in farming and the mercantile business. Married Latitia "Tishie" Fowlkes in 1867. In 1914 he was a cashier at Citizens

---

[764] Maney, *Surgeon's Log*, "20 July 1864"; Lawrence Wells, Cheatham Bivouac Application; Sistler and Sistler, *Davidson County Marriages 1838-1863*, 228; *Chattanooga Daily Rebel*, 27 July 1864.

[765] Porch, *Census of Davidson County: 1850*, 155; Dobson-Sides, *1860 Davidson County Census*, 341.

[766] Johnson, *1860 Census of Humphreys County*, 16.

[767] Maney, *Surgeon's Log*, "Stones River TN"; Dobson-Sides, *1860 Davidson County Census*, 626; Sistler and Sistler, *Davidson County Marriages 1838-1863*, 229; Smith, *Davidson County Naturalization Records*, 215.

National Bank of Waverly. Member of the Methodist Episcopal Church South, a Mason in the Waverly Lodge, and a member of the Alonzo Napier Camp No. 1390 of the United Confederate Veterans. Died 25 January 1923. Buried in the Wyly Cemetery, Waverly, Humphreys Co., TN.[768]

White, William King "Buck"; Fourth Corporal, Company H: Born 1832 in Tennessee. Relocated to Texas in 1852 before returning to Tennessee prior to the war. Sworn into service 14 May 1861 at Nashville. Elected fourth corporal, 10 June 1861. Sent to Lee Hospital at Columbus, GA., 30 September through 31 October 1864. Returned to Texas shortly after the war, residing at Aquila, Hill Co., TX. and later Waco, McLennan Co., TX. Served as a Methodist minister. Admitted to the Texas Confederate Home, Austin, TX., 12 April 1916. Died 5 July 1916. Buried in the Confederate field, Section 1, Row J, #43 of the Texas State Cemetery, Austin, TX.[769]

*White, William Marshall; Private, Company E, K: Born 1842 in Dickson Co., TN. Sworn into service 8 May 1861 in Company E at Nashville. Contracted measles while at Camp Cheatham. Age 20 on roll dated 16 August 1861 at Watauga Bridge, TN. Came down with pneumonia while at Haynesville in East Tennessee. Transferred to Company K, 1 May 1862 at Cumberland Gap, TN. Listed as a herdsman. The surgeon thought he may have suffered a slight stroke in the Battle of Lovejoy Station, GA., 2 September 1864. Surrendered with the Army of TN., 26 April 1865. Paroled 1 May 1865 at Greensboro, NC. Resident of White Bluff, Dickson Co., TN. A minister in the Missionary Baptist Church. Died 14 March 1925. Buried in the White Cemetery in Dickson Co., TN. Veteran Questionnaire vol. 5, p. 2178-9. Pension Application S1381.[770]

Whitley, T. N.; Private, Company B: Sworn into service 10 May 1861 at Nashville. Detached to quartermaster department at Morristown, TN., September through October, 1862. Age 26 on roll dated 25 June 1863 at Shelbyville, TN. Listed as deserting 23 December 1864 at Dalton, GA.

Wilkins, Carroll C.; First Corporal; Company E: Born c. 1839. Occupation: farmer. Sworn into service 18 May 1861 at Nashville. Discharged 4 June 1861 at Camp Cheatham.[771]

Willard, William W.; First Sergeant, Company D: Sworn into service 11 May 1861 at Nashville. Promoted to first sergeant by July 1862. Age 23 on roll dated 5 May 1863 at Shelbyville, TN. Killed in the Battle of Jonesboro, GA., 1 September 1864.[772]

Williams, Arrestes B.; Second Lieutenant, Company C: Born 16 September 1836 in Dickson Co., TN. Married Mary Street, 3 September 1856. Sworn into service 14 May 1861 at Nashville. Elected second sergeant at organization. Issued an Enfield rifle. Elected second lieutenant at reorganization, 1 May 1862. Age 25 on roll dated 1 May 1862. Resigned due to poor health, 17 June 1862. Eyes gray, hair black, complexion light, 5' 6". Died 27 June 1913. Buried in the Dickson Union Cemetery, Dickson Co., TN.[773]

Williams, E. L.; Private, Company G: Sworn into service 10 May 1861 at Nashville. Discharged for disability 16 December 1861.

Williams, Felix G.; Private, Company E: Born in Humphreys Co., TN., 3 April 1836. Sworn into service 18 May 1861 at Nashville. Age 24 on roll dated 16 August 1861 at Watauga Bridge, TN.

---

[768] Goodspeed Brothers, *Goodspeed's Histories of Montgomery, Robertson, Humphreys, Stewart, Dickson, Cheatham, Houston Counties*, 1283; White, "Veterans Questionnaire," 2177-78; Carnell, "Captain William I. White," 187; W. I. White, Tennessee Pension Application, 12320.

[769] Spence, *Travels*, June 4, 1861; Masters, "Story of Reagan Barr," 5-6; William K. White, Texas Confederate Soldiers Home Application; William K. White, Texas Confederate Pension Application.

[770] William M. White, Tennessee Pension Application, 1381; W. M. White, "Veteran Questionnaire" vol. 5, 2178-79; Garrett, *Dickson County Handbook*, 222; *Tennessee Death Records*, Tennessee State Library and Archives, www.tn.gov/tsla/history/vital1925-18.htm. (2 February 2002).

[771] Baker, *1850 Census for Dickson County*, 29.

[772] Maney, *Surgeon's Log*, "September 1864."

[773] Garrett, *Dickson County Handbook*, 222; McCauley, *Record Book, Company C*; Baker, *1850 Census for Dickson County*, 131.

Wounded in Kentucky. Wounded again in the Battle of Missionary Ridge, TN., 25 November 1863, being hit in the head by a shell fragment and shot twice in the right leg below the knee. Deserted 12 December 1864 near Nashville. Later took oath. Fair complexion, brown hair, grey eyes, 5'10". Resided at Beefrange, Dickson Co., TN. Died 24 May 1911.[774]

Williams, George Coleman; Private, Company C: Born 31 October 1846 in Dickson Co., TN. Sworn into service 14 May 1861 at Nashville. Discharged 25 July 1861. Age 18 on roll dated 8 May 1863. Died 9 March 1919. Buried in the Coleman Williams Cemetery, Dickson Co., TN.[775]

Williams, George Washington; Private, Company F: Born 27 September 1844 in Davidson Co., TN. Enlisted 18 May 1861 at Cedar Hill. Discharged 7 August 1862 at Tazewell, TN. Later served as a private in Company A, 8th Kentucky Mounted Infantry, Confederate. Resided in Logan Co., KY., where he died 6 October 1931. Pension Application Kentucky Application 1987 Logan (1912).[776]

Williams, Henry Andrews; Second Lieutenant, Company C: Sworn into service 14 May 1861 at Nashville. Age 24 on roll dated 8 May 1863. Wounded in the forearm, 31 December 1862 in the Battle of Murfreesboro, TN. Captured and sent to City Point, VA., on the James River. Later exchanged and rejoined the 11th Tennessee, 2 March 1863 at Shelbyville, TN. Later promoted from first sergeant to second lieutenant, 21 March 1864. Admitted to Catoosa Hospital, Griffin, GA., 22 July 1864. Wounded again 19 August 1864 near Atlanta, GA.[777]

Williams, James Richard "Red"; Private, Company C: Born 22 March 1844. Sworn into service 14 May 1861 at Nashville. Issued a minie musket. Listed as a teamster. Age 28 on roll dated 8 May 1863. Transferred to Company E, 10th Tennessee Cavalry, 1 August 1863.[778]

Williams, James R.; Second Corporal, Company F: Enlisted 18 May 1861 at Cedar Hill. Left in hospital at Versailles, KY. Captured, paroled, and went home. Later rejoined the regiment and was promoted to second corporal, 11 January 1862. Captured again at Andersonville, TN., 3 October 1863. Listed in U. S. Post and Prison Hospital at Alton, IL., 12 January 1864 with small pox.

Williams, John L.; Private, Company E: Captured at Ringgold, GA, 26 November 1863. Sent to Rock Island Prison, IL. Light complexion, brown hair, 6'4." Age 23 on roll dated 21 April 1864 at Rock Island, IL. Took oath and was paroled at Richmond, VA., 25 July 1865. Complexion, dark, dark hair, grey eyes, 5'8".

Williams, Joseph R.; Private, Company E: Born c. 1839. Occupation farmhand. Sworn into service on 18 May 1861 in Nashville. Discharged 15 June 1861 at Camp Cheatham.[779]

Williams, L. W.; Private, Company B: Sworn into service on 10 May 1861 at Nashville. Discharged 5 September 1861 at Knoxville, TN., by surgeon's certificate of disability.

Williams, Stephen T.; Private, Company E: Born c. 1840. Occupation: farmhand. Sworn into service 18 May 1861 at Nashville. Age 21 on roll dated 16 August 1861 at Watauga Bridge, TN. Killed at Kennesaw Mountain, GA., 21 June 1864.[780]

Willis, Benjamin F.; Private, Company H: Enlisted 3 February 1863 at Shelbyville, TN. Captured at Nickajack Creek, GA., near Marietta, 5 July 1864. Sent to Camp Douglas, IL. Discharged 12 May 1865. Complexion fair, black hair, grey eyes, 5'9".

*Wilson, Aubrey; Captain, Company G, B, Field & Staff: Born c. 1831 in Louisiana. Occupation: carpenter. Sworn into service on 10 May 1861 in Company G at Nashville. Promoted to second corporal by March 1862. Transferred to Company B at the reorganization, 1 May 1862. Promoted to fifth sergeant, 1 February 1863. Age 31 on roll dated 2 June 1863. Listed as captain of Company K, 2nd

---

[774] Felix G. Williams, Tennessee Pension Application, 6038.
[775] McCauley Camp 260, *Confederate Graves*, 53.
[776] Lynn, *Confederate Pensioners of Kentucky*, 249.
[777] *Chattanooga Daily Rebel*, 25 July 1864.
[778] McCauley, *McCauley, Record Book, Company C*; McCauley Camp 260, *Confederate Graves*, 53.
[779] Baker, *1860 Census for Dickson County*, 143.
[780] Maney, *Surgeon's Log*, "Kennesaw Mountain GA"

Tennessee Consolidated Infantry, April 1865. Surrendered and paroled with the Army of Tennessee, 26 April 1865.

Wilson, Daniel W.; First Sergeant, Company I: Occupation: farmer. Brother of Private John and First Lieutenant Samuel Wilson. Sworn into service on 20 May 1861 at Nashville. Age 19 on roll dated 6 May 1863. Promoted to fifth sergeant, 1 May 1862. Promoted to fourth sergeant, 25 April 1863. Later promoted to third sergeant then to first sergeant, 1 August 1863. Wounded slightly in the right ankle at Missionary Ridge, 25 November 1863. Sent to hospital at Marietta, GA. Paroled as part of 2nd Consolidated Tennessee Infantry at surrender. Resided at Watson, Desha Co., AR. Pension Application, Arkansas, Desha Co., 1915.[781]

Wilson, Gilbert R. "Dick"; Fifth Sergeant, Company C, E: Born in 1842 in Dickson Co., TN. Sworn into service 14 May 1861 in Company C at Nashville. Transferred to Company E, at the reorganization, 1 May 1862. Promoted to fifth sergeant by July 1862. Wounded in the arm at the Battle of Murfreesboro, TN, 31 December 1862. Captured 3 January 1863 at Murfreesboro. Sent to City Point, VA. Admitted to the General Hospital in Petersburg, VA., 2 April 1863 with a gunshot wound to the right arm.

Wilson, John D.; Private, Company I: Brother of First Seageant and First Lieutenant Samuel Wilson. Enlisted 1 April 1863 at Shelbyville, TN. Took oath 11 May 1865 at Nashville. Fair complexion, dark hair, blue eyes, 5'7".

Wilson, Samuel M.; First Lieutenant, Company I: Brother of Private John and First Seargeant Daniel Wilson. Sworn into service on 20 May 1861 at Nashville. Promoted from third sergeant to first lieutenant, 1 May 1862. Slightly wounded on the head in the Battle of Murfreesboro, TN, 31 December 1862. Age 20 on roll dated 8 May 1863. Wounded in the Battle of Franklin, TN, 30 November 1864. Resided at Tennessee Ridge, Houston Co., TN. Member of the Cumberland Presbyterian Church.[782]

Winn, John Henderson; Third Corporal, Company F: Born 19 January 1833. Enlisted 18 May 1861 at Cedar Hill. Elected third corporal, later went back to private. Listed as a pioneer. Captured on the second day of the Battle of Nashville, TN., 16 December 1864. Sent to Camp Chase, OH. Dark complexion, dark hair, grey eyes. Married Mary I. Ward, 1 December 1881. Died 29 May 1892. Buried in the Winn Cemetery, Cedar Hill, Robertson Co., TN.

Winn, John W. Jr.; Private, Company I: Born c. 1832. Occupation: farm laborer. Enlisted 20 June 1863 at Shelbyville, TN. Wounded slightly in the left hand during the Battle of Missionary Ridge, TN., 25 November 1863. Sent to hospital and captured. Sent to U. S. Prison in Louisville, KY. Took oath 19 June 1864. Complexion dark, hair light, eyes blue, 5' 9". Ordered to be released north of the Ohio River by order of Major General Thomas. Wife named Arena.[783]

Winn, William Hunley "Button"; Second Lieutenant, Company F: Born in Sumner Co., TN., 30 April 1828. Enlisted 18 May 1861 at Cedar Hill. Made third lieutenant in May 1861. Later promoted to second lieutenant. Listed as present but sick, December 1861, and on leave, 10 January 1862. Dropped from the roll 1 May 1862. He later organized a cavalry company of scouts, of which he was captain after joining General John Hunt Morgan at Gallatin. He was among a party of ten sent ahead to scout the raid into Ohio, but was captured while returning to Morgan's headquarters. He was held at Camp Dick Robinson, and later removed to Lexington, KY., then to Cincinnati, OH. and afterward to Camp Douglas, IL. He escaped in February 1864, and lived with a family sympathetic to the South in Carbondale, IL. Following the war, in 1867 he relocated to southeastern Kansas, and later was engaged in merchandising in connection with the construction of the Missouri, Kansas and Texas Railroad through the Indian nation. From 1872 until 1881, he lived in Dennison, TX., which became a boom town when the railroad arrived, and later served as its mayor. In 1881 he moved to El Paso, TX. and became an investor in mining and cattle interests. In 1892 he was elected county assessor and served until

---

[781] Maney, *Surgeon's Log*, "Missionary Ridge TN."
[782] Trogdon, "Interesting Letter."
[783] Maney, *Surgeon's Log*, "Missionary Ridge TN."

1898, later serving as general manager of the Western Abstract Company of El Paso, Inc. prior to his death on 15 May 1907 at age 79. Buried Evergreen Alameda Cemetery, El Paso, El Paso Co., TX.[784]

Winstead, Thomas H.; Private, Company A: Born 28 March 1839. Married Alice K. Wright. Occupation: farmer. Sworn into service on 10 May 1861 at Nashville. Discharged 28 October 1861 for disability. Died 16 August 1903. Buried in the Knight Cemetery, Humphreys Co., TN.[785]

Winters, John A.; Private, Company F: Born 18 November 1823. Resident of Robertson Co., TN. Enlisted 23 July 1861 at Camp Cheatham. Discharged at Tazewell, TN., 17 August 1862. Later took oath to avoid arrest. Died 23 November 1913. Buried in the Winters Cemetery, Robertson Co., TN.[786]

Witty, Horatio "Rash"; Second Sergeant, Company G: Born c. 1839. Listed as age 21 in 1860 census. Sworn into service 10 May 1861 at Nashville. Discharged 30 August 1861 for disability. Later joined McNairy's Cavalry. Occupation: Attorney. Died of a liver disease. Interred 30 May 1871 in the Nashville City Cemetery.[787]

Woodruff, Charles W.; Private, Company F: Occupation: farmer. Brother to Private William B. Woodruff, as well as first cousin of Private William Bennett Elliott. Enlisted 18 May 1861 at Cedar Hill. Sent to hospital at Knoxville, TN., 14 November 1862. Received multiple wounds in the Battle of Atlanta, GA., 22 July 1864. Right arm amputated at the middle third. Died from the wounds in August 1864.[788]

Woodruff, William B.; Private, Company F: Brother to Private Charles W. Woodruff, as well as first cousin of William Bennett Elliott. Enlisted 23 July 1861 at Camp Cheatham. Killed in the Battle of Franklin, TN., 30 November 1864, age 27. Buried in the McGavock Confederate Cemetery at Franklin, TN., section 54, grave 46.[789]

Woods, James; Private, Company G: Enlisted 3 June 1861 at Camp Cheatham. Deserted 24 April 1863.

Woodward, John D.; Captain, Company I: Born c. 1820. Occupation: farmer. Sworn into service on 20 May 1861 at Nashville. Elected second lieutenant. Promoted to captain, 1 June 1861. Resigned 1 August 1861.[790]

Work, John Holmes; Private, Company H: Enlisted 10 January 1863 at Shelbyville, TN. Listed as deserting when Chattanooga was evacuated, 8 September 1863, taking his gun and equipment.

Work, Robert J. "Dude"; Second Lieutenant, Company H: Born 8 August 1841. Occupation: farmer. Sworn into service on 14 May 1861 at Nashville. Appointed fourth corporal, 24 March 1862. Elected second sergeant 1 May 1862. Promoted to third lieutenant, then received a brevet commission to second lieutenant. Wounded in the left shoulder at Missionary Ridge, TN., 25 November 1863. Wounded in the right leg at New Hope Church, GA., 27 May 1864. Resigned 26 September 1864 and asked for transfer to cavalry. Given a medical discharge at Tuscumbia, AL. in 1864. Captured by Federals in Hickman Co., TN. upon his return home. Held prisoner near Waverly, TN. Took oath 2 December 1864 at Nashville. Complexion dark, eyes hazel, hair dark, height 5' 8". He would frequently show his leg

---

[784] Goodspeed Brothers, *Goodspeed's Histories of Montgomery, Robertson, Humphreys, Stewart, Dickson, Cheatham, Houston Counties*, 856; *Mayfield Weekly Messenger*, 17 May 1907.

[785] Fischer and Burns, *1880 Census of Humphreys County*, 67; Anderson, and Garrett, *Humphreys County, Tennessee, Cemetery Records* vol. 1, 75; Anderson, and Garrett, *Humphreys County, Tennessee, Cemetery Records* vol. 2, 211.

[786] John A. Winters, Tennessee Pension Application, 5623; Durrett, Williams, and Reid, *Robertson County Cemetery Records*, 213.

[787] *Nashville Daily Patriot*, 31 December 1861; Tennessee State Library and Archives. *Index to Interments in the Nashville City Cemetery, 1846-1962* (Nashville TN: Tennessee State Library and Archives, 1964) 87.

[788] Maney, *Surgeon's Log*, "Battle of Atlanta GA."

[789] Hudgins and Potts, *McGavock Cemetery*, 32.

[790] Johnson, *1860 Census of Humphreys County*, 78.

wound and remark, "look at what those damned Yankees did - shot me through the leg there, but, by God, they didn't get me, though." Married Lisa T. Bingham. Member of the County Court. Member of the Masonic order and of the United Confederate Veterans. Resided along Piney River. Served in the 47th Tennessee General Assembly 1891-93. Died 9 August 1920, one day after his 79th birthday. Buried with Masonic honors at Dickson Union Cemetery, Dickson, Co., TN.[791]

Wright, George; Private, Company A: Sworn into service 10 September 1861 at Cumberland Gap, TN. Listed as deserting 6 October 1862.

Wright, Monroe M.; Fourth Sergeant, Company H: Sworn into service 14 May 1861. Elected fourth sergeant 1 May 1862. Killed at the Battle of Murfreesboro, TN., 31 December 1862.

Wyatt, Christopher C.; Private, Company I: Born c. 1842. Brother of Second Lieutenant William M. Wyatt. Sworn into service on 20 May 1861 at Nashville. Died 10 July 1861 at home in Humphreys Co.[792]

Wyatt, William M.; Brevet Second Lieutenant, Company I: Born 1 October 1840 in Houston Co., TN. Brother of Private C. C. Wyatt. Sworn into service 3 May 1861. Brevetted second lieutenant, 1 August 1861. Resigned 1 October 1861 due to ill health. Later enlisted in the 10th Tennessee Cavalry. Captured and sent to prison at Rock Island, IL. Following the war he returned home to Bakerville, Humphreys Co., TN., and engaged in general merchandising and farming. Married C. J. Martin, 3 April 1872. Later married 2) Izora Stanfield. Politically a Republican and elected magistrate of the 12th district for six years. Served as editor and publisher of the *Bakerville Review*. Buried Bakerville Cemetery, Humphreys Co., TN.[793]

Wyly, Harris K.; Private, Company A: Born 11 November 1844. Son of wealthy merchant, planter, and slaveholder, John Wyly. First cousin to Major Hugh Ross Lucas. Enlisted 8 August 1861 at Camp Bateman. Home on furlough, 13–30 December 1861. Related by marriage to Alonzo Napier, who raised a cavalry unit in early 1862. He decided to join the cavalry and did so by providing a substitute and was discharged from the 11th Tennessee Infantry at Thorn Hill, TN., 19 June 1862. Enlisted as a private in Napier's Cavalry Battalion. Served as second lieutenant in Company D when the unit was reorganized into the 10th Tennessee Cavalry. Captured and held prisoner at Fort Donelson, TN., in early 1863. In a letter from prison, he wrote: "I am looking for the rope that is to make me dance in the air, but I have one consolation and that is they would never kill a truer patriot to his country." Paroled or escaped and returned to active duty. The Wyly home in Waverly was burned by the Federals, forcing the family to relocate to nearby Paris, TN., where he married Pocahontas "Poca" Bruce, 3 April 1865. Six days later, on 9 April, Wyly was attacked and killed by a force of Federal mounted infantry commanded by Lieutenant-Colonel E. C. Brott. Buried in the Wyly Cemetery, Waverly, Humphreys Co., TN.[794]

Wynn, John A.; Rank unknown, Company C: Fatally wounded in the Battle of Franklin, TN., 30 November 1864.[795]

Wynn, John Ellison; Private, Company F: Born 1841 in Trigg Co., KY. Resided in Caldwell Co., KY. Enlisted 18 May 1861 at Cedar Hill. Listed as a teamster. Sent with wounded to hospital at Rome,

---

[791] Garrett, *Dickson County Handbook*, 222; Maney, *Surgeon's Log*, "Missionary Ridge TN"; Maney, *Surgeon's Log*, "May 1864"; Lee Seifert Greene, *Lead Me On: Frank Goad Clement and Tennessee Politics* (Knoxville TN: University of Tennessee Press, 1982) 8; *Dickson County Herald*, 12 August 1920. R. J. Work, Tennessee Pension Application, 7999.

[792] Johnson, *1860 Census of Humphreys County*, 75.

[793] Goodspeed Brothers, *Goodspeed's Histories of Montgomery, Robertson, Humphreys, Stewart, Dickson, Cheatham, Houston Counties*, 1286; Johnson, *1860 Census of Humphreys County*, 75; Clifton, *1870 Census of Humphreys County*, 191; Fischer and Burns, *1880 Census of Humphreys County*, 159.

[794] Anderson and Garrett, *Humphreys County Cemetery Records*, 309; Smith, *Wyly Saga*, 68, 72-73.

[795] Daniel Grimes, Colored Man's Application for Pension.

GA. from Murfreesboro, 3 January 1863. Captured in 1864. Died in 1921. Buried in the Cedar Hill Cemetery, Princeton, Caldwell Co., KY. Pension Application Kentucky 1147 Caldwell (1912).[796]

Wynn, John Wesley "Wes"; Private, Company F: Born 1 November 1842 near Barren Plains, TN. Enlisted 18 May 1861 at Cedar Hill. In hospital just prior to 14 July 1864. Took oath 11 February 1865. Fair complexion, light hair, blue eyes, 5'10". Following the war he resided in Plainview, TX.[797]

Wynn, Samuel; Private, Company F: Enlisted 1 August 1862 at Cumberland Gap, TN. Left at the hospital at Versailles, KY., 6 October 1862. Captured, paroled, went home.

–Y–

Yager, Jacob; Private, Company E: Born in Wittenburg, Germany. Occupation: farmer. Sworn into service on 18 May 1861 at Nashville. Age 50 on roll dated 16 August 1861 at Watauga Bridge, TN. Discharged at Cumberland Gap, TN., 7 May 1862 on certificate of disability due to severe rheumatism and swelling in legs. Light complexion, 6', black eyes, gray hair.

Yates, Clayton H.; Third Sergeant, Company K: Born 14 February 1841 in Williamson Co., TN. Occupation: farmer. Sworn into service 25 May 1861 at Nashville. Age 21 on roll dated 15 August 1861 at Midway, TN. Promoted to fifth sergeant by July 1862, and fourth sergeant by January 1863. Wounded in the left shoulder near Atlanta, GA., 28 July 1864. Sent to hospital. Listed as deserting, 12 April 1865. Resided in Graves Co., KY., where he was a minister of the Methodist church. Died 31 May 1915. Buried in the Bethlehem Methodist Church Cemetery, Graves Co., KY. Pension Application Kentucky 1574 (1912).[798]

Yates, James H.; Corporal, Company H: Occupation: farmer. Sworn into service at Nashville on 14 May 1861. Served as nurse in hospital at Bean Station, TN., 1 November 1861 to March 1863. Appointed corporal, 10 June 1863. Listed in hospital at Columbus, GA., 30 September 1863 until 31 October 1863. Wounded through the left hand in the Battle of Atlanta, GA., 22 July 1864. Admitted to Qunitard Hospital, Griffin, GA., 22 July 1864.[799]

Yeatman, Henry Thornton Jr.; Sergeant-Major, Company K, Field & Staff: Born c1845 in Davidson Co., TN. Brother in law of Gen. James E. Rains. Sworn into service 9 May 1861 at Nashville. Age 19 on roll dated 15 August 1861 at Midway, TN. Transferred to the artillery where he served until 18 December 1862, when he became aide-de-camp to General James E. Rains. Following Rains' death, he joined the staff of General W. B. Bate and requested a commission in the regular army. Dark complexion, light hair, light eyes. He was living in Georgia in 1910.

Young, Archibald; Private, Company H: Enlisted 10 January 1863 at Shelbyville, TN. Captured at the Battle of Chickamauga, GA., 19 September 1863. Sent to U. S. Military Prison at Louisville, KY. Took oath 28 September 1863. Enlisted in the 48th Kentucky, U. S. Fair complexion, brown hair, hazel eyes, 5'5".

Young, B. F.; Private, Company A: Listed as deserter 17 June 1862 near Cumberland Gap, TN.

Young, Isaac Pavatt; Captain, Company I: Born 27 June 1838 in Humphreys Co., TN. Occupation: farmer. Sworn into service 20 May 1861 at Nashville. Elected second corporal at the organization. Elected captain at the reorganization, 1 May 1862. Wounded severely in both legs, 31 December 1862 at the Battle of Murfreesboro, TN. Captured 5 January 1863 at Murfreesboro. Sent to the penitentiary at Nashville, then to Camp Chase, OH., 27 March 1863. Forwarded to City Point, VA. for exchange, 29 April 1963. Rejoined command. Age 24 on roll dated 6 May 1863 at Shelbyville, TN. Suffered a wound on the left ankle in the Battle of Peachtree Creek, GA., 20 July 1864. Admitted to Ocmulgee Hospital,

---

[796] Lynn, *Confederate Pensioners of Kentucky*, 255.
[797] Jackson, "Letter to Parents," 14 July 1864; Yeary, *Reminiscences*, 826-28.
[798] Maney, *Surgeon's Log*, "28-31 July 1864"; Lynn, *Confederate Pensioners of Kentucky*, 256.
[799] Maney, *Surgeon's Log*, "Battle of Atlanta GA.;" *Chattanooga Daily Rebel*, 27 July 1864.

Macon GA., 22 July 1864. Wounded in the hip by a minie ball during the Battle of Franklin, TN., 30 November 1864, the ball remaining there until removed in 1882, by Drs. Brown, Slayden, and G. W. McMurray. Given a 60 day medical leave of absence from the Army of Tennessee at Tupelo, MS. by Special Order No. 14, dated 19 January 1865. Paroled 12 May 1865, at Meridian, MS. Following the war he returned to Humphreys Co. and engaged in the tanning business. Married America Edwards in December, 1865. One of his sons was named Gordon in respect of General George W. Gordon. Purchased a farm on Tumbling Creek in 1885. First joining the Cumberland Presbyterian Church, where he served as an elder, in 1886 he joined the Primitive Baptist Church, serving as clerk and remaining a member there until his death, 16 December 1909. Politically a Democrat. Buried at the Young Cemetery, Bold Springs, Humphreys Co., TN.[800]

Young, Jacob M.; Private, Company A: Enlisted 8 August 1861 at Camp Bateman. On 30 day sick furlough beginning 28 May 1862. Listed as a deserter 13 February 1863 and on roll dated 6 May 1863 at Shelbyville, TN., when listed as age 21.

Young, John B.; Private, Company A: Enlisted 1 September 1861 at Cumberland Gap, TN. Listed as a deserter 1 July 1862. Returned and reenlisted 18 February 1863 at Shelbyville, TN., Age 28. Died 17 April 1863 from febris typhoides at Academy Hospital, Chattanooga, TN. Buried in the Confederate Cemetery, Chattanooga, TN.

-Z-

Zachary, George W.; Private, Company D: Born c. 1844 in Kentucky. Enlisted 14 June 1863 at Shelbyville, TN. Captured at the Battle of Missionary Ridge, TN., 25 November 1863. Sent to U.S. prison at Louisville, KY., then to Rock Island, IL., 9 December 1863.[801]

---

[800] Maney, *Surgeon's Log*, "Stones River TN"; Maney, *Surgeon's Log*, "20 July 1864"; Goodspeed Brothers, *Goodspeed's Histories of Montgomery, Robertson, Humphreys, Stewart, Dickson, Cheatham, Houston Counties*, 1288; "Young, J.P." [sic., I.P.] *Confederate Veteran* vol. 18 no. 2 (February 1910) 88; Young, *Memoriam*.

[801] Dobson-Sides, *1860 Davidson County Census*, 719.

Appendix 1

2nd Tennessee Infantry Regiment (Redesignated 11th Tennessee)
First Organization
31 May 1861
Field & Staff

Colonel	James E. Rains
Lieutenant-Colonel	Thomas P. Bateman
Major	Hugh R. Lucas
Adjutant	Howell Webb
Quartermaster	Ephriam F. Cheatham
Surgeon	James M. Larkins
Assistant Surgeon	William B. Maney, M.D.
Chaplain	Rev. Fountain E. Pitts, D.D.
Acting Commissary of Subsistence	Jerome S. Ridley

Company A—The Hermitage Guards, Davidson County

Captain	John E. Binns
First Lieutenant	Benjamin W. McCann
Second Lieutenant	Alex R. M. McDaniel
Third Lieutenant	James L. Sloan

Company B—The Beauregard Light Infantry ("Bull Pups"), Davidson County

Captain	Samuel C. Godshall
First Lieutenant	Samuel D. Nichol
Second Lieutenant	Edward J. Guilford
Third Lieutenant	John E. Chandler

Company C—The Dickson Rifles, Dickson County

Captain	William H. Green
First Lieutenant	William J. Mathis
Second Lieutenant	William H. Roberts
Third Lieutenant	Sanford Hendricks

Company D—The Washington Guards, Robertson County

Captain	James A. Long
First Lieutenant	Martin V. Morris
Second Lieutenant	W. H. Winn
Third Lieutenant	Samuel J. Alley

Company E—The Dickson County Slashers, Dickson County

Captain	William J. Mallory
First Lieutenant	Robert A. W. James
Second Lieutenant	William M. Kirk
Third Lieutenant	Alexander Y. Brown

Company F—The Cheatham Rifles, Davidson County

Captain	J. Richard McCann
First Lieutenant	William T. Cheatham
Second Lieutenant	James Everett
Third Lieutenant	Edward W. Clark

Company G—The Waverly Guards, Humphreys County

Captain	Josiah Pitts
First Lieutenant	William I. White
Second Lieutenant	Thomas B. Traylor
Third Lieutenant	William M. Bowen

Company H—Thedford's Company, Dickson County

Captain	William R. Thedford
First Lieutenant	Franklin F. Tidwell
Second Lieutenant	Moses H. Meek
Third Lieutenant	Josiah Tidwell

Company I—The Hickman Guards, Hickman County

Captain	Phillip V. H. Weems
First Lieutenant	William C. Jones
Second Lieutenant	Richard C. Gordon
Third Lieutenant	Alexander H. Vaughan

Company K—The Gheber Guards, Humphreys County

Captain	John D. Woodward
First Lieutenant	Castillo M. Barfield
Second Lieutenant	Leroy Traylor
Third Lieutenant	William Wyatt

Appendix 2

11th Tennessee Infantry Regiment
Second Organization
1 May 1862
Field & Staff

Colonel	James E. Rains
Lieutenant-Colonel	George W. Gordon
Major	William R. Thedford
Adjutant	William J. Mathis
Quartermaster	H. R. Shacklett
Surgeon	William B. Maney, MD
Assistant Surgeon	W. J. Barron, M.D.
Chaplain	Rev. G. P. Jamison
Acting Commissary of Subsistence	Jerome S. Ridley

Company A—(Formerly Company G) Waverly Guards, Humphreys County

Captain	William I. White
1st Lieutenant	George D. Ridings
2nd Lieutenant	John McGill
3rd Lieutenant	Reuben F. Beasley

Company B—(Formerly Company F) The Cheatham Rifles, Davidson County

Captain	E. W. Clarke
1st Lieutenant	Samuel Stout
2nd Lieutenant	William Nichol
3rd Lieutenant	James R. Douglass

Company C—(Formerly C) The Dickson Rifles, Dickson County

Captain	William H. Green
1st Lieutenant	William H. McCauley
2nd Lieutenant	B. Williams
3rd Lieutenant	William M. Slayden

Company D—(Formerly Company A) The Hermitage Guards—Davidson County

Captain	John E. Binns
1st Lieutenant	R. M. McDaniel
2nd Lieutenant	Hugh Heverin
3rd Lieutenant	Lafayette Hunley

Company E—(Formerly E) The Dickson County Slashers, Dickson County

Captain	R. A. W. James
1st Lieutenant	Alexander Y. Brown
2nd Lieutenant	William Eleazer
3rd Lieutenant	Thomas Lane

Company F—(Formerly Company D) The Washington Guards—Robertson County

Captain	James A. Long
1st Lieutenant	James H. Darden
2nd Lieutenant	Thomas B. Jones
3rd Lieutenant	William H. Winn

Company G—(Formerly Company B) The Bull Pups, Beauregard Light Infantry—Davidson County

Captain	Edward J. Guilford
1st Lieutenant	James G. Stephens
2nd Lieutenant	Thomas Irwin
3rd Lieutenant	Michael J. Lawler

Company H—(Formerly I) The Hickman Guards, Centerville Guards—Hickman County

Captain	Philip Van Horn Weems
1st Lieutenant	Richard C. Gordon
2nd Lieutenant	Jacob H. Johnson
3rd Lieutenant	Ephraim A. Dean

Company I—(Formerly Company K) The Gheber Guards, Humphreys County

Captain	Isaac P. Young
1st Lieutenant	Samuel M. Wilson
2nd Lieutenant	Richmond "Richard" McCauley
3rd Lieutenant	William H. Baker

Company K—(Formerly Company H)—Dickson County

Captain	F. F. Tidwell
1st Lieutenant	David Rice
2nd Lieutenant	John W. Phillips
3rd Lieutenant	Aquilla Marsh

Appendix 3

"Camp Cheatham and the Boys"
By Sergeant W. Jerome D. Spence
3 July 1861, Camp Cheatham, Robertson County, Tennessee

Camp Cheatham is a lively place,
As all we fellows know,
And lively boys are stationed here—
Oh! Fellows ain't it so?

They curse and swear and rip and tear;
They cook and wash and eat,
The cooking's right, they eat a sight;
Their washing, O, it's neat.

Camp Cheatham is a lively place,
As everybody knows,
And fighting boys are ready here
To meet the coming foes.

They see their fun, they rip, they run
Until it's time to drill;
The roll they call, which finds them all,
At General Cheatham's will.

Camp Cheatham is a lively place,
And lively boys are here;
They ask not odds of mortal man—
Their equal they don't fear.

They've plenty of tin and no poor kin,
And friends a plenty too.
To cook and eat their bread and meat
Is almost all they do.

Camp Cheatham is a stirring place,
And stirring boys are here;
They ne'er put on their Sunday clothes,
For they're too nice to wear

Sometimes they wash, but then begosh,
The difference they can't tell—
They rear and curse and swear
And wash their clothes in—(well)

Camp Cheatham is the very place,
The "tactics" for to learn
A part they practice in the field,
But in the tents they yarn.

And in the tent each fellow's bent
To tell some courting spree
With the lovely lass in days to pass
A soldier's wife to be.

Camp Cheatham is the very place
To get your money back;
They'll teach you when to play the ace
To catch a fellow's jack.

At "Chuck-a-luck" and "seven-up"
They always put 'em through;
When done with this, they never miss
To get up something new.

Camp Cheatham boys and just such boys,
On whom the South depends
Will do the best that they can do
To try to meet the ends.

Should Northern foes, our way oppose
With shot and shell and steel;
Oh! Then 'twill be that Tennessee
Will into column wheel.

Camp Cheatham Boys are trusty boys;
They are ladies' fighting men.
They'll fight for you, till peace returns—
Oh! Then gals. Oh! Then!

Have something neat for them to eat,
For they are coming home
And marry you, to promise true;
Be ready when they come.

Appendix 4

Killed, Wounded, Captured, and Missing of the 11th Tennessee Infantry by Battle

Wildcat, KY. 21 October 1861

Name	Rank	Company	Disposition
Brown, James M.	Pvt.	E	Wounded
Brown, John	Pvt.	K	Wounded
Burns, William E.	Cpl.	D	Wounded
Gray, James	Pvt.	A	Wounded
Hansberry, John	Pvt.	G	Wounded
Scott, Robert T.	Pvt.	E	Wounded

Killed - 0
Wounded - 6
Captured - 0
Wounded and Captured - 0
Missing - 0
Total - 6

Tazewell, TN. 6 August 1862

Name	Rank	Company	Disposition
Gordon, George W.	Lt.-Col.	F&S	Captured

Killed - 0
Wounded - 0
Captured - 1
Wounded and Captured -
Missing - 0
Total - 1

Murfreesboro, TN. 30 December 1862

Name	Rank	Company	Disposition
Adams, J. I. J.	Pvt.	C	Wounded
Adams, William T.	Pvt.	C	Wounded
Andrews, Elijah S.	1st Corp.	A	Wounded
Baker, George W.	Pvt.	C	Captured
Baker, W. J.	Pvt.	C	Captured
Barr, James F.	Pvt.	H	Wounded
Baxter, William M.	Pvt.	H	Wounded
Beasley, Reuben F.	2nd Lt.	A	Wounded
Bibb, Epaminondas	Pvt.	H	Wounded
Biter, W. A. J.	Pvt.	C	Wounded
Brooks, Milton O.	2nd Lt.	G	Wounded and Captured

APPENDIX 4

Brown, W. J.	Pvt.	A	Captured
Brown, William J.	Pvt.	A	Captured
Bunn, William T.	Pvt.	A	Missing
Carroll, James J.	Pvt.	K	Wounded
Carter, Green W.	Pvt.	I	Captured
Chandler, Joseph K.	2nd Corp.	H	Wounded
Chandler, John H.	2nd Corp.	H	Killed
Chester, Claiborne	Sgt.	C	Wounded
Choate, John	Pvt.	A	Wounded
Clark, Edward W.	Capt.	B	Wounded
Clifton, Burill	1st Corp.	K	Wounded
Clohassey, John	Pvt.	G	Wounded
Coleman, George W.	1st Corp.	A	Wounded and Captured
Collins, Andrew	Pvt.	C	Captured
Conell, Joseph M.	4th Sgt.	D	Captured
Cooley, Mitchell	Pvt.	A	Wounded and Captured
Cooley, Robert W.	Pvt.	A	Wounded and Captured
Crawford, John E.	Pvt.	D	Wounded and Captured
Crosswell, Nimrod	Pvt.	I	Wounded
Crunk, William C.	3rd Corp.	E	Wounded
Darden, James P.	Pvt.	H	Wounded
Davis, C. J.	Pvt.	F	Captured
Dean, E. A.	2nd Lt.	H	Wounded
Dickson, Newton B.	1st Lt.	C	Captured
Douglass, James R.	2nd Lt.	B	Wounded
Dunn, A. J.	Pvt.	F	Captured
Echols, John S.	Pvt.	I	Killed
Eleazer, William D.	2nd Lt.	E	Wounded
Elliott, William	Pvt.	D	Wounded and Captured
Elliott, William M.	Pvt.	F	Wounded and Captured
Epps, George P. Y.	Pvt.	C	Captured
Fain, Tyree L.	3rd Lt.	E	Wounded
Flym, Martin	Pvt.	D	Captured
Freeman, George K.	Pvt.	C	Wounded and Captured
Gordon, George W.	Col.	F&S	Wounded and Captured
Graig, John C.	3rd Sgt.	K	Missing
Gray, William C.	Pvt.	C	Captured
Green, Michael	Pvt.	G	Killed
Gunn, Miles A.	Pvt.	F	Missing
Hale, Joseph D.	Pvt.	A	Wounded
Hanan, Michael	Pvt.	D	Wounded and Captured
Harvey, Onesiphorus	Pvt.	C	Captured
Hedgecock, Joseph	Pvt.	A	Captured
Henderson, Hugh H.	Pvt.	E	Captured
Hendrix, James	Pvt.	G	Wounded
Heverin, Hugh J.	2nd Lt.	D	Wounded
Hickey, Andrew	Pvt.	G	Wounded
Hornberger, Wiley	Pvt.	F	Wounded
Hudgins, Francis	Pvt.	E	Wounded
Jones, Samuel G.	Pvt.	H	Wounded and Captured
Jones, William C.	1st Sgt.	H	Captured

Lancaster, Samuel	Pvt.	H	Wounded
Larkins, Joseph H.	Pvt.	E	Wounded
Lawrence, Joseph B.	Pvt.	B	Wounded
Lawrence, William	Pvt.	E	Wounded
Lyons, Jeremiah	Pvt.	G	Wounded and Captured
Malia, Martin	Pvt.	G	Wounded
Maney, William B.	Surgeon	F&S	Captured
McCauley, William	Capt.	C	Wounded and Captured
McConnell, Joseph	4th Sgt.	D	Captured
McElroy, Samuel C.	Pvt.	D	Wounded
McKelvey, William	Pvt.	A	Wounded
Miles, William R.	Pvt.	F	Wounded
Miller, E. L.	Pvt.	H	Wounded and Captured
Miller, Willis D.	4th Sgt.	B	Wounded
Mobley, Benjamin	Pvt.	H	Wounded
Moore, Charles R.	Pvt.	I	Wounded and Captured
Napier, Robert H.	Pvt.	E	Wounded and Captured
Nichols, Griffin	Pvt.	H	Wounded and Captured
O'Neal, Henry	Pvt.	A	Wounded and Captured
Orm, John	Pvt.	G	Captured
Patterson, Joseph J.	Pvt.	C	Captured
Paterson, Joseph K.	Pvt.	H	Killed
Patterson, W. H.	Musician	C	Captured
Porch, William S.	Pvt.	C	Wounded
Price, W. Henry	Pvt.	I	Killed
Quinn, Michael	Pvt.	G	Mortally Wounded
Rains, James E.	Brig. Gen.	HQ	Killed
Randall, David A.	Pvt.	A	Captured
Reaves, William J.	Pvt.	H	Wounded
Redden, John W.	Pvt.	K	Wounded
Rees, John A.	Pvt.	G	Captured
Ridings, Elisha T.	Pvt.	A	Wounded and Captured
Ridings, George D.	1st Lt.	A	Wounded and Captured
Rochelle, Thomas J.	Pvt.	H	Captured
Rogers, George, E.	Pvt.	C	Captured
Rogers, James M.	Corp.	C	Wounded and Captured
Rosson, Joseph S.	3rd Sgt.	F	Wounded
Saunders, Adam	Unk	A	Killed
Scholes, Nathaniel	1st Sgt.	I	Wounded
Self, Abraham	Sgt.	C	Captured
Sensing, John H.	Pvt.	C	Killed
Sevier, James	Pvt.	D	Mortally Wounded
Shaver, Matthew	Pvt.	A	Wounded and Captured
Shaver, Michael Jr.	Pvt.	A	Missing
Skelton, Joseph P.	5th Sgt.	A	Captured
Smith, Thomas	Pvt.	B	Wounded
Smith, Thomas F.	Pvt.	H	Wounded and Captured
Stephens, James G.	1st Lt.	G	Wounded
Stevens, William M.	Pvt.	G	Captured
Street, David W.	Pvt.	C	Captured
Sutton, Joseph	Pvt.	D	Killed

APPENDIX 4

Tarkington, John H	4th Corp.	H	Wounded	
Taylor, John D.	2nd Lt.	E	Captured	
Tidwell, F. F.	1st Lt.	K	Wounded	
Webb, William C.	Pvt.	H	Mortally Wounded	
Whelan, John	Pvt.	G	Wounded	
Williams, Henry A.	Pvt.	C	Wounded	
Wilson, Gilbert R.	5th Sgt.	E	Wounded and Captured	
Wilson, Samuel M.	1st Lt.	I	Wounded	
Wright, Monroe M.	4th Sgt.	H	Killed	
Wynn, John E.	Pvt.	F	Wounded	
Young, Isaac P.	Capt.	I	Wounded and Captured	

Killed - 10
Wounded - 54
Captured - 31
Wounded and Captured - 25
Missing - 4
Total - 124

<u>Chickamauga, GA. 19-20 September 1863</u>

Allen, George	Pvt.	F	Wounded
Andrews, David L.	Pvt.	F	Wounded
Baldwin, John G.	Pvt.	F	Wounded
Balthrop, Gustavus J.	Pvt.	F	Wounded
Batts, Thomas J.	Pvt.	F	Wounded
Batts, William R.	Pvt.	F	Wounded
Bryant, Thomas R.	Pvt.	B	Wounded
Burk, Peter	Pvt.	G	Wounded
Burkhart, B. F.	Pvt.	E	Wounded
Carter, Joseph J.	Pvt.	G	Wounded
Coleman, George W.	1st Corp.	A	Wounded
Collins, Andrew	Pvt.	C	Killed
Connell, James M.	Pvt.	F	Wounded
Croswell, Nimrod B.	Pvt.	I	Wounded
Fain, Tyree L.	3rd Lt.	E	Wounded
Fuqua, William T.	Musician	A	Wounded
Gardner, Charles N.	Pvt.	F	Wounded
Gentry, David C.	Pvt.	K	Wounded
Gossett, William H.	Pvt.	F	Wounded
Gray, Samuel B.	Quart. Sgt.	H	Killed
Grimes, John P.	Pvt.	E	Wounded
Hannah, Benjamin F.	Pvt.	A	Wounded
Hornberger, Wiley W.	Pvt.	F	Wounded
Johnson, Granville Jr.	Pvt.	H	Mortally Wounded
Jordan, Berry M.	Pvt.	K	Killed
Kemp, John	5th Sgt.	H	Wounded
Lancaster, Jarrott S. J.	Pvt.	H	Killed
Larkins, Joseph H.	Pvt.	E	Wounded
McCauley, Richmond	2nd Lt.	I	Wounded
Miller, Willis D.	4th Sgt.	B	Killed
Northington, Samuel	1st Corp.	F	Wounded

Petty, Thomas B.	3rd Sgt.	H	Mortally Wounded
Pitts, Lewis L.	Pvt.	D	Wounded
Powell, Reynolds L.	2nd Corp.	F	Wounded
Ragsdale, Mathias W.	Pvt.	H	Captured
Redden, J. Liberty	Sgt.	K	Wounded
Reeves, F. J.	Pvt.	H	Wounded
Reynolds, William E.	Pvt.	C	Wounded
Rhodes, James H.	Pvt.	H	Wounded
Seaborn, Oliver	Pvt.	B	Killed
Sherrod, Richard T.	Pvt.	F	Killed
Southerland, John	Pvt.	H	Wounded
Stroud, Joseph W.	3rd Corp.	F	Mortally Wounded
Tidwell, F. F.	Capt.	K	Wounded
Tracy, Thomas	Pvt.	G	Wounded
Van Hook, J. W.	Pvt.	F	Mortally Wounded
Vineyard, Morgan H.	Pvt.	K	Wounded
Weaver, James R.	Sgt.	B	Wounded
Young, Archibald	Pvt.	H	Captured

Killed - 7
Wounded - 40
Captured - 2
Wounded and Captured - 0
Missing - 0
Total – 47

Missionary Ridge, TN. 25 November 1863

Adcock, Jesse W.	Pvt.	K	Wounded
Alderson, A. J.	3rd Corp.	E	Wounded
Anderson, John W.	Pvt.	B	Wounded
Austin, Calvin F.	Pvt.	K	Captured
Baggett, Stephen	Pvt.	A	Missing
Baker, James	Pvt.	B	Wounded
Baldwin, David W.	Pvt.	F	Wounded
Baldwin, John G.	Pvt.	F	Mortally Wounded
Bartlett, Alex L.	Pvt.	F	Wounded
Beasley, Francis M.	Pvt.	A	Wounded
Binkley, William H.	Pvt.	E	Captured
Brown, Alexander Y.	1st Lt.	E	Wounded
Browning, J. A.	Pvt.	I	Missing
Burchard, Abram V.	Pvt.	H	Captured
Caffrey, John	Pvt.	G	Missing
Capps, Sterling F.	4th Sgt.	K	Wounded
Chandler, Joseph K.	2nd Corp.	H	Wounded
Clark, James I.	Pvt.	D	Wounded
Collins, James	Pvt.	I	Wounded and Captured
Cooper, Oliver	Pvt.	D	Captured
Davidson, John W.	Pvt.	K	Missing
DeBow, H. B.	Unk.	Unk.	Captured
Dickson, William H.	Pvt.	C	Captured
Dogherty, Martin	Pvt.	G	Wounded

APPENDIX 4

Doughton, William C.	Pvt.	C	Wounded and Captured
Dunn, Edward	Pvt.	D	Wounded
Estes, Solomon	Pvt.	K	Killed
Ferguson, George S.	Pvt.	A	Wounded
French, Robert J.	Pvt.	I	Missing
Gafford, William J.	Pvt.	E	Captured
Gardner, Charles N.	Pvt.	F	Captured
George, James L.	Sgt.	H	Wounded
Goff, Patrick	2nd Sgt.	G	Wounded
Green, William H.	Major	F&S	Killed
Haile, George W.	Pvt.	A	Captured
Hale, Joseph D.	Pvt.	A	Wounded
Hannah, Benjamin F.	Pvt.	A	Wounded
Harvey, Onesiphorus	Pvt.	C	Captured
Hawkins, Martin	Pvt.	G	Captured
Hays, John	Pvt.	A	Captured
Heath, John	4th Corp.	E	Killed
Heverin, Hugh J.	1st Lt.	D	Wounded
Hudson, Robert A.	Pvt.	C	Captured
Hudson, William B.	Pvt.	C	Captured
Irwin, Thomas	1st Lt.	G	Wounded and Captured
Jackson, James P.	Pvt.	E	Wounded
Johnson, James	2nd Corp.	D	Wounded
Johnson, Peter	Pvt.	D	Wounded
Johnson, William	Pvt.	E	Captured
Jones, Joseph T.	Pvt.	G	Wounded
Jones, Lentulus	Pvt.	F	Wounded
Jones, William C.	2nd Lt.	H	Wounded
Keenan, Robert	Pvt.	G	Captured
Landers, Adam	Pvt.	I	Killed
Lawrence, Joseph B.	Pvt.	E	Wounded
Linzy, William H. H.	Pvt.	E	Wounded and Captured
Mayberry, B. F.	Pvt.	A	Wounded
Martin, George W.	Pvt.	H	Wounded
Martin, James T.	Pvt.	C	Wounded
Martin, Marshall R.	Pvt.	C	Wounded and Captured
Mathis, William J.	Adjutant	F&S	Wounded
Maury, John	1st Corp.	G	Killed
Mayberry, Frank	Pvt.	A	Wounded
McConnell, Joseph	3rd Sgt.	D	Wounded and Captured
McDaniel, Alexander R.	1st Lt.	B	Wounded
McIntosh, Green M.	Pvt.	B	Captured
Miller, Edward H.	5th Sgt.	B	Captured
Murphree, David D.	Pvt.	H	Captured
Musgraves, David	4th Sgt.	E	Wounded
Nichols, Griffin	Sgt.	H	Wounded
Nichols, Henry C.	Pvt.	C	Captured
O'Connor, ?	Unk.	C	Killed
Owen, Jesse L.	Pvt.	E	Wounded and Captured
Owens, James M.	1st Corp.	E	Captured
Parish, Thomas M.	4th Sgt.	F	Wounded

Poter, Columbus W.	Pvt.	A	Captured
Puckett, Andrew A.	Pvt.	G	Wounded
Randall, David A.	Pvt.	A	Captured
Redden, G. L.	Pvt.	K	Wounded
Redden, John W.	Pvt.	K	Wounded
Rhodes, James	Pvt.	H	Wounded
Rice, Daniel	Pvt.	C	Captured
Richardson, William T.	Pvt.	K	Captured
Rochelle, Thomas J.	Pvt.	H	Wounded
Rogers, John G.	3rd Corp.	A	Wounded
Schmittou, James O. L. V.	Pvt.	C	Captured
Scholes, Milton R.	Pvt.	I	Wounded
Skelton, James M.	2nd Lt.	C	Wounded
Skelton, Joseph P.	5th Sgt.	A	Wounded
Southerland, W. A.	1st Corp.	H	Captured
Stokes, Andrew J.	Corp.	C	Captured
Tarkington, John H. C.	4th Corp.	H	Wounded
Thompson, Francis M.	3rd Sgt.	K	Wounded
Thompson, J. Stewart	Pvt.	H	Wounded
Tracy, Thomas	Pvt.	G	Mortally Wounded
Weems, P. V. H.	Capt.	H	Wounded
Whelan, John	Pvt.	G	Captured
Williams, Felix G.	Pvt.	E	Wounded
Wilson, Daniel W.	1st Sgt.	I	Wounded
Winn, John W. Jr.	Pvt.	I	Wounded
Work, Robert J.	2nd Lt.	H	Wounded
Zachary, George W.	Pvt.	D	Captured

   Killed - 6
   Wounded - 54
   Captured - 30
   Wounded and Captured - 7
   Missing - 5
   Total – 102

Resaca, GA. 14 May 1864

Bowers, William D.	Pvt.	D	Killed
Gilman, Joseph W.	1st Sgt.	D	Wounded
Haile, William W.	Musician	F&S	Wounded
Kyle, William D.	Pvt.	B	Wounded
Robinson, A. J.	Pvt.	D	Wounded
Shortle, Thomas	Pvt.	G	Wounded
Stout, Andrew G.	Pvt.	D	Wounded
Weems, Corder T.	Pvt.	K	Wounded

   Killed - 1
   Wounded - 7
   Captured - 0
   Wounded and Captured - 0
   Missing - 0
   Total – 8

APPENDIX 4

Adairsville, GA. 17 May 1864

Baker, William L.	Pvt.		E	Wounded and Captured
Doherty, Martin	Pvt.		G	Wounded
French, George	3rd Corp.		I	Wounded
Garton, Moses	Pvt.		E	Wounded
House, William D.	Pvt.		K	Wounded
Jamison, Orville O.	4th Sgt.		I	Wounded
Larkins, Joseph H.	Pvt.		E	Wounded

Killed - 0
Wounded - 6
Captured - 0
Wounded and Captured - 1
Missing - 0
Total - 7

New Hope Church, GA. 27 May 1864

Baldwin, Samuel	Pvt.		F	Wounded
Barr, John H.	Pvt.		H	Wounded
Capps, Sterling F.	4th Sgt.		K	Killed
Cook, E. D.	3rd Sgt.		I	Wounded
Crim, Henry C.	4th Sgt.		A	Wounded
Cronan, Patrick	2nd Corp.		A	Wounded
Douglass, James R.	2nd Lt.		B	Mortally Wounded
Duke, John C.	Pvt.		G	Wounded
Freeman, George K.	Pvt.		C	Killed
Gentry, David C.	Pvt.		K	Mortally Wounded
Gordon, William H.	Pvt.		H	Killed
Gray, James M.	Pvt.		H	Wounded
Gray, William C.	Pvt.		C	Wounded
Hooper, Absolum B.	Pvt.		I	Wounded
Jones, John W.	4th Sgt.		B	Wounded
Lark, William	Pvt.		D	Wounded
Majors, John P.	Pvt.		K	Wounded
McKelvey, William	Pvt.		A	Killed
Redden, J. Liberty	Sgt.		K	Wounded
Rochelle, Thomas J.	Pvt.		H	Mortally Wounded
Skelton, Joseph P.	5th Sgt.		A	Killed
Slayden, John D.	Sgt.		C	Wounded
Warren, William J.	Pvt.		K	Wounded
Welch, John	Pvt.		G	Wounded
Work, Robert J.	2nd Lt.		H	Wounded

Killed - 5
Wounded - 20
Captured - 0
Wounded and Captured - 0
Missing - 0
Total - 25

Kennesaw Mountain, GA. 11-29 June 1864

Bumpass, Abe	Corp.	B	Killed, 11 June
Innis, J. T.	Pvt.	I	Wounded, 17 June
Redden, G. L.	Pvt.	K	Wounded, 19 June
Martin, George	Pvt.	H	Wounded, 19 June
Long, Martin F.	Pvt.	H	Killed, 19 June
Crow, John C.	Pvt.	K	Wounded, 21 June
Stewart, W. H.	Pvt.	K	Killed, 21 June
Eubanks, R. C.	Pvt.	E	Wounded, 21 June
Powell, J. W.	Pvt.	F	Wounded, 21 June
Jackson, W. T.	Pvt.	E	Wounded, 21 June
Smith, B. J.	Pvt.	C	Wounded, 21 June
Williams, Steve	Pvt.	E	Killed, 21 June
Trotter, Jordan	Pvt.	I	Killed, 21 June
Gorman, Mark	Sgt.	B	Wounded, 23 June
Larkin, James M.	Pvt.	E	Killed, 29 June

Killed - 6
Wounded - 9
Captured - 0
Wounded and Captured - 0
Missing - 0
Total - 15

Peachtree Creek, GA. 20 July 1864

Barr, John H.	Pvt.	H	Wounded
Bryant, Thomas R.	Pvt.	B	Wounded
Darden, Alfred B.	Pvt.	H	Wounded
Dickson, Newton B.	1st Lt.	C	Wounded
Fain, Tyree L.	3rd Lt.	E	Wounded
Garton, Moses	Pvt.	E	Wounded
Goad, Gustavus	Pvt.	D	Wounded
Hayes, Champion L.	Pvt.	C	Wounded
Henderson, Hugh H.	Pvt.	E	Wounded
Lane, Thomas	2nd Lt.	E	Wounded
Lynch, W. B.	Pvt.	B	Mortally Wounded
Manley, Benjamin F.	Pvt.	K	Wounded
Martin, Armistead	Pvt.	H	Mortally Wounded
Martin, George W.	Pvt.	H	Wounded
McClelland, James R.	Pvt.	C	Killed
McLemay, John	Pvt.	G	Wounded
McMahan, Allison W.	Pvt.	E	Wounded
Merrill, James C.	Pvt.	K	Killed
Morgan, Fred	Pvt.	F	Wounded
Nealey, Martin	Pvt.	G	Wounded
Newton, Wiley J.	Pvt.	F	Killed
Phillips, John W.	2nd Lt.	K	Wounded
Roland, William A.	Pvt.	F	Wounded
Rushing, John H.	Pvt.	I	Wounded
Southerland, John	Pvt.	H	Wounded
Stevens, William M.	Pvt.	G	Wounded

Weakley, William T.	5th Sgt.	C	Wounded	
Webb, J. H.	Pvt.	I	Wounded	
Wells, Lawrence	Pvt.	B	Wounded	
Young, Isaac P.	Capt.	I	Wounded	

Killed - 3
Wounded - 27
Captured - 0
Wounded and Captured - 0
Missing - 0
Total - 30

<u>Atlanta, GA. 22 July 1864</u>

Baldwin, Samuel P.	Pvt.	F	Killed
Bartlett, John H.	Pvt.	F	Wounded
Beasley, Reuben F.	2nd Lt.	A	Wounded
Bouglies, Victor	Sgt.	B	Killed
Bryan, Montgomery	Pvt.	F	Wounded
Clifton, Burill A.	1st Corp.	K	Wounded
Collins, Hazard	Pvt.	I	Wounded
Collins, Henry M.	Pvt.	I	Wounded
Corbett, Joseph M.	Corp.	B	Wounded
Croswell, C. N.	2nd Sgt.	A	Wounded
Dickson, John M.	Corp.	C	Wounded
Divaney, Matthew	2nd Lt.	G	Killed
Dogherty, Martin	Pvt.	G	Killed
Figg, Jason	Sgt.	B	Killed
Flaherty, Roger	Pvt.	G	Killed
French, George H.	3rd Corp.	I	Wounded
Gordon, George W.	Col.	F&S	Wounded
Gray, James M.	Pvt.	H	Captured
Greer, Daniel W.	Pvt.	F	Wounded
Gunn, Edward W.	2nd Sgt.	F	Wounded
Heverin, Hugh J.	1st Lt.	D	Wounded
Hogan, Martin	Pvt.	G	Wounded
Hunter, James P.	2nd Corp.	E	Killed
Jackson, Joseph W.	Pvt.	F	Killed
Johnson, Jacob H.	1st Lt.	H	Killed
Jones, Thomas B.	1st Lt.	F	Killed
Lawrence, William H.	Pvt.	E	Wounded
Mason, Benett	Pvt.	B	Wounded
McElyea, Marcus L.	4th Corp.	A	Wounded
McNeilly, Hugh J.	3rd Corp.	C	Killed
Nelson, Moses A.	1st Lt.	B	Wounded
Nichol, William C.	2nd Lt.	B	Wounded
Orm, John	Pvt.	G	Killed
Owens, Blythia	Sgt.	I	Wounded
Parker, James T.	1st Corp.	E	Wounded
Peaters, C. D.	Sgt.	I	Wounded
Polk, Henry A.	5th Sgt.	F	Wounded
Richardson, Andrew	Pvt.	E	Wounded

Richardson, William	Sgt.	E	Wounded
Robinson, A. Jack	Pvt.	D	Mortally Wounded
Rogers, John Gilbert	3rd Corp.	A	Wounded
Rooker, John W.	2nd Corp.	E	Wounded
Ruffin, Robert E.	Pvt.	F	Wounded
Schmittou, James L. V.	Sgt.	C	Wounded
Scholes, Nathaniel	1st Sgt.	I	Mortally Wounded
Shouse, Jacob W.	4th Sgt.	H	Wounded
Smith, Gus	Pvt.	B	Wounded
Stowers, John T.	1st Sgt.	B	Wounded
Teaster, Charles D.	5th Sgt.	I	Mortally Wounded
Weaks, William H.	Pvt.	I	Wounded
Weems, Corder T.	Pvt.	K	Wounded
Weems, P. V. H.	Major	F&S	Mortally Wounded
Woodruff, Charles W.	Pvt.	F	Wounded

Killed - 12
Wounded - 40
Captured - 1
Wounded and Captured - 0
Missing - 0
Total - 52

Near Atlanta, GA. 28 July – 18 August 1864

Dodson, Napoleon B.	Pvt.	C	Wounded, 28 July
Redden, John W.	Pvt.	K	Wounded, 28 July
Yates, Clayton	Sgt.	H	Wounded, 28 July
Lawrence, Joseph E.	Pvt.	E	Wounded, 29 July
Long, Alfred	Pvt.	E	Wounded, 31 July
Thompson, W. T.	Pvt.	K	Wounded, 31 July
Goad, Gustavus	Pvt.	D	Wounded, 31 July
Merrill, James	Pvt.	K	Killed, 31 July
Etheridge, William	Pvt.	K	Killed, 1 August
Welch, John	Pvt.	G	Wounded, 2 August
Smith, W. T.	Corp.	C	Wounded, 3 August
McCauley, George D.	Pvt.	C	Wounded, 4 August
Jackson, G. P.	Pvt.	E	Wounded, 4 August
Slayden, William	2nd Lt.	C	Wounded, 6 August
Jones, Clint	1st Lt.	H	Wounded, 6 August
McCollum, B. F.	3rd Lt.	H	Wounded, 11 August
Chester, John	Pvt.	C	Killed, 18 August

Killed - 3
Wounded - 14
Captured - 0
Wounded and Captured - 0
Missing - 0
Total – 17

Jonesboro, GA. 31 August – 1 September 1864

Beech, Thomas H.	2nd Lt.	D	Wounded
Flowers, James W.	Pvt.	F	Wounded
Gareo, R. William O.	Pvt.	I	Captured

APPENDIX 4

Harrison, Eugene A.	Pvt.	D	Wounded
Moore, Charles R.	Pvt.	I	Wounded
Baker, James	Pvt.	B	Wounded
Baker, William A.	Lt.	H	Wounded and Captured
Baker, William H.	2nd Lt.	I	Wounded
Ballard, Sam H.	Pvt.	H	Mortally Wounded
Balthrop, Gustavus	Pvt.	F	Mortally Wounded
Banks, Robert	Pvt.	E	Mortally Wounded
Butler, Joshua B.	Pvt.	K	Wounded
Caldwell, W. H.	4th Sgt.	I	Captured
Chandler, Joseph K.	2nd Corp.	H	Killed
Darden, George W.	Pvt.	F	Wounded
Darden, James H.	Capt.	F	Mortally Wounded
Dickson, John M.	Corp.	C	Wounded
Eubanks, Robert G.	Pvt.	E	Killed
Floyd, Harrison	Pvt.	H	Killed
Gilman, Joseph	1st Sgt.	D	Wounded
Kyle, William D.	Pvt.	B	Wounded
Long, James A.	Lt.-Col.	F&S	Mortally Wounded
Montgomery, Daniel	3rd Corp.	H	Wounded
Peach, Fountain E.	Pvt.	B	Captured
Richardson, M. Turner	Unk.	E	Killed
Ridings, George D.	1st Lt.	A	Wounded
Stewart, Nicholas P.	Pvt.	B	Mortally Wounded
Warfield, Henry C.	2nd Lt.	F	Wounded
Willard, William W.	1st Sgt.	D	Killed
Godwin, Reuben	4th Corp.	K	Captured
Hundley, Elisha T.	1st Corp.	D	Captured
O'Guinn, Robert	Pvt.	I	Captured
Rawley, Darius N.	4th Sgt.	D	Captured

    Killed - 5
    Wounded - 20
    Captured - 7
    Wounded and Captured - 1
    Missing - 0
    Total - 33

<u>Lovejoy Station, GA. 2-4 September 1864</u>

Austin, Charles D.	Pvt.	K	Wounded, 2 September
Burch, Thomas	Pvt.	H	Wounded, 2 September
Carter, Joseph J.	Pvt.	G	Killed, 2 September
Draughon, George W.	Pvt.	F	Killed, 2 September
Pullen, William C.	Pvt.	A	Wounded, 2 September
Schmittou, James L. V.	Sgt.	C	Wounded, 4 September
Tidwell, Silas	Pvt.	K	Killed, 2 September

    Killed - 3
    Wounded - 4
    Captured - 0
    Wounded and Captured - 0
    Missing - 0
    Total - 7

Franklin, TN. 30 November 1864

Name	Rank	Co.	Status
Atwood, T. H.	Pvt.	I	Wounded
Averitt, Paul	Sgt.	C	Wounded and Captured
Baker, George W.	Pvt.	I	Wounded and Captured
Baker, Wiley J.	Pvt.	C	Wounded
Barnes, James H.	Pvt.	F	Killed
Batts, Jeremiah	Capt.	F	Mortally Wounded
Batts, William R.	Pvt.	F	Wounded and Captured
Beech, Thomas H.	2nd Lt.	D	Killed
Brown, W. L.	Unk.	A	Wounded and Captured
Bunnell, Theodore A.	Pvt.	I	Wounded
Carbide, Joseph M.	Pvt.	B	Captured
Cook, E. D.	3rd Sgt.	I	Wounded
Corbett, Joseph M.	Corp.	B	Captured
Cronan, Patrick	2nd Corp.	A	Killed
Croswell, C. N.	2nd Sgt.	A	Killed
Dodson, Napoleon B.	Pvt.	C	Killed
Eubanks, Raford C.	Pvt.	E	Killed
Fitzgerald, Michael	Pvt.	G	Wounded and Captured
French, Cullen E.	Pvt.	I	Killed
French, George H.	3rd Corp.	I	Captured
Goff, Patrick	2nd Sgt.	G	Killed
Gordon, George W.	Brig. Gen.	HQ	Wounded and Captured
Gray, James F.	Pvt.	A	Killed
Gunn, Miles A.	Pvt.	A	Wounded
Halliburton, Charles	Pvt.	C	Wounded and Captured
Halliburton, Turner	Pvt.	C	Captured
Hogin, William M.	1st Sgt.	K	Captured
Hudgins, Francis M.	Pvt.	E	Wounded and Captured
Hurley, Jeremiah	4th Sgt.	G	Killed
Jackson, William T.	2nd Sgt.	E	Captured
Jamison, Orville O.	4th Sgt.	I	Wounded
Jamison, P. G.	Pvt.	I	Wounded
Jones, John Wesley	4th Sgt.	B	Wounded and Captured
Johnson, James	2nd Corp.	D	Wounded and Captured
Lawrence, William H.	Pvt.	E	Wounded
Lewis, James A.	Pvt.	A	Wounded
Mason, Bennet	Pvt.	B	Wounded
McAnally, Michael	Pvt.	G	Wounded and Captured
Menefee, James	Pvt.	B	Killed
Nelson, Moses A.	1st Lt.	B	Wounded
Newton, Henry W.	Pvt.	F	Wounded and Captured
Peck, John	Pvt.	B	Wounded and Captured
Powell, Reynolds L.	2nd Corp.	F	Killed
Puckett, Andrew	Pvt.	G	Captured
Quarles, Pinkney M.	Pvt.	F	Killed
Reeder, J. H. L.	2nd Corp.	K	Wounded
Reynolds, William E.	Pvt.	C	Captured
Ridings, Elisha T.	Pvt.	A	Wounded and Captured
Sayers, Charles P.	1st Sgt.	B	Wounded and Captured

APPENDIX 4

Sheridan, John	Pvt.	G	Wounded and Captured
Slayden, John	Sgt.	C	Captured (but escaped)
Smith, A. T.	Pvt.	B	Killed
Smith, James T.	Pvt.	B	Mortally Wounded
Smith, William J.	Corp.	C	Killed
Smith, Walter S.	Pvt.	A	Wounded
Sroffe, George W.	Musician	E	Wounded and Captured
Stokey, Montgomery A.	Sgt.	C	Killed
Taylor, Edmond D.	Pvt.	A	Wounded
Trogdon, Alfred W.	Pvt.	A	Wounded
Turner, George T.	Pvt.	C	Wounded and Captured
Weaks, William H.	Pvt.	I	Wounded and Captured
Weaver, Charles H.	Pvt.	B	Captured
Wilson, Samuel M.	1st Lt.	I	Wounded
Woodruff, William B.	Pvt.	F	Killed
Wynn, John A.	Unk.	C	Mortally Wounded
Young, Isaac P.	Capt.	I	Wounded

    Killed - 18
    Wounded - 20
    Captured - 10
    Wounded and Captured - 19
    Missing - 0
    Total – 67

<u>Nashville, TN. 15-16 December 1864</u>

Butler, Joshua B.	Pvt.	K	Wounded
Carroll, John	Pvt.	A	Wounded and Captured
Choate, Smith E.	4th Corp.	E	Captured
Darden, James P.	Pvt.	H	Captured
Flowers, James W.	Pvt.	F	Captured
Garner, George W.	Sgt.	H	Wounded and Captured
Glenn, Patrick	Pvt.	G	Captured
Goad, Gustavus	Pvt.	D	Wounded and Captured
Goodwin, J. M.	Pvt.	H	Killed
Gorman, Marcus	1st Sgt.	G	Wounded and Captured
Graig, James P.	Unk.	Unk.	Wounded
Guthrie, Roger	Pvt.	G	Captured
Hammon, Samuel	Pvt.	K	Captured
Harrison, Eugene A.	Pvt.	D	Wounded and Captured
Jones, Joseph T.	Pvt.	G	Captured
McLaughlin, Alex R.	1st Corp.	D	Captured
Newton, James M.	Pvt.	F	Captured
Nichols, Griffin	Sgt.	H	Captured
Peck, Giles	Pvt.	B	Captured
Shipp, James	Pvt.	H	Killed
Stout, Andrew G.	Pvt.	D	Captured
Ward, John H.	Pvt.	B	Captured
Welch, John S. G.	Pvt.	K	Wounded
Winn, John H.	3rd Corp.	F	Captured

    Killed - 2
    Wounded - 3

439

Captured - 14
Wounded and Captured - 5
Missing - 0
Total - 24

<u>Bentonville, NC. 21 March 1865</u>

Larkins, Joseph H.	Pvt.	E	Wounded
Weaver, James R.	Sgt.	B	Wounded

Killed - 0
Wounded - 2
Captured - 0
Wounded and Captured - 0
Missing - 0
Total - 2

Appendix 5

Members of the 11th Tennessee Infantry Held in Federal Prisoner of War Camps

Camp Chase, OH

Allen, Christian F.	Pvt.	F	
Averitt, Paul	Sgt.	C	
Banks, H. T.	Pvt.	G	
Batts, William R.	Pvt.	F	Died at Camp Chase
Brown, Wiley S.	Pvt.	K	Died at Camp Chase
Carroll, John	Pvt.	A	
Cooper, Charles	Pvt.	A	
Cruthers, J. M.	Pvt.	B	
Darden, James P.	Pvt.	H	
Echols, Robert M.	1st Corp.	I	
Edmonson, Henry C.	Pvt.	A	
Elliott, William C.	Pvt.	C	
Emery, N. R.	Pvt.	A	
Fitzgerald, Michael	Pvt.	G	
Flowers, James W.	Pvt.	F	
Garner, George W. F.	Sgt.	H	
Gordon, George W.	Col.	F&S	
Gorman, Marcus	1st Sgt.	G	
Gossett, William H.	Pvt.	F	
Gray, James M.	Pvt.	H	
Gunn, Miles A.	Pvt.	F	
Guthrie, Roger	Pvt.	G	
Halliburton, Charles	Pvt.	C	
Hammon, Samuel	Pvt.	K	
Hanan, Michael	Pvt.	D	
Harrison, Eugene	Pvt.	D	
Hooper, Absolom	Pvt.	I	
Hudgins, Francis M.	Pvt.	E	
Irwin, Thomas	1st Lt.	G	
Jones, George W.	Pvt.	F	
Jones, Joseph T.	Pvt.	G	
Lane, Abraham	Pvt.	G	
Marsh, William C.	Pvt.	C	
McAnally, Michael	Pvt.	G	
McCauley, William H.	Capt.	C	
McLaughlin, Alex. R.	1st Corp.	D	
Murphey, John R.	3rd Corp.	F	
Newton, James M.	Pvt.	F	
Nichols, Griffin	Sgt.	H	
Peck, James	Pvt.	D	
Proctor, William	Pvt.	F	
Ridings, Elisha T.	Pvt.	A	
Sayers, Charles P.	Musician	F&S	

Sheridan, John	Pvt.	G	
Sigel, Martin	Pvt.	A	
Smith, Elias P.	Pvt.	B	
Smith, Richard S.	1st Lt.	B	
Sroffe, George	Musician	E	
Stout, Andrew G.	Pvt.	D	
Taylor, John D.	2nd Lt.	E	
Thomas, Minor B.	2nd Lt.	K	Died at Camp Chase
Turner, George T.	Pvt.	C	
Weaks, William H.	Pvt.	I	
Wetmore, William C. S.	3rd Sgt.	B	
Winn, John H.	3rd Corp.	F	
Young, Isaac P.	Capt.	I	

Camp Douglas, IL.

Allen, Christian F.	Pvt.	F	
Anderson, Yeatman	Pvt.	B	
Blackburn, William H.	Pvt.	H	
Brown W. J.	Pvt.	A	
Brown, William J.	Pvt.	A	Died at Camp Douglas
Caffrey, John	Pvt.	G	
Caldwell, M. H.	4th Sgt.	I	
Carbide, Joseph M.	Pvt.	B	
Corbett, Joseph M.	Corp.	B	
Daughtry, George R.	Pvt.	G	
Davis, C. J.	Pvt.	F	
Dickson, James C.	Unk.	Unk.	
French, George H.	3rd Corp.	I	
Gaither, William B.	Pvt.	H	
Gallop, William T.	Pvt.	C	Died at Camp Douglas
Glenn, John	Pvt.	G	Died at Camp Douglas
Goodwin, Reuben	4th Corp.	K	
Halliburton, Turner H.	Pvt.	C	
Hannah, Benjamin F.	Pvt.	A	
Heckman, Charles E.	Hosp. Stew.	B	
Hogin, William M.	1st Sgt.	K	
Holland, William S.	Pvt.	A	
House, John W.	Pvt.	K	Died at Camp Douglas
House, William D.	Pvt.	K	
Hundley, Elisha T.	1st Corp.	D	
Jackson, William T.	2nd Sgt.	E	
Johnson, James	2nd Corp.	D	
Jones, George W.	Pvt.	F	
Jones, John W.	4th Sgt.	B	
Jones, William H.	Pvt.	B	
Keenan, Robert	Pvt.	G	
Lankford, Lawrence D.	Pvt.	K	Died at Camp Douglas
Lankford, Robert H.	Pvt.	K	Died at Camp Douglas
Luther, Newton J.	1st Corp.	K	
McCauley, George D.	Pvt.	C	
Menefee, Nicholas	Pvt.	B	

Mitchell, John W.	Pvt.	D	
Norman, Henry H.	Musician	F&S	
O'Guinn, Robert	Pvt.	I	
Osborn, John B.	Pvt.	A	
Patterson, Joseph J.	Pvt.	C	
Pitts, Lewis L.	Pvt.	D	
Proctor, William	Pvt.	F	Died at Camp Douglas
Puckett, Andrew A.	Pvt.	G	
Ragsdale, Mathias W.	Pvt.	H	
Randall, David A.	Pvt.	A	
Rawley, Darius N.	4th Sgt.	D	
Shaver, Matthew	Pvt.	A	Died at Camp Douglas
Sigel, Martin	Pvt.	A	
Skelton, Joseph P.	5th Sgt.	A	
Stevens, William M.	Pvt.	G	
Thomas, James D.	3rd Corp.	K	
Vaught, William	Pvt.	B	
Ward, John H.	Pvt.	B	
Weaver, Charles H.	Pvt.	B	
Webb, J. H.	Pvt.	I	
Willis, Benjamin F.	Pvt.	H	

Camp Morton, IN.

Adams, William T.	Pvt.	C	
Baldwin, James W.	Pvt.	F	
Banks, H. T.	Pvt.	G	
Bell, Alexander H.	4th Sgt.	K	
Binkley, James P.	Pvt.	E	
Bowker, Joseph A.	Pvt.	E	Died at Camp Morton
Brice, John	Pvt.	B	
Coleman, George W.	1st Corp.	A	
Crooker, Jacob P.	3rd Sgt.	G	
Crunk, William C.	3rd Corp.	E	
Flym, Martin	Pvt.	D	
Flynn, John J.	4th Sgt.	G	
Ford, Matthew W.	Pvt.	K	
French, Robert J.	Pvt.	I	
Goodwin, Henry H.	3rd Corp.	D	
Gray, George A.	Pvt.	K	
Gray, James	Pvt.	K	Died at Camp Morton
Gray, James W.	Pvt.	K	
Hedgecock, Joseph	Pvt.	A	
Hickey, Andrew	Pvt.	G	
Lyons, Jeremiah	Pvt.	G	
McCann, Benjamin W.	1st Lt.	D	
Napier, Robert H.	Pvt.	E	
O'Neal, Henry D.	Pvt.	A	
Orm, John	Pvt.	G	
Porch, William S.	Pvt.	C	
Rochelle, Thomas J.	Pvt.	H	
Smith, Richard S.	1st Lt.	B	

Smith, Thomas F.	Pvt.	H
Taylor, John D.	2nd Lt.	E
Traylor, Thomas B.	2nd Lt.	A

Fort Delaware, DE.

Collins, James	Pvt.	I
Crocker, John M.	Pvt.	B
Emery, N. R.	Pvt.	A
Gordon, George W.	Colonel	F&S
Hamilton, James G.	Pvt.	Unk
Irwin, Thomas	1st Lt.	G
Kilgore, Henry	Pvt.	H
Lucas, Hugh R.	Major	F&S
McCauley, Wm. H.	Capt.	C
Morgan, William B.	Pvt.	H
Pitts, Josiah H.	Capt.	A
Ridings, George D.	1st Lt.	A
Thomason, Benjamin W.	Pvt.	C

Fort Warren, MA.

Gordon, George W.	Brig. Gen.	HQ
Norvell, William	Pvt.	D

Gratiot Street, Saint Louis, MO.

Black, William A.	Pvt.	D
Crawford, John E.	Pvt.	D
Miller, Alexander C.	Pvt.	C

Johnson's Island, OH.

Bolton, John G.	Pvt.	A
Brice, John	Pvt.	B
Bryan, Martin W.	Sgt.	F
Pitts, Josiah H.	Capt.	A
Webb, Howell	Lt.-Col.	F&S

Point Lookout, MD.

Cathey, John	Pvt.	A

Rock Island, IL.

Alderson, A. J.	3rd Corp.	E	
Austin, Calvin F.	Pvt.	K	
Baggett, Stephen	Pvt.	A	
Brown, Alexander Y.	1st Lt.	E	
Brown, William F.	Pvt.	G	
Brown, William J.	Pvt.	A	Died at Rock Island
Burchard, Abram V.	Pvt.	H	
Caffrey, John	Pvt.	G	
Carothers, James H.	3rd Sgt.	H	

APPENDIX 5

Name	Rank	Co.	Notes
Cooper, Oliver	Pvt.	D	
Davis, J. T.	Pvt.	E	Died at Rock Island
Dickson, William H.	Pvt.	C	
Doughton, William C. Jr.	Pvt.	C	
Driscall, James	Pvt.	G	
Elliott, W. C.	Pvt.	C	
Gafford, James K. P.	Pvt.	E	
Gafford, William J.	Pvt.	E	
Gardner, Charles N.	Pvt.	F	
Haile, George W.	Pvt.	A	
Handlin, Thomas J.	Corp.	C	
Harvey, Onesiphorus	Pvt.	C	
Hawkins, Martin	Pvt.	G	Died at Rock Island
Hays, John	Pvt.	A	
Hudson, Robert A.	Pvt.	C	
Hudson, William B.	Pvt.	C	
Hutchins, William	Pvt.	D	
Johnson, William	Pvt.	E	
Jones, Samuel G.	Pvt.	H	
Keenan, Robert	Pvt.	G	
Linzy, W. H. H.	Pvt.	E	
Martin, James T.	Pvt.	C	
McConnell, Joseph	3rd Sgt.	D	
McIntosh, Green M.	Pvt.	B	
Miller, Edward H.	5th Sgt.	B	
Murphree, David D.	Pvt.	H	
Nesbitt, William J. A.	Pvt.	C	
Nichols, Henry C.	Pvt.	C	Died at Rock Island
Owen, Jesse L.	Pvt.	E	
Owens, James M.	1st Corp.	E	
Parks, Thomas P.	Pvt.	I	Died at Rock Island
Randall, David A.	Pvt.	A	Died at Rock Island
Rice, Daniel	Pvt.	C	
Richardson, William T.	Pvt.	K	
Roberts, William H.	2nd Lt.	C	
Rogers, Robert M.	Pvt.	B	Died at Rock Island
Schmittou, James L. O. V.	Pvt.	C	
Southerland, J. A.	1st Corp.	H	
Stokes, Andrew J.	Corp.	C	
Stuart, John M.	Pvt.	E	
Sudberry, David R.	Pvt.	C	
Whelan, John	Pvt.	G	
Williams, John D.	Pvt.	E	
Wyatt, William M.	2nd Lt.	I	
Zachary, George W.	Pvt.	D	

Appendix 6

Members of the 11ᵗʰ Tennessee Infantry On Rolls at the Surrender[1]

Name	Rank	Co.
Adcock, Jesse W.	Lt.	K
Adcock, M. V. B.	Musician	F&S
Alspaugh, Josiah C.	2nd Sgt.	K
Andrews, David L.	3rd Corp.	F
Atwood, T. H.	Pvt.	I
Austin, Charles	4th Sgt.	K
Baker, Charles	Pvt.	H
Baker, Wiley J.	Pvt.	C
Baldwin, David W.	Pvt.	F
Bartlett, John H.	Pvt.	F
Batts, John T.	Pvt.	F
Batts, Thomas J.	Pvt.	F
Bowles, M. W.	Pvt.	D
Brennon, Bartley	Pvt.	G
Brown James M.	1st Sgt.	C
Cathey, Morris R.	Pvt.	K
Clark, Edward W.	Capt.	B
Clifton, Burill A.	1st Corp.	K
Clifton, James K. Jr.	Pvt.	K
Collins, James	Pvt.	I
Cook, C. A.	Pvt.	I
Cook, E. D.	3rd Sgt.	I
Crim, Henry C.	4th Sgt.	A
Davidson, Green H.	Pvt.	K
Dickson, Newton B.	1st Lt.	C
Duke, John C.	Pvt.	G
Fain, Tyree L.	3rd Lt.	E
Ferguson, George S.	Pvt.	A
Ford, Jesse M.	Pvt.	E
Fuqua, William T.	Musician	A
Garton, Moses	Pvt.	E
Gooch, James W. M.	5th Sgt.	F
Greer, Daniel W.	Pvt.	F
Grimes, John P.	Pvt.	E
Grimes, Thomas J.	Pvt.	E
Gunn, Edward W.	2nd Lt.	F
Hale, Joseph D.	Pvt.	A

---

[1] At the end of the war the 11th/29th Tennessee was consolidated with other regiments to form the 2nd Consolidated Tennessee Infantry. Even though a soldier's name appears on a roster does not indicate that the soldier was actually present with the regiment at the time of the surrender.

APPENDIX 6

Harper, John H.	Sgt.-Maj.	F&S
Harris, Thomas J.	Pvt.	K
Harrison, Eugene A.	Pvt.	D
Hassell, Alfred B.	Pvt.	H
Hassell, Zebulon	2nd Corp.	H
Hayes, Champion L.	Pvt.	C
Hogan, Martin	Pvt.	G
Hudgins, Francis M.	Pvt.	E
Hunt, Andrew W.	Musician	F&S
Jackson, James P.	Pvt.	E
James, Robert A. W.	Major	F&S
Jordan, Benjamin M.	Pvt.	F
Kemp, John	2nd Lt.	H
Kyle, William D.	Pvt.	B
Larkins, Joseph H.	Pvt.	E
Lawrence, Belfield F.	Pvt.	E
Lawrence, Joseph B.	Pvt.	E
Luther, George M.	Pvt.	K
Malia, Martin	Pvt.	G
Maney, William B.	Surgeon	F&S
Manley, Benjamin F.	Pvt.	K
Manley, James	Pvt.	D
Martin, George W.	Pvt.	H
Mathis, John T.	Pvt.	E
Matthews, John T.	Pvt.	E
McCaleb, Thomas P.	Pvt.	K
McCauley, Wiley M.	1st Lt.	I
McCollum, Benjamin F.	2nd Lt.	A
McConnell, Joseph	3rd Sgt.	D
McDaniel, Alexander R. M.	1st Lt.	B
McDaniel, Jesse C.	2nd Lt.	B
McElyea, Marcus L.	4th Corp.	A
McNailus, James	Pvt.	G
Miller, H. C.	Pvt.	B
Mobley, T. J.	Pvt.	I
Moss, Thomas J.	Musician	A
Neblett, R. P.	Musician	F&S
Nelson, Moses A.	1st Lt.	B
Pullen, William C.	Pvt.	A
Randall, William H.	Pvt.	A
Reece, Griffith	Pvt.	K
Richardson, Andrew J.	Pvt.	E
Richardson, William T.	Pvt.	K
Rogers, George E.	Pvt.	C
Rogers, John G.	3rd Corp.	A
Roland, William A.	Pvt.	F
Savage, James R.	1st Sgt.	G
Schmittou, James L. V.	Sgt.	C
Scott, Robert T.	Pvt.	E
Sheppard, I. B.	Pvt.	K
Sherlock, John	Pvt.	G

447

Slayden, John D.	Sgt.	C
Stewart, Robert	Pvt.	B
Stout, Andrew G.	Pvt.	D
Street, David W.	Sgt.	C
Tarkington, John H. C.	4th Corp.	H
Thompson, William T.	Pvt.	K
Tidwell, Hickman C.	2nd Lt.	E
Totty, Thomas S.	Pvt.	E
Vineyard, Morgan H.	Pvt.	K
Walsh, Patrick	Pvt.	G
Warren, William J.	Pvt.	K
Weakley, William T.	5th Sgt.	C
Weaver, James R.	Sgt.	B
White, William M.	Pvt.	K
Wilson, Aubrey	Capt.	B
Wilson, Daniel W.	1st Sgt.	I

Appendix 7

Members Attending Postwar Reunions of the 11th Tennessee Infantry[1]

Name	Rank	Company	Reunion
Adcock, Jesse W.	Lt.	K	Nashville, 1904
Adcock, Martin V. B.	Musician	F&S	Bon Aqua Springs, 1885
Adcock, Thomas B.	1st Lt.	K	Bon Aqua Springs, 1885
Alspaugh, Josiah C.	2nd Sgt.	K	Nashville, 1904
Austin, Calvin F.	Pvt.	K	Bon Aqua Springs, 1885
Baldwin, James W.	Pvt.	F	Nashville, 1904
Batts, Thomas J.	Pvt.	F	Nashville, 1904
Binns, John E.	Col.	F&S	Bon Aqua Springs, 1885
Blackburn, William H.	Pvt.	H	Bon Aqua Springs, 1885
Bradley, Jefferson C.	Pvt.	H	Bon Aqua Springs, 1885
Brooks, Milton O.	2nd Lt.	G	Bon Aqua Springs, 1885
Brown, John J.	Pvt.	K	Bon Aqua Springs, 1885
Clifton, Burill A.	1st Corp.	K	Nashville, 1904
Clifton, James K. Jr.	Pvt.	K	Bon Aqua Springs, 1885
Dickson, John M.	Corp.	C	Nashville, 1904
Eleazer, William D.	Capt.	E	Nashville, 1904
Elliott, William	Pvt.	D	Nashville, 1904
Elliott, William M.	Pvt.	F	Nashville, 1904
Epps, George P. Y.	Pvt.	C	Bon Aqua Springs, 1885
Fielder, James K. P.	Pvt.	H	Bon Aqua Springs. 1885
Flowers, James W.	Pvt.	F	Nashville, 1904
Garner, George W. F.	Sgt.	H	Bon Aqua Springs, 1885
Garton, Moses	Pvt.	E	Bon Aqua Springs, 1885
Gordon, George W.	Brig. Gen.	HQ	Nashville, 1904
Graig, James P.	Unk.	Unk.	Bon Aqua Springs, 1885
Hall, Benjamin F.	Pvt.	K	Bon Aqua Springs, 1885
Hogin, William M.	1st Sgt.	K	Nashville, 1904
Hooper, William H.	Pvt.	H	Bon Aqua Springs, 1885
Jackson, James S.	Pvt.	E	Nashville, 1904
Jordan, Benjamin M.	Pvt.	F	Nashville, 1904
Lark, William	Pvt.	D	Nashville, 1904
Maney, William B.	Surgeon	F&S	Nashville, 1904
Mathis, William J.	Adjutant	F&S	Bon Aqua Springs, 1885
Matthews, John T.	Pvt.	E	Nashville, 1904
McCann, Benjamin W.	1st Lt.	D	Bon Aqua Springs, 1885
McCauley, John C.	Pvt.	C	Nashville, 1904
Phillips, John W.	2nd Lt.	K	Nashville, 1904
Redden, John W.	Pvt.	K	Bon Aqua Springs, 1885

---

[1] The 11th Tennessee held two post-war reunions. The first was at Bon Aqua Springs in Hickman County, TN on September 24, 1885. The second was in Nashville on June 14, 1904.

Rogers, John G.	3rd Corp.	A	Nashville, 1904
Roland, William A.	Pvt.	F	Nashville, 1904
Savage, James R.	1st Sgt.	G	Nashville, 1904
Shouse, Jacob W.	4th Sgt.	H	Bon Aqua Springs, 1885
Stokes, Andrew	Corp.	C	Bon Aqua Springs, 1885
Tarkington, George W.	Pvt.	K	Bon Aqua Springs, 1885
Tidwell, Franklin F.	Capt.	K	Bon Aqua Springs, 1885
Weems, Corder T.	Pvt.	K	Bon Aqua Springs, 1885
Welch, John	Pvt.	G	Bon Aqua Springs, 1885

Bibliography

<u>Primary Sources</u>
  <u>Letters, Diaries, and Manuscript Materials</u>
Allen, A. J. "Letter to Captain William Green." 10 November 1861. Possession of Lewis Hooper, Beaman Collection, Franklin TN.
Austin, C. F. "Letter to E. A. Reader." 5 November 1861. In Moore, John Trotwood. *Tennessee, Civil War Records – Middle Tennessee, Civil War Correspondence*. Nashville TN: Historical Records Survey June 1, 1939. Tennessee Historical Records Survey.
Barfield, Castillo. "Letter to Mollie." 4 November 1861. Abraham Lincoln Library and Museum, Lincoln Memorial University.
Black, Roy W., Sr. ed., "William J. Rodgers Memorandum Book." West Tennessee Historical Society Papers, vol. 9, 1955.
Bryant, James. "Letter to Miss Tennie." 22 February 1862. United State Military History Institute, Carlisle Barracks PA.
Chalaron, J. A. "Letter to Mary V. Nichols." 18 December 1897. Britt Collection, Box 3, File #10, Tennessee State Library and Archives.
Clark, E. W. "Letter to Mother." 26 August 1861. Clark Family Papers. Tennessee State Library and Archives.
Coble, Jesse. "Letter to Father and Mother." 26 August 1861. In Moore, John Trotwood. *Tennessee, Civil War Records – Middle Tennessee, Civil War Correspondence*. Nashville TN: Historical Records Survey June 1, 1939. Tennessee Historical Records Survey.
Coffee, Chatham. "May 27, 1864 - Battle of Pickett's Mill." *Memphis Daily Appeal* (Memphis TN), 12 June 1864.
Crook, W. J. "Letters to Hattie." W. J. Crook Papers, Kennesaw Mountain National Military Park.
Fielder, A. T. *Captain A. T. Fielder's Civil War Diary Company B 12th Tennessee Regiment Infantry C. S. A. July 1861 – June 1865*. ed. by M. Todd Cathey. Broken Arrow OK: Create Space, 2012.
Fitch, John. *Annals of the Army of the Cumberland: Comprising Biographies, Descriptions of Departments, Accounts of Expeditions, Skirmishes, and Battles; Also Its Police Record of Spies, Smugglers, and Prominent Rebel Emissaries... And Official Reports of the Battle of Stone River and of the Chickamauga Campaign*. Philadelphia PA: J.B. Lippincott & Co., 1864.
Francis, John Clark. Unpublished Manuscript. Francis-Martin Family Papers. Alabama Department of Archives and History.
Gale, W. D. "Letter to Wife after Hood's Defeat Before Nashville." 19 January 1865. Civil War Collection: Confederate Collection, Box 9, Letters, Folder 7, Gale William Dudley, Tennessee State Library and Archives.
"Gen. Gordon, Soldier, Statesman, Dead." From Gordon Collection, University of Memphis. Unknown Newspaper. 1 May 1910.
Gordon, R. C. "Letter to Miss Mary." 18 February 1862. Civil War Collection, Confederate, Box 9 #14, Tennessee State Library and Archives.
"H. R. DeBow." *Confederate Veteran* vol. 13 no. 10 (October 1905), 445.
Harder, William Henry. "Memoirs." Tennessee State Library and Archives, MF 574, 1 vol., 83.
Jackson, J. W. "Letters to Parents." Martha Farmer Anthony Collection. Tennessee State Library and Archives.
"James Polk Fielder." *Confederate Veteran* vol. 8 no. 7 (July 1900): 328.
"John M. Critz." *Confederate Veteran* vol. 25 no. 10 (July 1917): 324.
"Joseph W. Gilman." *Confederate Veteran* vol. 16 no. 3. March 1908: 137.
"Letter from Camp Cheatham." *Nashville Republican Banner* (Nashville TN). 2 July 1861.

Lowrey, Mark P. "Autobiography." Civil War Miscellaneous Collection. United States Army Military Institute, Carlisle Barracks, Pennsylvania.

Moscow Carter Interview. Unknown newspaper article in the McGavock-Cowan scrapbook, Carnton Plantation Archives.

Nichol, Bradford. "Civil War Memoir." Manuscript Collection MF 1627. Tennessee State Library and Archives.

Porter, George C. "Eleventh Tennessee." *Nashville Banner* (Nashville TN). Unknown date.

Pullen, William C. *Reminiscences of a Confederate Soldier*. Unpublished manuscript. Transcribed and edited by Mary McCrary.

R. M. Gray Reminiscences, 1867, Unpublished Manuscript, The Southern Historical Collection, The Louis Round Wilson Special Collections Library.

Rains, James E. "Letter to General Carter L. Stevenson." 14 May 1862. James E. Rains Service Record, Compiled Service Records of Confederate Soldiers Who Served in Organizations from the State of Tennessee. National Archives Microfilm Publications, Washington DC. M268 R163.

_____. "Letters to Wife." Manuscript Collection, James Edward Rains Letters 1861-1862. MF 64. Tennessee State Library and Archives.

Shipp, James, "Letters to Sister." In *Civil War Letters of Hickman County*, ed. By Carol Chessor. Genealogy Room, Hickman County Public Library, Centerville TN.

Skelton, James M., "Letter to A. B. Skelton." 5 November 1861. Possession of James M. Skelton, Evanston IL.

Sloan, William E. *Diary of William E. Sloan*. Tennessee State Library and Archives.

Smith, Frank H. "Interview with Col. M. B. Carter" in *History of Maury County* reproduced in Rick Warwick, comp. and ed., *Williamson County in the Civil War*. Nashville: The Heritage Foundation of Franklin and Williamson County, 2007.

Spence, W. Jerome D. *The Travels, Troubles, Pleasures, and Pastimes of Jerome D. Spence of Dunnington, Tennessee*. Unpublished diary 10 May - 25 November 1861. Copy of manuscript in possession of Gary W. Waddey.

Thedford, William. "Report of Operations and Casualties of the 11th Regt. Tenn. Inf. in the Battle of Murfreesboro 31 December 1862." Confederate States Army Casualties: Lists and Narrative Reports, 1861- 865. M836 R4, Tennessee State Library and Archives.

Trogdon, A. W. Trogdon, "Interesting Letter." *Waverly Sentinel* (Waverly TN). Unknown date.

Tuttle, John W. "Diary." Kennesaw Mountain National Battlefield.

White, W. K. "Letter to Parents." 18 January 1863. In *Waco Times-Herald* (Waco TX).

Yates, Clayton. "Reminiscences of the Civil War." *Daily Messenger* (Mayfield KY). Unknown date.

_____. "War Experiences." *Daily Messenger* (Mayfield KY). Unknown date.

_____. "War Reminiscences." *Daily Messenger* (Mayfield KY). Unknown date.

_____. "Article Four." *Daily Messenger* (Mayfield KY). Unknown date.

_____. "Further Reminiscences of the Civil War." *Daily Messenger* (Mayfield, KY). 28 April 1911.

_____. "Saved His Brigade." *Daily Messenger* (Mayfield KY). 4 November 1912.

_____. "Battle of Chattanooga." *Daily Messenger* (Mayfield KY). 12 November 1912.

Newspapers

Boston Daily Courier (Boston MA)
Chattanooga Daily Rebel (Chattanooga TN; Griffin GA)
Christian Advocate (Unknown Place)
Cincinnati Commercial (Cincinnati OH)
Cincinnati Gazette (Cincinnati OH)
Clarksville Leaf Chronicle (Clarksville TN)
Daily Messenger (Mayfield KY)
Hickman County News (Centerville TN)

Hickman Pioneer (Centerville TN)
Knoxville Register (Knoxville TN)
Louisville Courier Journal (Louisville KY)
Louisville Daily Journal (Louisville KY)
Memphis Commercial Appeal (Memphis TN)
Memphis Daily Appeal (Memphis TN)
Milwaukee Sunday Telegraph (Milwaukee WI)
Nashville Daily Gazette (Nashville TN)
Nashville Daily Patriot (Nashville TN)
Nashville Daily Union (Nashville TN)
Nashville Republican Banner (Nashville TN)
Nashville Union and American (Nashville TN)
Nashville Union and Dispatch (Nashville TN)
Nashville Weekly American (Nashville TN)
Review Appeal (Franklin TN)
Semi-Weekly Tobacco Leaf (Clarksville TN)
Waverly Sentinel (Waverly TN)

Microfilm, War Papers, and Periodicals

Alspaugh, Josiah C. "Reminiscences of Company A, 11th Tennessee." *Confederate Veteran* vol. 18 no. 11 (November 1910): 506.

"Autographs From An Old Album." *Confederate Veteran* vol. 32 no. 4 (1924): 131.

"Bivouac 18 A.C.S. and Camp 28, U.C.V." *Confederate Veteran* vol. 5 no. 11 (November 1897): 566-67.

Carnell, Reddick C. "Capt. William I. White." *Confederate Veteran* vol. 31 no. 5 (May 1923): 187.

Chapman, W. S. "A Boast and a Challenge." *Confederate Veteran* vol. 34 no. 8 (August 1926): 301-02.

Compiled Service Records of Confederate Soldiers Who Served in Organizations from the State of Louisiana. National Archives Microfilm Publications, Washington DC M320.

Compiled Service Records of Confederate Soldiers Who Served in Organizations from the State of Tennessee. National Archives Microfilm Publications, Washington DC M268.

Cook, John C. "A Boy at the Battle of Nashville." *The Taylor-Trotwood Magazine* (November 1909): 100-05.

Craig, R. J. "Obituary of Jerome B. Anderson." *Journal of the Tennessee Methodist Conference.* 1902: 41-42.

Crook, W. M. "W. M. Crook's Heroism at Franklin." *Confederate Veteran* vol. 5 no. 6 (June 1897): 303-04.

Deering, J. "Service with the Twentieth Tennessee." *Confederate Veteran* vol. 33 no. 1 (January 1925): 14-16.

"Dr. Thomas D. Thompson." *Confederate Veteran* vol. 25 no. 7 (July 1917): 323.

"Edward Hall Miller." *Confederate Veteran* vol. 30 no. 12 (December 1922): 472.

Eleazer, W. D. "Fight at Dead Angle in Georgia." *Confederate Veteran* vol. 14 no. 7 (July 1906): 312.

Figures, H. P. "A Boys Impressions of the Battle of Franklin." *Confederate Veteran* vol. 23 no. 1 (January 1915): 4-7, 44.

Gordon, George W. "The Famous Snowball Battle." In *Personal Record of the Thirteenth Regiment, Tennessee Infantry.* Edited by Alfred J. Vaughan. Memphis TN: Press of S.C. Toof & Co., 1897. Reprint, Memphis TN: Frank and Gennie Myers and Burke's Book Store, 1976.

_____. Manuscript. Unknown Occasion, Gordon Collection. University of Memphis.

Harris, Isham G. *First message to the Tennessee assembly, January 7, 1861.* Library of Congress. Public Acts of the State of Tennessee. Passed at the Extra Session of the Thirty-third General Assembly, for the year 1861. Published by Authority. Nashville TN: E. G. Eastman & Co., Public Printers, Union and American Office, 1861.

_____. *Reply to Simon Cameron, U. S. Secretary of War, April 15, 1861.* Isham G. Harris Papers. Tennessee State Library and Archives, Nashville TN.

_____. *Second Message to the Tennessee General Assembly, April 25, 1861*, Library of Congress. Public Acts of the State of Tennessee. Passed at the Extra Session of the Thirty-third General Assembly, for the year 1861. Published by Authority. Nashville TN: E. G. Eastman & Co., Public Printers, Union and American Office, 1861.

_____. *Isham G. Harris to Abraham Lincoln, April 29, 1861*. Abraham Lincoln Papers. Library of Congress. Series 1, General Correspondence. 1833-1916.

"Historic Records of Confederate Days." *Confederate Veteran* vol. 16 no. 2 (February 1908): 78.

Hutcheson, Joseph, "More About Gen. James E. Rains." *Confederate Veteran* 16 no. 8 (August 1908): 390-391.

"J. G. Miller." *Confederate Veteran* vol. 11 no. 7, (July 1903): 334.

"J.I.J. Adams." *Confederate Veteran* vol. 6 no. 11 (November 1898): 534.

"James I. Clark." *Confederate Veteran* vol. 9 no. 6 (June 1901): 274.

"John Jefferson Johnson." *Confederate Veteran* vol. 20 no. 9 (September 1912): 432.

Lincoln, Abraham. *Abraham Lincoln in Reply to Isham G. Harris, May 1861*, Abraham Lincoln Papers. Library of Congress. Series 1, Correspondence. 1833-1916.

Lowery, Mark P. *Autobiography*. Civil War Miscellaneous Collection, United States Army Military Institute, Carlisle Barracks, Pennsylvania.

"M. A. Nelson." *Confederate Veteran* vol. 21 no. 10 (October 1913): 503.

M'Amy. C. D. "Brave P.E. Drew and His Fate." *Confederate Veteran* vol. 2 no. 3 (March 1894): 85.

Maney, William B. *Regimental Surgeon's Log*. Confederate Collection, Manuscript Section, Box 18, Military Units Tenn. Inf. Regt. 11, Medical Records, Tennessee State Library and Archives.

McCauley, William H. "Tribute to a Federal Officer." *Confederate Veteran* vol. 7 no. 2 (February 1899): 72

_____. *Record Book, 11th Tennessee Infantry, Company C, Guns and Equipment*. Tennessee State Library and Archives. Army of Tennessee Records, Record Group 4, Box 3, series 5: Miscellaneous Material no.19.

"Members of Joe Johnston Camp, No. 94, Mexia, Tex. Deaths from July, 1911 to July, 1912." *Confederate Veteran* vol. 20 no. 12 (December 1912): 579.

"Memorial Addresses on the Life and Character of George Washington Gordon." Address of Mr. Sherwood of Ohio. University of Memphis, Memphis TN. Gordon Collection. National Archives Records Administration. *Compiled Service Records of Confederate Soldiers Who Served in Organizations from the State of Tennessee*. Washington DC: National Archives and Records Service, General Services Administration, 1960.

Office of the Commissioner for Marking Graves of Confederate Dead, comp., "Register of Confederate Dead Rock Island Illinois." Washington DC: War Department, 1912.

Order Book for Confederate Volunteers at Camp Cheatham. Tennessee Historical Society Miscellaneous volumes 1805-1918. Tennessee State Library and Archives.

Pirtle, Alfred. "Stone River Sketches." *Sketches of War History 1861-1865*. Papers Read Before Ohio Commandery, MOLLUS, 6 vols. Cincinnati OH: By the Commandery, 1888-1908.

"Preston G. Price." *Confederate Veteran* vol. 20 no. 11 (November 1912): 531.

"R. N.[W.] Cooley." *Confederate Veteran* vol. 11 no. 9 (September 1903): 422.

"Record of Gen. George W. Gordon." *Confederate Veteran* vol. 20 no. 9 (September 1912): 427-431.

Reunion Pamphlet of the 11th Tennessee Infantry of the C.S.A. June 14, 1904.

Shultz, B. F. "Lieut. A. H. Vaughan, Killed in the War." *Confederate Veteran* vol. 8 no. 12 (December 1900): 518.

Sowell, P. A. "Rev. John Wesley Rooker." *Journal of the Tennessee Conference* (1914): 69-70.

Tennessee Confederate Pension Applications. Tennessee State Library and Archives.

Texas Confederate Pension Applications. Texas State Library and Archives Commission.

"The Address of Gen. Gordon." *Confederate Veteran* vol. 8 no. 1 (January 1900): 6-12.

Thruston, Gates P. "Personal Recollections of the Battle In the Rear at Stones River, Tennessee."

Papers Read Before Ohio Commandery, MOLLUS, 6 vols. Cincinnati OH: By the Commandery, 1888-1908.
"Tributes to Gen. George W. Gordon." *Confederate Veteran* vol. 19, no. 10 (October 1911): 499.
"Turner Halliburton." *Confederate Veteran* vol. 6 no. 3 (March 1898): 110.
Turner, W. A. "Obituary of John G. Bolton." *Journal of the 79th Session Tennessee Conference of the Methodist Episcopal Church, South* (19-25 October 1892): 43-44.
United Confederate Veterans. "Tennessee Division Bivouac Records." 1862-1941. Tennessee State Library and Archives. Confederate Collection. Box 20, VII-D-1-2, Box 1, f. 5 and vol. II.
Watkins, L. J. "Address of Brig. Gen. James E. Rains." *Confederate Veteran* vol. 16 no. 5 (May 1908): 209-210.
Watkins, S. R. "Snow Battle at Dalton – Little Jimmie White." *Confederate Veteran* vol. 1 no. 9 (September 1893): 261-62.
Ward, John H. "The Eleventh Tennessee Infantry." *Confederate Veteran* vol. 16 no. 8 (August 1908): 420.
Weems, P.V.H. "Will, 22 July 1864." In *Hickman County Tennessee Wills*, edited by Oglia Dotson. Nunnelly TN: O. Dotson, 1983.
"Young, J.P." [*sic*., I.P.] *Confederate Veteran* vol. 18 no. 2 (February 1910), 88.

Books
Baker, Georgia L. *1850 Census for Dickson County, Tennessee with Index.* Nashville TN: Richland Press, 2001.
_____. *1860 Census for Dickson County, Tennessee with Index* rev. ed. Nashville TN: Richland Press, 2007.
_____. *1860 Census for Dickson County, Tennessee with Index.* Nashville TN: Richland Press, 1998.
_____. *1870 Census of Dickson County.* Nashville TN: Richland Press, 2001.
Bishop, J. W. *The Story of a Regiment; Being a Narrative of the Service of the Second Regiment, Minnesota Veteran Volunteer Infantry, in the Civil War of 1861-1865.* St. Paul MN: s.n., 1890. Reprint, St. Paul MN: North Star Press, 2000.
Clifton, Betty F. *1870 Census of Humphreys County, Tennessee: 1870.* Taylorsville CA: B.F. Clifton, 1979.
Copley, John M. *A Sketch of the Battle of Franklin, Tenn. With Reminiscences of Camp Douglas.* Austin: Eugene Von Boeckmann, Printer, 1893. Reprint edited by M. Todd Cathey. Broken Arrow, OK: Regimental Publishing, 2012.
Cotten, Michael. *The Williamson County Cavalry: A History of Company F, Fourth Tennessee Cavalry Regiment, CSA.* Goodlettsville TN: M. Cotten, 1994.
Cox, Jacob D. *The Battle of Franklin, Tennessee November 30 1864: A Monograph.* New York NY: Charles Scribner's Sons, 1897.
_____. *March to the Sea: Franklin and Nashville.* New York NY: Charles Scribners Sons, 1913.
Crumpton, Washington Bryan. *A Book of Memories 1842-1920.* Montgomery AL: Baptist Mission Board, 1921.
Dalton, Robert E. and Lynette H. Dalton. *Cheatham County Census: 1860.* vol. 1. Memphis TN: Robert E. Dalton and Lynette H. Dalton, 1986.
Dinkins, James. *Personal Recollections and Experiences in the Confederate Army by an Old Johnnie 1861 to 1865.* Cincinnati OH: R. Clarke Co., 1897. Reprint, Dayton OH: Morningside, 1975.
Dobson-Sides, Peggie. *1860 Davidson County, Tennessee, Census.* Nashville TN: P. Dobson-Sides, 2000.
Drake, Edwin L. ed. *The Annals of the Army of Tennessee and Early Western History.* Nashville TN: A. D. Haynes, 1878.
Dyer, Frederick H. "Seventy-Seventh Pennsylvania Regiment." In *A Compendium of the War of the Rebellion, Comp. And Arranged from Official Records of the Federal and Confederate Armies, Reports of the Adjutant Generals of the Several States, the Army Registers, and Other Reliable Documents and Sources.* Des Moines IA: The Dyer Publishing Company, 1908.

Dyer, Gustavus W., John Trotwood Moore, Colleen Morse Elliott, and Louise Armstrong Moxley. *Tennessee Civil War Veterans Questionnaires*. 5 Vols. Easley SC: Southern Historical Press, 1985.

Elliott, Sam Davis. ed. *Doctor Quintard, Chaplain C.S.A. and Second Bishop of Tennessee: The Memoir and Civil War Diary of Charles Todd Quintard*. Baton Rouge LA: Louisiana State University Press, 2003.

Evans, Clement A. *Confederate Military History: A Library of Confederate States History*. Vol. 10, Atlanta GA: Confederate Publishing Co., 1899. Reprint, Wilmington NC: Broadfoot, 1987.

Fischer, Marjorie H. and Ruth Blake Burns, *1880 Census, Humphreys County, Tennessee*. Vista CA: RAM Press, 1987.

Fitch, John. *Annals of the Army of the Cumberland Comprising Biographies, Descriptions of Departments, Accounts of Expeditions, Skirmishes, and Battles; Also Its Police Record of Spies, Smugglers, and Prominent Rebel Emissaries... and Official Reports of the Battle of Stone River and of the Chickamauga Campaign* 5th ed. Philadelphia, PA: J. B. Lippencott & Co., 1864.

Garrett, Jill K. *Census of Humphreys County, Tennessee: 1850*. Columbia TN: N.P. 1962.

Garrett, Jill Knight, and Catherine Kelly Gilliam. *1850 Census of Hickman County, Tennessee*. Columbia TN: 1967.

Harris, Bonnie P. *The Confederate Hospitals of Madison, Georgia: Their Records & Histories 1861-1865*. Buckhead GA: Bonnie P. (Patsy) Harris, 2014.

Hoffman, John. *The Confederate Collapse at Missionary Ridge: The Reports of James Patton Anderson and His Brigade Commanders*. Dayton OH: Morningside, 1985.

Johnson, Susy A. comp. *Census of Humphreys County, Tennessee: 1860*. Rosell IL: United States Census Office, 1976.

Jones, John William. *Christ in the Camp or Religion in the Confederate Army*. Richmond VA: B. F. Johnson & Co., 1887. Reprint, Harrisonburg VA: Sprinkle Publications, 1986.

Keil, F. W. *The Thirty-fifth Ohio Regiment: A Narrative of Service from August 1861 to 1864*. Fort Wayne IN: Archer Housh & Co. 1894.

Lane, Mills. *Dear Mother, Don't Grieve About Me: If I Get Killed, I'll Only Be Dead: Letters from Georgia Soldiers in the Civil War*. Savannah GA: Beehive Press, 1977.

Lindsley, John Berrien. *Military Annals of Tennessee: Confederate*. Nashville TN: J. M. Lindsley & Co., 1886. Facsimile of the first edition, Wilmington NC: Broadfoot Publishing, 1995.

Logsdon, David R., comp., *Eyewitnesses at the Battle of Franklin*. Nashville TN: Kettle Mills Press, 2000.

McMurray, William J., Josiah Roberts Deering, and Ralph J. Neal,. *History of the Twentieth Tennessee Regiment Volunteer Infantry, C.S.A*. Nashville TN: Publication committee, consisting of W.J. McMurray, D.J. Roberts and R.J. Neal, 1904. Facsimile reproduction, Nashville TN: Elder's Bookstore 1976.

Moore, John Trotwood. *Tennessee Records of Cheatham County, Marriage Liscence [Sic]*. Vol. A 1856-1897, Nashville TN: The Survey: Works Progress Administration, 1937.

Nashville City Directory. Marshall & Bruce Company, 1900.

Newlin, W. H. *A History of the Seventy-Third Regiment of Illinois Infantry Volunteers: Its Services and Experiences in Camp, on the March, on the Picket and Skirmish Lines, and in Many Battles of the War, 1861-65. Embracing an Account of the Movement from Columbia to Nashville, and the Battles of Spring Hill and Franklin*. Springfield IL: W. H. Newlin, 1890. Reprint, Denver CO: University of Denver.

Nisbitt, James Cooper. *Four Years on the Firing Line*. Chattanooga TN: Imperial Press, 1914.

Obreiter, John and David W. Reed. *The Seventy-Seventh Pennsylvania at Shiloh: History of the Regiment*. Harrisburg PA: Harrisburg Publishing Co., 1905.

Porch, Deane. *Robertson County, Tennessee, Census: 1850*. Nashville TN: Porch, 1968.

_____. *1850 Census of the City of Nashville, Davidson County, Tennessee*. Fort Worth TX: American Reference Publications, 1969.

"Register of Confederate Dead Rock Island Illinois." Compiled in the Office of the Commissioner for Marking Graves of Confederate Dead, War Department, 1912.

Roman, Alfred. *The Military Operations of General Beauregard In the War Between the States 1861 – 1865 Including a Brief Personal Sketch and a Narrative of His Services in the War With Mexico, 1846-8* vol. II. New York: 1884; Reprint, New York NY: Da Capo Press, 1994.

Scofield, Levi Tucker. *The Retreat from Pulaski to Nashville, Tenn.; Battle of Franklin, Tennessee, November 30th, 1864*. Cleveland OH: Press of the Caxton Co., 1909.

Sistler, Byron and Barbara Sistler. *1850 Census, Tennessee* vol. 1. Evanston IL: Byron Sistler and Associates, 1974.

_____. *1880 Census Hickman County, Tennessee*. Nashville TN: Byron Sistler & Associates, 1999.

_____. *Davidson County Marriages 1838-1863*. Nashville TN: Byron Sistler & Associates, 1985.

_____. *Early Middle Tennessee Marriages* vol. 1. Nashville TN: Byron Sistler and Associates, 1988.

_____. *1880 Census of Dickson County, Tennessee*. Nashville TN: Byron Sistler and Associates, 1993.

Smith, Frank H. "Interview with Col. M. B. Carter" in *History of Maury County* reproduced in Rick Warwick, comp. and ed., *Williamson County: Civil War Veterans Their Reunions and Photographs*. Nashville TN: The Heritage Foundation of Franklin and Williamson County, 2007.

Smith, Mary Sue. *Davidson County, Tennessee Naturalization Records: 1803-1906*. Nashville TN: Byron Sistler & Associates, 1997.

Spence, W. Jerome D. and David L. Spence. *History of Hickman County, Tennessee*. Nashville TN: Gospel Advocate Publishing Co., 1900. Reprint, Columbia TN: P-Vine Press, 1981.

Tarrant, Eastham. *The Wild Riders of the First Kentucky Cavalry. A History of the Regiment in the Great War of the Rebellion*. Louisville KY: Press of R.H. Carothers, 1894.

Thatcher, Marshall P. *A Hundred Battles in the West: St. Louis to Atlanta, 1861-1865, the Second Michigan Cavalry, with the Armies of the Mississippi, Ohio, Kentucky, and Cumberland with Mention of a Few of the Famous Regiments and Brigades of the West*. Detroit MI: by the Author, 1884.

United Confederate Veterans. *Biographical Sketches and Pictures of Company B, Confederate Veterans of Nashville, Tennessee*. Nashville TN: Foster & Webb, 1902; reprint Beverly Pearson Barnes, 1974.

United Daughters of the Confederacy, Thomas Stewart Easley Chapter No. 1814. *Hickman County, Tennessee United States Census, 1860*. Centerville TN: Thomas Stewart Easley Chapter No. 1814, United Daughters of the Confederacy, 1982.

United States War Department. *The War of the Rebellion: A Compilation of the Official Records of the Union and Confederate Armies*. Washington DC: 1882. Reprint, Gettysburg PA: National Historical Society, 1972.

Vance, Robert V. "Twenty-Ninth Regiment." In *Histories of the Several Regiments and Battalions from North Carolina in the Great War 1861-1865* edited by Walter Clark. Raleigh NC: E. M. Uzell Printer, 1901.

Vaughan, Alfred J. *Personal Record of the Thirteenth Regiment, Tennessee Infantry*. Memphis TN: Press of S.C. Toof & Co., 1897. Reprinted, Memphis TN: Frank and Gennie Myers and Burke's Book Store, 1976.

Watkins, Sam, *Co. Aytch*, rev. ed. Franklin TN: Providence House Publishers, 2007.

Williamson County Archives. *1860 Census of Williamson County, Tennessee*. S.l.: Williamson County Archives, 2003.

Willis, Laura, and Betty Sellers. *Stewart County, Tenn. Census of 1850*. Melber KY: Simmons Historical Publications, 2000.

Yeary, Mamie. *Reminiscences of the Boys in Gray, 1861-1865*. Dallas TX: Smith & Lamar, 1912. Reprint, Dayton OH: Morningside, 1986.

Young, John D. *In Memoriam: Life and Character of Captain I. P. Young*. Bold Spring TN: 1909.

Secondary Sources
Manuscript Materials
Luff, Pauline Williams. "A Confederate Military Record of Lieutenant Colonel William Thedford Together With His Descendants." Unpublished Manuscript. Genealogy Room, Dickson County Public Library, Dickson, TN.

Newspapers
Columbia Herald, Columbia TN
Dickson County Herald, Dickson TN
Waco Times-Herald, Waco TX

Microfilm, War Papers, Articles, and Periodicals
Barfield. Martha Hall. "John Hall Family." in *The Heritage of Dickson County, Tennessee 1803-2006*. Dickson County Heritage Book Committee. Waynesville NC: County Heritage Inc., 2007: 250.
Beasley, Barbara. "Jesse W. Adcock and the Civil War." in *The Heritage of Dickson County, Tennessee 1803-2006*. Dickson County Heritage Book Committee. Waynesville NC: County Heritage Inc., 2007: 150-51.
Blevins, Ernest Everett. "Howard Turner Meek Pioneer and Private Company K, 11th Tennessee Confederate States." in *The Heritage of Dickson County, Tennessee 1803-2006*. Dickson County Heritage Book Committee. Waynesville NC: County Heritage Inc., 2007: 315.
_____. "Moses Harvey Meek Pioneer and 2nd Lieutenant Company K, 11th Tennessee Confederate States." Dickson County Heritage Book Committee. Waynesville NC: County Heritage Inc., 2007: 316.
Brock, R. A. "Lost Opportunity at Spring Hill." In *Southern Historical Society Papers*, 524-41. Richmond VA: Virginia Historical Society, 1959.
Feis, William B. "The Deception of Braxton Bragg: The Tullahoma Campaign, June 23 - July 4, 1863." *Blue and Gray Magazine* (October 1992): 10-21, 46-54.
Fowler, Nolan. "Johnny Reb's Impressions of Kentucky in the Fall of 1862." *Register of the Kentucky Historical Society* 48 (July 1950): 205-15.
Gill, Ruth Clifton. "Pioneer Family of Burrel Alexander Clifton Jan. 18, 1842-July 5, 1919." in *The Heritage of Dickson County, Tennessee 1803-2006*, 190-91. Dickson County Heritage Book Committee, Waynesville NC: County Heritage Inc., 2007: 190.
Harris, Marian G. "Grymes (Grimes)." in *The Heritage of Dickson County, Tennessee 1803-2006*. Dickson County Heritage Book Committee, Waynesville NC: County Heritage Inc., 2007: 246-47.
Jones, Phillip Bradley. "Moses Meek." in *The Heritage of Dickson County, Tennessee 1803-2006*. Dickson County Heritage Book Committee. Waynesville NC: County Heritage Inc., 2007: 316.
Kincaid, Robert L. "Long Tom." Kentucky vol. 17 no. 4 (Winter 1963): 17-18.
"Letters to Jill. Letter from Mrs. H. P. Leeper, Nashville." *River Counties*. Jill Garrett ed. Vol. 3, 1974: 195.
Masters, Claire. "True Son of the Confederacy: The Story of Reagan Barr" *Waco Heritage and History* vol. 27 no. 1 Winter 1997: 5-13.
McDonald, Hunter. Unpublished Manuscript (4 January 1966 Nashville TN). Tennessee State Library and Archives Manuscript Division AC NO. 1132.
Mitchell, Enoch L. "Letters of a Confederate Surgeon in the Army of Tennessee to His Wife." *Tennessee Historical Quarterly*. vol. 5 no. 1: 60-81.
Patey, James G. *The Patey-Skelton Family*. Charleston SC: J.G. Patey, 2002.
"Philip Van Horn Weems, C.S.A., Hero of the Confederacy, Killed at Atlanta Was Beloved Kinsman." *Weemsana* (July 1983): 3, 6-7.
"Julia Marcum, Scott County's (and the USA's) Only Woman to Receive a Pension for Her Civil War Service." *Scott County Historical Society Newsletter* (Winter 1984): 3.

Shelton, William H. "Forbes Bivouac #21 of Clarksville." *Montgomery County Genealogical Journal* vol. 7 no. 1 (September 1977): 19-24.
Whittington, Barbara Clifton. "John J. Clifton." in *The Heritage of Dickson County, Tennessee 1803-2006*. Dickson County Heritage Book Committee. Waynesville NC: County Heritage Inc., 2007: 190-91.

Books
Adams, Charles. *When in the Course of Human Events: Arguing the Case for Southern Secession*. Lanham, Md.: Rowman & Littlefield Publishers, 2000.
Alexander, Hudson. *Physicians of Williamson County, A Legacy of Healing, 1797-1997*. Franklin TN: Bob Canaday, 1998.
Allen, David C. *Winds of Change: Robertson County Tennessee in the Civil War*. Nashville TN: Land Yacht Press, 2000.
Anderson, Gladys P. and Jill Knight Garrett, *Humphreys County, Tennessee, Cemetery Records*. Rev. ed. 2 vols. S.l.: Gladys P. Anderson and Jill Knight Garrett, 1978.
_____. *Humphreys County, Tennessee, Cemetery Records*. 2 vols. Columbia TN: s.n., 1966.
Anderson, Mary Sue. *Like Leaves on Trees*. Waverly TN: Privately Published, 1969.
Armistead, Sarah. *The Hassell Family of Hickman County and Their Descendants*. S.l.: Privately Published, N.D.
Armistead, Sarah Peery, Ova Lee Peery Sawyer, Lorraine Peery Russell, Penny Russell Boyer, and Theresa Tarkington-Kersey. *Tarkingtons of Tennessee: Genealogy of John G. Tarkington*. Brentwood TN: S.P. Armistead, 2001.
Beaudot, William J. K. *The 24th Wisconsin Infantry in the Civil War*. Mechanicsburg PA: Stackpole Books, 2003.
Bogle, Joseph and William L. Calhoun. *Historical Sketches of Barton's (Later Stovall's) Georgia Brigade, Army of Tennessee, C.S.A.* Dayton OH: Morningside, 1984.
Bowen, Mary Stewart and Melissa Snyder Bowen. *Perry County, Tennessee Cemetery Records*. Vol. 1. Linden TN: M.N. Bowen, 1992.
Bradley, Mark L. *Last Stand in the Carolinas: The Battle of Bentonville*. Campbell CA: Savas Woodbury, 1996.
_____. *This Astounding Close: The Road to Bennett Place*. Chapel Hill NC: University of North Carolina Press.
Bradley, Michael R. *Tullahoma: The 1863 Campaign for Middle Tennessee*. Shippensburg PA: Burd Street Press, 2000.
Brock, Reid, Thomas O. Brock, and Tony Hays. *Volunteers-Tennessee in the War with Mexico*. 2 Vols. Nashville TN: Kitchen Table Press, 1986.
Brown, Kent Masterson. *The Civil War in Kentucky: Battle of the Bluegrass State*. Mason City IA: Savas Publishing Company, 2000.
Burgess, Timothy L. *Confederate Deaths and Burials Nashville, Tennessee 1861-1865*. Nashville TN: Author's Corner, 2012.
Capt. W. H. McCauley Camp #260 Sons of Confederate Veterans, *Confederate Graves of Dickson County Tennessee Soldiers*. Dickson, TN: Dale's Quick Print, 2003.
Castel, Albert. *Decision in the West: The Atlanta Campaign of 1864*. Lawrence KS: University of Kansas Press, 1992.
Clayton, W. W. *History of Davidson County*. Nashville, Charles Elder, 1971.
Connelly, Thomas L. *Army of the Heartland*. Baton Rouge LA: Louisiana State University Press, 1967.
_____. *Autumn of Glory: The Army of Tennessee 1862-1865*. Baton Rouge LA: Louisiana State University Press, 1971.
Corlew, Robert Ewing. *A History of Dickson County, Tennessee*. Nashville TN: Tennessee Historical Commission, 1956.

Cozzens, Peter. *No Better Place to Die: The Battle of Stones River.* Urbana IL: University of Illinois Press, 1990.

Crute, Joseph H., Jr. *Confederate Staff Officers.* Powhattan VA: Derwent Books, 1982.

Dale, Frank. *Delaware Diary: Episodes in the Life of a River.* New Brunswick NJ: Rutgers University, 1996.

Daniel, Larry J. *Battle of Stones River the Forgotten Conflict between the Confederate Army of Tennessee and the Union Army of the Cumberland.* Baton Rouge LA: Louisiana State University Press, 2012.

Darnell, Anita Whitefield, Mary Lewis Roe Jones, Ann Evans Alley, Robert D. Davidson, and Cleo Hogan. *Cemetery Records of Montgomery County, Tennessee.* Clarksville TN: Ideal Publishing, 1965.

Daughters of the American Revolution, James Buckley Chapter. *Weakley County, Tennessee Cemetery Listings.* Vol. 2, Sharon TN: The Chapter, 1980.

Dotson, Olgia, comp. and ed. *Hickman County Tennessee Wills.* Nunnelly TN: O. Dotson, 1983.

Durham, Norman. *The Cagle Family of Hickman County, Tennessee.* Sanford NC: N.G. Durham, 1994.

Durrett, Jean M., Yolanda G. Reid, and Diane Williams. *Robertson County, Tennessee Cemetery Records.* Springfield TN: Y. G. Reid, 1987.

Eaton, Clement. *A History of the Southern Confederacy.* Free Press: New York NY: Collier-Macmillan: London, 1965.

Etowah County Centennial Committee. *History of Etowah County, Alabama.* Gadsden AL: Etowah County Centennial Committee, 1968.

Fiske, John. *The Mississippi Valley in the Civil War.* Boston MA; New York NY: Houghton, Mifflin and Co., 1900.

Fowler, John D. *Mountaineers in Gray: The Nineteenth Tennessee Volunteer Infantry Regiment C.S.A.* Knoxville TN: University of Tennessee Press, 2004.

Garrett, Jill Knight. *A History of Humphreys County, Tennessee.* vol. 2. Columbia TN: Jill Knight Garrett, 1963.

_____. *A History of Humphreys County, Tennessee: A Supplement.* N.P.: Fischer & Burns, 1988.

_____. *Dickson County Handbook.* Easley S.C.: Southern Historical Press, 1984.

Garrett, Jill Knight and Iris H. McClain, *Dickson County Tennessee Cemetery Records.* 2 vols. Columbia TN: s.n. 1967.

_____. *Old City Cemetery Nashville, Tennessee Tombstone Inscriptions.* Columbia TN: Jill Knight Garrett and Iris H. McClain, 1971.

_____. *Sacred to the Memory: Cemetery Records of Hickman County,* Part 1. Columbia TN: P-vine Press, 1982.

Garrett, Jill Knight and Marise Parrish Lightfoot. *The Civil War in Maury County, Tennessee.* Columbia TN: s.n., 1966.

Garrett, Jill Knight, Ruth Burns, and Iris H. McClain. *Dickson County, Tennessee, Cemetery Records.* rev. ed. 2 vols. Vista CA: Ram Press, 1991.

Garrett, Jill Knight, Virginia Wood Alexander, and Evelyn B. McAnally. *Confederate Soldiers and Patriots of Maury County, Tennessee.* Columbia TN: Capt. James Madison Sparkman Chapter, United Daughters of the Confederacy, 1970.

Gillum, Jamie. *Twenty-five Hours to Tragedy: The Battle of Spring Hill and Operations on November 29, 1864 Precursor to the Battle of Franklin.* Spring Hill TN: James F. Gillum, 2014.

Goodspeed Brothers. *Goodspeed's History of Maury, Williamson, Rutherford, Wilson, Bedford, & Marshall Counties of Tennessee.* Columbia TN: Woodward & Stinson, 1971.

_____. *The Goodspeed Histories of Montgomery, Robertson, Humphreys, Stewart, Dickson, Cheatham, Houston Counties of Tennessee.* Columbia TN: Woodward & Stinson, 1972.

_____. *The Goodspeed Histories of Lawrence, Wayne, Perry, Hickman & Lewis Counties of Tennessee.* Columbia TN: Woodward & Stinson, 1975.

Goodson, Gary Ray, Sr. *Georgia Confederate 7,000.* Shawnee CO: Goodson Enterprises, 1995.

Gordon, Bernice W. *Index to Confederate Cemeteries, Tennessee.* Memphis TN: United Daughters of the Confederacy, Tennessee Division, n.d.

Gowan, Phillip A. *Byrns/Jackson: A Record of Their Probationary State*. Vol. 3, Brentwood TN: P.A. Gowan, 1986.

Grady, Jamie Ault. *Bowens of Virginia and Tennessee; Descendants of John Bowen and Lily McIlhaney*. Knoxville TN: s.n., 1969.

Greene, Lee Seifert. *Lead Me On: Frank Goad Clement and Tennessee Politics*. Knoxville TN: University of Tennessee Press, 1982.

Haile, Dennis Dozier and James E. Garrett, Jr. *Tombstone Records of Cheatham County, Tennessee*. Nashville TN: Cata/List Services, 1987.

Hale, Will Thomas and Dixon Merritt. *A History of Tennessee and Tennesseans*. Chicago IL: Lewis Publishing, 1913.

Hamer, Philip May. *Centennial History of the Tennessee Medical Association*. Nashville TN: Tennessee State Medical Association, 1930.

Hess, Earl J. *Banners to the Breeze: The Kentucky Campaign, Corinth, and Stones River*. Lincoln NE; London GB: University of Nebraska Press, 2000.

Hickman County Historical Society. *Hickman County, Tennessee History 1807-1993*. Dallas TX: Taylor Publishing Company, 1993.

Hitt, Andrew P. *Short Life Sketches of Some Prominent Hardin Countians*. Savannah TN: Fundco, 1988.

Horn, Stanley F. *Tennessee's War: 1861-1865, Described by Participants*. Nashville TN: Tennessee Civil War Centennial Commission, 1965.

_____. *The Decisive Battle of Nashville*. Knoxville TN: University of Tennessee Press, 1986.

_____. *Army of Tennessee*. Wilmington NC: Broadfoot, 1987.

Hudgins, Helen H. and Helen Potts. *McGavock Confederate Cemetery*. Franklin TN: Franklin Chapter #14 United Daughters of the Confederacy, 1989.

Hughes, Nathaniel Cheairs. *General William J. Hardee: Old Reliable*. Baton Rouge LA: Louisiana State University Press, 1965.

Hughes, Nathaniel Cheairs and John C. Wilson. *The Confederate Soldiers of Hamilton County, Tennessee: An Alphabetical Listing of the Confederate Soldiers Who Lived at One Time in Hamilton County, Tennessee*. Signal Mountain TN: Mountain Press, 2001.

Jacobson, Eric, and Richard Rupp. *For Cause for Country: A Study of the Affair at Spring Hill and the Battle of Franklin*. Franklin TN: O'More Publishing, 2007.

Johnson, E. McLeod. *A History of Henry County, Tennessee: Descriptive, Pictorial Reproductions of Old Papers and Manuscripts*. Paris TN: McLeod, 1958.

Judd, Cameron. *The Bridge Burners*. Johnson City TN: Over Mountain Press, 1996.

Kelley, Sarah Foster. *West Nashville, It's People and Environs*. Nashville TN: West Nashville Founders Museum, 1987.

Kincaid, Robert L. *The Wilderness Road*. Indianapolis IN: Bobs Merrill, 1947.

Livingston, Donald L. *Fulton Countians in the Civil War: Biographical Sketches of the Men from Fulton Co., Kentucky, and Surrounding Area Who Participated in Our Nation's Civil War, 1861-1865: Unit Histories and Muster Rolls*. S.l.: D.L. Livingston, 1985.

Losson, Christopher. *Tennessee's Forgotten Warriors: Frank Cheatham and His Confederate Division*. Knoxville TN: University of Tennessee Press, 1989.

Lynn, Stephen Douglas. *Confederate Pensioners of Kentucky: Pension Applications of the Veterans & Widows, 1912-1946*. Baltimore, MD; Sebree, KY: Gateway Press 2000.

MacArthur, Douglas. *Reminiscences*. New York NY: McGraw-Hill, 1964.

Marsh, Helen Crawford, Timothy Richard Marsh, and Timothy J. Edwards. *Official Marriages of Bedford County, Tennessee, 1861-1880*. Vol. 1, Greenville SC: Southern Historical Press, 1996.

Massey, Ross. *Nashville Battlefield Guide*. Nashville TN: Tenth Amendment Publishing, 2007.

McBride, Robert Martin, Dan M. Robison, and Ilene J. Cornwell. *Biographical Directory of the Tennessee General Assembly*. Vol. 2 1861-1901, Nashville TN: Tennessee State Library and Archives, 1975.

McDonough, James Lee. *Stones River: Bloody Winter in Tennessee*. Knoxville TN: University of Tennessee, 1980.

———. *Nashville: The Western Confederacy's Final Gamble.* Knoxville TN: University of Tennessee Press, 2004.

McDonough, James L. and Thomas L. Connelly. *Five Tragic Hours: The Battle of Franklin.* Knoxville TN: University of Tennessee, 1983.

McDonough, James L. and James P. Jones. *War So Terrible: Sherman and Atlanta.* New York NY: W. W. Norton Company, 1987.

———. *War in Kentucky From Shiloh to Perryville.* Knoxville TN: University of Tennessee Press, 1994.

Montgomery County Historical Society, *Montgomery County, Tennessee, Family History Book 2000.* Paducah KY: Turner Pub. Co., 2000.

Nesbitt, William J. *The Primal Families of the Yellow Creek Valley.* Vanleer TN: W. J. Nesbitt, 1985.

———. *West from Edrom; an Account of the Nesbitt Family of Tennessee.* Warner Robins GA: s.n., 1968.

Obion County Genealogical Society. *Cemeteries of Obion County, Tennessee.* Vol. 2, Union City TN: Obion County Genealogical Society (Tennessee), 1986.

Parks, Joseph H. *General Edmund Kirby Smith C.S.A.* Baton Rouge LA: Louisiana State University Press, 1982.

Perrin, William H. *A History of Christian County, Kentucky.* Chicago IL: F. A. Battey, 1884.

Pitts, John A. *Personal and Professional Reminiscences of an Old Lawyer.* Kingsport TN: Southern Publishers, 1930.

Poole, Gregory, G. *Robertson County Obituaries and Death Records 1803-1930.* Nashville TN: Land Yacht Press, 1993.

Proctor, Irene Adams. *The Adams Family Kith and Kin: From Halifax County, Virginia to Yellow Creek Valley and Grices Creek, Houston County, Tennessee: A Narrative Account: History, Biography, Genealogy, and Legend.* Baltimore MD: Gateway Press, 2000.

Roy, Paul. *Scott County in the Civil War.* Huntsville TN: Scott County Historical Society, 2001.

Scaife, William R. *The Campaign for Atlanta.* Atlanta GA: William R. Scaife, 1985.

———. *The Campaign for Tennessee.* Atlanta GA: William R. Scaife, 1986.

Sifakis, Stewart. *Who was Who in the Confederacy: A Biographical Encyclopedia of More Than 1,000 Confederate Participants.* New York NY: Facts on File, 1988.

Sistler, Byron and Barbara Sistler. *Dickson County Tennessee Marriages 1857-1870.* Nashville TN: B. Sistler, 1988.

———. *Maury County Tennessee Marriages 1852-1867.* Nashville TN: B. Sistler, 1986.

Smith, Jonathan K. T. *The Wyly Saga.* Memphis TN: Padmoor Press, 1981.

Strange, Judith A. *The Tennessee Confederate Soldiers Home: Marching Out of the Midst into the Light: Roster One and Roster Two, The Tennessee Confederate Veterans Home.* Nashville TN: Tennessee Tracers Limited, 1996.

Sword, Wiley. *Embrace an Angry Wind: The Confederacy's Last Hurrah: Spring Hill, Franklin, and Nashville.* New York NY: HarperCollins, 1992.

Tennessee Civil War Centennial Commission. *Tennesseans in the Civil War: A Military History of Confederate and Union Units with Available Rosters of Personnel.* 2 vols. Nashville TN: Civil War Centennial Commission, 1964.

Tennessee State Library and Archives. *Index to Interments in the Nashville City Cemetery, 1846-1962.* Nashville TN: Tennessee State Library and Archives, 1964.

Todd, Joe L. *Tennessee's Confederate Veterans in Oklahoma.* Oklahoma City OK: Archives Division, Oklahoma Historical Society, 1996.

United Daughters of the Confederacy, Captain Thomas Stewart Easley Chapter. *Confederate Soldiers of Hickman County, Tennessee and Their Family Lines.* Centerville TN: Captain Thomas Stewart Easley Chapter #1814, United Daughters of the Confederacy, 1996.

———. *Hickman County, Tennessee Cemetery Records. Part 2.* Centreville TN: Captain Thomas Stewart Easley Chapter, 1814, United Daughters of the Confederacy, 1989.

Vaughan, Jack C. *Brigadier General Alfred Jefferson Vaughan's Brigade, Army of Tennessee Confederate States of America.* Grand Prairie TX: Major Jack C. Vaughan, 1959-60.

Warner, Ezra J. *Generals in Gray: Lives of the Confederate Commanders*. Baton Rouge LA: Louisiana State University, 1987.
Warwick, Rick. *Williamson County: Civil War Veterans Their Reunions and Their Photographs*. Nashville TN: The Heritage Foundation of Franklin and Williamson County, 2007.
Weatherbee, F. W. *Alabama Artillery Units and Their Organization within the Confederate Army*. Carrollton MS: Pioneer Pub. Co., 1991.
Welsh, Jack D. *Arkansas Confederate Pension Applications by Veterans of Tennessee Units*. Oklahoma City OK: J.D. Welsh, 1994.
_____. *Medical Histories of Confederate Generals*. Kent OH: The Kent State University Press, 1995.
_____. *Two Confederate Hospitals and Their Patients*. Macon GA: Mercer University Press, 2005.

Electronic Information
16th Ohio volunteer Infantry Regimental History-History of Company B, <http://www.mkwe.com/ohio/pages/c001.htm>.
"Biography of Isham G. Harris." TNGenNet Inc., http://www.tngenweb.org/bios/h/harris.html.
Cartwright, Thomas. *Thomas Cartwright's Battle of Franklin Guide*, Compact Disc Recordings, 2009.
Confederate Circle of Heroes, Evergreen Cemetery, Murfreesboro, Tennessee. http://www.tngenweb.org/rutherford/confed4.htm.
Crook, Wiley M. *Autobiography and Reminiscences*. http://web.utk,edu/~donahue/he-stuff/crook03.htm.
"Diary of William Warner Reid, Corporal, Company C, 16th OVI, 6 August 1862." <http://www.mkwe.com/ohio/pages/c001.htm>.
Dickenson, Elmer. "The Olsen Monument." http://kendallkin.org/records/military/civil-war-records/the-olson-monument.html.
Find-A-Grave Memorials. http://www.findagrave.com/cgi-bin/fg.cgi?page=gs&.Finn's Point National Cemetery Salem, Salem County, New Jersey, interment.net/data/us/ nj/salem/finns/.
Fraley, David. "Carter House Tour." Franklin, Tennessee.
"Letter to Tuscarawas Advocate." 16th Ohio volunteer Infantry Website, 15 August 1862. <http.//www.mkwe.com/ohio/pages/c001.htm>.
Long, Martin F. "Letter to Father." "In Their Own Words." 11th Tennessee Infantry Website. http://www.11thtennessee.com/oldsite/in_their_own_words.html.
Marchant, Peter. "Letter to Susan." 16 December 1864. Letters of Captain Peter Marchant, http.//www.geocities.com/Heartland/Hills/4427/letters.htm.
Mississippi Confederate Grave Registry, http://mscgr.homestead.com/.
Nelson, Jane Irish. Jane's Genealogy Jigsaw: Military Ancestors. http.//freepages.genealogy.rootsweb/~irishgirl/military/south/.
Oldham, Van Buren. "Diary." Special Collections. University of Tennessee at Martin. ed. Dieter Ullrich, http://www.utm.edu/departments/special_collections/E579.5%20Oldham/text/ vboldham_indx.php (20 August 2014).
Shiels, Damian. "Irish Colonels: Michael Magevney, Jr.; 154th Tennessee Infantry." http.//irishamericancivilwar.com/2011/03/21/irish-colonels-michael-magevney-jr-154th-tennessee-infantry/.
Tennessee Death Records, Tennessee State Library and Archives, www.tn.gov/tsla/history/vital1925-18.htm.
The American Civil War Overview, Chapter VI, the Western Theater: Bragg's Kentucky Campaign, http://www.civilwarhome.com/kentucky.htm.
West, Patricia A. Newsom Station / Newsom Mill, Williamson County, Tennessee, 2000, http://www.websitewiz.com/genealogy/pdf/ pl_newsom_mill.pdf.
Wolbach, Theodore David. "Camp and Field" articles of the 16th Ohio Volunteer Infantry. *Holmes County Republican*, 24 February 1881 through 17 August 1882. The 16th Ohio Volunteer Infantry Website http://www.mkwe.com/ohio/pages/H011-15.htm.

Index

1st Colored Brigade, 237
1st U. S. Cavalry Division, 279
2nd Brigade (aka Rains's Brigade), 87, 100
2nd Division, 195
3rd Division, 240
IV Corps, 161, 162, 200, 206
XIV Corps, 195, 248, 249
XV Corps, 194
XVI Corps, 189, 194
XX Corps, 248
XXIII Corps, 200, 205, 206, 217

A

A. J. Donnegan Cemetery, 404
Academy Hospital, 120, 336, 342, 355
Adairsville Road, 162
Adairsville, GA, 160, 161
Adairville, KY, 272, 337
Adams Cemetery, 330
Adams, Alice, 314
Adams, Fredonia, 298
Adams, Green, 53
Adams, J. I. J., 66, 113, 257, 426
Adams, Jeams, 257
Adams, L. A., 257
Adams, Lurana E., 263
Adams, TN, 21, 333
Adams, William T. "Pig", 113, 257, 426, 443
Adams/Nesbitt Cemetery, 367, 368
Adcock Cemetery, 258
Adcock, Jesse, W., 258, 430, 446, 449
Adcock, Martin Van Buren, 209, 258, 446, 449
Adcock, Thomas B., 236, 244, 258, 349, 373, 380, 449
Adkisson Cemetery, 259
Adkisson, James P., 259
Adkisson, Samuel W., 259
Adkisson, Thomas J., 259, 406
Agnew, I. P., 259
Aiken, Lillie S., 356
Akles, James, 259
Alabama, 2, 104, 151, 152, 164, 199, 200, 224, 238, 272, 306, 371
Alabama Troops - Artillery (Confederate): Eufaula Light Artillery, 86, 101, 102, 103, 104, 105; Lumsden's Battery, 238
Alabama Troops - Cavalry (Confederate): 2nd, 191
Alabama Troops - Infantry (Confederate): 16th, 49, 57; 19th, 146; 28th, 131; 29th, 238
30th, 86
Alabamian, 159, 179, 201
Albright, Adaline, 356
Albright, W. C., 259
Alderson, A. J., 259, 430, 444
Alderson, William L., 259
Alexander, Alex, 259
Alexander, Francis M., 260
Alexander, Robert P., 260
Alexander, TN, 216
Alf Richardson Cemetery, 258, 383
Alisonia, TN, 129
Allatoona Pass, GA, 163
Allen, Andrew J., 100, 101, 260
Allen, Benjamin, 260
Allen, Christian F., 260, 441, 442
Allen, E., 260
Allen, George, 183, 260, 429
Allen, Julius D., 260
Allen, Myrick R., 260
Allen, William B., 260
Allen, William D., 260
Allen, William, 23, 260
Alley, Benjamin M., 261
Alley, J. R., 261
Alley, Samuel J., 12, 261, 421
Alley, Sarah, 387
Allison, A. B., 261
Allison, Becky, 234
Allison, W. L., 261
Allsbrook, Alfred M., 261
Alonzo Napier Camp, 414
Alspaugh, Emily C., 383
Alspaugh, Josiah C., 13, 261, 446, 449
American, 1
An Authenticated History of the Bell Witch, 22
Anderson Cemetery, 318, 405, 407
Anderson Chapel Cemetery, 298
Anderson, Andrew O., 261
Anderson, C., 261
Anderson, Isaac C., 131, 261
Anderson, James F., 39, 261
Anderson, James H., 262
Anderson, Jerome B., 262
Anderson, John W., 262, 430

Anderson, Joseph B., 262
Anderson, Mary, 405
Anderson, William G., 262
Anderson, Yeatman, 87, 129, 262, 442
Andersonville, TN, 415
Andrews, Christopher, 262
Andrews, David L., 262, 429, 446
Andrews, Elijah S., 262, 426
Anglen, John W., 262
Anglin, A. J., 263
Anglin, Malinda, 297
Anglin, Martin Van Buren, 263
Anniston Cemetery, 334
Anniston, MO, 334
Antietam, MD, 185
Appalachian Mountains, 47
Aquilla, TX, 414
Arkansas, 2, 194, 195, 286, 293, 365, 370, 373, 376
Arkansas Troops - Infantry (Confederate): 2nd, 220
Arizona, 254
Army of Kentucky, 94, 101
Army of Northern Virginia, 130, 140, 143, 208, 248, 250
Army of Tennessee, 101, 103, 124, 126, 131, 143, 150, 151, 153, 159, 161, 162, 169, 176, 179, 183, 185, 186, 189, 193, 197, 199, 200, 202, 204, 209, 233, 243, 245, 246, 247, 249, 258, 259
Army of the Cumberland, 103, 186, 200
Army of the Mississippi, 97, 101
Army of the Ohio, 69, 96, 97, 186, 200, 205
Army of the Tennessee, 159, 188, 189, 193
Arnold, John, 263
Asheville, NC, 251
Ashland City, TN, 259, 378
Asylum Hospital, 268, 291, 294, 296, 317, 325, 336, 347, 396
Athens, TN, 143
Atkins, Thomas, 224
Atlanta Campaign, 159, 179, 196, 209, 253
Atlanta, GA, 142, 152, 163, 164, 172, 179, 183, 184, 186, 188, 190, 191, 192, 193, 195, 196, 197, 198, 199, 258, 259, 260, 261, 262, 264, 266, 268, 269, 271, 272, 273, 274, 276, 279, 280, 281, 284, 285, 286, 287, 288, 289, 290, 291, 292, 293, 294, 296, 297, 298, 299, 300, 301, 304, 305, 306, 307, 308, 309, 311, 312, 313, 314, 315, 316, 317, 318, 319, 320, 321, 322, 323, 326, 327, 329, 330, 331, 332, 333, 335, 336, 337, 338, 339, 341, 342, 344, 345, 346, 349, 350, 353, 354, 355, 356, 358, 359, 361, 362, 363, 364, 365, 366, 367, 368, 369, 370, 371, 372, 373, 375, 376, 377, 380, 382, 383, 384, 385, 386, 387, 388, 389, 391, 393, 394, 395, 396, 398, 399, 400, 401, 403, 404, 405, 406, 409, 410, 411, 412, 413, 415, 417, 419, 435, 436
Atwood, T. H., 263, 438, 446
Auburn, KY, 297
Augusta, GA, 247, 252, 260, 273, 282, 312, 355, 357, 376, 413
Augusta, OH, 286
Austin Cemetery, 261, 263
Austin, Calvin F., 72, 263, 430, 444, 449
Austin, Charles D. V. B., 263, 437, 446
Austin, George W., 263
Austin, M. V., 263
Austin, Margret, 304
Austin, Mary Z., 261
Austin, TX, 267, 350, 414
Averitt Cemetery, 264, 370
Averitt, Paul M. C., 263, 438, 441
Averitt, Walter, 264
B
Baggett, Stephen, 264, 430, 444
Bailey, John C., 264
Bailey, Louise, 367
Bailey, Matthew P., 264
Baker Cemetery, 265
Baker, Charles, 264, 446
Baker, George W., 220, 264, 265, 426, 438
Baker, James, 264, 430, 437
Baker, O. D., 264
Baker, O., 264
Baker, Robert S., 265
Baker, S. G., 265
Baker, Stephen, 265
Baker, Wiley J., 220, 264, 265, 438, 446
Baker, William A., 23, 37, 265, 437
Baker, William F., 265
Baker, William H., 265, 424, 437
Baker, William J., 265, 426
Baker, William L., 161, 266, 433
Bakerville Cemetery, 418
Bald Hill (see also Leggett's Hill), 184, 188, 189, 190
Baldwin, Captain Aaron P., 214
Baldwin, David W., 266, 430
Baldwin, Effie, 266
Baldwin, James W., 266, 443, 449
Baldwin, James Wesley, 266
Baldwin, John G., 162, 266, 429, 430

Baldwin, Samuel P. "Sam," 183, 266, 433, 435
Ballard, Sam Houston, "Hugh," 77, 266, 437
Ballinger, TX, 270
Balthrop, David, 267, 446
Balthrop, Gustavus J., 196, 267, 429, 437
Balthrop, Sarah S., 383
Balthrop, William T., 267
Bandana, KY, 385
Bank Hospital, 305
Banks, H. T., 267, 441, 443
Banks, Nathaniel P., 91
Banks, Robert, 267, 437
Banning, Henry B., 177
Baptist, 194, 258, 376
Barbboursville Home Guard, 50, 52
Barboursville, KY, 47, 50, 52, 53, 58, 70, 92, 94, 98
Barfield, Castillo, 12, 57, 61, 62, 63, 64, 65, 71, 267, 422
Barlow, KY, 385, 386
Barnes, James H., 267, 438
Barnes, John T., 267
Barnes, Martha A., 314
Barnes, Patia A., 385
Barr, James F., 113, 267, 268, 426
Barr, John H., 267, 268, 433, 434
Barren Springs, TN, 329
Barron, W. J., 268, 423
Barry, D. H., 52, 268
Barry, James T., 268
Barry, William A., 268
Bartlett Cemetery, 268, 269, 296, 314
Bartlett, Adeline V., 296
Bartlett, Alex L., 268, 430
Bartlett, James T. "Jim," 245, 268
Bartlett, John H., 191, 268, 435, 446
Bartlett, Polk, 162
Barton's Creek, 366
Barton's Station, 244
Bate, William B., 165, 166, 194, 202, 206, 226, 405, 419
Bate's Division, 188, 201, 202, 238
Bateman, Thomas P., 7, 9, 16, 19, 22, 36, 53, 54, 73, 79, 84, 269, 421
Bates, John, 269
Batson, Martha E., 299
Batson, Mary E., 389
Battle Creek, 129
Battle, Joel, 49, 50, 51, 52, 56
Battle's Regiment (aka 20th TN), 43
Batts, Benjamin F., 269
Batts, Emily F., 262

Batts, Jeremiah, "Jerrie," 2, 158, 197, 226, 233, 262, 269, 438
Batts, John T., 183, 262, 269, 446
Batts, Kate, 21
Batts, Thomas J., 270, 429, 446, 449
Batts, William R., 270, 429, 438, 441
Batts' Family Cemetery, 269, 376
Baxter, William M., 270, 426
Bean Station, TN, 78, 99, 100, 259
Bear Creek, 244
Beasley, Francis M., 270, 430
Beasley, Reuben F., 131, 270, 423, 426, 435
Beasley, William S., Jr., 270, 271
Beauregard Light Infantry (aka Bull Pups, See also Company G), 3, 4, 5, 7, 10, 11, 14, 185, 421, 424
Beauregard, P. G. T., 85, 199, 246
Beaver Dam, TN, 322
Beck & Meyers, 4
Bedford Co., TN, 401, 410
Beech, Stephen C., 436
Beech, Thomas H., 277, 436, 438
Beechville, TN, 336
Beefrange, TN, 410, 415
Bell Cemetery, 271
Bell Co., TX, 356
Bell Hotel, 83
Bell Witch, 21, 272, 376
Bell, Alexander H., 101, 271, 443
Bell, Charley (aka Charley Harris), 101, 271
Bell, James A., 22, 271
Bell, John I., 272
Bell, John, 21, 22, 376
Bell, Montgomery, 271, 272
Bell, Richard W., 22, 272
Bell, Rutha J., 271
Bell's Mill, TN, 234
Bellbuckle Gap, TN, 124
Belle Creole, 275
Belle Meade, 391
Belle Vue, 10
Belmont, MO, 49
Bennett's Farm, 250
Benton Co., TN, 348, 366
Bentonville, NC, 249, 323, 343, 348, 405, 411, 440
Berry, W. G., 272
Bethel Cemetery, 260, 269, 313, 314, 316, 402
Bethlehem Methodist Church Cemetery, 419
Bethpage Cemetery, 377
Bibb, Epaminondas, "Pam," 272, 426
Big Creek Gap, 47, 93
Big Hill, 95, 97, 98

Big Springs Cemetery, 272, 346
Big Springs Hospital, 260
Binkley, James P., 272, 443
Binkley, Joseph S., 272
Binkley, Mary A., 346
Binkley, William Henry, 272, 430
Binns, John E., 22, 29, 54, 77, 191, 197, 234, 236, 258, 273, 349, 380. 423, 449
Binns, Mary G., 273
Binns, William A., 273
Birchtree Township, MO, 368
Bird, John, 273
Bird's Mill, 140
Birmingham, Martin S., 273
Bishop, Judson W., 148
Bishop, William P., 249
Biter, William A. J., 273, 426
Bivins, Ashley B., 273
Black, Isaac, 50, 52
Black, William A., 273, 444
Black, William J., 274
Blackburn Cemetery, 312
Blackburn, William H., 273, 442, 449
Blackie Hospital, 302, 355
Blackwell, M., 274
Blackwell, Sarah, 282
Blackwell, William J., 274
Blair's Creek, 78
Blake, Elenora C., 280
Bledsoe County, TN, 59
Bledsoe, William T., "Tom," 274
Blevins, A. K., 167
Bloomfield, MO, 331
Blountsville, AL, 199
Boaz, Virginia, 322
Bold Springs, TN, 304, 358, 359, 382, 420
Bolivar, TN, 316, 383
Bolton, Rev. John G., 48, 102, 274, 444
Bon Aqua Springs, TN, 9, 190, 253, 258, 263, 273, 274, 275, 276, 277, 289, 298, 303, 305, 310, 311, 316, 321, 328, 353, 355, 380, 393, 399, 402, 406, 411, 412, 449, 450
Bone, John J., 274
Bone, Sarah E., 330
Boon, Mr., 24
Boone, Daniel, 99
Boston Harbor, 254
Bouglies, Victor, 274, 435
Boules Warf, 283
Boulevard de Godshall, 73
Bowen, William M., "Billy," 9, 10, 274, 383, 422

Bowers, William D., 160, 275, 432
Bowker, John A., 275
Bowker, Joseph A., 275, 443
Bowles, M. W., 275, 446
Bowling Green, KY, 292
Boyle, Patrick, 275
Boysen, Sergeant, 138, 139
Bradford, Mary, 4, 30, 35, 234
Bradley, Luther P., 201
Bradley, Jefferson C., 275, 449
Bradley's Brigade, 201
Bradley's Knoll, 201
Bradshaw, C. A., 79
Bragg Hospital, 318
Bragg, Braxton, 86, 92, 94, 95, 96, 97, 98, 99, 101, 102, 104, 108, 119, 120, 122, 124, 126, 128, 131, 142, 143, 145, 147, 185
Bragg's Corps, 248
Brake, James D., 275
Brake, Thomas W., 275
Branch, Alex, 275
Brandon, James C., 212
Brandy, TX, 338
Brann, Martin, 275
Branner's Cavalry Battalion, 53, 56
Brazell, Henry, 275
Brazelton, William, 57, 77
Brazelton's Cavalry Battalion (aka 3rd TN Cavalry Battalion), 60
Brazzell, James, 276
Brazzell, John J., 276
Brazzell, John, 276
Breckenridge, John C., 119
Breezy Hill, 205
Brennan, T. M., 3
Brennon, Bartley, 276, 446
Brennon, John, 276
Brice, John, 83, 276, 443, 444
Brick Church, 314
Bristol Co., KY, 386
Bristol, TN, 37, 259
Broad River, 248, 402
Broad Street, 4
Brock Field, 136, 137, 256
Brooks Cemetery, 372
Brooks, Milton O., 3, 5, 85, 276, 426, 449
Broom, Tennie, 354
Broughton, E. T., 237
Brown Aaron, 276
Brown, Alexander Y. "Sandy", 134, 276, 422, 424, 430, 444
Brown, John C., 26, 198, 200, 202, 204, 205, 206, 207, 224, 226, 233

Brown, Jackson J., 72, 277
Brown, James A., 277
Brown, James M., 67, 277, 426, 446
Brown, John J., 67, 277, 426, 449
Brown, Lucindy, 284
Brown, Mary, 321
Brown, Robert J., 277
Brown, Samuel, 12, 277
Brown, Thomas, 277
Brown, W. J., 278, 427, 442
Brown, W. L., 278, 438
Brown, Wiley S., 87, 129, 278, 441
Brown, William F., 278, 444
Brown, William J., 278, 427, 442, 444
Brown, William S., 23, 278
Brown's Division, 193, 201, 202, 207, 209, 237
Browning Cemetery, 274
Browning, John A., 278, 430
Browning, William J., 278
Brownlow, William G., 34
Browns Ferry, 131
Bruce, Jonathan M., 278
Bruce, Pocahontas, 418
Bruce, Thomas N., 278
Bryan, Edward W., 278
Bryan, Jake, "Colonel," 279
Bryan, James F., 279
Bryan, James M., 80, 82, 279
Bryan, Martin W., 279, 444
Bryan, Montgomery T., 279, 435
Bryant Cemetery, 403
Bryant, Ephraim, 279
Bryant, J. W., 279
Bryant, S. B., 279
Bryant, Thomas R., 279, 429, 434
Buchanan, Jane T., 314
Buckner Hospital, 260
Buckner, Simon B., 55
Buckner's Corps, 135, 136
Buell, Don C., 82, 85, 86, 94, 96, 97, 103
Buffalo Creek, 45
Buffalo River, 338, 345
Buford, Mary, 402
Bull Pups (aka Beauregard Light Infantry, See also Company G), 10, 11, 15, 16, 17, 18, 19, 24, 25, 27, 28, 36, 48, 50, 51, 61, 62, 64, 65, 66, 76, 421, 424
Bullard, William, 132, 279
Bullock, James M., 191
Bumpass, Abram B., "Abe," 69, 169
Bunn, William T., 280, 427
Bunnell, Theodore A., 280, 438

Burch, Thomas, 280, 437
Burchard, Abram V., 280, 430, 444
Burchard, William J., 69, 280, 347
Burditt, J. M., 168
Burgie, Mary E., 382
Burgie, Philah, 382
Burk, Peter, 281, 429
Burkhart, B. F., 281, 429
Burnett, E. F., 281
Burnett, Thomas J., 280
Burns, Bryant, 280
Burns, Caroline J., 367
Burns, TN, 5, 8, 12, 13, 252, 258, 261, 263, 277, 321, 323, 327, 361, 380, 401, 405, 406, 412
Burns, William E., 64, 67, 280, 426
Burnside, Ambrose, 143
Burnsville, GA, 410
Burnsville, MS, 403
Burton, John W., 281
Burton, N. G., 281
Bushwhackers, 74
Butler, Joshua B., 239, 281, 437, 439
Byrns, Joseph W., 333
C
C. D. Benson & Company, 4
C. E. Hillman, 6
Caesar, Julius, 163
Caffrey, John, 282, 430, 442, 444
Cagle, Charles B., 282
Cairo, IL, 6, 275
Caldwell Co., KY, 418, 419
Caldwell, William H., 282, 437, 442
Calhoun, GA, 161, 360
California, 125
Callender, John H., 2, 55, 61, 62, 64, 66, 67, 76, 86, 282
Callender, Thomas, 282
Calloway Co., KY, 341
Calus, Patrick, 282
Calvary Cemetery, 327, 332, 392
Camak, GA, 247
Camp Andy Johnson, KY, 47, 50
Camp Bateman, 418, 420
Camp Bradford, TN, 35, 36, 260
Camp Buckner, IL, 407
Camp Buckner, KY, 55, 56, 57, 272, 285, 304, 326, 332, 334, 338, 346, 354, 360, 364, 368, 369, 370, 389, 393
Camp Butler, IL, 364
Camp Chase Cemetery, 270
Camp Chase, OH, 122, 127, 260, 264, 267, 270, 278, 284, 286, 292, 295, 297, 302,

303, 306, 310, 314, 316, 317, 320, 321, 322, 324, 328, 330, 332, 336, 337, 342, 352, 355, 357, 360, 365, 368, 373, 377, 383, 388, 392, 393, 395, 396, 398, 399, 403, 404, 407, 408, 410, 413, 416, 419, 441
Camp Cheatham, TN, 14, 15, 18, 19, 21, 22, 24, 25, 26, 29, 30, 35, 258, 260, 262, 265, 266, 269, 276, 277, 278, 279, 283, 285, 286, 288, 289, 291, 293, 300, 301, 303, 306, 307, 309, 310, 312, 313, 317, 320, 321, 323, 326, 327, 329, 330, 331, 333, 334, 339, 343, 348, 349, 353, 354, 355, 357, 359, 360, 361, 362, 364, 365, 368, 370, 371, 372, 373, 374, 376, 377, 378, 384, 387, 388, 389, 392, 395, 396, 397, 398, 402, 404, 406, 407, 408, 409, 410, 413, 414, 415, 417, 425
Camp Crawford, TN, 44, 45
Camp Cummins, 357
Camp Dick Robinson, KY, 47, 48, 49, 69, 95, 97
Camp Douglas, IL, 153, 260, 262, 273, 278, 282, 283, 286, 292, 297, 298, 308, 310, 312, 314, 322, 323, 326, 328, 329, 331, 334, 335, 336, 338, 339, 342, 348, 356, 362, 363, 369, 370, 371, 372, 375, 377, 378, 379, 391, 393, 398, 404, 409, 411, 415, 416, 442, 443
Camp Foster, 40, 41
Camp Gannt, TN, 35
Camp Harding, TN, 9, 10, 12, 15, 18
Camp Morton, IN, 83, 257, 266, 267, 271, 272, 275, 276, 289, 294, 295, 307, 309, 314, 317, 326, 327, 349, 355, 366, 370, 371, 375, 384, 396, 403, 407, 443
Camp Rains, TN, 44
Camp Wildcat, KY (see also Wildcat, KY), 56, 59, 61
Campbell and McEwen Law Firm, 269
Campbell, C. E., 283
Cane Creek, 244
Cannon, Francis E., 377
Cannon, John T., 283
Cantey, James, 179
Cantey's Brigade, 159, 164
Capers, Ellison, 195
Capes, Elijah "Lige", 72, 283
Capps, Sterling F., 167, 283, 430, 433
Capps, William, 283
Carbide, James N., 283
Carbide, Joseph M., 283, 438, 442
Carnton, 206

Carol House, 147
Carolinas, 186
Carondelet, 235
Carothers Cemetery, 348
Carothers, Alice R., 397
Carothers, James H. "Tack," 9, 283, 444
Carothers, Rachel J., 347
Carper, John, 283
Carroll Co., OH, 286
Carroll Co., TN, 326
Carroll, James J., 283, 284, 427
Carroll, John A., 238, 439, 441
Carter Cotton Gin, 212, 216, 223, 224, 226
Carter House, 212, 218, 219, 220, 221, 222, 226, 230, 231, 256
Carter Smokehouse, 218
Carter, Captain Tod, 205
Carter, D. E., 284
Carter, Fountain B., 205
Carter, Green W., 284, 427
Carter, James, 47
Carter, John C., 165, 195, 202, 233
Carter, Joseph J., 28, 284, 429, 437
Carter, Moscow, 205, 219, 222
Carter, Sally Gault, 232
Carter, Samuel, 47
Carter's Brigade, 187, 207
Carter's Creek Pike, 206
Carter's Station, 36, 37, 268, 285, 293, 306, 314, 357
Carthel, Captain, 139
Caruthers, Robert L., 128
Casey, John, 284
Cash, Emma, 329
Cassville, GA, 162, 285
Castleman Cemetery, 390
Catawba Bridge, SC, 389, 402
Cathey, Archibald "Archy," 258, 284, 285
Cathey, Elias N., 284, 285
Cathey, James N., 284
Cathey, John, 284, 444
Cathey, Joshua C., 284, 285
Cathey, Martin, 285
Cathey, Morris R., 285, 446
Cathey, Samuel M., 125, 284, 285
Cathey, William J., 285
Catholic, 392
Catoosa Hospital, 191, 342, 415
Cavanaugh, James, 285
Cave Hill Cemetery, 262, 267, 397
Cearnall, John A., 26, 28, 285
Cedar Hill Cemetery, 419

Cedar Hill, TN, 5, 18, 24, 25, 183, 260, 261, 262, 266, 267, 268, 268, 269, 271, 273, 275, 278, 279, 286, 288, 291, 295, 296, 297, 300, 302, 303, 305, 306, 310, 313, 314, 316, 318, 319, 320, 324, 325, 329, 331, 332, 333, 336, 337, 345, 347, 362, 364, 365, 366, 367, 372, 375, 376, 378, 385, 386, 387, 392, 395, 401, 402, 415, 416, 417, 418, 419
Centerpoint Cemetery, 309
Centerville Academy, 337
Centerville Cemetery, 268, 270, 330, 397
Centerville Guards, 424
Centerville Hotel, 298
Centerville, TN, 7, 9, 10, 253, 267, 269, 270, 298, 329, 338, 365, 394, 397
Ceston, Charles A., 38, 285
Chalaron, J. A., 232
Chalmers, James R., 208
Chamber's Mill, 193
Chamberlain, Ambrose N., 18, 285
Chamberlain, D. P., 285
Chambers, Eugenia, 271
Chambers, John, 286
Chambers, Mary E., 353
Chandler Cemetery, 289
Chandler, James G., 286
Chandler, John E., 286, 421
Chandler, John H., 112, 286, 427
Chandler, Joseph K., 112, 427, 430, 437
Chandler, Margret, 289
Chandler, Spencer, 69
Chapman, M. G., 286
Chapman, W. S., 232
Charleston Harbor, SC, 3
Charleston, TN, 143, 144
Charlotte City Cemetery, 39, 287
Charlotte Road, 13, 252
Charlotte, NC, 247
Charlotte, TN, 5, 9, 39, 190
Chattahoochee River, 179, 182, 185, 186
Chattanooga and St. Louis Railroad, 312
Chattanooga Confederate Cemetery, 295, 325, 358, 420
Chattanooga Creek, 147
Chattanooga Valley, 149
Chattanooga, TN, 29, 35, 37, 39, 82, 86, 94, 96, 101, 120, 131, 132, 134, 140, 141, 142, 144, 159, 252, 253, 257, 259, 260, 261, 263, 264, 267, 268, 272, 274, 276, 277, 278, 279, 281, 283, 284, 286, 287, 290, 291, 292, 293, 295, 297, 299, 302, 304, 310, 312, 316, 318, 322, 323, 325, 326, 327, 330, 332, 333, 336, 338, 340, 341, 342, 344, 349, 352, 353, 355, 356, 358, 359, 362, 363, 365, 366, 367, 376, 379, 380, 381, 386, 387, 392, 393, 398, 400, 402, 404, 413, 417, 420
Cheairs, Martin, 202
Cheairs, Nathaniel, 204
Cheatham Bivouac, 268, 273, 286, 312, 327, 332, 337, 345, 350, 355, 359, 367, 370, 377, 379, 388, 391, 400, 403, 410, 411, 413
Cheatham Co., TN, 8, 236, 253, 259, 323, 334, 378, 391, 401
Cheatham Hill, GA, 170, 256
Cheatham Rifles (See also Company B), 4, 5, 9, 11, 14, 18, 19, 25, 27, 28, 29, 36, 37, 38, 39, 44, 45, 50, 51, 52, 54, 64, 79, 83, 422, 423
Cheatham, Benjamin F., 3, 11, 14, 108, 118, 123, 125, 126, 135, 136, 138, 139, 142, 151, 154, 156, 157, 161, 162, 164, 166, 170, 171, 175, 176, 179, 185, 186, 191, 197, 198, 200, 201, 202, 204, 205, 206, 208, 209, 228, 229, 230, 234, 235, 238, 239, 243, 244, 246, 247, 248, 249, 250, 251, 252
Cheatham, Edward S., 286
Cheatham, Ephraim F., 286, 421
Cheatham, Richard, 286
Cheatham, William T., 5, 27, 287, 422
Cheatham's Corps, 199, 201, 206, 233, 234, 235, 238, 246, 248
Cheatham's Division, 122, 126, 131, 132, 135, 136, 143, 151, 152, 153, 154, 156, 159, 160, 161, 163, 164, 169, 170, 178, 179, 181, 183, 185, 186, 188, 193, 194, 195, 197, 209, 237, 251, 283, 350
Cherokee, 246
Cherry Bottom, TN, 280
Cherry Street, 4
Cherry, Rev. S. M., 48, 92, 100, 102, 103, 111, 117
Chessor Cemetery, 282
Chessy, Matthew, 26, 287
Chester, Claiborne B., 287, 427
Chester, John A., 287, 436
Chester, Joseph, 287
Chester, NC, 248
Chicago, IL, 153
Chichester, Cyrus, 287, 349
Chickamauga Creek, 132, 133, 135
Chickamauga Station, 149

Chickamauga, GA, 134, 142, 143, 150, 186, 209, 256, 260, 262, 264, 266, 267, 270, 279, 281, 284, 289, 290, 291, 294, 304, 309, 310, 311, 316, 317, 319, 323, 329, 335, 338, 339, 341, 343, 354, 355, 357, 363, 369, 373, 375, 376, 378, 379, 380, 381, 389, 392, 396, 401, 405, 406, 408, 409, 411, 419, 429
Chimborazo Hospital, 306
Chitwood, TN, 43, 44, 47
Choate, John, 287, 427
Choate, Smith E., 287, 439
Chrisman, Lafayette C., 287
Christian Church, 259, 305
Christian Co., KY, 270, 299, 310, 319, 381
Church Street, 4
Church, Charles H., 287
Churchwell, William, 74, 75, 76
Cincinnati, OH, 399
Citronelle, AL, 293, 296, 349, 360, 385, 386, 392
City Hotel (Nashville), 32
City Point, VA, 127, 264, 265, 276, 278, 289, 290, 292, 298, 314, 316, 317, 326, 330, 337, 350, 355, 357, 364, 372, 384, 390, 401, 407, 415, 416, 419
Civil War, 201, 256
Claiborn Machine Works, 3
Claiborne County, TN, 77, 87, 395
Clardy, George W., 288
Clark, Edward W., 5, 27, 44, 86, 119, 251, 288, 422, 423, 427, 446
Clark, George N., 288
Clark, James I., 288, 430
Clarksville, TN, 253, 371
Clarksville, TX, 295
Clay, KY, 266
Cleburne Co., AR, 320
Cleburne, Patrick R., 94, 98, 104, 108, 115, 123, 171, 188, 189, 193, 194, 201, 202, 204, 207, 209, 212, 217, 220, 233, 254, 315
Cleburne's Division, 115, 128, 138, 169, 170, 171, 188, 195, 201, 206, 207, 209, 210, 212, 236
Cleveland, TN, 143, 260, 262, 356, 364
Cliffe, Dr., 66
Clifton Cemetery, 289
Clifton, Burill A., 72, 288, 427, 435, 446, 449
Clifton, James K., Jr., 271, 288, 446, 450
Clifton, Josiah W., 289
Clinch Mountain, TN, 87
Clinch River, 42

Clinton, TN, 42
Clohassey, John, 289, 427
Cobb, Howell, 355
Cobb, Tom, 162
Coble, Jesse, 39, 289
Coburn, John, 63
Cochran, John A., 289
Cochran, John F., 289
Cochran, Samuel, 289
Cockrill, Mark S., 42
Coffee, Chatham, 166
Cohen, William P., 289
Coke, Alexander, 358
Cole, William A., 307
Coleman, George W., 289, 427, 429, 443
Coleman, H. Clay, 289
Coleman, Jackie T., 363
College Hill Arsenal, 3
College Street, 4
Collier Cemetery, 290
Collier, Arthur, 289
Collier, Christopher, C., 290
Collier, Elizabeth, 386
Collier, George W., 290
Collins, Andrew, 290, 427, 429
Collins, Hazard, 290, 435
Collins, Henry M. C., 191, 290, 435
Collins, Insley, 290
Collins, James, 290, 430, 444, 446
Collins, Jones, 290
Columbia Pike, 201, 204, 206, 207, 208, 209, 212, 214, 215, 216, 217, 223, 224, 226, 230, 232
Columbia, TN, 123, 200, 204, 243, 268, 278, 295, 311, 315, 362, 369, 375, 392, 397
Columbus, GA, 247, 386, 419
Columbus, KY, 49
Columbus, MS, 365, 400
Combs, Arabella, 354
Commercial (Cincinnati), 93
Company A (See also Waverly Guards), 102, 112, 113, 118, 125, 131, 167, 173, 174, 200, 238, 241, 243, 245, 259, 260, 261, 262, 264, 270, 271, 274, 277, 278, 279, 280, 283, 284, 285, 287, 289, 290, 292, 293, 294, 295, 297, 299, 301, 303, 305, 308, 309, 313, 316, 317, 320, 321, 322, 323, 324, 326, 328, 329, 331, 335, 336, 338, 340, 341, 342, 345, 347, 350, 351, 352, 354, 358, 359, 360, 365, 366, 369, 370, 371, 373, 374, 375, 376, 377, 379, 383, 385, 387, 388, 391, 393, 395, 396,

397, 398, 403, 405, 407, 408, 409, 413, 415, 417, 418, 419, 420, 421, 423
Company B (See also Cheatham Rifles), 87, 97, 119, 137, 167, 169, 172, 173, 174, 191, 249, 259, 260, 261, 262, 264, 266, 268, 269, 273, 274, 275, 276, 279, 280, 281, 283, 284, 285, 287, 288, 291, 292, 293, 294, 295, 296, 298, 300, 301, 302, 304, 306, 307, 311, 312, 314, 316, 318, 320, 322, 323, 326, 327, 330, 333, 336, 337, 338, 339, 340, 341, 344, 345, 346, 349, 353, 356, 358, 359, 360, 362, 363, 365, 366, 367, 368, 370, 371, 372, 373, 375, 376, 379, 382, 384, 385, 387, 388, 389, 390, 391, 392, 395, 396, 398, 400, 402, 404, 409, 411, 413, 414, 415, 421, 423, 424
Company C (See also Dickson Rifles), 94, 113, 121, 131, 133, 134, 136, 140, 145, 146, 158, 159, 167, 172, 178, 179, 187, 189, 195, 196, 203, 206, 214, 220, 229, 233, 240, 241, 254, 255, 257, 259, 260, 261, 263, 264, 265, 267, 273, 274, 275, 276, 277, 279, 281, 285, 286, 287, 288, 290, 291, 295, 297, 298, 299, 300, 302, 303, 305, 306, 307, 308, 310, 311, 317, 318, 319, 321, 322, 323, 324, 325, 326, 327, 328, 330, 331, 333, 334, 339, 341, 343, 344, 348, 351, 352, 353, 356, 357, 358, 361, 362, 363, 366, 367, 369, 371, 372, 375, 378, 381, 382, 383, 384, 385, 387, 388, 390, 391, 393, 394, 395, 396, 398, 399, 400, 401, 403, 404, 408, 410, 412, 414, 415, 416, 418, 421, 423
Company D (See also Hermitage Guards), 160, 164, 173, 194, 196, 197, 238, 241, 257, 260, 262, 268, 271, 273, 275, 277, 279, 281, 282, 288, 289, 291, 292, 293, 295, 297, 299, 300, 302, 305, 306, 307, 308, 311, 312, 313, 314, 320, 322, 324, 327, 328, 329, 330, 331, 332, 333, 335, 336, 339, 340, 341, 342, 350, 351, 353, 355, 357, 358, 359, 360, 362, 363, 364, 369, 373, 375, 376, 378, 379, 380, 381, 384, 389, 390, 391, 392, 394, 396, 398, 399, 402, 409, 411, 412, 413, 414, 418, 420, 421, 424
Company E (See also Dickson County Slashers), 134, 137, 161, 164, 172, 175, 178, 249, 259, 261, 262, 264, 265, 266, 267, 272, 274, 275, 276, 281, 285, 287, 291, 295, 298, 300, 302, 304, 306, 307, 309, 310, 311, 316, 318, 319, 323, 326, 327, 330, 331, 332, 333, 334, 335, 338, 339, 340, 342, 343, 344, 346, 349, 352, 353, 354, 360, 361, 366, 367, 369, 370, 371, 372, 373, 376, 379, 382, 383, 386, 389, 390, 393, 398, 401, 403, 406, 408, 409, 414, 415, 416, 419, 422, 424
Company F (See also Washington Guards), 105, 108, 110, 132, 133, 137, 139, 144, 145, 146, 150, 158, 160, 161, 172, 183, 187, 191, 194, 196, 197, 207, 221, 222, 242, 256, 260, 261, 262, 266, 267, 268, 269, 270, 271, 273, 275, 278, 279, 286, 287, 288, 291, 295, 296, 297, 298, 300, 301, 302, 303, 304, 305, 306, 310, 313, 314, 316, 318, 319, 320, 321, 323, 324, 325, 329, 331, 332, 333, 336, 337, 338, 345, 347, 362, 364, 365, 366, 367, 368, 369, 372, 375, 376, 377, 378, 385, 386, 387, 392, 394, 395, 401, 402, 408, 410, 415, 416, 417, 418, 419, 422, 423
Company G (See also Beauregard Light Infantry aka Bull Pups), 87, 112, 160, 161, 174, 220, 239, 242, 257, 262, 264, 267, 273, 274, 275, 276, 278, 279, 281, 282, 284, 285, 286, 289, 291, 293, 294, 296, 297, 298, 299, 300, 301, 305, 306, 307, 312, 313, 314, 316, 317, 319, 320, 321, 323, 324, 326, 327, 329, 330, 331, 332, 335, 337, 338, 339, 340, 342, 344, 348, 349, 353, 354, 355, 356, 360, 361, 362, 363, 364, 366, 367, 368, 370, 372, 373, 374, 375, 376, 377, 378, 379, 380, 381, 382, 384, 388, 390, 392, 395, 398, 402, 406, 407, 409, 412, 413, 414, 415, 417, 422, 423, 424
Company H (See also Hickman Guards), 90, 107, 112, 113, 117, 133, 135, 136, 139, 140, 148, 167, 170, 187, 189, 190, 191, 241, 242, 260, 261, 262, 263, 264, 265, 266, 267, 268, 269, 270, 272, 273, 275, 277, 278, 280, 282, 283, 285, 286, 287, 289, 290, 293, 296, 297, 298, 301, 305, 307, 308, 309, 310, 311, 312, 313, 315, 316, 317, 318, 319, 323, 324, 325, 327, 328, 329, 330, 332, 335, 336, 337, 338, 339, 341, 345, 346, 347, 348, 349, 351, 352, 355, 357, 358, 362, 363, 364, 365, 368, 372, 373, 374, 375, 378, 379, 380, 381, 383, 384, 387, 392, 395, 396, 397, 400, 401, 402, 404, 405, 408, 411, 412, 414, 415, 417, 418, 419, 422, 424
Company I (See also Gheber Guards), 102, 108, 161, 167, 170, 172, 191, 194, 220,

INDEX

263, 264, 265, 266, 267, 271, 273, 276, 277, 278, 280, 282, 284, 289, 290, 291, 294, 297, 301, 302, 303, 304, 306, 307, 308, 309, 310, 311, 312, 314, 318, 321, 327, 328, 331, 332, 334, 335, 338, 339, 348, 349, 353, 357, 361, 363, 364, 370, 371, 372, 373, 374, 376, 377, 379, 382, 386, 387, 389, 393, 395, 398, 399, 403, 404, 405, 407, 409, 410, 411, 416, 417, 418, 419, 422, 424
Company K (See also Thedford's Company), 87, 93, 95, 96, 98, 111, 135, 136, 138, 161, 167, 170, 172, 209, 236, 239, 252, 258, 259, 261, 262, 263, 271, 272, 273, 275, 276, 277, 278, 279, 281, 283, 284, 285, 287, 288, 289, 293, 294, 295, 297, 303, 304, 305, 307, 309, 310, 311, 314, 316, 317, 318, 321, 322, 323, 324, 327, 329, 335, 338, 340, 342, 348, 349, 351, 352, 355, 361, 362, 363, 365, 373, 374, 376, 377, 379, 380, 381, 382, 384, 386, 390, 392, 397, 398, 402, 403, 404, 405, 406, 409, 410, 411, 412, 414, 419, 422, 424
Compton's Hill, 238, 239, 240
Concer Hospital, 293
Conell, Joseph M., 291, 427, 429
Confederacy, 82, 86, 130, 142, 152
Confederate government (aka Richmond), 45, 47, 176
Confederate Soldiers Home, 264, 278, 293, 302, 307, 337, 338, 343, 344, 345, 346, 355, 359, 360, 362, 363, 365, 367, 379, 391, 405
Confederate States of America, 9, 72
Confederate, 3, 4, 40, 41, 43, 49, 50, 51, 52, 58, 59, 60, 63, 68, 69, 73, 74, 75, 76, 77, 80, 82, 84, 85, 86, 87, 88, 91, 92, 93, 95, 96, 97, 103, 104, 105, 106, 107, 108, 111, 112, 119, 124, 125, 140, 142, 145, 146, 152, 154, 158, 160, 161, 163, 166, 169, 170, 172, 174, 175, 177, 178, 187, 190, 191, 193, 195, 196, 201, 202, 203, 206, 208, 211, 212, 213, 214, 216, 217, 218, 219, 220, 221, 222, 223, 226, 227, 228, 229, 230, 233, 235, 236, 237, 238, 239, 248, 249, 255
Conlan, Edward, 291
Conley, Austin, 291
Conley, John, 291
Connell, Hiram D., 291
Connell, James M., 291
Connell, John, 291

Connelly, Thomas L., 34. 204
Conners, Partick, 291
Connor, Patrick, 291
Conrad, Joseph, 215
Conrad's Brigade, 205, 206, 210, 211, 217
Conscript Act, 92
Cook, C. A., 291, 446
Cook, E. D., 291, 433, 438, 446
Cook, John F., 292
Cook, John, 235, 236, 238
Cooke Co., TX, 402
Cooke's Regiment (aka 59th TN Mounted), 86
Cooksey Cemetery, 387
Cooley, Mitchell M., 132, 292, 427
Cooley, Robert W., 292, 427
Coolidge, TX, 257
Cooper, Charles, 28, 29, 292, 441
Cooper, Oliver, 292, 430, 445
Cooter, John A., 78
Copley, John M., 224
Corbett, Joseph M., 292, 435, 438, 442
Corbitt, James A., 293
Corbitt, James N., 293
Corder, Moses P., 293
Corinth, MS, 82, 86, 244, 245, 246, 319, 380
Corlew, Elizabeth, 343
Corlis, Patrick, 293
Corn, P. S., 293
Cornel, Jonathan, 91
Cornwallis, Charles, 15, 381
Correy, Buck, 234
Coryell Co., TX, 296
Cosgrove, W. J. 293
Cotham, Martha, 296
Covington, GA, 333
Cowan's Station, TN, 129
Cox, Jacob D., 200, 205, 240
Cox, Samuel A., 293
Cox, William J., 293
Cracken, I. M., 132
Craighead, James B., 25
Crawford, Charles C., 293
Crawford, John E., 28, 293, 427, 444
Crim, Henry C., 293, 433, 446
Crim, James H., 293, 358
Crittenden, General George B., 80
Crittenden, Thomas L., 132
Critz, John M., 294
Crocker, J. G., 294
Crocker, John M., 294, 444
Cronan, Patrick, 167, 294, 433, 438
Crook, Wiley M., 207, 216, 240

Crook, William J., 154, 164, 171, 183, 241, 245
Crooker, Jacob, 294, 443
Cross Bridges, TN, 315
Cross Cemetery, 348
Cross, Henon, 382
Cross, Nathaniel, 315
Croswell, C. N., 294, 435, 438
Croswell, Nimrod B., 294, 427, 429
Crow, John C., 172, 295
Crow, Manley B., 295
Crowder, William H., 295
Crown Hill Cemetery, 317
Cruft's Division, 236, 237
Crunk, William C., 295, 427, 443
Crutcher, Betty C., 350
Cruthers, J. M., 295, 441
Cumberland Ford, 48, 49, 50, 52, 54, 55, 56, 67, 68, 69, 74, 81, 83, 94
Cumberland Furnace Cemetery, 263
Cumberland Furnace, TN, 263, 302, 325
Cumberland Gap, 47, 48, 49, 50, 68, 69, 70, 71, 72, 73, 74, 75, 76, 77, 78, 79, 80, 81, 82, 83, 84, 85, 86, 87, 88, 90. 91, 92, 93, 94, 97, 98, 99, 260, 261, 262, 266, 268, 271, 272, 273, 275, 276, 277, 278, 279, 280, 281, 284, 285, 290, 291, 293, 295, 297, 298, 300, 301, 302, 303, 304, 305, 306, 307, 308, 310, 311, 317, 319, 321, 325, 326, 334, 338, 339, 340, 341, 342, 346, 349, 352, 354, 355, 356, 357, 359, 363, 365, 366, 370, 373, 374, 375, 382, 383, 384, 388, 390, 393, 394, 395, 397, 400, 408, 409, 413, 414, 418, 419, 420
Cumberland Mountains, 34, 43, 44, 47
Cumberland Plateau, 129
Cumberland Presbyterian Church, 270, 312, 416
Cumberland River, 12, 49, 50, 52, 56, 68, 80, 82, 234, 235
Cumberland University Law School, 254, 315
Cumming's Brigade, 249
Cummings's Regiment (aka 19th TN), 52
Cunningham, H. D., 295
Cunningham, L. T., 3
Curren, Patrick, 295
Currin Vault, 120, 378
Curtis, John, 295
Curtis, S. J., 295
Curtis, Samuel, 295
Curtis, Sarah Jane, 407
Cuthbert, GA, 296, 310, 341
D

Dailey, Edward, 295
Daily Gazette (Nashville), 3
Daily Patriot (Nashville), 4
Daily Rebel (Chattanooga), 164, 179
Dallas Co., TX, 399
Dallas Road, 163
Dallas, GA, 163, 164
Dallas, TX, 392, 399
Dalton, GA, 132, 150, 151, 152, 154, 159, 183, 184, 199, 252, 277, 289, 313, 319, 322, 333, 341, 351, 363, 389, 392, 399, 414
Dalton, William M., 296
Dalton's Ford, 135
Damesworth, Margret, 334
Daniel Cemetery, 274
Danielsville, TN, 257
Danville, KY, 80, 95
Danville, TN, 328
Darden Cemetery, 297
Darden, Alfred B., 187, 296, 434
Darden, Charles B., 245, 296
Darden, George W., 2, 296, 437
Darden, Henry G., 296
Darden, James H., 108, 158, 162, 196, 296, 424, 437
Darden, James P., 296, 427, 429, 441
Darden, James P., 297
Darden, Thomas B., 245, 296, 297
Dark, Samuel T., 297
Daughtry, George R., 297, 442
Davidson County, TN, 1, 2, 4, 6, 8, 18, 19, 127, 236, 259, 266, 268, 269, 273, 277, 283, 286, 288, 292, 294, 312, 314, 323, 333, 336, 337, 338, 344, 346, 350, 351, 353, 355, 359, 362, 368, 369, 371, 375, 379, 388, 390, 391, 392, 394, 395, 415, 419421, 422, 423, 424
Davidson, Calvin, 297
Davidson, Dora, 322
Davidson, Edmond A., 297
Davidson, George C., 297
Davidson, Green H., 297, 446
Davidson, John W., 297, 430
Davidson, John, 297
Davidson, S. A., 40, 297
Davidson, Squire James, 12
Davis, C. J., 298, 427, 442
Davis, J. T., 298, 445
Davis, Jefferson (CS), 35, 142, 185, 197, 198, 405
Davis, Jefferson C. (US), 121, 195
Davis, John B., 298

Davis, Sam, 254, 315
Davis's Ford, 201
Dawson, Elizer, 326
Dawson, John W., 133, 140, 160
Dawson's Battalion Sharpshooters, 132, 133, 136, 137, 140, 318
Dead Angle, 171, 174, 175, 178, 180, 256
Dean, Ephraim A., 23, 191, 298, 424, 427
Deas, General Zachariah C., 146
Deas's Brigade, 147, 240
DeBow, H. B., 298, 430
DeBow, J. D. B., 30, 32
DeBow, John D., 298
DeBow's Review, 30
Decatur, AL, 186, 199
Decatur, GA, 188
Decherd, TN, 127
DeCourcy, Colonel John F., 87, 89
DeGarris, William, 298
Delaware River, 127
Delk, Samuel G., 275
Demopolis, AL, 152, 153, 214, 246
DeMoss, Mrs., 10
Dennison, TX, 416
Denver, TN, 23, 312, 314
Department of East Tennessee, 82, 85, 86, 87, 100
Department of the Interior, 254
Des Arc, AR, 320
Deshler's Brigade, 138
Devil's Elbow, 174
Dickens, Isaac W., 298
Dickens, Thomas P., 298
Dickson County Slashers (See also Company E), 5, 12, 18, 36, 64, 66, 79, 422, 424
Dickson County, TN, 5, 8, 12, 19, 72, 127, 220, 236, 244, 245, 252, 253, 257, 258, 261, 262, 263, 264, 265, 266, 267, 271, 272, 273, 274, 275, 276, 277, 278, 279, 281, 284, 285, 287, 288, 289, 295, 297, 298, 299, 300, 302, 303, 304, 307, 308, 309, 310, 311, 314, 318, 319, 321, 322, 323, 324, 325, 326, 327, 328, 330, 331, 332, 333, 334, 335, 338, 339, 340, 342, 343, 344, 345, 346, 349, 350, 351, 352, 351, 353, 354, 356, 357, 358, 360, 361, 363, 365, 366, 367, 368, 369, 370, 371, 372, 373, 375, 379, 380, 381, 382, 383, 384, 385, 386, 387, 388, 390, 391, 393, 394, 398, 400, 401, 402, 403, 404, 405, 406, 410, 411, 412, 414, 415, 416, 418

Dickson Rifles (See also Company C), 5, 12, 15, 19, 25, 26, 28, 29, 36, 41, 42, 66, 71, 79, 421, 423
Dickson, James C., 298, 442
Dickson, John M., 187, 298, 299, 435, 437, 449
Dickson, Newton B., 187, 298, 299, 427, 434, 446
Dickson, TN, 255, 263, 288, 297, 298, 299, 323, 328, 353, 373, 375, 380, 402, 409
Dickson, William H., 299, 430, 445
Dillan, Pat, 299
Dinkins, James, 226
Divaney, Matthew, 299, 435
Dixie, 21
Dixon Cemetery, 299
Doak, J. D., 299
Dobins, Byron, 299
Doctor's Creek, 97
Dodge, Granville, 189
Dodson, Napoleon B., 299, 436, 438
Dodson, Sarah, 347
Dog Creek Cemetery, 391
Dogherty, Martin, 161, 300, 430, 433, 435
Dominion State (See also Virginia), 25, 33
Donelson, Captain, 137, 139
Doney Stokes, 319
Donnegan, Arminta, 411
Dooley, Thomas, 300
Doolittle, Charles, 240
Doss, Captain, 41
Dossett, William, 300
Dotson, Thomas G., 300
Dotson-Brummit Cemetery, 300, 302
Doughton, William C., Jr., 300, 431, 445
Douglass, James R., 167, 300, 423, 427, 433
Douglass, Victor, 300
Drake, Joseph D., 300
Draughon, George W., 300, 437
Draughon, Virginia, 270
Dreux, Peter E., 152, 153, 214, 215, 226, 232
Driscall, James, 300, 445
Dromgoole, Mrs., 118
Duck River line, 124
Duck River, 119, 122, 125, 127, 201, 243, 267, 285, 363
Dudley, Harry F., 300
Dudley, Tennessee, 288
Duke, John C., 301, 433, 446
Duncan, Hannah F., 278
Dunlap Creek, 289
Dunn, A. J., 301, 427
Dunn, Ameila, 390

Dunn, Edward, 301, 431
Dunnagan, Tennessee, 351
Durham Station, NC, 250
Dyer Co., TN, 377
Dyer, Beverly, 181, 182, 192
Dyersburg, TN, 377

E

Eagleville, TN, 126
Eanes, John T., 301
Earlington, KY, 399
Easley, James D., 301
Easley, Warham D., 77, 301
East Point, GA, 193
East Tennessean, 59
East Tennessee and Virginia Railroad, 36, 39
East Tennessee, 29, 34, 35, 42, 43, 47, 50, 53, 76, 83, 102
Eastland, TX, 393
Eastside Cemetery, 280
Ebenezer Methodist Church Cemetery, 260, 357
Echols, John S., 301, 427
Echols, Robert M., 301, 441
Echols, Stephen C., 191, 301
Ector, Matthew D., 109
Ector's Brigade, 107
Ed Crockett Bivouac, 303, 329
Edgar, Joseph, 88
Edgefield and Kentucky Railroad, 12, 15
Edgefield, TN, 12
Edgewood Cemetery, 258, 390
Edgewood Cemetery, 406
Edgewood, TN, 257
Edgewood, TN, 406
Edmonson, Henry C., 441
Edmonson, John A., 48
Edwards Cemetery, 388
Edwards, America, 420
Edwards, R. H., 302
Edwards, Sophronia,
Edwards, Wiley, 302
Egan, James, 302
Egan, Michael, 302
El Paso, Co., TX, 417
El Paso, TX, 416, 417
Eldorado, KY, 96
Eleazer, William D. "Billy," 164, 175, 302, 346, 424, 427, 449
Elk River, 129, 393
Elliott, A. J., 302
Elliott, James, 302
Elliott, William B., 417
Elliott, William C., 302, 441, 445

Elliott, William M., 110, 303, 427, 449
Elliott, William, 302, 427, 449
Ellis & Moore, 3
Ellis Co., TX, 375
Ellis Mills, 372
Ellis, John M., 303
Ellis, Thomas J., 303
Elmwood Cemetery, 255, 292, 315, 329
Elsberry Ridge, GA, 164
Ely, A., 303
Emery, N. R., 303, 441, 444
Emery, William L., 303
Enon Cemetery, 326
Enoree River, 248
Episcopal Church Hospital, 384
Epps, George P. Y., 303, 427, 449
Erin, TN, 257, 351, 364, 370
Estes, Joshua G., 303
Estes, Solomon, 303
Estes, William G., 304
Estill Springs, TN, 127, 367
Etheridge, Mary, 358
Ethridge, William T., 304
Ethridge, William, 304, 436
Etowah River, 162, 163
Etowah, GA, 347
Eubanks, Raford C., 172, 304, 438
Eubanks, Robert G., 304, 437
Evans, J. C., 304
Everett, James, 5, 27, 28, 304, 422
Evergreen Alameda Cemetery, 417
Evergreen Cemetery, 270
Ewing, John A., 304

F

Fain, Tyree L., 137, 304, 427, 429, 434, 446
Fair Ground Hospital Number 1, 260, 261, 267, 272, 280, 281, 286, 291, 296, 301, 304, 307, 316, 319, 336, 339, 341, 349, 355, 359, 362, 364, 368, 370, 375, 380, 391, 395, 404, 410
Fair Ground Hospital Number 2, 258, 264, 267, 272, 281, 284, 285, 286, 291, 293, 297, 301, 307, 309, 314, 327, 329, 330, 332, 333, 337, 341, 356, 359, 366, 391, 400, 401, 405, 406
Fairview, TN, 325, 380
Fall & Cunningham, 4
Farley, John, 305
Farley, Thomas, 305
Farmington, KY, 309
Farrell, James, 305
Farrell, John, 305
Faw, G. O., 360

Fayetteville Road, 188
Fayetteville-Goldsboro Highway, 248
Federal government, 2, 6, 47
Federal, 3, 6, 45, 47, 49, 51, 52, 54, 56, 58, 61, 62, 64, 65, 71, 75, 80, 81, 83, 84, 85, 86, 88, 89, 92, 94, 96, 103, 104, 106, 110, 111, 113, 119, 121, 122, 125, 128, 130, 131, 132, 139, 140, 143, 145, 146, 147, 149, 151, 153, 159, 160, 162, 165, 166, 167, 168, 169, 172, 173, 174, 175, 176, 177, 178, 179, 181, 182, 186, 187, 188, 189, 191, 193, 196, 199, 200, 201, 202, 205, 206, 207, 209, 210, 211, 212, 213, 214, 217, 218, 219, 220, 221, 222, 223, 224, 225, 226, 227, 230, 234, 235, 236, 237, 239, 240, 245, 253, 256, 258
Feild, Hume, 157
Felts, Catherine M., 380
Ferguson Hall, 202
Ferguson, Clement M., 305
Ferguson, George S., 305, 431, 446
Ferguson, Jasper A., 305
Ferris, Martin, 305
Field, Susan, 358
Fielder, A. T., 250
Fielder, James K. P., 305, 449
Fields, James, 305
Fields, Samuel H., 305
Figg, Jason, 28, 306, 435
Finch, Emily J., 264
Finn's Point National Cemetery, 294
First Cumberland Presbyterian Church (Nashville), 3
Fisher, Wheless & Company, 7
Fishing Creek, 73
Fiske, John, 107
Fitzgerald, Edward, 306
Fitzgerald, James, 306
Fitzgerald, Michael, 306, 438, 441
Fitzgerald, Thomas, 306
Fitzgivens, E., 306
Fitzhugh, John A., 306
Fitzmorris, Patrick, 306
Fizer, Thomas, 26
Flaherty, Roger, 306, 435
Flarity, Patrick, 306
Flat Shoals Road, 188
Fleming, John, 306
Fleming, Patrick, 306
Flemings, Lawrence, 306
Fletcher, William J., 306
Flewellen Hospital, 285
Flint River, 193

Florence, AL, 199, 200
Florida, 2
Flowers, Cynthia A., 286
Flowers, James W., 194, 306, 436, 439, 441, 449
Floyd Hospital, 311, 321
Floyd House Hospital, 265, 267, 288, 299, 357, 358
Floyd, Harrison, 307, 437
Flym, Martin, 307, 427, 443
Flynn, John J., 174, 307, 443
Foard Hospital, 284
Folia, Thomas, 307
Foote, Flag Officer Andrew H., 82
Forbes Bivouac Number 21, 253, 280, 299, 305, 322, 357, 371, 386, 388, 394
Ford, Benjamin F., 307
Ford, Della J., 282
Ford, Jesse M., 307, 446
Ford, Matthew W., 307, 443
Ford, W. L. Grant, 26, 28, 307
Forrest Hills Cemetery, 259
Forrest, Nathan B., 153, 202, 204, 205, 390, 407
Forrest's Cavalry, 234
Forsyth City Cemetery, 412
Forsyth Co., GA, 412
Forsyth Co., NC, 261
Forsyth Confederate Cemetery, 347, 383
Forsyth, GA, 382, 393, 413
Fort Delaware, DE, 127, 383
Fort Donelson, TN, 82, 266, 281, 289, 302, 328, 356, 364, 387, 418
Fort Graham, TX, 351
Fort Granger, TN, 207
Fort Henry, TN, 82
Fort Leavenworth, KS, 388
Fort McHenry, MD, 308, 383, 385
Fort Negley, TN, 236
Fort Pulaski, GA, 332
Fort Rains, TN, 124
Fort Sumter, SC, 3
Fort Warren, MA, 254
Fortress Monroe, VA, 302, 308
Foster, General R. C., 16, 18, 23, 24, 25, 27, 28, 29, 356
Foster, William B., 308
Fowler, G. W., 308
Fowlkes, Gabriel, 98, 308
Fowlkes, Latitia, 413
Fowlkes, Mary, 312
Fowlkland, Lucy B., 191
Foy, Thomas, 308

Francis, Sarah E., 301
Frank Cheatham Bivouac Number 1, 253
Frankfort, KY, 55, 96, 376
Franklin County, TN, 127
Franklin Cross Roads, 278
Franklin Road (aka Franklin Pike), 106, 107, 238, 242, 243
Franklin, KY, 297
Franklin, TN, 176, 205, 206, 207, 211, 214, 217, 227, 228, 229, 230, 232, 233, 241, 243, 254, 256, 261, 263, 264, 265, 267, 269, 270, 271, 274, 278, 280, 283, 284, 292, 294, 297, 300, 304, 306, 307, 308, 311, 313, 315, 316, 317, 318, 319, 320, 321, 322, 324, 328, 330, 331, 334, 335, 336, 343, 344, 345, 350, 351, 353, 354, 355, 362, 367, 368, 373, 376, 377, 378, 380, 381, 383, 388, 389, 392, 394, 395, 396, 398, 399, 400, 403, 407, 408, 410, 411, 413, 416, 417, 418, 420, 438
Frazier, William G., 14, 18, 73, 74, 75, 308
Freeman, George K., 167, 308, 427, 433
Freeman, Samuel, 308
Freemont Church of Christ Cemetery, 344
French, Cullen E., 187, 308, 438
French, George H., 161, 308, 433, 435, 438, 442
French, Robert J., 309, 431, 443
Frizzell, William G., "Billy," 309
Fry, Colonel S. S., 80
Fullerton, Artemus, 66
Fulmer, Jesse, 109, 110
Fulton Co., KY, 340
Fuqua, Jesse J., 309
Fuqua, William T., 309, 429, 446
Fussell, Mazura E., 258
G
Gadsden, AL, 199
Gafford, James K. P., 309, 445
Gafford, William J., "Bud," 309, 431, 445
Gainesville, AL, 338, 369, 390, 407
Gaither, William B., 310, 442
Galaville, TN, 265
Gale, W. D., 239, 240
Gallatin City Cemetery, 386
Gallatin, TN, 416
Gallaway, Henry, 310
Gallop, William T., 310, 442
Galloway, J. W., 310
Gardner, Charles N., 310, 429, 430, 445
Gardner, Martha, 324
Gardner, Mary J., 402
Gareo, R. William O., 310, 436

Garfield, James, 282
Garland Co., AR, 373
Garland, Jesse, 310
Garner, George W. F., 77, 310, 439, 441, 449
Garner, Samuel W., 311
Garrard, Theophilus T., 56, 82
Garrett, Evaline R., 308
Garrett, James P., 311
Garrett, Joseph, 311
Garton, Moses, 271, 311, 433, 434, 446, 449
Gary, Peter, 311
Gatesville City Cemetery, 283
Gatesville, TX, 296
Gee, William K., 311
Gentry, David C., 167, 311, 429, 433
Gentry, Dr., 66
Gentry, Martha J., 361
George, James L., 106, 311, 431
George, Reverend, 191
Georgetown, KY, 376
Georgia Railroad, 187
Georgia, 2, 199, 200, 269
Georgia Troops – Artillery (Confederate); Yeizer's Battery, 86
Georgia Troops – Infantry (Confederate); 3rd, 83, 86 ; 3rd Battalion, 88, 101, 103, 105, 109, 114; 5th, 83; 9th Battalion, 102, 105, 106, 109, 110; 39th, 102; 42nd, 86, 101, 102, 103
Georgians, 154, 155, 156, 157, 159, 186, 198, 249
German, Daniel, 311
Gettysburg, PA, 130, 186
Gheber Guards (See also Company I), 6, 12, 23, 28, 35, 36, 46, 57, 60, 61, 76, 79, 85, 422, 424
Gibbons, Patrick, 312
Gibbs Cemetery, 334
Gibson Co., TN, 321
Giles County, TN, 23, 123, 262, 314, 379, 400
Gill, George W., 312
Gillmore, Nancy C., 403
Gilman, Joseph W., "Joe," 160, 196, 432, 437
Gilman, Thomas A., 312
Gilmer Hospital, 317
Gist, States Rights, 198, 233
Gist, W. W., 211
Gist, William H., 1
Gist's Brigade, 201, 202, 207
Glasgow, KY, 97
Glenn, John, 174, 312, 442
Glenn, Patrick, 312, 439

Glenn, Surgeon, 168
Glover, Joseph, 313
Goad, Delilah, 313
Goad, Gustavus, 241, 313, 434, 436, 439
Godshall, Samuel C., 1, 2, 3, 4, 5, 10, 11, 19, 24, 29, 36, 64, 313, 421
Godwin, Dr., 182
Godwin, J. M., 313
Godwin, Reuben, 437, 442
Goff, Anderson, 313
Goff, Patrick, 313, 431, 438
Goldsboro, NC, 248
Gooch, James W. M., 313, 446
Goodrich, J. P., 314
Goodwin, George M., 314
Goodwin, George, 314
Goodwin, Henry H., 314, 443
Goodwin, J. L. C., 314
Goodwin, J. M., 439
Goodwin, John, 314
Goodwin, Ruben, 314
Gordon, George W., 23, 24, 27, 35, 44, 46, 73, 79, 85, 88, 89, 90, 92, 97, 98, 99, 100, 101, 103, 109, 113, 114, 117, 120, 122, 127, 135, 136, 137, 140, 147, 150, 154, 155, 156, 157, 158, 166, 167, 170, 175, 177, 180, 181, 183, 189, 191, 192, 193, 195, 198, 200, 202, 206, 207, 208, 209, 210, 212, 213, 214, 215, 218, 221, 223, 224, 225, 226, 227, 228, 229, 232, 252, 253, 254, 256, 279, 314, 334, 335, 376, 404, 412, 420, 423, 426, 427, 435, 438, 441, 444, 449
Gordon, Pocahontas, 315
Gordon, Richard C. "Dick", 9, 70, 81, 315, 422, 424
Gordon, W. G., 316
Gordon, William Henry Harrison "Harry," 167, 314, 316, 433
Gordon's Brigade (until 15 August 1864 known as Vaughan's), 193, 194, 195, 196, 197, 201, 207, 208, 209, 211, 215, 216, 231, 233, 256
Gorman, Marcus, 239, 316, 439, 441
Gorman, Mark, 172, 316
Gorman, Patrick, 316
Gossett, John C., 316
Gossett, Robert, 184
Gossett, William H., 316, 429, 441
Gotton, James W., 316
Govan's Brigade, 194, 195, 220
Gower, Louisa J., 303
Grady, Rebecca, 279

Graham, Thomas, 91
Graham, William A., 181
Graig, James Polk, 316, 439, 449
Graig, John C., 316, 427
Granbury, Hiram, 233
Granbury's Brigade (see also Texas Brigade), 194, 210, 211, 212, 215, 217, 237
Granny White Pike, 5, 241, 242
Grant, Ulysses S., 49, 82, 85, 86, 129, 248
Gratiot Street Prison, 273, 293, 362, 444
Graves Co., KY, 309, 419
Gravitt, Andrew W., 17, 317
Gray, George A., 317, 443
Gray, James F., 64, 67, 317, 426, 438
Gray, James M., 317, 433, 435, 441
Gray, James W., 317, 443
Gray, James, 317, 443
Gray, Joseph, 317
Gray, Laura, 257
Gray, R. M., 88
Gray, Samuel B., 317, 429
Gray, William C., "Billy," 317, 427, 433
Great Britain, 126
Green Co., AL, 191
Green Co., AR, 305
Green, Michael, 317, 427
Green, Robert W., 317
Green, Samuel M., 318
Green, William H., "Bill," 5, 12, 19, 27, 29, 41, 79, 100, 133, 140, 150, 318, 421, 423, 431
Greene Co., TN, 348
Greensboro, GA, 311
Greensboro, NC, 101, 250, 259, 262, 265, 266, 268, 269, 270, 271, 275, 276, 292, 299, 302, 311, 314, 318, 319, 320, 323, 324, 325, 327, 330, 331, 333, 338, 343, 344, 346, 348, 350, 351, 353, 354, 367, 377, 380, 381, 382, 383, 385, 388, 392, 394, 401, 405, 406, 409, 414
Greenville, TN, 35, 47
Greenwood Cemetery, 272, 297, 307, 322, 339, 385, 386, 394, 399
Greenwood Methodist Church Cemetery, 346
Greer, Daniel W., 318, 435, 446
Greer, Richard T., 318
Gregg, J. P., 318
Grenada, MS, 299
Grenille, A. W., 318
Gresham House, 117
Gresham Lane, 106
Griffin Georgia Confederate Cemetery, 296, 412

Griffin, GA, 191, 196, 256, 267, 269, 276, 290, 294, 296, 299, 302, 316, 317, 342, 352, 359, 364, 369, 374, 376, 388, 393, 395, 412, 413, 415, 419
Griffin, William, 318
Griffis, Francis M., 318
Grimes, Daniel W., 318
Grimes, John P., 319, 429, 446
Grimes, Thomas J., 319, 446
Grimes, Thomas R., 77, 319
Grimmage, Mrs., 117
Griner, Lewis P., 319
Griner, W. J., 319
Grose, William, 110, 111
Grosvenor, Charles, 237
Grubbs, Joseph P., 319
Guenther's Battery (aka Battery H, 5th US Artillery), 110, 111
Guilford, Edward J., 319, 421, 424
Guitteau, Charles J., 282
Gum Springs, KY, 95
Gum Springs, TN, 273
Gunn Cemetery, 319, 410
Gunn, Edward W., 320, 435, 446
Gunn, Miles A., 320, 427, 438, 441
Gunn, William B., 320
Guthrie, KY, 279
Guthrie, Rodger, 320, 439, 441
Guy, John F., 320
Guy's Gap, TN, 124

H

Hadley, Jerome J., 320
Hadley, Mary, 234
Haffey, George W., 320
Haile Cemetery, 320
Haile, George W., 320, 430, 445
Haile, William Wallace, 70, 160, 320, 432
Hakewessell, Felix, 321
Hale, Joseph D., 321, 427, 431, 446
Hale, Rufus A., 321
Hale, Tennie J., 259
Hall Cemetery, 321, 380
Hall, Benjamin F., "Tobe," 321, 449
Hall, Joseph J., 321
Hall, Lieutenant, 221
Halliburton, Charles "Charley," 254, 321, 438, 441
Halliburton, John C., 321
Halliburton, Turner H., 254, 321, 322, 438, 442
Hamilton Chapel Cemetery, 388
Hamilton, James G., 322, 444
Hamilton, Lieutenant, 167
Hamilton, William A., 322
Hamlet, Robert, 322
Hammon Cemetery, 322
Hammon, Samuel, 322, 439, 441
Hampton, Wade, 248
Hanaford, Ebenezer, 110
Hanah, Joseph, 322
Hancock County, TN, 77
Handlin, John N., 322
Handlin, Thomas J., 323, 445
Hannah, Benjamin F., 323, 429, 431, 442
Hannah, Minnie, 254, 315
Hannan, Michael, 441
Hansberry, John, 67, 323, 426
Harbison, John M., 323
Harbison, John, 323
Hardee, William J., 101, 103, 104, 108, 142, 151, 162, 166, 169, 170, 179, 186, 187, 193, 195, 198, 248
Hardee, Willie, 248
Hardee's Corps, 105, 122, 124, 151, 162, 178, 188, 193, 194, 196, 198, 250
Hardeman Co., TN, 383
Hardin Co., KY, 278
Hardin Co., TN, 269
Hargrove, D., 323
Harker's Brigade, 174
Harlan Road, 83
Harlow, John, 323
Harmony Primitive Baptist Church Cemetery, 309
Harmony Primitive Baptist Church, 318
Harper, John H., 323, 447
Harpers Ferry Arsenal, 7
Harpeth River, 10, 205
Harrington Cemetery, 275
Harrington, Hannah, 324
Harrington, Mary J., 310
Harris, B. E. W., 323
Harris, Charley (aka Charley Bell), 101, 271
Harris, George, 323
Harris, Isham G., 1, 2, 3, 5, 6, 7, 8, 17, 34, 132, 286
Harris, John W., 167
Harris, Polly, 351
Harris, Thomas J., 323, 447
Harris, William, 323
Harrison, Eugene A., 194, 238, 324, 437, 439, 441, 447
Harrison, John M., 324
Harrison, Tobe, 324
Harrison, William H., 324
Harrodsburg, KY, 95, 96, 97

INDEX

Harry J. King, 246
Harvey, Lucy J., 273
Harvey, Onesiphorus S., 324, 427, 431, 445
Haslem, William B., 324
Hassell Cemetery, 325
Hassell, Alfred B., 324, 447, 324
Hassell, Artin, 325, 368
Hassell, Joseph H., 324, 325
Hassell, Ophelia, 283
Hassell, Zebulon, 325, 447, 324
Hawkins, George N., 325
Hawkins, Martin, 325, 431, 445
Hawkins, William F., 325
Hayes Cemetery, 325
Hayes, Champion L., 187, 325, 434, 447
Hayes, William A., 325
Hayes, William H., 325
Haynesville, TN, 29, 35, 40, 72
Hays, Eugenia, 408
Hays, John, 326, 431, 445
Hays, Silas, 326
Hazel Patch Valley, 61
Heads Freewill Baptist Church Cemetery, 303
Heath, Burril, 326
Heath, John, 326, 431
Heath, TN, 354
Heath, Zachary, 175
Heckman, Charles E., 326, 442
Hedgecock, Joseph, 326, 427, 443
Heiman, Adolphus, 18, 23
Helena, AR, 254, 315
Helpin, Lawrence, 326
Henderson, Colonel R. J., 101, 103
Henderson, Hugh H., 326, 427, 434
Hendrick, Sarah, 340
Hendricks, Sanford, 12, 326, 421
Hendrix, James, 326, 427
Hendrix, William A., 327
Henley, Thomas A., 327
Henressy, Nicholas, 327
Henry Co., TN, 322
Henry Hospital, 345
Henry, B. W., 118, 121
Henry, Patrick, 32
Henry, William H., 28, 29, 327
Herbison, Emma, 358
Hermitage Guards (See also Company D), 3, 4, 5, 7, 12, 15, 19, 22, 26, 28, 35, 36, 40, 41, 43, 44, 45, 54, 55, 64, 69, 79, 82, 84, 421, 423
Herring, Michael, 327
Heverin, Hugh J., 327, 423, 427, 431, 435
Hickerson, Mary F., 324

Hickey, Andrew, 327, 427
Hickey, Andrew, 327, 443
Hickman City Cemetery, 340
Hickman Countians, 90, 127
Hickman County Courthouse, 253
Hickman County, TN, 7, 9, 10, 19, 35, 39, 117, 135, 172, 252, 261, 263, 265, 267, 268, 269, 270, 272, 273, 274, 275, 276, 277, 278, 280, 282, 283, 284, 285, 286, 289, 290, 296, 298, 300, 301, 303, 304, 305, 308, 309, 310, 311, 312, 315, 316, 318, 319, 320, 321, 324, 325, 327, 328, 330, 331, 337, 341, 346, 347, 348, 351, 352, 353, 355, 356, 357, 358, 362, 363, 365, 368, 379, 380, 381, 384, 387, 392, 393, 394, 396, 397, 399, 402, 403, 404, 405, 406, 411, 412, 417, 422, 424,
Hickman Guards (See also Company H), 9, 10, 11, 14, 16, 17, 18, 19, 22, 23, 26, 37, 38, 39, 64, 69, 70, 72, 74, 77, 81, 253, 412, 422, 424
Hickory Guards, 335
Hicks, James H., 327
Higginsville, MO, 334
Hill Co., TX, 262, 414
Hilton, John B., 327
Hindman, Thomas C., 143
Hindman's Division, 131, 143
Hiwassee River, 143
Hogan, Martin, 327, 435, 447
Hogin, William M., 327, 438, 442, 449
Hogue, Mildred, 369
Holden Cemetery, 333
Holland, Susan, 328
Holland, William S., 174, 328, 442
Hollingsworth, Nannie, 259
Hollywood Cemetery, 320
Holmes, George M., 78
Holt, Isaac L., 328
Hood Hospital, 296, 341
Hood, John Bell, 185, 186, 187, 189, 193, 195, 196, 197, 199, 200, 201, 202, 203, 204, 206, 208, 209, 210, 227, 235, 238, 242, 246
Hood, Mary, 285
Hood's Corps, 164, 191
Hood's Division, 140
Hooker, Joe, 164
Hooper Cemetery, 328
Hooper, Absolom B., 167, 328, 433, 441
Hooper, John, 328
Hooper, Simeon H., 328
Hooper, William H., 328, 449

481

Hoosier Knob, 255
Hoover's Gap, TN, 124
Hopkins Co., KY, 399
Hopkinsville, KY, 381
Horn's Silver Band, 5
Hornbeak City Cemetery, 328, 329
Hornbeak, Eli A., 328, 319, 329
Hornbeak, Francis B., 329
Hornbeak, Samuel M., 329
Hornbeak, TN, 328, 329, 344
Hornberger, James P., 329
Hornberger, Wiley W., 245, 329, 427, 429
Horrigan, Timothy, 329
Hotchkiss, Charles T., 107
House, James W., 329
House, John W., 329, 442
House, William D., 161, 329, 433, 442
Houston Co., TN, 257, 290, 364, 370, 372, 383, 387, 393, 416
Houston-Whitworth Cemetery, 410
Howard, Oliver O., 161, 162, 193
Howe, Peter, 330
Howell Co., MO, 393
Howell, R. B. C., 313
Huddleston Cemetery, 280
Huddleston, Alice, 280
Huddleston, James H., 330
Huddleston, William Howell, 17, 330
Huddleston, Zianna, 280
Hudgins Cemetery, 330
Hudgins, Francis M., "France," 330, 427, 438, 441, 447
Hudson, David, 330
Hudson, Robert A., 330, 431, 445
Hudson, William B., 330, 431, 445
Huffman, William, 330
Huggins, A. J., 330
Hughes, Dr., 75
Hughes, Edward W., 331
Hughes, Frederick J., 331
Hughes, George W., 331
Hume, Alfred, 368
Humphreys County, TN, 6, 9, 12, 19, 21, 23, 62, 102, 127, 200, 236, 252, 253, 260, 265, 267, 271, 274, 276, 277, 278, 280, 287, 292, 293, 304, 305, 306, 309, 311, 312, 314, 320, 321, 323, 326, 327, 328, 334, 337, 338, 341, 345, 346, 347, 348, 351, 352, 356, 357, 358, 359, 365, 366, 370, 371, 374, 375, 376, 377, 382, 383, 387, 388, 389, 391, 394, 403, 405, 407, 410, 413, 414, 417, 418, 419, 420, 422, 423, 424

Hundley, Elisha T., 331, 437, 442
Hundley, John L., 331, 423
Hunt, Andrew W., 331, 447
Hunt, B. B., 331
Hunt, Millie, 362
Hunter, James P., 331, 435
Huntington, TN, 312
Huntsville, AL, 336
Huntsville, TN, 42, 43, 44
Hurley, James, 331
Hurley, Jeremiah, 331, 438
Hurricane Creek, 311
Hurricane Mills, TN, 405
Hurt, C. C., 233
Hust, Francis O., 332
Hust, John, 398
Hustburg, TN, 260
Hutchins, William, 332, 445
Hutchinson, James O., 332
Hutton, Zachariah D., "Zach," 332
Hyde, Joseph, 332

I

I. M. Singer Company, 4
Illinois, 176
Illinois Troops – Artillery (Federal): 2nd, 189
Illinois Troops – Infantry (Federal): 20th, 262
27th, 174; 36th, 218, 221
42nd, 115, 174
44th, 218; 51st, 174; 64th, 249; 72nd, 217
73rd, 218, 219, 221, 222, 226, 227
74th, 218; 79th, 139, 174
84th, 111
85th, 174
86th, 174
88th, 218
89th, 107
100th, 210
125th, 174
Indiana, 58, 62, 356
Indiana Troops – Infantry (Federal): 22nd, 174
32nd, 106
33rd, 63
36th, 110; 39th, 106; 40th, 210; 57th, 210, 214, 216
Indianapolis, IN, 317
Ingram, John, 208
Ingram, Martin V. B., 22
Innis, J. T., 170, 332
Iowa Troops – Infantry (Federal): 16th, 189
Ireland, 186, 258, 273, 291, 293, 301, 302, 305, 306, 307, 310, 312, 327, 332, 339,

349, 353, 355, 364, 366, 370, 392, 407, 409, 413
Irish Cemetery, 78, 409
Irwin, Thomas, 332, 424, 431, 441, 444
Island Number Ten, 82, 153
Itawamba Co., MS, 216
Iuka, MS, 244, 403
Ivey, W. O., 332

J
J. Warren Cemetery, 375
Jacksboro, TN, 43, 44
Jackson Cemetery, 319, 333, 365
Jackson Chapel Cemetery, 344
Jackson College, 123
Jackson Hospital, 300, 358, 397
Jackson, Andrew, 21
Jackson, Ellen, 334
Jackson, Epps, 333
Jackson, Green P., 333, 436
Jackson, James P., 333, 431, 447
Jackson, James S., 333, 449
Jackson, James, 333
Jackson, John, 144, 156
Jackson, Joseph W. G., "Jo," 183, 184, 333, 435
Jackson, Reverend Green P., 333
Jackson, Sanford Gilpin Marion, 132, 333
Jackson, Sylvanus, 333
Jackson, TN, 303
Jackson, William T., 172, 334, 438, 442
Jackson's Brigade, 135, 136, 154
James E. Rains Bivouac Number 4, 253
James Island, 346
James River, 127, 415
James, Robert A. W., 12, 334, 422, 424, 447
James, Thomas, 333
Jamestown, TN, 42, 80
Jamison, Orval, 161, 334, 433, 438
Jamison, Purvoyant G., "Gus," 48, 85, 127, 334, 423, 438
Jamison, William A., 334
Jane Jones Cemetery, 380
Jarnigan, T. C., 334
Jarrell Cemetery, 260
Jarrell, R. F., 335
Jeff Davis (Steam Boat), 152
Jefferson Co., KY, 282, 344, 397
Jefferson, Thomas, 282
Jenkins, Thomas G., 17, 335
Jennings, Edward, 335
Jentry, Thomas P., 335
Jobson, Livina, 292
John Benton Farm, 249

John's Hollow, 64
Johnson City, TN, 35
Johnson Creek, 319
Johnson, Andrew, 34
Johnson, Bushrod, 314
Johnson, Granville, 135, 136, 139, 429
Johnson, Jacob H. "Jake", 90, 92, 190, 335, 424, 435
Johnson, James S., 335
Johnson, James T., 335
Johnson, James, 335, 431, 438, 442
Johnson, John Jefferson, 335
Johnson, Peter, 336, 431
Johnson, Richard W., 106
Johnson, Thomas, 336
Johnson, William, 336, 431, 445
Johnson's Division, 106, 108
Johnson's Island, 374
Johnsonville, TN, 23, 236, 253, 292, 382, 387, 389
Johnston, Albert S., 85, 125
Johnston, Colonel, 125
Johnston, Joseph E., 150, 151, 157, 159, 160, 161, 162, 163, 169, 170, 179, 182, 185, 247, 248, 249
Johnston, Samuel M., 336
Jones Creek, 406
Jones Ferry, 248
Jones, Edward B., 336
Jones, F. A., 336
Jones, G. W., 405
Jones, George M., 336
Jones, George W., 336, 441, 442
Jones, Harris, 336
Jones, Jennie, 329
Jones, John A., 336
Jones, John W., 336, 433, 438, 442
Jones, Joseph T., 242, 337, 431, 439, 441
Jones, Lentulus A., 336, 337, 431
Jones, Samuel G., 23, 70, 77, 337, 347, 427, 445
Jones, Thomas B., 337, 424, 435
Jones, W. J., 337
Jones, William Clinton, 38, 72, 73, 112, 338, 422, 427, 431, 436
Jones, William H. H., 338, 442
Jones, William H., 140, 338
Jones, William S., 338
Jones, William W., 338
Jonesboro, GA, 193, 195, 196, 198, 264, 265, 266, 267, 271, 281, 282, 286, 296, 298, 304, 306, 307, 310, 312, 314, 324, 331,

341, 347, 363, 364, 370, 373, 379, 382, 383, 398, 410, 414, 436
Jonesboro, TN, 35
Jordan, Benjamin M., 183, 328, 447, 449
Jordan, Berry M., 338, 429
Jordan, Montgomery, 339
Joyce, Richard, 339
Joyce, Thomas, 339
K
Karney, Pat, 339
Keenan, Robert, 339, 431, 442
Keil, Captain F. K., 146, 149
Kelly, David C., 234, 235
Kemp, John, 429, 447
Kemp, Sarah, 404
Kemper Farm, 61
Kemper, Moses, 60
Kennesaw Line, 163, 170
Kennesaw Mountain, 170, 175, 179, 256, 280, 295, 304, 307, 312, 314, 316, 328, 332, 334, 338, 343, 347, 352, 353, 363, 369, 371, 375, 376, 379, 395, 398, 408, 415, 434
Kentucky and Edgefield Railroad, 183
Kentucky Military Institute, 152
Kentucky River, 96
Kentucky Road, 78
Kentucky State Militia, 55
Kentucky, 2, 14, 42, 43, 44, 45, 47, 49, 50, 53, 57, 71, 77, 80, 82, 86, 92, 94, 96, 97, 98, 99, 103, 384, 408
Kentucky Troops - Cavalry (Federal): 1st, 59, 66, 81
Kentucky Troops - Artillery (Federal): 1st Battery, 218
Kentucky Troops - Infantry (Federal): 3rd, 174, 176; 7th, 62; 12th, 240; 14th, 88; 23rd, 111; 28th, 210; 48th, 419
Kentucky Troops - Cavalry (Confederate): 12th, 369
16th, 278
Kentucky Troops - Infantry (Confederate): 8th Mounted, 415; 9th, 387
Karney, Pat, 339
Keenan, Robert, 339, 445
Kelleher, Patrick, 339
Kelly, Jeremiah, 339
Kelly, John, 339
Kemp, John, 339
Kennedy, John, 339
Kennedy, Patrick, 339
Kephart, Fountain E. P., 339
Kerley, E. R., 340

Kernell, Samuel H., 340
Kessell, Samuel A., 340
Ketelta, Captain, 109
Keys, James A., 340
Kidden, Dr., 182
Kilgore, Henry, 444
Kilpatrick, Judson, 194
Kimbro, George W., 340
King, Festus, 340
King, Martin (Company A), 340
King, Martin (Company G), 340
King, Thomas, 138, 139
King's Mountain, S C., 31
Kingston Springs, TN, 13, 23, 253, 323, 401
Kingston, GA, 162, 258, 322
Kingston, TN, 40, 41, 42
Kinsbro, J. C., 340
Kirby, Richard, 340
Kirk, Edmund, 106, 107, 108
Kirk, William M., 12, 340, 422
Kirkland, William H., 11, 14, 17, 340
Kleiser, Jonas M., 341
Knight Cemetery, 417
Knight, Thomas H., 341
Knights of Pythias, 257
Knott, James R., 341
Knox County, TN, 50, 269, 313, 314, 402
Knoxville, TN, 37, 39, 42, 45, 48, 55, 72, 73, 76, 78, 79, 82, 100, 143, 258, 261, 264, 266, 269, 271, 272, 273, 275, 278, 279, 285, 287, 291, 293, 296, 297, 300, 303, 304, 305, 307, 309, 310, 311, 313, 314, 316, 317, 319, 320, 322, 323, 325, 326, 331, 332, 336, 337, 338, 342, 346, 347, 348, 351, 353, 355, 356, 357, 360, 361, 362, 365, 366, 369, 370, 373, 376, 377, 385, 387, 391, 395, 398, 401, 402, 404, 408, 409, 415, 417
Kolb Farm, GA, 170
Ku Klux Klan, 254, 315
Kuhn, Lawrence, 26, 28, 29, 341
Kyle, William D., 160, 341, 432, 437, 447
L
Lafayette, GA, 131, 132, 134
Lagardo, TN, 374
LaGrange, GA, 152, 310, 395
Lancaster Pike, 95
Lancaster, George W., 17
Lancaster, Jarrott S. J., 341, 429
Lancaster, KY, 95, 97
Lancaster, Samuel M., 341, 428
Lancaster, Thomas C., 341
Landers, Adam, 342, 431

Landis, A. L., 57
Lane, Abraham, 342, 441
Lane, Colonel John Q., 210, 215
Lane, Jacob E., 342
Lane, Thomas, 342, 424, 434
Lane's Brigade, 205, 206, 210, 211, 212, 214, 217
Lankford, John N. H., 342
Lankford, Lawrence D. R., 342, 442
Lankford, Paralee, 390
Lankford, Robert H., 342, 442
Lankford, Sydney, 304
Lark, William, 342, 433, 449
Larkin, Joseph N., 343
Larkins, James M., 178
Larkins, James M., 25, 39, 55, 343, 421, 387
Larkins, Joseph H., 161, 162, 249, 343, 428, 429, 433, 440, 447
Larkins, Sarah, 353
Latham, John B., 343
Lauderdale Springs, MS, 374, 385
Laurel Creek Bridge, 53, 55, 58
Laurel Creek, 53, 56, 58
Lawler, Michael J., 344, 424
Lawrence Co., AR, 289
Lawrence, Belfield F., 344, 447
Lawrence, Joseph B., 344, 427, 431, 436, 447
Lawrence, William H. H., 344, 427, 435, 438
Lawrenceburg, KY, 96
Le Grande (Steam Boat), 153
Lea, Judge John, 238
Leak, James L., 344
Leake, Berry B., 5, 344
Lealand, 238
Leatherwood Cemetery, 272
Leatherwood Creek, 318
Leatherwood, TN, 272
Lebanon, KY, 80
Lebanon, TN, 254, 315
Lee and Gordon's Mill Road, 135
Lee and Gordon's Mill, 135
Lee Co., VA, 77
Lee Hospital, 386
Lee, Robert E., 130, 250
Lee, Stephen D., 191
Lee's Corps, 193, 194, 195, 204, 234, 238
Leech Cemetery, 370
Leek, Alfred H., 345
Leeper Cemetery, 345
Leeper, John H., 36, 345
Leggett, General Mortimer D., 189
Leggett's Division, 189
Leggett's Hill (see also Bald Hill), 184, 188

Leggitt, R. A., 345
Lenoir Station, TN, 101, 260
Lewallen, M. A. F., 285
Lewis Co., TN, 362
Lewis, James A., 345, 438
Lewis, William, 345
Lewisburg Pike, 206
Lexington, KY, 47, 55, 94, 416
Liberty Gap, TN, 124, 128
Liberty, VA, 384
Lick Creek Bridge, 36
Lilliard's TN Regiment, 49
Lincoln Co., TN, 279, 399
Lincoln, Abraham, 1, 3, 250
Lincolnites, 45, 70
Linden, TN, 381, 394
Linebaugh, Benjamin E., 345
Linzy, William H. H., 346, 431, 445
Little Beaver Dam Creek, 258
Little Lot, TN, 275, 402
Little Rock, AR, 268, 294
Lloyd, Margret J., 325
Lloyd, Sarah A., 391
Lobelville, TN, 345
Loftin, Thomas, 346
Logan Co., KY, 272, 297, 337, 365
Logan, John, 189
Logan's Crossroads, 80
Lomax, William E., 70, 346
London Road, 53, 56, 65
London, KY, 54, 58, 80, 95
Lone Oak, TN, 385
Lone Star Cemetery, 295
Long Blanche, 382
Long Cemetery, 347
Long Tom, 73, 87
Long, Alfred, "Alf," 346, 436
Long, Felix G., 346
Long, James A., 5, 12, 18, 19, 29, 105, 107, 110, 115, 127, 132, 144, 150, 158, 159, 189, 192, 193, 196, 347, 421, 424, 437
Long, James H., 347
Long, James Henry, Sr., 347
Long, James, 26, 28, 45, 346
Long, Martin F., 162, 172, 183, 347
Long, Samuel, 162
Longstreet, James, 140, 143
Longstreet's Corps, 143
Lonoke Co., AR, 282
Lookout Mountain, 132, 144
Los Angeles, CA, 362
Losson, Craig, 186, 209
Loudon Railroad Bridge, 37

Loudon, TN, 36, 40, 41, 42, 144, 279
Louisa Co., VA, 319
Louisiana, 2, 152, 214
Louisiana Troops - Artillery (Confederate):
  Bouanchaud's Battery, 232; Pointe
  Coupee Light Artillery, 152, 232
Louisville, KY, 8, 96, 97, 122, 254, 257, 344,
  382, 383, 385
Love, Jacob, 347
Lovejoy Station, GA, 196, 197, 263, 280, 284,
  300, 377, 388, 406, 414, 437
Lowe, Andrew J., 23, 77, 347, 357
Lowe, Henry, 348
Lowrey, Mark P., 194, 195, 201, 237, 240,
  241, 247
Lowrey's Brigade, 169, 194
Lucas, Hugh R., 6, 12, 19, 22, 24, 27, 36, 37,
  48, 65, 348, 418, 421, 444
Lundy, William T., 348
Lunn, John A., 348
Lunsford, James, 17, 348
Luther, Alonzo, 21
Luther, George M., 348, 447
Luther, Newton J., 21, 348, 442
Luther, Vernon, 21
Lyles, TN, 381
Lynch, W. B., 349, 434
Lynn Grove, KY, 341
Lynnville, TN, 243, 379
Lyons, Jeremiah, 349, 428, 443
M
Macey & Hamilton, 4
Mackall, William, 53
Macon, GA, 183, 188, 193, 247, 265, 267,
  274, 284, 285, 288, 293, 295, 296, 297,
  299, 301, 303, 308, 317, 328, 331, 334,
  338, 343, 349, 355, 357, 358, 360, 364,
  366, 368, 369, 383, 410, 411, 413
Madison, GA, 168, 261, 268, 291, 294, 296,
  297, 303, 311, 317, 325, 336, 339, 343,
  347, 355, 355, 355, 359, 364, 380, 383,
  384, 386, 386, 396, 398, 409
Magevney, Michael, 158, 183, 186, 187, 191,
  192
Magevney's Brigade, 189
Magnus, Gnaeus Pompeius, 163
Mahoney, James, 349
Mahoney, John, 349
Main Avenue, 73
Majors, John, 236, 244, 258, 349, 373, 380,
  433
Malia, Martin, 349, 428, 447
Mallard, Priscilla, 386

Mallory and Leech General Store, 349
Mallory, William J., 5, 12, 25, 26, 29, 36, 79,
  349, 422
Malugin, William G., 350
Mammoth Cave, 84
Manassas Junction, VA, 30, 87
Manchester, TN, 101, 102, 263, 285, 341
Maney, George E., 3, 4, 5, 8, 26, 157, 167,
  170, 171, 176, 185, 186, 189, 191, 193,
  350
Maney, Thomas, 350
Maney, William B., 86, 127, 169, 172, 190,
  274, 279, 293, 321, 350, 399, 421, 423,
  428, 447, 449
Maney's Brigade, 126, 136, 141, 154, 161,
  162, 171, 175, 178, 182, 187, 194
Maney's Sharpshooter Battalion, 132, 266,
  358, 398, 407
Manigault, General Arthur M., 326
Manley, Benjamin F., 351, 434, 447
Manley, Frank, 351
Manley, Hugh H., 351
Manley, James, 351, 447
Manley, Pat, 351
Maplewood Cemetery, 262
Marable Cemetery, 293, 351, 407
Marable, George W., 10, 351
Marane, Christopher C., 351
Marcum, Clayburn, 46
Marcum, Didama, 45
Marcum, Hiram, 45, 46, 408
Marcum, Julia, 45, 46, 408
Marcum, Minerva, 45
Marengo, 246
Marietta Confederate Cemetery, 266, 347
Marietta, GA, 169, 170, 172, 181, 258, 262,
  266, 268, 271, 272, 273, 284, 307, 310,
  317, 329, 332, 338, 342, 343, 347, 348,
  354, 355, 357, 393, 398, 404, 409, 415,
  416
Mariman, James, 59, 60
Marion Church Cemetery, 389
Maroney, Matthew H., 351
Marsh, Aquilla, 351, 424
Marsh, Edward J., 26, 28
Marsh, Elijah J., 351
Marsh, George W., 351
Marsh, James S., 352
Marsh, James T., 352
Marsh, Margret, 342
Marsh, William C., 352, 441
Martin Cemetery, 352
Martin Garton Cemetery, 311, 412

Martin, Armistead W. R., 77, 187, 352, 434
Martin, C. J., 418
Martin, Cave J., 352
Martin, G. T., 162
Martin, G. W., Jr., 352
Martin, George W., 170, 187, 352, 431, 434, 447
Martin, James Thomas "Tom", 147, 352, 431, 445
Martin, John (Company A), 352
Martin, John (Company G), 353
Martin, John S., 353
Martin, L. J., 352
Martin, Marshall Rudolph "Roff", 147, 353, 431
Martin, TN, 280, 329
Marvin, E. M., 386
Maryland, 2
Mason, Benjamin F., 353
Mason, Bennett, 353, 435, 438
Massey, William, 353
Massie, Rebecca E., 318
Mathis, John T., 353, 447
Mathis, William J. "Billy", 146, 149, 353, 431, 449
Mathis, William J., 12, 421, 423
Matlock, Pleasant, 29, 354
Matthews, Drewy N., 354
Matthews, John T., 354, 447, 449
Maurey Co., TN, 260, 269, 272, 281, 283, 297, 305, 310, 315, 318, 347, 355, 369, 381
Maury, John, 354, 431
Mauzy, Dr., 182
Maxey, William O., 354
Maxwell House Hotel, 400
May, Ann E., 257
Mayberry, Benjamin F., 64, 354, 431
Mayfield, GA, 247
Maynard, Horace, 34
Maysville, AL, 365
McAnally, Michael, 355, 438, 441
McArthur, Arthur, 218, 219, 220
McBride, James, 355
McCaleb, Alton, 355
McCaleb, J. B., 355
McCaleb, Thomas P., 355, 447
McCaleb, W., 355
McCall & Company, 4
McCann, Benjamin W., 5, 41, 355, 421, 443, 449
McCann, J. Richard "Dick", 2, 4, 5, 9, 19, 24, 50, 54, 64, 86, 356, 422

McCarty, William, 356
McCauley, George D. J., "Jeff," 356, 436, 442
McCauley, John C., 356, 449
McCauley, Richmond M., 137, 357, 424, 429
McCauley, Wiley M., 357, 447
McCauley, William H., 100, 113, 117, 121, 122, 127, 131, 257, 357, 423, 428, 441, 444
McClanahan, Anna, 308
McClanahan, Leander B., 357
McClanahan, Mortimer B., 357
McClelland, James R., 188, 358, 434
McClelland, Sarah, 274
McClenden, Jesse, 358
McCluggage, John, 88
McCollum, Benjamin F., 358, 436, 447
McCollum, Helen, 358
McConnell, Joseph, "Ive," 358, 428, 431, 445, 447
McCook's Brigade, 174, 176
McCook's Corps, 128
McCord, W. M., 358
McCown, Charles, 366
McCown, John P., 102, 103, 104, 109
McCown, Margret, 366
McCown's Division, 102, 103, 105, 107, 108, 109, 122, 126, 130
McCracken, M., 358
McCrary, John W., 358
McCrary, Joseph, 358
McCrary, Marquis L., 358
McCrary, Thomas L., 359
McCutcheon's Creek, 202
McDaniel, Alexander R. M., 79, 359, 421, 423, 431, 447
McDaniel, Jesse C., 87, 359, 447
McDonald, James H., 28, 359
McDonough, James L., 82, 204, 233
McDowel's Landing, 246
McDuffie, Lieutenant W. A., 102
McElhaney, James, 359
McElroy, Samuel C., 79, 359, 427
McElyea, Marcus L., 359, 435, 447
McEwen Cemetery, 280, 287
McEwen, Frances A., 311
McEwen, TN, 21, 277, 287, 304
McFarland's Gap, 132
McGavock Confederate Cemetery, 267, 294, 304, 308, 313, 317, 331, 378, 396, 399, 417
McGavock, Carrie, 206
McGavock, John, 206
McGill, Calvin, 360

McGill, John D., 360, 423
McGill, W. L., 360
McGuire, P., 360
McIntosh Cemetery, 383
McIntosh, Green M., 360, 431, 445
McIntosh, Mary, 383
McKelvy, William, 167, 360, 428, 433
McKenzie, TN, 326
McKinnon, James, 360
McLaughlin, Alex R., 360, 439, 441
McLemay, John, 360, 434
McLemore's Cove, 134
McLeod, Norman A., 360
McMahon, Allison W., 360, 434
McMahon, Byron, 361
McMillan, William L., 239
McMinn, Senona, 308
McMinnville, TN, 102
McMurray, G. W., 420
McMurray, J. A., 101
McNailus, James, 361, 447
McNair, Evander, 109
McNair's Brigade, 107
McNairy, Frank, 53, 57, 60
McNairy's (DuVal) Scouts, 297
McNairy's Cavalry Battalion (aka 1st TN Cavalry Battalion), 55, 61
McNamara, Patrick, 361
McNeilly, Hugh J., 361, 435
McNeilly, William D. "Dodd," 190, 361
McNichols, Charles W., 219, 221
McNutt, Alex D., 361
McPherson, James B., 159, 187, 188, 189
McTyer, Captain W. A., 101, 103, 104
Meadows, Sarah W., 389
Meadows, W. T., 361
Medical College Hospital, 259
Meek Cemetery, 361
Meek, Howard T., 361
Meek, Moses H., 8, 361, 422
Meeks, Major A. T., 220
Memphis and Charleston Railroad, 82, 85
Memphis, TN, 82, 123, 186, 254, 315, 335
Mendenhall, John, 119
Menefee, James, 362, 438
Menefee, Nicholas S., 362, 442
Mercer's Brigade, 194
Meridian, MS, 246, 360, 364, 371, 385, 386, 403, 404, 410, 420
Merrill, James C., 362, 434, 436
Merritt, James K. P., 362

Methodist Episcopal Church South, 269, 270, 274, 296, 299, 312, 315, 322, 330, 338, 347, 357, 374, 386, 394, 414
Methodist Publishing House, 77
Methodist, 9, 164, 191, 219, 257, 262, 266, 271, 314, 337, 378, 402
Mexican War, 1, 7, 123, 269, 275, 296, 301, 313, 324, 336, 348, 349, 350, 356, 374, 400
Mexico, 87
Michigan, 340
Middle Tennesseans, 19
Middle Tennessee, 85, 103, 130
Middleton, TN, 261
Midway Station, 36
Midway, GA, 247
Midway, TN, 258, 261, 262, 263, 271, 273, 276, 283, 284, 288, 294, 297, 317, 321, 322, 323, 329, 335, 340, 342, 348, 351, 352, 355, 361, 363, 365, 373, 374, 376, 379, 380, 381, 382, 384, 386, 390, 403, 404, 405, 406, 410, 411, 412, 419
Milan Cemetery, 327
Miles, Louisa, 345
Miles, William R., 110, 362, 428
Mill Creek Bridge, 249
Mill Creek Gap, GA, 159
Mill Springs, KY, 80
Milledgeville, GA, 247
Miller Co., AR, 281
Miller, Alexander C., 79, 362, 444
Miller, E. Luther, 362, 428
Miller, Edward H., 362, 431, 445
Miller, H. C., 363, 447
Miller, James G., 363
Miller, Joseph H., 363
Miller, Mary E., 363
Miller, Mary J., 371
Miller, S. B., 115
Miller, Willis, 25, 137, 363, 428, 429
Millwood Institute, 378
Millwood Institute, 8
Milton Scholes Cemetery, 389
Missionary Ridge Baptist Church Cemetery, 285
Missionary Ridge, TN, 140, 141, 144, 146, 149, 150, 159, 162, 172, 191, 209, 218, 258, 259, 262, 263, 264, 266, 268, 270, 272, 276, 278, 280, 282, 283, 285, 286, 288, 290, 292, 294, 297, 298, 299, 300, 301, 303, 305, 309, 310, 311, 313, 318, 320, 321, 323, 324, 325, 326, 327, 330, 332, 333, 335, 336, 337, 338, 339, 342,

344, 346, 352, 353, 354, 358, 359, 360, 362, 365, 366, 368, 369, 370, 371, 372, 375, 376, 377, 379, 380, 381, 382, 385, 388, 389, 391, 393, 397, 399, 402, 404, 406, 412, 413, 415, 416, 417, 420, 430
Mississippi Co., AR, 387
Mississippi Co., MO, 334
Mississippi River, 6, 86, 129, 152
Mississippi Valley, 86
Mississippi, 2, 48, 82, 91, 125, 151, 194
Mississippi Troops - Artillery: Turner's Battery, 240
Mississippi Troops - Infantry: 14th, 49 15th, 48, 49, 53, 54, 55, 56, 58, 63
Mississippians, 201
Missouri Troops – Infantry (Federal): 44th, 217
Missouri, 2, 26, 153
Mitchell, Ballard, 363
Mitchell, John W., 363, 443
Mitchell, Lawrence, 363
Mitchell, R. H., 363
Mitchner's Station, NC, 249
Mobile and Ohio Railroad, 82
Mobile, AL, 159, 160, 353, 386, 402
Mobley, Benjamin B., 363, 428
Mobley, T. J., 363, 447
Monterrey, Mexico, 123
Montgomery Co., TN, 260
Montgomery, AL, 152, 153, 247, 379
Montgomery, Daniel, 77, 363, 437
Montgomery, Martin, 280
Moody, Henry, 363
Moore Cemetery, 257
Moore, Charles, 194, 364, 428, 437
Moore, James, 364
Moore, Nancy, 257
Moore, William H., 364
Moore, William S., 192
Moran, Patrick, 364
Moreau, Christopher C., 77, 364
Morgan, Fred, 187, 364, 434
Morgan, George W., 86, 87, 92, 93, 94
Morgan, Hiram, 183, 364
Morgan, John H., 344, 416
Morgan, Robert J., 83
Morgan, Thomas J., 237
Morgan, William B., 444
Morgan's Regiment (aka 36th TN), 83
Moriarty, Patrick, 364
Morrill's Brigade, 189
Morris Island, SC, 332
Morris, G. J., 183, 364

Morris, Martin V., 12, 364, 421
Morrisett, Sally, 295
Morrisett, William R., 132, 365
Morrison, Allen, 365
Morristown, TN, 85, 307, 349, 398
Morrow Station Road, 193
Morton, James, 365
Moss, Pamela, 328
Moss, Rufus, 68
Moss, Thomas J., 365, 447
Motherspaw, Thomas, 218, 219
Mound Bottom, TN, 381
Mount Hope Cemetery, 274
Mount Juliet Cemetery, 390
Mount Olive Cemetery, 318
Mount Olivet Cemetery, 266, 268, 269, 273, 279, 282, 286, 288, 292, 312, 332, 337, 350, 351, 353, 355, 356, 368, 369, 373, 374, 379, 391, 394, 403
Mount Pleasant, TX, 300
Mount Vernon Road, 56
Mount Zion Baptist Church, 193
Mount Zion Cemetery, 324, 374, 410
Munford, H. H., 365
Murfreesboro Pike, 235, 237
Murfreesboro, TN, 88, 103, 107, 116, 117, 119, 120, 122, 123, 124, 125, 128, 130, 142, 209, 255, 257, 262, 264, 265, 267, 270, 271, 272, 273, 276, 278, 280, 281, 283, 284, 286, 287, 288, 289, 290, 291, 292, 293, 294, 295, 297, 298, 299, 300, 301, 302, 303, 304, 307, 308, 314, 316, 317, 318, 320, 321, 322, 324, 326, 327, 328, 329, 330, 337, 338, 341, 343, 344, 345, 349, 350, 355, 357, 358, 359, 360, 362, 363, 364, 366, 368, 370, 372, 375, 377, 378, 379, 380, 381, 383, 384, 385, 386, 388, 389, 390, 391, 393, 396, 398, 401, 402, 403, 405, 407, 411, 413, 415, 416, 418, 419, 426
Murphey, James G., 365
Murphey, John R., 365, 441
Murphree, David D., 365, 431, 445
Murphree, W. R., 365
Murpo, Melissa, 399
Murray, Artimesia, 270
Murrell, F. M., 365
Murrell, James C., 365
Murrell, Richard C., 365
Murrell, T. M., 366
Musgraves, David, 366, 431
Myatt, Burrell, 366
Myrtle Hill Cemetery, 289, 405

N

Nall, Rufus, 366
Nancy Creek, 184
Napier, Robert H., 366, 428, 443
Napier, Thomas A., 366
Napier, Victoria, 292
Narrows of the Harpeth, 259, 390
Nashville and Chattanooga Railroad, 39, 124, 237
Nashville and Northwestern Railroad, 10, 12, 13, 23, 236, 252, 253, 306, 321
Nashville Arsenal, 3
Nashville Chamber of Commerce, 253
Nashville City Cemetery, 120, 313, 353, 378, 379
Nashville Fairgrounds, 9
Nashville Penitentiary, 122
Nashville Plow Works, 3
Nashville Turnpike, 108, 109, 111, 112
Nashville, TN, 1, 3, 4, 5, 7, 8, 9, 10, 11, 12, 13, 14, 15, 19, 23, 25, 29, 30, 34, 35, 39, 43, 50, 53, 56, 69, 76, 82, 91, 103, 107, 118, 120, 122, 123, 184, 200, 201, 204, 235, 236, 237, 239, 243, 245, 252, 253, 257, 258, 260, 261, 262, 263, 264, 265, 266, 267, 268, 269, 270, 271, 272, 273, 274, 275, 276, 277, 278, 279, 280, 281, 282, 283, 284, 285, 286, 287, 288, 289, 290, 291, 292, 293, 294, 295, 296, 297, 298, 299, 300, 301, 302, 303, 304, 305, 306, 307, 308, 309, 310, 311, 312, 313, 314, 315, 316, 317, 318, 319, 320, 321, 322, 323, 324, 325, 326, 327, 328, 329, 330, 331, 332, 333, 334, 335, 336, 337, 338, 339, 340, 341, 341, 342, 343, 344, 345, 346, 347, 348, 349, 350, 351, 352, 353, 354, 355, 356, 357, 358, 359, 360, 361, 362, 363, 364, 365, 366, 367, 368, 369, 370, 371, 372, 373, 374, 375, 376, 377, 378, 379, 380, 381, 382, 383, 384, 385, 386, 387, 388, 389, 390, 391, 392, 393, 394, 395, 396, 397, 398, 399, 400, 401, 402, 403, 404, 405, 406, 407, 408, 409, 410, 411, 412, 413, 414, 415, 416, 417, 418, 419, 4439, 449, 450
National Peace Conference, 2
Naughton, Michael, 366
Nave, John J., 194, 366
Nealey, Martin, 366, 434
Neblett, R. P., 366, 447
Ned Merriweather Camp (UCV), 381
Neely, Margret V., 336
Neighbors, Jacob W., 367

Nelson, Moses A., 367, 435, 438, 447
Nelson, Thomas, 34, 40
Nelson, William, 94
Nesbitt, Joseph T., 66, 367
Nesbitt, Robert S., 367
Nesbitt, Semus O., 367
Nesbitt, William A., 367
Nesbitt, William J. A., 367, 445
Nevada, 254
New Hope Church, GA, 164, 168, 169, 179, 266, 268, 283, 291, 293, 294, 300, 301, 308, 311, 316, 317, 328, 336, 342, 349, 360, 379, 385, 393, 394, 410, 412, 417, 433
New Orleans, LA, 153, 268, 313, 381
New York, 286, 409
Newberry, SC, 247
Newman, Tazewell, 56, 63, 65
Newman's Regiment (aka 17th TN), 52
Newnan, GA, 260, 270, 318, 383, 385, 386
Newsom's Station, 259
Newton, Henry W., 368, 438
Newton, James, 242, 368, 439, 441
Newton, Wiley J., 187, 368, 434
Nichol, Bradford, 95, 368
Nichol, Samuel D., 5, 11, 16, 64, 65, 66, 76, 95, 368, 421
Nichol, William C., 51, 52, 64, 95, 190, 368, 423, 435
Nichols, Griffin, 242, 324, 368, 428, 431, 439, 441
Nichols, Henry C., 369, 431, 445
Nichols, Sallie, 289
Nicholson, Alex C., 217
Nickajack Cave, 131
Nickajack Creek, 273, 415
Nicks, Emma A., 391
Nisbet, Colonel James C., 155
Nix, James C., 369
Nolan, Levi H., 369
Nolen, Elizabeth J., 351
Nolensville Road, 105, 237
Noll, Nicholas, 369
Norfleet Cemetery, 318
Norman, Henry H., 369, 443
Normandy, TN, 101, 408
North Carolina, 2, 247, 250
North, 185
North Carolina Troops - Infantry (Confederate): 29th, 86, 101, 103, 105, 109, 110, 111, 113, 114, 115
Northington, Samuel, 369, 429
Norvell, William, 369, 444

Nunnelly, TN, 300
O
O' Brien, Michael, 370
O'Connell, John, 370
O'Connor, Ellen, 332
O'Guinn, Annie, 284
O'Guinn, James C., 370
O'Guinn, Mary, 324
O'Guinn, Robert N., 370, 437, 443
O'Leary, Tim, 370
O'Neal, Henry D., 370, 427, 443
O'Neal, Michael, 370
Oak Grove Freewill Baptist Church, 319
Oak Hill Cemetery, 318, 330
Oak Wood Cemetery, 399
Oak Woods Cemetery, 278
Oakland Cemetery (Atlanta, GA), 259, 264, 285, 291, 293, 294, 305, 314, 316, 323, 336, 373, 376, 401
Oakland Cemetery (Little Rock, AR), 294
Oakley, Cutis A., 369
Obion Co., TN, 328, 344
Ocmulgee Hospital, 265, 274, 284, 288, 293, 295, 296, 297, 301, 303, 308, 317, 331, 334, 338, 349, 357, 358, 360, 368, 369, 383, 392, 413, 419,
Oconee River, 247
Ohio River, 49, 94, 97, 260, 289, 351, 403, 416
Ohio Troops – Artillery (Federal):
Ohio, 54, 59, 99, 118, 176, 356, 416   ;
1st Light Artillery, 106, 217; 6th Battery, 214; 9th Battery, 91; 20th Battery, 223, 226
Ohio Troops – Infantry (Federal): 6th, 109, 110
15th, 107
16th, 88, 89
17th, 66
24th, 111
26th, 210, 211
35th, 146, 149
49th, 106, 107
50th, 215, 216
52nd, 174
64th, 174
65th, 174
90th, 136
94th, 111
97th, 210
98th, 177
100th, 215, 240
121st, 177

125th, 174, 218
Ohioan, 119
Ohioans, 88
Okolona, MS, 153
Old Barlow Cemetery, 386
Old State Hospital, 373
Oldham, Van Buren, 185
Oliver Hospital, 132
Oliver, James R., 249
Oliver, Mary, 321
Oliver, Olenthius D., 370
Olmstead, Colonel Charles, 194
Olson, Porter, 221
Omega, TN, 393
Oostanaula River, 160
Opdyke, Emmerson, 205, 218, 219, 226
Opdyke's Brigade, 218, 221
Orm, John, 370, 428, 435, 443
Orr, Carson T., 371
Osborn, William J., 371
Osborne, John B., 371, 443
Our Family Trouble, 22, 272
Overby, Lucinda, 275
Overton, John, 234
Owen, J. D., 371
Owen, Jesse L., 371, 431, 445
Owens, Blythia F., 371, 435
Owens, James M., 371, 431, 445
Owens, William, 371
Ozanne, John M., 283
P
Paducah, KY, 49, 262, 307, 312
Paige, Robert B., 371
Paine, Ora S., 254, 315
Palestine, TN, 362
Palmer, Joseph, 250
Palmer's Brigade, 250
Palmetto, GA, 197
Palmyra, TN, 273
Paluxy, TX, 372
Parish, Irvine, 162
Parish, Thomas M., 372, 431
Parker, Dan M., 372
Parker, James T., 372, 435
Parker, Leona, 328
Parkers Cross Road, 292
Parks, Thomas P., 372, 445
Parnell, John C., 372
Parrish, Robert A., 372
Parson's Battery, 111, 112
Parsons, E. B., 146
Patrick, J. B., 372
Patrick, Marsh M., 249

Patten, George W., 218
Patterson Cemetery #1, 372
Patterson, Joseph J., 372, 428, 443
Patterson, Joseph K., 372, 428
Patterson, W. H., 372, 428
Pea Patch Island, DE, 127
Peach Orchard Hill, 238
Peach, Fountain E., 373, 437
Peachtree Creek, 186, 188, 198, 268, 279, 296, 299, 305, 311, 313, 325, 326, 342, 349, 351, 352, 358, 360, 362, 364, 366, 368, 374, 385, 387, 396, 398, 410, 411, 413, 419, 434
Pearl, Edward, 373
Pease, George W., 250
Peaters, C. D., 373, 435
Peck, Giles, 373, 439
Peck, James, 373, 441
Peck, John, 373, 438
Peeler, Samuel, 373
Pemberton, John C., 102, 129
Pemberton, John, 373
Pembroke, KY, 310
Pennsylvania, 272, 400
Pennsylvania Troops – Infantry (Federal): 77th, 139
Pennymoore, VA, 381
Pentecost, A. M., 373
Perry Co., TN, 345, 381, 394
Perry, Marshall, 373
Perry, Thomas, 373
Perryville, KY, 96, 97, 123, 142
Peters, Dr. George, 201
Peters, Jessie McKissick, 201
Petersburg, VA, 248, 302, 385
Pettigrew Hospital, 358, 381
Pettis, Eagleston, 373
Pettus, May L., 330
Petty Cemetery, 290, 405
Petty, G. H., 236, 244, 258, 349, 373, 380
Petty, John M., 373
Petty, Magdaline K., 406
Petty, Milbury, 402
Petty, Thomas B., 373, 430
Phenix, J. C., 374
Phifer, TN, 370
Philadelphia, PA, 122, 381
Philbrook, Sam, 227
Phillips Co., AR, 350
Phillips, John W., 374, 424, 434, 449
Pigeon Hill, GA, 170
Pillow, Gideon, 49

Pim Hospital, 191, 269, 290, 294, 302, 364, 393, 395
Pine Mountain, GA, 169, 170
Pinewood Mills, 290
Pinewood, TN, 308
Piney River, 9, 418
Pinkston, John, 374
Pinkston, S. P., 374
Pirtle, Alfred, 111
Pitts, Fountain E., 9, 46, 48, 55, 74, 75, 85, 374, 421
Pitts, James B., 9, 55, 75, 374, 385
Pitts, Josiah, 6, 8, 17, 19, 29, 55, 62, 64, 259, 374, 421, 444
Pitts, Lewis L., 375, 430, 443
Pitts, Sophia, 374
Pittsburg Landing, TN, 82, 85
Plainview, TX, 419
Plant, John H., 375
Plant, TN, 365, 375
Plunkett Cemetery, 277
Plunkett, John W., 375
Poe, Mrs., 51
Polk Hospital, 289
Polk, Henry A., 375, 435
Polk, Leonidas, 49, 101, 123, 124, 125, 140, 142, 151, 152, 153, 166, 169, 170
Polk's (Lucius) Brigade, 171
Polk's Corps, 122, 127, 159, 164
Poore, John M., 375
Pope, John, 82
Porch, William S., 375, 428, 443
Port Royal, TN, 399
Porter, George, 194
Porter, James, 209
Porter, Samuel, 376
Poter, Charles P., 375
Poter, Columbus W., 375, 432
Poter, Thomas Y., 376
Potts, Fredoney, 325
Powder Springs Road, 183
Powel, I. W., 172
Powel, Samuel, 56
Powell River, 90, 92, 93
Powell, Betsy Bell, 22, 376
Powell, John W., 376
Powell, Joseph R., 376
Powell, R., 376
Powell, Reynolds L., 22, 222, 226, 256, 376, 430, 438
Powell, Wily, 183
Pratt, Henry P., 376
Precept, 254

Price, James, 376
Price, John R., 376
Price, Preston G., 43, 44, 53, 55, 164, 191, 376
Price, Richard, 377
Price, W. Henry, 377, 428
Priestly, Lafayette M., 377
Primm, William D. S., 377
Princeton, KY, 419
Proctor, Missouri F., 330
Proctor, William, 377, 441, 443
Provisional Army of the State of Tennessee, 11, 123
Puckett, Andrew A., 377, 432, 438, 443
Puckett, Sally, 377
Pulaski, TN, 243, 253, 254, 315
Pullen, Elmeda, 309
Pullen, James L., 377
Pullen, Sarah, 377
Pullen, William C., 241, 243, 245, 252, 309, 377, 437, 447
Purl, James, 167

Q
Quarles, Pinkney M., 378, 438
Quarles' Brigade, 224
Quinn, Michael, 378, 428
Quintard Hospital, 191, 265, 364

R
R & D Hospital, 332
Ragan Cemetery, 321
Ragsdale, Mathias W., 378, 430, 443
Rains Brigade (aka 2nd Brigade), 88, 101, 102, 103, 104, 105, 106, 107, 108, 109, 111, 112, 122
Rains House, 237
Rains, James E., 2, 4, 5, 8, 12, 19, 22, 23, 24, 25, 26, 27, 29, 30, 32, 35, 36, 37, 40, 41, 42, 43, 44, 46, 47, 49, 50, 53, 54, 55, 56, 61, 63, 65, 66, 71, 73, 74, 76, 77, 80, 81, 82, 83, 84, 85, 86, 87, 88, 91, 104, 107, 108, 110, 111, 113, 114, 116, 118, 120, 121, 124, 256, 260, 271, 273, 283, 378, 405, 419, 421, 423, 428
Rains, John, 4, 378
Rains, Lucinda C., 378
Rainsville, 73
Raleigh, NC, 122, 248, 250, 358, 381
Rally Hill Pike, 201
Randall, David A., 379, 427, 432, 443, 445
Randall, William H., 379, 447
Ransom, Thomas E., 194
Ratliff, William N., 379
Rawley, Darius N., 28, 379, 437, 443

Ray, A. W., 132, 379
Raymond, MS, 162
Readyville, TN, 102, 103, 260, 265, 283, 287, 300, 301, 305, 327, 333, 342, 364, 365, 370, 380, 386, 389
Rearden, Martin, 379
Reaves, James, 379
Rebel, 22, 50, 52, 57, 58, 59, 65, 75, 81, 83, 87, 89, 91, 93, 94, 99, 104, 105, 108, 109, 118, 121, 140, 142, 144, 146, 162, 171, 172, 174, 175, 176, 177, 204, 206, 208, 214, 215, 217, 220, 229, 237, 240, 250
Reconstruction, 253
Red River Baptist Church Cemetery, 310, 345
Redden, G. L., 170, 379, 432
Redden, J. Liberty, 379, 430, 433
Redden, John W., 236, 244, 258, 349, 380, 373, 428, 432, 436, 449
Reddick, John B., 380
Redoubt Number 1, 238
Redoubt Number 2, 238
Redoubt Number 3, 238
Redoubt Number 4, 238
Redoubt Number 5, 238
Reece, Griffith, 380, 447
Reed, W. M., 3
Reeder, John H. L., 380, 438
Reeder, Mrs. E. A., 72
Rees, John A., 380, 428
Reeves, Flavius J., 380, 430
Reeves, William J., 381, 428
Rehobeth Church Cemetery, 310
Reid, William, 89
Republican Banner (Nashville), 8, 22
Resaca, GA, 159, 161, 275, 312, 321, 341, 384, 387, 392, 399, 411, 432
Rest Haven Cemetery, 312
Revolutionary War, 381, 399
Reynolds, John, 380, 381
Reynolds, Robert D., 381
Reynolds, William E., 140, 145, 146, 147, 149, 158, 159, 178, 179, 188, 189, 190, 195, 196, 197, 203, 206, 207, 229, 233, 234, 240, 242, 255, 381, 430, 438
Reynoldsburg, TN, 366
Rhodes, Granville, M., 381
Rhodes, James, 381, 430, 432
Rhodes, Robert, 381
Rice Cemetery, 382
Rice, Daniel, 381, 432, 445
Rice, David H., 381, 424
Rice, Horace, 137, 152, 158, 166, 183, 191, 197, 199, 200, 212, 217, 221, 232

Rice, William B., 382
Rich, John R., 113
Rich, Peter, 382
Richardson, Andrew J., 382, 435, 447
Richardson, Benjamin W., 382
Richardson, M. Turner, 382, 437
Richardson, Sarah, 258
Richardson, William T., 383, 436
Richardson, William Turner, 382, 432, 445, 447
Richey, J. B., 389
Richmond (aka Confederate government), 34, 102, 143, 247
Richmond, KY, 94, 95, 284
Richmond, VA, 264, 279, 283, 300, 305, 306, 307, 310, 320, 352, 358, 371, 397, 415
Rickman, Wiley, 383
Riddleberger's Corner, 4
Ridings Cemetery, 345
Ridings Family Cemetery, 383
Ridings, Elisha T., 113, 114, 383, 437, 438, 441
Ridings, George D., 114, 118, 119, 383, 423, 428, 437, 444
Ridings, Sarah R., 345
Ridley, Jerome S., 36, 56, 98, 384, 421, 423, 428
Rienzi, MS, 246
Riley, Edward, 384
Riley, Michael, 384
Ringgold Road. 135
Rippavilla, 204
Rippey, Charles H., 136
River Road, 259
Riverside Cemetery, 267
Roberts Cemetery, 354, 384
Roberts, Albert, 61
Roberts, George W., 115, 116
Roberts, W. F., 384
Roberts, William H., 12, 384, 421, 445
Robertson County, TN, 2, 5, 12, 14, 18, 19, 21, 127, 162, 183, 197, 221, 222, 245, 267, 268, 269, 271, 278, 285, 286, 291, 296, 297, 302, 303, 310, 314, 318, 320, 329, 333, 345, 347, 364, 365, 375, 376, 385, 386, 399, 410, 416, 417, 421, 424, 425
Robertson, A. J., 384
Robertson, David L., 384
Robertson, Donia, 392
Robertson, H. H., 384
Robertson, Henry H., 55, 384
Robertson, James, 123

Robinson, A. J., 160, 432, 436
Robinson, James, 384
Robinson, W. D., 384
Rochelle, Thomas J., 167, 384, 428, 432, 433, 443
Rock Island Prison, IL, 259
Rock Spring Church, 134
Rock Springs Cemetery, 354
Rockcastle Hills, 56, 59, 61, 68, 69
Rockcastle River, 56, 59, 60, 95
Rockcastle, KY, 277, 317, 323, 374, 389
Rocky Face Ridge, GA, 159
Rogers, George E., 385, 428, 447
Rogers, James M., 113, 385, 428
Rogers, John G., 385, 432, 436, 447, 450
Rogers, Robert M., 385, 445
Roland, William A., 187, 385, 434, 447, 450
Rome, GA, 133, 265, 331, 349
Rome, Italy, 163
Rooker, Caleb, 331
Rooker, James B., 386
Rooker, James, 386
Rooker, John Wesley, 386, 436
Rose and Gordon Law Firm, 254, 316
Rose Hill Cemetery, 315
Rosecrans, William S., 69, 103, 118, 119, 128
Ross Hospital, 353, 356
Ross, William, 386
Rosson, Joseph S., 110, 386, 428
Rough and Ready, GA, 193, 407
Rough and Ready, KY, 96
Round Hill, 63, 65
Rousseau, Lovell, 108, 109, 111
Roy, William, 386
Royal Arch Masons, 257
Rubicon River, 163
Ruffin, Robert E., 386, 436
Runnells Co., TX, 270
Rushing, Clinton, 387
Rushing, John H., 187, 387, 434
Rushing, Missouri, 328
Rushing, William H., 387
Ruskin, TN, 330
Russell, Augustine M., 394
Russell, Mary S., 396
Russellville, KY, 345
Rust, J., 387
Rust, Lewis, 387
Rust, William H., 387
Rutherford Co., TN, 307, 333, 370
Rutherford Creek, 201, 243
Rye, Thomas, 387
S

S. P. Moore Hospital, 317
Salado Cemetery, 356
Salem, NJ, 294
Salisbury, NC, 249, 251
Salt River, 96
Saltillo, MS, 246
Samuel Vanleer & Company, 4
Sand Mountain, 199
Sanders, Robert W., 387
Sanders, Z. T., 387
Sangster, Mary, 282
Sartarem, Brazil, 374
Satterfield, John S., 387
Saunders, Liberty, 387, 388
Saunders, Robert W., 388, 387
Saunders, William V., 388, 387
Savage, James R., 388, 447, 450
Savage, Mary E., 388
Savage, Melinda, 368
Savannah River, 247
Savannah, TN, 269
Sayers, Charles P., 388, 439, 441
Schaffer, J. L., 69
Schmittou Cemetery, 375
Schmittou, James L. V. "Big Jim", 147, 388, 436, 437, 447
Schmittou, James O. L. V. "Little Jim", 147, 149, 388, 432, 445
Schoepf, Albin, 64, 66, 67
Schofield, John M., 186, 200, 201, 202, 203, 204, 205, 211, 216
Scholes, John T., 389
Scholes, Milton R., 102, 108, 389, 432
Scholes, Nathaniel R., "Nat," 12, 389, 428, 436
Scott Cemetery, 323
Scott Co., KY, 376
Scott Co., TN, 42, 43, 44, 45
Scott, Jo, 389
Scott, Robert, 67, 389, 426, 447
Scrivner, Alexander T., 389
Scrivner, John A., 389
Seaborn, Oliver, 389, 430
Seales, E. Holloway, 390
Seals, Absolum, 29, 390
Seals, Jacob, 390
Sears, John, 390
Self, Abraham, 390, 428
Self, J. W., 390
Selfe, C. J., 334
Selma, AL, 152, 153, 246, 366
Seminole War, 400
Sensing, John H., 390, 428

Sentinel Co., OK, 402
Sentinel, OK, 402
Sequatchie Valley, TN, 129
Sevier, James, 390, 428
Shacklett, Henry R., 87, 390, 423
Shacklett, TN, 391
Shady Grove, TN, 265, 318, 324, 368
Shaffer, Josiah L., 391
Shallowford Road, 140
Sharp & Hamilton, 3
Shaver, Jesse, 391
Shaver, Matthew M., 391, 428, 443
Shaver, Michael, Jr., 391, 428
Shea, John, 391
Shelby Medical College, 282
Shelbyville Pike, 119
Shelbyville, TN, 119, 120, 121, 122, 123, 124, 125, 126, 127, 128, 257, 259, 261, 262, 263, 264, 265, 266, 268, 270, 271, 272, 273, 274, 275, 276, 277, 278, 279, 280, 281, 282, 283, 285, 287, 288, 289, 290, 291, 293, 295, 296, 297, 300, 301, 303, 304, 305, 306, 307, 308, 309, 311, 312, 313, 314, 315, 316, 317, 318, 320, 321, 322, 323, 324, 326, 327, 328, 329, 330, 331, 332, 333, 335, 336, 337, 338, 340, 341, 342, 343, 344, 345, 346, 347, 349, 351, 352, 353, 354, 355, 356, 357, 358, 359, 360, 361, 362, 363, 364, 365, 366, 367, 368, 369, 370, 371, 372, 373, 374, 375, 376, 377, 378, 379, 380, 381, 382, 383, 384, 385, 387, 388, 389, 390, 391, 392, 393, 394, 395, 396, 397, 398, 399, 400, 401, 402, 403, 404, 405, 406, 407, 408, 409, 410, 411, 412, 413, 414, 415, 416, 417, 419, 420
Shelton, E. E., 295
Shelton, Georgia, 322
Shelton, John, 271, 391
Shelton, Lenora, 393
Shepard, Oliver L. 110
Shepard's Brigade, 109
Shephard, J. A., 392
Shephard, William, 392
Sheppard, I. B., 392, 447
Sherer, John D., 392
Sheridan, John, 220, 392, 442
Sheridan, Phil, 146
Sherlock, John, 392, 439, 447
Sherman, Frank, 161
Sherman, William T., 159, 160, 161, 162, 163, 170, 179, 184, 185, 186, 193, 199, 248, 249, 253

Sherrod, Richard T., 392, 430
Shiloh, TN, 123, 125, 350
Shipley, John, 233
Shipp, James, 22, 26, 35, 68, 241, 392, 439
Shipp, Parthenia, 392
Shivers, William H., 392
Shortle, Thomas, 160, 392, 432
Shouse Cemetery, 308
Shouse, Jacob W., 38, 191, 392, 436, 450
Shouse, Jennie, 402
Shreveport, LA, 394
Shropshire, Edward F., 102
Shultz, B. F., 78
Shy, William, 238, 239
Shy's Hill (see Compton's Hill)
Sigel, Martin, 393, 442
Sikes, James, 393
Sikes, William T., 393
Sills, Samuel, 393
Simmon, Nancy E., 265
Simpson Co., KY, 297
Simpson, George W., 393
Singleton, Mary E., 309
Skeift's Ferry, 248
Skelton, Abner B., 71
Skelton, James M., 71, 72, 257, 393, 432
Skelton, Joseph P., 167, 393, 428, 432, 433, 443
Slayden, Hartwell M., 393, 394
Slayden, John D., 220, 393, 395, 433, 439, 448
Slayden, TN, 375
Slayden, William M., 68, 75, 125, 241, 242, 287, 393, 394, 420, 423, 436
Sloan, James L., 40, 45, 79, 394, 421
Slocum, Henry W., 248, 249
Smith Co., TN, 389
Smith, Alexander, 395
Smith, Augustus T., 395, 439
Smith, B. J., 172, 395, 396
Smith, Beatty, 88
Smith, Edmund Kirby, 82, 83, 84, 86, 92, 93, 94, 96, 97, 98, 99, 100, 101
Smith, Elias P., 395, 442
Smith, Ella, 9
Smith, Gus, 191, 395, 436
Smith, J. T., 395
Smith, James A., 236
Smith, James T., 26, 28, 395, 439
Smith, James, 132, 395
Smith, Jasper, 395
Smith, John T., 395
Smith, Joseph T., 102, 106

Smith, Lewis, 395
Smith, Minor, 5
Smith, Oliver W., 395
Smith, Patrick S., 395
Smith, Preston, 123, 127, 132, 133, 135, 136, 137, 138, 139
Smith, R. J., 395
Smith, Richard S., 395, 442, 443
Smith, Thomas (Company A, B), 396, 428
Smith, Thomas (Company D), 396
Smith, Thomas F., 396, 428, 444
Smith, Thomas, 396
Smith, Walter S., 396, 439
Smith, William J., 396, 439
Smith, William, 396, 436
Smith's (Giles) Division, 188
Smith's Brigade, 122, 123, 125, 126, 128, 129, 132, 133, 135, 136, 138, 139
Smithfield, Depot, 248
Smithfield, NC, 248, 249
Smyrna, TN, 370
Snake Creek Gap, GA, 159
Snell, AR, 320
Snyder, Carrie, 230
Soard, H. A., 396
Soard, William J., 396
Soard, William, 396
Soldier's Friend Society, 25
Soldier's Home Cemetery, 293, 302, 307, 343, 346, 355, 359, 360, 362, 363, 365, 367, 391
South Carolina, 1, 247
South, 185, 252
South Carolina Troops - Infantry (Confederate): 16th, 154; 24th, 195
South Carolinians, 154, 195, 198
Southall, Rebecca, 350
Southerland Cemetery, 303
Southerland, John, 187, 396, 434, 445
Southerland, W. A., 396, 430, 432
Southside Cemetery, 305
Southside, TN, 299
Sparta, GA, 247
Spears, Samuel C., 397
Speer, Mary Ann, 268
Speight Cemetery, 300
Spence, David M. L., 397
Spence, John D., 397
Spence, William Jerome Dorris, 9, 17, 22, 39, 68, 71, 73, 75, 76, 397, 425
Spencer Mill, TN, 406
Spencer, Jesse, 397
Spencer, Thomas S., 132

Spencer, Thomas S., 398
Spicer, Clarissa, 401
Spillers, William, 398
Spotsylvania, VA, 286
Spring Hill City Cemetery, 202
Spring Hill, TN, 201, 205
Spring Hill, TN, 202, 243
Springfield Road, 28
Springfield, TN, 5, 14, 252
Sroffe, George W., 398, 439, 442
St. Cloud, 246
St. Louis Cemetery, 337, 344
St. Mary's Hospital, 310, 411
St., Louis, MO, 6
Stacy, Cora A., 305
Stanfield, Izora, 418
Stanfield, James F. M., 396
Stanley, David, 216
Statham, Winfield S., 56
Stennett, S. A., 332, 398
Stephens, James G., 174, 398, 424, 428
Steven's Brigade, 155
Stevens, William M., 398, 428, 434, 443
Stevenson, Carter, 85, 86, 87, 92, 94, 95, 96, 100, 102, 262, 278, 319, 384
Stevenson's Division, 94, 97, 98, 159
Stewart Co., TN, 263
Stewart Co., TN, 290, 381
Stewart, Alexander P., 187, 191, 239
Stewart, Charles, 398
Stewart, Michael, 398
Stewart, Nicholas P., 38, 398, 437
Stewart, Robert, 398, 448
Stewart, William H., 172, 398
Stewart's Corps, 186, 202, 204, 206, 234, 238, 248
Still, Sarah F., 295
Stokes, Andrew J., 399, 432, 445, 450
Stokey, Montgomery A., 214, 233, 399, 439
Stokey, William W., 94, 96, 113, 116, 133, 399
Stone, Elizabeth, 350
Stones River, 102, 103, 104, 105, 119
Stonewall Co., TX, 356
Stoney Point Church Cemetery, 274
Storey, W. C., 399
Stout Hospital, 168
Stout, Abraham, 399
Stout, Andrew G., 160, 241, 399, 432, 439, 442, 448
Stout, Dr. S. H., 168, 343, 399, 400
Stout, Ira A., 399
Stout, Phil A., 400

Stout, Samuel V. D., 400, 423
Stovall, M. A., 101, 103, 114
Stowers, John T., 400, 436
Strahl, Otho, 138, 198, 202, 233
Strahl's Brigade, 136, 138, 154, 165, 187, 201, 202, 207, 217, 224
Strasbourg City, France, 381
Stratton, John H., 400
Street, Andrew J., 400
Street, David W., 134, 400, 428, 448
Street, John C., 401
Street, Thomas M., 401
Street, William H., 401
Stroud, John W., 401
Stroud, Joseph W., 401, 430
Stroudsville, TN, 303
Stuart Cemetery, 277, 284, 401
Stuart, James M., 401
Stuart, John M., 401, 445
Stultz, Aaron, 26
Sturgeon Creek, 268
Sudberry, David R., 401, 445
Sugar Creek, 265
Sugg, Joseph H. L., 401
Sugg, Nathaniel R., 23, 401
Sullivan, S., 402
Sullivan, Timothy, 401
Summers Cemetery, 410
Summers, Margret, 410
Sumner County, TN, 8, 386
Sumter, Thomas, 32
Sutton, Joseph, 402, 428
Swayne, John, 402
Sweetwater, TN, 144, 278
Sycamore Landing, TN, 337
Sycamore Powder Mills, 378
Sykes, Robert, 402
T
Tallahachie Co., AL, 374
Talley, James A., 402
Tallulah, LA, 348
Taneyhill, Captain, 91
Tarkington, George W., 402, 450
Tarkington, John H. C., 402, 429, 432, 448
Tarrant, Eastham, 66
Tate, Louisa P., 342
Tatom, James K. P., 403
Tatom, Montgomery B., 403
Tatom, William B., 72, 403
Taylor, Edmund D., 403, 439
Taylor, James A. J., 403
Taylor, Joel T., 78
Taylor, John D., 403, 429, 442, 444

Taylor, Manoah, 403
Taylor, Mrs., 46
Taylor, Nancy, 257
Taylor, Richard, 246, 293, 296, 349, 358, 359, 360, 385, 386, 392, 402
Taylor, Skelton, 403
Tazewell, TN, 77, 78, 80, 87, 88, 92, 99, 268, 272, 275, 277, 278, 283, 284, 285, 287, 289, 291, 297, 299, 300, 302, 305, 306, 307, 309, 314, 318, 320, 321, 323, 325, 327, 328, 330, 331, 333, 334, 335, 339, 340, 344, 345, 346, 347, 348, 349, 351, 354, 355, 360, 361, 362, 363, 367, 369, 370, 371, 373, 375, 376, 377, 379, 381, 384, 386, 387, 389, 390, 392, 393, 395, 398, 401, 402, 403, 407, 408, 409, 409, 412, 415, 417, 427
Tearney, Bridget, 316
Teas, Margret, 403
Teaster, Charles D., 403, 436
Teaster, John T., 403
Temple Cemetery, 308
Tennessean, 2, 223
Tennesseans, 1, 3, 6, 24, 34, 54, 57, 62, 136, 149, 151, 154, 155, 156, 157, 175, 176, 177, 185, 210, 211, 212, 217, 218, 225, 249
Tennessee (Steamer), 41, 42
Tennessee Campaign, 199
Tennessee City, TN, 382
Tennessee General Assembly, 2, 5
Tennessee Hospital, 286
Tennessee Militia, 3
Tennessee Ridge, 290, 416
Tennessee River, 23, 36, 82, 85, 129, 131, 132, 199, 200, 236, 244, 253, 258
Tennessee State Capital, 9, 10
Tennessee State Legislature, 9
Tennessee, 1, 2, 3, 4, 6, 7, 14, 21, 24, 30, 31, 34, 39, 44, 47, 51, 71, 72, 74, 94, 99, 104, 105, 123, 128, 152, 154, 163, 171, 194, 200, 210, 223, 253, 254, 258
Tennessee Troops - Artillery (Confederate): Cockrill's Battery, 42; Mebane's Battery, 171; Rhett Artillery, 86; Rutledge Artillery, 42, 46, 53, 56, 63, 95, 295, 327, 368; Scott's Battery, 133, 137
Tennessee Troops - Cavalry (Confederate): 1st Battalion (aka McNairy's Cavalry), 49, 53, 56; 2nd Battalion, 49; 3rd Battalion (aka Brazelton's Cavalry), 49, 57, 77, 78, 79, 86; 4th, 49, 266, 391; 9th Battalion, 272, 285, 311, 324, 328, 329, 356, 357, 363, 402; 9th, 275, 311 ; 10th Battalion, 308, 321, 392; 10th, 277, 280, 309, 330, 344, 347, 358, 369, 375, 402, 405; 12th, 393
Tennessee Troops - Infantry (Confederate): 1st, 8, 14, 25, 28, 29, 126, 157, 161, 171, 175, 176, 177, 181, 256, 350, 378; 1st Regiment Consolidated, 250; 2nd (See also 11th Tennessee Infantry), 19, 24, 25, 26, 28, 421; 2nd Regiment Consolidated, 250, 251, 258, 259, 261, 262, 263, 264, 265, 266, 269, 270, 275, 276, 277, 279, 285, 288, 290, 291, 292, 297, 299, 301, 302, 305, 307, 309, 311, 314, 318, 319, 320, 321, 323, 324, 325, 327, 330, 331, 333, 338, 339, 341, 343, 344, 348, 351, 353, 354, 355, 357, 358, 361, 362, 363, 365, 367, 379, 380, 382, 385, 388, 392, 394, 398, 399, 401, 405, 406, 410, 411, 416, 446, ; 3rd, 14; 3rd Regiment Consolidated, 250; 4th, 48, 74, 79, 92, 100, 101, 318, 382; 4th Regiment Consolidated, 250; 5th, 308; 9th, 178, 185, 233
11th (See also 2nd Tennessee Infantry), 2, 4, 28, 29, 30, 35, 49, 50, 52, 53, 54, 55, 56, 58, 60, 61, 62, 63, 65, 66, 67, 68, 69, 72, 73, 74, 75, 76, 77, 79, 84, 85, 86, 88, 89, 90, 91, 92, 93, 95, 96, 98, 99, 100, 101, 102, 103, 104, 105, 107, 108, 109, 110, 111, 112, 113, 114, 115, 116, 117, 119, 120, 121, 122, 123, 125, 126, 127, 129, 131, 132, 133, 135, 136, 137, 140, 142, 143, 144, 145, 146, 147, 148, 151, 152, 154, 155, 157, 158, 159, 160, 161, 162, 163, 165, 166, 167, 169, 170, 171, 172, 173, 174, 175, 176, 177, 178, 179, 180, 181, 182, 183, 187, 188, 189, 191, 193, 194, 195, 196, 197, 199, 200, 201, 204, 206, 207, 209, 212, 213, 214, 217, 220, 221, 222, 226, 232, 233, 234, 236, 237, 238, 239, 240, 241, 242, 243, 246, 248, 249, 250, 251, 252, 253, 254, 256, 258, 261, 262, 263, 266, 270, 271, 273, 274, 275, 276, 277, 278, 279, 280, 281, 282, 285, 288, 289, 294, 298, 299, 302, 303, 305, 307, 308, 309, 310, 311, 314, 316, 318, 321, 322, 324, 325, 328, 333, 338, 342, 346, 350, 353, 354, 355, 356, 357, 363, 364, 367, 368, 374, 378, 380, 382, 381, 385, 387, 388, 393, 394, 397, 399, 402, 406, 407, 409, 411, 412, 413, 415, 418, 421, 423

INDEX

12th, 123, 126, 127, 132, 136, 137, 139, 144, 145, 146, 158, 165, 166, 167, 170, 171, 183, 189, 191, 207, 232, 236, 249, 250
13th, 123, 125, 132, 135, 136, 139, 146, 158, 160, 164, 171, 183, 189, 191, 207, 216, 236, 237, 240, 241, 245, 249, 250
15th, 344
17th (aka Newman's Regiment), 49, 56, 63, 65, 67
19th (aka Cumming's Regiment), 49, 80, 360
20th (aka Battle's Regiment), 49, 51, 56, 57, 58, 59, 61, 62, 63, 66, 67, 205, 238, 239
23rd, 115
27th, 171, 175, 176, 177, 181, 256
29th, 56, 58, 59, 63, 67, 68, 123, 132, 136, 146, 152, 158, 165, 167, 171, 172, 177, 183, 191, 197, 199, 200, 201, 204, 207, 212, 213, 214, 217, 221, 232, 234, 236, 238, 240, 241, 242, 243, 246, 248, 249, 250
30th, 85
34th, 49, 86
36th, 86
47th, 123, 132, 136, 137, 139, 144, 145, 146, 158, 165, 166, 167, 171, 183, 189, 191, 207, 236, 249, 250
49th, 224, 287, 300, 327, 328, 356
50th, 168, 250, 266, 274, 281, 354
51st, 207, 236, 245, 249, 250
52nd, 207, 236, 245, 249, 250
61st, 85, 374
63rd, 311
154th Senior, 123, 125, 132, 133, 135, 136, 139, 146, 158, 160, 154, 171, 183, 186, 189, 191, 207, 216, 236, 241, 245, 249, 250
Tennessee Troops - Cavalry (Federal): 2nd, 373
Tennessee Troops - Infantry (Federal): 8th, 240
Tennessee Troops (Mexican War): 1st, 123, 313, 336, 356
3rd, 123, 269, 349
Tennessee Troops (Militia): 97th, 320
Texas, 2, 263, 314, 372
Texas Brigade (see also Granbury's Brigade), 210
Texas State Cemetery, 414
Texas Troops - Cavalry (Confederate): 8th Cavalry (Terry's Texas Rangers), 167, 305, 316
Texas Troops - Infantry (Confederate): 1st, 185; 10th, 207

"The Thedford Song", 21
Thedford, William R., 5, 12, 13, 21, 29, 36, 85, 90, 100, 111, 114, 115, 116, 119, 122, 150, 404, 406, 422, 423
Thedford's Company (See also Company K), 8, 18, 21, 34, 36, 42, 64, 70, 72, 79, 422
Thoburn, Lieutenant, 215
Thomas, Charley, 51
Thomas, George H., 80, 162, 170, 186, 200, 201, 204, 236
Thomas, James D., 404, 443
Thomas, Minor B., 404, 442
Thomason, Benjamin W., 404, 444
Thompson, Francis M., 404, 432
Thompson, J. Stewart, 77, 404, 432
Thompson, James, 404
Thompson, John, 239, 404
Thompson, Samuel C., 405
Thompson, Thomas D., 38, 69, 405
Thompson, Thomas, 405
Thompson, William T., 405, 436, 448
Thompson's Colored Brigade, 236
Thorn Hill, TN, 290, 293, 327, 418
Thornton Cemetery, 265
Thruston, Gates P., 108
Tidwell, Benjamin O., 405, 406
Tidwell, Edmund M., 405, 406
Tidwell, Franklin F., 8, 79, 137, 191, 248, 249, 275, 405, 422, 424, 429, 430, 450
Tidwell, Hickman C., 271, 406, 448
Tidwell, Josiah, 8, 406, 422
Tidwell, Margret P., 263
Tidwell, Silas, 72, 406, 437
Tilford, Mary, 400
Tipton, H., 90
Tishomingo Co., MS, 403
Todd Co., KY, 279
Todd, John, 12
Todd, Mary Ann, 261
Totty, Nancy, 325
Totty, Thomas S., 406, 448
Tracy, Thomas, 406, 430, 432
Traveler's Rest, 234, 235
Traylor, Leroy, 12, 407, 422
Traylor, Thomas B., 407, 422, 444
Treanor, James, 407
Trenton, GA, 379
Trigg Co., KY, 418
Triune Road, 103, 104
Trogden, Caroline T., 407
Trogden, John W., 407
Trogdon, Alfred, 407, 439
Trotter, George W., 407

Trotter, Jordan, 172, 407, 407
Truett, Temperance, 324
Tuberville, Joseph L., 408
Tucker, Whil, 408
Tullahoma Campaign, 130
Tullahoma, TN, 119, 122, 124, 128, 130, 131, 260, 274, 322, 325, 336, 365, 377
Tumbling Creek, 297, 420
Tunnel Hill, GA, 403
Tupelo, MS, 246, 369
Turnbull, Mary J., 361
Turner, A. L., 408
Turner, Dillard, 408
Turner, George L., 408
Turner, George T., 408, 439, 442
Turner, Mary Ann, 320
Turnersville, TN, 291
Tuscumbia, AL, 244
Twining, Captain, 205
Tyler's Brigade, 182, 238
Tyner's Station, TN, 143
U
U. S. Military Prison, Louisville, KY, 259, 260, 261, 262, 263, 266, 267, 270, 272, 273, 275, 276, 278, 280, 281, 282, 283, 284, 290, 292, 293, 294, 295, 297, 299, 300, 301, 302, 303, 306, 307, 308, 309, 310, 312, 314, 316, 317, 320, 321, 322, 323, 324, 325, 326, 328, 329, 330, 331, 332, 334, 335, 336, 337, 338, 339, 340, 341, 342, 343, 345, 348, 349, 352, 355, 358, 360, 361, 362, 363, 364, 365, 366, 368, 369, 370, 371, 373, 375, 376, 377, 378, 379, 380, 382, 383, 384, 386, 388, 391, 392, 393, 395, 396, 397, 398, 399, 401, 419
Unaka Mountains, 34
Union Cemetery, 263, 288, 373, 402, 406, 414, 418
Union Chapel Cemetery, 292
Union City, TN, 310
Union Street, 4
Union, 1, 2, 3, 4, 21, 29, 34, 39, 40, 50, 59, 195
Unionist, 34, 35, 36, 37, 40, 41, 42, 44, 45, 47, 50, 52, 53, 54
Unionville Pike, 125
Unionville, NC, 248
United Confederate Veterans, 253, 254, 288, 292, 294, 303, 312, 315, 367, 381, 411, 414, 418
United States, 6, 91, 251

United States Troops – Artillery: 2nd, 189; 4th, 112
United States Troops – Infantry: 2nd, 309; 3rd, 367, 388; 6th, 409; 15th Battalion, 109, 110; 14th United States Colored, 237; 17th United States Colored, 237; 44th United States Colored, 199, 237
University of Nashville, 268, 273, 282, 350, 383
University of North Carolina, 315
University of Pennsylvania, 311
Ussery, Nathaniel T., 45, 46, 408
V
Vailes, William H. H., 408
Van Dorn, General Earl, 201
Van Hook, J. W., 408, 430
Van Pelt's Battery, 111
Vance, Colonel Robert B., 101, 103, 111, 114, 122
Vance's Brigade, 122
Vanleer, TN, 264, 274, 299, 325
Vaughan, Alexander H., 9, 38, 78, 80, 99, 408, 422
Vaughan, Alfred J., 125, 127, 135, 139, 140, 141, 142, 146, 147, 151, 157, 158, 160, 164, 165, 166, 169, 170, 171, 173, 174, 175, 176, 177, 178, 179, 181, 182
Vaughan's Brigade (after 15 August 1864 known as Gordon's), 143, 145, 146, 149, 151, 152, 153, 154, 158, 159, 160, 161, 162, 164, 166, 167, 169, 171, 183, 186, 191, 198, 240
Vaught, William E., 409, 443
Vera Cruz, Mexico, 123, 336
Vernon, TN, 9, 397
Verona, MS, 246
Versailles, KY, 96, 97, 98, 275, 276, 312, 335, 359, 369, 370, 387, 393, 400, 413, 415, 419
Vicksburg, MS, 86, 87, 102, 129, 130, 153, 262, 278, 325, 348, 356, 359, 409
Vineville, GA, 264, 359, 366
Vineyard Cemetery, 309
Vineyard, Morgan H., 409, 430, 448
Vining Station, GA, 181
Virginia Military Institute, 125
Virginia Road, 75
Virginia, 2, 25, 30, 35, 47, 91, 184, 186, 247, 259, 264
Virginia Troops - Infantry (Confederate): Mileham's Company, 86
Volunteer State (See also Tennessee), 2, 3, 243
Voss, J. E., 409

INDEX

W
W. H. Calhoun, 4
Waddle, A.M., 3
Wade, Captain C. N., 236
Waggoner, Calvin J., 409
Waggoner, Mary Ann, 292
Wagner, George, 205, 210, 212
Wagner's Division, 204
Walden's Ridge, TN, 262, 268, 281, 283, 289, 394
Walker, Francis, 171
Walker, John, 409
Walker, W. H. T., 136, 155, 185, 190
Walker's Division, 154, 155
Wall, John R., 409
Wallace, George, 409
Walp, Almira A., 380
Walsh, Patrick, 409, 448
Walsh, Patrick, 87
Walters, Frank, 409
Walthall's Division, 204
Ward, AR, 282
Ward, Hugh, 409
Ward, John H., 48, 97, 112, 119, 120, 409, 439, 443
Ward, William A., 410
Warfield, Henry C., 410, 437
Warren House, 195
Warren, Tom, 382
Warren, William J., 410, 433, 448
Warrior's Path, 94
Wartrace, TN, 124
Washington Co., AR, 397
Washington DC, 2, 6, 405
Washington Guards (See also Company F), 5, 12, 18, 19, 21, 36, 45, 79, 421, 424
Washington, George, 32
Watauga Bridge, 36, 39, 68, 265, 275, 276, 277, 281, 285, 287, 295, 300, 302, 316, 319, 326, 332, 333, 334, 339, 340, 342, 343, 344, 346, 349, 352, 353, 354, 361, 366, 367, 369, 370, 371, 372, 375, 379, 386, 389, 390, 401, 403, 406, 408, 409, 414, 415, 419
Watauga, TN, 36
Watkins, Sam, 176, 177, 181
Watkins, William M., 137, 158, 166, 183, 234, 236, 247
Watkins' Brigade (aka Vaughan's, Gordon's) 237, 238, 240, 241, 246, 249
Watson, AR, 416

Waverly Guards (See also Company A), 6, 9, 10, 11, 14, 16, 19, 22, 28, 29, 36, 54, 62, 64, 85, 422, 423
Waverly, TN, 252, 260, 278, 293, 321, 323, 328, 334, 338, 348, 356, 358, 374, 387, 394, 397, 405, 407, 413, 414, 417, 418, 422, 423
Waxahachie City Cemetery, 375
Waxahachie, TX, 375
Way Hospital, 263, 266, 271, 283, 285, 296, 299, 352, 358, 359, 364, 371, 385, 386
Waycross, GA, 190, 368
Waynesboro Road, 199
Waynesboro, TN, 123, 199
Waynick, George, 410
Wayside Hospital, 306
Weakley Co., TN, 280, 329, 330
Weakley, William T., 187, 410, 435
Weaks, William H., 410, 436, 439, 442
Weaver, Charles H., 411, 439, 443
Weaver, James R., 249, 411, 430, 440, 448
Webb, Aramathia, 313
Webb, Howell, 84, 85, 411, 421, 444
Webb, J. H., 187, 411, 435, 443
Webb, Norman, 411
Webb, Tabitha W., 410
Webb, William, 23, 411, 429
Webster Co., KY, 266
Webster, Mary C., 315
Weeks, W. H., 191
Weems Springs (see also Bon Aqua Springs), 355, 356
Weems, Anne B., 412
Weems, Corder T., 411, 432, 436, 450
Weems, Daniel, 412
Weems, George W., 412
Weems, Nathaniel Chapman, 190
Weems, Philip Van Horn, 9, 23, 29, 37, 38, 39, 70, 71, 127, 140, 148, 159, 167, 172, 189, 190, 197, 253, 273, 412, 422, 424, 432, 436
Weems, W. T., 412
Weems, William Loch, 412
Weems's Cemetery (Dickson Co.), 411
Weems's Family Cemetery (Hickman Co.), 190, 412
Weir, John, 194
Welch, James, 412
Welch, John S., 252, 412, 439
Welch, John, 412, 433, 436, 450
Wells, Lawrence, 413, 435
Wessyngton Plantation, 5
West Chickamauga Creek, 135

West Fork, KY, 319
West Nashville, 259
West Point (Military Academy), 122
West Point, GA, 152, 193
West Point, MS, 246, 411
West Tennessee, 26
Western Military Institute, 23, 314
Wetmore, Oldham B., 91, 413
Wetmore, William "Bill", 5, 16, 43, 91, 413, 442
Wharton's Texas Cavalry, 286
Wheat, Solomon, 413
Wheeler's Gap, 43
Whelan, John, 413, 429, 432, 445
White Bluff, TN, 13
White Bluff, TN, 303, 334, 336, 414
White Bridge Road, 259
White Cemetery, 406, 414
White Oak Creek, 301
White Oak Hospital, 385
White, Charles W., 132, 413
White, George W., 413
White, Jimmie, 157
White, Minnie, 267
White, William I., 9, 112, 127, 200, 252, 413, 422, 423
White, William K. "Buck", 23, 107, 111, 117, 414
White, William M., 414, 448
Whitley, T. N., 414
Whitney Memorial Park Cemetery, 263
Whitney, TX, 263
Whitton, AR, 387
Wigfall, Captain, 208
Wildcat, KY (see also Camp Wildcat, KY), 255
Wilder, Paul, 88
Wilderness Road, 47, 62, 71, 98
Wiley, Sil, 8
Wilkerson, J. B., 370
Wilkerson, Martha, 370
Wilkins, Carroll C., 414
Wilkinson Road, 108, 109
Will's Cemetery, 258
Willard, William W., 43, 196, 414, 437
Williams, Arrestes, 414
Williams, Charlotte, 386
Williams, E. L., 24, 25, 27, 414
Williams, Felix G., 414, 432
Williams, Francis, 287
Williams, George C., 415
Williams, George W., 415
Williams, Henry A., 415, 429
Williams, Hettie J., 274
Williams, James R., 415
Williams, James Richard, 415
Williams, John L., 415, 445
Williams, Joseph R., 415
Williams, L. W., 415
Williams, Mary J., 386
Williams, Steven T., 172, 415
Williamsburg, VA, 384
Williamson County, TN, 8, 269, 270, 274, 277, 298, 311, 312, 316, 325, 329, 336, 340, 350, 358, 372, 378, 380, 419
Williamson, John T., 236
Willich, August, 106, 107, 108, 130
Willich's Brigade, 106, 128
Willis, Benjamin F., 415, 443
Willow Mount Cemetery, 331, 342
Willow Springs Cemetery, 284
Wilmington, NC, 382
Wilson Co., TN, 390, 400
Wilson, AR, 308
Wilson, Aubrey, 415, 448
Wilson, Daniel W., 416, 432, 448
Wilson, Gilbert R., 416, 429
Wilson, John D., 416
Wilson, Read, 140
Wilson, Samuel M., 416, 424, 429, 439
Winchester, TN, 127
Winfield, TN, 43
Winn Cemetery, 416
Winn, Arena, 416
Winn, John H., 416, 439, 442
Winn, John W., Jr., 416, 432
Winn, William H., 12, 183, 416, 421, 424
Winstead Hill, 205, 206, 208, 209, 227
Winstead, Thomas H., 417
Winstead-Breezy Hill Range, 206
Winters, John A., 417
Wisconsin, 218, 219
Wisconsin Troops - Artillery (Federal): 1st Artillery, 89
Wisconsin Troops - Infantry (Federal): 20th, 271
24th, 146, 218, 227
Wiley, Artemis
Wither's Division, 126
Witty, Horatio, 16, 17, 417
Woltz, W. J., 177
Woodberry, TN, 102
Woodruff Co., AR, 376
Woodruff, Charles W., 417, 436
Woodruff, William B., 417, 439
Woods Valley, TN, 388, 391

Woods, James, 417
Woodson's Crossroads, 310
Woodward, John D., 12, 22, 29, 35, 417, 422
Woolslair, W. H. H., 139
Work, John H., 417
Work, Robert J., 17, 167, 417, 432, 433
Wright, Alice K., 417
Wright, George, 418
Wright, Luke E., 171
Wright, Marcus J., 198
Wright, Monroe M., 418, 429
Wright's Brigade, 136, 137, 154, 161, 162, 165, 182
Wyatt, Christopher C., 418
Wyatt, Josiah N., 192
Wyatt, William M., 418, 422, 445
Wyly Cemetery, 338, 394, 414, 418
Wyly, Harris K., 418
Wyly, Thomas K., 348
Wynn, John A., 418, 439
Wynn, John E., 418, 429
Wynn, John Wesley "Wes", 79, 97, 137, 138, 139, 145, 146, 149, 161, 183, 221, 419
Wynn, Samuel, 419

Y

Yager, Jacob, 419
Yale University, 8, 112, 378
Yandell Hospital, 306, 371
Yankee, 51, 56, 60, 62, 63, 65, 66, 80, 84, 87, 88, 89, 90, 92, 107, 108, 111, 112, 115, 116, 121, 134, 136, 140, 145, 146, 149, 153, 160, 166, 170, 174, 175, 177, 178, 181, 184, 193, 194, 195, 196, 197, 200, 202. 204, 205, 208, 212, 214, 216, 218, 221, 223, 225, 226, 229, 230, 231, 239, 240, 242, 252
Yarbrough, Lula, 356
Yarbrough, Martha, 260
Yarnell, Sergeant, 221
Yates, Clayton, 12, 34, 42, 95, 96, 98, 112, 114, 115, 135, 138, 145, 146, 255, 419, 436
Yates, James H., 191, 419
Yates, Roseanna, 411
Yeatman, Henry T., Jr., 419
Yeatman, Ida, 8, 378
Yell Co., AR, 365
Yellow Creek, 71, 322, 387
Young Cemetery, 304, 359, 420
Young, Archibald, 419, 430
Young, B. F., 419
Young, Isaac P., 85, 187, 220, 419, 424, 429, 435, 439, 442
Young, Jacob M., 420
Young, John B., 420

Z

Zachary, George W., 420, 432, 445
Zion Hill Cemetery, 377
Zollicoffer, Felix K., 2, 5, 34, 40, 42, 47, 49, 50, 52, 53, 55, 56, 57, 58, 59, 60, 61, 62, 65, 67, 68, 73, 80, 315
    Zollicoffer's Brigade, 48, 52, 61, 397

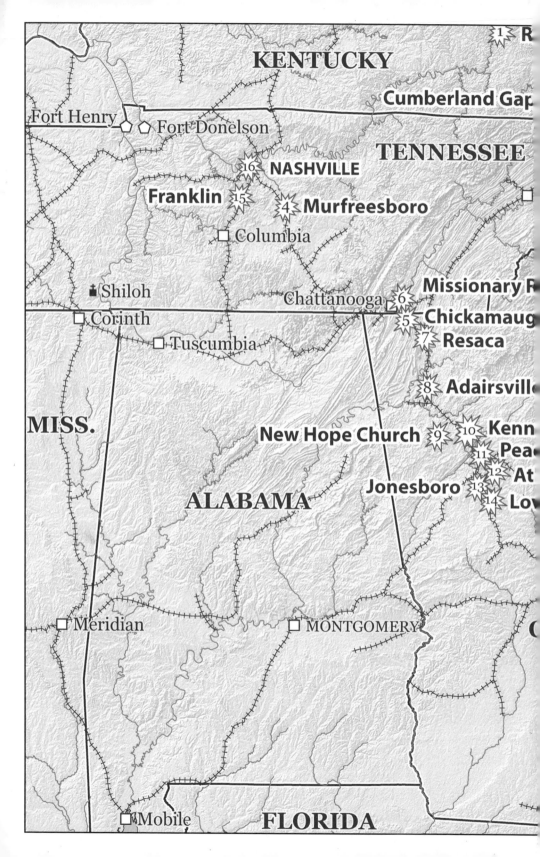